W9-CKR-763

FOR REFERENCE

Do Not Take From This Room

Ocean Currents
← Cool
← Warm

Tropic of Cancer

Equator

Tropic of Capricorn

Annual Precipitation

Inches	Centimeters
Over 80	Over 200
60–80	150–200
40–60	100–150
20–40	50–100
10–20	25–50
Under 10	Under 25

30°N

N

20°N

Port Sudan

Red Sea

ERITREA
Asmara

50°E

Mekele

Gulf of Aden

DJIBOUTI
Djibouti

Dese

10°N

Ethiopian Highlands
Harer
Hargeysa

Addis Ababa
Jima

ETHIOPIA

SOMALIA

Mbale

KENYA
Kisumu
Nakuru

0°

Mogadishu

Nairobi

Kilimanjaro
Moshi
Mombasa

Lake Victoria
Tanga
Dodoma

INDIAN

Zanzibar

Dar es Salaam

OCEAN

TANZANIA

COMOROS
Moroni

10°S

Antsiranana

Pemba

Nampula
Mahajanga

Blantyre

MOZAMBIQUE
Quelimane

Toamasina

Beira

Antananarivo

MADAGASCAR

20°S

Fianarantsoa

50°E

Toliara

30°S

Land Use and Resources

Percent Tree Cover
- More than 60%
- 30–60%
- 10–29%
- Less than 10%

Percent Cropland
- More than 60%
- 40–60%
- 30–39%

Sugarcane	Export crop
Maize	Domestic production
(Coffee)	Crop disrupted by war
Diamonds	Mineral

NEW ENCYCLOPEDIA OF

AFRICA

NEW ENCYCLOPEDIA OF

AFRICA

Volume 2

Dakar–Hydrology

John Middleton

EDITOR IN CHIEF

Joseph C. Miller

EDITOR

CHARLES SCRIBNER'S SONS
A part of Gale, Cengage Learning

Detroit • New York • San Francisco • New Haven, Conn • Waterville, Maine • London

BOCA RATON PUBLIC LIBRARY
BOCA RATON. FLORIDA

New Encyclopedia of Africa

John Middleton, Editor in Chief
Joseph C. Miller, Editor

© 2008 Gale, a part of Cengage Learning

For more information, contact
Charles Scribner's Sons
A part of Gale, Cengage Learning
27500 Drake Rd.
Farmington Hills, MI 48331-3535
Or you can visit our Internet site at
gale.cengage.com

ALL RIGHTS RESERVED
No part of this work covered by the
copyright hereon may be reproduced or
used in any form or by any means—
graphic, electronic, or mechanical,
including photocopying, recording, taping,
Web distribution, or information storage
retrieval systems—without the written
permission of the publisher.

For permission to use material from this
product, submit your request via Web at
http://www.gale-edit.com/permissions, or you
may download our Permissions Request form
and submit your request by fax or mail to:

Permissions Department
Gale
27500 Drake Rd.
Farmington Hills, MI 48331-3535
Permissions Hotline:
248-699-8006 or 800-877-4253 ext. 8006
Fax: 248-699-8074 or 800-762-4058

Since this page cannot legibly accommodate
all copyright notices, the credits constitute an
extension of the copyright notice.

While every effort has been made to ensure
the reliability of the information presented in
this publication, Gale, a part of Cengage Learning
does not guarantee the accuracy of the data
contained herein. Gale accepts no payment for
listing; and inclusion in the publication of any
organization, agency, institution, publication,
service, or individual does not imply endorsement
of the editors or publisher. Errors brought to the
attention of the publisher and verified to the
satisfaction of the publisher will be corrected in
future editions.

NEW ENCYCLOPEDIA OF AFRICA

John Middleton, editor in chief ; Joseph C. Miller, editor.
    p. cm.
        Includes bibliographical references and index.
        ISBN 978-0-684-31454-9 (set : alk. paper)
        ISBN 978-0-684-31455-6 (vol. 1 : alk. paper)
        ISBN 978-0-684-31456-3 (vol. 2 : alk. paper)
        ISBN 978-0-684-31457-0 (vol. 3 : alk. paper)
        ISBN 978-0-684-31458-7 (vol. 4 : alk. paper)
        ISBN 978-0-684-31459-4 (vol. 5 : alk. paper)
        Africa—Encyclopedias. Middleton, John, 1921-
    Miller, Joseph Calder.
        Title.

DT2.N48 2008
960.03—dc22   2007021746

ISBN-10:

0-684-31454-1 (set)
0-684-31455-X (vol. 1)
0-684-31456-8 (vol. 2)
0-684-31457-6 (vol. 3)
0-684-31458-4 (vol. 4)
0-684-31459-2 (vol. 5)

This title is also available as an e-book.
ISBN-13: 978-0-684-31557-7; ISBN-10: 0-684-31557-2
Contact your Gale representative for ordering information.

Printed in the United States of America
2 3 4 5 6 7 14 13 12 11 10 09 08

EDITORIAL BOARD

EDITOR IN CHIEF

John Middleton
Yale University

EDITOR

Joseph C. Miller
University of Virginia

ASSOCIATE EDITORS

Ann Biersteker
Yale University
Linguist, East/South Africa

Dale Eickelman
Dartmouth College
Anthropologist, North Africa

Sandra Greene
Cornell University
Historian, West Africa

Mark Horton
University of Bristol
Archaeologist, East Africa

Célestin Monga
World Bank
Economist

Kathleen Sheldon
University of California,
Los Angeles
Historian, Lusophone Africa

Aliko Songolo
University of Wisconsin
Literature, Francophone African
and Caribbean

Michael Watts
University of California, Berkeley
Geographer, West Africa

ADVISORS

J. F. Ade Ajayi
University of Ibadan,
Nigeria
Historian, West Africa

Boubacar Barry
CODESRIA, Dakar
Historian, West Africa

Catherine Coquery-Vidrovitch
University of Paris
Historian, Central and West Africa

James Currey
James Currey Publishers,
Oxford, U.K.
Publisher

Basil Davidson
University of Bristol, U.K.
Author, historian

Francis M. Deng
Sudan Peace Support Project
Director, lawyer,
diplomat

Joseph Harris
Howard University
Historian

Goran Hyden
University of Florida
Political scientist,
East Africa

Ali Mazrui
State University of New York,
Binghamton
Political scientist,
East Africa

Sally Falk Moore
Harvard University
Anthropologist, lawyer, East
Africa

V. Y. Mudimbe
Duke University
Philosopher, novelist, poet,
Central Africa

Roland Oliver
School of Oriental and African
Studies, University of London
Historian

Abdul Sheriff
Zanzibar Indian Ocean Research
Institute
Historian, East Africa

Wim Van Binsbergen
University of Leiden,
Netherlands
Anthropologist, philosopher,
Southern Africa

Jan Vansina
University of Wisconsin
Historian, Central Africa

CONSULTANTS

Kelly Askew
University of Michigan
Anthropologist, musicologist,
East Africa

Karin Barber
University of Birmingham
Historian, West Africa

Julia Clancy-Smith
University of Arizona
Historian, North Africa

Mamadou Diouf
Columbia University
Anthropologist, historian, West
Africa

Toyin Falola
University of Texas, Austin
Historian, West Africa

Richard Fardon
School of Oriental and African
Studies, University of London
Anthropologist, Central Africa

Gillian Feeley-Harnik
University of Michigan
Anthropologist, Madagascar

Peter Geschiere
University of Amsterdam
Anthropologist, Central Africa

Michelle Gilbert
Sarah Lawrence College
Art historian, West Africa

Jane Guyer
Johns Hopkins University
Historian, West Africa

Andrew Hill
Yale University
Paleontologist, East Africa

Michael Lambek
University of Toronto
Anthropologist, East Africa

George Nelson
University of Liverpool
Medicine, East/West Africa

Kimani Njogu
Twaweza Communications,
Nairobi
Director, linguist, East Africa

John Peel
School of Oriental and African
Studies, University of
London
Anthropologist, West Africa

Paul Richards
Wageningen University and
Research Centre,
Netherlands
Geographer, West Africa

Janet Roitman
University of Paris
Anthropologist,
Central Africa

Parker Shipton
Boston University
Anthropologist, East Africa

Thomas Spear
University of Wisconsin
Historian, East Africa

Dorothy Woodson
Yale University
Librarian, Africa

DA GAMA, VASCO. *See* **Gama, Vasco da.**

DAKAR. Dakar stands as the most populous city of the Republic of Senegal, with more than 1 million people in the city itself, or approximately 10 percent of the national population, and nearly 2.5 million residents in the urban area, according to 2004 figures. As the westernmost point on the African continent, Dakar serves as a gateway between West Africa, Europe, and the Americas. A rocky plateau on the Cape Verde peninsula, Dakar gained prominence in the twentieth century as the capital of French West Africa and one of the colony's most important commercial ports. Members of the Lebou ethnic group originally inhabited this region. They gave the fishing village the name Ndaxaru.

A French settlement had grown on Gorée Island, off the coast of the peninsula, since the seventeenth century. In the 1850s, officer Pinet-Laprade developed a plan for building a model colonial city. He envisioned Dakar as the new capital of the African empire and the most strategic location for commercial expansion in West Africa. In 1857 the governor approved of plans to pursue acquiring land for France and constructing a fort at Dakar. In addition, a steamship company acquired the rights to establish a route between France and Brazil with a stopover in Dakar. They began the construction of a new sea port to accommodate transatlantic travel. By the end of the nineteenth century, France completed plans to construct a railway linking Dakar to Saint-Louis, the Atlantic port city along the Senegal River. In 1902 France transferred the headquarters of the Government General of French West Africa from Saint-Louis to Dakar. This marked the end of the phase of territorial conquest and the beginning of the consolidation of French colonial rule.

The population of Dakar changed significantly in character between 1850 and 1960. The Lebou were not forcibly removed but remained on the outskirts of the plateau, since African housing was prohibited in that part of town. When a 1914 cholera epidemic swept through the town, African housing was burned and the inhabitants removed to an outlying village called Medina. French settlement increased significantly in the period between World War I and World War II. French shopkeepers, professionals, and agents for commercial firms moved to the city. Increasingly, Lebanese immigrants settled in Dakar and opened retail businesses making it the town with the largest number of Europeans and Lebanese in West Africa. The plateau grew with the creation of a Catholic cathedral, administrative buildings, hospitals, schools, and European residences. Residential segregation became a feature of urban planning, however. After World War II economic expansion led to the creation of middle- and upper-class neighborhoods along the coastal cornice beyond the Medina. With the end of colonial rule in 1960, Dakar became the capitol of the Republic of Sénégal. In the twenty-first century the city faces challenges familiar to many urban African environments: overpopulation, underemployment, and a decaying and outdated urban infrastructure. Yet Dakar continues to serve as one of the most vibrant, cosmopolitan, and strategically important cities on the African continent.

See also **Colonial Policies and Practices: French West and Equatorial Africa; Gorée; Saint-Louis; Senegal.**

BIBLIOGRAPHY

Clark, Andrew F., and Lucie Colvin. "Dakar." *Historical Dictionary of Senegal.* Metuchen, NJ: Scarecrow Press, 1994.

Cruise O'Brien, Rita. *White Society in Black Africa: The French of Senegal.* Evanston, IL: Northwestern University Press, 1972.

Johnson, G. Wesley. *The Emergence of Black Politics in Senegal: The Struggle for Power in the Four Communes.* Stanford, CA: Stanford University Press, 1971.

HILARY JONES

DANCE

This entry includes the following articles:
AESTHETICS
SOCIAL MEANING

AESTHETICS

Just as "There is no single entity called American Indian Dance" (Farnell 2003), there is no single entity called African Dance, nor can a single unit of dancing from the African continent be called by that name, because there are several thousand indigenous peoples living in Africa, each having their own distinct dances and ways of moving. The dances of urban Swahili-speaking peoples in Mombasa, or in Cairo, the *Sokodae*, the Ewe *Agbakɔ* the Venda, Lugbara death dances, the Nafana *Dance of the Bedu Moon*, are as different from each other as tap dancing is from Martha Graham technique. Just as there is no single entity called "African dance," no single aesthetic identifies or defines them all.

The dances of Africa may be ceremonial, sacred, political, or social, but in different ways, they all honor dancing as a major form of recognition, celebration, expression, healing, and communication.

All are representations of cultural and ethnic continuities as well as innovations. The dances affirm and perpetuate ways of life and beliefs that are important to the specific peoples to whom they belong. Some dances in Africa celebrate family, clan, or life-cycle events; some are seasonal (such as agricultural dances). Some dances are healing, some ward off evil, and some recall the particular events of (or prepare for) war. Dances and dancing, together with music, poetry, drama, weaving, painting, and sculpture, are embodiments of indigenous cultural values and identity.

During the colonization process in Africa, missionaries, governmental agencies, and western educators tried to suppress indigenous African practices, or they tried to bend these practices towards "assimilation." More recently, dances are manipulated and changed to satisfy international tourist industries. For colonizers, the dances of Africa were not "civilized," nor were they aesthetically pleasing. They were (often) considered time-consuming practices that interfered with a dominant culture's work ethic. Sometimes, dancing became a punishable offense. Many dances were subjected to prohibitions of some kind, with the result that some were "hidden." That is, they were performed on holidays belonging to the dominant culture's calendar, or they were performed when members of the dominant culture weren't aware of the performances.

A clear lack of correspondence between Western notions of aesthetics and African situations comes through examining Egyptian cinema and television, because there are many places in Africa where dancing is governed by the same hierarchy that governs musical performances throughout Islam, ranging from "legitimate/*halal*" through "controversial" to the "illegitimate/*haram*" or "forbidden" categories, not because of any intrinsic qualities of the music itself, but because it is associated with unacceptable contexts. Dancing, too, is condemned for the activities that often precede it (drinking; drug-taking), or follow it (illicit sex). "Egyptian filmmaking was ahead of [filmmaking] in other Arab speaking countries owing to its more advanced level of technological and economic development and to indigenous Egyptian nationalism" (Franken 1996, 270). Egypt's indigenous dances are frequently staged folklorically—with considerable European influence.

Ngoma (dances of the Swahili-speaking peoples of Mombasa, Kenya) are characterized by a stratified town culture of many centuries duration. *Waungwana* rituals and ceremonies, *lelemama* (an adult married women's dance), and *Maulidi* (recitations, with characteristic moves) are performed on important occasions, These are three of the status-laden activities performed throughout Swahili-speaking society. At the other end of the social scale are *uta* and *mwaribe*; both *watwana* (low status) dances.

In Ghana, the *Sokodae* commemorates the occasion when Dente (a high divinity) freed the Ntwumuru people from the Juabens (Ashanti), resulting in two sections of the dance (*Kowurobenye* and *Kumumuwuru*) being performed throughout the Krachi area of Ghana, known as the Krachi Flying Dance. *Sokodae* is considered to be in the hands of the chief who can command its performance for special occasions whenever he chooses. It is often performed for funeral occasions, such as the death of an *Asafohene* (head man). In this dance, the use of an extended metaphor of weaver birds communicates ideas about social relationships and divisions of labor Throughout Africa, dances can be seen as attempts to classify, categorize, and explain a people's attempts to embody their knowledge about life experience using movement, color, shape, and sound metonymically derived from other creatures and from nature.

There is no single aesthetic that identifies or defines the many dances of Africa:

> It is *assumed* that there is a general underlying metaphysical 'aesthetic' that is instantiated in both artistic and aesthetic experience. This vague assumption is usually taken to imply some sort of unspecified aesthetic *unity*. To repeat, rarely are any *reasons* given in favour of it, despite its implausibility. A unified 'aesthetic' is simply, and remarkably generally, assumed. (Best 1982, emphasis added)

On the whole, there is no distinction made regarding western dances between that which is artistic (meaning, purpose, insights) and aesthetic (elegance, beauty, ugliness, tragedy, comedy). Using this distinction, it would be easy to write about either characteristic of indigenous dances, provided one knows the language, classifications and categories of the people to whom the dances belong.

Tranceformations (Glasser 1996) is a contemporary South African choreographic work that draws inspiration from a deeply informed understanding of traditional San ritual practices. The bushman metaphor for trance is death. They describe the trance itself as half death, remarking on the similarity between the "dying shaman [in trance] and an antelope, especially an eland, dying from the effects of a poisoned arrow. Both the shaman and the eland tremble violently, stagger, lower their heads, bleed from the nose, sweat excessively and finally collapse unconscious" (Lewis-Williams and Dowson 1989, 50–51). These metaphors indicate states or movement descriptions that helped the dancers to depict the trance state physically and otherwise. The identification of San shamans with the eland and the central part elands occupy in the rock art and Bushman mythology provided main themes for *Tranceformations* (Glasser 1996, 302).

Katz, Biesele and St. Denis ask important questions about social change and the ownership and authenticity of dances when performance contexts change, saying that:

> The situation with the |Uihaba Dancers has changed dramatically. When the dance group was first formed and entered the government competitions, people of the |Kae|kae, especially the Ju|'hoansi, were quite pleased. Wearing traditional Ju|'hoan dance outfits, complete with leather garments, beadwork, and dance rattles, the troupe performed dances based on the traditional Ju|'hoan healing dance. The songs were based on both Ju|'hoan healing and initiation songs. However, there was no healing in the dance, nor any *!aia* or behavioral imitations of the *!aia* experience. As Xumi said, "There is no *n|om* in that |Uihaba dance. It's meant only as a dance."...By 1989 the Ju|'hoansi are no longer even "assistants." Their presence has become peripheral....Most devastating to the Ju|'hoan people, especially those who had eagerly supported the |Uihaba Dancers, is that the prize money won by the group in the competitions never leaves the school grounds....Is the |Uihaba dance group helping to preserve Ju|'hoan traditions, as the government seems to think? From the evidence in 1989, we are doubtful. The troupe, in fact, may be diluting the healing dance (Katz *et al* 1997, 77–79).

See also **Masks and Masquerades; Music; Religion and Ritual.**

BIBLIOGRAPHY

Blacking, John. "Songs, Dances, Mimes and Symbolism of Venda Girls' Initiations Schools." *African Studies* 28(1): 3–35 [Part 1]; 28(2): 69–118 [Part 2]; 28(3): 149–199 [Part 3]; 28(4): 215–266.

Blacking, John. "Songs and Dances of the Venda People." In *Music and Dance*, ed. David Tunley. Perth: University of Western Australia, 1982.

Chernoff, John M. *African Rhythm and African Sensibility*. Chicago: University of Chicago Press, 1979.

Evans-Pritchard, Edward E. "The Dance (Azande)." *Africa* 1, no. 1 (1928): 446–462.

Farnell, Brenda. "North American Indian Dance." In *The Dictionary of American History*, 3rd edition, ed. Stanley I. Kutler. New York: Scribner, 2003.

Franken, Marjorie. "Dance and Status in Swahili Society." *Journal for the Anthropological Study of Human Movement* 7, no. 2 (1992): 77-93.

Franken, Marjorie. "Egyptian Cinema and Television: Dancing and the Female Image." *Visual Anthropology* 8, no. 2–4 (1996): 267–286.

Glasser, Sylvia. "Transcultural Transformations." *Visual Anthropology* 8, no. 2–4 (1996): 287-311.

Glasser, Sylvia. "Is Dance Political Movement?" In *Anthropology and Human Movement: Searching for Origins*, ed. Drid Williams. Lanham, Maryland: Scarecrow Press, 2000.

Gore, Georgiana. "Textual Fields: Representation in Dance Ethnography." In *Dance in the Field: Theory Methods and Issues in Dance Ethnography*, ed. Theresa Buckland. New York: St. Martin's Press, 1999.

Katz, Richard; Megan Biesele; and Verna St. Denis. *Healing Makes Our Hearts Happy: Spirituality and Cultural Transformation Among the Kalahari Ju|'hoansi*. Rochester, New York: Inner Traditions International, 1997.

Lewis-Williams, David, and Thomas Dowson. *Images of Power. Understanding Bushman Rock Art*. Cape Town: Southern Book Publishers, 1989.

Middleton, John. "The Dance among the Lugbara of Uganda." In *Society and the Dance*, ed. Paul Spencer. Cambridge, U.K.: Cambridge University Press, 1985.

Mitchell, Clyde. "The Kalela Dance." *Rhodes Livingston Institute Papers* 27 (1956): 1–52.

Spencer, Paul, ed. "Dance as Antithesis in the Samburu Discourse." In *Society and the Dance*. Cambridge, U.K.: Cambridge University Press, 1985.

Williams, Drid. "The Dance of the Bedu Moon." *African Arts/arts d'afrique* 2, no. 2 (1968): 18–21.

Williams, Drid. "The Sokodae: A West African Dance." *Journal for the Anthropological Study of Human Movement* 7, no. 2 (1992): 114–138.

Williams, Drid. "The Cultural Appropriation of Dances and Ceremonies." *Visual Anthropology* 13 (2000): 345–362.

DRID WILLIAMS

SOCIAL MEANING

That a Zulu *ingoma* dance team performed at the start of the twenty-first century on a cobbled street in the English provincial city of Bath demonstrates that the world now provides opportunities for dances from Africa to be experienced far from that continent. But millennia before modern communications enabled such experience, the world had acknowledged the prominence of the dance in Africa. For example, at the courts of the early Egyptian pharaohs, the best dancers were said to be black Africans; similarly, Greek and Roman writings praised the dancing in northern parts of Africa. In the early Islamic world, the Prophet Muhammad's wife was said to have been spellbound by the dancing of some African slaves. In the mid-nineteenth century, the Scottish missionary and explorer David Livingstone (1813–1873) was so struck by what he saw of the dance among free men in the southern half of the continent that he equated it with their religion.

Such testimony shows both the longevity and the ubiquity of the dance's significance in Africa, but, for those who perform it in the twenty-first century, as well as for global audiences, appreciation of the dance tends to be primarily as a form of entertainment (at which Africans are often thought to excel because they have some innate "sense of rhythm.") More appropriate explanations must include the perspectives of the dancers, but they, too, typically stress the enjoyment and the relief provided by the dance in the often harsh conditions of African everyday life. Doubtless these psychological or cathartic elements do motivate those responding to the lure of the dance, but they tend to obscure its meaning in the specific, local contexts where it is typically performed. Studies of such contexts are available from different disciplines, including social anthropology, the principal source for this entry.

Looking first at the interactions between groups of musicians (often drummers in many parts

Zulu men in traditional costume, performing the foot-stomping, high-kicking dance.
The dance is performed in a row, with the men repeatedly raising their legs as high as possible and then bringing them down with a thunderous stomp that causes the ground to shake. The photos were taken in Zululand, now called KwaZulu/Natal (KwaZulu being the Zulu words meaning "home of the Zulus." © JASON LAURÉ

of Africa) and dancers, the performances clearly require intense cooperation between all participants, including onlookers, who together make a joint product that is itself a lesson in the virtues of collaboration. This lesson is partly recognized in the West African idiom, carried over into some African-American usage, that the dance "cools" all those who share in it. The term may seem odd, given the often frenetic physical activity involved, but it conveys the harmony achieved by performing together, a state sometimes believed to include the natural surroundings in which the dance is enacted—surroundings which may be hostile if not ritually treated through the dance.

This alleviating function of dance therefore featured prominently in older rituals affecting the vital concerns of whole communities, such as producing food, warding off epidemics, waging war, and concluding peace. The cooling idiom is also widely applied in Africa to curing sickness (which is considered to be "hot"). One form of curative dancing, which has proliferated in modern times, treats "spirit possession," an affliction that plagues individuals whose social status appears marginal or deprived and for whom receiving concentrated attention from others through the dance helps to improve their condition.

Although studies concerned mainly with performance (such as those of Joseph Nketia and John Miller Chernoff) assert that the "community dimension is perhaps the essential aspect of African music," they rarely analyze the social composition of the instrumental and dance groups whose performances the authors have observed and sometimes shared. To appreciate more fully this social dimension, one has to systematically answer key questions, such as when, why, and where dances are held, and, above all, who dances for whom at particular times and places. Summary answers to the first three questions are often provided from limited observations and straightforward inquiries: much dancing, particularly the more formal, organized kind, occurs at the life stages of initiation, marriage, and death. These milestones are very important, both for individuals and for the groups to which they belong, so an individual's passage through these stages must be socially supported and validated. Discovering how all this is achieved requires a more intimate knowledge of the prescribed ceremonial sequences into which the dancing must fit, as well as an understanding of the communal significance of the arenas where it is characteristically performed, such as in or around the central cattle-byre among the Zulu and other cattle-keeping peoples.

Answers to the remaining questions about the preexisting social categories and groups from which the dance teams are drawn can generally be found in the works of social anthropologists; relatively few published articles address these topics, however. For predominantly rural, traditional societies, the best readily available examples are John Middleton (1985) on the Lugbara of Uganda, Paul Spencer (1985) on the Samburu of Kenya, and John Blacking (1985) on the Venda of South Africa—all of which are included in a book with a valuable introductory survey by Spencer (1985) of the dance's functions based on ethnographies from many parts of the world. Kazuaki Kurita's innovative DVD, *Connections between the Nyakyusa and the Nkonde from the Viewpoint of Dance and Trade: with Video Data of Dances* (2005), is not in the same anthropological tradition, but it provides unprecedented detail on the interactions between dance teams who move around Nyakyusa and Nkonde territories, often crossing the international boundary between them and thus creating extensive new social networks.

Gender is the most general category for membership in African dance teams. The groups are often single-sex, such as the males that perform the mortuary dances after the death of a prominent, senior male among the Lugbara, or the warriors' dances among the Samburu; similarly, all-female groups are conspicuous in initiation ceremonies among the Venda. The division is immediately apparent to any observer, but to appreciate its full significance, one needs to know how gender roles are defined in a particular society. Where men and women perform together, their dancing and their singing may themselves express indigenous views of the relationships between the sexes, as for example in the *Sokodae* dance of the Ntwurumu people in Ghana. A division by age may also appear from inspection, but in societies like the Samburu, which have age-sets and age-grades, those systems must be understood to grasp what the status of "warrior" implies and how it is expressed in the dance.

Much more than a visual inspection is needed to show, as Middleton does, that the Lugbara male dancers at mortuary ceremonies belong either to patrilineages affiliated to that of the dead man or to kin categories created by marriages of female members of the dead man's group, such as sisters' sons (who in many African patrilineal societies assume special ceremonial and ritual functions for the groups of their mothers' brothers). A still more precise scrutiny reveals that the men's dancing serves to reemphasize, indeed reconstitute, the basic ties of descent and affinity which form Lugbara society. Included in that constitution is competition, as well as cooperation, between the component segments of the society and this, too, is expressed through the men's dance.

The manner of this dancing tries to contain the competition as well as to express it, but it does not always succeed. In some societies—for example, the Nuer, Lugbara, Samburu, and Zulu—fighting between the dance teams sometimes erupts, and initiations, weddings, and funerals can become violent occasions. Indeed, among the Zulu, specifically "to avoid fighting during ceremonies," the crushed roots and leaves of a particular medicinal plant are sprinkled around the homestead before the visitors arrive (Zobolo and Siebert 2005). But such disruptions are relatively unusual: innumerable dances are performed without them. Even when fighting occurs, it is often an expression of the group nature of the dance rather than of individual aggression, and therefore it must be understood largely in sociological terms.

Thus the dance very often expresses ordered opposition between the various component categories or groups that constitute the social system: those organized through descent, kinship, gender, age, residence, territory, and, particularly in modern urban conditions, tribal or ethnic affiliation. Sometimes the dance (and its accompanying song) may be almost the only way in which particular categories can emerge as players on the social scene, as in the striking case from Tamale, Ghana, where Dagomba children's dance groups are "unbelievably . . . known for singing witty political songs; several times they have been in trouble with local authorities and the national government, and their music is periodically banned" (Chernoff 1979). Such behavior is quite believable in the light of reports from all over the continent of "rituals of rebellion" in which otherwise "submerged" categories periodically appear to challenge the established order through such media as "licentious" dancing and "obscene" or "satirical" songs.

Typically, however, such challenges do not subvert that order. In fact, authorities often deliberately use the dance to reinforce their positions, organizing dances that assemble large crowds of people, thus demonstrating and reinforcing the status of those who called them together. Among the Venda, a dance "performance often expressed the political power of its sponsor." (Blacking 1985; see also Nketia 1975). At the same time, it helps to show that "a chief is a chief by the people," in the southern African saying, and he may be required to show his fitness to rule by dancing himself before his people (Chernoff 1979). This frequent association with leadership also reflects the need for preliminary planning, organization, and resources: even in the more egalitarian societies of Africa (such as the Nuer), formal public dances require considerable preparation by more senior people and the active support of many others. Among the Nyakyusa and Nkonde, men of ordinary origins may acquire status and influence that would not otherwise be available to them as teachers of the dance.

Dances therefore also show that those responsible for producing them have the necessary skills and means for success, while at the same time conveying to all participants the values and rewards of joint activity. Even the more informal dancing, going on all the time (especially at night) everywhere on the continent, is not only a spontaneous expression of high spirits, but also a process of teaching and learning, usually starting in infancy, that has important social implications.

Seen in such closer perspectives, the dance "cools" its participants by promoting, maintaining, or restoring harmonious relationships between them and with their environment, including those spiritual beings who are often believed to control it. But these irenic purposes do not exclude another major feature of African dancing, which is to express self-assertion, competition, and rivalry—even aggression and hostility.

The assertive, competitive aspects are apparent in the dance forms that encourage individuals to display their own skill and prowess, such as the dramatic *ukugiya* of the Zulu in South Africa (or *gaya* among the Venda) in which team members take turns executing demanding routines, often accompanied by their praise-names (*izibongo*) which are recited by themselves, by other team members, or by spectators. Such displays can showcase the best young male performers who may become leaders among their peers, not only in the dance but also in other social and political contexts. These competitions also give men a chance to display their attractions to young women, who often comprise most of the audience. Similarly, in their dances, young women may establish rank among themselves (particularly through composing songs for the dances) while showing their charms to potential suitors among the watching men.

In many traditional dances, the participants enhance their display by imitating striking features from the natural environment, particularly wild creatures or domestic animals (as in the classic case of the Nuer and other Nilotic peoples). The dancers also take whatever finery the environment offers them, such as skins, tails, feathers, shells, and paint, with which they make their costumes and color their bodies. Particularly in western Africa, the costume may include the masks that have acquired a global reputation as examples of African art, but largely away from the original context of those masquerades performed by associations with complex social, political, and religious functions in the communities where they occur.

Much of this competition and display has persisted through all the modern transformations of the dance in Africa. Both elements feature conspicuously in the dancing that emerged in the preindustrial coastal and inland towns of West Africa, where groups such as the Fante *asafo* companies were based on sections of the towns, and again in the remarkably similar *mbeni* teams that represented wards of the East African Swahili towns. Imitations of *mbeni* eventually spread over large parts of the interior, with the composition of the teams reflecting whatever social units were locally significant in both rural communities and in the new towns that emerged on the Copperbelt, where the version known as *kalela* became the subject of the first sustained sociological analysis of the dance (Mitchell 1956). Again, in South Africa, migrants from the rural areas to the new industrial and commercial centers created their own dance groups, such as the *ngoma* teams of the Zulu and the Venda. These teams emerged from preexisting "home-mate" ties between men from the same rural area of origin, and they often competed against each other in quite

elaborately organized public entertainments, attracting large audiences.

The example of similar dance groups among men of northern Sotho origins, working in Johannesburg and elsewhere, eventually influenced women with broadly similar ethnic backgrounds, who had also migrated to the towns, to organize and perform their own versions of such *kiba* dancing. This novel development enabled Deborah James (2000) to analyze the multiple and changing aspects of the female (as well as the male) experience of rural and urban life, as expressed through their songs, dances, and elaborate costumes. The wide appeal of their performances, transcending ethnic and social boundaries, culminated in the appearance of one group among the various musical acts celebrating the inauguration of President Nelson Mandela in 1994. So an originally local form of display and entertainment, devised by these women, reached national and international audiences.

At a different social level, beginning in the mid-twentieth century among the emergent African elites in cities like Johannesburg, the popularity of ballroom dance championships showed how competitive dancing established prestige and status for individuals. In the continent's innumerable bars and nightclubs, dancers now are not only "doing their own thing," but they are also often performing for the admiring attention of other patrons. They earn accolades through their skilful, stylish movements and also through the expensive, fashionable clothes that have replaced skins and feathers but communicate essentially the same message, because, as one Zairian participant remarked in a television interview, "Appearance is very important in Africa" (Chernoff 1979).

Finally, everything discussed in this entry suggests that the dance is simultaneously a conspicuous, dramatic, exciting display of individual prowess and skill as well as an ordered, regulated, cooperative assertion of group identity and cohesion. These and other functions account for much of the prominence and persistence of dance in Africa, noticed by so many observers over such a long period of time. The expanding influence of African dance throughout the rest of the modern world merits further study from a wider perspective that will probably provide, inter alia, other reasons for the presence of that Zulu team in Bath.

See also **Festivals and Carnivals; Johannesburg; Livingstone, David; Masks and Masquerades; Music; Spirit Possession.**

BIBLIOGRAPHY

Argyle, John. "Kalela, Beni, Asafo, Ingoma and the Rural-Urban Dichotomy." In *Tradition and Transition in Southern Africa*, ed. Patrick McAllister and Andrew Siegel. Johannesburg: University of the Witwatersrand Press, 1991.

Blacking, John. "Movement, Dance, Music, and the Venda Girls' Initiation Cycle." In *Society and the Dance: The Social Anthropology of Process and Performance*, ed. Paul Spencer. Cambridge, U.K.: Cambridge University Press, 1985.

Chernoff, John Miller. *African Rhythm and African Sensibility.* Chicago: University of Chicago Press, 1979.

Connections between the Nyakyusa and the Nkonde from the Viewpoint of Dance and Trade: with Video Data of Dances. Directed by Kazuaki Kurita. Rikkyo University, Center for Human Migration and Acculturation Studies, 2005.

Erlmann, Velt. *Nightsong: Performance, Power, and Practice in South Africa.* Chicago: University of Chicago Press, 1996.

James, Deborah. *Songs of the Women Migrants: Performance and Identity in South Africa.* New York: Columbia University Press, 2000.

James, Deborah. "Pedi Women's Kiba Performance." In *The World of South African Music: A Reader*, ed Lucia C. Amersham. Newcastle-upon-Tyne, U.K.: Cambridge Scholars' Press, 2005.

Levine, Laurie. *The Drumcafé's Traditional Music of South Africa.* Johannesburg: Jacana Media, 2005.

Lewis, Ioan. *Ecstatic Religion.* Harmondsworth, U.K.: Penguin, 1971.

Middleton, John. "The Dance among the Lugbara of Uganda." In *Society and the Dance: The Social Anthropology of Process and Performance*, ed. Paul Spencer. Cambridge, U.K.: Cambridge University Press, 1985.

Mitchell, Clyde J. *The Kalela Dance.* Rhodes-Livingstone Papers, no. 27. Manchester, U.K.: Manchester University Press, 1956.

Nketia, Joseph Hanson Kwabena. *The Music of Africa.* London: Gollancz, 1975.

Ranger, Terence. *Dance and Society in Eastern Africa, 1890–1970.* London: Heinemann, 1975.

Spencer, Paul. "Dance as Antithesis in the Samburu Discourse." In *Society and the Dance: The Social Anthropology of Process and Performance*, ed. Paul Spencer. Cambridge, U.K.: Cambridge University Press, 1985.

Spencer, Paul. "Introduction: Interpretations of the Dance in Anthropology." In *Society and the Dance: The Social Anthropology of Process and Performance*, ed. Paul Spencer. Cambridge, U.K.: Cambridge University Press, 1985.

Thomas, Jeffrey H. "Ingoma Dancers and Their Response to Town." M.A. thesis. University of Natal, Durban, 1988.

Wachsmann, Klaus. *Essays on Music and History in Africa.* Evanston, IL: Northwestern University Press, 1971.

Williams, Drid. *The Sokodae: A West African Dance.* London: Institute for Cultural Research, no. 7 Octagon Press, 1971.

Zobolo, Alpheus, and Stefan Siebert. "Establishing an Indigenous Knowledge Garden at the University of Zululand." *The Conservatory* (April 2005).

JOHN ARGYLE

DANQUAH, JOSEPH KWAME KYERETWI BOAKYE

(1895–1965). The Ghanaian lawyer and nationalist Joseph Kwame Kyeretwi Boakye Danquah is credited with influencing the choice of "Ghana" as the country's name after independence. Known to the people of Ghana as "J.B.," he is remembered as the principal opposition leader against Kwame Nkrumah and as a man who loved his people and the principles of democracy and individual freedom. He was born at Bepong, Kwahu, son of Emmanuel Yaw Boakye Danquah, the chief state drummer of Naha Amoako Atta II, Omanhene (paramount chief) of Akyem Abuakwa.

Born in Gold Coast (present-day Ghana) in December of 1875 to a prominent family, Danquah was educated at Basel Mission Schools at Kyebi and at Begoro in Akyem Abuakwa. in 1921 he went on to study at the University of London, becoming, in 1927, the first African to obtain a Ph.D. in philosophy from a British university. In addition, he took up the study of law. His wife, Mabel Dove Danquah (also of Gold Coast), was the first woman elected to an African legislature and a pioneer in West African literature.

In 1928, while still in London, Danquah published *Akim Abuakwa Handbook, Akan Laws and Customs and the Akim Abuakwa Constitution*, and *Cases in Akan Law*. On his return to the Gold Coast in 1931, he founded the *West African Times*, later the *Times of West Africa*. Danquah entered politics as one of the founders of the United Gold Coast Convention (UGCC) in 1947. On March 13, 1948, he, along with Francis Nwia Kofi Nkrumah and four other founding members of UGCC, was arrested and exiled to the Northern Territories. After rioting by students and others in protest of this action, the government was finally forced to relent and on April 12 reversed their decision, permitting Danquah and his colleagues to return home.

In 1949 Danquah became a member of the Coussey Committee appointed to consider constitutional reforms that might lead to political independence in the Gold Coast colony. The ties between Danquah and Nkrumah were broken because of disagreement over policy. In 1951 Danquah was elected to the Legislative Assembly for Akyem Abuakwa, the first rural member of the Gold Coast parliament. In 1954 and 1956 he lost elections in which he ran for the UGCC and the National Liberation Movement, respectively. In 1960, Danquah ran for the office of president against Nkrumah, who had held that office since Ghana's independence, but he captured only 10 percent of the vote. In 1961, Danquah was imprisoned under the Preventive Detention Act, which he had opposed vehemently in parliament. He was released on January 22, 1962, and chosen as president of the Ghana Bar Association but continued to attack the Nkrumah regime and was again arrested and imprisoned on January 8, 1964. In prison he was chained to the bare floor, given no food for days on end, and endured other severe mistreatment. On February 4, 1965, he died while still in prison, of a heart attack.

See also **Ghana: History and Politics; Nkrumah, Francis Nwia Kofi.**

BIBLIOGRAPHY

Akyeampong, H. K., comp. *The Undying Memories of a Gallant Man: Tribute to the Late Dr. Joseph Boakye Danquah, the Doyen of Ghanaian Politicians.* Accra: State Publishing Corporation, 1967.

Owusa-Ansah, David, and Daniel M. McFarland. *Historical Dictionary of Ghana*, Lanham, MD: Scarecrow Press, 2005.

GARY THOULOUIS

DAR ES SALAAM.   The port city of Dar es Salaam (the name means "haven of peace") is the largest city in Tanzania and, until 1996, it was the nation's capital. Although the official capital is now the more centrally located city of Dodoma, Dar es Salaam continues to be Tanzania's preeminent city and many of the government's more important facilities and administrative offices remain there.

Archaeological evidence indicates that fishing and agricultural villages occupied the area as early as the eighth century. Dar es Salaam was created by Swahili Arabs who came from the Benadir coast (modern Somalia) in the seventeenth century. They consolidated several fishing villages clustered around a large and safe harbor and named the new urban settlement Mzizima (which means "healthy town"). The real growth of the city did not begin until Sultan Sayyid Majid of Zanzibar built a palace and a few buildings there in the late 1860s. In 1862 the sultan changed the name of the city to Dar es Salaam. By 1867 the population of the town was about 900.

The German East Africa Company set up a trading station in Dar es Salaam in 1888. In 1891 the German government named Dar es Salaam the capital of its colony of German East Africa, and began constructing administration buildings, a Catholic cathedral, a Lutheran church, and a casino. As a colonial capital, the city was the administrative headquarters of a territory that extended 600 miles west to Lake Tanganyika and included the modern states of Rwanda and Burundi. At the beginning of the twentieth century the Germans also built a railroad from Dar es Salaam along the northern caravan route to Tabora, with branches going to Lake Tanganyika and Lake Victoria.

The British captured Dar es Salaam in 1916, and the German colony was assigned to the city after World War I as the League of Nations mandated territory of Tanganyika. The city spread out from around the harbor, especially after 1930, when the British built the Selander Bridge to make the northern suburbs more accessible. Growth continued after World War II, and during the Korean War (1951–1953) the city expanded as a result of a boom in the local sisal industry. According to the 1957 census, 128,742 people lived in Dar es Salaam, of whom nearly 75 percent were African and nearly 20 percent were Indian. Three-quarters of the population were Muslim.

Tanganyika became independent in 1961, and it joined with Zanzibar in 1964 to form the United Republic of Tanzania, with Dar es Salaam as the national capital. In 1974 Dodoma was proposed as a more suitable capital, and the government began moving in 1980. The Chama Cha Mapinduzi, Tanzania's ruling party during the pre-1995 one-party state, established its party headquarters in Dodoma, but legislative and administrative functions remained in Dar es Salaam. One year later, Dodoma was officially declared the new capital, but a total relocation of government offices has been deemed too expensive to complete.

Dar es Salaam's main market is called Kariakoo. The market is located near the center of town, near most of the government buildings. The industrial districts are concentrated along the rail lines near the main station and adjacent to the southern end of the harbor. Foreign embassies line the road leading north from the city, and the University of Dar es Salaam, the national university, is at the furthest reaches of the municipality in the north, about 7.5 miles from the center.

By 2004 Dar es Salaam and its suburbs had an aggregate population of 3.8 million. Private business have grown; roads have been widened and repaved; and night clubs, casinos, restaurants—even a luxury Sheraton hotel—have opened, all signs of Dar es Salaam's growing, albeit modest, prosperity. However, the city has also suffered some serious setbacks, including the 1998 terrorist attack on the U.S. embassy there.

See also **Archaeology and Prehistory: Historical; Colonial Policies and Practices: German; Nyerere, Julius Kambarage; Tanzania.**

BIBLIOGRAPHY

Freeman-Grenville, G. S. P. *The New Atlas of African History.* New York: Simon and Schuster, 1991.

Loire, Georges. *Gens de mer à Dar-es-Salaam.* Paris: Karthala, 1993.

Thomas F. McDow

DARFUR. *See* **Sudan: Wars.**

DE KLERK, FREDERIK WILLEM

(1936–). Frederik Willem De Klerk was born in Johannesburg on March 18, 1936. His father, Jan de Klerk, had been a cabinet minister and president of the Senate of the then Union of South Africa. De Klerk graduated B.A. and L.L.B. (cum laude) from Potchefstroom University for Christian Higher Education in 1958. He was an attorney at Vereeniging (1961–1972), where he was active in the National Party (NP). He was elected member of Parliament for Vereeniging in the by-election of 1972 and was returned, unopposed, in the general election of 1974. From April 1978 de Klerk held cabinet portfolios that included Posts and Telecommunications; Mining, Environmental Planning, and Energy; Home Affairs; and National Education. He became head of the NP in February 1989 and was elected president of South Africa in September 1989, serving until April 1994. De Klerk was co-recipient, with Nelson Mandela, of the Nobel Peace Prize in 1993, owing to the ending of minority rule in South Africa that the two negotiated.

Prior to becoming president in 1989, de Klerk was something of an unknown quantity. Over the years, he underwent a gradual political conversion from an overcautious approach to politics to fearless entrepreneurship, from ultraconservatism to outspoken enlightenment (*verligtheid*), from ideological correctness to open, critical pragmatism and realism. He came of age, politically, in an era in which he felt himself neither shackled to the baggage of past National Party commitment to absolute racial separation (apartheid) nor historically bound to continue what became outdated policies. De Klerk sought advice from civilians rather than the military, which was a sea change for South Africa at the time. Faced by growing violence by Africans excluded from the political process and by growing international isolation, he embarked on the most radical period of political reform the nation had experienced.

No other NP leader had broken so fundamentally with party orthodoxy. De Klerk permitted peaceful mass demonstrations by extra-parliamentary groups; in October 1989, he released eight long-term prisoners belonging to the African National Congress (ANC); on February 2, 1990, he started negotiations on South Africa's future with the ANC, the Pan-Africanist Congress, the South African Communist Party, and allied organizations representing formerly excluded African and Asian residents of the Republic. On February 11, 1990, de Klerk released Nelson Mandela, the near-legendary ANC leader and martyr, from prison; subsequently, he initiated several meetings between the government and the ANC on the transitional process that led to the Groote Schuur Minute (May 1990) and the Pretoria Minute (August 1990). He also headed the government delegation to the Convention for a Democratic South Africa (December 1991–December 1993), the constitutive assembly that charted a democratic course for the nation's future. In May 1994 he became second executive-deputy president in the resulting government of national unity, from which he resigned in June 1996 to reposition the NP (which he still led) for the next election in 1999. In 2004 he quit the party, however, when it announced that it would merge with the ANC, and declared that he would be seeking a new political base from which to work.

Through the efforts of de Klerk and others, the South African state dismantled apartheid in a relatively short period of time, thereby opening the path to socioeconomic reconstruction and reconciliation, and devising a new political order in which race has no role in determining life chances of citizens. Knowing at the outset that these actions would do away with the exclusive hold on political power that he and the NP had previously enjoyed, he nonetheless used his party office to pursue this course from a position of relative strength.

See also **Apartheid; Mandela, Nelson; South Africa, Republic of: Society and Cultures.**

BIBLIOGRAPHY

De Klerk, Willem. *F. W. de Klerk: The Man in His Time.* Johannesburg: J. Ball, 1991.

Gastrow, Sheila. *Who's Who in South African Politics.* London and New York: Has Zell Publishers, 1993.

Hayes, S. V., ed. *Who's Who of Southern Africa, 1995/96.* Edison, NJ: Hunter Publishing Inc., 1995.

DENIS VENTER

DEATH, MOURNING, AND ANCESTORS.

Among the many paradoxes of death is that people cope with this universal experience in so many different ways. Africanist scholars have made significant contributions to our understanding of the universality and particularity of death and mourning by studying how people define the concepts of life and death and relate them to their ideas and practices of personhood or identity, embodiment, and the creating and breaking of social ties; how funerals are connected to the economic and political dynamics of families, communities, ethnicities, and nations; and how, through their handling of death and mourning, people attempt to resolve the problems of evil, injustice, and other intractable ethical and moral issues. The diversity of African practices since prehistoric times testifies to the long-standing awareness and interest of people throughout the continent in how one can comprehend the ultimate mystery of life: death. People in Africa have their share of explanations for the origins of death in the world and for the deaths of specific individuals, explanations that range from the philosophical, proverbial, apocryphal, theological, or mythical to the social and somatic. Case studies show that people usually draw on many ways of trying to understand the personal, social, and cosmic catastrophes involved in death. A Rwandan saying expresses the social complexity of death in these words: People who die are not buried in a field, they are buried in the heart.

DEATH, MOURNING, AND IDENTITY

The publicity or secrecy that surrounds death, and our knowledge of this sensitive topic, testifies to its intimate connections with ideas of identity and body, relations of power and authority, and theories of evil and injustice, wealth, and poverty. Thus, for some people—such as the Lugbara living in northwestern Uganda and northeastern Democratic Republic of the Congo in the 1950s—death was a familiar experience and given great importance. The Lugbara then lived in densely populated rural settlements where deaths occurred daily and publicly, in that they were known, if not witnessed. Their funeral rites— longer and more elaborate than rites for birth, puberty, or marriage—involved large numbers of people beyond the immediate family and lineage of the deceased. The publicity of the funeral was essential to the transformation of the dead person into a spirit whose name would be remembered by his or her living descendants for many generations after. Important elders, male and female, were commemorated in fig trees that were planted at the heads of graves, and in small slabs of granite, sometimes put together to form house-like structures. The trees and stones served as shrines where the descendants of the dead could continue to consult them. The most senior elders lost their ties to any one location and became merged with Adroa, the Creator. Lugbara mortuary rites, which could extend over many years, enacted the relationship between human beings and the Creator while contributing to the power of the living people who served as intermediaries.

Other people, such as the Mbeere of Kenya, who lived in small, dispersed, and highly mobile settlements before British colonial rule in Kenya, left corpses in the surrounding bushland with little ceremony. Yet the Mbeere began to develop elaborate funerals in the 1920s, together with new ways of reckoning kinship and ancestry, in response first to the British government's requirement in 1930 that they bury their dead, and then in response to shifts in land-tenure regulations from corporate groups to individuals in the late 1960s. The new burials became landmarks testifying to the ownership of the territories in which they were located. The visible memorials also served as tributes to the authority of particular leaders and the political and economic strength of their supporters.

Urbanites in contemporary Nigeria and Ghana, crowded among strangers, may read all about the

Two trees in a coastal village in northwestern Madagascar, dedicated to ancestors. The trees, known as *togny* ("calm," or "peaceful"), are established when a living person raises a particular tree as a place of supplication or remembrance (*fangatahana* or *fahatsiarovana*). PHOTOGRAPH BY GILLIAN FEELEY-HARNIK, APRIL 1973

deaths and burials of prominent citizens in long, detailed obituaries in the daily papers. Although some readers dismiss these obituaries as obnoxious junk journalism, others support them as the deserved rewards of good citizens; variations in class, ethnicity, and religion contribute to the diversity of views. Wealthy people can place obituaries in all the media, from television and radio to full-page announcements with pictures in the daily and weekly papers, whereas poor people who cannot afford the cost of preserving bodies in hospitals or mortuaries rely mainly on radio. Muslims who must bury their dead within hours also prefer radio announcements. They are reluctant to reproduce images of the deceased in newspapers or television, and tend to have different values of worldly success than those displayed in most of the written accounts.

In Nigeria, as in Cameroon, Ghana, Bénin, Botswana, Kenya, and elsewhere, death notices provide details concerning burials, which have become increasingly important occasions for creating and consolidating relations among surviving family, friends, patrons, and clients. In the ensuing months and years, notices called In Memoriam may commemorate the dead. These longer accounts enable surviving kin to celebrate their rising social status through the so-called career path of the deceased. Contemporary Nigerian obituaries express ideologies of individualism and consumerism related to recent historical events, such as the oil boom of the 1980s. Yet there, as elsewhere, the publicity surrounding the deaths of community leaders also draws on older ideals of individual political and economic initiative. The Giriama of coastal Kenya, for example, have long celebrated the entrepreneurial prowess of their renowned traders, who are commemorated in carved hardwood posts as models of "what fellow Giriama have been, and can be" (Parkin 1991).

Our scholarly knowledge of death, mourning, and ancestry in Africa suggests a similarly complex mix of celebrated, overlooked, and hidden ideas and practices, reflecting diversities of interests among participants and observers alike. Most of the published studies come from West and Central Africa and from Madagascar, then East Africa. Until the abolition of apartheid in South Africa in 1994, there were relatively few studies from Southern Africa. Yet recent historical research shows that dignifying

death in funerals was the commonest way of asserting their humanity and cultural autonomy for residents of Bulawayo in colonial Southern Rhodesia (present-day Zimbabwe) since the 1890s and for Basotho mineworkers in South Africa in 1890–1940.

Thus, consideration of the social, spiritual, and political-economic issues involved in publicizing some deaths entails equal attention to why other deaths may seem to have been forgotten. Beginning in the 1980s, Nuer military leaders of the Sudanese People's Liberation Army began to gain the cooperation of new recruits and civilian villagers by persuading them that their killing in Sudan's civil war carried no risk of the pollution associated with intraethnic homicide in local feuding. Sharon Hutchinson (1998) argues that "the fluctuating strength of politico-military power networks in the region has varied directly in relation to ordinary people's willingness to accept, however reluctantly, that some slain relatives will be consigned to a kind of social and spiritual 'oblivion'." In post-genocide Rwanda, resettled villagers have adopted a kind of amnesia in order to deal with particular memories and to avoid renewed conflict, a strategy that may risk perpetuating the violence by leaving its social sources unexamined and thus circumstances unchanged.

Scholars may draw on personal, as well as professional, knowledge of home regions and family histories in accounting for African funerary practices. Specialists in the study of religion may have degrees in theology or serve in religious institutions. Nationalist debates can complicate disciplinary, theological, and methodological differences in research. Despite the antiquity of Islam in Africa, little has been published on Islamic funerals and mourning practices until recently, when debates over orthodoxy, prompted by the increasing presence of Wahhabi reformists, have inspired studies of death rituals in the Comores, East Africa, and Mozambique.

Religious pluralism throughout Africa is thus an important area for further research. The Bwiti religion of the Fang people in Gabon, now spread into Equatorial Guinea and southern Cameroon, draws on their past ideas and practices concerning death, mourning, and burial, in dialogue with the views of missionaries and government officials, to create a new path of birth and death celebrated in the nightlong liturgies in the chapels through which Bwiti members seek new visions of community and tranquility. Conversion affects both individuals and their communities. Funerals may be the main occasions in which people's several religious and political loyalties are finally sorted out, as in "the sudden death of a millionaire," described by Michelle Gilbert (1988). The arrangements for his burial and commemoration mobilized the populations of the two rival towns to which the deceased belonged by kinship, marriage, and political-economic ties, as well as by rival affiliations to the Presbyterian Church and the non-Christian deity of his father. His conversion was completed only after his death, when the Presbyters claimed him as their convert because they had succeeded in burying him. With his conversion, his hometown and primary kin affiliations were also decided. In other cases, such as with residents of Mochudi in Botswana, people strive for funeral services conducted by several clergy jointly. Recent scholarship shows that funerals in urban Botswana are critical to maintaining civil conduct more broadly, as participants strive to prevent differences from becoming irreconcilable by emphasizing the mutuality of their emotions.

CHANGING RELATIONS OF IDENTITY THROUGH LIFE AND DEATH

Studies of death and mourning in Africa show that an understanding of death requires an understanding of how people conceive of their lives as individuals and in their manifold relations with others. Indeed, individuals' identities are never formed in isolation but derive from their particular relations with others, including nonhuman beings, throughout life and continuing through death. Death severs ties but also creates new relations between the living and the deceased person. The cosmology of the Dogon of Mali is still one of the most famous examples of the complexity of such views, leading to continuing study. According to the Dogon, people have at least eight dimensions, referred to by some scholars as souls. Every child is born with twin female and male aspects related to fertility and bodily strength, one of which is chosen when the other is removed with a part of the genitals (the prepuce or clitoris) at initiation. Children acquire other aspects of their identity from the names they acquire from their patrilineal or matrilineal kin or their peers, including two aspects of so-called

intelligent souls associated with knowledge and will and with *nyama*, the life force that permeates the cosmos; two aspects of shadow souls linked to their place of birth; and praise names associated with their clan and community. As the naming suggests, these aspects of personhood are the substance of social relations, incorporated into a person's bodily being as she or he matures, and also into shrines where people may themselves make offerings for their own or for their family's well-being, of which their own is a part.

The Dogon conceive of death in terms of these dynamic aspects of identity that derive from a person's relations to other people and beings. Only Amma, the creator of life, can bring death by separating the intelligent soul from the body and strangling it. The strangled soul joins the life force, which has left the body through the breath, in the corpse's hair and eventually in its shroud. The relatives of the deceased are able to take the soul and life force from the shroud and put them with the other aspects of the person into a clay shrine called the womb of Amma. In the shrine, the reassembled dimensions of the person can receive the nourishment it needs to regain enough strength to be able to journey back to the creator. The deceased person, but especially his or her life force, continues to nurture the descendants. The deceased person's journey back to Amma may take years to complete, because the concluding sacrificial ritual (*dama*), in which masked dancers relive the event in which death originated, are so elaborate and costly that they are held only after several deaths have occurred.

Funerals take many different forms, varying even in the same community according to differences in such factors as age, gender, ethnicity, class, religious affiliation, and the nature of the death itself. Sudden and untimely deaths are commonly considered bad deaths, warranting a minimal funeral or none at all, whereas longevity, community service, and wealth are widely celebrated. Who buries whom and where the burial occurs vary according to how people reckon their nearest of kin. For example, among the matrilineal Akan peoples of Ghana, grown children should bury their fathers; a husband should pay for the coffin and grave of his wife, but only her father can bury her. Yet complications inevitably arise, including disputes over whether people have proven to be real kin in practice. Susan Reynolds Whyte (2005) argues that, despite the greater attention to the burials of elite men, "it is the burials of ordinary women...that are often most controversial." For example, in contemporary Bunyole in eastern Uganda, where a married woman should be buried at her husband's home, debates may arise over which husband, the nature of their union, whether she was still married when she died, and other such questions. With the onset of the AIDS pandemic, as ever more afflicted women have returned to their natal homes for care, their natal kin now claim the right to bury these women, based on "arguments of affection."

Across such differences, funerals generally involve the preparation of the corpse by washing and other means and its separation from living people, usually by burial. The funeral may coincide with the ritual transformation of the dead person into an ancestor who will remain a social presence even after the living separate from the dead, give thanks to their fellow mourners, and reenter their everyday lives. The length of these stages varies widely, according to different philosophies of the course of death as well as different interests and capacities for preserving the corpse long enough for kin and friends to gather immediately or for later services, an interval prolonged by the widespread use of morgues.

At the end of a funeral, whether it has taken hours, days, weeks, or months, all participants are expected to cleanse themselves. The association of death with filth is widespread in Africa, as elsewhere, though moderated in some areas by Christianity. Typically, pregnant women and young children are considered to be so vulnerable to the deadly filth of death that they are forbidden to attend funerals. Yet other categories of people may be required to handle the filth of death. Just who is expected to do such work—for example, to wash and sometimes shave the body, clean out its orifices and sometimes expel the excrement, cut the fetus from the womb of a woman who died in childbirth (lest the survivors risk sterility or the birth of sickly children), dig and fill the grave or keep it clean later—is a critical issue, serving to illuminate relations of power and authority in other aspects of life. Among the Kaguru of Tanzania, the deceased's *watani*, particularly people related by marriage who have license to joke about

the most forbidden topics, do all this work. The death duties of the *watani* link Kaguru ideas and practices concerning human mortality to the tensions they associate with sexuality and marriage, processes through which the dead are reborn. Among the Kasena of Ghana and Burkina Faso, the *bayaa*, or burial expert, must go through a long arduous initiation before he is allowed to "make death pregnant with life" (Abasi 1995). Such work is now widely commercialized throughout Africa. In Soweto, for example, there has been a tremendous growth of funeral parlors since the 1950s, especially since the spread of HIV/AIDS. Although burial societies have also grown in number, the enormous costs of funerals—for example, in urban Ghana and Cameroon—have provoked intense debates about the morality of many contemporary practices.

Funerary ritual in Africa illuminates the ways in which people achieve their identities as moral beings through the give and take of their relations with others, especially relatives and friends, and how these identities—changing throughout life—are disaggregated and reassorted through giving and receiving in the events of death, burial, mourning, and afterlife. Some people, such as the Dogon of Mali, the LoDagaa of northern Ghana, and the Yoruba of Nigeria, have developed eschatologies involving long, arduous journeys to distant spiritlands, sometimes (as among the LoDagaa) including final judgments on the character of the deceased by Na'angmin, the highest of the deities. Among Muslims in Mayotte, the annual *kuitimia* ritual on behalf of deceased forebears is performed during the month of the pilgrimage to Mecca (*hajj*), opening the passage between the living and the dead for the exchange of prayers and blessings, as well as likening the rigors of the pilgrimage to a kind of living death that may bring about spiritual rebirth.

Similar to the Yoruba and the Igbo (Ibo) and many peoples of Madagascar, but unlike the Lugbara, for example, the Tallensi (Talensi) of the Volta region of Ghana hold that every person has his or her unique destiny, acquired prenatally but closely influenced by the destinies of the child's parents and eventually his or her guardian ancestors. For the Tallensi, destiny is realized on earth, in relations among the living and between the living and the deceased kin who have become their ancestors. Questions of fate, mortality, and responsibility are to be resolved through the interventions of ancestors in the lives of the living.

FUNERALS AND THE CREATION OF ANCESTORS

In the nineteenth century, Africa was stereotyped as the location of cults of the dead, also called ancestor worship. Scholars of the time interpreted such phenomena as the earliest evolutionary stages of religious practice, beginning in small-scale societies based on kinship and ending with world religions in large-scale societies based on contractual relations. Subsequent research has shown that respect for ancestors is widespread and that such evolutionary schemes are unfounded. One of the first insights from the study of African rituals of death and mourning was to confirm the general observation that death alone does not create ancestry. Anthropologist Meyer Fortes's (1906–1983) study of the Tallensi of Ghana in 1945 showed that the Tallensi make a clear distinction between a dead person and an ancestor, as the term was translated for their named, dead forebear whose continuing presence defines the structural positions of his or her descendants in social life. Here, as elsewhere, unmarried or childless people, orphans, the very poor, suicides, criminals, and former slaves, people who have died bad deaths, and those who have died from bad diseases (such as leprosy or elephantiasis) are unlikely to be remembered as ancestors. In contemporary Cameroon, where the spread of Christianity has led to greater acceptance of formerly stigmatized categories of people, ancestors have proliferated as a result. However, a person who has not buried his or her parent well, and who is therefore regarded as a foolish or useless person, is still likely to be socially forgotten.

Fortes wanted to retain the phrase *ancestor worship* to show the similarity of Tallensi practices of serving ancestral forebears to those of the ancient Romans and contemporary Chinese. He also wanted to distinguish all these from the practices of other African peoples such as the Tiv of central Nigeria and the Nuer of the Sudan, who used genealogies of ancestors as social maps of relations among their living descendants but did not emphasize their interaction in everyday life.

Two contemporaneous studies of death and ancestry on the Lugbara and on the LoDagaa confirmed the importance of ideas and practices concerning death and ancestry in political and economic relations among living people. Yet both showed that the importance of ancestry was not limited to domestic life separated from politics. They showed how the powerful elders who actually mediated between living people and their ancestors operated across these domains, thus weakening still further the evolutionary theories of development from kinship to contract in which the notion of ancestor cult had originated. The Lugbara elders who mediated between living people and their forebears were attempting to resolve social contradictions inherent even in the smallest communities and in their own multiple roles as, for example, fathers, husbands, brothers, uncles, or nephews of people living or dead, political representatives of the community, owners of land or cattle, and so on. Thus their interpretations of ancestral intervention, for example in deaths or disputes over land shortages in their densely populated settlements, were never entirely free of the suspicion that they were speaking for themselves rather than for the ancestors representing larger collectivities.

Lugbara recognize several kinds of deceased forebears carefully distinguished by different words in their own language. Efforts to establish common grounds for comparative research on death, mourning, and ancestry in Africa have been fraught with definitional debates over whether to use vernacular terms or translations, and if so, which equivalent terms. Further ethnographic and historical research, together with an intellectual shift away from the dominance of Western models in comparative research, has led most scholars to reject the worship analogy, arguing that the terms *respect* or *veneration* would be more accurate. Similar debates concern whether to use such translations as ancestors, *ancêtres*, the living dead, ghosts, spirits, wraiths, forebears, progenitors, shades, or *Seelen* or retain the vernacular terms.

Precision is essential for understanding the paradoxically embodied disembodiment of ancestral beings, if that is even the most fruitful way to think about their conditions in various circumstances. For example, the Luo of Kenya regard ancestors as whole beings, not as disembodied spirits. Scholars are increasingly trying to understand the phenomena of death and mourning according to the participants' own theories of language and sensory experience. Tombs are usually the fullest statements of these relations. But tombs may be serial (as in first and second burials), and, as the ethnography of Madagascar shows in the most detail, people are constantly transforming them. Furthermore, tombs are almost always associated with numerous other forms and places of continuing interaction between living and ancestral beings, including shrines in the home, neighborhood, or elsewhere; stories, genealogies, or histories, encountered orally through living people or in books; in the phenomenon of spirit possession; in subsequent generations of children who may be named for their ancestors and in whom the ancestral spirits may be believed to be reborn; and in inherited property, known in Zimbabwe as tears of the dead; or in the conception of the Nzima of Ghana of the work of the dead continuing across generations, which is realized in such inheritances as plantations or orchards. The presence of ancestors in everyday life may thus constitute what has been called a veritable landscape of names.

The ancestral screens of the Kalabari people of Rivers State in Nigeria give material and aesthetic form in sculpture to the people's ideas and practices concerning death and ancestry. Most of the screens were made in the early twentieth century, then given to the British colonial government to save from destruction by a local missionary. The carved screens are memorial portraits of the deceased heads of trading houses in the city-state of New Calabar in southern Nigeria. The Kalabari call these memorials *duein fubara* (foreheads of the dead). Their focus on the forehead derives from their conceptions of the several intersecting dimensions of spiritual and other forces or states of being that make up a living person. Among the most important of these are *so*, destiny or will, *tamuno*,

Antandroy tomb in southern Madagascar. The tomb, which is about 40 meters long by two meters high, was built in 1971 to be visible from the main road between the east and west coast port towns of Taolañaro and Toliara. It is crowned with the horns of the cattle sacrificed to feed workers during the months-long burial rites. PHOTOGRAPH BY ALAN HARNIK, 1972

life force, and *teme*, the fixed spirit controlling a person's behavior, which is thought to reside primarily in the forehead. In death, the teme leaves the body; in cases of possession, the teme of an ancestor or other spirit enters the body of another. Only through the humanly carved duein fubara are Kalabari able to locate spiritual beings and control them. Barley (1988) discusses whether Kalabari drew their inspiration for these images from the famed bronze plaques depicting sixteenth-century Bénin royalty, or from early portrait photography as practiced in West Africa. The photographic portraits and now videotapes that are such a prominent feature of contemporary funerals in many parts of Africa warrant similar study.

Ekiti Yoruba woman, from rural southwestern Nigeria, holding an *ere ibeji*. This *ere ibeji*, or wood carving, was made to represent her deceased twin daughter. It was made by the late Ekiti carver, Omo Agbegbileye ("He who carves wood with fame and fortune"). PHOTOGRAPH BY ELISHA P. RENNE, JULY 1999

ANCESTRY AND GENDER

The gendered dimensions of death, mourning, and ancestry in Africa present a complex picture. Some scholars have suggested that because of women's involvement in childbirth, they become associated with human mortality and thus constitute a kind of natural foil against which men may create social illusions of eternal life through such figures as ancestors. Perhaps because so many of the studies of ancestry in Africa have focused on the importance of ancestral sanctions in legitimating the authority of living office holders, men do appear to be dominant in these contexts. Yet among the Lugbara of Uganda, and the Luo and Luyia of Kenya, and many others, women are also recognized as ancestors, and elder women past childbearing age may exercise considerable authority in their households and communities. Among the Jola (Diola) of the Lower Casamance region of Senegal, there are no hereditary offices for women or men, just as there were not among the Lugbara. Women marrying into patrilineal households nevertheless exercise considerable power as intermediaries with spirit-shrines (not identified with particular ancestors) essential to the survival of whole communities.

The large funerals and obituaries that are such a striking dimension of contemporary Nigerian politics also support the predominance of men in government and the professions. Male corpses are kept longer than female corpses in the mortuaries, contributing to larger crowds of mourners at their burials. Similarly, most of the obituaries for men are longer and more costly than those for women; yet the relationship is reversed among Igbo-speakers. Among the Igede of Nigeria, men predominate in public life, but women who are survived by their children are given burials fully comparable to those of men who have died good deaths. Furthermore, both Igede women and men compose the dirges that are a characteristic feature of Igede funerals, with men's dirges "disordered, less philosophical, [and] shorter" than those of women (Ogede 1995). Women predominate in the organization and serving of food and the display of donations in Ghanaian funerals. Women are everywhere in Africa, as elsewhere, the principal mourners of the dead. In Botswana's women-centered burial societies (*diswaeti*), their ritual assumption of common dress (*kapeso*) marks their power to regenerate gender and familial relations torn by death from AIDS, as well as redefine "practices of spirituality across denominational affiliation and Tswana humanism" (Ngwenya 2002).

Recent research, focusing on the different kinds of formal and poetic speech that the Hemba people of Democratic Republic of the Congo associate with women and men, shows that their modes of speaking are not considered opposite, but complementary. Thus, in Hemba funerals, men's oratory and women's singing and dancing, and their different forms of direct and indirect speech, are carefully interwoven in order to deal with the difficulties raised by deaths, especially involving cause-of-death accusations. Similar gendered divisions of labor in rituals of death and ancestry have been documented in Madagascar, where people reckon descent through both women and men. Here, the predominance of women and men in different aspects of funerals, spirit possessions, and ancestral healing rituals is more clearly linked to how people conceptualize the different roles of women and men in contributing to the birth and growth of children.

The prominence of women as mourners throughout Africa and their role in rites of death and ancestry require more research if their productive and reproductive relationships involved in these rites are to be better understood. The study of burial shrouds may prove to be a surprisingly fruitful source of new understanding because of the near-universal associations between cloth and wealth, cloth and flesh, and clothing as one of the most eloquent forms of nonverbal speaking. Through burial cloths, the fleshly dimensions of a person may be subtly renewed in the transformation of the corpse into an ancestor, conceived as a kind of rebirth. Among the Bunu Yoruba of Nigeria, until recently, women wove the cloths that were critical to bringing children into the world, while men wove on women's looms the one kind of red cloth that was critical to the transformation of a chief into an ancestor. Men's semen and women's blood comes together in their rebirthing of ancestors as living human beings.

DEATH AND POLITICAL MOVEMENTS

Studies of the radical changes in kinship and gender relations in contemporary Africa have made scholars more sensitive to the political and economic

Body of the deceased, Abonnema, Rivers State, southern Nigeria. During the day and night before burial, when mourners visit to pay their respects, the body is displayed in a series of rooms in the family house. Each room has its own distinctive name and cloth decorations. With each move, the body itself is redressed. PHOTOGRAPH BY ELISHA P. RENNE, MARCH 1985

dimensions of death, birth, and ancestry on a national, even global scale. Throughout Africa, people recognize that deaths are likely to come earlier and more often to the poor and less powerful. A saying from Madagascar puts it bluntly: *Olo misy vola velona, olo tsisy—maty!* (People with money live, people without, die!). Together with restrictions on what are considered proper unions, which may transform children into bastards, restrictions on funeral rites and mourning are among the most powerful ways, short of enslavement, to transform people into socially nonexistent persons, stripped of their generational ties to others, having no past as well as no future. African ethnography shows that this obliteration of the deceased may happen in different ways: through the enforcement of social codes of burial for different classes of people, or—in a monetary economy—by pricing proper burials so high that poor people cannot afford them.

Whereas earlier studies clarified the role of funerary rituals and ancestors in resolving the social and moral contradictions of life in local communities, more recent studies have attempted to link these to participants' larger circumstances and to the injustices involved in colonial and postcolonial relations among ethnicities and nationalities. The conceptual bridge between the analysis of intimate interpersonal relations and national politics derives from scholars' increasing recognition of the power of governments to affect their citizens' most elemental experiences of death and birth, through systemic political-economic inequalities in such areas as housing, schooling, and public health. Thus death and ancestry are as much national as personal issues. This nationalizing of the person through the rituals of death is evident in the formation of burial societies. In Africa, people started forming burial societies when they migrated into colonial cities in the early twentieth century. Many have been in existence for decades. Burial societies help to ensure a proper burial by prevailing cultural standards, as well as offering many other social benefits related to health, employment, and mutual aid.

Historically, the link between death rituals and political activism is most evident in the prominence of ancestral figures in nationalist movements during the nineteenth and twentieth centuries. Intensive efforts by outsiders to sever people's relations to their kin and communities have provoked major uprisings, led by people often described as prophets who were inspired by ancestral figures. The so-called Xhosa cattle-killing movement of 1856–1857, the Matabele rebellion, and the Mbuya Nehanda-inspired uprisings in Mashonaland at the close of the last century, the Chilembwe uprising in Malawi at the beginning of this century, the Malagasy uprising of 1947–1948, and the guerrilla war that led to the formation of Zimbabwe exemplify the importance of ancestors in contributing to political unification.

Ritual *zebu* sacrifice. A Betsimisaraka man from a village in the Mananara-Nord region of Madagascar has raised enough money to stage a ritual *zebu* sacrifice in obligatory tribute to his deceased father and brother. PHOTOGRAPH BY GENESE SODIKOFF, 2001

Ancestors are central to contemporary land claims in Madagascar, South Africa, Lesotho, and several other countries in Africa.

In *The Dead Will Arise: Nongqawuse and the Great Xhosa Cattle-Killing Movement of 1856–7* (1989), Jeffrey Brian Peires shows how the Xhosa uprising started in British Kaffraria in Southern Africa shortly after the British established the military colony after more than two decades of armed combat with the Xhosa. Despite their losses, the Xhosa began in the 1850s to regroup yet again under the leadership of prophets inspired by Xhosa ancestors. The prophets' exhortations to Xhosa to forego internal differences and prepare for ancestral intervention by sacrificing their cattle coincided in 1853–1856 with an epidemic of lung sickness, introduced from Europe, which began to devastate their herds. In 1856–1857, a fifteen-year-old girl, Nongqawuse, speaking for Xhosa ancestors, proclaimed that the cattle were dying as a result of the Xhosa's deadly quarrels among themselves. If they would sacrifice all their cattle and cease cultivating, she said, they would bring about a miraculous rebirth of the Xhosa people and their herds. The Xhosa themselves debated whether the orphaned Nongqawuse truly spoke for the ancestors, as some other well-known female political leaders in the region did, or merely for her uncle and guardian, Mhala, who led the campaign. Some Xhosa refused to follow the ancestral injunction, but a desperate majority eventually complied. As a result of the slaughter, an estimated 40,000 persons died of starvation, and an equal number were driven into forced labor on the British farms now occupying the Xhosa's best pasture lands.

Struggles over the corpses of prominent people are another common form of political action on a national scale. French colonial officials chose the dead of night to move the remains of revered former rulers of Madagascar from a rural cemetery to a guarded enclosure inside the capital city of Antananarivo to make sure the Malagasy people would not use them to inspire revolt against French rule. In the 1920s, French authorities cut short the burial ceremonies of an important former ruler of a coastal domain from a year to three months, then forbade his reburial because of similar fears that his followers would use these events to generate political opposition to their rule. Fifty years later, in the 1970s, the first president of the Malagasy Republic finally granted permission for the ruler's reburial in order to gather local support for his own reelection campaign.

During the same decade, General Idi Amin of Uganda tried to gain political support from the Ganda, the country's largest ethnic group, by bringing back the body of their former *kabaka*, or ruler, from Great Britain, where he had died in exile. Amin staged a public viewing in the park where Uganda's independence ceremonies had taken place a decade earlier, followed by a major state funeral in the capital's cathedral. But when the kabaka's heir tried to legitimate his own succession to office by giving the body its final burial in the Baganda royal tomb, General Amin dismissed the action as an empty ritual. In South Africa, the funeral in 1983 of James Arthur Calata (1895–1983), an Anglican Canon involved in the African National Congress (ANC) since 1930, helped to revive widespread opposition to apartheid throughout the Eastern Cape. One of Nelson Mandela's first acts after becoming president of post-apartheid South Africa in 1994 was to start negotiating with the French government for the return of what remained of the famed Hottentot Venus (her brain, genitals, and bones) after Cuvier's (1763–1832) dissection of her body at the Musée de L'Homme in Paris 187 years earlier. The burial of Sara Baartman on August 9, 2002 (National Women's Day), at Hankey, eastern Cape Province, was attended by thousands of mourners, including Mandela's successor, President Thabo Mbeki.

The burial of a prominent lawyer, Silvanus Melea Otieno (1931–1986), sparked a nationwide controversy in Kenya that was finally decided in court. His patrilineal kin, who demanded the right thereby to bury him in the Luo homeland of Siaya, claimed Mr. Otieno as a Luo. Yet Mr. Otieno, as many of his contemporaries, had married into a different ethnic group. Virginia Edith Wambui Otieno, his Gikuyu wife, and her lawyers argued that the spouse had the greater right to decide the place of burial. The judge's decision in favor of Mr. Otieno's patrilineal kin (male and female) accorded with the views of a majority of Kenyans, who continue to give priority to relations of descent over marital relations in reckoning inheritance. Yet the widow's challenge to

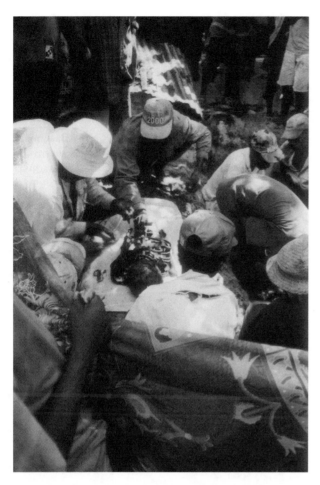

Residents of coastal village in Mananara-Nord district of Madagascar performing the manokatra ritual. In this ritual, the skeleton of an ancestor is exhumed. Since the ancestor here is male, women attending the ritual are prohibited from seeing the skeleton, as men unwrap the cloth shroud (*lamba*) and count the bones to confirm none have been stolen from the grave. PHOTOGRAPH BY GENESE SODIKOFF, 2001

the court also illustrates the new ways in which Kenyans are attempting to rethink their relations of kinship, gender, and marriage, and where customary and common law should prevail.

Based on several such cases in Cameroon in 2001, some argue that the politics of belonging, epitomized in funerals, must also be understood in terms of changes in the government's new constitution of 1996 emphasizing new minority and autochthonous identities, while obscuring the pan-ethnic civic identities based on language which had begun to challenge them. Two recent studies have focused on death, burial, and mourning as a way of elucidating what has seemed to some oppressed citizens to

be the social death of the nation in Kinshasa during Mobutu's Second Republic and in contemporary Nairobi.

ANCESTORS AND POPULAR CULTURE

The vitality of ancestors in interpersonal relations, domestic life, and national culture has long been evident in fiction writing, and now increasingly in new theories of psychological counseling and social work. Several authors have made the road a potent image of the vicissitudes of birth, death, and rebirth in contemporary Africa. Linking hometowns, cities, and nations past and present, the riverine roads see much traffic between living, dead, and ancestral beings, sometimes conveyed in coffin-like vehicles.

The *ogbanje* (in Igbo), *abiku* (in Yoruba), or *donkor* (in Fante/Twi)—a wayward spirit who keeps visiting as a newborn child only to die back again into the spirit world—is a central character in much of West African fiction, for example, in Buchi Emecheta's (b. 1944) *The Slave Girl* (1977), where she is called Ogbanje Ojebeta, which translates to "this regular visitor who has been visiting for a long time," and Ben Okri's (b. 1959) *The Famished Road*, 1991, where the *abiku* is named Lazaro. Chenjerai Hove's (b. 1956) vision of the cyclical relations between the living, the dead, the unborn, and the newborn is set in the political context of Zimbabwe's war of independence, from which so many young people were never to return home. He dedicated his novel *Bones* (1988), the fictional life story of Marita, whose only son dies fighting in the Zimbabwean Liberation Army, to "the women whose children did not return, sons and daughters, those who gave their bones to the making of a new conscience, a conscience of bones, blood and footsteps."

Stanlake Samkange's (1922–1988) *The Mourned One* (1975) is a story about a dead man in colonial Zimbabwe. Samkange explains at the beginning— quite ironically, it seems by the end—that he got the story from his now-dead kinsman who did "meritorious service" as a guard in Her Majesty's Prison, Harare. In retelling the story of Lazarus Percival Ockenden, whom his mother renamed Muchemwa, "The Mourned One," after colonial Zimbabwean authorities executed him for a rape he did not commit, Stanlake Samkange resurrects his dead kinsman's dead prisoner as an ancestor to be mourned by all his fellow citizens who fought for the liberation of

Zimbabwe. Yet great controversy now surrounds Heroes' Acres, the national monument to the war, built near Harare with help from North Korea. The individual tombs of named Heroes so outnumber the one tomb of the Unknown Soldier that the monument appears to reproduce the political inequalities the war was meant to abolish. In Cameroon, novelist Pabé Mongo (b. 1948) (*Nos Ancêtres les Baobabs*, 1994) uses popular slang to satirize newly rich Cameroonian politicians and businessmen who claim to exemplify ancient ideals of reciprocity between the living and the dead while pursuing their own self-interest. Rather than rooting themselves in ethical ancestral practices and nourishing and sheltering their descendants as the great leaders of the past did, modern *baobabs* strive for their own elevation by rooting themselves in mountains of gold.

Whereas Chinua Achebe (b. 1930) was one of the first to portray *ogbanje* in his fiction (*Things Fall Apart*, 1958), Chinwe C. Achebe (his wife) has drawn on the work of the Igbo-speaking Nigerian healers of the Enugu area to make popular ideas and practices concerning ogbanje more widely known to clinicians trained in European and American methods of counseling and social work. Chinwe Achebe decided to carry out her study after a sixteen-year-old student asked for her help in dealing with the pain and bewilderment she had been feeling since her secondary-school days in being treated as an ogbanje who might return at any moment to the spirit-world from which she had come. Chinwe Achebe argues that understanding a client's worldview in its full complexity is essential to better healing practices in the cosmopolitan world of contemporary Nigeria, a view confirmed in later research at the Lagos Teaching Hospital.

Among the Kaguru, the hostility of religious and government officials to what they labeled superstition had forced the Kaguru to be extremely secretive, especially with outsiders, about the ancestral ideas and practices that they considered to legitimate their existence. Studies of death, mourning, and ancestry in Africa have shown that such rites are not limited to elucidating how people conceive of the great cosmic problems of the human condition. They are intimately involved with the social identities of living people and thus most vulnerable to the processes of marginalization and subordination by which people are transformed into nonpeople. Although we may never fathom the ultimate mysteries of death, continued study may help contribute to an ever greater respect for the dignity of living human beings.

See also **Achebe, Chinua; Amin Dada, Idi; Baartman, Sara; Initiation; Kinship and Descent; Madagascar: Religion in; Mandela, Nelson; Masks and Masquerades; Mbeki, Thabo; Nongqawuse; Prophetic Movements; Religion and Ritual; Sudan: Wars.**

BIBLIOGRAPHY

Abasi, Augustine Kututera. "*Lua-lia*, the 'Fresh Funeral': Founding a House for the Deceased Among the Kasena of North-East Ghana." *Africa* 65, no. 3 (1995): 448–475.

Achebe, Chinua. *Things Fall Apart*. London: Heinemann, 1958.

Achebe, Chinwe. *The World of the Ogbanje*. Enugu, Nigeria: Fourth Dimension Publishers, 1986.

Ahmed, A. Chanfi. "Rites de mort aux Comores et chez les Swahili: Entre Islam savant et culture locale." *Journal des africanistes* 72, no. 2 (2002): 187–201.

Appiah, Kwame. Anthony. *In My Father's House: Africa in the Philosophy of Culture*. New York: Oxford University Press, 1992.

Arhin, Kwame. "The Economic Implications of Transformations in Akan Funeral Rites." *Africa* 54, no. 3 (1994): 308–322.

Barley, Nigel. *Foreheads of the Dead: An Anthropological View of Kalabari Ancestral Screens*. Washington, DC: Published for the National Museum of African Art by the Smithsonian Institution Press, 1988.

Beidelman, Thomas O. *Moral Imagination in Kaguru Modes of Thought*. Bloomington: Indiana University Press, 1986.

Bloch, Maurice. *Placing the Dead: Tombs, Ancestral Villages and Kinship Organization in Madagascar*. New York: Seminar Press, 1971.

Bloch, Maurice. "Death, Women, and Power." In *Death and the Regeneration of Life*, ed. Maurice Bloch and Jonathan Parry. Cambridge, U.K.: Cambridge University Press, 1982.

Buckley-Zistel, Susanne. "Remembering to Forget: Chosen Amnesia as a Strategy for Local Coexistence in Post-Genocide Rwanda." *Africa* 76, no. 2 (2006): 131–150.

Cohen, David William, and E. S. Atieno Odhiambo. *Burying SM: The Politics of Knowledge and the Sociology of Power in Africa*. London: James Currey, 1992.

Cohen, David William, and E. S. Atieno Odhiambo. *The Risks of Knowledge: Investigations into the Death of the Hon. Minister John Robert Ouko in Kenya, 1990.* Athens: Ohio University Press, 2004.

Coplan, David B. "Land from the Ancestors: Popular Religious Pilgrimage along the South Africa-Lesotho Border." *Journal of Southern African Studies* 29, no. 4 (2003): 977–993.

Dennie, Garrey Michael. "Flames of Race, Ashes of Death: Re-Inventing Cremation in Johannesburg, 1910–1945." *Journal of Southern African Studies* 29, no. 1 (2003): 177–192.

de Witte, Marleen. *Long Live the Dead!: Changing Funeral Celebrations in Asante, Ghana.* Amsterdam, Askant Academic Publishers, 2001.

de Witte, Marleen. "Money and Death: Funeral Business in Asante, Ghana." *Africa* 73, no. 4 (2003): 531–559.

Dieterlen, Germaine. *Les âmes des Dogon.* Paris: Institut d'ethnologie, 1941.

Drucker-Brown, Susan. "The Grandchildren's Play at the Mamprusi King's Funeral: Ritual Rebellion Revisited in Northern Ghana." *Journal of the Royal Anthropological Institute* 5, no. 2 (1999): 181–192.

Durham, Deborah, and Frederick Klaits. "Funerals and the Public Space of Sentiment in Botswana." *Journal of Southern African Studies* 28, no. 4 (2002): 777–795.

Emecheta, Buchi. *The Slave Girl.* New York: G. Braziller, 1977.

Evers, Sandra. "Trumping the Ancestors: The Challenges of Implementing a Land Registration System in Madagascar." In *Competing Jurisdictions: Settling Land Claims in Africa*, eds. Sandra Evers, Marja Spierenburg and Harry Wels. Leiden, the Netherlands: Brill, 2005.

Feeley-Harnik, Gillian. *A Green Estate: Restoring Independence in Madagascar.* Washington, DC: Smithsonian Institution Press, 1991.

Fernandez, James W. *Bwiti: An Ethnography of the Religious Imagination in Africa.* Princeton, NJ: Princeton University Press, 1982.

Fortes, Meyer. *The Dynamics of Clanship Among the Tallensi, Being the First Part of an Analysis of the Structure of a Trans-Volta Tribe.* London: Oxford University Press, 1945.

Gilbert, Michelle. "The Sudden Death of a Millionaire: Conversion and Consensus in a Ghanaian Kingdom." *Africa* 58, no. 3 (1988): 291–314.

Glazier, Jack. *Land and the Uses of Tradition Among the Mbeere of Kenya.* Lanham, MD: University Press of America, 1985.

Goody, Jack. *Death, Property and the Ancestors: A Study of the Mortuary Customs of the LoDagaa of West Africa.* London: Tavistock, 1962.

Griaule, Marcel. *Dieu d'eau: Entretiens avec Ogotemmêli.* Paris: Fayard, 1975.

Grootaers, Jan-Lodewijk, ed. *Mort et maladie au Zaïre.* Paris: L'Harmattan, 1998.

Hove, Chenjerai. *Bones.* Harare, Zimbabwe: Baobab Books, 1988.

Hutchinson, Sharon. "Death, Memory, and the Politics of Legitimation: Nuer Experiences of the Continuing Second Sudanese Civil War." In *Memory and the Postcolony*, ed. Richard Werbner. London: Zed Books, 1998.

Ilechukwu, Sunny T. C. "Ogbanje/Abiku: A Culture-bound Construct of Childhood and Family Psychopathology in West Africa: The Ogbanje/Abiku Syndrome: A Case Study of an Interface between a Culture-bound Concept and Modern Psychiatry." *Psychopathologie africaine* 23, no. 1 (1990–1991): 19–60.

Jindra, Michael. "Christianity and the Proliferation of Ancestors: Changes in Hierarchy and Mortuary Ritual in the Cameroon Grassfields." *Africa* 75, no. 3 (2005): 356–377.

Jua, Benedict Nantang. "The Mortuary Sphere, Privilege and the Politics of Belonging in Contemporary Cameroon Grassfields." *Africa* 75, no. 3 (2005): 356–377.

Klaits, Frederick. "The Widow in Blue: Blood and the Morality of Remembering in Botswana's Time of AIDS." *Africa* 75, no. 1 (2005): 46–62.

Kriger, Norma. "The Politics of Creating National Heroes." In *Soldiers in Zimbabwe's Liberation War*, eds. Ngwabi Bhebe and Terence Ranger. London: James Currey, 1995.

Lambek, Michael. *Knowledge and Practice in Mayotte: Local Discourses of Islam, Sorcery, and Spirit Possession.* Toronto: University of Toronto Press, 1993.

Lawuyi, Olatunde Bayo. "The Social Marketing of Elites: The Advertised Self in Obituaries and Congratulations in Some Nigerian Dailies." *Africa* 61, no. 2 (1991): 247–263.

Liberski, D., and C. Henry, eds. Special issues on *Le deuil et ses rites, I, II, III: Systèmes de pensée en Afrique noire* (1989, 1991, 1994).

Maloka, Tshidiso. "Basotho and the Experience of Death, Dying, and Mourning in the South African Mine Compounds, 1890–1940." *Cahiers d'études africaines* 38, no. 149 (1998): 17–40.

Maseko, Zola, and Gail Smith. *The Return of Sara Baartman.* Johannesburg, South Africa: Black Roots Pictures, 2003.

Matobo, Thope. "The Socio-Economic Role of Burial Societies and Money Lending Clubs in the Informal Sector in Lesotho." *Lesotho Social Science Review* 4, no. 1 (1998): 51–67.

Matsunyane, Kgomotso, Robby Thorpe, and David Jammy. *Heavy Traffic.* Cape Town, South Africa: Day Zero Film and Video, 2001.

Maupeu, Hervé, and Yvan Droz. *Les figures de la mort à Nairobi: une capitale sans cimetières.* Paris: L'Harmattan, 2003.

McCall, John C. "Rethinking Ancestors in Africa." *Africa* 65, no. 2 (1995): 258–262.

Middleton, John. *Lugbara Religion: Ritual and Authority among an East African People.* London: Published for the International African Institute by the Oxford University Press, 1960.

Mongo, Pabé *Nos Ancêtres les Baobabs.* Paris: L'Harmattan, 1994.

Ngwenya, Barbara Ntombi. "Gender, Dress and Self-Empowerment: Women and Burial Societies in Botswana," *African Sociological Review* 6, no. 2 (2002): 1–27

Ngwenya, Barbara Ntombi. "Redefining Kin and Family Social Relations: Burial Societies and Emergency Relief in Botswana." *Journal of Social Development in Africa* 18, no. 1 (2003): 85–110.

Noret, Joël. "Morgues et prise en charge de la mort au Sud-Bénin." *Cahiers d'études africaines* 44, no. 176 (2004): 745–767.

Ogede, Ode S. "Context, Form, and Poetic Expression in Igede Funeral Dirges." *Africa* 65, no. 1 (1995): 79–96.

Okot p'Bitek. *Religion of the Central Luo.* Nairobi: East African Literature Bureau, 1971.

Okri, Ben. *The Famished Road.* London: J. Cape, 1991.

Parkin, David. *Sacred Void: Spatial Images of Work and Ritual Among the Giriama of Kenya.* Cambridge, U.K.: Cambridge University Press, 1991.

Pavanello, Mariano. "The Work of the Ancestors and the Profit of the Living: Some Nzema Economic Ideas." *Africa* 65, no. 1 (1995): 36–56.

Peires, Jeffrey Brian. *The Dead Will Arise: Nongqawuse and the Great Xhosa Cattle-Killing Movement of 1856–7.* Johannesburg, South Africa: Ravan Press, 1989.

Rakotsoane, Frances C. L. "The Impact of African Holistic Cosmology on Land Issues: A Southern African Case." *Journal for the Study of Religion* 18, no. 1 (2005): 5–15.

Ranger, Terence O. "Dignifying Death: The Politics of Burial in Bulawayo." *Journal of Religion in Africa* 34, no. 1/2 (2004): 110–144.

Renne, Elisha P. *Cloth That Does Not Die: The Meaning of Cloth in Bùnú Social Life.* Seattle: University of Washington Press, 1995.

Samkange, Stanlake. *The Mourned One.* London: Heinemann Educational, 1975.

Schwartz, Nancy. "Active Dead or Alive: Some Kenyan Views about the Agency of Luo and Luyia Women Pre- and Post-mortem." *Journal of Religion in Africa* 30, no. 4 (2000): 433–467.

Smith, Daniel Jordan. "Burials and Belonging in Nigeria: Rural-Urban Relations and Social Inequality in a Contemporary African Ritual." *American Anthropologist* 106, no. 3 (2004): 569–579.

Soyinka, Wole. *The Road.* London: Oxford University Press, 1965.

Tetelman, Michael S. "The Burial of Canon J. A. Calata and the Revival of Mass-based Opposition in Cradock, South Africa, 1983." *African Studies* 58, no. 1 (1999): 5–32.

van Beek, Walter E. A. "Dogon Restudied: A Field Evaluation of the Work of Marcel Griaule." *Current Anthropology* 32, no. 2 (1991): 139–167.

van der Geest, Sjaak. "Between Death and Funeral: Mortuaries and the Exploitation of Liminality in Kwahu, Ghana." *Africa* 76, no. 4 (2006): 485–501.

Werbner, Richard P. *Tears of the Dead: The Social Biography of an African Family.* Harare, Zimbabwe: Baobab Books, 1992.

Whyte, Susan Reynolds. "Going Home? Belonging and Burial in the Era of AIDS." *Africa* 75, no. 2 (2005): 154–172.

GILLIAN FEELEY-HARNIK

DEBT AND CREDIT

This entry includes the following articles:
INTERNATIONAL TRADE
ENTRUSTMENT

INTERNATIONAL TRADE

One of the most intriguing paradoxes of contemporary economics is the fact that Africa's external trade has become an insignificant player in world trade. It is estimated that the continent accounts for barely 1 percent of global gross domestic product (GDP, the most basic measure of a country's economic welfare) and about 2 percent of world trade. Its share of global manufactured exports is almost zero. During the last three decades of the twentieth century, the continent lost market shares in global trade—even in traditional primary goods—and failed to diversify its economies. While other formerly colonized regions of the world in Asia or Latin America have been able to adopt the path of structural transformation from agriculture to manufacturing and services—a process typically associated with economic development—Africa remains almost totally dependent on the export commodities of its colonial era, despite their low income elasticity and declining and volatile terms of trade (a measure of the volume of imports that a given quantity of exports can command).

Yet, Africa has been at the heart of international trade even in precolonial times. Nubia and Ethiopia even had trade routes north to the Mediterranean world. For most of the first millennium CE, the Axumite kingdom (in modern Ethiopia) had a prosperous trade empire on the East Coast (around the Horn of Africa). Axum had trading links going as far as the Byzantine Empire and India. The introduction of the camel by Arab conquerors of North Africa in the seventh century opened increased an ancient trade across the Sahara. The profits from this commerce in gold and salt led to the creation of a series of powerful empires in the western Sahel such as the kingdom of Ghana and the Mali and Kanem-Bornu empires. A prosperous maritime trade also developed along the east coast of the continent as Swahili traders exported gold, ivory and slaves across a trading region that spanned the entire Indian Ocean region. Portuguese traders went around the west coast of the continent in the fifteenth century and began to trade directly with Guinea. Other European traders soon joined them. This led to a rapid rise in export-led prosperity in that region, which soon became home to a number of flourishing states, such as the kingdom of Benin-Dahomey and the Ashanti Confederacy. However, this wealth was dominated by the slave trade and vanished with the abolition of slavery and the later European colonization of almost the entire continent.

The patterns of African involvement into world trade (especially since the late nineteenth and twentieth centuries) and the nature of the relationship between the continent and the West have made the colonial order an important variable of African economic performance. Indeed, four centuries after the beginning of that relationship and five decades after independence, the basic organization, structure, and performance of most African economies have not changed much. They still rely mostly on primary commodities for foreign exchange and for a large share of their government revenues.

It is estimated that about 25 percent of world merchandise trade consists of primary commodities. More than fifty developing countries—many of them in Africa—depend on three or fewer commodities for more than half of their merchandise export earnings. Reliance on commodities for increasing national income is not a bad development strategy in itself—countries like Australia or even the United States have done so successfully over the course of their history. But sticking to that pattern of growth for several centuries in face of evidence of declining marginal gains, little structural transformation, high price volatility and all the major external shocks associated with it raises questions about its appropriateness for most African countries.

Both short-term and long-term commodity price fluctuations are important determinants of development in the world economy. The study of 140 years of commodity price data shows that prices have trended broadly downward, but that such trends are small and variable, especially in comparison with the large variability of the prices of various commodities. Markets of primary products have exhibited changing patterns of instability, much greater since the late twentieth century. Analyzing commodity price cycles, empirical studies conclude that price slumps tend to last much longer than price booms, with the severity of positive or negative changes in prices being unrelated to their duration. This unpredictability makes policy prescription for African countries that rely on a few commodity prices particularly difficult. Even more worrisome is the observation that shocks to commodity prices are usually long lasting, with half-lives typically in excess of five years—which complicates the search for the appropriate policy and institutional response to smooth the effects of such shocks.

Other empirical studies have identified as the key determinants of price fluctuations for non-oil commodity prices the supply of commodities on the world market (which is strongly affected by climatic variability and subsidies), the real exchange rate of the U.S. dollar, and world industrial production. In macroeconomic terms, the impact of constantly changing prices in African countries is better captured through their effects on the terms of trade.

Terms of trade shocks have had a big impact on fluctuations in national output and the real exchange rate—especially for countries operating within the CFA (Communauté financière d'Afrique, former French colonies) zone. Even temporary terms of trade shocks have a large impact on private saving and the current account balance. In fact, there seems to be a correlation between shocks and reduced national consumption, investment, and innovation. Finally, several studies have established a clear link between the evolution of the real price of commodity exports and the real exchange rate—a key indicator of external competitiveness for small open economies of sub-Saharan Africa.

What explains Africa's costly disconnection from the world trade networks in which she has been deeply involved for centuries? Two broad schools of thought have attempted to explain why international trade has failed to spur growth in the African context: one includes proponents of a neoclassical perspective like A. G. Hopkins, who argue that a market system initially failed in Africa because domestic resources were not sufficient to spur the growth of effective demand. It was constrained on the one hand by the low density of population and on the other hand by the high cost of transportation. Thus, the first phase of international trade could not act as an engine of growth because the slave trade, besides being criminal and immoral, created only a very small export sector, one that had few beneficial links with the rest of the economy. There was a turning point the beginning of the nineteenth century when trade became more legitimate and more intense, as a large number of small producers and traders challenged warrior entrepreneurs who had dominated the scene up to that time. This shift in the structure of export-producing firms was sustained throughout several decades by some internal dynamics in African societies (the emergence of a very industrious class of local entrepreneurs), and the increasingly important restrictions of colonial powers across the continent. However, by the end of the nineteenth century, this new economy of small entrepreneurs suffered a major setback. Economic and political factors like a prolonged fall in the price of palm oil and groundnuts after 1860 and desperate attempts by the oligarchs of the slave-trade networks to maintain their grasp

on the economy led to a general economic crisis. Furthermore some poor business practices on the part of indebted trading firms eventually encouraged colonialism; in response to declining profit margins, monopolies became popular and business relations more politicized. Colonial powers felt compelled to become more involved in the ruling of these territories.

The second school of thought, which comprises substantivists, Marxists, and dependency theorists, offers a completely different economic history of Africa. It tends to reject the notion that underdevelopment could be the natural, initial stage of any society, and sees Africa's current low productivity as the distorted result of European hegemony that has been imposed over the world since the fifteenth century. It affirms African capability and business sense but stresses its limitations in the context of these externally imposed constraints. According to Walter Rodney, a leading advocate for this group, the logic of capitalist accumulation is to mobilize forces of production to the point where the concentration of ownership lies in ever fewer hands, which then produces a high level of inequalities of wealth and power. Rodney argues that prior to European penetration African societies were at various stages of development, from communalism to a "transitional" stage "below class-ridden feudalism." Thereafter, European-generated activities created underdevelopment. Specifically, the external domination of merchant capital through the slave trade, unequal exchange, and the destruction of domestic economies (especially handicraft production and trade) promoted development in Europe and mostly misery and inequality in Africa.

While these views are not mutually exclusive, it appears that well before the nineteenth century, Africa had established strong trading networks based on the exchange of locally produced agricultural and industrial goods. As noted by G. A. Akinola, "Africa was Europe's trading partner, not its economic appendage." Colonialism ended that balance. An important step in doing so was to wrest control of trade from middlemen, like the Swahili states of the eastern African coast, and powerful magnates, like Ja Ja, king of the Niger Delta state of Opobo. Indeed, several of the wars resisting European penetration in the Lower Niger, in eastern Africa, and in the Congo Basin were precipitated by European measures to take control of trade. The subsequent colonial boundaries and the smothering of precolonial industries through the flooding of African markets with European consumer goods contributed to the export-import orientation of the colonial economy—still a dominant feature of African economies today. Encouragement was, however, given to the growth of cash crops like cocoa, peanuts, coffee, tea, and cotton, organized so as to ensure that a colony specialized in one major crop, such as cocoa in the Gold Coast and Côte d'Ivoire, peanuts in Senegal and the Gambia, and cotton in Uganda. Even in those areas, European firms or prosperous merchants and produce buyers stood between the African producer and the world market, and skimmed off most of the profit. For most African countries, the main challenge ahead is still to diversify their economies (that is, getting away from the trap of commodity exports) and to create conditions for generating value-added domestically.

See also **Aid and Development; Economic History; Money; Slave Trades; Trade, National and International Systems.**

BIBLIOGRAPHY

Agénor, Pierre-Richard, et al. "Macroeconomic Fluctuations in Developing Countries: Some Stylized Facts." *World Bank Economic Review* 14, no. 2 (2001): 251–285.

Borenzstein, Eduardo, et al. *The Bahavior of Non-Oil Commodity Prices.* Occasional Paper no. 112. Washington, DC: International Monetary Fund, 1994.

Cashin, Paul, and Alasdair Scott. "Booms and Slumps in World Commodity Prices." *Journal of Development Economics* 69 (2002): 277–296.

Cashin, Paul, and C. John McDermott. "The Long-Run Behavior of Commodity Prices: Small Trends and Big Variability." *IMF Staff Papers* 49, no. 2 (2002): 175–199.

Cashin, Paul; Hong Liang; and C. John McDermott. "How Persistent Are Shocks to World Commodity Prices?" *IMF Staff Papers* 47, no. 2 (2000): 177–217.

Fage, John D. *A History of Africa*, 4th edition. London: Routledge, 2002.

Hoffmaister, Alexander; Jorge Roldos; and Peter Wickham. "Macroeconomic Fluctuations in Sub-Saharan Africa." *IMF Staff Papers* 45 (1998): 132–160.

Hopkins, A. G. *An Economic History of West Africa.* London: Longman, 1973.

Monga, Célestin. "Commodities, Mercedes-Benz, and Structural Adjustment: An Episode in West African Economic History." In *Themes in West Africa's History*, ed. Emmanuel Akyeampong. Athens: Ohio University Press, 2005.

Rodney, Walter. *How Europe Underdeveloped Africa.* Washington, DC: Howard University Press, 1982.

World Bank. *Can Africa Claim the 21st Century?* Washington, DC: World Bank. 2000.

CÉLESTIN MONGA

ENTRUSTMENT

Loans and entrustments are part of human life in any part of Africa as elsewhere. Credit, in the sense of a loan, refers to the transfer of a good or service between persons or groups on the understanding that the recipient(s) will later return some quantity of the same or another good or service. In another usage, the term implies one party's trust or confidence that another will repay debts or satisfy obligations when due. Credit and the debt it implies can involve intimates or strangers. Many of their forms are nonmonetary, hard to quantify, or not strictly economic in nature. Calling these entrustment and obligation allows more scope for social, political, religious, aesthetic, and emotional considerations. An entrustment, however, need not always be returned to its source but may be expected to be passed along instead to some third party, as for instance in serial inheritance, in which one can satisfy a perceived obligation to a parent or ancestor by handing along something to one's own progeny in turn.

Numerous African languages (including some of European origin) use the same word for *borrow* as for *lend*, suggesting an emphasis on the social relationship and not just on mere possession by an individual or on the object itself. Land, animals, tools, water, food, money, labor, and even humans themselves are among the many things lent and borrowed, or entrusted in subtle ways not explicitly identified as loans in a commercial sense. Long-distance monetary credit has become increasingly important since the mid-twentieth century with the rise of international development finance agencies. A cause and an effect of troubled economic conditions in many parts of Africa has been rising financial indebtedness to external lenders ill acquainted with the needs, values, and capacities of African populations. But much local experimentation has been occurring to find new financial and other fiduciary solutions.

DOMESTIC AND LOCAL ENTRUSTMENT AND OBLIGATION

Whereas some theorists have supposed that economies evolve along a continuum of increasing complexity from barter to cash to credit, probably no African society ever existed for long without some kind of borrowing and lending or without other kinds of entrustment. Among foraging people in past and present (for instance among San or "Bushman" groups in southern Africa, Hadza in eastern Africa, or Twa in Central Africa), the immediate sharing of gathered foods and hunted meat, within and between families or multifamily bands, has often been deemed necessary both to prevent spoilage and loss to living animals, and to maintain mobility. Here as elsewhere, credit and debt shade into gift exchange (and into theft, too), even though the same people may engage in market or other economic life in other contexts.

Among herding and agropastoral people, entrusting animals to friends and neighbors for the short or long term (a practice observed most everywhere from Senegal to Somalia) cements bonds of special friendship and helps to even out unequal endowments of pasturage, labor, and milk among households or multi-house homesteads. In this way animal-sharing partnerships help accommodate the shifting needs of families at different points in their life cycles.

Similarly, the sharing or entrustment of children between households or homesteads and the caring of children by older child kin or neighbors play a bigger part in African settings almost continent-wide, at least in rural areas, than in many parts of the world. Customs of shared parenting befit languages whose kin terminology identifies parents with their siblings by use of the same terms, or children with those children's cousins as "brothers" or "sisters." Many, probably most, African languages classify at least some collateral kin together in this broad and inclusive way, bringing them semantically closer together and making the movement of children between homes seem more normal and natural. A practice of delegating child care to older children under supervision or to grandparents also befits contexts where women have many children but also are charged with heavy duties of farm work. Growing up in entrusted care helps prepare children for the give-and-take between homes in later life among rural Africa's

main forms of "insurance" and "social security." In times and places of crisis (as in the present HIV/AIDS epidemic, which has thinned out the generation of young parents in large parts of eastern and southern Africa), child entrustment becomes especially important. It does, however, subject some children to abuse or neglect, for instance by foster or stepparents who deliberately or inadvertently favor their own biological children. In extreme cases child fosterage can merge into slavery.

Among farming and herding peoples alike, exchanges of labor are practiced almost continent-wide in small interfamily gatherings or in much larger, and usually less frequent, work parties. Typically the sharing of food and drink is a part of these; poorer people may rely on such occasions for an important part of their diet, but they are sometimes exploited for their work. The larger work parties in agrarian settings are widely deemed to be dying out—and in inland fishing communities with diminished catches they are for sure—but real history on this is hard to sort from nostalgic and imaginative memories of collective action and solidarity.

Other common longer-term transactions include payment for school fees for younger kin, who are expected to reciprocate or pass on help once financially established later in life. Wage workers paid in cash but lacking bank accounts may as often request delayed payment as they do advances, to let their savings accumulate beyond their own temptation or the claims of kin and neighbors.

The kinds of ceremonies and sacred events that anthropologists study have seldom been objects of economic inquiry in Africa, but they have fiduciary dimensions, if not also financial ones, no less than social and spiritual ones. Ceremonial exchanges of food or work may or may not involve strict accounting of debts. The process of marriage over most of Africa south of the Sahara involves protracted payments of goods, services, or both. Typically the payments or transfers are made mainly from a groom's to a bride's family in exchange for rights or interests in a woman (bridewealth) and her offspring (childwealth); but even where so, it is common that some other transfers, usually adding up to less, also move from bride's family to groom on the same or other occasions. In some eastern and southern African societies marriage debts or obligations, incurred mainly in livestock, may last many years or even several generations; thus entrustments and obligations are heritable. In some societies, for instance in western Kenya, marriage payments or a portion thereof may be demanded back upon divorce. Sexual unions outside wedlock seem more often than not to involve a net flow of goods or economic favors from male to female partners; under some circumstances the latter's participating can be construed as reciprocation of sorts. Parents who invest in their children commonly expect the latter to reciprocate not just directly by caring for them in their old age (and in some societies by sacrificing to them after death), but also indirectly by bearing and providing for descendants who will remember them as ancestors and keep their names alive.

Funerals and other mortuary celebrations are other important occasions of financial and fiduciary transfer, involving wide networks of kin and acquaintances as they do in visiting and feasting that can last many days and serve many social, spiritual, and aesthetic functions. But even where written accounts are kept, as for funeral contributions in the Lake Victoria/Nyanza basin, reciprocity is not always strictly pursued or enforced. Sacrifice of animals to ancestors or divinity, during rites of transition like marriages and funerals or during times of general crisis like drought, is sometimes understood and discussed in an idiom that partakes of and "borrows" from the sphere of transactions between humans themselves. Sacrifices may be explicit attempts to obligate or incur reciprocity (for instance in rain or healthy crops) in a way resembling a contract, or humbler measures just to ingratiate or propitiate in a looser way with such practical benefits nonetheless in mind. Or they may be understood as thanks, payback, or mere sharing, to continue a longer-term relationships with ancestors, other spirits, or divinity.

The sharing of blood or other human or animal bodily fluids in the formation of "blood brotherhood" or similar bonds, across lines of lineage, clan, chiefdom, or ethnolinguistic grouping, has in the past provided a basis for trust in long-distance trading partnerships crisscrossing the continent, and in associated agreements for protecting travelers. After long being assumed to be disappearing, such practice has been revived as common libations of blood or plant substances in times of civil crisis, for instance among early twenty-first century Acholi in Uganda during soldier initiation and bonding rituals or in postconflict homecomings and reconciliation, a practice and form of justice debated locally and internationally.

All these diverse forms of entrustment and obligation, many of which are both economic and symbolic in nature, mean that practically no one on the continent is without some sort of existing debts and obligations, a fact seldom fully appreciated by foreign financiers arriving with new offers of credit. Once borrowers have put loan money to sacred uses like marriage or funeral contributions, they may not be able to take it out to return to distant or foreign lenders without local opprobrium.

Concentric exchanges of gifts, tributes, or taxes, and redistributions outward to the needy or favored, characterize centralized polities of all sorts and sizes, including chiefdoms, monarchies, and democratic states. They also typify religious communities, including Muslim and Christian ones, whose adherents engage in tithing and other authorized forms of taxation or charity. These practices can function as credit and debt in that some who give to a central authority or a collectivity also receive from it at other times, albeit without strict equivalence. Relief and development agencies have attempted to emulate or adapt the principle in many parts of the continent, for instance in setting up food banks. More than a few African political leaders in new nation-states have expanded older, more local ways of tribute collection into nationwide taxation and extortion without assuming the kinds of reciprocal and redistributive obligations formerly incumbent upon headmen, chiefs, or other leaders or their clients. Foreign bank accounts, by helping them do so, drain local economies.

Self-help contribution clubs are found across Africa, as in many places around the world. Among these, rotating saving and credit associations (or ROSCAs) are a popular institution among women (and less often among men) of many towns and cities, and among traders and the lower-level salariat. Often based on rural models of rotating labor exchange, these groups go by many names, including merry-go-round, *tontine* (French), *esusu* (Yoruba), and *djanggi* (Bamileke). In the simplest and most common version, the group meets at weekly or monthly intervals, each member contributing a fixed amount to a common pot, which one member takes home until each has had a turn. For members who take their turns early in the cycle the group provides credit, and for those who take later turns the group provides savings—all in the same transactions. The occasion of a meeting may serve as a celebration. Elaborations of the rotating contribution club variously involve interest payments, variable contributions, insurance, and lottery. Savers find that belonging to a club lets them refuse day-to-day demands of kin or neighbors on their resources without appearing antisocial. But contribution clubs appear to work best where members have other, nonfinancial interconnections or common interests (kinship, neighborhood, age-set ties) to bind them together, and where they are of comparable wealth or incomes. Such associations have proved most effective for non-farm uses, as farmers of a community tend to want to deposit and to withdraw all at the same times of the agricultural cycle. In rural Africa, rotating and other contribution clubs appear most important as a means of saving and lending in forest areas of the central and western regions, where tsetse prevents the use of large animals. In some documented cases in Cameroon, rotating saving and credit associations have transformed into formal banks on imported models.

Traders, shopkeepers, and others practice moneylending and credit in cash and kind throughout the continent, and supplier credit is common in industry and commerce, postdated checking being one easy method among many. Generally, however, Africa's rural moneylending is less important and socially problematic than southern Asia's. In many parts of inland eastern and southern Africa, loans in cash or kind do not conventionally involve interest charges. Such charges appear to be more common practice in parts of West Africa and coastal areas long monetized, and they occur even where prohibited by religious or secular law.

ATTEMPTS AT REGULATION, SACRED AND SECULAR

Islamic law (*shari'a*), which is important in the northern half of the continent and isolated communities farther south, has much to say about financial custom. Morally based, it condemns lending at interest (deemed usury or a form of *riba*, unjustified gain), gambling, speculation, and transactions with unequally shared information—all classed as *haram*

(things prohibited) or *gharar* (sin). African Muslims are familiar with legal devices (*hiyal*; singular *hila*) for evading strictures about interest and usury, for instance by reconstruing interest as service charges (a practice of some Islamic banks) or by redesignating loans as sales and counter-sales. Some Muslims justify such measures by calling the sacred obligation (*fard*) to provide for one's family a higher duty. The laws of finance and their interpretations and breaches are topics of debate across northern Africa and wherever else there are Muslims.

There is no simple way to distinguish usury from fair lending in African contexts, or to prevent it. Rapid currency inflation and devaluation in many African countries have spurred high-interest moneylending, particularly around cities. Usury and pawn-brokering laws copied over from European statutes (for instance, in Kenya, Nigeria, and the Gambia) have proved ineffective in controlling it. Usually they fail to account for currency instabilities and have been ignored in financial practice if not also in court. In rural communities researched in Kenya, the Gambia, and elsewhere, many people prefer to conceive of interest more as a timeless ratio or a stepwise seasonal increment than as a steady rate. That is, if time is money, it is not so always or everywhere.

EXOGENOUS CREDIT AND DEBT

European-style commercial banking has penetrated Africa unevenly. Even in parts of West Africa exposed to long-distance trade and monetary commerce for centuries, many rural Africans remain involved with banks only infrequently or indirectly. Their reasons are mixed and complex. They variously include currency inflation; rules about literacy or minimum deposits; other ethnic, sex, and class discrimination by the institutions; demands for bribes; and uncertainties about political control or surveillance. In times of rapid inflation, money is something to spend or to convert to harder currency before it loses value. In times and places of more stable currencies, rural dwellers and townspeople have commonly entrusted some of their earnings to known local deposit takers—usually senior persons with reputations to uphold and ones solvent enough to resist temptations—to keep it from being begged or demanded away.

Like other forms of "development aid" and emergency relief in Africa, financial credit has swung with international fashion. Early-twentieth-century colonial policies varied and vacillated between measures designed to protect African people from unscrupulous money lenders (real or imagined), and loans and grants to them to promote favored cash crop and livestock enterprises of interest to the European powers. Meanwhile, financial credit for European settler farmers in East Africa proved a mixed blessing, helping them establish lucrative cash cropping enterprises but bankrupting many in the Great Depression of the 1930s and other economic downturns.

As many African nations gained formal independence from European colonial powers in the late 1950s and early 1960s, international agencies stepped in with hands-on community development projects for rural Africans, often attempting to combine financial with other forms of intervention. The 1970s and early 1980s saw larger-scale, "integrated" agricultural development programs replicated in many African countries, generally funded by the World Bank, the U.S. Agency for International Development, and other large agencies based outside the continent. These programs represented attempts to provide packages of hybrid seeds, fertilizers, and pesticides on loan to people deemed too poor to afford them for themselves, usually through government channels. Led by supply more than demand, and commonly scaled in the tens of millions of dollars, these programs usually required little of their supposed beneficiaries, and thus instilled little local commitment. Complex and administratively cumbersome, these programs often foundered through managerial problems like rising input costs, unsuited input combinations, graft and diversion of funds, inappropriate timing of disbursements, and marketing bottlenecks and disincentives. Usually heavily subsidized, these loans tended to be devoured by powerful persons rather than their intended beneficiaries. At international, national, and local levels, funds were allocated as much for political patronage as for increasing production or consumption. They did, however, contribute to the spread of hybrid varieties and of cash crops, for better or worse.

In the 1980s, 1990s, and early 2000s, most international programs to extend financial services into the African countryside were much more modest in scope and design. Their financiers sought to avoid government intermediaries. Typical were smaller microfinance programs channeled through private voluntary agencies to reach small-scale entrepreneurs, sometimes with training programs. Some organizations have used self-help groups like rotating saving and credit associations as models or as building blocks, attempting to build in savings as a prerequisite for borrowing and sometimes freeing credit from requirements of use within a particular sector like agriculture or manufacturing. While international financiers continued to consider credit a good thing, many by now deemed it more important to mobilize savings locally, in addition to or instead of.

LOAN SECURITY AND OTHER ISSUES

Debates on lending strategies revolve around several recurring issues. Is it best to lend to individuals or groups, in cash or kind, for restricted or unlimited purpose (and if restricted, then for production or consumption)? Some of these turn out to be false dichotomies. Those who cannot consume, for instance, cannot produce. And loans can be issued to individuals but groups made collectively responsible for their repayment.

A recurrent question throughout the past century has been what kind of guarantees or security would ensure loan repayments. More than a few parts of Africa south of the Sahara have witnessed human pledging or pawning traditions, whereby persons in positions of relative power could offer poorer or weaker kin—usually women or children—as collateral for loans from persons better off. The resulting debt bondage has sometimes been associated with indigenous forms of slavery and also with the Atlantic and Indian Ocean slave trades; it took conspicuous forms in areas accessible to the West African coast. Colonial authorities' eventual attempts, in the nineteenth and twentieth centuries, to prohibit or discourage slavery within Africa dampened the practices of pawnship and debt bondage but did not entirely stamp them out.

Over most of the region, local rules and custom lodge land tenure in kinship and community membership and thus have long prohibited or discouraged land mortgaging (though land pledging has been long practiced in some parts, notably in parts of what is now Ghana). Nonetheless, numerous African colonial governments, beginning at the turn of the century, experimented with small-scale programs to title rural land as "freehold" (i.e., private, alienable) individual property, often partly to render it usable as collateral for loans. The best-known attempt has been Kenya's nationwide land registration program, part of the Swynnerton Plan that passed into law in 1957. It has failed to make credit broadly accessible to the rural public. New mortgage loans anyway mean burdensome debts, dangers of permanent dispossession and dislocation, and cause for sporadic unrest when lenders attempt to foreclose. In this nation's case and others, the promise of future loans scarcely justifies an attempt to reform basic property rights, though the point is sometimes debated.

Other means of loan security include peer group pressure, loan guarantees, and liens on crops, salaries, buildings, or durable chattels such as trade goods, vehicles, or farm machinery. Cattle, in eastern and southern Africa, tend to be too charged with important cultural meanings to be attachable as collateral for loans. No single method of securing loans can suit all African contexts. Knowledge of personal character and contacts, linkage of credit to saving, and gradually incremental lending—the methods most like established local practice—have generally succeeded best.

DEBTS AND RESENTMENTS

Credit for farming or herding is risky, particularly where these depend on unreliable rains and markets, as they do in most of agrarian Africa. Mortgages, or deadlined pledges, only compound the hazards for borrowers. While often necessary, borrowing is at least as likely to impoverish as to enrich; and the demoralizing effects of indebtedness on work cannot be measured. The past century's overlay of institutional credit on local and indigenous entrustments and obligations among rural Africans has generally disappointed borrowers and lenders alike, leaving a legacy of debts and resentments. Some public and private agencies continue, however, to explore more sensitive and appropriate forms of formal financial intermediation through self-help and capillary banking, links between commercial banks and aid agencies, and other strategies. Meanwhile, African people across the continent have continued to adapt their own fiduciary strategies—not all of which involve money or banks—to uncertain economic and political conditions.

See also **Agriculture; Death, Mourning, and Ancestors; Disease: HIV/AIDS, Social and Political Aspects; Family; Islam; Kinship and Affinity; Labor; Law: Islamic; Marriage Systems; Religion and Ritual; Secret Societies; Slavery and Servile Institutions; World Bank.**

BIBLIOGRAPHY

Adams, Dale, and Delbert A. Fitchett, eds. *Informal Finance in Low-Income Countries.* Boulder, CO: Westview, 1992.

Ardener, Shirley, and Sandra Burman, eds. *Money-Go-Rounds: The Importance of Rotating Savings and Credit Associations for Women.* Oxford, U.K., and Washington, DC: Berg Publishers, 1996.

Bourdillon, Michael F. C., and Meyer Fortes, eds. *Sacrifice.* London and New York: Academic Press, 1980.

Comaroff, John, ed. *The Meaning of Marriage Payments.* New York: Academic Press, 1980.

Falola, Toyin, and Paul E. Lovejoy, eds. *Pawnship in Africa: Debt Bondage in Historical Perspective.* Boulder, CO: Westview, 1994.

Ferguson, James. *The Anti-Politics Machine: "Development," Depoliticization, and Bureaucratic Power in Lesotho.* Minneapolis: University of Minnesota Press, 1994.

Gambetta, Diego. *Trust: The Making and Breaking of Cooperative Relations.* Oxford: Blackwell, 1988.

Gluckman, Max. *The Ideas in Barotse Jurisprudence.* New Haven, CT: Yale University Press, 1965.

Goody, Esther. *Parenthood and Social Reproduction: Fostering and Occupational Roles in West Africa.* Cambridge, U.K.: Cambridge University Press, 1982.

Goody, Jack, and S. J. Tambiah. *Bridewealth and Dowry.* Cambridge, U.K.: Cambridge University Press, 1973.

Gulliver, P. H. *The Family Herds.* London: Routledge and Kegan Paul, 1955.

Guyer, Jane I., ed. *Money Matters: Instability, Values and Social Payments in the Modern History of West African Communities.* Portsmouth, NH: Heinemann, 1995.

Guyer, Jane I., and Endre Stiansen. *Credit, Currencies and Culture: African Financial Institutions in Historical Perspective.* Uppsala: Nordic Africa Institute, 1999.

Hart, Keith. "Kinship, Contract, and Trust: The Economic Organization of Migrants in an African City Slum." In *Trust: Making and Breaking Co-operative Relations,* ed. Diego Gambetta. Oxford: Blackwell, 1990.

Kuper, Adam. *Wives for Cattle: Bridewealth and Marriage in Southern Africa.* London: Routledge and Kegan Paul, 1982.

LeVine, Robert A., et al. *Child Care and Culture: Lessons from Africa.* Cambridge, U.K.: Cambridge University Press, 1996.

Mannan, M. A. *Islamic Economics: Theory and Practice.* Lahore, Pakistan: Sh. Muhammad Ashraf Publishers, 1983.

Nabudere, Dani Wadada. *The Crash of International Finance Capital.* Harare, Zimbabwe: Southern Africa Political Economy Series (SAPES) Trust, 1989.

Robertson, A.F. *The Dynamics of Productive Relationships: African Share Contracts in Comparative Perspective.* Cambridge, U.K.: Cambridge University Press, 1987.

Robinson, Marguerite. *The Microfinance Revolution.* Washington, DC: World Bank, 2001.

Seidman, Ann. *Money, Banking and Public Finance in Africa.* London: Zed Books, 1986.

Shipton, Parker. *The Nature of Entrustment: Intimacy, Exchange, and the Sacred in Africa.* New Haven, CT: Yale University Press, 2007.

Tegnaeus, Harry. *Blood Brothers: An Ethno-Sociological Study of the Institution of Blood-Brotherhood with Special Reference to Africa.* Stockholm: Ethnographical Museum of Sweden, 1952.

Von Pischke, J. D. *Finance at the Frontier: Debt Capacity and the Role of Credit in the Private Economy.* Washington, DC: World Bank, 1991.

Von Pischke, J. D.; Dale W. Adams; and Gordon Donald; eds. *Rural Financial Markets in Developing Countries.* Washington, DC: World Bank, 1983.

White, Lawrence H., ed. *African Finance.* San Francisco, CA: ICS Press, 1993.

PARKER SHIPTON

DEBT BONDAGE. *See* Debt and Credit: Entrustment.

DÉBY ITNO, IDRISS

(1952–). Born in Fada, Chad, Déby was the son of a goat herder. The young Déby (he added Itno to his name in 1990) attended the officers' training school in N'Djamena, Chad's capital, and received further military training in France. He came back to Chad in 1976.

An army officer, Déby cast his lot with Hissène Habré (b. 1942), one of the regional leaders in a civil war fought from 1979 to 1982. Habré became president in 1982 and the next year made Déby the armed forces commander in chief. Déby smashed a Libyan-backed insurrection in the north in 1984 and drove Libyan troops out of Chad in 1987. But in 1989 Habré suspected Déby of plotting a coup. Déby fled to neighboring Sudan and there organized the Patriotic Salvation Movement that overthrew Habré in December 1990.

Déby became provisional president in February 1991. A long-delayed constitution was adopted by referendum in 1996, and Déby was elected to a five-year presidential term that year and again in 2001, although both elections witnessed fraud and other abuses. The human rights environment under Déby was poor as security forces committed extrajudicial killings, abductions, torture, and other abuses, and journalists critical of the government were arrested; even so, the situation was not as bad as during Chad's previous, unelected regimes.

Relations with Libya improved under Déby, but after Sudanese rebels and their supporters from the Darfur region began fleeing into eastern Chad in large numbers in 2003, Chad–Sudan relations deteriorated. The completion of an oil pipeline in 2003 brought Chad significant oil revenues, but in the summer of 2006, Déby challenged foreign oil companies over Chad's share of oil money and expelled two of the three firms involved. A constitution ratified by a 2005 referendum, widely believed to be fraudulent, ended the two-term limit for presidents, and in May 2006, Déby was elected to a third term.

See also **Chad.**

BIBLIOGRAPHY

Eriksson, Hans, and Björn Hagströmer. *Chad: Towards Democratisation or Petro-dictatorship.* Uppsala, Sweden: Nordiska Afrikainstitutet, 2004.

Massey, Simon, and Roy May. "Commentary: The Crisis in Chad." *African Affairs* 105, no. 420 (2006): 443–449.

Nolutshungu, Sam C. *Limits of Anarchy: Intervention and State Formation in Chad.* Charlottesville: University Press of Virginia, 1996.

MICHAEL LEVINE

DECOLONIZATION.

No neat line separates a "colonial" era from a "postcolonial" situation. In the decade and a half after World War II, "colonialism" was a moving target, not a fixed object. And the aims of political activists in different parts of Africa were not limited to the single goal of producing independent states, each the expression of a particular national sentiment. Some dreamed of a pan-African nation embracing oppressed people of color wherever they had ended up, others of turning empires into a Euro-African community stripped of colonial inequality. Instead of seeing a stolid colonialism leaving determinant legacies to a present-day Africa divided into nation-states, one should remember the possibilities, the hopes, the struggles, and the disappointments that Africans experienced along the way.

The challenge to colonial regimes at the end of World War II should be seen from both an African and a worldwide perspective. France, Britain, and other colonial powers, aware of the weakness and discredit spawned by the war and of the assertiveness of colonized people realized that their empires would have to change. That awareness presented African leaders with alternatives, within and outside colonial systems. Political movements drew on olderhistories of mobilization within Africa: on

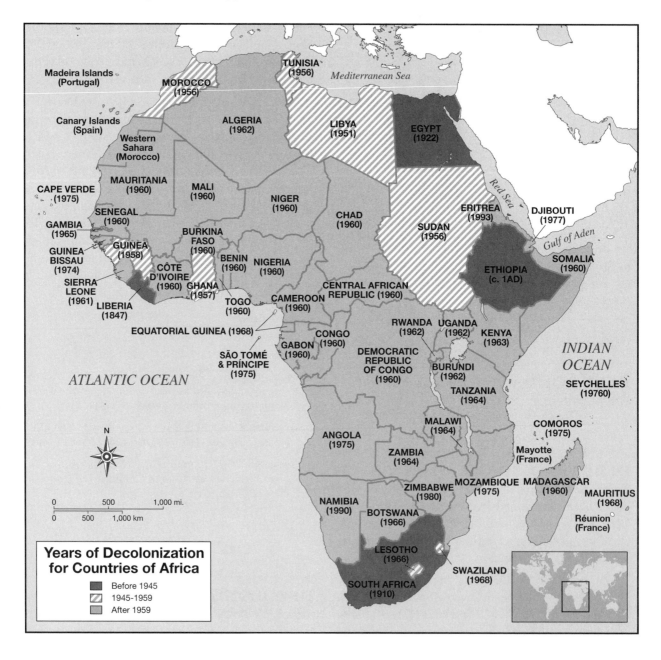

Years of Decolonization for Countries of Africa

- Before 1945
- 1945-1959
- After 1959

pan-African connections dating to the late nineteenth century, on antifascist and anticolonial coalitions that came together after the Italian invasion of Ethiopia in 1935, on local and regional resistance movements that had erupted in rural areas ever since the colonial conquests, on labor organizations that had multiplied since the late 1930s, and on educated and professional activists who kept challenging colonial regimes in courts, in the press, and in the colonial legislative councils. Up until the 1940s, colonial regimes had been able to weather such challenges, in large part because of their own limited transformative ambitions and the compartmentalization of much of rural Africa into ethnically defined administrative units.

THE OPENING

A colonial crisis began with recovery from the depression of 1929, as African workers returned to employers who were slow to raise wages and to cities with virtually no social services. A wave of strikes began in the British Copperbelt in 1935, engulfing entire towns. Other waves rose along railroads in the Gold Coast and in ports in Kenya, Tanganyika, and elsewhere. An even bigger wave struck the British West Indies. The limited communications channels and the isolated islands of capitalist production in colonial Africa proved vulnerable, even if Africa remained primarily rural and agricultural. The British at last accepted, in the Colonial Development and Welfare Act of 1940, the need to use metropolitan resources to restore social peace and provide minimally acceptable social services to vulnerable areas. Then came the war—to which Africans contributed their bodies and their labor, and from which they received little in return. British Africa in particular faced new waves of strikes, and officials lost the initiative as each concession led to further demands. In French Africa, parallel developments occurred after the war—including major strikes and urban conflicts between 1945 and 1948—to which new development programs were in part a response.

The international context had also changed. France's loss of Indochina and the Netherlands' loss of Indonesia to the Japanese led to a revolutionary situation when the powers tried to repossess their colonies after Japan's defeat in 1945. They never fully succeeded, unable to conquer

growing movements for independence and radical social transformation in those countries, while India achieved a negotiated decolonization in 1947. Such revolutions set out alternatives of which both colonial rulers and political leaders in Africa were aware. Meanwhile, colonial ideologies became less convincing in metropoles as well as in the colonies, as Nazism and the war discredited the smug self-confidence that many in Europe once had in the naturalness of the white man's rule. Reconciling Europe's need for African resources—greater than ever in the era of postwar reconstruction—with the political necessity of putting a progressive face on imperial systems defined an opening for demands on European powers. For France and Britain, the idea of "development" seemed to offer an answer: this approach would provide an influx of metropolitan capital and knowledge, improved infrastructure, European industrial and agricultural techniques, and better services. Development would therefore both increase output for the Europeans and raise the standard of living for Africans.

Portugal and Belgium, in different ways, tried to join the development bandwagon without making any political concessions. South Africa was buffeted by some of the same emancipatory winds as the rest of Africa, and one can see parallels in the labor and political movements there and in colonial Africa in the years after the war, particularly in the great gold mine strike of 1946 and more radical currents in the African National Congress. But after the Afrikaner-dominated National Party won the election of 1948, policy took a different direction: toward aggressive economic development combined with draconian policing of African political activities, tighter restrictions on their owning land, and careful control over Africans' movements between country and city. State strategies intended to foster economic development while denying Africans' political voice would collapse dramatically in the case of the Belgian Congo and persist somewhat longer in Portuguese Africa and South Africa.

MOBILIZATION AND AFRICAN SOCIETY

If one can sense the vulnerability of European powers in the postwar years, one also needs to understand the multiple ways in which Africans mobilized and the diverse objectives which they sought by the 1940s. There were attempts to make chiefdoms more influential, efforts by urban migrants to strengthen their communities of origin, and attempts to combat threats to the spiritual health of local communities. Christian or Muslim movements crossed cultural boundaries. Pan-Africanists, from the Americas as well as Africa, came together in a conference in Manchester in 1945 to demand the global liberation of people of color.

While formally organized political parties were not the only locus of political mobilization, they were crucial in bringing together different modes of protest, bridging the gap between literate elites and peasants and workers. In Nigeria and the Gold Coast, older elite organizations turned into mass parties, not only enrolling individuals but also linking together networks and organizations. In French Africa, the *Rassemblement Démocratique Africaine*, organized in 1946, was notable for grouping political parties in individual territories into a party that represented French Africa as a whole.

Social action was necessarily political, and political action invariably had social implications. In the 1945–1950 strike wave, unions in French Africa kept transforming French insistence that colonized and colonizers were part of a single, transoceanic France into demands that all workers in the colonies receive the same pay and benefits as their counterparts in Europe. Although political leaders saw workers as a constituency and unions saw political action as useful to their cause, a tension grew between the idea of equivalence among workers and solidarity among the Africans of many backgrounds who were united in the nationalist movements. Similarly, one must consider a wide variety of issues of concern to peasants—intrusive colonial agricultural projects, land appropriation, below-market prices paid to farmers by colonial crop marketing boards—in all their specificity, while recognizing that every success any movement had contributed to a general sense of empowerment.

Nationalist leaders like Kwame Nkrumah or Leopold Senghor were "machine politicians" in the best sense of the term. They could draw on a common sense of frustration and denigration at the hands of the colonial state. Yet such coalitions were as fragile as they were, for a time, powerful.

THE LIMITS OF COLONIAL CONTROL

France and Britain sought to contain movements within carefully constructed boundaries. In certain brutal ways, they succeeded; notably, in the French repression of an armed insurrections in Sétif in Algeria (1945), and in Madagascar (1947) and in the later but longer effort of the British against the Mau Mau rebellion in Kenya (1952–c. 1958). They set certain limits, primarily with regard to demands for independence that arose before European governments were ready to respond to them and forms of political action that they regarded as violent, as communistic, or as primitive.

British and French governments tried to mold political change in characteristically different ways. Both realized they had to give Africans—or at least elite Africans—a voice in the political process, hoping to confine protest within certain controllable institutions. The French in 1946 abandoned their old distinction between subject and citizen, declared all people in their colonies to be citizens with equal civil rights, and—although suffrage only gradually moved toward universality—with the right to elect members of legislatures, including the *Assemblée Nationale* of France itself. The British did the opposite, hoping to channel educated colonial subjects toward participation in local councils or to a much lesser extent in legislative councils in each territory—with no representation at all in the British parliament. Neither power succeeded in binding political activity the way it wanted. Instead, both country's attempts unleashed waves of mobilization, campaigning, and escalating demands for fuller participation and for material resources to be channeled to constituents.

The holding of elections prompted politicians to attempt to exploit whatever social ties they had. In Nigeria, the Gold Coast, and Senegal, teachers, civil servants, and wage workers already constituted political blocs. In French Equatorial Africa, the weakness of colonial education efforts and the fragmented nature of colonial society meant that politics created its own social base: the first generation of politicians competing in the postwar elections used patronage resources to build a clientele. Since such vertical ties tended to link politicians with people to whom they had regional or ethnic ties, electoral politics fostered an ethnicizing logic.

Meanwhile, other forms of political connection—from pan-Africanism to Muslim brotherhoods—received no such representation nor encouragement. In the case of Algeria, the French extension of citizenship to Muslim Algerians proved to be too little too late, subverted by well-organized French settlers and repudiated by much of the nationalist leadership. When the National Liberation Front (FLN) began an armed struggle in 1954 and the French government—insisting that Algeria, unlike West and Equatorial Africa, was an integral part of the French Republic—began a brutal campaign of repression, the situation became polarized. The FLN was riven by factionalism and its leadership underwent repeated purges. With extensive use of torture and collective punishment of suspected rebels, France achieved a measure of military success, but it lost the political war. The pace of political change elsewhere, the influence of newly independent African and Asian countries in international organizations, and the fear of the United States that die-hard defense of colonial interests would compromise the struggle against communism put mounting pressure on France to find an exit strategy, and by 1962 it had done so. Fighting among FLN factions promptly began, however, and celebrations of liberation were short-lived.

Meanwhile, in other parts of Africa, governments had to steer a narrow pathway between the danger of anticolonial revolution—such as the armed struggles in Kenya, Cameroon, and later in much of southern Africa—and the costs of meeting escalating demands by African politicians who operated within the institutional framework of postwar colonialism. The very interest of Great Britain and France in excluding extremists gave the moderates more room to maneuver, and leaders like Kwame Nkrumah and later Jomo Kenyatta successfully combined mass support with enough demonstrated respect for existing economic and political institutions to trade in the label of "dangerous demagogue" for that of "responsible moderate."

The spirit of making claims—by workers for wages equal to those of workers from Europe, by war veterans for equal pensions, by students for equal access to educational opportunity, by farmers for a fair share of the world market price for their crops—trapped Britain and France in a spiral of demands they were not prepared to meet.

From the late 1940s, leaders in British Africa were pushing the envelope on territorial politics, demanding internal self-government followed by independence. In French Africa, the empire-wide framework was being turned by leaders like Senghor into a demand that was radical in a different way: for making the administrative unit of French West Africa into a federation of territories, with a federal parliament and a federal executive, while turning the French empire into a confederation: a union of autonomous states that choose to stay together for mutual benefit. By the 1950s, and particularly among students, the slogan of independence would be heard increasingly in French Africa, but until the very end of the 1950s, the desire for autonomy was part of a spectrum of opinion about how to transform the unequal structures of empire into some form of layered sovereignty, in which Africans could both exercise power at home and retain a voice in a multinational Francophone confederation.

As early as 1951 or 1952, officials in France and Great Britain were complaining about the results of the development drive. Heavy expenditure of public funds was failing to produce private investment; the inadequate infrastructure was choking on the new supplies coming in; the lack of trained personnel and the strength of African trade unions in ports, mines, and railways was driving up labor costs; and African societies were being stubbornly resilient in the face of newfound colonial aspirations to change the ways they produced and lived. In fact, this was the great era of expansion of exports such as copper, cocoa, and coffee from Africa—the most impressive of the colonial era.

But the dynamism of African export economies was more chaotic and conflictual than the Eurocentric image of harmonious and controlled development that had been conceived by officials. The development project did not do the political work of satisfying its colonial subjects: Development efforts created more conflicts than they resolved. For example, when white or black farmers used land more intensely, they cracked down on tenants—a major cause of the Mau Mau rebellion in Kenya. Even the authors of the success stories of the late-colonial era—such as prosperous West African cocoa farmers or operators of transportation fleets—used their gains to challenge

European-owned firms or to support politicians that criticized colonial rule.

By 1956 or 1957, French and British governments and elements of the press were doing something they had not done before: coldly calculating the costs and benefits of empire. Familiar images of colonial ideology reappeared: an Africa of vast, untamed space inhabited by backward people—remote from the images of the citizen or of the economic man with which European elites associated. The two governments began to think about extricating themselves from the continent. Part of the postwar thinking about development eased the imaginative transition: Development had become a universal possibility, one dependent on European know-how and funds, so that European elites could expect that Africans would follow a path that would keep them in close and dependent relationship to Europe. But there was an element of cynicism too: a desire for African governments, not European ones, to assume the responsibility for handling the complications of change.

African politicians had built their power bases within the territories defined by the colonial powers seventy years earlier. These boundaries and the institutions of state provided the basis for negotiated decolonization, marginalizing other kinds of affinities and aspirations. With the Sudan and the Gold Coast leading the way—acquiring independence in 1956 and 1957, respectively—followed by Nigeria, French Equatorial and West Africa, and the Belgian Congo in 1960, and other British colonies (except for Southern Rhodesia) by 1964, the die was cast. The independence of Algeria in 1962 marked the fact that France and Britain, like their former colonies, were now more national and less imperial than they had ever been before.

In international circles, decolonization created new norms, with countries like India that had gained independence earlier making use of the United Nations and other organizations to chip away at the seeming normality of colonial empire. Political movements in mandated territories such as Cameroon or Tanganyika gained access to these sponsoring groups even before independence, and as more countries left empires, those states added a collective voice to anticolonial politics, such as those expressed at the Bandung conference of 1955 and the All Africa People's Congress in Ghana in 1958. Meanwhile, the United States

and the Soviet Union tried to capture the development ideal for themselves, and to seek allies among the newly independent states and demonstrate the respective superiority of their capitalist or communist models. For a time, such processes gave elite groups of anticolonial or postcolonial politicians room to maneuver: to assert a predominantly national interest in the development process and seek to balance old colonial powers and new world powers against each other.

A WORLD OF NATIONS?

The world was coming to consist of juridically equivalent nation-states, and self-determination had gone from an idea honored mainly in the breach to a standard whose violation turned the last bastions of white domination (Portuguese Africa, Southern Rhodesia, and South Africa) into pariah states. By 1975, 1980, and 1994, respectively, the specifically colonial and racial nature of those white-settled polities had been repudiated. Decolonization—emerging out of local and global political struggles—redefined the meaning of sovereignty worldwide.

But the brave new world of nation-states also had its limits. Decolonization did not end social or political inequality or equalize the uneven power to determine the categories of political analysis. It would be a mistake to see colonialism either as a phenomenon that could be turned off like a television set—with all problems instantly turned into African responsibilities—or to define a colonial legacy that determined Africa's fate. The anxieties and the brittle repressiveness of new African rulers reflected as much their appreciation and fear of the diverse movements they had built as their inability to confront the divisions in society which the colonial regimes had encouraged. Both colonial regimes and their independent successors were gatekeeper states, facing great difficulty routinizing the exercise of power outside of capital cities, communications links, and commercial or mining centers, best able to manipulate the interface between inside and outside. Their great fear was that political movements would draw on connections to social groups independent of the regime, within and beyond their borders. Postcolonial gatekeeper states were perhaps better able than colonial states to forge relations of clientelism, but in the absence of external, coercive power coming from without, they were extremely vulnerable to any attempt to contest access to the gate itself. Cycles of coups and military governments, as well as of repression of citizen action, began shortly after decolonization.

One must keep in mind the political dynamics that ended up creating an Africa of brittle gatekeeper states. But one should remember as well the many futures imagined by Africans since the 1940s and the many forms in which mobilization took place. In less than two decades after World War II, colonial empires went from an ordinary fact of political life to the embodiment of illegitimate power, and the idea that Africans could rule themselves went from inconceivable to ordinary. This rapid reversal hopefully tells one as much about Africa's future as about its past.

See also **Aid and Development; Independence and Freedom, Early African Writers; Kenyatta, Jomo; Neocolonialism; Nkrumah, Francis Kwia Kofi; Senghor, Léopold Sédar; United Nations.**

BIBLIOGRAPHY

Allman, Jean Marie. *The Quills of the Porcupine: Asante Nationalism in an Emergent Ghana.* Madison: University of Wisconsin Press, 1993.

Anderson, David. *Histories of the Hanged: Britain's Dirty War and the End of Empire.* New York: Norton, 2005.

Bayart, Jean-François. *The State in Africa: The Politics of the Belly.* London: Longman, 1993.

Berman, Bruce, and John Lonsdale. *Unhappy Valley: Conflict in Kenya and Africa, Book Two: Violence and Ethnicity.* London: James Currey, 1992.

Bernault, Florence. *Démocraties ambiguës en Afrique Centrale: Congo-Brazzaville, Gabon: 1940–1965.* Paris: Karthala, 1996.

Birmingham, David, and Phyllis Martin, eds. *History of Central Africa: The Contemporary Years since 1960.* London: Longman, 1998.

Bonner, Philip, Peter Delius, and Deborah Posel, eds. *Apartheid's Genesis, 1935—1962.* Johannesburg: Ravan, 1993.

Chafer, Tony. *The End of Empire in French West Africa: France's Successful Decolonization?* Oxford: Berg, 2002.

Connelly, Matthew. *A Diplomatic Revolution: Algeria's Fight for Independence and the Origins of the Post–Cold War Era.* New York: Oxford University Press, 2002.

Cooper, Frederick. *Decolonization and African Society: The Labor Question in French and British Africa.* Cambridge, U.K.: Cambridge University Press, 1996.

Cooper, Frederick. *Africa since 1940: The Past of the Present.* Cambridge, U.K.: Cambridge University Press, 2002.

Mazrui, Ali, ed. *General History of Africa: Africa since 1935.* Berkeley: University of California Press for UNESCO, 1993.

Mbembe, Achille. *On the Postcolony.* Berkeley: University of California Press, 2001.

Ranger, T. O. "Nationalist Historiography, Patriotic History and the History of the Nation: the Struggle over the Past in Zimbabwe." *Journal of Southern African Studies* 30 (2004): 215–234.

Shepard, Todd. *The Invention of Decolonization: The Algerian War and the Remaking of France.* Ithaca, NY: Cornell University Press, 2006.

FREDERICK COOPER

DEMOGRAPHY

This entry includes the following articles:
OVERVIEW
FERTILITY AND INFERTILITY
MORTALITY
POPULATION DATA AND SURVEYS

OVERVIEW

Among the social sciences, with the possible exception of economics, demography has most assiduously sought to develop uniform measures of social behavior and methods that may be applied universally to societies across time and space. And while scholars in many fields express concern about insufficient sources of information, demographers studying populations in both the present and the past seem particularly preoccupied by the lack of data—perhaps because the field defines "useful" facts and measures in very specific ways.

Demography emerged as an international science with the founding of the International Union for the Scientific Study of Population in 1928 and the intensifying attention accorded population growth after World War II. Divergent definitions, measures, and methods to assess population change converged, so that by the beginning of the independence era in Africa in the late 1950s, professional demographers everywhere spoke a common language and engaged in research on similar topics whose results were designed to be comparable. United Nations agencies, other international institutions, foundations, and western countries such as the United States, France, and the United Kingdom fostered and financed the development of an international demography.

CONTEMPORARY AFRICAN DEMOGRAPHY: CENSUSES, SAMPLE SURVEYS, AND METHODS

Demographic studies of Africa, African countries, and individual populations echo and underscore these concerns. The greatest challenge for African demography in the modern era has indeed been the shortage of demographic data as defined by the field at large. Initial concern in the 1960s and 1970s focused on the limited number of national censuses for African countries and the much smaller number of countries for which there existed several censuses, necessary for analyses of the evolution of populations through time. The modern census is the classic demographic operation, designed to collect information simultaneously about all people within a clearly defined territory (most often a nation-state). By this definition, there have been virtually no censuses in Africa—although in the late nineteenth and early twentieth centuries, authorities in many European colonies often referred to partial and imperfect enumerations as censuses.

Recognizing problems posed by limited personnel and poor infrastructure, however, African censuses conducted over several days have become the norm, and procedures and methods have been developed to assess inaccuracies introduced by mobility. By 2000, at least one census had been conducted in almost all African countries. New concerns, however, focus on the growing number of countries and regions afflicted by war, upheaval, and refugee flight, conditions that undermine efforts to conduct new censuses.

To fill the census data gap, demographers developed sample surveys, aimed at collecting data on specific demographic phenomena from smaller populations statistically representative of national populations. French colonial demographers pioneered sample survey methodology in Africa in the late colonial period. The largest series of sample surveys were the international World Fertility Survey of the 1970s and 1980s, and the American-funded Demographic and Health Surveys, which began in the late 1980s and continued into the twenty-first century. These series of surveys targeted fertility behaviors and their "proximate determinants," or factors that influence childbearing. Smaller numbers of sample surveys in Africa have gathered information about mortality and migration, although their numbers have increased since the mid-1990s. In the 1990s a regional series of migration surveys (*Reseau migration et urbanization en Afrique de l'Ouest*) also collected data on mobility in eight West African countries. Other coordinated migration studies have been done in southern Africa. In the late twentieth century, continuing high levels of infant and child mortality in Africa led to more studies of mortality. The HIV/AIDS epidemic, which affects Africa more than any other continent, has stimulated mortality and morbidity surveys, along with study of their proximate determinants.

In light of inadequate information, demographers of Africa have made important contributions to the field by developing techniques for the analysis of imperfect data. Sample surveys were a response to this need. The multiple-round survey—repeated visits to people in a sample to chart the evolution of births and child development—is another methodological contribution of African demographic studies. Given the ever-growing bodies of population data available for other parts of the world and despite progress in data collection in Africa, however, many demographers would probably still consider the continent to be demographically underdeveloped.

CONTEMPORARY AFRICAN DEMOGRAPHY: CONCEPTS, MODELS, AND THEORIES

Beyond deficiencies of data, African demographers have also struggled with how to apply, adapt, and ultimately broaden concepts, models, and theories conceived for societies elsewhere—notably in Europe and North America. For example, elsewhere in this encyclopedia, Jack Caldwell notes that conventional demographic definitions of marital status do not reflect the forms and processes of many African marriage systems. Similarly, understandings of the family derived from research in western nations do not accurately reflect core domestic units in Africa, which may include near and more removed relatives as well as other people. Demographers working on Africa have responded to these differences by elaborating and contextualizing the concept of the household. In an effort to understand the reasons for continued high levels of child bearing in Africa, Caldwell pioneered the concept of the reversal of intergenerational flows of wealth (from parents-to-children to children-to-parents) that afforded security to parents in their later years. Africanist demographers also developed methods to study the demographic characteristics of nomads who do not have a fixed residence.

The Demographic Transition.

Beyond concepts, demographers of Africa have raised important questions about two fundamental demographic models and theories. The first is the demographic transition. Often termed a theory, but more accurately referred to as a model, since it describes a process without identifying precise causes or predicting timing, the model of the demographic transition was formulated by historical demographers of Europe. It describes the preindustrial or premodern era as a time of high fertility, high mortality, and hence slow population growth. Industrialization, urbanization, and, eventually, the spread of public health measures led to a drop in mortality. But fertility remained high, prompting great population growth. Eventually, fertility began to drop—as new "modern" values and changing economic interests favored smaller families. Following World War II, demographers who were alarmed about rapid population growth in the nonwestern world, including Africa, posited that this European model could be used to understand rapid demographic growth outside the West.

The stages of this European model raised the question of what development measures might be taken to slow the population explosion in the developing world, since the transition was intimately tied to modernity. Since then, demographic studies of the developing world have been preoccupied with fostering the demographic transition and predicting when it will begin. Indeed, it is true that birth rates have dropped—dramatically in some cases—in much of the developing world, although the combinations of reasons for the decline seem to differ from one place to another.

In Africa, however, high fertility has been very persistent, leading to debates about whether African societies would ever make what was also considered to be a transition to modernity. In another example of "African exceptionalism," demographers began to suggest that only Africa would resist the transition. At first, international demographic institutions and their researchers focused on the cause for this peculiarly African problem, rather than analyzing the persistence of high birth rates in African terms. Beginning with Zimbabwe in the mid-1980s, however, fertility rates began to fall across the continent, although at a slow pace. Nonetheless, fertility in Africa south of the Sahara remains the highest in the world. African experiences suggest that the reasons for the transition are very complex and the demographic transition is not necessarily a path to modernity as previously understood.

Modernization Theory.

More than the other social sciences, demography has clung to modernization theory. The demographic transition, for example, was not only intended to bring smaller families, but also to set up social institutions that resembled those of western nations. African demographic experiences illustrate that social change is more varied than modernization theory predicts. For example, modernization is usually paired with urbanization, and both trends are accompanied by declines in family size and the practice of polygyny. In West African cities, however, fertility levels have dropped, but only slowly, and polygyny levels remain astonishingly high. Lineage solidarity trumps the unity of the nuclear family. Moreover, fertility may well have increased in the early twentieth century, even though this era is associated with colonial rule and modernization. Young people in many areas do seem to be more independent, however, due to the effects of education and labor migration. New communications technologies allow greater interaction with migrants and others living elsewhere in Africa and abroad, presenting alternative models for social and family life. Tabutin and Shoumaker (2004) underscore the increasing diversity of demographic behavior in sub-Saharan Africa, an indication that the uniformity predicted by modernization theory is more a hindrance than a help in understanding the demography of contemporary Africa.

African Historical Demography.

African demography has been extraordinarily ahistorical, despite the fact that some of the most eminent demographers of the continent have been pioneers in European historical demography. This inconsistency stems, once again, from lack of data—or at least data that allow the calculation of the indices and measures that are the stock and trade of contemporary demography. Funding priorities in African demography also heavily favor research on contemporary population. Nonetheless, a few demographers and historians have continued to try to uncover sources (such as several hundred early censuses from the Portuguese colony of Angola, or parish registers from the nineteenth century in West Africa) that would permit conventional studies in historical demography. Others have identified new kinds of sources or have attempted to apply methods to adjust imperfect contemporary data to available historical materials, such as the censuses of the former French and British colonies.

Finally, scholars of Africa have suggested interdisciplinary approaches to analysis that should yield important insights into the historical evolution of African populations, even if they do not produce the conventional demographic indices. For the most part, demographers of Africa express interest in the historical demography of the continent, but few have engaged in such research. Ironically, then, just as western historians in the first half of the twentieth century claimed that Africa had no history because many of the conventional sources of historical study did not exist, some twenty-first-century demographers suggest that Africa has no demographic history because conventional demographic sources are not plentiful.

See also **Disease: HIV/AIDS, Social and Political Aspects.**

BIBLIOGRAPHY

Cordell, Dennis, and Joel W. Gregory. "Historical Demography and Demographic History in Africa: Theoretical and Methodological Considerations." *Canadian Journal of African Studies/Revue canadienne des ètudes africaines* 14, no. 3 (1980): 389–416.

Cordell, Dennis, and Joel W. Gregory, eds. *African Population and Capitalism: Historical Perspectives.* Madison: University of Wisconsin Press, 1994.

Fetter, Bruce, ed. *Demography from Scanty Evidence: Central Africa in the Colonial Era.* Boulder, CO: Lynne Rienner Publishers, 1990.

Kuczynski, R. R. *Demographic Survey of the British Colonial Empire,* Vol. 1: *West Africa.* London: Oxford University Press, 1948.

Kuczynski, R. R. *Demographic Survey of the British Colonial Empire,* Vol. 2: *East Africa, Etc.* London: Oxford University Press, 1949.

Lamptey, Peter R.; Jami L. Johnson; and Marya Khan. "The Global Challenge of HIV and AIDS." *Population Bulletin* 61, no. 1 (March 2006):1–24.

Locoh, Thérèse, and Véronique Hertrich, eds. *The Onset of Fertility Transition in Sub-Saharan Africa.* Liège,

Belgium: International Union for the Scientific Study of Population, 1994.

Tabutin, D., and B. Schoumaker. "The Demography of Sub-Saharan Africa from 1950s to the 2000s: A Survey of Changes and a Statistical Assessment." *Population-E,* 59, nos. 3–4 (2004): 457–556.

Zuberi, Tukufu; Amson Sibanda; and Eric Udjo; eds. *The Demography of South Africa.* Armonk, NY: M.E. Sharpe, 2005.

DENNIS D. CORDELL

FERTILITY AND INFERTILITY

Africa presents paradoxes with respect to levels of fertility and infertility. Whereas certain countries of Africa have among the highest levels of fertility in the world, others have had among the fastest fertility reductions in the late twentieth and early twenty-first centuries. Africa is also the world region with the highest levels of both fertility and infertility, because social, economic, and cultural structures that favor large families also tend to give rise to patterns of sexual mobility that expose individuals to risk of sterility.

The characterization of fertility and infertility is the product of demographic, public health, and reproductive health interests. Demographically, fertility indicates the average number of live children born per woman, and infertility refers to the absence of live children born to women. In the health field, "sterility" is also used to refer to the underlying condition of an infertile person, not observable in demographic terms.

HISTORY

As far as is known, fertility has been high in Africa since the development of settled agriculture. But high fertility has been accompanied by high mortality due largely to communicable diseases; thus African populations grew slowly. Mortality declined in Africa during the twentieth century, notably after World War II, and population growth increased accordingly. Mortality in Africa remains higher than in other regions and having in fact risen as a result of HIV/AIDS, it can decrease substantially more. Fertility decline due to the practice of modern contraceptive methods has also lagged behind other regions. For these reasons, the downturn in population growth estimated by the United Nations (UN) to have begun in Africa in the 1990s occurred a quarter of a century after other regions and is proceeding more slowly.

Sexually transmitted diseases, some of which can cause irreversible reproductive pathology in women, introduced sterility to African populations. It is likely that sexually transmitted diseases came to Africa with European and West Asian explorers beginning in the mid-fourteenth century and spread inland from coastal settlements along waterways and trade routes. Non-Africans encountered indigenous levels of sexual toleration ranging from permissive to restrictive. Slavery aggravated disease transmission due to behavioral change associated with the displacement of people, the disruption of the social order, and sexual exploitation. Until the 1980s gonorrhea was the main cause of infertility, but since then, chlamydia increased to account for a larger share of sterility-inducing disease and is now the leading cause of infertility.

LEVELS AND TRENDS IN FERTILITY

Fertility assessment comes from survey research and indirect estimation using census data. Information on trends since World War II derives from a pioneering assemblage of case studies for the 1950s and 1960s by William Brass and others, the participation of fourteen countries in the *World Fertility Survey* in the late 1970s and early 1980s (Bénin, Cameroon, Côte d'Ivoire, Egypt, Ghana, Kenya, Lesotho, Mauritania, Morocco, Nigeria, Rwanda, Senegal, Sudan (North) and Tunisia), and the execution in forty countries of the ongoing *Demographic and Health Surveys* since the mid-1980s.

According to United Nations assessments, the average fertility of women in 2000– 2005 in continental Africa ranged between 2.0 and 7.9 live births, with a regional average of 5.0 (see Table 1). Countries with the highest fertility rates (over 6.5 live births) are found in Western Africa (Burkina Faso, Guinea-Bissau, Liberia, Mali, Niger, Sierra Leone), Eastern Africa (Burundi, Uganda), and Middle Africa (Angola, Chad, Democratic Republic of the Congo). Countries in Southern and Northern Africa have the lowest fertility, ranging from 2.8 to 4 live births in Southern Africa (Botswana, Lesotho, Namibia, South Africa, Swaziland, Zimbabwe) and 2.0 to 4.5 in Northern Africa (Algeria, Egypt, Libyan Arab Jamahiriya, Morocco, Sudan, and Tunisia).

Among the countries with lowest fertility, some have undergone remarkably rapid fertility declines. In Northern Africa, live births fell by two-thirds between 1970–1975 and 2000–2005 in Algeria and Tunisia, equivalent to more than four births per woman in each case, and by one-third—over two births—in Sudan. Similarly, in Southern Africa, live births fell by over one-third—or just over two births—in Lesotho over the same period. African islands display both moderately high fertility (Comoros and Madagascar) and low fertility (Mauritius, Réunion). In Cape Verde, live births fell by nearly half between 1970–1975 and 2000–2005 to under four births per woman.

Fertility is determined by a combination of biological and behavioral factors that are fully identified, which are the occurrence of sexual intercourse (coital frequency), sterility, breastfeeding, abstinence, abortion, and contraceptive practice. Determinants vary in importance by country. For African countries, fertility was generally high until the 1980s because marriage was universal and there was little birth prevention aside from the indigenous practice of postpartum abstinence (abstention from intercourse for a long period after delivery). Other nonmodern methods of contraception include withdrawal (coitus interruptus) and periodic abstinence (rhythm), as well as folk or traditional methods for which there is no evidence of effectiveness. Factors that now determine variability in fertility from country to country include the persistence of postpartum abstinence, the prevalence of pathological or acquired sterility and resulting infertility, and the rising use of modern contraceptive methods, including hormonal contraception, sterilization, condoms, and IUDs.

POSTPARTUM ABSTINENCE AND FERTILITY REGULATION

Although some African countries have markedly high fertility, women have fewer births than the biologically possible maximum because fertility is significantly lowered by prolonged breastfeeding and postpartum abstinence. Breastfeeding suppresses the physiological capacity to bear children for part of its duration, and abstinence lasting as long as breastfeeding, or longer, guarantees that total fertility will be effectively dampened. These practices are recognized as means to protect newly

Fertility and infertility in Africa (continental countries), 2000–2005

Region	Average fertility*	Range of fertility	Countries with highest fertility (6.5 live births or more)	Countries with fertility at or below average for all Africa (5.0 live births)	Estimated range of infertility prior to the 1990s**	Average contraceptive practice***	Range of contraceptive practice	Countries with contraceptive practice at or above average for the region
Middle Africa	6.3	4.0–6.8	Angola, Democratic Republic of Congo	Cameroon, Central African Republic, Gabon	15–30	5	2–12	Gabon, Cameroon, Central African Republic
West Africa	5.9	4.4–7.9	Burkina Faso, Guinea-Bissau, Liberia, Mali, Niger, Sierra Leone	Gambia, Ghana, Senegal	3–10	8	2–13	Ghana, Togo, Gambia, Nigeria, Senegal
Eastern Africa	5.7	5.0–7.1	Burundi, Uganda	Kenya, United Republic of Tanzania	10–14	17	4–32	Kenya, Malawi, Zambia
Northern Africa	3.3	2.0–4.5	None	All	4–9	42	7–54	Algeria, Egypt, Morocco, Tunisia
Southern Africa	2.9	2.8–4.0	None	All	3–4	51	26–55	South Africa
All Africa: • range • average		2.0–7.9 5.0			3–30	20	2–55	

*average number of live births per woman of childbearing age (15–49 years)
**percent of women childless at age 45–49 years (or 45 years and over in the case of the early World Fertility Survey)
***percent of women of childbearing age (15–49 years) using a modern method, latest available year

SOURCE: United Nations. *World Population Policies 2005*. New York: United Nations, 2006. Available from http://www.un.org/esa/population/publications/WPP2005/Publication_index.htm; Frank, Odile. "Infertility in Sub-Saharan Africa: Estimates and Implications." *Population and Development Review* 9, no. 1 (March 1983); World Fertility Survey, multiple years. Available from http://opr.princeton.edu/archive/wfs/; and Demographic and Health Surveys, multiple years. Available from http://www.measuredhs.com/.

Table 1.

born children from the harmful effects of short birth intervals, rather than to reduce the number of births: they are generally practiced explicitly to regulate, but not reduce, fertility.

Breastfeeding is a mainstay of nutrition and child survival. Social patterns for breastfeeding and abstinence durations probably long ago settled at equilibrium points that traded off higher fertility for the support they gave child survival. Historical information suggests postpartum abstinence was typically long (over a year) in Western Africa and shorter (under a year) in Eastern Africa. Abandonment of the practice is associated with education, urbanization, and detachment from tradition. As breastfeeding without abstinence results in earlier next pregnancies, abandonment can cause fertility increases in the short term. More generally, the effect of abandonment has been to offset the concurrent rising practice of contraception, delaying the onset of fertility decline.

No discussion of fertility in Africa is complete without mention of the effects of the HIV/AIDS epidemic. Women living with HIV/AIDS have lower coital frequency and more other sexually transmitted infections linked to infertility, and experience more fetal loss than other women These factors together reduce their fertility by as much as 25 to 40 percent when compared to other women. Population fertility is also lowered by the large numbers of premature deaths of women of childbearing age. In the late 2000s, because a minority of women who are HIV-positive know it, few women alter their behavior on the basis of their HIV status (whether positive or negative), or due to fear of HIV/AIDS. Several major impacts on fertility could occur in future, however, which may or may not be intended. These include large-scale increases in condom use to prevent HIV transmission that indifferently lower fertility; declines in breastfeeding designed to avert mother-to-child transmission (whether the risk is known or suspected) that increase fertility; and decreases in postpartum abstinence intended to lower the motivation for extra-marital sexual activity, which can also increase fertility.

INFERTILITY

Infertility has not been assessed as systematically as fertility. Existing data suggest that primary infertility (the proportion of all women who pass through the childbearing years without a live birth) reached about 10 percent of women in Africa south of the Sahara at least until the 1980s and 1990s. A larger proportion of women—often twice as many—experienced secondary infertility, having unintentionally had very few births by the end of childbearing. Highest primary infertility (roughly 15–30% of women childless) was found in Middle Africa (Angola, Cameroon, Central African Republic, Congo, Gabon, Democratic Republic of the Congo [formerly Zaïre]); primary infertility was intermediate (10–14% of women childless) in Eastern Africa (United Republic of Tanzania, Zambia), and low (fewer than 10% women childless) or absent (3% or fewer women childless) in Western Africa (see Table 1). There is less documentation on infertility in Southern and Northern Africa, but available data imply it was low or absent in the countries of both regions.

Information on trends in infertility comes from successive surveys designed to measure fertility, with the possibility of measurement bias. On that basis, there is evidence that infertility has declined, but it may have resulted more often from serendipitous treatment due to the wider availability of antibiotics than from specific diagnosis and treatment. Persistence of infertility even at low levels (for example, 7%–8% of women childless in Middle Africa in 1995–2000) is consistent with poor health infrastructure, a low priority for diagnosis and treatment of nonfatal conditions, and the advent of disease strains resistant to first-line antibiotics. Furthermore, the course of the HIV/AIDS epidemic in the region supports the contention that the sexual patterns that underlie all sexually transmitted infections are not changing favorably on a large scale.

THE INTRODUCTION OF MODERN CONTRACEPTION

After World War II demographers, development assistance foundations, and the health community became aware that declining mortality rates had begun to result in substantial population growth in developing countries. Policy to address population growth emerged with both a socioeconomic focus (to alter the demand for high fertility) and a programmatic focus (to increase the presence, acceptability, and adoption of family planning). Generally, however, family planning and contraceptive practice are often viewed as the principal—or only—policy avenues to lower fertility and population growth. Most countries of Africa were late to view population growth as undesirable and to establish family planning programs on that basis. Health betterment provided the initial political motive for family planning.

According to latest national reports to the UN, seven of forty-eight continental countries had adopted a policy to lower fertility and gave direct support to access to contraceptive methods by 1976 (Botswana, Ghana, Kenya, Lesotho, South Africa, Swaziland, Uganda), and thirty additional countries had adopted similar policies by 2005. Of the eleven remaining countries, seven had no stated policy on fertility levels (six of them reported nevertheless providing direct or indirect support to family planning programs), three reported a policy to maintain fertility levels (including South Africa that altered its policy after 1996), and only one country reported a policy to raise fertility. Of the last four countries, only two reported providing no support to family planning programs. As a result, by 2005, virtually all African countries provided some degree of support for family planning. It is noteworthy that six of the countries that had either no policy on fertility or a policy to maintain or raise fertility levels are in the former high infertility belt in Middle Africa, where there is some persistence of infertility.

ADOPTION OF CONTRACEPTIVE PRACTICE

Once contraceptive methods are introduced and their availability is assured, contraceptive adoption is a dynamic process. Estimates of prevalence of contraceptive practice are nevertheless often made at long intervals, because they rely on fertility surveys that are expensive and complex undertakings. Statistics for African countries indicate that more than half of women of childbearing age practice a modern method of contraception in South Africa and Zimbabwe (55% and 50%), and in Algeria, Egypt, and Tunisia (50%, 54%, and 51%); up to and over one-third in Morocco as well as Botswana, Kenya and Lesotho (42%, 39%, 32%, and 30%), and more than a quarter in Libyan Arab Jamahiriya, Malawi, Namibia, and Swaziland (26%

each). The proportion of women is from one in six to one in four women in Zambia, Uganda and the United Republic of Tanzania (23%, 18%, and 17%), over 13 percent in Ghana, and about 12 percent in Gabon. Elsewhere, one woman in ten (or fewer) reports practice of a modern method. Countries with the highest prevalence tend, as expected, to have the lowest fertility, but because contraceptive adoption is accompanied by reduced postpartum abstinence and shortened breastfeeding, fertility decline is observed to be delayed in some countries of Africa relative to other regions reporting the same levels of contraceptive practice.

MOTIVATION TO LIMIT FERTILITY

Historical observations and experience in other regions of the world underscore the contribution of social and economic factors, such as increasing education and income, and of institutional and structural change in the advent of a population-wide decline in family size. Better survival prospects for infants and small children due to improved living conditions are also implicated. Specific underlying causes for irreversible progression from mortality decline to fertility decline, as depicted by demographic transition theory, are, however, fundamentally unknown. Debate thereby arises over the influence of family planning programs: whether a preexisting "unmet demand" for family limitation is revealed, or a new demand is triggered by the promotion of contraceptive practice. Historical evidence that fertility declined prior to modern contraceptive practice in European populations that relied on withdrawal, abstinence, and abortion also carries weight.

Structural arguments stress the complementary role of family planning: before fertility declines, the reasons children are needed must first erode. Pronatalist factors in Africa cited by specialists include customary net wealth flow to parents. Others underline the differential benefits of parenthood for women and for men. Whereas women may derive their sole access to resources through children, men may acquire status and power from large lineages. Women may nevertheless still carry the major economic responsibility for childrearing, which creates a motivation to lower fertility once access to resources can be assured in other ways, notably due to education and greater legal and social autonomy. In addition, an institution particular to Africa, child fostering, relieves the consequences of infertility as well as the burden of large families, and disconnects the costs of childrearing from the act of chilbearing. The presence and fear of infertility may themselves discourage interference in childbearing.

Accordingly, economic opportunities for women, female education, and, more generally, "empowerment" of women are often invoked as main sources of motivation to lower family size. Others argue that desires for lower family size and willingness to practice contraception can occur as a result of the diffusion of such ideas, or by means of their legitimation within social networks. Evidence from African countries reporting fertility decline suggests that programs are tapping a demand created by concurrent structural change. Regardless of opinion on fertility decline, however, there is broad agreement that family planning programs should promote condom use in Africa because of the unique potential for HIV/AIDS containment afforded by that contraceptive method.

See also **Childbearing; Disease; Sexual Behavior.**

BIBLIOGRAPHY

Bongaarts, John, and Robert G. Potter. *Fertility, Biology, and Behavior: An Analysis of the Proximate Determinants.* New York: Academic Press, 1983.

Brass, William, et al. *The Demography of Tropical Africa.* Princeton, NJ: Princeton University Press, 1968.

Caldwell, John C. "Toward a Restatement of Demographic Transition Theory." *Population and Development Review* 2 (1976): 321–366.

Cleland, John, and Christopher Wilson. "Demand Theories of the Fertility Transition: An Iconoclastic View." *Population Studies* 41 (March 1987): 5–30.

Demographic and Health Surveys. Available from http://www.measuredhs.com/.

Frank, Odile. "Infertility in Sub-Saharan Africa: Estimates and Implications." *Population and Development Review* 9, no. 1 (March 1983).

Frank, Odile. "The Demand for Fertility Control in Sub-Saharan Africa." *Studies in Family Planning* 18, no. 4 (1987): 181–201.

Frank, Odile. "Sterility in Women in Sub-Saharan Africa." *International Planned Parenthood Federation Medical Bulletin* 21, no. 1 (1987): 6–8.

Frank, Odile. "The Childbearing Family in Sub-Saharan Africa: Structure, Fertility, and the Future." Policy, Research, and External Affairs Working Paper 509. Washington, DC: World Bank, 1990.

Frank, Odile, ed. "Historical Epidemiology: Mortality Decline, and Old and New Transitions in Health." *World Health Statistics Quarterly* 51, no. 2–4 (2000).

Frank, Odile. "Abstinence." In *The Encyclopedia of Population*, ed. Paul Demeny and Geoffrey McNicoll. New York: Macmillan, 2003.

Frank, Odile, and John Bongaarts. "Behavioural and Biological Determinants of Fertility Transition in Sub-Saharan Africa." *Statistics in Medicine* 10 (1991): 161–175.

Page, Hilary J., and Ron J. Lesthaeghe, eds. *Child-Spacing in Tropical Africa: Traditions and Change.* London: Academic Press, 1981.

United Nations. *HIV/AIDS and Fertility in Sub-Saharan Africa: A Review of the Research Literature.* New York: United Nations, 2002.

United Nations. *World Contraceptive Use 2003.* New York: United Nations, 2004. Available from http://www.un.org/esa/population/publications/contraceptive2003/wcu2003.htm.

United Nations. *World Population Policies 2005.* New York: United Nations, 2006. Available from http://www.un.org/esa/population/publications/WPP2005/Publication_index.htm.

United Nations. *World Population Prospects: The 2004 Revision.* New York: United Nations, 2005. Available from http://esa.un.org/unpp.

World Fertility Survey. Available from http://opr.princeton.edu/archive/wfs/.

ODILE FRANK

MORTALITY

OVERVIEW

Historically, mortality was high in Africa, and the introduction of European clinical medicine in the colonial era probably reduced it little, so that high levels of mortality persisted until the mid-twentieth century. Following World War II, the situation was substantially altered by changes in standards of living, levels of education, implementation of effective public health strategies and interventions—for example, the eradication of smallpox by 1977—and advances in clinical medicine, notably the advent of antibiotics. As a result, mortality in Africa steadily declined between 1950 to the mid–1980s, so much so that concerns arose over the population growth

that resulted and that would intensify as long as fertility did not also decline.

At the same time, irregular and often sluggish economic and social development, competing priorities for public expenditures, and conflicts held the decline to a slow pace, and the gap between Africa and other developing regions widened. Since that time, progress on mortality has simply lost ground, essentially due to the HIV epidemic and AIDS, as well as the inability to sustain efforts to control malaria, persistent failures of economic growth and social development, conflict and population displacement, and crises of subsistence on a large scale due to complex emergencies. There are, nevertheless, wide variations within the continent with respect to the path of economic growth and development, and the course of mortality.

ESTIMATES AND INDICATORS OF MORTALITY

Mortality is the collective characterization of deaths of individuals in a population due to all causes. Mortality levels are estimated from population censuses, surveys, and vital registration (birth and death certification). Although registration is operational in a few countries, mortality assessment in much of Africa still relies on indirect estimation derived from population censuses by applying model life tables. Life expectancy at birth is a useful indicator of mortality as it sums up mortality at different ages of either sex or both sexes at a given period. Another good indicator is infant mortality, which provides a specific picture of the survival of newborns in the first year, and is sensitive to political, economic, social, and epidemiological factors, as well as the quality of prenatal and delivery healthcare.

In recent years, household surveys designed to research a range of maternal and child health issues—particularly in resource-poor settings—have provided a rapidly growing pool of statistically well-founded information on mortality of children under five years, thereby providing a third means to document trends in African mortality. Under-five mortality in Africa is sensitive to communicable diseases (such as respiratory infections, malaria and diarrheal diseases) and to the level of immunization coverage for vaccine-preventable diseases of childhood such as measles. It is also affected by undernutrition, related in turn to underlying economic and social conditions, the presence of endemic malaria, and the prevalence of HIV.

PERIOD BETWEEN 1950–1955 AND 1985–1990

Communicable diseases have long been and still are the major causes of death in Africa. Each year at present, HIV/AIDS causes over 2 million deaths, malaria over 1.1 million deaths, and tuberculosis about 350,000 deaths. Tuberculosis has increased in Africa due to co-morbidity with HIV, and reduction of tuberculosis deaths has been slowed by drug resistance. Groups of other infectious diseases, notably diarrheal diseases and respiratory infections, together cause an estimated 1.8 million deaths. Among noncommunicable conditions, cardiovascular diseases as a group comprise the major cause, being responsible for about 1 million deaths per year. The major infectious causes of death for children under five years after the first month are acute respiratory infections, malaria, HIV/AIDS, diarrheal diseases, and measles (severe infections, birth asphyxia and prematurity are the three leading causes of death in the first month).

Average life expectancy at birth for all Africa is estimated to have stood at about 38 years in 1950–1955, and to have lengthened to 51½ years by 1985–1990 (see Table 1). A large part of these low levels of life expectancy was due to high average infant mortality that is estimated to have declined from about 180 to 107 deaths per 1,000 births over the period. From the outset, however, the situation was generally better in Northern and Southern Africa than in Eastern, Middle, and Western Africa (although less so for Northern Africa with respect to infant mortality), and the gains in Northern and Southern Africa were also greater. Life expectancy increased by 16–19 years in Northern and Southern Africa between 1950 and 1990, and exceeded 60 years by 1985–1990. During the same period, it was extended by only 11–12 years in the other regions, to a level barely reaching 50 years. Similarly, by 1985–1990, infant mortality in Southern Africa had fallen to half, and in Northern Africa to three-quarters of the level in Eastern, Middle, and Western Africa.

PERIOD AFTER 1985–1990

After 1985–1990, mortality decline in Africa entered a period of stagnation and reversal of a type that has rarely been documented in such a large, culturally diverse, and geographically dispersed population (see Table 2). Moreover, the phenomenon is age-related, given that infant mortality continued to improve, even if slowly, whereas overall mortality worsened. The situation with regard to infant mortality has not been uniform, however, and infant

---

Mortality indicators in Africa and African regions, 1950–1955 and 1985–1990, in descending order of mortality level in 1950

(life expectancy rounded to the nearest year and infant mortality*)

| Region/Year | Mortality indicators, 1950–1955 and 1985–1990 | | | | | |
| | Life expectancy (years) | | | Infant mortality (deaths per 1000 births) | | |
	1950–1955	1985–1990	Difference	1950–1955	1985–1990	Difference
Southern Africa(1)	45	61	+16	104	53	−51
Northern Africa(2)	42	61	+19	185	78	−107
All Africa	38	52	+13	179	107	−72
Eastern Africa(3)	37	50	+12	179	109	−70
Western Africa(4)	36	48	+11	188	124	−64
Middle Africa(5)	36	47	+11	187	119	−68

*Small discrepancies may occur due to the rounding

(1) Botswana, Lesotho, Namibia, South Africa, Swaziland

(2) Algeria, Egypt, Libyan Arab Jamahiriya, Morocco, Sudan, Tunisia, Western Sahara

(3) Burundi, Comoros, Djibouti, Eritrea, Ethiopia, Kenya, Madagascar, Malawi, Mauritius, Mozambique, Réunion, Rwanda, Seychelles, Somalia, Uganda, United Republic of Tanzania, Zambia, Zimbabwe

(4) Benin, Burkina Faso, Cape Verde, Côte d'Ivoire, Gambia, Ghana, Guinea, Guinea-Bissau, Liberia, Mali, Mauritania, Niger, Nigeria, Senegal, Sierra Leone, Togo

(5) Angola, Cameroon, Central African Republic, Chad, Congo, Democratic Republic of the Congo, Equatorial Guinea, Gabon, São Tomé e Príncipe

SOURCE: United Nations. *World Population Prospects: The 2004 Revision.* New York: United Nations, 2005. Available at http://esa.un.org/unpp/.

Table 1.

Mortality indicators in Africa and African regions, 1985–1990, 1995–2000, and 2005–2010, in descending order of mortality level in 1950

(Life expectancy rounded to the nearest year and infant mortality*)

| Region/Year | Mortality indicators, 1985–1990, 1995–2000, 2005–2010 | | | | | |
| | Life expectancy (years) | | | Infant mortality (deaths per 1000 births) | | |
	1985–1990	1995–2000	2005–2010	1985–1990	1995–2000	2005–2010
Southern Africa(1)	61	58	43	53	45	40
Northern Africa(2)	61	65	68	78	53	38
All Africa	52	50	50	107	99	89
Eastern Africa(3)	50	46	47	109	98	86
Western Africa(4)	48	47	47	124	117	108
Middle Africa(5)	47	43	45	119	125	110

*Small discrepancies may occur due to the rounding

(1) Botswana, Lesotho, Namibia, South Africa, Swaziland

(2) Algeria, Egypt, Libyan Arab Jamahiriya, Morocco, Sudan, Tunisia, Western Sahara

(3) Burundi, Comoros, Djibouti, Eritrea, Ethiopia, Kenya, Madagascar, Malawi, Mauritius, Mozambique, Réunion, Rwanda, Seychelles, Somalia, Uganda, United Republic of Tanzania, Zambia, Zimbabwe

(4) Benin, Burkina Faso, Cape Verde, Côte d'Ivoire, Gambia, Ghana, Guinea, Guinea-Bissau, Liberia, Mali, Mauritania, Niger, Nigeria, Senegal, Sierra Leone, Togo

(5) Angola, Cameroon, Central African Republic, Chad, Congo, Democratic Republic of the Congo, Equatorial Guinea, Gabon, São Tomé e Príncipe

Table 2.

mortality is estimated to have also worsened in Middle Africa between 1995 and 2000. According to current projections, infant mortality is expected to continue to decline in most regions–albeit at a remarkably reduced and almost stagnant pace in most cases—indicating that only modest improvements are expected in underlying conditions.

With respect to overall mortality, improvements in life expectancy halted after 1985–1990, and the favorable upward trend was replaced by a downward trend. By 1995–2000, life expectancy had fallen 1–4 years across most of Africa. Northern Africa was the exception with an increase of four years. The deterioration was due to the impact of the HIV epidemic on adult mortality and on under-five mortality. It occurred against a background of slowed gains in economic growth and social development, resurgence of malaria that is also a major cause of mortality in children under five, and the occurrence of conflicts. Over that period, a series of conflicts disrupted societies and economies, thereby undermining the living standards and the health status of substantial populations, as well as also directly causing deaths. Transmission of HIV from mother to child at delivery and through breastfeeding contributed to the slowing in infant mortality decline and to an increase in under-five mortality. This is estimated to have persisted until 2005 in countries heavily affected by AIDS, particularly in Southern Africa and Zimbabwe, until efforts to control the transmission of HIV from mother to child began to be effective.

PERIOD FROM 1995–2000 TO 2005–2010
Current projections for 2005–2010 imply that life expectancy will continue to lengthen in Northern Africa and start to recover in Eastern, Middle and Western Africa by regaining 1–2 of the years lost (see Table 2). In Southern Africa, however, life expectancy is anticipated to still fall and to do so sharply. The projected loss of fifteen years in life expectancy over the short period (1995–2000 to 2005–2010) reflects the drastic situation in the countries most affected by HIV and AIDS. In this region, where the proportion of the adult population estimated by UNAIDS to be living with HIV reached between 19 and 33 percent in 2005, millions of people are expected to die each year even with increased access to antiretroviral therapy as currently projected. In Southern Africa, the numbers of deaths per year more than doubled between 1990–1995 and 2000–2005, from below 400,000 to nearly 900,000, as the number of people with AIDS grew. Because AIDS now likely causes the

majority of adult deaths of men and women, the total number of deaths per year is projected to exceed 1.1 million by 2005–2010, even though infant and child mortality are already relatively low by African standards, and even if, as is projected, the coverage of access to antiretroviral therapy reaches at least 40 per cent.

IMPLICATIONS

The mortality patterns and expected trends in Africa have implications not only for trends in fertility and population growth, but also for policy. Among other factors, declining infant mortality is beneficial to fertility decline, because survival of infants has both a biological and behavioral influence on childbearing decisions. To the extent that the overall health situation in Africa continues to be poor and the levels of infant and child mortality remain high and diminish only slowly, the decline in fertility will accordingly be retarded, as will reductions in the resulting population growth. Yet slower population growth has been linked to a better pace of economic growth and potential for social development. In this way, despite the high levels of mortality, positive population growth is expected to continue throughout Africa for some decades because of the persistence of high levels of fertility.

Accordingly and paradoxically, improved health and lower mortality are one of several preconditions to lower fertility and population growth, and thereby improve prospects for development. With regard to policy, current mortality levels point to the persistent inadequacy of development planning, governance, government budgets, and health infrastructure, as well as overall economic growth. Increased public investment in health systems is called for, but strides in education, gender equity, and access to decent jobs must also be made, so that both the supply of health and the demand for health may serve to improve the public health and lower the mortality of African populations.

See also **Death, Mourning, and Ancestors; Healing and Health Care.**

BIBLIOGRAPHY

Adjuik, Martin, et al. "Cause-specific Mortality Rates in Sub-Saharan Africa and Bangladesh." *Bulletin of the World Health Organization* 84, no. 3 (2006): 181–186.

Brass, William, et al. *The Demography of Tropical Africa.* Princeton, New Jersey: Princeton University Press, 1968.

Frank, Odile, ed. "Historical Epidemiology: Mortality Decline, and Old and New Transitions in Health." *World Health Statistics Quarterly* 51, nos. 2–4 (2000).

Hill, Kenneth. "Making Deaths Count." *Bulletin of the World Health Organization* 84, no. 3 (2006): 162.

Joint United Nations Programme on HIV/AIDS (UNAIDS). *Report on the Global AIDS Pandemic.* Geneva: UNAIDS, 2006.

Lopman, Ben A., et al. "Assessing Adult Mortality in HIV-1 Afflicted Zimbabwe (1998–2003)." *Bulletin of the World Health Organization* 84, no. 3 (2006): 189–195.

United Nations. "Manual X: Indirect Techniques for Demographic Estimation. (United Nations publication, Sales No. E.83.XIII.2)." 1983. Available from http://www.un.org/esa/.

United Nations. "World Population Prospects: The 2004 Revision Population Database." 2005. Available from http://esa.un.org/unpp/.

World Health Organization (WHO). *The World Health Report 2004: Changing History.* Geneva: WHO, 2004.

World Health Organization (WHO). *The World Health Report 2005: Make Every Mother and Child Count.* Geneva: WHO, 2005.

ODILE FRANK

POPULATION DATA AND SURVEYS

In the second half of 2005 Africa's population was estimated as 900 million or one-seventh of that of the world. Because Africa's annual population growth rate of 2.2 percent was almost double that of the world, its numbers were projected to grow by 2100 to around 2,250 million or one-quarter of global numbers. By that time it is expected that population growth everywhere in a world of 9 billion will be almost stationary.

These figures disguise the demographic differences between North and Sub-Saharan Africa that are revealed in Table 1. Figures for southern Africa are also shown because in recent decades this area has become demographically distinct.

Table 1 shows that North Africa constitutes only one-fifth of the whole continent's population. Its death rate is lower and its birth rate much lower, yielding a modest annual growth rate. Southern Africa and North Africa have both experienced a marked fertility transition in recent

African demography 2005					
	Population (millions)	Birth rate[1]	Death rate[1]	Annual natural increase[2]	Total fertility rate[3]	Life expectancy at birth[4]
North Africa	190	26	7	1.9	3.2	66
Sub-Saharan Africa	698	40	17	2.3	5.4	46
Africa	888	37	15	2.2	4.9	49
Southern Africa*	52	24	18	0.6	2.8	46

*Included above with Sub-Saharan Africa
(1) Per thousand population per year
(2) Percent
(3) Average number of lifetime births per woman at current rates
(4) Years

Table 1.

decades and so both record similar birth rates. In contrast, largely because of AIDS, southern Africa has a much higher death rate, which may soon lead to a decline in population numbers.

Ancient Egypt held censuses from before 3000 BCE but nothing remains. The Roman Empire held regular censuses. Some figures remain for its Africa province (western North Africa). Sufficient records are extant from Egyptian censuses of the first three centuries CE that they have provided the best analysable data of the demographic situation in the Roman Empire.

Before the twentieth century there were no reliable figures on the continent's population. Seventeenth century guesses were the basis of estimates until around 1950. Thus it was assumed that there were around 100 million people for centuries until about 1900. This assumption ignored various possibilities of growth, especially the introduction of new crops such as corn and manioc from the Americas and new types of yam from Asia. It seems likely that the early seventeenth century population was no more than 50 million. Even now the best estimates prior to 1950 are those based on the backward projection of post–World War II censuses. There are still no firm figures for some countries, notoriously Nigeria which may include more than one-seventh of the continent's population.

Nevertheless, the census was to prove a necessity for African administration. It was the sole source of comprehensive data on a range of matters which, in more statistically developed regions, were gathered by other routine administrative methods.

The poor censuses during most of the colonial period are explained by a lack of both financial and human resources. The amount spent per capita on censuses in Anglophone Western Africa multiplied in the thirty years after 1931 by a factor of up to 100, far in excess of inflation. Later censuses have depended for their success on great numbers of educated enumerators, particularly schoolteachers, a resource not available in the earlier period. There was often resistance to the census, most often because of the fear that it would identify people for the poll tax.

THE EARLY MODERN CENSUSES

Sub-Saharan Africa. Although the British Colonial Office decided that censuses should be carried out in British territories beginning in 1871, nineteenth-century censuses were largely confined to such areas as Lagos Colony, the Gambia, the Colony in Sierra Leone, and the large "native reserves" in Southern Africa that became Lesotho and Swaziland. The situation changed after the turn of the century, and, starting in either 1901 or 1911, most British colonies held decennial censuses in the first year of each decade, as did Britain. They were joined by Portuguese colonies with the taking of a census in Mozambique in 1940 and in Angola, São Tomé, and Principe in 1950. In that same year the Spanish colonial administration carried out a census in Spanish Guinea (present-day Equatorial Guinea).

These were not censuses in the modern sense. R. R. Kuczynski calculated that five-sixths of the population supposedly counted in the nineteenth century was only estimated. Usually at best the censuses were little more than head counts, and as late as the 1921 census of the Northern Territories of the Gold Coast (present-day Ghana), much of the counting was done by villages sending in calabashes of beans representing men, groundnuts women, and stones children. The only well enumerated populations were resident Europeans and, to a lesser extent, Asians. The French colonies carried out no censuses until well after World War II. In all colonies there were local administrative counts, often based on village population registers; these were used for estimates, and appear to have formed a significant part of the British colonial censuses. They reached their high point in the card-index system of the Belgian Congo (present-day Democratic Republic of the Congo) in the 1950s.

North Africa. Full censuses in the sense of enumerating the indigenous as well as the colonial population were mostly a phenomenon of the twentieth century. The partial exception is Egypt where decennial censuses began in 1897, improving until 1917, and continuing to 1947. In French colonial territories the first real censuses were held in Algeria in 1906, and in Morocco and Tunisia in 1921. In Tunisia the 1936 census set new standards. In Libya the Italian administration held the first census in 1931.

THE EMERGENCE OF THE MODERN CENSUS
After World War II, the census began increasingly to be seen as a necessary instrument for development planning and as an essential part of the preparation of colonies for independence, particularly when the enumeration was also used to prepare lists of voters. In British West Africa the 1950 census of Lagos was used as a trial for the 1952–1953 census of the whole of Nigeria, which was staggered over time to allow skilled personnel and other resources to be moved from one region to another. The 1948 censuses of Uganda, Kenya, Tanganyika (now part of Tanzania), and the Gold Coast (present-day Ghana) were landmarks. In each of them a simple census was complemented by a longer questionnaire administered to a subsample. Although administrative lists were undoubtedly consulted during the censuses, the latter proved their worth by enumerating considerable more people than were on the lists.

A new emphasis on censuses around the developing world led to an increasing United Nations role in setting standards and providing experts. A key event was its publication in 1954 of *A Handbook of Population Census Methods*, which provided procedural guidelines and lists of essential and important questions to be included. The first African census to meet these requirements was held in Ghana in 1960, with a post-enumeration survey or supplementary sample survey held three months after the main census. This showed that independent African countries could carry through a modern census. However, limited resources meant that, although the census volumes appeared within a few years, the post-enumeration results were not available until 1971.

Similar censuses were held later in the 1960s in Nigeria, Kenya, Tanzania, and Uganda, while Francophone countries continued to rely on administrative censuses compiled from local records, increasingly supplemented by demographic sample surveys. However, in 1971 the United Nations Population Commission established the African Census Program, funded by the newly established United Nations Fund for Population Activities (UNFPA). During the rest of the decade censuses were held as part of this program in twenty-two sub-Saharan African countries, including eleven Francophone ones. Similar programs were undertaken in the 1980s and 1990s, so that by 1990 at least one census had been held in every sub-Saharan country, with Chad being the last country to complete a census. South Africa held its first census in 1904 (although component parts of the country had held much earlier ones) and continues to conduct regular censuses, although undercounts apparently occurred in 1993, probably because of the volatile political situation.

There were still problems, as shown by the Nigerian censuses of 1962, 1963, and 1973. Over-enumeration could occur because of ethnic and political rivalries or because promised resources would be based on population counts. Some countries, such as Liberia in 1962 and the Central African Republic in 1965, suppressed censuses, apparently on the grounds that smaller populations were revealed than their national prestige demanded. This was expected by many to be the fate of the 1993 Nigerian census after the coup late that year, but this did not occur.

In North Africa regular censuses were carried out in the years after World War II: In Egypt six censuses were held from 1947 to 1996, in Tunisia six from 1946 to 2004, in Algeria seven from 1948 to 1998, in Morocco five from 1960 to 2004, and in Libya five from 1954 to 1995.

In the whole continent the 2000 census round (broadly defined as 1996–2005) has been carried out in forty-one of the fifty-seven recognized territories, are reportedly planned in eleven more, and apparently will not take place in five. The five defaulters are Djibouti, Liberia, Sierra Leone, Somalia, and Western Sahara (totally two percent of the continent's population), mostly explained by war or civil unrest.

PROBLEMS IN THE INTERPRETATION OF AFRICAN CENSUS DATA

Much demographic analysis depends on accurate age statement. In one sense, age is important in many African cultures because of the formation of age cohorts as males reach maturity and because of strongly held concepts of seniority in relationships. Nevertheless, age cohorts may be broad and overlapping, as traditional societies did not observe birthdays or identify people by exact age. As a result, age statement is worse than in any other world region. This in turn accounts for the imprecision in fertility, mortality, and growth estimates. Even the 1960 census of Ghana, the most educated country of tropical Africa, showed three- or fourfold differences in the numbers of people enumerated at successive single-year ages, although five-year age groups were much more regular.

Pre–World War II censuses tended to use four or five major age groupings, or even just divide the population into men, women, and children. Since 1960 there has been an almost universal attempt to collect single-year age data, but success in this effort depends very much on the achievement of near-universal schooling. Observation of enumeration in 1969 in southwest Nigeria showed that only 43 percent of males and 34 percent of females even attempted to report their own age, and the majority of estimates came from the enumerators or other people. Experiments with the use of

historical calendars to assist the memory have done little to improve the situation.

Problems with defining marital status in Sub-Saharan Africa have made the analysis of marriage very difficult. Minor variations in the wording of a survey or census question can result in striking differences in the proportion reporting that they have ever been married. In Botswana, for instance, the contrast is between 96 and 30 percent for twenty- to twenty-four-year-old women in two successive surveys. Part of the problem is that in many societies getting married has traditionally been a continuing process rather than an instantaneous one; part is that practices are changing. The first Anglophone census to attempt to obtain marriage data was taken in 1957 in Tanganyika, where men were asked how many wives they had. Current marital status was first asked for in the 1960 Ghana postcensus enumeration survey. The data are still inadequate for establishing trends satisfactorily. If marriage questions are asked, then a question on polygyny should be included, but answers can be misleading where polygyny is illegal, as in the Democratic Republic of the Congo or South Africa.

In the absence of adequate vital registration data, and with a growing interest after World War II in fertility rates, attempts were made in the 1948 censuses of British East Africa and Ghana to obtain information on births. Questions were asked in East Africa on the total number of live births to each woman and on her births within the previous twelve months. The information was clearly inaccurate because, from what is known of the timing of family-building, the responses to the two questions were incompatible for the whole society. Efforts were also made to obtain mortality data by seeking information on deaths over the previous year and on the numbers of children women had lost. These data too usually appeared to be implausible.

African censuses have frequently sought information on ethnicity, mother tongue, religion, literacy, education, and physical condition. Ethnicity and religion are invaluable social measures, but they have been increasingly charged with causing internal competition and conflict and both were omitted from the 1993 Nigerian census. Literacy is very sensitive to the measure used, as is shown by the fact that in Nyasaland (present-day Malawi) the

1945 census recorded a literacy level only one-eighth of that reported by the 1931 census. Data on physical condition were thought to be related to the needs of colonial plantation and mining economies and disappeared from the postindependence censuses, although they subsequently began reappearing in some surveys because of an increased interest in health.

VITAL REGISTRATION

Efforts have been made for almost two centuries to enforce the registration of births and deaths, but, as most of the population does not need passports or seek employment where birth certificates are needed, usable systems exist nowhere. Sierra Leone declared registration compulsory in 1801, the Gambia in 1845, Lagos in 1892, selected towns of the Gold Coast in 1912, and other Nigerian towns in 1926.

Only in some island colonies did registration ever exceed 90 percent. Lagos has been quoted as a success story because birth registrations yielded plausibly high fertility levels, but the evidence seems to be that, while many Lagos births were not registered, other babies from outside Lagos were registered as born in the city so that the children would later be eligible to attend the city's schools. Research in Ghana showed that registration officials accepted birth registration from all applicants and had no clear idea of the boundaries of the registration district, thus making it impossible to calculate birth rates by comparing registration and census population data. In South Africa vital registration for Whites has been complete for all of the twentieth century and for Indians and Coloureds since the 1940s, but it is still far from complete for the black population.

An alternative approach to state registration was to make it a responsibility of Native Administrations. This was done with considerable success from 1904 in the kingdom of Buganda and by 1930 in most of Uganda. A similar approach was adopted in Northern Nigeria early in the twentieth century and in some cities, notably Katsina, a high level of coverage was achieved. The nearest approach to complete national registration appears to have developed in the Belgian Congo in the 1950s. Nowhere have such systems been successfully used for demographic analysis.

In the early 1970s several projects were organized with external help to establish dual record schemes whereby data could be obtained from at least two different sources (e.g., a registration system and periodic surveys), so that births and deaths could be estimated from the degree of overlap between the two systems. Experience in Morocco, Liberia, and Malawi yielded estimates of fair quality, but the schemes were too expensive to continue and did not meet the legal and other needs for which national registration systems are usually employed.

NEW DEMOGRAPHIC METHODS AND DATA COLLECTION SYSTEMS

The problems of obtaining plausible fertility and mortality estimates from African census and other population data were so challenging that they gave rise to new methodologies. The resultant demographic analytical approaches have been widely applied to contemporary data from developing nations and historic data from developed countries. Faced with incomplete data of the 1948 East African censuses, beginning in 1953 William Brass published papers on how to obtain acceptable fertility estimates from biased retrospective birth reporting. Beginning in 1956 he made available his methodology on estimating child mortality from retrospective reporting of child deaths. Later, methods were devised for estimating adult mortality from information on whether the respondents' parents (or, in some cases, other relatives) were still alive. An alternative approach to fertility estimation, requiring only information on the age structure of populations, was developed by Ansley Coale using stable population models that he and Paul Demeny published in 1966. At the Princeton University Office of Population Research, these three and others applied their methods to African census and survey data in the first attempt to obtain demographic estimates for the whole of Tropical Africa.

SAMPLE CENSUSES AND POST-CENSUS SURVEYS

Southern Rhodesia (present-day Zimbabwe) conducted a sample census in 1948, and sampling was also used in the 1955–1956 Sudan census. Post-census sample surveys were undertaken in Uganda, Kenya, Tanganyika, and the Gold Coast in 1948. The sample censuses were more expensive than anticipated and subsequent evidence suggested that they underestimated population numbers compared with full censuses. The post-census surveys allowed information on fertility, mortality, and migration to be collected through multiple questions.

FRANCOPHONE DEMOGRAPHIC SURVEYS, 1954–1961

In the absence of censuses, French colonial administrators, supported by French statistical and demographic agencies, carried out ten demographic surveys in French sub-Saharan African colonies between 1954 and 1961. A demographic survey was also carried out by the Belgian administration in the Belgian Congo in 1955–1957. Some of these surveys attempted to be representative of whole countries but others chose restricted and unrepresentative areas. The relatively small scale of the enquiries allowed a density of demographic questions and an intensity of fieldwork that permitted the new demographic analytical techniques to be fully used.

The most detailed analyses of Princeton University Office of Population Research's African Project of the early 1960s, published in 1968 as The Demography of Tropical Africa, concentrated on these surveys, although less detailed analyses were also carried out on the censuses from Anglophone countries and Portuguese colonies. For the first time, it was possible to map estimated fertility levels for much of sub-Saharan Africa. The pattern was one of high fertility, six or more live births per woman, with the level rising to more than eight in a significant number of populations. But areas of Africa were revealed where a considerable proportion of women—almost half in some districts—had never borne a child, with resultant total fertility rates under four. The largest area of pathological sterility of this type was in central Africa, embracing Gabon, Río Muni, and considerable parts of northern Democratic Republic of the Congo, the Central African Republic, southwest Sudan, and Cameroon. The analyses also showed that much of sub-Saharan Africa had infant mortality rates of more than two hundred per thousand live births (i.e., 20% of babies died in the first years of life). Consequently, life expectancy at the time of birth was below thirty-five years and often below thirty years.

WORLD FERTILITY SURVEY, 1980–1984

The World Fertility Survey (WFS) was an international program of demographic surveys (collecting mortality as well as fertility data), supported by the United Nations Fund for Population Activities as well as many national governments and other organizations. It originated in 1972, but all the African surveys were carried out in the early 1980s so as not to interfere with the 1970 African census round. The program provided standardized questionnaires and analysis, as well as a great deal of technical assistance. Surveys were held in North Africa in Algeria, Morocco, Tunisia, and, in sub-Saharan Africa in Kenya, Lesotho, Senegal, Cameroon, Ghana, Bénin, Côte d'Ivoire, and Nigeria, and also in Mauritania and northern Sudan. The surveys had a good coverage of the North Africa and the West African coast but a very limited coverage elsewhere.

The program published its own reports and analyses, which were supplemented in professional journals. Only one book concentrated on the region: *Reproduction and Social Organization in Sub-Saharan Africa*, edited by Ron J. Lesthaeghe (1989). This book used the World Fertility Surveys and a range of other sources to map marriage patterns, showing significant regional differences in age at first marriage (women marry earliest in the savanna regions of Western and Central Africa; men marry latest in western Africa, especially in the far west, where the gap between spouses is typically more than nine years). Patterns of polygyny were also shown, with the proportion of wives in polygynous marriages exceeding 40 percent from Senegal to the western part of the Democratic Republic of the Congo, except for the small minority of matrilineal areas; the rates were 30 percent in Eastern Africa and below 20 percent in most of Southern Africa.

DEMOGRAPHIC AND HEALTH SURVEYS FROM 1986

A new international demographic survey program, the Demographic and Health Surveys (DHS), funded by the United States Agency for International Development (USAID), published its first African survey report in 1985 and by the end of 2005 had issued reports on three North African countries (Egypt, Morocco and Tunisia) and thirty sub-Saharan African countries. The new program focused on fertility levels more than on the determinants of these levels, and on contraception and various health measures. A major publication in 1994 was The Population Dynamics of Sub-Saharan Africa, arising from a National Research Council of the National Academies of Sciences and Engineering research project with the same title, directed by Samuel Preston. The project was able to confirm that fertility had begun to fall in all North African countries covered and in four sub-Saharan African countries, Botswana, Zimbabwe, Kenya and Ghana, as had the fertility of black South Africans a decade earlier. It also drew together childhood mortality data showing levels and trends for most sub-Saharan African countries. It appears that child mortality fell steeply from at least 1945 until 1980 and that adult mortality had also improved.

In some countries there had been four or five surveys, thus giving a continuing picture. Between 1950 and 1980 life expectancy at birth increased from forty-one to fifty-five years in North Africa and similarly from thirty-six to forty-seven years in sub-Saharan Africa. Thereafter trends diverged. In the next twenty years life expectancy rose another eleven years in North Africa and, because of the failure of economic development and the impact of the AIDS epidemic, remained stationary below the Sahara.

FERTILITY CONTROL
The first surveys of fertility and family planning had been carried out in the early 1960s as part of the KAP (Knowledge, Attitudes, and Practice of Family Planning) survey program. Fertility control was also a component of the WFS and DHS surveys as well as more specialized programs such as the Contraceptive Prevalence Surveys (CPS) and the PAPCHILD surveys in Tunisia and Libya. In the 1950s few couples of reproductive age used contraception, but by 2000 the level of use of modern contraception was 43 percent in North Africa (compared with 58 percent in industrialized countries) and 13 percent in sub-Saharan Africa. Nevertheless, in the latter region levels exceeded 50 percent in Southern Africa and 30 percent in Kenya. Fertility was falling persistently in North and Southern Africa, Kenya and Ghana, as well as in most sub-Saharan African cities.

In conclusion, North African demographic data are comparable with those of other parts of the developing world but those of sub-Saharan Africa are less secure. The major advance in census-and-survey-taking has been electronic data storage and the availability to analysts of sample or survey data in this form. Such data have enabled a great deal of demographic analysis of countries included in the World Fertility Surveys and the Demographic and Health Surveys.

See also **Childbearing; Death, Mourning, and Ancestors.**

BIBLIOGRAPHY

Brass, William, et al. *The Demography of Tropical Africa.* Princeton, NJ: Princeton University Press, 1968.

Caldwell, John C., and Chukuka Okonjo, eds. *The Population of Tropical Africa.* New York: Columbia University Press, 1968.

Caldwell, John C., et al., eds. *Population Growth and Socioeconomic Change in West Africa.* New York: Columbia University Press, 1975.

Evalds, Victoria K. *Union List of African Censuses, Development Plans, and Statistical Abstracts.* Oxford: Hans Zell, 1985.

Foote, Karen A.; Kenneth H. Hill; and Linda G. Martin; eds. *Demographic Change in Sub-Saharan Africa.* Washington, DC: National Academy Press, 1993.

Ominde, Simon H., and Charles N. Ejiogu, eds. *Population Growth and Economic Development in Africa.* London: Heinemann, 1972.

Page, Hilary J., and Ron Lesthaeghe, eds. *Child-Spacing in Tropical Africa: Traditions and Change.* London: Academic Press, 1981.

Pinfold, John R., ed. *African Population Census Reports: A Bibliography and Checklist.* Oxford: Hans Zell, 1985.

Tabutin, Dominique, and Bruno Schoumaker. "The Demography of Sub-Saharan Africa from the 1950s to the 2000s: A Survey of Changes and a Statistical Assessment." *Population* 59, no. 3–4 (2004): 457–556.

United Nations. *Population Prospects: The 2002 Revision.* New York: United Nations, 2003.

Van de Walle, Étienne; Patrick O. Ohadike; and Mpembele D. Sala-Diakanda; eds. *The State of African Demography.* Liège: International Union for the Scientific Study of Population, 1988.

Van de Walle, Étienne; Gilles Pison; and Mpembele D. Sala-Diakanda; eds. *Mortality and Society in Sub-Saharan Africa.* Oxford: Clarendon Press, 1992.

JOHN C. CALDWELL

DESCENT. *See* **Family; Kinship and Descent.**

DESERTIFICATION, MODERN.

Since the early decades of the twentieth century, people have been concerned with long-term ecological and climatic changes affecting productivity and usefulness of rangelands and croplands in drylands (arid, semiarid, and dry subhumid areas). These changes, variously referred to as desertification, desertization, degradation, or desiccation, have emerged as a major environmental and development issue in the drier parts of Africa. Much of the attention has been directed to the West African Sahel, a region affected by recurrent periods of drought and famine, which conjures up the image of desertification most commonly used in the media: one of an advancing Sahara Desert, irreversibly destroying pastures and farmland. Views on desertification, however, have changed throughout time. And while debate about the causes, extent, and permanence of desertification is still unresolved, the picture of a constantly advancing desert is obviously inappropriate, as is the common understanding that desertification is the result only of irrational land use practices. Satellite remote sensing has been instrumental in persuading scientists to reassess, if not challenge, societal perspectives of desertification by indicating the extreme year-to-year fluctuations in rainfall and in vegetation productivity inherent to drylands.

Prior to the end of the nineteenth century, inhabitants of arid and semiarid areas in many parts of Africa had learned how to cope with a variable climate from one year to the next. Pastoral populations had worked out, by persuasion or by coercion, interactions with settled farm populations in the wetter areas. Sometimes their arrangements were the result of war, in which slave populations were left to cultivate the land to produce foods for the nomadic people in the dry season and fodder for livestock in the event that drought conditions resulted in shortage of pasture. With the advent of colonial rule and the European powers' competition for African colonies came international borders, as well as a call for the end of slavery in the region. Old seasonal migration routes for pastoralists and their herds were often blocked by those borders. Social arrangements created by the wartime victors of precolonial times to ensure food availability were disrupted.

Although early reports on desertification date back to colonial times (e.g., Henri Aubreville's *Climate, Forests and Desertification in the Dry Forests of Africa*, published in 1949), the phenomenon did not receive much attention until the late 1960s, when an unusually long and severe drought caused a regional environmental crisis and extensive human suffering across the Sahelian zone of sub-Saharan Africa. Africa was called the "Dark Continent" in the 1800s because of the mysteries it held for European explorers. At the beginning of the twenty-first century, it could be called the "dry continent." In addition to all the political, economic, and cultural problems confronting Africans, recurring and prolonged drought episodes in Africa have taken a major toll on the continent's inhabitants, livestock, and development plans. It is difficult to lead a country towards economic development when the climatic conditions are unfavorable: respond to the recurring emergencies will always take precedence over achieving long-term development goals.

DESERTIFICATION AND DROUGHT

Most people relate drought to the amount of rainfall expected in a given area for a given period of time. Yet, because it can be viewed from the perspectives of different academic disciplines, drought has many definitions. Thus, there are agricultural, meteorological, and hydrological droughts. To a farmer, the timing of rainfall is most important in relation to the moisture needs of the particular crop being grown, whereas to a hydrologist, the total amount of rainfall may be more important so that water may be stored in reservoirs to support human activities.

About two-thirds of the African continent can be categorized as drylands. These regions are characterized not only by recurrent drought periods, but also by low annual rainfall amounts in most years and by extreme year-to-year rainfall variability. As a rule, the lower the annual rainfall totals, the higher the variability; that is, a few heavy rainy years are outweighed by a larger number of below-average rainfall years.

The West African Sahel serves as one of the most dramatic examples of climate variability worldwide. During the past one hundred years, the Sahel experienced devastating drought periods between 1910 and 1914, between 1941 and 1943, and between 1968 and 1997, separated by short rainfall recoveries. Since 1997, a positive trend in rainfall has been observed in the Sahel, with the wettest years being 1998, 1999, 2003, and 2005. While the drought years of 1983 and 1984 affected almost the entire continent, different dryland regions of Africa showed contrasting rainfall characteristics. East Africa and the Horn of Africa suffered devastating droughts from 2002 to 2004, and Southern Africa was affected by major droughts in the early 1990s. Ecosystems respond to drought with an overall decline in productivity, including vegetation stress, loss of green vegetation cover, decreases in streamflow, and the drying out and cracking of soil surfaces.

While both drought and desertification lead to declines in ecosystem productivity, the latter implies irreversibility. According to page 4 of the official text of the 1996 United Nations Convention to Combat Desertification (UNCCD), desertification is defined as "land degradation in arid, semiarid, and dry sub-humid areas resulting from various factors, including climate variations and human activities." Land degradation refers to reductions in vegetation cover and soil fertility and can lead to accelerated soil erosion. Given their relatively low biological potential, the deserts are less prone to desertification than are the semiarid drylands. Also, the latter support higher population densities, which intensifies the economic impacts of desertification.

Desertification is a creeping environmental degradation with low-grade, incremental changes over time. Today's landscape looks like yesterday's, and tomorrow's appears similar to today's. Yet, over time, a crisis in the landscape becomes visible. Desertification is often accelerated during periods of drought. As drought renders large areas of land temporarily unproductive for farming or for use as pasture, increased land use pressure is shifted to neighboring areas that are less affected by drought. Fallow periods are shortened and livestock densities are increased. As a result, vegetation and soil become degraded, sometimes irreversibly. Vegetation recovery after a drought period is a good indication of whether the observed changes in vegetation cover are a temporary outcome of drought or are part of an irreversible process of desertification.

Hope for early warning and response to drought has been generated by greater scientific understanding since the 1970s of global atmospheric and ocean circulation dynamics that drive interannual and decadal rainfall variability. In the forecasting of droughts in Africa, attention since the 1980s has focused on a phenomenon known as El Niño Southern Oscillation (ENSO, popularly referred to as El Niño), which can be described as quasi-periodic changes in sea surface temperatures and sea level pressure in the equatorial Pacific thousands of miles away. These changes, though originating in the Pacific Ocean, have global repercussions called "teleconnections" and have been associated with droughts in southern and northeastern Africa. These teleconnections—linkages between climate events in widely separated regions—hold a great potential for forecasting droughts several months in advance and providing policy makers with the opportunity to prepare for, as well as mitigate, the effects of recurrent drought. Governmental and nongovernmental organizations in the Horn of Africa, western Africa, and southern Africa have successfully used El Niño information. Since the 1990s anomalies related to the North Atlantic Oscillation (NAO) and the Pacific Decadal Oscillation (PDO) have also been cited as possible causes of rainfall variability at different time scales and in different locations.

DESERTIFICATION AND CLIMATE CHANGE
Although rainfall fluctuations are a normal part of the climate in drylands, and recurrent drought is expected and planned for in many areas of Africa, the occurrence of prolonged droughts over large areas might indicate a regional or global desiccation trend. The last two decades of colonial rule in West Africa (i.e., the 1940s and 1950s) coincided with a wet period in the Sahel. Annual rainfall decreased sharply, however, from the 1960s until the end of the twentieth century. The great Sahelian droughts, which lasted from the late 1960s until the mid-1990s, have been unprecedented in the history of the region. Unfortunately, the new leaders of the independent nations had to cope with this extended dry period, and its human and environmental impacts, in addition to the challenges of governing their newly formed nations.

Whether this long and severe drought period has been part of a normal multidecade climate variability or a trend associated with twentieth-century global climate change is not yet sufficiently understood. Africa is about 0.9 degrees Fahrenheit (0.5 degrees Celsius) warmer than it was a century ago: an increase that corresponds approximately to the rate of warming experienced globally. Yet there is no simple correlation between temperature and rainfall, and scenarios remain highly speculative. Some areas in southern Africa might get drier, while other regions in East Africa might actually get wetter. Some scientists suggest that rainfall variability will increase and droughts and floods will become more extreme. Regardless of its impact on rainfall, however, warming will place additional stress on water resources through increased evaporation and transpiration rates. This development might exacerbate the impacts of droughts and increase the risk of desertification, as soils dry out and as the hot, dry seasons become longer.

Different parts of Africa will experience different influences of global warming on local and regional ecosystems. Some will likely benefit from a changing climate. Others are expected to suffer greatly because of increased temperature, high evaporation rates, decline in soil moisture, and reduced vegetative cover, which leaves soils exposed to wind and water erosion. It is important to keep in mind that computer modeling of changes in rainfall amounts, location, and timing is extremely difficult, and drought prediction is as much an art as it is a science.

DESERTIFICATION AND SOCIETY

Since 1945 many important demographic changes have worsened the severity of the impacts of drought and desertification. As populations have increased, people have been leaving the rural areas for urban centers in search of a better life. They have also been moving into marginal areas because the best agricultural land has already been put into production. Putting marginal areas under the plow inevitably increases the likelihood of drought-related crop failures, not because of an increase in frequency or intensity of droughts, but as a result of the inherent drought susceptibility of dryland margins. This process has been referred to as "drought follows the plow" (Glanz 1994).

Even though there is no conclusive evidence that the total area threatened by desertification is on the rise in Africa, the number of people affected has surely risen as the continent's population increases and expands into marginal areas. Socioeconomic factors such as poverty, political or cultural marginalization, and unfavorable land tenure relationships make societies or groups within societies vulnerable to the effects of droughts, thereby forcing them to resort to adopting unsustainable land use practices that increase desertification.

Although overgrazing, overcultivation, and deforestation have been portrayed as almost inevitable consequences of population growth, some success stories have emerged throughout the African drylands in places where population growth has been accompanied by improvements in human and ecological well-being. Certainly, favorable political and infrastructural circumstances facilitate the transition from degradation to sustainable agricultural intensification, as has been the case for Machakos, Kenya. There, population growth allowed implementation of labor-intensive soil and water conservation as well as income diversification. Similar situations have been reported in the Kano region in Nigeria and the Central Plateau of Burkina Faso.

Traditional land use systems, which incorporate shared risk distribution through social relations and the timely movement of livestock herds, have been adapted to a high degree to cope with the uncertainties imposed by variability in the environment. Nevertheless, since the 1990s they have often been discredited as inappropriate, outdated, or even as damaging to the environment. The strengths of these systems, however, such as their flexibility in adaptation to changing environmental and economic conditions, have also been recognized and have begun to form the basis for novel approaches to coping with desertification.

DESERTIFICATION AND DRYLAND ECOLOGY

When desertification became a widely discussed issue in the 1970s, the equilibrium paradigm prevailed in much ecological thinking and guided most land management policy. This paradigm builds on the assumption of an optimal level of, or climax, vegetation for each particular site that is in equilibrium with climate and soil and can be perturbed by changes in land use intensity or climatic fluctuations and change. Equilibrium thinking implies that a climax vegetation can be achieved and maintained in rangelands through the adoption of an equilibrium grazing policy with prescribed stocking rates. Viewed from this perspective, desertification is a result of overstocking a rangeland beyond its carrying capacity or of overcultivating farmland.

While the equilibrium paradigm might still be a valid approach to describe vegetation dynamics in humid environments, particularly those with a less variable climate from year to year, its applicability to highly variable arid and semiarid environments has since been challenged. Most contemporary scholars view arid rangelands in sub-Saharan Africa as being nonequilibrial environments, governed by variability and unpredictability of the timing of adverse climatic episodes, such as recurring severe droughts. These episodes result in discontinuous and possibly nonreversible transitions between alternative stable states, for example grassland and shrubland. Equilibrium in a dryland environment cannot simply be restored by prescribing lower stocking densities. Variability of precipitation might be the major control for both the livestock population and for vegetation dynamics (rather than vegetation dynamics being primarily controlled by the number of animals grazing). Pastoralists must "track" the seasonal and interannual variations in vegetation as best as they can in order to keep their livestock alive. Mismatches (e.g., too many livestock combined with a drought-induced loss in vegetation) can be fatal to the herders as well as to their herds.

The nonequilibrium paradigm in rangeland ecology has important implications for the current understanding of desertification. The number of animals that can be sustained in arid and semiarid environments is not static but highly variable; therefore, an equilibrium policy with prescribed stocking rates (unless it is fixed at a low level of animals regardless of the level of abundance of vegetation available) does not help to prevent or to combat desertification. Neither do management strategies that fail to accommodate resource variability and promote fundamental changes in the environment, such as desertification. Thus, pockets of desertification are frequently found around settlements and well sites, where high animal concentrations prevail year-round. By contrast, using variable stocking rates might be a better way to seize

climate-related opportunities and evade hazards in arid and semiarid environments. This strategy is not new. In fact, it has been practiced by African pastoralists over centuries: during drought years, they expand into infrequently used areas.

INSTITUTIONALIZATION OF DESERTIFICATION

The prolonged, intense, and devastating droughts that affected the Sahel in the late 1960s and 1970s, and the resulting widespread environmental degradation and human suffering, prompted the United Nations to host a Conference on Desertification (UNCOD). It intended to develop a plan of action to combat desertification. The conference, held in Nairobi, Kenya in 1977, brought together scientists and policy makers and marked the beginning of the institutionalization of desertification. Since then, desertification has been featured in major environmental conferences and conventions. In 1996 an institution uniquely devoted to the desertification issue was founded: the United Nations Convention to Combat Desertification (UNCCD).

It can be argued that the upsurge in the interest in desertification following UNCOD has been driven more by politics than by science, and that its effects will sort out accordingly. Indeed, the institutionalization of the desertification issue has attracted international attention and given support to many dryland nations that they otherwise would not have received. In addition to national governments, scientists have benefited from greater funding opportunities for desertification research.

Since the early 1990s, as new technological detection methods (particularly remote sensing) have been applied over longer periods of time, desertification skeptics have argued that the total global area affected by irreversible desertification is considerably smaller than initial estimates suggested. While this might be viewed as good news, many African nations continue to struggle with the impacts of drought—a struggle that could be exacerbated by global climate change. The claim that the area affected by irreversible desertification is smaller than initially estimated might adversely influence policies by reducing aid from donor governments to help national and local authorities cope with the consequences of desertification processes, especially the interactions between land degradation and drought episodes. This development could have fatal consequences—particularly for the poor, whose livelihoods are periodically threatened by the uncertainties of dryland environments.

See also **Climate; Ecology; Ecosystem; Kalahari Desert; Sahara Desert; Western Sahara.**

BIBLIOGRAPHY

Briske, D. D.; S. D. Fuhlendorf; and F. E. Smeins. "Vegetation Dynamics on Rangelands: A Critique of the Current Paradigms." *Journal of Applied Ecology* 40 (2003): 601–614.

Fairhead, J., and M. Leach. *Misreading the African Landscape; Society and Ecology in a Forest-Savanna Mosaic.* Cambridge, U.K.: Cambridge University Press, 1996.

Field, John Osgood, ed. *The Challenge of Famine: Recent Experience, Lessons Learned.* West Hartford, CT: Kumarian Press, 1993.

Glantz, Michael H. "Global Warming and Environmental Change in Sub-Saharan Africa." *Global Environmental Change* 1, no. 4 (1992): 183–204.

Glantz, Michael H. "Forecasting El Niño: Science's Gift to the Twenty-First Century." *EcoDecision* (April 1994): 78–81.

Glantz, Michael H. *Currents of Change. El Niño's Impact on Climate and Society.* Cambridge, U.K.: Cambridge University Press, 1996.

Glantz, Michael H. *Climate Affairs: A Primer.* Covelo, CA: Island Press, 2003.

Glantz, Michael H., ed. *Drought and Hunger in Africa: Denying Famine a Future.* Cambridge, U.K.: Cambridge University Press, 1987.

Glantz, Michael H., ed. *Drought Follows the Plow.* Cambridge, U.K.: Cambridge University Press, 1994.

Grainger, Alan. *The Threatening Desert: Controlling Desertification.* London: Earthscan in association with United Nations Environment Program, 1990.

Herrmann, S. M., and C. F. Hutchinson. "The Changing Contexts of the Desertification Debate." *Journal of Arid Environments* 63 (2005): 538–555.

Hulme, M., et al. "African Climate Change: 1900–2100." *Climate Research* 17 (2001): 145–168.

Johnson, P. M., K. Mayrand, and M. Paquin, eds. *Governing Global Desertification: Linking Environmental Degradation, Poverty and Participation.* Aldershot, U.K.: Ashgate, 2006.

Monod, Theodore, ed. *Pastoralism in Tropical Africa.* London: Oxford University Press, 1975.

Mortimore, M. *Roots in the African Dust: Sustaining the Sub-Saharan Drylands.* Cambridge, U.K.: Cambridge University Press, 1998.

Mortimore, M., and W. M. Adams. *Working the Sahel: Environment and Society in Northern Nigeria.* London: Routledge, 1999.

Thomas, D. S. G., and N. J. Middleton. *Desertification: Exploding the Myth.* Chichester, U.K.: Wiley, 1994.

Tiffen, M., M. Mortimore, and F. Gichuki. *More People, Less Erosion: Environmental Recovery in Kenya.* Chichester, U.K.: John Wiley, 1994.

Tiffen, M., and M. Mortimore. "Questioning Desertification in Dryland Sub-Saharan Africa." *Natural Resources Forum* 26 (2002): 218–233.

Tucker, Comptom J.; Harold E. Dregne; and W. W. Newcomb. "Expansion and Contraction of the Sahara Desert from 1980 to 1990." *Science* 254 (1991): 299–301.

Tucker, C. J., and S. E. Nicholson. "Variations in the Size of the Sahara Desert from 1980 to 1997." *Ambio* 28, no. 7 (1999): 587–591.

Watts, Michael. *Silent Violence: Food, Famine, and Peasantry in Northern Nigeria.* Berkeley: University of California Press, 1983.

STEFANIE HERRMANN
MICHAEL H. GLANTZ

DESERTIFICATION, REACTIONS TO, HISTORY OF (C. 5000 TO 1000 BCE).

Africa: the cradle of humankind, and the cradle of humankind's enormous ingenuity when confronted by an oft-perverse Nature. Perhaps no other peoples demonstrate this essentially optimistic conclusion than did Africans when responding to the surprises and stresses—and opportunities—of desertification during the latter part of the Holocene period. Long lagging behind other parts of the globe in the production of high-resolution palaeoclimate sequences, now African climate change begins to be documented at intercentury, interdecadal, and interannual timescales. Data come not just from deep ocean and coral cores, but also increasingly from terrestrial contexts linked to archaeological records of settlement, environmental exploitation, and regional abandonments.

A fine series of orbital-resolution deep-ocean sediment cores off Cape Blanc, Mauritania, the

Congo River mouth, and Angola allow us to tie African trends with spans of greater than many thousands of years to the ultimate drivers of global climate: eccentricities in the earth's orbit. However, archaeologists have impatiently awaited the human-resolved palaeoclimate data now coming from lake cores (especially the long rain-gauges of Ghana's Lake Bosumtwi or South Africa's Tswaing Crater), the Kilimanjaro glacial cores, from stable light isotope records in southern African stalagmites, and even from ecofacts (such as pollen and botanical remains) derived from the dense net of well-dated, stratified sites now available from South Africa, the eastern Sahara, the Chad Basin, and Mali's Middle Niger.

The upshot of all these new data: many parts of the African continent did, indeed, undergo a general drying trend after roughly 5000 BCE (in keeping with orbital shifts in insolation [amounts and geometry of sunlight hitting various latitudes] and with global-scale atmospheric and oceanic processes). But humans adapted to the higher-resolution hues and flavors of that drying—the irregularity of shifts characterizing intercentury or interdecadal change, the recurrence of abrupt short-term shifts, and the creation of environmental mosaics (spatial patchiness). In the context of these human resolution, hues and flavors of changes in the continent's climate, archaeologists are uncovering a spectrum of Africans' adaptations that go far beyond the standard set of prehistoric responses to desertification, risk, and uncertainty—that is, mobility, storage, intensification, and exchange.

This is not to say, of course, that mobility and migration were not among the African responses during the period 5000–1000 BCE. However, it is one thing to say that peoples sought out new lands where they might retain an older way of life (a standard view of Late Stone Age responses), and another to document migration and mobility as components of radically new strategies. Three classic migration scenarios show the subtlety of the African response. Stable rains from about 8500 to 5300 BCE blessed upper Egypt, Lower Nubia, and the larger eastern Sahara, but then the rains began a fairly rapid, steady retreat 497 miles to the south, with essentially hyperarid conditions in place by 3500 BCE. Gone were those early Holocene pluvial conditions that allowed a widespread sedentary life, with pottery and locally domesticated cattle. With the

post-5300 readjustment a uniquely African form of food production took shape, contrasting with the Near East model of earlier nomadic hunters and gatherers shifting to sedentary settlements of pottery-using, mixed livestock-keeping cereal farmers. In Africa earlier sedentary, pottery-producing hunting and fishing cattle-keepers increasingly became nomadic cattle herders (and gatherers, without cereal farming). In less than two millennia these herders and their descendants then moved out successfully across the Sahara and far south into eastern Africa. Others left the desert to become the first Nile Valley farmers (the first villages in the Fayum and Delta appeared approximately 5000 BCE), who imported western Asian cereals and small stock to achieve steady population increases. However (and contrary to older ideas of predynastic and earliest Old Kingdom abhorrence of the desert), it is possible that the first push to social stratification and (eventual state) unification came not from those parts of the Valley most in contact with western Asia but instead from upper Egyptian polities (Hierakonpolis, This, and Naqada) that persisted in a desert ethos of trade, extensive contact, and mineral exploitation far into the western desert and south to middle Nubia.

In contrast to hyperarid northeast Africa's contrarian cattle herding response to desertification, in southern Africa foragers seem to have moved away both from mobility and, curiously, from food production. Exploitation there through the middle Holocene might be generalized as extensive and expedient as peoples followed the movements of large ungulates; contrast that emphasis on hunting with the compartmentalized social and exploitation landscape in place after a climatic mode shift at between 3200 and 2700 BCE. The dense net of stable light isotope data and ecofacts in excavated contexts mentioned earlier show that not only does the interior of the subcontinent become so inhospitable that some argue for complete cessation of occupation, but also that coastal areas and those at the overlap of the summer and winter rainfall zones in the vicinity of what is now the Kalahari Desert submitted to abrupt rainfall changes. In the face of this, people developed the anti-Neolithic. In some cases (KwaZulu Natal and perhaps the far western Cape), archaeologists can trace peoples' seasonal rounds (visits to the same seasonal resource zones each year). More common was a distinct reduction in movements amounting to near-sedentarism as growing populations turned to a concentration upon small package resources—tortoise, fish, small bovids (antelope), and shellfish—allowing greater predictability of resources overall. Add to this concentration on relatively high-yielding localities the apparent fire management of root and tuber-bearing geophytes, the definition of discrete groups (with new rules for expressing ethnicity in, for example, rock art), and exchange relations among them, along with new storage technologies.

New storage technologies, more efficient food processing tools (including pottery), and the adoption of domesticates developed locally or imported from afar are, of course, well-known ways to at least delay the need to flee areas under desertification. An interesting technological addition to this repertoire came at the end of this period, from the Tripolitanian arid steppes from the North African coast south to the Saharan limits (the Roman *limes)* of Punic-Libyan and then Romano-Libyan settlements. The extensive United Nations Educational, Scientific and Cultural Organization (UNESCO) Libyan Valleys Survey documented the innovations in floodwater-based agriculture (dependent upon dams built across seasonal watercourses) that allowed surpluses to be extracted from this predesert zone.

Ultimately, however, climatic unpredictability, desertification, and mobility go hand in glove— which is not to say that such environmentally encouraged mobility is monolithic. Although not a case of classic desertification, the rapidly improving command of the vegetation sequences within Nigeria's Benue region/southern Cameroonian Bantu-homeland, and Congo Basin of the onset of aridity (at roughly 3500 BCE—fragmentation of the forest) and high oscillations of precipitation after 2000 BCE, throws new light on the circumstances of the Bantu expansion. It is possible to correlate (logically never an argument for exclusive causation) the first pulse of the Bantu-speakers south toward the deepest rainforest of the Basin and along the Atlantic coast with the onset of abrupt subcontinental dry spells (including deep lake regressions in the homeland). The second pulse into the interior of the Basin after 1000 BCE coincided with a profound disturbance of

the forest, in part climatically based and partly aggravated by entering settlers' slash-and-burn agriculture practices. Likewise, detailed geomorphology and archaeology in the southern Lake Chad basin documents the tentative exploration at around 2000 BCE by seasonally mobile pastoralists of the rich *firgi* lands left behind by a receding lake. After the area experienced full terminal lake stage recession, this group was replaced by semi-permanent and, shortly thereafter, by sedentary farmers who rapidly increased in population and in agricultural competence.

Another desertification-propelled mobility and regional abandonment in far western Africa in this era led to one of Africa's most famous and distinctive forms: composite ethnic urbanism. Saharan peoples began a long, drawn-out flight (around 4400 BCE) with arid episodes disrupting the Sahara's second Holocene pluvial stage, intensifying after approximately 2200. Among these peoples' final refuges were the floodplains of the Senegal and upper Niger Rivers. The Middle Niger proved to be a spawning ground for niche specialization—an innovative use of a highly variable, undoubtedly unpredictable but rich mosaic dune and fluvial landscape that gave rise, ultimately, to sub-Saharan Africa's earliest urbanism. Entering onto a landscape of high risk, and higher potential, the Middle Niger peoples took desertification and abrupt climate shifts in stride, responding by intensive ethnic-based production of local ecosystem knowledge. Each ethnic group possessed specialized knowledge of how a particular crop, animal, or suite of related resources might thrive or be best exploited under different climatic circumstances, including which might be domesticated. All groups were linked together in tight networks of contractual expectations of goods and services—a classic buffering mechanism underlain by obligations of mutual aid. Successful niche specialization led to ever higher populations living in massive, if composite settlements that, by the mid first millennium BCE or earlier, became true cities.

Africa's innovative responses to desertification must be reckoned with in any worldwide discussion of collapse and sustainability in response to the unstable climates of the five millennia before the Common Era. Collapse (reversion of a social or political system to a less complex state) was hardly seen as eastern Saharan peoples flocked to the upper Egyptian and lower Nubian Nile valleys (indeed, where one of the world's great archaic states emerged), or entered into increasingly specialized, mutual-aid relationships with other niche specialists along the Middle Niger (where one of the world's seven original, fully indigenous urban civilizations emerged). Sustainability—maintaining the system that produce valued goods and services for as long as they are valued—is just another name for the move to exploit small package resources in an increasingly compartmentalized South African landscape, and for the efficient colonization of the firgi lands left behind as Lake Chad receded. Climate change, including desertification, should not be considered the mother of African innovation, but at times it may have been the hand that rocked the cradle.

See also **Bantu, Eastern, Southern, and Western, History of (1000 BCE to 1500 CE); Climate; Ecology; Egypt, Early; Indian Ocean, Africa, History of (1000 BCE to 600 CE); Interlacustine Region, History of (1000 BCE to 1500 CE); Madagascar and Western Indian Ocean, History of (Early to 1500); Northeastern Africa, Classical Period, History of (1000 BCE to 600 CE); Northwestern Africa, Classical Period, History of (1000 BCE to 600 CE); Nubia; Technological Specialization Period, History of (c. 19,000 to 5000 BCE); Western Desert and Margins, History of (1000 BCE to 600 CE).**

BIBLIOGRAPHY

Brunk, Karsten, and Detlef Gronenborn. "Floods, Droughts, and Migrations. The Effect of Late Holocene Lake Level Oscillations and Climate Fluctuations on the Settlement and Political History in the Chad Basin." In *Living with the Lake. Perspectives on History, Culture and Economies of Lake Chad*, eds. Matthias Krings and Editha Platte. Cologne, Germany: Köppe, 2004.

Friedman, Renée, ed. *Egypt and Nubia: Gifts of the Desert*. London: British Museum Press, 2002.

Kuper, Rudolf, and Stefan Kröpelin. 2006. "Climate-Controlled Holocene Occupation in the Sahara: Motor of Africa's Evolution." *Science* 313, no. 5788 (2006): 803–807.

Marret, Fabienne; J. Maley; and James Scourse. "Climatic Instability in West Equatorial Africa during the Mid- and Late Holocene." *Quaternary International* 150 (2006): 71–81.

McIntosh, Roderick. *Ancient Middle Niger: Urbanism and the Self-Organizing Landscape*. Cambridge, U.K.: Cambridge University Press, 2005.

McIntosh, Roderick. "Chasing Dunjugu over the Mande Landscape: Making Sense of Prehistoric and Historic Climate Change." *Climates of the Mande*. Special Segment of *Mande Studies* 6 (2005): 11–28.

Mitchell, Peter. *The Archaeology of Southern Africa*. Cambridge, U.K.: Cambridge University Press, 2002.

Tainter, Joseph A. "Problem Solving: Complexity, History, Sustainability." *Population and Environment* 22, no. 1 (2000): 3–41.

RODERICK J. McINTOSH

DESERTS. *See* **Desertification, Modern; Ecosystems: Deserts and Semi-Deserts.**

DIASPORAS

This entry includes the following articles:
OVERVIEW
INSTITUTIONS
MUSIC
RELIGIONS
ARTS
RE-AFRICANIZATION

OVERVIEW

The African diaspora has three key dimensions: dispersion from Africa, settlement abroad, and a physical or psychological return. The dispersion establishes points of departure that indicates the cultural areas from which Africans originated, whereas settlement deals with the locations, adjustments, and identities of the dispersed Africans, their descendants, interactions, and adjustments abroad; and return includes physical returns, nostalgia, and the use of the idea of Africa to accomplish or fulfill certain political, cultural, or other objectives. The diaspora concept thus establishes the continuity of African peoples and their history, and requires researchers and others to explore the history of Africa itself from the variety of available sources.

Although for many centuries Africans migrated abroad voluntarily as merchants, sailors, soldiers, entertainers, and adventurers, the most significant legacies common to Africa and its diaspora are the domination of blacks by Europeans and North Americans who perceived themselves to be superior and thus claimed privileged positions in Africa and abroad. Africa's depopulation, although a disruptive element for its societies, was a critical source for population growth in the Americas; those who survived the trauma contributed significantly to the development of their new homelands in the Americas, Europe, and Asia, and established a presence abroad that fueled a continuous redefinition of identity, struggle, and the assertion of freedom worldwide.

THE AFRICAN DIASPORA IN ASIA

In ancient times, Africans both willingly traveled and were involuntarily taken across the Red and Mediterranean Seas and the Indian Ocean. They interacted with Arabs in Egypt, Sudan, and across the Red Sea, and shared common values and customs. Africans settled on the Arabian peninsula and in the Persian Gulf region long before the area succumbed to the Roman Empire. Their descendants in Asia became known as Siddis and Habshis. Although the Arabs established a multi-racial/ethnic empire in the seventh century, they held views of blacks as inferior beings. A number of early black poets in Arabia revealed this in their poetry.

As early as 694 CE, enslaved and free Africans in today's Iraq launched a freedom movement, and a larger one in 868, both of which affirm the existence of sizable African settlements. In 868, some 15,000 people followed Rihan Ibn Salih, an enslaved African, and established the independent state of Dawlat al-Zanj. The people there worked in gangs clearing the salt marshes for the cultivation of rice, sugar, and wheat, and they also tended, date plantations that supplied the molasses industry, or coconut groves.

The expansion of Islam from the seventh century fostered a large and sustained movement of Africans abroad as free and enslaved people. The well-known African Bilal ibn Rabah (c. 578–c. 638) became the first chanter of the Islamic call to prayer, and a number of Africans fought with Muhammad in Arabia; others continued the struggle across Persia and into India. In 711 CE, when the Arabs conquered Sindh in Pakistan, Africans fought on both sides. One of them, Siddi Shiya

Habshi, is revered in Sindhi literature as a heroic resister against Islam during that period.

Over time, communities of Africans emerged in a number of Arabian and Persian towns and cities: Giddah, Hodeida, Mecca, Mocha, Aden, and Makulla in the Red Sea area; Muscat, Sur, Basra, Sharjah, Bushire, Lingeh, and Bandar Abbas on the Persian Gulf, and inland at Shiraz. They worked as merchants, dockworkers, clerks, and as agricultural laborers on sugar and date plantations, and the salt marshes. Other communities emerged in Balochistan of today's Pakistan and Iran.

Enslaved Africans were also found in China. One authority on slavery, Wilbur Martin (1967), wrote that "dark skinned slaves, certainly negroid, were popular" there and such references to them go back to the fourth and fifth centuries. He attributed their presence to Arab traders, who propagated Islam in China after 651. It is estimated that thousands of Arabs and Persians brought hundreds of Africans when they settled in Canton and Yang-chou. By the sixteenth century, bonded African crews served on Portuguese vessels that went to Gao in India, Macao in China, and Nagasaki in Japan; African soldiers also fought with Portuguese forces against the Persians, and at Macao against the Dutch.

The largest number of enslaved Africans in Asia was settled in India. Ibn Battuta (1304–c. 1368), the great world traveler, journeyed from northern India to Ceylon between 1333 and 1342 and observed Africans working as administrators, guards, and sailors scattered across wide stretches of that subcontinent. They had varied experiences in the region. Jalal-ud-din Yaqut, for example, was the royal stable master and companion for Queen Razia (d. 1240) of the thirteenth-century Delhi sultanate. In Gujarat, large numbers of Africans served in Muslim armies at least from the thirteenth century. And when the Bahmani kingdom in northwest India reached its peak under Bahman Shah I in the late fourteenth and early fifteenth centuries, several Africans rose to prominent positions in the army and the administration. In Bidar, the Bahmani capital, the Habashi Kot, an Ethiopian fort with tombs of African nobles, remains. In northeast India, several African slaves seized power in the fifteenth century, whereas several others seized control of Janjira Island and were eagerly sought as allies by the Dutch and English in the sixteenth and seventeenth centuries.

In a few cases, one can trace specific Africans from their original homes to areas in Asia. Malik Ambar (1550–1626), for example, was captured in Ethiopia by Arabs and sold in Baghdad, where he learned Arabic and became a clerk. Later he was sold to Indians who took him to the Deccan Peninsula in central India. There he became a soldier, organized a revolt, and seized control of Ahmednagar, which he ruled from 1601 to 1626. During that time he founded towns, constructed canals and roads, and fostered trade, scholarship, and the arts. He demonstrated an identity with Africa in some of the art he commissioned, and employed Africans, Arabs, Indians, and Persians at his court. Ambar and the Siddis of Janjira periodically joined forces against Indian and European foes. The tomb of Malik Ambar now stands in Maharashtra state in India. Another enslaved African, Siddi Sayed, obtained his freedom, became a prosperous merchant, and in 1573 built a mosque in Ahmadabad, an Indian city with an estimated 5,000 Africans at the time. Several European experts have praised this mosque, which still stands, as comparable to architecture in medieval Greece.

The power of gunpowder, the compass, and the caravel gave Europe control of the seas and thus world trade that enabled Portuguese explorers to extend their voyages along the western coast of Africa. They established political and commercial relations with a number of African rulers, most notably in the Kongo in 1485. When Vasco da Gama (c. 1469–1524) rounded the southern tip of Africa in 1498, he found a system of commercial relations between the east African coast and the offshore islands, Arabia, and Asia. He continued his voyage to India and established an all-water route to Asia.

This development, combined with the Atlantic phase of exploration by Christopher Columbus (c. 1451–1506), ushered in a new era of world relations generally, and, in particular, internationalized the slave trade. The possibility of owning sugarcane plantations in the Canary Islands and São Tomé e Príncipe led to the development of a slave trade from the African mainland to those offshore islands where plantation economies with slave labor had been established prior to the voyage of Christopher Columbus.

The sixteenth century witnessed Europeans and Arabs competing in a vigorous trade in goods and slaves in East Africa and Asia. The Arab-conducted slave trade to Asia continued through the nineteenth century, when Europeans were abolishing such trade. The city of Karachi in the 1830s reportedly imported up to 1,500 African slaves annually, and Africans functioned in a variety of roles. Hosh Mohammad, also known as Hoshu Sheedi, gained fame as a soldier defending Sindh against the British in the late eighteenth century. Articles, stories, and poems pay homage to him. Zahur Shah Hashmi and Murad Sahir became noted poets; Mohammad Hashim Rangooni, a dramatist; Mohammad Jharak, a singer; and Banal Dashtiari, a poet and writer.

Mohamed Siddiq Mussafar, a sheedi/African descendant, described local conditions in the Karachi area in *The Eye-Opening Account of Slavery and Freedom* (1951), written in Urdu. He referred to a percussion instrument, known as the *masendo*, as being of African origin and a symbol of Afro-Sindhi identity. He also discussed conditions in the nineteenth century, including the situation of United States blacks, to whom he frequently referred as freed shindi brothers. He praised the works of Frederick Douglass (1818–1895) and Booker T. Washington (1856–1915). Mussafar recognized the global presence of African people and their contributions to other societies. Omar Khalidi wrote in his introduction to *Hyderabad, After the Fall* (1988), that Habshi musicians still play the tambura bowl (lyre) throughout the Persian Gulf states. In parts of Sind and Balochistan, Habshis annually celebrate the *Waghu Mela* (Crocodile Festival). Swahili is still spoken in scattered parts of central India and Gujarat. And the feelings of kinship with continental Africans prompted the 1973 visits by Habshis to Kenya, Uganda, and Tanzania to explore common interests. Thus, the legacy of the slave trade continues to inspire efforts for psychological, physical reunion, and cooperation.

The trade in Africans across the Red Sea and the Indian Ocean became an international phenomenon as the Portuguese took shipments to the Persian Gulf and India and to China and Japan; the Dutch shipped slaves to India and Indonesia; the French took them to India and the Mascarene Islands; the British transported them to India, Mauritius, and China; and the United States took shipments. As the nineteenth-century restrictions on the Atlantic Ocean slave trade increased after 1807 when the British outlawed the trade, the Portuguese relied more heavily on East Africa for cargoes to Brazil and Cuba. Meanwhile, Muslim Arabs and Indians continued their trade out of Zanzibar and neighboring areas to parts of Arabia and farther east.

During the early nineteenth century, a number of free Africans continued to settle in various parts of Asia. Some came as merchants, others accompanied Asians for whom they worked in East Africa, still others were children of Asians who had settled along the east African coast from Somalia to Tanzania. Over the centuries these free and enslaved Africans adopted aspects of Asian culture while maintaining much of their own.

Although not part of the slave trade, the convict-labor system of Britain had the effect of creating an African diaspora in Australia from the late eighteenth to the middle of the nineteenth centuries. This dispersion was part of the British policy of peopling their colonies with convicts, many of whom were guilty of vagrancy laws that disproportionately affected blacks who could not find employment because of racial discrimination. Although Africans seem to have composed a small proportion of those shipped there, they arrived in Australia along with other blacks from the Caribbean, South Africa, and Mauritius.

THE AFRICAN DIASPORA IN EUROPE
Commercial contacts between Europeans and Africans developed from antiquity in southern Europe and northern Africa around the vicinity of Carthage and Egypt, and fostered urban growth and attracted merchants from Sudan, the Sahara, and the Nile Valley. This commercial interaction resulted in an accelerated migration in and out of the continent. In addition, the Muslim campaign across northern Africa and into Iberia and neighboring areas from the eighth century augmented the African presence there. Muslims continued to dominate the Mediterranean Sea up to the fifteenth century, during which time Arabs and Europeans captured, bought, and sold Africans. Many of these Africans appear to have come from Tunis and Cyrenaica in Libya, an important North African slave entrepot for the traffic from Sudan. Africans were

shipped to Barcelona, Genoa, Naples, Turkey, and the Middle East.

A number of free and enslaved Ethiopians visited and settled in parts of Europe during the medieval period. The Crusaders encountered several Ethiopian monks in Jerusalem and Egypt. This was the time when the Zagwe kings of Ethiopia (1137–1270) were reaching out for connections with western Christendom. When the Crusaders lost Jerusalem in 1244, Ethiopia, as an established Christian state since the fourth century, became even more attractive to Europeans and was sought as an ally against the Muslims. It was during the thirteenth century in particular that a number of Ethiopians visited Milan, Venice, Bologna, Rome, Aragon, and Portugal. Rome and Aragon reciprocated by sending monks and craftsmen to Ethiopia. In addition, Ethiopian envoys participated in the Council of Constance in 1418, and Deacon Peter of Ethiopia spoke at the Council of Ferrara-Florence in 1441.

Important as those developments were, however, the era of the greatest dispersion of Africans to the western hemisphere began in the fifteenth century with the exploration of the world by the Portuguese, the Spanish, and other Europeans. The lucrative caravan trade in gold between Sudan and northern Africa intensified, largely because southern Europe depended heavily upon this source; this became a powerful motive for exploring Africa in the fifteenth century. As Christian forces in Iberia pushed the Muslims back into northern Africa, more Europeans developed direct links with that caravan trade that led to larger numbers of Africans visiting and settling in several European cities. Some of those Africans were trained and used by the Portuguese and other European explorers as interpreters and guides in the exploration of Africa.

Over the next five hundred years, Africa was drawn closer into the increasing European-dominated world economy, providing markets and resources, including Africans themselves. The Portuguese, disappointed by the small amounts of gold they obtained in Africa, increasingly turned to the acquisition of manpower in the form of slaves. Eventually, more and more Africans were enslaved or became menial laborers in Portugal and Spain. In 1444, a company was established in Lagos, Portugal, to engage in the slave trade. That year

Prince Henry (b. 1394), the Church of Lagos, the Franciscans of Cape Saint Vincent, and various European merchants appropriated some 240 bonded Africans. In 1448 Portugal initiated regular trade in goods and Africans with Arguin, off the coast of Mauritania. In Portugal, enslaved and free Africans worked in mines, factories, and construction, on farms, as guards, soldiers, domestics, couriers, stevedores, and concubines. They lived in Lisbon, Barcelona, Cadiz, Seville, and Valencia. The Spanish took Africans to the Netherlands. Over time, a number of African merchants and rulers came to rely on European goods, and that increasingly dictated that they collaborate in the slave trade.

After William Hawkins sailed to West Africa in 1530, more and more Africans were taken to England. Despite the observation of Queen Elizabeth I in 1556 that there were too many blackamoors in the country and that they should be returned to Africa, the numbers continued to grow. From the eighteenth century, West Indian planters and military officers on home leave brought enslaved Africans with them, and by the nineteenth century the number of Africans in England had increased to an estimated 15,000, mostly poor and unwelcome. Some of them became free and worked with English abolitionists, and several helped to launch a 1787 program to settle Africans in Sierra Leone.

From the fifteenth century, Africans also were seen in France. Although a royal court proclaimed that France did not permit slavery, the institution emerged there. Both enslaved and free Africans lived in Anjou, Lyons, Orleans, Nantes, Marseilles, Toulon, and Paris. They worked as servants, menial laborers, pages, and entertainers. From the seventeenth century, Africans arrived in larger numbers as France acquired a greater share of the slave trade. Royal policy also allowed the French in the Americas to bring their enslaved Africans back with them. By the eighteenth century, some 2,000 Africans were estimated as living in France.

Other parts of Europe became residences for Africans, enslaved and free. Some joined the small communities of Ethiopian monks and other Africans in Venice, Rome, and neighboring cities along the northern Mediterranean rim; there were Africans along the southern Adriatic coast of Yugoslavia. The city of Ulcinj in particular had a

number of Africans who, in the sixteenth and seventeenth centuries, worked as seamen on ships in the Strait of Otranto. The slave traders also took Africans to Sicily, Cyprus, and the southern Iberian coast.

Little is known about African settlers in eastern Europe in this period. However, it is clear that the Ottoman Turks carried Africans into southeastern Europe as soldiers and bureaucrats. That the great Russian poet, Aleksander Pushkin (1799–1837), whose great-grandfather was of African descent, was reexported from Turkey to Russia, suggests the possibility of others following this route. Some Turks of African descent engaged in collecting data about their enslaved past will no doubt help to fill these pages of history.

The status of Africans in Europe was precarious. Whereas laws in Europe did not recognize slavery, European colonial laws did. Consequently, enslaved Africans brought to France and Britain, for example, often were kept as slaves. The Mansfield court's decision in England of 1772, stating that Africans in England could no longer be held legally as slaves, represented the beginning of a new era. From the early nineteenth century, the European powers gradually abolished the slave trade and legally clarified the status of Africans as free people.

A small group of African students also resided in Europe, especially from the middle of the eighteenth century when more African rulers sent their sons to Europe to learn the languages and commercial skills needed to conduct business more effectively with Europeans. Missionaries in Africa sent African students for education in Europe, as well. These students included Anton Armo, who studied at the University of Halle and the University of Waltenberg, became a philosopher, and returned to teach in the Gold Coast, now Ghana; Philip Quaque (b. c. 1741) and Jacobus Capitein (c. 1717–1747) of the Gold Coast, who returned home to work as teachers and missionaries; Ottobah Cugoano (b. c. 1750), whose *Thoughts and Sentiments on the Evil and Wicked Traffic of the Slavery and Commerce of the Human Species* (1787) stirred debate about the slave trade; and Ignatius Sancho (1729–1780), whose posthumously published letters confirm him as an important spokesman for African freedom and dignity in Africa and the diaspora. Several other Africans in

Europe addressed the issue of freedom, and engaged in a dialogue with the Europeans who became prominent in the abolition of slavery and the revolutionary struggles for democracy. Ethiopian monks and other Africans broadened European knowledge about the Middle East and northeastern Africa, and played an active role in bridging the eastern and western cultures.

THE AFRICAN DIASPORA IN THE AMERICAS

Although there was an African presence in the Americas prior to the slave trade, it was that trade that led to the greatest dispersion of Africans. At least an estimated twelve million Africans were in the Americas by 1800: some two million in the United States (approximately four million by the late nineteenth century) and three to four million in Brazil, which continued the slave trade until 1888, resulting in many millions more. Whereas the largest communities of people of African descent now reside in Brazil and the United States respectively, there are sizable numbers throughout the Caribbean, Central and South America. Haiti, Jamaica, Barbados, and several of the Caribbean islands, as well as Panama and Belize, contain majority populations of African descent. Africans participated in the exploration of the United States and contributed to the exploration of Canada and Central and South America.

Major ports of entry for enslaved Africans in South America were Salvador and Rio de Janeiro in Brazil, Montevideo in Uruguay, and Buenos Aires in Argentina. From Uruguay and Argentina, sixteenth century overland caravans of captive Africans passed through the Mendoza region and across the rough Andes Mountains to Valparaiso and Santiago in Chile. The northern route led principally to Cartagena, Colombia, across Panama, and southward to Quayakill, Ecuador, and Callao and Lima in Peru. These Central and South American bonded Africans worked primarily in agriculture, in gold and silver mines, and as pearl divers, especially in Venezuela.

Most of these Africans came from the area of today's Ghana eastward to the Cameroons and from the area around the mouth of the Congo River; sizable numbers also arrived from East Africa. The resistance at those initial points of enslavement was an affirmation of identity and a struggle for freedom. The fight began at the point of capture, continued

on the slave ships, in the slave markets abroad, and in enslavement. Although Africans often were caught at random, sold, and packed on ships, each shipload included some captives who spoke the same or related languages, frequently came from the same areas in Africa, and, in a number of cases, were captives from the same ethnic group. These factors facilitated communication, as several examples of collaboration in slave mutinies aboard ships confirm. A reexamination of some of those mutinies reveals that Africans conspired for days to plan revolts. Research also has shown that some of the cooks aboard slave ships were African women who sometimes had social relations with European crewmen and then conveyed to the enslaved African men information that helped to facilitate conspiracies and mutinies.

As debilitating as the slave ship experiences were, Africans cultivated friendships there that lasted into the system of enslavement in the Americas. Evidence of the development of a group identity is provided by a number of terms from the ships that survived in bondage, and were equivalent to the terms for a friend or compatriot. These relationships no doubt facilitated the beginning of a synthesis of African culture aboard ship, during enslavement, and beyond.

During the seventeenth and eighteenth centuries, many slaves adopted the terms African and Ethiopian as labels, and there are several examples of Africans striving to retain their ethnic names. Although local customs and legal codes in the Americas often forbade them to speak African languages or to practice their religion and culture, many of them, in their limited private lives, did. In time, however, they learned European languages and established parallel institutions: African churches, African schools, and African lodges. Too seldom studied, especially in the North American experience, is the extent to which those institutions incorporated African ideas and traditions. African lodges reflect not only Western influences but also the African tradition of secret societies like the *poro* and *sande* along the West African coast, from which many of the enslaved Africans in the Americas originated. Margaret Creel (1988) makes a strong case in this regard for links between the offshore islands of South Carolina/Georgia and Sierra Leone/Liberia. Judith Carney

(2001) has also demonstrated the critical link between the Guinea coast from which Africans transferred rice cultivation and culture to the Americas, South Carolina in particular.

The black churches, schools, lodges, and other institutions in America drew upon both African and Western traditions, as group identity was molded in the diaspora. Those institutions, especially the churches and schools in the United States, utilized their African and Western values, skills, and ideas in efforts to educate Africans in the Caribbean, Europe, and Africa itself. A number of blacks, including Frederick Douglass, articulated a group identity and traveled abroad to promote freedom for blacks in the wider diaspora. Like Douglass, Andre Reboucas (1838–1898) in Brazil became a tireless abolitionist. Alexander Crummell (b. 1819), William McNeil Turner, Alexander Walters (b. 1858), Edward Wilmot Blyden (1832–1912), and others promoted ideas of pan-African unity before the concept became formalized.

The persistence of language, traditional beliefs and practices, relationships cultivated aboard the slave ships, and bonds developed abroad provided a strong base for freedom movements, several of which led to the establishment of communities of fugitive slaves, known as *quilombos*, *palenques*, or Maroons. The fight for dignity and freedom was represented in several ways: in the sixteenth and the seventeenth century Venezuela insurrections of Negro Miguel in 1552 and among black pearl divers in 1603; the establishment of Palmares as a separate community in 1605 that lasted until 1694 in Brazil; the Maroon War in Jamaica in 1725 and the signing of a treaty in 1739 between Britain and Captain Cudjoe from the Gold Coast; the resistance in Guyana under the Caromante leader Adoe in the 1740s and Cuffy in the 1760s; and the sixteenth century community in Mexico known as Coyula, led by Gaspar Yanga and described as resembling Guinea. Similar freedom movements occurred in Cuba, Panama, Colombia, Peru, Suriname, and the Leeward and Windward Islands. And there were many smaller revolts, including the uprising led by Nat Turner (b. 1800) and Gullah Jack that saw a collaboration between African and diaspora leadership in the United States.

A most successful freedom struggle by diaspora Africans that clearly reflected the combination of African and Western cultures occurred in Haiti. In 1791, Boukman (d. c. 1791), an African who bound his followers with voodoo rituals and African-style secret oaths, mobilized Haiti's African masses against the slave masters. He was joined by the diaspora-born Christian Toussaint L'Ouverture (c. 1743–1803), who organized the guerrilla war that led to the independence of Haiti in 1804. Haiti thus became the second republic in the Americas and a symbol of African freedom in the diaspora. Although isolated by the major powers, the United States in particular, and thus destined to poverty, the Haitian example nonetheless continues to inspire other black freedom movements. In more recent times, Haitians returned to the continent to assist Africans in their independence struggles and educational and economic development.

These and other freedom movements reveal the nascent African nationalism that developed among diaspora Africans in the Americas. Their aims were not simply vengeance and escape; they sought the establishment of control over their communities to promote their values, aspirations, and traditions. Even under alien control these objectives were pursued and survived to varying degrees: in Cuba, where the Efik-derived African secret societies still survive; in Trinidad, Colombia, and elsewhere, where the Yoruba-derived *shango* is practiced; and in Brazil, where the Yoruba-derived *orisa* persists. There also are isolated groups whose cultures seem hardly to have been affected by colonial and contemporary rule in the diaspora, including the Boni, Djuka, Saramacca, and Akwa of Surinam, and the descendants of Maroons in Jamaica, Haiti, Cuba, and Santo Domingo, areas that deserve more intensive field and archival research.

The Arab, European, and American slave trades from Africa converged during the age of European exploration and made the dispersion and settlement of Africans abroad global. Despite centuries of inhuman ordeals, descendants of those Africans maintained a sense of their African identity that fueled their struggle for freedom and justice. And in the process, African descendants in Asia, Europe, and the Americas contributed to economic and cultural development in those areas and extended their influence to Africa itself.

THE RETURN PHENOMENON

The return phenomenon is a strong indicator of diaspora identity with the homeland, or place of origin. Return movements have been a major part of the link between Africa and members of its diaspora. The return represented both a longing to rejoin family and friends and to redeem Africa, as well as a reaction against the many obstacles to inclusion in host societies to which, over the years, they made significant contributions and were the only societies many of the returnees knew firsthand.

Chief Justice Mansfield's decision in the 1772 Somerset's Case in England, and the influx of Africans who had been liberated because they had fought with England during the American War of Independence, resulted in a significant increase in the size of the black community, especially in London. Consequently, abolitionists pursued the idea of resettling Africans in Africa, where it was hoped that a society founded on the basis of European and North American ideas would lead to the restriction of the slave trade, the spread of Christianity, and the expansion of western trade. Africans in London joined the effort as a way to gain freedom and return home. Finally, in 1787, a group of over 400 Africans and a few English women left Britain to found a new society on land acquired from a Temne ruler in Sierra Leone. This appears to have been the first sustained effort to repatriate Africans to Africa, although not to the specific areas from which they originally came. Other blacks came from Nova Scotia and Jamaica. In addition, once the British had outlawed the slave trade in 1807, Sierra Leone became the base for the British West Africa Squadron that patrolled the West African coast to enforce abolition treaties signed by the several powers. Africans recaptured and liberated by that Squadron were settled in Sierra Leone that, by the middle of the century, had an estimated population of 70,000.

Because the first settlers had come from England and its colonies in the Americas, they knew English and had a sense of western society. They enrolled in the mission schools, and some sent their sons and daughters to English universities. This desire for a western education, and the missionaries' belief in education to civilize and Christianize Africans, led to the founding of Fourah Bay College by the Church

Missionary Society in 1827, which became a regional center for western education, especially for training teachers and missionaries. In 1841, Edward Jones, believed to be the first African American college graduate in the United States, was named president of Fourah Bay College.

Those pioneer settlers, however, regarded themselves as elites to both the indigenous and recaptured Africans led to internal conflicts that continue in the early twenty-first century. However, as the recaptured Africans began to outnumber the western groups and accepted Christianity and western education, the gulf between these two groups narrowed, intermarriages occurred, and earlier distinctions diminished. By the middle of the century, a new group emerged, the Krio, representing a blend of Christian and African beliefs, western and African cuisine, and speaking Africanized English. The Krio helped to forge links in West Africa that broadened the horizons and expanded channels of communication beyond local societies and thus contributed to a growing awareness of African nationalism and pan-Africanism.

In the United States a return movement also developed. Africans petitioned for freedom prior to the American War of Independence and expressed determination to return to Africa. The first major organized effort began with Paul Cuffe (1759–1817), a black shipper in Rhode Island, who took some thirty-eight settlers to Sierra Leone in 1815, thus demonstrating the feasibility of black resettlement. Within a few years, European Americans chose colonization as a serious means of ridding the country of free blacks. Thus, in 1816, religious leaders, politicians, and planters organized the American Colonization Society for resettlement in Africa. The federal government gave benevolent encouragement and in 1819 passed a bill authorizing funds for the American navy to seize any American slave vessel, return the slaves to Africa, and provide for their welfare. These efforts led to the founding of Liberia in 1821. Thereafter, free blacks from the United States and slaves captured on the seas were taken to Liberia as settlers. By 1867 nearly 20,000 had settled there. Of that number, 13,000 came directly from the United States, over 4,500 of whom had been born free. Some 350 also came from Barbados.

In comparison with Sierra Leone, two points are especially significant. First, although the overall number of Liberian settlers was much smaller, the great majority of them had previously resided in the United States. Second, whereas most of the settlers were poor, several were educated and had owned property in the United States. Thus, the Liberian settlers retained a special attachment to the United States and patterned many institutions after American ones. In 1847 the settlers declared their independence and Joseph Roberts (1809–1876), a former slave from Virginia, as president.

With independence, Liberia devoted serious effort to devising a viable political system, out of which emerged the one-party system that, it was hoped, would unify the people. But real unity was a long way off. As in Sierra Leone, the settlers, known as Americo-Liberians, assumed an elitist attitude toward the indigenous Africans and dominated positions in business, education, government, and the churches. Unlike in Sierra Leone, Liberia was independent and formulated its own policies that included attempts to assimilate native Africans through the educational system. The school population became overwhelmingly indigenous and gradually opened up opportunities to some of the Vai, Kru, Grebo, and others. But the numbers were small, and progress was slow, with some areas not affected at all by these efforts.

Still, Liberia was unique. It became the second African country to be internationally recognized as independent (after Ethiopia), and the only one with diaspora leadership. Precisely because it was unique, Liberia became a symbol of hope for the salvation of African peoples. Its Declaration of Independence noted that the Liberians had been inhabitants of the United States, where they had been denied their rights and privileges; Liberia's constitution proclaimed the objective of providing a home for the dispersed children of Africa. Several well-known African Americans went to Liberia and made significant contributions: John Russwurm (b. 1799) founded the first newspaper, Lott Carey (b. 1780) left a successful business position in Richmond, Virginia, to become a missionary, John Day left North Carolina and became a teacher and later a chief justice. The renowned Edward Wilmot Blyden made great contributions as principal, ambassador to England, secretary of state, editor, professor, and later president of the University of Liberia. He emphasized the importance of African languages and culture and developed ideas about the importance of a synthesis of African and western culture. The nineteenth century also witnessed return movements from Brazil and Cuba to Nigeria, Bénin, Togo, and Ghana. These returnees also made contributions to West African culture and development.

A number of individual African Americans from the United States and the Caribbean—missionaries, businesspeople, teachers, and others—applied their skills for the general betterment of Africans. Many started schools and medical stations in different parts of Africa, and provided scholarships for Africans to study in African-American schools, including Lincoln University in Pennsylvania, Howard University in Washington, D.C., and Fisk University in Tennessee. Notable among the organizations that provided education and medical assistance in Africa was the African Methodist Episcopal Church, particularly in western, central, and southern Africa. That church and others had a significant impact on African cultural, political, and economic development. With help from individuals and churches, many African students received an education in the United States that prepared them for professions in Africa and elsewhere.

Although it was much smaller, the diaspora in Europe had a similar impact. During the colonial period in Africa, many Africans migrated to the imperial countries for employment and education. The result was that, from the early twentieth century in particular, a new wave of Africans and blacks from the French-speaking Caribbean area—particularly Martinique, Guadeloupe, and Haiti—joined the earlier diaspora and expanded the black presence in France; blacks from Jamaica, Trinidad, Barbados and other English-speaking areas in the Caribbean increased their presence in England; and blacks from Suriname migrated to Holland. These later diasporas in Europe were smaller and did not witness the rigid racial discrimination prevalent in the United States. They therefore did not attract national or international attention as did those in the United States where racial discrimination was more blatant and relations more tense. However, the diasporas in Europe did maintain a consciousness of their African identity and joined their American cohorts in pan-African activities.

A small return movement also occurred from Asia to Africa. British suppression of the slave trade in the Indian Ocean led to the establishment of small communities in Aden, Bombay, and the Seychelles Islands. Only a few hundred resettled along the east African coast, mostly in Freretown, Kenya. This community of ex-slaves came largely from captured Arab dhows and,various parts of Asia, and settled in Nasik, India where missionaries taught them English and western culture; they also learned some Indian languages. In Kenya, the British colonizers recruited them as low-level civil servants and teachers. Over time these returnees became an elite group similar to those in Sierra Leone and Liberia. However, their influence was limited because they were a smaller group in a concentrated area and did not have the sustained influence of a mobilized diaspora abroad. However, a delegation of Siddis from India did visit Kenya, Uganda, and Tanzania in 1972 to consult on common interests.

For the western diaspora, however, the several threads of identity motivated Henry Sylvester Williams (b. 1869) of Trinidad and W. E. B. Du Bois (b. 1868) of the United States to convene the first Pan-African Congress in London in 1900 to consider issues common to Africa and its diaspora. They addressed issues of human rights (broadly defined), as well as social, economic, and political equity. Significantly, this was the time of a nadir for many African peoples—legalized inequality and racial violence in the United States diaspora, and colonial suppression in Africa. But historical identity and cultural expression remained viable seeds that continued to germinate and ultimately flourished from the second decade of the twentieth century. It could be seen in the Harlem Renaissance, Negrismo, Négritude, the Universal Negro Improvement Association, pan-Africanism, and the Black Studies movement. They fired the movement for greater freedom in the diaspora, and independence for Africa.

The African diaspora is global and dynamic phenomenon. The last decades of the twentieth century, for example, witnessed a larger wave of migration of Africans and Caribbean blacks, many of whom were more educated than earlier immigrants, in search of employment, education, and political freedom in the western countries. The historical diaspora, based on the slave trade and enslavement, identified with Africa as a continent. However, the more recent diaspora has a committed consciousness of independent African countries and have established their own social groups with publications in their ethnic languages, businesses that cater largely to their compatriots, and have become increasingly vocal on national and international issues that relate to their national homelands, as well as their adopted countries. All of this suggests the evolution of a more dynamic presence within the African diaspora and the wider world, with the potential for greater research and reorientation of world history.

See also **Blyden, Edward Wilmot; Du Bois, W. E. B.; Gama, Vasco da; Ethnicity; Immigration and Immigrant Groups; Slave Trades; Slavery and Servile Institutions; Travel and Exploration.**

BIBLIOGRAPHY

Andrews, George Reid. *Afro-Latin America, 1800–2000.* New York: Oxford University Press, 2004.

Bastide, Roger. *African Civilizations in the New World,* trans. Peter Green. New York: Harper and Row, 1971.

Beraud-Villars, Jean Marcel Eugene. *Les Touareg au pays du Cid; les invasions almoravides en Espagne aux XIe et XIIe siècles.* Paris: Plon, 1946.

Berlin, Ira. *Slavery and Freedom in the Age of the American Revolution.* Urbana: University of Illinois Press, 1986.

Berlin, Ira.*Generations of Captivity: A History of African-American Slaves.* Cambridge, MA: Belknap Press, 2004.

Blakely, Allison. *Blacks in the Dutch World: The Evolution of Racial Imagery in a Modern Society.* Bloomington: Indiana University Press, 1993.

Boxer, Charles R. *The Dutch Seaborne Empire, 1600–1800.* New York: Knopf, 1965.

Boxer, Charles R. *The Portuguese Seaborne Empire, 1415–1825,* 2nd rev. edition. Manchester, U.K.: Carcanet Press, 1991.

Cambridge History of China. 15 vols. Cambridge, 1978–1994.

Carney, Judith. *Black Rice: The African Origins of Rice Cultivation in the Americas.* Cambridge, MA: Harvard University Press, 2001.

Chauhan, Raghu Raj Singh. *African's in India: From Slavery to Royalty.* New Delhi, India: Asian Publication Services, 1995.

Creel, Margaret W. *A Peculiar People: Slave Religion and Community-Culture among the Gullahs.* New York: New York University Press, 1988.

Cunha, Manuela Carneiro da. *Negros, estrangeiros: os escravos libertos e sua volta Africa.* Sao Paulo, Brazil: Brasiliense, 1985.

Debrunner, Hans Werner. *Presence and Prestige: Africans in Europe: A History of Africans in Europe Before 1918.* Basel, Switzerland: Basler Afrika Bibliographien, 1979.

Goveia, Elsa. *Slave Society in the British Leeward Islands at the End of the Eighteenth Century.* New Haven, CT: Yale University Press, 1965.

Harris, Joseph E. *The African Presence in Asia: Consequences of the East African Slave Trade.* Evanston, IL: Northwestern University Press, 1971.

Harris, Joseph E. *Repatriates and Refugees in a Colonial society: The Case of Kenya.* Washington, DC: Howard University Press, 1987.

Harris, Joseph E. *Global Dimensions of the African Diaspora.* 2nd edition. Washington, DC: Howard University Press, 1993.

Harris, Joseph E. "Expanding the Scope of African Diaspora Studies." *Radical History Review* 87 (Fall 2003).

Hunwick, John, and Eve Troutt Powell, *The African Diaspora in the Mediterranean Lands of Islam.* Princeton, New Jersey: Markus Wiener, 2002.

Levine, Lawrence W. *Black Culture and Black Consciousness: Afro-American Folk Thought from Slavery to Freedom.* New York: Oxford University Press, 1977.

Lewis, Bernard. *Race and Slavery in the Middle East: An Historical Enquiry.* New York: Oxford University Press, 1990.

Martin, Gaston. *L'ère des négriers, 1714–1774. Nantes au XVIIIe siècle*, New edition. Paris: Karthala, 1993.

McCoy, Shelby. *Negroes in France.* Frankfort: University of Kentucky Press: 1961.

Mullin, Michael. *Africa in America: Slave Acculturation and Resistance in the American South and the British Caribbean, 1736-1831.* Urbana: University of Illinois Press, 1992.

Northrup, David. *Africa's Discovery of Europe.* New York: Oxford University Press, 2002.

Pescatella, Ann. *The African in Latin America.* New York: Knopf, 1975.

Rout, Leslie B. *The African Experience in Spanish America, 1502 to the Present Day.* Cambridge, MA: Cambridge University Press, 1976.

Sadiq Ali, Shanti. *The African Dispersal in the Deccan.* New Delhi, India: Orient Longman, 1996.

Toledano, Ehud R. *The Ottoman Slave Trade and Its Suppression, 1840-1890.* Princeton, New Jersey: Princeton University Press, 1982.

UNESCO. *The African Slave Trade from the Fifteenth to the Nineteenth Century.* Paris: UNESCO, 1979.

Verlinden, Charles. *L'esclavage dans l'Europe médiévale.* Bruges, Belgium: De Tempel, 1955.

Walker, Sheila S., ed., *African Roots/American Cultures: Africa in the Creation of the Americas.* Lanham, Maryland: Rowman and Littlefield Publishers, 2001.

Wilbur, Clarence Martin. *Slavery in China during the Former Han Dynasty, 206 B.C.–A.D. 25.* New York: Russell and Russell, 1967.

JOSEPH E. HARRIS

INSTITUTIONS

In the early twenty-first century, the term "African diaspora" is most commonly associated with the social formations that emerged in the Americas as a consequence of the transatlantic slave trade. Between the early sixteenth century and the last quarter of the nineteenth century, more than 10 million Africans were forcefully removed to the Americas as slaves. This process had momentous consequences for the cultural history of those New World societies that engaged in the slave trade. But it was neither the first massive displacement of continental Africans to other parts of the world, nor did the ending of the slave trade and the protracted processes of emancipation bring an end to demographic flows out of Africa.

The trans-Sahara trade had brought sub-Saharan Africans to the Mediterranean for more than a millennium before the fifteenth century, when the Portuguese commenced their first slaving expeditions down the West African coast. Africans served in Roman armies as far north as contemporary England; the Islamic conquest of the Iberian Peninsula brought thousands of Africans to southwestern Europe. By the thirteenth century there is good evidence for African population movements (both slaves and, to a lesser extent, free) toward Asia Minor, the Arabian peninsula, and the Black Sea and Caucasus regions of present-day Russia, Iran, and Central Asia, as well as the Indian subcontinent and Sri Lanka. With the beginnings of Spanish, Portuguese, and Dutch colonial ventures in Africa, Southeast Asia, and East Asia, African populations were evident even in Indonesia, the Philippines, and China. Not all of these movements resulted in a permanent (or even temporary) consolidation of an African diasporic consciousness or institutionally distinct, or socially recognized, African diasporic communities. But in some cases, such communities did develop as in the case of the contemporary Sidi communities in India or that of the Ethiopian Beta Israel in Palestine.

During the era of European colonial expansion, Africans circulated through different European empires as seafarers and conscripted soldiers, as colonial civil servants and as migrant dockworkers. The end of formal colonial rule frequently set in motion migratory processes towards the former metropoles that led to the consolidation of diasporic identities and institutions based primarily on common experiences of racial marginalization. Beginning in the 1970s, many African states experienced increasing levels of economic and political crises due to warfare, the imposition of structural adjustment programs, or misrule by cleptocratic regimes. One of the consequences of this was intensified movement into the global north and the emergence of major African urban centers outside the continent in such cities as London, Paris, Brussels, New York City, Washington, D.C., and Toronto.

In the early twenty-first century, African asylum seekers and other refugees, exiled political dissidents or followers of ousted regimes, professionals, artists, and athletes are operating on a more or less permanent basis in Europe and North America, as are more mobile entrepreneurs, illegal *sans papiers*, and other groups in the global African diaspora. These individuals and groups oftentimes form highly self-conscious communities abroad or operate within tightly knit transnational networks. They also often exert significant economic and political influence upon their homelands in Africa.

In many cases, the local institutions and far-flung networks integrating these new African diasporas are beginning to come into empirical and analytical focus. The best known cases in the early twenty-first century include Sudanese, Somalian, Ethiopian, and Sierra Leonian refugees in North America; the Senegalese Mouride trading networks in the United States and Italy; Nigerian or Kenyan diaspora(s) in Britain; migrants and refugees from the two Congos in Paris and Brussels; and, to a lesser extent, the Mozambiquan, Angolan, and Cape Verdean presence in Portugal (and probably in Brazil as well).

Bringing these (by no means clearly distinct) historical phases of the African diaspora under one analytical framework represents a formidable task. It is, thus, not at all clear whether the term diaspora is equally applicable to such groups as African-descended slaves in Islamic Spain, Mamluk soldiers and administrators in the Ottoman empire, slaves on Caribbean sugar plantations, colonial intellectuals sojourning in Oxbridge or Paris, and Sudanese Lost boys in Toronto. And what of the African diasporas within Africa itself: from the centuries-old Hausa trading diasporas scattered across much of West Africa, to Sudanese refugees in Kenya, and on to Senegalese middleman diamond traders in Democratic Republic of the Congo and Nigerian drug lords in Johannesburg? Does extending the label of African diaspora to all of these variegated population movements and social formations yield valid generalizations, or does the use of the term diaspora for all of these cases simply distort their specificities and suggest spurious commonalities? Answers to these questions are not readily apparent.

Nevertheless, a focus on the historical African diaspora in the Americas may at least reveal how the study of other African diasporas—both those much older and much newer—may help to direct inquiries into such questions. During the centuries in which the slave trade linked American plantation regions with West Africa, the New World became a contact zone where people hailing from a wide variety of cultures interacted under variegated and changing historical conditions. What all of them brought to the New World encounter were varying amounts of knowledge about what all of them experienced, albeit in ways deeply affected by the manner in which they became incorporated into emerging political and economic regimes based on racial slavery: the need to adapt such cultural knowledge to the options and constraints of new and oftentimes rapidly changing social environments.

There was nothing mechanical about the Atlantic transfer of African cultures. Although the significance of an African contribution to the cultural heritage of the Americas is beyond dispute, the study of the historical links between Africa and the Americas is fraught with problems: the ways in which enslaved Africans managed to transform parts of the cultural knowledge they carried across the Atlantic into collective practices; the reasons some practices and not others proved viable under conditions of slavery; the manner in which such incipient new social institutions eventually stabilized into transgenerationally viable African American traditions; and the transformations that were wrought upon these practices and institutions in the process: None of this is accessible to easy generalization. As a result, the question of how to assess and explain continuities and ruptures in transatlantic cultural transmission has been subject to considerable debate.

In the early twenty-first century, the existence in the Americas of practices, institutions, and ideological complexes evidencing varying degrees of semblance to African cultural forms is well documented. These range from place names and other lexical items in regional vernaculars, to foodways, musical idioms, proverbs and folktales, decorative styles, modes of personal adornment, belief systems, and ritual practices. In terms of geographic distribution, areas formerly characterized by extensive slave-based plantation economies—such as the Caribbean, Brazil, and parts of the Atlantic littoral of southern continental America—represent the historical heartland of African-influenced New World cultures. However, postemancipation migrations, more recent international population shifts, and processes of appropriation of African American cultural complexes by populations of non-African descent, have led to the diffusion of strongly African-influenced cultural forms far outside their geographical and social locations of origin.

Yet, despite a wealth of descriptive data, in most instances the historical processes that led to the emergence, continuity, and transformation of such forms are far from adequately known. Does one speak of African cultural institutions in the diaspora, or rather of African American diasporic institutions? In posing such a question, one also has to define "Africanness" as a historical problem rather than an "essence."

Mere resemblances between African and African American social and cultural forms thus do not prove historical relations between them. Such resemblances may be based on continuities, or represent independent developments determined by local structural conditions. In the absence of historical evidence about the transmission and reproduction of African cultural elements in the New World, it is difficult to rule out either convergence or parallelism. In several instances, the origins of certain New World cultural forms (for example, the North American banjo, the Haitian pattern of stable extramarital sexual unions known as *plaçage*, or the Trinidadian institution of the ninth night wake) can be traced to Africa or to Europe. What is more, mere attributions of origin do not elucidate the history of institutions in terms of how the cultural forms that integrate them are put to social use over time.

These questions and concerns are not just of academic interest, but are also of political import. Claims that certain New World institutions are of African derivation have always been linked to conceptions of African American identity, the place of African-descended peoples in New World societies, and the representations of "Africanness" in the public definition of New World national cultures. As a result, it is hardly surprising that the question of how to assess and explain continuities and ruptures in transatlantic cultural transmission continues to incite controversy.

Though historical records are replete with references to forms of slave behavior judged by contemporary observers to be of African derivation, systematic inquiry into the African backgrounds of African American cultures commenced only around the turn of the twentieth century. Since then, two sharply divergent approaches tended to characterize this field of inquiry. The position prevailing in the 1940s was that slavery and its aftermath (with its continued social and economic marginalization of people of African descent) had obliterated whatever African cultural elements slaves had originally carried to the Americas. One of the leading exponents of this view was the black sociologist E. Franklin Frazier (1894–1962), who believed that contemporary forms of African American social behavior were the result of an incomplete assimilation of the norms of European American culture by African Americans barred from full participation in American social life.

The anthropologist Melville J. Herskovits (1895–1963) reversed this line of argument by explaining the formal characteristics of contemporary African American cultures not in terms of New World structural conditions, but of African cultural antecedents. Proceeding from the assumption that present similarities in form indicate prior historical connections, Herskovits interpreted differences on the American side as incrementally measurable deviations from the results of putatively normal cultural dynamics in Africa. Such deviations, in turn, were explained by varying degrees of acculturative pressure brought to bear on Africans and their descendants under New World slave regimes. Contrary to previous approaches assuming initial cultural loss, Herskovits thus proffered the idea of a continuity of African cultural knowledge and practices. Though partly eroded or modified, elements of original African heritage (Africanisms) could be detected in the behavior and thought of contemporary African Americans.

Formalistic approaches such as that advocated by Herskovits have yielded convincing results in cases where morphological correspondences between New World phenomena and potential African equivalents are pronounced enough to warrant ethnically precise attribution of African origin not only to single cultural elements but to whole complexes. The divination systems practiced in Cuban *regla ocha* (also known as Santeria) and Brazilian *Candomblé*, for instance, represent New World variants of the Yoruba *ifa* and *merindilogun* oracles. Likewise, the conception and ritual manipulation of power objects termed *prenda* or *nganga* in the Cuban *reglas de congo* closely correspond to ideas and practices concerning *minkisi* recorded among the Kongo and other Bantu-speaking groups of western central Africa.

Still, unless the path of cultural transmission can be traced in sufficient historical detail, identifying Africanisms by morphological criteria raises considerable methodological and theoretical problems. The morphological characteristics of cultural complexes found in contemporary African American societies are oftentimes too unspecific to facilitate the identification of a single African source, or, alternatively, are too ambiguous to allow more than tentative attribution of African derivation. A case in point is the longstanding debate about whether certain African American forms of sociality, such as the so-called matricentric family, economic practices such as male peasant marketeering or higglering, and forms of customary land tenure such as family land are determined by New World structural conditions constraining the behavioral options of African Americans or are primarily shaped by the carryover of African ideologies about kinship, gender roles, and inheritance.

Perhaps the most critical deficiencies of formalistic approaches are of a theoretical nature. For apart from the comparisons upon which these approaches rest presupposing the absence of cultural change in Africa, they fail to historicize cultural transmission and change as social processes. Hence, they have a tendency to obscure the possibility of independent development of similar forms on both sides of the Atlantic (such as through functionally determined convergence), and to preclude an understanding of the role of creativity, synthetic processes, and conscious efforts at re-Africanization in African American culture-building.

Such issues had been raised by Jamaican anthropologist Michael G. Smith (1921–1993) as early as the late 1950s. Yet a theoretical formulation superseding the rigid dichotomy between structural and formalistic approaches was achieved only in 1976 with the publication of Sidney Mintz and Richard Price's influential essay, *An Anthropological Approach to the Afro-American Past: A Caribbean Perspective* (republished as *The Birth of African-American Cultures: An Anthropological Perspective* in 1992). Partly basing their argument on conclusions derived from Price's research on the Maroons of Suriname, Mintz and Price argued that the emergence and development of African American cultures was theoretically inseparable from the processes by which enslaved Africans—as initially entirely desocialized individuals—forged viable social institutions. At the same time, they emphasized the likelihood that such institutions arose from synthetic processes (involving not only elements of diverse African cultures but of European American ones, as well), and continued to be shaped less by the precepts of any single African tradition than by creative adaptations to the historical challenges presented by particular New World social environments.

In the late twentieth century, Mintz and Price's rapid early synthesis, or Creolization, model gained wide acceptance. Its attractiveness lies in that, although acknowledging the importance of Africa in the making of African American and, indeed, New World cultures, it avoids the ahistoricism and mechanistic conceptions of cultural dynamics characteristic of formalistic approaches to African American cultural history. On the other hand, its emphasis on the synthetic character of African American cultures makes it difficult to account for cases where Creolization processes resulted in greater stability of form than this model would tend to predict. Though it is too early to gauge the likelihood of another revisionist turn, several studies have indicated the need to reevaluate the possibility that certain New World social conditions may have strengthened, rather than undermined, the adaptive viability of African models of sociality.

In this respect, a line of inquiry that directs its attention to the interconnected nature of cultural change on both continents appears promising. Integrating findings of Africanist historiography on the articulation of African social formations with an Atlantic political and economic system emerging since the fifteenth century, such studies both transcend the assumptions of African cultural stability characteristic of formalist approaches and shed new light on the supralocal factors involved in processes of African American culture building. In several instances it may be argued that the supposedly aboriginal African prototypes of New World forms and institutions were themselves already the products of processes operative on an Atlantic scale. This type of reasoning was first used in the context of linguistic hypotheses about the origin of New World Creole languages in West African–Portuguese Creole idioms developed in the context of the coastal trade. It has since been independently proposed by historians and anthropologists concerned with the interrelations between larger economic conjunctures and the historical dynamics of local social and cultural formations on both sides of the Atlantic.

In addition, recent research on processes of re-Africanization has shed new light on the question of continuity. Here the focus is on the continuous contacts between certain areas of the Europe and the Americas and West Africa after the end of the slave trade (as are well documented in the case of Brazil), but also of the deliberate replenishment of traditions from the ethnographic literature on Africa (as is attestable for African American religious formations in Cuba, Brazil, and the United States), and the arrogation of certain representations of

Africanness in the absence of historically demonstrable links (as in the case of the identification of the Jamaican Rastafarian with Ethiopia that is unequivocally derived from biblical and, perhaps, other European sources). All these phenomena depart radically from the notion of an unbroken line of tradition connecting present-day African American cultures with (ideally specifiable) African prototypes. But they also do not readily yield to conceptions of the evolution of African American cultures out of synthetic processes characterizing the earliest stages of African American social formation.

Yet attributing Africanness to forms and institutions arising out of such processes of re-Africanization that is a recent development is more than a matter of supporting claims to ancestrality for what are, historically speaking, invented traditions, whether such claims are made in an overtly politicized fashion or not. Just as the criteria on which a good part of the scholarly ascriptions of African derivation to New World cultural institutions have been based must be evaluated in terms of the social and ideological context of their pronunciation, so must such public claims to Africanness be analyzed not just on political, but theoretical grounds. Given the history of Western notions of "tradition" and "ancestrality" there is no reason why one should not judge deliberately introduced social and cultural forms modeled after images of Africa (rather than transmitted from Africa in an unbroken line of tradition) as somehow less genuine. Rather, their existence should stimulate research in the history of the social and intellectual conditions in which they emerged that have fostered their emergence and encourage a thorough rethinking of the conceptual apparatus on which our inquiries have hitherto been based.

The same holds for the still far from well developed study of the cultural impact of recent African migrations to Europe and the Americas, as well as the rapidly growing literature on the diffusion of diasporic cultural forms to Africa (music, satorials, styles of comportment, forms of political mobilization, etc.), and that on the effects of "return" movements (most notably in the case of U.S. African American "roots-tourism") on social and political arrangements on the continent itself. The extent to which the new African diasporas are emerging in recent decades, and the globalization of cultural forms coded as African, can still be captured by the analytical frameworks developed in the study of the historical African diasporas produced by the slave trade and postemancipation regimes of racial inequality is a question that, as of now, still awaits sustained inquiry.

See also **Creoles; History of Africa; Immigration and Immigrant Groups; Slavery and Servile Institutions.**

BIBLIOGRAPHY

Berlin, Ira. *Many Thousands Gone: The First Two Centuries of Slavery in North America.* Cambridge, MA: Belknap Press of Harvard University Press, 1998.

Besson, Jean. *Martha Brae's Two Histories: European Expansion and Caribbean Culture-Building in Jamaica.* Chapel Hill: University of North Carolina Press: 2002.

Brown, David H. *Santería Enthroned: Art, Ritual and Innovation in an Afro-Cuban Religion.* Chicago: University of Chicago Press, 2003.

Fikes, Kesha, and Alaina Lemon. 2002. "African Presence in Former Soviet Spaces." *Annual Reviews of Anthropology* 31: 497–524.

Gilroy, Paul. The Black Atlantic: Modernity and Double Consciousness. Cambridge, MA: Harvard University Press, 1993.

Harris, Joseph. E., ed. *Global Dimensions of the African Diaspora.* Washington, DC: Howard University Press, 1993.

Herskovits, Melville. *The Myth of the Negro Past.* New York: Harper and Brothers, 1941.

Hunwick, John, and Eve Troutt Powell, eds. *The African Diaspora in the Mediterranean Lands of Islam.* Princeton, NJ: Markus Wiener Publishers, 2002.

Jayasuriya, Shihan, and Richard Pankhurst, eds. *The African Diaspora in the Indian Ocean.* Trenton, NJ: Africa World Press, 2001.

Koser, Khalid, ed. *New African Diasporas.* London: Routledge, 2003.

Lovejoy, Paul E. "The African Diaspora: Revisionist Interpretations of Ethnicity, Culture and Religion Under Slavery." *Studies in the World History of Slavery, Abolition, and Emancipation* 2, no. 1 (1997): 1–24.

Matory, James Lorand. *Black Atlantic Religion: Tradition, Transnationalism and Matriarchy in the Afro-Brazilian Camdomblé.* Princeton, NJ: Princeton University Press, 2005.

Mintz, Sidney W., and Richard Price. *The Birth of African American Culture.* Boston: Beacon Press, 1992.

Palmié, Stephan. *Wizards and Scientists: Explorations in Afro-Cuban Modernity and Tradition.* Durham, NC: Duke University Press, 2002.

Smith, Michael Garfield. *The Plural Society in the British West Indies.* Berkeley: University of California Press, 1965.

Thornton, John Kelly. *Africa and Africans in the Making of the Atlantic World, 1400–1680.* Cambridge, U.K.: Cambridge University Press, 1992.

STEPHAN PALMIÉ

MUSIC

The diffusion of African music outside Africa is linked to the slave trade and the development of African-American communities in the Americas. Using diverse regional traditions, enslaved Africans began to invent original musical forms before 1800, and over time decisively influenced all genres of popular music. In turn, African-American music encouraged young urban Africans to create the modern forms of dance music known commercially as World Music. European and Asian music were influenced by the growing popularity of modern African urban music and enriched by contributions from musicians of African origin.

Africans in the New World came from culturally and musically diverse areas. Many who came from the same region were dispersed, and the conditions they endured prevented them from performing music as it was played in Africa. African music began the protracted processes of creolization, which varied by the region in the Americas. The social organization of enslavement—including the relationship between masters and slaves, the proportion of Africans to non-Africans, and the presence of Africans sharing the same language—as well as the physical environment (important for instrument making) also varied by region. Consequently, although creolization processes were similar everywhere, their musical outcomes differed greatly.

African-American creole musical forms resulted from the innovative blending of musical elements taken from European popular and religious music of the seventeenth, eighteenth, and nineteenth centuries with various African musical elements—becoming a form of musical "pan-Africanism in exile."

Three traits are hallmarks of African-American music. The first is the systematic contrametricity of

African rhythms. Contrametricity is the dissociation between the metrical pulse, or "beat," and the rhythmical accents. It is highly probable that "swing," which stands as one of the main features of African-American music, derives from the adaptation of contrametricity to the European alternation of a strong beat and a weak beat (which African music ignores). A second is the cyclical construction of musical pieces, which allows both for repetition and variation. This gave birth to the original techniques of ornamentation and improvisation often heard in African-American music. The third is the predominance of "thick," or overtone-rich sounds.

In some places, African instruments were preserved or reconstructed: drums and types of sanza (hand pianos) are used in the West Indies (the Jamaican rumba box is one example), xylophones on the Caribbean coast of South America, musical bows in Brazil. New instruments were invented, such as the banjo, in which a skin-covered (African) soundbox is paired with a flat neck, probably borrowed from the guitar or even the bandora—a type of lute very popular in Great Britain and Europe during the sixteenth and seventeenth centuries. Often, African-American musicians simply adopted European

musical instruments because they were forbidden to make their own. European instruments were also chosen because their mastery by slaves demonstrated an ability to play instruments considered legitimate by the owners.

African music thus gave birth to a wealth of African-American musical forms. In the United States and North America, it contributed to the development of a musical universe that became a fertile field for innovation. From creole music, which probably appeared in the seventeenth century but remain largely undocumented, stemmed minstrel songs, spirituals, and the music that would later be called blues. Minstrel show music, then that of vaudeville, formed the roots of classic blues, jazz, and country and western. Spirituals gave birth to gospel. Jazz, or Great Black Music, evolved into a variety of styles, some of which were infused with impressions of or borrowings from African musical forms (Duke Ellington's "jungle" style; Art Blakey's drumming; Randy Weston's compositions; several free jazz musicians' musical conceptions).

In Central and South America and in the West Indies, music retained more creole forms, with stronger African retentions (although hardly devoid of

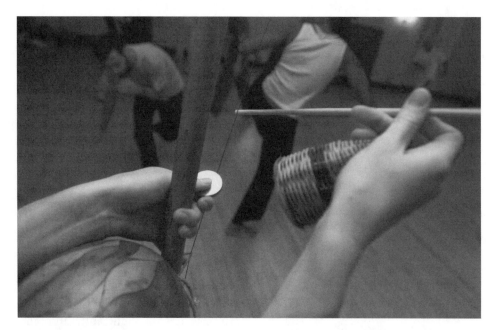

A musician plays the berimbau during a game of capoeira, a Brazilian martial art, Chicago, 2002. The single-stringed percussion instrument comes from Angola and is one of five instruments played during the game. The musician strikes the string with a thin stick while shaking the caxixi, the basket shaker shown in the musician's right hand. The sound from the string resonates in the hollowed-out gourd at the bottom of the berimbau. © AP IMAGES

Jazz greats Duke Ellington and Louis Armstrong meet at New York's Madison Square Garden after a tribute to Ellington, February 1970. "Duke Ellington has always been my man of music," wrote Armstrong in the liner notes to *Louis Armstrong and Duke Ellington*, an album they did together in 1961. © AP IMAGES

European influences) at one end, and more European forms (although African and Indigenous influences are never absent, except in local renditions of European "classical" music) at the other. In places where groups of Africans that shared the same language could exert a strong influence, specific African retentions were prominent and frequently linked to religious rituals (voodoo in Haiti; santeria in Cuba; candomble in Brazil). In regions where small pockets of descendants of Africans lived in isolation, genres characterized by singing to the accompaniment of drums, and linked to dancing, also retained African elements (maroon music in Jamaica; gwo ka in Guadeloupe; music of the palanques in Columbia, and quilombos in Brazil).

The more creole forms were the basis on which innovations developed, often spurred by European elements (especially in the domain of harmony) or by other African-American music (jazz influences played an important role in the invention of new styles: modern calypso with sparrow in Trinidad and Tobago; bossa nova in Brazil; several Cuban styles; rhythm and blues nourished the imagination of the creators of ska and reggae in Jamaica). Indeed, many musicians from Central and South America and the West Indies played jazz, often introducing into it flavors from the creole music of their country (Monty Alexander, Jamaica; Hermeto Pascoal, Brazil; Gato Barbieri, Argentina; Alain Jean-Marie, Guadeloupe; William Cepeda, Puerto Rico; Paquito D'Rivera and Gonzalo Rubalcaba, Cuba). All popular musical forms (songs, dance music, carnival music) in the Americas derived from creole innovations, nurtured by African musical memories, and also sometimes by indigenous Amerindian elements. Present-day salsa, for example, has incorporated elements of American (North and South) and West Indian musical styles.

More academic musicians did not, however, remain deaf to the richness of creole and African-influenced music. Louis-Moreau Gottschalk in North America (who was also sensitive to West Indian and Southern American music), Ignacio Cervantès in Cuba, and Ernesto Nazareth in Brazil used rhythmic patterns and melodic contours characteristics of creole music to compose original "classical" works. Many other American and European composers of great renown have lent an interested ear to African-American music: George Gershwin, Aaron Copland, Leonard Bernstein, Igor Stravinsky, Claude Debussy, Darius Milhaud, and Kurt Weill. Indeed African-American composers such as Harry T. Burleigh, R. Nathaniel Dett, and William Grant Still also incorporated ingredients they found in spirituals, blues, ragtime, and jazz.

African-American music began to be recorded on a large scale in the 1920s. After World War II, some of these recordings became available in Africa, where they attracted a great interest among city dwellers. Musicians searching for self-expression that also displayed their sophistication and modernity adopted elements of African-American music and mixed them with traditional forms that had already been altered by the urban experience and the

Vodún celebration surrounding Assumption Day. Followers of Vodún dance as they are possessed by spirits in the village of Sucry, Gonaives, Haiti, August 15, 2001. The blood on the women's clothing is from a goat that was sacrificed earlier. © AP IMAGES

development of broadcasting. New musical styles emerged in different regions of Africa (highlife, rumba, marabi). This melding of African-American and African music was repeated several times, stimulated by the evolution of popular music on both sides of the Atlantic.

When European-American rock and pop began to decline in the 1970s and 1980s, some artists and producers turned to non-European music for fresh inspiration, only to discover modern, urban, popular, and somewhat "Americanized" African music. They used African pop music or musicians to give their productions new color and vitality. African performers entered the world music market that developed in the 1980s and 1990s. Today a few African musicians and singers are international pop stars, with followings in Europe, Asia, and North America. The first big African "hit" on the international pop market was "Soul Makossa," a single by Manu Dibango (1972).

Rock singer and producer Peter Gabriel was instrumental in promoting African music. King Sunny Adé and Fela Anikulapo Kuti of Nigeria, Salif Keita, Ali Farka Toure, and Mory Kante of Mali, Touré Kunda of Sénégal, and Thomas Mapfumo of Zimbabwe are famous all over the world; and the controversial

Graceland album and tour organized by Paul Simon—despite the boycott of apartheid South Africa—gave South Africans Ray Phiri and Ladysmith Black Mambazo worldwide fame. African instruments, such as xylophones, lamellaphones (sanza/mbira) and djembe drums (which have become international symbols of African music), are widely used by non-African musicians, and are taught in many American, Asian, and European music schools.

There are salsa groups in India, where Bollywood music has incorporated African American influences, and one can hear jazz musicians in Shanghai. African, West Indian, and African-American music are quite popular in Japan, as are reggae and ska; Japanese jazz musicians such as Yosuke Yamashita and Akira Sakata are renowned worldwide. Africa is part of a universal pop world, and if one considers both the influence of African American music and the success of contemporary African music, one realizes that there is not one form of pop music anywhere in the world that does not owe something to Africa.

As early as the fifteenth century, authentic African music had been described by European travelers, traders, explorers, and missionaries. However, before the invention of sound recording and the development of ethnomusicology as a full-fledged discipline, it had far less influence on music worldwide. In the early twenty-first century a few contemporary composers began to draw on traditional (orally transmitted) African musical forms. A few composers—such as Luciano Berio, György Ligeti, and Steve Reich—have discovered African music through ethnomusicological studies that reveal its polyrhythmic intricacy, the richness of its timbre, and complex forms. A younger generation studied African music in Africa, and have incorporated their experiences in their music. Philip Glass, Frank Denyer, and Jean-Louis Florentz represent this new attitude toward African music.

Music from or affected by Africa can be heard everywhere. Without African influence, jazz, rock, pop, salsa, reggae, and rap would not sound the way they do. Even in the field of written academic music, African influence, although certainly weaker than in popular music, is not negligible.

See also **Adé Sunny; Creoles; Keita, Salif; Kuti, Fela; Ladysmith Black Mambazo; Music; Popular Culture; Vodún.**

BIBLIOGRAPHY

Bergman, Billy. *African Pop, Goodtime Kings.* Polle, Dorset, U.K.: Blanford Press, 1985.

Ekueme, Lazarus E.W. "African Music Retentions in the New World." *The Black Perspective in Music* 2, no. 2 (Fall 1974): 128–140.

Erlmann, Veit. *Music, Modernity, and the Global Imagination, South Africa and the West.* New York: Oxford University Press, 1999.

Kebede, Ashenafi. *Roots of Black Music: The Vocal, Instrumental and Dance Heritage of Africa and Black America.* Englewood Cliffs, NJ: Prentice Hall, 1982.

Martin, Denis-Constant. "Filiation or Innovation? Some Hypotheses to Overcome the Dilemma of Afro-American Music's Origins." *Black Music Research Journal* 11 (1991): 19–38.

Martin, Denis-Constant, and Olivier Roueff. *La France du jazz, musique, modernité et identité dans la première moitié du XXe siècle.* Marseille: Parenthèses, 2002.

Maultsby, Portia K. "Influences and Retentions of West African Musical Concepts in US Black Music." *Western Journal of Black Studies* 3, no. 3 (Fall 1979): 197–215.

Natale, Oscar. *Buenos Aires, Negros y Tango.* Buenos Aires: Peña Lillo Editor, 1984.

Nketia, J. H. Kwabena. "The Study of African and Afro-American Music." *Black Perspective in Music* 1, no. 1 (Spring 1973): 7–15.

Shain, Richard M. "Roots in Reverse: Cubanismo in Twentieth-Century Senegalese Music." *International Journal of African Historical Studies* 35, no. 1 (2002): 83–101.

Storm-Roberts, John. *Black Music of Two Worlds.* New York: William Morrow, 1974.

Tenaille, Frank. *Le swing du caméléon, musiques et chansons africaines, 1950–2000.* Arles: Actes Sud, 2000.

Toussaint, Godfried. *Classification and Phylogenetic Analysis of African Ternary Rhythm Timelines.* Available at http://cgm.cs.mcgill.ca/~godfried/rhythm.html.

Van der Merwe, Peter. *Origins of the Popular Style: The Antecedents of Twentieth-Century Popular Music.* Oxford: Oxford University Press, 1989.

Wa Mukuna, Kazadi. *Contribuição Bantu Na Música Popular Brasileira.* São Paulo: Global Editora, 1979.

Waterman, Richard Alan. "African Influence on the Music of the Americas." In *Acculturation in the Americas,* ed. Sol Tax, 207–218. New York: Cooper Square Publishers, 1967.

DENIS-CONSTANT MARTIN

RELIGIONS

The Africans bound for the plantations, mines, and workshops of the Americas embarked primarily from the western African coast between present-day Senegal and Angola, and in smaller numbers from present-day Mozambique. Among the ten million or so who reached the Western Hemisphere, some began their odyssey as Muslims or Christians, many as worshipers of local gods and ancestors, and more than a few as practitioners of hybrid religions. They and their American cultural descendants have carried forth a complex legacy; various self-described African religions have spread beyond any single race, and the practices of many Christians of all colors appear to reflect African influence as well.

EXPLICITLY AFRICAN RELIGIONS

Religions in which most worshipers identify their beliefs and practices as African include, in Brazil: Macumba, Batuque, the Nagô and Jeje nations, or sects, of Candomblé, and Tambor de Minas; in Cuba: Santería (Regla de Ocha), Palo Mayombe, and Abakuá; and, in Haiti: Sèvi lwa, or voodoo. All of these religions venerate gods with easily recognizable counterparts in specific West and west-central African societies. For example, Sango and Ogun are worshiped in Nigeria and Bénin, their counterparts Xango and Ogum in Brazil, Changó and Oggún in Cuba, and Chango and Ogou in Haiti. There are of course exceptions. The goddess Ezili in Haiti has no direct and obvious African counterparts. Central to most of these religions are typically West African patterns of initiation, spirit possession, animal sacrifice, and divination.

The Cuban Abakuá society and the Brazilian Egum society feature masquerades, or divine spirits animating full-body masks. Both the Egum and Cuban Palo Mayombe priesthoods venerate the dead. Complex African-inspired forms of ancestor veneration also continue prominently in Carriacou, an island in the southeastern Caribbean, and among the Suriname Maroons, descendants of escaped slaves in that country.

THE CONDITIONS OF AFRICAN RELIGIONS' SUCCESS

Some have attributed the success of self-described African religions in certain regions to the alleged gentleness of Latin American slavery. Although few recent historians would support that allegation, a number of other historical factors seem relevant. Such religions have flourished disproportionately in sugar-producing and predominantly Roman Catholic regions, especially where either forced or voluntary migration from Africa continued well into the late nineteenth or early twentieth century. Because sugar production tended to require a high ratio of labor to management, when crop prices remained high and the price of imported slaves relatively low, managers favored importation over the rearing of slave children to replace those who died from disease and overwork. Therefore, sugar-producing regions tended to host large and constantly refreshed African populations relatively uninfluenced, until a late date, by a sizable European cultural presence.

SYNCRETISM: A MULTIPLICITY OF SOURCES

Nonetheless, European culture was inevitably influential. Beyond the obvious material control that European immigrants exercised over African bodies, the European folk-Catholic logic of multiple sacred beings and of bargaining with them must have seemed familiar to polytheistic Africans, who often came to identify their gods with Catholic saints. Because white authorities often feared African religion as a potential focus of rebellion or instrumentality of vengeance,

Africans are said to have camouflaged the real object of their devotion behind a Catholic saint's name or image. However, later generations integrated important aspects of Catholic ritual, affect, mythology, and symbolism into their devotions. To this day, most contemporary practitioners of Candomblé and Santería, for example, consider themselves Roman Catholic as well. Moreover, many of these syncretic religions were influenced by the nineteenth-century French mystic Allan Kardec—also known as Hippolyte Léon Denizard Rivail (1804–1869)—whose writings became popular among the Latin American bourgeoisie and thus entered into the dialogue that produced these religions.

The vocabulary and practices of the west-central African peoples such as the Kongo are important references in Candomblé, Angola, Palo Mayombe, Sèvi lwa, and the black North American magical and divinatory practices called conjure, hoodoo, and voodoo. The religious vocabulary and practices of Ghanaian Akan-speakers appear to be influential among the Suriname maroons and in Caribbean magical practices known as *obeah*.

Among all the African cultures, the *orisa*-worshiping Nigerian Yoruba and the *vodún*-worshiping Béninese Fon provide the largest proportion of sacred references among the self-described African religions of the Americas. The imperialism of the Oyo Yoruba and of their former Dahomeyan vassals produced unusually uniform pantheons across large African populations. These populations supplied a disproportionate part of the nineteenth-century slave market, partly because the early nineteenth-century collapse of the Oyo Empire precipitated a flood of these peoples into the Americas during the latest period of the slave trade. In contrast with the incoming central African captives, these West Africans were often preferred in urban trades that allowed them some autonomy of earnings and movement. Ongoing pilgrimage and commerce between specific African regions and Latin America after the abolition of the slave trade helps to explain the exceptional success of certain African traditions, such as the worship of the Yoruba-affiliated orisa gods, in the Americas.

New Meanings of Orisa Worship. Despite the clear proliferation of practices without obvious European precedents, indigenous claims of devotion to African religions should not always be taken literally. Significantly, worshipers' conception of Africanness in a post-slavocratic American society endows their sacred spirits with powers and meanings different from the ones that African worshipers attribute to theirs. Indeed, West African Yoruba *orisa* worshipers are more likely to describe their gods as in the mountain, in the river, Nupe (that is, of a neighboring African people), Muslim, or from Mecca than as African; for them, little is sacred or awesomely powerful about Africanness.

Even when they are focused on Africa, religious practices in the Americas are rooted in American infrastructures of kin networks, political relationships, laws, economic structures, and medical practices. Not only is the safety of religious practice and the authority of religious leaders guaranteed by non-African means, but these African religions in America are shaped by the different forms of resistance they encounter and the diverse problems they are called upon to solve. For example, the typical client of a modern Nigerian *orisa* priest is a woman seeking healing from infertility. The most common single complaint of the Candomblé client is material misfortune or mental illness of an origin that priests diagnose as spiritual; people with mental and physical problems of a material nature are usually sent to a psychiatrist or physician. Africans and their American cultural descendants have mobilized their similar religions in the service of different political projects. For example, initiation into the pre-nineteenth-century Sango priesthood of the Yoruba served to create a body of viceroys, administrators, and messengers for the Oyo imperial palace. In the twentieth-century Brazilian Candomblé, similar initiations have served to create a familial sense of solidarity among people whose families slavery had destroyed and whose subsequent order of solidarity and sustenance—the plantation—had been disrupted by abolition and the late-nineteenth-century decline of the sugar industry.

Implicitly African Religion. Popular writers, indigenous theologians, and social scientists have attributed African roots to a range of beliefs and practices that practitioners may not classify as African. For example, the Haitians' purchase and ritual creation of spirits called *points* follow ethnographically documented precedents in African sorcery but are classified by Haitians as inimical to the

conventions of Guinea, or Africa, because *points* serve selfish and individualistic goals rather than the collective interests sanctioned by the ancestors. Brazilian Umbanda venerates the *orixás*, gods with Yoruba names that have been borrowed from Candomblé Nagô, but many middle-class practitioners are anxious to attribute Umbanda to ultimately non-African and racially superior sources. Practitioners of the popular Candomblé de Caboclo in Brazil worship the spirits of Brazilian Indians and explicitly identify their devotion as Brazilian, unlike the African Candomblé Nagô. However, they still worship by means of animal sacrifice and spirit possession that are atypical of Brazilian Indian religion.

The distinctive importance of dance and of being filled with the Holy Spirit in various African American Protestant denominations—such as the Trinidad Shouters, Jamaican Revivalism, and black North American Baptists and Pentecostals—may be seen as extensions of the role of sacred dance and spirit possession in the religions of Africa. Other observers have discussed the African content of conjure, voodoo, and hoodoo, which clearly owe a great deal to European folk beliefs as well. Practitioners' conceptions of the geographical origins of their religions appear to vary across regions and across generations.

Secondary Migrations and the Black Atlantic Dialogue. The self-described African religions of the Americas have spread from their earliest venues to broaden and integrate a sacred dialogue around the Atlantic perimeter. For example, at the end of the eighteenth century, the Haitian Revolution prompted the migration of slave owners, slaves, and free people of color to Cuba and Louisiana, where they influenced local religions. Some Afro-Brazilians traveled to West Africa on the late-nineteenth-century eve of its colonization by the French and the British, sometimes precisely in order to be initiated in African religions. They brought back not only religious information but also African nationalist inspirations. The 1915 U.S. invasion of Haiti nurtured a libelous print and film literature on voodoo, transforming it into evidence that the oppressed are truly savage and therefore deserve to be oppressed. And, much to the chagrin of animal-loving North Americans, Cubans fleeing the 1959 revolution carried Santería and Palo Mayombe, with their sacrificial traditions, not only to Puerto Rico and mainland Latin America, but to the United States mainland as well.

This secondary migration was a boon for many North American black nationalists who adopted Afro-Cuban religion as their own lost spirituality and proceeded to strip it of its Roman Catholic accretions. Two sets of developments have in turn led many Brazilians, Cubans, and Haitians to do the same. First, ever since the late nineteenth century, scholarly books, from which many practitioners seek additional information about their religions, have tended to focus on and give honor to the African survival. Second, the independence of various African nations and the activism of North American black nationalists have, since the 1960s, inspired much respect for black cultural resistance in the Americas. Thus, an ongoing international history has transformed the local practice and meaning of these traditions.

When compared with forms of economic and political organization, religious practices are among the most conspicuous of sub-Saharan Africa's contributions to American civilization. They stand second only to Africa's musical contribution. Yet what appears African in the American religions has transformed and been transformed by much that appears European or Amerindian. In any given American region, the dialogue among diverse African, European, and Amerindian religious traditions is shaped by a lengthy history of politics, migration, production, and, indeed, professional research.

See also **Divination and Oracles; Music; Religion and Ritual; Secret Societies; Slave Trades; Vodún.**

BIBLIOGRAPHY

Brown, David H. *Santería Enthroned.* Chicago: University of Chicago Press, 2003.

Brown, Karen McCarthy. *Mama Lola: A Vodou Priestess in Brooklyn.* Berkeley: University of California Press, 2001.

Clarke, Kamari. *Mapping Yoruba Networks.* Durham, N.C.: Duke University Press, 2003.

Cosentino, Donald J., ed. *The Sacred Arts of Haitian Vodou.* Los Angeles: University of California, Los Angeles Fowler Museum of Cultural History, 1995.

Johnson, Paul Christopher. *Secrets, Gossip, and Gods: The Transformation of Brazilian Candomblé.* Oxford: Oxford University Press, 2002.

Larose, Serge. "The Meaning of Africa in Haitian Vodu." In *Symbols and Sentiments,* edited by Ioan Lewis. London: Academic Press, 1977.

Long, Carolyn Morrow. *Spiritual Merchants: Religion, Magic, and Commerce.* Knoxville: University of Tennessee Press, 2001.

Matory, J. Lorand. *Black Atlantic Religion: Tradition, Transnationalism, and Matriarchy in the Afro-Brazilian Candomblé.* Princeton, N.J.: Princeton University Press, 2005.

Thompson, Robert Farris. *Face of the Gods: Art and Altars of Africa and the African Americas.* New York: Museum for African Art, 1993.

Vega, Marta Moreno. *The Altar of My Soul: The Living Tradition of Santería.* New York: One World/Ballantine, 2000.

J. LORAND MATORY

ARTS

Europe from 1725 to around 1907 construed art beyond the West as savage or primitive. Western-imagined primitive art embodied the hieroglyph (as opposed to Western phonetic script), the grotesque (as opposed to Western classicizing norms of beauty), and, finally, the ornamental (meaning patterns purely decorative, devoid of meaning). All of these attributes were supposed opposites to the classical ideal.

Europeans and Americans of European descent had a difficult time sensing the importance and reality of authentic African-influenced American art behind the grimacing, grotesque mask of minstrelsy, both in the North American form and in the similarly stylized, grimacing countenances of blacks as portrayed in the art of Pedro Figari (1861–1938) in Uruguay. It was all too easy in the racist past to take these negative mimes as real, masking the possibility of a serious history of art.

For a world-famous twentieth-century example of the problem, consider the aesthetic gigantism in the dress of Carmen Miranda (1909–1955), the well-known Brazilian film star of the 1930s and 1940s. Her oversized, exaggerated Yoruba *orisa* beads and fruit-piled headdresses caricatured the elegant, small color-coded beads worn by black women in Bahia that proclaimed their allegiance to certain Nigerian goddesses and gods, as well as their carefully balanced market head-trays.

The concept of the grotesque not only blocked appreciation of the art of the descendants of Africans in the Americas, but minstrelsy even became an art style of its own. Similarly, white America did not bother with niceties of distinction, between the correct phonetic script and the inferior syllabaries and ideographies in the world beyond the West. Africans were considered to come from totally illiterate areas. If they were thought not to have writing of any form of their own whatsoever, it was logical to assume that the myriad gestures of Kongo sculpture carried no intrinsic meaning, either, to say nothing of the art of gesture among descendants of Kongo in the Americas. This, too retarded the study of deep meaning and deep form in African-influenced art in the Western Hemisphere.

The bedrock of the dilemma was hyperracism. But scholarly exaggeration of the fragility of African cultures when confronted by Western cultures discouraged research. Some scholars maintained as late as the 1960s that as a matter of course no African social structure survived the Middle Passage. In reality, wherever Kongo cultural influence is strong in the Americas—Brazil, Haiti, and Cuba—dance societies with a king and queen of Kongo at their head can be found, along with shadow governments and shards of past glory, concealed in play. Creolized equivalents to these figures, such as the Simbi Makaya and Reine Kongo, also exist in Haitian vodún.

Additionally, the continuity of the male leopard society (Ngbe) of Nigeria's Ejagham, in its counterpart Afro-Cuban leopard society (Abakua), suggest structural and aesthetic continuations. Finally, there are arguments for the influence of Igbo (Ibo) religious political structure on the rise of similar structures among traditional black church hierarchies in Virginia, a state known to have absorbed Igbo captives in the colonial period. The truth of Africanisms in the diaspora is thus more various than previously thought.

It was once assumed that the policy of slaveholders in separating the tribal groups to prevent interplantation modes of insurrectionary communication worked against the reestablishment of African art and philosophy in the Western Hemisphere. This assertion comes perilously close to depending on a slaveholder's understanding of African linguistics in order to build theories about African American cultural continuities. In fact, the close cognation between the various Bantu language-speaking groups thrown together on the plantations—persons from the Kongo and Angola areas—meant that the formation of a cultural lingua franca, especially in terms of worship, could covertly emerge and persist.

A historian of Central Africa has begun to dismantle the argument that cultural weakness derived from inability to communicate across tribal lines. Did slaveholders carefully separate Ijesha from Ketu, or Mbundu from Kongo and Tu-Chokwe, because the slaveholders spoke their languages and were in a position to know that Ijesha and Ketu, or Kongo and Mbundu, could communicate through cognates? It is doubtful. Yoruba, Dahomeyans, and Kongo, all coming from intense monarchical traditions with pride in heritage and origin, kept their sectors of the plantations and the cities as determinedly—if covertly—Yoruba, Dahomeyan, and Kongo as they could.

But even those who admitted the theory, if not the fact, of African art in the Americas were confused by narrow Western classical definitions of art itself as painting and sculpture, objects framed on walls, and things marking the center of a plaza or a thoroughfare. This rendered invisible, initially at least, the powerful contribution of African women's multistrip dress as transformed into multistrip piecework among black women of the United States and Suriname. But even when noted, such works were believed to be crafts, not the fine arts that they really are. Finally, the great gift of Africans in the Western Hemisphere of reinventing themselves, with found objects and found concepts, meant that the creolization together, say, of Fon, Yoruba, Kongo, Roman Catholic, and Masonic elements in the formation of Haitian *veve*, blazons rendered on the ground to call the gods from Africa to the Caribbean, announced a fabulous dialectic of tradition and developmental brilliance. Veve thus require scholars to think three-dimensionally, through all the sources, in order to comprehend inventive realities, astonishing in the midst of poverty and deprivation.

YORUBA ATLANTIC ART

When the Haitian Revolution deprived Europe after 1804 of a main source of sugar, sugarcane was planted in northeast Brazil and in the provinces of Havana and Matanzas in Cuba. Simultaneously, the ports of the Yoruba coast, in present-day Nigeria and the Republic of Bénin, were filling up with captives who ultimately were sent to labor in the new sugar plantations in the Caribbean and Brazil. These captives resulted from Fulani and Dahomeyan military incursions, plus serious internal strife—Ibadan Yoruba against the Ekiti Yoruba, Egba Yoruba against Ijebu Yoruba—and they were marched to Badagri, Lagos, and Porto Novo, where Brazilian and Cuban slavers or their agents were waiting for them. After a horrific voyage, survivors found themselves working without pay in the cane fields of Cuba and Brazil or, if they were luckier, in the town houses of Bahia, Havana, and other cities.

However, slavers were unaware that the ships brought to Cuba carried not mentally passive captives but women and men in whose minds, unfathomed and unpoliced, burned an intense and abiding spirituality. So the Yoruba, one of the world's major civilizations, with a history of urbanism and sophistication of art and philosophy long predating penetration of their coast by Europeans, hardly constituted a fragile culture, easily crushed by captivity and enslavement. They had always been dispersive, spreading their ways and their religion over centuries, for example, to the west among the Fon, as well as in the ancient city of Edo (Benin City), and to the southeast of their linguistic area. At first covertly, and then increasingly openly after slavery was abolished in Cuba and Brazil in the 1880s, the Yoruba remembered and served their ancient goddesses and gods with art, dance, and music. This involved continuities in using the body as art—hard, stern, bulging-eyed masks worn by persons possessed by the spirits of hard deities such as Ogun, lord of blacksmithing. Or it involved eyes-shut visages worn by persons possessed by cooler spirits, such as the goddesses of certain rivers, Osun and Yemoja.

The importance of spirit possession as one of the cardinal values of the Yoruba civilization is mirrored in the exorbitant eyes and pursed lips of an early Cuban-Yoruba drum-mask, now in the Museum of Music in Havana, dating from the last quarter of the nineteenth century. There is a similar masking of the face of a woman carved for Creole Yoruba in Bahia on a wooden ritual pedestal for the Yoruba goddess of the sea, now in the Museum of Afro-Brazilian Art in Bahia.

From these starting moments evolved whole lines of continuity, linking together laterite mounds for the Nigerian Yoruba trickster god, Eshu-Elegba, with concrete pillar-figurines in Havana and Rio; irons for the deity Ogun in both Nigeria and the Yoruba New World; thundergod axes; statuettes for twin spirits; riverine goddess fans and cosmologized crockery arrangements; spectral-robed ancestral inquisitors in the Republic of Bénin, on the island of Itaparica, and in a suburb of Rio in Brazil; and strangely pierced bowls for deities of pestilence and moral vengeance, linking Nigeria to the Yoruba New World. In the process the art and iconography of the Yoruba deities, the *orisa*, in brilliant mixtures of specificity and inventive genius, anchored the rise of a truly world religion.

EJAGHAM ATLANTIC ART

The impact of the visual and choreographic arts of the Ejagham of southwestern Cameroon and southeastern Nigeria in the Western Hemisphere is essentially expressed in the Cuban provinces of Havana and Matanzas. Though more research is needed to confirm this, it is possible that Ejagham influence was also a formative factor in the rise of graphic writing systems elaborated among the Njuga and Aluku black Maroons (descendants of runaway slaves) in eastern Suriname and westernmost Guyana.

The Ejagham long ago developed the male society called Ngbe (leopard) to refer to all that was hardy, brave, and sovereign. Ngbe, called Ekpe among Ejagham-influenced Igbo, Ibibio, and Efik in and around the notorious slaving port of (Old) Calabar, near the mouth of the Cross River, was possessed of an expansionist dynamic—it spread up and down the Cross River. There it established a reputation as an ultimate source for justice and right decisions in the field of human conflict.

From its putative origins among the Ejagham, Ngbe spread with its sounding drum connoting order and justice, associated with Abasi, God himself. There were masked messengers of the sounding drum called *okum ngbe* (images for the sacred leopard), with skin-covered staffs of office, one in particular entitling a leader to respond in words to the rumbling of the sacred voice behind the Ngbe screen. In addition, Ngbe and other societies once used and elaborated a complex writing system, pictograms, and signs collectively called *nsibidi*, after a root term, *sibi*, meaning cruel or bloodthirsty. Nsibidi also referred to a society of executioners, summoned in cases necessitating capital punishment. Associated with leadership and one of the diacritical marks of ultimate decision making, the power of life and death, nsibidi and the jurisprudentially oriented Ngbe society were admired by the neighbors of the Ejagham and spread far and wide up and down the Cross River. The coming of Ngbe and nsibidi writing to western Cuba in the wake of the slaving ties between Calabar and sugar termini in western Cuba, such as La Habana, Matanzas, and Cárdenas, was a dramatic instance of the traveling power of associative values of manhood and prestige among strong men who secretly refused to be coerced into a European-dominated life.

Whereas membership in Ngbe on the Cross River guaranteed a traveling member lodging and respect in other villages, in western Cuba membership served as a kind of a proto-labor union. Abakua (the Afro-Cuban creole form of Ngbe) could assure employment on the docks of Havana, where many of the foremen and other workers were members of the society.

Ejagham art is famed for skin-covered heads and striking realism, and though that particular art apparently did not pass through the hostile filter of Cuban slaving, certain echoes did. There are in the Museum of Guanabacoa, for example, splendid examples of skin- or fur-covered staffs of office (*itones*) very similar to those of the Cross River. Indeed, certain *nkame* (chants, incantations) remembered among members of the leopard society in Cuba—there called Abakua, after the name for the Ejagham in Calabar, Abakpa—make reference to the calling back of spirits from the other world by means of consecrated skin.

Blacks in Cuba creolized the Ejagham writing system into a related body of signs called *ereniyo* or *anaforuana*. The last and great Afro-Cubanist, Lydia Cabrera, compiled an impressive volume documenting the existence in Cuba as of 1959 of some 512 signs. Some anaforuana stem from ancient Ejagham contexts of communicative focus, for instance, the funeral. When an important person dies in Ejagham country, members of the nsibidi society may chop down trees in the back of their houses as a sign that death has arrived. Or, they may fire volleys at palm branches so that the latter drop downward, again as a sign of death. Downward-dropping palm leaves, the nsibidi sign of death in Nigeria, creolized into downward-drooping branches as a sign of death in the anaforuana system of signs in western Cuba. Further creolization brought in new elements to the tradition, clear-cut borrowings from the language of Western blazonry in the formation of blazon- or shield-like signs of local membership. Considerable overlaps with Kongo cosmograms also occurred, reflecting the fact that many members of Abakua were simultaneously *paleros* (Kongo-Cuban coreligionists).

The dress of the masked messengers of the leopard drum of justice as creolized in Cuban Abakua (there called *ireme*, an Afro-Cubanization of the Efik term for body or masked person, *idem*) retained a systematic resemblance to the Ngbe prototype. It consisted of a conical headdress, raffia mane—broomstraw substituted for this element in Cuba—and raffia cuffs at wrists and ankles. The checkerboard, perhaps the deepest symbol of the spotted pelt of the leopard in Ejagham Ngbe symbolism, was ingeniously kept alive by the use of checked gingham in the making of the ireme costume in Cuba. In the process the costume became, as one Cuban scholar put it, one of the deepest manifestations of the folklore of the island.

KONGO ATLANTIC ART

The massive importation of captives from the Kongo-Angola area, approximately 40 percent of the ten million or so Africans landed in the Americas between 1550 and 1870, had a resounding impact. It resulted in the establishment of distinct Kongo-influenced traditions of visual art in the Americas. The Regla de Mayombe (domain of the followers of the faith of Mayombe), one of the most important groups of the northern Kongo, exists in Cuba, as do other Kongo-influenced religious groups.

The first core element of Kongo-Cuban art and worship is the *nkisi*, or *prenda* (literally, pledge). This is a three-legged iron cauldron in which are inserted various pieces of symbolic wood, iron, and other objects. Each inserted object is a visual and/or sonic pun on spiritual action, as desired by the supplicant: horseshoes, that the charm travel for the owner; mercury in vials, that it travel as fast as quicksilver; hooked wood, that it bring in good luck and ward off evil, and so forth.

The second element is the *vititi menso* (roughly, the leaves of vision; literally, herbs of the eyes), a horn filled with medicine stoppered with a visionary mirror. This object echoes the strong presence of *minkisi lumweno*—mirror medicines or mirror bundles—in the classical religious art of Kongo. The third element is the *lucero*, a conical mound of concrete or some other substance enlivened with inserted cowrie eyes and mouth, standing guard over the worshiper's altar. The lucero indicates the Creole independence of the Kongo-Cuban visual realm, for it is actually an interpolation of the imagery of the Yoruba trickster in Cuba, Echu. Its name, however, indicates conceptual continuity from Kongo. Lucero means morning star. The role of the lucero, as a household guardian, matches the traditional Kongo view of certain stars as spirits that guard the way.

Kongo visual impact is equally strong in Haiti, where there is a whole class of figured medicine bundles, some with clairvoyant mirrors at the belly precisely in the manner of classical central African statuary, called, significantly, *pacquets kongo* (kongo sachets). These are formally and linguistically distinguished from less elaborate wrapped charms, which may or may not come from Yoruba and Dahomeyan traditions. The latter critically lack the specifically Kongo characteristics of the plume of plenitude at the top, a long stem (the secret navel, bringing down blessings and power from God), and the swelling belly, filled with cemetery earth and other substances, embedding the spirit and telling it what to do.

GLOBALIZING DIASPORA

On the Black Pacific side—Peru, Ecuador, the Colombian Chocó, western Panama, and the Costa Chica south of Acapulco in Mexico—whole realms of sub-Saharan-influenced architecture, music, dance, and dress await their proper study and estimation. For example, the presence of masked riders with beaded veils in a town in black Ecuador cries out for tracking a possible line of Yoruba influence. Kongo visual impact in Peru may go back for several centuries. Colombia, with an immense but understudied black population, possibly conceals several veins of creolized African architectural form and practice,

particularly among the stilt-house traditions of the Chocó, reminiscent of Ganvie and other stilt-house tidal towns on the coast of western Africa.

New and much-needed attention is being focused upon the sociocultural and aesthetic links between Africa and the Indian Ocean world. Historians and archaeologists have long noted the evidence of ancient trade and slaving networks that linked the Arabian peninsula, the continent of Africa, and various regions of Asia (Chinese pottery shards found upon the East Africa coast, designs on traveling Swahili travel chests for instance). Studies from the late twentieth century have sought to broaden significantly the paradigm of diaspora, unearthing wide-ranging evidence of diasporic practices in everything from so-called Afro-Omani arts, to retentions and reformations of languages and customs intricately linked to spirit possession cults and Sufism, to music, dance, and performance. Similar work is also being conducted by a host of scholars on the long existing sub-Saharan African diaspora in the North African/ Mediterranean world, particularly as it pertains to religious performance practices and other artistic traditions brought to their new homes by both enslaved and free Africans.

POSTCOLONIALISM AND DIASPORIC SUBJECTIVITIES

It is common in the early twenty-first century to hear the term "diaspora" applied interchangeably with expatriatism, exile, migrancy, and transnationalism. Contemporary African diasporic arts are defined in part by the legacies of cultural retentions and their reworkings that date from the age of slavery, and in part by a broader postmodern condition of rootlessness. As the dismantling of colonialism brought mass migrations to the former metropoles, large and impressive diasporic communities formed. Scholars began to understand diasporic experiences as those that could be chosen, claimed, and performed. Many artists within a contemporary diaspora move multiple times, a practice that allows researchers to question a politics of representation that often seeks to link identity to place and aesthetics. Artists such as Yinka Shonibare (b. 1962), Rachid Koraichi (b. 1947), and Wangechi Mutu (b. 1972) question essentialist assumptions and reclaim ways in which Africa is framed within contemporary discourses.

This contemporary emphasis on subjectivity in the face of displacement and emplacement had its roots in the modernist period (corresponding to colonialism and the era of its dismantlement) during which many of the continent's intellectuals, artists, and future statesmen gathered together within a cosmopolitan diaspora that gave them space to reflect upon and articulate modernist senses of identity and nationhood. Indeed, the broader pan-Africanist artistic and political reflections on double-consciousness and subjectivity would not have had such a profound impact had they not been nurtured within the crucible of diaspora.

The field is open, not closed. Research in this new century will refine understanding of the phenomena of spiritual rootedness—tradition, fused with creole expansiveness and developmental brilliance and ingenuity. These processes have been so clearly central to the diasporic histories in the Americas. They will also produce more global and contemporary understandings that reflect the multiple waves and varieties of movement, both forced and chosen, within, beyond, and back to the African continent.

See also **Architecture; Art; Arts; Benin City; Creoles; Dance; Lagos; Masks and Masquerades; Music; Porto Novo; Religion and Ritual; Slave Trades; Slavery and Servile Institutions; Spirit Possession; Vodún.**

BIBLIOGRAPHY

Alpers, Edward. "Recollecting Africa: Diasporic Memory in the Indian Ocean World." *African Studies Review* 43, no. 1 (2000): 83–99.

Brown, Karen McCarthy. *Tracing the Spirit: Ethnographic Essays on Haitian Art.* Seattle: University of Washington Press, 1995.

Cabrera, Lydia. *Anaforuana: Ritual y simbolos de la iniciacion en la sociedad secreta Abakua*, 2nd edition. Miami: Ediciones Universal, 2001.

Connelly, Frances S. *The Sleep of Reason: Primitivism in Modern European Art and Aesthetics, 1725–1907.* University Park: Pennsylvania State University Press, 1995.

Farrell, Laurie Ann. *Looking Both Ways: Art of the Contemporary African Diaspora.* New York: Museum for African Art, 2003.

Powell, Richard. *Black Art: A Cultural History.* London: Thames and Hudson, 2002.

ROBERT FARRIS THOMPSON
REVISED BY ELIZABETH HARNEY

RE-AFRICANIZATION

The term "re-Africanization" is used by some anthropologists to describe the efforts of many practitioners of African American religions to trace the African ancestries of their beliefs and rituals. This process can be observed throughout the New World, especially in Brazil and in the United States. It constitutes the latest stage in the development of these religions.

In Brazil the Afro-Brazilian religious field contains various practices, such as Umbanda and Candomblé, which, as colonial creations, are the result of syncretism involving Catholicism, spiritism, native, and African religions. According to some, all of these syncretic religions are organized a continuum, in which practitioners are transitioning from one religion to the other, usually closing their religious career with affiliation in a Candomblé house. It is thought that this evolution in the practitioners' career defines the passage from a "syncretic" variant such as Umbanda to a more "African" one such as Candomblé. This belief is founded upon years of anthropological research in Brazil, which has erroneously proclaimed Ccandomblé in its Nago (Yoruba) forms as the "purest" religion within the field, the closest to its African origins.

This emphasis on Yoruba origins itself rests on premises about a re-Africanization process. If Candomblé is the result of syncretism, some practitioners believe a search for the "original" Yoruba forms of the religion are required in order to practice it in the "purest" and most "traditional" way. In Brazil, re-Africanization manifested itself in different ways. In Salvador de Bahia beginning in the late nineteenth century, re-Africanization took the form of a fight against syncretism. For the practitioners, the idea was to purify Nago Candomblé from its Catholic influences. Inspired first by Afro-Brazilian travelers to Nigeria in the mid- to late nineteenth century and reinforced by the work of anthropologist Roger Bastide's "theory of the mask," they believed that syncretism between Catholic saints and Yoruba gods was superficial and that the early practitioners were using the Catholic saints to hide the actual gods they were worshiping. Getting rid of the mask (the Catholic saints) would then necessarily mean reconnecting with the "real gods:" the Yoruba ones. In doing so, they tried to purify Candomblé, applying a process of re-Africanization that also accentuated the power of prestigious Bahian houses within the Afro-Brazilian religious field. This intellectually constructed Africa then became the latest legitimising source of these religions.

Africanized practitioners have since looked to Africa, especially Yorubaland, as the true source of theological knowledge. They have taken courses in Yoruba languages and culture; they are learning Ifa divination, a technique that had disappeared from Brazil; and are acquiring books on this particular mythology. Cultural centers and shrine houses have been welcoming students from Nigeria, who sometimes became authorities defining the religious "dogma." For these Brazilian devotees, re-Africanization has meant searching for the roots in Africa and looking for the tradition there.

Nevertheless, searching for the "real religion" in Africa does not necessarily mean that postcolonial Africa has become, for the re-Africanized practitioners, the land of tradition. In the United States, the re-Africanization process was born out of the encounter of African Americans promoting cultural nationalism by converting to Afro-Cuban religions, mostly Santería, a faith that (like Candomblé) is considered as one of the "purest" form of African religious practices in Cuba. However, as the coworship of African Americans and Latinos in the same shrine houses became complicated, numerous African Americans began, in the 1960s, to develop their own religion that they referred to as "Yoruba" or orisha-voodoo. As with Brazilian practitioners, many believers soon began to travel to West Africa. Some of them even underwent initiations as priests in Yorubaland.

In the early twenty-first century, worshipers of the Yoruba religion in the United States tend to assert their independence from both their Cuban and their Nigerian initiators. Indeed, Oseijeman Adefunmi, the father of the Yoruba movement, has sometimes been extremely critical of the Nigerians involved in the religion and of their actions toward African Americans. He has not hesitated to condemn the effects of colonialism on Yoruba culture in Africa and has contended that what was left of that culture was the equivalent of a bastardization of African and Western cultures. For Oseijeman Adefunmi, the search for Yoruba culture should therefore not only be conducted in Africa but also in its reproduction in the United States where believers claim to have been able to recreate its "essence."

In this search within the diaspora for a "real" African tradition can be found one of the main effects of the re-Africanization process: the discovery of a literature specialized in Africa and African American cultures that the believers study in order to recreate what they consider as their lost faith. Books, anthropological and missionary literatures, are thought as holding the real tradition. Its growth does not rely exclusively on oral transmission anymore. The tradition stays alive if the believer studies it and incorporates it in his or her everyday life and in his or her innovated rituals.

Re-Africanization also deeply modified the self-perception of African American religious believers. While emphasizing the unique African-ness of religions such as Candomblé and Santería, it has created, in believers, an awareness of belonging to a trans-national community of worshippers. Re-Africanization has minimized the historical and religious particularities of African-American religions and claimed the existence of a world religion that is worshiped by individuals who are considered participants in a global African cultural heritage. Using the Internet, meeting at international conferences, Cuban practitioners, Brazilians, African Americans from the United States and many more come together in their search for legitimation. At the meso level, the impact of re-Africanization is still strong. In the United States, for example, alongside the Yoruba movement, other groups have appeared claiming the necessity for their members to go back to their "ancestral religion." In the early twenty-first century, the Akan movement as well as various Kemetic groups have become popular "African-based" religions that may be soon challenging the hegemony of Christianity and Islam in urban communities.

See also **Anthropology, Social, and the Study of Africa; Religion and Ritual; Vodún.**

BIBLIOGRAPHY

Capone, Stefania. *La quête de l'Afrique dans le candomblé: Pouvoir et tradition au Brésil.* Paris: Karthala, 1999.

Frigerio, Alejandro. "Re-Africanization in Secondary Religious Diaporas: Constructing a World Religion." *Civilisations* 51, no. 2 (2004): 39–60.

Gregory, Steven. *Santeria in New York City: A Study in Cultural Resistance*. New York: Garland Publishing, 1999.

Matory, J. Lorand. "The English Professors of Brazil: On the Diaporic Roots of the Yoruba Nation." *Comparative Study in Society and History* 41, no. 1 (1999): 72–103.

Palmié, Stephan. "Against Syncretism: 'Africanizing' and 'Cubanizing' Discourses in North American Orìsá Worship." In *Counterworks: Managing the Diversity of Knowledge*, ed. Richard Fardon. New York: Routledge, 1995.

PAULINE GUEDJ

DIKE, KENNETH ONWUKA

DIKE, KENNETH ONWUKA (1917–1983). The pioneer Nigerian historian and university administrator Kenneth Onwuka Dike was born in eastern Nigeria and educated there and in Ghana, Sierra Leone, and the United Kingdom. His influential book *Trade and Politics in the Niger Delta, 1830–1885* (1956) derived from his London University Ph.D. thesis. After two years teaching at University College in Ibadan, Nigeria, he undertook a survey of government records throughout the then colony that led to the establishment of Nigeria's National Archives, which he later directed. He returned to Ibadan in 1954, becoming professor of history at University College in 1956 and principal in 1960.

During 1960–1966 the range of the college's departments, its research activities, and its student enrollment were all substantially increased; in 1962 it became an independent university and Dike was named vice-chancellor. However, the communal rivalries that led to the Nigerian civil war made it impossible for Dike to continue at Ibadan, and in 1967 he left, hoping to plan a new university in eastern Nigeria. The war and its aftermath aborted this scheme, however. In 1971 he accepted an invitation to become Harvard's first professor of African history. By this time he had a considerable international reputation, based in part on his role in instituting the International Congress of African Studies, which he chaired from 1962 to 1967. From 1964 to 1975 he was vice-chairman of the International African Institute (London), and from 1965 through 1966 he was chairman of the Association of Commonwealth Universities. His last years were spent in

Kenneth Onwuka Dike (1917–1983), with his wife. Dike was the first Nigerian vice chancellor as well as a professor of history at the University of Ibadan, Nigeria. He is pictured here after receiving the honorary degree of Doctor of Laws at the University of Aberdeen, Scotland, July 18, 1961. © BETTMANN/ CORBIS

his homeland as the first president of the Anambra State University of Technology. He died in 1983.

See also **Education, School: Overview.**

BIBLIOGRAPHY

Afigbo, A. E. K. O. *Dike and the African Historical Renascence*. Owerri, Nigeria: RADA, 1986.

Alagoa, Ebiegberi Joe. *Dike Remembered: African Reflections on History*. Nigeria: University of Port Harcourt Press for Historical Society of Nigeria, 1998.

Animalu, Alexander O. E. *Life and Thoughts of Professor Kenneth Onwuka Dike*. Nsukka, Enugu State: Ucheakonam Foundation, 1997.

Dike, K. Onwuka. *Study of African History: The Present Position*. Addis Ababa: 3rd International Congress of Africanists, 1973.

J. D. FAGE

DINGISWAYO (c. 1770–c. 1816). Dingiswayo was the last paramount chief of the Nguni confederation prior to the rule of Shaka, and prior to European settlement in southeastern Africa. It is legend that, after spending time wandering through the countryside in what is now Natal as a young man, Dingiswayo returned home on horseback to kill his brother, who had succeeded their father as chief, because he believed his brother was not the rightful ruler. Dingiswayo's subsequent reign was marked by his beginning of a process of unification of several related chiefdoms into a military confederation, a process continued by Shaka to great success.

Dingiswayo appointed a number of subchiefs, including Zwide of the Ndwandwe and Sobhuza I of the Swazi, to serve beneath him in the organization of a rapidly expanding Mtetwa population. He introduced a new, successful military structure in which young men, grouped by age, spent much time with one another preparing for the circumcision that entitled them to be warriors, thus inspiring bonds of camaraderie among them that would shape them into trusted companions for military endeavors. Within this framework, Dingiswayo sent Shaka, who had become a leader within the Mtetwa forces, to lead an army to take the throne of the Zulu, a small community within the confederation, after his father had died. Dingiswayo was killed in 1816 by adherents of his rival, Zwide, who had set a trap for him. After a brief decline of the Mtetwa army, Shaka assumed the paramount chieftaincy and once again unified a new federation under his own assumption of the Zulu kingship.

See also **Shaka Zulu; Sobhuza I and II; Southeastern Africa, History of (1600 to 1910).**

BIBLIOGRAPHY

Argyle, John. "Dingiswayo Discovered." In *Social System and Tradition in Southern Africa: Essays in Honour of Eileen Krige*, ed. William John Argyle and Eleanor Preston-Whyte. Cape Town; New York: Oxford University Press, 1978.

Roberts, Brian. *The Zulu Kings*. New York: Charles Scribners Sons, 1974.

Weir, J. "'I Shall Need to Use Her to Rule': The Power of 'Royal' Zulu Women in Pre-Colonial Zululand." *South African Historical Journal* 43 (2000): 3–23.

SARAH VALDEZ

DIOGO, LUÍSA DIAS (1958–). Luísa Dias Diogo, prime minister of Mozambique from 2004, was born in Tete province, where she was raised and educated through secondary school, earning a degree at Escola Comercial de Tete (Tete Commercial School) in 1974. She moved to Maputo and began working for the ministry of finance while earning her degree in economics at Universidade Eduardo Mondlane in 1983. She became a ministry department head in 1986, and was named national budget director in 1989. She continued her education by correspondence, completing a master's degree in finance economics from the University of London in 1992.

Diogo left government for the World Bank in Maputo from 1993 to 1994, but following

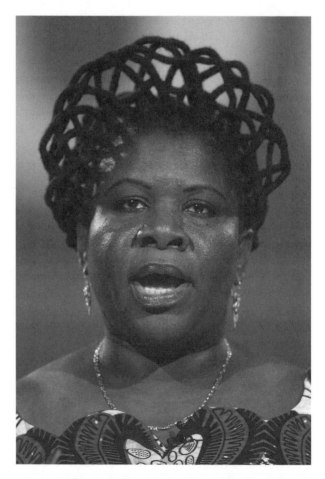

Luísa Dias Diogo (1958–) speaks at the annual Labour Party conference, September 2005, Brighton, England. Diogo, Mozambique's first female prime minister, represents the Liberation Front of Mozambique, which has been ruling the country since 1975. PETER MACDIARMID/GETTY IMAGES

Mozambique's first multiparty elections in 1994 she took the post of deputy finance minister. In 1999 she became minister of finance, a post she retained after she was named prime minister by President Joaquim Chissano in February 2004. She continued as prime minister in the government of Armando Guebuza, though he named a new minister of finance. While she is a member of the ruling party, Frelimo, she is the first Mozambican prime minister who was not part of the generation that fought for liberation from the Portuguese; she is also the first female prime minister in Mozambique. She and her husband, lawyer Albano Silva, have three children.

See also **Mozambique; World Bank.**

BIBLIOGRAPHY

Brown, Mark Malloch. "Luisa Diogo: Advocate for Africa." *Time* 163, no. 17 (April 26, 2004): 60.

Rolletta, Paola. "Mozambique: Small Portraits of Big Women." *New African* 435 (December 2004): 52–53.

KATHLEEN SHELDON

DIOP, ALIOUNE (1910–1980). Alioune Diop was born in Saint-Louis, Senegal, and educated in the French colonial system. He received his bachelor of arts degree in literature in 1931, then went to the University of Algiers to study philosophy. He worked as a professor and represented Senegal in the French Senate; in Paris in 1947 he founded *Présence africaine*, the most influential French-language journal of literature and culture concerned with Africa. As its name implies, the journal (which later spawned a publishing house of the same name) reflected an attempt to remedy the invisibility of Africa on the world stage—the "disinherited" status of Africans—through nothing less than a redefinition of the continent. Diop's introduction to the first issue ("Niam n'goura") was remarkable for its tactfulness: he managed to suggest a quiet revolution in the representation of Africa and to lay the groundwork for a persistent, diverse, and successful anti-colonialism. His work was closely associated with the idea of négritude, but *Présence africaine*, as Diop wrote, was "not subservient to any philosophical or political ideology." Diop also founded the Société Africaine de Culture and played a leading role in organizing the first and second International Congress of Black Writers and Artists (in Paris, 1956, and in Rome, 1959), as well as the First World Festival of Negro Arts, in Dakar (1966), and the (Second) Festival of Black and African Arts and Culture, in Lagos (1977), known as FESTAC.

See also **Literature and the Study of Africa; Senegal: Society and Cultures.**

BIBLIOGRAPHY

Coats, G. "From Whence We Come: Alioune Diop and Saint-Louis, Senegal," *Research in African Literatures* 28 (4) (1997): 206–219.

Diop, Alioune. "Niam n'goura; ou, les raisons d'étre de *Présence africaine*." *Présence africaine* 1 (1947): 7–14.

Grah Mel, Frédéric. *Alioune Diop, le bâtisseur inconnu du monde noir*. Abidjan, Côte d'Ivoire: Presses universitaires de Côte d'Ivoire; Paris: ACCT, 1995.

Kesteloot, Lilyan. *Black Writers in French: A Literary History of Negritude*, trans. Ellen Conroy Kennedy. Washington, DC: Howard University Press, 1991.

Mudimbe, V. Y., ed. *The Surreptitious Speech: "Présence africaine" and the Politics of Otherness, 1947–1987*. Chicago: University of Chicago Press, 1992.

CHRISTOPHER L. MILLER

DIOP, CHEIKH ANTA (1923–1986). The eminent twentieth-century Senegalese African scholar and Pan-Africanist political leader Cheikh Anta Diop was born in Diourbel, Senegal, on December 23, 1923, to a Muslim Wolof family. His devotion to his mother, Maguette Diop, the peasant setting of the black African Mouride Islamic sect, and his early Qur'anic schooling gave Diop a solid African foundation that counterbalanced his education in the French colonial school system and the completion of a bachelor's degree in Senegal.

Diop went to Paris in 1946 to pursue graduate studies in physics and became involved in the African students' anticolonial movement for independence. He helped launch the first Pan-African Student Congress in Paris in 1951. In 1956 Diop participated in the First World Congress of Black Writers and Artists in Paris and attended the second congress in Rome in 1959. These movements and congresses laid the foundations for important post-1945 ideological arguments for African liberation, including Négritude, Marxism, and Pan-Africanism.

Deeply influenced by his firsthand experiences of the richness of traditional African cultures and histories, Diop started research into the origins of civilization in Africa during his studies in Paris. The scope, depth, and imaginative interdisciplinarity of his inquiries expanded as the political climate of anti-racist and anti-colonialist discourses intensified in Europe, Africa, and the Americas. In 1951 the Sorbonne could not assemble a jury to hear his first doctoral thesis, which argued that ancient Egypt was a black African civilization. In 1960 Diop finally received his *docteur ès lettres* after a defense before a panel of specialists in sociology, anthropology, and history—which has become famous because of public interest in his work and the unheard-of array of specialists he faced at the defense. Diop returned to Senegal in 1960 and set up a carbon-14 dating laboratory at the Institut Fondamental d'Afrique Noire (IFAN) to continue his research and political activism.

In 1961 and 1963 he created political opposition parties in Senegal, the Bloc des Masses Sénégalaises and the Front National du Sénégal. In 1976 he founded the Rassemblement National Démocratique (RND), whose official journal was *Siggi*, and later *Taxaw*, a Wolof-language publication.

An accomplished historian, physicist, archaeologist, Egyptologist, and linguist, Diop set out his theories in four texts, the titles of which together summarize his ideas. These works, originally published in French, are: *The African Origin of Civilization: Myth or Reality* (1974); *The Cultural Unity of Black Africa: The Domains of Patriarchy and of Matriarchy in Classical Antiquity* (1978); *Precolonial Black Africa: A Comparative Study of the Political and Social Systems of Europe and Black Africa, from Antiquity to the Formation of Modern States* (1987); and *Civilization or Barbarism: An Authentic Anthropology* (1991). Diop's main agenda was the definition and reconstruction of colonially fragmented African identity. This led him to consider the scientific, theoretical, and philosophical legacy of ancient black Egypt to classical Greece, as well as the historical relationships

of Islam, Christianity, and Judaism to Egyptian religious thought. He was an optimistic thinker who in place of the barbarism of colonial conquest and imperialism hoped for a new philosophy of reconciliation in which all nations could join hands to build a true planetary civilization.

Diop believed that gender and the ideology of race were central issues in understanding the differences between European and African state formations. Those civilizations with female-centered societies were, for him, the most humane civilizations. He claimed that the matriarchal regimes he identified were African in origin; he saw patriarchy as the engine that drove European racism, imperialist conquests, and expansion. African studies should be grounded in the Egyptian classics, he argued, and in unity, and with knowledge and confidence, Africans, including those in the diaspora, could repeat their great historical achievements.

In 1966 at the first World Festival of Negro Arts in Dakar, Senegal, Cheikh Anta Diop was honored with W. E. B. Du Bois as "the scholars who exerted the greatest influence on Negro thought in the twentieth century." In 1980 he was appointed professor in the faculty of arts of the University of Dakar, where he taught ancient history. In 1982 he received the highest award for scientific research from the Institut Cultural Africain (ICA). In 1985 Atlanta mayor Andrew Young invited Diop to Georgia, and April 4, 1985, was proclaimed "Dr. Cheikh Anta Diop Day." Diop died in Dakar on February 7, 1986, and was survived by his widow, Louise Marie Diop-Maes, and their sons.

See also **Afrocentrism; Egypt, Early; History and the Study of Africa; Senegal: Society and Cultures.**

BIBLIOGRAPHY

Diop, Cheikh Anta. *Towards the African Renaissance: Essays in African Culture and Development, 1946–1960*, trans. Egbuna P. Modum. London: Karnak House, 1996.

Gray, Chris. *Conceptions of History: Cheikh Anta Diop and Theophile Obenga*. London: Karnak House, 1989.

Van Sertima, I., ed. *Great African Thinkers: Cheikh Anta Diop*. New Brunswick, NJ: Transaction Books, 1986.

IFI AMADIUME

DIOUF, ABDOU (1935–). Born in the railroad town of Louga and educated in Saint-Louis, Senegal, Diouf completed his secondary education at the Lycée Faidherbe there. He began university studies in Dakar and received a degree (*licence*) in public law and political science from the Faculté de Paris. In 1960, the year of Senegalese independence, he earned a diploma (*brevet*) from the colonial training institute, the École Nationale de la France d'Outre-mer. After his return to Senegal, his career advanced rapidly, and by 1963 he was assigned to the office of President Léopold Sédar Senghor. He remained close to Senghor throughout the 1960s and was named prime minister in 1970, a post he held for the next decade.

Upon Senghor's resignation on January 1, 1981, Diouf succeeded him as president of the Republic of Senegal. He was reelected to five-year terms in 1983 and 1988 and to a seven-year term in 1993. Diouf was responsible for much of Senegal's political liberalization, but he also presided over a degenerating economy. His early popularity eroded significantly over time, and he faced escalating popular unrest and confrontation in urban Senegal. Like that of his mentor Senghor, Diouf's foreign policy was characterized by close ties with France and high-profile visibility in such international forums as the Organization of African Unity (OAU), the Organization of the Islamic Conference (OIC), and Francophone organizations. In 2000 he lost his bid for re-election to Abdoulaye Wade. He moved with his family to France. In 2002 he assumed the secretary-generalship of the International Francophone Organization, succeeding Boutros Boutros-Ghali in the office.

See also **Organization of African Unity; Senegal: History and Politics; Senghor, Léopold Sédar.**

BIBLIOGRAPHY

Diop, Momar Coumba, and Mamadou Diouf. *Le Sénégal sous Abdou Diouf: État et société*. Paris: Karthala, 1990.

Ndiaye, Falilou; Manfred Prinz; and Alioune Tine. *Visages publics du Sénégal: 10 personnalités politiques parlent*. Paris: L'Harmattan, 1990.

LEONARDO A. VILLALÓN

DIRECT RULE. *See* **Colonial Policies and Practices.**

DISEASE

This entry includes the following articles:
VIRAL AND INFECTIOUS
CLIMATE AND DISEASE
SEXUALLY TRANSMITTED
INDUSTRIAL
HIV/AIDS, MEDICAL ASPECTS
HIV/AIDS, SOCIAL AND POLITICAL ASPECTS

VIRAL AND INFECTIOUS

Infectious diseases have always been responsible for the majority of deaths in sub-Saharan Africa. This remains the case in the early twenty-first century, in spite of an increasing burden of morbidity due to noncommunicable disease (e.g., cardiovascular disease, diabetes, and cancer) in urban populations. The burden of infectious diseases in Africa falls most heavily on young children. They are exposed frequently to the many endemic infectious diseases and, as they grow older, develop a degree of immunity that prevents further infection or reduces the severity of the consequent illness.

INFECTIOUS DISEASES AND CHILDHOOD MORTALITY

In the 1950s Ian McGregor and colleagues carried out a unique series of studies on the demography of four typical rural villages in the West Kiang District of the Gambia. They found that more than 40 percent of live-born infants died before their fifth birthday. As in most of sub-Saharan Africa, malaria due to *Plasmodium falciparum* was endemic in these villages. During the rainy season, 90 percent or more of children aged less than five years were found to have malaria parasites in their blood. McGregor concluded that malaria was the main cause of death among children in this age group. Epidemics of measles with extremely high death rates were also documented (Billewicz and McGregor 1981).

The conditions described by McGregor and colleagues in Gambian villages prevailed at the time in most of sub-Saharan Africa, and there is no reason to believe childhood mortality rates were unusually high in the Gambia. Subsequent studies in The Gambia and elsewhere, many of them conducted by McGregor's successor as director of the Medical Research Council Laboratories in The Gambia, Brian Greenwood, confirmed and augmented his findings.

Most children in Africa die at home, and when, as often happens, the cause of death is unknown, "verbal autopsies," in which relatives are asked about the symptoms that preceded death, may give some pointers. However, there are several problems with this informal system. One is that the symptoms of several diseases overlap, for example, malaria and pneumonia, which is another common cause of death in young children, produce similar symptoms. It is therefore difficult to determine the cause of death. A further problem is that some infections, such as malaria and measles, depress the immune system, thereby increasing vulnerability to other infections. As a result, it is possible that a patient who has died from pneumonia would not have done so if he or she had not previously been infected with malaria. Reducing the rate of malarial infection would therefore reduce the death rate even though malaria is not itself the immediate cause of death. This has been demonstrated to be the case in a 1991 study carried out by Brian Greenwood and colleagues (Alonso et al. 1991). Infections also precipitate malnutrition in vulnerable populations, especially children around the time of weaning, and this also increases the risk of illness and death.

As previously discussed, it is often difficult to identify the cause of death in African children due to the lack of medical observation. The proportion of deaths attributable to a particular disease can be estimated by measuring the reduction in mortality that follows the introduction of an effective prevention program. In their 1991 study Greenwood and colleagues showed that the provision of insecticide-impregnated bed nets to prevent malaria transmission reduced mortality by almost 40 percent in Gambian children aged less than five years. It was therefore possible to deduce that malaria had been an important contributor to child mortality. Greenwood and colleagues subsequently showed that vaccination against the two commonest bacterial

causes of pneumonia in children, *Haemophilus influenzae* type b and *Streptococcus pneumoniae*, each reduced mortality by more than 10 percent in this age group (Cutts et al. 2005, Mulholland et al. 1997). Following identical logic it was again possible to deduce that these bacteria had been responsible for a significant proportion of child deaths.

Before the introduction of vaccination in the late 1970s, measles was an important cause of death in Africa. In isolated rural populations few if any people were immune, and mortality during epidemics was high in all age groups. In urban populations most people are exposed in early childhood. Attack rates remain high where vaccine coverage is suboptimal. The chance of dying during an attack of measles is very much higher in Africa than in Europe. A series of studies in Guinea-Bissau documented the fact that the risk of death was almost ten times higher among secondary cases in a household than in individuals infected outside the home (Aaby 1985). Review of historical records confirmed that, in the past, the same phenomenon had been observed in Europe. The conclusion was that the chance of death depends on who infects the victim: If it is someone with whom an individual shares a room, he or she is exposed to a large inoculum of measles virus, and this causes a more severe attack with a greater chance of dying than if an infection were obtained from a passerby in the street. Thus the high mortality due to measles in Africa is a consequence of overcrowding, exacerbated in some cases by malnutrition.

NONFATAL ENDEMIC INFECTIOUS DISEASES
There are numerous nonfatal endemic infectious diseases that are the cause of a great burden of disease and disability among the populations of many African countries. These diseases generally have the greatest affect on rural populations and, in some cases, their prevalence has fallen as a result of increasing urbanization but also due to successful control programs. The following section focuses on four of the major endemic infectious diseases that afflict Africa; three of these four have, at least in some areas, been successfully controlled as a result of mass treatment campaigns in the second half of the twentieth and early twenty-first centuries.

Yaws. Yaws is a skin disease caused by the bacterium *Treponema pallidum*, which is also responsible for causing syphilis. Whilst syphilis is sexually transmitted, in the case of yaws the infection is spread by skin-to-skin contact, which is most common between children. In the past, before effective treatment was widespread, it used to be a common cause of disfiguring skin ulcers and deformities in the hot, humid regions of Africa. However, in other climates it was less common, and in the Sahel and other dryer regions, it was not yaws, but a similar disease, endemic syphilis or bejel, that was endemic, being transmitted under conditions of poor hygiene, possibly by shared use of drinking vessels.

There have been several examples of confusion involving yaws, syphilis, and bejel. The reasons for this are that there are great clinical similarities between bejel and syphilis; moreover, the serological test developed by August Wasserman in the early 1900s to identify venereal syphilis did not distinguish between the three diseases caused by *T. pallidum*. An important example of this confusion can be found in Uganda in the early twentieth century. The colonial authorities viewed a severe outbreak as a major epidemic of venereal syphilis. The colonial government, alarmed at what appeared to be a serious threat to the population of the Uganda Protectorate, commissioned an investigation to be led by Colonel Lambkin, of the Royal Army Medical Corps. The Commission reached the alarming conclusion that 50 percent of the population of Buganda, and 90 percent of the Ankole Kingdom, were infected with venereal syphilis and that the entire population of the Protectorate could be threatened. This opinion was endorsed by the missionary Dr. Albert Cook who had been operating at Mengo Hospital in Uganda since 1897. However, a great deal of debate has arisen around this conclusion, and has led some experts to question whether there was in fact such an epidemic.

The element that was said to have sparked the epidemic in the early years of the twentieth century was the relaxation in traditional morals and social control systems as a result of the introduction of Christianity. The new religion allowed a greater liberty for women, thereby producing a group of immoral women who are the villains of the original story. However, it is this conclusion that has been challenged. The exact details that justify this revision

of the traditional history are too extensive to be dealt with in depth, but the conclusion reached is that it seems more likely that this was in fact endemic syphilis or yaws, and that these diseases had been present for generations; there was therefore probably no epidemic instigated by free women. That yaws and syphilis had been prevalent in the region for some time is suggested by the fact that the Banyoro people appear to have invented a method for infecting young children by wrapping them in clothes smeared with discharges from patients with skin lesions in order to prevent more severe disease in later life. This widespread practice is unlikely to have been introduced in the one generation since the arrival of Europeans, and it can therefore be reasonably used to support the conclusion. This is similar to the practice of variolation used in Europe before vaccination became available, in which infants were exposed to smallpox by wrapping them in blankets used by smallpox cases.

Soon after the discovery of penicillin in the 1940s it was found that *T. pallidum* was exquisitely sensitive to the drug. In the 1950s and 1960s yaws mass treatment campaigns were undertaken in many African countries with the support of the World Health Organization (WHO), in which whole populations received penicillin injections. This was so successful that yaws was eliminated from most of Africa, and in the early twenty-first century is a rare disease. This campaign, along with the elimination of smallpox, is considered one of WHO's greatest achievements. For many African communities it was their first contact with Western medicine, and it has been suggested that its effectiveness accounts for the preference for injectable over oral medication still found in some parts of Africa.

Onchocerciasis (River Blindness). Onchocerciasis is caused by a filarial worm, Onchocerca volvulus, which is transmitted by biting flies of the Simulium genus. Because these flies breed in fast-flowing rivers, the disease occurs along the banks of such rivers, mainly in mountainous regions of West Africa. The adult worms live in nodules under the skin, and produce large numbers of progeny, known as microfilariae, which migrate to the skin and eyes. In the skin they cause dermatitis, which can be intolerably itchy, and in the eyes they cause damage that may lead eventually to blindness. In severely affected villages almost the entire adult population may be blind, leading to the abandonment of large areas of fertile farmland as populations moved away from the rivers.

Initial attempts to control onchocerciasis by spraying rivers with insecticide were unsuccessful. Since the 1980s a program of community-based mass treatment with the drug ivermectin has had an enormous impact on the disease. Ivermectin was developed by the American pharmaceutical company Merck for the treatment of parasitic diseases of cattle. When it was found to be effective against onchocerciasis, the company was persuaded to donate the drug for mass treatment campaigns, and undertook to provide as much as was needed, for as long as it was needed. Substantial funds were obtained from the World Bank, and the Onchocerciasis Control Program was set up in Ouagadougou to direct the mass treatment campaign. Since the mid-1980s many million doses have been given, usually by village health workers or community volunteers. The drug is safe, has few side effects, and is particularly popular with communities that receive it because of its efficacy against a variety of parasitic diseases, from intestinal worms to scabies.

Trachoma. Trachoma is the leading infectious cause of blindness. It is caused by a bacterium, *Chlamydia trachomatis*, which is transmitted from eye to eye in communities where hygienic standards are poor. It is largely confined to poor rural African communities living in arid conditions, especially in Ethiopia, Sudan, and the countries of the Sahel. The prevalence of trachoma has declined in many African countries since the mid-1980s as a result of urbanization and improved living standards and, since the late 1990s, mass treatment with the antibiotic azithromycin, which has been shown to be highly effective when high levels of coverage are achieved. The manufacturer of azithromycin, the American pharmaceutical giant Pfizer, agreed to donate 135 million doses of the drug to trachoma control programs. Like ivermectin, it is well received by communities receiving mass treatment, because it has a broad spectrum of activity against many infectious diseases, including malaria and sexually transmitted infections.

Schistosomiasis (Bilharzia). Schistosomiasis, sometimes called Bilharzia after the German physician Theodor Bilharz who first described it, is caused by a trematode worm that resides in the veins surrounding the bladder or bowel. The female worm produces eggs continuously for many years, which pass through the walls of the bladder or bowel, causing inflammation and bleeding. If the eggs are excreted into fresh water they hatch, producing free-living larvae, which parasitize particular species of snail. The life cycle is completed when a second larval stage is released from the snail, and penetrates the skin of a human bathing in the water.

More than 100 million Africans suffer from schistosomiasis. Involvement of the bladder by Schistosoma haematobium leads to bleeding; in some rural African communities blood in the urine is so common that it is not considered abnormal. Damage to the bladder can eventually lead to bladder cancer or to kidney failure. The eggs of Schistosoma mansoni damage the liver. When the infection is heavy, this can lead eventually to cirrhosis of the liver, which is fatal in some cases.

Like the other endemic diseases, schistosomiasis can be treated with a single dose of a drug that is safe and relatively free from side effects. Campaigns to deliver mass treatment with this drug, praziquantel, to schoolchildren in disease-endemic areas have accelerated in the early twenty-first century with generous support from the Bill and Melinda Gates Foundation. Treatment for schistosomiasis is often accompanied by treatment for soil-transmitted helminths, such as hookworm, which are endemic in many parts of Africa and can cause anaemia and malnutrition.

EPIDEMIC INFECTIOUS DISEASES

The impact of epidemic diseases is more dramatic than that of endemic infectious diseases, even when they kill fewer people. This is because epidemic diseases tend to kill adults as well as infants, often in large numbers over a short time period, leading to greater social and economic disruption. Africa is unique in having suffered major epidemics of sleeping sickness in the twentieth and twenty-first centuries, because this disease does not occur in other continents. The Sahel region has also been afflicted by several huge epidemics of bacterial meningitis in the twentieth century, which occur every ten to fifteen years, toward the end of the dry season.

Sleeping Sickness. African sleeping sickness was well known to European slave traders in West Africa in the eighteenth century, who sometimes referred to it as the "negro lethargy." The English physician Thomas Winterbottom, who worked in Freetown in the 1790s, described the enlarged cervical lymph nodes that are a characteristic sign of the disease, and reported that slave traders were aware that this sign was a harbinger of early death.

A major epidemic of sleeping sickness, which is universally fatal unless treated, occurred in Uganda in the early years of the twentieth century, decimating populations in central Uganda, especially close to the shores of Lake Victoria and on islands in the lake; some individuals saying that "[t]hese were the most important epidemics in colonial Africa, and provoked greater intervention in the lives of ordinary Africans than any other disease" (Doyle 2000, p. 430). In Busoga District, more than 20,000 people were reported to have died of the disease in 1902. Albert Cook described the impact of the epidemic in 1907: "It is most melancholy visiting the shores or islands of the lake. Where six or seven years ago was a contented and relatively dense population, today reigns desolation and sadness, the empty and fallen huts being rapidly lost in the overgrowth of tropical vegetation" (p. 27).

When the epidemic began, the cause of the disease was unknown, though it was generally believed to be infectious in origin. It was suggested by some that the disease had been introduced to Uganda from West Africa by Henry Stanley's trans-African expedition, though others believed it had been introduced by Sudanese troops. In 1902 the British government, alarmed by Patrick Manson's warning that the disease could spread to India, supported the Royal Society in establishing the first Sleeping Sickness Commission to investigate the cause of the disease. This three-man commission was able to disprove Manson's theory that it was due to a filarial worm, but failed to definitively identify the cause. Aldo Castellani, an Italian member of the Commission, found Trypanosome parasites in the cerebrospinal fluid of some patients, and proposed that this was the cause. This was subsequently confirmed by Colonel David Bruce, who led the second Sleeping Sickness Commission.

The organism was named, after him, *Trypanosoma brucei.* He showed that it was transmitted by the bite of the tsetse fly, Glossina palpalis, which breeds in scrub land along the shores of lakes and rivers.

It is not clear why there should have been a major sleeping sickness epidemic on the shores of Lake Victoria at this time, but a plausible theory is that the epidemic resulted from changes in farming practices brought about by colonialism. However, another possibility is that it was not the arrival of foreign trypanosomes in Uganda that provoked the epidemic, but rather that there was endemic trypanosomiasis prior to the arrival of Europeans in Uganda and the high number of cases was due to the changes taking place in Uganda at the start of the twentieth century. The epidemic caused many deaths in Kenya and Tanganyika as well as in Uganda. In Uganda, it has been suggested that the change from a communalistic system of agriculture to a capitalist system, in which large tracts of land came to be owned by individuals, led to changes in the way in which land was cultivated, with increasing areas of scrub vegetation in which tsetse flies could breed. Movement of people, for example to work as laborers on plantations, may have spread the disease to new areas.

In 1902 the authorities in Uganda had proposed that the epidemic should be controlled by segregation of sleeping sickness patients on Buvu island in Lake Victoria, or in a "concentration camp" near Kisumu. However, this plan was not implemented, as the Colonial Office was unwilling to allocate the necessary funds. Identification of the insect vector suggested an alternative method of sleeping sickness control: destruction of its habitat through removal of vegetation, or transfer of populations living near the lake shore to areas where the fly did not breed.

In 1905 Hesketh Bell became commissioner for the Ugandan Protectorate. At least 200,000 people had died of sleeping sickness in Uganda in the previous five years, out of a total population of 3.5 million. He decided that the only way to control the epidemic was to compulsorily resettle the entire populations of the islands and lake shore in tsetse fly–free areas at least two miles from the Lake. Remarkably, this evacuation was peacefully completed by 1910. The adverse impact on trade and agriculture was profound and long lasting, but

Eradicating tsetse flies. An Ethiopian cattle farmer explains how his cows are suffering from bovine trypanosomiasis, a disease that attacks the blood and nervous system of livestock, in Ghibe Valley, 115 miles southwest of Addis Ababa. The parasite that causes the disease is transmitted by tsetse flies, which are only found in Africa. AP PHOTO/OBED ZILWA

the epidemic was eventually brought under control, although sleeping sickness remains endemic in Uganda in the early twenty-first century.

Meningococcal meningitis. Meningitis is an infection of the meninges, the membranes that cover the brain and spinal cord. It can be caused by a variety of bacteria and viruses, which are spread from person to person by the respiratory route (coughing and sneezing). A bacterium called *Neisseria meningitidis,* or the meningococcus, continues to cause major epidemics of meningitis in the Sahel region of Africa. These were first reported in the medical literature in the early twentieth century. For example, an epidemic was described in

Sokoto, in northern Nigeria, in 1921, in which 45,900 people died in the course of a few months.

Lapeyssonnie has described the geographical extent of the African "meningitis belt," which extends from the Gambia in the West to Kenya and Ethiopia in the East, and is bounded by the Sahara desert to the North, and the more humid regions to the South; epidemics have not been recorded in areas where the average annual rainfall exceeds forty-three inches. Within the meningitis belt, epidemics of meningococcal meningitis occur each year towards the end of the long dry season, with a major epidemic every ten years or so. Between 1949 and 1951, for example, 239,000 cases were reported in the countries covered by his report (Niger, Nigeria, Haute Volta, Chad, and Sudan), with 44,100 deaths.

It has proved difficult to control these epidemics. Before effective antibacterial drugs became available in the 1940s, more than 70 percent of cases of meningococcal meningitis died, and many survivors were left with disabilities such as blindness or deafness. Antimicrobial treatment has greatly reduced the mortality, but it must be administered early, because mortality is high in the first few days of the illness. This presents logistical problems in the dispersed, mainly rural communities in which these epidemics occur, although single dose treatments, which can be given to outpatients in rural health centers and dispensaries, have greatly reduced mortality since the 1970s. A vaccine has been available against the strain responsible for most major epidemics, serogroup A, since the 1970s, but it is not effective in young children, and its protective effect lasts only a few years. Moreover recent epidemics have been caused by different serogroups, for example the W135 strain that has also caused epidemics among pilgrims attending the haj. Improved vaccines against this and other strains of meningococcus, with a longer protective efficacy, are available in the early twenty-first century. It is possible that when they are widely deployed in populations with a high burden of infection, new mutants will be selected against which these vaccines are not effective.

See also **Children and Childhood: Infancy and Early Development; Healing and Health Care; Slave Trades; World Bank.**

BIBLIOGRAPHY

Aaby, Peter, et al. "High Measles Mortality in Infancy Related to Intensity of Exposure." *Journal of Pediatrics* 109 (1985): 40–44.

Alonso, Pedro L., et al. "The Effect of Insecticide-Treated Bed Nets on Mortality of Gambian Children." *Lancet* 337 (1991): 1499–1502.

Billewics, William Z., and Ian A. McGregor. "The Demography of Two West African (Gambian) Villages, 1951–1975." *Journal of Biosocial Sciences* 13 (1981): 219–240.

Binkin, N., and J. Band. "Epidemic of Meningococcal Meningitis in Bamako, Mali: Epidemiological Features and Analysis of Vaccine Efficacy." *Lancet* 2 (1982): 315–317.

Cook, Albert. "On Sleeping Sickness as Met in Uganda, Especially with Regard to Its Treatment." *Transactions of the Society of Tropical Medicine & Hygiene* 1 (1907): 25–43.

Cutts, Felicity T., et al. (Gambian Pneumococcal Vaccine Trial Group.) "Efficacy of Nine-Valent Pneumococcal Conjugate Vaccine against Pneumonia and Invasive Pneumococcal Disease in The Gambia: Randomized, Double-Blind, Placebo-Controlled Trial." *Lancet* 365 (2005): 1139–1146.

Davies, John N. P. "The History of Syphilis in Uganda." *Bulletin of the World Health Organization* 15 (1956): 1041–1055.

Decosas Joseph, and John B. Koama. "Chronicle of an Outbreak Foretold: Meningococcal Meningitis W135 in Burkina Faso." *Lancet Infectious Diseases* 2 (2002): 763–765.

Doyle, Shane. "Population Decline and Delayed Recovery in Bunyoro, 1860–1960." *Journal of African History* 41 (2000): 429–458.

Foege, William H. "Feasibility of Eradicating Yaws." *Rev Infect Dis.* 7, Supp. 2 (1985): S335–S337.

Lapeyssonnie, Louis. "La meningite cerebro-spinale en Afrique." *Bulletin of the World Health Organization* Supp. 28 (1963): 2–114.

Mabey David, Anthony Solomon, and Allen Foster. "Trachoma Seminar." *Lancet* 362 (2003): 223–229.

Molyneux, David H.; Peter J. Hotez; and Alan Fenwick. "Rapid-Impact Interventions: How a Policy of Integrated Control for Africa's Neglected Tropical Diseases Could Benefit the Poor." *Public Library of Science Medicine* 2 (2005): e336.

Mulholland, Kim, et al. "Randomized Trial of Haemophilus influenzae type-b Tetanus Protein Conjugate Vaccine for Prevention of Pneumonia and Meningitis in Gambian Infants." *Lancet* 349 (1997): 1191–1197.

Musere, Jonathan "African Sleeping Sickness: Political Ecology, Colonialism, and Control in Uganda." In *Studies in African Health and Medicine*, Vol. 5. Lampeter, Wales: Edwin Mellen Press, 1990.

Omura, Shiko, and Andrew Crump. "The Life and Times of Ivermectin—A Success Story." *Nature Reviews in Microbiology* 2 (2004): 984–989.

Soff, Harvey G. "A History of Sleeping Sickness in Uganda." Ph.D. diss. Syracuse University, New York, 1971.

Solomon, Anthony W., et al. "Mass Treatment with Single-Dose Azithromycin for Trachoma." *New England Journal of Medicine* 351 (2004): 1962–1971.

DAVID MABEY
WILLIAM MABEY

CLIMATE AND DISEASE

The role of climate in disease dynamics has become a subject of increasing interest in the early twenty-first century, particularly in Africa, which is generally acknowledged to have a heavy disease burden. Although controversy remains over how human activities might be driving climate variability and change, it is generally agreed that global climate is changing and there is an increasing need to understand the potential outcomes of such changes on diseases and health.

AFRICA'S CLIMATE

Africa's climate is often described as both varied and varying. It is varied in the sense that it encompasses a wide range that spans from the moist, humid region through the semiarid Sahel to the hyperarid climate of the Sahara and Kalahari Deserts. The continent also has a mild Mediterranean climate in the northern part and a temperate climate on the mountainous regions. Africa's climate is also varying because all these climates exhibit differing degrees of temporal variability, particularly with regard to rainfall. Extreme climatic events such as droughts and floods occur frequently, effecting huge economic losses and introducing serious health implications. Observational records in the past century show that Africa has been warming, and this warming is projected to increase in the future, with a consequent rise in sea level and variable effects on precipitation. In some areas, the warming is associated with increased precipitation whereas in other areas it is expected to cause a significant decline in rainfall. This climatic pattern plays a major role in determining the ecology and habitat of disease vectors in the continent.

CLIMATE AND HUMAN DISEASES IN AFRICA

Characterizing the sensitivity of infectious diseases to climate is complex, as climate is only one factor among many that can influence the occurrence of infectious diseases, particularly in Africa. Many human diseases in Africa are affected directly or indirectly by weather and climate (see Table 1). These links may be spatial, with climate affecting distribution; temporal, with weather affecting the timing of an outbreak; or relate to the intensity of an outbreak. There are several causal pathways for outbreaks—vector-borne diseases, water- and food-borne diseases, airborne and heat-related diseases, and extreme climate events. However, it should be noted that

although these diseases are climate sensitive, human activities also contribute to their spread, particularly for the diseases that require human and livestock hosts. For instance, the movement of humans and livestock has contributed to the resurgence and spread of some diseases to areas where such diseases had previously been controlled. An example is the resurgence of malaria and tuberculosis in previously controlled areas and the 2007 outbreak and spread of rift valley fever in some parts of Kenya.

Vector-borne Diseases. Vector-borne diseases are the most common climate-influenced human diseases in Africa. Most notable among these vectors are mosquitoes, flies, and ticks.

Mosquito-borne diseases. Malaria is a potentially life-threatening disease caused by four related species of the protozoan parasite *Plasmodium*: *Plasmodium falciparum, P. vivax, P. malariae, and P. ovale.* It is transmitted from human to human through the bite of an infected anopheles mosquito. Unlike in other parts of the world, Africa's malaria mosquitoes are almost exclusively human-biters, and this fact enhances the chain of human-to-human transmission. It is estimated that in 2005, about 343 million clinical attacks of malaria had likely occurred in Africa; 209 million would have been among children aged less than five years. Malaria is a major cause of death (over 950,000 deaths annually) in Africa. It is also a significant indirect cause of deaths in the continent, where malaria-related maternal anemia in pregnancy, low birth weight, and premature delivery cause about 75,000–200,000 deaths per year in sub-Saharan Africa. The anemia frequently requires blood transfusions. Transfusion screening systems remain rudimentary in many sub-Saharan countries, contributing to the transmission of human immunodeficiency virus (HIV) through infected blood supplies. Ten to fifteen percent of overall HIV infections and as much as 25 percent of pediatric infections in sub-Saharan Africa result from blood transfusions, mainly for the treatment of severe malaria and sickle cell anemia.

Major endemic regions include most of sub-Saharan Africa except the Sahara and Kalahari Deserts and South Africa (see Figure 1). Recent reports have shown the emergence of malaria in

Common infectious diseases in Africa and their sensitivity to climate

Disease	Transmission	Evidence for inter-annual variability	Climate-epidemic link	Strength of temporal climate sensitivity
Influenza	Airborne transmission	xxxxx	Decreases in temperature associated with epidemics	+ +
Cholera	Food and Waterborne Transmission	xxxxx	Increases in land and sea surface temperature as well as El Niño events associated with epidemics	+ + + + +
Malaria	Transmitted by bite of female *anopheles* mosquito	xxxxx	Changes in temperature and rainfall associated with epidemics	+ + + + +
Meningitis	Airborne Transmission	xxxx	Increases in temperature & wind speed and decreases in humidity associated with epidemics	+ + +
Lymphatic Filariasis	Transmitted by the bite of female *Culex, Anopheles, Aedes* and *Mansonia* mosquitoes	—	Temperature, rainfall and humidity determine the geographical distribution of vectors and diseases`	+ +
Leishmaniasis	Transmitted by the bite of female phlebotomine sand flies	xx	Increase in temperature and rainfall associated with epidemics	+ + +
Schistosomiasis	Waterborne transmission involving an intermediate snail host	x	Increase in temperature and rainfall can affect seasonal transmission and distribution	+
African Trypanosomiasis	Transmitted by the bite of male and female tsetse flies, *Glossina spp.*	xxx	Changes in temperature and rainfall may be linked to epidemics	+ +
Onchocerciasis	Transmitted by female simuliid black flies	x	Evidence for climate effects on spatial distribution and seasonal vector biting rates but not temporal variation in disease	—
Dengue	Transmitted by the bite of female *Aedes* mosquitoes	xxxx	High temperature, humidity and rainfall associated with epidemics	+ + +
Rift Valley Fever	Transmitted by the bite of female culicine mosquitoes	xxx	Heavy rains and flooding associated with warm ENSO events associated with onset of epidemic	+ + +
Yellow Fever	Transmitted by the bite of female *Aedes* and Haemagogus mosquitoes	xxxx	High temperature and heavy rain associated with epidemic	+ +

SOURCE: World Health Organization. *Using Climate to Predict Infectious Disease Epidemics.* Geneva. World Health Organization, 2005; Wilkinson, P. *Climate Change and Infectious Disease in Africa and the UK. Infectious Diseases: Preparing for the Future.* U.K.: World Health Organization, Office of Science and Innovation, 2006.

Table 1.

previously malaria-free areas such as the Kenyan highlands. The frequent malaria epidemics recorded there are due to the low immunity in the area. Modeling studies show that areas with low suitability for malaria transmission could become highly suitable by 2080 with climate change. Under warmer conditions mosquitoes develop faster, and the parasite also multiplies more rapidly. However, the role of climate on malaria transmission and epidemics is highly contested as some studies argue that it is the poor malaria control strategies and drug resistance that would be the most determining factors than climate parameters. Nevertheless, it is obvious that temperature and precipitation, acting through other socioeconomic and environmental variables, are important in explaining the occurrence of malaria in Africa.

Dengue is a viral disease transmitted to humans by *aedes sp.* mosquitoes mostly in tropical and subtropical areas. Most dengue infections are self-limiting, but a small portion develops into a more serious illness—dengue hemorrhagic fever/dengue shock syndrome (DHF/DSS)—characterized by spontaneous hemorrhage. Fatality rates in untreated DHF/DSS can be as high as 50 percent. Dengue is primarily an urban disease and over the years there has been an unprecedented increase in the global incidence and geographic range of dengue and the primary

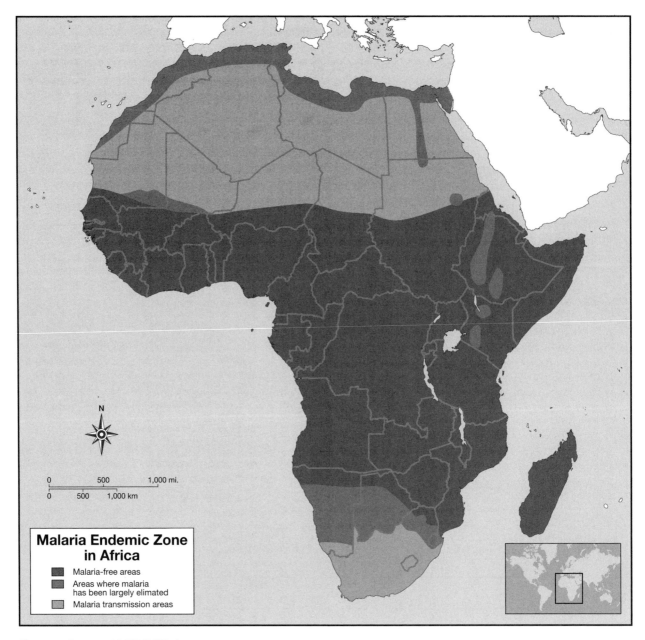

Figure 1. COURTESY UNEP/GRID-ARENDAL

mosquito vector. In Africa, the disease occurs year-round but has a seasonal peak that occurs in the months of high rainfall and humidity. Almost all sub-Saharan African countries, except Sudan, South Africa, Chad, Niger, Mali, and Mauritania are currently at risk for contracting the dengue virus. Countries with recorded epidemic dengue activity include Lesotho, Mozambique, Angola, Nigeria, Côte d'Ivoire, Burkina Faso, Senegal, and the Gambia. Some modeling studies have projected a net increase in the latitudinal and altitudinal range of dengue with

climate change. The latitudinal increase results from a projected increase in rainfall and temperature in the Sahel, as well as projected temperature increases in the East African highlands, creating a suitable habitat for mosquito vectors that transmit Dengue. The highlands particularly, were not at risk of Dengue.

Yellow fever is a viral disease native to tropical Africa. It is transmitted by at least fourteen species of mosquito—the entire genus *Aedes*—that breed in tree holes and other natural cavities. Humans can be infected if bitten by infected mosquitoes.

One kind of mosquito that is closely associated with human habitation is the peri-domestic form of *Ae. aegypti*, a species that readily breeds in water jars and other man-made containers. The endemic zone of yellow fever in Africa extends from the southern borders of the Sahara to Angola. The disease occurs in a wide variety of habitats and its epidemiology is correspondingly complex. However, yellow fever is a highly seasonal disease and heavy rain and high temperature are associated with epidemics in the continent. Since 1985, there has been a resurgence of yellow fever epidemics in Africa with occurrences in Senegal, Guinea, Liberia, Côte d'Ivoire, Ghana, Togo, Bénin, Nigeria, Cameroon, Gabon, Angola, Democratic Republic of the Congo, Sudan, and Kenya.

Rift Valley fever (RVF) is transmitted by the bite of female *Culex* mosquitoes that breed in flooded low-lying habitats, and has only been identified in Africa. It affects primarily domestic livestock but can be passed to humans if they are exposed to the blood or other body fluids of infected animals. This can happen during the slaughtering or handling of infected animals or during the preparation of food. The disease is more common in rural areas but occasional outbreaks in urban areas have also been reported. Although the disease is widespread in Africa, as of the early twenty-first century the endemic countries are Sudan, Egypt, Kenya, Mozambique, Senegal, Madagascar, South Africa, Lesotho, Swaziland, Mozambique, Zambia, and Namibia.

Outbreaks of RVF in Africa are characterized by distinct spatial and temporal patterns that are largely influenced by climate. Heavy rains and flooding are particularly associated with onset of the disease, and outbreaks are positively associated with warm El Niño Southern Oscillation (ENSO) events. People with Rift Valley virus infections typically have a flu-like illness with fever, weakness, back pain, dizziness, and weight loss. Sometimes, the infection can cause hemorrhage (severe bleeding), encephalitis (inflammation of the brain), or severe eye complications. Outbreaks of RVF in recent years have been accompanied by bans on livestock trade between the Middle East and the greater Horn of Africa since the 1997/1998 El Niño event, and has cost the greater Horn of Africa an estimated loss of about US$300–$500 million annually. Some parts of Kenya have experienced an outbreak of Rift Valley Fever, which started in the northern parts of

Kenya and spread to the central and southern parts, largely through livestock and human movements.

Lymphatic Filariasis (*Elephantiasis* or LF) is caused in Africa by the parasitic threadlike worm, *Wuchereria bancrofti*, and is transmitted to humans through the bites of female *Culex, Anopheles Aedes* and *Mansonia* mosquitoes. Humans are the definitive host for this parasite and there is no animal reservoir. The spread of this disease is therefore largely influenced by human movement. LF can lead to painful and disfiguring chronic enlargement of the arms, legs, and genitals in people of all ages and in both sexes, and of the breasts in women. In 2002 the World Health Organization estimated that about 120 million people worldwide were infected by LF, and one-third of them were in Africa. Most sub-Saharan countries are endemic. This disease is often called elephantiasis because of the physical appearance of the swollen limbs in those most severely affected. The acute and chronic manifestations of the disease can cause severe physical and psychological disability in affected people. The disease can also have a significant economic impact in endemic communities because some of the disabilities may lead to reduced productivity.

Temperature, rainfall, and humidity determine the geographical distribution of vectors and diseases. However, changes in the distribution of the disease in the continent in recent decades have not been driven predominantly by climatic variables but by large-scale agricultural development projects that have shifted the nature and quantity of water sources and potential mosquito breeding sites.

Fly-borne diseases. Onchocerciasis (*River blindness*) is transmitted by female *simuliid* black fly and is largely found in sub-Saharan Africa. Onchocerciasis is often called "river blindness" because of its most extreme manifestation, blindness, and because the black fly vector abounds in fertile riverside areas, which frequently remain uninhabited for fear of infection. Estimates by the World Health Organization show that out of some 120 million people worldwide who were at risk of onchocerciasis in 2002, 96 percent were in Africa. A total of 18 million people are infected with the disease of which 99 percent are in Africa. The onchocerciasis endemic belt falls within the humid tropical rainforest zone and covers about thirty countries in Africa. With the Onchocerciasis Control Programme (OCP) of the World Health Organization, it was expected that almost 300,000 cases of blindness would have been prevented in the 11 countries in the OCP zone by 2000. However, this has not been the case as more countries have become endemic.

African Trypanosomiasis (*Sleeping sicknesses*) is a systemic disease caused by a parasite that is transmitted to humans by the bite of the tsetse fly. There are two types of African trypanosomiasis—the West African, transmitted by the *T. b. gambiense*, and the East African variety, transmitted by the *T. b. rhodesiense*. The disease is prevalent in tropical Africa only (north of South Africa and south of Algeria, Libya, and Egypt). The number of infected people in Africa is estimated to be 300,000—500,000, and the disease is estimated to cause an annual death of about 50,000 people. Climatic variables that partly explain the occurrence of the disease include changes in land surface temperature and rainfall. Other non-climatic issues such as cattle density and vegetation patterns are also relevant factors that explain the occurrence of epidemics.

Leishmaniasis is caused by the bite of female phlebotomine sand flies. In Africa, the current distribution of the disease is largely dependent on the distribution of the principal sand fly vectors, which in turn are determined by climatic and environmental factors. Epidemics are often associated with increases in temperature and heavy rainfall. Endemic zones cover the countries of Ethiopia, Kenya, Sudan, Uganda, Somalia, Namibia, and all the countries in northern Africa and the sub-Saharan savanna, causing an estimated 9,000 deaths per annum.

Waterborne and Food-borne Diseases. Exposure to waterborne and food-borne pathogens can occur via drinking water (associated with fecal contamination), seafood (due to natural microbial hazards, toxins, or wastewater disposal), or fresh produce (irrigated or processed with contaminated water). Climate influences the transport and dissemination of these microbial agents through rainfall and runoff, and the survival and/or growth through such factors as temperature.

Cholera is caused by the infectious bacterium *V. cholerae*. Primarily a waterborne disease, cholera is an epidemic that may be enhanced by secondary transmission. In Africa, cholera is the fourth most important infectious disease both in terms of morbidity and mortality. More than 80 percent of the total cholera cases worldwide occur in the continent. Since the 1990s, epidemics have been reported in Djibouti, the Horn of Africa, and Mozambique. In 2002, case fatality ranged from 0.2 percent in South Africa to 11.78 percent in Mali of reported infections. The death rate is highest among children between two and four years of age. The transmission of many diarrheal diseases shows strong seasonal variation that may be associated with rains and flooding that occur during ENSO. In Africa, epidemics are associated with seasonal increases in sea surface temperature and excessive rainfall. However, sanitation and human behavior are probably more important determining factors. With increased sea-surface temperatures as projected by most climate models, it is likely that there may be an increase in cholera epidemics, particularly in Africa where the relative weakness in disease surveillance and reporting systems hampers detection and control of cholera epidemics.

Schistosomiasis (bilharzias) is a waterborne disease caused by a trematode flatworm that requires an intermediate snail host. Most infections occur in childhood. Temperatures and land use largely determine the distribution of schistosomiasis in Africa. The disease is common throughout sub-Saharan Africa, the Nile River Basin, and in Madagascar. Studies in the early twenty-first century, however, show that the distribution of the disease may be increasing mainly because of the expansion of irrigation projects and population movements.

Airborne and Heat-Related Diseases. Meningococcal meningitis is an airborne bacterial disease and more than 425 meningitis epidemics have been documented in Africa since the mid-nineteenth century. A meningitis epidemic hits West Africa every year, affecting 25,000 to 200,000 people, particularly children. The endemic zone, popularly referred to as the meningitis belt, covers the Sahel and south of this region and extends from northern Uganda and the eastern part of Democratic Republic of the Congo, through the Great Lakes and the Rift Valley regions to Malawi and northeastern

Mozambique, and from northeastern Mozambique west and south to include other parts of southern Africa. These are areas with 12–43 inches of mean annual rainfall. Epidemics have been rarely reported from the humid forested or coastal regions, even when neighboring areas are severely affected. These epidemics show a characteristic association with season. They normally start early in the dry season, build to a peak at the hottest and driest time of the year, and then abate rapidly with the onset of the rains. The most important climatic factors associated with meningitis epidemics are increase in temperature, wind speed, and low humidity.

Influenza is caused by a range of viral pathogens, directly transmitted between humans. Weather and climate could also affect health through exposures to biologic agents, including aeroallergens and microbiologic agents. For example, many allergies exhibit a seasonal pattern, reflecting pollen releases and levels in the air. This seasonality suggests that climate variability and weather may play a role in the amount and timing of such releases and consequent health outcomes. Influenza epidemics in Africa normally occur during the cold season and are thus associated with lower temperatures.

Heat stroke is often caused by heat waves, which are sporadic but recurrent in many parts of Africa. Elevated temperatures during summer months, particularly in Africa's drylands, are associated with excess morbidity and mortality. Exposure to extreme and prolonged heat may lead to heatstroke, a condition characterized by a body temperature of 105 degrees Fahrenheit or higher, and altered mental status. In 2006 at least sixty people were reported to have died of heat stroke within a week in the northeastern city of Maiduguri in Nigeria. This resulted from an intense heat wave, with temperatures of between 131 and 140 degrees Fahrenheit in the area.

Other Climate-Related Diseases. Malnutrition is also related to climate. About 200 million people on the continent are undernourished, and the number is expected to increase by almost 20 percent from the beginning of the twenty-first century. In more than a dozen African countries, the rate of undernourishment is above 40 percent. The result is that more than one-third of African children are stunted in their growth and must face a range of physical and cognitive challenges not faced by their better-fed peers. It is estimated that malnutrition is the major risk factor underlying more than 28 percent of all deaths in Africa (some 2.9 million deaths annually). For Africa, the continuing human costs of inadequate food and nutrition are enormous. International efforts to address this and other developmental problems in the developing countries led to the declaration of the Millennium Development Goals in 2000. Malnutrition is directly affected by food availability, food access, and food utilization. Climate variability, such as periods of drought and flood, directly or indirectly affect all three components. Recent models estimate that by the 2050s, an additional 12 million people in the continent could be at risk from hunger as a result of falling crop yields.

Yaws is caused by a *Treponema pertenue*, a microbe that is temperature and humidity dependent. The disease is limited to the wet and humid coast of western Africa, and has been largely eradicated through a World Health Organization campaign to give penicillin to its victims. A similar organism is responsible for non-venereal syphilis, a sickness that causes skin and bone lesions; the outbreaks are distributed in the borders of the Sudan savanna in western Africa. During the prolonged absolute dry season, the lesions on affected people heal or shrink.

CLIMATE-RELATED LIVESTOCK DISEASES

Whereas some of the diseases discussed above, such as Trypanosomiasis and Rift Valley Fever, impact both humans and livestock, some climate-sensitive diseases affect only livestock. Livestock is an important component of Africa's economy, contributing significantly to its GDP, as well as playing a major role in achieving food security. The following are some climate-influenced diseases that affect livestock in Africa.

Peste des Petits Ruminants (PPR) is an acute, contagious, viral disease of small ruminants, especially goats (which are of great economic importance in many parts of Africa). The sickness is transmitted mostly by aerosol droplets between animals in close contact. However, the appearance of clinical PPR is often associated with the onset of the rainy season or dry cold periods, a pattern that may be related to viral survival. It is estimated that climate change could encourage the stocking of small ruminants rather than large animals, and this may imply an increase in PPR to regions that are currently risk-free.

African Horse Sickness (AHS) is a lethal infectious disease of horses caused by a virus transmitted by *Culicoides* biting midges. Large outbreaks of AHS in the Republic of South Africa over the last 200 years are associated with the combination of drought and heavy rainfall brought about by the warm phase of the ENSO.

Other diseases transmitted by tsetse flies and by ticks, such as anaplasmosis, babesiosis, and East Coast fever, impose a tremendous burden on African livestock. Ticks, as ectoparasites, are a further direct burden. Many aspects of the vectors' life cycles are sensitive to climate, and spatial distributions.

See also **Climate; Desertification, Modern; Ecosystems; Healing and Health Care: Hospitals and Clinics; Kalahari Desert; Sahara Desert.**

BIBLIOGRAPHY

Baylis, Matthew, and Andrew Githeko. "The Effects of Climate Change on Infectious Diseases of Animals." *Foresight: Preparing for the Future.* London: Office of Science and Innovation, 2006.

Benson, Todd. *Africa's Food and Nutrition Security Situation. Where Are We and How Did We Get Here?* Washington, DC: International Food Policy Research Institute, 2004.

Hulme, Mike, et al. "Global Warming and African Climate Change." In *Climate Change and Africa*, ed. Pak Sum Low. Cambridge, U.K.: Cambridge University Press, 2005.

Indeje, Matayo, et al. "Predictability of the Normalized Difference Vegetation Index in Kenya and Potential Applications as an Indicator of Rift Valley Fever Outbreaks in the Greater Horn of Africa." *Journal of Climate* 19, no. 9 (2006): 1673–1687.

Malaney, Pia; Andrew Spielman; and Jeffrey Sachs. "The Malaria Gap." *American Journal of Tropical Medicine and Hygiene* 71, Suppl. 2 (2004): 141–146.

Reiter, Paul. "Climate Change and Mosquito-Borne Disease." *Environmental Health Perspectives* 109 (2001): 141–161.

Rose, Joan B., et al. "Climate Variability and Change in the United States: Potential Impacts on Water and Food-borne Diseases Caused by Microbiologic Agents." *Environmental Health Perspectives* 109 (2001): 211–220.

Wilkinson, Paul. "Climate Change and Infectious Disease in Africa and the UK." *Infectious Diseases: Preparing for the Future.* London: Office of Science and Innovation, 2006.

World Health Organization. *The World Health Report 2004.* Geneva, Switzerland: World Health Organization, 2004.

World Health Organization. *Using Climate to Predict Infectious Disease Epidemics.* Geneva, Switzerland: World Health Organization, 2005.

ANTHONY OKON NYONG

SEXUALLY TRANSMITTED

Which sexually transmitted diseases (STDs) were introduced or originated where and when in Africa is a matter of speculation and dispute. In South Africa early European historians stated that syphilis was unknown among the Africans. It might have been the increased contacts between immigrants and local people at the diamond and gold mines that first led to the spread and increase of syphilis. The Zulu, who previously had no name for the disease, called it "the disease of the white men" or "the disease of the town." The treponemal diseases, which include syphilis and yaws, probably had a common ancestor that may have originated in equatorial Africa. Certainly yaws was endemic in large parts of Africa, but transmission was by direct, nonsexual contact facilitated by crowding, poverty, and poor community hygiene and clothing. The lesions were often mistaken for syphilis by early health workers, as was another variant of syphilis: endemic syphilis, which occurs in some sub-Saharan areas and also is transmitted by direct skin lesion or saliva contact and not by sexual contact. The early descriptions of very high rates of syphilis, for example in Uganda, may well have been due to some of this confusion.

Improvements in housing and clothing, as well as the yaws campaign established by the United Nations in the 1950s, based on mass penicillin treatment, almost eradicated these endemic treponemal diseases. The endemic syphilis, called *bejel* in Arabic, was most common among the nomadic people of Chad, Niger, Mali, and Senegal but is becoming less prevalent; the endemic syphilis in some other countries has mostly disappeared. However, there has been an increase in incidence of sexually transmitted syphilis due to *Treponema pallidum*.

Gonorrhea must have a long history, although many attribute its arrival to Europeans or to the movement of people accompanying the slave trade. Both syphilis and gonorrhea usually have names in the local languages, although there is much confusion with other conditions, such as, in some areas, hernia or schistosomiasis. The various diseases causing genital ulcers or discharges are often not distinguished in local traditional medicine. Nor were they differentiated very clearly by early biomedical practitioners from Europe.

The pattern of clinical presentation of complications has of course changed since the discovery and use of effective treatment—first the arsenicals for syphilis in 1910, then penicillin and the sulfonamides in the early 1940s. Before these, cardiovascular syphilis and urethral stricture due to gonorrhea were common in the medical wards. Undiagnosed and untreated pelvic infection with blockage of the fallopian tubes and sterility also was common and probably gave rise to a band of low fertility that stretched from Gabon to Uganda; this complication is still all too common.

DEMOGRAPHY AND FREQUENCY OF STDS

In Africa, which has a broad-based population pyramid, a high proportion of the population is in the age groups most affected by sexually transmitted disease: men twenty to thirty years old and women fifteen to twenty-five years old. In most countries in Africa the majority (80%) of the population is rural, but there is an increasing rate of urbanization. The urban areas grow rapidly from an influx, initially of men seeking employment; this leads to an imbalance of the sexes, with younger men outnumbering women, thus setting the stage for prostitution and the creation of a reservoir of a small number of infected women infecting a larger number of men. In urban clinics a majority of male STD patients name prostitutes as their source of infection, and men constitute the majority of diagnosed patients.

The level of STD infection in a country is usually estimated by incidence (new cases per year) and prevalence (number of cases at a given point or period of time). Exact information is patchy, often questionable, and most often from urban clinics.

Comparable estimates over long periods of time are seldom available. However, it is evident that STDs are hyperendemic in many countries, with varying percentages of pregnant women having serological evidence of syphilis (4–20%) and bacteriological evidence of gonorrhea (5–20%) and trichomoniasis (10–14%). Clinic rates are high for syphilis and gonorrhea, and rates per 100,000 are many times those seen in Europe or America. Prevalence in rural areas is also high: 9 percent for gonorrhea in Teso men in Uganda and 18 percent in women. In Zambia STDs are the third most frequent reason for visiting a clinic and can rank with malaria as one of the major public health problems.

MOVEMENT AND MIGRATION

Some of the early studies of migrant labor and family health in South Africa pinpointed migrant labor and population movement to towns as an important factor in the increasing incidence and prevalence of syphilis. The movement of armies, cross-border trade of smugglers and petty traders, and the movement of truck drivers in relation to the spread of HIV have been investigated; these movements existed decades earlier and were related to the spread of all STDs.

Movement also occurs at specific times: town workers return to their home villages on the weekends, holiday makers congregate at coastal towns or resorts at certain times or seasons, college students return home for vacations. People move from towns to rural areas for funerals and ceremonies and celebrations. There are records of increased STD incidence related to these movements and times.

There are social and psychological aspects to movement and migration—moving to town is often movement away from relatives and pressures for conformity. The return home of migrant mine workers with money to spare calls for relaxation and beer drinking.

WOMEN AND CHILDREN

The diagnosis of STDs is much easier in men, who usually present for treatment to medical practitioners (including traditional ones) with the early, more identifiable signs and symptoms. In women diagnosis is more difficult for several reasons and often delayed until complications further obscure the diagnosis. The initial sores may not be visible externally; discharge may not be regarded as abnormal; modesty and fear of ridicule, stigma, and rejection may prevent seeking treatment. Often women present with secondary syphilis, with latent syphilis detected during routine blood testing in pregnancy, or with acute and chronic pelvic infections from gonorrhea or chlamydia. This pattern is common throughout Africa in both urban and rural areas. Use of traditional healers often leads to further delays before obtaining effective antibiotic treatment from a clinic.

STDs in pregnant women have grave consequences for infants. Conjunctivitis of the newborn due to gonorrhea or chlamydia infection can lead to blindness, and these two infections can also produce respiratory complications. Congenital syphilis is all too common, with a rate of up to 4–10 per 1,000 live births in some urban areas. Unfortunately, occurrence of these preventable conditions often is not reported. The frequency of STD in the mother being transmitted to the fetus or newborn is being made more evident by the human immunodeficiency virus (HIV).

In many African societies women have a period of postpartum sexual abstinence while breastfeeding. A husband sometimes pursues extramarital sex during this period and acquires STD. The problems of severe complications of acute pelvic inflammation in women and of infections of their infants are episodic, but they can generate lifelong problems. Scarring of the fallopian tubes may lead to ectopic pregnancy, which can be fatal, or cause sterility, a condition with very serious social implications in a society that values fecundity. A sterile woman is often divorced or has no status, and the social and emotional consequences are disastrous for her.

The problems for women and children need to be stressed because they are rooted in the position of women in society and their lack of power to negotiate safer sexual activity. In many countries women are left in rural areas while husbands seek work in towns—and sometimes return with STD. Rural women are poor and can seldom raise funds for treatment. In the early 2000s women increasingly go to towns—often to periurban informal settlements where many set up woman-headed households. Whether the setting is urban or rural,

women who are poor and have less education may have few options for earning a living and may be forced to resort to prostitution or beer brewing.

Several studies have shown that married women are at risk of STD from their husbands. In Ethiopia women married to their first and only sexual partners had high rates of STD: gonorrhea, 40 percent; chlamydia, 54 percent; syphilis, 19 percent (serology); herpes, 33 percent; chanroid, 13 percent; and pelvic inflammatory disease, 47 percent—levels approximately half those in prostitutes, from whom the infections possibly were acquired by the husbands.

STD AND COMMERCIAL AND TRANSACTIONAL SEX

In Africa commercial sex is an important factor in the transmission of STD. Commercial sex workers operate in many settings: urban streets, bars and guest houses, brothels, discos, customers' rooms. The poorer ones often have many partners per twenty-four hours at low prices, whereas the more elite prostitutes cater to fewer, more wealthy clients—often in hotels. Very high rates of all sexually transmitted diseases (including HIV) are found in sex workers with many clients because even if they have medical checks and treatment, they are infrequent and reinfection is likely. With the fear of AIDS, many men now seek out younger and younger girls in the anticipation that they will not be infected. Street children, with the number of girls increasing in the larger cities, are now involved in sex work.

Prostitution is the only alternative to destitution for many women, but there are numerous factors leading to this activity: teenage pregnancy, lack of school fees, abandonment by a husband, divorce. In particular localities, the client availability is also a factor—the truck stops and army bases provide a steady flow of customers.

However, in a 1992 study of prostitutes and their clients in the Gambia, a differing picture emerges of prostitutes. They have a higher-than-average standard of living, require use of condoms (80%), are often mobile, and have clients of low educational and occupational status.

In rural and urban areas transactional sex is also common; immediate financial remuneration is not demanded, but sex is provided for other rewards— a job, a raise in monthly pay, a new dress, payment of rent, a good time with drinks and dancing. This type of relationship can operate between sexual partners at all levels of society, from university students to laborers. Many concubines or mistresses fall into this category.

The wide variety of sexual and marital relationships in the urban situation in Kampala and its suburbs was well described by Aidan Southall and Peter Gutkind in their 1957 study. Broken marriages (34% of the married population), "free marriages," occasional lovers, concubines and prostitutes, the mix of ethnic affiliations and occupations, the overcrowding, and the continuing social change were in evidence. The relationship of these factors to STD can be constructed.

BELIEFS AND TRADITIONAL PRACTITIONERS

Traditional healers are available in almost every village or urban area, and there are several branches of the art. The term "traditional practitioners" is preferred in South Africa because it embraces traditional birth attendants and traditional surgeons or circumcisers. All of the categories, whether they are diviners diagnosing through ancestral spirits, herbalists, midwives, surgeons, or specialists in particular diseases, see large numbers of patients with STDs.

Some STDs are considered bewitchments—for example, the Xhosa believe pubic lice are a bewitchment responding only to traditional medicine. Some are considered "African diseases" responding best to herbs. The beliefs about causes of STD and the reliance on traditional healers are closely linked: the Swazi (like many other African peoples) consider diseases transmitted by sexual intercourse as being Swazi illnesses best treated by their own healers. This is because the underlying beliefs are that a man or husband has treated a woman with a Swazi medicine to ensure fidelity, and that if she has sex with a man other than her husband, she will transmit a disease. Other beliefs are that certain Swazi taboos were not observed, thus leading to disease. From such beliefs, on which the traditional healer bases his diagnosis and treatment, it is clear that a clinic doctor or nurse might not be considered to have the correct local treatment or the correct insight into social relationships. Unfortunately, there is no evidence that traditional treatment is effective, considering the increasing rates of infection.

A large proportion of persons with STDs seek traditional cures either initially or after failure of Western medicine—which has become all too frequent with resistance of gonorrhea and chlamydia to commonly available drugs. When traditional healers publish or display advertisements of their skills and remedies, invariably they include STDs and sterility—using local traditional terms or biomedical terms.

In some countries, such as Zimbabwe and Malawi, traditional birth attendants have been trained to send pregnant women to a clinic to get immunization against tetanus and at the same time to have blood taken for serology for syphilis. These birth attendants are at risk for contracting infections, including HIV, because they rarely use gloves.

SEXUALITY AND BEHAVIOR

Beginning in the 1940s, anthropologists researched many aspects of many communities in Africa, but very little was written about the most intimate and private aspect of behavior: sexuality and sexual practices. Kinship relationships and patterns of marriage were recorded, often in great detail, but it was only with the arrival of AIDS that social scientists started to investigate sexual behavior in Africa. Sexual activity in many parts of Africa starts early, and life skills or sexuality education must start in primary school if HIV and STD transmission is to be prevented. Many social scientists have emphasized the importance of the powerless, subordinate position of women and the dominance of men as decision makers as factors in the transmission of STD. This is because women cannot negotiate the use of a condom and men can expect their sexual demands to be met in many situations. For example, a young girl might have difficulty refusing the sexual advances of an older man. Newly circumcised youths, now regarded as men, often feel empowered to test their sexual performance.

One of the features of family life in most areas of Africa is the extreme reluctance to discuss sexual matters. Reference to the sexual organs is taboo between parents and children, so that sexual knowledge and behavior are learned in peer groups rather than within the family. Knowledge of STDs and their prevention may thus be quite limited, especially among girls.

In some societies age of marriage is a factor. Men get married much later than women, having first to establish a home, a job, or their herd of cattle—but this gives them more time for extramarital sex and the acquisition of STD. In societies where there is polygyny, the difference of ages between husband and wives may lead to extramarital relationships, and once STD is introduced, it can circulate within the family.

Although it seems generally acknowledged that practices other than conventional heterosexual intercourse are less common in Africa (than, for example, in Europe or America), it has become evident through some detailed behavioral research that heterosexual oral and anal sex is not unknown and that homosexuality and bisexuality also exist in many societies—but are concealed or channeled in specific settings.

Much of the contemporary research has evaluated the use of condoms; it is clear that they are not liked by most men and that health workers and women have difficulty in getting men to accept their use. In some areas of Africa (the Gambia; Nigeria; and Nairobi, Kenya) prostitutes have been successful in advocating their use and even in getting men to accept inspection for STD before use of the condom. In northern Tanzania condoms, which are used, are distributed on the pillows of beds in guest houses by the women workers.

THE DISEASES

The lack of adequate laboratory facilities and the reliance in clinics and health centers on nurses and medical assistants with less clinical training than doctors necessitated a new approach to management of the many sexually transmitted diseases. Another limitation in the average clinic in Africa has been the large number of patients—hence short consultation times—and the lack of effective drugs. When it became clear that diseases often occurred together and that clinical features were not specific, it was apparent a new form of management was needed. The World Health Organization has helped to establish a "syndromic approach" to the diagnosis and management of STD in most countries. In this approach, based on epidemiological evidence (and sensitivity to drugs), the most effective combination of drugs is used to cover all the diseases included in the syndrome. For example, the syndrome "genital

ulcer" can include syphilis and chancroid, so management covers both; similarly, "urethral discharge" can include gonorrhea and chlamydia, so treatment should cover both. The syndromes and management have been refined into algorithms and wall charts, and staffs have been trained to deal with genital ulcer, urethral discharge, vaginal discharge, acute lower abdominal pain, acute scrotal swelling, conjunctivitis in the newborn, and swelling of the inguinal glands.

Syphilis, one of the best-known and readily treatable conditions, is still a major and, in many areas, an increasing problem. Its frequency could be reflected in incidence rates—the number of new cases in a particular period—but with the syndromic approach, primary syphilis would not always be distinguished from other forms of genital ulcer. The incidence of other stages—for example, secondary and tertiary syphilis—is essentially available only from clinics and hospitals with good laboratory facilities.

Chancroid, the other infection frequently causing genital ulceration, is sometimes claimed to be more common in uncircumcised men, and it is often overlooked in women. Its association with painful abscesses in the lymph glands in the groin is a feature distinguished by some communities. The sensitivity to antibiotics changes, and clinics do not always have the most effective drugs. The newer drugs are expensive and liable to theft if there is poor control or mismanagement.

Urethral and vaginal discharges are the most common symptoms of STD in Africa, but accurate community-based figures are difficult to obtain because many patients go to several traditional healers or private practitioners. Failure of treatment means that patients move around, seeking a cure. Symptomless infections are frequent, so there is constant transmission by people who have no complaints. However, even those with symptoms do not always refrain from sexual activity.

Many of the less documented STDs are very widespread. Pubic lice, for example, are common but are not easy to see on a dark skin (although the nits and scratching are more prominent). Genital herpes with recurrent episodes is also common, as is trichomoniasis infection. Papilloma virus infection, now linked with cervical and penile cancer, is common but has not yet become feared.

STD RESEARCH IN AFRICA

Much of the early STD research was descriptive and often based on institutional care—to analyze the personal, time, and place variables of patients seeking treatment. As penicillin resistance of gonococci became apparent, research entered a phase of properly controlled treatment trials. In some countries, such as Uganda, community-based surveys were undertaken to determine the epidemiology of STD. This research had to be multidisciplinary with laboratory, clinical, and demographic aspects combined. In these surveys the importance of symptomless infections first became evident. The ethical aspects of surveys and informed consent for taking specimens have become important.

With the advent of AIDS and the realization of the critical importance of STDs in facilitating HIV transmission, research has become very sophisticated with laboratory, clinical, sociological, anthropological, psychological, and statistical teamwork.

Thomas Barton's 1991 annotated bibliography of sexuality and health in sub-Saharan Africa includes 2,065 references gleaned by extensive library and database consultation. In the introduction the author brings out some of the limitations of scope, the deficiencies in the literature, and unreliability of much of the statistics. This single article on STD in Africa has little hope of showing either the variety or the broad patterns of factors related to the distribution, determinants, deterrents, and consequences of these diseases in the varied societies of a continent. The available research does, however, show that the long-existing, widespread, and increasing epidemic of STD and its social, behavioral, and economic causes set the stage for the rapid spread of the HIV.

STDs have been an underestimated and growing problem of epidemic proportions over a long period. It has taken the arrival of HIV/AIDS as a new, lethal sexually transmitted condition to arouse administrative action; STDs have moved from being dealt with as a clinical service activity to being part of a national control program linked with HIV/AIDS. The need for STDs to be included in maternal and child health and reproductive health programs is also evident.

STDs, previously of concern largely to clinicians and epidemiologists, are a health problem requiring the skills of many disciplines, the resources of many sectors, and effective communication if control is to be accomplished. Social scientists, pharmacists, health economists, teachers, social workers, communication specialists, and parents are now becoming involved.

The greatest difficulties of control are to be found in poorer communities, such as the periurban informal settlements and the remote rural villages. It is here that effective treatment is less accessible or poorly used while the educational, social, and economic basic causal factors are operating.

See also **Children and Childhood: Infancy and Early Development; Healing and Health Care; Prostitution; Sexual Behavior; United Nations.**

BIBLIOGRAPHY

Antal, George M. "The Epidemiology of Sexually Transmitted Diseases in the Tropics." *Clinical Tropical Medicine and Communicable Diseases* 2, no. 1 (1987): 1–16.

Arya, O. P.; A. O. Osoba; and F. J. Bennett. "Epidemiology of Sexually Transmitted Diseases." In *Tropical Venereology*. 2nd edition. Edinburgh: Churchill Livingstone, 1988.

Barton, Thomas George. *Sexuality and Health in Sub-Saharan Africa: An Annotated Bibliography*. Nairobi, Kenya: African Medical and Research Foundation, 1991.

Duncan, M. E., et al. "A Socioeconomic, Clinical, and Serological Study in an African City of Prostitutes and Women Still Married to Their First Husband." *Social Science and Medicine* 39, no. 3 (1994): 323–333.

Green, Edward C. "Sexually Transmitted Diseases, Ethnomedicine, and Health Policy in Africa." *Social Science and Medicine* 35, no. 2 (1992): 121–130.

Parry, E. H. O., ed. "Sexually Transmitted Diseases." In *Principles of Medicine in Africa*. 2nd edition. Oxford: Oxford University Press, 1984.

Pickering, H., et al. "Prostitutes and Their Clients: A Gambia Study." *Social Science and Medicine* 34, no. 1 (1992): 75–88.

Southall, Aidan W., and Peter C. W. Gutkind. *Townsmen in the Making: Kampala and Its Suburbs*. 2nd edition. Kampala, Uganda: East African Institute of Social Research, 1957.

F. JOHN BENNETT

INDUSTRIAL

Industrial development in Africa, as in Europe and America, has carried with it significant health costs. These costs are normally defined by occupational health and safety experts in terms of the direct health consequences of worker exposure to specific hazardous processes, materials, or environmental conditions associated with the work place. A more comprehensive measurement of industrial health costs, however, would also include an assessment of the impact of industrial development and the creation of an industrial work force on ecological relationships, environmental conditions, and patterns of sickness and health in the areas surrounding industrial centers. The environmental destruction caused by oil drilling in large regions of the Niger Delta is evidence of this indirect cost.

This entry reviews the direct costs of industrial production associated with mining, large-scale agriculture, and manufacturing industries. The health costs of small-scale farming, herding, and fishing, as well as informal industries, while real, are not examined. In addition, the entry focuses on workers in general and does not distinguish between male and female workers. Female workers, however, are often at greater risk due to their employment in low-skill, seasonal, and undercapitalized industries. Finally, it must be noted that the occupational health risks of workers in sub-Saharan Africa often go unreported for these reasons:

1. They often result from exposure to substances that only produce symptoms years after exposure;

2. Workers who retire to rural homes seldom have access to health services capable of diagnosing such conditions;

3. Industrial health monitoring, legislation, and enforcement are underdeveloped;

4. Countries dependent on foreign capital to industrialize are hesitant to impose tight controls on industries for fear of reducing industry profits and willingness to invest;

5. Surveillance responsibilities are frequently left to the companies themselves. While large industries often employ medical personnel to treat their workers, they are seldom trained in occupational health. Smaller industries, moreover, seldom have the resources to provide medical care and therefore do not monitor their employee's health. These conditions have produced a backlog of undiagnosed industrial disease. For example, a 2002 survey of retired mine workers in the

Transkei region of South Africa revealed that 64 percent suffered from tuberculosis with or without silicosis. Few of these had been previously diagnosed or compensated. Similar results were reported for ex-mine workers in neighboring Botswana.

MINING

The health costs of industrial employment in mining industries, and particularly the gold mining industry in southern Africa, have been well documented. Aside from industrial accidents, mine workers have been subject to a wide range of industrial diseases. Lack of ventilation and excessive dust produced by machine drills and blasting resulted in high levels of silicosis among both black and white gold miners during the early years of this century. Black workers also suffered from a range of infectious diseases, including tuberculosis, pneumonia, hookworm, typhoid, and meningitis, due to the poor conditions under which they were forced to work and live. Nutritional problems, including scurvy, and heat stroke also threatened black workers' health.

The worst of the conditions affecting the health of black miners were largely eliminated by the 1950s. Yet accidents have continued to occur. Between 1991 and 2001, the gold mines claimed 3,496 lives in accidents. Black workers still suffered tuberculosis rates ranging from eleven to twenty-four hundred cases per one hundred thousand workers per year in the late 1990s. Asbestos miners in southern Africa suffer from high levels of asbestosis, mesothelioma, and lung cancer. The asbestos industry was largely unregulated for most of the twentieth century and relied heavily on women and child labor until the 1980s. The health effects of asbestos mining have not been limited to workers, but spread to the worker's families who were exposed to the dust which coated the worker's clothing.

AGRICULTURE

Irrigation agriculture, introduced in many parts of Africa after World War II, produced simplified ecosystems in which parasites and other disease vectors achieved high densities. When combined with inadequate sanitation, irrigation projects contributed to high rates of schistosomiasis among irrigation workers and their families. Similarly, the expansion of rice-growing areas in western Kenya and cocoa areas in Ghana have created new breeding zones for *Anopheles gambiae* mosquitoes and altered the epidemiology of malaria. Recognition of the impact of large-scale irrigation on disease ecologies encouraged international donor agencies, such as the U.S. Agency for International Development (USAID) and the World Bank, to evaluate the environmental impact of their funded projects. Yet agriculture workers, many of whom are women, frequently also suffer from other conditions associated with long working hours, low wages, lack of protective clothing, inadequate housing and sanitation, and unclean water supplies. Eighty-one percent of sugar workers surveyed in Kwazulu, South Africa in 1993 reported having suffered an acute traumatic injury.

Farm workers are also exposed to toxic substances, including fertilizers and pesticides. Pesticide use has increased dramatically in Africa since the 1990s, reflecting increased levels of pesticide resistance and the need for more frequent spraying. Vegetable farmers in Bénin are spraying their cabbages twelve to twenty times a season, compared with only three sprays in the mid-1990s. Several multinational companies that operate plantations in Africa also produce pesticides. Faced with restrictions on the use of toxic products in the United States and Europe, these companies sell their banned pesticides to their African projects.

MANUFACTURING

Industrial accidents are the most widely reported direct health cost of manufacturing employment. Respiratory illnesses are the most frequently reported nonaccident problems. The widespread development of textile industries in Africa following World War II and the lack of enforcement of industrial health regulations in these plants made byssinosis (which results from inhalation of vegetable dust) a common respiratory problem. Forty-five percent of textile workers surveyed in the mid-1990s in southwest Ethiopia suffered from byssinosis.

Respiratory problems resulting from industrial exposure to asbestos occur in many nonmining contexts. Moreover, the dry nature of many manufacturing processes (e.g., milling) and the more concentrated and refined nature of asbestos products make exposure to asbestos in manufacturing more dangerous than in mining. The number of those exposed while mixing and using insulation compounds, doing building work, working with asbestos textiles, repairing brakes and clutches, and so forth, is difficult to determine.

Industrial workers in Africa are also exposed to a long list of chemicals, metals, and gases. One of the most pervasive problems is lead poisoning, especially prevalent in lead acid battery factories. Other substances, which are not in themselves toxic, can, under conditions of industrial employment, be unhealthy. For example, prolonged exposure to pineapple juice, such as occurs among female canning factory workers in Swaziland, can lead to skin ulceration.

The adverse working conditions in African factories are not all related to exposure to toxic materials. As in mining and agriculture, long hours, lack of sanitation facilities, low pay rates, absence of protective clothing, and insecurity of employment take a heavy toll on both the physical and mental well-being of the factory worker and may indirectly contribute to industrial accidents.

See also **Healing and Health Care; Labor: Industrial and Mining; Metals and Minerals; Production Strategies; World Bank.**

BIBLIOGRAPHY

Livingston, Julie. *Debility and Moral Imagination in Botswana.* Bloomington: Indiana University Press, 2005.

Loewensen, Rene. *Modern Plantation Agriculture, Corporate Wealth and Labour Squalor.* London: Zed Books, 1992.

McCulloch, Jock. *Asbestos Blues: Labor, Capital, Physicians, and the State in South Africa.* Oxford: James Curry, 2002.

Packard, Randall. "Workplace, Health and Disease in Sub-Saharan Africa." *Social Science and Medicine* 28, no. 5 (1989): 475–496.

Packard, Randall. *White Plague, Black Labor: Tuberculosis and the Political Economy of Health and Disease in South Africa.* Berkeley: University of California Press, 1989.

RANDALL M. PACKARD

HIV/AIDS, MEDICAL ASPECTS

Scientists discovered the global epidemic (pandemic) known as acquired immunodeficiency syndrome (AIDS) in 1981. Within its first decade, researchers and clinicians predominantly from industrialized countries and regions (e.g., the United Kingdom, the United States, and Western Europe) collaborated on research to identify the populations most at risk for developing the numerous infections and malignancies characteristic of this disease syndrome of impaired cellular immunity. The opportunistic infections (OIs, as they take advantage of a weakened immune system) and cancers comprising AIDS were occurring in individuals in the absence of known immunosuppressive causes (e.g., prior chemotherapy). Despite contentious debate at times, researchers have maintained a near-unanimous consensus since the mid-1980s that infection with a retrovirus, subsequently referred to as the human immunodeficiency virus (HIV), is the principal cause of the disease.

By the 1990s AIDS had become "the most studied disease in human history" (Webb 1997, 1); giving rise to a veritable industry of specialized healthcare, HIV/AIDS-specific journals, national and international conferences, and global activism. Since the discovery of AIDS, more than 25 million people have reportedly died of the disease, mortality equivalent to that of the devastating worldwide Spanish flu epidemic of 1918–1920. According to the Joint United Nations Program on HIV/AIDS (UNAIDS), "an estimated 33.4 million–46.0 million people worldwide were living with the HIV at the end of 2005" (2006, 8).

BIOLOGY AND PATHOLOGY OF HIV/AIDS

In June 1981 the U.S. Centers for Disease Control (CDC) received a physician's report of a handful of men in California with profound immune deficiency and in advanced stages of disease with rare cancers and infections. This report catalyzed a search for additional patients with similar clinical characteristics in large cities throughout the United States, the United Kingdom, and European countries. Within just a few years international researchers had identified major populations ("risk groups" initially included homosexual men, hemophiliacs, heroin addicts of injection drug users, and Haitians) that appeared to be at highest risk for developing the disease syndrome of AIDS. As research on the disease evolved over time, and new AIDS cases were discovered among transfusion recipients, as well as heterosexual partners

and/or infants of the previously identified risk groups, research quickened on finding a viral cause of the disease.

Soon after 1983–1984, scientific consensus coalesced around a particular retrovirus (HTLV-III, LAV, or ARV, later renamed HIV) as the likely infectious cause of AIDS. By 1985, when a blood test to detect antibodies to the new retrovirus became widely available, scientists redefined transmission risk factors for the disease as the exposure to blood or body fluids from an individual with viral antibodies, or from an antibody-positive mother to her child ("vertical," or mother to child transmission, MTCT). Shortly thereafter, this retrovirus was officially renamed HIV, and in 1987 France and the United States signed an international treaty to resolve financial disputes pertaining to diagnostic tests and assign credit for discovery of the virus (Grmek 1990).

For industrialized countries in the West, the availability of an HIV-antibody or "screening" test rapidly enabled transfusion blood products to be tested and discarded if they showed evidence of the virus; provided additional evidence for advocating the use of condoms and sterile needles to interrupt transmission during sex or injection use respectively; and spurred research on anti-retroviral drugs (ARVs). The presence of HIV antibodies in the blood or body fluids of the majority of AIDS cases who have been tested also accelerated, and continues to sustain, research on ARVs, barrier methods to prevent HIV infection (such as male and female condoms, microbicides), and research and development on an HIV vaccine (not yet developed as of 2006).

BIOLOGY OF HIV/AIDS

There are two major types of the Human Immunodeficiency Virus, HIV-1 and HIV-2. This article deals solely with the retrovirus HIV-1 (abbreviated throughout this text as HIV), which has spread globally to almost every country in the world, and is considered to be the "etiologic (causal) agent" of the AIDS pandemic. (HIV-2 is largely geographically contained within the region of western Africa, and has yet to be associated with widespread human morbidity or mortality.)

Despite its relatively simple genetic structure, HIV's "adaptability" and mutability means that different strains of the virus can arise from within an HIV-infected person, a factor that has also frustrated attempts to find consistently effective antiretroviral (ARV) treatment regimens, as long-term treatment with ARVs can be subject to problems of drug "resistance" or failure. Since the late 1990s, combinations of ARVs have been developed for treating AIDS, and the opportunistic infections (OIs) associated with the disease. These treatments are commonly referred to as highly active antiretroviral therapy (HAART), and as of 2006 there are twenty-nine approved pharmaceutical therapies for HIV/AIDS available for use in industrialized countries (their use is limited in many developing countries).

"Currently, HIV-1 viruses fall into three separate groups, the main group (M), the outlier group (O), and the non-M/non-O group (N). Viruses in the M group cause the vast majority of HIV-1 infections in the world" (Essex et al. 2002, 268), and this group contains nine genetically distinct subtypes (or "clades": A-K). While HIV-1 type B is dominant in the Americas and Europe, there are at least five known subtypes present on the African continent, and nearly as many present in India; viruses can also combine into hybrid types. This genetic diversity therefore complicates research and development on effective drug therapies and/or a vaccine, as it lends geographically distinct epidemiological profiles for the epidemic in different regions (Mayer and Pizer 2005, 21–22).

PATHOLOGY OF HIV/AIDS

Because AIDS is characterized by a lengthy incubation period, the course of the disease has been divided into various stages. The Initial Phase is marked by infection with HIV-1. Phase II is characterized by a "window" period when an individual host is HIV infected but has not yet produced HIV antibodies that can be detected in current laboratory tests (i.e., the host does not test HIV-positive). During Phase III a "latent" period ensues, during which an individual now tests positive for HIV-1 antibodies (i.e., is HIV-positive), but is largely asymptomatic (few overt clinical signs of the disease AIDS). During this period, which can reportedly last from eight to fifteen years (median ten years' incubation from HIV infection to AIDS in the West), the HIV-positive host can transmit the virus in blood or body fluids, or while giving birth or breastfeeding a child.

Scientists do not completely understand the mechanism(s) by which HIV-1 causes AIDS. However, the virus is highly trophic for (attracted specifically to) critical cells of a host's immune system and is believed to cause AIDS by impairing the host's immune response to disease agents and/or by killing key cells of the immune system such as CD4 t-helper cells, (which help to control infections), or other hypothesized mechanisms.

In the absence of a "cure" for the disease, the last stage of AIDS is manifest when a person develops one or many clinical signs of the disease, which can include: a low CD4 t-cell count; the emergence of rare cancers (Kaposi's sarcoma/KS) or pneumonias (*Pneumocystis carinii* pneumonia/PCP); reactivation of latent infections, such as tuberculosis (TB) or herpes; the acquisition of new infections due to lower host immunity (cryptosporidium, thrush); or the loss of significant weight ("wasting" or "slim disease").

The prevalence, type, and number of OIs and malignancies that define an AIDS diagnosis has changed since the early 1980s, and can differ by the geographic location (place), sex, and age of the AIDS case (e.g., pediatric AIDS or PAIDS differs from adult AIDS), as well as by the route of exposure to HIV/AIDS (transmission "risk factors"). In industrialized regions such as the United Kingdom, the United States, and Europe, AIDS is defined as a disease syndrome comprising more than twenty different OIs or malignancies, and/or a low CD4 t-cell count in the presence of a positive HIV-antibody test.

In contrast, in some low-resource countries in Asia or in sub-Saharan Africa (SSA), and in instances where HIV-antibody tests are not widely available, an AIDS diagnosis can be based on clinical diagnoses of "two major signs and one minor sign of AIDS, or the existence of generalized Kaposi's sarcoma" (Essex et al. 2002, 300). In settings where neither primary health care nor OI prophylaxis are widely available, for example in SSA, the most frequent infections among persons living with AIDS (PLWA) are tuberculosis, as well as high rates of co-morbidity with malaria.

GLOBAL SPREAD OF THE DISEASE

During the initial years of the epidemic, AIDS cases numbered in the thousands and were reported predominantly from major metropolitan areas of Western industrialized countries and from within the 4-H risk groups previously noted. However, as the HIV-antibody test entered into widespread use for screening populations, the disease was increasingly recognized among the heterosexual partners of persons at high risk, their children, and recipients of blood products. By the mid-1990s, "1.3 million cumulative AIDS cases had been reported from 193 countries," although the magnitude of the pandemic was assumed to be many times greater, given the unknown number of HIV infections and possible AIDS case underreporting (Quinn 1996, 99). Since the early 1990s, sub-Saharan Africa has been reported as the region with the greatest burden of the disease; however, the epidemic has great geographic heterogeneity—within nations, across regions, and throughout the African continent.

Global data on HIV/AIDS should be interpreted cautiously, as estimates of the population living with the disease are subject to constant revision, and often data from small or unrepresentative samples (e.g., urban or STD or prenatal clinics) have been inappropriately extrapolated to provide estimates of overall HIV/AIDS prevalence at the country level, especially in low-resource settings. The 2006 UNAIDS report acknowledges these methodological errors of past years, and has thus reduced HIV/AIDS prevalence data for many developing countries. Moreover, in light of limitations of the data, as well as low population rates of HIV voluntary counseling and testing (VCT) and possible urban biases for HIV testing, UNAIDS currently reports plausibility bounds (a range of minimum and maximum estimated values) for each country/region's HIV/AIDS prevalence (proportion of the adult population currently living with the disease), and HIV/AIDS incidence (new cases occurring within a specific time period, typically one year). This article retains the use of plausibility bounds for describing the epidemiology of HIV/AIDS, as estimates can range widely. In 2006 UNAIDS estimated that "[33.4 million–46.0 million] people worldwide were living with HIV at the end of 2005 ... [3.4 million–6.2 million] became newly infected with HIV, and an estimated [2.4–3.3 million] lost their lives to AIDS. Overall, the HIV incidence rate is believed to have peaked in the late 1990s and to have stabilized subsequently" (UNAIDS 2006, 6).

The global prevalence of HIV is currently estimated to be 1 percent, and has reportedly leveled off or declined throughout the world, with the exception of Eastern Europe and southern Africa (UNAIDS). However, there is great inter- and intranation variability above and below this figure: In Asia (a total of 5.7 million–12.5 million cases), more than two-thirds of all HIV cases are located in India, and China has reported 390,000–1.1 million HIV cases, the majority of the latter among injection drug users (IVDUs). The epidemic is "relatively limited" in other regions, such as Indonesia and Pakistan, and throughout the Middle East and North Africa (UNAIDS 2006, 9–10).

There are rising rates of new HIV infections in Eastern Europe and the former Soviet Union but HIV cases remain predominantly concentrated in the Russian Federation and Ukraine where IVDU is the major transmission risk factor. Throughout Latin America, there are approximately 1.2–2.4 million PLWAs; 30 percent of whom live in Brazil. This region is notable for pioneering the public health strategy of universal access to HIV/AIDS treatment and care, and has promoted the production and distribution of generic pharmaceuticals to developing nations. Outside of SSA, the Caribbean is the second most affected region in the world; HIV prevalence ranges from more than 2 to 3 percent in heavily affected countries such as Haiti and Trinidad where AIDS is reportedly the "leading cause of death among adults (15–44 years)" (UNAIDS 2006, 9). For the African continent as a whole, UNAIDS estimates HIV prevalence at approximately 6 percent (4%–7% of adult men and women between the ages of fifteen and forty-nine years are living with HIV), or six times the level of global HIV prevalence.

EPIDEMIOLOGICAL RISK FACTORS AND GEOGRAPHIC DISTRIBUTION OF HIV/AIDS IN AFRICA

In UNAIDS's annual report on the epidemic (2006), sub-Saharan Africa remains the region with the greatest global burden of HIV/AIDS. Approximately 21.6 to 27.4 million persons, or roughly two of every three persons living with HIV/AIDS in the world, reportedly reside in SSA. Across the continent however, the HIV/AIDS epidemic is characterized by great geographical heterogeneity: HIV prevalence in North Africa (excluding Sudan) remains below 0.1 percent, and some countries in West Africa (such as Senegal or Nigeria) report adult HIV prevalence in the range of 1–4 percent. In contrast, some public prenatal clinics in South Africa have reported that one-third (30%) of all women attending are living with HIV (UNAIDS 2006, citing 2004 data), with even higher HIV sero-prevalence reported among pregnant women at surveillance sites in contiguous countries, such as Botswana, Lesotho, and Swaziland.

Central, East, and southern African countries have historically reported the greatest proportion of their populations infected with HIV/AIDS, as well as the largest absolute number of HIV/AIDS cases, the greatest number of female AIDS cases, and consequently the largest number of pediatric AIDS cases in the world. In SSA, approximately 12 million children have lost one or both parents to the disease, comprising 90 percent of the world's AIDS orphans (UNAIDS).

While the epidemic appeared to be most intense in Central and East Africa during the 1990s, HIV prevalence stabilized in these regions in the late 1990s and since declined to 2 percent (Eritrea), 3 percent (Rwanda), or approximately 7 percent of the adult population (Burundi, Kenya, Uganda; UNAIDS 2006). Some of these declines in the epidemic have been driven by revisions in surveillance reporting techniques, while Kenya and Uganda may have benefited from coordinated HIV/AIDS prevention, education, and behavioral change campaigns, and/or access to ARV therapies.

Most epidemiological research on risk factors for HIV/AIDS in SSA has attributed the preponderance of infections in the region to heterosexual transmission (approximately 75–85%). MTCT transmission of HIV either perinatally and/or during breastfeeding is next in importance, with a relatively small proportion of infections attributed thus far to unsafe blood transfusions and/or unsterile needle use or IVDU. High rates of STD prevalence, numerous sexual partners, and the absence of male circumcision are also hypothesized as facilitating risk factors in regions with intense HIV/AIDS epidemics. As young women in many low-resource countries throughout SSA and Asia appear to have the greatest vulnerability for acquiring HIV/AIDS, these regions consequently have a high rate of vertical (MTCT) HIV transmission to their newborn children.

POSSIBLE RESPONSE STRATEGIES

The epidemiological profile previously described has historically led most HIV/AIDS interventions in SSA to focus largely on ABC ("Abstinence, Be Faithful, Condomize") prevention and education campaigns that focus on changing sexual behavior, and widespread Voluntary Counseling and Testing (VCT) initiatives.

Globally, research has concentrated predominantly on developing more effective ARVs, barrier methods (e.g., microbicides), and a vaccine to prevent HIV/AIDS. However, the unstable nature of HIV has defeated early optimism, and at this time "it is difficult to judge how long it will take to develop an HIV vaccine that is safe, efficacious, and practical for worldwide use" (Mayer and Pizer 2005, 162).

In the early twenty-first century, a growing number of advocates have also called for widespread distribution of affordable (or free) ARVs to treat populations with HIV/AIDS in resource-constrained countries. Advocates of this approach argue that HIV/AIDS prevention and treatment are inextricably linked in combating the epidemic, as the effective use of ARVs can reduce HIV transmission from mother to child, and may reduce sexual transmission as the probability of HIV transmission increases with higher levels of virus in blood and body fluids. In addition, ARVs can improve the quality of life for PLWAs and slow progression of the disease (thereby reducing hospital costs, maintaining household productivity, and ensuring families remain intact). Despite such advocacy however, targets for distributing ARVs established by the UNAIDS Declaration of Commitment on HIV/AIDS (2001), the Millennium Development Goals, and the "3 by 5" initiative (to treat three million PLWAs with ARVs by 2005) have not yet been met.

RESPONDING TO THE HIV/AIDS EPIDEMIC WITH STRATEGIES TO IMPROVE PUBLIC HEALTH

While environmental public health strategies have historically been the most successful interventions for preventing infectious diseases and sustainably improving the health of populations, these strategies have yet to be fully employed in global initiatives combating the HIV/AIDS epidemic. John Snow's classic epidemiological study of a cholera outbreak in London in the 1800s exemplifies such an approach, as he demonstrated that one could curtail an infectious epidemic prior to fully understanding the specific causal agent. In analogous fashion, shortly after the discovery of AIDS in the United States, grassroots activists and community-based organizations (CBO) initiated health education campaigns about safe(r) sex, seeking to change normative behaviors and expectations in populations at risk. Subsequently, activists distributed free condoms and clean needles for IVDU and advocated in earnest for their widespread availability and use, sometimes in defiance of the law or public sentiment in major cities of the industrialized world. In later years, patient-led organizations imported experimental drug therapies to treat the disease, established community-led clinical trials of promising treatments, and vigorously challenged the status quo of biomedical research, clinical trials, and pharmaceutical development.

In recent years, PLWAs and public health policymakers in Brazil, India, and South Africa have been vigorous advocates for expediting access to more affordable patented pharmaceuticals, while defending their rights to manufacture or import generic drugs. These efforts however, fall far short of coordinating a political constituency to counter systemic "structural violence," which in turn produces local and global social inequalities that create and sustain the dynamics of most infectious disease epidemics, including the HIV/AIDS epidemic. In seminal work on the epidemic in SSA and other low-resource regions by Farmer (1999), Stillwaggon (2006), and other researchers have contextualized HIV/AIDS risk behaviors by examining the structural vulnerabilities created by migrant labor systems, transactional sex relationships, and other socioeconomic dynamics.

Strategically, this research on the social production of disease, or the political ecology of epidemics, directly implicates poverty and the profound deprivation of basic needs and primary health care in low-resource countries as generative causes of HIV/AIDS. From this vantage point, AIDS is but one of several emerging or resurgent epidemics signifying a collapse of global public

health care and infrastructure in recent decades, especially profound in transition countries of the former Soviet Union and in developing countries of Asia, the Caribbean, and sub-Saharan Africa.

Analytically, multifactorial theories of disease empirically ground these theories of disease causation by providing specific evidence of discrete biological mechanisms by which intercurrent infections (or co-factors) amplify the HIV/AIDS epidemic. Epidemiological studies have demonstrated that co-factors such as STDs, malaria, worm infestations, and common deficiencies related to poverty (malnutrition, protein deficiency, and poor sanitation) degrade host immunity and/or amplify HIV infection. By identifying the additive effects of co-factors (that vary by place and population), multifactorial models of AIDS may help to explain the relative ease of HIV transmission in transition and developing countries and the striking geographical variability of the HIV/AIDS epidemic both globally and locally.

This model extends the strategic response to HIV/AIDS to include multisectoral programs to ensure basic needs, deliver public health care and prevention services, and improve the health, welfare, and disease ecology of vulnerable populations. Such an approach implies significant and sustained levels of international and national investment (including significant debt relief), but is still feasible and within the means of a global health coalition. As Eileen Stillwaggon (2006) argues, "HIV/AIDS is indeed a development issue" (p. 14), and ensuring basic needs in developing countries would have significant spillover or positive social and economic externalities for communities and nations.

Expanding HIV/AIDS prevention, education, and access to affordable treatments and care for PLWAs is critically important for combating the pandemic. However, in the absence of more systemic change, much of this effort may be what Stillwaggon called "too little, too late" (p. 179). As Meredith Turshen demonstrated in her study of the successful disease eradication campaign against smallpox (1967–1979), international coalitions can indeed succeed in extinguishing a single disease agent, and yet fail to improve "world health . . . [because] all the old problems that cause poverty and ill health were left untouched and the health services functioned no better afterward" (1989, 155).

See also **Demography: Mortality; Healing and Health Care; Sexual Behavior.**

BIBLIOGRAPHY

Asamoah-Odei, Emil, et al. "HIV Prevalence and Trends in Sub-Sahara Africa: No Decline and Large Subregional Differences." *Lancet* 364 (July 3, 2004): 35–40.

Clarke, Loren K., and Malcolm Potts, eds. *The AIDS Reader: Documentary History of a Modern Epidemic.* Boston, MA: Branden, 1988.

Essex, Max, et al., eds. *AIDS in Africa*, 2nd edition. New York: Kluwer Academic Press, 2002.

Farmer, Paul. *Infections and Inequalities: The Modern Plagues.* Berkeley: University of California Press, 1999.

Grmek, Mirko D. *History of AIDS: Emergence and Origin of a Modern Pandemic.* Princeton, NJ: Princeton University Press, 1990.

Joint United Nations Program on HIV/AIDS (UNAIDS). "2006 Report on the Global AIDS Epidemic." Geneva, Switzerland: UNAIDS, May 2006. Available from http://www.unaids.org/en/hiv_data/2006globalreport/default.asp.

Mayer, Kenneth H., and H. F. Pizer, eds. *The AIDS Pandemic: Impact on Science and Society.* San Diego: Elsevier Academic Press, 2005.

Packard, Randall, and Paul Epstein. "Medical Research in Africa: A Historical Perspective." In *AIDS: The Making of a Chronic Disease*, ed. Elizabeth Fee and Daniel M. Fox. Berkeley: University of California Press, 1992.

Poku, Nana K., and Alan Whiteside, eds. *The Political Economy of AIDS in Africa.* Burlington, VT: Ashgate Publishing Company, 2004.

Quinn, Thomas C. "Global Burden of the AIDS Pandemic." *Lancet* 348 (July 13, 1996): 99–106.

Sonnabend, Joseph. "The Debate on HIV in Africa: Letter to the Editor." *Lancet* 355 (June 17, 2000): 2163.

Stillwaggon, Eileen. *AIDS and the Ecology of Poverty.* New York: Oxford University Press, 2006.

Turshen, Meredith. *The Politics of Public Health.* New Brunswick, NJ: Rutgers University Press, 1989.

Webb, Douglas. *HIV and AIDS in Africa.* Chicago: Pluto Press, 1997.

Yong Kim, Jim, et al. *Dying for Growth: Global Inequality and the Health of the Poor.* Monroe, ME: Common Courage Press, 2000.

MICHELLE COCHRANE

HIV/AIDS, SOCIAL AND POLITICAL ASPECTS

Between 1980 and 2000, the HIV/AIDS epidemic outpaced every prediction with the speed and scale of its spread in eastern and southern Africa. It reached and sustained prevalence in adult populations of over 20 percent in six countries—a level that implies that almost half of all adults will contract HIV in their lifetimes. Epidemiological and social scientific research into the causes and implications of the epidemic has lagged well behind the scale of the crisis. Broad-brush explanations for the region's exceptional vulnerability—such as poverty—are increasingly superceded by more specific epidemiological factors, while official appeals to political will and leadership remain routine.

Various factors determine a population's vulnerability to HIV/AIDS. Sociobiological factors include male circumcision (a powerful protective factor, the significance of which has been overlooked for years) and the prevalence of other sexually transmitted infections (in turn linked to functioning health services). Socioepidemiological factors include the level of concurrent long-term sexual partnerships, which allow for the onward transmission of HIV during the short postexposure period of its maximum infectivity. In turn these risks are determined by wider socioeconomic and political factors, notably poverty, gender relations and population mobility.

It is striking that times of political transition, which tend to involve mobility and the revision of social norms, are empirically associated with increased rates of HIV. The AIDS epidemic has coincided with Africa's liberalization and democratization. The striking parallel between South Africa's political transition, including the opening of its borders and the dismantling of restrictions on internal movement, and the spread of HIV is a case in point. However, crisis and disruption is not always associated with increased incidence of HIV. Despite often being linked to impoverishment, forced displacement and high levels of gender-based violence, armed conflicts do not always contribute to increased levels of HIV transmission. To the contrary, remote populations in conflict-stricken Angola and Southern Sudan appear to have been protected from exposure to HIV. Postconflict reconstruction appears to be increasing the risk of HIV in these populations, as refugees return home, trade routes open up, and combatants are demobilized.

African governments' response to the HIV/AIDS epidemic has mostly been slow and half-hearted. The Ugandan government's early recognition of its HIV/AIDS epidemic (in 1986) is exceptional, and five years after African heads of state committed themselves to increasing their health budgets to 15 percent of expenditure, at the Abuja Summit on HIV/AIDS and other infectious disease in April 2001, only Botswana has met the target. Democratic governments have been no more energetic than authoritarian ones. This failure is commonly attributed to lack of political will. More precisely, it appears to reflect the absence of political incentives for effectively responding to AIDS. In democratic countries, electors have not made AIDS a priority, as reflected in the overwhelming vote for the African National Congress in South Africa's April 2004 election, despite President Thabo Mbeki's denial that HIV causes AIDS and his government's slow pace in instituting AIDS programs. In turn this reflects the low priority given to responding to AIDS by African publics, as measured in the Afrobarometer public opinion surveys. AIDS consistently ranks lower than other issues such as employment, education and crime in voters' priorities. This is an outcome both the host of other pressing problems afflicting Africans and the enduring level of denial surrounding the issue of HIV/AIDS.

Denial should be seen as more than a simple refusal to acknowledge AIDS, but instead as the construction of an alternative normality that encompasses AIDS. People living in situations of very high risk—such as mineworkers and sex workers in South African townships—find means of normalizing AIDS so that it is just one peril among many in their lives. In many communities, the HIV/AIDS epidemic has coincided with a rapid increase in accusations of sorcery. In others, funeral rites have become more elaborate, which appears to derive from people's attempt to sustain a cosmic moral order amid the eschatological crisis caused by so many adults dying premature and "bad" deaths.

AIDS activists have played a leading role in impelling national and international responses to AIDS, and shaping that response. South Africa's Treatment Action Campaign is the most sophisticated and successful activist organization. While using tactics borrowed from the anti-apartheid struggle including civil disobedience and legal challenges, the TAC frames its challenge to the South African government as an attempt to enforce the rights enshrined in the new constitution. It is a reformist movement, not a revolutionary one. In other countries, AIDS activists have focused on battling against stigma, denial and discrimination, on promoting women's rights, and on increasing resource flows to AIDS projects.

International AIDS organizations have recognized the role of African activists. The Global Fund to fight AIDS, tuberculosis, and malaria includes African people living with HIV and AIDS on its board and insists on civil society participation in the country coordinating mechanisms whereby projects are assessed. Such mechanisms have ensured that human rights, gender equity and participation are at the center of official responses to HIV/AIDS, and that democratic norms have been strengthened in the international AIDS effort in Africa. Activists have been instrumental in bringing down the price of anti-retroviral drugs and ensuring that governments are committed to major programs of treatment. The funds and capacity involved will change the nature of government in Africa, intruding into citizens' lives.

Some writers have predicted the collapse of African governments, the overthrow of democracy and the eruption of conflict on account of AIDS. Empirical evidence suggests real but more modest impacts. AIDS is assailing the capacities of governance institutions—including political parties, electoral commissions, departments of health and education, and national armies. The level of human resource attrition in these institutions can jeopardize their basic functioning, leaving the delivery of services under strain. In situations of intersecting stresses related to the outmigration of professionals and other social and economic crises, institutions can even become paralyzed. The loss of a key individual can cripple an organization or even a government. But governments are proving remarkably resilient, demonstrating their ability to meet threats to their survival. For example, armies and security forces have taken measures to reduce their exposure to AIDS, through mandatory testing of conscripts, selective provision of treatment to officers and specialists, and structuring their human resources management so as to leave them with sufficient human resources to continue functioning.

HIV/AIDS is leaving millions of orphaned children. This is a human tragedy of immense proportions, made worse by individual trauma, stigma, and the vulnerability of orphans to loss of assets and exploitation. But there is no evidence that Africa is being overwhelmed by a crisis of unsocialized orphans who threaten the social order. African kinship structures have cared for the great majority of orphans, albeit at a cost that is borne mostly by poor women. The continent's greater-than-expected capacity for coping with the orphan burden is linked to the fact that most African societies already had extremely extensive and under-recognized fostering mechanisms, including distant kin hosting school children and parenting systems adapted to the absence of fathers who are migrant workers. HIV/AIDS has changed and intensified patterns of distress among orphans, by increasing the number of double orphans (who have lost both parents) and creating great hardship where high prevalence of HIV intersects with other stresses such as drought or unemployment.

International institutions have been at the forefront of the response to AIDS in Africa. AIDS was the first disease to gain its own specialized UN agency, UNAIDS. Reflecting their origins in liberal internationalism, UNAIDS and other multilateral agencies have promoted a response to AIDS based upon individual responsibility rather than collective action. Non-governmental organizations have been favored over state service provision, voluntary compliance with norms over coercion. The Republican administration in the United States has become Africa's largest AIDS donor, with the President's Emergency Program for AIDS Relief (PEPFAR). This shares the multilateral agenda of supporting NGOs and liberal values, but is also strongly colored by a moral agenda that includes an emphasis on abstinence and a strong opposition to condoms. As AIDS funding grows to become 15 percent or more of official development assistance to Africa, donor dependency becomes entrenched and foreign agendas become embedded in the continent's public policy. AIDS interventions are supporting democracy, but only of a very specific kind.

In contrast to the high level of scientific expertise on HIV and the development of technologies for monitoring the progress of the infection in an individual patient, epidemiological and social scientific tools for analyzing and monitoring the epidemic remain rudimentary. For example, HIV incidence—the number of new infections—is the main measure of the course of the epidemic and the marker of the success or failure of HIV/AIDS policies and programs. Nowhere in Africa is HIV incidence measured, and instead policymakers rely on the much less reliable indicator of prevalence, the overall number of infected people. Without much better systems for evidence and monitoring, public policy will remain hampered and political incentives for action will stay obscured.

See also **Healing and Health Care; Mbeki, Thabo; Political Systems; Sexual Behavior.**

BIBLIOGRAPHY

Afrobarometer. "Public Opinion and HIV/AIDS: Facing Up to the Future?" Afrobarometer Briefing Paper No. 12, April 2004.

Barnett, Tony, and Alan Whiteside. *AIDS in the Twenty-First Century: Disease and Globalization.* London: Macmillan, 2002.

Campbell, Catherine. *Letting Them Die: Why HIV/AIDS Prevention Programmes Fail.* Oxford: James Currey, 2003.

de Waal, Alex. *AIDS and Power: Why the Epidemic is Not a Political Crisis—Yet.* London: Zed Books, 2006.

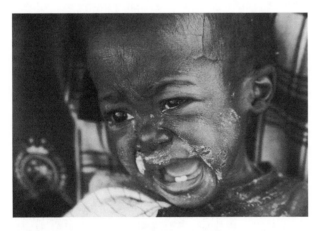

AIDS in Swaziland. A young child with AIDS cries at her home near Magomba, Swaziland, August 2002. The girl's mother is also dying from the disease, which already has claimed her father's life. The family, including three other siblings, is cared for by the eldest of the household, a teenaged son. AP PHOTO/SCHALK VAN ZUYDAM

Heald, Suzette. "The Absence of Anthropology: Critical Reflections on Anthropology and AIDS Practice in Africa." *Learning from HIV and AIDS*, ed. George Ellison, Melissa Parker, and Catherine Campbell. Cambridge, U.K.: Cambridge University Press, 2003.

Heywood, Mark. "Shaping, Making and Breaking the Law in the Campaign for a National HIV/AIDS Treatment Plan." In *Democratizing Development: The Politics of Socio-Economic Rights in South Africa*, ed. Peris Jones and Kristian Stokke. Leiden: Martinus Nijhoff Publishers, 2005.

Strand, Per; Khabele Matlosa; Ann Strode; and Kondwani Chirambo. *HIV/AIDS and Democratic Governance in South Africa: Illustrating the Impact on Electoral Processes.* Cape Town: IDASA, 2005.

ALEX DE WAAL

DIVINATION AND ORACLES.

There is practically no community in black Africa that does not know divination, an institution attuned to people's basic assumption that the fundamental order of things lies in the invisible, the otherworldly. Divination and its clients see the otherworldly realm as underpinning the this-worldly social-symbolic order and holding the key to the individual's fate, good or bad, here and now. Despite the availability of cosmopolitan technology and biomedicine (which assume that reality is sheer matter, i.e., something constructed and/or indeterminate) to which the well-to-do have ready access, the historical African religions, for their part, as well as widespread Christianity and Islam, underscore most African people's sense of the world as fundamentally reaching out human knowledge and mastery. In the case of a lasting disempowerment or affliction (insoluble conflict, disaster, exceptional loss, lack of income, chronic illness, misfortune, threat of death, or difficult decisions concerning the foundation of a house, marriage, or divorce or migration opportunities), people in uncertainty may call upon a diviner's keen sense of offering new insights into the enmeshed ancestral, societal, ethical determinants of their lives, so as to stir up their existence. Recourse to divination may even be linked to critical political or communitarian decisions, the struggle over scarce economic resources, warfare, and similar conflicts.

The divinatory consultation or oracle works toward identifying remedial or preventive measures to be taken and thereby provides stepping stones for empowerment and a temporality of prospect and peace of mind. Sometimes, however, the diviner's involvement may actually exacerbate the conflict or indeterminate situation. Indeed, a diviner's role may be that of the trickster, namely, one of ambivalent speech or apparent deception, in order better to reveal and address the problem. Public scepticism toward the diviner or power struggles among elders and family factions may detract from the authority or acceptability of an oracle's findings. While diviners reject suggestions that they themselves are sorcerers, they tend not to discourage their client's depressive belief in sorcery. That diviners have only occasionally aspired to positions of public leadership also shows the extent to which divination remains beyond political power.

KINDS OF DIVINATION AND ORACLES

In black Africa the continuum of geomantic and shamanistic divination implies cross-world communication and knowledge not otherwise attainable. Diviners are perceived as mechanisms of spiritual forces that have been selected for this role at birth or identified through name-giving, through recovery from a particular illness, or by descent relations; many are endowed with a charismatic personality. Through elaborate professional training and initiation, diviners-to-be become members of trans-local cults, sodalities, or lodges. Divination basically concerns a rather stable and culturally relevant body of expert production of etiological hermeneutics. Divinatory perception—and here a punctual observation from a psychoanalytic perspective—traces a kernel of forces or fate at the heart of human experience that escapes conventional understanding and other mainstream human control yet is perceptible through its effects.

Divination in Africa is always to some degree mediumnic in that the oracle and the divinatory tools, if not the entranced shamanic diviner him- or herself, establish heightened sensorial awareness of, and communication with, what is defined as an otherworldly realm of unforeseeable and invisible forces diagnosed as being coactivated by spirits, ancestral sanction, sorcery, or spell, determining one's fate. The divinatory oracle utters the message from a beyond preceding the thought out or domesticated. By singling out a sorcerer, a transgression, or an ancestral wrath, the oracle makes the source of the problem both localizable and particular. The oracle thereby helps to name the as yet unclarified ominous dimension in the lived world, and disentangle its destabilizing effect in the client's subjectivity of introjected, self-ensorceling anger and destructive desires. Divination senses out the subject's and group's inner fields of unruly, unnameable, and undomesticated forces, drives, impulses, sensations, wants and imaginaries and relocates the client in these fields at a point sheltering him or her in sheer possibilities he or she can tap again from so as to intersubjectively reengage in the struggle for a better life.

It could be argued that the effect of the consultation (due to the divinatory techniques and overall ambiance) comes out of the client's unnoticed switching from active and controlled sensorialist rationality seeking tangible evidence for his or her condition and future, on the one hand, to an unfocused, uncensored and somehow unprecedented openness or receptivity to new insights. Such disposition may inspire a new relation to oneself and others, as well as life-changing decisions. This turnover is perhaps all the more effective if the mind is in a humble and unfocused disposition and when the censorship of sensorialist rationality is turned off, like in dream, in an introspective mood induced by the oracle or the charitable distribution of ritual offerings (as recommended by the diviner of Islamic tradition).

Divinatory apparatus and practices appear to be common over very large areas. Shamanic divination operates via mediumship and dream and with the aid of divinatory vehicles such as the divining shrine, whereas geomantic divination deploys a basket, tray, ladle, or cup, enticing a set of icons or moves whose configurations are to be decoded: a grid of cowry shells, marked tablets, or some other figure, these being icons of the articulation points of society and life. While manipulating the divinatory vehicles, and/or reciting the verses or questions suggested by the oracular grid, diviners apply, in strictly prescribed ways, an interpretational strategy appropriate to the local worldview,

symbolic references, and social organization. The grid enables the diviner to work through a set of questions, or lends meaning to the visionary information or the configurations of the divinatory vehicles, in an interplay of past with present and of bodily, social, and cosmological fields (health, human dispositions, the client's web of social relations, the predicaments of a postcolonial globalizing world, sorcery, or relations with the deceased, ancestors, or spirits). In some traditions, as among the Nyole of eastern Uganda, a dialogue between diviner and client creates a socially acceptable and ordered interpretation of seemingly chaotic divinatory messages. The diviner's decoding of these messages is compared to the actions of an animal making an imprint, the ideogram formed by the nerve pattern on the underside of a leaf or the shell of a groundnut or other leguminous plant, or to weaving.

John Pemberton III and Wim Van Binsbergen offer in-depth interregional and historical comparative studies of divination. A shift in interpretation in the 1990s led to new perceptions of divination as a hermeneutics, a mode of world-making, or a process of regeneration, whereas former approaches had been stymied by the modernist and positivist preoccupation with whether divination provides valid knowledge of reality in the form of factual propositions. Several authors have classified most of the African divination forms as either geomantic or rather shamanic. The particular space-time set-up that is involved in cultivation, pastoralism, external (long-distance) trade, and/or in conquest and political centralization, especially when going hand in hand with Arabic literacy and geometry, has favored the spread of *geomantic* divination. Van Binsbergen demonstrates how much the latter is an offshoot of the millennia-old civilizations of the ancient Near East, cross-fertilized by ancient developments of science in the Indus valley and ancient China, and sophisticated by a later offshoot from the same stem: the Islamic civilization. He traces how Arabic geomantic science—an early example of globalization—became a central feature of Islamic high civilization, extending even beyond Islam both along the Indian Ocean and the coasts of Byzantium, to the Latin West, and across most of Africa and Madagascar, and via the trans-Atlantic slave trade, around the Caribbean and on the Latin American west coast.

Most widespread geomantic techniques attested in various parts of the African continent since the sixteenth century are the cowrie-shell and dream divination (in Islamic West Africa), the *Bilumbu, Fa, Hakata, Hamba, Ifa, Sikidy* and so many akin forms of divination (respectively along Luba, Fon, Shona, Chokwe, Yoruba, or Malagasy cultural traditions), or the *sangoma* tablet divination in southern Africa, as well as the *mankala* board games. In cowrie-shell and tablet divination, the seemingly at random, divinatory-borne manipulation of divinatory tools or tokens over a geometric layout of lines or holes may act as an oracular grid inducing the divinatory analysis. In many *mankala* board games, the mechanical, chess-like, gaming rules may do without reference to otherworldly realm. Tablet divination turns distant time and space (or the elsewhere and otherwise) into a geometry of here and now co-occurring or intersecting paths of causes or antecedents and effects.

While the natural sciences and usual mathematics would conclude that the results of cowry-shell, tablet, and Mankala geomantic techniques are determined by chance, local actors consider them to be activated and guided by invisible forces. The diviner establishes the divinatory theme according to information a client reveals concerning his or her needs or motivation for the consultation. The diviner then decodes the position or movement of an array of divinatory vehicles, and further interprets the social relevance in dialogue with the client. These divinatory vehicles are manipulated in front of the client while standardized verses or questions about causes, relationships, and events are uttered, depending on the configuration of objects. The ostensibly neutral quality of the divinatory vehicles permits the diviner to deny personal involvement in the social and otherworldly forces at stake. Elsewhere, the client may be the interpreter, as in Ifa divination among the Yoruba of Nigeria, whereas the Sissala client in northern Ghana is expected to examine personally the divinatory apparatus while being asked a series of yes/no questions. Among the Chagga-speaking people of Kilimanjaro, the perspicacious tuning in of the divinatory objects and the everyday activity of dwelling around production and reproduction, with the client's subjectivity and affliction, both allows for and results from an unprecedented "seeing through" at the heart of neighborhood relationality.

Scholars have distinguished three types of shamanic divination depending on whether it is produced by possession trance, by strict-shamanic trance, or by a trance-like or heightened state of consciousness. The first category is widespread and involves spirit appropriation of the diviner, who relays or even acts out the message sent by the possessing spirit or deity. Spirit mediums may be associated with a shrine of an interregional cult, such as Ngombo (spread across the Congo-Lunda belt in the southwest of the Democratic Republic of Congo, southeast Angola, and northwest Zambia) or Mwali in southeast Africa. In the second category, the shamanic diviner is believed to initiate visionary contact with the spirit. He or she either recounts this visionary journey or transduces the actions of the spirit in his or her body through a particular alteration in his or her sensory capacities.

It could be argued that this type of divination is being reappropriated in multiethnic (peri-) urban cultures throughout Africa by many of the Christian healing churches and new Christian-borne movements of the Holy Spirit. While speaking in the name of the Holy Spirit, Christian diviner-prophets surreptitiously coalesce this Christian entity with the ancestral spirits (though often overtly diabolized) summoned to participate in the healing process of the most afflicted church members. The shifting power of the Holy Spirit–Ancestor is all the more effective by virtue of its encompassing capacity to animate, re-energize and recapture life forces. That the divining art of these prophets tends to slide into moral prophecy focussing on individual strivings demonstrates the extent to which the perception and explanation of misfortune and divinatory practice increasingly reflect a spirit of entrepreneurship that is spurred by the multiethnic and commoditized urban context. The third type of divination is distinct in that diviners or seers here develop heightened sensorial or dreamlike visionary capacities.

There are yet other self-arbitrating forms of guilt divination or ordeal. The ordeal extends the shamanic divination into a self-arbitrating proof of guilt. One subcategory involves the diviner's coercion of an invisible force to configure items in tablet or basket divination or provoke friction or other movement among the divinatory apparatus (rubbing horn, cowry shells, board, or stick; divining cords, listening or detective horn, rattle, axe handle, bones, gourd of medicine, roots, nut shells, coins, etc.) or the reactions of a poisoned fowl to the diviner's yes/no questions. Omens and forms of hunt intended to interrogate the spirits or recently deceased relatives constitute another subcategory.

NATURE AND JURAL ASPECTS OF THE DIVINATORY PROCESS

A subtle transaction between diviner, spirits, divinatory vehicles, and clients produces a picture throwing a particular but unforeseeable light on the client's identity and social network, making possible an authoritative rereading and intervention in the problem at hand. Though most divinatory traditions operate at the margins of the local political power structure, some clearly serve to support high political office or regulate power relations between families.

Geomantic and shamanic divination are more of a birthing process than an arbitration; a hermeneutics of disorder more than a discourse of truth; and an art of counselling rather than a factual, causal, or ethical inquiry. Unlike the judicial council, shamanic and geomantic divination is not an exercise of redressive power or domination. Divinatory revelation stands to the jural council of elders as dreamwork to representational and discursive argument, as "speaking from the heart" or "from the womb" stands to the rhetorical reassertion of power relations in the masculine order of seniority.

The diviner disavows authorship of vision and judgment and asserts that whatever message he or she may be voicing stems from the divinatory forces at work in him or her, or in the divinatory media. The diviner is a medium who simply transmits or utters the divinatory message. In some cases the diviner is not even conscious of what he or she is saying and requires an assistant to translate his or her esoteric discourse for the client; under these conditions the divinatory séance is without dialogue. In the Lobi area of southeastern Burkina Faso, the diviner's spirit has no tongue but communicates through hand gestures.

SOCIAL CONTEXT

A critical distinction must be made between the oracle proper and the social use of it, namely the instance of divination and the subsequent interpretation, in a family council, of the divinatory assertions. Diviners are expected not only to justify their claims by offering criteria substantiating both their skills and the source of their knowledge but also to demonstrate their impartiality. Divination entails the basic assumption that human relations can be at the origin of affliction. Divinatory aetiologies consider misfortune as the consequence of a tear in the social fabric. The diviner's verdict offers a possible grid for how to reweave the damaged strands in the agnatic, uterine, and matrimonial weave of social reciprocity and reintroduce clients into an order of discourse and exchange. In other words, the oracle achieves its aims through the foundational discourse that the diviner and the clients exercise publicly in the fashion laid down by tradition.

The oracle's ultimate purpose is the transformation of disarray into the order of exchange that forms the basis of meaningful-being-in-the world. The divinatory encounter and consultation enhance the client's openness to the outside world and the invisible realm, and contributes to the innovative shaping of the condition of the subject in the contemporary, postcolonial life-world. The divinatory oracle relativizes its own aetiology, leaving room for individual freedom and genuine initiative in the moral space. Insofar as it establishes multiple links between the misfortune and various social and axiological (cosmological) registers of meaning (the social organization, the rule of exchange, offences, curses, persecutions, spirits), the oracle domesticates impending doom and an inauspicious destiny.

Most divination witnesses to a postcolonial, open-minded intercultural encounter and science-sharing between and across North and South in the twenty-first century's processes of globalization and economic marginalization. Van Binsbergen, a Dutch professor of intercultural philosophy at Erasmus University Rotterdam and director of research at the Africa Study Center in Leiden, describes his becoming a *sangoma* diviner in Francistown (Botswana). Since his initiation he has practiced tablet divination in southern Africa and in the Netherlands, where he devised a computer program for *sangoma* consultation with him worldwide by Internet. Numerous African diviners or diviners initiated in an African divinatory art, at work in the North with clients from many African and non-African cultural horizons, invite one most forcefully to rethink, in and from a variety of divinatory knowledge productions and ways of subject formation, one's by definition limited and biasing modes of understanding reality and representation, meaning and agency, culture and power, as well as place and time or locality and belonging.

See also **Death, Mourning, and Ancestors; Religion and Ritual; Symbols and Symbolism.**

BIBLIOGRAPHY

Adler, Alfred, and Andras Zempleni. *Le Bâton de l'Aveugle: divination, maladie et pouvoir chez les Moundang du Tchad.* Paris: Herman, 1972.

Anderson, David, and Douglas Johnson, eds. "Diviners, Seers and Prophets in Eastern Africa." Spec. issue, *Africa* 61, no. 3 (1991).

Bascom, William. *Sixteen Cowries: Yoruba Divination from Africa to the New World.* Bloomington: Indiana University Press, 1980.

Bastide, Roger. "La divination chez les Afro-Américains." In *La Divination,* Vol. 2, ed. André Caquot and Marcel Leibovici. Paris: Presses Universitaires de France, 1968.

Devisch, René. "Perspectives on Divination in Contemporary Sub-Saharan Africa." In *Theoretical Explorations in African Religion,* ed. Wim van Binsbergen and Matthieu Schoffeleers. London: Routledge and Kegan, 1985.

Devisch, René. "Parody in Matricentred Christian Healing Communes of the Sacred Spirit in Kinshasa." *Contours: A Journal of the African Diaspora* 1 (2003): 171–198.

Devisch, René, and Claude Brodeur. *The Law of the Lifegivers: The Domestication of Desire.* Amsterdam: Harwood Academic Publishers, 1999.

Jaulin, Robert. *La géomancie: Analyse formelle.* Paris: Mouton, 1966.

Kassibo, Bréhima. "La géomancie ouest-africaine: formes endogènes et emprunts extérieurs." *Cahiers d'Etudes Africaines* 128, no. 38 (1992): 541–596.

Kuczinski, Liliane. *Les Marabouts Africains à Paris.* Paris: CNRS Editions, 2002.

Myhre, Knut Christian. "Divination and Experience: Explorations of a Chagga Epistemology." *Journal of the Royal Anthropological Institute* 12 (2006): 313–330.

Peek, Philip, ed. *African Divination Systems.* Bloomington: Indiana University Press, 1991.

Pemberton, John III, ed. *Insight and Artistry in African Divination: A Cross-Cultural Study.* Washington, DC: Smithsonian Institution Press, 2000.

Retel-Laurentin, Anne. *Oracles et Ordalies chez les Nzakara.* Paris: Mouton, 1969.

Turner, Victor. *Revelation and Divination in Ndembu Ritual.* Ithaca, NY: Cornell University Press, 1975.

van Binsbergen, Wim. *Intercultural Encounters: African and Anthropological Lessons toward a Philosophy of Interculturality.* Münster, LIT Verlag, 2003.

Winkelman, Michael, and John Peek, eds. *Divination and Healing: Potent Vision.* Tucson: University of Arizona Press, 2004.

RENÉ DEVISCH

DIVORCE. *See* **Marriage Systems.**

DJEBAR, ASSIA (1936–). Assia Djebar is the pen name of Fatima-Zohra Imalayen, Algeria's foremost female writer. Of Berber ancestry, she was born near Algiers and benefited from advanced education because her father was a school teacher. In 1954 she went to Paris to study; the next year she became the first North African woman to be admitted to the prestigious École Normale Supérieure de Sèvres. But in 1956 she took to the streets of Paris with other students to demonstrate solidarity with Algeria's struggle for independence (1954–1962). Instead of taking her final exams, she produced her first novel, *La soif* (Thirst, 1957). Sought by the French police, she and her husband escaped to newly independent Tunisia in 1958, where she continued to write and work as a political activist. From Tunis she went to Rabat in 1959 to work with Algerian refugees in Morocco; there she obtained a teaching post at the national university.

Out of her Moroccan period came a collection of poems, a play, and a third novel, *Enfants du nouveau monde* (*Children of the New World*), published in Paris in 1962 and translated into English in 2005. Since 1957 she has produced more than twenty literary and artistic works—fiction, essays, film scripts, and poetry. Her works often portray women's political coming of age in colonial, wartime, and

Algerian writer Assia Djebar (1936–). Algerian novelist, translator, and filmmaker Assia Djebar shows off her sword in the Paris library of Académie Française, before giving a speech to a formal audience, June 22, 2006. Djebar became the first-ever North African woman to join the ranks of the "immortals" upon being inducted into France's most prestigious cultural institution a week prior to the event. AFP/Getty Images

postcolonial eras. Djebar has held teaching posts in the United States and Europe. In 2006 she was awarded the Académie Française medal for francophony.

See also **Algeria: History and Politics.**

BIBLIOGRAPHY

Djebar, Assia. *Children of the New World: A Novel of the Algerian War.* Trans. Marjolijn de Jager, afterword by Clarisse Zimra. New York: Feminist Press, 2005.

Mortimer, Mildred. "Fantasia: An Algerian Cavalcade." In *World Literature and Its Times*, Vol. 2: *African Literature and Its Times*, ed. Joyce Moss. Detroit: Gale Group, 2000.

JULIA CLANCY-SMITH

DJIBOUTI, REPUBLIC OF.

The ministate of Djibouti historically has generated significant international interest due to its strategic location straddling the Strait of Bab al-Mandab and bordering the larger nations of Ethiopia, Somalia, and (since 1993) the Republic of Eritrea. The French established Djibouti as a protectorate in 1885. The railway linking Addis Ababa in Ethiopia and Djibouti City, Djibouti's capital, was built in 1917, spurring growth that led to modern Djibouti. Known then as French Somaliland, the citizens voted in a referendum in 1967 to maintain the territory's relationship with France, after which the name was changed to the French Territory of the Afars and Issas. Allegations were made, however, that the French had rigged the vote by expelling pro-independence Somalis from the country prior to the vote. This, as well as political pressure from the Organization of African Unity and domestic French concerns, pushed the French colonialists to grant the Republic of Djibouti political independence in 1977.

The topography of Djibouti is mostly a barren, flat landscape composed of black volcanic rock, the harsh beauty of which is broken by a series of mountain ranges, particularly in the north. An often torrid climate, most notably during the dry *khamsin* season (May to September), in which the temperature can reach as high as 113 degrees Fahrenheit, once led travelers to call the country the hell of Africa.

Djibouti's only marketable mineral resource is salt that is extracted from deposits in the Lake Assal region. The small amount of arable land means that almost all agricultural products must be imported, at great cost to the local economy. Djibouti produces only about 3 percent of its food requirements. Limited development of the manufacturing and industrial sectors also ensures heavy reliance on the import of consumer products. These problems are compounded by an unemployment rate ranging from 40 to 70 percent of the national workforce, recurring budget deficits since 1982, and the burden of thousands of illegal economic migrants and political refugees from neighboring countries.

The most vital aspects of Djibouti's economy is its roles as a service provider and as a regional trading center, based upon its modern international

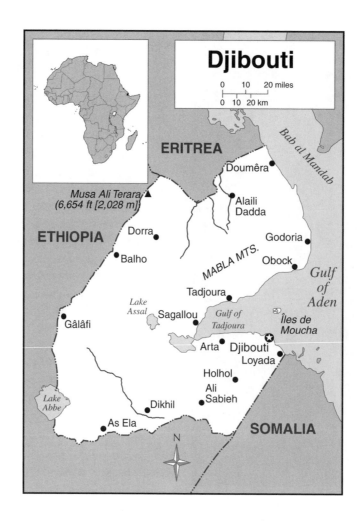

port, the 483 mile–long railroad that links Ethiopia's capital of Addis Ababa with Djibouti City, and the French, German, and American military personnel who reside on military bases within the territory. These sources make up approximately 80 percent of Djibouti's economy. Djibouti contains the largest French military base outside of French soil, as well as a United States military base that was founded in 2002 and is the headquarters for U.S. counterterrorism activities in the Horn of Africa. Due to its strategic location, Djibouti is currently the largest recipient of U.S. development aid in sub-Saharan Africa. Both the French and American militaries pay a substantial amount in taxes to the government of Djibouti for use of its land, which is an important source of revenue for the nation. The country remains heavily reliant on French foreign assistance and military presence, as France has a security agreement with Djibouti that commits France to protecting Djibouti's territorial

sovereignty from external threats. In addition, Djibouti maintains a national army that reached is height in 1993 during its civil war of 15,000 soldiers. In accordance with peace accords, the government has worked to demobilize some of its soldiers, making the current estimate around 5,000. The government of Djibouti is also working to improve its tourist industry and to attract international commercial capital in order to make Djibouti a regional banking center.

Djibouti is an ethnically diverse country of about 496,374 people (2007) in which the majority of the population is urban and Muslim. Due to its proximity to the Arabian Peninsula, Djibouti was the first region in Africa to become predominantly Muslim. Arabic and French are the official languages, though Somali and Afar are also commonly spoken. As indicated by the preindependence name of Territory of Afars and Issas, these peoples are the dominant ethnic groups that historically inhabited the territory, and are the most dominant political cleavages in postindependence Djibouti. A subgroup of the Somali peoples of the Horn of Africa, the Issas, constitute the largest ethnic group and inhabit the southern third of the country below the Gulf of Tadjoura and east of the Djibouti-Addis Ababa railway. The Afars are the second-largest ethnic group and inhabit the northern two-thirds of the country above the Gulf of Tadjoura and west of the railway. The remainder of the population is divided among four major recently-arrived groups living largely in Djibouti City: Gadaboursis and Isaaks (also subgroups of the Somali) who migrated from northern Somalia during the twentieth century; Arabs, particularly Yemenis, who work primarily in the commercial sector and number about 12,000; and roughly 5,000 French nationals working at nearly all administrative levels of the government, about 3,000 of which are French military personal. Approximately 84 percent of the population currently lives in urban areas, and about 12 percent continue to live nomadically.

Djibouti's politics have been dominated since independence by President Hassan Gouled Aptidon, an octogenarian Issa politician, and his ruling party, the Rassemblement Populaire pour le Progrès (RPP; Popular Assembly for Progress), which derives the majority of its support from the Issa community. Aptidon held strong control over the central government throughout the 1980s after having made the RPP the only legal political party in the country in 1981. Growing dissatisfaction with this state of affairs within the Afar community reached a turning point in November 1991 when the Front pour le Restauration de l'Unité et la Démocratie (FRUD; Front for the Restoration of Democracy), a military force of approximately 3,000 Afar guerrillas, launched a sustained military offensive designed to topple the Gouled regime.

A process of political reform designed to defuse this Afar-based military offensive then commenced. Reforms included the writing of a new constitution, the opening up of political space to allow for four legal political parties, and the holding of multiparty legislative and presidential elections in 1992 and 1993. These elections were significantly marred, however, by electoral fraud and a FRUD-inspired boycott heeded by approximately 50 percent of the voting-age population (primarily within the Afar community). As expected by most foreign observers, Aptidon and the ruling RPP declared victory in these elections and subsequently launched a military offensive in July 1993 that broke the back of the FRUD guerrilla insurgency. The government then signed a peace accord with a minor faction of the FRUD in 1994, co-opting factional leaders into the government and splitting FRUD. In the few years that followed, Aptidon became ill, allowing his longtime chief of staff and head of security forces, Ismaël Omar Guellah, to consolidate power. Guellah ran as the RPP's candidate in the April 1999 presidential election that he won easily against Moussa Ahmed Idriss, the opposition candidate.

Guellah, then, became Djibouti's second president in 1999. Ahmed Dini, the leader of the militant faction of FRUD, returned to the country the next year, which officially ended the civil war of the 1990s. The government and Dini signed a formal peace accord in 2001 that called for a demobilization of the insurgency and government troops in preparation for parliamentary elections in 2002. Eight political parties contested the January 2003 elections, the first election following the expiration of the four party limit mandated under the 1992 constitution. These parties fell into one of two blocks, the first being the Union pour la Majorité Présidentielle (UMP) or the pro-government coalition that included the RPP, and the second being the opposition block, called the Union pour une alternance démocratique (UAD), which was headed by Dini. The UAD suffered a devastating blow, though, as it failed to win a majority in any district despite winning 37 percent of the total vote. Because of this, the UMP won all the seats in the National Assembly. The UAD planned protests, citing fraud in the electoral system, but the government banned any protests. The Constitutional Court also rejected the UAD's case. Few international observers were present for these polls, and those who were did not publicly challenge the results.

The opposition suffered another blow in 2004 when Ahmed Dini died, leaving the opposition with no clear leader or candidate to challenge Guellah in the 2005 presidential elections. Because of this, the opposition boycotted the elections, and Guellah won an easy, uncontested election. The RPP then won the majority of seats in the Djibouti City and the five regional assemblies in elections held in March 2006, giving the president and his party nearly total political control over the country. This power monopoly

République de Djibouti (Republic of Djibouti)

Population:	496,374 (2007 est.)
Area:	23,000 sq. km (8,880 sq. mi.)
Official languages:	French, Arabic
Languages:	Somali, Afar, Arabic, French
National currency:	Djibouti franc
Principal religions:	Muslim 94%, Christian 6%
Capital:	Djibouti (est. pop. 320,000 in 2006)
Other urban centers:	Ali Sabieh, Dikhil, Tadjoura, Obock
Average annual rainfall:	less than 127 mm (5 in.)
Principal geographical features:	*Mountains:* Moussa Ali, Malba Mountains *Lakes:* Lac Assal, Lac Abbé
Economy:	*GDP per capita:* US$1,000 (2006)
Principal products and exports:	*Agricultural:* fruits, vegetables, goats, sheep, camels, animal hides *Manufacturing:* agricultural processing *Mining:* salt extraction Economy is based primarily on services and commerce.
Government:	Independence from France, 1977. Constitution approved, 1992. Republic. President is elected to a 6-year term, with 2-term maximum. The 65 deputies of the Assemblée Nationale elected for 5-year terms. Suffrage is universal. President appoints prime minister and Council of Ministers. For purposes of local government there are 6 districts (cercles).
Heads of state since independence:	1977–1993: President Hassan Gouled Aptidon 1999–: President Ismaël Omar Guelleh
Armed forces:	President is commander in chief. Armed forces are in the process of being downsized. *Army:* 8,000 *Navy:* 200 *Air force:* 200 *Paramilitary:* 1,200 *Foreign forces (French):* 2,600
Transportation:	*Rail:* 97 km (60 mi.), the Djibouti segment of the Addis Ababa–Djibouti railroad, operated by Chemin de Fer Djibouto-Ethiopien. *Port:* Djibouti *Roads:* 2,900 km (1,800 mi.), 13% paved *National airline:* Air Djibouti *Airports:* International facilities at Djibouti Airport. About 12 other small airports and airstrips throughout the country.
Media:	No daily newspapers; 5 nondailies. No book publishing. Radio and television service provided by Radiodiffusion-Télévision de Djibouti. 3 radio stations, 1 television station.
Literacy and education:	*Total literacy rate:* 46.2% (2006 est.). Free, universal, and compulsory education has not been introduced. No institutions of higher learning.

may threaten Djibouti's delicate peace, as the RPP's Afar ally, the FRUD, also did poorly in the 2006 elections and may resume its violent insurgency if it continues to feel powerless in the political sphere. The opposition also has little media access, and journalists who do not practice self-censorship are reportedly often harassed by the government security service. The next parliamentary elections are due in January 2008, and the next presidential election is slated for April 2011.

Djibouti maintains good relations with the international community and with its neighbors for the most part. It is a member of the United Nations, the African Union, the Common Market for Eastern and Southern Africa (Comesa), the Intergovernmental Authority on Development (IGAD), and the League of Arab States. The government officially remains neutral over the conflict between Ethiopia and Eritrea, though President Guellah has close ties to the ruling party in Ethiopia and Djibouti derives much of its economy from the export of Ethiopian goods. Djibouti in fact has benefited substantially from the Ethiopian-Eritrean wars because of the large increase in Ethiopian goods being exported through Djibouti's port instead of through Eritrea. Eritrea had cut off ties to Djibouti in the late 1990s but reestablished them in 2000 after Libyan mediation. Eritrean and Djiboutian officials now meet annually to address cooperation between the two nations. Regarding Somalia, Djibouti officially supports a united Somalia and does not recognize Somaliland, though Somaliland has maintained a diplomatic mission in Djibouti since 2003 and the two sides maintain several security agreements.

Regional disputes have attracted thousands of refugees to Djibouti, primarily from Somalia and Ethiopia. In 2004, the U.N. Refugee Agency (UNHCR) estimated the number of refugees in Djibouti at around 27,000. In addition, Djibouti attracts a significant number of illegal immigrants who come looking for work. The government sees them as a burden on its already stretched social service system and in July 2003 ordered that all illegal immigrants be expelled from the country. At the time, the number was estimated at 100,000 persons. The vast majority heeded the order at the time, but authorities believe that many returned after the expulsion crisis died down.

See also **Addis Ababa; Djibouti City; Ethiopia, Modern; Organization for African Unity; Postcolonialism; Somalia.**

BIBLIOGRAPHY

Djibouti Country Profile 2006. London: Economist Intelligence Unit, 2006.

Schraeder, Peter J. "Ethnic Politics in Djibouti: From 'Eye of the Hurricane' to 'Boiling Cauldron.'" *African Affairs.* 92, no. 367 (1993): 203–221.

Shilling, Nancy A. "Problems of Political Development in a Ministate: The French Territory of the Afars and Issas." *Journal of the Developing Areas.* 7 (1973): 612–634.

Tholomier, Robert. *Djibouti: Pawn of the Horn of Africa*, trans. Virginia Thompson and Richard Adloff. Metuchen, New Jersey: Scarecrow Press, 1981.

PETER J. SCHRAEDER
REVISED BY NANCY RHEA STEEDLE

DJIBOUTI CITY. The capital city of the republic of the same name, Djibouti is situated on the Horn of Africa, bordered by Somalia, Ethiopia, and Eritrea. The city of Djibouti lies at the mouth of the Red Sea, on a strip of semidesert land measuring 14,291 square miles, in a position of great strategic significance at the narrowest strait between Europe, the Mediterranean, and the Indian Ocean

and Asia, via the Suez Canal. The port attracts many citizens of the country into the city, creating one of the highest ratios of urbanization in Africa. Whereas the national population was estimated at 716,800 in 2004, 624,600, or nearly 87 percent, lived in Djibouti city or its immediate environs. This is, in part, a function of the extreme rates of unemployment in the country as a whole, where between 40 and 50 percent of the labor force in the countryside cannot find work.

In 1887 France began building the city of Djibouti on land settled by Issas and Somalis, in an attempt to counter the British presence at Aden, across the Bab el Mendab strait in (now South) Yemen. There followed an influx of immigrants from the neighboring states (Somalia, Ethiopia, and Eritrea), along with Yemeni Arabs, and people from the Djibouti hinterland. With the completion of a railroad and port in the city this influx grew, as people were attracted by the hope of employment opportunities and wealth creation. Immigration from countryside to city continued long after actual work opportunities had been exhausted.

Although a wide variety of ethnic groups share the city, they live segregated lives, reinforcing the distinctions among them. In the late twentieth century, these ethnic divisions contributed to significant unrest. An uprising among the Afar (who constitute 35% of the population) resulted in a decade of violence, which was concluded only with the signing of a peace accord in 2001. The city's economic contributions, although constituting the lion's share of the nation's gross national product (GNP), have not been enough to keep Djibouti from falling into arrears with its international loan debt.

See also **Djibouti, Republic of.**

BIBLIOGRAPHY

La Commission du Centenaire de Djibouti. *Centenaire de première ville de Djibouti.* Djibouti: Imprimerie Nationale Djibouti, 1987.

Thompson, Virginia, and Richard Adloff. *Djibouti and the Horn of Africa.* Stanford, CA: Stanford University Press, 1968.

UNIDO, Regional and Country Studies Branch. *Djibouti: Economic Diversification through Industrialization.*

New York: United Nations Industrial Development Organization, 1989.

United Nations Economic Commission for Africa. *Socio-economic Aspects of Poverty (Case Study: Djibouti)*. New York: United Nations Economic Commission for Africa, 1981.

MARTHA HANNAN

DOCTORS. *See* **Healing and Health Care: Medical Practitioners.**

DOMESTIC GROUPS. *See* **Family; Household and Domestic Groups; Kinship and Descent.**

DOMITIEN, ELIZABETH (c. 1920–2005). Elizabeth Domitien, who served as prime minister of the Central African Republic (CAR) from 1975–1976, was Africa's first and the world's fourth woman prime minister. Given CAR's political history of one-party autocratic rule, detailed information about Domitien's life is limited. Domitien was born between 1920 and 1925 in Oubangui-Shari in the period of French colonial rule. As a child, Domitien attended a missionary school in Brazzaville, Congo. By the time she served as prime minister, Domitien was a leading businesswoman in agricultural production, export trade, and domestic commerce. Domitien's economic activities resulted in her leadership of significant business organizations. She founded the Central African Commerce Society that exported coffee beans and was the head of the Association of Male and Female Sellers of the Central Market in the capital city Bangui. Domitien's formal political activities began with the momentum towards African independence from colonial rule.

Domitien joined the Social Evolution Movement of Black Africa (MESAN) in the 1950s and was a leading public speaker for the party. In 1965 the head of the country's armed forces, Lieutenant Jean-Bédel Bokassa, overthrew the civilian government in a coup and proclaimed himself as president, field marshal, and emperor of the country.

Domitien became the vice-president of MESAN in 1969 and was a political ally who aided Bokassa in his rise to power. In 1975, Bokassa appointed Domitien as prime minister, along with five other women in his cabinet. In 1976, Bokassa dismissed Domitien. In 1979, French soldiers seized the national palace when Bokassa was abroad and declared that he was no longer president. David Dacko's (1930–2003) new government imprisoned Domitien and other allies of Bokassa. Domitien was released in 1981, withdrew from formal politics, and died in 2005.

See also **Bokassa, Jean-Bédel; Central African Republic.**

BIBLIOGRAPHY

Binoua, Josué. *Centrafrique: L'instabilité permanente*. Paris: L'Harmattan, 2005.

Decalo, Samuel. *Psychoses of Power: African Personal Dictatorships*. Boulder, CO: Westview Press: 1989.

Français, Jean. *Le putsch de Bokassa: histoire secrete*. Paris: Harmattan, 2004.

Kalck, Pierre. *Central African Republic: A Failure in De-Colonisation*. New York: Praeger, 1971.

Opfell, Olga S. *Women Prime Ministers and Presidents*. Jefferson, NC: McFarland & Co., 1993.

Titley, E. Brian. *Dark Age: The Political Odyssey of Emperor Bokassa*. Montreal: McGill-Queen's University Press, 1997.

United Nations. *Le droit et la condition de la femme en République centrafricaine*. Addis-Ababa, Nigeria: Organisation des Nations Unies, Commission économique pour l'Afrique, 1985.

RACHEL JEAN-BAPTISTE

DOUALA. Douala is the economic capital of Cameroon. Its port accounts for the great bulk of the country's maritime activity (crude oil, timber, coffee, cocoa, and cotton are the principal exports) and is a primary site for export of goods from Chad and the Central African Republic. Since its inception, Douala has been a city dominated by trade. As early as 1472, local communities were in contact with European merchants—first Portuguese, then British, German, and French—serving as intermediaries between the coast and the interior that was rich in ivory, slave, and rubber. In this context,

Douala chiefs played a central role, and the city came to be named after them.

Initially a fishing village, by the nineteenth century Douala had grown into a thriving town. From 1901 to 1916, it served as capital of the German Kamerun protectorate. As a result of the Versailles Treaty ending World War I, it fell to the French. Under French rule, the capital was moved to Yaoundé. Douala, however, continued to thrive. Rural migration, primarily from the densely populated western highlands, played a key part in its development. In the early twenty-first century, 75 percent of Douala's inhabitants trace their origins to the highlands. Absent reliable census data, the city's total number of residents is unclear. Estimates range from 1.8 to 4 million, with an overwhelming majority of persons under the age of 40. The city has five elected mayors, all who report to an official named by the head of state.

See also **Cameroon; Yaoundé.**

BIBLIOGRAPHY

Gouellain, René. *Douala, ville et histoire.* Paris: Institut d'ethnologie, Musée de l'homme, 1975.

Mainet, Guy. *Douala: Croissance et servitudes.* Paris: L'Harmattan, 1986.

Séraphin, Gilles. *Vivre à Douala. L'imaginaire et l'action dans une ville africaine en crise.* Paris: L'Harmattan, 2000.

DOMINIQUE MALAQUAIS

Nigerian sculptor Sokari Douglas Camp works with a welding torch in her London studio, October 1995. Douglas Camp's work, which draws on her childhood memories of southern Nigeria, has questioned traditional assumptions about African art. AP PHOTO/MAX NASH

DOUGLAS CAMP, SOKARI (1958–).

The Nigerian sculptor Sokari Douglas Camp was born in the Kalabari town of Buguma, Nigeria. Educated in Britain, she returned home regularly, and the imagery of life in the eastern Niger Delta is strongly evident in her work. She uses contemporary techniques to create larger-than-life-sized painted steel figurative sculpture that draws on her varied experiences in Nigeria and Britain. Her monumental, open-work figures convey volume and mass through empty spaces: It is as if she sews in space with welded steel. Some of her constructions are motorized. All capture the moment with vitality, excitement, and a sense of delight. Many of her pieces are autobiographical. Most concern performative aspects of Kalabari cultural festivals or rites, and male masqueraders, drummers, and women in the audience are caught with an amused and penetrating observer's eye. Her inventive and bold work is sometimes playful, always serious, occasionally shocking. Douglas Camp returns to Kalabari themes repeatedly. Other subjects she has addressed include street life in South London, multiple identities, women, and contemporary politics—the militant Islamist Osama bin Laden, the Nigerian activist and writer Ken Saro-Wiwa, the Nigerian musician Fela Kuti, Nigeria's arms trade, and conflict in the Delta over oil. While the Nigerian topics she often portrays have led her to be viewed in the West as an African artist, Douglas Camp is a British citizen whose powerful work blurs such boundaries and manifests a sophisticated Western aesthetic.

Douglas Camp attended the California College of Arts and Crafts (1979–1980); the Central

School of Art and Design, London (1980–1983) where she received her bachelor's degree; and the Royal College of Art, London (1983–1986), where she received her master's degree in sculpture. A prolific artist who exhibits in solo and group shows in the United States, England, and Europe, she has had many large-scale public commissions and received numerous honors, including Commander of the British Empire (CBE). Douglas Camp is married to an English architect, has two daughters, and lives in London.

See also **Arts: Sculpture.**

BIBLIOGRAPHY

Oguibe, Olu. "Finding a Place: Nigerian Artists in the Contemporary Art World." *Art Journal* 58, no. 2 (Summer 1999): 30–41.

MICHELLE GILBERT

DOW, UNITY (1959–). Botswana lawyer and human rights activist Unity Dow was appointed in 1998 as her country's first woman High Court Judge. She is a founder-member of Women and Law in Southern Africa (WLSA), a member of International Women's Rights Watch, and founder of Botswana's first women's legal counseling center. She was elected to the International Commission of Jurists in 2004 and to its Executive Committee in 2006. Dow studied law at the University of Botswana and Swaziland, with two years at the University of Edinburgh. As a lawyer Dow won important advances in law regarding rape, child support, and married women's property rights. She came to prominence in Botswana through her successful legal challenge to the discriminatory Citizenship Law of 1982/1984, which denied women citizens married to foreigners the right to pass on their citizenship to their children, but allowed men to do so. Frustrated with government resistance to arguments for its change, Emang Basadi! (Stand Up, Women!), the leading Botswana women's rights group, and WLSA joined with Dow to pursue her pathbreaking suit. The 1991 Citizenship Case victory was a significant catalyst for the Botswana women's rights movement. It resulted in reforms of other discriminatory laws, programs by Emang Basadi! to recruit and train female political candidates, and numerous appointments of women to high offices.

Dow has also written four novels focused on gender, justice, and power: *Far and Beyon'*, *The Screaming of the Innocent*, *Juggling Truths*, and *The Heavens May Fall*.

See also **Human Rights; Literature.**

BIBLIOGRAPHY

Armstrong, Alice, and Welshman Ncube, eds. *Women and Law in Southern Africa*. Harare: Zimbabwe Publishing House, 1987.

Holm, John, and Patrick Molutsi, eds. *Democracy in Botswana*. Athens: Ohio University Press, 1989.

Van Allen, Judith. "'Bad Future Things' and Liberatory Moments: Capitalism, Gender and the State in Botswana." *Radical History Review* 76 (2000): 136–168.

JUDITH IMEL VAN ALLEN

DRAMA. *See* Theater.

DREAMS AND DREAM INTERPRETATION. The evolutionist paradigms of early European observers have contributed a great deal toward misunderstanding dreams in Africa. Central to the evolutionist paradigm was the dichotomous distinction between scientific "Western thought" and mystical "primitive thought." European scholars speculated that Africans confused dreaming and waking realities, or valued dreams more than waking perceptions.

In 1871 E. B. Tylor suggested that it was from the attempts of "primitives" to come to terms with dream experiences that the ideas of the spirit and soul arose. The experience of the dream self that wanders about at night gave humans an idea of their own duality. The appearance of the dead in dreams suggested that the soul had an after-life. For Tylor, a belief in spiritual beings was the central idea of religion.

Psychoanalysts, such and Sigmund Freud (1856–1939) and Carl Jung (1875–1961), continued to use dreams as a means of constructing Africans as "the other." They perceived the dreams of Westerners as analogous to the walking realities of Africans: dreams were an indication of the "savage world" within the Western person that had to be subdued and civilized.

In the early twenty-first century this binary distinction between scientific and primitive mentalities is seen as a Western fiction. The most decisive break with evolutionism occurred among anthropologists who sought to demonstrate the universality of the deep psychoanalytic processes. In 1958 S. G. Lee examined the manifest content of the dreams reported by subjects at a hospital in Zululand, South Africa. His evidence confirms Freud's hypothesis that dreams express wish fulfilment and unresolved conflicts in the dreamer. However, Lee's research also shows the importance of social influences on dreams. He recorded significant differences between the dreams reported by men and women. Men's dreams of owning large herds of superb cattle and of lovemaking were pleasant wish-fulfilment dreams. Men also dreamt of beer-drinking, feasts, and fighting. In contrast, women dreamt of babies, snakes, still water, and flooded rivers. Newly married brides and women with a record of marital infertility tended to dream of babies, and these dreams were of a wish-fulfilling nature. Dreams of water were also associated with childbirth. (The Zulu word *isiZalo* refers to both the uterus and the river-mouth.) Women who had already borne a few children, and whose wish for further offspring was not as strong, dreamed of still water. Married women with considerable experience of childbirth, had nightmares about flooded waters. These dreams indicate a fear of the economic pressure of further childbearing that could not be overtly expressed.

Anthropological studies of religion occasionally refer to dreams. For example, Axel-Ivar Berglund's *Zulu Thought-Patterns and Symbolism* (1989) outlines the Zulu belief that the ancestors reveal themselves to their descendants through dreams, bringing good news and showing the dreamers where to locate lost cattle. During the first months of pregnancy, the ancestors could announce the sex of an expected child. Dreams of green and black snakes, and of buffaloes, indicate a boy; those of puff adders and of crossing rivers show that the child would be a girl. As servants of the ancestors, diviners are called to their profession by incomprehensible dreams, such as vomiting snakes. Dreams teach diviners about their practice and about herbs.

Studies of the independent church movement also provide expansive sociological consideration of dreams. They often focus on the narration and interpretation of dreams as public performances during church services. In 1973 S. R. Charsley found that members of a Pentecostal-type church in Uganda perceived dreams as "messages from God" about what had happened and what should happen. A decade later, R. Curley highlighted the different social roles of "conversion" and "reconfirming" dreams in a fundamentalist church in Cameroon. Conversion dreams showed vulnerability prior to the conversion and physical strength thereafter. They were used as personal charters to claim full church membership and provided a "repository of striking images" that helped to establish religious truth. Reconfirming dreams were about spiritual power, such as healing the sick, and testified to the active spiritual life of the dreamer. Their narration often had a competitive aspect and expressed rivalry between title holders in the church.

Late-twentieth-century interest, as evident in M. C. Jedrej and Rosalind Shaw's collection *Dreaming, Religion, and Society in Africa* (1992), focuses on dreams as sites of cultural meaning. In that work L. Holy shows that for the Berti of Dafur, in the Sudan, dreams do not indicate the innermost desire of the dreamer but rather what the dreamer would get. Though the Berti saw dreams as intensely personal, they use complex, culturally shared, frameworks for interpreting them. Dreams are believed to be in code, and they have to be decoded in terms of the indices and the symbols they contain. Indices are signs that show only one form of a general class. For example, owning a goat is one way of getting rich. Therefore, to dream of a goat indicates wealth and prosperity, although it may not actually be acquired thorough ownership of goats. Dream symbols are recognizable because they are objects used in everyday waking life. These symbols can be interpreted literally or in terms of a reversal of content; they can have either a positive or a negative value; or they can carry a general or a specific message.

In conclusion there is no single, all-encompassing framework for the study of dreams in Africa. Instead, there has been a variety of concerns, including the social contexts of dreams, their symbolism, the hermeneutics of dream interpretation, and the uses of dreams as sources of ideas that structure identities and experiences. Most important have been the recognition that the images provided by dreams are filtered through the prisms of local cultural traditions and that they reflect human mental processes no different from other dreamers elsewhere in the world.

See also **Christianity; Divination and Oracles; Religion and Ritual; Spirit Possession; Symbols and Symbolism: Animal.**

BIBLIOGRAPHY

Berglund, Axel-Ivar. *Zulu Thought Patterns and Symbolism.* London: Hurst and Company, 1989.

Charsley, S. R. "Dreams in an Independent African Church." *Africa* 43, no. 3 (1973): 244–257.

Curley, R. "Dreams of Power: Social Process in a West African Religious Movement." *Africa* 53, no. 3 (1983): 20–38.

Holy, L. "Berti Dream Interpretation." In *Dreaming, Religion, and Society in Africa*, ed. M.C. Jedrej and Rosalind Shaw. Leiden: E. J. Brill, 1992.

Lee, S. G. "Social Influences in Zulu Dreaming." *Journal of Social Psychology* 47 (1958): 265–283.

Tylor, E. B. *Origin of Religion*, Vol. 2: *Primitive Culture* [1871]. New York: Harper Torchbooks, 1958.

ISAK NIEHAUS

DROUGHT. *See* **Climate; Desertification, Modern.**

DRUMS. *See* **Languages; Musical Instruments.**

DU BOIS, W. E. B. (1868–1963). William Edward Burghardt Du Bois, an African-American of mixed blood, was born in Great Barrington, Massachusetts. He attended Fisk University in Nash-ville, Tennessee, in 1888, then attended Harvard to earn a master's degree (1891) and then a Ph.D. (1895). Du Bois emerged in the early twentieth century as a vigorous advocate of equal rights for American blacks. In 1909 he founded with black and white American liberals the National Association for the Advancement of Colored People (NAACP).

During the 1920s and the 1930s, Du Bois organized Pan-African congresses. He campaigned assiduously against the philosophy of "back to Africa" preached by Marcus Garvey. He also attacked Booker T. Washington's accommodationist philosophy of black progress.

Known as the Father of Pan-Africanism, Du Bois was a prolific writer. His books include *The Souls of Black Folk* (1903), *The Negro* (1915), *Color and Democracy* (1945), and *The World and Africa* (1947). Du Bois later identified with mainstream Marxism-Leninism. In 1963 he became an expatriate, adopting Ghana as his home. He died there later in the same year, at the age of ninety-five.

See also **Garvey, Marcus Mosiah; Literature.**

BIBLIOGRAPHY

Legum, Collin. *Pan-Africanism: A Short Political Guide*, rev. edition. New York: Praeger, 1965.

Lewis, David Levering. *W. E. B. DuBois—Biography of a Race, 1868–1919.* New York: H. Holt, 1993.

Lewis, David Levering. *W. E. B. DuBois—The Fight for Equality and the American Century, 1919–1963.* New York: H. Holt, 2000.

Nordquist, Joan, comp. *W. E. B. Du Bois, A Bibliography.* Santa Cruz, CA: Reference and Research Services, 2002.

Rudwick, Elliott M. *W. E. B. Du Bois: Propagandist of the Negro Protest.* Philadelphia, University of Pennsylvania Press, 1968.

Vincent, Theodore G. *Black Power and the Garvey Movement.* Berkeley, CA: Ramparts Press, 1971.

Young, Alford A., Jr., et al. *The Souls of W.E.B. Du Bois.* Boulder CO: Paradigm Publishers, 2006.

OLUTAYO ADESINA

EARLY HUMAN SOCIETY, HISTORY OF (C. 50,000 BP TO 19,000 BCE).

By 50,000 years ago, as human beings, *Homo sapiens sapiens* began their expansion out of Africa and into the rest of the world, they had already fully evolved all the capabilities that their descendants have today. They had the same capacities for language, thought, and invention. They strived for material survival, built structures of thought that gave meaning to their lives, and sought recognition and acceptance from their fellows. But they carried out their lives within overall frameworks of knowledge and belief very different from those of nearly anyone today. This entry focuses on Africa, but much of what is said likely applies to human beings everywhere at that ancient point in time.

All human beings of the period 50,000–19,000 BP were food collectors. They supplied their food needs by gathering edible wild plant foods and by hunting animals. Scholars know from a wide array of examples from later eras of history that women were the chief gatherers of plant foods. Throughout most of the tropics and the temperate zones, women were thus the suppliers of the majority of the calories of the diet, with their work providing the steady, predictable daily source of sustenance. Men would have been the hunters of animals. Their success would have depended in part on their individual skills as hunters; even more, it would have depended on the vagaries of the movement of animals about the landscape. Many a time hunters would have come back empty handed simply because the game was somewhere else that day.

Communities living in seashore areas often gathered shellfish, and communities with access to rivers, lakes, and seaside areas may also have engaged in fishing. Both women and men, it appears, would have participated in these kinds of activities.

The vast majority of, if not all, people at 50,000–19,000 BP lived in very small-scale social and residential units. Bands of around twenty-five to forty people were probably the characteristic local unit across most of Africa. Each band would have had a recognized territory for its activities. Each band would normally have belonged to a wider network of bands, all of which spoke the same language or various dialects of the same language. Linguists have found that, to be viable and persist in use, a language normally requires from around four hundred up to a few thousand speakers. With twenty-five to forty people per band, the typical language community of the era 50,000–19,000 BP would thus have included a minimum of fifteen to twenty bands, each with its own recognized gathering and hunting territory.

Population densities, even in favorable savanna environments, would have been exceedingly low in those eras. There did not yet exist anywhere in the world the intensive and specialized kinds of gathering and hunting, such as those found in California of three hundred years ago, that could sustain densities of as much as two to three persons per square mile. Probably everywhere before 19,000 BP, even in the most favorable conditions, human population densities were less than one person per square mile and, in many regions, far lower than that. The combined lands of a typical group of bands speaking the same language must usually have extended across 10,000 or more square miles. In poor environments with much lower population densities, a grouping of bands, with a total population of several thousand, might have been scattered across 100 times as much land. This is the kind of situation, for example, that held true for the Paiute of the mid-nineteenth-century Great Basin of North America and for the Western Desert Aborigines of Australia right up to the mid-twentieth century.

Unilineal kin institutions, with lineages and clans, did not yet exist in the human societies of 50,000–19,000 BP. Studies from several scholarly disciplines have proposed that the core social unit in the gathering and hunting band of that time may have been a kin group of a different sort—a coalition of close female relatives, consisting of grandmothers, their daughters, and their daughters' children. These female kin groups were matrilocal; the band coalesced around them. Anthropologists James O'Connell, Kristen Hawkes, and Nicholas Blurton Jones have established that just such female coalitions operated in the Hadza gathering and hunting society of Tanzania in the 1980s and 1990s. Historian Christine Ahmed-Saidi has described the same matrifocal institution among Bantu-speaking farming peoples of East-Central Africa. In this region, a specific word (*bumba*) for the female matri-kin coalition has been in use for at least 1,500 years and may trace back to the still earlier proto-Savanna Bantu language of 3,000–4,000 years ago.

Coalitions of close female kin would have enhanced human adaptation for survival in several basic ways. Grandmothers helped with the gathering of food for women burdened with as yet unweaned children, and they also helped by taking care of weaned children. Cooperative multigeneration female kin groupings thus freed up time for women to go about the tasks of providing the great majority of the food that sustained life in the band, while supporting the reproductive success of the group as a whole and enhancing the survival chances of their children. Men gained access to marriage and reproduction with women of these coalitions, and to the women's regular and ongoing subsistence productivity, through being able to provide—although in much more variable and intermittent fashion—gifts of meat from the hunt. Meat provides additional nutrients enhancing the health and survival of children, and thus good hunters would have been attractive mates to the female kin group.

Can one extrapolate the existence of this sort of institution, as these scholars have done, to the period 50,000–19,000 BP and before? The first developments in Africa of unilineal kin institutions appear to have taken place as early as 10,000 years ago in at least two different parts of the continent. The reconstructed kin terminologies in the Nilo-Saharan family imply the existence of matriliny in one branch of that family at a period that can be dated from well-established archaeological correlations to around 10,000 BP. As for the Niger-Congo family, over forty years ago the scholar George Peter Murdock made a compelling case that the speakers of this family followed matrilineal descent rules far back in their history, probably back to the proto-Niger-Congo era of also perhaps 10,000 or more years ago. That the earliest unilineal descent groups in Africa were matrilineal favors the idea that the first lineages and clans evolved out already existing, but smaller-scale, female-based descent groups. The matrikin coalitions would seem to fit this requirement. That still does not reach back to 50,000 to 19,000 BCE, although it does shorten the gap somewhat. Whether matrikin coalitions were a common basis of local society in Africa before 19,000 BCE remains an intriguing issue for future investigation and debate.

What can one say about the inner life of those times? How did peoples of the era 50,000–19,000 BP understand their place in the universe? The evidence of art and archaeology strongly suggests that the original human religion was shamanism. In this belief system existence is biaxial: it has two realms, the concrete world of everyday experience and a parallel realm of spirit. The surface of the earth forms the interface between the two realms. The shaman was the religious and medical practitioner who tapped into the world of spirit for the benefit (or sometimes the ill) of human beings. Shamans, as scholars discovered from the relict preservation of this religious system here and there around the world, were people able to drive themselves into a state of trance. The trance experience transported them into the spirit realm, there to connect up with spirit power and bring it back into the everyday world in which their society lived.

The indirect archaeological evidence of shamanism goes far back in time. As cognitive archaeologist David Lewis-Williams has noted, the earliest known human symbolic markings, from 77,000 years ago in Blombos Cave, South Africa, already consist of geometric figures resembling those that are characteristically "seen" by people in the early stage of entering into a trance. The rock art of southern Africa, dating as early 27,000 BP, as well as the rock art of Europe of the next 15,000 years, similarly seem to have had the trance experiences of shamans as their principle subject. In this later art, however, scholars discover fuller and more complex presentations of the images that inhabited the shamans' minds when they were in states of trance. The specific spirit figures, animals, and other images of this art differed in different parts of the world because humans everywhere have been historical beings: over time they have developed different myths and associated images to convey their experiences of the two realms.

But the shamanistic traditions also abounded in common structural features and imageries rooted in the psyches of all human beings. For example, the rock surfaces on which early humans painted held special numinous significance as a boundary zone between the concrete world of everyday life and the realm of spirit. In different parts of the world can be found cases where the painters depicted an animal as emerging from a crack in the rock, in other words, as a spirit animal passing from the one world into the other.

Burial of the dead is another custom of the period 50,000–19,000 BP probably originally linked to the shamanistic division of existence into corporeal and spirit realms. Burial penetrated the earth's surface, putting the deceased into the realm of spirit. An alternative early practice in some regions, also connected to shamanistic beliefs, was to lay the deceased to rest out in the open. The Iraqw of Tanzania, for example, formerly laid their dead out in the bush for the hyenas to find, believing that the hyena transported the spirit of the dead person to the world of spirit. Plains Indians of North America similarly laid their dead out in the open but placed them on low wooden frameworks.

At least two materials, ochre and quartz, had special significance for early human societies in Africa as well as elsewhere. The earliest known

human symbolic markings, from Blombos Cave, were etched in ochre, and people in many early societies used ground ochre for ceremonial body markings or to decorate ceremonial objects. Quartz crystal apparently took on magical significance for early humans in widely separate parts of the world, including Africa, between 50,000 and 19,000, because of the ways in which it refracted light.

Much more remains to be learned about the worldviews and ideas of early humans in Africa and elsewhere in that early age. Scholars have raised provocative proposals about the nature of society, culture, and belief in those times, and exciting new discoveries remain ahead.

See also **Archaeology and Prehistory; Kinship and Descent; Prehistory; Technological Specialization Period, History of (c 19,000 to 500 BCE).**

BIBLIOGRAPHY

Hawkes, Kristen; James F. O'Connell; and Nicholas Blurton Jones. "Hunting and Nuclear Families: Some Lessons from the Hadza about Men's Work." *Current Anthropology* 42 (2001): 681–709.

Lewis-Williams, David. *The Mind in the Cave: Consciousness and Origins of Art.* London: Thames and Hudson, 2002.

O'Connell, James F.; Kristen Hawkes; and Nicholas Blurton Jones. "Grandmothering and the Evolution of *Homo erectus.*" *Journal of Human Evolution* 36 (1999): 461–485.

CHRISTOPHER EHRET

EASTERN AFRICA AND INDIAN OCEAN, HISTORY OF (1500 TO 1800). The eastern African coast has been an intermediate zone of exchange and interaction between continental Africa and the maritime world of the Indian Ocean at least from the beginning of the Christian era. From such interaction between Africa and the Indian Ocean emerged the Swahili civilization that was mercantile, cosmopolitan, and urbane, extending from southern Somalia to northern Mozambique, the Comoro Islands and northwestern Madagascar. These exchanges did not give rise to any mythical Zenj Empire, but to a series of Swahili city-states threaded together by the monsoons and coastal trade routes. The

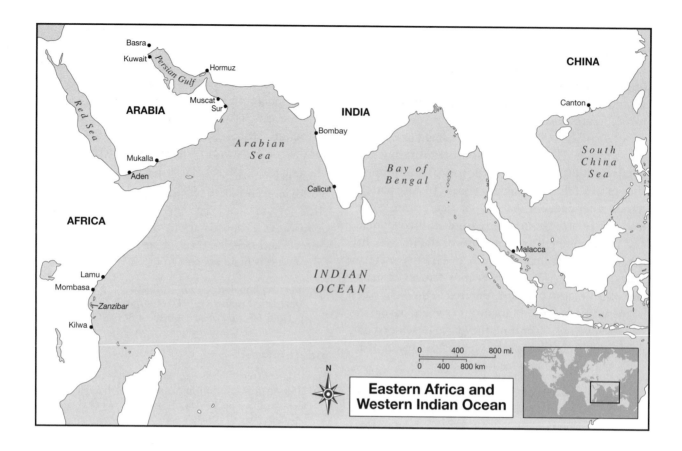

Eastern Africa and Western Indian Ocean

civilizations shared a common culture and the Swahili language, itself basically a Bantu language but with numerous words taken from Indian Ocean languages. The residents of the region also shared a belief in Islam, which had not only become central to Swahili society but had also become the prevailing faith of many of their mercantile partners all across the Indian Ocean. This syncretic Islam integrated features of the folk religions from the areas all around the littoral of the Indian Ocean.

According to the archaeologist Neville Chittick, the Indian Ocean was by 1500 "arguably the largest cultural continuum in the world" (1980, 13). It was a genuine *mare liberum* (open sea where all may trade freely), an arena of social and cultural interaction from the Swahili coast to the Indonesian archipelago. Not even the Chinese, who sent a series of expeditions as far as eastern Africa at the beginning of the fifteenth century, had tried to establish hegemony over the region. Commerce in this area was dominated by different nationalities at different times: the Persians in the pre- and early Islamic periods, the Arabs during the high Islamic

period, and the Gujarati Indians by the early sixteenth century. All the littoral peoples, however, had participated in trade and had developed a sophisticated network of seaborne interactions with strategically located port city-states all around the rim of the Indian Ocean. The researcher Tome Pires, who surveyed the Indian Ocean at the beginning of the sixteenth century, noted traders from Kilwa, Malindi, Mogadishu, and Mombasa at Malacca in Malaysia in the early sixteenth century. (1967, 46–47). Before the nineteenth century the hinterland of the northern Swahili towns was confined largely to a narrow coastal belt that was hemmed in by the *nyika* (wilderness), but Portuguese source from the early sixteenth century hints at commercial contacts among Kilwa, Mombasa, and Malindi with the "Monemugi" in central Tanzania. Further south the hinterland extended deep through the Zambezi valley into the plateau region of Zimbabwe, which was rich in gold and ivory (Strandes, 95).

When the Portuguese entered the Indian Ocean, they found a prosperous mercantile civilization along the Swahili coast. Although there is evidence

146

of local production of glass beads and cotton goods, by the sixteenth century Indian textiles "clothed virtually the whole littoral and far inland in the Indian Ocean" (Pearson 2000, 40). Barbosa remarked that "the kings of these isles live in great luxury; they are clad in very fine silk and cotton garments, which they purchase at Mombasa from the Cambay merchants." (Freeman-Grenville 1962, 133). Swahili architecture was impressive; a contemporary European visitor compared the mosque at Kilwa with that at Cordoba in Spain. By then the coastal mercantile economy was bifocal. Mombasa—with a population of 10,000—dominated in the north, because it was the most convenient port for the monsoon dhows bringing Indian textiles from Gujarat. In the south, Kilwa—with a population of 4,000—controlled the gold trade from Zimbabwe (Strandes, 88, 90). Numerous other Swahili city-states also competed for trade in such commodities as ivory.

THE VASCO DA GAMA EPOCH

In 1498 the Portuguese inaugurated what the scholar K. M. Pannikar has dubbed "the Vasco da Gama epoch of history" (1959, 12). They imported the European system of armed trading to destroy the preexisting network of free trade through the Red Sea and the Persian Gulf, and divert it to their own artery around the Cape of Good Hope. They embarked on their crusade "to conduct war with the Muslim and trade with the heathen" (Strandes, 56) and sacked city-states that resisted, such as Kilwa, Zanzibar, and Mombasa. They manipulated local rivalries to divide and rule the fragmented Swahili merchant class, buttressing Malindi against Mombasa. They imposed tribute and a *cartaz* (pass) system over trade in essential commodities, such as gold and ivory, to pay for their pepper in India. They concentrated on the island of Mozambique as a base to capture the gold trade from Zimbabwe and to provision their vessels en route between Europe and India. Modern scholars, however, argue that Portuguese domination during this period has been exaggerated. With their limited human and financial resources, the Portuguese were unable to control the whole system of commerce in the Indian Ocean. Their restrictive monopoly either killed the gold and ivory trade or drove it underground. After the first violent overture, they settled within the prevailing economy and were eventually swallowed by it.

Swahili resistance along the coast of Mozambique was based partly on their deep penetration into the interior. As many as ten thousand Muslims were said to be trading in the interior, and they were able to divert trade to Angoshe, within a stone's throw of Mozambique, with active encouragement from Kilwa and Mombasa. Smarting from the cumbersome Portuguese monopolies and oppression, the Swahili welcomed the Turks in the 1580s, forcing the Portuguese to build Fort Jesus from 1593 and move their puppet ruler from Malindi to Mombasa. This development merely sharpened the contradiction between the Muslim Swahili and their Portuguese overlords, leading to a revolt by the Christianized ruler of Mombasa who reverted to Islam in 1631. The standard-bearer of this resistance was Pate in the Lamu archipelago, which had developed as a center of Arab and Indian shipping and had successfully forged commercial links with the interior using the Tana River corridor. Not just an isolated local phenomenon, Swahili resistance also resonated with the wider Indian Ocean movement. In 1650 the Omanis finally expelled the Portuguese from Muscat and encouraged the Swahili to rebel. Portuguese rule ended when a combination of Swahili and Omani forces captured Fort Jesus in 1698.

SWAHILI RENAISSANCE IN THE EIGHTEENTH CENTURY

Although Oman left behind a garrison in Fort Jesus under the Mazrui governors, this Persian Gulf state was undergoing a fundamental socioeconomic and political revolution that was to transform it from a theocratic Imamate into a mercantile Sultanate. The prolonged interregnum permitted a renaissance of the Swahili coast during the eighteenth century, when Swahili commerce flourished. Trade focused on less ostentatious commodities that had long been exchanged between the east African coast and the Persian Gulf region: food grains and mangrove poles in exchange for dates, dried fish, and Muscat cloth. More lucrative was the carrying trade in the western Indian Ocean dominated by the Omanis, exchanging African ivory for Indian cloth and beads. Many of the Swahili city-states also tried to extend their hinterlands during this period. In the case of Mombasa, the Mazrui governors attempted to indigenize their power base that came to rest on an intricate hierarchy of relationships between themselves, the rival

Swahili confederacies of Mombasa, and a system of patronage that linked them with the Mijikenda "tribes" of the immediate hinterland, who supported the commercial prosperity of the city.

In addition, there was a revival of building and cultural activities all along the Swahili coast. In many Swahili city-states, an increasing number of Hadhramis from south Yemen were quickly assimilated. They spearheaded the movement to deepen Islamic learning, and some of them became noted Swahili literary figures. Most of the numerous Arabic loanwords in the Swahili language also began to be absorbed during this period. The Lamu archipelago emerged as the religious and cultural heartland of the coast, although Islam was still largely confined to the coastal towns.

GENESIS OF ZANZIBAR AND THE OMANI COMMERCIAL EMPIRE

The eighteenth century also laid the foundation for Zanzibar to emerge as the center of a vast commercial empire during the following century. Oman evolved into an expansionist commercial power, carrying trade as far as the Bay of Bengal and threatening to capture the lucrative China trade. The expansion of date production in Oman created a demand for slaves, who were also used as domestics and as sailors and pearl divers in the Persian Gulf. The number of slaves sent to the north from Africa probably amounted to about three thousand per year. More portentous, however, was a new demand for slaves from the French islands in southwestern Indian Ocean, where the Atlantic system of a slave plantation economy had extended. In 1776 a Frenchman, Morice, signed a treaty with Kilwa to supply one thousand slaves per year, but by the 1780s, an average of two thousand slaves were being exported annually. Unable to dislodge their Mazrui rivals from Fort Jesus, the new Busaidi dynasty of Oman reasserted control over Kilwa and chose Zanzibar as the capital of their future commercial empire.

See also **Eastern African Coast, History of (Early to 1600); Indian Ocean, Africa, History of (1000 BCE to 600 CE).**

BIBLIOGRAPHY

Berg, Fred J. "The Swahili Community of Mombasa, 1500–1900." *Journal of African History* 9, no. 1 (1968): 35–56.

Chaudhuri, K. N. *Trade and Civilization in the Indian Ocean: An Economic History from the Rise of Islam to 1750.* Cambridge, U.K.: Cambridge University Press, 1985.

Chittick, Neville. "East Africa and the Orient: Ports and Trade before the Arrival of The Portuguese." In *Historical Relations Across the Indian Ocean*, ed. C. Mehaud. Paris: UNESCO, 1980.

Filesi, Teobaldo. *China and Africa in the Middle Ages*, trans. David L. Morison. London: Frank Cass, 1972.

Freeman-Grenville, G. S. P. *The East African Coast: Select Documents.* Oxford: Clarendon Press. 1962.

Freeman-Grenville, G. S. P. *The French at Kilwa Island.* Oxford: Clarendon Press, 1965.

Horton, M., and J. Middleton. *The Swahili.* Oxford: Blackwell, 2000.

Levtzion, Nehemia, and Randall L. Pouwels, eds. *The History of Islam in Africa.* Oxford: James Currey, 2000.

Pannikar, K. M. *Asia and Western Dominance.* London: George Allen and Unwin, 1959.

Pearson, Michael N. *Port Cities and Intruders: The Swahili Coast, India and Portugal in the Early Modern Era.* Baltimore, MD: Johns Hopkins University Press, 1998.

Pearson, Michael N. "The Indian Ocean and the Red Sea." In *The History of Islam in Africa*, ed. Nehemia Levtzion and Randall L. Pouwels. Oxford: James Currey, 2000.

Pires, Tome. *The Suma Oriental of Tome Pire*, ed. Armando Cortesão. Liechtenstein: Kraus Reprint, 1967.

Pouwels, Randall L. "The East African Coast, c. 780 to 1900." In *The History of Islam in Africa*, ed. Nehemia Levtzion and Randall L. Pouwels. Oxford: James Currey, 2000.

Sheriff, Abdul. *Slaves, Spices, and Ivory in Zanzibar.* London: James Currey, 1987.

Strandes, Justes. *The Portuguese Period in East Africa*, trans. J. F. Wallwork. Nairobi, Kenya: East African Literature Bureau, 1961.

ABDUL SHERIFF

EASTERN AFRICAN COAST, HISTORY OF (EARLY TO 1600).

The many towns and associated hinterland communities of the eastern African coast share broad cultural commonalities that emerged in the context of what came to be called Swahili civilization. This emergence took place in the first millennium CE. Swahili culture was created along a narrow coastal strip of some 1,553 miles, from modern Somalia southward to Mozambique and incorporating Kenya's Lamu archipelago, Tanzania's offshore islands of Pemba, Unguja (Zanzibar), and Mafia, the Comoros Archipelago, and northwestern Madagascar. The early history of the coast is known largely through archaeological research, augmented by a few historical documents and interpretations drawn from historical linguistics. In the centuries immediately prior to the founding of Swahili settlements, the coast was home to a low-density array of smaller-scale societies with lifeways built around pastoralism and mixed farming and fishing. These groups shared material culture and linguistic connections with groups farther to the interior, rather than having strictly coastal affinities. The production and use of distinctive ceramic types, such as Urewe and Kwale wares, exemplify the shared coastal and interior horizons for the Late Stone and Early Iron Ages.

Archaeological work at sites dating to the first half of the first millennium CE, including Ras Hafun in Somalia and Unguja Ukuu in Tanzania, provide evidence of relatively small farming and fishing settlements, some with impressive trade ties beyond the coast. The first written document pertaining to the coast is a merchants' guide titled *The Periplus of the Erythraean Sea*. It was written in 40 CE by a Greek sailor who described encounters with coastal groups and trade along the Red Sea, Eastern African, and Indian shores while employed in a Roman ship. His text includes references to places that have been identified as Ras Hafun and Pemba Island, and to Rhapta, the Romans' southernmost port of trade thought to be on the central Tanzanian coast. Rhapta's inhabitants are described as under the authority of the governor of the port of Muza in the southwestern Arabian peninsula. Subsequent documents and archaeological evidence have not confirmed this depiction. Exported goods included ivory and rhino horns from the interior and nautilus and turtle shells from the coast, and imports included metal weapons and tools, glass, and some foods.

Another second-century documentary source is Ptolemy's *Geography*, a compilation of Greco-Roman knowledge containing sailing coordinates for coastal locations (with few similarities to those in the *Periplus*). Both documents are consistent with archaeological evidence that at least some of the coastal Early Iron Age populations had already participated in trade and social relations with commercial societies from the Mediterranean and Indian Ocean rims. The documentary record is then largely silent until the end of the millennium, when Arab and other first-person accounts become available.

THE FORMATION OF SWAHILI SOCIETY

The early Swahili maintained many of the cultural practices of the pastoral and farming/fishing peoples on the coast and nearby mainland from whom they were derived. But, by the sixth to tenth centuries CE, archaeological evidence reveals a Swahili lifeway that, in total, was distinct from earlier or neighboring groups, despite ongoing continuities. Its characteristics include use of Tana Tradition or Triangular Incised Ware ceramics; technologies such as iron smelting and boat construction; the building of round and rectangular earth and thatch houses; household economy based on millet agriculture, husbandry, and fishing; obtaining imported goods including glazed ceramics, glassware, silver and copper jewelry, and stone and glass beads from the Persian Gulf and beyond; and evidence for conversion to Islam from the eighth century onward.

The settlement of the coast by people with this archaeological signature marks a transition from the previous mosaic of groups, who disappear from the archaeology of the coast but remain in the interior. The vast majority of settlements with Swahili characteristics were on the beachfront or within twelve miles of the coast, and a few others have been identified up to several hundred miles to the interior, such as Dakawa in Tanzania.

Islam grew to great importance in coastal life. The earliest evidence to date for its practice is seen in the excavated remains of an eighth-century timber mosque at Shanga in the Lamu archipelago. A series of mosques of increasing size and formality were subsequently superimposed. This sequence attests to contacts, by at least this time, between Eastern Africans (proto- or early Swahili) with Muslim traders or missionaries. Earlier understandings of the formation of Swahili society presumed that large-scale Arab and Persian immigration colonized the coast for the purpose of developing trading opportunities. Conversion of coastal peoples was seen as part of this presumed wave of immigrants. Archaeological and linguistic evidence now points convincingly to a model of the African origins of Swahili culture. However, this model freely acknowledges that small numbers of immigrants arrived throughout Swahili history, and that an openness to select foreign influences was fundamental to Swahili life.

By the ninth century, economic connections between eastern Africa and the Middle East had grown in scale to include the export of thousands of slaves from the African interior. The slaves were transported through coastal centers including Unguja and Pemba Islands to destinations in present-day Iraq where they were employed in drainage projects at the head of the Gulf of Basra. In 868 CE, a massive slave uprising known as the Zanj Revolt weakened the Caliphate based in Basra and eventually led to a downturn in interest in slaves from Swahili sources. The revolt is an indication of the presence and influence of Africans in Asia at that time. However, neither the exchange of goods in and out of the region, nor the export of slaves and the Zanj revolt, provide more than a glimpse into the full texture of the relationship between eastern Africa and various parts of Asia in the first centuries of Swahili history.

The spiritual transformation of the coast had sweeping effects, but these were neither uniform nor rapid. Representatives of several Islamic sects gained influence in different areas. Conversion took place gradually and irregularly and did not eclipse, but rather incorporated, local spiritual practices. By about 1200 CE, however, all larger Swahili settlements and many smaller ones featured mosques as centerpieces of Islamic practice and community organization.

THE EMERGENCE OF STONETOWNS

The wealth and power of the Swahili towns waxed in the eleventh to fourteenth centuries, as measured by the scale and number of settlements and their material culture. Numerous villages became more substantial settlements, increasing greatly in size and functions, and expanding trade relationships with polities in the African interior and along the Indian Ocean shores. Building in stone became an important medium of Swahili cultural expression and the hallmark of elite dwellings and public and ritual structures within settlements. In the ninth century, Swahili elites adopted a method of mortared limestone construction that originated on the Red Sea shores. The technology included detailing buildings with finely carved coral arches, niches, and geometric elements made when fresh coral was still soft. The carved blocks were then allowed to dry and harden, after which all were plastered into smooth surfaces together with the limestone.

The resulting architecture—bright, elaborated, multistoried, and more permanent than structures of earth and thatch—may have been critical to anchoring the relationships of certain Swahili lineages with important foreign traders. Ethnohistorically, such houses acted as customs houses and provided lodging for visiting merchants, helping to cement their elite owners' credibility as business partners, and contributing to the prosperity of the towns and regions at large. This relationship may be suggested for earlier centuries as well, although all settlements with stone houses cannot be assumed to have had direct ties with international merchants. Although earth and thatch architecture continued to characterize villages and remained abundant even in the new larger settlements, called stonetowns, the stone architecture alone became the basis for modern archaeologists' and historians' initial reconstructions of Swahili society.

Many of the Swahili settlements have been described as urban (some call them city-states or states) marked by complex relations with rural settlements in their local countrysides. Such centers differed in their internal class structures and political styles, with two kinds of government becoming most common in later centuries, and known ethnohistorically. One emphasized a single leader, elevating him far above the majority of the town dwellers. This was called the Shirazi mode of dominance, from claims that such authorities made to Persian connections through the city of Shiraz. Other towns emphasized a larger class of elites with less distance between social tiers. This was known as the Waungwana mode of dominance, referencing the class of elites. Coastal regions became more distinct from one another with localized historical trajectories. The shared, distinctive visual signatures of Swahili towns and their hinterlands past and present are compelling, but also tend to overshadow important differences between regions along the coastline.

Major stonetowns that have been investigated archaeologically include Shanga, Manda, and Gede in Kenya; Chwaka, Ras Mkumbuu, Tumbatu, and Kilwa in Tanzania; and Mahilaka in Madagascar. Certain urban centers created epic histories, passed down orally and ultimately formalized as written chronicles; the best-known histories of this sort are from Lamu and Pate in Kenya and Kilwa in Tanzania. The chronicles, as well as other external and internal sources, often discuss sociopolitical relationships such as those seen in the deep ties between the Swahili and interior peoples, marriage alliances with Indian Ocean families, and acts of generosity by local leaders toward their populations.

As in the earlier phase of coastal settlement, life in the stonetowns included farming (with rice becoming important in addition to millet) and fishing, craft production, the active practice of Islam and the presence of religious specialists, and long-distance trade both to the interior and throughout the Indian Ocean region. Gold obtained through trade with societies of the Zimbabwe Plateau came to be one of the most important exports from the coast, along with ivory, iron, animal products, and mangrove poles. Imports continued to feature ceramics from far afield, including East Asia, Southeast Asia, and Southwest Asia; a wide range of personal items such as beads and other jewelry; cloth; and copies of the Qur'an and other texts. Copper and silver coins were minted in some of the largest centers, such as Kilwa. Rock crystal and other stone was worked into beads and traded, and iron continued in importance locally while copper alloys were increasingly added to local production.

SHIFTS IN COASTAL POWER

1600 CE does not mark a sharp historical break in the life of the Swahili towns and villages except in the way that the effects of Middle Eastern and European colonizers were increasingly felt from the sixteenth century onward. Portuguese ships rounded the Cape of Good Hope to reach the eastern African coast for the first time in 1498. The early Portuguese in the region have not been the focus of much study, although their sixteenth-century presence is known from documentary sources and, in some cases, from architecture at Malindi, in Zanzibar town, elsewhere on Unguja and Pemba Islands, and at Kilwa. Their limited settlement and cultural impact is not well understood in the early twenty-first century and future study is warranted. At a regional level, their aggressive naval intrusions in the Indian Ocean are credited with contributing to the long-term decline of Swahili autonomy and power. The construction of Fort Jesus in Mombasa in 1593 was the most striking architectural presence the Portuguese achieved in this period. They were evicted from that site in 1698 after a long siege that ended the first phase of their colonialism on the Swahili coast. Sections of the coast came under immediate attack from Omani Arabs, however, such that from 1498 onward the Swahili struggled against unwanted incursions of various scales and levels of success. Swahili urban and rural life prevailed throughout, although disruptions in long-distance trade and losses of regional autonomy weakened the strength of the entire coastal system, and its ties to the interior and the Indian Ocean.

The coast was not united under a single political authority at any point until the Omani Sultanate colonized the region in the early nineteenth century.

See also **Archaeology and Prehistory; Eastern Africa and Indian Ocean, History of (1500 to 1800); Eastern African Coast, History of (Early to 1600); Indian Ocean, Africa, History of (1000 BCE to 600 CE); Prehistory: Eastern Africa.**

BIBLIOGRAPHY

Allen, James de Vere. *Swahili Origins.* London: J. Currey, 1993.

Casson, Lionel. *The Periplus Maris Erythraei.* Princeton, NJ: Princeton University Press, 1989.

Chami, Felix A. *The Tanzanian Coast in the First Millennium AD: An Archaeology of the Iron-Working, Farming Communities.* Uppsala, Sweden: Societas Archaeologica Upsaliensis, 1994.

Chittick, H. Neville. *Kilwa: An Islamic Trading City on the East African Coast.* Nairobi, Kenya: British Institute in Eastern Africa, 1974.

Freeman-Grenville, Greville Stewart Parker. *The East African Coast: Select Documents from the First to the Earlier Nineteenth Century.* Oxford: Clarendon Press, 1962.

Garlake, Peter S. *The Early Islamic Architecture on the East African Coast.* London: Oxford University Press, 1966.

Horton, Mark. *Shanga: The Archaeology of a Muslim Trading Settlement on the Coast of East Africa.* London: British Institute in Eastern Africa, 1996.

Horton, Mark, and John Middleton. *The Swahili.* London: Blackwell, 2000.

Insoll, Timothy. "The East African Coast and Offshore Islands." In *The Archaeology of Islam in Sub-Saharan Africa.* Cambridge, U.K.: Cambridge University, 2003.

Juma, Abdurahman. *Unguja Ukuu on Zanzibar: An Archaeological Study of Early Urbanism.* Uppsala, Sweden: Societas Archaeologica Upsaliensis, 2004.

Kirkman, James S. *Men and Monuments on the East African Coast.* London: Lutterworth Press, 1964.

Kusimba, Chapurukha M. *The Rise and Fall of Swahili States.* Walnut Creek, California: AltaMira, 1999.

Nurse, Derek, and Thomas Spear. *The Swahili: Reconstructing the History and Language of an African Society, 800–1500.* Philadelphia: University of Pennsylvania Press, 1985.

Pouwels, Randall. *Horn and Crescent: Cultural Change and Traditional Islam on the East African Coast, 800–1900.* Cambridge, U.K.: Cambridge University Press, 1987.

ADRIA LAVIOLETTE

ÉBOUÉ, ADOLPHE-FÉLIX-SYLVESTRE

(1884–1944). Éboué was born in Cayenne, French Guyana, in South America. His education at a select school of colonial administration ensured his future professional success in France's colonies, and friendships he made there, notably with the Senegalese statesman Blaise Diagne, were vital to his career. Éboué adopted French manners and attitudes and rose high (although slowly) in the French colonial administration. He served in Oubangui-Chari in French Equatorial Africa, one of the poorest places on earth, from 1909 to 1931. In 1917, while traveling by ship to France to try to enlist in the French army, he was forced to stay over in Gabon to await the ship on which he had booked passage. There he was denied a hotel room because of the color of his skin, for racism was deeply entrenched in the port city of Libreville. Historians have suggested that he and many other Creoles chose to settle in the hinterland of what is now the Central African Republic to avoid the racism of the coast.

Éboué returned to the Caribbean to serve as colonial governor in Martinique from 1932 to 1934, back to Africa in the French Soudan (western Africa) from 1934 to 1936, and back again to a premier post in the Caribbean in Guadeloupe from 1936 to 1938. In 1939 he fell afoul of political rivals and was forced to return to obscure Oubangui-Chari. This demotion would, however, place him squarely in the path of history and allow him to serve France during World War II in a way that would have been thought impossible just a few years previously.

It was during World War II that Éboué became famous. He brought the colonies of French Equatorial Africa and Cameroon into the war on the side of Charles de Gaulle's Free French. His loyalty was particularly important to the Allies, because all other French colonies in northern and western Africa, as well as Somalia and Madagascar, were supporting the Nazi-allied Vichy regime. In 1949, de Gaulle showed his enduring gratitude for Éboué's aid in a time of need by ensuring that Éboué would be buried in the Panthéon of heroes in Paris, an honor that only Éboué, of all France's African citizen-subjects, has ever received.

See also **Colonial Policies and Practices: French North Africa; Creoles; Decolonization; World War II.**

BIBLIOGRAPHY

Castor, Elie. *Félix Éboué: Gouverneur et philosophe.* Paris: Editions L'Harmattan, 1984.

Weinstein, Brian. *Éboué.* New York: Oxford University Press, 1972.

ALEXANDER GOLDMAN

ECOLOGY

This entry includes the following articles:
HUMAN ROLES
MODERN ISSUES

HUMAN ROLES

In a sense, the entire world consists of a mosaic of ecosystems, some large and some small. Overall, Africa has a number of prominent ecosystems, all of which have included human elements that have had varied effects upon their respective environments.

TROPICAL RAIN FOREST

The tropical rain forest straddles the Equator in a belt around the world. Africa still has a considerable portion of its own tropical rain forest stretching from Mali, Gabon, Cameroon, Congo Brazzaville, and Democratic Republic of the Congo (DRC). Characteristically, the tropical rain forest consists of a shallow top layer of fertile and well-watered soil closely packed with tall trees. These trees provide a canopy leaving other plants that protrude beyond the canopy. Others are condemned to form a carpet of low-lying plants that only get an opportunity to rise above the ground level when the tall trees die and fall or are burnt down by either human or other natural phenomena like lightning.

Tropical rain forests constitute the largest variety of both plant and animal species living together in an intricate relationship. It has a constant temperature and high (almost daily) rainfall, which leads to high humidity and dense vegetation that gives the ecosystem its unique water and nutrient cycle.

Apart from providing a huge gene pool that is second to none, tropical rain forests also provide a stabilizing influence on world climate. Deforestation can and does lead to devastating erosion of forest soils and nutrients, and pollution of the supporting river system such as the Congo and the Amazon Rivers. It also leads to changes in rainfall patterns over wide areas. Tropical rain forests are probably the biggest absorbents of carbon emissions and are thus acting as buffers against global warming. Deforestation counteracts this function.

In the original lifestyle of the human inhabitants of the African tropical rain forest, stretching particularly from Cameroon to DRC, the pygmies were hunter-gatherers hunting primarily for food. However, with modernity and so-called civilization, the result is an accentuated desire to acquire money. It is no longer the pot that matters. It has now acquired a sinister edge of bushmeat trade. Myths have grown about special medicinal or aphrodisiac features of bushmeat. This is leading to a severe depletion of animal—particularly primate—populations in the rain forests.

An additional factor in the depletion of the rain forest primate fauna has been the change in their habitat. Again, this is due to the cutting down of trees and the depletion of the vegetative cover.

Gorillas, as a prime example of an African tropical rain forest primate, are now regarded as an endangered species.

Logging, not an old African pursuit, offers jobs to the native inhabitants of these tropical rain forests who innocently abandon their forest habits and drift into the townships that have grown around the edges of the forest. Meanwhile, loggers who bring bulldozers and other heavy vehicles are practicing a one-sided decimation of the tropical rain forest without any reseeding or providing cover for the dirt roads opened up for transporting the hewn wood.

THE AFRICAN SAVANNA

North and south of the tropical rain forest belt are the savannas that are really tropical grasslands. Being situated where they are, they go through periods of rainfall and periods of drought. As the monsoons that bring the rains move up and down the tropical belt, so do the wild animals that inhabit these areas.

The nomadic pastoralists have for centuries followed the rainfall patterns of the African savanna to provide pasture for their animals—cattle, sheep, and goats, to which some of the indigenous nationalities have also added camels. It is not pastures alone that the nomadic pastoralist wants for his animals. He is also after water.

Domestic livestock for the nomadic pastoralist is not merely a source of living by providing meat and milk and blood to them. They also constitute wealth. Wealth, by its nature, means that the more one has, the more one wants. In the ecological equation of the African savanna, the fine balance between the desire for wealth and the carrying capacity of the grazed lands has unfortunately led to a severe degradation of the savanna. It is being transformed into semiarid and, later, arid lands. In due course, an outbreak of rinderpest or East Coast fever leads to a mass death of livestock but the relevant lessons are unfortunately not learnt.

THE AFRICAN DESERTS

Overgrazing of the African savanna by both wild and domestic livestock in combination with deforestation are the main causes of desertification. The use of trees for providing firewood and the growth of human populations have undoubtedly contributed significantly to desertification. Tropical rain forests are being whittled at the edges and turned into African savanna, the savanna is being overgrazed and turned into semiarid lands, and semiarid lands are becoming arid lands and eventually deserts. But humans are not the only players in this ecological transformation equation. Climate change—particularly global climate change—has also been a factor. Thus, the world's largest desert—the Sahara—has been a victim of such global climate change.

Human beings have contributed little to the formation of the Sahara and Kalahari Deserts. What people have done, however, is to adapt to their conditions to exist over a number of centuries, if not millennia. The Arabs and Berbers of the Sahara have a number of ways in which they have modified their lifestyles to survive in the world's largest deserts. Equally, though, the San of Kalahari have their own adaptations. It would be not be possible in this brief survey to recount even a few of these adaptations to desert life, but they are well worth looking up.

OTHER AFRICAN ECOSYSTEMS

Other African habitats must be mentioned. There are the mountain forests that have not only provided refuge for the likes of the mountain gorilla but have also provided shelter for the Kikuyus who were constantly wary about their traditional enemies, the marauding Maasai. Cleared patches of forests provided fertile lands for the agricultural Kikuyus and allied cousins the Akamba, although the latter have remarkable adaptations to surviving in the semiarid lands.

The coastal peoples of the eastern seaboard of Africa are the Swahili. They have traditionally not only exploited the mangrove swamps but also have built and sailed dhows up and down the entire eastern seaboard and across the Indian Ocean to the North and the East.

The coral reef off East Africa provides not only a spectacular concentration of species of marine life but also has provided food for the coastal Swahili for millennia. The Swahili provide an excellent example of a people adapted to living in typical tropical coastal lowlands. Of late, a threat to the coral reefs has come from three different sources: dynamiting to enable catches of large numbers of fish; fine sediment being taken by the eastward-flowing rivers smothering the corals; and sewage from the growing concentration of tourist hotels along the beautiful beaches of East Africa.

The human roles in the African ecology have, in the initial phases, been of a creative interaction with that ecosystem. The pygmies of the tropical rain forest, the Khoes of the Kalahari Desert, the Tuaregs of the Sahara Desert and, in a sense, the Swahilis of the eastern seaboard have all been examples of nondestructive adaptation to their specific habitats. Increasingly, these and other groups are coming under pressure to pursue practices that threaten the total or partial integrity of a number of ecosystems.

Growth of human populations means that, increasingly, only those animals and plants that are conserved within national parks and national reserves would continue to gain respite from extinction for now, but not forever.

The need to feed these rising human populations also means that there is more intensified agricultural activity—increasing use of inorganic fertilizers and the consequent outflow of nitrogenous materials—which lead to eutrophication of drainage basins and lakes. Such is the case of Lake Nakuru in the heart of the Rift Valley.

The cutting down of trees for firewood leads to progressive desertification, whereas growing industrialization in many parts of Africa means a growing threat of industrial waste and carbon emissions. But many parts of Africa are also becoming dumping grounds for industrial wastes from first world countries.

With new oil reserves being increasingly discovered on the African mainland and associated offshore areas, oil pollution becomes a real threat. Add to these the threat of global warming.

There is growing consciousness the world over that a blinkered-vision pursuit of economic progress oblivious of environmental concerns will surely lead only to irremediable destruction of the biosphere that sustains all of humanity.

See also **Agriculture; Archaeology and Prehistory; Climate; Demography: Population Data and Surveys; Desertification, Modern; Ecosystems; Forestry; Frontiers; Human Evolution; Land: Reform; Land: Tenure; Peasants; Plants; Sahara Desert; Wildlife.**

BIBLIOGRAPHY

Cairncross, Frances. *Costing the Earth: The Challenge for Governments, the Opportunities for Business.* Boston: Harvard Business School Press, 1992.

Carwardine, Mark. *The WWF Environment Handbook.* London: Macdonald Optima, 1990.

Davidson, Joan. *How Green Is Your City?: Pioneering Approaches to Environmental Action.* London: Bedford Square Press, 1988.

Durrell, Lee. *The State of the Ark.* London: Bodley Head, 1986.

Jenner, Paul, and Christine Smith. *The Environmental Business Handbook.* London: Euromonitor, 1989.

Johnston, Ronald. J. *Environmental Problems: Nature, Economy and State.* London: Belhaven, 1989.

Pretty, John. N. *Regenerating Agriculture: Policies and Practice for Sustainability and Self-Reliance.* London: Earthscan, 1995.

Simpson, Struan. *The Times Guide to the Environment: A Comprehensive Handbook to Green Issues.* London: Times, 1990.

Tesar, Jenny. *Threatened Oceans.* New York: Facts On File, 1991.

Tudge, Colin, ed. *The Encyclopedia of the Environment.* London: Christopher Helm, 1988.

Turner, R. Kerry, ed. *Sustainable Environmental Management: Principles and Practice.* London: Belhaven Press, 1988.

World Commission on Environmental and Development. *Our Common Future.* Oxford: Oxford University Press, 1987.

MOHAMED HYDER

MODERN ISSUES

NO CONSERVATION WITHOUT PEOPLE

Ecology is a social issue; there can be no conservation (sustainable management of biological resources) without the conscious effort of people as social agents. Earlier attempts to develop environmental policy in Africa tended to put the cart before the horse, seeking to isolate and protect biological resources (such as forests) because they were thought to be in a "natural" state (untouched by human concerns); "ecology" and "social issues" were judged to be poles apart. But the more science has revealed about the depth of human evolutionary history in Africa, the less likely it seems one will find any areas in the continent not affected by long-term human occupancy. In 1973 P. W. Richards, a leading expert on the botany of the African tropical rain forests, concluded that "primeval" rain forest, unmodified by human action, was no more than a fiction as far as Africa was concerned. Yet significant tracts of the continent are properly described as "wilderness," rich in biological resources, and it is a legitimate objective for environmental policy to consider the proper use and management of these areas.

Where genuine wilderness areas occur in Africa today, it is generally for one of three reasons: human inhabitants have withdrawn from the land; communities have ring-fenced and protected environmental resources of special interest; or people have consciously striven to create new "natural resources." There is emerging consensus that the key to effective environmental policy in Africa, as elsewhere in the world, is to align human interests and biological resource management objectives. Thus, it is useful to start by considering in what ways human agency has shaped, and even created, present biological resource endowments in Africa.

Withdrawing from Marginal Land. Some marginal areas have reverted to wilderness as a result of unsustainable previous use. Parts of the southern border of the Sahara, in the western African Sahel, proved especially fragile when agricultural land use was intensified in the modern period. For example, unwise investment in cattle-watering facilities led, on occasion, to overgrazing with subsequent, mostly highly localized, desertification (permanent loss of vegetation cover). In other cases, large-scale irrigation schemes (in Mali and Sudan, for example) have proved troublesome and expensive to maintain, and few, if any, donors are willing to consider investing in such projects without very careful consideration of possible adverse effects on the environment (e.g., salinization of soils) or health (e.g., spread of schistosomiasis).

Much of the Sahara's present barren loneliness, however, is not the result of agricultural mismanagement but a human response to long-term changes in humidity associated with the periodic waxing and waning of the polar ice caps. During a wetter phase some ten thousand years ago, even the central Sahara was inhabited by hunting and fishing peoples, some of whom may have practiced early forms of agriculture. Descendants of the people who founded these early civilizations, however, evacuated these areas in response to desiccation, following the rainfall belts as they shifted southward.

Abandonment of settled and cultivated land is not limited to the dry Sahel, however, but is a feature of some wetter areas as well. Many forest reserves were created in the colonial period on tracts of land earlier emptied of their human populations not by climatic change but by slave raiding, warfare, and epidemics (e.g., the periodic upsurge of sleeping sickness, a debilitating and ultimately fatal disease affecting both cattle and humans, transmitted by the bite of tsetse flies). Conflicts among the volatile polities of the African forest belt in the nineteenth century appear to have been partly a reaction to the intensification of often violent and anarchic overseas trading activities (including the slave trade) in the period prior to formal colonial annexation.

A good example is the complex sequence of wars that engulfed the city-states of southwestern Nigeria during much of the nineteenth century. Here, established political elites vied for power and control of trade routes with new military-mercantile factions, resulting in the sacking of several established towns and the abandonment of cultivated tracts of farmland surrounding them. It was into these abandoned tracts that the early colonial foresters stepped. The patchwork of reserves carved by the colonial Nigerian forestry department in these war-devastated areas was, for some of the main losers in the Yoruba civil wars of the nineteenth century, one of their lasting memorials. For example, the site of Owu, a thriving, large Yoruba town in the early nineteenth century, is reserved forest in the early 2000s.

Reservation was undertaken mainly to protect timber for logging interests against the inroads of farmers seeking to recover their land, rather than for reasons of biological conservation. But a good number of these early colonial acquisitions were, in fact, more suited to small-scale farming activities than to logging; it is these forests, taken out of circulation by colonial fiat but not subsequently exploited by the commercial timber industry, that provide a resource of great interest to a new generation of conservationists interested mainly in protection of biodiversity. Given that biodiversity is sometimes seen as the residue of nature not yet "consumed" by human activity, it is ironic to note that the value of these reserves as stores of biodiversity is, at times, more a consequence of their long and checkered history of human use than of their being intrinsically rich in plants and animals.

The Gola Forest on the border between Sierra Leone and Liberia is a good case in point. Adopted by the Royal Society for Preservation of Birds in 1990 as its first overseas nonmigratory bird conservation project, on account of exceptional species richness, the Gola reserves in Sierra Leone were first delimited in the 1920s. According to historical sources, however, they were not forest at all but a tract of farmland regularly exploited by border-zone communities in the early to mid-nineteenth century. The region was then emptied of its population by a sequence of local wars fought by rival border-zone warrior chiefs. These local "big men" were struggling to secure their positions within volatile trading networks, in a region already being pulled apart by the rival activities of colonial commercial interests in Freetown and Monrovia.

Not long after the imposition of British colonial rule, this empty border region, now rapidly reverting to forest, was delimited as a sequence of reserves, to protect its timber from farmers edging back toward their ancestral settlement sites. It seems likely that some part, at least, of the richness of Gola's bird species is a product of this checkered settlement history. Regrown from forest islands, tree-crop plantations, garden plots, and fallow thickets, the Gola reserves constitute a patchwork of many different vegetation types conducive to the survival of a larger number of bird species than might be found in a more uniform if nondescript forest.

"Ring Fencing" of Valued Wilderness. Africa is a continent, historically, of relatively low population pressure on land. This has limited the more general need for elaborate, labor-intensive systems of agriculture such as those found in the rice lands of Southeast Asia, though there are many localized instances of such development. Nor has there been much development of private landed property, an essential feature of the pattern of agrarian and agro-technological change in western Europe. In the early twenty-first century African cultivators tenaciously retain, and often for good technical reasons in hard and variable environments, elements of shifting cultivation as the basis for their farming activities. Gathering and hunting also remain quite significant to household budgetary and subsistence strategy. Outside advisers on environmental policy, used to different property rights regimes in their own countries, have been hostile to the idea of shifting cultivation. Part of this hostility is based on a misconception. It was once understood that these footloose systems of land resource exploitation in traditional Africa operated according to a system of communal landownership. Theoretically inclined outsiders were quick to predict Africa's vulnerability to the "tragedy of the commons"—degradation that results from lack of control over "free riders" on land that nobody owns.

In point of fact, however, Africa's land-tenure systems are rarely if ever "communal," in the sense of allowing unrestricted access to all comers. The more normal pattern is group ownership, land controlled by corporations to which entrance is governed by strict membership conditions. These landholding corporations—kin groups or sometimes entire villages—will, given the chance, protect their collective interest with vigor. Strangers entering a village may not necessarily pay rent, but they will be granted use rights over land, or access to forest for hunting, only after full public acknowledgment of family ownership. In many cases, land modifications with long-term implications (such as irrigation or tree-crop planting) are strictly limited to members of the landholding group. An outsider may be excluded permanently from such activities, or qualify for inclusion only after demonstrating a durable sense of local commitment (e.g., by marrying a member of the landed family). Elaborate arrangements may be in force to share the products of hunting and gathering with representatives of the landowning group. Among the Mende of Sierra Leone the paramount chief is *ndo mahei* (chief of the land), and a hunter in the forest is required to acknowledge this authority by sharing with the chief specified parts of any large animal killed. Modernity is no excuse. A tractor driver who ran into and killed a buffalo while plowing grassland for a government rice-farming scheme had to report the event to the paramount chief without delay and offer up the requisite parts of the animal.

Separate schemes of corporate ownership may cover the management of land, water, and tree-crop, and forest (or wilderness) resources. Tree tenure, for example, may operate independently of land tenure. Although African corporate land-tenure principles are sometimes considered a brake on commercialization, because land sales can be achieved only after intensive negotiations across an entire group, there is little hard evidence that, of themselves, these arrangements are unsuited to the sustainable management of natural resources. In fact, just the reverse appears to be the case. The ring fencing of a natural forest may be that much more thorough when all eyes and ears in the village are alert to abuse by outsiders. Additionally, since corporate ownership derives from the continuity of the local residential community over time, stakeholders are predisposed to take the sustainability of land resources seriously. Typically, African villagers still tend to put the matter in terms once used by the Oni of Ife (in western Nigeria) addressing the British colonial authorities in Nigeria at the turn of the century: that land management is an issue for the ancestors, the living, and the members of the community yet to be born.

This sense of history and commitment to the future health of the resource base in the long term is often expressed in the vigorous survival, throughout rural sub-Saharan Africa, of ideas about "ancestral blessing." Even success in the modern sector—at school, for example—is assimilated to the moral economy of ancestral goodwill. (At the very least, successful education is seen to be dependent on parental foresight, which in turn creates the obligation to "think ahead" for one's own descendants.) Villagers on the move in their wilderness areas are constantly alert for signs of previous occupation (old kola trees in the forest, long-forgotten grave sites, surface artifacts indicating former settlement) and will note these as "belonging to the ancestors," finding them rich in reassurance that people recognizably similar to themselves have already passed this way. This encourages the thought that only through the foresight of these earlier tenants is it possible to enjoy the benefit of forest resources today. Thus, members of the present generation, so long as they can see themselves being invoked and called to account by their descendants, have an obligation to think about the state in which they leave the land. Ritual activities at ancestral sites in the forest are part of a continuing process through which village communities lay claim to wilderness as a landscape shaped by human activity over the long term.

The Unmaking and Remaking of Natural Resources.

There seems little doubt that in some cases rapid increase in population can engulf existing and relatively stable land-management procedures. But there is still much disagreement among experts as to how, exactly, this kind of destabilization occurs in specific instances—whether, for example, "weight of numbers" causes physical collapse of delicate ecosystems (in ways documented in nature by ecologists working with nonhuman populations), or whether a crisis of population pressure mainly causes institutional breakdown. (An example would be the attempt, by some authorities, to explain ethnic warfare in Rwanda as a result of land hunger in one of Africa's most densely populated countries.)

Even less clear is whether there is a general crisis of overpopulation in Africa. Africa is the least densely populated continent, and the one with the highest current rates of population increase. But these facts can be accounted for in two ways. Present high rates may represent a disaster in the making for a continent with poor soils and complex but fragile ecosystems equipped to sustain only a thin scatter of human settlement. But equally, these high present rates of increase may be, historically, no more than the result of a "catching up" exercise after a sequence of demographic disasters in the nineteenth century.

Although historical demography in Africa is in its relative infancy, a number of such disasters have been clearly delineated. Some can be traced, ultimately, to the aggressive way in which foreign (colonial and pre-colonial) commercial interests exploited natural resources, especially in the equatorial belt of tropical Africa during the latter half of the nineteenth and first two decades of the twentieth century. Slave raiding, forced labor, and rapid proliferation of networks of long-distance trade all had their impact by removing people from their communities, diverting labor from subsistence production, and (through social dislocation) fostering the spread of epidemics. Demographers still identify a belt of chronic low fertility in equatorial Africa that coincides with areas exploited by the colonial concession companies, where long-distance, forced labor migration and community breakdown went hand in hand with the rapid spread of venereal disease. The pattern is repeating itself in the spread of HIV/AIDS in the same region, with similar demographic consequences.

The difficulty in resolving the issue of what constitutes a "proper" or "safe" or "sustainable" level of population density across the African continent arises from the facts that the historical data are only patchily available, and that "carrying capacity" (the number of people a region can support without the biological resource base suffering irreversible damage) is not an absolute figure but varies according to climate, soils, technology, and level of economic development (to name but four possible factors).

This is why a number of authorities are in favor of viewing population pressure (within limits) as a resource rather than as a problem. According to this school of thought (originating in the work of Danish economist Ester Boserup), Africa provides a number of good examples of positive feedback between population and resources. These are instances in which, historically, the potential of a rural landscape has remained dormant due to shortage of people and labor, but where rapid improvement begins to take place once population density passes a certain critical threshold.

Contemporary scholarship provides a number of impressive examples of this phenomenon of land improvement "from within." A study of Machakos District in Kenya, drawing on historical data, aerial photographs, and careful on-the-ground fieldwork with farmers, shows clearly that an area where disaster might have been (and indeed was) predicted, given earlier unsatisfactory land-management practices combined with high and uncontrolled rates of population increase, is actually a thriving, successful region of intensive, small-holder agriculture. Population pressure is the key factor (it is argued) in explaining this success.

Some will counter that sustainably managed landscapes of intensive agriculture, however desirable in themselves, are far from being the crux of the ecology-society issue in Africa today. The real focus of concern, as far as conservationists are concerned, is "wilderness" resources, which in the nature of things are among the first casualties of intensive agriculture in regions of high population density, however stable and sustainable these forms of agriculture might be as farming systems.

It is of great interest to note, therefore, that there are some carefully researched case studies of local management of landscape resources in Africa indicating a positive role for peasant farmers in supporting, and even enriching, the local biota, even where there is no population pressure incentive to do so. In a low-population-density sector of the forest-savanna transition in the Republic of Guinea, research shows that farmers actively (and consciously) create conditions for the expansion of "natural" forest at the expense of the less productive savanna grassland. They do this for a mixture of reasons, but one important factor is to trigger the more favorable cycle of soil recovery associated with fallow land under forest. Careful perusal of historical data and aerial photographs suggests that some of the forest in this part of western Africa, far from being in retreat over several centuries, as assumed by many experts on the region, is actually advancing as a result of this human managerial action.

IS THE COMMUNITY APPROACH SUFFICIENT?

Although a siege-mentality approach to the protection of reserves from the hungry hordes still prevails in some quarters, as the main plank in environmental policy, the general mood among conservationists in Africa has begun to change. It is now more widely recognized that a strongly "pro-nature, anti-people" environmental policy (at times dependent on the use of quasi-military force) is ineffective and may even be counterproductive. In any war, the enemy tends to raise its game and quickly acquires the methods and weapons deployed against it. The highly publicized battles between conservationists and increasingly sophisticated big-game poachers in parts of eastern and central Africa are a clear sign that the draconian approach is getting out of hand. The perspective outlined above—that nature is in significant respects the product of human management of the African landscape over many millennia—points to a different kind of environmental policy, in which the stress is on understanding, and working with and through, the perspective of resource users. One practical fruit of this new alliance between environment and development is the attempt to manage biological resources through an active network of local

stakeholders. The assumption is that these stakeholders have direct interests in protecting natural resources and thus will supply the necessary buffers against abuse by outside operators.

How does this community approach work and how likely is it to succeed? Community-oriented conservation is based on two key preliminary steps—correct identification of local stakeholders, and accurate assessment of the significance of the stake they hold in the resource base as presently used. If resource use is to be changed (if farmers are to be prevented from cutting new farm sites in a forest reserve, or cattle herders are to be banned from certain areas of a national park because cattle and big game don't mix), sustainable alternative uses have to be devised. These have to be at least as attractive to the stakeholders as the uses they are required to forgo. A process of bargaining is then required to secure agreement about alternative uses and compensation.

Typically, a community conservation agreement might include the following:

- Provision for maintenance of local rights to resource exploitation where these involve non-destructive activity (such as the gathering of wild foods or the trapping of small game within forest reserves);
- Commitments concerning employment (as forest guards and game wardens, etc.) and the extent to which these jobs will be reserved for local people;
- Plans to raise revenue from ecotourism, with provision to reinvest some portion in locally beneficial development activities (e.g., rehabilitation of local schools or provision of a health facility);
- Assistance with activities intended to compensate for productive opportunities lost or forgone (e.g., farmers might be assisted, through supply of extension advice, credit, and other modern inputs, to adopt permanent-field agriculture outside the reserve boundaries as a replacement for shifting cultivation within it).

Community-focused approaches to conservation and management of environmental resources now have the right relationship between horse and cart. They start with the people and their interests and problems. But whether this cart can move—indeed, whether a horse-drawn cart is an appropriate contraption for the modern world—is still to be addressed in formulating and implementing this kind of environmental policy in Africa.

The outstanding questions, and perhaps key area of weakness, facing community-focused approaches to conservation, are What is the community? and Who is local? Are all citizens, de facto, considered to be stakeholders in national conservation projects, or only local residents? Which local residents count (or count most)? Does the bargaining focus mainly upon indigenes with "ancestral" land claims, or are the "floaters" who drift to the edges of settled society (and are therefore sometimes found in large numbers around "boundary wildernesses") also to be included?

That these questions have not yet been tackled with the seriousness they deserve stems from the often rather unrealistic pictures that prevail concerning the sociology of the areas at the focus of attention in environmental policy documents. It has been popularly assumed that because areas of special environmental significance are in the back of beyond, they are in some way socially conservative, mainly populated by long-established groups of indigenes. At times, these populations are fondly regarded as "rooted" repositories of traditional ecological wisdom.

The idea of the "noble savage" must be put aside immediately. The concept of forest peoples living in harmony with nature, dependent on technology little modified since the Stone Age, is a highly controversial conceptual import from the Amazon, with little if any relevance to Africa. Forest gatherer-hunters, never more than a tiny element in equatorial Africa and entirely absent in western Africa, prove on closer inspection to be fully conversant with the modern world and to be in large measure integrated with it (in some cases even to be products of social changes associated with modernity).

A second idea, with more scholarly support, is the notion that the frontier of agricultural settlement in Africa is populated by "neoconservative" groups (by contrast with the alleged social "dynamism" of the North American frontier in the nineteenth century). The argument is that frontier zones in Africa (where, in the early twenty-first century, conservationists mark out their sites of special scientific interest) are in many cases peopled by the descendants of groups who sought refuge from struggles provoked by international trade rivalry and the opening up of Africa to the modern world. The idea is that, thrust to the margins of society, these cultural "refugees" sought to re-create, on the frontier, ideal versions of "old" African society they had lost at home. The rich indigenous knowledge of environmental resources often found in forest-edge communities is well accounted for by this idea.

Most wildernesses of interest to conservationists in Africa are home to at least some communities fitting this neoconservative picture. Not surprisingly, environmental policymakers tend to seek out such groups as natural allies in pressing the case for environmental resource management through community participation.

But neoconservative groups are often only one (and in some cases an increasingly minor) element in wilderness-edge society. Other important groups have to be placed in the picture if participatory approaches to management of natural resources are ever to become sustainable reality. Understanding these other groups requires attention to some of the main features of social change in African states since independence from colonial rule.

Since the mid-1970s, most African states have experienced steady economic decline, a weakening of state institutional structures, and (perhaps most notably) an enormous rise in the proportion of young people in the population. Over half of all Africans are currently under the age of eighteen. It is a mistake to think that these youngsters all drift to the cities. Rising rates of urban unemployment now impel many to move in the other direction, toward frontier areas where social regulation is loose, state supervision weak, and the economy, based on "off-limits" income-generating activities such as smuggling, illicit mining and logging, and drugs, very lively. Where the state and formal economy can no longer offer employment, frontier wildernesses may be the only places to find work.

How to handle the ingress to wilderness areas of young and unemployed people blocked from advancement in the more formal reaches of the economy is a major problem not yet addressed by environmental policymakers in Africa. It largely escapes the agenda of those who favor the participatory approach.

In simpler cases the focal problem is land rights for migrants. Unless incomers have a stake in the local community, they are unlikely to show much regard for traditional sanctions keeping local resource use within limits. Procedures for social incorporation tend to break down, however, where (as in the East Usamabara reserves in northeastern Tanzania) some villages comprise 75 percent or more migrants. In many mixed communities weighted toward incomers, traditional leaders have given ground to a younger generation of migrant activists. In extreme cases, this has meant ceding control to insurgent groups with few local roots and little, if any, interest in the agenda of sustainability. The Revolutionary United Front (RUF), operating in and around the Gola Forest reserves in Sierra Leone, is one such group.

As with Shining Path in Peru or RENAMO (Resistência Nacional Moçambicana) in Mozambique, education, unemployment, and the frustrations of youth seem more important in explaining adherence to the movement than the appeal of the RUF's (largely opaque) political ideology. Rounding up considerable numbers of partly educated youngsters in urban slums and the diamond fields of eastern and southern Sierra Leone and transporting them to forest "academies" along the Liberia-Sierra Leone border, the RUF leadership trained its conscripts to fight with a minimum of equipment and external backup. Navigating the forest tracks and living off the land, armed at times with nothing more than knives and a few wooden replica "guns" and wearing stolen army fatigues, these young guerrillas (some barely teenagers) have spread terror and confusion to all parts of the country. Groups of young rebels materialize apparently at will, murdering local leaders and torching villages of no conceivable strategic or material significance.

If the RUF is correctly characterized as a movement expressive of the anger of frustrated youth, then it is clear that its use of forest camps to retrain its captives, and hide its lengthy roster of Western hostages, is more than tactics. It is also a profound challenge to the politics of environmental resource conservation in Africa. The RUF seeks to invert the normal relationship between metropolis and periphery and show that real power, in a resource-scarce world, lies with those who have learned to make do and survive in remote wilderness regions. As much as anything, it is the Western conception of the tropical rain forest "reserve" that the RUF

holds hostage. The vulnerability of Africa's wilderness areas to these new and violent kinds of social movement points to the conclusion that there can be no sustainable participatory management of natural resources in remote regions without parallel progress toward a fairer global distribution of metropolitan resources.

See also **Aid and Development; Desertification, Modern; Disease: HIV/AIDS; Ecosystems; Forestry; Frontiers; Land; Peasants; Sahara Desert; Soils; Wildlife.**

BIBLIOGRAPHY

Adams, Johnathan S., and Thomas O. McShane. *The Myth of Wild Africa: Conservation without Illusion.* New York: Norton, 1992.

Guyer, Jane, and Paul Richards. "The Social Shaping of Biodiversity: Perspectives on the Management of Biological Variety in Africa." *Africa: Journal of the International African Institute* 66, no. 1 (1996): 1–13.

Kopytoff, Igor, ed. *The African Frontier: The Reproduction of Traditional African Societies.* Bloomington: Indiana University Press, 1987.

Leach, M., and M. Fairhead. "The Forest Islands of Kissidougou: Social Dynamics of Environmental Change in West Africa's Forest-Savanna Mosaic." Report to ESCOR, Overseas Development Administration, 1994.

Martin, Claude. *The Rainforests of West Africa: Ecology, Threats, Conservation.* Trans. Linda Tsardakas. Basel, Switzerland: Birkhäuser Verlag, 1991.

Richards, Paul. *Fighting for the Rain Forest: War, Youth, and Resources in Sierra Leone.* Portsmouth, NH: Heinemann, 1996.

Tiffen, Mary; Michael Mortimore; and Frank Gichuki. *More People, Less Erosion: Environmental Recovery in Kenya.* New York: John Wiley, 1994.

PAUL RICHARDS

ECONOMIC COMMUNITY OF WEST AFRICAN STATES (ECOWAS).

The Economic Community of West African States (ECOWAS) is a regional grouping that was formally created in May 1975 with the ECOWAS Treaty. With the withdrawal of Mauritania in 1999, ECOWAS now comprises fifteen countries. Eight are members of the West African Economic and Monetary Union (WAEMU)—Bénin, Burkina Faso, Côte d'Ivoire, Guinea-Bissau, Mali, Niger, Senegal, and Togo. The other seven ECOWAS countries are Cape Verde,

Gambia, Ghana, Guinea, Liberia, Nigeria, and Sierra Leone. In 1993, the ECOWAS Treaty was revised to accelerate the process of integration and establish an economic and monetary union to stimulate growth and development in West Africa. To this end, the treaty sets the following objectives: (i) the removal of customs duties for intra-ECOWAS trade partners having equivalent effect; (ii) the establishment of a common external tariff; (iii) the harmonization of economic and financial policies; and (iv) the creation of a single monetary zone.

The ECOWAS institutions include: the Executive Secretariat, the Authority of Heads of State and Government, a Council of Ministers, and a Fund for Cooperation, Compensation, and Development. In addition, the institutions also include a Parliament, an Economic and Social Council, and a Court of Justice.

ECONOMIC AND SOCIAL BACKGROUND

The region is highly fragmented. The 245 million inhabitants (2002) are unevenly distributed among countries, with Nigeria accounting for half of the population and half of the regional aggregate and several countries having less than a million people. The region is roughly one-third desert, one-third Sudano-Sahelian with rather irregular rainfall, and one-third humid and more favorable for agricultural production. Nearly half of the area comprises landlocked countries. Internal distances as well as distances to core markets (about 50% greater than East Asia) are enormous and transport infrastructure networks are only partially interconnected between countries—because they had been originally conceived to serve colonial interests rather than the region's—and are generally poorly maintained. As a result, infrastructure costs are among the highest in the world: electricity and international telephone costs average, respectively, 4.5 and 4 times higher than in the Organisation for Economic Co-operation and Development (OECD) countries, and 2 and 2.5 times higher than in Latin America.

The fifteen ECOWAS countries have a combined GDP roughly the size of Ireland's. Most of the countries' economies are undiversified and highly dependent on agriculture. ECOWAS' exports consist mostly of a limited range of agricultural commodities. All countries but Nigeria are net oil importers. As a result, ECOWAS countries are highly vulnerable to external shocks of international market price fluctuations. Manufactured exports are negligible. The relatively narrow range of activities—especially in industry—does not offer much scope for intra-industry trade within the region. As a result, intraregional trade as a share of total trade remains marginal at some 10 percent reflecting the lack of complementarities of economies.

All countries in ECOWAS display poor social indicators. The proportion of population in absolute poverty (less than 1 US dollar per day) is above 50 percent for the subregion, but around 10 percent in the more urbanized coastal, humid zone, and about 60 percent in the largely rural Sahelian zone.

REGIONAL INTEGRATION: ACHIEVEMENTS AND ISSUES

Against this background, since 2000 ECOWAS has made significant efforts to advance its integration agenda in West Africa by: (i) accelerating trade integration; (ii) deepening sectoral policies; and (iii) creating a West African monetary zone.

With a view to establish a common market of goods, WAEMU countries formally established a customs union on January 1, 2000. At the same time, following a ten-year transitional period, the ECOWAS Free Trade Area officially entered into effect in 2000. Its application remains challenging, however, in part because the process of licensing products meeting the rules of origin criteria (similar to those of the WAEMU) remain cumbersome, and the original fiscal compensation mechanism was poorly designed and underfinanced.

Integration of infrastructure services—transport, power, and telecommunications—has been considered sector by sector. A number of transborder power projects for electricity transmission and natural gas transport, most notably the Powerpool, have been launched.

Establishing a common finance market has also proved challenging. Current payments, as well as capital movements, are free within the WAEMU zone. However, in practice, it has not been easy. Payments across currency zones via formal channels are still extremely difficult and lengthy, reflecting differences in banking systems and practices and extremely weak currency clearing arrangements. Established years ago by ECOWAS, the West African Clearing House has not functioned, mainly because governments failed to honor their obligations to provide foreign exchange. At the same time, the creation of ECOBANK in the early 1990s, probably the most efficient institution for money transfers across the subregion, has demonstrated the potential for greater financial integration by the private sector.

A common market for people has been probably the most advanced aspect of integration within ECOWAS. Migrations inside the region have been a feature for centuries, and the regional treaties enshrine the principles of the free movement and right of residence in any of the ECOWAS countries for all member citizens. There are no visa requirements for ECOWAS citizens to travel within the zone. Meanwhile, episodes for xenophobia and recrimination in parts of the region have led to the return of large number of immigrant workers, most recently from Côte d'Ivoire, where citizens from neighboring countries are still required to obtain immigrant documents.

In the area of business environment, ECOWAS has launched various initiatives to improve a business environment, including tax harmonization. The WAEMU countries have agreed to a set of identical business laws under the treaty obligations of Organisation pour l'Harmonisation du Droit des Affaires en Afrique (OHADA). A common investment code exists within the WAEMU, with a view to establishing a secure environment, equally and automatically applicable to all domestic and foreign private businesses throughout the region.

ECOWAS countries have pushed the integration of water management, and formed the West African Conference on Integrated Water Resources Management in 1998. They formulated a West Africa Water Vision and a Regional Action Plan, covering national integrated water management programs, water resource reconstruction programs in countries damaged by wars, education and awareness campaigns, and institutional structure for monitoring and coordinating the policies and actions to improve water resource management.

Monetary integration has also been a major preoccupation for ECOWAS member states. In April 2000, five non-WAEMU members of ECOWAS (The Gambia, Ghana, Guinea, Nigeria, and Sierra Leone) agreed to create a second monetary zone (West Africa Monetary Zone, WAMZ), with a common currency (the eco), and a flexible exchange rate regime as a prelude to a larger monetary union of all ECOWAS countries. Work is underway for the introduction of the eco, for improvements of the payment system, for creation of the West African Central Bank (WACB), and for creation of the regional banking supervision authority. However, the process of creating a unique monetary zone within the West Africa region has stalled. The merger of the two zones has, in early 2007, not been done. The creation of a unique monetary zone set in July 2006 has not materialized. Beyond the renewed political commitment of ECOWAS leaders, the calendar set forth to create a unique monetary zone appears too optimistic in view of the large differences in the degree of economic structures of ECOWAS countries, which are highly dissimilar in terms of shocks and fiscal needs.

CHALLENGES

Recent estimates reveal that, over the decade 1995–2004, half of the ECOWAS countries, including Côte d'Ivoire, the Gambia, Guinea, Guinea-Bissau, Niger, and Togo, were considered no growth or slow growing countries, with an annual GDP growth ranging between -2.4 percent and 2.0 percent. In this context, reducing poverty and more broadly achieving the Millennium Development Goals (MDGs) is a daunting challenge for the region. Indeed, despite the implementation of national Poverty Reduction Strategies (PRSes), progress toward achieving the MDGs has been slow. A joint study by the ECOWAS Secretariat and WAEMU Commission stresses that a number of ECOWAS countries will not achieve the goals if the current macroeconomic trends were to be maintained. In particular, it would take twenty-five years to achieve the objective of reducing poverty by half within the region if the current average annual reduction rate of about 1 percent is to be maintained.

See also **World Bank.**

BIBLIOGRAPHY

Masson, Paul, and Catherine Pattillo. *Monetary Union in West Africa (ECOWAS)*. IMF Occasional Paper No. 204, 2001.

Masson, Paul, and Catherine Pattillo. *Monetary Union in West Africa: An Agency of Restraint for Fiscal Policies?* IMF Working Paper No. 01/34, March 2001.

Monga, Célestin. "A Currency Reform Index for Central and Western Africa." *The World Economy* 20, no. 1 (1997): 103–126.

The West African Economic and Monetary Union: Recent Development and Policy Issues. IMF Occasional Paper No. 170, January 1998.

EMMANUEL PINTO MOREIRA

ECONOMIC DEVELOPMENT. *See* Aid and Development.

ECONOMIC HISTORY.

Because of Africa's extensive and often notorious involvement in international circuits of trade, colonialism and postcolonial crisis, economics has always played a role in accounts of the continent's history. The challenge of such historiography is to write it in African terms; that is, treating Africans as agents rather than objects of developmental projects by outsiders and understanding local economic change in a way that considers both the internal conditions of Africa and the impact of unavoidable engagement with more affluent external partners.

ECONOMIC HISTORY, PRE-1900

Africans managed to provide for themselves and to trade with the outside world long before coming under European rule. Thus there can be little question about the existence of an early economy. Beyond such a simple observation, however, the history of this subject remains deeply entangled in controversy. Scholars continue to dispute how much real information they have about the early African economy, what kind of changes were taking place within it, and by what standards or models of growth one should evaluate its development. Relations between Africans and outsiders are the most visible sector of early commerce, but it is not at all clear how much weight should be given to them in analyzing the internal African economy and its eventual subjugation to colonial domination as well as postcolonial crisis and dependency.

Agriculture. Until well into the twentieth century most Africans produced their own food supplies, a condition that is sometimes labeled "subsistence" and equated with economic stagnation. In an absolute sense both of these terms are inaccurate because people who consume their own products can still provide a surplus to exchange for other goods. At the same time there can be varying degrees of productivity that allow for increased populations, higher standards of living, and more advantageous participation in markets. But before comparing early Africa with other parts of the world—specifically, those that traded with Africa—it is necessary to consider what is known about the changes in production and the growth of exchange within the continent.

If one begins Africa's economic history with the development of domesticated food production, particularly agriculture, this seems to have occurred somewhat later in most of sub-Saharan Africa than in other parts of the Old World. The conditions for this change in Africa were not the "natural" or perceived advantages of controlling food supplies but rather the pressures of severe environmental change connected to the desiccation of the Sahara. Cattle were domesticated in the Sahara by the seventh millennium BCE and diffused southeastward all the way to the Cape without any noticeable connection to agriculture. Cultivated plants seem to have spread from the Sahel region in West Africa, beginning in the late second millennium BCE and reaching southern Africa by the first centuries CE. Whether or not there was any influence from earlier domestication in Mediterranean societies, the changes in Africa all involved species of cattle and varieties of plants (millet, sorghum, rice, yams, and oil palm) indigenous to the sub-Saharan portion of the continent.

At almost the same time that Africans shifted toward domesticated food production, they began to smelt iron and copper for making tools, weapons, and decorative or ritual goods. Thus, by the beginning of the Common Era, the African economy displayed a wide variety of productive occupations with a potential for mutual exchange. In fact, there is evidence for very early markets among farmers and cattle keepers, and between the general population and those groups occupying such specialized niches as hunting, fishing, iron- or (more rarely) copperworking, and the production of salt. However, the internal geography of Africa placed formidable limitations upon the expansion of this trade. Given the smooth outline of the African coast, a relatively small part of the continent's territory has access to the sea. Most internal rivers can be used for transport only over short stretches, and much of the terrain south of the Sahel is extremely unhealthy for large domesticated animals, thus limiting their use for either carrying goods or drawing wheeled vehicles. Indeed, the wheel and rotary motion are generally absent from early African technologies, not because they were unknown (wheeled vehicles entered but did not cross the Sahara in ancient times) but because they were not adaptable to local conditions.

It is relatively easy to trace the beginnings of animal and plant domestication and the location of exchange systems, but the more controversial issue in this internal economic history is the question of intensification of production. Did the adaptation of new technologies and the stimulus of exchange opportunities lead to further developments in efficiencies of production, yielding higher rates of return? Most agricultural systems in precolonial Africa used extensive swidden (slash and burn) methods. These involved high ratios of land to labor; few inputs such as fertilizer, irrigation, or ridging and terracing; and use of single tracts of land for only a few years in succession, followed by long fallow periods. There were many exceptions to this low-investment strategy, and there were movements by groups between intensive and swidden agriculture.

The lack of major changes in African food production systems after the initial shifts to domestication can be explained by the relationship between the costs of such transformations and the pressures or incentives for undertaking them. Transportation barriers represented one such cost involved not in production itself but rather in the reduction of incentives to provide large surpluses of unmarketable goods. Most of the African goods that entered international markets were items that could bear high transport costs and were not directly linked to food production systems. Soil and rainfall conditions in much of Africa also discouraged intensive cultivation, as European colonial agronomists would discover to their chagrin.

Demographic pressure, which might have induced efforts at greater intensification (although, as modern experience has again shown, not necessarily successful ones), was relieved by the availability of open lands for settlement by excess populations. In

any case, populations seem to have grown more slowly in tropical Africa than in portions of the world with environments less hospitable to disease-bearing organisms. Furthermore, a not insignificant portion of the population was taken out of the region by the Islamic and European slave trades. (Between 800 and 1900 CE, around 20 million people were actually exported, and mortality between capture and time of exit has been estimated at another 4 million, to say nothing of "collateral damage" in the process of usually violent enslavement.)

It is also possible to explain an absence of intensified production through the operation of social institutions and cultural values that favored "wealth in people" over the accumulation of goods and capital. Individual Africans who did accumulate property, rather than redistribute it to their community and dependents, were often accused of witchcraft, that is, appropriating the goods, reproductive powers, and even lives of others. Such practices and beliefs certainly had a life of their own and did inhibit economic development. But it is difficult to imagine a value system of this kind without the material limitations on land use and slave-trade experiences of precolonial Africa.

Significant trade between Africa and the external world began well after the shift to Iron Age agricultural production within the continent, and the initiative for such contacts seems to have come from outside. West and south Asian seafarers made commercial voyages to Africa's Indian Ocean coast as early as the second century CE, and regular camel caravans (replacing unsuccessful wheeled vehicles) began to cross the Sahara sometime between the sixth and the eighth centuries. Europeans entered west and East African trade during the fifteenth century, opening up new Atlantic frontiers while stimulating further growth of established Mediterranean and Asian routes. The pioneering Portuguese oceanic voyages introduced international commerce to the hitherto isolated South African subcontinent.

Almost all of the points of contact with long-distance external trade were built upon previous internal systems. Historians know little about East African commerce prior to the very early arrival of Indian Ocean sailing ships, but there is ample evidence of regional trade across the southern edges of the Sahara before that desert became a highway to the

Mediterranean. Likewise, most of the sites where commerce developed along the Atlantic coast had been settled by groups engaged in fishing and the extraction of sea salt for purposes of trade with the interior. Even the peoples of southern Africa, who had not adopted either agriculture or metallurgy, were already engaged in commerce among themselves as well as with the Bantu-speaking Iron Age peoples to their north when Europeans settled at the Cape of Good Hope in the 1650s.

Except for the Khoe and San, the internal economies of most peoples along the Atlantic littoral were not radically altered by external of trade with North Africans, Asians, and Europeans. Because of high transport costs, the goods exported from Africa did not draw on existing food production systems, nor did manufactured imports overwhelm or transform local craft technologies.

Outside contact did bring about the diffusion of, as opposed to commerce in, new food crops that added to the productive capacities of African farmers. Perhaps the most transformative of these was the plantain, which arrived via the Indian Ocean sometime very early in the Common Era and became the staple starch source for a number of high-rainfall areas in east and west-central Africa. These regions—not widespread but often historically significant—could thus support relatively dense populations and in some cases, such as Buganda, sophisticated political development. Other food crops were added to the existing agricultural systems, increasing their capacities for supporting local populations and provisioning itinerant merchants but not intensifying local land use in the same way as had the introduction of plantains, a tree that, under the right tropical conditions, could be maintained for many years on the same terrain. These crops included coco yams (taro, macabo) from Asia, which supplemented indigenous yams as a starch source in forest areas, and maize, peanuts, and cassava (manioc), introduced from the Americas to both forest and savanna zones. Cotton, a nonfood plant whose commercial importance as an export (it was produced and consumed locally much earlier) developed later in the nineteenth century, entered the West African Sudan as a result of trans-Saharan trade.

The large-scale export of slaves was damaging to African economies in many ways beyond the demographic and cultural issues discussed above. These included an emphasis on warfare rather than production as a source of wealth; the movement of vulnerable communities to more defensible but less commercially favored locations; and disease exposure and reduced fertility among forcibly transported populations even within the continent. However, the internal organization of these enterprises more closely resembled the small-scale family farms of the rest of Africa than the gang labor and mechanized processing systems of New World sugar and cotton plantations. The availability of slaves and the limits on the capacity of their owners to coerce them into unfamiliar work routines may actually have reduced the incentive to adopt new technology in these regions of Africa.

International Commerce. The story of early Africa's participation in the world economy is centered around the export of three commodities: gold, slaves, and vegetable oils. Other goods such as ivory, tropical hardwoods, tree gums, cloves, and wild rubber played important but lesser roles. Africa's entire range of major exports was made up of raw materials rather than manufactured goods.

During the era of the medieval trans-Saharan and Indian Ocean trade, circa 1000–1500, Africa probably achieved its most prominent international economic position as a key source of the gold that enabled thriving commercial growth around the Mediterranean and in South Asia. Gold continued to be the main object of the first European merchants in western and eastern Africa, but during the sixteenth and seventeenth centuries African supplies diminished just as alternative sources of bullion were opened up in Latin America. The gold of South Africa, later the world's leading supplier in the twentieth century, could not be extracted with the technology available to Africans or Europeans in the early era.

Slaves formed an important, if far from the dominant, portion of medieval African trade with the Maghreb and Asia. Europeans entered this commerce, at first in proportions similar to the Eastern slave traders, but eventually exporting Africans to the plantations of the Americas at rates unprecedented in world history. As the European slave trade diminished and then ceased during the nineteenth century, the Islamic slave trade reached its highest point; these exports of people to Asia came to an end just before (or in some cases after) the colonial period.

At the time that the Atlantic slave trade ended in the mid-nineteenth century, new efficiencies in oceanic transport as well as the increased consumer demands of industrializing Europe created a major foreign market for African agricultural commodities, mainly palm oil and peanuts (also sought for their oil). However, as the nineteenth century progressed, African vegetable oils faced increasing competition from petroleum and Asian vegetable oils; as a result, their prices stagnated and then, in the 1870s and 1880s, went into sharp decline.

In return for these commodity exports, African merchants and producers received a wide range of manufactures from northern Africa, Asia, and Europe. Most prominent among these at all times were textiles, followed by metal goods of various sorts, shells and beads, and weapons (horses and armor from across the Sahara, firearms and munitions from Europe). Some of these goods competed directly with the production of African handicraft manufacturers, who usually could not operate on the same scale and range as their Asian and European competitors. But often the two sets of industries complemented one another, and gross production in Africa increased.

Africans imported foreign textiles both as finished products and as raw materials for their own systems of weaving and garment manufacture, which suffered from bottlenecks in the spinning of cotton yarn and the dyeing of cloth in colors other than the blue derived from local indigo. African wrought iron (and perhaps steel in some cases) was superior in quality to European imports but could not be produced in comparably large quantities. However, metal goods suitable to local markets could be made by African smiths with the unshaped iron bars that constituted a major import item in regions short of hardwood charcoal for smelting. Likewise, beads, but particularly Indian Ocean cowry shells, served not only as consumer items for Africans but also as currencies, which greatly aided internal exchanges over greater distances. The one major example of internationally competitive African industry existed in the cities of the western and central Sudan, such as Timbuktu and Kano, whose textiles and leather

goods were regularly exported into and across the Sahara.

On the eve of colonization in the 1880s, the sub-Saharan African economy thus displayed a number of contradictory tendencies. Most of the population continued to live in rural villages, probably linked in some way (e.g., the use of cowrie currency) to continental and international markets but little aware of these contacts and shielded from major changes by transport barriers and the sufficiency of local production for most daily needs. In quantitative terms, Africa had undergone considerable economic growth but without the transformation that would allow it to market anything except raw materials in a world economy growing even more rapidly. Africans had been increasingly incorporated into this economy and proved willing to export whatever would bring them the imports they desired, including slaves. Yet, after the Atlantic slave trade was abolished and prices for "legitimate" vegetable oil exports declined drastically, even the Africans most engaged in overseas trade often refused to provide export goods. With the advent of colonial rule these choices between autonomy, transformation, and subjugation to international dependency would become far more difficult.

COLONIAL AND POSTCOLONIAL ERAS

One of the most frequently stated justifications for imposing European control upon African territory was the need to "open up" the continent by removing previous barriers to economic development. And from about 1900 commerce did grow almost everywhere due to a more secure political environment (the *pax colonialana*) and the introduction of new transport infrastructure. Colonialism provided the possibilities for major economic growth through the provision of a more secure political environment in which little male labor was needed for defense, contracts could be enforced, and transport costs reduced through the introduction of new infrastructure. However such improvements were costly and European governments were generally unwilling to invest very heavily in their new African territories. Thus improvements were much delayed and various expedients were taken to provide them as cheaply as possible.

One such policy—echoing contemporary neoliberal practices—was the granting of large territorial concessions (sometimes entire colonies) to private entrepreneurs who, in return for monopoly trading and mineral extraction rights, were expected to stake out territorial claims, provide administrative services, and construct railroads. The results, most enduringly and notoriously in the Belgian Congo, French Equatorial Africa, German Cameroon and Portuguese Mozambique, were disastrous. The costs and gestation periods of serious development were well beyond available means so that concessionaires usually focused on gathering wild products, especially rubber, often using very violent methods.

Eventually railways did get built, accounting for around one-fifth of the total foreign capital investment into Africa up to the mid-1930s. These projects were often politically grandiose and economically unviable, saddling the local administrations with a high debt burden. However, they did dramatically reduce the costs of transport to the interior. For example, the opening of the railway to Uganda lowered prices per ton to about one-seventh of their level using porterage.

Export-led Growth, 1900–1960. The provision of a peaceful political environment and rail transportation was sufficient to induce export-led growth for more than sixty years, a process that transformed much of the continent. However, this long export-led growth phase suffered two severe interruptions. Between 1929 and 1934 the value of world trade contracted by two-thirds. Africa suffered a less severe decline than the world average, in part because one of its major exports, gold, rose in price relative to everything else. Even so, its exports fell by 48 percent. During World War II there was a further massive disruption of trade flows. The engine for export-led growth varied by region: mineral extraction in southern and central Africa, peasant agriculture in western and parts of eastern Africa, and pockets of settler/plantation agriculture.

Mineral extraction was highly successful and accounted for around a third of all foreign investment into Africa up to the mid-1930s. By then Africa had virtually the entire world market in diamonds and cobalt; around half the world market in gold, chromite, and phosphate; and about a fifth of the world market in copper, manganese, and asbestos. From the mid-1930s the industrial sector also grew rapidly in the major mineral economies: South Africa, Zaire, Zimbabwe, and Zambia. The mining-manufacturing economy created a demand for food which in turn stimulated peasant production.

A second model of export-led growth was that based on large-scale commercial agriculture, whether undertaken by settlers or, more rarely, by plantations. This proved much slower to develop as an engine of growth than mineral exports, partly because it required more locally specific knowledge. For example, in Kenya the settler/plantation economy experienced limited growth in the first half of the century. Even so, by the 1920s around a quarter of the African labor force was employed in the labor market. In the range of produce for which much of African agriculture was suited, there was little evidence for any economies of scale. Anything that large farms could do could therefore be done at least as competitively by small farms. Faith in scale economies, however, did not want. Lever Brothers made huge plantation investments in Zaire during the 1930s, which were never competitive. Later, these same myths would appear in the public sector, justifying the Groundnuts Scheme of the colonial authorities, the communal farming initiative of the Tanzanian government, and restrictions on subdivision in Kenya.

In large parts of Africa, especially western Africa, a third model delivered growth, namely the commercialization of peasant agriculture. African peasants proved adept at innovating into the newly introduced commercial crops even when this required substantial irreversible investment. In northern Nigeria the low-cost annual crop of groundnuts was rapidly taken up, but more remarkably in the southern parts of western Africa and the highlands of eastern Africa tree crops spread rapidly. Tree crops are almost irreversible investments and they do not yield income for some years after planting. They therefore require confidence, liquidity, and farsightedness. As these crops were adopted, living standards rose and the incomes generated high savings rates both at the level of the household and for the economy as a whole. For example, by the time of independence, Ghana, the leading peasant economy, had accumulated large foreign-exchange reserves, while Nigerian cocoa farmers were found to have savings rates of around 40 percent during good years.

In each of these types of economies, the primary impetus for growth spawned a secondary growth of African entrepreneurship in the service, transport, and manufacturing sectors. However, African enterprises grew in number rather than in scale. With rare exceptions (mainly in road transport), African entrepreneurs did not build large-scale businesses. This is partly because most large firms start large, and Africans lacked the necessary access to both education and finance. In western Africa the indigenous communities had long experience in trade and urbanization, so that much of the new transactions generated by cash crop income were from the start in the hands of Africans. By contrast, in eastern Africa prior to 1900 trade had been very limited and commerce became the domain of Asian immigrants. In eastern Africa the towns, which were primarily trading places for the agricultural population, became largely immigrant economies.

By around 1950, when the first national accounts become available, African economies had two radically different structures depending upon whether export growth had been in agriculture or minerals. In the mineral economies of South Africa, Zimbabwe, Zambia, and Zaire, mining and manufacturing accounted for 30 to 50 percent of national income, with agriculture typically contributing only around 25 percent. By contrast, in Ghana and Nigeria, agriculture accounted for nearly 70 percent of national income. There was one feature that both types of economy had in common: In none of these countries did the share of government in national income reach 10 percent.

Neither system had raised per capita incomes close to developed-country levels. Setting per capita income in Britain in the early 1950s at 100, that in South Africa was 33, Zimbabwe 20, Zambia 15, Ghana 12, Zaire 9, and Nigeria, Kenya, and Uganda 7. Because national accounts do not exist for early years, any estimate of the growth of these economies over the first half of the century is speculative. However, one can see even more disparities among nonmineral economies with less developed export sectors, so that, using the same comparative

scale, per capita incomes in Tanzania and Malawi during the 1950s come, respectively, to 4 and 2.

In South Africa and Zimbabwe, and to a lesser extent Zambia, the high averages, in the range of 15–33, are influenced by a large nonindigenous population so that much of the growth was attributable to and accrued to immigrants. However, in Ghana and Zaire immigrant populations were negligible, and these countries by 1950 constituted the most successful examples of export-led growth attributable to the indigenous population, the former driven mainly by agriculture and the latter by minerals. The comparison of Ghana and Zaire in 1950 with Tanzania and Malawi suggests that at their best each of these models might raise an economy from the 2–4 range to the 9–12 range over half a century. The implied annual growth rate of around 2.5 percent in per capita incomes would be comparable with the growth of many developing countries in postwar years.

The two-plus decades between World War II and independence witnessed very high growth rates for African economies. During this time terms of trade for primary exports remained generally favorable and Africa increased its production of such commodities as coffee, cocoa, tin and antimony. Moreover Britain and France dramatically raised their levels of public development investments, driven by a combination hope and fear: hope about African potential and economic planning in general; fear of anticolonial nationalism on the Asian model and the future of their own national economies if left to fend by themselves in a world dominated by the United States and the Soviet Union. However, the African development schemes—especially massive agricultural projects—did not turn out well, terms of trade shifted after the early 1950s Korean War boom, and European economic strategy shifted from colonialism toward the Common market/European Union.

Within Africa, colonial export-led growth, even when economically successful, was not always benign. Coercion was often used to increase the supply of African wage labor for estates and mines and to increase sales of crops. In South Africa and Zimbabwe this was supplemented with restrictions on access to land. Earnings of the unskilled were broadly equivalent to earnings in agricultural self-employment, or possibly somewhat lower. This produced a pattern of high turnover and return migration among unskilled workers, whether on estates or in mines and manufacturing. In Zaire and Zambia a smaller skilled elite received much higher wages and was employed on a long-term basis. In South Africa this process was arrested in the mid-1920s and again in the 1940s by the political opposition of the Afrikaner community, which feared for its own position. Real wages of Africans appear to have been no higher in 1960 than early in the century as a result of these controls. Other than in South Africa, coercive labor laws were gradually reversed. During the 1950s, pressure from the colonial authorities, together with that from African unions, and the politics of transition to independence, forced urban wages up for the unskilled by means of minimum-wage laws. But even such a positive development opened an earnings gap between the urban and rural labor force, which was to be a major problem for independent governments.

Independence: From Development to Structural Adjustment. African independence was not viewed at the time as a major economic event. The foreign trading and manufacturing firms did not, on the whole, oppose the independence movements, an indication that they did not anticipate significant economic change. In the short term this confidence was justified: In the early postindependence years most African economies continued to grow fairly rapidly on the basis of export-led growth models as well as continued aid from both Western and Eastern Cold War blocs. During the 1960s the volume of African exports increased by 6 percent per annum and per capita gross domestic product (GDP) grew at around 2 percent per annum.

Continuing urban-rural wage disparities as well as very rapid expansions in education induced a growing percentage of African populations to move into cities and peri-urban areas. In some economies the stock of the labor force with secondary education increased by 20 percent per annum during the 1960s. This conjunction of enormous increases in the supply of labor appropriately skilled for urban work together with a massive increase in urban wages pushed the labor market into a radical disequilibrium: youth unemployment became a central policy issue. There was therefore a political need to generate urban employment. "Incomes policies" were enacted whereby the government negotiated with unions and employers for wage

moderation in return for employment expansion. These policies proved ineffective and were abandoned. Thereafter, there was strong pressure on government for fiscal expansion. In the colonial period any such pressures had been contained by supranational currency boards that prevented governments from printing money. In Francophone Africa these boards persisted and indeed succeeded in containing fiscal deficits. In Anglophone and Lusophone Africa they were dismantled soon after independence, in part because the incentives provided by Britain were much smaller than those provided by France.

As spending pressures increased, government budgets other than those in the Franc Zone tended to move into deficit, and this produced incipient balance-of-payments crises. An example is the experience of Kenya during the early 1970s. The new minister of finance, a graduate of the London School of Economics, adopted a Keynesian strategy of increasing the fiscal deficit to take up the supposed slack in the economy. This produced a payments crisis the following year. The government then faced a choice familiar to many high-spending governments between fiscal retrenchment, devaluation, or trade restrictions. The Kenyan government, like many other African governments, chose to impose trade restrictions. As these policies cumulated, exchange rates became highly overvalued, with foreign exchange being rationed by the central bank, various ministries, and the presidency. Overvaluation, the central economic policy of most African governments, had powerful implications for income redistribution, exports, and government revenue.

The major beneficiaries of overvaluation were importers, often urban consumers. The rents involved were sometimes enormous. For example, in Nigeria during the early 1980s the official exchange rate was for a while barely a quarter of the market-clearing rate, so that close to three-quarters of oil revenues came to be allocated as rents to those to whom the cheap foreign exchange was assigned. The policy of overvaluation constituted an implicit tax on exports. Additionally, some governments continued with and increased the explicit taxation system that colonial governments had introduced through marketing boards. This provided governments in the agricultural economies with an enormous increase in incomes. The equivalent in the mineral economies was more usually provided by nationalization. In both types of economies other than in Francophone Africa, these sources of revenue were supplemented by deficit financing. The government's share of national income, which had been below 10 percent in 1950, rose rapidly. For example, in Ghana the share of government consumption in GDP doubled between 1950 and 1968.

The combination of implicit and explicit taxation severely reduced the domestic profitability of exporting. In the agricultural export economies there was a transfer from peasants. In the mineral economies it was a transfer from the mining sector, which was itself nationalized by the government. In the latter case government revenues were thus directly undermined. In the former, government revenues were initially augmented by high rates of taxation, so that in addition to importers, a second group of beneficiaries (though sometimes the same people) were the recipients of government expenditure. However, as high taxation led to export contraction, the revenue base was eroded. Thus, in both cases the high taxation of exports eventually undermined government revenue, and so the state began to wither away. Spectacular instances of this process are Ghana and Uganda, where by the early 1980s the government accounted for a lower share of national income than in 1950.

Because import controls prevented fiscal laxity from spilling over into a payments deficit, domestic inflation ensued. Some governments attempted to suppress inflation through price controls. Where they were enforced, these controls created shortages of goods at official prices with an illegal market emerging on the sidelines. This parallel market operated at a disadvantage even in relation to the nonlegal transactions that had occurred in the precolonial economy: Transactions were not just unenforceable but liable for punishment. In some countries the deterioration in food markets that this control regime produced gave rise to periodic famines, most notably in Ethiopia during the 1980s, where the punishment of those who stored or traded food transformed localized harvest declines into consumption collapses. In others, the range of consumer choice narrowed drastically as shops became empty of goods. This decline in

the range of choice lowered living standards as consumption expenditure became less efficient in meeting wants.

Most significantly, the high taxation of exports ended and indeed reversed the process of export-led growth. Africa's shares in world and developing-country exports started to decline after the mid-1960s. This decline was not simply relative, it was absolute. In aggregate, agricultural-export volumes reached a peak in 1968 and thereafter fell fairly continuously so that by 1980 they were only two-thirds of their 1968 level. This aggregate performance conceals considerable diversity. In Ghana, the most successful of the export-agriculture economies, the volume of exports peaked in 1965 and by 1980 had fallen by 60 percent. In Uganda they peaked in 1970 and by 1980 had fallen by 43 percent. In Tanzania they peaked in 1973 and by 1980 had fallen 15 percent. By contrast, Kenya sustained quite rapid growth in agricultural exports during this period.

The faltering of the agricultural-export economies from the mid-1960s was accentuated by the oil shock of 1973, which produced a powerful transfer within the continent from agricultural to oil exporters. By the mid-1970s most of the agricultural economies had declining export earnings due to a combination of falling volumes and worsening terms of trade. This decline was temporarily relieved by booms in most agricultural prices during the late 1970s, most notably in coffee, tea, and cocoa. As these booms receded during 1978–1979, the agricultural economies were further hit by a second intracontinental transfer to the oil producers following the 1979 oil price increase. Thus, between the mid-1960s and 1980 the agricultural-export economies suffered a severe reversal as declining export volumes and declining prices combined to lower export earnings. Agricultural-export economies in Asia shared the decline in world prices, but were generally able to compensate for this by volume growth and diversification.

The mineral economies fared rather better, though again performance was highly varied. Zambian and Congo exports peaked between 1969 and 1975 but by 1980 had fallen by 40 to 28 percent, due partially to declining world copper demand. In contrast, Botswana achieved the highest sustained growth rate in the world, based on expansion of diamond exports. Because of petroleum discoveries, several countries switched from agricultural exports to mineral exports, most notably Nigeria and Cameroon. These oil economies commonly fell victim to "Dutch disease," whereby growth of mineral exports tended to make other exports uncompetitive through appreciation of the real exchange rate. Nigeria is the classic example, with the growth of the oil economy leading to a collapse of the former agricultural-export economy as resources were transferred from that sector to the sectors producing internationally non-tradable goods and services. In principle this is an efficient reallocation of resources. However, it became problematic in three ways. First, the decline of agricultural exports directly hit large sections of the peasant population, whereas oil income directly accrued to the government and the beneficiaries depended upon the pattern of public spending. Hence, the oil booms were periods of massive redistributions of income between economic classes. Second, because the period of high net oil incomes was rather short, the resource shift out of the non-oil export sector soon needed to be partly reversed. Because the classes that had benefited from oil spending were politically influential, this reversal was met with opposition. Third and most remarkable, the export-led growth model was for the first time unsuccessful in achieving its most basic feature: It failed to be a source of overall growth in the economy. Nigeria had a high investment rate out of oil income, but this investment had a chronically low rate of return. By 1980 output was no higher than had the economy simply sustained its pre-oil growth rate.

Hence, by 1980 both the agriculture- and the mineral-based export economies were in trouble. In aggregate, per capita GDP first stagnated and then began to decline. From 1973 to 1980 it declined on average by 0.1 percent per annum whereas South Asia grew at 2 percent per annum. Economic performance of both types of economy continued to deteriorate during the first part of the 1980s. From 1980 to 1987 per capita GDP declined at the annual rate of 2.6 percent, whereas in South Asia it grew at 2.8 percent.

The accelerating decline in economic growth after 1965 coincided with an acceleration in the rate of population growth as infant mortality rates fell because of basic improvements in public health. This created increasing pressure on land, which had until the midcentury been plentiful in most areas.

Low population density and unpredictable environmental assets had produced shifting cultivation and communal property rights. Commercialization during the first half of the century and rising population density thereafter produced a switch to settled agriculture with a consequent need for greater input intensity and private property rights. The switch to input dependence, in order to preserve fertility under shorter fallow periods, was hindered by government regulation of many rural transactions such as transport, fertilizer, and produce. Some rural economies, such as Uganda and Tanzania, experienced a retreat back into subsistence during the time when rising labor/land ratios should have implied greater market integration. Property rights evolved as social conventions slowly changed. Governments variously attempted to accelerate or retard the emergence of private marketable rights. For example, in Tanzania private rights were removed by the state, which nationalized agricultural land and created a nonmarket allocation system through village committees. By contrast, in Kenya the government assisted the emergence of private rights through land registration. However, over a period of thirty years the rate of land sales was similar and unchanging in Kenya and Tanzania, suggesting that the remit of the state in rural property rights was not so much de facto as de jure. This is an example of the gap between legislation and the actual framework governing African transactions.

Conditionality. By the mid-1980s four forces for change were building within African governments. First, their tax bases were withering away so that they could no longer meet the claims of the patronage systems that the public sector provided. Second, they were highly exposed to external shocks, and in the early 1980s there was a considerable deterioration in the terms of trade due to a decline in export prices. Third, debt to donors had accumulated and this provided donors with leverage which they became increasingly willing to use. Fourth, they were becoming unpopular with the broad mass of the population.

In the short term the most effective of these forces was the donors. During the colonial period Africa was not heavily indebted. Public borrowing was limited by the fiscal conservatism of the authorities and private debt by the limited collateral available. This situation changed rapidly during the commodity booms of the 1970s. Internationally, banks were highly liquid and willing to lend and donors channeled huge resources to Africa. Public net capital flows to Africa, which had been around $50 million per annum in the interwar period and around $300 million in 1945–1960, had grown to around $2,000 million per annum by 1976–1979. As African economies deteriorated during the 1980s, net aid flows fell, and the accumulated stock of debt usually became unmanageable given the decline in export earnings. Governments faced the choice of default or rescheduling and often alternated between the two. The donors used rescheduling negotiations as an opportunity to insist upon a set of policy reforms labeled "structural adjustment."

Structural adjustment programs (SAP) mark a second postcolonial era. Their base in African economic failure was reinforced, after 1989, by the end of the Cold War and its concern for maintaining the support of African regimes whatever their domestic shortcomings. The major components of SAP were currency devaluation (to encourage exports and cut imports); removal of price controls (to encourage local food production); and privatization (to get governments out of unproductive enterprises and achieve fiscal balance; the latter also meant cuts in social expenditures). These neoliberal programs were not popular among African elites and mass consumers and have not (with the partial and perhaps unrepresentative exception of post-Apartheid South Africa) produced very positive results in terms of increased exports or foreign direct investment (FDI). In fact Africa's share of FDI has declined since 1980 and what there is has been heavily concentrated in enclave extractive enterprises (as well as a growing criminal sector). Some of the failure of SAP may be attributed to the unwillingness or incapacity of corrupt African regimes to implement them. However, it can also be argued that economic development on this basis has no real precedent, particularly in the case of Asian ex-colonies, which have made the move to industrialization.

African growth during the first sixty-five years of the twentieth century was narrowly based on agricultural and mineral exports. It was often coercive and spasmodic. Nevertheless, this is the only model for growth that has proved successful in orthodox terms. The late colonial and immediate postindependence experiments with industrialization and public-sector expansion contributed, by the late 1970s, to widespread economic crisis. Since the 1980s Africa has been simultaneously marginalized in the global economy and ever more integrated into it through the impositions of neoliberal SAP, the proliferation of technologies such as mobile phones (one of the few sources of legitimate private fortunes) and the movement of an increasing portion of its skilled and unskilled labor force into international migration. Whether or not all this suggests some new model for measuring economic "success" is something not easily discerned from the record of even the relatively proximate past.

See also **Agriculture; Aid and Development; Capitalism and Commercialization; Colonial Policies and Practices; Economics and the Study of Africa; Ivory; Labor: Migration; Money; Plantation Economies and Societies; Production Strategies; Slave Trades.**

BIBLIOGRAPHY

African Economic History. Published semiannually from 1976 to 1983 and annually since 1983.

Austen, Ralph A. *African Economic History: Internal Development and External Dependency.* London: Currey, 1987.

Deane, Phyllis. *Colonial Social Accounting.* Hamden, CT: Archon Books, 1973.

Ferguson, James. *Global Shadows: Africa in the Neoliberal World Order.* Durham, NC: Duke University Press, 2006.

Hailey, William M. *An African Survey: A Study of Problems Arising in Africa South of the Sahara.* New York: Oxford University Press, 1957.

Hopkins, Antony G. *An Economic History of West Africa.* London: Longman, 1973.

Lovejoy, Paul E. *Transformations in Slavery: A History of Slavery in Africa.* Cambridge, U.K.: Cambridge University Press, 2000.

Mkandawire, Thandika, and Charles C. Soludo. *Our Continent, Our Future: African Perspectives on Structural Adjustment.* Ottawa: International Development Research Center, 1999.

Prest, Alan R., and I. G. Stewart. *The National Income of Nigeria, 1950–51.* London: H. M. Stationary Office, 1953.

Shaw, Thurstan, et al. *The Archaeology of Africa: Food, Metals, and Town.* London: Routledge, 1993.

Sutton, J. E. G. "Toward a History of Cultivating the Fields." *Azania* 24 (1989): 98–112.

Thornton, John. *Africa and Africans in the Making of the Atlantic World, 1400–1800.* Cambridge, U.K.: Cambridge University Press, 1998.

van de Walle, Nicolas. *African Economies and the Politics of Permanent Crisis, 1979–1999.* Cambridge, U.K.: Cambridge University Press, 2001.

World Bank. *Adjustment in Africa: Reform, Results, and the Road Ahead.* New York: Oxford University Press, 1994.

Wrigley, C. C. "Aspects of Economic History." In *Cambridge History of Africa*, Vol. 7, *1905–1940*, ed. John Donnelly Fage and Roland Oliver. Cambridge, U.K.: Cambridge University Press, 1986.

Zeleza, Paul Tiyambe. *A Modern Economic History of Africa*, Vol. 1: *The Nineteenth Century.* Dakar: Codesria, 1993.

RALPH A. AUSTEN

ECONOMIC SYSTEMS. An enormous variety of experiences and possibilities characterized African economic systems at the beginning of the twenty-first century. Small village communities continued to till the soil and raise goats, sheep, cows, and chickens using the same techniques of their grandfathers, renewing all the while traditions of social solidarity and hospitality that have characterized rural Africa for centuries. Overhead, however, multinational corporations owned and operated by African nationals organized transcontinental air travel, microwave and satellite transmissions, and cell phone networks. Africa globalized with the rest of the world, though in different ways. Exports of goods and services stagnated even as migration generated new diaspora communities (often illegal as Europe and the United States erected obstacles to legal migration). Imports of new technologies failed to surprise jaded villagers who realized that MP3 files had already replaced their still-fresh compact disc collections.

International assistance networks, for provision of services from health care to peace keeping, became important institutions in most countries. Some countries collapsed in civil war, while others continued to build asphalt highways that hastened regional integration.

One generalization was pertinent and increasingly self-evident at the close of the first decade of the twenty-first century: African economic systems were intimately linked to increasingly unstable and violent mechanisms for regulating political power. The problem of ensuring political order repeatedly spilled over into the economic realm, impeding ordinary persons from earning a living and bringing investments to fruition.

The seriousness of the problem of political order was manifest in the sheer number of violent civil conflicts in Africa. About half of the countries in sub-Saharan Africa experienced at least one year of civil war after 1980, and more often experienced sustained civil conflicts that lasted many years, even decades. These included Angola, Burundi, Chad, Congo (Kinshasa and Brazzaville), Côte d'Ivoire, Eritrea, Ethiopia, Guinea-Bissau, Liberia, Mozambique, Namibia, Rwanda, Senegal, Sierra Leone, Somalia, South Africa, Sudan, Uganda, and Zimbabwe. Sudan, for example, saw civil war in the south from 1983 to 2005, and also war in the western region of Darfur at low intensity over much of the period and then catastrophically violent in the period from 2003 to 2007, spilling over into Chad and Central African Republic. The Democratic Republic of the Congo, formerly Zaire, saw civil war, including incursions by numerous neighboring states, over the decade from 1994 to 2004. Somalia saw warlord rule and conflict even within Mogadishu, the capital city and largest urban area of the country, for the period from 1991 to 2005. Rwanda saw a genocidal slaughter of perhaps 800,000 persons in six months in 1994. Côte d'Ivoire experienced a brief, year-long spasm of violence in 2002 that resulted in partition of the country, with the north ruled by rebel forces.

Civil conflicts significantly hampered the viability of formal, large-scale organization of economic activity. The mid-sized city of Bouaké, in Côte d'Ivoire, was largely abandoned in the civil war of 2003. Freetown, the capital of Liberia, was invaded by Rwandan Patriotic Front (RPF) forces during the height of the conflict. Southern Sudan saw virtually no building for twenty years, as northern military forces repeatedly bombed southern infrastructure including schools and hospitals. Civil conflicts also generated large numbers of internally displaced persons. These internal and external refugees grew increasingly reliant on an international system of aid delivery, that itself became an integral component of many economic systems across the continent. Observers coined or resuscitated terms to describe these economies characterized by violent and dysfunctional polities: warlord economies; collapsed or failed states; aid-dependant states; and refugee economies. Understanding the systems that regulated economic life for ordinary persons in these economies involved investigation of blood diamonds, transnational arms flows, money laundering, compassion fatigue, and the political economy of international military intervention and nonintervention.

Political processes were not always the bane of economic development in Africa. At independence in the 1960s, much hope rested on state-directed transformation and investment. The colonial powers had imposed economic systems designed to provide raw materials and profits to favored enterprises, whether colonial planters, processors, trading firms, or small manufacturers. Cotton, cocoa, and coffee in West Africa were the clearest examples; African producers were at the bottom of a colonially controlled commodity chain. In temperate zones, such as Kenya and South Africa, the exploitation of tea plantations and mining operations was directed by white settlers. Populations were displaced and regulated to serve the colonial enterprises. In colonies without high-value export crops or mineral resources, agricultural commodities were produced by small farmers using few purchased inputs. Farmers were taxed indirectly by monopolies that distributed desirable consumer goods (such as soap, sugar, radios, and bicycles).

These economies were to be transformed after independence through heavy state involvement in economic activity. Agriculture in particular was targeted, as well as industrial processing of agricultural commodities. Sudan, for example, launched Operation Breadbasket, an ambitious complex of agricultural investments intended to open and mechanize the vast and underutilized clay plains of central Sudan. Tanzania, likewise, collectivized scattered hamlets and resettled villagers in larger centers, and sought to mechanize large agricultural areas. Many countries passed agrarian reform laws declaring all land property of the state. Other sectors were similarly transformed. Mines were nationalized, and petroleum revenues appropriated by the state, for the benefit of the people. Governments launched development banks to finance state-controlled industries and services. In some countries, revolutionary leaders inspired by socialism and allied with the Soviet Union proposed far-reaching transformations.However, overall, implementation of state-led development was similar across the continent, if only because the capacity of newly independent states to project their project across the national territory was limited.

The intellectual justifications and political economy explanations of these programs were twofold. First, political elites in newly independent regimes felt that peasant farming and a small colonially oriented bourgeoisie would neither modernize nor invest quickly enough to generate a large surplus that could fuel rapid industrialization and pay for expensive urban infrastructure. Second, the new elites that inherited colonial power had seen how the state could be used to generate economic advantage by "clients" of the "patrons" holding state office. The precarious political position of the postindependence governing classes impelled them to attempt to extract and control as much advantage as possible from the power of the state.

The transforming project of many postindependence elites succeeded in only a handful of countries. Botswana was the clear star performer, with gross domestic product (GDP) per person growing by 6 percent annually over the period from 1980 to 2004. Literacy rates for youth improved from an already high level of 70 percent in 1980 to 90 percent in 2005. (Literacy for youth in Burkina Faso, by contrast, barely reached 20 percent.) Hundreds of miles of road infrastructure were built, most notably the trans-Kalahari highway. This growth occurred even as the HIV/AIDS epidemic lowered life expectancy to thirty-five years and resulted in more than 60,000 orphans by 2005. The government moved aggressively to combat the epidemic and its effects, committing to education, women's empowerment, and free distribution of anti-retroviral therapy for HIV-positive persons.

Post-apartheid, the African National Congress government of South Africa likewise revealed itself to be a prudent manager of the national economy, pursuing cautious policies during the decade after 1994 despite the temptations of retaliatory nationalization following the peaceful transition to majority rule. GDP per capita remained steady in this period fraught with tension. One policy that contributed strongly to social peace and the sense of commitment to the continuity of the South African state and its economic institutions was the extension of state pensions to the black population following the transition. The resulting transfer of purchasing power to the elderly empowered key persons in society and benefited the health and schooling of their grandchildren.

For most African countries, however, the increasingly state-centric economic systems that emerged after independence proved fragile in the face of global economic shocks of the 1970s and 1980s. Oil prices rose following OPEC's cartelization of the market. Interest rates on foreign loans rose in response to the global recession, collapse of the Bretton Woods system of fixed exchange rates, and Latin American debt crisis. Shaky political regimes became beholden to international lending authorities such as the International Monetary Fund and the World Bank, which diagnosed state intervention as the problem, and conditioned further lending during the 1980s and 1990s on state disengagement. The famous Structural Adjustment Programs (SAPs) of the period proved disastrous, as multilateral lenders failed to realize, at best, the precarious political equilibria of most countries, or, at worst, were complicit in the massive corruption that exacerbated the economic woes of the countries under their surveillance.

African economies saw declines in many measures of well-being, over the quarter century from 1980 to 2004. Life expectancy at birth remained below fifty years, and declined in numerous countries in southern Africa largely due to the HIV/AIDS epidemic (which may have been preventable through effective public action) and little progress in reducing deaths attributable to diarrhea, malaria, and tuberculosis. By 2004, most countries had only about one-half of births attended by skilled health personnel, and consequently infant and maternal mortality were very high. Gross national income

(GNI), the value of goods and services produced by nationals of a country in a year, declined for almost half of African countries from 1960 to 2000, when measured in inflation adjusted dollars and on a per-person basis.

By the 1990s there was no longer a single African experience. Three groups of countries could be distinguished.

The first included those countries that experienced modest growth without civil conflict, after the 1980s. These included countries that emerged from the downturns and political instability of the 1980s with more open political systems and economic stability, with states pursuing more modest interventions in the economic sphere. Such was the case for a number of West African states, including Burkina Faso, Ghana, Mali, and Senegal. Mozambique, Uganda, and Rwanda likewise returned to a semblance of tenuous normalcy following the conflicts of the 1980s and 1990s. Many countries in southern Africa likewise remained politically stable and saw modest economic development, even as the HIV/AIDS pandemic devastated the quality of life.

A second group included the oil exporters, both old and new, that continued to experience grave difficulties in integrating the wealth from oil exports into a dynamic economy; they were afflicted by the "natural resource curse." Many saw large increases in GDP, though the equitable distribution of oil revenues typically remained scandalously deficient. Equatorial Guinea was the prime example: GDP grew fantastically from 1995 to 2005 as oil companies invested billions of dollars to exploit offshore fields, but the ordinary citizen benefited little from the growth. Corruption grew exponentially. Riggs Bank, a prominent Washington, D.C., bank, was fined $25 million by U.S. regulators for collusion with government officials in Equatorial Guinea, including the president, to steal hundreds of millions of dollars of public money. Similar situations were apparent in two other new oil exporters, Chad and Sudan. Sudan began exporting oil in 1999, but the unwillingness of the ruling elite to share the benefits of oil revenues led to uprisings and horrific retaliation by government militias in the marginalized region of Darfur. The Darfur crisis spilled over to Chad and rebel groups threatened the military regime of

Idriss Déby, who abnegated on promises to use oil revenues for antipoverty programs.

Finally, Africa's largest oil exporter and most populous country, Nigeria, teetered for decades between extremely corrupt military rule and disordered informalization of economic activity. The Nigerian oil economy, insulated from local politics in most countries, became fully politicized, with local militia groups organizing armed takeovers of drilling platforms in desperate bids to secure promised community development funds. Elections set for 2007 were the major hope for a return to political stability and transparent governance.

A third group included those countries that remained mired in political crisis, with consequent economic retrogression. These included Guinea, Liberia, Sierra Leone, Côte d'Ivoire, Somalia, Ethiopia, and Eritrea. Fiscal and monetary policy sometimes exhibited stunning breakdowns, most starkly in the case of Zimbabwe, where inflation topped 1,000 percent per year in 2006, and formal sector activity ground to a halt.

There was also considerable variety across economic sectors and systems. The majority of people in Africa continued to derive most of their livelihood from the agricultural sector. Agriculture accounted for only about 20 percent of value added in the region, but 60 percent of the population resided in rural areas. Technical change and new crop varieties transformed some agricultural regions, even as agriculture overall stagnated with the breakdown of marketing infrastructure that accompanied state collapse and civil conflict. In West Africa, peasant farmers proved adept at transforming agricultural practices: pineapple exports grew rapidly in Ghana; cotton farmers continued to earn substantial income, even as U.S. and European Union production subsidies negatively impacted world prices for cotton; shea butter, largely collected and processed by women, became a major export for use in creams and lotions.

In East Africa, the cut flower industry grew rapidly, serving the European market. In Central Africa, new varieties of cassava spread throughout the region, leading to increased yields and less production risk. But there were also agricultural failures on the continent. Zimbabwe's botched takeover and redistribution of commercial white farmers led to a 30 percent drop in agricultural output from 2000 to 2005. Farmers in Burkina Faso had initial successes exporting green beans to Europe, but undependable air cargo services and more complex food regulations in the European Union led to stagnation in the sector.

Agriculture depends heavily on systems of rural land tenure, and these were in continuous flux across the continent. After the state arrogated to itself ultimate title over land, it became apparent that most states had neither the capacity nor the restraint to encourage efficient use of land and fairly resolve disputes. Communal and traditional tenure systems continued to thrive, even as farmers increasingly came to understand their rights to particular plots of land as private rights. In the 1990s, partly at the behest of international donors, states began experimenting with decentralization and communalization of land tenure, with varying effects and experiences across the continent.

Telecommunication services saw stunning growth across the continent as cell phone licenses were granted to private entrepreneurs, and as Internet cybercafés responded to a large demand for connectivity. Mobile phones began penetrating rural areas, where a significant minority of the population derived large benefit from the ability to coordinate or save face-to-face meetings. By 2005 approximately 10 percent of the population was using mobile phone services.

African economies, with the exception of South Africa, continued with small and inefficient industrial sectors despite the investments of the postindependence decades, and these largely stagnated during the 1980 to 2005 period. Bottling plants, industrial tanneries, soap manufacturing, and plastics facilities operated at extremely low levels of capacity and efficiency. Investment in new equipment generally yielded low returns, and many multinational manufacturing concerns shuttered or sold their African operations. Instead, informal workshops became the modest growth engines of urban agglomerations, recycling metal and wood for small-scale production and construction.

Systems of corruption in public office became the focus of considerable attention during the 1990s. The World Bank and other international organizations made good governance a central plank in lending and assistance to the continent, and conducted extensive research documenting and analyzing the strong link between corruption and poor economic performance. Corruption audits, for example, revealed tremendous misallocation of public funds for schooling and antipoverty funds. In Uganda, an audit estimated that only 13 percent of the funds allocated for schools reached the intended recipients; the remaining funds could not be properly accounted for. Audits in Ghana, Tanzania, and Zambia likewise found that more than 50 percent of allocations disappeared.

International prioritizing of good governance led regimes across the continent to at least pay lip service to new standards of transparency and accountability. There were, however, few cases of successful anticorruption efforts. Corruption scandals rocked the Daniel arap Moi government of Kenya, and the Mwai Kibaki government that succeeded Moi ostensibly carried the election because of an anticorruption platform. Kibaki's anticorruption czar, John Githongo, released a report detailing the corrupt activities of government ministers. The report read like a primer on state corruption, named names, and provided documentary evidence. But Githongo was rebuffed by the president and subsequently sought asylum in the United Kingdom. In Nigeria, transition from the corrupt military leader Sani Abacha to the elected President Olesegun Obasonjo was likewise accompanied by a perception of Obasonjo as a corruption fighter. After five years of rule most observers felt Obasonjo had not been able to deflect the state from its corrupt ways. The anticorruption organization Transparency International continued to rank African countries at the bottom of their corruption index. Only Botswana, South Africa, and Namibia scored in the top one-third of countries around the globe, and Ghana and Burkina Faso were the only other African countries in the top 100.

There was also variation across the continent in women's place in economic systems. Women in many regions of the continent continued to be denied rights to self-ownership in both national and local juridical settings. The rights of women in family law, especially in inheritance of assets, remained as brakes on women's abilities to invest and profit from their entrepreneurial talents, even as they were a major source of poorly remunerated farm and household labor. But progressive policies toward women in Botswana and South Africa, and continued prominence of women entrepreneurs in West Africa, pointed the way for unleashing a largely untapped potential.

The beginning of the twenty-first century saw three major incipient changes likely to significantly affect African economic systems. First, as China and India developed, the scale economies from urban agglomerations in those countries (concentrations of skilled labor, second-hand factory equipment, deep knowledge bases of financial intermediaries) meant that prices of their exported industrial products continued to decline. African economies were likely to face continued difficulties in developing industrial sectors. The opportunity to import consumer goods at low prices, however, would generate significant benefits and increases in real income for the average African consumer. Also, the rapid economic development in China and India meant that entrepreneurs in those countries were increasingly seeking foreign investment opportunities in Africa. Indeed, by 2005 there was considerable evidence that Indian and Chinese diaspora networks and multinational corporations were expanding rapidly in Africa.

Second, trade liberalization offered significant opportunities across the continent. The United States encouraged textile growth through its Africa Growth and Opportunity Act (AGOA). The ending of the Multi-Fiber Agreement, the international quota system for textiles, while initially favoring China, would eventually come to favor African producers. The World Trade Organization sponsored global talks to liberalize trade in agricultural commodities, known as the Doha Round, which held the potential to end the harmful subsidies and protectionist policies of the United States and Europe.

Third, Africans themselves had been migrating out of the region in accelerating numbers, and new immigrant communities in Europe and North America were generating large remittance flows back to the region. Money transfer firms such as Western Union and Moneygram expanded throughout the region. The diasporas were also creating a new generation of Africans of dual nationalities, educational backgrounds, and outlooks. This new generation was likely to significantly globalize African economies, in positive ways, though there remained the danger that the "brain drain" could reinforce the cycle of political instability and economic stagnation seen in many countries.

The three new constituencies—new investors from China and India, exporters operating in a more liberalized global marketplace, and African diaspora communities— together had the potential in many countries to reverse the downward political-economic spiral, and reinforce in other countries the process of consolidating equitable economic growth.

See also **Agriculture; Brazzaville; Déby Itno, Idriss; Disease: HIV/AIDS, Social and Political Aspects; Economic History; Globalization; International Monetary Fund; Kibaki, Mwai; Kinshasha; Labor; Moi, Daniel arap; Obasanjo, Olusegun; Sudan: Wars; Poverty; Women: Women and the Law; World Bank.**

BIBLIOGRAPHY

Collier, Paul, and Anke Hoeffler. "Greed and Grievance in Civil War." *Oxford Economic Papers* 56, no. 4 (2004): 563–595.

Fafchamps, Marcel. *Market Institutions in Sub-Saharan Africa: Theory and Evidence.* Cambridge, MA: MIT Press, 2004.

Mkandawire, P. Thandika, and Charles Soludo. *Our Continent, Our Future: African Perspectives on Structural Adjustment.* Trenton, NJ: Africa World Press, 1999.

Sender, John. "Africa's Economic Performance: Limitations of the Current Consensus." *The Journal of Economic Perspectives* 13, no. 3 (1999): 89–114.

MICHAEL KEVANE

ECONOMICS AND THE STUDY OF AFRICA.

At the time most African countries became independent, Africa was not seen by economists as particularly different from other parts of the developing world. In fact, many thought it was at an advantage, often enjoying levels of gross domestic product (GDP) per head quite a bit higher than those recorded for, say, India or China. Moreover, most of Africa had inherited from colonization institutions and infrastructure thought to be prerequisite for growth. The prognosis for Africa was thus fairly optimistic and, until the mid-1970s when African growth faltered, it seemed in agreement with the facts.

Consequently, the early period of economic research on Africa is characterized by concerns about how to manage rapid growth and the structural transformation of African economies that was to ensue. The focus was on absorptive capacity (could Africa absorb all the foreign investment?), structural transformation (how to ensure that workers and entrepreneurs had the qualifications required to switch from traditional to modern sectors and modes of production), and urbanization (how to generate the revenue necessary to provide the infrastructure and social services required by a rapidly growing urban population).

During this period most of the emphasis was on macro and sectoral issues. This body of research is perhaps best exemplified by the 1986 work of Hollis Chenery and his team at the World Bank. According to the Keynesian policy views of the time, the state was expected—and encouraged—to take a proactive role in the economy. The rapid Africanization of the public sector was seen as normal and the nationalization of many sectors of the economy as potentially beneficial.

In the shadow of the dominant macroeconomic discourse, a strong tradition of fieldwork-based microeconomic research was also taking roots in the continent. Although economic fieldwork resembles anthropology in many respects and has often borrowed ideas and methods from it, the emphasis on surveys and statistical analysis is inherited from agricultural economics. During this period much of the microeconomic work in Africa was indeed undertaken by economists seeking to understand agricultural markets and technology adoption. The behavior of African farmers was understood as rational but severely constrained by poverty, ignorance, and missing markets.

These efforts were to have a long-lasting influence on economics, not only on methods— the heavy emphasis on the collection of survey data has become a distinguishing feature of development economics everywhere—but also on economic thought. Early theorizing on the behavior of farming households led to subsequent applications to home production and intra-household welfare allocation and developed and developing economies alike. Gary S. Becker was particularly influential in expanding the domain of economics to the family and in opening the debate on the scope and limits of altruism in shaping human behavior. His contribution is nicely summarized in his 1981 *Treatise on the Family*. The "small but efficient" hypothesis did not go completely unchallenged, however. Some economists proposed what scholars of the twenty-first century might call behavioural interpretation of individual choices, such as bounded rationality and myopic strategies.

In the wake of the oil shocks and debt crises of the early 1980s, African economies faltered and lost their growth impetus. This initiated a long period of fiscal crises and foreign exchange shortages. African governments encountered problems to fund public services, including essential services such as health care and basic education. Many African countries found themselves having to adopt structural adjustment programs, with mixed success. This sequence of events triggered a massive academic and popular literature on the causes of Africa's growth failure and on the merits of structural adjustment programs.

From the point of view of economists working on Africa, the structural adjustment debate was mostly a sterile one. Adjusting their structure is what economies have to do when they go bankrupt. Countries that implement a structural adjustment program thus normally experience a decline in welfare and public services compared to those that do not. The purpose of structural adjustment programs, however, is to set the conditions for recovery. The real question is whether structural adjustment programs implemented in Africa served their purpose; that is, created the conditions for growth at the smallest possible social cost. In the 1980s the policy debate was dominated by the so-called Washington consensus—a liberal policy agenda emphasizing market liberalization and seeking to undo the excesses of the two previous decades in terms of state interventionism in the economy. As a result, many structural adjustment packages were designed in a dogmatic way with little consideration for local conditions. Economics' general consensus seems to be that many structural adjustment programs were poorly designed by donors and poorly implemented by African governments. The end result was a social cost higher than necessary and a delayed resumption of growth in the continent. In spite of these failings, structural adjustment

may nevertheless have set the stage for resumed growth at least in some African countries. Indeed several of the African countries with the highest rates of growth since the mid-1990s had implemented structural adjustment programs beforehand.

The debate on the causes of slow economic growth in Africa was sparked by Robert J. Barro who, in a well-known 1991 article, showed that standard determinants of growth could not account for Africa's experience—hence the need to include an "African dummy" in cross-country growth regressions. Africa no longer was a continent like any other, it had become a place where standard theory does not apply. This triggered a flurry of articles seeking to explain the African dummy. What was wrong with Africa? Various explanations were tried: from colonial heritage to geography, from weak institutions to bad governance and conflicts. In 2002 Daron Acemoglu, Simon Johnson, and James A. Robinson made an influential contribution to this literature by showing that much of Africa's poor performance can be explained by weak institutions. So doing, they effectively joined hands with a voluminous micro-economic literature studying institutions and their failings in Africa and elsewhere.

After a decade dominated by debates around the Washington consensus, the late 1990s saw a renewed policy interest in poverty alleviation. On the research side, this interest translated in a number of books and articles focusing on macro determinants of poverty. In 2002 David Dollar and Aart Kraay set the tone of the debate by arguing that growth is good for the poor and that large-scale durable poverty alleviation can only be achieved by fostering growth. Their views have been criticized as overly simplistic, but no economist would dispute that the massive poverty reduction that took place in China, for instance, is a by-product of rapid growth.

Literature from the first decade of the 2000s has also focused on the effectiveness of aid in promoting growth and alleviating poverty. The debate is dominated by two diametrically opposed views, those of Sachs and Easterly. In *The End of Poverty*, 2005, Jeffrey Sachs argues that much of Africa is in a poverty trap and that only a massive injection of foreign aid to the continent can meet the Millenium

Development Goal of drastically reducing poverty in the world. In his 2006 book William Easterly argues instead that aid has largely been ineffective in Africa and that it may even be an obstacle to growth and poverty reduction because of the perverse incentives it generates in recipient countries. What Africa needs is to build good institutions and governance. Injecting massive amounts of aid, Easterly says, would only make this objective harder to achieve. Both camps have sought to marshal statistical evidence in support of their views. Sachs supporters point out the successes of aid in East Asian countries—notably Taiwan and South Korea. Easterly supporters note that China and India started at the same level of development as Africa but have done much better while receiving much less aid per capita.

The renewed policy emphasis on poverty has had a profound influence on the direction taken by microeconomic research. Much recent microeconomic work in Africa takes the form of applied welfare analysis. Because in the 2000s many countries have to prepare a national poverty assessment in preparation to negotiations with donors, issues surrounding the measurement of poverty have gained renewed prominence. Some methodological advances have been made, particularly in the design of poverty maps. Further progress remains hampered by the lack of comparative, comprehensive surveys in many African countries. Impact assessment based on experimental designs and randomized trials is rapidly becoming a strong focus of empirical research in Africa, much of the data collection taking place in collaboration with nongovernmental organizations. Microeconomists have also begun incorporating elements of behavioral psychology in their research design, slowly moving away from the rational agent paradigm. Works by Edward Miguel and Michael Kremer (2004), Esther Duflo (2006), Marianne Bertrand and colleagues (2005), and Abigail Barr and colleagues (2005) are representative of these new trends.

Much of the economic debate on Africa has been dominated by non-Africans. This is largely a reflection of the small number of African economists publishing in Western academic journals; however, organizations such as the African Economic Research Consortium, funded by the World Bank and other donors and assisted by a number of European universities, have accomplished valuable work. In addition, there is extensive participation of African researchers in the 2000 World Bank report on Africa, *Can African Claim the 21st Century?*, and a growing number of African authors publishing in the *Journal of African Economies.*

While Africans may not have contributed much to economic debate yet, economics as a discipline has learned a lot from the study of Africa. The continent has been the deathbed of many theories and policy prescriptions developed for other parts of the world—from neo-Keynesian state interventionism to Washington-consensus laissez-faire. As pointed out by Collier in 1993, economists have had to enrich their paradigm so as to account for the specific realities of the continent. This has led to more emphasis on institutions and governance, geography and historical heritage, political economy and state capture, ethnicity and networks—all topics that had long been the focus of attention of social scientists but were traditionally ignored (or downplayed) by economists. As a result, the study of Africa has brought economics closer to other social sciences.

See also **Economic History; World Bank.**

BIBLIOGRAPHY

Acemoglu, Daron, Simon Johnson, and James A. Robinson. "Reversal of Fortune: Geography and Institutions in the Making of the Modern World Income Distribution." *Quarterly Journal of Economics*, 117, no. 4 (November 2002): 1231–1294.

Barr, Abigail, Magnus Lindelow, and Pieter Serneels. "To Serve the Community or Oneself: The Public Servant's Dilemma." Policy Research Paper Series No. 3187. Washington, DC: World Bank, 2004.

Barro, Robert J. "Economic Growth in a Cross-Section of Countries." *Quarterly Journal of Economics* 106, no. 2 (May 1991): 407–443.

Bauer, P. T. *West African Trade: A Study of Competition, Oligopoly and Monopoly in a Changing Economy.* Cambridge, U.K.: Cambridge University Press, 1954.

Becker, Gary S. *A Treatise on the Family.* Cambridge, MA: Harvard University Press, 1981.

Bertrand, Marianne, et al. *What's Psychology Worth? A Field Experiment in the Consumer Credit Market.* New Haven, CT: Economic Growth Center, Yale University, 2005.

Chenery, Hollis; Sherman Robinson; and Moshe Syrquin. *Industrialization and Growth: A Comparative Study.* New York: Oxford University Press, 1986.

Collier, Paul. "Africa and the Study of Economics." In *Africa and the Disciplines: The Contributions of Research in Africa to the Social Sciences and Humanities.* New York: Oxford University Press, 1993.

Dollar, David, and Aart Kraay. "Growth Is Good for the Poor." *Journal of Economic Growth* 7, no. 3 (September 2002): 195–225.

Duflo, Esther. *Understanding Technology Adoption: Fertilizer in Western Kenya, Evidence from Field Experiments.* Cambridge, MA: Department of Economics, Massachusetts Institute of Technology, 2006.

Easterly, William. *The White Man's Burden: Why the West's Efforts to Aid the Rest Have Done So Much Ill and So Little Good.* New York: Penguin, 2006.

Elbers, Chris; Jean O. Lanjouw; and Peter Lanjouw. "Micro-Level Estimation of Poverty and Inequality." *Econometrica* 71, no. 1 (January 2003): 355–364.

Fafchamps, Marcel. *Market Institutions in Sub-Saharan Africa.* Cambridge, MA: MIT Press, 2004.

Jones, William O. *Manioc in Africa.* Stanford, CA: Stanford University Press, 1959.

Miguel, Edward, and Michael Kremer. "Worms: Identifying Impacts on Education and Health in the Presence of Treatment Externalities." *Econometrica* 72, no. 1 (January 2004): 159–217.

Sachs, Jeffrey. *The End of Poverty.* New York: Penguin, 2005.

Stiglitz, Joseph. *Globalization and Its Discontents.* New York: Norton, 2003.

World Bank. *Accelerated Development in sub-Saharan Africa: An Agenda for Action.* Washington, DC: World Bank, 1981.

World Bank. *Can African Claim the 21st Century?* Washington, DC: World Bank, 2000.

MARCEL FAFCHAMPS

ECOSYSTEMS

This entry includes the following articles:
COASTAL ENVIRONMENTS
DESERTS AND SEMI-DESERTS
MONTANE ENVIRONMENTS
SAVANNAS
TROPICAL AND HUMID FORESTS

COASTAL ENVIRONMENTS

The most important ecosystems for African coastal-dwellers are those associated with open rocky and sandy shores, coral reefs, deltas, estuaries, and lagoons. Seawater temperature is one of the key factors that governs the distribution pattern, composition, and biological diversity of those ecosystems, which are dominated by seagrasses, mangroves, kelp (brown seaweeds), and corals. Other regional and local factors that play an important role include upwelling of colder nutrient-rich water, geology, shore topography, wave exposure, and high turbidity linked to lowered salinity due to seasonal discharge from major rivers. These factors, as well as the absence of shallow rocky banks or shoals and lowered seawater temperatures during the last Pleistocene glaciations, are linked to the absence of reef-building corals in tropical West Africa and its offshore islands. Spillage of oil has become an ever more important factor in West Africa, where it has been responsible for environmental degradation, especially the loss of mangrove in the Niger Delta. Development of new oil fields off the shores of countries such as Mauritania, Gabon, Angola, and Equatorial Guinea will further damage inshore ecosystems along the West African coast.

CORAL REEFS

These biologically diverse ecosystems extend northward along the East African coast, from latitude 20 degrees south to the Red Sea, reaching as far north as the Gulf of Suez. Reef-building corals grow where the seawater temperature does not normally fall below 56 degrees Fahrenheit and rise above 86 degrees Fahrenheit. Some of the most well developed reefs are associated with the offshore islands, with those of the Seychelles being some of the most extensive in the world. Indian Ocean islands, like Aldabra, are coral atolls, parts of roughly circular reefs developed around a central lagoon. Along much of the East African coast and its larger offshore islands, inshore reefs, known as fringing reefs, are often mixed with "patch reefs" formed over irregularities in shallower parts of the seabed. Sometimes reefs are interrupted by major rivers that discharge freshwater and sediment into the sea. In Mozambique there are many such rivers, resulting in a coast dominated by deltas and muddy banks with fringing reefs confined mostly to offshore islands.

Coral diversity is highest along the seaward margin of reefs. Often the most common coral genus in shallower areas is *Acropora* and many so-called boulder corals are more commonly

Seaweed farm at Jabiani on the island of Zanzibar. Seaweed is an important crop in many parts of Africa, where it is collected or grown in relatively wave-sheltered coastal areas. Grown at this farm is the Eucheuma denticulatum, an important source of the seaweed polysaccharide known as iota-carrageenan. © M.D. GUIRY (ALGAEBASE)

encountered in deeper water. Often landward of fringing reefs lie sheltered lagoons whose sandy floors are commonly carpeted by seagrasses and green siphonaceous algae. Commonly backing these lagoons are areas of mangrove trees.

Toward the end of the twentieth century the phenomenon of "coral bleaching," the loss of the algal component from coral polyps, became more frequent. In the late 1990s a mass bleaching event resulted in the death of corals throughout the Indian Ocean, although the more important tourist reefs in the northern parts of the Red Sea escaped. It was caused by periods of prolonged above-average maximum surface seawater temperature. Strictly local events also degrade or kill coral reefs; these include pollution from industry, agricultural run-off, mining, tanker traffic, domestic effluent, and ship groundings. Deterioration of East African reefs is also caused by=increased flushing of sediments into coastal waters due to mangrove destruction, agricultural malpractice, and inland deforestation and logging. Overexploitation of shells, corals, and dynamite fishing all pose threats to reefs. Modern fishing methods are more destructive than traditional ones and can

lead to the incidental capture of dugongs, turtles, and small reef fishes.

Coral reefs protect the coastline against waves and storm surges, prevent erosion, contribute to the formation of sandy beaches, and provide safe anchorages. Reefs are also important breeding and nursery grounds for commercially important fish and a habitat for the spiny lobster. Increasingly, reefs are becoming major tourist attractions, and recreational activities related to ecotourism are generating considerable income for countries such as Egypt, the Seychelles, Kenya, and Tanzania. Reef management is most developed in these countries where several protected marine areas exist. There are few protected areas for offshore islands except for the Seychelles, with several marine protected areas including the island of Aldabra.

LAGOONS

Those lagoon ecosystems not associated with coral reefs are usually inhospitable environments for most marine organisms because of widely fluctuating salinities and extensive areas of mud or sediment. Lagoon systems are very extensive in

Coral reef scene in the northern part of the Red Sea. The extraordinary diversity of corals is evident along with the presence of other reef-associated organisms. These reefs are the most biologically diverse and economically important ecosystems bordering the Red Sea, as well as the Indian Ocean coast of East Africa and offshore islands. PHOTOGRAPH BY DAVID GEORGE

the Gulf of Guinea region of West Africa, where an outer fringing zone of salt-tolerant herbs commonly gives way to an inner one of mangroves extending down to the permanent level of the open water. The prop-rooted mangrove *Rhizophora* characterizes those lagoons that are connected permanently to the sea, and on its roots are zones of attached organisms. Lagoons having no permanent connection to the sea only contain the white mangrove (*Avicennia germinans*), which often grows at the highest levels of seasonal flooding. Isolating sandbars are occasionally breached naturally or artificially by the local fishing communities. In lagoon systems microorganisms comprise the free-living plankton, and many are associated with the muddy lagoon floor and other mud- or sediment-covered surfaces. Mollusks and polychaete worms commonly live on the bottom sediments of lagoons, along with the air-breathing fish known as the mudskipper.

The lagoons and other waterways of the vast Nile Delta have profoundly changed since closure of the Aswan High Dam in 1964. There is no longer an annual flooding, and the famous papyrus swamps have largely disappeared. Sediment and a large volume of nutrient-rich flood water coming down the River Nile no longer reaches the delta, so the waters of the southeastern Mediterranean are now less fertile. The coastal lagoons have become more saline due to erosion of their seaward margins, and dense phytoplankton blooms develop, caused by nutrient-enrichment from fertilizer run-off and dumping of wastewater and sewage sludge.

Lagoons are important habitats for adult fish and essential spawning and nursery grounds for many economically important marine fish. Several species of shrimp and prawn depend on lagoons and mangroves. Over the past decade, however, the livelihood of those who fish the lagoons of the Gulf of Guinea coast has been threatened by the spread of the water hyacinth, a very invasive floating aquatic weed. An increasing threat to lagoons comes from draining or infilling to reclaim land for building. Lagoons along the Gulf of Guinea coast, such as those close to Abidjan (in Côte d'Ivoire), are particularly threatened by the cutting of channels, extraction of gravel, building of dikes, pollution by insecticides and chemical fertilizers, as well as by the influx of domestic and industrial wastewaters. These lagoons, and those elsewhere in Africa, are important wildlife sanctuaries, especially for migrating birds.

MANGROVE OR MANGAL

These ecosystems of salt-tolerant, evergreen trees and bushes are most common in sheltered deltas, estuaries, and lagoons along the tropical and subtropical coasts of Africa. One of the most extensive mangrove areas in Africa is the Niger Delta, where the trees cover approximately 14,000 square miles and commonly reach seventeen feet in height. The fringing coral reefs of eastern Africa allow mangroves to grow along the open coast. In southern Mozambique, the island of Madagascar gives sufficient protection to allow extensive mangrove development on the offshore banks of river-derived sediments. In West Africa mangroves lie between Mauritania in the north and Angola in the south. They are more widely distributed in East Africa, with mangroves extending northward from the Gonabie River (32°55') in South Africa to the Gulf of Suez.

The arching prop roots of mangrove trees, such as *Rhizophora*, and the vertical "breathing" roots of *Avicennia*, provide attachment surfaces for seaweed and various animals. In western Africa there is a simple zonation of mangrove vegetation, with *Rhizophora* species dominating where tidal influences are strong, followed inland by *Avicennia germinans*, and then grasses such as *Paspalum vaginatum*. Mangrove tree diversity is much greater in East Africa, and the zonation pattern there is more complicated.

Mangroves protect shorelines from storm damage and coastal erosion as well as stabilize them and their nearby riverbanks. By trapping sediment in the mangroves' network of roots, they build up mud banks leading to land reclamation. Mangroves are an important local resource in supplying wood products for building, boat and fish-trap construction, medicines, dyes, and fuel. Crabs, oysters, prawns, and fish are the principal sea foods harvested in mangrove and lagoon ecosystems.

In the early twenty-first century, the mangrove ecosystem is under serious threat throughout Africa, having been cleared or modified for shrimp farming, oyster growing, rice cultivation, and solar salt production, or reclaimed for agricultural use and for urban and industrial development. Oil spillages have caused considerable damage to mangrove areas, particularly in the Niger Delta, where there have been over four thousand oil spills between 1960 and 2006. One of the most visible consequences of such spills has been the loss of mangrove trees. Damage to mangroves is also caused by changes in freshwater regimes, often related to reduced river inflow into delta systems due to damming or land-use changes in the catchments.

SALT MARSH, SEAGRASS, AND SANDY BEACHES

Salt marsh ecosystems are dominated by low-growing, salt-tolerant grasses, sedges, and succulent plants that cover muddy banks at and above mid-tide levels, where they often come to form a distinct series of zones. Widely distributed plants like *Spartina*, *Puccinellia*, *Salicornia*, and *Sueda* are common at extreme high-tide levels. Along the temperate south and west coasts of South Africa, salt marshes are within estuaries; further to the north in Mozambique, they are frequently confined to mangrove margins. Salt marsh vegetation is developed in West Africa on the more wave-sheltered southern side of the Cap Blanc Peninsula in Mauritania, but otherwise it is more common along the Mediterranean coast of north Africa.

The grass-like herbaceous plants, the "seagrasses," often form the dominant ecosystems on sand and mud in shallow, wave-protected habitats. In tropical western Africa, seagrasses are rare, with *Halodule* and *Cymodocea* the two most frequently encountered genera. The most extensive seagrass beds in West Africa are in fully marine estuaries along the Angola coast and on the Mauritanian side of the Cap Blanc peninsula.

Seagrasses are widespread and more diverse in East Africa, where extensive submarine meadows grow over sandy intertidal flats and on the floor of shallow coastal lagoons, especially those landward of fringing coral reefs. Often they are very extensive in the Red Sea, although only *Halophila* and *Halodule* are present in its more northerly parts. Very extensive beds occur along the Mediterranean coast of North Africa, where *Posidonia oceanica* is often the dominant grass. In East Africa seagrasses show a characteristic zonation pattern, with some intertidal and others growing to a depth of about eleven yards.

Seagrass beds are highly productive. They act as important nursery grounds for fish and crustaceans and provide food and shelter for many other organisms. The creeping stoloniferous stems and rhizoids of the seagrasses are important in stabilizing the seabed, but these are threatened in many areas by siltation, prawn trawling, and seaweed farming.

Sandy beach ecosystems in many parts of Africa are often too mobile to support plants or those animals that form stable burrows. Animals associated with sand are usually below the surface at low tide and occupy different zones. The beach area influenced only by wave splash and spray is frequently characterized by air-breathing crustaceans (ocypod or ghost crabs); the middle intertidal often by small crustaceans; and the junction with subtidal is sometimes subdivided into a "subtidal fringe" dominated by two mollusks (*Donax* and *Gastrosaccus*), a transition zone almost devoid of animals, and an outermost turbulent zone, where increased stability results in greater animal diversity.

STRAND AND SAND DUNES

Strand ecosystems develop above the high tide mark and are recognized throughout Africa by the presence of a few salt-tolerant plants. These areas are frequently subdivided into a pioneer community to the seaward of the beach and a much denser and more diverse community away from the beach. The pioneer community includes grasses and sedges with underground stems along with other plants whose stems straggle along the surface and have succulent leaves. Various upright perennials grow toward the landward limit of the zone, and these extend into a much wider second zone: the main strand zone. On the landward side there is sometimes an evergreen shrub zone of prostrate or semiprostrate plants that become trimmed into a

wedge shape by the prevailing wind. The main strand zone and evergreen shrub zone has often been disturbed in the tropics by agriculture and the widespread planting of coconut palms.

Sand dune ecosystems are rare along the Gulf of Guinea coast of West Africa, with genuine dunes confined only to a small area of Ghana. They are very extensive in drier parts West Africa, such as along the coasts of northern Senegal, Mauritania, Western Sahara, and Morocco in the north and southern Angola and Namibia in the south. In eastern Africa they are common along parts of the Kenyan and Somalian coasts as well as along much of the Red Sea coast. Mobile dunes are usually fixed by sand-binding plants whose creeping underground stems are like those growing in the pioneer zone of the strand. Behind these are more stable dunes possessing a wider variety of plants, including many of those forming the strand vegetation.

INTERTIDAL ROCKY SHORE ECOSYSTEMS

The gradient in physical stress experienced by rocky shore organisms on rocky shores during low tide results in them coming to occupy distinctive zones. These are more telescoped on wave-sheltered shores and extend vertically upward by several yards where wave action is severe. The degree of exposure of shore organisms to wave action determines their height, the width of the zones, and the composition and biodiversity of the communities.

Similar types of organisms often characterize the same shore level in different parts of Africa, although the genera and species are not necessarily the same. Small snails are usually at the uppermost level on shores influenced by wave splash or spray. The intertidal is usually divisible into zones: a lower one dominated by encrusting calcareous red algae ("coralline algae"), except in the temperate region of South Africa where there are barnacles and "fleshy" algae, along with an upper barnacle-dominated zone. The junction of the intertidal and subtidal is recognized in many tropical areas by the uppermost limit of black sea urchins and the brown seaweed *Sargassum*, and in the temperate areas by especially large brown seaweeds known as kelps.

Local people harvest shellfish such as mussels, oysters, limpets, and barnacles from rocky shores.

Shell collectors frequent the east coast of South Africa in search of cone shells and cowries. Rocky-shore seaweeds are not widely used in Africa as food, although red seaweeds are harvested commercially in various countries including Namibia, South Africa, Kenya, Tanzania, and Senegal. Information on seaweeds that are harvested in Africa and those of potential importance on the continent is contained in the Web site *SeaweedAfrica*.

See also **Forestry; Production Strategies; Wildlife.**

BIBLIOGRAPHY

Day, J. H., ed. *Estuarine Ecology: with Particular Reference to Southern Africa*. Cape Town, South Africa: A. A. Balkema, 1981.

Field, J. G., and C. L. Griffiths. "Littoral and Sublittoral Ecosystems of Southern Africa." In *Intertidal and Littoral Ecosystems*, Vol. 24: *Ecosystems of the World*, ed. Arthur C. Mathieson and P. H. Neinhuis. New York: Elsevier, 1991.

Hughes, R. H., and J. S. Hughes. *A Directory of African Wetlands*. Gland, Switzerland and Cambridge, U.K.: IUCN, 1992.

John, D. M., and G. W. Lawson. "Littoral Ecosystems of Tropical West Africa." In *Intertidal and Littoral Ecosystems*, Vol. 24: *Ecosystems of the World*, ed. Arthur C. Mathieson and P. H. Neinhuis. New York: Elsevier, 1991.

John, D. M.; C. Lévêque; and L. E. Newton. "Western Africa." In *Wetlands of the World: Inventory, Ecology, and Management*, ed. Dennis F. Whigham, Dagmar Dykyjová, and Slavomil Hejn'y. Dordrecht: Kluwer, 1993.

Lawson, G. W. *Plant Ecology in West Africa: Systems and Processes*. New York: Wiley, 1986.

Lawson, G. W., and D. M. John. *The Marine Algae and Coastal Environment of Tropical West Africa*, 2nd edition. Berlin: J. Cramer/ E.Schweizerbart'sche, 1987.

Lipkin, Y. "Life in the Littoral of the Red Sea (with remarks on the Gulf of Aden)" In *Intertidal and Littoral Ecosystems*, Vol. 24: *Ecosystems of the World*, ed. Arthur C. Mathieson and P. H. Neinhuis. New York: Elsevier, 1991.

Richmond, M. D. *A Guide to the Seashores of Eastern Africa and the Western Indian Ocean Island*. Zanzibar, Tanzania: SIDA/Department for Research Cooperation, 1997.

SeaweedAfrica. Available from http://www.seaweedAfrica.org

Spalding, M. D.; C. Ravilious; and E. P. Green. *World Atlas of Coral Reefs* Berkeley: University of California Press, 2001.

White, F. *The Vegetation of Africa: A Descriptive Memoir to Accompany the UNESCO/AETFAT/UNSO Vegetation Map of Africa*. Paris: UNESCO, 1983.

DAVID M. JOHN

DESERTS AND SEMI-DESERTS

More than half of the surface area of the African continent is arid (desert or semideserts). Deserts and semideserts are generally defined as areas of high aridity or, more specifically, with low ratios of precipitation (P) to potential evapotranspiration (PE), as affected by temperature and insolation (exposure to and strength of the sun's rays). Aridity increases as one moves north and south of the equator, with a large fraction of deserts and semidesert ecosystems on the continent found between 15 and 30 degrees north and south latitude—areas affected by descending dry air on the poleward sides of the tropical circulation systems commonly referred to as Hadley cells.

A major anomaly to this pattern is the drier than expected region in East Africa from the Horn south into the central portion of Kenya and Tanzania (Somali-Masaii) at 0 to 10 degrees north latitude. The Sahara and Namib deserts represent the most arid portions of the continent with their aridity indexes (P/PE) spanning the hyperarid (less than 0.03) to arid (0.03 to 0.20) range. Other areas, such as the Sahel lying just south of the Sahara, the Somali-Masaii region in East Africa, and the Karoo and Kalahari deserts of Southern Africa, are best seen as semideserts having aridity indexes ranging from the arid (0.03 to 0.20) to semiarid (0.20–0.50).

There is a strong relationship between mean rainfall, mean vegetative cover/production, and vegetative structure across dryland regions of the continent. Both scientific definitions derived from climate parameters (aridity index) and popular understandings of deserts and semideserts have been strongly shaped by perceptions of what a desert should look like visually—sparse vegetative cover and simple structure (grassland/bushland/steppe). Common understandings of what a desert or semidesert should look like in terms of structure and vegetative cover have contributed to the persistent confusion around environmental change in dryland regions more generally, and terms such as desertification more specifically.

Simply put, deserts are generally characterized as supporting very sparse or no ephemeral herbaceous vegetation. Lignaceous vegetation (trees and shrubs) is generally found within small patches of more persistent soil moisture in small areas receiving higher rainfall (elevated rock outcrops); higher concentrations of runoff; or higher water tables (wadis). Semideserts are often viewed as having a steppe or bushland vegetation, a mix of herbaceous vegetation, and widely scattered bushes and short trees—an intermediate structural vegetative category between desert and dry savanna. With increased soil moisture, steppe/bushland grades into dry savanna with a structure characterized by grassland with widely spaced taller trees. Clear separations between these vegetation formations are difficult to discern at regional and national scales.

MAJOR DRYLAND REGIONS

There are three major dryland regions (deserts and associated semideserts) on the continent of Africa. The Sahara desert is the largest desert in the world (8–10 million square kilometers or 3.09–3.86 million square miles), stretching eastward from the Atlantic Coast to the Red Sea, and from the Atlas Mountains southward to the Niger Bend in the west, and from the Mediterranean to the Ethiopian Highlands in the east. It is also one of the hottest regions of the world with average daily maximum temperatures exceeding 95 degrees Fahrenheit across a large fraction of its surface (increasing from north to south). Rainfall in the southern Sahara (less than 4 inches/year) and the semidesert region (4–20 inches/year) lying just south (the Sahel) is influenced by the movement of the intertropical convergence zone (ITCZ) and occurs during the summer months with a monomodal distribution. Conversely, the northern Sahara and semidesert oriregion lying just north has a Mediterranean climate. The rain falls during the winter with a monomodal distribution and a contrasting floristic composition.

The semidesert region of East Africa extends from the Horn of Africa through parts of Ethiopia and northern Kenya. Named deserts include the Danakil, Ogaden, and Chalbi. A distinctive feature of the East African drylands is their relative proximity to the equator compared to the Sahara and the Southern African drylands. Although the seasonal distribution of rainfall is similar to that observed for the Sahel at their northern extent in the Danakil and drylands of the Horn, rainfall distribution in East African drylands lying within 0–6 degrees north of the equator are bimodal. This results in rainy seasons of longer duration than areas elsewhere in dryland Africa receiving similar annual rainfall.

The driest area of southern Africa is the Namib Desert, a 75–124 mile-wide strip of land lying between the Atlantic coast and the western edge of the interior plateau of Southern Africa (Great Escarpment) in the southwest (primarily in Namibia). The climate of the Namib is affected not only by its latitude but also by the cold Benguela ocean current that runs along the coast. A steep gradient of rainfall and temperature exists from the coast inland (annual average maximum daily temperature of 63 degrees Fahrenheit with rainfall often less than 0.4 inches/year) to the edge of the escarpment (annual average maximum daily temperature of 86 degrees Fahrenheit with 4 inches/year).

The other drylands of Southern Africa generally lie on the interior plateau of Southern Africa (2,625–3,937 feet above sea level) and therefore, similar to the Namib, have cooler temperatures than the Sahara and associated semideserts. The Kalahari is a semidesert region lying north of the Orange River (extending north into southern Angola) and stretching west to east from the mountains of central Namibia to the highlands of eastern Botswana. Rainfall is highest in the north (20–31 inches/year) and lowest to the southwest (8 inches/year). It consists largely of a sedimentary basin overlain by deep sands that promote infiltration, leading to few permanent surface water bodies (besides river-fed inland deltas and swamps to the northwest) and a north-to-southwest gradient of tree to bush savannas. The Karoo lies south of the Kalahari and east of the Namib in South Africa. In its northern portion, summer rainfall varies from 16 inches in the east to 6 inches in the west. To the south toward the coast, 4–12 inches/year fall during the winter months. The Karoo is a semidesert biome with a unique floristic composition including a large diversity of succulents.

DRYLAND ECOLOGY

Despite the strong correlation of rainfall with vegetative composition and structure across the continent, biogeographic variation at subregional scales is strongly influenced by recent rainfall history, edaphic conditions, and human land-use history. Understandings of deserts and semideserts based on vegetative cover often diverge from categories derived simply from climatic parameters. This confusion has contributed to the conceptual problems concerning environmental change. For example, the use of the term "desertification," which, despite attempts to regularize it, has commonly been used to refer to shifts from vegetated to denuded states—shifts that occur on a seasonal and interannual basis with regularity in dryland Africa but that are often seen to be persistent and anthropogenic in the nonscientific literature. Due to the high spatiotemporal variability of rainfall in dryland areas of Africa, it is difficult to document persistent vegetative changes and their cause.

Most dryland areas of Africa have experienced long historic periods of more humid conditions associated with significant soil weathering. This is especially the case for the semiarid areas lying just south of the Sahara desert. An underlying sedimentary rock formation combined with this climate history has resulted in infertile soils that constrain biological productivity. If these areas receive more than 10–14 inches of rainfall infiltration, nutrient availability becomes more limiting to vegetative growth. Across such rainfall gradients, vegetation in the dryer areas, although sparse, is of generally higher nutritive quality for grazing animals. In southern Africa, vegetation in drier areas, the sweet veld, is of higher quality than the sour veld of more humid areas. The fact that vegetation of higher forage quality is often found in areas that lack permanent water bodies has played an important role in shaping seasonal longer-range movements of wild ungulates and pastoralist-managed domestic livestock in dryland Africa.

Desert and semidesert environments represent some of the most difficult in the world for the persistence of life. Plant and animal life have evolved a wide range of adaptations to survive under these conditions. Adaptations to the highly dynamic and harsh conditions of dryland environments include morphological, physiological, and behavioral modifications to reduce the use and loss of moisture (skins more impermeable to water, more water-efficient physiologies and temperature control, water storage, small leaves of plants) and to escape periods of extreme aridity (dormancy, drought deciduous, animal behavior). For example, the extreme aridity and high temperatures experienced in the Sahel and Sahara region explains the dominance of annual plants in its herbaceous strata—seeds that are more resistant to desiccation than plant parts. In the coastal Namib, a significant fraction of moisture comes through fog and plants, and animals there show remarkable adaptations to capture it.

Compared to other arid regions of the world, the species richness of African drylands is high, particularly in Southern Africa. Species richness of the Namib, Kalahari, and Karoo is particularly high with few phytogeographical connections to the Sahara and East African dryland ecosystems at the generic and specific levels. The clear separation of the Sahara and East African flora from those of the south reflects not only contemporary differences in climate and soils but also contrasting biogeographical histories. The unique biodiversity in Southern Africa is all the more remarkable given what is generally seen as a relatively young flora.

HUMAN SETTLEMENT AND LAND USE

The aridity of desert and semidesert environments is a major constraint to human habitation and agricultural production. In true deserts, human desert-based livelihoods are centered on the micropatches of higher soil moisture. Outside of these patches, crop agriculture is impossible and animal husbandry is extremely difficult to sustain. Therefore, livelihoods are strongly tied to trade—economic surpluses gained through the transport of goods, trade, and the state-sponsored and illegal taxation of these trade flows.

More generally, the steep ecoclimatic gradients associated with the desert-semidesert-savanna transitions, although shifting over time, have arguably played an important role in the development of ecologically specialized trade networks during the precolonial era that persist to the present.

As one moves into the semidesert zone, annual average rainfall and length of the rainy season increases. Semidesert areas have been defined on a continental scale as those areas receiving on average 4–16 inches/year. Given the high risk of crop failure from year to year, crop agriculture is only practiced in the moister third of semidesert areas. Millet is the major rainfed crop in these areas (outside of irrigated areas) and given the high spatiotemporal distribution of rainfall, farmers will often seed widely dispersed fields in order to seek a harvest. There are significant interregional differences in where the cultivation limit falls. In East African drylands that experience bimodal rainfall patterns, cultivation generally fails at annual rainfall levels supporting crop agriculture in West Africa, because sparse rainfall in East African drylands is spread across a longer rainy season. Moreover, it has been argued that, at comparable rainfall levels, rainfall in East and Southern Africa is more variable from year to year due to the influence of the El Niño southern oscillation on these regions' rainfall. As a result, the climatic risk for crop agriculture is higher in East Africa and Southern Africa. Therefore, the reliance on pure pastoralism is higher than in areas receiving similar long-term average rainfall to areas lying south of the Sahara.

Pastoralism, a variously mobile form of livestock husbandry, represents a major productivity strategy particularly suited to the high spatiotemporal variability of rainfall and vegetative productivity in dryland Africa. Hunter-gathering strategies share these advantages although it is much less common—the most notable case being the !Kung San who utilize the highly diverse Kalahari ecosystem. Major domestic livestock raised in dryland areas include camels, cattle, sheep, and goats. The degree of livestock mobility and integration with crop agriculture have been historically highly variable at household to regional levels. Studies since the mid-1980s have generally noted a decline in livestock mobility and increased reliance on agriculture among pastoralist ethnic groups across dryland Africa.

See also **Climate; Desertification, Modern; Ecology; Kalahari Desert; Sahara Desert; Salt; Soils; Water and Irrigation.**

BIBLIOGRAPHY

Adams, William Mark; Andrew S. Goudie; and Anthony R. Orme, eds. *The Physical Geography of Africa*. Oxford: Oxford University Press, 1996.

Cloudsey-Thompson, John L., ed. *Sahara Desert*. Oxford: Oxford University Press, 1984.

Ellis, Jim, and Kathleen A. Galvin. "Climate Patterns and Land-Use Practices in the Dry Zones of Africa." *BioScience* 44, no. 5 (1994): 340–349.

Middleton, Nick, and David Thomas, eds. *World Atlas of Desertification*. New York: United Nations Environment Programme, 1997.

Niamir-Fuller, Maryam, ed. *Managing Mobility in African Rangelands*. London: Intermediate Technology Publications, 1999.

Penning de Vries, Frits W. T., and M. A. Djitèye, eds. *La productivité des pâturages sahéliens*. Wageningen, the Netherlands: Centre for Agricultural Publishing and Documentation, 1982.

Thomas, David S.G., and Paul A. Shaw. *The Kalahari Environment*. New York: Cambridge University Press, 1991.

White, Frank. *The Vegetation of Africa; A Descriptive Memoir to Accompany the Unesco/AETFAT/UNSO Vegetation Map of Africa*. Paris: United Nations Educational, Scientific and Cultural Organization, 1983.

MATT TURNER

MONTANE ENVIRONMENTS

Sub-Saharan Africa does not have a long, high mountain range like the Andes, the Rocky Mountains, or the Himalaya. In fact, most of Africa is fairly flat and low, but the eastern part of the continent from northern Ethiopia to South Africa has a series of elevated regions, often separated by great distances. Smaller highland areas exist in western Africa. During the Miocene period, starting approximately 25 million years ago, sections of eastern Africa underwent tectonic uplift and rifting. Some of these areas, such as the Ethiopian Highlands and the Rwenzori Mountains, were pushed to heights well above the tree line, while others, such as the Drakensberg complex in South Africa, the Eastern Arc mountain system in Tanzania and Kenya, and Mlanje in Malawi, remained low enough to be mostly forested (although many are largely deforested in the early twenty-first century). In association with this uplift, the region became volcanically active. The highest mountain in Africa, Mount Kilimanjaro (5,895 m; 19,340 feet) in Tanzania, remains a dormant volcano. Mount Kenya (5,199 m; 17,058 feet), the second highest, is an extinct volcano. The Virunga Mountains in

Rwanda and Democratic Republic of Congo remain active, as do some other centers. There are fundamental biological differences between the older uplift mountains, which often have great biodiversity and high endemicity, while the more recent, often more spectacular, isolated volcanoes are biologically more depauperate and have fewer endemics.

The uplifting of the eastern part of the continent and the formation of a series of volcanoes drastically changed not only the geomorphology of the continent but also its climate and associated soils, ecosystems and potential for human habitation, and resource availability. The formation of the mountains has resulted in a highly fragmented region with tremendous landscape heterogeneity, varying from deserts to rain forests, from cool montane regions to hot coastal plains, from nutrient-rich volcanic soils to old, impoverished ones. Rainfall in the mountains is an important source of fresh water in a generally arid area, and feeds rivers and lakes throughout the region and beyond. Some of this water is used for irrigation in dry downstream areas, or for hydroelectric power generation, but it remains a limited resource and must be used wisely.

The east African mountains, high enough to be glaciated on Kilimanjaro, Mount Kenya and Rwenzori, and often isolated from other montane areas by wide stretches of low plains, have developed a set of unique ecosystems forming zones of different vegetation types. Of these the Afroalpine ecosystem above the tree line is the most distinctive in both appearance and climate. The landscape is often dominated by the massive rosettes of giant groundsels (genus *Dendrosenecio*) and lobelias, whose highly unusual growth forms are adapted to the harsh environment with its daily cycle of ambient temperature change, which has been referred to as "summer every day, winter every night"; nocturnal frosts are the norm. An example of adaptation to this daily temperature oscillation is *Lobelia deckenii* subsp. *keniensis* on Mount Kenya. This plant grows into a large rosette that traps a rainwater among its leaves. This water retains residual heat to protect the central growing core from the daily temperature extremes of the alpine environment. At night the ambient surface temperature

may drop to below -10°C (14°F), but the growth tip in the middle of the rosette remains unfrozen.

What makes this system even more interesting is that there are a number of insect species whose larvae live and develop in this relatively temperate and predator-free water. Most terrestrial insects in the Afroalpine zone have evolved freeze tolerance or "antifreeze" in their body fluids. Some larger insects, such as grasshoppers and beetles, have evolved wingless forms, an adaptation to life in a relatively small, suitable, high-altitude area surrounded by hostile low-altitude habitat. Many of the mammals typical of the Afroalpine zone, such as the rock hyrax, shrews, mole rats and other rodents, live in burrows, while larger species such as the Common Duiker often have longer coats than normal.

Below the treeline, the forested Afromontane zone is less dramatic and not as accessible as the Afroalpine zone, but is more important in terms of rainfall catchment, forest resources and overall biodiversity. Most Afromontane forests show high degrees of ecological complexity, with vegetation types varying by altitude and in response to natural and human disturbance. Rainfall is the most important factor in determining vegetation type, and different aspects of the mountain often have widely contrasting forest communities that may even have their own endemic species. Temperature-related phenomena, such as the daily formation of a cloud-belt, are also important in determining ecosystem type and composition.

The upper part of the forest, often in the cloud belt, exemplifies the diversity and complexity of an ecosystem that is often rich in bryophytes, ferns and herbaceous plants. The dominant tree here is usually *Podocarpus milanjianus*, but as its seedlings are shade-dependent it arrives late in a post-disturbance succession, particularly after fire. Burning stimulates a mass germination of the giant heather *Erica excelsa*, which grows rapidly to 10 meters tall but soon senesces. Among them are seedlings of *Hagenia abyssinica*, which grow up to form massive trees with wide-spreading limbs. They often survive in 'parkland' forest in which grazing herbivores, especially buffalo, maintain a sward of close-cropped grass and herbs that inhibits tree establishment. *Podocarpus* germinates under maturing *Erica* and when mature provides shelter for its own seedlings. It also grows with the Afro-montane bamboo, *Yushania alpina*, which has its own cycle of growth and development followed by flowering and dieback over approximately forty years. *Podocarpus* seedlings develop at times when the bamboo is reduced in stature. Both *Podocarpus* timber and bamboo are valuable forest products and are often illegally harvested.

At lower altitudes Afromontane forests are dominated by a diversity of broad-leaved trees, although camphor *Ocotea usambarensis*, pillarwood *Cassipourea* and olives *Olea* species are often common, dependent on the physical characteristics of the site. Much lower-altitude montane forest has been destroyed by human settlement and agriculture, or replaced by plantations of exotic timber species. Further degradation occurs through grazing within forest boundaries, subsistence hunting and firewood collection. Fragmentation of forests is also a serious threat to the integrity of their biodiversity, especially apparent in the species-rich Usambara mountains where many forest patches are too small to support larger mammals and birds that may be important in seed dispersal and maintenance of the full forest ecosystem. Among well-known horticultural plants originating in Afromontane forests are the African Violet (*Saintpaulia* spp.) and Busy-lizzie (*Impatiens walleriana*).

The Afromontane ecosystem supports a diverse fauna, and traditionally also has functioned as a refuge for lower-altitude plains animals during periods of drought. A wide range of mammals—from very large herbivores such as elephant and buffalo to the mountain gorilla, monkeys, hyrax, rodents and insectivores—occur in montane forests, as does a rich avifauna. Hunting and range restrictions have reduced the numbers of most of these species, and many populations are now effectively isolated from others by the agricultural zones at the base of the mountains, or fragmented into small pockets of forest.

Montane environments are not static. Over geological time they are subject to uplift and erosion, and the varying patterns of climate change at both local and global scale. The current high biodiversity and endemicity of eastern African mountains reflects both this and the more local climatological and disturbance phenomena. Some older

mountains, such as Rwenzori and Usambara, have acted as refugia for forest organisms in dry periods associated with global glaciation, and typically have higher biodiversity and endemicity than recent volcanic mountains, many of which are believed to have lost their forest cover at such times. Recolonization has been by overland migration and especially from long-distance dispersal with birds and the wind being the principal vectors.

The comparative isolation of many mountains has also led to increased speciation and rapid evolution of organisms 'marooned' on their slopes without a genetic link to other populations. A conspicuous example can be found among the giant lobelias, represented by about fifteen species and eight subspecies in the east African mountains; many of these are endemic to single mountains. Because of their mobility and size, birds and larger mammals show much lower levels of speciation and endemism. Smaller mammals and invertebrates, however, also show the development of species flocks and high levels of endemism. For instance, the flea *Ctenophthalmus cophurus* is encountered as three separate subspecies, one on rodents on Kilimanjaro and two on Mount Kenya, one of which is found in the Afromontane zone on rodents, the other exclusively on shrews and mole shrews in the Afroalpine zone.

The comparatively wet and fertile lower slopes have always attracted humans to African mountains, and they are often surrounded by large, high-density human populations living in urban centers as well as in more traditional villages. Where formerly smaller communities existed in a sustainable balance with the forest and its products, expanding populations put ever greater demands on its resources: water, timber, fuel and other forest products, and on the soil. The clearance of forest for crops such as coffee and tea, and in drier areas for grain and pyrethrum production, has led to the loss of biodiversity and the increased risk of degradation of land and water supplies through erosion. Most governments in eastern Africa have policies aimed at halting further inroads into the remaining forest and improving land-use practices in all upper watersheds. The problem remains, however, because enforcement is poor and population pressure is still mounting. Climate change poses another challenge as rainfall patterns alter, often leading to diminution of rainfall. The glaciers on Kilimanjaro, Mount Kenya and Rwenzori are rapidly receding due to rising temperatures and diminished precipitation, and are expected to disappear within the next few decades.

The Afroalpine ecosystem is harsh and of low productivity, and has not been permanently settled by humans, although domestic stock is sometimes grazed above the treeline. However, the zone is one of incredible beauty, challenge, and interest, with scenery ranging from the dramatic pinnacles and cliffs of the Simien massif in Ethiopia to the flower-covered grassy slopes of the Drakensberg, via the glacier-capped dome of Kilimanjaro. In consequence, several of the mountains have become major tourist attractions; Mount Kenya alone attracts close to twenty thousand visitors per annum, and despite turbulence in Rwanda and Democratic Republic of Congo, the remaining populations of the mountain gorilla are the focus of an important tourist trade. Adventure travel and ecotourism to the mountains is both a benefit and a problem; revenue helps conserve such areas, but tourism often leads to environmental degradation of sensitive montane habitats.

Tourism, maintenance of watershed integrity, and the preservation of biodiversity can be integrated, but the demands of local people for fuelwood and bushmeat, the interests of land-hungry farmers and international forest-product corporations are a serious challenge to the long-term preservation of Afromontane ecosystems. Much support from international nongovernmental environmental organizations is necessary to help African governments establish and enforce policies that will secure the future protection of these unique and valuable ecosystems.

See also **Ecology; Geography and the Study of Africa.**

BIBLIOGRAPHY

Coe, M. J. *The Ecology of the Alpine Zone of Mount Kenya.* The Hague: Junk, 1967.

Grimshaw, J. M. "Disturbance, Pioneers and the Afromontane Archipelago." In *Chorology, Taxonomy and Ecology of the Floras of Africa and Madagascar*, ed. C.R. Huxley, J. M. Lock, and D. F. Cutler. Kew: Royal Botanic Gardens, 1998.

Harmsen, Rudolf; J. R. Spence; and William C. Mahaney. "Glacial Interglacial Cycles and Development of the Afroalpine Ecosystem on East African Mountains." *Journal of African Earth Sciences* 12 (1991): 513–523.

Lovett, J. C., and S. K. Wasser. *Biogeography and Ecology of the Rain Forests of Eastern Africa.* Cambridge, U.K.: Cambridge University Press, 1993.

Mahaney, William C., ed. *Quaternary and Environmental Research on East African Mountains.* Rotterdam: A. A. Balkema, 1989.

Newmark, W. D., ed. *The Conservation of Mount Kilimanjaro.* Cambridge, U.K.: International Union for Conservation of Nature and Natural Resources, 1991.

Young, Truman P. "High Montane Forest and Afroalpine Ecosystems." In *East African Ecosystems and Their Conservation*, ed. T. R. McClanahan and T. P. Young. New York: Oxford University Press, 1989.

RUDOLF HARMSEN
REVISED BY JOHN M. GRIMSHAW

SAVANNAS

Savannas are the quintessential vegetation of Africa. Over half the African land surface is covered by savannas, and more than half the world's savannas are found in Africa. The origin of the word is apparently Caribbean or South American, meaning a marshy grassland with a few scattered trees, but it is in the twenty-first century most widely used to mean a tropical vegetation type that is co-dominated by trees and grasses, but neither to the exclusion of the other. The grasses overwhelmingly have the C4 photosynthetic pathway. This includes a wide range of tree and grass combinations, from near-desert grasslands with scattered low shrubs to tall, dense woodlands bordering on tropical forests. The popular image of an African savanna, consisting of a grassland dotted with occasional umbrella-thorn trees and herds of large game, represents only one of many types. Where greater botanical precision is needed, a specific term should be used and defined: for instance "grassland" if the tree cover is less than 5 percent, "wooded grassland" for between 5 and 20 percent, "grassy woodland" between 20 and 40 percent, "woodland" between 40 and 60 percent and "forest" above 60 percent. Other than grasslands and forests, all of the above are variants of the broad 'savanna' ecosystem type.

Savannas occur, worldwide, where a hot wet seasons of three to nine months' duration alternates with a warm dry seasons. Generally there is a single dry season, in "winter," but in monsoonal climates, there may be two "rainy seasons" per year, separated by dry periods. During the extended dry season the grass becomes sufficiently dry to support frequent fires; this is an important (but not exclusive) factor in preventing complete dominance by trees. Mixed tree-grass ecosystems may also occur on periodically flooded soils, a condition that disfavors trees; on soils with a high concentration of toxic minerals; or in areas where forests have been partially cleared by humans.

The African savannas have been strongly shaped by human actions, over a long period of time. From at least a million years ago until modern times, this interaction has consisted of setting fires, cutting trees, collecting food-plants and hunting wildlife. Since about five thousand years ago, it has included the grazing of domestic livestock. Seasonal aridity and low fertility kept many southern and eastern African savannas from becoming a major location of crop agriculture until the twentieth century. The major expansion of savannas, as evidenced by the rapid increase in traces of C4 grass in ocean sediment cores, is thought to have occurred about 5 million years ago, which predates the evolution of hominids and is speculated to be associated with the establishment of the early Pliestocene climate pattern, globally-declining atmospheric CO_2 levels and an increase in fire.

TYPES OF AFRICAN SAVANNA

Savannas can be classified in three ways: floristically (by the plant species which they contain); structurally (by the height and cover of the vegetation layers); and functionally (by their ecological attributes). Fortunately, in Africa these three approaches agree at their highest levels. Functionally, there are two main types and some intermediates and outliers. The first main type occurs on infertile soils receiving 24 to 71 inches of rainfall per year. The tree layer is dominated by the legume subfamily Caesalpinioideae, which includes the species referred to as *miombo*. They have relatively large leaflets (more than a few centimeters in diameter) and no thorns. The tree cover is typically greater than 30 percent and the trees taller than 20 feet. The grasses grow in dense tufts up to 6 feet tall and are unpalatable except when young. The second

main type occurs on more fertile soils, between 14 and 31 inches of rainfall (the upper limit is about 24 inches on sandy soils). The tree layer is dominated the legume subfamily Mimosoideae (the acacias), which are thorny and have tiny leaflets. The tree cover is variable, but may be low, and the trees are often short. The grasses are typically less than 3 feet tall, palatable even when dry, and form "lawns" under intense grazing.

The distinction between the "broad-leafed" savannas of moist, infertile areas and the "fine-leaved" savannas of arid, fertile areas is reflected in many other features, including the grass tribes, the number and types of mammals, insects and birds, the frequency of fires, and the density of human population, so it is worth exploring its origin.

Broad-leaved savannas occupy the remnants of the oldest African geomorphological surfaces, principally on the elevated interior plateau composed of granite-like rocks. The geology, combined with millions of years of weathering under moist, warm conditions, has resulted in acidic soils, often sandy, with low a nutrient content, lacking particularly in phosphorus and nitrogen. Following the disintegration of Gondwanaland and the several subsequent events of continental warping and uplift, more recent surfaces have developed, notably in the major river valleys. These landscapes are lower, hotter, drier and more fertile, both because they have been exposed to a shorter and less intense period of weathering, but also because the underlying geology is more favorable, consisting of basic lavas and sediments. They were colonized by the acacias, giving rise to the fine-leaved savannas. The fertile savannas were the areas that supported the greatest human populations prior to the twentieth century. The widespread occurrence of the cattle disease *nagana* and sleeping-sickness in humans, both caused by trypanosomes transmitted by the tsetse fly, also kept the human and livestock population low in the moist savannas.

Very arid areas support savannas dominated by trees of the genus *Commiphora*, and moderately arid, infertile soils are dominated by the genus *Combretum*. A large area of hot, arid land on fertile but poorly permeable soils in southern Africa is dominated by a single species, the mopane tree.

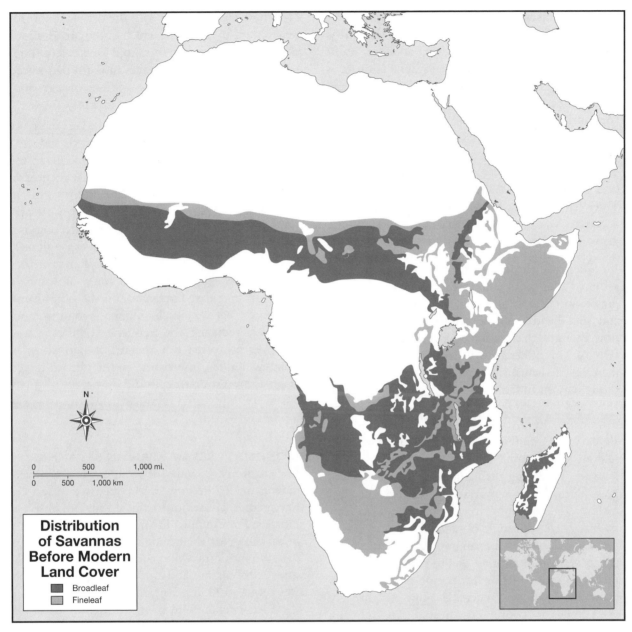

R. J. SCHOLES, BASED ON WHITE, F. *THE VEGETATION OF AFRICA*. NATURAL RESOURCES XX. PARIS: UNESCO, 1980

Eastern and southern African savannas contain similar sets of species, but West African savannas differ somewhat. The "Guinean" savannas of West Africa correspond in general terms with the "broad-leaved" category, while the "Sudano-Sahelian" savannas correspond with the "fine-leaved" group. The rainy season in West Africa is generally shorter (but not necessarily drier) than in southern Africa, which results in a higher proportion of annual grasses. West Africa has a longer history of intensive use by pastoralists and crop farmers, which further promoted annual grasses and fewer trees.

SAVANNA ECOLOGY

In other climates, either trees or grasses come to dominate the landscape, but in savannas both persist as mixture. One theory to explain the coexistence, outlined by Hienrich Walter in *The Ecology of Tropical and Subtropical Vegetation* (1971) is that trees are deeper-rooted than grasses and therefore use a different water resource. There is some validity in this idea, but the degree of root separation is insufficient for it to be the only factor. It is more likely that the seasonal variation in water supply, a central feature of the savanna climate, is directly and indirectly responsible for the coexistence. Trees, due to their longevity, large bulk (permitting the storage of water and carbohydrates) and deep-rootedness, are able to grow very rapidly at the beginning of the wet season, starting even before the onset of the rains. Grasses reach peak production only after several weeks of growth. Trees have another opportunity for near-exclusive access to water and nutrients at the end of the growing season.

The early theories of co-existence in savannas assumed that the relative proportions of trees and grasses were stable and in balance with the climate and soil. Field evidence suggests otherwise. It is now thought that savannas, like many other ecosystems, are inherently variable. The tree cover increases if disturbances that serve to retard tree growth are excluded. Fire is the main such disturbance, which works in conjunction with browsing by mammalian herbivores (especially large ones, like elephants or giraffes) and clearing by humans. Fire seldom kills savanna trees, it simply keeps young trees from escaping the flame zone. Once they do, grass growth is suppressed, fires become less intense, and the woody cover increases. Two contradictory trends can be observed in African savannas. In areas of high human population density, the tree cover is disappearing as a result of clearing for fuelwood, construction timber or croplands, and browsing by goats. Where clearing and fire are prevented, or continuous heavy cattle grazing reduces the fuel available for fires, the tree cover typically increases, eventually threatening the sustainability of cattle ranching.

Grass growth in savannas is directly related to the amount of rainfall during the growing season, but the slope of the relationship is controlled by soil fertility. Above 24 inches per annum rainfall, there is a large difference in the mammal herbivore carrying capacity of the broad-leaved and fine-leaved savannas. The mammalian herbivore carrying capacity of fine-leaved savannas continues to rise with increasing rainfall, up to about 125 lbs per square mile at 47 inches, while in broad-leaved savannas it levels off at about 8000 lbs/mi^2 above

24 inches. This has to do with the dry-season nitrogen content of the grass, which in the broad-leaved savannas falls below the threshold for efficient ruminant digestion. The tree leaves in the broad-leaved savannas contain high concentrations of digestion-inhibiting chemicals (principally tannins).

The frequent fires in broad-leaved savannas are mostly set by pastoralists or hunters, to induce a brief flush of more palatable grass attractive to the game they seek, or are accidental consequences of slash-and-burn agriculture. The herbivores in broad-leaved savannas consume less than 10 percent of the plant production; the rest decomposes or is burned. The resulting smoke is a globally important source of methane, atmospheric particles and the trace gases that form lower-atmosphere ozone. In fine-leaved savannas, on the other hand, herbivores eat a much higher proportion of the grass, reducing the frequency of fires. Large mammals are often not the major herbivores in savannas. Rather, insects may prevail; broad-leaved savannas are prone to episodic outbreaks of caterpillars, and fine-leafed savannas to swarms of grasshoppers or locusts.

ECONOMIC USES OF AFRICAN SAVANNAS

The economic benefits of savannas are generally underestimated because the key ecosystem services they provide are seldom reflected in formal-sector statistics. For example, the majority of Africans rely on savannas for their supply of domestic energy. The amount of fuelwood consumed per household varies with climate and fuel availability, but averages about 1100 lb per person per year. Where the wood has been cleared from the vicinity of settlements and must therefore be transported, it is usually first converted to charcoal, which has a higher energy content per unit mass.

Timber is cut from savannas for the construction of dwellings and livestock pens, as well as for the manufacture of household and craft items. Many savanna plants are used for food, fibre or medicine. Honey is an important savanna product, mostly locally consumed. Several insect species, including termites, grasshoppers and caterpillars, form a valued protein sources for human consumption. Game is increasingly scarce outside protected areas, but was historically an important source of protein for people. Small mammals and birds still fill this need in many areas.

Many savanna trees produce high-value hardwoods, but the low stature of the trees, their crookedness and early branching limit the size of the boards that can be cut from them. Trees favored for craft carving (ebony, for instance), have become scarce in most areas.

The formal or commercial economy in savannas is largely based on cattle and tourism (plus crop agriculture in areas where the original savanna has been cleared). The most-visited game parks in Africa are located in savanna regions. Together with savanna-based commercial hunting, wildlife-related tourism is a major foreign-currency earner in many East and Southern African countries. The majority of Africa's 100 million cattle graze in savannas. The offtake of meat products is relatively low, for a variety of cultural and technical reasons, but the ownership of livestock confers many other benefits, such as asset accumulation, milk and draft power.

Crop agriculture is extensively practiced in landscapes that were formerly savanna-covered, especially in West Africa, even where the rainfall is low and erratic. In the infertile savannas, various forms of ash-fertilisation agriculture are practiced (also known as "slash-and-burn," or swidden agriculture). For instance, in the *chitemene* system in Zambia branches are lopped off over a wide area, dragged to a central area and burned. This permits a few crops of maize to be grown. If the cutting cycle is sufficiently long to permit nutrient regeneration (a decade or more), the practice is sustainable. Cutting cycles have shortened, and the land productivity decreased as the population density has increased over the past century. In parts of southern and eastern Africa, the restriction of traditional African farmers to limited and often marginal areas by the land demands of commercial farmers (particularly European settlers during the colonial period) contributed to this trend.

The technical potential for crop production in the moist savanna regions of Africa using modern agricultural technology—in particular, fertilizers, mechanization, biocides, and new crop strains—is high, and sufficient to reverse the current lack of food security of many Africans. On the negative side, the rates of conversion of moist savannas into cultivated lands, and of land degradation in arid savannas, are already high, and are projected to accelerate in the next fifty years, with adverse consequences for biodiversity and the global climate.

See also **Agriculture; Ecology; Forestry; Plants; Soils.**

BIBLIOGRAPHY

Bourliere, Francois. *Tropical Savannas.* Amsterdam: Elsevier, 1983.

Cole, Monica. *The Savannas: Biogeography and Geobotany.* London: Academic Press, 1986.

Huntley, Brian. J., and Brian. H. Walker. *Ecology of Tropical Savannas.* Berlin: Springer, 1982.

Scholes, Robert. J., and Brian. H. Walker. *An African Savanna: Synthesis of the Nylsvley Study.* Cambridge, U.K.: Cambridge University Press, 1993.

R. J. SCHOLES

TROPICAL AND HUMID FORESTS

The tropical and humid forests of Africa extend across the tropical belt of the continent and south to north from the South African Cape to the Ethiopian highlands. Forests are defined as a continuous stand of trees with a more or less closed canopy. They are often structured in layers with a canopy, mid-storey, shrub, and ground layer. When the humidity is high the canopy can support dense growths of epiphytes such as orchids and ferns. Plants also reach light in the canopy by being lianas, strangling figs, or hemi-parasites such as mistletoes. Because of dense shading caused by other layers the ground layer can be sparse making undisturbed forests open and easy to walk through, but disturbed forests and forest edges can be tangled and difficult to penetrate. Canopy heights vary from 164 feet in well-developed low and mid-elevation forests, with emergent trees approximately 200 feet tall, to stunted 6.5 to 10-feet-tall elfin mist forests on high mountains. Generally, the canopy is about 98 feet. Closed canopy forests occur when rainfall exceeds about 60 inches a year without a prolonged dry season.

A few parts of Africa have rainfall of greater than 59 inches per year, such as the mountains of eastern Tanzania and the western African coast, with Mount Cameroun having an exceptionally high rainfall of more than 394 inches a year. However, in general, humid forests in Africa grow under an annual rainfall of about 79 inches and experience a marked dry season, though the

Usambara mountains of eastern Tanzania have two rainy seasons a year and so the climate is perhumid with more than four inches of rain in every month of the year. Forest occurs from sea level up to altitudes of 11,155 feet on the highest tropical mountains. Under natural conditions upper forest limits are determined by the elevation at which frost occurs regularly during the cold season. Because higher elevations are cooler, closed canopy forest can occur on mountains under lower rainfall than in the hot lowlands, such as the dry Juniper forests of the east African mountains which can grow under an annual rainfall of 31.5 inches.

The main area of forest in western and central Africa, the Guineo-Congolian forest, extends in a band around the equator from the western edge of Africa bordered by the Atlantic Ocean to the high ridge of mountains running north-south along the Albertine Rift. This includes the vast tract of forest in the Zaire basin that grows on an alluvial plain and includes extensive swamps. On the western edge of the Zaire basin the forest block covers the Precambrian crystalline uplands of Gabon and Cameroon and the volcanic Mount Cameroon before extending to the Niger Delta and Nigeria. The western limb of the Guineo-Congolian forest, from Ghana to Guinea, is separated from the larger eastern part by the dry Dahomey Gap. The northern limits are determined by increasing aridity toward the Sahara Desert and dry harmattan winds from the desert can reach the rainforest, intensifying the dry season. The Guineo-Congolian forests spill over the Albertine Rift mountains to the Lake Victoria basin, but are separated from forests in eastern Africa by an arid corridor that runs over the central African plateau from the Horn of Africa to the Namib desert.

Eastern and southern Africa forests are much more restricted in extent than those of western and central Africa. Apart from the tropical eastern African coast, areas of high rainfall are associated with mountains so the forests are found on the disjunct mountain blocks that rise out of the coastal plains or form the edges of the eastern African rifts and the Ethiopian uplands. There are essentially four main types of distribution patterns of forest plants. First, many species are of restricted distribution, being found only in a limited number of sites. These are narrow range endemics and they

are clustered in a few areas which are termed biodiversity hotspots. The main African forest biodiversity hotspots are the Eastern Arc and Coastal Forests of eastern Africa, forests of the Albertine Rift and forests in the high rainfall area of Cameroon and Gabon. Second, forest plants can be distributed throughout the extent of the Guineo-Congolian forests with some of these West African species also occurring in eastern Africa. Third, the coastal forests of eastern Africa have a distinct flora; and fourth, the tropical high mountains have an Afromontane flora that comes down to lower altitudes in the south African Cape. Together with altitude and rainfall, these four distribution patterns are used as the basis for African forest vegetation classification systems and have their origins in geological and climatic history.

GEOLOGICAL AND CLIMATIC HISTORY

To understand distribution patterns of African forest plants it is necessary to go back in time to the break-up of the super continent Gondwana during the Jurassic period. At this time Africa was at the center of Gondwana and about 18 degrees south of its present position. As Gondwana fragmented, South America moved away from the West African coast and India and Australia moved away from the eastern African coast. Fossil evidence suggests that a pan-African rainforest extended from east to west across what is the present-day Sahara desert. As Africa moved north it closed the Tethys Sea, which had previously separated Gondwana from the northern Laurasian supercontinent, creating the Mediterranean Sea in the Miocene period. During the northward movement the equatorial belt moved relatively southward together with the pan-African rainforest. Closure of the Tethys Sea resulted in an increasing drying of northern Africa and consequent compression of the northern limits of the pan-African forest. Further aridification of Africa during the Pliocene and uplift of the central African plateau split the pan-African rainforest into the larger western Guineo-Congolian forests and the smaller eastern African forests.

Evidence for these geological and climatic changes can be seen in the present-day distribution of African forest plants. West African–South American connections are represented by about one hundred lowland rainforest plant genera. Ancient links between eastern Africa and other former parts of Gondwana are evidenced by the Eastern Arc monotypic endemic genera of Neohemsleya and Platypterocarpus, which have links to montane plants in Asia and Mexico respectively. Platypterocarpus is considered to be extinct following forest clearance in the West Usambara mountains in the 1960s. Remnants of the pan-African forest can be seen in the many connections between the western and eastern Africa forests, particularly on the Eastern Arc mountains. For example, the tall rainforest tree genus Allanblackia is present in both east and west. It has indehiscent fruits that weigh up to 15 pounds. No mode of long dispersal across the dry central Africa plateau can be envisaged suggesting that this plant is the relict of a formerly more extensive forest. In southern Africa there is fossil evidence from the Miocene of forest plant families no longer found on mainland Africa, but which still occur on Madagascar. This suggests that past climate changes in the south African Cape resulted in the loss of formerly more extensive forest.

The Pleistocene period was characterized by a series of about twenty glacial advances that were associated with cool dry conditions in the tropics. For example, in the last glacial maximum about 18,000 years ago it is thought that African forests were much reduced in extent and restricted to small areas termed "refugia." Africa has been described as the "odd-man out" in terms of species richness of its tropical forest because it contains many fewer species than the rainforests of South America or Indo-Malaysia. One theory to explain this difference is that massive extinctions of rainforest species occurred during Pleistocene climate fluctuations and that the forest refugia coincide with the present-day hotspots of forest biodiversity. Alternatively, patterns of species richness in African forests compared to other continents have been explained by the fact that African rainforests are in general much drier that those elsewhere, and that Africa did not experience the massive mountain building resulting from the break-up of Gondwana that occurred in the Andes and throughout Indo Malaysia and Oceania. Mountain building creates many new habitats and fertile soils, which under conditions of high rainfall are associated with species richness.

More controversial is the role that Sahara may have played in changes of extent of the Guineo-Congolian forests. Forests of the Zaire basin grow on sand and it is possible that this originated from a greatly extended Sahara desert during periods of drier climate. West African forests dominated by the oil palm Elais guineensis are also thought to result from past climate change, though they may also result from human influence. Thus the African rainforests may be very dynamic, expanding and contracting in response to global climate changes. Modelling of the potential impacts of future climate variation on African vegetation has revealed that similar changes may occur in response to global warming.

HUMAN HISTORY

Present-day forest limits are largely determined by human influence. Fire is a dominant ecological factor in the African landscape and there is evidence for human use of fire dating back 1.8 million years ago. Much of what is open woodland in Africa is climatically suitable for closed forest. For example, when fire is excluded from woodland in Zambia, forest species regenerate. On high mountains ericaceous heath is thought to be a result of repeated burning, and there are charcoal horizons dating to 12,000 years ago in cores taken from southwest Ugandan montane swamps. This suggests that both upper and lower forest limits are largely determined by fire rather than climate.

Generally, it is considered that major forest clearance did not start until after 5,000 years ago, when there is evidence for agricultural development, but there is no reason to exclude human-induced fire as a factor for tens of thousands of years prior to that. Human influence may have been extensive in the past: charcoal horizons 3,000 years old have been found in the currently undisturbed Ituri Forest of Zaire, forests in Nigeria grow over former sites of habitation, as do forests in coastal Kenya and montane Tanzania.

The forest provides many useful products: animals for skins and food, saplings for building, palms for weaving, wood for tools and household utensils, medicines, and honey. In present-day central Africa, the forest peoples supply forest products to farmers outside the forest zone in trade for goods not available within the forest. In eastern Africa there are historical records of forest peoples, but those people groups are not present in modern times. With the advent of European migration and administration within the last few hundred years, timber became the main forest product. Forest reserves with central government legal control were established. Existing forest management systems of shifting cultivation, periodic clearance for dry-season grazing, and maintenance of protected areas for cultural reasons were, in many cases, supplanted for timber production or watershed protection. This change in emphasis generally profited people remote from the forest areas rather than those affected by day-to-day management of the forest, who had benefited from the previous management regime.

Since the late twentieth century, local participation, conservation of biodiversity, and sustainable utilization have become major management issues, though how effectively they can be implemented remains to be seen. Estimates of management costs incurred by local people involved in joint forest management schemes indicate that it is the poorest people who carry the greatest burden and it is richer people who gain more benefits. The effectiveness of local management for biodiversity conservation has also been questioned. A study on the success of conservation efforts in African rainforests found that protected area success was not correlated with employment benefits for the neighboring community, conservation education, conservation clubs, or with the presence of integrated conservation and development programs. Rather, success is associated with strong public support, effective law enforcement, low human population densities, and substantial support from international donors.

Deforestation rates in West Africa are estimated to be about 2.3 percent. This is half the rate in the 1980s, but still high in a global context. The main causes of deforestation are commercial logging, high population density, rapid population growth, armed conflict, and population displacement. Most timber exports are from Ghana and Côte d'Ivoire, primarily as sawn wood and veneer. Central Africa has lower population densities, more extensive and remote forest than West Africa with a correspondingly lower deforestation rate of about 0.2 percent a year. However this is likely to change as tropical timber resources elsewhere become exhausted and more roads are built into the forested interior. Gabon, Cameroon, and the Democratic Republic of Congo are major exporters of tropical timbers, mostly as raw logs rather than processed timber as in the case of West Africa. The area of forest in southern and eastern Africa is much less than in west and central Africa and most forest is administered under protective forest reserves. However, locally rates of deforestation can be high due to proximity to cities, plantation development, building of communication links, and social factors such as labor migration and refugee settlement.

See also **Climate; Ecology; Forestry.**

BIBLIOGRAPHY

Burgess, Neil D., et al., eds. *Terrestrial Ecoregions of Africa and Madgascar: A Conservation Assessment.* Washington, DC: Island Press. 2004.

Davis, Stephen D.; Vernon H. Heywood; and Alan C. Hamilton; eds. *Centers of Plant Diversity*, Vol. 1: *Europe, Africa, South West Asia, and the Middle East.* Cambridge, U.K.: IUCN, 1994.

Fishpool, Lincoln D. C., and Michael I. Evans, eds. *Important Bird Areas in Africa and Associated Islands: Priority Sites for Conservation.* Cambridge, U.K.: Pisces Publications and Birdlife International, 2001.

Hall, John B., and Mike D. Swaine. *Distribution and Ecology of Vascular Plants in a Tropical Rain Forest: Forest Vegetation in Ghana.* The Hague: Springer. 1981.

Hamilton, Alan C. *Environmental History of Africa: A Study of the Quaternary.* London: Academic Press. 1982.

Lovett, Jon C., and Samuel K. Wasser, eds. *Biogeography and Ecology of the Rain Forests of Eastern Africa.* Cambridge, U.K.: Cambridge University Press, 1993.

Oates, J. F. *Myth and Reality in the Rain Forest: How Conservation Strategies Are Failing in West Africa.* Berkeley: University of California Press, 1999.

White, Frank. *The Vegetation of Africa: A Descriptive Memoir to Accompany the UNESCO/AETFAT/UNSO Vegetation Map of Africa.* Paris: UNESCO, 1983.

JON C. LOVETT

EDUCATION, SCHOOL

This entry includes the following articles:

OVERVIEW

Education in sub-Saharan Africa takes three institutional forms:

1. The socialization of children in domestic and community settings, through their guided participation in work, ritual, and everyday social activities, under the supervision of parents, older siblings, and other adults;

2. Qur'anic schooling, that is, religious instruction at the homes of Islamic religious scholars or in community settings of Muslim communities; and

3. Western schooling, that is, bureaucratically organized instruction in buildings dedicated to education, with standardized spatial arrangements, curricula, teaching procedures, teacher training, and examinations supervised by an administrative hierarchy.

Education in Africa changed enormously during the twentieth century. At the beginning of the century, virtually all African children were socialized at home and in the community, and for a majority, there was no other form of education. Those raised in the Muslim communities of the Sahel, the Sudan, and the East African coast also attended Qur'anic schools. Christian missionaries introduced Western-type schools in the European colonial territories, but only a small fraction of children attended them. By the end of the century, however, Western schooling prevailed in many places, and Qur'anic schooling had also expanded, largely within regions north of the equator. The socialization of children was altered not only by their school attendance but also by a multitude of socioeconomic and cultural factors affecting the homes and communities in which education took place.

The education of African children in domestic and community settings was, and is, different from school learning. It included their acquisition, through early and continued participation, of the skills involved in agriculture, animal husbandry, hunting and gathering, and food processing, often from their older siblings. The labor-intensive domestically organized agriculture of the sub-Saharan region demanded child labor, in tasks ranging from caring for infants to carrying water and herding sheep and goats, in order to free adults for heavier or more skilled work as well as contributing directly to food production. This required that children learn such tasks at an early age, often by the time they were five years old.

In addition to learning skills, the children assumed responsibilities and were expected to take them seriously. Respect for elders was high on the parental agenda for culturally defined virtues that children were to acquire. This was true of most of the agricultural and pastoral societies, less so of the hunting and gathering peoples of Southern Africa. Other virtues were also variable: for example, gregariousness was valued more among African peoples with clustered settlements and homesteads, less among those with dispersed settlement and separate households, and this affected the socialization of children from the start.

Initiation ceremonies for boys and/or girls, at or before puberty, formed the centerpiece of education in some but not other African communities, and this variation occurred within areas of East Africa where initiation, usually with ritual circumcision, defined the cultural identity of one group as contrasted with others who had no initiation. In Kenya, for example, the Kikuyu, Maasai, Nandi-Kipsigis (Kalenjin), Gusii, and other peoples held male and female initiation ceremonies for children or adolescents, and the anticipation of these ritual transitions played the part of an organizing principle for their prior education. Yet there were neighboring peoples, notably the Luo of the Lake Victoria region, who organized their children's socialization without these ceremonial transitions, achieving an equally strong sense of ethnic and gender identity. On the other side of the continent, the secret societies in Liberia (such as among the Gola, Kpelle, and Vai peoples) and Sierra Leone (such as among the Mende, Sherbro, and Temne peoples) organized lengthier and more formal training, often referred to as bush schools, in gender-specific virtues, and the peoples with bush schools lived next to other peoples who did not have them.

Thus differing skills, virtues, and practices were involved in the societies of the sub-Saharan region, but indigenous education generally fostered the child's development of social responsibility and local cultural identity along with knowledge and practical competence. The average eight-year-old had extensive knowledge of local flora and fauna, could perform a large proportion of the tasks essential to adult living, and was capable of acting responsibly and assuming the moral attitudes of adults to a degree that is striking from a Western perspective. This was accomplished without schools but by participation in the domestic economy and local community at an early age.

Western-type schools introduced a contrasting model of education: outside the home and beyond parental control, with age-segregated groups in school buildings where specially trained adults taught a standard curriculum, including literacy and numeracy skills, through verbal instruction. This bureaucratic Western schooling, initially introduced by Christian missionaries, spread massively in sub-Saharan Africa during the second half of the twentieth century. Great Britain, France, and Belgium expanded the school systems of their African colonies to a moderate degree between 1945 and 1960. But when the colonies gained political independence (roughly from 1957 to 1964) leaders saw universal schooling as an imperative for modern nationhood and membership in the United Nations. With advice and financial help from the wealthy countries of Europe and North America and United Nations agencies, the new nations of Africa embarked on unprecedented programs of educational expansion.

Table 1 shows (with crude and somewhat inflated estimates) that the two decades after 1960 saw large increases in primary school enrollments and less (though proportionately greater) expansion of secondary school enrollments. As primary schooling pushed toward universality, secondary school remained an elite attainment. By 1980, the adult literacy rate (the proportion of those fifteen or older who had attended five years of school) for males reached the 50 percent mark, whereas females trailed far behind. Yet these rates continued growing, and by 2000–2004, 71.6 percent of males and 53.9 percent of females were estimated to be literate.

This can be seen as an impressive achievement, especially considering African population growth during that period, in which the number of children was increasing so rapidly that it took more resources each year to educate the same proportion of children. Furthermore, in the 1980s and early 1990s the lagging African economies and the

Selected educational statistics for sub-Saharan Africa, 1960–2000			
Sub-Saharan Africa	1960	1980	1995–1999
Male primary school Enrollment ratio (gross)	47	70	80
Female primary school Enrollment ratio (gross)	24	45	67
Male secondary school Enrollment ratio (gross)	3	10	28
Female secondary school Enrollment ratio (gross)	2	8	22
Adult literacy rate (male)		50	64
Adult literacy rate (female)		29	46

SOURCE: UNESCO Statistical Yearbooks.

Table 1.

Structural Adjustment Programs imposed by international agencies created severe hardships for governments and parents alike, with a direct impact on education budgets and school facilities. Despite these obstacles and the damage to school quality, African school expansion continued, and the primary school enrollment ratios (gross) reached 89 percent for males and 78 percent for females by 1997–2000.

However remarkable this numerical expansion of Western-type schooling in Africa over a forty-year period, there are few who take satisfaction from it for several reasons. First of all, school quality is generally acknowledged to be poor (and in many places, declining), with crowded classrooms, inadequate facilities (lack of seats, blackboards, and textbooks), and unqualified and often absent teachers. As the school population grew, the pressure increased on a system already stretched beyond its breaking point. Second, dropout rates are high, even from primary schools, and relatively few children go further. Comparisons with other world regions show sub-Saharan Africa to be lagging behind. In analyses of world education, Africa is a problem case, with progress in primary schooling for girls as one accomplishment that stands out. In any event, for better or worse, the expansion of Western-type schooling has transformed the experience of African children in a relatively short period of time.

Qur'anic education also expanded during the same period, though largely within the areas where

Qur'anic schools already existed. A major reason for the expansion was the continuing conversion of non-Muslims to Islam, even in countries such as Senegal and regions such as Northern Nigeria where Muslims had long been in power but that had substantial populations practicing indigenous religions. As the population of Muslims grew, there was a demand for more schools to teach the Qur'an to young children, beginning in the preschool years and continuing when they are school-aged, after which a small proportion went on to a *madrasa* or secondary school.

In the typical Qur'anic school, known as *makaranta* in northern Nigeria and Ghana, children learn to recite and memorize the Qur'an in Arabic, no matter what their native language, through group chanting or individual repetition of verses as well as writing them in Arabic script. The teacher, known as *mallam* or *marabout*, also instructs the children in how to conduct daily prayers and teaches them about the Prophet's life and other aspects of Islam. His instruction and discipline are regarded as their moral and religious training. The training often takes place at his home or in the shade of a tree near a main road or on the premises of a mosque. These are not government schools, nor are they funded, controlled, or standardized by the government, even in countries where Muslims are in the majority, and information about their numbers and enrollments is often not systematically recorded. The rural mallam is paid by the parents of his pupils, some of whom (only boys) also contribute their labor to his remunerative enterprises.

Many children in Muslim communities of northern Nigeria, Ghana, Senegal, Guinea, Mali, and Niger attend both government schools and Qur'anic schools. They may attend the makaranta when they are three to five years old and then start government school at the normal age, continuing their Qur'anic study before or after secular school on a typical day. But there are also integrated schools, known as *Islamiya* in northern Nigeria, that are organized similar to Western schools but include Islamic learning, and these are increasingly favored by parents. The enrollments at these schools have increased as the quality and physical condition of government schools have declined, and they are also considered safer environments

for girls, who outnumber boys in many of them. In some cases the schools are subsidized by international Islamic philanthropies. Parents in West Africa, as elsewhere in the developing world, have proved willing to take their children out of free government schools they regard as inadequate and enroll them in private schools that require fees but are perceived to be superior.

African education during the 1980s and 1990s was affected by many disruptive forces: the AIDS pandemic that left children without parents, civil wars in some regions that turned boys into soldiers and other children into refugees, and poverty resulting not only from disease and war but also from economic stagnation, population growth, and political corruption. These disruptive forces affected all three kinds of African education, for all depend on stability and resources to function effectively. Yet the disruption was not uniform through sub-Saharan Africa and added further to the great diversity of educational conditions and practices on the continent. In the twenty-first century, African parents are more inclined than ever to define their hopes in terms of their children's education, and they remain determined to take advantage of the educational opportunities in their local, national and even international environments. The rebuilding and reform of educational institutions in sub-Saharan Africa is recognized as a priority by most governments and the international agencies that assist them.

See also **Education, University and College; Initiation; Labor: Child; Literacy; United Nations.**

BIBLIOGRAPHY

Benoliel, Sharon. *Strengthening Education in the Muslim World*. (PPC Issue Working Paper No. 1). Washington, DC: USAID, 2004.

Fortes, Meyer. *Social and Psychological Aspects of Education in Taleland*. International African Institute Memorandum No. XVII, 1938.

Iddrisu, Abdulai. *The Growth of Islamic Learning in Northern Ghana and Its Interaction with Western Secular Education*. Africa Development 30: 53–67, 2005.

Peshkin, Alan. *Kanuri Schoolchildren*. New York: Holt, Rinehart and Winston, 1972.

Read, Margaret. *Children of their Fathers: Growing Up among the Ngoni of Nyasaland*. New Haven, CT: Yale University Press, 1960.

Serpell, Robert. *The Significance of Schooling: Life-Journeys in an African Society.* New York: Cambridge University Press, 1993.

ROBERT A. LeVINE

ANGLOPHONE CENTRAL AND SOUTHERN AFRICA

Since 1990 African educational initiatives have been dominated by Education for All (EFA). EFA was the systematic response of the world community to an emerging crisis of access to and quantity and quality of education. At the Jomtien (Thailand) conference of 1990, delegates drew up the World Declaration of Education for All, affirming the right of every child, youth, and adult to an education that would meet their basic learning needs, including "learning to know, to do, to live together, and to be." (UNESCO, *Learning: The Treasure Within* [1996]). A host of subsequent policy documents and conference declarations further reaffirmed the key principle that education was the key to ending poverty in Africa in a context where many countries were facing a crisis of public service provision. Thirty of the thirty-four countries classified by the United Nations as having low human development were located in sub-Saharan Africa, and of these, most were in Central and Southern Africa. Yet by 2000, when the Dakar conference reported on the progress of EFA in Africa, the results were not promising. By 2006 there was considerable evidence of a further decline in educational participation. Although many countries had improved access at primary levels and had narrowed the gender gap that had favored boys over girls, only some 50 percent of children were in school. With regard to literacy rates, adult education, secondary, tertiary and technical education, there were alarming shortfalls regarding access and quality, with serious implications for future development prospects.

While the above picture gives an important overview of the educational circumstances of the majority of the population early in the twenty-first century, significant differences exist among the various national education systems. The South Africa and Southern Rhodesia (Zimbabwe) settler states had provided privileged education for whites. Africans' access to secondary education was often confined to those groups able to gain preferential access to missionary education from an early date.

Poorer states failed to provide meaningful, quality education for all.

COLONIAL ERA
Until the 1920s, the colonial state neglected educational provision, a situation tempered only to a degree by Christian missionary involvement from the early nineteenth century. By the early twentieth century, a network of flagship mission schools and supplementary "bush schools" flourished throughout Central and Southern Africa. This system emphasized the importance of Christian education and the broad need to promote rural economic development for the majority.

Educational reform based on recommendations for the adaptation of the curriculum to the African rural context originated in the Phelps Stokes Commission reports on *Education in Africa* (1922–1924) and the British Colonial Office's Advisory Committee on Native Education in Africa's policy document on *Educational Policy in British Tropical Africa* (1924). The missionary/government/settler/nationalist debate about African education raised question about the aims of basic education, access, curriculum goals, the relationship between education and work, rural education, gender issues, vocational education, and the accommodation of African culture and language. These policies were further developed in the 1930s and 1940s, and they emerged as a significant aspect of the African political agenda after World War II just prior to independence. By the mid-twentieth century, the British Colonial Office reports on *Mass Education for African Society* (1943) and on *Higher Education in the Colonies* (1945) paved the way for the mass expansion of educational provision. Parallel developments took place in French colonial policy. The era of independence marked a belated spurt of activity in relation to public service provision at all levels, with increasing local involvement in educational provision. In the era of *uhuru,* or African independence, the responsibility for education gradually fell to the new national governments, and in an era of optimism, prosperity, and rapid expansion, UNESCO played an increasing role in policy development.

POSTCOLONIAL ERA
Independent Anglophone Central and Southern Africa saw a massive but brief expansion of educational provision in the 1960s and 1970s. Enrollment

rates increased from 46 percent in 1970 to 77 percent in 1980 but declined progressively thereafter. The extension of secondary and higher education was based on assumptions by the new planning experts about the need for modernization. Despite strong claims for a curriculum that prepared youth for the social and economic challenges of life in rural Africa, governments' well-intentioned attempts to reform the formal academic curriculum—such as those from the adapted education movement of the 1920s, African socialist models put forward by President Julius Nyerere of Tanzania (*Education for Self Reliance*) and the Patrick van Rensburg's *Brigades: Education with Production* in Botswana and Zimbabwe—were viewed with suspicion by the majority of ordinary people, who were struggling to put their children through school so they could land government jobs or employment in the formal (i.e., cash-paid) economy. These market considerations help to explain the extraordinary durability of colonial forms of education and curriculum well into the era of national independence.

While most of former colonial Africa was transforming its education system to accommodate the tremendous demands for access and the creations of new formal curricula that reflected a new African identity (African literature, African history), the settler states of the South were engaged in a last-ditch stand to defend the colonial order and white educational privilege. Rhodesia and South Africa pursued segregated education policies to perpetuate different educational universes along racial and ethnic lines. After the National Party victory in 1948, the educational policy of the Union of South Africa shifted in line with apartheid ideology, creating separate education structures for those whites who spoke English and those who spoke Afrikaans. The establishment of the Bantu Education Department in 1953 (and later the Departments of Coloured and Indian Education, in addition to the various Homeland Education Departments) entrenched the black/white education division for the next forty years. The new system established mass education for all for the first time, but the objective of Bantu Education was to create an inexpensive educational system attuned to indigenous cultures, African languages, and life in the rural areas at a distance from an urban labor market, where it was feared that educated blacks would come into competition with whites.

Although the policy worked in form, by enforcing separate educational provision for the separate races and restricting access by blacks to a wide range of jobs and opportunities, there was little deviation from the curriculum inherited from the colonial era. What distinguished black schools from white schools was not the content of the curriculum but the relative wealth of resources in the former compared to the latter, which translated into poor levels of literacy and limited access to science and mathematics in African schools. A new policy regarding the language of instruction in black high schools, which required black students to accept Afrikaans as language of instruction in some subjects, led to ongoing resistance culminating in the Soweto uprising of 1976. This marked a key moment of political change for the apartheid regime. Thereafter, the De Lange Committee of Enquiry into the *Provision of Education in the RSA* (1981) introduced a period of educational reform (1981–1994) based on global models. The emphasis now changed from education for racial and cultural awareness to the provision of skills for work in the modern sector, in keeping with the needs of a modern industrial economy that was seeking to compete internationally.

THE ERA OF STRUCTURAL ADJUSTMENT POLICIES

During the 1980s system-wide education reform became widespread in Africa through the policies of two major donors: the World Bank and the United States Agency for International Development (USAID). These organizations aimed to create greater equity in educational provision, but they faced daunting challenges, such as the decline of many African economies due to rising oil prices and downturns in commodity prices; the destabilization of the region as a result of the wars of liberation in the Portuguese colonies, Zimbabwe, Namibia and South Africa; and the dwindling reserves of hard currency associated with the global Debt Crisis. These issues meant that many of the poor countries, which eventually formed a coalition called the Southern African Development Community (SADC), had difficulty maintaining the levels of social welfare, health, and educational services of the immediate postcolonial era.

Structural adjustment policies, usually brokered by the World Bank or the International

Monetary Fund to cope with the African debt crisis, aimed at introducing neoliberal norms for budgeting and were to inform educational strategies throughout the region from the 1980s. The provision and the quality of education came sharply under threat, and poor and rural populations absorbed the brunt of the crisis. Where the central government was increasingly constrained to cut its social expenditure, even when committing itself to EFA, the solution to education provision seemed to be offered by the strategy of cost recovery, where the local communities and parents (the consumers) were required to pay considerable amounts for the limited education provided. They often faced bills for the building or upkeep of the school, for textbooks and materials, and demands to supplement the salaries of teachers. At the same time, school curricula and educators were increasingly controlled from the center in order to meet the needs of the efficiency or assessment criteria that were part of the new management packages required to monitor the effects of reform as the region incorporated global trends in educational policy.

In Zimbabwe and Lesotho, schools suffered from these changes and from the economic meltdown. Quality systems were fatally eroded. In Malawi, the election promises of the new democratic government that came to power after 1997 with regard to EFA proved to be hollow. Namibia and Botswana, with their small populations and relatively full coffers, fared better than their neighbors.

After 1994, democratic South Africa embarked on a massive development of educational policy aimed at the redress of the injustices of apartheid education. Many of the changes remain highly controversial. They incorporated many international trends in regard to school governance (decentralization) such as progressive curriculum reform, which attempted to move away from content-based learning and promote a constructivist perspective of knowledge (Curriculum 2005) through Outcomes-Based Education (OBE) a National Qualifications Framework [NQF]) and a South African Qualifications Authority (SAQA). The introduction of a wide variety of initiatives geared to the improvement of "human resource capacity" reflected many of the global changes in educational policy that had become a feature of neoliberal politics. Poverty alleviation through education competed with a strong push to promote economic competitiveness in the modern sector. A race-based educational policy was gradually giving way to an emphasis on market forces in education. Choice, meaning access to quality education for those who could afford it, came to replace race as a means of selection for the limited places available in quality secondary and higher education. The problems of educational equity and EFA remained, however.

The history of modern education systems in the region is both heroic and tragic. What was achieved with limited resources is hugely impressive; yet too few students have reaped the benefits of education by becoming employed in the modern economic sector or by sustaining a life of dignity in the rural areas. Although the demise of a racially selective education associated with the settler states of the south has opened the door for African advancement in the elite schools and institutions, education reformers still must promote educational opportunity for the majority and link that reform to significant benefits in life chances. The crafting of educational policies sensitive to local dynamics and regional politics in a context starved of economic resources continues to present considerable challenges. The tendency to craft policies like EFA that are high on rhetoric and low on political and economic analysis points to the need for a sober assessment of educational priorities.

See also **Apartheid; Colonial Policies and Practices; De Klerk, Frederik Willem; Education, University and College; International Monetary Fund; Literacy; Literature; Mandela, Nelson; Nyerere, Julius Kambarage; Socialism and Postsocialisms; Verwoerd, Herdrik French; World Bank.**

BIBLIOGRAPHY

Association for the Development of Education in Africa (ADEA). *Formulating Education Policy: Lessons and Experiences from Sub-Saharan Africa.* Paris: Author, 1995.

Chisholm, Linda, ed. *Changing Class: Education and Social Change in Post-Apartheid South Africa.* New York: Zed, 2004.

Chisholm, Linda; Shireen Motala; and Salim Vally; eds. *South African Education Policy Review, 1993–2000.* Sandown, South Africa: Heinemann, 2003.

Fiske, Edward B., and Helen F. Ladd. *Elusive Equity: Education Reform in Post-Apartheid South Africa.* Washington, DC: Brookings Institution Press, 2004.

Graham-Brown, Sarah. *Education in the Developing World: Conflict and Crisis.* London: Longman, 1998.

Human Sciences Research Council. *Human Resources Development Review.* Pretoria, South Africa, 2004.

Kallaway, P., ed. *Education under Apartheid.* New York: Peter Lang, 2002.

King, Kenneth, and Lene Buchert, eds. *Changing International Aid to Education.* Paris, UNESCO/NORRAG, 1999.

Moulton, Jeanne; Karen Mundy; Michel Welmond; and James Williams; eds. *Educational Reforms in Sub-Saharan Africa: Paradigm Lost?* Westport. CT: Greenwood, 2002.

PETER KALLAWAY

ANGLOPHONE EASTERN AFRICA

Anglophone eastern Africa historically refers to territories that, after the partition of Africa, were designated as territories of the British East Africa Protectorate. These were Kenya, Uganda, Zanzibar, Northern and Southern Rhodesia (Zambia and Zimbabwe), and Nyasaland (Malawi). Tanganyika (present-day Tanzania) was a German territory until the end of World War I, when it became a mandated British territory. The contemporary reference to eastern Africa, however, now denotes Kenya, Uganda, and Tanzania, as the other countries are usually classified as part of Central Africa.

EDUCATION IN THE COLONIAL PERIOD

British imperial education policy in eastern Africa was shaped by three principle concerns. The first involved the felt need to educate the natives about their own environment and culture. The second concern focused on educational content, and put greater emphasis throughout the colonial period on vocational and technical training. The third concern, which had to do with secondary education policy, emphasized direct government control so as to limit the number of schools and to firmly control the educational content provided. This was in order to avoid the creation of an intellectual proletariat, a situation that was believed to have led to the collapse of British imperial rule in India. The primary emphasis during the early years, however, was on basic and vocational education (provided mainly by missionaries, with indirect government support). The content of the education provided and the manner in which it was organized aimed to help combat the perceived African characteristics of indolence and depravity.

The elementary education system consisted mostly of catechumate village and central schools. Most village schools had four classes. Above the village schools were central schools that had additional classes so students could complete the primary school course. The education provided at the central schools could then lead to yet another course in teacher training, or to secondary school. Elementary and primary education expanded rapidly in the interwar period and this, in turn, led to the opening of secondary schools. Government interest in teacher education was modeled after the Jeans method of teacher training, in which selected African teachers and their wives were taught not only how to teach but also to become community leaders. Jeans teachers were supposed to travel to different localities to help teach and supervise other teachers, while also transforming the village schools into community centers. A typical example of such a school was the Jeans School of Kabete in Kenya. Only in the late 1930s were there efforts to provide grants to missionaries to establish centers for the training of lower primary and elementary school teachers.

Secondary Education. Similar to elementary education, the provision of secondary education for Africans was the responsibility of missionaries. In Kenya and Zimbabwe, although the missionaries were generally in favor of beginning some form of secondary and higher education as a means of appeasing African demands for better education, the necessary funds to do so were lacking. Uganda was the first to see the establishment of a secondary school when a high school was opened at the beginning of the twentieth century. In Kenya, however, it was not until the late 1920s that secondary education was provided. In 1926 an organization called the Protestant Alliance used funds donated by the East African War Relief Fund to start the Alliance High School in Kikuyu. This was followed by Kabaa High school for Catholics in 1930. Subsequently, junior secondary schools in Kenya were opened at Maseno and Yala in 1939 and 1940, respectively. In Zambia, the first secondary school was opened at Munali in 1938.

By the end of World War II, the number of secondary schools within the region had significantly increased. In Tanzania, the main secondary schools by 1950 included Tabora, St. Andrews,

Minaki, and St. Francis, Pugu. In Malawi after World War II, the government established secondary schools at Dedza and Mzuzu, and churches established secondary schools in Blantyre and Zomba. In Zimbabwe, no secondary school was opened until 1946, at Goromanzi near Harare (then Salisbury).

Higher Education. The first approach to the development of higher education was through the establishment of regional university colleges affiliated to the University of London. Makerere became the first such institution established in 1922, although it was not upgraded to a degree awarding institution until 1950. The establishment of regional higher education institutions was prompted by the recommendations of the 1943 Elliot Commission that advised the colonial government that the development of universities was an inescapable corollary of any policy leading to the achievement of self-government. The University College at Salisbury (Zimbabwe) was set up in 1953. A second approach to the providing of higher education opportunities focused on the establishment of University colleges in each of the countries, which were then linked to the regional university. Kenya saw the development of the first of these institutions with the opening of the Royal Technical College of East Africa (RTC) in Nairobi. Based on the recommendations of the 1949 Willoughby commission the RTC was designed as a technical and commercial institute to provide courses leading to the Higher National Certificate offered in Britain, and to prepare matriculated students, through full-time study, for university degrees in engineering and allied subjects not provided at Makerere. The East Africa High Commission established the college in 1954 after obtaining a Royal Charter. In 1963, the Royal College, Nairobi became University College, Nairobi and constituted the Federal University of East Africa together with Dar es Salaam and Makerere University Colleges.

Technical Education. Official policy stressed the value of industrial education despite student preferences for a more purely academic education. And individual colonial governments demonstrated a preference for these kinds of schools by supporting missionary efforts to provide technical education and by establishing their own technical training schools, such as the Native Industrial Training Depot in Kabete, Kenya, the Kampala Technical School in Uganda, and the Dar es Salaam Technical Institute in Tanzania. Makerere College remained at the apex of technical education, especially in Uganda before it obtained university status in 1950. The 1961 opening of the Kenya Polytechnic in Nairobi expanded opportunities for technical education in Kenya.

THE POST-INDEPENDENCE PERIOD

The Policy Context. Educational developments in Anglophone postcolonial East Africa have been influenced by a combination of forces. First, the leadership of the nationalist parties that formed the first governments at independence had an ideological commitment to provide mass education. They sought to address the high illiteracy rates, and to provide a stronger human resource base that could then be used for the development in the new nations. The second influential force was the United Nations Educational, Scientific and Cultural Organization (UNESCO)-sponsored Addis Ababa conference of African ministers of education in 1961. The conference set targets for African governments to achieve. These goals included the establishment of universal primary education, and a 30 percent transition rate from primary to secondary education by 1980.

Primary Education. Since independence, primary education has developed in roughly four phases. The first phase, beginning in 1960, was marked by attempts at Africanization of the school curriculum and the removal of school levies to increase enrolments. During this period, the curriculum in all the countries was basically academic, aimed at providing general literacy skills. The second phase saw a return to a more vocational-oriented curriculum. Vocationalization was a response to the emerging school leaver unemployment problem. The aim was to have primary school graduates engage in self-employment in the rural agricultural sector. The third phase, from the late 1970s to the end of the millennium, marked a period of uncertainty and decline of enrolments and quality. The global recession of the 1970s and the oil crisis within the same period eroded the capacity of governments to continue financing the expansion of free primary education. A significant development in all the countries within the period was the emergence of a diversified private primary education sector.

The last phase, from the end of the 1990s and the start of the new millennium, has seen concerted efforts to redress the above problems. With the assistance of donors and a significant provision of national resources, all the countries of the region have in place new policy frameworks for the expansion and provision of primary education to meet Education for All (EFA) targets (reiterated at the 1990 Education for All world conference in Thailand). The influx of pupils to schools has, however, not been accompanied by commensurate expansion of facilities. Teacher quality is still a problem, much as is the provision of quality materials. The development of nonformal schooling for populations who miss out on formal education is not well entrenched in government policy and has been left largely to nongovernmental organizations (NGOs). HIV/AIDS poses a serious challenge to enrollments and teacher effectiveness. The future of primary education in the region largely depends on the extent to which the governments can develop the capacity to address these problems.

Secondary Education. Secondary education was meant to educate and supply the middle-level personnel required to service the economy. At the 1961 Addis Ababa conference, the countries involved were required to achieve a 30 percent transition rate from primary to secondary education by 1980. Efforts to achieve this goal differed from country to country based on the emphasis each country gave to the expansion of primary education. By 1968, Kenya and Rhodesia had achieved a transition rate of 20 percent each; Zambia had 35 percent, and Tanzania and Uganda had 13 percent and 10 percent, respectively. The countries developed a system of high quality secondary schools that admitted students from all regions of the countries based on agreed quotas. Initially, each country's government subsidized entry into these schools, such that fees in the better-equipped secondary schools of the region were low compared to the poor quality district secondary schools. From the 1980s all the countries embarked on reforms to vocationalize the secondary school curriculum as a response to the school leaver unemployment problem. Technical secondary schools were supposed to stream

students toward their future occupations, provide them with better practical skills to address the unemployment problem, and fulfill the notion of integrating mental and manual labor. Emphasis in strengthening the teaching of science and mathematics as preparation for professional courses at the universities has also been common.

Higher Education. Higher education within Anglophone postcolonial East Africa consists of two segments. The first includes middle-level colleges founded in the immediate postcolonial period, during the days of the East African Community, and after. They include national polytechnics, vocational training centers, and research and policy analysis institutions. The latter segment includes institutions that came into being from the mid-1980s in all the countries for purposes of supporting research and policy analysis in the government and private sector. The second segment consists of universities. The development of universities in the region was influenced by British policy during the late colonial period of establishing regional universities attached to the University of London so as to control quality. The regional university system collapsed by 1977, however, in favor of national universities. Thereafter, university education developed in three different directions. First was the expansion of national university capacities during much of the 1980s and 1990s. This was driven largely by political than economic considerations. Second came the growth of private universities and third, the semi-privatization of public universities in the 1990s. These developments have raised concerns about issues of social responsibility and the role of university education in promoting social equity and quality. Lastly, there has been a return to regional approaches in the provision of university education, with the revival from the mid 1990s of the Inter-University Council for East Africa (IUCEA), and support for the movement and exchange of students within the region.

CONCLUSIONS

In reviewing educational developments in postcolonial Anglophone East Africa, it is clear that individual governments have taken a number of common approaches even as they diverged on specific issues: After initial attempts at Africanization, postcolonial governments returned to the colonial logic of providing education designed to help students adapt to new circumstances. There has also been a return to an approach that pays attention to market forces when providing education services. This is evident in the steady growth of private education institutions that tend to exacerbate regional and socioeconomic inequalities. And finally, all have sought to link education to employment.

See also **Addis Ababa; Blantyre; Colonial Policies and Practices; Disease: HIV/AIDS; Education, University and College; Literacy; Nongovernmental Organizations.**

BIBLIOGRAPHY

Berman, Edward H., ed. *African Reactions to Missionary Education.* New York: Teachers College Press, 1975.

Buchert, Lene. *Education in the Development of Tanzania: 1919–1990.* London: James Currey, 1994.

Furley, W., and T. Watson. *A History of Education in East Africa.* New York: NOK, 1978.

Kurian, George T., ed. *World Education Encyclopedia.* New York: Facts on File, 1988.

Lewis, J.E. "The Ruling Compassions of the Late Colonial State: Welfare Versus Force, Kenya, 1945–1952." *Journal of Colonialism and Colonial History* 2, no. 2 (2001): 1–35.

Mwnakatwe, John M. *The Growth of Education in Zambia since Independence.* Lusaka, Zambia: Oxford University Press, 1968.

Oliver, Roland, and Anthony Atmore. *Africa since 1800.* London: Cambridge University Press, 1967.

Sifuna, Daniel N. *Development of Education in East Africa: The Kenyan Experience.* Nairobi, Kenya: Initiatives, 1990.

Whitehead, Clive. "The Historiography of British Imperial Education Policy, Part II: Africa and the Rest of the Colonial Empire." *History of Education* 34, no. 4 (2005): 441–454.

DANIEL N. SIFUNA
IBRAHIM O. OANDA

ANGLOPHONE WESTERN AFRICA

The Gambia, Ghana, Nigeria, and Sierra Leone share a common colonial past within the former British Empire but in addition to them, Liberia is discussed in this entry as part of "Anglophone" western Africa since the lingua franca in Liberia is English, although its historical metropolitan orientation is to the United States.

EDUCATIONAL BEGINNINGS AND DEVELOPMENT

Although European missionaries made various attempts in the seventeenth and eighteenth centuries to found schools along the coast, these efforts were short-lived. It was not until the era of mission expansion in the nineteenth century (and acceptance of the "scientific" belief that Africans were human and therefore had souls to be saved, and practical abilities and intellects to develop) that more persistent efforts to educate West Africans were made. Sierra Leone, however, has a different educational history. As a freed-slave settlement, rather than as a trading and administrative center) and as a result of the British government's early involvement there, government schools in Sierra Leone have a longer history than elsewhere along the coast but in all of Anglophone Western Africa, missionaries played a significant part in the establishment of Western education. Missionaries in west Africa wanted literate functionaries for the church as well as members of congregations; but with expanding commercial opportunities along the coast during the latter part of the nineteenth century, they found great difficulty in keeping those they had trained within the churches.

Only with the growth and consolidation of colonial territories through the nineteenth century, did the British government gradually give some attention to the provision of education and not only provide its own schools, but also establish an inspectorate to monitor standards in all schools. Until the 1940s the schooling provided was along the lines of British primary education, and schools still tended to be sited either in towns or near mission stations. Secondary education provision was restricted to a handful of elite schools throughout British West Africa.

Although Liberia's metropolitan orientation is to the United States rather than Britain, the history of the establishment of education there is similar to the other Anglophone states, with the missions leading the way and government following in their wake. While the ex-British colonies adopted the British primary and secondary school system, education in Liberia followed the American model, consisting of a series of grades leading through elementary and junior high school to senior high school. Liberia, like Sierra Leone, was founded as a settlement for manumitted slaves. In terms of the dominant ideologies of both states, this led to a distinct separation between those descendants of the slaves (Creoles) who lived on the coast and formed an elite—which from the beginning set a premium on "civilization," a part of which was becoming educated—and the indigenous populations of the hinterlands, which were regarded by the Creoles as backward and not "civilized." This distinction has had consequences for political leadership and development in both states. In the Gambia, Ghana, and Nigeria, education was slower to acquire a positive value, and generally such value evolved gradually with the perception of a link between education and opportunities for social and economic advancement.

From the 1920s there were frequent debates among colonial policymakers as to the nature and type of education which was to be developed and supported in west Africa. Mission teachers had tended to assume that education should involve a thorough training in literacy and numeracy as well as some development of practical skills; secondary and higher levels of education were not initially favored. From the 1920s to the 1940s, however, the formal establishment of government secondary schools and the beginnings of the opening up of access to secondary education, even though still limited, made very clear the strong local demand for academic rather than practical or vocational training. This demand was linked both to opportunity and status considerations. There was a far greater chance of becoming wealthy and being considered a member of an elite through becoming a lawyer or doctor than through building up a carpentry business or gaining a scientific knowledge of farming.

INDEPENDENCE

With the move toward self-rule and independence in the 1950s, educational provision in the Anglophone west African states expanded. New nations needed not only highly educated leaders but also a Western-educated and -skilled populace if they were to take their places in the world. In Liberia, Sierra Leone, and the Gambia, the expansion in educational provision was extensive if gradual, but in Ghana and southern Nigeria moves toward universal primary education necessitated both a vast increase in

infrastructure and a focus on the training of many more teachers. Attempts to accomplish this met with varying degrees of success. In Ghana nominally there has been universal primary education since 1961, but in spite of major efforts in the south of the country, it was not until 1976 that a concerted attempt was made to bring primary education to children in both the northern and southern parts of Nigeria.

Throughout the whole region, hinterland areas were less well served by Western schools than those along the coastal areas. Historically, the dominance of Islam in the inland and more northerly areas has meant that the Christian missionaries (the pioneers of Western education in many cases) there had had less success in winning converts and school pupils. In the case of northern Nigeria, Christian missionaries were not allowed to proselytize until the 1940s–1950s, when government schools were being established, and the take-up of Western education has always been less in the north than the south. Providing a Western education in the north, and persuading parents to send their children (both girls and boys) to schools was expensive; the Nigerian federal government's major campaign to introduce universal primary education throughout the country could be effectively operationalized only after revenues from oil grew enormously in the 1970s.

In spite of the rhetoric of universal primary education in Nigeria and Ghana, recent figures on school enrollment throughout the region show that universality has not been achieved at the primary level, and the enrollment rates drop away at the secondary level, particularly for girls (see Table 1).

Enrollment, gross (2002–03)

Country/Level	The Gambia	Ghana	Liberia	Nigeria	Sierra Leone
Pre-primary	18	45	43*	12	4**
Primary girls	84	75	103	107	65
Primary boys	86	82	103	132	93
Secondary girls	28	36	24	32	22
Secondary boys	41	43	37	40	31

*Figures for Liberia are for 1998–9
**Figures for Sierra Leone are for 2000–01

SOURCE: http://www.uis.unesco.org/profiles (accessed in November 2005).

Table 1.

Pupil-teacher ratio, primary (2002–03)

Country/Level	The Gambia	Ghana	Liberia	Nigeria	Sierra Leone
	38	31	38	42	37

SOURCE: http://www.uis.unesco.org/profiles (accessed in November 2005).

Table 2.

Educational spending (2002–03)

Country/Level	The Gambia	Ghana	Liberia	Nigeria	Sierra Leone
% of GDP	2.8	4.1	na	na	3.7
% of Government spending	3.9	na	na	na	

SOURCE: http://www.uis.unesco.org/profiles (accessed in November 2005).

Table 3.

Figures for the teacher/student ratio at the primary level are given in Table 2.

CONTEMPORARY ISSUES

Throughout the postindependence period, political rhetoric about and spending on education have fluctuated as governments have changed and economic fortunes have varied. Recent levels of spending on education, when measured as a proportion of the GNP (see Table 3), are still very low, although figures are largely based on estimates where they do exist.

In general, there has been a move away from the British system in Nigeria and Ghana, while the Gambia and Sierra Leone retained it until the millennium. The functions of the West African Exams Council (WAEC), founded in 1951 to moderate the secondary school intermediate and advanced level School Certificates (and whose examinations' standards were accepted by European and North American tertiary institutions as entry qualifications) have changed from moderating common examinations to those of quality assurance and probity across several systems. In Liberia schooling has nominally continued along the American model

with only a small number of students graduating from high school through the years of the civil war.

All of the countries considered here are, to a greater or lesser degree, undergoing economic reform. For those free of the tragic waste of civil war this has meant educational reform; for wartorn Liberia and Sierra Leone, facing not only economic restructuring, but also the mammoth tasks of reconciliation and rehabilitation, the established systems have only in the early twenty-first century come under the scrutiny of reformers. Nigeria first moved away from the British system (the elementary cycle was too long) in the 1970s as part of its thrust toward indigenization, but Ghana's educational reforms were undertaken under the auspices of the World Bank. In the Gambia, only in 1988–1989 was the age for starting primary school lowered from eight to seven and only then was consideration given to introducing a shift system into secondary schools to increase the number of students to which they cater. In 1990, however, the country began to plan major restructuring: the Gambia set out its plans for restructuring between 1998 and 2003.

Whatever the underlying rhetoric for reforms in each state, what is emerging is a shortening of the first cycle (primary and junior high school), together with attempts to widen access and improve completion rates. At the same time, there has been a vast increase in preprimary provision throughout the region since the mid-1990s. The introduction of cost-recovery measures in education has meant that although primary education might be nominally free, parents must pay for equipment, and communities often have to provide the buildings. Increases in cost, whether actual or perceived, tend to militate against the widening of access and the improvement of completion rates. Beyond the first cycle, students who want to go on are channeled into either an academic or more practical orientation. Earlier arguments about the relative merits of academic and vocational training are subsumed in that the new first cycle training tends to have a more practical orientation than its predecessors; only later might students go on to specialize in academic subjects. This has had consequences both for teacher training (which now tends to be exclusively post-second cycle) and for university entrants, whose academic standards, some suggest, are falling. Although the new systems do represent attempts to widen the access to education, overall what they offer to most students represents a leveling down of opportunity; the majority will have a chance for basic education and training for work, at most.

EDUCATION FOR ALL

In the wake of the millennium development goals (MDGs), the major donors have been concerned with the implementation of plans under the heading Education for All by 2015. The goal is in effect a concrete statement of plans already in existence in the states under consideration here. The problems in implementation remain the same, mainly financial, but also logistical. Thus Ghana set in motion its policies for Free Compulsory Universal Basic Education (FCUBE) enshrined in its 1992 Constitution, in September 2005, with backing from donors. But one result has been that urban primary schools in particular are grossly overcrowded and some children found no place available for them to learn.

Girls' education is also being discussed and not only because of its association with MDGs. All of the Anglophone west African states have much lower proportions of girls than boys in primary education, and the sex ratio favors boys more as one goes through secondary to tertiary education. In Islamic areas the number of girls attending Western schools is even smaller. While the proportional disparity may in itself be considered an injustice, further impetus to improving the opportunities for girls to attend school comes from the strong positive associations found between women's education and the health of children and also between women's education and small family size. Both health and population size have enormous lobbies in their wake, large enough to promote positive attention to the provision of education for girls and their successful completion of it, or at least of the first cycle, so as to gain functional literacy. Whether or not Education for All is achievable throughout the region, however, remains a moot point.

See also **Christianity; Colonial Policies and Practices; Creoles; Education, University and College; Gender; Literacy; Postindependence; Slavery and Servile Institutions; World Bank.**

BIBLIOGRAPHY

Abernethy, David B. *The Political Dilemma of Popular Education: An African Case.* Stanford, CA: Stanford University Press, 1969.

Bray, Mark. *Universal Primary Education in Nigeria: A Study of Kano State.* London: Routledge and Kegan Paul, 1981.

Fafunwa, A. Babs. *History of Education in Nigeria.* London: Allen and Unwin, 1974.

Foster, Philip. *Education and Social Change in Ghana.* London: Routledge and Kegan Paul, 1965.

Gay, John, and Michael Cole. *The New Mathematics and an Old Culture: A Study of Learning among the Kpelle of Liberia.* New York: Holt, Rinehart, and Winston, 1967.

Hilliard, F. H. *A Short History of Education in British West Africa.* London: T. Neslon, 1957.

Stephens, David, ed. Spec. issue, *International Journal of Educational Development* 20, no. 1 (January 2000).

Subbarao K., and Laura Raney. *Social Gains from Female Education: A Cross-National Study.* World Bank Discussion Papers, no. 194. Washington, DC, 1993.

UNESCO. *Statistical Yearbook, 1996.* Paris: UNESCO, 1996.

LYNNE BRYDON

FRANCOPHONE CENTRAL AFRICA

As in other African regions, education in central Africa is characterized by a dual system. A traditional (indigenous) component coexists with the Western-style schooling instituted during the colonial period.

Traditional education is the prevailing system. While its success in terms of skills training is largely undocumented, it is nevertheless recognized that African economies—even the Western-type economy transplanted in the region during the colonial period—draw a sizable part of their skilled manpower from this system. Agricultural, masonry, carpentry, and other skills are equally acquired through it.

In spite of its relative importance, traditional education has been largely ignored in modern education policies. The belief, popularized in human capital and economic development theories since the 1950s, that the Western type of education is a more effective mechanism for achieving social and economic development led to massive investments in schooling. In the 1960s and 1970s, the proportion of national budgets allocated to schooling was generally around 20 percent in most countries. The actual level of public resources invested in this system is, however, much higher. For example, while primary education is ostensibly free, an important part of school expenses is being borne by parents; they are asked to construct schools and to pay for teaching materials and equipment for their children. Moreover, some of the training expenses incurred outside of the ministries of education are not included in national education accounts; it is therefore estimated that schooling and training expenditures represented as much as 40 percent of the national budgets in some countries during the 1960s and 1970s.

Schooling is organized mainly by the government. There was a relatively large private church-sponsored education sector (partially financed by the state) before the 1960s in some countries, but this sector has either disappeared completely, as in countries where education was nationalized, or its importance has diminished because of the considerable expansion of the public sector. The private sector's share in enrollments has tended to rise as schooling has been denationalized in most countries. However, this growth derives also from the emergence of private profit-making schools; in general, these schools are of low quality because they are, in most cases, created by entrepreneurs with limited interest and experience in education.

The heavy investment in education and training led to a dramatic rise in enrollments in all countries during the 1960s and 1970s. While these enrollments tended to fall during the late 1980s, some of the countries appear close to achieving universal primary education in quantitative terms. In 1986 the gross primary enrollment rates (including repeaters) reached 114 percent in Congo, 107 percent in Cameroon, 98 percent in Zaire, and 126 percent in Gabon. The rates were lower in some countries (67 percent in Rwanda, 59 percent in Burundi, and 43 percent in Chad) mainly because of their low starting point. The enrollment rates were even higher at the secondary and higher-education levels in relative terms; in some countries, about 20 percent of secondary-age young people are in school, while the rate is close to 2 percent for those of higher-education age. The improved access to education has led to a greater participation of women in education. In most countries, the proportion of girls at the primary level is almost equal to that of boys; however, girls tend to leave the school system much earlier than boys. Schooling is also increasingly accessible to rural children; however, in this case too, rural children leave earlier than urban children. Therefore, while access to education has become more equitable, inequalities of access have not been eradicated.

The impressive expansion of enrollments has been accompanied by a high degree of inefficiency. For example, at the primary level, only about half of the students in a given cohort reach the terminal year. Among those who do so, as few as 10 percent complete the cycle without repeating grades. The situation is similar at the secondary and higher-education levels.

The high internal inefficiency of the school systems is attributed to a variety of factors. First, the level of allocations to education has generally fallen since the 1970s. The resources directed at the primary level have fallen even more substantially because the allocations to the secondary and higher-education levels have been increased while the overall education budgets were either reduced or frozen at existing levels. In 1986 the annual per-student expenditure at the primary level was less than fifty dollars in most countries.

Second, available resources are used mainly to pay teacher salaries. Less than 5 percent is invested in educational material and equipment. Thus, not only do students lack the necessary learning tools, but existing infrastructures have deteriorated considerably and are overcrowded. In some countries, the pupil-teacher ratio is as high as 200 to 1 in poorly equipped and maintained classrooms.

Third, the curricula, teaching materials, and training methods are largely unadapted to the African learning environment. For example, it is estimated that less than 10 percent of the population functionally master the French language; yet French is the language of instruction even at the primary level. Fourth, many teachers are unqualified, either because they have not attained the appropriate academic levels or because they lack adequate training in education.

The external efficiency of the education systems appears also to be rather low. There is a high rate of unemployment even for those with education because the public sector is no longer able to provide jobs. Another reason for this high unemployment is that the school systems do not appear to be producing the kind of skills needed in the private sector or which could contribute to the expansion of this sector. Moreover, the low external efficiency can equally be attributed to the fact that the school systems inherited from the colonial period appear to be generally irrelevant to the indigenous social and economic environment. In most cases, children are sent to school not because of what they could bring into their indigenous environment in terms of skills but of what they need to leave it.

Since the public sector will probably be unable to provide employment to the majority of those coming out of the school systems for the foreseeable future, the irrelevancy of the education system with respect to both the private economic sector and the indigenous economic systems appears to be one of the principal problems facing the education systems in central African countries.

See also **Education, University and College; Family: Economics; Literacy; Research: Overview.**

BIBLIOGRAPHY

Bobb, F. Scott. *Historical Dictionary of Zaire.* Metuchen, NJ: Scarecrow Press, 1988.

Capelle, Jean. *L'éducation en Afrique à la veille des indépendances.* Paris: Editions Karthala, 1990.

Cissé, Samba Yacine. *L'éducation en Afrique à la lumière de la Conférence de Harare.* Paris: United Nations Educational, Scientific, and Cultural Organization (UNESCO), 1985.

Decalo, Samuel. *Historical Dictionary of Chad.* Metuchen, NJ: Scarecrow Press, 1987.

Erny, Pierre. *L'enfant et son milieu en Afrique noire: Essai sur l'éducation traditionnelle.* Paris: Payot, 1972.

Gardinier, David E. *Historical Dictionary of Gabon.* Metuchen, NJ: Scarecrow Press, 1981.

Omo-Fadaka, Jimoh. "Education and Endogeneous Development in Africa." *Prospects* 12, no. 2 (1982): 261–268.

Thompson, Virginia, and Richard Adloff. *Historical Dictionary of the People's Republic of the Congo.* Metuchen, NJ: Scarecrow Press, 1984.

United Nations Educational, Scientific, and Cultural Organization (UNESCO). *Les politiques de l'éducation et la formation en Afrique sub-saharienne.* Paris: UNESCO, 1987.

United Nations Educational, Scientific, and Cultural Organization (UNESCO). *Rapport mondial sur l'éducation, 1991.* Paris: UNESCO, 1992.

World Bank. *Education in Sub-Saharan Africa: Policies for Adjustment, Revitalization, and Expansion.* Washington, DC: World Bank, 1988.

MIALA DIAMBOMBA

FRANCOPHONE WESTERN AND INDIAN OCEAN AFRICA

Politically, the region of Africa south of the Sahara was governed by European colonial powers from in the mid- to late nineteenth century. Most of the countries began gaining independence in the 1960s, with Namibia as the last to do so in 1991.

Whether it was the British or French colonial rule, Africans ended up marginalized. The French, compared to the British, were prepared to treat Africans as equals as long as they learned to speak French properly, adopted the values of French culture, and obtained a sufficient level of education. The French colonial system aimed at preparing a small group of *Auxilliaires d'administration*, or évolués, a group of Africans chosen by the French colonial masters as assistance to help run the colonial administration. As a result, in order to obtain the French standard of equality, Africans had to give up who they were as Africans and assimilate to French values. As the Francophone countries gained independence, thus, this attitude had to be reversed, and as such, there were clashes among the alienated Africans who assumed a "French identity" and the Africans who wanted to get rid of French identity and remain Africans.

The Francophone western and Indian Ocean African countries over the years have had to contend with a colonial legacy, in addition to increasing populations, heavy urbanization, low economic growth, civil wars, ethnic violence, education issues, limited health care delivery, and the AIDS pandemic and other diseases.

NONFORMAL EDUCATION SYSTEMS (ISLAM)

Apart from European colonization, the greatest influence in Africa has been Islam, which spread from North Africa in the seventh century and then swept across the Sahara, down the east coast of Africa, and to Indian Ocean. When Islam came to the African societies, people were intrigued, puzzled, and perhaps even bewildered. But the Africans were seldom hostile, in part because of the small numbers of their citizens involved. Islam in Africa was principally established along important trade routes. Gradually these small Muslim trading communities grew in size and influence and led to Africans in the local communities converting to Islam. Many of these converts, however, continue to practice their old religions because they see no conflict between the two religions.

But with time, Islam has gently broken away from the old religions, insisted on reform, and demanded a break with the old customs. With time the Islamic reformers sanctioned those communities and coverts still mixing Islam and African customs because they demanded absolute royalty. The leaders of the Muslim community envision that, for Islam to continue, steps must be taken to teach the religion to their children and to support schools and Islamic scholars. This results in teachers and educators taking responsibility for Islam becoming active in such communities. However, the French colonial authorities feared this propagation of Islam might undermine their clout and might incite the Africans against the spread of Islam, and so they decided to send troops to check this trend. The French were determined and demanded that Muslims should become loyal subjects of the colonial empire. Instead, Muslims became antagonized by colonial rule. Despite these problems, Islamic schools (madrassas) continue to operate in former French colonies.

FORMAL EDUCATION

During the colonial period in Africa, the European missionaries introduced and implemented a Western model of education. The primary agenda of the two dominant Christian denominations (Protestants and Catholics) was evangelism and antislavery. The colonial educational strategies included training in reading, writing, and scripture. During the colonial era, access to education was restricted and controlled, as were curricular subjects and the duration of study. African education was geared toward the roles deemed appropriate by the colonial masters. Sons of chiefs had privileged access to schooling because such practice served both the religious and political agendas of those in power.

The education systems of these countries in the modern era are a reflection of their colonial heritage. This is indicative of examinations and certification systems, mediums of instruction, and curricular systems. Many see education as the means to better life, a perception supported by the rise of educated citizens to leadership positions at the time of independence. Education was viewed as a basic right of citizenship and as the ultimate fruit of independence. Governments saw the importance of education as prerequisite for not only building modern, productive economies, but also for building national unity. Campaigns were mounted to Africanize national civil services by replacing Europeans with newly educated African citizens, and this served the twin purpose of meeting both economic and popular demands. Some of the countries have piloted alternatives, such as education for self-reliance in Tanzania and the mass adult literacy programs in Mozambique.

After independence, the ministries of education in the countries were saddled with the responsibilities for the provision, management, inspection, and support of pre-primary, primary, secondary, and vocational schools, universities, and teacher and other training institutions. Their educational systems were based on French and British models. Classes were taught in French and English. The systems were highly centralized and so most governments used this centralization to develop a sense of national identity and to ensure control over resources allocations. Most of the countries made education compulsory, and although the duration varies for each country, six to eight years are most common.

African educational systems expanded immensely in the first years of independence. Primary school enrollments rose greatly, which in turn brought in many schooling opportunities to some segments of the population that had no previous access to formal education. However, it was not egalitarian. Most national education systems served only less than half percent of the school age populations as indicated in the tables. It also typically favored urban populations.

In sub-Saharan Africa, the general regional average information of the participation in education for girls and boys, on average, 67 percent of boys and 63 percent of girls of the relevant ages are enrolled in primary education. The region accounts for 39 percent of the world's out-of-school children. Fifty-two percent of these are girls. The average number of years a child will spend in school increased from 6.6 in 1999 to 7.6 in 2004, according to UNESCO Institute for Statistics.

Bénin. Four percent of children are enrolled in pre-primary school. Seventy-two percent of girls and 93 percent of boys are in primary school, of which 49 percent of children complete a full course. As of 2004, the pupil-to-teacher ratio in primary schools was 52 percent.

Burkina Faso. Thirty-five percent of girls and 46 percent of boys are in primary school. Eight percent girls and 11 percent boys are in secondary school. Two percent of the population is receiving a higher education. Twenty-nine percent of children complete a full course of primary education. As of 2004, the pupil-to-teacher ratio in primary school was forty-nine.

Cameroon. Twenty percent of children are enrolled in pre-primary school. Five percent of the population is obtaining a higher education. Sixty-three percent of children complete a full course of primary education, and 17.2 percent of government spending goes to education. In 2004, the pupil-to-teacher ratio in primary school was fifty-four.

Central African Republic. Two percent of children are enrolled in pre-primary school. Primary enrollment as of 1991 was 63 percent male and 41 percent female. Secondary enrollment as of 1991 was 16 percent boys and 6 percent girls. As of 2004, no data was available for the pupil/teacher ratio.

Chad. As of 2002, 71 percent of boys and 47 percent girls were enrolled in primary school. In 1999, 11 percent of boys and 3 percent of girls were enrolled in secondary school. Twenty-nine percent of children complete a full course of primary education. As of 2004, the pupil-to-teacher ratio in primary school was sixty-nine.

Comoros. Three percent of children are enrolled in pre-primary school. In 1999, 54 percent of boys and 45 percent of girls were enrolled in primary school. Two percent of the population is obtaining a higher education. Fifty percent of children complete a full course of primary education, with 24.1 percent of the government spending going to education. In 2004, the pupil-to-teacher ratio in primary school was thirty-five.

Republic of the Congo. Six percent of children are enrolled in pre-primary school. Based on the data in 1991, 82 percent boys and 77 percent of girls were enrolled in primary school. Sixty-six percent of children complete a full course of primary education, and 12.6 percent of government spending goes to education. As of 2004, the pupil-to-teacher ratio in primary school was eighty-three.

Côte d'Ivoire. In 2002, 3 percent of boys and 3 percent of girls were enrolled in pre-primary school. In 2002, 52 percent boys and 37 percent girls were enrolled in primary school. At the same time, 26 percent boys and 15 percent girls were enrolled in secondary school. For university enrollment in 1999, 10 percent of males and 3 percent of females were enrolled. Slightly more than 21 percent of government spending goes to education. The pupil-to-teacher ratio was forty-two in 2004.

Democratic Republic of the Congo. In 1991, 61 percent boys and 48 percent girls were enrolled in primary school. By 1999, 24 percent of boys and 12 percent of females were enrolled in secondary school. In 2004, the pupil-to-teacher ratio in primary school was twenty-six.

Djibouti. Two percent of children are enrolled in pre-primary school. Twenty-nine percent of girls and 36 percent of boys are in primary school. Fifteen percent of girls and 22 percent of boys are in secondary school. Two percent of the population is in university. About 20.5 percent of government spending goes to education. By 2004, the pupil-to-teacher ratio in primary school was thirty-four.

Gabon. As of 2002, 14 percent of children were enrolled in pre-primary school. In 1991, 85 percent of boys and 85 percent of girls were enrolled in primary school. For university attendance in 1999, 9 percent males and 5 percent females were enrolled. The government spends 9.6 percent of its budget on education. The pupil-to-teacher ratio in primary schools in 2004 was thirty-six.

Guinea. Six percent of children are enrolled in pre-primary school. Fifty-eight percent of girls and 69 percent of boys are in primary school. Fourteen percent of girls and 28 percent of boys are in secondary school. Two percent of the population is in university. Forty-eight percent of children complete a full course of primary education, and 25.6 percent of government spending goes to education. The pupil-to-teacher ratio in primary schools in 2004 was forty-five.

Madagascar. Ten percent of children are enrolled in pre-primary school. Eighty-nine percent of girls and 89 percent of boys are in primary school. In 1999, 11 percent boys and 11 percent girls were enrolled in secondary school. Three percent of the population receives a higher education. Forty-five percent of children complete a full course of primary education. About 18.2 percent of government spending goes to education. The pupil-to-teacher ratio in primary schools was fifty-two in 2004.

Mali. By 2002, 1 percent of children were enrolled in pre-primary school. Forty-three percent of girls and 50 percent of boys are in primary school. For secondary enrollment in 1991, 7 percent boys and 4 percent girls were in school. Two percent of the population was enrolled in higher education. Forty-four percent of children complete a full course of primary education. The pupil-to-teacher ratio for primary schools was fifty-two in 2004.

Niger. One percent of children are enrolled in pre-primary school. Thirty-two percent of girls and 46 percent of boys are in primary school. Five percent of girls and 8 percent of boys are in secondary school. One percent of the population obtains a higher education. Twenty-five percent of children complete a full course of primary education. The pupil-to-teacher ratio in primary schools was forty-four in 2004.

Senegal. Six percent of children are enrolled in pre-primary school. Sixty-four percent of girls and 68 percent of boys are in primary school. Thirteen percent of girls and 18 percent of boys are in secondary school. Five percent of the population pursues higher education. Forty-five percent of children complete a full course of primary education. The pupil-to-teacher ratio in primary schools was forty-three in 2004.

Togo. Two percent of children are enrolled in pre-primary school. Seventy-two percent of girls and 85 percent of boys are in primary school. As of 1999, 27 percent boys and 12 percent girls were enrolled in secondary education. For university attendance in 1999, 5 percent males and 1 percent females were enrolled. Sixty-six percent of children complete a full course of primary education, with 13.6 percent of government spending going to education. The pupil-to-teacher ratio in primary schools was forty-four in 2004.

OVERVIEW OF ACADEMIC PROGRAMS (CURRICULUM), POLICIES, AND STRUCTURE

The failure to align education policies with the nature and the culture of society developed contradictory results that still affect many African countries' education system: the youth completed primary education but could not be accommodated in secondary school due to restricted space, and neither could they find the vocational occupation that they trained for due to the limited industry. Other problems of education systems included students dropping out, fewer opportunities for women, overcrowding and urbanization, and disillusionment among people with the governments' reform efforts that have yielded failures and increased poverty. These conditions, coupled with political and religious differences, led to conflicts that face these countries today. Brain drain has became prominent because people who obtained higher education are not able to find working conditions in Africa which they can use their skills. Despite these problems, there has been nothing done to radically restructure the educational systems to meet the educational, political, and economic needs of these countries.

So much attention is focused on reform rather than restructuring, with least attention given to important variables of the system such as curriculum, pedagogy, or teacher training. Teachers and students, policy makers, coordinators of courses, administrators, financiers, parents, and other members of the communities outside of the immediate educational setting play important roles in shaping functional and productive academic programs. The situation is complex and dynamic, driven by social and technical forces outside the unique circumstances of each country. Undoubtedly, these countries are characterized by enormous diversity in terms of size, economic structure, governance, social factors, and level of development of the education systems, yet they encounter many common challenges. These include continuously low levels of economic development and high rates of population growth. Although some efforts were made to change the curriculum, they were mainly cosmetic because the formal schooling remained French and the notion of development was based on Western, industrialized society, an orientation in conflict with the rural and agrarian African societies. The rationale for this strategy is the neoclassical model of economic growth, which considers human capital (quantity of labor and labor productivity) to be the main determinants for long-term growth. Therefore, these countries should be viewing and reforming their education systems based on education for whom and education for what.

From the 1980s much of Africa, including the Francophone western and Indian Ocean African countries, was in economic crisis. Most countries suffered a decline in real per capita income and living standards that fell back to or below 1960s levels. The impact of such a crisis continued to be felt in education, where many of the countries' governments were unable to sustain previous levels of funding. Of biggest concern to these nations has been the consequences of civil conflict, natural disasters, political instability, public debt burdens, and poverty.

Toward the end of the twentieth century and from the beginning of the twenty-first century, the Francophone African countries devised means to overcome the social, educational, political, and economic problems facing their nations. The different approaches and intervention tactics resulted in varying degrees of success. Early efforts of educational reform from the 1960s to 1970s focused on changing from a French-oriented to African-oriented system that was quantitative in nature and that emphasized manpower development for industrial growth and developed a system that was reflective of local needs but at the same time compatible with the French system. During this period Francophone Africa, as well other African countries, viewed education as the main vehicle for economic development. Thus, more funding was directed to education.

Although governments of these nations continued to build schools to meet the demands of growing populations, inadequate resources contributed greatly to a decline in the quality of education offered. The governments then turned to external funding to help finance the costs of education. It is taken for granted in most of these countries that any type of education reform will require external support. Additionally, many of these countries have undertaken structural adjustment reform programs as prescribed by World Bank and International Monetary Fund that limit government spending on social services such as education, and the influences of foreign funding agencies have grown over the years. Increased external control over the planning and running of their educational systems perpetuates the nations' poverty and dependence on external funding, both capital and recurrent.

External indebtedness has hindered economic development and poverty reduction in this region. Although per capita growth rates have recently been on an upswing in some of the countries, they have yet to make any substantial impact on poverty.

According to a 1997 United Nations estimate, projections point to a slowdown in population growth worldwide, but in this region the population growth remains high. For example, in 2007 one person in three is of primary- or secondary school age, as compared with only one in five in Latin America and Asia, and one in six in many European and North American countries, according to education statistics from the United Nations Educational, Scientific and Cultural Organization (UNESCO). The high rates of demographic growth are negatively affecting education resources and making it difficult to sustain current enrollment rates in schools.

Most governments in the 1980s allocated an increasing proportion of their educational budgets to primary and secondary education, and have decreased budgetary allocations to higher education. Most of the countries earmarked between 80 to 90 percent of their recurrent education budget for teachers' salaries, leaving little for teaching and learning materials. This lack of materials and other essentials contributed to the declining quality of schools in most of the countries.

There seems to be some progress toward education planning that has evolved since the early years of independence when planning was in principle solely guided by the intervention called social demand. This term became meaningless once governments made education compulsory, and this new requirement created a legal demand for schooling. In the 1970s most of the governments in Africa experimented with manpower planning, reflecting their view that the future was predictable and that an education system could be designed to fulfill labor market needs. However, as developmental economists and agencies such as the World Bank and the International Monetary Fund have come to exercise greater control and influence over these nations, the countries' overall economic planning and investment analyses for education have become prominent. In addition, educational policymaking in these countries draws increasingly on the findings of educational research. Yet since the economic crises of the 1980s, critics have noted that African education systems, although expanding quantitatively, have failed to bring about higher employment rates, more equitable societies, or more accountable governments. The narrowing of education reform agendas to fit the neoliberal economic policies prescribed by foreign assistance agencies has generated increasing dissatisfaction among the Africans.

The emphasis on efficiency, critics argue, comes at the expense of equity and to accountability to internal constituents—in other words, the citizens and the students. This critique has in turn generated greater appreciation for the complexity of educational problems that included poor retention rates, low achievement, high drop out rates, and a lack of adequate finances in almost all the countries. As a result, this problems should not be seen strictly as internal efficiency problems but as deeper issues that must be better understood if education in Francophone and Indian Ocean African countries is to improve and subsequently have an impact on the labor market.

See also **Colonial Policies and Practices; Disease: HIV/ AIDS; Ethnicity; International Monetary Fund; Literacy; Postcolonialism; Warfare: Civil Wars; World Bank.**

BIBLIOGRAPHY

Appiah, Kwame Anthony, and Henry Louis Gates. *Africana: The Encyclopedia of the African and African American Experiences.* New York: Basic Civitas Books, 1999.

"Council for the Development of Social Science Research in Africa." Available from http://www.codesria.org.

Crandell, D. *CultureGrams 2004 World Edition Cultural Reports for Africa*, Volume 111. Lindon, UT: Axiom Press, 2003.

Johnson, Robert C. "Educational Change in Francophone Africa." *The Journal of Negro Education* 56. no. 3 (1987): 265–281.

United National Educational, Scientific and Cultural Organization Institute for Statistics. "Global Education Digest 2004." Available from http//www.uis.unesco .org/.

P. Masila Mutisya
Revised by Apollos Goyol

MUSLIM AFRICA

Muslims place primary significance upon the preservation and transmission of their religious heritage as revealed in the Qur'an and recorded in the prophetic traditions (*hadith*) and other classic religious texts. Therefore, education and educational institutions occupy an essential place in the fabric of Islamic religious culture.

The Qur'anic school for basic religious education is the classic Islamic educational institution, attended by Muslim children throughout sub-Saharan Africa, and elsewhere in the Muslim world. The curriculum includes learning the fundamental elements of Islamic religious obligation, such as how to perform ritual ablution and to pray, as well as to recite at least some verses of the Qur'an. The better students, or those whose parents have decided they should continue their studies, may learn to recite the entire Qur'an. During this stage of schooling, students are also taught to read and write the Arabic alphabet. Because the maternal language of most African children is not Arabic, their studies in the early years inevitably focus on rote memorization, rather than understanding.

Parents place their children in Qur'anic school primarily to fulfill their religious obligations, but also so they become educated in the broader sense of the term. Discipline is normally strict and children are expected to submit completely to the authority of the teacher. Children also are expected to perform work around the teacher's house and to labor in his fields. This process of socialization also serves a religious purpose. Combined with the memorization of Qur'anic texts, the constantly reinforced expectation to manifest humility toward one's teacher (and to the text of the Holy Qur'an) may eventually be transformed into a more conscious and cultivated understanding of what it may mean to submit oneself to God.

These early educational experiences are essential to the development of the forms of religious devotionalism that have been characteristic of Islam in sub-Saharan Africa for so many centuries. The word "Islam" literally means submission in the Arabic language, and the idealized image of the holy person (usually male) was of a learned, humble, and devout individual totally committed to serving God. The foundations of this religious persona are established in the Qur'anic school. Even that the Qur'an is learned initially by rote without understanding the text contributes to this process, because young students are expected to concentrate fully on how the text is recited. Not only must the recitation be precise and correctly follow one of several accepted versions of chanting, but the Qur'an itself must be accorded the respect that is its due. The overall objective of the Qur'anic school, then, may be described as the inscription of the text of the Qur'an on the student's mind and body.

The relatively few students who continue their studies beyond the Qur'anic school proceed to the 'ilm, or majlis, school. 'Ilm is the Arabic word for knowledge or learning, connoting that, at this stage, students will begin to devote attention to the substantive content of the texts they study. They also undertake the formal study of Arabic language and grammar. 'Ilm school usually begins with small but standard works of theology, for example on the attributes of God and the prophet Muhammad, and jurisprudence, for example on the regulations concerning ablution and prayer. The complexity and sophistication of the texts studied progresses as competence in the Arabic language improves. More advanced students study *hadith*, the collected traditions of the Prophet, other classics of religious law, and ultimately *tafsir*, the interpretation of the Qur'an. It is significant that tafsir is undertaken during the advanced stages of study because only mature scholars are thought to be capable of understanding and properly interpreting sacred text.

Both teaching and learning are highly individualized. There is no formal or standardized curriculum that outlines an obligatory course of study. Most students read the same major texts, although not necessarily in the same order. Also, some variation is to be found between regions where the Maliki legal school predominates (most of western and Sudanic Africa) and where there is a Shaf'i presence, as in parts of eastern Africa.

Advanced students often study with several different teachers in order to benefit from instruction with experts in a particular specialization. They usually study a single book at a time, and the procedure follows closely the way in which the Qur'an was learned. Each day a prepared passage of the book is read with the teacher, who translates if necessary and explains the content. If adequate competence in the book is demonstrated, the teacher can issue a certificate (*ijaza*) authorizing the student to teach it. A student may also repeat the study of a particular book with more than one teacher, thus deepening his knowledge of the subject. It is through this process that future teachers are trained.

During the twentieth century, and especially since the 1940s, Muslim education in Africa has been affected by a wide range of contemporary influences that have increasingly marginalized Qur'anic and 'ilm schools. The challenge has come not only from state-supported forms of secular schooling but increasingly from modernized Islamic educational institutions, referred to as Islamiyya schools or *madrasas* (the Arabic word for school). Madrasas are characterized by their founders' efforts to reformulate the transmission of Islamic religious knowledge in the light of contemporary pedagogical principles.

Perhaps the most visible changes have occurred in the spatial organization of the teaching enterprise. In the Qur'anic schools, children sit on mats on the ground, grouped in a somewhat disorderly fashion around the teacher; in the majlis, the teacher receives his students in the mosque or his own home. The madrasa, however, even in its simplest form, physically resembles a Western-style school. It is organized into classrooms with blackboards, and students sit in rows at desks. There is a single teacher for each class who gives lessons according to a fixed syllabus that every pupil must follow, in contrast to the individual attention given to each child in the Qur'anic or 'ilm school.

In the Qur'anic school, children write out the verses they are learning on a wooden slate with a reed; majlis students do the same, unless they have access to a copy of the book they are studying. In the madrasas, pupils use notebooks, ballpoint pens, and textbooks.

The language of madrasa instruction varies. It is common practice everywhere for children to be taught Arabic as a foreign language from their first year. Students learn to speak, read, and write Arabic at a relatively young age, giving them quicker and more direct access to the sources of Islamic knowledge. This is a significant departure from the Qur'anic practice, in which access to advanced knowledge is limited both by the hierarchical structure of religious scholarship and by students not learning Arabic early in their program of studies.

The differences between the practices of literacy in Qur'anic schools and madrasas have deep ideological ramifications. Emphasis on rote memorization in the Qur'anic schools inculcates the notion that the word in and of itself, as properly recited or written, is both sacred and efficacious, not only for purposes of worship but also, for example, in the form of amulets, for magical uses. In madrasas, on the other hand, literacy is taught as a skill or a tool, and the word is ideally a transparent vehicle for meaning. For pupils in the Qur'anic system, the proper recitation of the sacred word in Arabic is at least as important as its content. For students in madrasas, the content is primordial. Ultimately, the two systems foster different kinds of religious sensibilities in their respective students.

The early pioneers of the madrasa movement sought to employ new pedagogical methods to Islamic religious studies. With time, however, some madrasas began to include secular subjects in their curricula, which is perhaps one of the most significant breaks with the Qur'anic system of education. The majlis and 'ilm schools are vocational only in the sense that they prepare their students for religious roles within society. The objective of the elementary Qur'anic school, however, is to provide the foundations of religious education for children

who would normally be expected to seek their economic livelihood in nonreligious occupations, the training for which would have to be found elsewhere, usually in some form of apprenticeship.

Western-style schooling in the late-twentieth century is explicitly job oriented, and the educational programs of those madrasas that have incorporated secular subjects are designed to prepare their students for contemporary employment in a similar manner as secular schools, albeit with a significant element of religious education included in the syllabus. The burgeoning popularity of madrasas among African Muslims is partly due to failure of state-sponsored schooling. Structural adjustment programs imposed by aid donors on African nations stipulated drastic cuts in government bureaucracy and in social services. State schools suffered from dwindling resources while the population of school-age children mushroomed. Immediately after independence in the 1960s, a major attraction of diplomas from state schools was that they qualified holders for jobs in the civil service. As such jobs became scarcer and less lucrative, Muslim parents of school-age children found themselves increasingly drawn to madrasas. Many devout Muslims were already suspicious that state schools indoctrinated pupils with values, whether secular or Christian, incompatible with Islam. Madrasas isolated pupils from such extraneous ideologies and taught them such skills as simple mathematics and literacy in European languages, invaluable in the rapidly expanding informal sector of the economy.

As the number of madrasa schools has increased, African governments have sought to regulate them. Although many madrasas have retained private status, funded by school fees, others have received both government recognition and financial support, as has been the case for some Islamiyya schools in Nigeria. Even if governments are not officially sympathetic to religious schooling, they have realized that Muslim schools can make a significant contribution to achieving national educational policy goals by providing more school places for children.

For these reasons, Muslim parents often prefer to send their daughters to a madrasa than to a state school. Female enrollment often exceeds 50 percent in the elementary years in madrasas. A much smaller proportion of girls continues into

Graduation ceremonies at the École Franco-Arabe (Franco-Arabic School) in Korhogo, Côte d'Ivoire, 1985. The École Franco-Arabe is a typical example of the new style of Muslim education in Africa. The curriculum includes instruction in French and secular subjects as well as Arabic and religion. During graduation ceremonies, each student reads a passage from Qur'an to assembled guests. PHOTOGRAPH BY ROBERT LAUNAY

secondary education, and only a tiny percentage advance to postsecondary levels. Education is, however, one of the fields in which Muslim women are finding contemporary employment opportunities. Evidence suggests that some women have played an important role in the Qur'anic system, but only rarely have they obtained public recognition and status for their scholarly attainments.

The madrasa system continues to expand in most parts of sub-Saharan Africa and has developed vocational, secondary, and even university-level institutions in different parts of the continent. In some countries—for example, Nigeria—the success of the movement has spawned the demand for programs of Islamic studies in state secondary schools and in universities.

The continuing success of the madrasa movement has been won, in part, at the expense of the Qur'anic system, which nonetheless persists and even interacts with madrasas in some contexts. But the Qur'anic schools and the madrasas are each embedded in different socioeconomic sectors of the contemporary African political economy. The madrasas, whether privately or publicly funded, are fully integrated into the contemporary cash economy. They are often large institutions with modern facilities, their administrations are necessarily highly bureaucratized, and their staff consists of salaried employees. Although their curricula retain an important element of religious content, the driving force in the growth of many of these schools has been to provide their students with an alternative Islamic path to further education and employment.

By contrast, the Qur'anic system is more compatible with a communal socioeconomic base. Most Qur'anic schools are single-teacher operations, organized according to the personal decisions of the teacher. There is no bureaucratic structure and none is required. Qur'anic schoolteachers derive economic benefit from their teaching, usually in the form of gifts from parents and labor from their students, but they do not charge fees as such. No teacher or scholar who operates within this system would ever cite economic gain as a justification for teaching; virtually without exception, they claim to teach in order to serve God. Furthermore, the religious devotionalism nurtured by the Qur'anic system is not found among the aims and objectives of madrasa teaching, where religious knowledge is transmitted as any other subject in a broader educational curriculum.

See also **Aid and Development; Asma'u, Nana; Islam; Labor: Child; Literacy; Literature: Islamic.**

BIBLIOGRAPHY

Boyd, Jean. *The Caliph's Sister: Nana Asmau, 1793–1865, Teacher, Poet, and Islamic Leader.* London: F. Cass, 1989.

Brenner, Louis. *Controlling Knowledge: Religion, Power and Schooling in a West African Muslim Society.* Bloomington: Indiana University Press, 2001.

Cissé, Seydou. *L'enseignement islamique en Afrique noire.* Paris: L'Harmattan, 1992.

Ndiaye, Mamadou. *L'enseignement arabo-islamique au Sénégal.* Istanbul, Turkey: Centre de recherches sur l'histoire, l'art et la culture islamiques 1985.

Reese, Scott S., ed. *The Transmission of Learning in Islamic Africa.* Leiden, the Netherlands: Brill, 2004.

Reichmuth, Stefan. "New Trends in Islamic Education in Nigeria." *Die Welt des Islams* 29 (1989): 41–60.

Sanankoua, Bintou, and Louis Brenner, eds. *L'enseignement islamique au Mali.* Bamako, Mali: Editions Jamana, 1991.

Sanneh, Lamin. *The Jakhanke Muslim Clerics: A Religious and Historical Study of Islam in Senegambia.* Lanham, MD: University Press of America, 1989.

Santerre, Renaud. *Pédagogie musulmane d'Afrique noire: L'école coranique peule du Cameroun.* Montreal, Quebec: Presses de l'Université de Montreéal, 1973.

Sperling, David C. "Rural *Madrasas* of the Southern Kenya Coast, 1971–92." In *Muslim Identity and Social Change in Sub-Saharan Africa,* ed. Louis Brenner. Bloomington: Indiana University Press, 1993.

Wilks, Ivor. "The Transmission of Islamic Learning in the Western Sudan." In *Literacy in Traditional Societies,* ed. Jack Goody. Cambridge, U.K.: Cambridge University Press, 1968.

LOUIS BRENNER
REVISED BY ROBERT LAUNAY

EDUCATION, UNIVERSITY AND COLLEGE

This entry includes the following articles:

OVERVIEW

Higher education has a much older history in Africa than is generally realized. It long antedated the establishment of Western-style universities in the nineteenth century. The history of universities and colleges can be divided into various phases, beginning with the institutions created among some of Africa's ancient civilizations, followed by the institutions that emerged under colonial rule, and finally the postindependence era, a period of unprecedented growth during which the bulk of contemporary Africa's universities were established. Given this long, complicated history, Africa's universities and colleges are remarkably diverse in their structure and organization, mission, and roles.

HIGHER EDUCATION AND UNIVERSITIES IN ANCIENT AFRICA

The origins of higher education in Africa including universities and colleges as communities of scholars and learning can be traced to three institutional traditions: first, the Alexandria Museum and Library; second, the early Christian monasteries; and third, the Islamic mosque universities established following the spread of Islam in northern and western Africa.

The Alexandria Museum and Library was established in the third century BCE in Egypt. It grew to become the largest center of learning in the ancient world. The complex is estimated to have housed more than 200,000 volumes, and supported up to 5,000 scholars and students. This was a large research institution, and many of the leading Egyptian and other African as well as Greek, Roman, and Jewish scholars of the ancient world studied or worked there at some point in their lives. The library gradually declined as buildings were destroyed by fire, its holdings looted in times of warfare, and scholars left due to political instability in the twilight years of the Roman Empire. Alexandria left a rich legacy of scholarship covering a wide range of fields from mathematics and the sciences to philosophy and religion.

It was also in Egypt, one of the earliest centers of Christianity in the world, that monasteries first developed in the third century CE. Tens of thousands of Christians gathered in the monasteries in the Egyptian desert not only to escape the exactions of Roman rule, but also for a life devoted to spiritual contemplation. The monasteries and the monastic orders that regulated them provided important spaces for reflection, writing, and learning. The idea and institution of monasteries spread to other parts of Africa, as well as to parts of the world as far as Britain and Georgia in Europe and Persia and India in Asia, out of which some universities later developed.

This was the case in Ethiopia, for example, where Christianity was introduced in the fourth century CE. Following the establishment of Christianity as a state religion a monastic educational system was introduced that included higher education, which grew from the period of the Zagwe dynasty (1100–1270). Higher education was largely restricted to the clergy and nobility. At the bottom of the system was the *Qine Bet* (School of Hymns), followed by the *Zema Bet* (School of Poetry), and at pinnacle was an institution called *Metsahift Bet* (School of the Holy Books) that provided a broader and more specialized education in religious studies, philosophy, history, and the computation of time and calendar, among various subjects.

It is the third tradition, Islam, which gave Africa its first higher education institutions that have endured to the present. Indeed, Africa claims distinction as the center of the world's oldest Islamic universities and some of the world's oldest surviving universities. The first was Ez-Zitouna madrassa in Tunis founded in 732. Next came al-Qarawiyyin mosque university established in Fez in 859 by a young migrant female princess from Qairawan (Tunisia), Fatima Al-Fihri. The university attracted students and scholars from Andalusian Spain to West Africa. Then in 969 Al-Azhar mosque university was founded in Cairo, the same year that the city was founded, by the Fatimid dynasty from the Maghreb. It came to be regarded as the most prestigious center of Islamic education and scholarship and attracted the greatest intellectuals of the Muslim world, including Ibn Khaldun, the renowned historian who taught there and lived in Cairo from 1382 until 1421 when he died. Another major early Islamic university was Sankore mosque university in Timbuktu, founded in the twelfth century, where a wide range of courses were taught, from theology, logic, astronomy, and astrology to grammar, rhetoric, history, and geography. Islam also arrived early in Ethiopia and

Ethiopian Muslims developed higher education institutions in the form of madrassas

The legacy of the ancient Islamic university for modern Africa is threefold. First, many of the Islamic universities have survived to the present, although they have undergone major changes over the centuries, including the introduction of secular, technical and professional fields of study, processes that accelerated during the course of the twentieth century. This is true of three of the four universities previously mentioned—Sankore being the sole exception. Second, new Islamic universities have been created in several countries from Sudan to Uganda, especially as state control of universities loosened and privatization of higher education gained momentum. Third, as Y. G-M. Lulat argued, "The modern university that was brought to Africa by the colonial powers is as much Western in origin as it is Islamic. The Europeans acquired from the Muslims five elements that would be absolutely central to the foundation of the modern Western university. First, they acquired a huge corpus of knowledge that the Muslims had gathered over the centuries.... Second, they learned rationalism from the Muslims, combined with ... the secular, investigative approach typical of Arab natural science. The third practical element was an elaborate and intellectually sophisticated disciplinary map of knowledge. The Muslims provided the Europeans a body of knowledge that was already divided into a host of academic subjects that was very unfamiliar to the Europeans" (2003, 16). Fourth, the Europeans learned the notions of individual scholarship from the Muslims, and fifth, they borrowed the idea of the college.

HIGHER EDUCATION AND UNIVERSITIES IN COLONIAL AFRICA

The establishment of Africa's modern Western-style colleges and universities can be traced back to the early nineteenth century. They were mostly started by missionaries and largely concentrated in the expanding European settler colonies of South Africa and Algeria, and in Sierra Leone and Liberia newly established territories of African diaspora resettlement. The first was Fourah Bay College founded in Sierra Leone in 1826 and more than three decades later, in 1862, came Liberia College.

The two institutions became the beacons of West Africa's bourgeoning colonial intelligentsia and its nascent nationalism. Edward Blyden, the renowned Pan-Africanist scholar-activist was actively engaged with both colleges. In addition, there was a series of smaller colleges in Liberia, including the College of West Africa (for teacher training) established in 1838, the Hoffman Institute (a vocational college) founded in 1889, and a divinity school founded in 1897. The last two were later amalgamated and upgraded in 1951 into Cuttington University College.

In the meantime, in South Africa segregated institutions were set up beginning in 1829 with the South African College in Cape Town (later the University of Cape Town), which mostly catered to the English settlers. In 1866 a college for the Afrikaner settlers was created called the Stellenbosch Gymnasium (renamed Stellenbosch College in 1881, then Victoria College in 1887, and finally Stellenbosch University in 1918). A small college for Africans, the Lovedale Institution, was created in 1841, which was increasingly modeled on African American industrial and vocational colleges in the United States. Then in 1873 the University of the Cape of Good Hope (renamed the University of South Africa in 1916) was established initially as an examining body before it became one of Africa's and the world's leading distance education providers.

As in South Africa, in French Algeria higher education was largely confined to the settler population. It began with the establishment of the School of Medicine in 1857, followed in 1879 by the creation of four specialized schools of medicine, pharmacy, sciences, letters, and law, which merged to form faculties of the University of Algiers in 1909. Another French colony where higher education started in the late nineteenth century was Madagascar where the Antananarivo Medical Training Academy was established in 1896.

It was not until the twentieth century following the European conquest of the continent that colonial universities spread to the rest of the continent. Two countries escaped colonization, Liberia and Ethiopia, but both sought to modernize their educational systems. In Liberia, where American models were popular, Cuttington University College was created in 1949 with support from the

Protestant Episcopal Church, and Liberia College destroyed by fire in the late 1940s was reconstituted into the University of Liberia in 1951. The brief Italian occupation of Ethiopia from 1935 to 1941 shocked Ethiopia into embarking on a drive for educational modernization. In 1949, the government created Trinity College, which was granted a charter in 1950 under the name of University College of Addis Ababa, and renamed Haile Selassie University in 1961. In the 1950s and early 1960s "a number of small colleges and post-secondary institutions were opened by the Ethiopian Government, often with the assistance of external agencies" (Ajayi 1995, 64).

In colonial Africa, the development of higher education remained limited until after World War II because the authorities were generally suspicious of and opposed to the modern educated African elite and their nationalist demands for equality and freedom, and colonial civil servants feared African competition. Africans seeking higher education were often forced to go abroad including the imperial metropoles themselves. During this period higher education was limited to the British and French empires, virtually none was provided in Belgian and Portuguese Africa.

The first colonial university college in Northern Africa was the Gordon Memorial College founded in the Sudan in 1902, renamed Khartoum University College in 1951 and Khartoum University at independence in 1956. A decade later, in 1912, the Islamic Institute was founded; it became a college in 1924 and was renamed the Omdurman Islamic University in 1965. In Egypt, Cairo University was founded in 1908 despite the opposition of the colonial authorities. It grew to become one of the largest universities in Africa, with a student population at the turn of 2000 of 155,000 students and more than 5,500 faculty members and instructors. In 1938 the university formed a branch in Alexandria, which later became Alexandria University in 1942.

In South Africa, a new era in higher education began with the establishment of the Inter-State Native College in 1916, later renamed the University College of Fort Hare in 1951. Fort Hare became a magnate for not only black South African students but also for African students from across Southern Africa as attested by its list of alumni who include such nationalist leaders and presidents as Nelson Mandela of South Africa, Seretse Khama of Botswana, and Robert Mugabe of Zimbabwe.

In several colonies a number of colleges were founded before the war that functioned largely as secondary schools or technical schools before they were converted after the war into university colleges. Examples from the British colonies include Makerere Government College established in Uganda in 1921 first as a vocational school before it was turned into Makerere University College in 1948. In Nigeria Yaba Higher College was set up in 1932, which served for years as the country's only higher education institution. In Ghana there was the Government Training College, which was formally opened in January 1927 and renamed the Prince of Wales School and College, Achimota. Among its most famous instructors was Dr. Kwegyir Aggrey, the famous educator, and its alumni include Kwame Nkrumah who obtained his teacher's certificate from the college in 1930. These colleges were often affiliated with and provided courses, examinations, and qualifications from British universities.

In the French colonies, higher education was hampered by the preference among both the colonial authorities and the African elites, spawned by the policies and ideology of assimilation, for higher education in the metropole. Moreover, missionary provision of education was quite limited, which undermined the development of primary and secondary education that could feed into higher education. The institutions of higher education established before the war included the French Western Africa Medical Training Institution founded in 1918 in Dakar, the William Ponty School established in Gorée in 1903 that provided some medical training and teacher training, schools of marine engineering and veterinary medicine in Gorée and Bamako, respectively, and a polytechnic also in Bamako.

It was not until the end of World War II that more systematic efforts were undertaken by colonial governments to establish higher education. In the British colonies the new era started with the establishment of university colleges in Nigeria (Ibadan in 1947), Ghana (Legon in 1948), Sudan (Khartoum in 1949 from merger of the Gordon

Memorial College and the Kitchener Medical School), and Uganda (Makerere was upgraded in 1949). In addition, in Kenya the Royal Technical College was established in Nairobi in 1951, and further south the University College of Salisbury was formed in 1953 and renamed two years later as the University College of Rhodesia and Nyasaland. Meanwhile, Fourah Bay became the University College of Sierra Leone. Most of these new or upgraded university colleges served as regional universities and were affiliated with and awarded degrees of the University of London.

After the war French universities set up a few overseas campuses in the colonies. The University of Paris established Institutes of Higher Studies in Tunis in 1945, and together with the University of Bordeaux in Dakar in 1950 and Antananarivo in 1955 that became the University of Dakar in 1957 and the University of Antananarivo in 1960, respectively. In Algeria access to the University of Algiers for Algerians was expanded slightly, although by the time of the Algerian revolution in 1952 there were only 1,000 Algerian university graduates. In the rest of the French colonial empire university education had to await independence.

The Belgians in the Congo followed the French practice as the Catholic University of Louvain established the Lovanium (little Louvain) University Center in 1949, with which it became affiliated in 1954, whereas the state created the Official University in 1956 in Lubumbashi. Lovanium also catered for students from Rwanda and Burundi. In the Portuguese colonies higher education lagged behind until the turn of the 1960s. In Angola, institutions to train priests were formed in 1958 in Luanda and Huambo, followed by the establishment in 1962 of two General University Studies in Angola and Mozambique as branches of the Portuguese university system that were converted in 1968 into the Universities of Angola and Lourenço Marques, respectively.

In the meantime, in South Africa where apartheid had been established in 1948 and Namibia then under South African occupation, higher education became even more racially segregated than before. South African blacks were no longer allowed to attend the "white" universities without securing special government approval and separate universities were created for Africans in the so-called self-governing homelands and for Coloreds and Indians in the major cities. By 1994, the year that ushered in the country's first democratically elected government, there were thirty-six higher education institutions in South Africa consisting of twenty-one universities and fifteen technikons, of which nineteen were for whites, two for Coloureds, two for Indians, and thirteen for Africans. Higher education was far better resourced for whites than for the other races with the Africans at the bottom. In Namibia, college education started as late as 1980 with the establishment of the Academy for Tertiary Education, followed in 1985 by the formation of the Technikon of Namibia, and the College for Out-of-School Training.

GROWTH AND TRANSFORMATION AFTER INDEPENDENCE

Decolonization was a staggered process as African countries got independent at different times, but the bulk of them did so in the 1950s and 1960s. Colonial rule left behind very few universities and colleges; the majority of countries did not even have a single university, so that one of the key challenges for the new independent states was to establish or expand their higher education systems. Also, because the few existing universities were patterned on European models and were rather elitist there was the need to make them more relevant to Africa's developmental needs and sociocultural contexts and more accessible to students of different social backgrounds.

Across Africa the growth in higher education after independence was nothing short of spectacular. The new states embarked on ambitious development programs in which universities were seen as central for national prestige, training a highly skilled labor force, and creating and reproducing a national elite. The new national universities were quite diverse and flexible in their structures and models. On the whole, they were much larger in size than their colonial predecessors, broader in their missions, and they expanded their disciplinary and curricula offerings from the arts and social sciences to include professional fields of study such as business, medicine and engineering, and they incorporated graduate programs.

In 1960, often considered as the year of African independence, there were an estimated 120,000 students in African universities; the number jumped to 782,503 in 1975 and to 3,461,822 in 1995. Similarly, the number of universities grew from less than three-dozen in 1960 to more than four hundred during the same period. In the early 2000s, tertiary education exists in all African countries, although the systems vary enormously in terms of size and levels of development and internal differentiation. For example, in 1995 the largest concentration of university students was in Egypt (850,051), followed by South Africa (617,897), Nigeria (404,969), Algeria (347,410), and Morocco (294,502) (World Bank 2000, 111). Between them the five countries accounted for nearly three-quarters of African students in universities. In contrast, there were twenty-three countries with fewer than 10,000 university students in 1995.

There were also sharp gender differences in terms of access to higher education. While several countries had managed to attain gender parity at the primary and secondary levels by 2000, very few had managed to do so at the tertiary level. The exceptions were Botswana, Lesotho, Swaziland, Namibia, and South Africa. Females made up 34 percent, 22 percent and 12 percent of primary, secondary, and tertiary level students across the continent as a whole. The gender gap also manifested itself in fields of study and faculty distribution. Women were concentrated in the humanities and social sciences, while they were grossly underrepresented in the sciences and most of the professional fields. As multiethnic, sometimes multiracial, and invariably class societies, access to university education in African countries was further differentiated according to ethnicity, race, and class, as well as, in some cases, religious and cultural affiliations. Class became increasingly salient as the African middle classes grew after independence, in many cases thanks to the establishment or expansion of university education itself, and sought to reproduce themselves.

The rapid expansion of education across the continent not only led to a massive improvement in the African human capital stock, it also laid the institutional basis for the social production of African intellectual capacities and communities. But Africa remained the least educated continent in the world, with a tertiary gross enrollment ratio of less than 5 percent, as compared to 10 percent

for the low- and middle-income countries and 58 percent for the high-income countries. The challenges facing African higher education deepened with the imposition in the 1980s and 1990s of draconian structural adjustment programs (SAPs) by the international financial institutions including the World Bank that led to severe government cutbacks in social expenditures, including education, especially for higher education whose rates of social return were deemed by the supporters of neoliberalism to be lower than for primary education.

Thus from the 1980s even as the number of colleges and universities continued to expand, tit became increasingly evident that the higher education system in many countries was in crisis, which was expressed in declining state funding, falling instructional standards, poorly equipped libraries and laboratories, shrinking wages, and faculty morale. Faculty increasingly resorted to consultancies or they became part of the "brain drain" as they sought refuge in other sectors at home or universities abroad. The costs of teaching, research, and Africa's capacity to produce highly skilled human capital was predictably high.

There were other responses to the crisis besides increasing academic labor migration. One was the proliferation of regional research networks, the growth of an academic nongovernmental organization (NGO) sector. Examples include the Dakar-based Council for the Development of Social Science Research in Africa (CODESRIA), and the Nairobi based International Institute of Insect Physiology and Ecology (ICIPE). These organizations and networks provided crucial support for basic and applied research, both individual and collaborative, and offered training, internships, and fellowships to graduate students.

Another response was seen in the explosion in private universities and the privatization of programs and funding sources in public universities, both of which were manifestations of the growing liberalization of African higher education. The private universities can be distinguished in terms of their institutional types (their status—not-for-profit and for-profit; identity—religious and secular; and focus—business, Christian, or Islamic), programs and levels, staffing and funding, and governance structures and regulation. While these universities faced numerous challenges, by the beginning of the

2000s they had begun to outstrip the number of public universities in some countries, a development that profoundly and permanently altered the terrain of higher education.

From the late 1990s African leaders, educators, researchers, and external donors became increasingly aware of the challenges facing African higher education and the need for renewal if the continent was to achieve higher rates of growth and development and compete in an increasingly knowledge intensive global economy. The reform agenda has centered on five broad sets of issues, even if expressions of concern have yet to be matched by the provision of adequate resources. First, the need to examine systematically the philosophical foundations of African universities is widely recognized. Included in this context are issues pertaining to the principles underpinning public higher education in an era of privatization, the conception, content and consequences of the reforms currently being undertaken across the continent, and the public-private interface in African higher education systems.

The second set of issues center on management, how African universities are grappling with the challenges of quality control, funding, governance, and management in response to the establishment of new regulatory regimes, growing pressures for finding alternative sources of funding, changing demographics and massification, increasing demands for access and equity for underrepresented groups including women, and the emergence of new forms of student and faculty politics in the face of democratization in the wider society. Third, there are pedagogical and paradigmatic issues, ranging from the languages of tuition in African universities and educational systems as a whole to the dynamics of knowledge production—the societal relevance of the knowledge produced in African higher education systems and how this knowledge is disseminated and consumed by students, scholarly communities, and the wider public.

Fourth, the role of universities in the pursuit of the historic project of Africa nationalism: decolonization, development, democratization, nation-building and regional integration is under scrutiny. Included in this regard are questions of the uneven and changing relations between universities and the state, civil society, and industry, as well as the role of universities in helping to manage and resolve the various crises that confront the African continent from civil conflicts to disease epidemics including HIV/AIDS. Also, the part universities have played and can play in future to promote or undermine the Pan-African project is of great interest as African states, through the African Union, renew their efforts to achieve closer integration within Africa and between Africa and its diasporas.

Finally, there is the question of globalization, the impact of trends associated with the new information and communication technologies, the expansion of transborder or transnational provision of higher education, and trade in educational services under the General Agreement on Trade in Services (GATS) regime. Critical in this context for Africa is the changing role of external donors from the philanthropic foundations to the World Bank and other international financial institutions and multilateral agencies. The impact of these trends on African higher education and vice-versa are of utmost importance and provide one area of fruitful collaboration between researchers from Africa and other world regions.

See also **Alexandria; Blyden, Edward Wilmot; Cairo; Cape Town; Dakar; Disease: HIV/AIDS, Social and Political Aspects; Egypt, Early; Globalization; Gorée; Khama, Seretse; Luanda; Lubumbashi; Mandela, Nelson; Mugabe, Robert; Nkrumah, Francis Nwia Kofi; Timbuktu; Tunis; World Bank.**

BIBLIOGRAPHY

Addae-Mensah, Ivan. "The Independence of the African University on the Third Millennium." Paper Presented during the African University Day Lecture Series at the University College of Education, Winneba, November 12, 1999.

Ajayi, J. F. Ade, et al. *The African Experience with Higher Education.* London: James Currey, 1995.

Lulat, Y. G.-M. "The Development of Higher Education in Africa: A Historical Survey." In *African Higher Education: An International Reference Handbook,* ed. Damtew Teferra and Philip G. Altbach. Bloomington: Indiana University Press, 2003.

Lulat, Y. G.-M. *A History of African Higher Education from Antiquity to the Present: A Critical Synthesis.* Westport, CT: Praeger, 2005.

Meena, R. "Women's Participation in Higher Levels of Learning in Africa: Interventions to Promote Gender Equity." Paper presented at the Carter Lectures 2001,

"Governance and Higher Education," University of Florida, Gainesville, March 22–25, 2001.

Sall, Ebrima, ed. *Women in Academia: Gender and Academic Freedom in Africa.* Dakar: Codesria, 2000.

Samoff, Joel, and Carrol Bidemi. "The Promise of Partnership and Continuities of Dependence: External Support to Higher Education in Africa." Report presented at the African Studies Association Annual Meeting, December 2002.

Sawyerr, Akilagpa. "Challenges Facing African Universities: Selected Issues." Report presented at the African Studies Association Annual Meeting, December 2002.

Teferra, Damtew, and Philip G. Altbach, eds. *African Higher Education: An International Reference Handbook.* Bloomington: Indiana University Press, 2003.

World Bank. *Higher Education in Developing Countries: Peril and Promise.* Washington, DC: World Bank, 2000.

Zeleza, Paul Tiyambe. *Rethinking Africa's Globalization,* Vol.1: *The Intellectual Challenges.* Trenton, NJ: Africa World Press, 2003.

Zeleza, Paul Tiyambe, and Adebayo Olukoshi, eds. *African Universities in the Twenty-First Century.* Dakar: Codesria, 2004.

PAUL TIYAMBE ZELEZA

CENTRAL AFRICA

Higher education in the thirteen countries constituting Central Africa was greatly neglected or restricted during the colonial period. The colonizing powers—Britain, France, Belgium, and Portugal—were unquestionably responsible for this situation. On the other hand, there was little effective demand from Africans for the provision of higher education locally. The impetus for the establishment of any colleges and universities during the colonial period was compounded of various other pressures acting in isolation or together in different places and circumstances. These colleges and universities were open to anyone, but the opportunities for Africans to meet entry qualifications were practically nil or extremely limited.

In some areas, resident officials and settlers sought higher education for their children locally and influenced the founding of colleges and universities. This occurred with the sizable resident European population in the Katanga copper-mining region of Zaire and the State University of Lubumbashi in 1956, the European settlers in Rhodesia and the University College of Rhodesia and Nyasaland,

and the Portuguese officials and settlers in Angola and Mozambique and the Universities of Luanda (later Agostinho Neto) and Lourenco Marques (later Eduardo Mondlane).

Other institutions were established as a result of religious and ethnic rivalries in the colonizing country, such as the Belgian Catholic Lovanium University in Kinshasa in 1954 and the Protestant University of Kisangani in 1955, while those who believed it was wrong to encourage religion-based universities in Africa were greatly instrumental in the creation of the State University of Lubumbashi. In other cases outside agencies had an influence, as when the United Nations Mandated Territories Commission sought university education for the mandated territories of Rwanda and Burundi and partly dictated the location of the Lubumbashi institution.

In the absence of such special circumstances, however, the colonizing nations did not set out to establish institutions of higher education in their colonies. The Francophone countries in Central Africa without their own university institutions used the Center of Higher Education in Brazzaville, the Congo, set up in October 1959 (renamed the Foundation for Higher Education in Central Africa in 1962). This was facilitated by a cooperation agreement concerning higher education concluded between France and Chad, the Congo, Gabon, and the Central African Republic. These African countries subsequently established their own national universities at various times.

Each colonial power imposed its own pattern of higher education on the institutions it did sponsor. However, the two essential characteristics of the colonial colleges and universities in Central Africa, as elsewhere in the continent, were the search for equivalence with European university standards and the attendant control of both curriculum and personnel, enforced through various forms of tutelage by the British, French, or Belgian universities, as the case may have been. This lack of autonomy clearly denied the African institutions the freedom and flexibility to develop and grow as they wished in response to the real needs of the communities and countries in which they existed. The Universities of Zambia and Malawi, established after independence, avoided this experience by beginning as universities in their own right.

The postcolonial era has witnessed a tremendous development and expansion of higher education in Central Africa. Apart from numerous other institutions, there were some twenty universities in the region in 1996–1997 compared to only four before 1960. Only one country, São Tomé e Príncipe, does not have a university of its own. Thus, the Francophone countries that previously depended on the Foundation for Higher Education in Central Africa have since established their own universities. When the Federation of Rhodesia and Nyasaland broke up in 1963, independent Zambia and Malawi forsook their shared institution in Harare and established their own universities in 1964 (Malawi) and 1965 (Zambia). After their independence in 1975, Angola and Mozambique each reorganized and developed its university for new roles. Many countries in the region now have more than one university. Even so, the demand for higher education continues unabated everywhere, although the ordinary people do not look to colleges and universities for the solution of their everyday problems.

Apart from the Africa-wide problems of declining quality in the face of expanding student numbers, financial constraints, and the stagnation and deterioration of physical resources, the trauma of political turmoil, civil war, and ethnic conflict leading to genocide has attended some of the countries in the region, thereby grossly, even violently, disrupting the life and functioning of colleges and universities there. The most outstanding examples are Zaire immediately after independence, Angola and Mozambique under prolonged internal armed conflict subsequent to independence, and Rwanda and Burundi in the wake of ethnic violence in the 1990s.

Common to all the higher education institutions in the region is the idea that they are essential tools of national development. Indeed, the universities have produced the skilled human resources required to staff and manage public and private institutions, replacing expatriates and permitting growth. The growing perception of the importance of science and technology is reflected in the establishment of new and separate universities of science and technology, such as those in Zambia, Zimbabwe, and Gabon.

Higher education institutions have done remarkably well in indigenizing academic and other senior staff. But gross gender inequality prevails. No woman has ever served as a university vice-chancellor, rector, or president in the region, few women are on the faculty, and the student population is preponderantly male.

See also **Kinshasa; Kisangani; Knowledge: Research; Lubumbashi; Mondlane, Eduardo Chivambo; Neto, Agostinho.**

BIBLIOGRAPHY

Ajayi, J. F. Ade, Lameck K. H. Goma, and Ampah G. Johnson. *The African Experience with Higher Education*. Athens: Ohio University Press, 1996.

Assié-Lumumba, N'Dri Thérèse. *Higher Education in Francophone Africa: Assessment of the Potential of the Traditional Universities and Alternatives for Development*. AFTHR Technical Note 5. Human Resources Division, Technical Department, Africa Region. Washington, DC: World Bank, 1993.

Coleman, James S., and David Court. *University Development in the Third World: The Rockefeller Foundation Experience*. New York: Pergamon Press, 1993.

Conference on the Development of Higher Education in Africa. *The Development of Higher Education in Africa*. Paris: United Nations Educational, Scientific, and Cultural Organization (UNESCO), 1963.

LAMECK K. H. GOMA

EASTERN AFRICA

Higher education in East Africa has undergone profound expansion since the liberalization of the university sector in the early 1990s. Multilateral donors emphasize the twin need for public investment in universities and for generating funding from student fees. Several countries have adopted a technocratic reform agenda. This has focused on strengthening university governance and management, expanding student numbers, legislating the foundation of private universities, promoting cost-sharing (such as spaces for privately-sponsored students), commercializing research, and improving academic salaries. There is growing policy convergence, and throughout the region there is concern about access and equity (especially equal opportunities for women), and interest in sustaining quality. Most governments have up-to-date university information available on the Internet.

Higher education in eastern Africa dates back to the period of British rule. In 1945, the Asquith

Commission was appointed to promote the development of universities in the colonies, and Makerere College in Uganda became the University College of East Africa in 1949. The Royal Technical College, Nairobi, was opened in 1954, and in 1961 the University College of Dar es Salaam was established. Later that year these three colleges became constituent colleges of the University of East Africa, an initiative that lasted until the dissolution of the East African community in 1970. More than thirty-five years later, much has changed. There are more than fifty public and private universities in these three countries alone, most founded during or since the 1990s. There has also been a growth in the number of teacher-training and technical colleges.

KENYA

Kenya has six public universities and one constituent college. In 1970 the University of East Africa was dissolved and the University of Nairobi was created. Its two constituent colleges, Kenyatta University College, established in 1972 to train graduate teachers in all disciplines, and Egerton College, were both granted full university status in the mid-1980s. Moi University was founded at Eldoret in 1984 as a technological university. Founded in 1981, the Jomo Kenyatta College of Agriculture and Technology became an independent university in 1994. Maseno Teachers College became a constituent college of Moi University in 1990. A sixth public university, the Western University College of Science and Technology was similarly registered in 2002. All non-scholarship students in public universities pay fees, often drawing on loans available from the Higher Education Loans Board.

The public universities have been unable to meet the growth in student demand, leading to the creation of fourteen private universities and to many Kenyan students studying in Uganda and Tanzania (estimated to be 30,000 in 1999). In 1985 the Commission for Higher Education was established to coordinate and regulate higher education in Kenya. The total number of students in all Kenyan universities in 2004–2005 was about 92,000, up from 60,000 in 2000.

UGANDA

Makerere University College (1949) became a full-fledged university in 1970. Its student numbers expanded dramatically between 1995 and 2005,

by which point there were almost 30,000 full- and part-time students. It has significant strengths in the arts, social sciences, education, law, agriculture, and medicine. There are three other public universities in Uganda. Mbarara University of Science and Technology, was founded in 1989. Kyambogo University (previously the National Teachers College) and Gulu University were registered in 2003. Three accredited private universities have religious foundations: the Islamic University at Mbale, Uganda Martyrs University, and Nkozi Christian University. A further thirteen private institutions are provisionally licensed by the National Council of Higher Education.

TANZANIA

The University of Dar es Salaam was established in 1970, and is one of eight public universities, including Sokoine University of Agriculture (established in 1984) and the Open University of Tanzania. Total student enrolment in public universities in 2004–2005 was 34,000. By 2006, the Ministry of Higher Education had accredited eleven private universities (total enrolment 3,500) and four technical colleges. Total university enrolment increased from 17,500 in 2000–2001 to 37,500 in 2004–2005, two thirds of whom are men.

ETHIOPIA AND ERITREA

The first college-level institution was the University College of Addis Ababa, established in 1950 at the initiative of the government. The Commission of Higher Education was formed in the early 1960s and led to the creation of a unified Addis Ababa university with the faculty of education (1962), the law school (1963), and the medical college (1965) as constituent institutions. In 1999 it had 12,000 registered students. Along with many technical colleges, there are two other state universities and four private universities.

The University of Asmara (now in Eritrea) was chartered in 1968, and its original goal was to prepare students for university study in Italy. Four thousand students were registered in 2000, and the university has relied heavily on returning Eritrean expatriates to fill faculty vacancies

SOMALIA

Higher education began in 1954 when the Italian government established institutes of law, economics, and social studies as satellites of the University of Rome. These became the nucleus of the Somalia National University after independence. Its operations have been heavily affected by the years of civil war. The private Mogadishu University was founded in 1997. Many Somalis still go abroad, particularly to Italy, for higher education. The number of female students in higher education is negligible.

MAURITIUS, RÉUNION, AND MADAGASCAR

Mauritius has one public university, established in 1965, that offers programs in medicine, education, agriculture, and engineering. In 2000 it had an estimated population of 4,800 students, almost all of Mauritian origin. In a comparatively affluent economy, the university has been unable to accommodate demand, and many students go to either Britain or South Africa for higher education.

The University of Réunion is styled after the French education system. It is the only one on the islands and offers both undergraduate and postgraduate programs in education, journalism, sport science, and social sciences.

Madagascar, which uses both French and Malagasy as the media of instruction in higher education, currently has six public universities—Toliary, Toamasina, Antsiranana, Mahajanga, and Fianarantsoa, and fifteen private universities. Enrolments in the public universities halved during the 1990s.

ISSUES FACING HIGHER EDUCATION IN EAST AFRICA

The public universities in East Africa today face similar dilemmas. Despite talk of institutional transformation, the massive expansion in university places has placed heavy demands on teaching staff, library resources, and academic infrastructure. A concern with quality has led to the creation of national higher education commissions. A determination to address gender inequalities in university participation has led some institutions to introduce controversial affirmative action policies with lower cutoff points for admission for women, often leading to gender tensions on campuses. Privately sponsored students benefit from lower entrance requirements, leading to discrimination by economic status. Retaining high quality academic staff remains a major problem, and many faculty depend on consultancy work to survive. Targeted donor funding circumscribes academics' research topics and agendas. Finally, student unrest and strikes continue to affect universities.

See also **Addis Ababa; Colonial Policies and Practices; Dar es Salaam; Islam; Nairobi.**

BIBLIOGRAPHY

Samoff, Joel, and Bidemi Carrol. *From Manpower Planning to the Knowledge Era: World Bank Policies on Higher Education in Africa.* Paris: United Nations Educational, Scientific and Cultural Organization Forum on Higher Education, Research and Knowledge, Division of Higher Education, 2003.

Sicherman, Carol. *Becoming an African University: Makerere 1922–2000.* Trenton, NJ: Africa World Press, 2004.

Task Force on Higher Education and Society. *Higher Education in Developing Countries: Peril and Promises.* Washington, DC: The World Bank, 2000.

Teferra, Damtew. and Philip G. Altbach, eds. *African Higher Education: An International Reference Handbook.* Bloomington: Indiana University Press, 2003.

CHACHA NYAIGOTTI-CHACHA
REVISED BY DAVID MILLS

NORTHERN AFRICA

In North Africa as in other parts of the Muslim world, a powerful and often flexible tradition of Islamic higher education co-existed with European styles of education from the nineteenth century onward. Many of the students and scholars whom Egypt's Muhammad 'Ali (late 1760s–1849) and other rulers sent to Europe on educational missions from the 1820s onward were graduates of *madrasas*, an Arabic term that simply means "place of study." Many students on these missions had studied at the great mosque-universities of al-Azhar in Cairo, the Qayrawan in Tunisia, and the Qarawiyin (Fez) and Yusufiyya (Marrakesh) mosque-universities (*jami'as*) in Morocco. As elsewhere in the Muslim majority world, these institutions played, and in some cases continue to play, an important cultural and institutional role in the religious, political, and social imagination of Egypt and North Africa.

Historically, a *madrasa* is a place where the young first learn to memorize and recite the Qur'an, but since the early Islamic centuries the term has also signified a place of advanced religious learning. *Madrasas* have produced religious leaders capable of playing major roles in sustaining—and constraining—the authority and legitimacy of rulers. Because of this, Egypt's Muhammad 'Ali in the 1820s confiscated most of the revenues from the pious endowments (*waqfs*), an action that severely reduced the autonomy of men of learning (*'ulama*). Recognizing the prestige and political influence of the learned elite the French, soon after invading Algeria in 1830, destroyed a widespread system of religious education by seizing the *waqf* revenues. Until the 1930s in Morocco, all religious education was funded entirely by *waqf* endowments. The larger endowments were then taken over by the French Protectorate government, although many smaller local *madrasas* continued to be privately funded.

THE *MADRASA* LEGACY IN HIGHER EDUCATION

Madrasa education has often been described as fixed and static, but in the nineteenth century it was dynamic and flexible in a variety of contexts. Religious scholars were often selected by Egypt's Muhammad 'Ali to take part in the educational missions sent to Europe to learn non-religious subjects. In Morocco as well, the nineteenth century was a period of intellectual ferment for scholars and students at its mosque-universities.

Unfortunately, those who knew *madrasa* education best have been its fierce critics. Writing with a first-hand knowledge of the Qarawiyin of eighty years ago, the distinguished French historian and Arabist Évariste Lévi-Provençal (1894–1956) claimed that the domestication of the memory involved in *madrasa* education deadened the student's sense of inquiry to the point that the knowledge and comportment of twentieth-century men of learning could be assumed "without fear of anachronism" to be exact replicas of four centuries earlier. This also reflected the views of many Muslims who received a European-style education, such as the influential Sorbonne-educated Egyptian intellectual (and Minister of Education from 1950–1952), Taha Husayn (1889–1973).

In the latter part of the nineteenth century, mathematics, engineering, and astronomy were reintroduced as taught subjects at the leading mosque-universities throughout North Africa. Men of learning (*'ulama*) associated with the government were in the vanguard of the reform movement, the goal of which was a rededication to the values that made the Islamic community (*umma*) great in the past.

Through personal and collective effort (*ijtihad*) and a renewed discipline of self and society through education and control (*nizam*), the *'ulama* considered that Islamic society would become revitalized and offset the European challenge, at the same time accepting useful contemporary innovations. To achieve this goal, religious scholars were sent on foreign missions to pursue studies, including military science, in Egypt and Europe. For example, Morocco's sultan, Mawlay Hasan I (r. 1873–1894), strongly encouraged scholars imbued with modernist, reform-minded ideologies derived from studies in the Arab East, primarily Cairo and Mecca. He took a personal interest in the debates of the men of learning and encouraged *madrasa* education. His concern for higher religious studies was integrally linked to his efforts to strengthen the precolonial Moroccan government. Although Morocco fell under French colonial rule in 1912, the colonial government relied on *madrasa* graduates for administrative posts as late as the 1940s, when the graduates of colonial schools finally became available in sufficient numbers.

The style of learning exemplified by *madrasa* students continued to be the most popularly respected form of knowledge, shaping the language of politics and political action. Leading graduates played a significant role in legitimizing Morocco's precolonial rulers and also played significant, if not always willing, political roles as spokesmen for the community in times of conflict between royal authority and subjects.

Even after the 1930s, reform-minded *madrasa* graduates played a similar role with colonial authorities, making the Qarawiyin stand out as a hotbed of resistance to various objectionable French-inspired actions. In seeking to limit the influence of the Qarawiyin in 1931 and the Yusufiya in 1939, the French cleverly used the some of the same language as the reformers of the nineteenth century, seeking to bring "order" (*nizam*) to its curriculum and to regulate who was to teach.

REFORM AND RESISTANCE

Colonial authorities throughout North Africa and Egypt consistently diminished the significance of the *madrasa* tradition of higher learning. One reason was that mosque-universities had no formally defined body of students or faculty, administration, entrance or course examinations, curriculum, or unified sources of funds. Teachers in Morocco were not formally appointed, although some held royal decrees (*dahirs*) that provided them with recognition and specified emoluments.

Former teachers in Morocco regarded with amusement the efforts of French colonial officials to determine its "responsible" leaders and to treat it as a corporate entity analogous to a medieval European university. Although teachers did not act as a formal collectivity, several older and respected *shaykhs* served as informal spokesmen for their colleagues. Because of their recognition by the wider community, these individuals also controlled the distribution of gifts given by wealthy or powerful individuals to the community of learning.

As in any educational system with diffuse, implicit criteria for success and where essential skills were not fully embodied in formal learning, the existing elite was favored. Students from wealthy or influential families had initial advantages in securing useful ties, for they continued to be enmeshed in their families' networks of kinship, friendship, and patronage. Reformist *shaykhs* drew students into questioning the relation of Islam to contemporary society. Reformist teachings fit well within the prismatic nature of Islamic learning.

The principal achievement of the reformers of the 1920s and 1930s was to introduce material into lesson circles that men of learning had privately acquired in the houses of the elite: Qur'anic exegesis, theology, history, geography, mathematics, classical poetry, and literature (*adab*). The reformers argued that these topics were as much a part of the religious sciences as the more conventional subjects.

FROM ELITE TO MASS HIGHER EDUCATION

Although mosque-university education was in principle open to all, in practice it was only the established elite who could reach its highest levels. In addition, knowledge of the language of the colonizer or, in the case of Egypt, of the dominant European power, became an important means of achieving success. Yet such institutions were largely confined to an elite few. Cairo University, founded in 1908 and later to become the largest university in Africa (200,000 undergraduates in 2005) remained a selective, elite institution until the 1950s. Likewise, Algeria's Université d'Alger, founded in 1909, accepted only a highly restricted number of "indigenous" students, and Morocco's

first public university—there are sixteen in the early twenty-first century—was founded only in 1958, two years after the end of French colonial rule. At the outset, all these universities and their counterparts elsewhere were accessible primarily to an elite.

For the most part, mass higher education is a recent phenomenon in the Middle East. It began in earnest only in the 1950s in Egypt and later elsewhere. In Egypt the number of primary school pupils more than doubled in the decade following the 1952 revolution. Corresponding increases in secondary and university-level education began a decade later. The timing of educational expansion varies for other parts of the Middle East. Major educational expansion in Morocco, for example, began after independence in 1956, accelerated in the 1960s, and in the early twenty-first century struggles to keep up with the rate of population growth. From 1957 to 1992, university enrollment grew from 1,819 to 230,000 students, and again doubled by 2005. Fifty times as many women in Morocco are being educated today as in the early 1960s.

Yet this expansion of numbers is not matched by educational quality. In Morocco, Arabization programs of the 1970s were implemented before adequate textbooks and qualified instructors were trained. Philosophy was eliminated from the secondary school and university curriculum and replaced with "Islamic Studies," again with unqualified instructors or texts. The "Arabization" encouraged the elite to leave the state secondary and university system for private schools where French (and English) were adequately taught, leaving the public schools to those unable to pay for this alternative. In other North African countries, state-sponsored education has reached a similar impasse. The *Arab Human Development Report* for 2003 heavily criticizes the general failure of Arab educational institutions to encourage the creation of a knowledge-based society and to develop institutional frameworks that allow both women and men to realize their full potential as citizens and contribute more to their societies. Critical thinking exists, but authorities often severely constrain its dissemination and use in public discussion, and the lack of investment in higher education also limits its quality.

See also 'Ali, Muhammad; Cairo; Colonial Policies and Practices; Islam.

BIBLIOGRAPHY

Berque, Jacques. "Dans le Maroc nouveau: Le role d'une université Islamique." *Annales d'Histoire Economique et Sociale* 10 (1938): 193–207.

Eickelman, Dale F. *Knowledge and Power in Morocco: The Education of a Twentieth-Century Notable.* Princeton, NJ: Princeton University Press, 1985.

Eickelman, Dale F. "Mass Higher Education and the Liberal Imagination in Contemporary Arab Societies." *American Ethnologist* 19 (1992): 1–13.

Reid, Donald Malcolm. *Cairo University and the Making of Modern Egypt.* Cambridge, U.K.: Cambridge University Press, 1990.

Vermeren, Pierre. *École, elite et pouvoir au Maroc et en Tunisie au XXe siècle.* Rabat-Ryad, Maroc: Alizés, 2002.

Waardenburg, Jean-Jacques. *Les universités dans le monde arabe actuel.* Paris: Mouton, 1966.

DALE EICKELMAN

SOUTHERN AFRICA

By first decade of the twenty-first century, post-school education in Southern Africa had changed dramatically. The growth and establishment of new public institutions, the closure or conversion of colleges, the combination of institutions through mergers and incorporations, the rise of local and international private higher education, and the emergence of new forms of education delivery, together redefined the landscape of postsecondary education provision in southern Africa.

The historical origins of southern African universities are diverse. Some universities were direct products of colonial rule (Angola, Mozambique); a few were established by white settler regimes (Southern Rhodesia, later Zimbabwe; South Africa); several were direct creations of the post-1948 apartheid government (South Africa, Namibia); some emerged as regional cooperatives (the University of Botswana, Lesotho, and Swaziland); and others were first created to embody the vision of independent, postcolonial states (Zambia, Malawi).

Over time, the older universities in southern Africa redefined their missions, broadened their programs and became more inclusive in response to improved institutional status, changing political

conditions, and new social challenges of developing countries.

The oldest higher education initiatives of the region often started as colleges (e.g., the University of Cape Town started in 1829 as the South African College) or as specialized programs (e.g., training for Catholic priests in Angola in 1958) or as general studies programs which functioned as branches of metropolitan universities (e.g., courses offered since 1962 by Portuguese universities in Mozambique for settler children).

The former high commission territories, Botswana, Lesotho and Swaziland, initially sought to provide university education through regional cooperation; accordingly, the University of Botswana, Lesotho and Swaziland (UBLS) was established in 1963 from the Pius XII Catholic University College based in Roma, Lesotho, with degrees initially awarded by the University of South Africa. In the course of time, each of the three countries established their own, autonomous universities thereby severing the link with apartheid South Africa and creating autonomous institutions in these new states.

Nowhere is the colonial imprint of higher education more firmly established that in the former Portuguese colonies of southern Africa, Angola and Mozambique. In Mozambique, the program of general education studies evolved into the University of Lourenco Marques (1968) and was renamed at independence as Eduardo Mondlane University (1975). In Angola, the Estudos Gerais Univeritarious de Angola was established in 1962 as part of the Portuguese university system; it was later established as the Universidade de Luanda in 1968. Under the postcolonial government, the institution was renamed as the Universidade de Angola 1979 and later as the Universidade Agostinho Neto in 1985, after the first president of the Republic.

While other African governments were establishing the first universities of the *postcolony*, the apartheid government in South Africa was moving in a completely different direction, and established a range of "tribal colleges" (later universities) designed, by race and ethnicity, to train the growing number of postschool black youth outside of the established white universities. The logic of apartheid extended into the Windhoek Academy in South West Africa (present-day Namibia), but in 1993 the new government established the University of Namibia even though many students from this country study in South Africa.

Despite their changing character and mission over time, all these universities bear an unmistakable European character reflected in dominant curriculum orientations, ceremonial rituals such as graduation, preferred languages of instruction (Portuguese and English), and patterns of institutional interaction and partnership with western institutions.

In the course of the 1990s, higher education in southern Africa was to change dramatically a result of three main factors: the growing number of high school graduates, the growing openness of developing markets in the post–Cold War era to the rest of the world, and the declining fiscal capacity of state institutions to respond to increasing demand.

First, there was the explosion of private institutions in countries that for many years had only a single public university. Angola and Mozambique instituted at least five new private universities in each country; Zimbabwe created five new "church-related" universities; and at one time in South Africa at least fourteen transnational universities, such as Australia's Bond and Monash, had applied for registration as private providers of higher education.

Second, there was the reorganization of state institutions for greater efficiency, capacity and equity. This was expressed by creating multi-campuses of a single university in underserved areas (Malawi), expanding program offerings within institutions (Namibia), converting colleges and technical institutions such as polytechnics or technikons into universities of technology (Zimbabwe), closing or merging existing institutions (South Africa), and creating expansive and supporting networks within the region to support student training (Lesotho).

Third, there was the establishment of new kinds of institutions or institutional arrangements to deliver higher education through open and distance learning. While the University of South Africa used to be the major supplier of then correspondence-type education, there are now a host of private and public providers of online and distance education. Sometimes the capacity for distance education is created within existing public institutions (Botswana); sometimes through public-private partnerships (South Africa), and sometimes through the creation of specialized institutions for distance learning (Zimbabwe).

In this dynamism that characterizes higher education in southern Africa in the twenty-first century, old problems remain, new opportunities emerge, and unexpected dilemmas threaten.

The problem of state funding capacity for higher education lies at the root of the malaise of many universities in the region; the symbolic status invested in having a national university has in many cases outweighed the intellectual contribution and productive capacity of these institutions. On the other hand, the end of apartheid has created study opportunities for Southern African Development Community (SADC) students within some of the better resourced and more prestigious South African universities. Rather than continue to channel students at great cost to Europe and North America, some South African universities have become more attractive options. Yet, is there not the real danger that South Africa could become the new metropole as it offers more and more programs within several regional nations and draws thousands of students from their poorer neighbors into South African universities?

See also **Cape Town; Cold War; Colonial Policies and Practices.**

BIBLIOGRAPHY

Jansen, J. D., ed. *Mergers in Higher Education: Lessons Learned in Transitional Contexts.* Pretoria, South Africa: University of South Africa Press, 2002.

Teferra, Damtew, and Philip G. Altbach, eds. *African Higher Education: An International Reference Handbook.* Bloomington: Indiana University Press, 2003.

JONATHAN D. JANSEN

WESTERN AFRICA

The origins of higher-education institutions in West Africa are historically rooted in the French and British colonization of countries, although this subregion already had a tradition of indigenous Islamic education and related institutional formations that predated Western colonization. In both French and British colonies, official policies for the provision of higher education did not exist until after World War II, although public debates on the need for a higher institution of learning had emerged since the 1870s. French and British policies for higher education in their colonized territories were very different in character.

French policy in West Africa, and indeed in its other colonies, has been described as assimilationist, aimed at the creation of a "black elite" with modern metropolitan values and culture. British policy on higher education, by contrast, was understood and interpreted as cultural adaptation, reflecting systematic adjustments to local political and social institutions and the creation of an educated class rooted in their own culture. Notwithstanding the different trajectories, the overriding purpose was remarkably similar across the two colonial systems: higher education was developed to promote the adjustment of local populations to the needs of the colonial powers; it sought the dissemination of modern modes of thought and common patterns of behavior among a select number of Africans whose values and views conformed with—and therefore made it easy for them to serve the needs of—the colonial administration.

The first generation of British universities and colleges in West Africa began with Fourah Bay College (Sierra Leone), established by the Church Missionary Society (CMS) in 1827, followed in the 1930s by Yaba College in Nigeria. Achimota College in Ghana, then called the Gold Coast, was initially established as a higher secondary school but later became a first-class coeducational school and college. Fourah Bay College played a transformative role in higher education in the subregion, as it was its only institution of higher learning for almost a century. Beginning in the 1950s, the Asquith Colleges, including those in West Africa (University College, Ibadan; University College of the Gold Coast), were established. The French established the Institute for Higher Studies in Dakar, Senegal (1950), which was upgraded to a university status around 1957. Both British and French institutions of this era were linked to universities in Britain and France and adhered to the curriculum and traditions of their metropolitan affiliates. Church missionary organizations were very influential in both territories, acting in partnership with metropolitan universities in the West. This influence was particularly evident at the Fourah Bay College in Sierra Leone, where the Church Missionary Society was very effective in expanding the religious focus in the educational curricula.

A significant impact of the Christian mission in West Africa was in the training and leadership development of early West African educators. Notable among them were Edward Wilmont Blyden, a Liberian educator who in the 1870s had begun to call for the expansion of higher education in West Africa, and James Emmanuel Kwegyir Aggrey, an early-twentieth-century Ghanaian educator who graduated from Livingstone College, in North Carolina. Aggrey played a major role in shaping education in sub-Saharan Africa as a member of the Phelps-Stokes Commission, an international task force aimed at improving education for Africans. In 1927, as co-founder and vice-principal of Achimota College, he was instrumental in making the college a coeducational institution, stressing the need for the education of girls.

Most West African countries gained independence in the 1950s and 1960s, and postcolonialism provided a new context for higher education in the subregion. The establishment of higher-education institutions was regarded as a key element in the postcolonial national development project. The most notable feature of that period was the rapid expansion in the number of institutions and students, as countries rapidly strove to train a cadre of young African professionals to fill the void left by foreign civil servants who had served in the colonial administration. The primary purpose of these universities was to graduate political officials, agriculturists, government administrators, secondary-school teachers, and health personnel.

Another impetus for higher educational expansion was economic development. Postcolonial leaders in West Africa and elsewhere on the continent saw modern education as the single most important lever for economic growth, expecting it to contribute to national development efforts by helping Africans develop and manage their resources and thus contribute to alleviating poverty among the majority. National governments accordingly invested substantial resources in the establishment and development of higher-education institutions with the expectations that they would serve the public interest by providing the necessary leadership for material and social development.

The postcolonial environment also afforded a degree of autonomy that had not been present in the earlier period, which encouraged some governments to look beyond the British and French models of higher education. Such was the case with the University of Nigeria, Nsukka, and Njala University College in Sierra Leone, established in the 1960s along the lines of the land-grant university model in the United States. For most countries in the subregion and elsewhere, however, the vestiges of the colonial curriculum model—liberal arts and the basic sciences—remained, with higher education catering to a relatively small number of students. Admission was based on examination results and courses were related to the requirements of the civil service. Student populations were predominantly male. Studies were full-time and fully funded by the state. University management was highly centralized and hierarchical.

SOCIOPOLITICAL CONSEQUENCES AND REACTIONS AND INDEPENDENT GOVERNMENT POLICIES

Higher-education institutions in West Africa, as in other parts of the region, have historically been shaped by the transformations in the social and political economies of the nation-states and local communities in which they are embedded. After independence, concerns about the role of higher education in national development gradually increased, in part fueled by a growing impatience with the liberal arts and basic science emphasis of higher institutions inherited from the colonial era. There were increasingly strong sentiments among emerging African educators that higher-education institutions should contribute more directly to the social, cultural, and economic development of their region. The notion of the "developmental university" and the relevancy of education to the region's development goals emerged in this context.

Early optimism about higher education's developmental role in West Africa and other parts of the region was tempered in the 1970s and 1980s by the virtual collapse of most national economies in these decades following changes in the international terms of trade and subsequent structural adjustment policy implementations. The economic crisis led to significant declines in the real value of university budgets. Declines were even more significant in previous French colonial (Francophone) countries than elsewhere. The states retreated from supporting the universities, leading to major student protests in many countries in the subregion. In contrast to the early independence period, many governments, weakened by ongoing economic crisis, came to see the university as a threat to internal stability. Higher-education institutions in this era experienced dramatic deterioration in both public and financial support. Universities and colleges struggled to redefine and reposition themselves in the emergent social conditions.

INTERNATIONAL INFLUENCES AND INVOLVEMENT

Postindependence West Africa witnessed growing international influence in higher education policy through expanded involvements of agencies and institutions from countries such as the United States, Union of Soviet Socialist Republics, Sweden, China, and Canada, although these relationships waned significantly at the height of the economic crisis in the mid–1980s. Rekindled international interest in the early twenty-first century has been manifested through a variety of partnership modes with higher education institutions worldwide. International agencies such as UNESCO and lending institutions such as the World Bank, as well as private foundations (including the Carnegie Foundation, the Rockefeller Foundation, and the Ford Foundation) have expanded their programs in West Africa, funding research that has increasingly shaped higher educational policy in the region. Notwithstanding these international and private influences on higher education in post-independence Africa, West Africa has remained unique in the low number of private colleges compared to those in Eastern, Southern, and Central Africa.

See also **Aggrey, James; Christianity; Dakar; Islam; Prophetic Movements; Postcolonialism.**

BIBLIOGRAPHY

Samoff, Joel, and Carrol Bidemi. "The Promise of Partnership and Continuities of Dependence: External Support to Higher Education in Africa." *African Studies Review* 47, no. 1 (2004): 67–133.

Sawyerr, Akilakpa. "Challenges Facing African Universities: Selected Issues." *African Studies Review* 47, no. 1 (2004): 1–59.

UNESCO. *UNESCO and the United Nations Economic Commission for Africa: The Development of Higher Education in Africa … Report of the Conference, September 3–12, 1962.* Paris: UNESCO, 1963.

Whitehead, C. "Education in British Colonial Dependencies, 1919–1939: A Re-appraisal." *Comparative Education* 17, no. 1 (1981): 71–80.

MARGARET M. KROMA

EGYPT, EARLY

This entry includes the following articles:
PREDYNASTIC
OLD AND MIDDLE KINGDOMS
NEW KINGDOM
LATE AND PTOLEMAIC
ROMAN AND BYZANTINE
ISLAMIC

PREDYNASTIC

In one of the most important developments in the history of Africa, the first steps toward food production were initiated in its northeast corner. The area, now occupied by Egypt and Sudan, was the arena for initial attempts to keep cattle from an African stock. It was also the area that hosted the beginnings of cultivating cereals and of herding sheep and goats introduced from Southwest Asia.

Cattle keeping became prominent in the tenth millennium BP (Before Present). Several communities in the eastern Sahara began to experiment with the intensive utilization of local grasses, including millet and sorghum. By 7,800 years ago, sheep and goats, originating in Southwest Asia, began to appear in Northeast Africa in sites that are geographically wide apart. The remains of these animals have been found along the Red Sea coast and in several places in the Eastern Sahara. By 6,800 years ago, village communities that cultivated wheat and barley, grains also from southwest Asia, and kept cattle, sheep, goats, and pigs became evident along the margin of the Nile Delta.

These beginnings of agriculture, which eventually became the most influential elements in the African economy over the next millennia, were apparently due to climatic upheavals that punctuated the wetter climate that prevailed as the last Ice Age ended. African communities along rivers, lakes, and favorable tropical and subtropical habitats continued to pursue hunting and food gathering, with the addition of fishing and fowling. But in semi-desert areas of Southwest Asia, stressful climatic conditions made it better to begin exploiting and domesticating certain food resources (such as sheep, goats, wheat, and barley). By the ninth millennium BP, communities began to subsist more heavily on food production, instead of hunting and foraging. A short episode of global cooling 8,200 years ago, and a period of unsettled climatic conditions that followed until 6,800 years ago, were crucial in the dispersal of domesticated plants and animals from their original habitat in Southwest Asia to Northeast Africa.

Between 7,000 and 5,000 years ago, successive social, political, and economic transformations ultimately led to the rise of a state society in Egypt. The foundation of this transformation was the inception of farming in the Nile Valley and the Delta.

The earliest evidence of farming communities in the Nile Valley dates to 6,800 BP at Merimde Beni Salama in the Delta (Lower Egypt). In Upper Egypt (southern Egypt), the earliest farming communities appeared in the Badari region about 6,400-6,200 BP. Sites in this region contain a ceramics suite referred to as the Badarian, with definite African connections. In Upper Egypt, distinctive pottery types are also used to identify three successive ceramic assemblage zones: Nagada I (or Amratian), 5,800 to 5,500 BP; Nagada II (or Gerzean), 5,500 to 5,300 BP; and Nagada III (Protodynastic), 5,300 to 5,000 BP. In the Delta, a zone called Maadi-Buto predated late Nagada II. Pottery sequence and other archaeological remains in Upper Egypt document a continuous cultural development.

The political transformation from farming communities to a state society in Egypt was primarily a result of successful alliances between neighboring villages in combating the difficulties of early agriculture. Nile floods were highly erratic. The earliest farmers were faced with droughts, over-flooding, and destruction of natural dikes. Initially, bonds of kinship and social ties provided a basis for intercommunity food exchange, to gain food security. Shrines and ceremonial centers emerged to enhance group solidarity. Subsequently, alliances led to the emergence of chiefdoms that were later consolidated and expanded to form petty kingdoms and principalities. This stage was achieved in Nagada II, as indicated by the tomb of a prominent chief or king at Hierakonpolis, dated about 5,500 BP.

The emergence of kings and chiefs was linked to the development of a belief in cosmic forces responsible for the generation (birth) and regeneration (resurrection) of life. Cows, already sacred in the African Sahara as indicated by elaborate cow burials, became life-giving deities, and kings became identified with bulls. The iconography of deities on decorated Nagada II pottery showed the cow goddess at the top of the palette associated with Narmer (5,000 BP), the founder of a unified Egypt. Cows eventually came to represent many of the earliest Egyptian goddesses, who were symbols of birth, nurturing, and protection. Local political centers in the Nile Valley were, in addition, identified with local cult standards and centers. Many of these centers developed into towns with large cemeteries.

Both at Nagada and at Hierakonpolis, the cemeteries initially included a few large, elaborate tombs with numerous objects in the grave, indicative of a powerful and wealthy elite. The elite later separated their burial grounds from the main cemeteries, and the tombs became progressively larger through time. This was a prelude to the building of monumental mastabas and pyramids that served as the tombs of the pharaohs during the Old Kingdom.

The production of religious objects and items for the elite stimulated both trade and crafts. Maadi, a site at the apex of the Delta, was a station for overland trade with the Near East, while Buto, eventually overshadowing Maadi, handled sea trade. Hierakonpolis in the south was a center for trade with Nubia. Copper and gold jewelry, alabaster vases and other objects made from fine rocks and minerals, gemstones, and faience were common grave goods in the tombs of the elite.

By about 5,400 BP, Nagada and Hierakonpolis were amalgamated into a single kingdom under rulers from the south. Later they extended their power to Abydos, further north. Simultaneously, local Delta cultures were being replaced by elements from Upper Egypt during the late Nagada II period. This is well illustrated by burial customs

Fragment of the Bull Palette from Abydos, late Naqada II Period (c. 3200-3100 BCE: Louvre Museum E.11255). Such palettes, nominally used for the grinding of pigments for make-up, were common during the late Predynastic times. Many have implicit or explicit references to warfare. Here, the bull almost certainly represents a king attacking enemy cities, possibly before the unification of Egypt during the 1st Dynasty. PHOTOGRAPH BY AIDAN DODSON

and pottery at Minshat Abu Omar in the East Delta. Subsequently, by approximately 5,200 BP, the first steps toward a politically unified Egypt were undertaken, as shown by the tombs of great kings at Abydos. The unification, which led to a single nation-state under Narmer (5,000 BP), was the culmination of political alliances and military confrontations.

The development of kingship was closely linked with a religious ideology, which combined elements from different districts in Egypt. In historical times, every king was identified with the god Horus, represented by a falcon. Osiris, a god who was considered the first king of Egypt, was Horus's father. Horus was also affiliated with Isis, a goddess who retained the role of the predynastic cow goddess as a nurturing and protective mother. The political and religious development of predynastic Egypt is among Africa's great contributions to the world. Following the indigenous development of pastoralism in the Sahara, settlers in the Nile Valley undertook a series of actions that concluded in the rise of dynastic Egyptian civilization. The developments in Egypt were also enriched by a continuation of cultural interactions between the Nile Valley settlers and their neighbors. Many similarities between Egypt and other African societies are related to this common past, a common heritage of which Egypt is an integral part. The cultural continuity with an African substratum and the strong historical cultural interactions between Egypt and other African societies clearly demonstrates that Africa was the cradle of the Egyptian civilization.

See also **Agriculture: Beginnings and Development; Archaeology and Prehistory; Ceramics; Climate; Death, Mourning, and Ancestors; Kings and Kingdoms; Metals and Minerals; Nubia; Political Systems: Chieftainships; Prehistory.**

BIBLIOGRAPHY

Hoffman, Michael A. *Egypt before the Pharoahs: The Prehistoric Foundation of Egyptian Civilization.* Austin: University of Texas Press, 1991.

FEKRI HASSAN

OLD AND MIDDLE KINGDOMS

The transition from predynastic culture to pharaonic civilization took place during the Early Dynastic Period, c. 3000–2686 BCE. During this period, the kings of the First and Second Dynasties ruled over a united Egypt from a capital they established at Memphis. A central administration and hierarchical society, dominated by the king, was solidified, and the supremacy of the king can be seen in the ever-larger royal funerary complexes built at Abydos.

The Old Kingdom that followed was the first great flourishing period of pharaonic civilization. The Old Kingdom consisted of Dynasties 3 through 6, and lasted from approximately 2686 to 2125 BCE. An intervening period of approximately 140 years, in which there was decentralization, civil war, and famine, separated the Old Kingdom from the Middle Kingdom, the second great period of pharaonic civilization. This chaotic era, called the First Intermediate Period, ended when a Theban king, Nebhepetre Mentuhotep (c. 2055–2004 BCE) forcibly reunited Upper and Lower Egypt. This began the Middle Kingdom, which lasted from about 2055–1650 BCE and consisted of the late Eleventh Dynasty down through the Thirteenth Dynasty.

THE OLD KINGDOM

The rule of the king was absolute and based on his divinity as descendent of the sun god Re and son of Osiris, the king of the underworld. The king became divine at the time of his coronation, and periodic rituals renewed his divinity. The job of the king was to maintain cosmic order, and the king was high priest in the cult of every god. Under the king, an official called the vizier was in charge of all governmental and judicial matters and was assisted by a circle of high officials. In the earlier part of the Old Kingdom, these were all relatives of the king. Officials called nomarchs, who ruled a nome (administrative district), paralleled the central administration on the local level. The nomarch's main job was the collection of taxes in the form of grain, or human labor. The nomarchs also conscripted soldiers when necessary; in the Old Kingdom troops were used mainly in expeditions to quarries or foreign lands. Egyptians traveled to Byblos in Lebanon for cedar, the land of Punt (usually accepted as the coast of Somalia or Eritrea) for incense and myrrh, and Nubia and Sudan for ebony, leopard skins, elephant tusks, and other exotic goods. Harkhuf (c. 23rd century BCE), a Sixth Dynasty nomarch of Elephantine in the south of Egypt, made four expeditions south into Lower Nubia and also the land of Yam in the Dongola Reach. On his last trip he brought back a dancing pygmy for King Pepy II (c. 2278–c. 2184 BCE) who, at that time, was about eight years old. The king sent a letter to Harkhuf that the nomarch had copied on the façade of his tomb, entreating him to take care of this pygmy.

Pyramid building was a prominent characteristic of the Old Kingdom. The first pyramid was the Step Pyramid at Sakkara, built by King Djoser (c. 2667–2640 BCE) in the Third Dynasty, the first example of a pyramid and also of monumental architecture in stone. The Step Pyramid Complex developed out of the earlier royal burials at Abydos, where a squared mound covered the burial and a separate, large, rectangular enclosure provided space for royal rituals. By the Fourth Dynasty, the stepped pyramid had developed into a true pyramid, as seen best in the famous pyramids at Giza.

In the Fifth Dynasty, pyramid building continued, although on a much reduced scale. Rather than a massive pyramid protecting the king's body for his afterlife, each Fifth Dynasty king also built a sun temple complex, connecting his afterlife with the eternal cycle of the sun. By the time of the Sixth Dynasty, pyramid texts carved in the burial chambers of the royal pyramids ensured that the king awakened from death and joined the gods in heaven.

THE MIDDLE KINGDOM

The Twelfth Dynasty, a line descended from Amenemhet I (c. 1985–1956 BCE), who usurped the throne but was later assassinated, makes up the greater part of the Middle Kingdom. A new royal residence was built south of Memphis at Itja-tawy, close to the Fayum. The kings of this dynasty built most of their pyramids in this area, and also reclaimed large tracts of agricultural land in the Fayum. Kings were still interred in pyramids, but the structures began to be constructed of mud brick cased in stone. There was a resurgence of literature and art in the Twelfth Dynasty, although much of it served as propaganda for the king.

King Senusret I (d. 1926 BCE) built the earliest temple of the god Amun at Karnak, as well as an exquisitely carved processional chapel, the White Chapel. This king also began a chain of fortresses on the open plain by the river in the northern part of Lower Nubia. These forts guarded the routes that left the river, and served as administrative and trade centers. By regnal year five, Senusret I had constructed the massive fortress of Buhen, complete with ditches, glacis, barbicans, and ramparts; perhaps as many as three hundred soldiers were garrisoned there.

Senusret III (c. 1956–1911 BCE) completed the line of fortresses down through the rugged reaches of southern Lower Nubia to the end of

Obelisk of King Senusret at Matariya, ancient Heliopolis. This obelisk is almost the sole standing element of the great temple of the sun god Ra in the city. It stood with its now-fallen mate in front of the gateway of the temple. PHOTOGRAPH BY AIDAN DODSON

Desert fortress at Buhen, Egypt. The ancient Egyptian settlement of Buhen's fortress was likely constructed during the rule of Senusret III, around 1860 BCE. Evidence at the site suggests the Egyptians stayed there for about 200 years, until they were forced to move due to immigration from the south. © ROGER WOOD/CORBIS

the Second Cataract. At the fortress of Semna, Senusret III set up a boundary stela boasting: I have made my boundary farther south than my father's. His group of forts guarded the shipping route, and the plan of each had been modified to fit the rocky terrain along the river's edge.

These forts not only protected Egypt's southern border but also secured the trade route up through Lower Nubia to Egypt. The indigenous population of Lower Nubia at this time, called the C-Group, seems to have been pastoral and posed no physical threat. Perhaps it was the more distant Kerma culture, located above the Third Cataract, that was a growing threat, for when Egyptian control over Lower Nubia waned at the end of the Middle Kingdom, the Kerma culture moved north and seized these forts.

See also **Architecture: Monumental; Death, Mourning, and Ancestors; King Lists and Chronologies; Kings and Kingdoms; Namibia.**

BIBLIOGRAPHY

Adams, William Y. *Nubia: Corridor to Africa.* London: Allen Lane, 1977.

Edward, David. N. *The Nubian Past: The Archaeology of the Sudan.* London: Routledge, 2004.

Kemp, Barry J. "Old Kingdom, Middle Kingdom and Second Intermediate Period in Egypt." *The Cambridge Ancient History of Africa*, vol. 1. Cambridge: Cambridge University Press, 1982.

Lichtheim, Miriam. *Ancient Egyptian Literature*, vol. 1. *The Old and Middle Kingdoms.* Berkeley: University of California Press, 1973.

O'Connor, David, and Andrew Reid, eds. *Ancient Egypt in Africa.* Portland, OR: Cavendish, 2003.

Shaw, Ian, ed. *The Oxford History of Ancient Egypt.* Oxford: Oxford University Press, 2000.

Trigger, Bruce G. *Nubia under the Pharaohs.* London: Thames and Hudson, 1976.

Williams, Bruce B. "Serra East and the Mission of Middle Kingdom Fortresses in Nubia." In *Gold of Praise: Studies on Ancient Egypt in Honor of Edward Wente.* Chicago: Oriental Institute, 1999.

LISA SABBAHY

NEW KINGDOM

The New Kingdom (the Eighteenth through Twentieth Dynasties, c. 1550–1070 BCE) is one of the best-known periods of Egyptian history. Marked by extensive interaction with the country's neighbors, the period is defined by diplomatic interaction with equals, the military domination of client states, and imperialist domination of subject peoples. Among the equals were the Mesopotamian states of Assyria and Babylon, the north Syrian polity of Mitanni, and the Hittites of Anatolia; the clients were many of the small city-states of Syria-Palestine. In contrast, Nubia—the southern part of modern Egypt and the northern part of modern Sudan (anciently referred to as Kush)—was the subject of wholesale domination and attempted absorption.

During the Old and Middle Kingdoms, much of Nubia had been exploited for its mineral resources, with a system of frontier fortresses-cum-trading posts established around the Second Cataract in Twelfth Dynasty times. During the Second Intermediate Period, however, an independent Nubian state, known as the Kerma Culture, had been established and had at least once carried out a deep military penetration of Upper Egypt, as recorded in an inscription at El-Kab found in 2003.

The Kushites were allied with the Palestinian Hyksos kings, who ruled Lower Egypt during c. 1650 to 1550 BCE, and were thus attacked as part of the Theban Seventeenth Dynasty's liberation of Egypt from the Hyksos. Egyptian forces were successful, seizing the whole of Nubia and installing its own viceroy who reported directly to the Egyptian pharaoh. Nubia played an important role in Egypt's economy, not only because of its own reserves of gold and produce, but also because it served as a conduit for trade to and from central and southern Africa, including the provision of slaves. In addition, free Nubians served in the Egyptian police force, becoming so ubiquitous that the name of their tribe, the Medjay, became synonymous with the word "policeman."

In the wake of the expulsion of the Hyksos by the Eighteenth Dynasty founder, Ahmose I, Egypt foreign policy became much more aggressive, with most kings during the first part of the dynasty conducting military campaigns into Syria-Palestine. As a result of the expeditions of Thutmose I and III, a network of client-states was created, stretching up into the northern part of Syria.

Trading activities included expeditions to the country known as Punt. Scholars have debated its exact location, but it certainly lay on the African shore of the Red Sea, most probably comprising parts of eastern Sudan, Eritrea, and Ethiopia. The country was a source of many native exotica, as well as material traded from further inland. A major mission to Punt took place under the female king Hatshepsut, which was commemorated in her mortuary temple at Deir el-Bahari, Western Thebes.

The proceeds of this trade, together with the tribute exacted from the vassal-states, combined with the resources derived from Nubia to provide for a buoyant Egyptian economy. This abundance allowed for large-scale state building activity, including the construction of such great temples as those of Amun at Thebes and Ptah at Memphis, together with the elaborate royal tombs in the Valley of the Kings at Western Thebes. The richness of the material found in tombs of the period gives a clear indication of the prosperity of the times.

As well as those in Egypt, major temples were also erected in Nubia, as far south as Gebel Barkal (ancient Napata), which had become the capital

Statue of Thutmose III from the Temple of Karnak, c. 1479–1425 BCE. Thutmose III was responsible for the greatest extension of Egypt's political dominion, from northern Syria to the 4th Cataract of the Nile in Sudan. © SANDRO VANNINI/ CORBIS

of the whole Nubian province. Further north, notable monuments included the temple at Soleb, built by Amenhotep III, and the rock-cut sanctuary at Abu Simbel, the work of the Nineteenth Dynasty king Ramesses II. These marked settlements intended to cement Egyptian authority in the area,

Village of Deir el-Medina at Western Thebes, home of the workmen who built the royal tombs of the New Kingdom pharaohs in the nearby Valley of the Kings. Begun by Thutmose I, it was occupied until the latter part of the 20th Dynasty, and documents from the village are an important source for our understanding of society during the New Kingdom. The slopes in the foreground housed the workmen's tombs. Their places of worship were at the far left. PHOTOGRAPH BY AIDAN DODSON

which was reinforced by the co-option of local princes into the Egyptian administration, who adopted Egyptian names and mores. Late in the Eighteenth Dynasty, King Akhenaten carried out a short-lived religious revolution, in which the ancient pantheon of deities was replaced by a single sun god, the Aten. Soon after his death, however, orthodoxy was restored under Tutankhamun, and Akhenaten was written out of history. With the extinction of the old royal line soon afterward, a series of three army generals took the throne, the last of whom, Ramesses I, founded the Nineteenth Dynasty.

The first part of the new dynasty saw renewed military activity in Syria-Palestine by Sethy I and Ramesses II, where the Hittites threatened Egyptian hegemony. After the Battle of Qadesh, however, there was a rapprochement, culminating in a peace treaty between the two powers, which henceforth became allies. The seven-decade reign of Ramesses II saw public works on a spectacular scale; nevertheless, his siring of more than one

hundred children may have sown the seeds of family conflict that was to bring his dynasty to a premature end.

The latter years of the Nineteenth Dynasty and the following Twentieth Dynasty saw a gradual decline in Egypt's standing, probably beginning with the civil conflicts that followed the death of Ramesses II's successor, Merenptah. The collapse of a number of Near Eastern states through the invasion of the Peoples of the Sea from the Aegean region during the latter part of the twelfth century BCE also contributed to the gradual disintegration of Egypt's northern areas of control, although two separate attempted invasions of Egypt itself were repulsed by Merenptah and Ramesses III, second king of the Twentieth Dynasty. Internal economic problems gathered pace later in this dynasty, giving rise to law-and-order issues that included the wholesale robbery of tombs at Western Thebes and a potential division of the kingship between the north and south of Egypt in the early tenth century.

Egyptian control of Nubia also came to an end around the same time through a civil war between the Viceroy of Nubia and the High Priest of Amun at Thebes. This conflict cut Egypt off from its principal source of gold and African produce, further contributing to its economic and political difficulties. The fallout from this strife led to an institutionalized north-south division during the succeeding Twenty-First Dynasty (beginning the Third Intermediate Period), with a king, nominally of the whole of Egypt, reigning in the northern city of Tanis, but a quasi-royal high priest and army leader controlling most of Upper Egypt from Thebes.

See also **Death, Mourning, and Ancestors; King Lists and Chronologies; Kings and Kingdoms; Nubia; Slave Trades.**

BIBLIOGRAPHY

Cline, Eric H., and David O'Connor, eds. *Thutmose III: A New Biography.* Ann Arbor: University of Michigan Press, 2006.

Dodson, Aidan, and Dyan Hilton. *The Complete Royal Families of Ancient Egypt.* London and New York: Thames and Hudson, 2004.

Freed, Rita E., et al., eds. *Pharaohs of the Sun: Akhenaten, Nefertiti, and Tutankhamen.* Boston: Museum of Fine Arts, 1999.

Kitchen, Kenneth A. *Pharaoh Triumphant: The Life and Times of Ramesses II, King of Egypt.* Warminster: Aris and Phillips, 1982.

Kozloff, Arielle P., and Betsy M. Bryan. *Egypt's Dazzling Sun: Amenhotep III and His World.* Bloomington: Indiana University Press, 1992.

Manley, Bill. *Penguin Historical Atlas of Ancient Egypt.* London: Penguin Books, 1996.

Murnane, William J. *The Road to Kadesh: A Historical Interpretation of the Battle Reliefs of King Sety I at Karnak.* Chicago: University of Chicago Press, 1990.

Redford, Donald B. *Egypt, Canaan, and Israel in Ancient Times.* Princeton, NJ: Princeton University Press, 1992.

Shaw, Ian, ed. *The Oxford History of Ancient Egypt.* Oxford: Oxford University Press, 2000.

Trigger, B. G., et al. *Ancient Egypt: A Social History.* New York: Cambridge University Press, 1983.

Vernus, Pascal. *Affairs and Scandals in Ancient Egypt,* trans. David Lorton. Ithaca, NY: Cornell University Press, 2003.

AIDAN DODSON

LATE AND PTOLEMAIC

From the Late to Ptolemaic Period (c. 747–30 BCE), Egypt came under the direct and indirect control of other states, to the south (Kush), to the northeast (Assyria and Persia) and to the north (Macedonian and Greek). The changing political circumstances are reflected in the ruling houses (dynasties) of Egypt and cultural and economic life of the land.

Egypt was ruled by the Kushite (a state to the south of Egypt based at Napata in modern Sudan) king Piankhy (Piye) from circa 747–716 BCE. He saw himself as the upholder of the cult of the Egyptian god Amun who also had a temple in the Kushite capital at Gebel Barkal (Napata). Piankhy was the first of the Egyptian ruling Dynasty 25 (c. 747–656 BCE) who merged their African background and respect for Egyptian culture successfully. They achieved political control in southern Egypt through the office of the God's Wife of Amun and their economic power was based on control of the Nubian gold mines and agricultural produce from the Nile Valley to the south of Egypt. King Tanwetamani, however, could not withstand the first Assyrian invasion of Egypt in 671 BCE. The sacking of the great Egyptian cities and temples in a second Assyrian invasion by Assurbanipal in 663 BCE effectively ended Kushite power in Egypt. The Kushite kings retreated back to Gebel Barkal and ultimately to Meroe, beyond the confluence of the White and Blue Niles.

The Egyptians regrouped under the northern Delta leaders of whom King Tefnakhte of Saïs and his successors proved to be the strongest. Under King Necho and then King Psamtek I, Dynasty 26 (c. 664–525 BCE) reestablished a united Egypt with a ceremonial center at Saïs and administrative control based at Memphis, both in northern Egypt. The religious power and economic estates of the temple of the god Amun at Thebes in southern Egypt were brought under Saïte control by "marrying" Saïte princesses to the god Amun. Their long-lived line of God's Wives ensured a stable dynasty of dedicated god's servants loyal to the north of Egypt, but with economic control of southern Egypt. In addition, strategically placed military forts controlled the eastern Egyptian Delta and the northern river mouths on the Mediterranean coast. A Greek trading center was

Ruins of the temple of Amun at San el-Hagar (Tanis), the capital of Egypt for much of the Third Intermediate Period. Much of the stonework for the city was brought from Piramesse, the resident city of the late New Kingdom, which had been abandoned when the adjacent channel of the Nile Delta dried up. Its place was taken by San, which continued to be a significant city into Roman times. PHOTOGRAPH BY AIDAN DODSON

established at Naukratis in northwestern Egypt circa 660 BCE to effect the control of trade between the Greek mainland and colonies and Egypt. The army was strengthened by the use of Ionian and Carian mercenaries, some of whom settled in Egypt. In order to pay the foreign soldiers coinage was introduced for the first time in Egypt, creating the potential for a Mediterranean economic system based on currency. The Persian invasion of Egypt in 525 BCE put an end to this successful dynasty, which had introduced a new administrative and religious script, demotic, and used an artistic renaissance to enhance the legitimacy of the northern kings.

Egypt became a province of the Achaemenid Empire based in Persia (Iran) from circa 525 BCE and, although later Egyptian tradition regarded the Persian rulers as cruel unbelievers, it seems that King Cambyses (c. 525–522 BCE) ensured the continuation of the traditional Apis bull burials at Memphis and King Darius I (c. 522–486 BCE) built at least one temple at El-Hibis in Khargeh Oasis. A Nile–Red Sea canal was completed in his reign and twenty-four ships sailed from Egypt to Persia laden with gifts via the canal at its opening. The Egyptians made alliances with Athens and

Sparta in Greece in order to achieve independence again from circa 404 BCE. Within Egypt, however, the situation seems to have been one of intense rivalry between noble families, based at important cities through the Delta and Nile Valley, for example King Amyrtaios of Dynasty 28 (c. 404–399 BCE) ruled from Saïs and at Mendes there was a strong line of kings including Nepherites I and Hakoris (Dynasty 29, c. 398–378 BCE). According to the *Demotic Chronicle*, a text composed circa 200 BCE, only the most pious and honest rulers could achieve political success, perhaps a comment upon the quality of the Late Period kings.

Dynasty 30 (c. 378–341 BCE) represented the last native Egyptian rulers at the town of Sebennytos in the north of Egypt, who continued the policies established in Dynasty 26. They embarked upon an active temple building program and also donated shrines to many cult centers, most important of which is the Saft el-Henneh shrine. The dynasty promoted the cult of the goddess Isis by building temples at Behbeit el-Hagar, in the Delta and at Philae, in Aswan. The founder of the dynasty, King Nectanebo I, had been a general and, together with his son Teos, embarked upon an ambitious foreign

Island of Philae, the sanctuary of the goddess Isis, just south of Aswan. First begun during the Late Period and largely built during Ptolemaic times, the temples remained in use until the very end of paganism. The last dated hieroglyphic inscription was carved there in 394 CE. PHOTOGRAPH BY AIDAN DODSON

policy against the Persians. Another general, King Nectanebo II, usurped power during their absence from Egypt on a military campaign, but he was eventually deposed by the second Persian invasion in circa 343 BCE. King Artaxerxes III governed Egypt from Persia as a province in order to exploit the strong resource base there. The defeat of the Persians at the Battle of Issus in circa 333 BCE by Alexander the Great brought Egypt into the Macedonian Empire and, at his death, Egypt passed into the hands of the general Ptolemy Lagus who quickly established himself as king Ptolemy I and began a dynasty that lasted until the death of Cleopatra VII in 30 BCE.

The Ptolemies ruled from a newly founded city and harbor at Alexandria on the northwestern edge of the Delta, reflecting a familiarity with Hellenistic Mediterranean culture rather than strong Egyptian traditions. Nevertheless, in order to manage effectively the agricultural resource base of Egypt, the Ptolemies behaved much as previous Egyptian rulers by commissioning temples, founding new cities and reorganizing the rural administration

throughout the Nile Valley and Egypt. The political situation in the eastern Mediterranean meant that conflicts with neighboring countries brought Egypt into the increasingly powerful sphere of Rome. To the south of Egypt, the area of about 75 miles from Aswan to Maharraqa were put under the direct control of one of the generals of Ptolemy I and known as the Dodekaschoinos. The area formed a frontier buffer zone and corridor allowing access to the gold mines at Wadi Allaqi. Ptolemaic kings built temples in this zone and the buildings were then embellished by indigenous Kushite rulers. The Temple of Isis at Philae was an important shared cult center between Egypt and the Kushite heartland. This cooperative religious spirit did not always extend to the political sphere and there were revolts during the reigns of Ptolemy V and VI. The Great Procession held by Ptolemy II Philadelphus in Alexandria in 274 BCE displayed elephants, slaves, great amounts of gold and leopards as representative of the African wealth of the Ptolemaic dynasty. After the defeat of Anthony and Cleopatra VII at the Battle of Actium in 30 BCE, the Romans redrew the southern border of Egypt at Aswan and awarded the kingdom of Kush the status of a client kingdom under the control of a viceroy (tyrannus).

See also **Alexandria; Cleopatra VII; King Lists and Chronologies; Kings and Kingdoms; Nubia; Queens and Queen Mothers.**

BIBLIOGRAPHY

Bowman, Alan K. *Egypt after the Pharaohs, 332 BC–AD 642: From Alexander to the Arab Conquest.* Berkeley: University of California Press, 1986.

Morkot, Robert. *The Black Pharaohs: Egypt's Nubian Rulers.* London: Rubicon Press, 2000.

Mysliwiec, Karol. *The Twilight of Ancient Egypt: First Millennium B.C.E.*, trans. David Lorton. Ithaca, NY: Cornell University Press, 2000.

Welsby, Derek A. *The Kingdom of Kush: The Napatan and Meroitic Empires.* London: British Museum Press, 1996.

PENELOPE WILSON

ROMAN AND BYZANTINE

The Roman province of Egypt (Aegyptus) dates from 30 BCE, with the defeat and death of the last Ptolemaic ruler, Cleopatra, and her consort, Mark Antony, by Octavian (from 27 BCE, known as Augustus). The province was then ruled directly under imperial authority from Rome by a viceregal governor, known as the prefect, on account of its strategic importance as one of the major producers of grain for the Roman Empire. Throughout the Roman Empire, the culture and language of Egypt was respected, provided supplies of grain continued to sail from Alexandria. However the period saw an increasing adoption of Hellenic culture and styles. Coptic, a direct descendant of ancient Egyptian, was widely spoken in the countryside whereas Greek and Demotic were used in correspondence. Initially temples continued to be erected in the pharaonic style, and Augustus was even on occasions shown as a pharaoh as, for example, on the temple reliefs at Kalabsha. Prosperous new areas of settlement were opened up, particularly in the Fayyum, and the empire sought out new resources to exploit, such as natron from the western desert (used in glass making and mummification), gold from Nubia or marbles, especially Imperial Porphyry, from the Eastern desert. Of particularly significance was the Red Sea, which provided a sea route to East Africa and India, and where the Romans established ports, as well as desert routes, with way stations between the Nile River and coast.

After 30 BCE, the Romans, under the first prefect (who was also a poet and friend of Virgil), Gaius Cornelius Gallus, moved to secure the Nile Valley as far as Aswan, but it was the expedition in 23 BCE of the third prefect, Gaius Petronius into Nubia that led to the establishment of a permanent southern frontier, originally intended to be at Qasr Ibrim (Primis) but shortly moved north to Hiera Sykaminos, fifty miles south of Aswan. Pliny recorded an expedition at the time of Nero in 61 CE, which was reputed to have reached Meroe in the Sudan, although its purpose may have been more exploratory than military. Effective control of the Red Sea coast, which had been overrun by Beja nomads, dates to time of Claudius (41–54 CE). The first 150 years of Roman rule was generally stable and prosperous. The most famous imperial visits were those of Hadrian (130–131 CE), who founded a town named Antinoopolis, in memory of his drowned homosexual companion, Antinous. However, from the second century onward there were a series of revolts; the first mounted by the Jewish community (115–117), followed by the somewhat mysterious Boukoloi War. In essence these revolts by the Egyptians were attempts to resist excessive taxation and support rival imperial claimants; the general insecurity led to a decline in agricultural productivity. Further revolts took place in 193, 261, 270, 293, and 297 CE.

Another cause for concern was the freedom to follow their own religion. The plurality of gods and sects, which dates to pharaonic times, were generally tolerated, while the imposed Greco-Roman religion never spread beyond the urban areas; there was, however, considerable fluidity between the two belief systems. But there were also numerous minority groups: Jewish communities mostly in Alexandria, Gnostics in middle Egypt, and Manichaean groups in the Western Desert and Fayyum. But the most important were the Christians, who became increasingly numerous from the third century CE. Alexandria was the major center for the development of Christian theology, especially under Clement and Origen. In this period were major persecutions, under imperial edict, most famously those by Decius (c. 249–251) and Diocletian (303), whose martyrs are still

Red Monastery (Deir el-Ahmar) at Sohag. The monastery originally was built during the fifth century CE, but it has been rebuilt on more than one occasion since. The building is dedicated to St. Bishoi, and its church is extensively decorated with paintings. PHOTOGRAPH BY AIDAN DODSON

commemorated in the twenty-first century by the Coptic Church. The legalization of Christianity throughout the empire from 311 to 313 led to the rapid expansion of the Egyptian Church. Initially many temples were converted, such as at Luxor, or ancient religious sites reused, such as at Dendera. New basilicas were also constructed at sites like such as Hermopolis Magna (El-Ashmunein) and Abu Minas.

Another important development was monasticism, whose roots lay in the period of persecutions, but became important in the fourth century, where withdrawal from the Nile Valley into the desert became a spiritual alternative to martyrdom. Many of these early monastic sites are still active communities today, especially in the Wadi el-Natrum, and including the very early monasteries of St. Antony and St. Paul in the Red Sea Hills. A few sites, such as the White and Red Monasteries at Sohag, or Saint Simeon's Monastery at Aswan, are remarkably complete monuments and provide more archaeological details. The site of Abu Minas has been extensively excavated as a pilgrimage and monastic town in the desert to the west of Alexandria. In parallel to the growth of Christianity

was the progressive closure of pagan centers, especially after the Theodosian edict of 390. The only temple to remain was the Temple of Isis at Philae, kept open to appease the Nubians (who remained steadfastly pagan) until closed by Justinian around 540, and converted by him into a church in 553.

Byzantine Egypt is considered to date from the foundation of Constantinople in 330, as the new capital of the Roman Empire, and Alexandria emerged as the Eastern Empire's second city. This was a period of increasing control by the Church, and the survival of remarkable manuscripts, textiles, and paintings in the arid desert conditions attest to the cultural achievements of this period. There were also major doctrinal arguments initially around the Arian heresy (from 318 onward), and later the Monophysite controversy (from 381), the doctrine of which still defines the Coptic Church as distinct from most of the rest of Christendom. Byzantine Egypt was characterized by excessive bureaucratic control—as is evidenced from the survival of numerous papyri—and increasing unpopularity of the ruling authorities in Alexandria. Egypt fell briefly to a Persian occupation between 619 and 622, but the Arab armies of Amr ibn al-As were able to drive out the Byzantine garrisons from 639 to 642, such as

Christian cross carved in the temple of Isia at Philae. The temple was converted to a church after the fall of paganism. Similar conversions are found in temples throughout Egypt. PHOTOGRAPH BY AIDAN DODSON

various parts of modern Alexandria, especially at Kom el-Dikka, with its well-preserved roman theater. Investigation of the desert sites include a Roman settlement at Ismant el-Kharab in the Daklah oasis, with rare traces of a Manichaean community, the Red Sea ports of Berenice and Quseir al-Qadim (Myos Hormos), the Byzantine fort of Abu Shar'ar, and the quarry complexes at Mons Porphyrites and Claudianus. Beyond the frontier into Nubia, the fortress and temple town of Qasr Ibrim contains numerous papyri (some dating to the Roman occupation of 23 BCE, including a poem by the prefect Gallus), Coptic manuscripts, textiles, basketry, and an immense range of other organic materials.

See also **Alexandria; Christianity; Cleopatra VII; Nubia; Warfare: Internal Revolts.**

BIBLIOGRAPHY

Bard, Kathryn A., ed. *Encyclopedia of the Archaeology of Ancient Egypt.* London: Routledge, 1999.

Bowman, Alan K. *Egypt after the Pharaohs: 332 BC–AD 642 from Alexander to the Arab Conquest,* 2nd edition. New York: Oxford University Press, 1990.

Ellis, Simon P. *Graeco-Roman Egypt.* Aylesbury: Shire Publications Ltd., 1992.

Horton, M. "Africa and Egypt: New Evidence from Qasr Ibrim." In *Egypt and Africa,* ed. W. V. Davies. London: British Museum Press, 1991.

Kamil, Jill. *Coptic Egypt, History and Guide.* Cairo: American University in Cairo Press, 1987.

Maxfield, Valerie, and David Peacock. *Mons Claudianus: Survey and Excavation 1987–1993,* Vol. 1: *Topography and Quarries.* Paris: Institut Français d'Archéologie Orientale, 1997.

Maxfield, Valerie, and David Peacock. *The Roman Imperial Quarries: Survey and Excavation at Mons Porphyrites 1994–1998,* Vol. 1: *Topography and Quarries.* London: Egypt Exploration Society, 2001.

Peacock, David. "The Roman Period (30 BC–AD 311)." In *The Oxford History of Ancient Egypt,* ed. Ian Shaw. New York: Oxford University Press, 2000.

Peacock, David, and Lucy Blue. *Myos Hormos: Quseir al-Qadim, Roman and Islamic Ports on the Red Sea,* Vol. 1: *The Survey and Report on the Excavations.* Oxford: Oxbow Books, 2006.

Spencer. A. J. *Excavations at El-Ashmunein III: The Town.* London: British Museum Press, 1993.

Watterson, Barbara. *Coptic Egypt.* Edinburgh: Scottish Academic Press, 1988.

those occupying Babylon (Old Cairo). Although Alexandria was briefly retaken in 645, from 646 Egypt was a Muslim state, although it retained and tolerated a sizable Christian minority.

The archaeological evidence for everyday life, as well as trade and society, is better preserved in Egypt than anywhere else in the Roman Empire. The survival of papyri hoards in the dry desert soils, of which the most famous are from Oxyrhynchus, include letters, details of commercial transactions, and also literary and religious materials. Mummified burials in the Fayyum contain mummy portraits that give a very intimate view of the ordinary Roman Egyptians. There have been major excavations of several Roman towns, most notably in the Fayyum at Keranis (undertaken by the University of Michigan in the 1920 and 1930s), at El-Ashmunein in Middle Egypt, and in

Wendrich, Willeke, and Steven E. Sidebotham. *Berenike 1999–2000*. Los Angeles: Cotsen Institute of Archaeology, 2006.

MARK HORTON

ISLAMIC

Between 650 and 1350, Egypt, which had been a province of the Roman and Byzantine Empire for seven hundred years, turned from a province of the new Arab empire into the seat of an empire in the Nile valley, Palestine, and Syria. In addition, it turned from a predominantly Christian country into a mainly Muslim one, and from speaking Coptic and Greek into speaking Arabic. At the same time it became a hub of the new Islamic world, developing from the original point of entry of Islam into Africa into the focal point of communication with northern, Saharan, and Sudanic Africa, and between the Mediterranean and the Indian Ocean. After its conquest in 740–742 by ʿAmr ibn al-ʿAs, who founded Fustat, the origin of Cairo, in place of Alexandria as the capital of the country, its political history divides into periods of roughly a hundred years, under the Umayyads, 661–750; the ʿAbbasids, 750–868; the Tulunids and Ikhshidids, 868–969; the Fatimids, 969–1074; the late Fatimids, 1074–1171; the Ayyubids, 1171–1250; and the Mamluks, 1250–1517.

Under the Umayyads and ʿAbbasids, Egypt was a province of their empire, but became independent under the Tulunids and then the Ikhshidids, dynasties founded by Turkish governors appointed by Baghdad. In 969 Egypt was conquered by an invasion from North Africa that brought the Fatimids to power. The Fatimids aimed to replace the ʿAbbasids as rulers of the Arab empire, but were obliged to be content with that of the Ikhshidids in Egypt and Syria. At al-Qahira, the palace city outside Fustat that gave its name to Cairo, they created a grand ministerial regime that in 1074 was taken over by the army. While Syria and Palestine were lost to the Seljuks and the Crusaders, its mainly Armenian commanders ruled almost continuously until Egypt was conquered from Syria in 1169 in the course of the conflict with the Crusaders. Power was then taken by Saladin, who abolished the Fatimid dynasty in 1171, and went on to annex Syria and finally Jerusalem in 1187. The Ayyubid dynasty that he founded ruled a family empire based upon Egypt until it was taken over by the Mamluks. These so-called slave soldiers were Turks recruited as boys into the Ayyubid armies, who in 1250 murdered the heir to the Egyptian throne, then defeated the Mongol invaders of Syria at the battle of ʿAyn Jalut in 1260, and finally expelled the Crusaders in 1291. Their commanders became Sultans of a centralized empire that was the greatest power in the region until the Ottoman conquest in 1517.

The basis for this Egyptian empire was the revenue from the agriculture of the floodplain of the Nile below Aswan, whose collection and allocation was the chief concern of government. Collection on behalf of the Umayyads and ʿAbbasids provoked a series of peasant rebellions in the eighth and ninth centuries; tax farming then became the norm, offering a means of investment in the land, until land tax farms were used from 1074 onward like fiefs to maintain the army. Under this fiscal regime, the tribal Arab warriors settled in the country became the nucleus of a growing Muslim population in town and country, whose rate of reproduction gradually turned the Coptic Christian majority into a small minority without the necessity of mass conversion. Meanwhile the country became entirely Arabic speaking. With independence, it also became prosperous, partly because of the intercontinental trade and pilgrimage routes that passed through Alexandria and Cairo, one of the greatest cities of the mediaeval world.

The conquest of North Africa and Spain from Egypt, from 670 to 715, created a route to and from the west that rapidly branched south across the Sahara to the Central and Western Sudan. Egypt then became the focal point of communication between the western and eastern halves of the Islamic world, crowded each year by the pilgrimage to Mecca. The pilgrimage was a major event, which in the fourteenth century drew Ibn Battuta from Morocco and Mansa Musa from Mali. The Christian pilgrimage to Jerusalem from Nubia and Ethiopia likewise passed down the Nile through Egypt, whose various rulers strove to assert their superiority to the Nubian Christian kingdom of Muqurra through the Baqt ("Pact"), a tributary agreement dating from the seventh century. The agreement covered an important slave trade, which provided Egypt with black slave soldiers, and the black eunuch Kafur, who ruled Egypt as regent for the Ikhshidids from 947 to 968. Nubian control of the valley south of Aswan was weakened from the ninth century onward by the gold rush into the Wadi 'Allaqi in the desert to the east, which drew in warrior Arab tribes from Egypt. As these tribes migrated further and further south, pressure upon Muqurra from the Fatimids, Ayyubids and Mamluks culminated in the early fourteenth century in the accession of one of their chiefs to the throne at Dongola, and the rapid disappearance of the kingdom.

See also **Alexandria; Cairo; Islam; Labor: Conscript and Forced; Mansa Musa; Nubia; Pilgrimages, Islamic.**

BIBLIOGRAPHY

Fage, J. D., and Ronald Oliver, eds. *The Cambridge History of Africa*, Vol. 2: *From c. 500 BC to AD 1050.* Cambridge, U.K.: Cambridge University Press, 1977.

Lane-Poole, Stanley. *A History of Egypt in the Middle Ages* [1901]. London: Frank Cass, 1968.

Petry, Carl F., ed. *The Cambridge History of Egypt*, Vol. 1: *Islamic Egypt, 640–1517.* Cambridge, U.K.: Cambridge University Press, 1998.

MICHAEL BRETT

EGYPT, MODERN

This entry includes the following articles:
GEOGRAPHY AND ECONOMY
SOCIETY AND CULTURES
HISTORY AND POLITICS

GEOGRAPHY AND ECONOMY

Egypt's geography is dominated by the flow of the Nile River through the Sahara Desert on its way north from Ethiopia and Central Africa to the Mediterranean. Much of the economic activity of the country is located in or very near the Nile Valley. The floor of the valley consists of extremely fertile agricultural land, comprising about 3.5 percent of Egypt's land area. There has been some spread of agriculture into nearby desert areas. The desert areas are also used for housing, some industries and military installations, and recreation, particularly along the Mediterranean and Red Sea coasts. Rainfall is negligible, especially away from the Mediterranean.

Egypt's total area is 386,662 square miles, it has a coastline of 1,522 miles, and the elevation ranges from below sea level in several places to Mount Catherine in Sinai at 8,625 feet. In July 2007 its population was estimated at about 80 million people, with a growth rate of 1.75 percent. The life expectancy is about seventy-one years, and the literacy rate is about 58 percent for those over fifteen. Women have a higher life expectancy and men a higher literacy rate.

The highly productive Egyptian agriculture represents about 15 percent of the gross domestic product, and absorbs about 32 percent of the labor force. Farming is based on year-round irrigation, and the land supports on average two crops per year. Crops include cotton, rice, maize, wheat, fruits and vegetables and clover used for animal fodder. Domestic animals include water buffalo, cattle, sheep, goats, and camels. Most families keep poultry. Farmers raise animals as a source of capital growth, use them for work, and consume dairy products.

Land is privately owned, and most farmers own small amounts, averaging around 2.5 acres. There are also some large estates. The unit of production is the farm family, which incorporates the gender division of labor. Men do most of the work in the fields, although in some areas women also are involved, and relate the family firm to the market and government; women raise poultry and care for the household including the dairy animals. Machinery has largely replaced animal traction, but still much work is done by hand. Most farm families have nonagricultural sources of income, either salaried jobs, small businesses, or are employed as day laborers.

Somewhat over half the population is urban, located particularly in Cairo whose inhabitants are about one-quarter of the total. Industries include textiles, food processing, chemicals, cement production, and light manufacturing. After an effort in the 1950s and 1960s to develop heavy industries, typically in the public sector, there was a switch to light industry, often initiated by local entrepreneurs. The hydrocarbon sector (oil and natural gas) is expanding; the extraction areas are along the Red Sea. The industrial sector currently represents about 36 percent of gross domestic product (GDP) and employs about 17 percent of

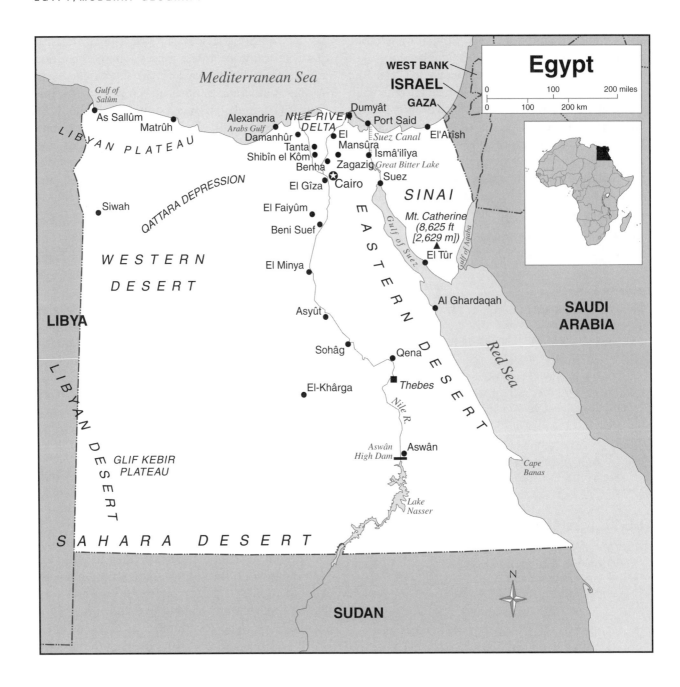

the labor force. More prominent economically than either agriculture or industry is the service sector, which represents about 49 percent of GDP and 51 percent of the labor force. Tourism, both visits to the historical sites and recreational tourism along the coasts, is a growing element in the service sector, although it is vulnerable to political events. Government is also a major employer, although the policy of guaranteeing all graduates a government job has largely been scrapped and there is some effort to streamline the official work force. There is also a very large informal sector of small-scale

enterprises and vendors, often based on a single person or a family. Unemployment, particularly of high school and college graduates, has been a problem.

Egypt also benefits from two other income streams: remittances from Egyptians working abroad, and tolls from the Suez Canal. The first goes to individual families, and second to the public treasury. Egyptian men have sought work in the Arab oil countries, but also increasingly in the West. In the early twenty-first century, more money was remitted from the United States than from Saudi Arabia.

Overall, the GDP in a good year grows at about 5 percent. The figure is responsive both to government policies and to the international conjuncture. Poverty remains (about 20% of the population is below the official poverty line) and the substantial government subsidies have become a form of entitlement, sometimes referred to in terms of a social contract.

The growth of the population and the economy has also put strains on the environment, and Egypt confronts serious problems in that domain. Air quality and noise levels in the crowded cities are problematic, although the biggest issues for the country as a whole are water issues. Most of Egypt's share of Nile water is used for agriculture. By 2006 Egypt reached the point where per capita availability of renewable fresh water is below the threshold for water scarcity, and the problem is aggravated by water pollution from sewage, industrial effluents, and agricultural pesticides. Continued growth of tourism along the coasts is threatened by degradation of the marine and coastal environments. The health and other costs of this pollution have not been calculated, but awareness of the dangers is high. Egypt is characterized by a growing population in a crowded environment, and careful husbanding of resources will be necessary in the future.

See also **Cairo; Economic Systems; Nile River; Sahara Desert; Tourism.**

BIBLIOGRAPHY

Hopkins, N.S.; S. R. Mehanna; and S. el-Haggar. *People and Pollution: Cultural Constructions and Social Action in Egypt.* Cairo: American University in Cairo Press, 2001.

Ibrahim, Fouad, and Barbara Ibrahim. *Egypt: An Economic Geography.* London: I. B. Tauris, 2003.

Said, Rushdi. *The River Nile: Geology, Hydrology, and Utilization.* Oxford and New York: Pergamon, 1993.

NICHOLAS S. HOPKINS

SOCIETY AND CULTURES

Egypt is often used as a metaphor to convey multiple messages about its social and cultural conditions and potential. The glory of its past as the great civilization of the ancient Near East stands in strong opposition to the twenty-first century's visible poverty of large parts of its population and its economic dependence on foreign investment and support. This mixed message corresponds to the contemporary dialogue between civilizations. Egypt stands poised between Islam and the West. As part of the "heartland" of Islam, it is deeply anchored in religious history; it is also a strongly secularized and Westernized society, overburdened with economic problems. In Western philosophies of history, Egypt incorporates both the "oriental" model of a nature-bound, static society and, at the same time, its basic historical role as a primary cultural source of Europe and modern Western civilization. Comparative analysis of civilizations today links the pharaohs' Egypt to the rise of monotheism, in a way detracting from its former image as a purely pagan contrast to early Christianity.

Egypt also has a dual image as a bastion of Islamic orthodoxy and a birthplace of Islamic modernism that has greatly influenced the Arab and Islamic worlds. The boundaries of the varying images of Egypt are also set by geographical and historical factors: the valley of the Nile limits the possibility for human settlement and yet the self-affirming powers of one of the oldest civilizations is the very gift of the Nile and its beauty, which traverses desert lands from deep inside Africa all the way to the Mediterranean basin.

EARLY MODERN STRUCTURAL HERITAGE

Following the French Napoleonic invasion (1798–1801), modern Egypt began with the reign of Muhammad 'Ali (1805–1848) and his early attempts at industrialization. Between the 1850s and the 1920s, a small industrial sector based on the processing and export trading of the Egyptian cotton emerged. The decline of the cotton crop during and after the 1930s limited later attempts to transform Egypt from a subsistence economy to a diversified modern one. Despite all its shortcomings, Egypt is a highly developed country in contrast to many other African and Middle East countries. Egypt's modern fate has always been intrinsically linked to developments in Europe, and since the 1977 peace treaty with Israel, it has come under increasing American political and cultural influence. A substantial part of the country's intellectually and technically sophisticated elite is trained in France, Britain, and the United States.

Arab Republic of Egypt

Population:	80,335,036 (2007 est.)
Area:	1,001,450 sq. km (386,662 sq. mi.)
Official language:	Arabic
Languages:	Arabic, English, French
National currency:	Egyptian pound
Principal religions:	Muslim 94%, Coptic Christian and other 6%
Capital:	Cairo (est. pop. 16,000,000 in 2006)
Other urban centers:	Alexandria, Aswan, Asyut, Port Said, Suez, Ismailia
Annual rainfall:	203 mm (8 in.) at the coast to 25 mm (1 in.) in the south
Principal geographical features:	*Mountains:* Mount Helal, Mount Serbal, Gebel Elba, Gebel Sherif, Mount Sin Bishar, Mount Sinai *Rivers:* Nile *Lakes:* Great Bitter, Lake Moeris, Serbonian Bog, Mariout, Nasser, Toshka, Paralus *Other:* Saharan Desert, Libyan Desert, Isthmus of Suez
Economy:	*GDP per capita:* US$4,200 (2006)
Principal products and exports:	*Agricultural:* cotton, rice, corn, wheat, beans, fruits, vegetables, cattle, water buffalo, sheep, goats *Manufacturing:* textiles, food processing, chemicals, pharmaceuticals, hydrocarbons, cement, metals, light manufactures *Mining:* gold, zircon, iron ore, phosphate, limestone
Government:	Independence from the United Kingdom, 1922. Constitution, 1971; amended 1980 and 2005. Republic. President elected for 6-year term (unlimited number of terms) by popular vote. Bicameral system consists of the People's Assembly or Majlis al Sha'b (454 seats: 444 elected by popular vote, 10 appointed by the president; 5-year terms) and the Advisory Council or Majlis al-Shura (consultative role only; 264 seats: 176 elected by popular vote, 88 appointed by the president; 6-year terms). President appoints prime minister and cabinet. For purposes of local government, there are 26 governorates.
Heads of state since independence:	1953–1954: President Muhammad Naguib 1956–1970: Colonel Gamal Abdel Nasser 1970–1981: Field Marshal Anwar Sadat 1981–: President Mohammed Husni Mubarak
Armed forces:	The armed forces consists of an army, navy, air force, and air defense command with a combined membership of 450,000. Compulsory 3-year service.
Transportation:	*Rail:* 5,063 km (3,146 mi.) *Waterways:* 3,500 km (2,175 mi.), including Nile River, Lake Nasser, Alexandria-Cairo Waterway, and Suez Canal *Ports:* Alexandria, Damietta, El Dekheila, Port Said, Suez, Zeit *Roads:* 92,370 km (57,396 mi.), 81% paved *National airline:* Egypt Air *Airports:* International facilities at Cairo and Luxor; 85 other smaller airports in the country
Media:	There are more than 500 newspapers, most independent. State-controlled ERTU operates most of the more than 50 radio stations. 98 television stations.
Literacy and education:	*Total literacy rate:* 58% (2006). Education is free and compulsory for ages 6–15. Postsecondary education provided by 13 major universities and 67 teacher colleges.

Despite the high decree of urbanization and cultural Westernization, Egypt figures in modern discourse as an exemplar of agrarian societies and as one of the first bureaucratic states, a model based on the idea of Egypt's role in ancient history as described by the German sociologist Max Weber (1864–1920). In varying intensity, this model also prevails in interpretations of Egypt's modern society and culture that include characteristics such as an inability to expand settled areas, dependence on the Nile and a need to regulate and organize irrigation, collective work, the absence of private landholdings, strong ties to the village community, and the absence of conditions for individualism. Accordingly, there is a symbolic survival of the "pharaoh" in modern political discourse about Egypt, signifying a prevailing, almost absolutist concept of the state and the centralization of authority, which since the late 1970s has increasingly become threatened by militant revivalist groups and political Islam.

THE INFLUX OF VILLAGERS TO CITIES

Egypt's modern society and culture has long been characterized by a strong divide between a highly

Westernized and intellectualized urban middle-class and the agricultural cultivators (*fellahin*) of rural Egypt. Numerous Western and Egyptian studies depict their strategies for survival under modern conditions and their lifestyle. A 2000 edition of Winifred S. Blackman's *The Fellahin of Upper Egypt*, first published in 1927, with a new introduction by an Egyptian anthropologist, suggests the continued cultural importance of the rural popular mentality and lifestyle in Egypt. The ways this "type" reinvents itself in urban quarters in Cairo is a central theme in many of the novels of Naguib Mahfouz. Similarly, the Egyptian vocalist Umm Kulthum combines classical Arabic music with a popular Egyptian style and has become one of the most beloved singers in Egypt and in the Arab world.

In contrast to the remaining cultural and imaginary differences between the fellahin and the townspeople and the separations between rural and urban space, between the realms of popular life worlds and civil institutions, and despite official 1999 census figures that classify 60 percent of the population as employees in the agricultural sector, geographers have observed an increasingly accelerated trend toward reduction of the social and spatial disparities in Egyptian society. Villages and rural areas, specifically in the Nile Delta region north of Cairo, are rapidly becoming urbanized. To the contemporary observer, it seems likely that the rural city centers in the Nile Delta, including Banha, Tanta, and Damanhur, could integrate into a new Mediterranean metropolis, with Cairo and Alexandria at their edges. This urbanization process has resulted from population increases and new patterns of mass mobility, consumption, and communication.

THE MAKING OF MODERN ISLAM

Since the 1880s, when it became linked to the Pan-Islamic activism of Jamal al-Din al-Afghani (1838–1897), Egypt emerged as the center of Islamic reform and modernism. Figures like Muhammad ʾAbduh (1849–1905) and Rashid Rida (1865–1935), using their journal *al-Manar* (the lighthouse) as a vehicle, advised Muslim scholars all over the world—including those in China, the Malay world, and Africa—on how to deal with modernity. They also helped to turn the al-Azhar-University and the academy of Dar al-ʾUlum in Cairo into leading centers of modern Islamic learning. Through these institutions, Egypt contributed much to the modern self-understanding of Islamic intellectualism and political Islam. Since its foundation in 1928, the Muslim brotherhood played an active part in the main events of Middle East political history of the twentieth century. The brotherhood's type of Islam continues to dominate substantial arenas of the Muslim world, including Egyptian society and culture. Despite the challenges of religious modernism, however, every year millions of Egyptians from all social strata return annually to their saints. These regional pilgrimages make the recurrent return to popular culture an important increment in religious and national self-confidence.

See also ʿAli, Muhammad; Islam; Mahfouz, Naguib; Urbanism and Urbanization.

BIBLIOGRAPHY

Assmann, Jan. *Moses the Egyptian: The Memory of Egypt in Western Monotheism.* Cambridge, MA: Harvard University Press, 1997.

Ayrout, Henry. *The Egyptian Peasant.* Boston: Beacon Press, 1968.

Baer, Gabriel. *Studies in the Social History of Modern Egypt.* Chicago and London: University of Chicago Press, 1969.

Denis, E. "Les échelles de la densifications: Le peuplement de l'Égypte de 1897 à 1996." *Revue de Géographie de Lyon* 73, no. 3 (1998): 183–202.

Denis, E. "La question méridionale égyptienne: Gérer ou réduire les disparité;s sociospatiales." *Méditerranée* 1, no. 2 (1999): 45–56.

Gilsenan, Michael. *Saint and Sufi in Modern Egypt: An Essay in the Sociology of Religion.* New York: Oxford University Press, 1973.

Hegel, Georg W. F. *Philosophie der Weltgeschichte. Zweiter Band: Die orientalische Welt.* Leipzig: Felix Meiner, 1923.

Hopwood, Derek. *Egypt. Politics and Society 1945–1984.* Boston: Unwin Hyman, 1985.

Ikram, Salima. "Introduction." In *The Fellahin of Upper Egypt,* ed. Winifred S. Blackman. Cairo: American University Press, 2000.

Kepel, Giles. *The Prophet and the Pharaoh: Muslim Extremism in Egypt.* London: Al-Saq Books, 1985.

Mabro, Robert, and Samir Radwan. *The Industrialization of Egypt: 1939–1973. Policy and Performance.* Oxford: Clarendon Press, 1976.

Mayeur-Jaouen, Catherine. "Holy Ancestors, Sufi Shaykhs and Founding Myths: Networks of Religious

Geography in the Central Nile Delta." In *Yearbook of the Sociology of Islam*, Vol. 5: *On Archaeology of Sainthood and Local Spirituality in Islam Past and Present: Crossroads of Events and Ideas*, ed. Georg Stauth. Bielefeld: transcript, 2004.

Mayeur-Jaouen, Catherine. *Histoire d'un pélrinage légendaire en Islam: Le mouled de Tanta du XIIIe siècle à nos jours.* Paris: Éditions Flammerion, 2004.

Ruthven, Malise. *Islam in the World.* London: Penguin Books, 2000.

Said, Edward. *Freud and the Non-European.* London: Verso, 2003.

Stroumsa, Guy G. "Cultural Memory in Early Christianity: Clement of Alexandria and the History of Religions." In *Axial Age Civilisations and World History*, ed. Johann P. Arnason, S. N. Eisenstadt, and Björn Wittrock. Leiden and Boston: Brill, 2005.

Weber, Max. *Agrarian Sociology of Ancient Civilizations.* London and New York: Verso, 1988.

GEORG STAUTH

HISTORY AND POLITICS

The modern history of Egypt has been one of gradual emergence from a series of foreign rulers into national self-government. In 1798 the French army under Napoleon conquered Egypt and maintained themselves for about three years. This ended the 600-year-long period of Mamluk and Ottoman rule. The presence of the French army was the first major influence from a modernizing Europe, and it foreshadowed what followed. After the French departure, an Ottoman officer, Muhammad 'Ali, took power by force and overcame his many rivals. He ruled from 1805 to 1849, although his efforts to expand outside Egypt were blocked by the European powers. His descendents continued to occupy the throne of Egypt until 1952, while recognizing Ottoman suzerainty.

Muhammed 'Ali developed his military and industrial force not least by calling on European, primarily French, technical assistance. This pattern of dynastic rule with the help of individual Europeans continued for about thirty years after his death. During this time the Suez Canal was built, the irrigation system was improved, and cotton was introduced as a major cash crop. But by the end of this period, the dynasty was weakened by debt and mismanagement, and the colonial drive among European powers had increased. In 1882 the British took charge of Egypt, without,

however, making it a formal colony. Sovereignty remained with the Ottomans, so it functioned like a veiled protectorate.

The outbreak of war in 1914 found the British and the Ottomans on opposite sides, so the quasi-colonial power had to find a new formula consecrating the separation of Egypt from the Ottomans. In this juncture, Egyptian nationalists raised their voices to argue for independence, and there was a brief revolt in 1919 reflecting both elite and peasant discontent. One of the leaders of this rebellion was Sa'ad Zaghlul, who was first exiled and then brought back to take charge of the government. A constitution was prepared and approved in 1923 that represented the first step back toward an independent Egypt. Egypt was governed by a parliamentary regime under King Fuad, but with reserved powers for the British. In 1936 a new treaty with the British restored more of Egypt's sovereignty, and allowed it to join the League of Nations and to exchange diplomatic representatives. However, before this could be consolidated, World War II broke out, and Egypt became too important strategically to be left on its own. British tutorship returned in the form of a close control of the young king Farouk by the British ambassador. Politics during this period was often described as a three-cornered fight between the palace, the British residence, and the dominant political party, known as the Wafd.

After World War II nationalistic army officers grew increasingly unhappy with this arrangement, and in particular with the poor Egyptian showing in the first confrontation with Israel in 1948, and this led to a coup d'état to overthrow King Farouk in 1952. The Free Officers, as they were known, established a republican regime in 1953. Shortly one of the officers, Gamal Abdel Nasser, emerged as the dominant figure. Although initially somewhat oriented toward the liberal model, by the end of the 1950s the regime opted for a socialist model that had the advantage of concentrating power in the hands of the state. This choice reflected both domestic reasons the international conjuncture. Egypt began to nationalize industry and commerce (and the Suez Canal company) and to extend the land reform, which had begun immediately after the coup in 1952. Thus the coup itself evolved into a revolution, which attempted to change the class basis of the Egyptian policy by sidelining the old elite in favor of a new younger generation. The final moment of overt colonialism was the evacuation of Egyptian territory by the British army in 1954.

Nonetheless, developmental success was not immediately forthcoming, and some of the political capital was lost in an ill-advised intervention in Yemen in the mid-1960s and then the disastrous war with Israel in 1967. It became impossible to pursue the socialist policy, even with the help of the Soviet bloc, and the older elite gradually began to return to Egyptian politics. Abdel Nasser himself died prematurely in 1970, and was succeeded by his vice president, Anwar Sadat. The trend toward a more liberal economy continued, and at the same time Sadat succeeded, through the 1973 war and subsequent negotiations, in recovering the Sinai peninsula, which had been under Israeli rule. Sadat was pushing to make peace with Israel, but was losing touch with the country when he was assassinated in 1981 and was in turn succeeded by his vice president, Husni Mubarak. At the start of the twenty-first century, Mubarak is still president, the Soviet Union has disappeared, there is a cold peace with Israel, and the economy is still trying to recover from its brief period of socialism.

The political scene in Egypt is dominated by the government and a dominant government-created party, the National Democratic Party. Other parties have been created, but have not had much success. The main political opposition is centered in the Islamic movement, represented by the Muslim Brotherhood. However, the brotherhood is not allowed to be a party, or even to have full legal existence. In the 2005 parliamentary elections, candidates affiliated to the Muslim brotherhood won about 20 percent of the seats, despite ferocious opposition from the legal system and the security forces. In parliament they behave like a party, caucusing, raising issues, and stressing coordination. It is hard to know how much of their support is because of the brotherhood's articulation of Muslim values, and how much is because they are the most credible alternative to the government party. The Muslim Brotherhood represents essentially the same class background as the dominant party. The government, consisting mostly of technocrats, is basing its claim

to success on its ability to manage the economy, especially in a period of globalization. The main problems facing the country are poverty and joblessness; overpopulation that consumes considerable government resources; an ineffective educational system; various forms of pollution including air, water, and noise, and environmental conservation; dealing with an economy that is not wholly a market economy because various vested interests block the transition; and an uncertain transition to democracy.

See also **'Ali, Muhammad; Farouk, King of Egypt; Fuad, King of Egypt; Mubarak, Husni; Nasser, Gamal Abdel; Sadat, Anwar al-; World War II.**

BIBLIOGRAPHY

al-Sayyid-Marsot, Afaf Lutfi. *Egypt's Liberal Experiment: 1922–1936.* Berkeley: University of California Press, 1977.

Beinin, Joel, and Zachary Lockman. *Workers on the Nile: Nationalism, Communism, Islam, and the Egyptian Working Class, 1882–1954.* Princeton, N.J.: Princeton University Press, 1987.

Ibrahim, Saad Eddin. *Egypt, Islam, and Democracy.* Cairo: American University in Cairo Press, 1996.

Owen, Roger. *Lord Cromer: Victorian Imperialist, Edwardian Proconsul.* New York: Oxford University Press, 2004.

NICHOLAS S. HOPKINS

ELMINA. Elmina (Edina, in Akan) is a town originally located along a small promontory on the south-central Atlantic coast of Ghana (formerly the Gold Coast) with a population of 21,103 (2000 census). Its origins are obscure, but in the 1470s Portuguese mariners encountered a settlement of Akan-speaking people at this site, where they successfully purchased gold mined by inhabitants of the inland districts. In 1482, with local permission, they built a fortification that they named Castelo de São Jorge da Mina (the Castle of St. George of the Mine}, at the tip of the promontory. A new settlement arose alongside the fort. The lucrative gold trade attracted the attention of other European powers. In 1637 forces of the Netherlands' West India Company and local allies successfully assaulted the fort and ejected the Portuguese. Renamed St. George d'Elmina, the fort became the headquarters of the Dutch on the west coast of Africa until the later nineteenth century. The adjacent town, now known as Elmina to Europeans and as Edina locally, remained politically autonomous of the Dutch, though in the course of the eighteenth century it became allied politically and commercially with the inland Asante empire.

Through its mainland and overseas connections, Elmina became a major center of the trades in gold and slaves until the early nineteenth century, and the largest town on the Gold Coast. A Dutch census of 1858 counted 3,350 houses and estimated a population of 18,000–20,000, organized into ten named sociopolitical units (*asafo*) under a king (Edinahen). A small, cosmopolitan community of Euro-Africans, many bearing Dutch patronyms, dominated trade in the nineteenth century. In 1872 the Dutch ceded the fort to the British. The Edina government refused to accept the British claim of authority; consequently, British forces destroyed the town in June 1873. The old town site was abandoned and a new one was built on the mainland opposite the promontory, where it stands today. The dilapidated ruins of a few nineteenth century merchant houses are all that remain of the town's former glory, whereas the refurbished fort attracts international tourists as a monument to the transatlantic slave trade.

See also **Ghana: Geography and Economy.**

BIBLIOGRAPHY

DeCorse, Christopher. *An Archaeology of Elmina: Africans and Europeans on the Gold Coast, 1400–1900.* Washington, DC: Smithsonian Institution, 2001.

Feinberg, Harvey. *Africans and Europeans in West Africa: Elminans and Dutchmen during the Eighteenth Century.* Philadelphia: American Philosophical Society, 1989.

Hair, Paul Edward Hedley. *The Founding of the Castelo de São Jorge da Mina: An Analysis of the Sources.* Madison: University of Wisconsin African Studies Program, 1994.

Vogt, John. *Portuguese Rule on the Gold Coast, 1469–1682.* Athens: University of Georgia Press, 1979.

Wartemberg, J. Sylvanus. *Sao Jorge D'Elmina. Premier West African European Settlement. Its Tradition and Customs.* Ilfracombe, England: Arthur Stockwell, 1951.

Yarak, L. "Elmina and Greater Asante in the Nineteenth Century." *Africa: The Journal of the International African Institute* 56, no. 1 (1986): 33–52.

LARRY W. YARAK

EMECHETA, BUCHI (1944–). The internationally acclaimed Nigerian novelist Buchi Emecheta was educated at the Methodist Girls' High School (Lagos). Born Florence Onyebuchi ("Nnenna") Emecheta, the young girl yielded to family pressures and married Sylvester Onwordi when she was only sixteen. In 1962 she emigrated to England where she still lives. As a child she was inspired by the stories told by her aunt; later when she studied English literature she vowed to become a story-teller herself. In her autobiography (*Head above Water* [1986]) and her novels, Emecheta draws on details of her family's life in Africa (*The Bride Price* [1976], *The Slave Girl* [1977], and *The Joys of Motherhood* [1979]) and those of her own experiences as a working-class immigrant and an ill-treated wife, who wrote her first novel while working as a librarian and, after her divorce, went on the dole to support her five children (*In the Ditch* [1972] and *Second-Class Citizen* [1974]).

Nigerian novelist Buchi Emecheta (1944–). At age 22, Emecheta left her husband and earned a degree in sociology in the hopes of supporting her five children and her love of writing. JERRY BAUER

Because her heroines face difficult circumstances, some Western readers have been inclined to project their own feminist views onto her work, a political alignment Emecheta herself declines. Emecheta's geopolitical views are presented in *Destination Biafra* (1982, a novel about the Biafran War) and *The Rape of Shavi* (1985, a fable about colonialism). She also writes children's books and holds a degree in sociology.

See also **Literature: Women Writers, Northern Africa; Literature: Women Writers, Sub-Saharan Africa.**

BIBLIOGRAPHY

Fishburn, Katherine. *Reading Buchi Emecheta: Cross-Cultural Conversations.* Contributions to the Study of World Literature, 61. Westport, CT: Greenwood Press, 1995.

KATHERINE FISHBURN

EMIN PASHA. *See* **Schnitzer, Eduard.**

ENDOGAMY. *See* **Kinship and Affinity; Marriage Systems.**

ENERGY

This entry includes the following articles:
DOMESTIC
ELECTRIFICATION
INTERNAL COMBUSTION ENGINE
PETROLEUM AND DERIVATIVES

DOMESTIC

Wood fuel—including both fuelwood and charcoal—accounts for more than 90 percent of residential energy consumption in most of sub-Saharan Africa. Wood fuels also provide most of Africa's total primary energy consumption. According to the Food and Agriculture Organization of the United Nations (FAO), Africa has the highest per capita wood fuel consumption in the world. Consumption of petroleum products and other energy sources is increasing with urbanization and economic development, but wood fuel, particularly charcoal, is still important for domestic use in Africa's rapidly growing cities and towns.

While it is difficult to generalize accurately about Africa, there are certain common patterns: People have long relied on solar energy and wood fuel due to their low cost and ease of use. Although easily overlooked, solar energy's importance is evident in everyday tasks such as drying foodstuffs, hides, and clothing. Like energy from the sun, fuelwood was customarily regarded as a free good in most parts of the continent. A major misperception is that Africans mainly obtain their wood fuel by cutting down forest trees. In reality, they generally collect deadwood or prunings from forests and fields. Indeed, foresters have come to acknowledge that African wood fuel supplies often originate from "trees outside forests"—woody plants found in cultivated areas, bush fallows, and pastures.

In many African societies, means for conserving culturally valued trees have been embedded in local systems of land tenure, religious beliefs, and agroforestry practices. These practices and beliefs have not always been sufficient to maintain a sufficient stock of trees, and in areas such as the Ethiopian north-central highlands, rural communities rely on cow dung as their primary cooking and heating fuel. Crop residues also serve as seasonally important fuel sources in many places. Women, sometimes helped by children, usually hold responsibility for gathering wood or other organic fuels, mainly for cooking in open fires or small stoves. Some wood is used for heating space or water, for evenings in Africa are often chilly, particularly for elderly people. In the past, log fires were often lit as a precaution against predatory animals or human enemies at night. In the early twenty-first century, it is increasingly common to find kerosene lamps, candles, or, in urban centers, electricity, used after sundown.

In the midst of the mid-1970s petroleum price rises, Erik Eckholm's *The Other Energy Crisis* (1975) dramatically drew attention to widespread firewood shortages in Africa and other developing areas. The Food and Agriculture Organization (FAO), World Bank, and other organizations added to the perception of crisis by issuing at the time analyzes about a widening "fuelwood gap":

Current or future fuelwood demand were portrayed as requiring over-cutting of forest resources. The Sahel and mountainous areas of Africa, for example, were depicted as being already in acute scarcity, with over-cutting unable to meet present demand. Dire forecasts predicted severe environmental and social consequences for most of the continent if the fuelwood gap continued.

International donors, national agencies, and nongovernmental organizations (NGOs) launched numerous interventions aimed at augmenting supplies through tree planting (often in plantations or wood-lots) or by tighter controls on tree cutting. To a lesser extent they tried to influence demand by introducing fuel-efficient stoves or new energy sources, such as biogas. Most efforts proved highly disappointing. By the 1980s, many studies appeared challenging key assumptions behind the supposed fuelwood gap and its associated interventions, especially the notions that wood fuel demand was a major cause of deforestation, or that it was outpacing supply. What was once "crisis" became seen as yet another example of error in international development planning and practice. During the 1990s, research and analysis on wood fuel issues declined substantially.

With global petroleum prices again on the rise, it is worthwhile reexamining sources of misunderstanding in the misperceived fuelwood crisis. Top-down planning strongly contributed to it: Officials did not understand that trees are an integral part of complex cultural landscapes and cannot be isolated from other rural realities. They failed to distinguish, for example, between wood fuel shortages due to lack of trees versus scarcity experienced because of socioeconomic concerns such as household labor shortages or exclusion arising from privatized tenure rights. Concerns with aggregate national demand often masked significant differences within countries regarding access to fuel. In particular, the difficulties of obtaining fuel are harshest for Africa's poor and landless, as well as for many dwellers on arid and semiarid lands.

Officials and planners frequently believed that villagers were passive, naturally cooperative, and would work together for a common good unilaterally defined from above. They not only underestimated local capacity to act (including to resist) and the role of incentives, but also the diverse range of interests that often existed regarding land and forestry resources within communities. Little attention was paid to crucial questions of who would weed, water, and thin the seedlings and trees and guard them against both livestock and people. When officials did consult local people, it was usually only the men; the women, who would be expected to do most of the work, were ignored. There were many other problems: For example, nurseries were mostly centralized and thus inefficient because of difficulties in transporting seedlings; rainfall was frequently inadequate—tree-planting is relatively easy when annual rainfall exceeds forty inches, but when it is less than twenty-four millimeters, tree survival rates are low.

Several responses followed the failure of the woodlots. Farm forestry strategies encourage people to plant trees for their own purposes on their own land, and they often rely on decentralized tree nurseries whose stock often includes indigenous species. Management of common property forests and woodland has received greater attention, with efforts aimed at strengthening local institutional capacity. Overall, participatory or community forestry strategies have moved into the mainstream of the forestry profession, and many countries have implemented various forms of decentralization, aiming to increase the role of communities and local authorities in managing forest and tree resources. These policies and programs have met with varied success, sometimes fostering local empowerment, but other times resulting in conflicts or in little change at all (or worse yet, in the further marginalization of local forest users).

Many obstacles are evident. Conflicting interests within communities or across resource user-groups are often underestimated, making it harder to organize or maintain collaborative arrangements. Elites can dominate local institutions, thwarting widespread representation. Women often lack opportunities to participate or share fully in benefits. Pastoralists have been underrepresented or neglected. Intrusive state rules and requirements can make local empowerment difficult, while reinforcing central control. National policy frameworks may not allow participatory activities to move beyond the pilot stage, and they sometimes have yet to provide secure roles for NGOs, some of which have promoted successful tree-planting efforts.

Reports issued by FAO and the Center for International Forestry Research since 1999 call for a reappraisal of African wood fuel issues. The role of charcoal is especially singled out for more attention, given the context of rapid urbanization. Although fuelwood comprises the largest part of wood fuels, charcoal production is increasing all over Africa. In contrast to fuelwood, charcoal is a relatively recent innovation as a domestic fuel; it had long been widely used in forges by metal-smiths. Nearly all charcoal is produced in rural areas, but consumed in urban areas. Its production is a specialized occupation: Making charcoal involves skill and care, and sometimes good wood is wasted by beginners. The best charcoal is made from hardwoods, such as *Combretum spp.*, *Securidaca longipedunculata*, and *Terminalia spp.* In some places these valuable trees have disappeared, resulting in a poorer quality of charcoal.

Charcoal has been called "the forester's public enemy," and governments have attempted to ban its production. Sellers have usually been able to circumvent such measures. In some regions, charcoal has become known as "the poor man's cash crop" because many landless peasants try to obtain some income from this source. The demand comes mainly from middle- and lower-income urban families, as the richer people have electricity or gas. Given charcoal's importance both in terms of urban demand and rural livelihoods, some foresters call for solutions that involve careful analysis of its complex socioeconomic context, including labor and technological constraints faced by producers.

Apart from tree-planting, two other approaches to solving the wood-fuels problem must be mentioned: conserving fuel and using alternative fuels. The typical open, three-stone African fire is inefficient in terms of heat loss. Analysts have been surprised, however, by how simple economy measures such as building a smaller fire, protecting it from wind, or extinguishing it quickly after use, can raise efficiency. Since the late 1970s several improved stoves have been introduced, some successfully: for instance, the British organization Intermediate Technology promoted the construction and distribution of Upesi stoves in western Kenya. Most charcoal is burned in round metal stoves, called jikos, and improved models have been introduced in east Africa. Improved charcoal kilns are also being tried out, all in an attempt to conserve fuel. Where these innovations have proved successful, it is because the manufacturers worked with local people and took their needs and lives into account. When local people rejected an innovation, it was not necessarily because they were conservative, ignorant, and resistant to change, as is sometimes claimed. The proposed innovation may not have fitted in with other inescapable demands on the people, or they may not have been able to afford the risk, small as it might seem to an outsider, because their economic margins were so slim.

Other fuels besides wood and charcoal are utilized for domestic purposes. Animal dung is heavily used in Lesotho and Ethiopia; crop residues are frequently used, especially in Malawi. Both of these are lower quality fuels than wood, and earlier analyses usually emphasized that both could be better used for enriching soil quality. Research by Peter Dewees and other shows that arguments often underestimate the labor and other costs involved in doing so, while overestimating the expected return. Commercial energy products, including electricity, gas, and paraffin, are too expensive for most Africans, although they may use small amounts of paraffin (kerosene). One exception is Zimbabwe, where electricity is common in homes in the main cities. Experiments have been done with many other fuels—biogas, solar energy, wind energy, methanol, and ethanol—but with little success as of the early twenty-first century. In some cases the technology is nineteenth century; in others the energy is too expensive or it is inappropriate for local needs. Overall, there still appears to be no immediate alternative to wood fuels for domestic use in Africa.

See also **Desertification, Modern; Family; Forestry; Land: Tenure; Nongovernmental Organizations; Production Strategies; World Bank.**

BIBLIOGRAPHY

Amous, Samir. *The Role of Wood Energy in Africa.* Rome: Food and Agriculture Organization of the United Nations, Forestry Department, 1999.

Arnold, Michael, et al. *Fuelwood Revisited: What Has Changed in the Last Decade?* Occasional Paper No. 39. Jakarta: Center for International Forestry Research, 2003.

Brown, David. *Principles and Practice of Forest Co-Management: Evidence from West-Central Africa.*

European Union Tropical Forestry Paper No. 2. Brussels: European Commission, 1999.

Dewees, Peter. "The Woodfuel Crisis Reconsidered: Observations on the Dynamics of Abundance and Scarcity." *World Development* 17, no. 8 (1989): 1159–1172.

Food and Agriculture Organization of the United Nations. *State of the World's Forests, 2005.* Rome: Food and Agriculture Organization of the United Nations, 2005.

Girard, Philippe. "Charcoal Production and Use in Africa: What Future?" *Unasylva* 53, no. 211 (2002): 30–34.

Ribot, Jesse. *African Decentralization.* Program on Democracy, Governance and Human Rights, Paper No. 8. Geneva: United Nations Research Institute for Social Development, 2002.

DAVID BROKENSHA
A. PETER CASTRO

ELECTRIFICATION

Sub-Saharan Africa, the region with the highest levels and the most rapidly rising percentages of the population in poverty, also has the least access to modern energy. Since late 1980s, the absolute number of the poor in sub-Saharan Africa (SSA) has grown five times more than in Latin America and twice that in South Asia. Since the mid-1990s, not only has SSA lagged behind globally in gross domestic product (GDP) per capita, but also in the mid-1990s, electricity consumption (see Figure 1). The levels of electricity consumption are strikingly low at 126kWh/capita (kilowatt hours per capita) or 150 times that in industrialized countries. Further, in the 1990s, the average per capita consumption of modern energy in Africa was less than 300 kilograms of oil equivalent (kgoe), or approximately 50 percent of the global average.

After five decades of rural electrification, less than 5 percent of the rural population has access to the central grid in SSA and new connections barely keep pace with population growth (see Table 1). The patterns of regional energy production and consumption are far from uniform, however. North Africa is heavily dependent on oil and gas, the Republic of South Africa on coal and nuclear energy while in the rest of SSA biomass (charcoal, fuelwood, dung, and crop residues) supplies 70 to 90 percent of energy demand. The Republic of South Africa accounts for 50 percent of installed electricity generation in the continent. Moreover, energy use and energy investments in SSA are clearly mismatched. Despite serving a minority, large-scale conventional energy sectors (electricity and petroleum) receive the bulk of energy investments. This is at the expense of the abundant, mature and cost-effective small-scale renewable energy technologies (RETs) such as micro-hydro, solar energy, and improved biomass cookstoves. Many studies in SSA and elsewhere demonstrate strong empirical linkages between RETs and a wide range of the United Nations (UN) Millennium Development Goals (MDGs), including reduced child and maternal mortality, poverty alleviation, improved education and health services.

INNOVATIVE REGULATORY TOOLS FOR EXTENDING RURAL ELECTRIFICATION IN AFRICA

Sub-Saharan Africa, like many other least-developed countries (LCDs), has spent over a decade implementing a standard reform package aimed at creating competitive markets in the power sector. Implementation of these reforms raised many hopes, not the least of which was increased access to rural electrification. After nearly two decades of implementation, the results are disappointing, however. Improvements in electricity access, quality, reliability, and affordability have not materialized as expected. A number of international and national factors and processes underlie the failed promise of reforms in sub-Saharan Africa. First, while reforms in Organization for Economic Cooperation and Development (OECD) countries were limited to the power sector and supported by strong and functional economic and political systems, reforms in non-OECD countries, SSA inclusive, were economy-wide; overlaid on weak and dysfunctional economic and political institutions. This led to mismatched expectations and capabilities in the latter.

Additionally, while reforms improved financial and technical performance in certain utilities (e.g., Tanzania), researchers have contested the international indicators (e.g., customer-employee and electricity sales-employee ratios) used to measure such success. Given the monopolistic power supply conditions in developing countries, employee performance has limited effect on customer's choice. Moreover, using consumption average to rate utility performance created negative incentives toward

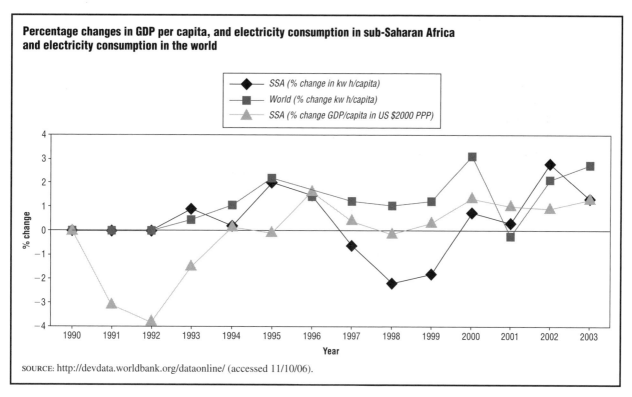

Percentage changes in GDP per capita, and electricity consumption in sub-Saharan Africa and electricity consumption in the world

Legend:
- SSA (% change in kw h/capita)
- World (% change kw h/capita)
- SSA (% change GDP/capita in US $2000 PPP)

SOURCE: http://devdata.worldbank.org/dataonline/ (accessed 11/10/06).

Figure 1.

Electrification rates in selected sub-Saharan African countries

Country	% of total population below the poverty line[1]	Electricity use per capita (kWh)	Electrification level (%)			Traditional energy as % total energy consumption
			Rural	Urban	National	
Malawi	54		<1	46	6	82
Ethiopia	76	24	<1	12	3	93
Eritrea		44	2		18	66
Mozambique	78	48	1	18	9	93
Sudan		49			31	
Benin		54			25	90
Tanzania	51	62	1	26	9	95
Congo		70			20	75
Nigeria		89			45	
D.R. Congo		90			8	
Angola		92			5	
Botswana	33		8		26	
Zimbabwe	41		19	80	41	60
Namibia			15			
Zambia	86		2	25	18	78
Uganda	55		1	20	4	92
Kenya	47	104	4	46	15	78
South Africa		3800	50	84	67	

(1) Defined by national poverty references using PPP of $1/day

SOURCES: World Bank. *African Poverty at the Millennium – Causes, Complexities and Challenges.* Washington, DC: World Bank, 2001; AFREPREN/FWD. *AFREPREN/FWD Energy database.* AFREPREN/FWD, Nairobi, 2002; Ministry of Energy Kenya. "Study on Kenya's Energy Demand, Supply and Policy Strategy for Households, Small Scale Industries and Service Establishments." Final Report by Kamfor Ltd. Nairobi, 2002. Entries with no data reflect either the lack of reported information, or cases where published estimates differ significantly.

Table 1.

rural areas where demand is generally low and dispersed. The reforms also justified massive retrenchment and a steep rise in tariffs, by as much as 300 percent in Ghana, for example; triggering social and political unrests. By narrowly focusing on cost-recovery and finance, the standardized reform menu lacked the appropriate breadth and sequence required to address important social and public goals such as electrifying the poor-both urban and rural. Further, instead of lowering the cost of electricity supply, thus increasing demand, breaking up of public monopolies, and liberalizing generation and distribution has had the opposite effect.

In the post-reform period, rural energy service suppliers in Africa will be very different from the large national utilities with which most governments are traditionally familiar. Given the right incentives and institutional framework, individual entrepreneurs, small companies and industries, nongovernmental organizations and local communities are likely to catalyze and dominate the liberalized rural electricity markets in the future These players may be inexperienced with electricity, and constrained by capital and technical skills. Yet, the profit motive and ability to manage costs are likely to compensate for any deficiency in technical knowledge and finances. The Urambo Electric Consumer's Cooperative in Tanzania is a promising example; it performs better than the national utility, Tanganyika Electricity Company (TANESCO), in terms of lower operation and maintenance costs, setting and enforcing cost-reflective tariffs and improved customer service.

In Latin America, South Asia, and SSA, the emerging rural electricity suppliers can be grouped in three broad models: concessions, cooperatives, and dealers. In the concession model, the entity or concessionaire is granted a franchise to supply power for a profit. Supply can take different forms: distribution or generation or generation and distribution. Also, concession can either be exclusive or nonexclusive. The former is time bound, with the concessionaire enjoying exclusive right to supply to a predetermined geographic territory. Producing and/or distributing goods and services for its members, a cooperative is a commercial enterprise created to serve the interests of its members. Electric cooperatives pioneered rural electrification in the United States in the 1930s. Dealers sell (and often) maintain energy equipment such as solar photovoltaic (PV) and related components to rural customers. Dealers face many challenges including stiff competition, limited cash flow, limited access to credit and low purchasing power of rural customers. Successful models in Kenya and Sri Lanka have penetrated and grown through existing dealer networks, retail businesses, and personal relationships. These networks help in lowering the per-unit costs because many costs are spread over a wide range of retail products. Through cash sales and check-off system, the rural middle-class, notably tea and coffee farmers and salaried government employees such as teachers, have provided a critical market for solar PV in Kenya.

Africa stands to gain the most by drawing from vast experience and lessons gained in South Asia and Latin America on how to seed and grow rural electricity markets while protecting private investments. A number of innovative regulatory tools have demonstrated success in these regions. Examples include licensing; standards and guidelines; metering; tariffs and out-put based contracting. Licensing is a standard regulatory tool for restricting access to an industry. Licensing can vary from a lengthy and costly bureaucratic nightmare to a simple one-stop process. Generation and distribution in rural India is license-free; rural generation and distribution below 1MW and 0.5MW (megawatts) is license-exempt in Nepal and Uganda, respectively.

Despite power sector reforms, conventional technical standards inherited or adopted from Europe and the United States are still enforced for rural electrification in most African countries. Reducing the size of poles and increasing the distance between poles (long span) can dramatically cut costs. In El Salvador, for example, the long span is 295 feet as opposed to 442 feet in many other countries. Given the low loads in rural areas, switching transmission from three-phase to single phase can be economical. Many rural towns in the United States, with much higher loads than many urban areas in Africa, continue to be served cost-effectively by single-phase power. Further, the Single Wire Earth Return (SWER) systems are the cutting edge technology for rural electrification in many countries such as Australia, Canada, New Zealand, Brazil, India, Tunisia, Botswana, South Africa and Namibia.

Conventional metering is inappropriate for rural Africa for, at least, two reasons. The transaction and administration costs of installing and reading meters and bills preparation by far exceeds the corresponding revenue generated because of low demand, subsidized tariffs and scattered rural population. Additionally, unlike the large-scale utilities, distributed generation systems operated by rural electricity suppliers are likely to be too capacity-constrained to meet temporary peak demands. This problem can be easily solved by metering on the basis of instantaneous power consumed (kW) rather than cumulative consumption (kWh). Customers are then charged for a preset maximum power per month and circuit breakers, which are much cheaper than normal meters, are used to enforce load limits.

Getting tariffs right is essential if rural electricity markets are to emerge and grow in Africa. Common claims that rural people cannot afford the true cost of electricity can be misleading. Through wide use of batteries to power lights, TV and radio, a sizeable proportion of rural people have demonstrated willingness and ability to pay for improved energy services in the order of three to ten dollars per kWh. In setting tariffs, the regulator must therefore ensure that private rural electricity suppliers receive a reasonable return on investment. This is not an argument against subsidies, however. If directed at capital investments rather than operating costs, combined with cost-reflective tariffs, technology-neutral subsidies could make a positive difference in rural electrification.

Linking subsidies to concrete outputs is another institutional innovation suitable for the energy sector in Africa. Introducing supply competition through output-based contracting for rural electrification has increased electricity access while lowering costs in Cape Verde, Chile, and South Asia. Under this system, private companies bid to supply rural electricity services to selected areas at least cost. Payment of subsidies and/or renewal of contracts (by government or donors) are conditional on meeting pre-determined targets (e.g., number, rate and cost of connections). Active participation of the beneficiary community through financial or labor contributions, local management and in the contract renewal processes can lower costs further, enhance monitoring of targets and improve service delivery.

Wheeling-and-dealing and net-metering are additional transmission constraints facing rural electricity suppliers. Despite two decades of reforms, transmission and pricing mechanisms and rules are heavily skewed in favor of utilities with steady and predictable flow of power. This presents a serious setback to rural suppliers operating and/or considering investing in highly variable renewable sources such as solar, wind, micro-hydro and co-generation. Moreover, metering systems have not been adjusted to measure two-way flow. Consequently, rural industries (e.g., tea and sugar factories operating micro-hydro and co-generation DGs, respectively) are unable to sell electricity to the national grid when they have surplus generation while buying back during low generation seasons. Another major disadvantage is the pricing of transmission services. Utilities charge a flat transmission fee irrespective distance wheeled, congestion and line losses incurred. Uniform transmission pricing fails to reward rural suppliers located closer to their demand centers for lowering line losses and cost of power supply vis-à-vis state owned utilities.

THE UNMET PROMISE OF RENEWABLE ENERGY IN AFRICA

In 1981 Africa hosted the first international conference on New and Renewable Sources of Energy in Nairobi. As the world faced unprecedented high petroleum energy prices, Africa, as elsewhere in the world, embraced the strong optimism and vision for transition to renewable energy sources. While important initiatives have since been taken, notably in biomass and solar energy, the promise of renewable energy in Africa remains largely unmet.

Biomass Energy and Co-generation. The renewable energy conference played a key role in launching programs for research, design, and dissemination of improved household woodstoves in the region. Designed to improve both combustion and heat transfer efficiencies, about three million improved household woodstoves have been disseminated in over ten African countries (see Table 2). Most of the improved stoves have been adopted in urban households and therefore dissemination to rural areas needs to be aggressively pursued.

In 2001, 400,000 premature deaths, especially for women and children, in SSA or 25 percent of such deaths globally, were attributable to indoor

Dissemination of improved household woodstoves in sub-Saharan Africa

Country	Improved household stoves disseminated
Botswana	1,500
Malawi	3,700
Zimbabwe	20,880
Sudan	28,000
Ethiopia	45,000
Eritrea	50,000
Uganda	52,000
Tanzania	54,000
South Africa	1,250,000
Kenya	1,450,000
Total	2,955,080

SOURCE: AFREPREN/FWD. *AFREPREN/FWD Energy database.* AFREPREN/FWD, Nairobi, 2002.

Table 2.

air pollution from biomass use. This mortality trend is projected to reach 10 million by 2030. Rapid transitions to sustainable charcoal production and use have the potential to prevent three million deaths, however. Moreover, biomass fuels, particularly the charcoal trade, are a vital source of livelihoods and employment to millions of people in Africa. In Kenya, for example, charcoal trade provides direct employment to about 200,000 people, supports roughly 2.5 million livelihoods, with women playing a significant role in production, distribution, and selling.

In SSA, cogeneration provides substantial opportunities for producing electricity and/or process heat, cost-effectively and in environmentally friendly manner. Various forms of biomass, notably sugar cane waste (bagasse) could be used. Sugar is a major agricultural export crop in many countries such as Ethiopia, Madagascar, Malawi, Mozambique, Swaziland, Zambia and Zimbabwe. Mauritius already meets 20 percent of its total electricity demand from bagasse-based cogeneration; estimates show that 16 other SSA countries could meet significant proportions of their current electricity demand through this process

Solar Energy. For lighting, rural households in Africa spend an overwhelming amount on kerosene, a fuel that delivers poor and very costly lighting services. The cost per useful lighting energy services

($/lumen-hour of light) for kerosene lighting is 3,000 times higher than for compact-fluorescent light. This makes solar PV an increasingly important alternative for cleaner and cheaper lighting services. In addition to lighting services, demand for "connective power" by the rural middle class—i.e., electricity to power television, radios, cellular telephones phones—are the key socioeconomic uses driving the solar PV in rural Africa. In Kenya, solar electrification has outpaced grid connection with cumulative sales of solar home systems in excess of 200,000 units and growing at 18 percent annually.

Debates about solar PV in SSA revolve around cost, equitable access and potential for productive uses to generate income and contribute to poverty reduction. Of primary concern is the high cost of the technology. The cost of a typical household PV system (40-50W$_p$) can be as high as 200 percent of the GNP per capita of most SSA counties (see Table 3). The PV cost estimates could even be higher considering that rural incomes are much lower than the national average GNP per capita in SSA. Through better-quality lighting, solar PV has enabled important but modest income-generation activities in Africa. However, the amount of power delivered by typical solar home systems is insufficient for mechanical applications such as agro-processing, irrigation, welding, and carpentry. These productive uses account for over 50 percent of off-farm income and employment in rural Africa.

The high costs combined with the market-driven dissemination approach have decidedly kept solar PV beyond the reach of the majority rural poor. The richest 10 percent own 50 percent of all solar PV systems in rural Africa. Another important observation is that the small size PV systems affordable to rural middle-class households deliver less than one-tenth of the electricity (about 30kWh/year) used by an average grid-connected rural household.

Fuel-based lighting is another major concern in Africa. Apart from delivering low quality lighting at high cost, extensive fuel-based lighting is also a major source of greenhouse gases (GHGs). Used four hours a day, a typical kerosene lantern emits over 100 kilograms of GHGs into the atmosphere each year. But rapid penetration of cost-competitive cleaner alternatives such as solar PV and solid-state white light-emitting diode (WLED) is constrained

GNP per capita and cost of household solar PV system

Country	GNP per capita	Estimated cost of solar PV system (40-50W$_p$) US$	% of estimated cost of solar PV system per GNP per capita
Zambia	330	1200	364
Uganda	310	1037	335
Eritrea	200	600	300
Kenya	350	620	177
Lesotho	570	1000	175
Zimbabwe	610	800	131

SOURCE: Karekezi, S., and W. Kithyoma. "Renewable Energy Strategy for Rural Africa: Is a PV-led Renewable Strategy the Right Approach for Providing Modern Energy to the Rural Poor of Sub-Saharan Africa?" *Energy Policy* 30 (2002): 1071-1086; Jacobson, A., and D. M. Kammen. "Engineering, Institutions, and the Public Interest: Evaluating Product Quality in the Kenyan Solar Photovoltaics Industry." *Energy Policy* (2006).

Table 3.

by substantial subsidies extended to kerosene and propane fuels by African governments. In addition to creating price distortions, encouraging fuel diversion and adulteration into the transport sector, fuel subsidies divert scarce public resources from critical pro-poor social services such education and health.

Heating Energy Services. Electrification commands the largest share of rural energy projects and funding in Africa as in other developing countries. While electricity is important for rural development, studies have shown that heating energy—which is too costly to provide with electricity—is crucial particularly for cooking and income generation. In many parts of SSA, women travel for 6–8 hours each day collecting sparsely distributed fuelwood for their cooking needs. Heating energy is also crucial for many rural industries and microenterprises such as beer brewing, brick-making, food processing. These enterprises are the primary sources of rural and urban livelihoods, particularly for women in Africa And in many parts of SSA, charcoal and fuelwood dominate the available heating energy mix.

Emphasis on heating fuels has the advantage of opening food micro-enterprises as a significant market niche for improved energy services. Greater attention to heating energy and switching to more efficient heating fuels like LPG would have

twofold impact: first, enhance the profitability and employment in the heat-intensive micro-enterprises and industries; second, substantially reduce the aggregate woodfuel consumption in urban areas, thus lowering losses in forest cover in ecologically fragile savanna lands where charcoal is commonly produced in Africa.

See also **Children and Childhood: Infancy and Early Development; Production Strategies; Women: Women and Urbanism.**

BIBLIOGRAPHY

Bailis, R.; M. Ezzati; and D. K. Kammen. "Mortality and Greenhouse Gas Impacts of Biomass and Petroleum Energy Futures in Africa." *Science* 308 (2005): 98–103.

Cabraal, A.; D. F. Barnes; et al. "Productive Uses of Energy for Rural Development." *Ann Rev Environ Resources* 30 (2005): 117–144.

CORE International. *Zambia: Regulating Rural Electrification Experiences and Lessons; Learned Report Prepared for the United States Agency for International Development.* CORE International, Inc., 2005.

Jacobson, A. "Connective Power: Solar Electrification and Social Change in Kenya " *World Development* 35, no. 1 (2007): 144–162.

Karekezi, S. "Poverty and Energy in Africa—A Brief Review." *Energy Policy* 30, nos. 11–12 (2002): 915–919.

Wamukonya, N. "Power Sector Reform in Developing Countries: Mismatched Agendas." *Energy Policy* 31 (2003): 1273–1289.

Williams, J. H., and R. Ghanadan. "Electricity Reform in Developing and Transition Countries: A Reappraisal " *Energy* 31 (2006): 815–844.

World Bank. *Reducing the Cost of Grid Extension.* Washington, DC: World Bank, 2000.

CHARLES KIRUBI
DANIEL M KAMMEN

INTERNAL COMBUSTION ENGINE

In Africa there is a vast field of study that has only partially been systematically researched or analyzed. Since the start of the twentieth century this field has become so pervasive as to have become unnoticed as a simple fact of everyday life, much as the clothes that one wears, and the food that one eats. This is the field of the interaction between people and the Internal Combustion Engine (ICE). Internal combustion engines are those in which motive power comes from the explosion of vapor—usually a petroleum distillate—in a cylinder, and are to be found in virtually every generator, pump, motorcar, train, boat, and bus on Earth.

In the early twenty-first century the majority of Africans live in sprawling urban conglomerates that are serviced by water, electricity, and transport, all dependent on ICE technology. Likewise, Africa's export earnings, be they in mining, agriculture, or industry, are thoroughly dependent on ICE technology, and deeply vulnerable to the vagaries of world markets in technology, commodities, and oil. ICE technology.

The introduction of ICE technology is arguably the single most important factor for change in Africa in the twentieth century. In sub-Saharan Africa, with the exception of sectors of the Sahel and southern Africa, tsetse flies and African horse sickness made the use of working animals in transport and agriculture impossible, and dictated dependence on human power. Consequently, ICE technology was of greater consequence in Africa than elsewhere on earth, if only because it entailed a radical transformation from human powered society to externally powered society.

In dealing with ICE technology there has been a tendency to see it as being the domain of the political and economic elite, yet its impact stretches far beyond the elite and into the everyday lives of people in the smallest villages at the farthest reaches of African states. Though it is the stereotypical Wabenzi—the rich Mercedes car owner—who is known beyond Africa, it is the motorcycle, bus, mammy- and pickup truck that truly traverse African states, and accelerated the already extensive travel of Africans.

Motorized travel led to new ways of seeing and dealing with the world. True, the introduction of railways also had a tremendous impact on African societies. However, from the 1940s onward the train dwindled in importance, and came to be almost totally superseded by buses and trucks. The extensive shantytown that has developed on the tracks of the shunting yards of Ghana railways in downtown Accra is a graphic example of this decline. In addition, in contrast to the motor vehicle, the train is bound to run on the tracks laid

out for it. The train does not allow for the initiative of a single individual or a small group of people. The capital input is such that it requires state funding and is quite simply beyond the finances of small entrepreneurs, whereas the purchase of a motorcycle, taxi, or truck is not. In addition, there has been a tendency to see Africa as predominantly rural. Yet Africa is highly urbanized in sprawling cities that are often serviced solely by motor vehicles that are powered by ICE technology. Indeed, the continent may possess but a minute proportion of the world's motor vehicles, yet it is precisely because of the scarcity of transport that they assume such importance in so many fields of human experience.

ICE technology radically changed African economies. The increased mobility of people, products, raw materials (from labor to iron ore), information, goods, and services led to the development of new economies. In the formal economy the introduction of ICE technology as a power source for motor vehicle led to the development and accessing of new markets, as well as the establishment of a completely new economy centered on motor vehicles. New entrepreneurial and technical skills were developed as petrol stations and automotive workshops came to be established. New companies were created that transported people and goods, from small single taxi companies to enormous freight enterprises. The presence of motor vehicles necessitated the development of roads, which in turn led to further economic development. The increased accessibility stimulated and allowed for the development and exploitation of resources that had been hitherto neglected; mining, agriculture, and industry all received a boost. In addition, apart from being a major pollutant, motor vehicles also caused extensive environmental degradation through strip-mining, logging, and forest clearance, as well as topsoil loss and soil exhaustion through large scale mechanized farming practices. Further, the economic expansion and increased mobility led to the development of not only the itinerant migrant laborer but also the daily commuter—people essential to Africa's formal economies but heavily dependent on the taxi and bus services of the informal economy.

Studies have sought to examine the impact of transport in the formal economy. However, little has been done on the relationship between motorized transport and the informal economy in which the majority of Africans make a living. The impact of the ICE technology in the informal economy has primarily been in the service industry. African bus stations and transport depots are unthinkable without the myriad services provided by transport touts, food and drink salespeople, prostitution, informal bars, puncture repairmen, welders, bush mechanics, and many more. Along the road villagers peddle handicrafts, agricultural produce, chickens, fish, and more, as well as bushmeat and charcoal for city dwellers. New forms of corruption and taxation have developed along African roads, and in many countries roadblocks have become an important source of income for underpaid civil servants. Associated with the informal economy is the flourishing trade in secondhand cars, which has developed in the last twenty years of the twentieth century between Europe and West Africa, and Japan and Central Africa. Vehicles written off in Europe and Japan are shipped to Africa where they have long and productive careers. Apart from the development of new African entrepreneurs, the secondhand car industry has also led to the establishment of numerous middlemen and interlopers essential to the trade.

ICE technology in transport led to the collapse of other forms of economic enterprise. Old trade routes lost their importance. Portage- and animal-drawn freight came to be superseded. The service industries that had developed to cater for these now defunct routes and forms of transport ceased to exist. Similarly, during periods of extensive economic decline, communities that have come to depend on the motor vehicle and its roads can be struck by economic ruin.

More than on any other continent, ICE technology-driven vehicles, be they cars, trucks, motorcycles, boats, or airplanes, gave form, content, and unity to states created by colonial whim. The introduction of ICE technology has had a tremendous impact on politics in Africa, transforming both the state as well as the manner in which politics is conducted. The colonial state and later the nation-state came to rely heavily on motor vehicles for the extension and enforcement of its control, both at a symbolic level as well as at a functional level. Motor vehicles became indispensable to the

running of the state, and came to be used at all levels of government, from tax collection to education, from health care to border patrols. With roads and motor vehicles, the African state spreads its message and seeks to enforce its will. ICE technology has led to the development of new forms of warfare in Africa, such as the Technicals of Somalia and the Toyota wars of Chad.

ICE technology also allowed for the development of novel ways of politicking. Africans have sought to enforce political change through the boycotting of bus services, and the enforcement of a complete ban on all forms of motorized transport. Many political rallies in Africa would be unthinkable without the party faithful bussed in from outlying areas or the political leaders standing in open-backed cars.

ICE technology determines Africa in more ways than mobility alone. Its cities, in which the majority of Africans live, would not be able to exist without water pumps, electricity generators, and transport, all of which are powered by ICE technology. In African states where the steady supply of water and electricity have long ceased to be the domain of the state, elites employ their own water pumps and electricity generators, thereby guaranteeing access to potable water, air conditioning, and a whole host of other things necessary for comfortable living and status. Seen in this light, it is clear that ICE technology is central to the issues of status and power in Africa. In addition, apart from observing the manner in which people interact with ICE, one also observes the manner in which social relations between people are shaped by ICE in Africa.

See also **Disease; Labor: Transport; Transportation; Urbanism and Urbanization; Women: Women and Urbanism.**

BIBLIOGRAPHY

Berry, Sara S. *From Peasant to Artisan: Motor Mechanics in a Nigerian Town.* Boston: African Studies Center, Boston University, 1983.

Beuving, Joost. "Contonou's Klondike: A Sociological Analysis of Entrepreneurship in the Euro-West African Secondhand Car Trade." PhD diss. University of Amsterdam, 2006.

Due, John F. "The Problem of Rail-Transport in Tropical Africa." *The Journal of Developing Areas* 13, no. 4 (1978/79): 375–393

Gewald, Jan-Bart. "Missionaries, Hereros, and Motorcars: Mobility and the Impact of Motor Vehicles in Namibia before 1940." *International Journal of African Historical Studies* 35, no. 2–3 (2002): 257–285.

Grieco, Margaret, et al. *At Christmas and on Rainy Days: Transport, Travel and the Female Traders of Accra.* Aldershot, U.K.: Avebury, 1996.

Moriarty, Patrick, and Clive S. Beed. "Transport in Tropical Africa." *Journal of Modern African Studies* 27, no. 1 (1989): 125–132.

Schivelbusch, Wolfgang. *The Railway Journey: The Industrialisation of Time and Space in the 19th Century.* Los Angeles: University of California Press, 1987.

Urry, John. *The Tourist Gaze: Leisure and Travel in Contemporary Societies.* London: Sage, 1990.

Urry, John. *Sociology beyond Societies: Mobilities for the Twenty-first Century.* London: Routledge, 2000.

Urry, John. "The 'System' of Automobility." *Theory, Culture and Society* 21, no. 4–5, (2004): 25–39.

Wainaina, Jemimah. "The 'Parking Boys' of Nairobi." *African Journal of Sociology* 1, no. 1/2 (1981): 7–45.

World Bank. *Accelerated Development in Sub-Saharan Africa: An Agenda for Action.* Washington DC: World Bank, 1981.

World Bank. *Adjustment in Africa: Reforms, Results, and the Road Ahead.* Oxford: Oxford University Press, 1994.

JAN-BART GEWALD

PETROLEUM AND DERIVATIVES

The considerable wealth in hydrocarbons in parts of the Gulf of Guinea coastal region—from Mauretania to Angola—has prompted substantial investment in oil production since the 1960s. The expansion of this activity over the intervening years, despite some recurring political instability in Angola and Nigeria, has helped to turn this subregion into one of the world's major oil-producing zones. Nigeria and Angola are both likely to remain the leading producers in sub-Saharan Africa for the foreseeable future, and continuing new offshore finds in the early 2000s have enhanced the importance of Angola, Gabon, and Nigeria as suppliers to the world market. As of the end of 2004 the region's oil producers accounted for nearly 5 percent of world-proven reserves. This represents a 110 percent increase over the preceding twelve years, a period in which world proven reserves increased by only 12 percent.

Since the end of its long-running civil war in 2002, Angola increased its production to more than 450 million barrels per year in 2005, a figure that is expected to increase to more than 600 million barrels per year by 2008. Exploration continues in several offshore blocks south of the traditional center of production off the northern provinces of Cabinda and Zaire. Nigeria continues to be the largest producer at more than 960 million barrels per year in 2005 and is expected to remain in first place though expected rates of increase in its more mature oil fields are somewhat lower than those in more recently discovered areas. The substantial reserves of oil in Sudan are being exported at a rate of approximately 130 million barrels per year, according to 2005 statistics, after years of difficulty in exploitation due to civil war.

Through 2005 few of the existing sub-Saharan African oil-producing countries—namely Angola, Cameroon, Congo, Côte d'Ivoire, Gabon, Nigeria, and Zaire—were able to capitalize on the potential developmental benefits of increased national incomes from oil. On the one hand, the political and economic systems of those countries were inefficient in distributing income, and on the other hand the instability of oil prices led to overambitious development plans—leaving a burden of foreign debt as heavy as anywhere in the world and no developmental benefits to show for it. Furthermore, all of these countries suffer to some degree from the constellation of economic distortions called the "resource curse" in which large flows of mineral-derived income cause economic distortions that tend to cause non-oil sectors to stagnate. The most illustrative example of all of these problems is in Nigeria, which since the 1960s has undertaken numerous policy changes in largely unsuccessful efforts to stimulate a development process, arousing an unresolved debate in Nigerian political, business, and academic circles about the causes and solutions of the country's development crisis.

The prospect of oil wealth in Nigeria since the 1970s helped to exacerbate preexisting social, political, and economic stresses and stirred fierce domestic competition for the new revenues available to the state. Angola is in some ways an even more extreme example, given the much higher degree of oil dependence there compared to Nigeria. Complicated by the effects of the pre-existing civil war, Angola is nevertheless an example of how large (relative to the economy) flows of oil revenue can cause government and private sector activity in the sectors to wither, while oil becomes the center of political and economic power and effort.

Although oil revenues and policy have not been the only issues affecting national stability, the more significant oil-producing countries have all witnessed destabilizing political struggles and increasingly unstable economic conditions. Cameroon, Congo, Gabon, and Zaire have all experienced difficult transitions to multi-party democracy since 1990. The communities directly affected by oil production, such as the Ogoni people of Nigeria, began to demand a greater share of royalties and better environmental management of onshore production areas after 1990 and the ongoing civil unrest has continued to the present time and has become severe enough in the Niger Delta to threaten oil production and to provoke visible effects in world oil markets. These issues are likely to become even more prominent in the years ahead as production is boosted in response to higher prices while developmental benefits remain slow to materialize for those most directly affected in production zones. However, given the fact that much of the newer production in Angola, Nigeria, and other countries is located in offshore fields, there is reason to believe that there are limits to the extent to which such local unrest can interfere with exports. Indeed, Angola is an example of a country in which an extremely destructive civil war did not cause offshore oil production to suffer.

For many years from the 1970s through the 1990s fluctuations in international market prices had a mixed impact upon the African oil industry as a whole. Whereas world oil price increases cause proportionately more financial hardship to non-oil producers than they bring benefits to the countries producing crude oil, the producers themselves suffer widespread hardship when oil prices fall. Unexpected revenue losses help to dislocate government expenditure and provoke a wider economic instability. However, substantial price increases to more than $70 per barrel in 2005 and 2006 have presented exporters with a huge unexpected windfall that has presented them with an opportunity to significantly change their economic conditions. Nigeria has responded to this by paying off virtually all of its foreign debt, while Angola has been less successful in this area. Other countries have largely continued their previous patterns of revenue management, with correspondingly little change in results.

North Africa is the most important area in terms of oil consumption. Algeria, Libya, and Egypt account for almost 60 percent of Africa's total consumption. South Africa accounts for an additional 14 percent and the remaining 26 percent is spread between all the other countries. Throughout sub-Saharan Africa as a whole, the rise in consumption of petroleum fuels has been gradual, in line with the modest economic growth patterns evidenced throughout the region. Though non-commercial fuels such as firewood account for more than half of total energy consumption in sub-Saharan Africa, petroleum products nevertheless represent the most important source of commercial energy in the area, covering 45 percent of requirements on average in sub-Saharan Africa, rising to 60 percent if South Africa (which has significant coal reserves) is excluded. An increasing amount of foreign earnings are devoted to energy purchases by those countries lacking their own resources, well above the one-third of total earnings used for this purpose in 1994.

Statistically, the output of the region's oil-producing countries far exceeds sub-Saharan Africa's consumption requirements of petroleum products. Sub-Saharan Africa is thus a net exporter of crude oil, but most countries of eastern and southern Africa have tended to buy their supplies, of both crude oil and refined products, from the Middle East. The major African producers generally send their crude oil directly by tanker to Europe and the Americas, holding back only the amounts required to fulfill local demand. Since 2000 there has been additional demand for African crude oil from Asia and the Far East, especially India and China. China has made a particular effort to become directly involved in oil producing countries, both bidding for drilling rights and providing large amounts of foreign aid.

The region's major petroleum-products consumer, South Africa, consumes almost 500,000 barrels per day of oil of which a bit more than half is imported, according to 2003 statistics. Nigeria, the next biggest consumer, accounts for approximately 310,000 barrels per day.

Nigeria and South Africa are the dominant refining centers in sub-Saharan Africa, with installed refining capacities of around 440,000 and 520,000 barrels per day, respectively. In South Africa's case the leading domestic energy company, Engen, is a major supplier of refined products to neighboring countries in southern Africa. By contrast, Nigeria's imports refined products since poor efficiency of its refining operations limits production to about half of installed capacity. Elimination of subsidies in 2004 resulted in widespread strikes, though production was not affected. However, theft and vandalism of pipelines and other facilities remains widespread. Indeed, so-called bunkering of Nigerian oil has become a significant problem, as have pipeline fires and explosions resulting from attempts by the population to tap into pipelines directly.

Environmental concerns are a major driving factor in the unrest suffered in many on-shore production areas, most prominently among the Ogoni in the Niger Delta of Nigeria. Increased rates of various types of sickness caused by the widespread pollution with oil-derived contaminants have been documented in this area and are widely thought to affect production areas in other countries as well. Efforts to clean up these areas have moved only slowly though international oil companies have been under increasing international pressure to make progress in this regard.

Fuel shortages have occurred at one time or another in most African economies but can be considered a perennial feature of weak commercial and physical infrastructures. Shortages are also inevitably occasioned by acute political instability and civil war, which occur periodically in many parts of the continent. Even in the most stable countries, high levels of inefficiency have been diagnosed in sub-Saharan Africa's petroleum-products industry, at the various stages of procurement, refining, and distribution. These inefficiencies are variously blamed on the high level of government involvement, the low priority given to commercial considerations, the continent-wide shortage of foreign exchange, inefficient technical management of refineries, and the poor transport infrastructure. The landlocked countries are inevitably subject to very high transport charges.

Under pressure from the World Bank and Western governments, African states have reversed many earlier economic policies that aspired to increase state ownership and control. Nigeria's government-owned oil company, Nigerian National Petroleum Corporation, has gradually moved toward accommodating higher levels of foreign ownership though these production sharing agreements have yet to become dominant in the industry. A wide variety of contractual arrangements exist in the African oil market, with a consequent variation in the share of oil revenues enjoyed by governments as opposed to oil companies. International pressure from the World Bank and International Monetary Fund (IMF) has also been brought to bear on internal oil subsidies that are a significant factor in the chronic budget deficits of many producers including the two largest, Nigeria and Angola. Attempts to eliminate these subsidies has provoked civil unrest in both of these countries at times in the past and the current extremely high international market prices has had the somewhat paradoxical result of increasing the implicit subsidy to the internal market even though retail prices have been increased.

See also **Disease; Ecology; International Monetary Fund; Labor: Trades Unions and Associations; Production Strategies; Sudan: Wars; Trade, National and International Systems; Warfare: Civil Wars; World Bank.**

BIBLIOGRAPHY

Auty, Richard. "Patterns of Rent-Extraction and Deployment in Developing Countries: Implications for Governance, Economic Policy and Performance." Paper prepared for the Poverty Reduction and Economic Management Unit (PREM) Seminar, World Bank, Washington DC, April 27, 2004.

Bandlien, Einar H. "Oil in SADC: May We See More Producers Than Angola?" *SADC Energy* 10, no. 27 (1993): 53–58.

Cuneo e Associati. *Petroleum Products Supply and Distribution in Sub-Saharan Africa: Executive Summary.* Milan: Cuneo e Associati, 1993.

Forrest, Tom. *Politics and Economic Development in Nigeria.* Boulder, CO: Westview Press, 1995.

Kyle, Steven. "The Interaction of Social and Regional Structure with Macroeconomic Trends—The Political Economy of Angolan Growth in the Long Run." *Review of African Political Economy* 32, nos. 104–105 (2005): 269–293.

Kyle, Steven. "The Politics of Oil and the Aftermath of Civil War in Angola." Working Paper No. 2005–2006. Dept. of Applied Economics and Management, Cornell University, October 2005.

Lewis, Peter. "Getting the Politics Right: Governance and Economic Failure in Nigeria." *Crafting the New Nigeria: Strengthening the Nation*, ed. Robert I. Rotberg. Boulder, CO: Lynne Rienner, 2004.

Mazraati, M., and S. M. Tayyebi Jazayeri. "Oil Price Movements and Production Agreements" *OPEC Review* (Sept. 2004).

Mistry, Percy S., ed. *Economic Integration in Southern Africa*, Vol. 2. Abidjan, Côte d'Ivoire: n.p., 1993.

Panter-Brick, Keith, ed. *Soldiers and Oil: The Political Transformation of Nigeria*. London: Cass, 1978.

RICHARD M. SYNGE
REVISED BY STEVEN KYLE

ENTEBBE. With a population of 100,000, Entebbe, Uganda's third largest town, is situated 25 miles south of the capital city Kampala. Its position on a peninsula jutting into Lake Victoria made it a water transport crossroads, an ideal landing for boats from Europe and later an international airport. As the seat (ntebbe) of the guardian of the Kabaka's war canoes, Entebbe was a marine headquarters and center of trade and war in precolonial times.

Entebbe developed from a garrison post established in 1893 to the seat of the colonial government when Uganda became a British Protectorate in 1894; its altitude—at 3,760 feet—provided a perpetual moderate summer for the British. From 1905 to 1958 Uganda was administered from Entebbe rather than from Kampala. The presence of the state house, the residence of the governor, turned Entebbe into a colonial powerhouse, and the city became the center of rituals and leisure activities. The government printers, the Ministry of Health, and the botanical gardens are still located there.

See also **Uganda: History and Politics.**

BIBLIOGRAPHY

Nsimbi, Michael B. *Waggumbulizi*. Kampala, Uganda: Uganda Bookshop, 1952.

Thomas, H. B., and Robert Scott. *Uganda*. London: Oxford University Press, 1935.

CHRISTINE OBBO

ENVIRONMENT. *See* **Climate; Ecology; Ecosystems.**

EPICS AND EPIC POETRY. *See* **Literature: Epics and Epic Poetry.**

EQUATORIAL GUINEA

This entry includes the following articles:
GEOGRAPHY AND ECONOMY
SOCIETY AND CULTURES
HISTORY AND POLITICS

GEOGRAPHY AND ECONOMY

The Portuguese have had a significant geographical impact in the Gulf of Guinea since the end of the fifteenth century. The discovery of the volcanic island of Annobón (6.75 square miles), just south of the equator, came before the islands of Fernando Po (named after the man who discovered it, present-day Bioko), Corisco, Elobeyes, Mbañe, and others. Portugal regarded the mainland territory that lay opposite these as belonging to the Portuguese. Under the Ildefonso Treaty, confirmed by the Pardo Treaty (1778), Spain was given the islands and coasts of the Gulf of Guinea, from the Niger Delta to the Ogoowe, in exchange for a plot of land in what would later become Brazil.

As a result of Spain's weak hold on the Gulf of Guinea, the English, French, and Germans seized large parts of it. This trend has persisted into the twenty-first century with the claims of Gabon over the islands of Corisco and Mbañe, under pressure from oil producers. Following the Treaty of Paris between Spain and France, in 1900 Spain retained a small piece of land (approximately 10,800 square miles), sandwiched between Cameroon, Gabon, and the islands of Fernando Po (Bioko) and Annobón. On October 12, 1968, the Spanish colony gained independence under the name Equatorial Guinea. The new country consisted of a mainland province (Río Muni) of 10,036 square miles, and a coastal province (Bioko and Annobón) of 791

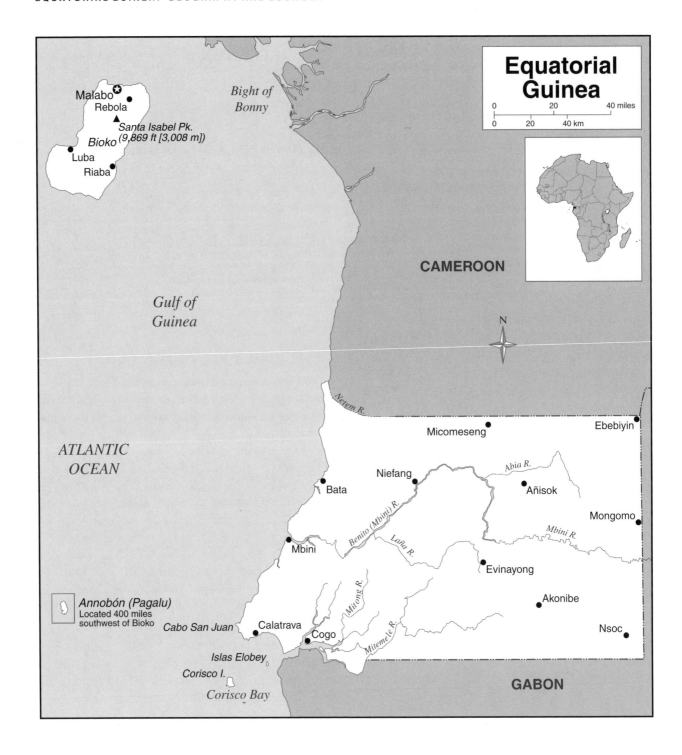

square miles and was under the presidency of Francisco Macias Nguema (1924–1979), a member of the Esangui clan of the Fang tribe from the town of Mongomo (east of Río Muni).

The mainland territory is basically a plateau, some 1,640 feet in elevation, but it rises in the south (toward Gabon) and is studded with several steep peaks (each almost 3,937 feet high), the most

well known of these being the Piedra de Nzas, which is popular with tourists. The Ntem River (or Rio Campo) and the Río Muni River (or Utamboni), respectively, irrigate the northern and southern borders of the country. The widest river in the country, the Mbini (or Rio Benito), runs through the center of the province but is only navigable for about twelve miles. The climate on the mainland, hot and humid with frequent thunderstorms, favors the growth of dense jungles wherein elephants and gorillas reside. Bioko and Annobón are also hot and humid and, because they are volcanic islands, have especially fertile soil. Bioko offers the only natural harbor in the entire country at Malabo, the site of the capital.

The Spanish colonial government developed a thriving economy for Spain, based on the export of timber, cocoa, coffee, and palm oil. But that economy was devastated in the forty years after independence by the regime of two dictators and did not regain the prosperity of the Spanish period until the recent discovery of oil off Malabo and Río Muni. However the majority of the population still lives below the poverty line, despite US$3 billion per year in oil revenues and record economic growth. Timber, especially okoume, remains the country's most important vegetal export, followed by cocoa, 90 percent of which is grown on Bioko, but the volume produced is far smaller than at the time of independence. Tuna from the waters off Annobón and shellfish from offshore Bioko represented another major export before independence, but the fishing industry was destroyed in the 1970s; it is still carried out mainly by Asian pirate vessels and by European ships on the basis of agreements signed with the European Union.

The country has a potential economic resource in its reserves of gold, iron, thorium, manganese, tantalum, and uranium, but so far they remain unexploited. The present government looks primarily to the economic potential of petroleum, currently extracted by U.S. companies ExxonMobil (which accounts for 70% of the country's production), Marathon Oil, AmeradaHess and Noble Energy, as well as others from Malaysia, Australia, South Africa, Japan, and the People's Republic of China. The third largest sub-Saharan oil producer, the country produced 420,000 barrels per day in 2005. Oil production is set to peak in 2008 at 508,000 barrels per day. Equatorial Guinea's total proven oil reserves are estimated at 1.1 billion barrels. A liquefied natural gas plant, established at Malabo, began production in 2007, at a rate of 3.4 million metric tons processed per year. Petrol and gas reserves should last until 2030. An Autonomous Free Zone with a deepwater port is under construction at Luba in the west of Bioko for regional hydrocarbon activities.

As a result of hydrocarbons, Equatorial Guinea's GDP in 2006 rose to US$50,300 per capita, but this rise did not reflect any real improvement in people's welfare, as the bulk of the revenues were appropriated by the ruling clan: at the end of 2006, Obiang Nguema's (b. 1942) personal fortune was estimated at US$600 million. Hydrocarbon activities offer jobs mostly to foreigners (such as Americans and Filipinos). Three-quarters of the population live on less than US$2 per day. After two decades in which France and Spain were dominant, Equatorial Guinea has fallen under the American sphere of influence. Secret payments by American companies led in 2004 to the Riggs Bank (Washington) scandal, uncovered by a U.S. Senate inquiry: US$700 million had been secreted away by Obiang Nguema and his relatives. Subsequently, American oil payments were made secretly to offshore bank accounts. Marathon Oil and Noble Energy have committed US$8.3 million to support malaria programs for Bioko Island.

In 2004 there was an attempted coup (the Wonga Coup) by sixty South African mercenaries instigated by British businessmen and politicians; it failed, but showed that the virtual U.S. monopoly over oil extraction was under threat. Hence the overtures of the George W. Bush administration to Obiang Nguema, who was welcomed in Washington in April 2006 and described by Secretary of State Condoleezza Rice as a friend of the United States. In 2006, the eldest son of the dictator, Teodorín Nguema Obiang (b. 1971), minister of agriculture and forestry, with an annual salary of US$60,000, purchased a mansion in Malibu, California, for US$35 million. In 2004 tiny Equatorial Guinea was the recipient of $3.1 billion in direct U.S. investment (in 2005, it was $1.7 billion). However the dictator is increasingly distrustful of the United States, and this has influenced his strengthening of relations with South Korea, Malaysia, the Philippines, and the People's Republic of China. New hydrocarbons laws were adopted in November 2006, after the increase of both petrol prices and benefits from oil companies. Royalty taxes were raised from 10 percent to a minimum of 13 percent, with minimum state holdings in both oil and gas operations at 20 percent.

U.S. Secretary of State Condoleezza Rice (right) listens to Teodoro Obiang Nguema Mbasogo, president of Equatorial Guinea, Washington, D.C., April 2006. Equatorial Guinea is one of the smallest countries in continental Africa, and the smallest United Nations member from the continent, though it is one of the largest producers of oil in Africa. © AP IMAGES

The development of this "Kuwait of the Gulf of Guinea" was essentially offshore, both in capital and labor. This oil mirage prompted a rural exodus, causing (1) a food-supply deficit that made imports from neighboring countries indispensable and (2) dramatic urban unemployment, in the absence of a manufacturing sector. The current regime intends to make the country a hub of the Gulf of Guinea. As for its stated priorities of the development of schools and health centers, as well as agricultural activities, these remain largely fictitious. The increase in revenues—fueled by massive foreign investments in the oil and gas sectors—has resulted in the diversion of a substantial part of the public treasury overseas.

See also **Colonial Policies and Practices: Spanish; Ecosystems.**

BIBLIOGRAPHY

Fegley, Randall. *Equatorial Guinea: An African Tragedy.* New York: P. Lang, 1989.

Liniger-Goumaz, Max. *Small Is Not Always Beautiful: The Story of Equatorial Guinea.* Totowa, NJ: Barnes and Noble Books, 1989.

Historical Dictionary of Equatorial Guinea, 3rd edition. Lanham, Maryland: The Scarecrow Press, 2000.

U.S. Department of State. *Equatorial Guinea. Country Report on Human Rights Practices, 2006.* Washington, DC, March 2007.

MAX LINIGER-GOUMAZ

SOCIETY AND CULTURES

The majority of Equatorial Guinea's 551,201 inhabitants are of Bantu origin. The Fang, the ethnic group indigenous to the mainland Río Muni (10,036 square miles) constitute the great majority of Equatorial Guinea's population (approximately 90%). The Fang are also one of the major ethnic groups in Gabon, with smaller numbers in the south of Cameroon. Exogamous clans based on patrilineal kinship groups characterize the traditional social-political structure of Fang society. Exogamy favors alliances between different clans. The Fang settlements in the rain forest originated from a common ancestor who was known for his mythical capacities to overpower dangerous wild animals.

República de Guinea Ecuatorial (Republic of Equatorial Guinea)

Population:	551,201 (2007 est.)
Area:	25,993 sq. km (10,036 sq. mi.)
Official languages:	Spanish, French
Languages:	Spanish, French, pidgin English, Fang, Bubi, Ibo
National currency:	CFA franc
Principal religions:	nominally Christian and predominantly Roman Catholic 94%; animist
Capital:	Malabo (est. pop. 100,000 in 2006)
Other urban centers:	Bata, Luba, Moca, Nietang, Evinayong
Annual rainfall:	2,000 mm (79 in.)
Principal geographical features:	*Mountains:* Crystal Mountains (Monte Chocolate, Piedra de Mzas, Monte Mitra, Monte Chime). Mount Malabo on the Island of Bioko. *Rivers:* Mbini (Río Benito), Ntem (Río Campo), Río Muni *Islands:* Bioko, Pagalu (formerly Annobón), Elobey Grande, Elobey Chico, Corisco
Economy:	*GDP per capita:* US$50,300 (2006)
Principal products and exports:	*Agricultural:* coffee, cocoa, rice, yams, cassava (tapioca), bananas, palm oil nuts, livestock, timber, fish *Manufacturing:* sawmills, food processing, soap factories *Mining:* oil
Government:	Independence from Spain, 1968. Constitution approved in 1968, replaced in 1973. New constitution in 1982, replaced in 1991. Political parties legalized in 1992. Civilian dictatorship. President is head of state and of government, elected (since 1982) by universal suffrage for 7-year term. President appoints the Council of Ministers, under the prime minister. National legislature consists of 100-member Cámara de Representantes del Pueblo (house of representatives), elected for 5-year terms by universal suffrage. For purposes of local government there are 7 provinces, each with 2–7 districts headed by local councils.
Heads of state since independence:	1968–1979: President Francisco Macias Nguema 1979-: President Brigadier General (ret.) Teodoro Obiang Nguema Mbasogo
Armed forces:	President is commander in chief. *Army:* 1,400 *Navy:* 200 *Air force:* 120 *Paramilitary:* 400
Transportation:	*Ports:* Malabo, Luba, Bata, Río Benito, Kogo *Roads:* 2,880 km (1,790 mi.), 12% paved *Airlines:* Spain's Iberia Airlines and Cameroon Airlines provide international service. Compañia Ecuato-Guineana de Aviación provides domestic service. *Airports:* International airports at Bata and Malabo
Media:	Main periodicals: *Ebano, Poto-poto, Africa 2000, Hoja Parroquial, La Verdad,* and several irregularly produced periodicals. No publishing industry. There are 3 government-operated radio stations and 1 television station.
Literacy and education:	*Total literacy rate:* 62% Education is free, universal, and compulsory for ages 6–14. Higher education facilities include a teacher-training school at Malabo, an agricultural school, and two centers (at Malabo and Bata) administered by the Spanish Universidad Nacional de Educación a Distancia.

The Fang are predominantly subsistence farmers and hunters well known for constructing ritual masks, drums, harps, xylophones, and sculptures of wood and iron. The Fang are divided into sixty-seven clans. President Teodoro Obiang Nguema belongs to the Esangui clan from the Mongomo region in Río Muni. The Esangui clan dominates the political power structures of the state and the ruling party PDGE (*Partido Democrático de Guinea Ecuatorial*). Three smaller ethnic groups on the coast of Río Muni and the coastal islets of Corisco (9 square miles) and the Great and Little Elobeys (1.5 square miles) are the Ndowé (also called *playeros*), the Kombe (some 3,000 each), and the Bujebas (some 2,000). Due to migration, since independence the Fang have gradually also become the dominant group on the island of Bioko (784 square miles; formerly Fernando Pó).

The Bantu-speaking Bubi, comprising approximately 50,000, are the autochthonous ethnic group on Bioko. Archaeological data of Bioko confirm local settlements with pottery as early as c. 560 CE. Traditionally Bubi society was endogamous and organized in matrilineal descent groups. The village chief, called *Bötúkku*, was assisted by a council of elders. Above this organization existed the spiritual power of the *Abba*, the supreme priest of Bubi religion. A Bubi king locally known as *Böbítáari* ruled the entire island.

The Fernandinos, an Anglophone creole community on Bioko, are descendents of Sierra Leonean Krios—who arrived with the British and who operated an antislave trade base from 1827 to 1834 in the main port on Fernando Pó—and recaptives that were settled by the British navy on the island. In the early twentieth century many Fernandinos had become wealthy cocoa farmers. In the nineteenth century they occupied many coastal lands, pushing the Bubis into the interior of the island. At that time the Fernandino community never exceeded 1,500. The approximately 2,000 Annobónense on the small island of Annobón (6.75 square miles) are a creole population descended from African slaves brought in the sixteenth century by the Portuguese from São Tomé. Their economic mainstay is artisan fishing. Fernando Pó and Annobón had nominally been Spanish since 1788, when they were ceded to Spain as part of the Treaty of El Pardo by the Portuguese, who had discovered the islands in the fifteenth century. In 1858 the Spanish decided to effectively occupy the islands, while 1926 marked the beginning of the colonization of Río Muni that had become a protectorate in 1885.

The capital Malabo (formerly Santa Isabel) on Bioko, with an estimated population of 100,000 (including suburbs), is the main economic and administrative center. The capital is named after Malabo Löpèlo Mëlaka, a local Bubi who ruled from 1904 until his death in 1937. A second noteworthy town on Bioko is Luba in the south. Bubi villages are located in the eastern and western regions of the island. The port of Bata is the only urban center on the mainland. Administratively, the country is divided into seven provinces: Bioko Norte, Bioko Sur, and Annobón for the two islands; Centro-Sur, Kié-Ntem, Litoral, and Wele-Nzas for the mainland and the coastal islets. Fang-Ntumu is the language spoken by those living in the northern part of Mbini, while Fang-Okah is spoken by those in the south. The two languages are mutually unintelligible. The Bubi speak six dialects, all of which are also distinct. The Anglophone Fernandinos speak a form of Krio called Fernandino or Porto that became the lingua franca on Bioko. The local language on Annobón is Fa d'Ambu, a Portuguese-based creole that is closely related to the Lungwa Santome, the majority creole spoken on São Tomé. Spanish and French are both official languages.

Resident foreigners come predominantly from Cameroon, Gabon, and Nigeria. The literacy rate is 83 percent. There are three state-owned FM radio stations and one television station operating in the country, but there is no daily newspaper. The majority of the population (about 94%) is nominally Roman Catholic, while traditional African religions are also widely practiced. Since the early twentieth century Bwiti has been the monotheistic syncretic religion of the Fang that has incorporated and transformed many Christian concepts. The syncretic Bwiti has largely replaced the Biere, the Fang's traditional ancestral cult.

See also **Creoles; Kinship and Descent; Literacy.**

BIBLIOGRAPHY

Boleká, Justo. *Aproximación a la história de Guinea Ecuatorial.* Salamanca: Amarú Ediciones, 2003.

Sundiata, Ibrahim. *Equatorial Guinea: Colonialism, State Terror, and the Search for Stability.* Boulder, CO: Westview Press, 1990.

GERHARD SEIBERT

HISTORY AND POLITICS

From the middle of the nineteenth century until the beginning of the twentieth, Spain entrusted the control of its possessions in the Gulf of Guinea to the *Infantería de Marina* (Marine Corps), from which all its governors were drawn, and to the Claretian missionary order (Brothers of the Immaculate Heart of Mary), in the light of the privileged church-state relationship. From 1923 to 1930, and then from 1939 until independence in 1968, the Spanish dictators Joaquin Primo de Rivera (1870–1930) and Francisco Franco Bahamontes (1892–1975) ruled the colony. In 1960, under pressure from Fang nationalists and the ONU, the colony obtained a statute of autonomy. On October 12, 1968, Equatorial Guinea achieved independence from Spain under the authority of a Mongomo Fang, Francisco Macias Nguema, who was democratically elected in August.

Following an attempted coup by the minister of foreign affairs, Ndongo Miyone, in March 1969, Macias Nguema (1924–1979) established a reputation for gross violations of human rights, including both the torture and murder of political opponents. As a result, more than 100,000 of the people of Equatorial Guinea went into exile, including the majority of intellectuals. On August 3, 1979, Teodoro Obiang Nguema Mbasogo (b. 1941, commander of the army, governor of Bioko, and director of the prison of the capital) deposed his uncle, the president. Macias Nguema was sentenced to death and shot by the Moroccan guard of Obiang Nguema. The observers from the International Commission of Jurists emphasized that Obiang Nguema's elimination of the first nguemist dictator would absolve neither him nor any other accomplices of responsibility for their crimes against the people of Equatorial Guinea. Obiang Nguema installed the single Partido Democrático de Guinea Ecuatorial (PDGE), in 1987. In 1993 he authorized a dozen political parties, most of them the handiwork of senior figures in the regime. Since then a number of parties in exile have emerged, principally in Spain. The appearance of a democratic system enabled the country to attract investments by Spain, France, and the United States. In 1995, the country joined the CFA franc zone. Macias Nguema had surrounded himself with Cuban soldiers for protection, whereas Obiang Nguema relies upon Moroccans.

The population of Equatorial Guinea was estimated in 2007 to be 551,201 (the government claims more than 1 million), including 41.7 percent under the age of fifteen; it consists primarily of Bantu peoples: the Fang make up the majority in Río Muni and are relatives of the Fang of Cameroon and Gabon; the Ndowe dominate along the mainland coast. There are Bayele Pygmies along the Cameroon border. On the island of Bioko, the Bubi have predominated historically, but in recent years an influx of Fang from the mainland has begun to shift the local demographic balance. Bioko is also inhabited by Protestant Creoles, descendants of migrants from various parts of western Africa and of former slaves, called Fernandinos, who were resettled on the island by the British in the nineteenth century. The people who live on Annobón Island are mainly of Angolan ancestry. Ninety-four percent of the population is Catholic; 4 percent are Protestant; and 2 percent are Animist. Islam is almost entirely absent. Equatorial Guinea is the only Hispanophone country in sub-Saharan Africa, but at the end of the twentieth century French was adopted as a second national language.

Primary education in Equatorial Guinea is free and is supposed to be compulsory. In fact, the national public school system is incapable of educating all the school-age children. Two-thirds of children are not registered at birth. In 2004, 62 percent of children attended primary school, and 26 percent went to secondary school. At the primary school level, the pupil/teacher ratio is around 43, but often is as high as 90. There are several institutions of higher learning in Malabo: a National University, a school of administration, a teacher-training college, and an agricultural school. Internationally these institutions are considered to be of an inadequate standard. In 2005, a proportion of total government expenditure, 1.6 percent was allocated to teaching, whereas those for health were 1.5 percent. The literacy rate is 70 percent among those aged 15–24, and 62 percent among the adult population as a whole. There is a branch of the Spanish Universidad de Educacion a Distancia, two French cultural centers, and a Spanish cultural center.

Despite national revenues of $1.97 billion in 2005 (for a population of 540,000)—90 percent from hydrocarbons—in 2006 the United Nations Council on Trade and Development (UNCTAD) included Equatorial Guinea in a list of the 50 least developed countries. Life expectancy is decreasing: 49.1 years in 2001, 43.3 in 2005.

As a result of the legislative elections held on April 25, 2005, the Democratic Party of Equatorial Guinea (PDGE, led by Obiang Nguema) and its allies hold 98 percent of the seats in the monocameral parliamentary system (two seats are occupied by the Convergencia para la Demócracia Social, CPDS, the only democratic party allowed). At the end of 2002, Obiang Nguema—who rules by decree—was reelected president for a new seven-year term with 97 percent of the vote, despite persistent reports of his poor state of health. In 2006, a conference of the University for Peace (Nairobi), affiliated to the United Nations, recalled that Radio Malabo had broadcast songs warning citizens that they would be killed if they spoke out against the regime, and described Obiang Nguema as the God of the country, holding complete power over everyone and everything.

In 2006 Equatorial Guinea was judged to be one of the ten most corrupt states in the world (by Transparency International, Global Witness, Heritage Foundation, among others). The U.S. State Department and the Department of Energy, the International Monetary Fund (IMF), and several nongovernmental organizations (NGOs), including Amnesty International and Freedom House, all came to the same conclusions: serious electoral fraud; poor government human rights record; arbitrary arrests, incommunicado detention, torture of opponents by government officials; corruption in the judicial system; lack of good governance; lack of transparency in public finances and oil production; and misappropriation of revenue by the government were responsible for growth without development in Equatorial Guinea. The State Department also stated that Equatorial Guinea is a transit destination country for women and children trafficked for forced labor.

The country's infrastructure is old and second rate, and only partially renewed by Moroccan, South African, and Chinese companies. The regime does not permit trade union activity. Power cuts, a grave shortage of drinkable water, and a lack of medical institutions complete the picture. The country's dozen airlines have been banned from European airspace in 2006, including the two presidential aircrafts, because they fail to conform to the requirements of the International Civil Aviation Organization (ICAO). Furthermore, the country has no newspapers except for one monthly governmental review (journal), printed in Spain. The New York-based Committee to Protect Journalists includes Equatorial Guinea in its 2006 ranking of the world's top five most censored countries. The only independent periodical in the country is *La Verdad*, published for the time being by the Convergence for Social Democracy (CPDS) party.

In July 2006, the dictator Obiang Nguema appointed a new fifty-eight-member government, the majority of the previous cabinet and Fang from Río Muni, including eleven direct relatives. As for the PDGE, they proposed Obiang Nguema for a fourth seven-year term from 2009; however there are marked internal family tensions between supporters of Teodoro Obiang Nguema and his elder son Teodorín Obiang Nguema (b. 1971), playboy and minister of agriculture and forestry.

See also **Colonial Policies and Practices; Creoles; International Monetary Fund; Media: Journalism; Nongovernmental Organizations; United Nations.**

BIBLIOGRAPHY

Klitgaard, Robert E. *Tropical Gangsters: One Man's Experience with Development and Decadence in Deepest Africa.* New York: Basic Books, 1990.

Liniger-Goumaz, Max. *United States, France and Equatorial Guinea: The Dubious Friendships.* Geneva, Switzerland: Les Editions du Temps, 1997.

Liniger-Goumaz, Max. *La Guinée équatoriale, opprimée et convoitée: aide-mémoiré d'une démocrature, 1968–2005.* Paris: L'Harmattan, 2005.

Roberts, Adam. *The Wonga Coup: Guns, Thugs and a Ruthless Determination to Create Mayhem in an Oil-Rich Corner of Africa.* New York: Public Affairs, 2006.

U.S. Bureau of Democracy, Human Rights and Labor. "Equatorial Guinea." In *Supporting Human Rights and Democracy.* Washington, DC: The U.S. Record 2005–2006.

MAX LINIGER-GOUMAZ

EQUIANO, OLAUDAH (c. 1745–1797).

Now best known by his pen name, Olaudah Equiano virtually single-handedly founded the genre of the African-American slave narrative when he published *The Interesting Narrative of the Life of Olaudah Equiano, or Gustavus Vassa, the African. Written by Himself* in London in March 1789. *The Interesting Narrative* is a spiritual autobiography, captivity narrative, travel book, adventure tale, slavery narrative, economic treatise, apologia, and argument against the transatlantic slave trade and slavery. Equiano's autobiography established many of the literary conventions employed in subsequent slave narratives. Since the early 1970s historians, literary critics, and the general public have come to recognize Equiano as one of the most accomplished English-speaking writers of his times, and unquestionably the most accomplished author of African descent. Several modern editions of his autobiography are available in the early twenty-first century.

The literary status of *The Interesting Narrative* has been acknowledged by its inclusion in the Penguin Classics series. Excerpts from the book appear in almost every anthology and on nearly all Internet sites covering American, African American, British, and Caribbean history and literature of the eighteenth century. The most frequently excerpted sections are the early chapters on his life in Africa and his experience on the Middle Passage, the trip across the Atlantic to the Americas that enslaved Africans endured. Indeed, it is difficult to think of any historical account of the Middle Passage that does not quote his eyewitness description of its horrors as primary evidence. Interest in Equiano has not been restricted to academia: He has been the subject of television shows, films, comic books, and children's books. The story of Equiano's life has become part of African, African American, Anglo American, African British, and African Caribbean popular culture.

Equiano writes that he was born into an Igbo ruling class family in 1745 in what is now southeastern Nigeria, and was kidnapped and enslaved at around the age of eleven. Then, he says, he was taken to the West Indies for a few days before being brought to Virginia and sold to a local planter. Michael Henry Pascal (d. 1787), an officer in the British Royal Navy, soon bought him from the planter and took him to England in 1757. Recent biographical discoveries, however, cast doubt on Equiano's story of his birth and early years. Baptismal and naval records say that he was born in South Carolina sometime between 1745 and 1747. If they are accurate, he must have invented his African birth, and thus his much-quoted account of the Middle Passage on a slave ship. Other recently discovered evidence proves that he first reached England in December 1754, which would make him significantly younger when he came under Pascal's control than he claims if he had indeed been born in 1745 or 1747. On the other hand, all surviving archival and published records from the period after 1754 attest to Equiano's astoundingly accurate memory of his life once he arrived in England. The truth

Olaudah Equiano (c. 1745–1797). Equiano published his autobiography in 1789. It was one of the earliest examples of published writing by an African author.

about the place and date of his birth may never be known.

Pascal renamed his new slave Gustavus Vassa, after the sixteenth-century Swedish nobleman who led his people in a successful revolt against Danish rule, and who consequently became the first king of an independent Sweden. Slaves were often given ironically inappropriate names of powerful historical figures, such as Caesar and Pompey, to emphasize their subjugation to their masters' wills. Throughout his life, Pascal's slave retained the name Vassa in private and public, even after he either reclaimed or assumed the name Equiano in print in 1789. Gustavus Vassa is the name found on his baptismal record, his marriage certificate, legal documents, his private correspondence, and his will.

Equiano served under Pascal in the Seven Years' War (1756–1763) and expected to be freed at its conclusion. Equiano's high expectations at the close of the war were not unwarranted. By the end of 1762 he had spent nearly half of his life aboard royal naval vessels. Because the Navy forbade slavery on its vessels, his status as Pascal's slave had been effectively hidden. One can understand why Equiano might have thought of his enslaved status as merely nominal. His freedom of movement appears to have been no more limited than that of other officers' servants, who were legal minors, though not chattel slaves. Unlike most slaves, Equiano was out of his owner's sight for months at a time, and during their time together Equiano had come to consider Pascal as a father figure. But for reasons unknown, Pascal reneged on his promise of freedom and sold Equiano into West Indian slavery at the end of 1762. There, Robert King, a Quaker, bought him.

Fortunately, the education Equiano had received in the schools aboard the larger Royal Navy ships he had served on rendered him too valuable an asset to be wasted doing the kinds of backbreaking agricultural labor most slaves endured. Because of Equiano's literacy and mathematical skills, King employed him in his intercolonial commerce between the West Indies and British North America. Service at sea on Royal Navy and commercial vessels gave Equiano an extraordinary vantage point from which to observe the world around him. His social and geographical mobility exposed him to all kinds of people and levels of society. He was able to comment on the range of types of slavery in the British colonies only because his own enslaved condition was so atypical. His convincing account of Africa was derived at least in part from the experiences of others, he tells his readers, that he encountered during his many travels in Britain, the Caribbean, and North America.

Equiano purchased his freedom from King in 1766 with the money he saved from shrewd business deals. He remained in King's employ for another year and made several more trading trips to Georgia and Pennsylvania. Between 1767 and 1773, Equiano, now based in London, worked on commercial vessels sailing to the Mediterranean and the West Indies, and commented on all the versions of slavery, white and black, he observed. A combination of necessity and desire led him to spend a total of more than ten years of his life on the water. Once he was a free man he repeatedly returned to the sea. His apparent wanderlust led him to join his friend and former employer, Dr. Charles Irving, on an expedition to the Arctic unsuccessfully seeking a Northeast Passage in 1773. Equiano's desire for fame and adventure almost cost him his life when ice nearly crushed the expedition's wooden ships.

During the 1770s he worked as a domestic servant in London between commercial voyages to North America and the Mediterranean. During one of these voyages on October 6, 1774, Equiano experienced what he considered to be the most important event in his life: In Cadiz, Spain, he was reborn as a Christian. While back in London in 1774, Equiano also had his first involvement with challenges to the legal status of slavery and the transatlantic slave trade. Two years earlier, the abolitionist Granville Sharp (1734–1813) had succeeded in getting William Murray, 1st Earl of Mansfield (1705-1793), to rule that no slave in England could legally be forced back into slavery in the West Indies. When Equiano's friend John Annis, a former slave, was kidnapped by his former owner to be sent back to the Caribbean to be sold, Equiano sought Sharp's help to save him. They were unable to act in time, however. Although Equiano was not yet an abolitionist himself, his attempt to save Annis brought him into contact with the initial phase of the movement.

Soon again growing restless, in 1775–1776 he helped in a short-lived attempt to establish a plantation in Central America, acting as buyer and driver (overseer) of the black slaves and hoping for success as a Christian missionary. Frustrated by having failed to convert any of the natives and disgusted by the behavior of his fellow overseers, at the beginning of 1777 he returned to London, where he once again went into domestic service. In 1779, the Bishop of London rejected his petition to be ordained and sent to Africa as a missionary. Equiano's acquaintance with Sharp and his interest in going to Africa led to a different kind of mission, however.

During the late 1780s, Equiano became increasingly involved with Thomas Clarkson (1760–1846), James Ramsay (1733–1789), Granville Sharp, and others in efforts to help his fellow blacks, with the project to resettle the black poor in Sierra Leone, and with the drive to abolish the African slave trade. In 1786, the British government hired Equiano to be in charge of provisions for the projected settlement in Sierra Leone of destitute African, African American, and East Asian residents of London. Many of them were Black Loyalists, some of the tens of thousands of former slaves who had fled their owners during the American Revolution to accept the British offer of freedom to any slave of the rebellious colonists. When the defeated British evacuated their troops in 1783, thousands of now-free blacks were taken to Canada and hundreds to England. Besides overseeing supplies for the settlers, Equiano was also to be the British government's representative in dealing with local leaders in Africa. One of Equiano's reasons for publishing his autobiography was his desire to justify his conduct in the project because he had been relieved of his duties after a dispute with a fellow employee while still in England. Exactly when Equiano turned against the transatlantic slave trade and the institution of slavery in unknown, but in 1788 he published hostile newspaper reviews of proslavery books and argued in print for racial intermarriage and against slavery. He also collaborated with Quobna Ottobah Cugoano (c. 1757–c. 1801) and other self-styled Sons of Africa in public protests against the transatlantic slave trade.

The timing of the publication of *The Interesting Narrative* in 1789 was no accident. Organized and sustained opposition to the transatlantic African slave trade was a recent development when the autobiography first appeared. Abolition of the slave trade had become a truly popular cause only during the previous five years, especially after the founding of the Society for Effecting the Abolition of the Slave Trade in London in 1787. During the eighteenth century, abolition almost always referred to eradication of the trade. The term rarely included the much smaller number of people openly calling for emancipation, eradication of the institution of slavery. Opponents of slavery became generally known as abolitionists only after the transatlantic slave trade become illegal in 1807. Mainly through the efforts of the philanthropist Thomas Clarkson, the organized opposition to the African slave trade gathered and published evidence against the infamous practice from 1787 on. Responding to the growing public interest in abolition, in February 1788 King George III (1738–1820) ordered an investigation into British commercial relations with Africa, and the nature of the

slave trade. During the following session of Parliament, the House of Commons began to hear testimony on the slave trade. Much of the evidence gathered dealt with conditions in Africa and during the Middle Passage. Equiano attended some of the hearings, but his own offer to testify was rejected.

Publishing his *Interesting Narrative* allowed Equiano to present in print the positive image of Africa and Africans he was not permitted to give in person before Parliament, as well as to give a first-person account of the Middle Passage and West Indian slavery told from the victim's point of view. Prior to 1789 the evidence and arguments against the slave trade had come from white voices alone. The only published black witnesses were clearly fictitious. In *An Essay on the Slavery and Commerce of the Human Species* (London 1786), Equiano's future subscriber Thomas Clarkson acknowledged the desirability of hearing the victim's point of view. Initially, not even black opponents of the trade recognized the rhetorical power an authentic African voice could wield in the struggle. When Equiano's African friend, collaborator, and future subscriber Quobna Ottobah Cugoano published *Thoughts and Sentiments on the Evil and Wicked Traffic of the Slavery and Commerce of the Human Species* in London in 1787 he chose not to describe Africa or the Middle Passage in much detail. Equiano, however, recognized that what the antislave trade movement needed most in 1789 to continue its momentum was precisely the kind of account he supplied, a story that corroborated and even explicitly drew upon earlier reports of Africa and the trade by some white observers, and challenged those of others. He also knew that, two years earlier, Cugoano had missed his chance to give such an account.

Reviewers praised Equiano's *Interesting Narrative* as a remarkable achievement. Some of the book's great popularity must be attributed to the timing of its initial publication at the height of the movement in Britain to abolish the slave trade. His first reviewers acknowledged the significance of the first-hand perspective of the book, which greatly influenced the development of the nineteenth-century African American slave narrative. Equiano's *Narrative* offered the only account by a former slave of slavery in Africa and on the Middle Passage, as well as in the West Indies, North

America, the Mediterranean, the Middle East, and Britain. Equiano's pre-publication advertisements for the book and supervision of the publication and distribution of nine British editions between 1789 and 1794 make him an important figure in the history of book publishing. During his lifetime unauthorized editions and translations appeared in Holland (1790), New York (1791), Germany (1792), and Russia (1794).

A genius at self-representation and self-promotion, Equiano defied convention first by writing his autobiography, and then by publishing, marketing, and distributing it himself. Publication of his *Interesting Narrative* enabled him to reclaim the social status, equivalent to that of a British gentleman, he says that he had lost when he was enslaved. Having raised himself from poverty and obscurity to international fame, Equiano epitomized a self-made man who profited from marketing that image of himself. He rose from being a piece of property in the eyes of the law to become the wealthiest person of African descent in Britain. He offered his own life as a model for others to follow. Equiano's personal conversions and transformations from enslaved to free, pagan to Christian, and proslavery to abolitionist, anticipated the changes he hoped to make in his readers, as well as the transformation he called for in the relationship between Britain and Africa. He became the first successful professional writer of African descent in the English-speaking world. By retaining the copyright to his autobiography, he maintained control over his tale, which enabled him to make changes in every one of the nine editions he published of his autobiography. The 311 names on the subscription list to his first edition, ranging from the Prince of Wales to the unidentified Mrs. Hogflesh, demonstrates that he was a master of political and social networking. By the ninth edition, the number of subscribers had grown to more than 1,400. Equiano was a pioneer in the development of the promotional book tour, traveling throughout England, Ireland, and Scotland to sell his book and promote the abolitionist cause. He did very well by doing good.

Equiano also defied convention by marrying on April 7, 1792, Susannah Cullen (d. 1796), an Englishwoman, in Cambridgeshire. He made sure that his racist opponents knew he had done so by announcing his wedding in every subsequent edition of his autobiography. He and his wife had two daughters, the younger of whom, Joanna (b. 1795), survived her parents to inherit in 1817 the sizeable estate worth £950 in 1817, equivalent in 2006 currency to approximately £100,000, or nearly $200,000. Equiano's marriage anticipated the commercial union he advocated between Africa and Europe. His will, in which he identifies himself as a gentleman, demonstrates that he had achieved the economic and social status he sought throughout his life when he died on 31 March 1797.

Through a combination of natural ability, accident, and determination, Equiano seized every opportunity to rise from the legal status of being an object to be sold by others to an international celebrity, the story of whose life became his own most valuable possession. Once free from enslavement, his every action reflected his repudiation of the constraints bondage had imposed on him. As if to flaunt his liberty, he traveled the world virtually at will, recognizing the sea as a bridge rather than a barrier between continents and people. His freedom gave him the chance to move socially, economically, religiously, and politically, as well as geographically. Having known what the loss of liberty entailed, once free he took as much control of his life as he could, even revising the events in it to make a profit in a just cause.

Print allowed him to resurrect not only himself publicly from the social death enslavement had imposed on him, but also the millions of other diasporan Africans he represented. By combining his own experiences with those of others he refashioned himself as the African. Rejected in his attempts to be sent by Europeans to Africa as a missionary or diplomat, through his *Interesting Narrative* Equiano made himself into an African missionary and diplomat to a European audience. In the recreation of his own life he forged a compelling story of spiritual and moral conversion to serve as a model to be imitated by his readers.

Unfortunately, Equiano did not live to see the abolition of the slave trade. The political triumph of the abolitionist cause in 1807 came ten years too late for him to celebrate. It might not have come that soon, however, had he not contributed to the cause by so skillfully and creatively fashioning the story of his life to put a speedy end to a traffic that was both cruel and unjust. He gave the abolitionist cause the African voice it needed. The role he played in the last mission of his life entitled him to accept the name of a European liberator of his people ironically given him in slavery. He had transformed himself into the cosmopolitan citizen of the world he called himself.

See also **Literature and the Study of Africa; Slavery and Servile Institutions.**

BIBLIOGRAPHY

Carretta, Vincent. *Equiano, the African: Biography of a Self-Made Man.* Athens: The University of Georgia Press, 2005.

Equiano, Olaudah. *The Interesting Narrative and Other Writings,* revised edition, ed. Vincent Carretta. New York: Penguin Books, 2003.

Equiano, Olaudah. *The Interesting Narrative of the Life of Olaudah Equiano, or Gustavus Vassa, the African. Written by Himself,* 2nd edition, ed. Robert J. Allison. 2 vols. New York: Bedford/St. Martin's, 2006.

VINCENT CARRETTA

ERITREA

This entry includes the following articles:
GEOGRAPHY AND ECONOMY
SOCIETY AND CULTURES
HISTORY AND POLITICS

GEOGRAPHY AND ECONOMY

Eritrea, located in Northeast Africa, borders the Red Sea in the north and east, Djibouti in the southeast, Sudan in the west and northwest, and Ethiopia in the south. Its total area is approximately 46,842 square miles and its total land boundaries are about 1,012 miles long. Eritrean boundaries with Djibouti, Ethiopia, and Sudan extend to 70 miles, 566 miles, and 375 miles respectively. Its coastline is approximately 1,367 miles long; there are more than 350 islands and archipelagos

(including Dahlak Kebir, Dohul, and Norah) to the southern part of the Red Sea and thereby Eritrea borders with the Yemen. Eritrea is located in a geopolitical position at one of the world's busiest maritime and commercial routes, the Red Sea.

Eritrea comprises several contrasting geographical zones: the Eastern Escarpments, the Eastern Coastal Plains, the Central and Northern Highlands, and the Western Lowlands. The Red Sea coastal plains extend in a long tail-like prolongation from the port of Massawa and the Gulf of Zula to Djibouti. They constitute part of the huge Danakil Depression, which comprises extensive sand and salt plains and lakes. Some parts of this arid zone sink 230 ft or more below sea level. In contrast, the adjacent Eastern escarpment forms steep-walled, rugged mountains. The western part of the country is characterized by steep and gentle slopes, and the vast plains of Barka. The central highlands are largely tablelands marked by high mountains rarely covered by vegetation; their plains are nonetheless fertile agricultural areas. The highest mountain Emba Soyra (9,902 feet high) is located on the southern part of the plateau. The plateaus form a major watershed between the Red Sea and the western drainage basins. The three major rivers (the Mereb, the Baraka, and the Anseba) rise in this region and flow west and northwest. The northern highlands are characterized by lofty mountains and arid climate.

There is remarkable climatic difference among the diverse geographical zones of the country. The highlands have temperate climate throughout the year while the lowlands are scorched by blazing heat for most of the year. Rainfall also varies depending on the altitude. While the annual average distribution of rainfall on the plateau ranges between 19 and 27 inches, in most parts of the lowlands annual rainfall ranges between 4 and 16 inches. The temperature of most lowland zones is arid and semiarid. The distribution of rainfall and vegetation types markedly varies throughout the country. The drainage systems originate from the plateau and northern highlands. Most of the rivers (which are important resources of water for seasonal irrigation; and for human as well as livestock consumption) drain towards the Red Sea, the western lowlands and the Danakil Depression.

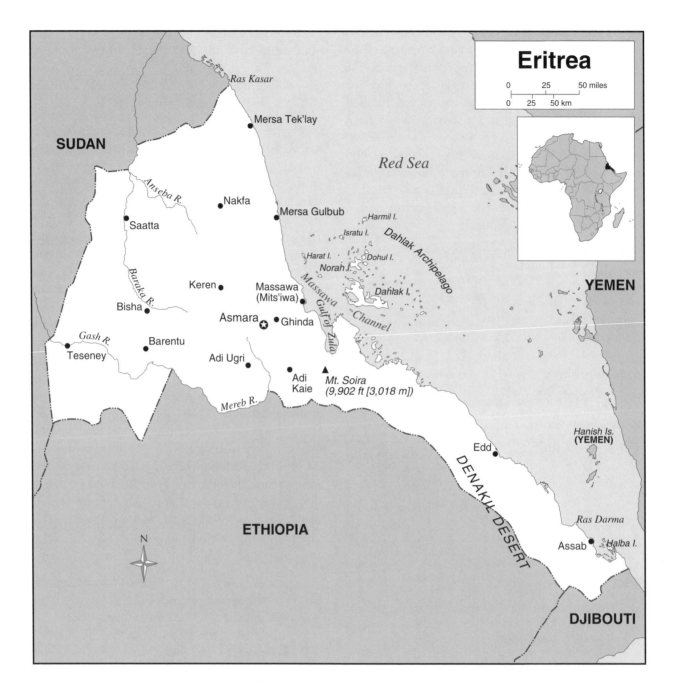

The Eritrean economy is largely based on subsistence agriculture. About 80 percent of the total Eritrean population depend on subsistence farming and herding. During the Italian colonial occupation (1890–1941), the economy was augmented by a slight industrialization, infrastructural development, and commercial farming. The colonial economy which was governed by a segregation policy and racial discrimination marginalized the majority of the people. The Eritrean economy showed a short-term boom necessitated by the ongoing wars in the Middle East and Horn of Africa during the British Military Administration (BMA; 1941–1952). However, the economy also showed sharp fluctuations followed by a serious deterioration during the postwar periods (1945–1952). The economy during the federal period (1952–1962) showed further worsening, particularly in the industrial sector. The Ethiopian occupation and liberation struggle (1962–1991) period was characterized by extensive military conflicts and massive destruction of the economic resources. Particularly during the Derg regime (1974–1991), the general economy was transformed into socialist orientation in which most of the private sectors were nationalized. Military atrocities over the human and livestock resources of the country were accompanied by acute environmental degradation that led to severe droughts and famine throughout the 1970s and 1980s. Land degradation, soil erosion, deforestation, and depletion of water sources are among the acute environmental problems of the country.

Independent Eritrea (since 1991) inherited a ruined economy. The Eritrean government embarked on new development plans that were directed towards rebuilding the economy of the country. Building up of educational, transport, medical infrastructures, afforestation and land and soil conservation were some of the top priorities of the governmental policies. Although the gross domestic product (GDP) showed dramatic increase from below 1 percent to 8.2 percent between years 1991 and 1998, it again showed sharp decrease to 1 percent between 1999 and 2004. The sharp decrease of GDP is attributed to the bad effects of Eritrean-Ethiopia border conflict which broke out in 1998. The war (1998–2000) and the unsolved border tensions have crippled the general economy weakening the potentials of export income and badly affecting domestic agricultural production. However, due to Eritrea's rich human resource both in the diaspora (which injects hard currency) and the organized domestic labor force, the country continues to develop its infrastructure, including transportation, education, modern agriculture, and industries.

See also **Climate; Ecosystems; Livestock; Production Strategies: Agriculture; Transportation: Shipping and Ports; Water and Irrigation.**

BIBLIOGRAPHY

Abdul-Haggag, Y. *A Contribution to the Physiography of Northern Ethiopia*. London: np., 1961.

Berhane Woldemichael, and Ruth Iyob. "Reconstruction and Development in Eritrea: An Overview." In *Post Conflict Eritrea: Prospects for Reconstruction and Development*, ed. Alemseged Tesfay and Martin Doornbos. Asmara: Red Sea Press, 1991.

Gebre, Hiwet Tesfagiorgis. *Emergent Eritrea: Challenges of Economic Development*. Asmara: Red Sea Press, 1991.

Killion, Tom. "The Eritrean Economy in Historical Perspective." *Eritrean Studies Review* 1 (1996): 91–118.

Murtaza, Niaz. *The Pillage of Sustainability in Eritrea, 1600s–1990s: Rural Communities and the Creeping Shadow of Hegemony*. Westport, CT: Greenwood Press, 1998.

Zemhret, Yohannes. "Nation Building and Constitution Making in Eritrea." *Eritrean Studies Review* 1 (1996): 154–166.

MUSSIE TESFAGIORGIS

SOCIETY AND CULTURES

Eritrea formally came into existence in 1890, and in the years that followed, a series of border treaties in respect of neighboring Sudan, Ethiopia, and French Somaliland (Djibouti) gave the Italian colony its modern form. In common with most African colonial territories, it was a wholly artificial creation, and encompassed considerable cultural, social and religious diversity, as it does to the present day. Officially, Eritrea comprises nine distinct ethnic and/or linguistic groups, although some of these have closer historical and cultural ties than others, while none is completely homogeneous. Several inhabit distinct ecological zones, and have consequently developed particular economic systems, which has tended to reinforce "ethnic" or "tribal" uniqueness.

Two broad distinctions have defined Eritreans' view of themselves and others' perceptions of them. The first is between communities living in the highlands (*kebessa*) and those in the lowlands (*metahit*), although again there is considerable diversity within these zones. The second is between Christian (broadly highland) and Islamic (both highland and lowland) populations. The Orthodox Christian Church dates to the fourth century in the Eritrean region, and was part of the Ethiopian Orthodox Church until independence, whereupon it separated to function as a self-governing church in communion with the Coptic Church of Egypt. Islam is held to have come to Eritrea during Muhammad's lifetime, in the early seventh century, and in the twenty-first century the vast majority of Eritrean Muslims are Sunnis.

The largest ethno-linguistic grouping are the Semitic Tigrinya speakers, who are predominantly sedentary farmers inhabiting the three former provinces of Hamasien, Serae, and Akele Guzay in the *kebessa*. The majority are Orthodox Christian, while there are minorities of Catholics and Protestants—

the consequence of earlier European missionary activity—and of Muslims, known as *Jiberti*. Historically and culturally linked to Tigray in northern Ethiopia, the Tigrinya have long dominated highland and subsequently national politics, while they have also constituted a significant proportion of urban traders and businessmen in more recent times; in large part this is a reflection of the fact that the Tigrinya region is by far the most urbanized in the country. The Tigrinya have often been seen—correctly—as the shapers of national destiny, and certainly this is how many see themselves. They were exposed to more colonial influences than any other group in Eritrea, and found themselves divided over the future of the territory in the 1940s and 1950s; but by the beginning of the 1970s a group of Tigrinya had laid the foundations of the Eritrean People's Liberation Front (EPLF) which, while to some extent recruiting outside the highlands, became dominated by the Tigrinya.

The other sizable group in terms of population are the predominantly Muslim Tigre, also speaking a Semitic language, who inhabit a swathe of territory from the western lowlands, across the northern mountains, and onto the northern coastal plains. Most are herders and seasonal farmers, and in the early twenty-first century Tigre-speakers are found in Massawa, and also in highland towns such as Ghinda and Keren, and in the area of Nakfa. The Tigre are divided into several groups, including the Beni Amer, Marya, and Mensa, and these provided the Eritrean Liberation Front (ELF) with some of its earliest fighters in the 1960s.

Along the southeastern coast and on the adjacent Red Sea islands are the Afar (Danakils), Cushitic-speakers who straddle the Ethiopian border and whose clan-based society is based around herding, trade and fishing. Throughout their history they have been responsible for the creation of independent sultanates, doubtless in part contributing to their reputation as the archetypal "warrior people"; the deserts they inhabit constitute one of the most inhospitable environments on earth. Their history has nonetheless been characterised by divided loyalties, despite periodic pan-Afar nationalist movements and the unity provided by Islam: While the Afar of the northern Eritrea Danakil desert have long gravitated toward

Massawa, and contributed fighters to both the ELF and EPLF, others further south have been oriented toward the Ethiopian sultanate at Aussa.

The Cushitic-speaking Bilen are located in the Keren area, known historically as the Bogos region, and are both Muslim and Christian (mostly Catholic). Both herdsmen and farmers, many early ELF fighters were Bilen; society is structured around clans, which are politically decentralised and in which authority is vested in clan elders. To the northwest, the Muslim Hedareb inhabit the western Barka lowlands, speak a Hamitic language, and are to be found among sections of the Tigre-speaking Beni Amer. They are also known as Beja or Tu-Bedawi—Beja-speakers are also to be found across the border in Sudan—and historically they are pastoralists, although some have become engaged in agriculture since the early twentieth century.

Also found in the western lowlands are the Nara, Nilotic farmers who keep cattle, inhabiting the region to the east of the Gash River. Their Islamic faith was largely imposed following the Egyptian occupation of the area in the mid-nineteenth century, and they were also involved in the liberation struggle from its earliest stages. Historically, they have a hostile relationship with the Kunama, who inhabit the southwest lowlands and the Barentu area, on the Ethiopian border. The Kunama are also Nilotic, in the early twenty-first century primarily herdsmen and farmers, and although there has been some conversion to either Christianity or Islam, many continue to adhere to local beliefs. The Kunama have had an ambivalent relationship with the liberation movements, and thus with the independent Eritrean state: Their historic hostility toward the Nara and the Beni Amer—both of which were involved in the struggle for independence—partly explains this, and successive Ethiopian governments have found in the Kunama willing recruits in the war against both the ELF and EPLF, and more recently the government in Asmara.

The Cushitic-speaking Saho inhabit the southern highlands below Asmara, and the escarpment down to the southern Massawa hinterland. Most are Muslim, and are herders and seasonal farmers. They are loosely organized into several "tribes," and historically have been engaged in conflicts with the Tigrinya over access to farming and pasture land. Finally, the Arabic-speaking and Muslim

Eritrea

Population:	4,906,585 (2007 est.)
Area:	121,320 sq. km (46,842 sq. mi.)
Official language:	No official language
Languages:	Afar, Arabic, Kunama, Tigre, Tigrinya, Italian
National currency:	Birr
Principal religions:	Christian 50%, mostly Orthodox, Muslim 48%, indigenous beliefs 2%
Capital:	Asmara (est. pop. 435,000 in 2006)
Other urban centers:	Keren, Assab, Massawa, Afabet, Tessenie, Mendefera, Dekemhare, Adekeieh, Barentu, Ghinda
Annual rainfall:	483–686 mm (19–27 in.) in southern highlands; 100–360 mm (4–14 in.) in eastern lowlands; 100 mm (4 in.) in Danakil Depression
Principal geographical features:	*Mountains:* Western Highlands, Eritrean Highlands, Malad, Ramlo *Rivers:* Gash, Mereb, Baraka, Anseba *Other:* Danakil Depression, Dahlak Islands
Economy:	*GDP per capita:* US$1,000 (2006)
Principal products and exports:	*Agricultural:* sorghum, lentils, vegetables, corn, cotton, tobacco, coffee, sisal, livestock, goats, fish *Manufacturing:* food processing, beverages, clothing and textiles, salt, cement, commercial ship repair *Mining:* copper, gold, oil
Government:	Independence from Ethiopia, 1993. Transitional government since that time. In 1993, a National Assembly was established as a transitional legislature. The Transitional National Assembly comprises 75 members of the People's Front for Democracy and Justice (PFDJ) and 75 additional popularly elected members
Heads of state since independence:	1993–: President Isayas Afeworki
Armed forces:	300,000 during border war with Ethiopia; in the process of demobilization
Transportation:	*Rail:* 306 km (190 mi.) *Ports:* Massawa, Assab *Roads:* 4,010 km (2,494 mi.), 21% paved. *National airline:* Eritrean Airways *Airports:* Asmara International Airport. 16 other smaller airports and airstrips.
Media:	Main periodicals: *Eritrean Profile, Hadas Eritrea, Chamber News, Trade and Development Bulletin*. One government-controlled television station.
Literary and education:	*Total literacy rate:* 58.3% (2003). Many schools destroyed during the war, but the EPLF established schools in areas it controlled. These educated civilians and all soldiers. Postsecondary education provided at the University of Eritrea and the Institute of Science and Technology.

Rashaida, along the northern and central coast, are the most recent ethnic immigrants to Eritrea, arriving from the Arabian peninsula in the course of the nineteenth century. They are mostly traders and pastoralists.

Exact statistics are currently impossible to come by, but together, the Tigrinya and Tigre make up between 80 and 90 percent of a population of 4.9 million. Most estimates place the Tigrinya at something around 50 percent. The remaining seven ethno-linguistic groups, therefore, constitute tiny minorities. Muslims and Christians are roughly equal in number, at close to 50 percent each. There is no official language in Eritrea, but Tigrinya and Arabic—and to some extent English—are the languages of government and public life. Much celebrated in tourist and other official literature, Eritrea's

ethnic diversity nonetheless has yet to be thoroughly addressed in legal and constitutional terms.

See also **Ethnicity; Languages; Linguistics, Historical.**

BIBLIOGRAPHY

Longrigg, Stephen H. *A Short History of Eritrea*. Oxford: Clarendon Press, 1945.

Ministry of Information, State of Eritrea. *Eritrea: A Country Handbook*. Asmara: Ministry of Information, 2002.

Nadel, Siegfried F. *Races and Tribes of Eritrea*. Asmara: British Military Administration, 1944.

Pateman, Roy. *Eritrea: Even the Stones Are Burning*. Trenton, NJ: Red Sea Press, 1998.

Pool, David. *From Guerrillas to Government: The Eritrean People's Liberation Front*. Oxford: James Currey, 2001.

Trevaskis, Gerald Kennedy Nicholas. *Eritrea: A Colony in Transition 1941–1952*. New York: Oxford University Press, 1960.

RICHARD REID

HISTORY AND POLITICS

In the mid-twentieth century, Eritrea was one of the first colonies in postwar Africa to grapple with the issue of decolonization. At the time, national sovereignty was not the obvious or inevitable option it would later become, and there were as many Eritreans who favored independence as those who chose union with Ethiopia. Few would have imagined at the time that Eritreans would eventually become engaged in one of Africa's most bitter and prolonged wars of national liberation in the name of a common identity.

As a territorial entity, Eritrea is the direct product of Italy's imperial expansion between 1869 and 1890. Prior to the 1860s, its constituent peoples had been part of a wider Red Sea world, connected by culture and commerce if not always by political affiliation. In the first half of the twentieth century, the construction of the Italian colonial state, and the process of social, economic, and cultural transformation that it initiated, profoundly reshaped the relationship of the territory's peoples to each other.

The Italians had initially planned to turn Eritrea into a settler colony. But following a peasant rebellion and defeat by Ethiopian forces at the Battle of Adwa in 1896, they were forced to abandon these plans. Eritrea was instead designated to become part of the Italian commercial empire and this provided the impetus for the construction of a relatively extensive rail and road infrastructure connecting various settlements. A light industrial sector emerged that by the 1930s had turned Eritrea into the most industrialized zone of northeast Africa. But colonial education policy was extremely conservative and there were fewer than one thousand students enrolled in modern educational institutions when Italian rule collapsed in 1941. The upshot of sixty years of Italian rule was that while the territory was materially integrated as never before, the state's educational policy and its divide and rule strategy had circumvented the emergence of a widespread sense of Eritrean-ness.

The British invasion and occupation of Eritrea (1941–1952) profoundly affected the growth of Eritrean political culture. When the war ended in 1945, Arabic and Tigrinya had emerged as the respective literary languages of Muslims and Christians, each possessing vernacular newspapers and administrative representation. Two main political blocs subsequently emerged—the Muslim League advocating independence and the Unionist Party advocating amalgamation into Ethiopia—and the stage was set for a bitter contest over the future of Eritrea.

A self-conscious Eritrean nationalism appeared at this time but from its inception it was hindered by cultural and linguistic divides, and for some time remained the notion of a very small group in the urban areas. It gained an initial following in the Muslim towns where reaction to the prospect of being absorbed into the Ethiopian empire-state galvanized the population. It acquired a mass form following the social revolt of the plebeian Tegra against the tributary system in the Muslim lowlands. The relaxation of political controls in the mid-1940s permitted a coalescence of these two trends that culminated in a simultaneous call for social and national emancipation. Meanwhile, in the Christian highlands, the forces of nationalism took longer to develop. There, the Orthodox Church had served as the bulwark of the call for union with Ethiopia and it took several years of imperial state repression and the fracturing of a common ethno-religious identity before a major shift in cultural and political allegiances would take place.

The Paris Peace Treaties at the conclusion of World War II had mandated the victorious Allied Powers—the United States, the Union of Soviet Socialist Republics, Great Britain, and France—to determine the future of the former Italian colonies. Unable to reach a consensus, the Allies handed the matter over to the newly formed United Nations (UN). A UN Commission of inquiry was set up to canvas the views of Eritreans and, in the context of internal rivalry and external great power manipulation, the General Assembly passed a resolution in 1950 federating Eritrea with Ethiopia.

From the start, the federation proved unworkable. Ethiopia was an empire ruled by an absolutist monarchy that was hostile to any semblance of democracy. Eritrea's UN-drafted constitution and its democratic provisions was anathema to the monarchy. Over the next decade (1952–1962), the Ethiopian state systematically dismantled the democratic freedoms Eritreans enjoyed. Political parties, independent associations, and labor unions were suppressed. The once vibrant Eritrean press was muzzled and Eritrea's two administrative languages—Arabic and Tigrinya—were replaced by Amharic, the official language of Ethiopia. In 1959 the Eritrean flag was lowered and it was followed three years later by the formal abrogation of the federation and the annexation of Eritrea into the Ethiopian Empire.

In response, nationalist politicians initially put most of their energies into international appeals for redress against the disabling of Eritrea's autonomy. By the late 1950s, confronted with an increasingly intransigent autocratic order, the nationalist movement's main impetus of activity shifted to armed opposition. The efforts of the Eritrean Liberation Movement (ELM) at political mobilization were soon outflanked by the emergence of the Eritrean Liberation Front (ELF), which emphasized the exclusive efficacy of armed struggle and commenced operations in September 1961. In the subsequent decade, the nationalist movement went through a series of internal crises culminating in the breakaway formation of the Eritrean Peoples Liberation Front (EPLF). A new generation of Christian Eritreans had by then begun affirming their nationalist credentials. This represented an unprecedented extension of nationalist politics, which now embraced all Eritreans regardless of faith or ethnicity, and a more deeply rooted sense of Eritrean-ness was fostered in the crucible of a three-decades-long war of national liberation (1961–1991).

By May 1991 the end of the Cold War isolated the already besieged Ethiopian regime and provided the EPLF, the hegemonic nationalist movement, with an auspicious opportunity to liberate Eritrea and initiate the process of fashioning the emerging state institutions. The formal declaration of independence came two years later on May 24, 1993, following a UN-supervised referendum.

The transition to statehood and the prevalent sense of peace worked to mobilize popular expectations behind a vision of reconstruction that incorporated strong ideals of democratic citizenship and social justice. Once the initial euphoria of liberation had settled, however, political power seemed less susceptible to popular control and the space for creative politics was constrained. In the society at large, there was a general retreat to the concerns of the everyday as the jubilation of 1991 gave way to

the hard labor of reconstruction. The onset of the tragic war with Ethiopia (1998–2000) further threatened to reduce the promise of national liberation, and unmasked the authoritarianism latent in the nationalism articulated by the EPLF. The period after the conclusion of this war marks a transition to a different kind of political landscape in which the regime finds itself confronted with a popular longing for democratic rights and a representative government.

See also **Cold War; Colonial Policies and Practices; Menelik II; Mengistu, Haile Mariam; Nationalism; United Nations.**

BIBLIOGRAPHY

Iyob, Ruth. *The Eritrean Struggle for Independence: Domination, Resistance, Nationalism 1941–1993.* Cambridge, U.K.: Cambridge University Press, 1995.

Negash, Tekeste. *Italian Colonialism in Eritrea, 1882–1941: Policies, Praxis, and Impact.* Stockholm: Uppsala University, 1987.

Pool, David. *From Guerrillas to Government: The Eritrean People's Liberation Front.* Athens: Ohio University Press, 2001.

Trevaskis, G. K. N. *Eritrea: A Colony in Transition 1941–52.* New York: Oxford University Press, 1960.

Yohannes, Okbaghzi. *Eritrea: A Pawn in World Politics.* Gainesville: University of Florida Press, 1991.

FOUAD MAKKI

ETHIOPIA, ART. See **Art, Regional Styles: Ethiopia.**

ETHIOPIA, MODERN

This entry includes the following articles:
GEOGRAPHY AND ECONOMY
SOCIETY AND CULTURES
HISTORY AND POLITICS

GEOGRAPHY AND ECONOMY

Ethiopia is a landlocked country in the Horn of Africa. It borders with Eritrea to the north, Djibouti to the northeast, Somalia to the east,

Kenya to the south, and Sudan to the west and northwest. Its total area is 435,071 square miles.

Ethiopia is one of the oldest countries in the world. Its territorial extent has varied over the millennia of its existence. In the ancient times it remained centered in the northern part of the modern state around the city of Aksum, which was first an imperial capital and later became a holy city of Ethiopian Christendom. The present territory was consolidated during the nineteenth and twentieth centuries as a result of a conquest that this indigenous empire state undertook in the face of European colonialism.

PHYSICAL GEOGRAPHY

Ethiopia's topography is one of the most rugged in Africa. Five topographic features can be distinguished: the Western Highlands, Western Lowlands, Eastern Highlands, Eastern Lowlands, and the Great Rift Valley. The Western Highlands are the most extensive and the rockiest component of Ethiopia. The most spectacular portion of the northern massifs form the roof of Ethiopia with elevations as high as Mount Ras Dashan—the highest mountain in Ethiopia at 15,157 feet.

The Western Lowlands stretch north-south along the Sudanese border and include the lower valleys of the Blue Nile, Tekeze, and Baro Rivers. Situated at around 3,300 feet, these lowlands have been too hot to attract dense settlement. The Great Rift Valley with its scattered lakes and active volcanoes divides the Highlands and the Lowlands. In its first part in the northeast, the valley floor widens into a funnel shape as it approaches the Red Sea. This is a relatively flat area with occasional volcanic cones, some of which are active. The Danakil Plain, with a depression dropping as low as 380 feet below sea level, is located here. These conditions—high temperatures and lack of moisture—make the northeast Great Rift Valley unattractive for settlement. However, the southwest section is a narrow depression of higher elevation. It contains several lakes that form Ethiopia's internal drainage basin for many small rivers. This part of the Great Rift Valley is one of the most productive and settled parts of the country.

The Eastern Highlands are much smaller, still with impressive peaks at Batu (14,127 feet) and Mount Chilalo (13,575 feet). The Eastern Lowlands gently extend from the Eastern Highlands and roll through the country until reaching the Somali border. This area incorporates the regions of Ogaden and Haud with the rivers, Shebele and Genale, that moderate the desert conditions.

Because Ethiopia is located in the tropical latitudes, its areas of lower elevation experience climatic conditions typical of tropical savanna and desert. However, the relief plays a key role in moderating temperatures so that higher elevations experience weather typical of more moderate climate. The north part of the Western Highlands experiences irregular rainfall, whereas the southern part enjoys rain year-round. The Eastern Lowlands get some rain twice per year, in April–May and October–November. The driest of all regions is the Danakil Plain, which receives less than twenty inches and sometimes none at all.

ECONOMY

With only about 12 percent of the population living in urban centers, most Ethiopians inhabit rural areas. In the northern highlands, peasants have been using the plough for centuries to grow cereals. They eat pancake-like bread made with *teff*—an indigenous staple grain—that is served with a spicy sauce or a thick stew. In the culturally and climatically different southwest, the population uses the stem of a false banana tree (*ensete*) to provide dough for a bread-like product. It is mashed and left in the ground to ferment. Agriculture contributes to half of Ethiopia's gross domestic product. The most important form of agricultural activities is subsistence farming that produces most of the staple grains such as teff, wheat, barley, oats (on the cooler plateaus), sorghum, maize, millet, and pulses such as chickpeas, peas, beans, and lentils. Farm plots are usually small and range from 1.2 to 2.5 hectares.

Soil erosion is a serious problem in Ethiopia, particularly in the northern provinces that have been settled and used for agriculture for millennia. The population density has caused major damage to the soil, which has affected its organic and chemical nutrients and the natural vegetation cover.

Another type of agriculture is cash-cropping. The main cash crop is coffee, which is native to Ethiopia and provides more than 50 percent of foreign-exchange earnings. Cultivation of a mild drug, *chat*, has become almost equally important. Popular especially with the Muslim population,

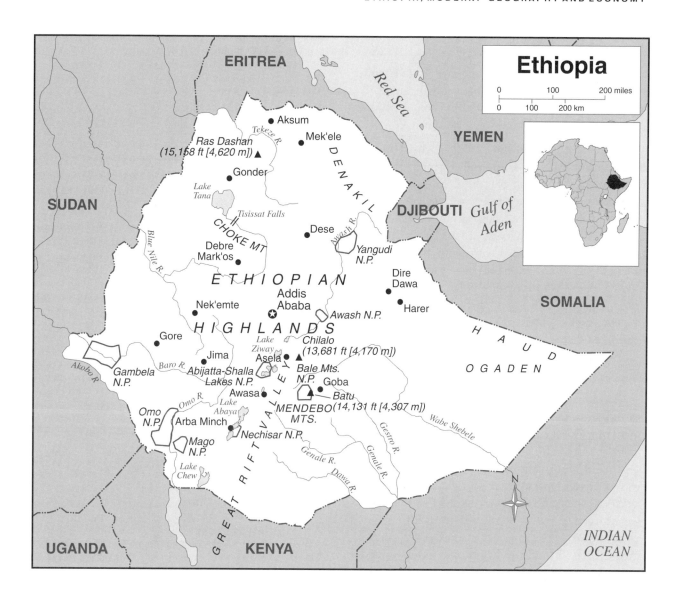

chat is grown mainly in Harar in the east and is widely exported to Djibouti, Yemen, and Somalia. Subsistence livestock rearing is important in the peripheral lowlands of Ethiopia. Families keep large herds as the cattle migrate each season in search of grazing and water. The livestock provide hides and skins that are also an important export. The remaining agricultural export commodities consist of oilseeds and vegetables. Manufacturing and transport equipment account for almost three-quarters of the value of imports. This situation leaves Ethiopia's balance of payments negative for many years.

HISTORICAL PERSPECTIVE AND THE LAND ISSUE

Under Emperor Haile Selassie (c. 1892–1975), Ethiopia's economy developed considerably. The production of cash crops such as coffee advanced at the same time that manufactured goods such as textiles and footwear were established. The revenues were used to improve communication and modernize urban centers. However, the emperor did not sufficiently address the issue of needed land reform. In 1974, fuelled by a severe drought in the north of the country, a series of mutinies took place in the capital. Junior army people who blamed the government for the country's economic problems and social inequality led the revolts. These events resulted in the deposition of Haile Selassie. The Derg regime that ruled from 1974 until 1991 promised to bring radical change to what was described as feudal and exploitative administration. Initially known as the Provisional Military Administrative Council (PMAC) and later promulgating itself as the Workers' Party of Ethiopia, the Derg instituted a Soviet-style government. It abolished the lineage-based land-tenure system that was traditional, especially in the northern plateau, and nationalized all means of production including land, housing, and industry.

The Green revolution (1979) focused on collectivization of the land and formed Peasant's Production Co-operatives. Equitable distribution of land among the members of the cooperatives led to smaller plots, overcultivation, land degradation, and declining harvest. In order to feed the urban population, the government tried to force the peasant's associations to deliver grain at below-market prices—a disastrous policy that led to the 1984 famine. The mid-1980s famine further impelled collectivization. The government embarked on forced resettlement and villagization as part of a national program to combat drought, avert famine, and increase agricultural productivity.

Resettlement, the regime's long-term solution to the pressing drought problem, involved the permanent relocation of about 1.5 million people from the drought-prone areas of the north to the south and southwest. The population in these areas was relatively sparse, and so-called virgin, arable land was plentiful. Beginning in 1985, peasants were forced to move their homesteads into planned villages that were clustered around water, schools, medical services, and utility supply points in order to facilitate distribution of those services. Many peasants fled rather than acquiesce to the relocation that generally proved highly unpopular. Additionally, the government in most cases failed to provide the promised services. Far from benefiting agricultural productivity, the program caused a decline in food production.

In the early twenty-first century, modern manufacturing contributes only about 7 percent of the GDP of Ethiopia. The products include processed food, textiles, tobacco, leather, footwear, and chemical products. Despite soil erosion, overgrazing, and deforestation, Ethiopia's most promising resource seems to be its agricultural land. Most of the reserve land is in the areas with favorable climatic conditions for intensive agriculture. Also, better management of grazing lands and breeding of livestock could meet the demands of internal and external markets.

See also **Addis Ababa; Asmara; Haile Selassie I; Harar; Massawa; Mengistu, Haile Mariam.**

BIBLIOGRAPHY

Bruce, John W.; Allan Hoben; and Dessalegn Rahmato. *After the Derg: An Assessment of Rural Land Tenure Issues in Ethiopia.* Madison: University of Wisconsin, 1994.

Göricke, Fred V. *Social and Political Factors Influencing the Application of Land Reform Measures in Ethiopia.* Saarbrücken: Verlag Breitenbach, 1979.

Hansson, Göte. *The Ethiopian Economy 1974–94: Ethiopia Tikdem and After.* London: Routledge, 1995.

Rahmato, Dessalegn. *Agrarian Reform in Ethiopia.* Trenton, NJ: Red Sea Press, 1985.

Tadesse, Zenebework, ed. *Environment and Development in Ethiopia: Proceedings of the Symposium of the Forum for Social Studies, Addis Ababa, 2000.* Addis Ababa, Ethiopia: The Forum, 2001.

Teferra, Daniel. *Social History and Theoretical Analyses of the Economy of Ethiopia.* Lewiston, NY: Edwin Mellen Press, 1990.

Wolde-Mariam, Mesfin. *An Introductory Geography of Ethiopia.* Addis Ababa, Nigeria: 1972.

Wolde-Mariam, Mesfin. *Rural Vulnerability to Famine in Ethiopia: 1958-1977.* Dew Delhi, India: Vikas Pub. House, 1984.

Wubneh, Mulatu Yohannis Abate. *Ethiopia: Transition and Development in the Horn of Africa.* Boulder, CO: Westview Press, 1988.

IZABELA ORLOWSKA

SOCIETY AND CULTURES

The 1994 national census gives some indication of the ethnic diversity of Ethiopia and the importance of the Oromo and Amhara in defining identity. In a nation containing over seventy ethnic groups, Oromo constituted 32.1 percent of a population that at the time was approximately 53.1 million, while Amhara made up 30.1 percent of the population. Other sizable ethnic groups and their percent of the population included Tigrean (6.2%), Somali (5.9%), Gurage (4.3%), Sidama (3.5%), and Welaita (2.4%). However, the rigid ethnic boundaries used in conducting a census do not reflect the flexibility of identity in Ethiopia.

Ethnic identity in Ethiopia has been a historically fluid category that has shifted with changes in political power. The group that was politically dominant during the twentieth century, and for much of the past one thousand years, is known to the outside world as the Abyssinians, and within Ethiopia as *Habesha*. The term Abyssinian encompasses two linguistic and geographic groups, Amhara and Tigrean, and it has been widely used by scholars to refer to the Orthodox Christians living in what is present-day northern Ethiopia. The unification of the Orthodox Christian Abyssinian empire and the military conquest of what is present-day southern and western Ethiopia that began in the late nineteenth century is one of the key factors in defining ethnic identity in modern Ethiopia. Although other ethnic groups participated in this military expansion, it has been primarily associated with the Amhara, meaning that the Amhara have occupied a peculiar position of dominance within ethnic relations during the past one hundred years.

The ethnic category of Amhara has expanded or contracted depending on the context, and it has been argued that Amhara identity is based less on biological descent than the performance of particular cultural traits. The two most relevant aspects of Amhara culture for assimilation have been religion and language. Historically, being an Amhara has been nearly synonymous with being an Orthodox Christian. The Amharic language, which is the national language of Ethiopia, is also an important source of identity. In the conquered regions, unless individuals adopted these traits, they were stigmatized and exposed to harsh forms of economic exploitation.

Ethiopian Orthodox Christians generally have not used missionaries as a means of converting non-Christians. Instead, conversion to Orthodox Christianity and assimilation to Amhara culture has occurred on the basis of political and military might. Largely because of a complicated system of land tenure based on bilateral descent that was forced upon them at the time of the conquest, subjugated groups found it necessary to assimilate in terms of religion and language in order to access political and economic goods. Fluency in Amharic provided some ability to engage in the litigation that was necessary to claim rights to land within the new system.

Conversion to Orthodox Christianity enabled one to avoid some of the worse forms of discrimination, as the prejudices of the northerners could not be as easily applied to other Christians. While the northerners certainly adopted some linguistic and cultural traits, on the whole the exchange of culture moved from the politically dominant Amhara to the subjugated groups. That said, the process of assimilation was never complete, and ethnicities with distinct identities, often defined partially in opposition to the Amhara, continue to exist even in areas with a strong Amhara presence.

Interaction among ethnic groups has been limited by Ethiopia's unique geography. For the most part, northern expansion did not extend beyond the highland plateau that forms much of Ethiopia. Lowland areas in the extreme south, east, and west of the country have largely been occupied by pastoralists, shifting cultivators, and hunter-gatherers. While land that was suitable for the plow agriculture practiced by the Amhara was often appropriated, the mobility of local ethnic groups enabled them to avoid direct subjugation and extensive interactions with the northerners.

Although the Oromo are the largest ethnic group in Ethiopia, their importance in shaping modern notions of ethnicity has not always been acknowledged. The Oromo emigrated from the south in the sixteenth century, and their current geographical location, covering much of central Ethiopia as well as areas in the north and south, had been more or less established by the beginning of the nineteenth century. In contrast to the Amhara, the Oromo have had a long-standing practice of quickly absorbing and assimilating conquered groups rather than ruling over them. In some cases the assimilation appears to have been total, while in others, dominated groups continued to maintain distinct ethnic identities while adopting some aspects of Oromo culture, such as religion.

Scholars disagree about the degree to which conquered groups affected Oromo culture. For example, early in the eighteenth century in the Gibe Valley region in what is present-day southwestern Ethiopia, the primarily pastoral Oromo adopted the more sedentary agriculturally based mode of subsistence practiced by the groups they had conquered. It has also been argued that

Women selling handwoven baskets on the outskirts of the main market in Jimma, Ethiopia, a city of approximately 120,000. The baskets, called *messob*, are used for storing *injera*, a pancake-like bread that is the staple food of most Ethiopians. PHOTOGRAPH BY ALISE OSIS

Oromo in this region borrowed their political system from subjugated groups living in the Gibe Valley, but the current consensus among scholars is that the transition from an age-grade system known as *gada* to a monarchy was based primarily on the internal dynamics of Oromo society.

In the twenty-first century, the Oromo people are spread over a large region of Ethiopia that includes a variety of natural environments that lead to different modes of subsistence. While Oromo are united by a common language, they practice different religions including Islam, Orthodox Christianity,

A farmer plowing in the highlands of southwestern Ethiopia with his son. The ox-drawn plow has been used for farming in Ethiopia for centuries. This method is the norm for much of the 85 percent of Ethiopia's population who live in rural areas. Typical crops grown in this manner include maize, sorghum, barley, and tef, a grain used to make injera. PHOTOGRAPH BY ALISE OSIS

Protestant Christianity, and the worship of their traditional sky god, Waqa. This means that in some areas, like the Gibe Valley region, assimilation to the Oromo norm has involved conversion to Islam, while in other areas it has not.

The introduction of ethnic federalism after the fall of the Marxist "Derg" government in 1991 has further transformed the process of defining ethnic identity. Under ethnic federalism, Ethiopia is divided into eleven states—two cities and nine regions—based primarily on historic ethnic boundaries. States have a broad range of power covering education, economic development, health, police forces, and legal courts, and they may conduct government business and education in the language of their choice.

Whereas in the past individuals had good reason to assimilate to Amhara, or especially during the eighteenth and nineteenth centuries to Oromo norms, under ethnic federalism political and economic incentives have been created for individuals to identify with the ethnicity of the region in which

they reside. For example, individuals who speak Oromo have a better chance of obtaining government employment in the Oromo region. Furthermore, within some states, particular ethnicities are given control over the local government in smaller regions called *waredas*. Allocating resources according to ethnicity has led to more attention being focused on the ethnic identities of others. This system has given rise to debates over the authenticity of ethnic identity that serve to critique the system of ethnic federalism as a whole, or to question the rights of particular groups or individuals.

While ethnicity has been the dominant trope for understanding societies and cultures in modern Ethiopia, it is also possible to categorize societies based on a loose combination of linguistic families, modes of production, and religion. Northern Ethiopia is inhabited by Orthodox Christian plough cultivators who speak the Semitic languages of Amharic and Tigrinya. Eastern Ethiopia is predominantly occupied by Afar and Somali people who are generally nomadic pastoralists, practice

Federal Democratic Republic of Ethiopia

Population:	76,511,887 (2007 est.)
Area:	1,126,829 sq. km (435,071 sq. mi.)
Official language:	Amharic
Languages:	Tigrinya, Arabic, Guaragigna, Oromigna, English, Somali, Amharic
National currency:	Birr
Principal religions:	Ethiopian Orthodox Christian 40%, Sunni Muslim 45%–50%, Protestant 5%, remainder indigenous beliefs
Capital:	Addis Ababa (est. pop. 5,000,000 in 2006)
Other urban centers:	Dire Dawa, Nazret, Gondar, Dessie, Mekelle, Bahir Dar, Jimma, Awassa
Annual rainfall:	2,640 mm (104 in.) in southwest; 100 mm (4 in.) in the Danakil Depression
Principal geographical features:	*Mountains:* Ahmar Mountains, Dejen, Chilalo, Abuna Yosef, Batu, Guna, Bada, Guge, Ras Dashan, Ch'ok'e, Simen, Abuye Meda *Lakes:* Abbe, Abaya, Abiata, Ch'amo, Langano, Turkana, Shala, Chew Bahir, Tana, Ziway *Rivers:* Abay (Blue Nile), Akobo, Atbara, Awash, Baro, Dawa, Fafan Shet, Genale, Gilo, Omo, Segen, Wabe Shebele, Tekeze, Wabe Gestro. *Other:* Great Rift Valley, Dallol Depression, Danakil Depression, Somali Plateau
Economy:	*GDP per capita:* US$1,000 (2006)
Principal products and exports:	*Agricultural:* cereals, pulses, coffee, oilseed, cotton, sugarcane, potatoes, qat, cut flowers, hides, cattle, sheep, goats; fish *Manufacturing:* food processing, beverages, textiles, leather, chemicals, metals processing, cement *Mining:* gold; natural gas and iron mining is under development
Government:	Never a colony, briefly held by Italy 1935–1941. Constitution approved in 1987, suspended in 1991. New federal constitution approved 1994. After the emperor was deposed in 1974, a Marxist-Leninist military regime ruled the country until the 1991 revolution. Elections were held in 1992, won by the Ethiopian People's Revolutionary Democratic Front (EPRDF). Under the 1994 constitution, 548-member Council of People's Representatives elected for 5-year terms by popular vote. State councils from the 9 ethnic-group-based administrative regions have limited powers, including appointing the 117-member Federal Council for 5-year terms. Following legislative elections, the party in power designates the prime minister, who has full executive power. Prime minister appoints Council of Ministers, subject to approval of the Council of People's Representatives. The Council of People's Representatives elects the president, a largely ceremonial office.
Rulers since 1930:	1930–1974: Emperor Haile Selassie (excluding the years 1936–1941) 1974–1977: Provisional Military Administrative Council, led by Gen. Aman Andom (1974), Brig. Gen. Tafari Benti (1974–1977) 1977–1991: Lt. Col. Mengistu Haile Mariam 1991–1995: Acting President Meles Zenawi 1995–: Prime Minister Meles Zenawi 1995–2001: President Negasso Gidada 2001–: President Girma Woldegiorgis
Armed forces:	The Ethiopian National Defense Forces (ENDF) comprises about 200,000 personnel, including ground forces and an air force.
Transportation:	*Rail:* 681 km (422 mi.) Ethiopian segment of the Addis Ababa-Djibouti railway *Roads:* 36,469 km (22,661 mi.), 19% paved *National airline:* Ethiopian Airlines *Airports:* International facilities at Addis Ababa and Dire Dawa. Airports for internal flights at regional capitals and towns. 84 airports and airstrips in total.
Media:	Main periodicals: *Addis Zemen, Ethiopian Herald, Al-Alam, Ye Ethiopia Dimiz, Ethiopia Today, Hibret, Abyotawit Ethiopia, Addis Tribune, Addis Zimit, Meskerem, Birhan Family Magazine, Ethiopian Trade Journal, Ethiopia Review, Tinsae.* 8 radio stations, 1 television station.
Literacy and education:	*Total literacy rate:* 43% (2003). Public education is free up to the college level. Four junior colleges for agriculture, education, and animal health; University of Addis Ababa, Alemaya University of Agriculture, and Institute of Agricultural Research.

Islam, and speak languages of the Cushitic family. Although central-southwestern Ethiopia contains a diversity of religions and language families including the Cushitic-speaking Sidamo, Semitic Gurage, and Omotic Kafa, the region is united by the hoe-based cultivation of the enset, or false banana plant. These peoples are sometimes referred to as enset cultures because cultivation of enset structures many of their daily and seasonal activities.

The Omotic family of languages is the most diverse in Ethiopia, containing about fifty distinct languages and cultures. Omotic speakers live primarily along the Omo River in south and southwest Ethiopia. They include pastoralists as well as grain and enset cultivators, and they are not united by a common religion. The pastoral Nuer and the sedentary cultivator Anuak both speak languages belonging to the Nilo-Saharan family and inhabit the western border of Ethiopia. The Cushitic-speaking Oromo are spread throughout Ethiopia and practice plough-based agriculture, enset culti-vation, and pastoralism. Almost all Ethiopian soci-eties also contain craft workers, such as potters, tanners, or blacksmiths. These trades were officially banned during the "Derg" regime; practitioners remain highly stigmatized and form a group that resembles a distinct caste. In many cases, they are forbidden from intermarrying with others or own-ing land.

A final cultural group that is emerging in con-temporary Ethiopia is based around urban centers. With the exception of the Semitic-speaking Muslim Harari, who have developed their culture in the city of Harar in Eastern Ethiopia, all Ethiopian cultural groups have their historic roots in rural environ-ments. In the early twenty-first century, however, approximately 15 percent of the population live in urban areas and they share a relatively cohesive culture that may be described as urban Ethiopian. Urban Ethiopian culture is characterized by fluency in Amharic (although often as a second language), religious piety, a high level of respect for guests and formality in interpersonal interactions, and a belief in the importance of education. Consumer habits are important for urban residents, who generally dress conservatively and enjoy eating injera (a flat spongy bread made from the grain *tef*), drinking coffee, and listening to contemporary Ethiopian and international music. All of these traits are found in rural areas as well, but in cities they form a coherent set of behaviors that extend across lin-guistic or religious boundaries. Urban Ethiopians generally have a relatively high amount of contact with the international Ethiopian diaspora, which has a significant influence on their economic and cultural activities.

See also **Harar; Urbanism and Urbanization.**

BIBLIOGRAPHY

Asmarom, Legesse. *Gada: Three Approaches to the Study of an African Society;* New York: Free Press, 1973.

Baxter, P. T. W.; Jan Hultin; and Allesandro Triulzi; eds. *Being and Becoming Oromo: Historical and Anthropo-logical Enquiries.* Lawrenceville, NJ: Red Sea Press, 1996.

Donham, Donald. "Old Abyssinia and the New Ethiopian Empire: Themes in Social History." In *The Southern Marches of Imperial Ethiopia: Essays in History and Social Anthropology,* ed. Donald Donham and Wendy James. Cambridge, U.K.: Cambridge University Press, 1986.

Freeman, Dena, and Alula Pankhurst, eds. *Peripheral People: The Excluded Minorities of Ethiopia.* Lawrenceville, NJ: Red Sea Press, 2003.

Hassen, Mohammed. *The Oromo of Ethiopia: A History 1570–1860.* Cambridge, U.K.: Cambridge University Press, 1990.

Hoben, Allan. *Land Tenure among the Amhara of Ethiopia.* Chicago: University of Chicago Press, 1973.

James, Wendy; Donald Donham; Eisei Kurimoto; and Alessandro Triulzi; eds. *Remapping Ethiopia: Socialism and After.* Oxford: James Currey, 2002.

Levine, Donald. *Wax and Gold: Tradition and Innovation in Ethiopian Culture.* Chicago: University of Chicago Press, 1965.

Levine, Donald. *Greater Ethiopia: The Evolution of a Multiethnic Society.* Chicago: University of Chicago Press, 1974.

Turton, David, ed. *Ethnic Federalism: The Ethiopian Experience in Comparative Perspective.* Oxford: James Currey, 2006.

DANIEL MAINS

HISTORY AND POLITICS

The nineteenth century in Africa was marked by European colonial conquest. Ethiopia not only withstood the colonial onslaught but also managed to revive its monarchy and increase its territory in size. The restoration of the Ethiopian monarchy began in the mid-1850s with the rise to power of the charismatic leader Dejazmach Kassa, later Emperor Téwodros II (1855–1868). The revival drew heavily on the unifying ideology of the Solomonic state, whose kings traced their lineage to 1270 and beyond to biblical origins.

The ideology of the Solomonic state, which also constituted the myth of national origin, revolved around the belief that the Hebrew Ark of Covenant was transferred in accordance with God's will from ancient Jerusalem to the Ethiopian city of Aksum. It was based on the sense of unique-ness of Ethiopian rulers and their subjects as God's chosen people and was crucial in shaping a distinct and unifying identity. The Solomonic ideology was a powerful force in the revival and survival of this indigenous monarchy. The body of symbols asso-ciated with the national ethos enabled cultural legitimacy for the society as a whole and for those with a privileged position within it. This ideology, deeply embedded in Orthodox Christianity, was further reinforced and disseminated by the Church.

Téwodros brought to an end the era known as the Era of the Princes (1769–1855). Following a series of successful battles against competing regional lords, Dejazmach Kassa had himself crowned Téwodros II. This event was of great significance for the monarchy as it set a precedent of assuming imperial throne by a nonmember of the Solomonic lineage and hence set new rules for succession.

Téwodros, together with his successors Yohannis IV (1872–1889) and Menelik II (1889–1913) comprise the so-called Neo-Solomonic line of emperors, and their reigns symbolize a change in the established rules governing succession. These changes enabled the successful unification of semi-autonomous regions under the leadership of the emperor and consequently enabled Ethiopia to withstand colonial powers.

Téwodros was surrounded by the aura of reform and progress. Foreign observers often commented on his daring attempts to increase his revenues in order to create a stable national army. However, his policies were extreme and resulted in alienating the nobility. Overall, Téwodros proved unable to find a peaceful basis for his rule and sustained his claim to the imperial office mainly through coercion. Increasingly alienated by his own people and disappointed by the lack of response from the British court, Téwodros imprisoned a British envoy, together with a few other Europeans. In 1868 he committed a suicide at his fortress of Meqdela, surrounded by a British expeditionary force that had been sent to free the hostages.

This British expedition was aided by a northern ruler, Dejazmach Kassa Mircha (b. 1837) who facilitated its passage inland. On the way back, the withdrawing army left Kassa with considerable military equipment. He gradually established his rule and the remaining regional rulers submitted to him. Inspired by Téwodros's pioneering example, Kassa aspired to the imperial throne and was crowned Yohannis IV.

Yohannis IV faced a number of foreign threats during his reign. In 1868, Egypt took over from the Ottomans the Red Sea port of Massawa and began to expand into Ethiopian territory. Between 1875 and 1876, Yohannis successfully dealt with the encroaching Egyptian army. He faced the Egyptians in two main battles, at Gundet in November 1875 and at Gura in March 1876. A peace agreement was signed in 1884, in what is known as the Treaty of Adwa. However, the Egyptians withdrew from the Red Sea coast only to be replaced by Italy, which was secretly encouraged by Britain to occupy the port of Massawa. Italian presence on the Red Sea coast later led to the establishment of the colony of Eritrea. Mahdist Sudan was another intruder against whom Yohannis had to defend his western border. The Mahdists launched a *jihad* against Christian Ethiopia, and the two countries fought a number of battles between 1885 and 1889. In March 1889 at Metemma, Yohannis was mortally wounded. During his reign, Yohannis not only managed to subdue other regional rulers but also engaged them in the governing process by reviving the hierarchical structures of power.

His successor, Menelik II, could therefore almost immediately concentrate on expanding Ethiopian borders. This policy provided him with necessary resources such as gold, ivory, musk, coffee, hides, and slaves to obtain modern weapons and munitions necessary to equip the imperial army. However, Menelik also had to face European attempts at establishing a colony. The treaty of amity and commerce that Menelik signed with the Italians at Wuchale in 1889 proved controversial. Although the Amharic text of article 17 of the treaty read that Menelik could, if he wished, call upon the services of Italian authorities in his communication with other powers, the Italian version made this obligatory, by which Ethiopia in effect was made Italy's protectorate. Eventually, the Italians crossed the boundary separating their colony of Eritrea, created in 1889, and entered Ethiopian territory to exert pressure on Emperor Menelik. In response, Menelik declared national mobilization. On March 1, 1896, the battle Adwa took place, the result of which was a spectacular Ethiopian victory over the Italian forces. In the Treaty of Peace, signed on October 26, 1896, at Addis Ababa, Italy recognized independence of Ethiopia.

Menelik used the revenues from the periphery to modernize the new capital. He commissioned first modern schools, hospitals, a number of key roads, and a railway between Addis Ababa and Djibouti. The new capital also benefited from setting up telephones, a postal system, the first modern bank, and a hotel.

Having had no male heir of his own, Menelik wanted his grandson to succeed him. Lij Iyasu (1887–1935) took over in 1913, but proved unpopular mainly due to his favorable treatment of Muslims whom he attempted to integrate into the administration. In 1916 the Christian elite accused Iyasu of heresy and subversion and replaced him with Menelik's daughter Zewditu (1876–1930). Ras Teferi, the son of the cousin of Menelik, was appointed a regent, which was an unprecedented power arrangement. By 1928 Zewditu nominated Teferi king (*nigus*), and after her death in 1930 he was crowned Emperor Haile Selassie. In July 1930 the emperor had a constitution drafted that secured his prerogative delegate authority to an appointed and bicameral parliament, among other modern institutions.

The state modernization process that Haile Selassie carried out for the first time in history took away the armies from regional rulers and created armed forces under the emperor's command. He rewarded the notables with important government posts and grants of land. Carefully chosen officials, whose appointments could have been withdrawn at any time, governed the provinces on behalf of the emperor. Thus the former might of provincial governors was largely reduced.

Emperor Haile Selassie engineered Ethiopia's entry to the League of Nations in 1923, hoping that the collective security would protect Ethiopia from aggression. However, Italy had colonial ambitions in the Horn of Africa that received justification after a clash between an Ethiopian patrol with an Italian garrison at the Wolwol oasis in the southern region of Ogaden. Shortly after, in October 1935, Italian forces crossed Ethiopian borders. During the seven months of the Italo-Ethiopian War, the Italian command used air attacks and poison gas in order to break Ethiopian resistance. Consequently, between 1936 and 1941 Ethiopian was joined with the Italian colonies of Eritrea and Italian Somaliland to form Italian East Africa. During that time the Italians managed to dominate most cities, towns, and caravan routs, with fierce

Ethiopian resistance concentrated in the countryside. After Italy joined the World War II in 1940, Britain recognized Haile Selassie as a full ally. As a result, a combined army of Ethiopian and British troops liberated Ethiopia. On May 5, 1941, the emperor, who spent the occupation period in Britain, triumphantly returned to Addis Ababa.

During the Cold War period, Haile Selassie aligned himself with the West. His close ties with the United States helped him to recover, in 1952, the former colony of Eritrea that provided access to the Red Sea. Addis Ababa was also chosen to be headquarters for both the United Nations Economic Commission for Africa and the Organization of African Unity. Despite revision to the constitution in 1955 that led to the creation of an elected lower house of parliament, the emperor preserved his power to decree and his authority to appoint the government. The emperor and the state apparatus that he controlled failed to respond to calls for reforms instigated by certain groups within the educated elite. Students began to express their demands for change and in December 1960, the imperial bodyguard attempted a coup. The crisis of Haile Selassie's administration was further affected by the ongoing rebellion in Eritrea and the Somali borderlands. Also, the dramatic increase of imported oil in 1973 negatively affected the Ethiopian economy, already badly strained by the arms expenditure. A radical student movement emerged in Addis Ababa that identified the emperor and his landowning oligarchy as the agent of imperialism.

In 1974, series of mutinies began under the leadership of junior officials forcing some resignations of government officials. Severe famine in the overpopulated north made the situation worse for the government. In June of that year, the representatives of the mutinies organized themselves as a military Committee of the Armed Forces, Police, and Territorial Army (known as *Derg*). Mengistu Haile Mariam was elected its chairman. The Derg proceeded to dismantle the monarchy's institutions and to arrest Haile Selassie's close adviser and confidantes. Consequently, in September 1974 the Derg deposed the emperor. That November, Mengistu's faction within the Derg prevailed. Committed to Soviet-style socialism and determined to drive moderates from the Derg, this group instigated the removal of its first chairman,

General Aman Andom, and a few other Derg members who were executed on 23 November. The bloodshed continued that evening, which became known as "Bloody Saturday," and as many as sixty members of the old regime were executed. Subsequently, Mengistu installed a revolutionary socialists government.

Mengistu's years in office were marked by a totalitarian-style government and the country's massive militarization, largely financed by the Soviet Union and assisted by Cuba. Accordingly, in April 1976 Ethiopia abrogated its military assistance agreement with the United States and expelled American military missions. In 1977 Mengistu was faced with the Somali encroachment into to the Ogaden region, in pursuit of its irredentist claims to the ethnic Somali areas in Ethiopia. With the assistance of a massive Soviet arms airlift and Cuban combat forces, Ethiopian forces withstood the attack. In an attempt to sustain the regime, thousands of suspected enemies were tortured and killed between 1977 and 1978 in what became known as the Red Terror. Under Soviet pressure and hoping that a civilian party would be able to gain a degree of control over the population, the Workers' Party of Ethiopia (WPE) was established in 1984 and a new Soviet-style civilian constitution was submitted to a popular referendum in 1987. In September 1987, in accordance with this new constitution and with Mengistu as president, the country was renamed the People's Democratic Republic of Ethiopia.

The regime's later collapse was hastened by droughts that affected around eight million people, as well as by insurrections, particularly in the northern regions of Tigray and Eritrea. In 1989, the Tigrayan People's Liberation Front (TPLF) merged with other ethnically based opposition movements to form the Ethiopian People's Revolutionary Democratic Front (EPRDF). By April 1991, all of Eritrea was under the control of the Eritrean People's Liberation Front (EPLF) and the forces of EPRDF advanced on Addis Ababa. Consequently, Mengistu fled the country to Zimbabwe, where he received asylum.

In July 1991, the EPRDF and other political groups established the Transitional Government of Ethiopia (TGE) with an aim to engineer a new constitution and elections. The new government announced the reorganization of the country as a federal state divided into regions along ethnic lines as a way of acknowledging ethnic diversity. It soon became clear, however, that ethnically based regional governments were expected to be politically and ideologically affiliated with the EPRDF. In June 1992, the OLF withdrew from the government and in March 1993 members of the Southern Ethiopia People's Democratic Coalition also left the government. In May 1993 Eritrea, following a referendum, declared its independence.

In 1992, the EPRDF managed to carry out elections, which overall failed to provide them with a genuine popular mandate. The consensus of international observers was that the conditions for open political competition did not exist in Ethiopia at the time. In 1994 the Ethiopian parliament approved a new constitution that formed a bicameral legislature and a judicial system. Ethiopia's second multiparty election was held in May 2000. Meles Zenawi was once again elected as prime minister in October 2000. In October 2001, Girma Wolde-Giorgis (b. 1924) was elected president and remains in his office as of 2007.

In the early twenty-first century, Ethiopia's overall economy is recovering from years of mismanagement. However, the country continues to be affected by ethnic strife. The relations between Ethiopia and Eritrea deteriorated rapidly in 1998, and a border dispute leading to a war erupted between the two countries. An agreement was reached in December 2000, but the economic consequences of this bloody conflict seriously disturbed Ethiopia's recovery in terms of the social and economic achievements of previous decades.

See also **Addis Ababa; Aksum; Cold War; Eritrea: History and Politics; Ethiopia and the Horn, History of (1600 to 1910); Ethiopia and Vicinity, History of (600 to 1600 CE); Haile Selassie I; Menelik II; Mengistu, Haile Mariam; Organization of African Unity; Téwodros.**

BIBLIOGRAPHY

Beyene, Taddese; Richard Pankhurst; and Shiferaw Bekele, eds. *Kasa and Kasa: Papers on the Lives, Times and Images of Tewodros II and Yohannes IV (1855–1889).* Addis Ababa: Addis Ababa University, Institute of Ethiopian Studies, 1990.

Caulk, Richard, ed. "*Between the Jaws of Hyenas*": *A Diplomatic History of Ethiopia, 1876–1896*. Wiesbaden, Germany: Harrassowitz, 2002.

Donham, Donald, and Wendy James, eds. *The Southern Marches of Imperial Ethiopia*. Cambridge, U.K.: Cambridge University Press, 1986.

Marcus, Harold. *Haile Selassie I: The Formative Years, 1892–1936*. Lawrenceville, NJ: Red Sea Press, 1995.

Marcus, Harold. *The Life and Times of Menelik II: Ethiopia, 1844–1913*. Lawrenceville, NJ: Red Sea Press, 1995.

Pankhurst, Richard. *History of Ethiopian Towns from the Mid-Nineteenth Century to 1935*. Stuttgart, Germany: Franz Steiner Verlag Wiesbaden, 1985.

Rubenson, Sven. *The Survival of Ethiopian Independence*. London: Heinemann, 1976.

Tibebu, Teshale. *The Making of Modern Ethiopia, 1896–1974*. Lawrenceville, NJ: Red Sea Press, 1995.

Zewde, Bahru. *A History of Modern Ethiopia, 1855–1991*. Oxford: James Currey, 2001.

Zewde, Bahru, and Siegfried Pausewang, eds. *Ethiopia: The Challenge of Democracy from Below*. Uppsala, Sweden: Nordiska Afrikainstitutet, 2002.

IZABELA ORLOWSKA

ETHIOPIA AND THE HORN, HISTORY OF (1600 TO 1910).

At the dawn of the seventeenth century the Christian kingdom of Ethiopia found itself struggling to recover from the convulsions of the preceding century. The wars of Ahmad Grañ and the movement of the Oromo people had forced the state to retreat progressively northwards. After nearly a century of meandering, it finally came to settle at Gondär, a commercial center located to the north of Lake Tana. The founding of Gondär as the imperial capital in 1636 marked the beginning of a new chapter in the history of the region. Although a shadow of the medieval empire that it had come to replace, the Gondärine state saw a flourishing of the arts and crafts and the growth of a distinctively urban culture. The castles that still bedeck the city and constitute a great tourist attraction are living testimony of the new trends that emerged in the realm of architecture. Religious art, in the form mainly of icons, also attained new levels of refinement.

RETREAT AND ISOLATION

Yet the Christian kingdom remained a truncated edition of the sprawling medieval empire. The occupation of Massawa by the Ottoman Turks in 1557 had closed it off to the outside world. Contributing as well to the isolation of the Christian kingdom was the reorientation of its foreign policy in the seventeenth century. Establishing themselves in the country in the wake of the Portuguese military expedition that had helped the Christian kingdom defeat Ahmad Grañ, missionaries of the Order of the Society of Jesus (commonly known as the Jesuits) had applied themselves to the task of converting the country to Catholicism with singular zeal. The ensuing civil war induced the converted emperor, Susenyos (r. 1608–1632), to abdicate in favor of his son, Fasiladas (r. 1632–1667). Fasiladas not only expelled the Jesuits in 1632 but also shut the doors of the empire to Europeans of any ilk, cultivating instead friendly relations with the traditional Islamic enemies in the Arabian Peninsula.

The doctrinal challenge represented by the Jesuits provoked an internal debate within the Ethiopian Orthodox Church. Hence, in the ensuing two centuries, the Church was rent into factions advocating conflicting interpretations of the divine and human nature of Jesus Christ. These doctrinal controversies were not only of theological significance. They came to be aligned with warring regional lords, thereby giving ideological nourishment to the prevalent political rivalries. As the regional lords vied for supremacy, the "King of Kings" was reduced to a mere puppet with depleted financial and military resources. The divisions, often attended by bloody conflicts, persisted until they were formally resolved in 1878 at the Council of Boru Meda, presided by Emperor Yohannes IV (r. 1872–1889).

"ZAMANA MASAFENT"

This period of Ethiopian history, lasting from the last quarter of the eighteenth century to the coronation of Emperor Téwodros in 1855, is popularly referred to as the "Zamana Masafent" (Era of the Princes). It saw the rise of powerful regional lords in the provinces of Gojjam, Shawa, Simen, and Tegre (a designation including the Eritrean highlands as well as present-day Tegray). Enjoying a status of *primus inter pares* in this political constellation were the Yajju princes (also known as the

Yajju dynasty). From their base in Dabra Tabor, to the southeast of the imperial capital, Gondär, these lords of Oromo origin exercised considerable control over the crown and bore the much-coveted title of *Bitwaddad* ("the most favored").

Elsewhere in the region, a number of principalities had emerged through varied processes of state formation. Of these, the ones of longer pedigree and relatively elaborate institutions were the Omotic kingdoms of Yam (formerly known as Janjaro) Kafa, and Walayta. To the northwest of these kingdoms, a number of Oromo monarchical states had emerged by the first half of the nineteenth century. These included the Gibe monarchies of Limmu-Ennarya, Jimma Abba Jifar, Gera, Gomma and Guma as well as the Leqa Oromo principalities to the north, Qellam and Naqamte. On the Ethio-Sudanese borderland were the sheikhdoms of Aqoldi (Asosa), Beni Shangul, Gubba and Khomosha, all products of the superimposition of a Watawit aristocracy of Sudanese origin over the indigenous inhabitants, the Berta and Gumuz. Another Islamic center not only of political power but also of Islamic culture and learning arose in the east in the form of the city-state of Harar. The pastoralist Somali in the southeast presented a more fragmented political landscape, whereas their Cushitic kin to the north, the Afar, had managed to evolve a sultanate in the central portion of their region.

The dawn of the nineteenth century brought new challenges and opportunities to the region. Europe, spurred on by the Industrial Revolution and a resurgence of missionary activity, expanded into the African interior with renewed energy. Exploration went hand in hand with the signing of treaties of commerce and the establishment of consular posts. By this time, the Iberian powers of the sixteenth and seventeenth centuries had receded into the historical twilight, having been replaced on the world stage by the rising powers of Britain and France.

Yet in the first half of the nineteenth century, expansion of a more threatening nature to the region came not from Europe, but from a reinvigorated Egypt. In the wake of the expulsion of the forces of Napoleon from Egypt, an Albanian adventurer by the name of Muhammad 'Ali had removed the Mamluk rulers and inaugurated his own dynasty. His reign was marked, among other things, by vigorous expansion along the Nile and the Red Sea. A power more aggressive than the moribund Otttoman Empire thus came to encircle the Ethiopian region.

RESURGENCE

The person who epitomized more than any other the response to both challenges—Egyptian and European—was Kasa Haylu, made more famous in history by the name Téwodros that he assumed on his ascent to the throne in 1855. Border skirmishes with the Egyptians shaped his world outlook and stirred in him an abiding interest in military modernization. Defeat by the Egyptians in 1848 was followed by a series of brilliant military victories over the lords of the "Zamana Masafent." From 1852 to 1855, he subdued one warlord after another. The defeat of *Ras* Ali II, the Yajju prince, at the Battle of Ayshal (June 29, 1853) effectively marked the end of the "Zamana Masafent." But the coronation of Kasa Haylu as Emperor Téwodros II of Ethiopia had to wait until February 8, 1855, when he defeated *Dajjazmach* Webe, the powerful ruler of Semen and Tegre. Téwodros followed this up with the subjugation of Wallo and Shawa, the southernmost province of historic Ethiopia.

His program of reunification of the empire was intertwined with his policy of instituting administrative and military reforms. But his attempts at modernization were vitiated both by the Emperor's own caprice and inconsistency and the opposition of well-entrenched interests like the Orthodox Church. The problem was compounded by the interminable provincial rebellions that checkered his eventful reign. As if his domestic travails were not enough, Téwodros had a troubled relationship with foreigners that precipitated his downfall. The quest for modernization—both military and nonmilitary—made him turn to the Europeans, particularly the British, for technical assistance. Frustrated at the lack of positive response, he turned against them, detaining the British consul, Captain Cameron, and a number of missionaries, as well as Hormuzd Rassam, the envoy sent to negotiate their release. In reaction to that the British sent in 1867 a 32,000-strong force led by Sir General Napier with the objective of liberating the captives and punishing Téwodros. By then, the forlorn Emperor had shut himself in his mountain stronghold, Maqdala. There, in April 1868, in an act of defiance that was to enshrine him as an icon to posterity, Téwodros shot himself as the victorious British troops rushed in to capture their big prize.

A year after the death of Téwodros, an event occurred that contributed to intensifying both Egyptian and European interest in the Horn of Africa. The opening of the Suez Canal in 1869 transformed the Red Sea from a backwater to a major international passage to India. The acquisition of coastal possessions as coaling stations or trading posts became a major preoccupation of European powers. Thus, the Italians came to acquire Assab, the French Obock and Tajurah, and the British Zeila and Berbera—footholds that evolved, respectively, into the colonies of Eritrea, French Somaliland, and British Somaliland. Of these powers, none was more determined than the new state of Italy not only to acquire a coastal stronghold but also to push on to the interior. This Italian drive was to have its dénouement in the historic Battle of Adwa in 1896.

But the immediate threat to Ethiopia came not from Italy but from Egypt. Khedive Ismail (r. 1863–1879) went about ensuring Egyptian control of the Nile waters with greater energy and determination than any of his predecessors. This resulted not only in the extension of Egyptian power into the equatorial reaches of the Sudan but also in an equally aggressive expansion into the Ethiopian highlands. After occupying Bogos (in present day Eritrea) in 1872, Ismail sent an expedition that took hold of the Harar city-state in October 1875. Simultaneously, a larger military force was dispatched into the northern Ethiopian highlands, but it was routed at the Battle of Gundat (November 16, 1875) by the Ethiopian force led by Emperor Yohannes IV. In a bid to reverse this humiliating defeat, the Egyptians sent an even more formidable force led by veterans of the American Civil War. But that force suffered a similar fate at the Battle of Gura (March 6–7, 1876).

As it turned out, the military defeats in Ethiopia contributed to the downfall of Khedive Ismail in 1879 and the British occupation of Egypt in 1882. The simultaneous outbreak of the Mahdist movement in the Sudan plunged Ethiopia into a new round of hostilities that eventually claimed the life of Emperor Yohannes himself. In the east, the Italians used Massawa, which they had acquired in 1885 through the good offices of the British overlords of Egypt, as a springboard for their expansion into the interior.

Although they suffered a major defeat at the Battle of Dogali (January 25, 1887), this did not deter them from pushing further inland. As a matter of fact, when Emperor Yohannes met his death at the Battle of Matamma (March 9, 1889), the Italians took advantage of the power vacuum thus created to advance briskly to the highlands and proclaim their colony of Eritrea in January 1890.

TERRITORIAL EXPANSION AND STRUGGLE FOR INDEPENDENCE

The formidable task of checking Italian expansion fell on the shoulders of Emperor Menilek, Yohannes's successor. Until 1889 Menilek had focused his attention on the expansion of his ancestral kingdom, Shawa. Continuing and amplifying a process that had been initiated by his ancestors, he was able to forge an empire of unprecedented magnitude. Between 1876 and 1890, he had managed to incorporate the Gurage, the Oromo kingdoms of southwestern Ethiopia, the fiercely independent Arsi Oromo in the southeast, and the commercially important city-state of Harar. The process continued in the following decade, bringing into Menilek's empire the ancient Omotic kingdoms of Walayta and Kafa, the sheikhdoms of the Ethio-Sudanese borderland, the Borana Oromo and the Somali-inhabited Ogaden.

This expanded power base not only made Menilek's succession to the throne automatic, but it also gave him the resources with which to counter Italian colonial expansion. Yet at the beginning the relationship between Menilek and the Italians was far from inimical. Indeed, while Emperor Yohannes was confronting the Italians in the north, Menilek was cultivating friendly relations with them. A series of treaties and agreements in the 1880s culminated in the Treaty of Wechale, which Menilek and the Italians signed in May 1889, a couple of months after the Emperor's ascent to the throne. Wechale marked both the high point of their amicable relations and the beginning of the hostilities that had its dénouement at the Battle of Adwa. Not only did the Italians take advantage of the divergence between the Italian and Amharic versions of Article XVII of that treaty to declare a protectorate over Ethiopia, but they also contravened the territorial circumscriptions of Article III to encroach on Ethiopian territory.

The campaign of Adwa was a protracted affair. In effect, it could be said to have begun with the rebellion against Italian colonial rule by *Dajjazmach* Bahta Hagos of Akkala Guzay (in southeastern Eritrea). This spilled over into armed clashes between the Italians and *Ras* Mangasha Yohannes, the hereditary ruler of Tegray. Italian advances deep into the heart of Tegray finally left Menilek with no other option but to mobilize his forces. At the head of some 100,000 troops, most of them equipped with modern firearms, he headed north to deal with the invading Italian forces. The Italians were first defeated at Amba Alage (December 7, 1895), a mountain stronghold in southern Tegray; then forced to surrender their well-nigh impregnable fortress in Maqale, the Tegrean capital, to which Ethiopian troops had laid siege from January 7 to 21, 1896; and finally met their biggest defeat at the day-long Battle of Adwa (March 1, 1896).

Adwa guaranteed the political independence of Ethiopia, thereby giving it a unique place in colonial Africa and inspiring Black Nationalism both on the continent and among the African diaspora. The neighboring colonial powers had no other choice but to recognize that independence. The final years of the nineteenth century were thus characterized by a rush of European powers to establish diplomatic relations (the Italian, French, and British legations were all set up in 1897, in that order) and delimiting their colonial boundaries with Ethiopia, a process that began in 1897 and was finally concluded in 1908. Menilek was at an apogee of power and glory that few other Ethiopian rulers had thitherto enjoyed.

But things began to change after he suffered in 1906 the first stroke that announced his lingering death. Although he tried to smooth the succession process by appointing ministers in 1907 and designating his grandson, Iyyasu, as his heir to the throne in 1909, these acts could not prevent the eruption of a power struggle among various contenders. The removal of his powerful spouse, Taytu, from the palace in 1910 was only one episode in a long saga that attained its finale with the coronation of Tafari as Emperor Haile Sellassie I in 1930.

See also **Ahmad ibn Ibrahim al-Ghazi (Ahmad Grañ); Colonial Policies and Practices: Italian; Ethiopia and Vicinity, History of (600 to 1600 CE); Fasiladas; Haile Selassie I; Massawa; Menelik II; Mengistu, Haile Mariam; Susneyos; Téwodros.**

BIBLIOGRAPHY

Caulk, Richard. *"Between the Jaws of Hyenas": A Diplomatic History of Ethiopia (1876–1896)*. Wiesbaden: Harrassowitz, 2002.

Crummey, Donald. *Priests and Politicians: Protestant and Catholic Missionaries in Orthodox Ethiopia 1830–1868*. Oxford: Clarendon, 1972.

Gabre-Sellassie, Zewde. *Yohannes IV of Ethiopia: A Political Biography*. Oxford: Clarendon, 1975.

Marcus, Harold. *The Life and Times of Menelik II. Ethiopia 1844–1913*. Oxford: Clarendon, 1975.

Rubenson, Sven. *The Survival of Ethiopian Independence*. London: Heinemann, 1976.

Zewde, Bahru. *A History of Modern Ethiopia 1855–1991*. Athens: Ohio University Press, 2001.

Bahru Zewde

ETHIOPIA AND VICINITY, HISTORY OF (600 TO 1600 CE).

The sixth century found the Aksumite kingdom, which had its center in northern Ethiopia, at the apogee of its power and glory. It had developed as a maritime commercial power, on par with the Byzantine and Persian empires. Its adoption of Christianity in the fourth century had made it a natural ally of Byzantium in the latter's struggle with Persia for global preeminence. Over the succeeding centuries, successive Aksumite kings pushed the frontiers of the kingdom until it included large parts of present-day Eritrea and eastern Sudan, as well as the Arabian coast of the Red Sea. In 525, King Kaleb of Aksum (c. 520) led a naval expedition to southern Arabia to punish the Jewish king, Dhu Nuwas (c. 520), who had massacred the Christian inhabitants of Najran. Yet, as so often happens in history, the apogee of Aksumite power contained within it the seeds of decline.

THE RISE OF ISLAM

At the end of his successful naval campaign, Kaleb had installed a general by the name of Abraha (r. 525–570) as his viceroy. In 570, Abraha, who had established his capital at San'a (present-day Yemen), suffered a major military defeat in his campaign to subdue Mecca. That year was also the year of the birth of the Prophet Muhammad, whose new religion, Islam, was to reconfigure the world in such a decisive manner. Initially, though, relations between the Muslims and the Aksumite state were anything but hostile. Indeed, when Muhammad and his followers faced persecution from the powerful Quraish aristocracy of Mecca, he urged some of his followers to seek asylum in Aksum, whose ruler had a reputation for generosity. This pilgrimage (*hijra*) was a minor edition of the major Hijra that the Prophet himself was obligated to make from Mecca to Medina in 622.

The Aksumite king, variously known as Ella Saham or Ashama b. Abjar, did receive the refugees with open arms, and gave them shelter and freedom to exercise their new religion. He was apparently impressed by the affinity of their religious tenets with the fundamentals of his own Christian faith so much so that there has grown a tradition of the king, immortalized by Muslims as Ahmad Najashi, having embraced Islam. The Prophet's famous injunction not to touch the Abyssinians (Ethiopians) unless provoked by them is attributed to his sense of gratitude for the hospitality of the Aksumite king.

Soon, however, relations turned rather sour. The rivalry between the Aksumite port of Adulis and the Arabian port of Jeddah led to skirmishes on the Red Sea. Arabian control in the early eighth century of the Dahlak Islands, just off the Adulis coast, spelled the end of Aksumite hegemony over the Red Sea. On a more fundamental plane, the expansion of Islamic power across much of the Near East and North Africa effectively cut off Aksum's commercial lifeline with the Mediterranean world. That, coupled with uprisings from the subjugated peoples of Agaw and Beja, contributed to the decline and eventual eclipse of Aksum. For some time, the Aksumite kingdom was forced to move its capital southward into the Ethiopian interior.

What followed was a period of flux and uncertainty. So little is known about the intervening two or three centuries that they have been commonly referred to as the Dark Ages, in a manner analogous to the characterization of a similar period of European history. Yet, it appears to have been of formative significance for the evolution of the entities that took their final shape in the medieval period. In the tenth century, however, an event of almost apocalyptic significance occurred when a

female warrior by the name of Gudit (c. 960, also known as Yodit and Esat) led a devastating attack on what was left of the Aksumite kingdom, ransacking churches and monasteries and killing all those who stood in her way.

THE ZAGWE KINGDOM

It was only around the middle of the twelfth century that the Ethiopian state reemerged under a new dynasty known as the Zagwe. This is believed to have been derived from Agaw, the name of the Cushitic people who had been subjugated by the Aksumites but had risen to preeminence with the decline of Aksum. The capital of the Zagwe was known as Adafa, now more popularly known as Lalibäla, after the most famous of the Zagwe kings. Although the territory that they controlled was a truncated version of the Aksumite kingdom, the Zagwe pursued an active foreign policy, reestablishing the contacts with the Eastern Mediterranean world that had been severed in the preceding centuries.

The Zagwe rulers attained eternal fame with the construction of the monolithic churches that have now come to be recognized as UNESCO World Heritage sites. Devout Christians that they were, the Zagwe rulers are believed to have tried in this way to replicate the Christian Holy Land (Jerusalem); there was even a river christened Jordan (Yordanos) flowing between the different groups of churches. There were eleven churches in all, clustered in three groups. The largest of them all was dedicated to Madhane Alam (Holy Savior) whereas the most accomplished, St. George, was shaped in the form of a cross and stood alone in the west. These monolithic churches constitute the apex of a fairly long tradition of rock-hewn churches that was prevalent in post-Aksumite Ethiopia, notably in many parts of present-day Tegray.

Their architectural accomplishment notwithstanding, the Zagwe had a short lifespan. They were beset with the problem of royal succession from inside and political opposition from outside. That opposition was ideologically anchored on a tradition that gained widespread acceptance at the time and bound legitimate royal succession with the lineage of King Solomon and Queen Sheba, represented by their son, Menilek I. The Zagwe rulers, who were alleged to be not descendants of

Menilek I, were portrayed as usurpers. It was such opposition that brought to power a local chieftain by the name of Yekunno Amlak (r. 1270–1285), who claimed direct descent from the last Aksumite king. In 1268, Yekunno Amlak defeated the last Zagwe king, Yetbarak, and inaugurated what has come to be known in history as the Solomonic dynasty, a dynasty that came to an end only with the overthrow of Emperor Haile Sellassie in 1974.

MEDIEVAL ETHIOPIA AND THE HORN

Historians of Ethiopia have characterized the period from 1270 to about 1600 as medieval. This, more than anything else, is to signify its intermediate position between the ancient and the modern. It was a period that witnessed an unprecedented territorial expansion of the Ethiopian state. It was also a period characterized by literary and artistic effervescence and official and unofficial contacts with a Europe that was emerging from its medieval insulation.

Initially centered in the Amhara region in southern Wallo, the locus of power of the medieval state gradually shifted southward to northern Shawa. Although the town of Dabra Berhan served as imperial capital for a number of successive rulers, the tradition of continuous campaigning favored what has come to be known as the roving capital. Incorporating a number of new territories in the south and southeast, as well as controlling a good deal of the Aksumite empire including the highlands of what eventually became Eritrea, the Ethiopian state foreshadowed in many ways the modern empire-state created by Emperor Menilek II in the last quarter of the nineteenth century.

The foundations of the medieval empire were laid by Emperor Amda Tseyon (r. 1314–1344). He incorporated the independent kingdom of Gojjam, campaigned as far as the coastal region in present day Eritrea, and pushed his rule into the southern state of Damot. He also established his paramountcy over the string of Muslim states that had emerged in the southeast along an important trade route that linked the coast to the southwest. The leader of these states was the Sultanate of Ifat, ruled by a dynasty (the Walasma) that originated at about the same time as the Solomonic dynasty. Amda Tseyon's chronicle, the first of its genre in Ethiopian history, gives a graphic and highly embellished account of his campaign in this region. Medieval state power attained its peak during the reign of Emperor Zara Ya'iqob (r. 1434–1468). A sovereign who has a number of theological treatises to his credit, he was a kind of philosopher-king who did not shrink from a policy of ruthless persecution to ensure religious orthodoxy.

European interest in the Ethiopian region and its rulers originated with the legend of Prester John, accounts of whose fabulous wealth and formidable military power had begun to percolate from the Middle East, most probably through returning Crusaders. After a long quest for the location of this Christian priest-king, who was valued as a potential ally against the Muslim enemy, European attention focused on the Christian kingdom of Ethiopia. Tentative diplomatic exchanges in the fourteenth and fifteenth centuries assumed a more vigorous character with the emergence of Portugal as a global power with ambitions of dominance in the eastern hemisphere. Although the Crusades had by then become a matter of the past, the Iberian state was still keen to have a Christian ally in its struggle against the Ottoman Empire, its rival for dominance. Portuguese contacts with the Ethiopian state culminated in the sending in 1520 of an official mission, whose journey across the country has been recorded for posterity by the chaplain of the mission, Francisco Alvarez (c. 1465–c. 1540). Interestingly, Alvarez entitled his invaluable account *The Prester John of the Indies.*

THE UNRAVELING

Alvarez's account gives a vivid picture of the medieval Ethiopian empire on the eve of its collapse. In less than a decade after the Portuguese mission, the empire suffered the first of two major blows that heralded its eclipse. The first assault came from the Muslims, who had appeared to be so effectively subdued by the Christian state by the mid-fifteenth century. Toward the end of that century, however, a more militant brand of leadership had appeared in Adal, the successor state to Ifat that had emerged on the Harar plateau. No person embodied this change of leadership more dramatically than the young Imam Ahmad ibn Ibrahim al Ghazi (more popularly known as Ahmad Grañ, or the left-handed), who galvanized the nomadic Afar and Somali who had their own existential reasons for expansion, into a *jihad* (holy war) against the Christian Ethiopian kingdom. He defeated the

Emperor Lebna Dengel (r. 1508–1540) at the Battle of Shembera Kure, some forty-three miles southeast of present-day Addis Ababa. In a series of brilliant and breathtaking military campaigns that followed the historic battle, Grañ was able to sweep across much of the Christian highlands. It required the intervention of a Portuguese relief force of some four hundred led by Christopher da Gama (c. 1516–1542), son of the famed voyager Vasco da Gama, to defeat Grañ and save the Christian kingdom.

But no sooner had the Christian kingdom recovered from the wars of Ahmad Grañ than it faced a challenge of even more enduring consequences. This was the movement of the Oromo people from their original homeland in the southern highlands across much of the Ethiopian plateau until they had reached as far as the Sudanese border by the beginning of the eighteenth century. There is no consensus among historians as to what precipitated this major movement, although it is commonly attributed to overpopulation. Whatever its genesis, the movement was swift and overwhelming. It could be said to have been facilitated to a considerable degree by the mutual exhaustion of both the Christian and Muslim powers in the wars of the second quarter of the sixteenth century. By the end of the Oromo movement, the Muslim state of Harar had been reduced to a walled city-state and the Christian kingdom had been forced to retreat to the highlands around Lake Tana.

See also **Ahmad ibn Ibrahim al-Ghazi (Ahmad Grañ); Aksum; Ethiopia and the Horn, History of (1600 to 1910); Haile Selassie I; Islam; Menelik II; Northeastern Africa, Classical Period, History of (1000 BCE to 600 CE); Zara Ya'iqob.**

BIBLIOGRAPHY

Ahmed, Hussein. "Aksum in Muslim Historical Traditions." *Journal of Ethiopian Studies* 29, no. 2 (1996).

Hable Sellassie, Sergew. *Ancient and Medieval Ethiopian History to 1270.* Addis Ababa, Nigeria: United Printers, 1972.

Hassan, Mohammed. *The Oromo of Ethiopia: A History.* Cambridge, U.K.: Cambridge University Press, 1990.

Kaplan, Steven. *The Monastic Holy Man and the Christianity of Early Solomonic Ethiopia.* Wiesbaden, Germany: Franz Steiner Verlag, 1984.

Munro-Hay, Stuart. *Aksum: An African Civilisation.* Edinburgh: Edinburgh University Press, 1991.

Tamrat, Taddesse. *Church and State in Ethiopia 1270–1527.* Oxford: Clarendon Press, 1972.

Zewde, Bahru. *A Short History of Ethiopia and the Horn.* Addis Ababa: Department of History, 1998.

BAHRU ZEWDE

ETHIOPIAN CHURCHES. *See* **Christianity: African Instituted Churches.**

ETHNICITY

This entry includes the following articles:
OVERVIEW
CENTRAL AFRICA
EASTERN AFRICA
NORTHERN AFRICA
SOUTHERN AFRICA
WESTERN AFRICA

OVERVIEW

A term adopted in the social sciences only in the 1960s, ethnicity highlights the relationships between different ethnic groups and is best defined as thinking and acting in ethnic categories. Ethnic groups both encompass and transcend families, and assert a collective identity and/or are defined by outsiders as a group. Yet in any case, the criteria demarcating group boundaries are variable and refer to only a small part of the total cultural repertoire that an ethnic group often shares with its neighbors. Ethnic community ideologies, however, generally claim that members of the "we-group" share their entire culture, ancestry, language, history and are rooted in a specific territory.

Ethnicity in Africa today appears as something of a paradox. On the one hand, anthropologists and historians agree that much of precolonial Africa did not consist of "tribes" or ethnic groups with clear-cut cultural, linguistic and politico-territorial boundaries of the sort attributed to them by colonial authorities and some early ethnographers. Rather, these societies were characterized by mobility, overlapping networks, multiple group memberships and the context-dependent drawing of boundaries. Only rarely did precolonial community ideologies resemble eighteenth- and nineteenth-century European ideas about "nations." Most African communities defined themselves by neighborhood, kinship, or loyalty to a political authority, not necessarily by common language and culture. Many precolonial states were multiethnic entities, whose present-day ethnonym was a common name that referred only to their shared acceptance of the ruler, not to shared origins or language. Stateless groups were bound together (and to surrounding states) by overlapping ties of kinship and religious and economic networks, as well as political alliances, secret societies, or age groups. However they seldom developed a group consciousness beyond the kin group and the locality. In most cases, ethnic community ideologies developed only in interaction with European ideas about "tribes," brought to Africa by missionaries and colonial officers.

On the other hand, ethnic ideologies are by now firmly entrenched in Africa. Whether "tribalism" is valued as the preservation of cultural tradition or decried as nepotism, it is ubiquitous in public political discourse. The dominant view in popular discourse is contrary to that espoused by constructivist scholars: ethnic groups count not as recent creations but as the relics of a distant past. However, although many Africans insist on the long histories of their respective ethnicities, the actual boundaries, designations, and cultural values defining the groups are matters of heated debate.

Since the 1970s the terms "ethnicity" and "ethnic group" have superseded problematic terms like "tribalism," "race," or "tribe." Like other key terms in the social sciences and history, they are at once categories of scholarly analysis and of political practice, belonging not only to the theoretical repertoire of scholars but also to the vocabulary of chiefs, politicians, local intellectuals, labor migrants, and social movements. Unlike other cornerstones of group cohesion such as class, religion, or political membership, ethnicity is a category defined by no specific criterion. It may draw on origin, descent, any number of social and cultural traits, language, region, membership in (or opposition to) a polity or religion, or any combination of these. Yet it need not involve any of these. This kaleidoscopic quality is why ethnicity, while having immense power to command subjectivities and to generate very real

sociopolitical effects, is also a "shadow theatre" (Bayart, 41). Thus while ethnic discourses argue in an essentialist manner and naturalize social relationships, the "content" of any particular ethnicity is historically contingent. It is the product of particular—mainly political—contexts and of the material history has made available. Its power rests precisely on this inherent contradiction: ethnic identifications claim to be primordial and nonnegotiable, creating permanent bonds, stability, and security (as well as instability and insecurity among those excluded); at the same time, the boundaries of the communities created and the associated traits and practices are malleable and can be adapted to specific interests and contexts.

Ethnicities emerge only in the plural, typically within the same colonial or nation-state, against which they contrast each other. But ethnicity also exists in relation to various other identity-constituting criteria from which it draws some of its content, or which serve as alternative identifications, such as class, education, religion, or rural versus urban loyalties. Because ethnicity itself is not only fluid, but fluidly connected to these nonethnic bases of identification and commonality, understanding the dynamics of ethnic groups and boundaries requires considering the wider context.

THE COLONIAL "INVENTION" OF ETHNICITY

The apparent historical continuity of contemporary ethnicities at least partly resulted from the fact that when colonial administrators, missionaries, and anthropologists attempted to classify and geographically fix African "tribes," they mapped them onto existing toponyms and group names. Prior to colonialism these names often referred to professional groups or political associations rather than to culturally or linguistically distinct, rigidly defined ethnic communities. Some ethnonyms common today were originally simply autonyms meaning "people"; others were exonyms—sometimes derisive—used by neighbors, merchants, or conquerors. Which names entered colonial maps and ethnographies ultimately depended upon the African interpreters and local elites who assisted the colonial authorities. Ethnic categories, as a system of differences, were often (re)defined by colonial officials depending on their

THE LAND AND HUMAN ACTIVITY

Fires in the Okavango Delta, Botswana. Herders seeking to stimulate the growth of fresh grass risk contributing to the northward spread of the Kalahari Desert, here viewed looking northwestward (upstream) from the shuttle, *ATLANTIS*. © CORBIS

TOP LEFT: **Rhino poached for horn.** This white rhinoceros, an endangered species, has been killed by poachers solely for its horn, which is ground and used in Asia in traditional cures for sexual dysfunction. Poaching is but one form of conflict in a region where elephants and other large species roam vast expanses of land needed by growing human populations. © MARTIN HARVEY/CORBIS

BELOW: **Coral reef in the Red Sea.** African marine waters boast an extraordinary diversity of life. Coral has been prized as a regal ornament by some African cultures. PHOTOGRAPH BY DAVID GEORGE

TOP RIGHT: Victoria Falls. Mosi-oa-Tunya (The Smoke That Thunders), on the Zambezi River, which separates Zambia and Zimbabwe, is among the world's most dramatic waterfalls and a World Heritage Site. Here as elsewhere, political tensions often threaten Africa's reliance on tourists drawn by its spectacular natural features. © TIBOR BOGNAR/CORBIS

BELOW: The Blue Nile at Tisisat Falls, Ethiopia. Water and silt carried down from highland Ethiopia by the world's longest river have supported dense populations and innovative technologies in the lower valley of the Nile since long before pharaonic Egypt. © DIEGO LEZAMA OREZZOLI/CORBIS

TOP LEFT: Ice field on Kilimanjaro. Glacial melting on Africa's highest mountain (19,340 feet) has been variously attributed to climate change, solar radiation, and latent volcanism. © PAUL SOUDERS/CORBIS

BOTTOM LEFT: African penguins near Cape Town. These birds have been treated and cleaned by volunteers after suffering damage from an oil slick thought to have been created by vessels illegally flushing bilges off southern African coasts. © MIKE HUTCHINGS/REUTE CORBIS

BELOW: City ramparts, Taroudant, Morocco, with peaks of the Atlas Range in the background. These mountains separate Africa's Mediterranean northern littoral from the Saharan world to the south. © WALTER BIBIKOW/JAI/CORBIS

TOP LEFT: Planting rain forest seedlings. Sustainable forest management is a priority in Africa, after decades of highly destructive timbering by international corporations. Farmers employ various strategies to preserve their threatened resources. This Cameroonian program enlists local youth in a program of reforestation. © KEVIN SCHAFER/CORBIS

MIDDLE LEFT: Wangari Maathai. The Kenyan winner of the 2004 Nobel Peace prize here points out invasive forest species near Cape Town. Colonial regimes introduced numerous species from their Asian colonies. © NIC BOTHMA/EPA/CORBIS

BELOW: Farmers in Ghana. Abiba Gyarko poses with son and hired workers on her rented seven-acre farm. Her tomatoes must compete in the market with canned imports from subsidized European farms. © GIDEON MENDEL/ACTIONAID/CORBIS

TOP RIGHT: Vineyards near Stellenbosch, South Africa. The Mediterranean-type climate of the western Cape Province favors agriculture and allows for the export of wines and other products to the world market. © JON HICKS/CORBIS

BOTTOM RIGHT: Zebu cows in Chad. *Bos taurus indicus*, introduced from India, is common in the Sahel for its tolerance of extreme conditions. Nevertheless, overgrazing threatens the region with the prospect of further desertification. © MICHAEL MARTIN

BELOW: Gas flare in Nigeria. Fuel is often scarce in Africa. Urhobo villagers have had to appropriate the heat from Shell Petroleum's gas flares to cook manioc despite the danger that the fumes pose to their health. Exploitation of Africa's abundant petroleum resources poses environmental and social challenges. © ED KASHI/CORBIS

BOTTOM RIGHT: Traffic in Port Harcourt. Africans are increasingly urbanized and subject to universal problems of overcrowding and traffic jams. Although Nigeria is one of the world's leading exporters of petroleum, its lack of refining capability and foreign exchange causes chronic gasoline shortages. © GEORGE STEINMETZ/CORBIS

Takai dancers at the National Festival of Arts and Culture, Washington, D.C., November 2006. The Takai dancers come from Dagbon, one of the largest Northern Ghanaian precolonial states. The boots they wear refer to their cavalry, which was important in precolonial warfare. Their huge smocks, which they whirl around in dancing, point to wealth and connectedness with Islam (though they are not necessarily Islamic). PHOTOGRAPH BY CAROLA LENTZ

strategic and bureaucratic requirements. The Dagara in present-day northern Ghana, for example, were divided into "Lobi" and "Dagaba," despite sharing a language and cultural practices, because one group was more difficult to pacify than the other. But colonial officials also identified certain "tribes" as particularly suited for military service or work in the mines. Colonial officers thus effectively created categories to administer.

Early colonial ideas concerning African "tribes" incorporated late-nineteenth-century evolutionist and diffusionist arguments, as well as European nationalist concepts. Colonial officers believed that from birth to death every African belonged to a single "tribe," distinct in its physiological, linguistic, and cultural features, which inhabited a particular territory governed by a council of elders or a chief. Tribes were ascribed a fixed place in the natural evolution of political communities toward larger scales: families joined together as clans, clans as tribes, and finally tribes as nations. The tribe thus constituted not only a classificatory instrument but also a model political order. Chieftaincies and districts were therefore supposed to reflect the ethnic boundaries. In practice, however, congruence between ethnicities and "native states," as British colonial administrators called the chiefdoms, was impossible. In fact, usually it was not the imagined "tribes" that formed chieftaincies, but rather chieftaincies formed for political reasons were retroactively given an ethnic label.

Gologo dancers at the National Festival of Arts and Culture, Washington, D.C., November 2006. The "naked" and war-like Gologo dancers, from Tongo in the Upper East Region of Ghana, have to be understood in direct contrast to the Takai dancers. They perform at the same festival, and they come from a pre-colonially "stateless" society. They were known as skilled warriors and reputed to be "anarchic" and aggressive. Today they invert these stereotypes into a positive self-presentation. PHOTOGRAPH BY CAROLA LENTZ

Africans actively participated in this colonial "invention" of "tribes." Colonial intelligence depended on African informants who exerted a certain degree of control over the knowledge gained by colonial officials, influencing the drawing of ethnic boundaries and administrative practices in their own interests. While colonial officials needed efficient administrative units, Africans too wanted action groups, which were larger and more effective than the kin group or the local settlement. Sometimes, ambitious individuals on the margins of these communities promoted themselves as representatives of the colonial categories. Chiefs, early mission school students, and male elders played central roles in naming and distinguishing ethnic groups and in codifying customs and norms presented as "traditional" and "tribal." However, what historian Bill Bravman has shown for the Taita in Kenya also holds for other cases: new ethnic identities quickly became the objects of struggle in the cultural politics of defining proper identity and behavior—struggles in which not only elders, but also young men, Christian (or Muslim) converts and women engaged.

Although the colonial "invention" of tribes tied into complex and locally variegated models of belonging and differed in precolonial states and in segmentary societies, "ethnicization" processes, colonial and postcolonial, share four features. First, ethnic recategorization usually occurred in contexts of social inequality, which they stabilized or legitimized. Second, cooperation between colonial authorities and local cultural intermediaries led to the interweaving of European with local models of belonging. Consequently, new practices, symbols, and histories became "tradition," while older elements were adapted and transformed through codification into "customary law" and other processes of inscription. Although colonial categorizations appeared more rigid than precolonial modes of belonging, in reality they were, and are, also subject to continuous debate and negotiation.

Third, inculcated through everyday (administrative) practice, the new identities eventually appeared natural. Finally, the reasons for the initial creation of ethnicities could differ from the reasons for which they continued to be meaningful. For example, ethnic categories and forms of self-understanding created in the colonial context also provided labor migrants with a much-needed sense of security and means of solidarity among actual strangers, and later they became the idiom through which political claims were made against the postcolonial state. They also were used to establish moral communities to dispute social inequities and norms of reciprocity.

ETHNICITY, LABOR MIGRATION, AND URBANIZATION

For African labor migrants membership in these colonially created, or redefined, ethnic groups became one of the most important resources for finding work, a place to live, and for obtaining emergency assistance. For socializing and celebrating, too, people gravitated to those speaking the same language and following similar customs. An appeal to shared membership in an ethnic group more effectively mobilized people to attend funerals or other *rites de passage* than appeals to kinship or shared village origins. In many cities and mines, employers, local chiefs and the colonial administration also expected migrants to join together under "tribal headmen," who were to mediate between migrants and employers or hosts. In past decades such headmen have been largely replaced by voluntary associations, in which migrants from one region join together for mutual support but also work toward the development of the home region. Ethnicity continues to be an important basis for solidarity when away from home.

Not only labor migrants but also traders and practitioners of other occupations use ethnicity as an economic resource, especially in the informal sector. Well studied is the case of West African Hausa merchants, who used their cultural and religious differences to maintain their monopoly over the long-distance trade in kola nuts and cattle. Where economic activity and ethnic identity are closely connected, ethnic "conversion" often occurs; that is, individuals change ethnic identities to engage in a particular occupation.

In the 1950s and 1960s a series of innovative studies by British social anthropologists examined the relationship between ethnicity and labor migration in towns of the Rhodesian copper belt and South Africa. These studies emphasized the flexibility and manipulability of ethnicity in the urban context. Urban ethnic categories often differed from those of the rural "tribes," having been created anew by migrants or their employers to suit their respective needs. Later studies showed how migrants brought these new categories back to the rural settlements, changing the colonial "tribal" order. By observing ethnic affiliation over an extended period, the fluidity and context-dependency of its boundaries become apparent. In early-twentieth-century southern Ghana, for example, all migrants from the north of the colony joined under a single tribal headman, behaving as if one ethnic group. As the number of labor migrants grew, so did the pressure to subdivide. Consequently smaller groups formed around new tribal headmen creating new "tribes"—a process often sparked by conflicts between group members and existing headmen. Similarly, as the number of potential members in an ethnic association grows, fragmentation becomes more likely. Depending on the situation and the vested interests, however, more inclusive affiliations may continue to be mobilized.

POLITICAL ETHNICITY

Growing ethnic awareness and the integration of groups into the state are not mutually exclusive, as many recent studies have shown. On the contrary, recourse to ethnic identity was and is a useful strategy to demand benefits from the state for one's own group. But why is competition over education, income, status, infrastructure, and political influence often expressed in terms of ethnic and not class or religious conflict? This tendency has partly to do with the territorial unevenness of modernization, which distributed valued goods such as education and infrastructure inequitably. Colonial ethnicization cast such differences as favoritism for particular ethnic groups vis-à-vis others. Moreover, less well-off members pressure the educated elites of their ethnic group to provide jobs, access to education, and better infrastructure back home. Political scientists suggest that this accountability to constituents is why elites only seldom formed a pan-ethnic, national ruling class, and instead compete among

Nandom Naa and fellow chiefs at the Kakube cultural festival, November 2006. The Kakube festival, held in the Lawra District, Upper West Region, Ghana, is another cultural festival at which local ethnic identities are "performed" and standardized through dance and music with a jury judging the competition between various local dance troupes. PHOTOGRAPH BY CAROLA LENTZ

themselves for resources for their home regions. Moreover, in democratic systems ethnic groups comprise an important source of votes, which turns the state into a clientelistic system in which ethnicity is instrumentalized, a phenomenon the literature sometimes calls "political tribalism." In any case, ethnicity is a common explanation for political discrimination, underdevelopment, and civil war, even when other factors such as the economy and demography are patent.

However, where ongoing economic crisis and institutional weakness lead to a state's having fewer resources to distribute, political ethnicity can also work to strengthen regional autonomy. Understanding ethnicity simply as a political resource used by elites in competing to claim from the state

the "goods of modernity" would certainly be reductionist.

THE MULTIDIMENSIONALITY OF ETHNICITY
Even if processes of colonial ethnicization and postcolonial ethnic transformations share similarities, it is impossible to derive a general theory of ethnicity in contemporary Africa, since the genesis and transformation of ethnic identities is historically and regionally specific. But whatever its specific trajectory, ethnicity can fulfill various functions and take on many meanings. Ethnicity can be an idiom of personal and collective identity, associated with home ties and cultural roots. It can engender a moral community within which the less well-off members and their elite brethren

contend over the redistribution of resources and the providing of mutual assistance, as John Lonsdale's work on "moral ethnicity" shows. Finally, ethnicity may be deployed as an idiom of political mobilization and making demands on the state. Ethnic ideologies assert that identity is natural and immutable. Its power rests upon the emotional force of kinship and origins that are carried over and applied to larger communities. But only because it conceals that it is in fact open to multiple interpretations and negotiation is ethnicity for so many different people emotionally attractive and strategically efficient. Where such negotiation is forcefully prevented ethnic ideologies also lead to exclusion, hardship, insecurity, and death.

See also **Colonial Traditions and Inventions; Colonialism and Imperialism; Kinship and Affinity; Warfare.**

BIBLIOGRAPHY

Amselle, Jean-Loup, and Elikia M'bokolo, eds. *Au coeur de l'ethnie. Ethnies, tribalisme et état en Afrique.* Paris: La Découverte, 1985.

Bayart, Jean-François. *The State in Africa: The Politics of the Belly.* London: Longman, 1993.

Bates, Robert H. "Ethnic Competition and Modernization in Contemporary Africa." *Comparative Political Studies* 6 (1974): 457–484.

Berman, Bruce. "Ethnicity, Patronage and the African State: The Politics of Uncivil Nationalism." *African Affairs* 97 (1998): 305–341.

Berman, Bruce; Dickson Eyoh; and Will Kymlicka; eds. *Ethnicity and Democracy in Africa.* Oxford: James Currey, 2004.

Bravman, Bill. *Making Ethnic Ways: Communities and Their Transformations in Taita, Kenya, 1800–1950.* Oxford: James Currey, 1998.

Cohen, Abner. *Custom and Politics in Urban Africa: A Study of Hausa Migrants in Yoruba Towns.* Berkeley: University of California Press, 1969.

Epstein, A. L. *Politics in an Urban African Community.* Manchester: Manchester University Press, 1958.

Fardon, Richard. "'Crossed Destinies': The Enlarged History of West African Ethnic and National Identities." In *Ethnicity in Africa: Roots, Meanings and Implications,* ed. Louise de la Gorgondière et al. Edinburgh: Center of African Studies, 1996.

Jenkins, Richard. *Rethinking Ethnicity: Arguments and Explorations.* London: Sage, 1997.

Lentz, Carola. "'Tribalism' and Ethnicity in Africa: A Review of Four Decades of Anglophone Research." *Cahiers des Sciences Humaines* 31 (1995): 303–28.

Lentz, Carola. *Ethnicity and the Making of History in Northern Ghana.* Edinburgh: Edinburgh University Press, 2006.

Lonsdale, John. "The Moral Economy of Mau Mau." In *Unhappy Valley: Conflict in Kenya and Africa,* eds. Bruce Berman and John Lonsdale. Oxford: James Currey, 1992.

Mitchell, Clyde. *The Kalela Dance: Aspects of Social Relations among Urban Africans in Northern Rhodesia.* Manchester: Manchester University Press, 1956.

Ranger, Terence. "The Invention of Tradition in Colonial Africa." In *The Invention of Tradition,* ed. Eric Hobsbawm and Terence Ranger. Cambridge, U.K.: Cambridge University Press, 1983.

Tonkin, Elizabeth et al., eds. *History and Ethnicity.* London: Routledge, 1989.

Vail, Leroy, ed. *The Creation of Tribalism in Southern Africa.* Oxford: James Currey, 1989.

Young, Crawford, ed. *The Rising Tide of Cultural Pluralism: The Nation-State at Bay?* Madison: University of Wisconsin Press, 1993.

CAROLA LENTZ

CENTRAL AFRICA

IDEOLOGY OF ETHNICITY IN CENTRAL AFRICA

In the postcolonial nation-states of Central Africa, black African social actors identify themselves as members of particular "tribes," or "ethnic groups," or the equivalents of these terms in African and European languages in local use. Such ethnic groups tend to be felt as a tangible reality. They are claimed to organize major aspects of the individual's life in the field of language, expressive and ritual culture, kinship, production, and reproduction. Allegiance and opposition in traditional and modern politics are considered to be largely determined along ethnic lines. National territory is often seen as parceled out in contiguous sections, each of which forms an ethnic group's rural home area administered by a traditional ruler (chief, headman). The natural habitat of ethnic identity is therefore thought to be "the village home," a category implying purity, meaningfulness, and order.

This view is largely nostalgic. Significant ethnic processes in Central Africa evolve not only in a rural context but also in towns, bureaucracies, and national political circles; they involve, among others, born urbanites organizing themselves through dyadic network contacts and formal organizations rather than through historic localized groups. Moreover, massive twentieth-century social change in the rural areas has blurred the distinction between town and countryside.

This local ideology of ethnicity must form our point of departure. It resonates with the views held by European travelers, administrators, Christian missionaries, employers of African labor, and anthropologists active in Central Africa throughout the colonial period. Colonial administration partitioned African territories into strictly demarcated units thought to possess, through "tribes," a unique culture and indigenous sociopolitical organization allegedly underpinned by centuries of inescapable tradition. In their selection and diocesan administration of certain areas, and their codification of local languages for education and Bible translation, Christian missions reinforced the illusion of tribal identity. Central African intellectuals and politicians perpetuated this understanding by articulating their own ethnicities; "inventing" tradition in the form of ethnohistory, ethnic festivals, and folklorization; and supporting reinstatement of traditional leadership as a focus for ethnicity.

Anthropology also adopted the tribal illusion. It was only in the 1960s that the concept of "tribe" was subjected to profound criticism as a Eurocentric and reified designation of an ethnic group, and ethnic differentiation began to be viewed as a sociopolitical process. In the twenty-first century anthropologists understand Central African ethnicity to be constructed and situational. Late-twentieth-century research shows how many ethnic names, or ethnonyms, in Central Africa originated in colonial practices. Whereas the "tribe" was once thought to sum up a total, bounded, and localized culture, ethnicity has come to be stressed to be only one among several primary structural principles in Central African societies.

ETHNICITY AND ETHNICIZATION

Ethnicity poses great analytical difficulties because it is operative in many social and political contexts where it displays varying and contradictory dimensions. "Ethnicity" in Central Africa today can refer to, among other things, a system of social classification that is ostensibly rigid yet depends on flexibility and manipulation at the level of both ethnic groups and individuals; a structure for the definition and interaction of subnational power groups making up the national polity; a system of social inequality; and a strategic network for redistribution. It constitutes the local folk theory of political causation in addition to being an ideology justifying inequality and violence vis-à-vis other ethnic groups. This multidimensionality makes for the complex ethnic dialectics of Central African societies and renders these dialectics unpredictable.

Definitions are a first step toward managing this complexity. An "ethnic group" is an explicitly named set of people. Within a given social field there are more than one such set, but only a finite, usually limited number are distinguished. The numerically largest set in the social field is of considerable demographic scope; other sets may be quite small. The membership of a set is in principle ascriptive—that is, determined by birth. Within the set, people identify with one another and are identified by others on the basis of a few historically determined and historically changing ethnic "boundary markers," including ethnonym, language, historic forms of leadership, modes of production, selected cultural traits, and sometimes selected somatic characteristics such as skin color, hair texture, facial characteristics, and deliberate human interference with the body's appearance, both reversible (for example, hairstyle) and irreversible (for example, scarification).

"Ethnicity" is the way in which the wider social field is economically, politically, and culturally structured in terms of a multiplicity of such ethnic groups in interaction. "Identity" is the self-image that members of any social category construct as members, on the basis of identification and of stereotyping both among themselves and among outsiders. Identity tends to be situational, multiple (since every social field consists of many intersecting social categories), strategic, and subject to historical change. This applies to ethnic identities no less than to gender, class, and professional, religious, and other identities. Socialization early in life, as well as social control, propaganda, and taking consciousness in adulthood, may cause a specific identity to become so deeply entrenched in the personality as to produce a fixed, self-evident vision of reality, no longer consciously negotiated in social contexts. "Ethnicization" marks the process by which ethnic identity becomes a militant political idiom taking precedence over an individual's other identities, as a basis for political action. "Culture" comprises the total combination of attributes a human individual acquires as a member of society.

Ethnonyms tend to be nested. Local groups that are clearly distinguished at the regional level may be merged at the national level in the face of nonmembers of either group. If either local group is of higher status, such merging amounts to ethnic "passing" on the part of members of the group considered inferior. Ethnonyms are segmentary, shifting, situational, and manipulable, and so are ethnic boundary markers. The history of ethnic groups within a social field includes the capricious pattern of the emergence, distribution, and redistribution of boundary markers including ethnonyms. For instance, in the region straddling Angola, Zaire, and Zambia, male circumcision serves as a boundary marker between groups (the Lunda, Ndembu, Luvale, Mbunda, Chokwe, and Luchazi, for example) associated with the widespread Lunda complex of language and political and ceremonial culture, as against other yet related groups such as Nkoya and Mbwela, who practiced circumcision until the nineteenth century.

Throughout Central Africa language plays a major role as an ethnic boundary marker. This springs partly from the codification of African languages since the nineteenth century but also more in general from language's capability of encoding and displaying identity or alienness in social interaction. More than any other feature of institutionalized culture, language is encoded in formal rules the infringement of which (by nonnative speakers, for example) immediately causes puzzlement, ridicule, rejection, or a breakdown of communication among listeners and readers. Language for the native speaker tends to be the last refuge of owning and belonging, of competence and identity. However, such emotive appeal presupposes ethnicization; without this factor, the role of language as an ethnic boundary marker is attenuated by Central Africa's widespread multilingualism.

The tribal model and ethnicization erroneously equate ethnic identity with a total culture embracing all aspects of human life, instead of with selected cultural items serving as boundary markers. In Central Africa, a specific cultural package encompassing all aspects of human life is seldom limited, in place and time, to a specific ethnic group; usually it has a much wider distribution. For instance, in the savanna belt of south Central Africa, scores of ethnic groups have been distinguished, one next to the other, since the nineteenth century, yet the distribution of patterns of production, reproduction, and signification shows such an underlying unity that one should speak of one large culture region. Within this far-reaching regional continuity, distinct ethnic groups have distinguished themselves by relatively minor cultural items marking ethnic boundaries.

Ethnicization entails the construction of ethnonyms to mark ethnic boundaries and the redefinition of local culture so as to offer distinctive boundary markers. The cultivated sense of a shared history lends meaning to experiences of powerlessness, deprivation, and estrangement, and kindles hope of improvement through ethnic self-presentation. The ethnonym and the principle of ascription then produce for the members of society an image of a bounded, particularist set of solidary people. The vulnerable individual's access to national resources and to the formal organization (state, industry) controlling them becomes the object of group action. In postcolonial Central Africa, ethnicization increasingly has included cultural politics. Sets of people are restructured as ethnic groups by the designing of a cultural package, which in its own right constitutes a major stake in the negotiations with the outside world. One dissociates from rival ethnic groups at the local and regional scene through a strategic emphasis on cultural and linguistic elements; at the national level one competes for the state's political and economic prizes via the state's recognition of the ethnically constructed cultural package. New inequalities emerge within the ethnic group. The mediation takes place via ethnic brokers who are best positioned to exploit the opportunities at the interface between the ethnic group and the outside world. Asserting the "traditional," "authentic" (but in fact newly reconstructed) culture is seen as an important task and becomes a source of power and income for the brokers. Ethnic associations, publications, and festivals constitute general strategic instruments in this process.

Ethnicization restructures individuals' perceptions of time and space. It creates social meaning by offering to the members of Central African societies a folk theory that enables them to impose a sense of spatial localization and temporal continuity on the otherwise bewildering fragmentation and heterogeneity of their postcolonial experience. Individuals not only frame selected items of their regional culture within the boundaries of their ethnic group and within their image of "home," but also project these items onto a glorified past. Political, judicial, and moral relations are underpinned by reference to the virtual, dreamed village, the evocation of which (in urban ritual, ethnic festivals, and political demonstrations embellished by traditional costumes, ceremonial weapons, and traditional leaders) enables people to derive symbolic comfort from their communion with mythical images and provides a basis for ethnic leaders' mobilizing appeal.

Ethnicity displays a remarkable contradiction between inescapability and constructedness, which largely explains its great societal potential. As a classification system, ethnicity offers a logical structure, which is further ossified through ascription and which presents itself as unconditional, bounded, inescapable, and timeless. This is what made early researchers of Central African ethnicity stress primordial attachments. However, the social praxis of ethnicity, as ethnicization, implies flexibility, choice, constructedness, and change. Together, these entirely contradictory aspects constitute ethnicity, which is able to disguise strategy as inevitability. This dialectics renders ethnicity particularly suitable for mediating, in processes of social change, between social contexts that are of a fundamentally different structure. Because of this internal contradiction, ethnicity offers the option of strategically effective particularism in a context of universalism and hence enables individuals, as members of an ethnic group, to cross otherwise nonnegotiable boundaries and to create a foothold or niche in structural contexts (such as cities and bureaucracies) that would otherwise remain inaccessible.

ETHNICITY AND SOCIAL CONFLICT IN CENTRAL AFRICA

Ethnicity is rarely a mere classification system of parallel groups operating at the same level of power, esteem, and privilege. It usually implies an element of vertical subordination: ethnic group membership is a status position in a hierarchy of politico-economic power and prestige, and ethnicization aims at improving the position of the entire ethnic group; failing empowerment of the group, an individual may try to pass singly to a more highly placed group by the adoption of new boundary markers (a different ethnonym, language, dress style, world religion, and so on). Ethnic formulations govern conflicts over social inequality in the society.

Though ethnicity is not as dominant and independent a factor in Central African society as ethnic actors (and many outside analysts) claim it to be, it has established itself as the Central African political folk theory, and all major social conflicts assume ethnic manifestations. This is possible because of ethnicity's unique capability of being manipulated by ethnic and political brokers; its suggestion of inescapability; its focus on ethnonyms, which makes actors reduce complex structural issues to identified social groups; and its spatial and temporal imagery (evoking, for example, the idealized village home), which renders ethnic constructs highly persuasive. The appeal by ethnic brokers to historic ethnic symbols emulating precolonial contradictions of competition (pastoralists versus agriculturalists, lords versus clients) suggests that the conflict is rooted not in contemporary power relations but in precolonial, perennial, intergroup conflicts, and hence is unsolvable.

Redefining circumstances in essentialistic, primordialist ethnic terms transforms social conflicts into nonnegotiable standoffs that inevitably result in violence, especially given the poverty and erosion of many postcolonial states in Central Africa, which render states prizes instead of arbiters in social conflict. Ethnicization turns class conflict into ethnic conflict over control of the state, and having captured the state, an ethnic group seizes its political and military resources to further its own aims. With the global availability of sophisticated weaponry, ethnic conflicts easily precipitate into large-scale violence, of which the 1994 tragedy in Rwanda is only one example from Central Africa. While the cultural and mass psychological factors in such events should not be ignored and the unique historicity of events makes a systematic explanation difficult, ethnicity is largely a template for class conflict.

PRECOLONIAL AND COLONIAL ETHNICITY IN CENTRAL AFRICA

Ethnicity in Central Africa has been greatly influenced by intergroup processes within political arenas defined by the colonial and postcolonial state. However, many ethnonyms and other boundary markers undoubtedly have a precolonial origin.

Ethnic groups as defined above are too prominently and consistently represented in oral traditions to be explained away as mere projections of colonial or postcolonial realities into a precolonial past (although such projections do occur). Moreover, the same ethnonyms appear in documents generated in the nineteenth and early twentieth centuries, before colonial administration could have made an impact. However, the various genetic and proper names for groups thus distinguished by precolonial Central Africans must have lacked the standardization and territoriality imposed with colonialism. Their dimensions diverged: named political units constituting precolonial state systems did not coincide with linguistic clusters, but probably did reflect ecological specializations of agriculturalists, pastoralists, hunters, fishermen, and petty commodity producers. Precolonial states, as systems integrating ecological diversities, were usually multiethnic: one dominant ethnic group among several other ethnic groups, several languages, and an underlying regional culture.

Ethnonyms in precolonial times may reflect rejection of a central state or regional cult (as did those of the Tonga and Kwangwa, for example), designating groups "tired of subservience," as found repeatedly in Zambia, Malawi, and Zimbabwe. Of course, such structural designation precludes any genetic link between groups thus named. In addition, outside of the context of the state, ethnonymic practices reflected ecological specializations, for example, by distinguishing between hunter-gatherer Pygmies and agriculturalist Bantu-speakers in Zaire, and between Khoesan-speaking hunter-gatherers and Bantu-speaking agriculturalists and pastoralists in Zambia, Botswana, and Namibia. Here both ecological specialization and language served as ethnic boundary markers. The historic ecological opposition between pastoralism and agriculturalism has provided the imagery (if nothing more) for the most violent ethnic conflicts Central Africa has seen in postcolonial times, in Rwanda and Burundi.

If ethnicity in Central Africa has definite precolonial antecedents, the most obvious form in which colonial ethnicity has presented itself—as a hierarchical structure of geographically bounded, mutually exclusive ethnic, linguistic, religious, political, and administrative units administered by traditional rulers who became colonial officials—does not. The impact of European colonization on ethnicity and identity in Central Africa has been felt in a number of structural contexts.

ETHNICITY IN FORMAL ORGANIZATIONS

In modern formal organizations (state bureaucracies, industrial and commercial enterprises, and voluntary associations including churches, political parties, and ethnic associations), ethnicity emerges as the specific social format in which individuals negotiate between the universalist legal rules and statuses as defined within the formal organization, and their individual and group goals of economic survival, material appropriation, prestige, interpersonal power, and the acquisition of a political following. When of two interacting partners one is an official in the organization, ethnic identification often persuades the official to divert resources for unofficial means. Ethnicity then amounts to a structure of redistribution and patronage, which undermines the universalist principles of the formal organization but at the same time informally ties a significant section of the population both to the redistributing official and to the organization—and ultimately to the state.

The situationality of ethnicity means that only in certain contexts is a display of ethnic exclusiveness acceptable, and even then under specific conditions (in secret, in private, or during leisure time). Outside these contexts universalism is the norm, and there the migrant, job seeker, or client merges inconspicuously into the background of urban and formal-organizational mass society, submitting to generalized styles of dress and conduct, and using a lingua franca instead of a minority home language, the ticket to ethnic solidarity.

Before independence, industrial officials in Central Africa were mainly European and Asian expatriates; this introduced an ethnic factor, both between the expatriates and the local Africans and among expatriates from different parts of the world. African labor has been one of the largest problems of local economies; initially the solution was found in recruitment across considerable distances, which (even against the background of extended regional cultures) made for considerable linguistic, social, and cultural diversity at the towns, mines, and plantations where migrants converged. Urban ethnicity emerged under such conditions. The labor market features niches reserved for specific ethnic groups, exemplifying chains of redistribution between town and countryside. Some of today's ethnonyms (Nyamwezi, for example) are derived from the colonial labor market. Initially, industrial social control was exercised on a rural ethnic basis, by "tribal elders," in line with managerial fictions of the "target worker," "the bachelor labor migrant," and the "temporarily displaced villager," but this situation soon became unacceptable to urban and industrial workers developing a worker's class consciousness. In Central Africa, therefore, industrial conflicts tended to be expressed as ethnic conflicts.

The struggle for independence in Central African countries comprised not only the emergence of political parties (often with an ethnic or regionalist element) striving for constitutional reform, but also a distinct ethnic conflict: between a dominant white group of European ancestry controlling the colonial state, its bureaucracies, industry, and large-scale agriculture on the one hand, and on the other the African population, regardless of ethnic composition. Independence marked a replacement of white personnel by black, and in the latter's rallying for access and control, ethnicization played a major role.

Voluntary organizations in Central Africa may be implicitly or explicitly organized on an ethnic basis; of this tendency the standard example is ethnic organizations aiming at the presentation of ethnic identity through music, dance, and annual festivals, and through furthering of traditional leadership. In a multiethnic environment they offer people the opportunity of creating refuges of ethnic particularism, as a basis for effective dyadic network relationships between individuals. The colonial and postcolonial state's intense fear of monoethnic

group activity has led to a paucity of such associations in Central Africa. Frequently, voluntary formal organizations can be seen to function in a multiethnic manner, in reflection of the fact that everyday life, especially in towns but increasingly also in rural areas, is multiethnic. Voluntary associations of a recreational, sportive, and religious nature provide a usable model of the wider society and teach people to operate within the latter.

Christian churches furthered ethnic and regionalist particularism; however, this was often balanced by such nationalist and antiracialist orientation as Central African adherents derived from their churches' cosmopolitanism. The same point applies to Islam, a major presence in the northeastern and eastern parts of Central Africa. As a result, world religions and their formal organizations constitute the least ethnically divided domain in postcolonial Central Africa. Many congregations are multilingual in their rituals, and whereas ethnic conflicts (and those between Africans and non-Africans) may contribute to congregational fission, in general the adherents' ethnic particularism yields to religious universalism.

ETHNICITY IN URBAN CONTEXTS

The towns of Central Africa, products of the imposition of colonial administration and of the capitalist mode of production, have served as laboratories of multiethnic social life. African townspeople have shaped converging forms of urban life, molding the multiethnic and multilingual influx of migrants into viable urban societies where, with the aid of a lingua franca, formal and informal norms of conduct, patterns of experience, and sources of identification and mobilization are widely shared across ethnic and regional divisions. On this basis towns have asserted themselves in the face of the modern state and the declining postcolonial economy.

A widespread academic opinion stresses the increasing irrelevance, in the urban situation, of historic, rural-derived forms of social organization (kinship, marriage, and "traditional" politics and ritual). Here the Kalela dance, studied by J. Clyde Mitchell (*The Kalela Dance*, 1956) offers the classic paradigm, emphasizing how at the city boundaries, elements of rural society and culture may be selectively admitted onto the urban scene, yet undergo such a dramatic transformation of form, organization, and function that their urban manifestations must be understood by reference to the urban situation alone. Or, in H. Max Gluckman's famous words, "the African townsman is a townsman." He is "not a displaced villager or tribesman[but is]'detribalised' as soon as he leaves his village." The pioneering research by Mitchell and A. L. Epstein on the Zambian Copperbelt in the 1950s viewed urban ethnicity principally as a classification system for the management of dyadic network contacts and marital choices in town—an exclusively structural feature, not a vehicle for cultural continuity between rural and urban areas. Whereas Mitchell's later work developed the theory of urban ethnic categorization, Epstein abandoned the earlier position. He elaborated on the emotive aspects of identity as deriving from a sense of collective history, and from identification between (alternate) generations. He asserted that the private urban domain of the household, kinship, and sexuality was informed by cultural orientations from the migrants' distant rural homes.

This issue is elucidated by subsequent research on kinship rites, life-crisis rites, and historic African rituals in town. What is reproduced in such urban rituals is not an ethnically specific distinctive set of practices (although ethnicization pretends otherwise), but the overall cultural orientation of the wider region. The rural-derived practices bring to bear historic-cultural meaning and the attending cosmological orientation upon the culturally fragmented urban existence, in order to complement such symbolic orientation as derives from the modern state, the capitalist economy, world religions, and global consumer culture. Underneath the multiplicity of ethnic labels circulating in town, institutionalized modes of interethnic discourse (joking relations, funerary friendship) and marriage also mediate this joint substratum. Historic African cults, syncretistic cults, and independent Christian churches in town, which tend to be transethnic, derive much of their appeal from the way in which they articulate and transform this historic substratum and thus recapture meanings for urbanites who have loosened their direct contact with rural culture.

ETHNICITY IN RURAL CONTEXTS

In late-twentieth-century Central Africa, the urban-rural distinction has become less clear. Formal organizations exist in rural areas, and many

of the patterns of ethnicity discussed above are therefore also found there. Through rural-urban links (migration, marriage, part-time farming, ritual, and healing), many Central Africans participate both in urban and in rural life, and ethnicity provides strategic connections between these structurally different settings.

The colonial project sought to turn rural Central Africa into a patchwork quilt of "tribes," but never succeeded. Although in many countries the administration of rural areas is partly in the hands of traditional rulers whose authority is defined territorially, chiefs' areas today are not homogeneous in terms of the inhabitants' ethnic and economic characteristics; they include national and international ethnic strangers, primary rural producers, as well as representatives of all sorts of national-level formal organizations. The rural areas are involved in processes of class formation, in which the increasing scarcity of land as an agricultural resource leads to ethnic conflict because of the link between ethnic groups, traditional rulers, and land allocation. For such ethnic confrontations, as well as for the contest over scarce resources trickling down from the central state and from international development agencies, local and regional politics constitute an arena; the players include traditional rulers, ethno-political brokers conversant with urban and national-level conditions, and nonlocals pursuing supralocal political and economic concerns.

As small agricultural producers, equipped with the power to vote and usually with personal knowledge of urban conditions at the political center, peasants also play a role. Their view of politics tends to be dominated by ethnicity as a folk political theory. Here they are inspired by a collective sense of rural deprivation in the course of a shared colonial and postcolonial history. Expecting to extract, from state, party, and individual politicians, goods and services that until the late twentieth and early twenty-first centuries have been denied them, peasants give voting support to politicians who involve them in and through ethnicization. Politicians, often with a local background but through their education and careers involved beyond the local level, are often in collusion with local intellectuals, ethnic associations, and traditional rulers.

Provided ethnicization leads to recognition from the center (in the fields of expressive culture and traditional leadership) and an allocation of material benefits, it often results in increased regional and national integration. The view of ethnicity as invariably politically divisive and centrifugal cannot be supported. However, if local ethnicization is systematically frustrated or if the rural area is near a national border across which ethnic identification is cultivated with other groups sharing the same regional culture, then the conditions may be building up for secessionism, one of the most obvious spatial expressions of ethnicized intrastatal conflict, and one feared by Central African governments.

ETHNICITY IN THE POSTCOLONIAL STATE

The postcolonial state is far from a fixed and static bedding through which ethnic processes flow. On the contrary, the resilience of ethnic phenomena in Africa and worldwide reflects the erosion of the nation-state, internally by regional and local pressures and externally by the global economy and the changing international political order. If wealth flows from the state, ethnicity provides a network to redistribute it; if the state can no longer deliver, ethnicity provides counterstructures for such things as security, distribution, and assertion of group rights.

In Central Africa, national politics has a regionalist rather than an ethnic bias. Many small ethnic groups coalesce into a few regional power blocs; the latter operate at the national level, in shifting factional arrangements striving for control over the state. In Zambia, for instance, this process has now given rise to "mega-ethnic groups" such as the "Nyanja" (marked by a simplified version of the Chewa language as lingua franca) and the "Bemba." The latter name no longer primarily designates one among many other ethnic groups in the country's northeast, but has come to be mainly used for an ethnic composite encompassing the entire northern part of the country, which since 1930 has provided the bulk of labor migrants to the Zambian Copperbelt towns whose urban lingua franca, Bemba (more than the rural ethnic group of the same name), gave the block its name. Ethnic boundary markers between the constituent ethnic groups are shed and even their ethnonyms become obsolete.

The emergent mega-ethnic group, though largely a national-level political construct, begins to coincide with the underlying regional culture. This process will continue to define ethnicization in Central Africa into the twenty-first century.

The increase of scale in ethnicization is partly brought about by national elites who in the absence of the political expression of existing class and religious cleavages in national politics appeal for voter support to the ethnic folk theory of politics. In the 1970s and 1980s, one-party and military rule in Central Africa had as one of its major rationalizations the avoidance of ethnicization in the national political field. The elite sought to borrow from the underlying regional culture symbols of authority with nationwide appeal. A case in point is President Mobutu Sese Seko's drive for *authenticité* in Zaire. In other Central African postcolonial states, however, historic African symbols were combined with or supplanted by North Atlantic, Christian, and Islamic ones in the bricolage of national symbolism. With the general reinstitution of multipartyism in the 1990s, however, the explicitly ethnic element in Central African politics has greatly increased and occasionally (as in Rwanda in 1994) assumed genocidal proportions.

CULTURAL RECONSTRUCTION AND THE LIMITS OF ETHNIC MANIPULATION

Is there a limit to the manipulative capacity of ethnicity in Central Africa? Here it is useful to distinguish between a person's identification with a particular ethnic group and its regional and national trajectory in terms of political and economic power, prestige, and intergroup conflicts, and a person's cultural orientation, which is usually shared by many people belonging to a vast region comprising various ethnic groups.

Culture organizes the worldview, including fundamental conceptions of the body, time, space, causation, hierarchy, morality, legality, and relations between genders and between generations, and between the human, natural, and supernatural worlds. Invested in symbolic contents rather than in boundaries and their markers, the identity produced by such an overall cultural orientation does not have a name and may be termed existential, as against contrastive identity, which distinguishes the members of named ethnic groups through contrasting boundary markers.

Ethnicization, therefore, amounts to a conceptual and organizational focusing or framing, so as to make a social contradiction or conflict capable of being processed within the available technologies of communication, bureaucratic organization, and political representation.

The emergence of ethnic associations is one example of such framing at the organizational level. Individuals and groups can and do readily drop certain ethnic boundary markers and adopt others (a different language, ethnonym, or puberty rite, for example) without fundamentally affecting their overall cultural orientation; however, the process of ethnicization, and the intercontinental response it generates, condemns (unjustifiably) any such strategic shift (discouraging the use of a minority language for educational and judicial reasons, for example, or of puberty rites for medical reasons) as a denial of existential identity and an infringement of human rights.

By contrast, such assaults on existential cultural identity as the imposition of colonial rule, world religions, and the capitalist mode of production have affected the people of Central Africa profoundly, but not initially at the level of their specific ethnic group affiliations. However, after religious, therapeutic, and military responses, ethnicization has tended to emerge as a powerful secondary response to threatened destruction of existential identity. This has often produced new ethnic groups as the obvious focus for taking consciousness and for political action. It is a standard strategy of ethnicization to present the wider regional culture as eminently peculiar to one's own ethnic group; the emergence of megaethnic groups must also be seen in this light. Ethnicization thus becomes a strategy in the struggle not only for political and economic power, but particularly for the rebuilding of an eroded worldview within new boundaries, the reconstruction of existential identity through contrastive identity. The actors engage in a social process that allows them, by the management of boundaries and the positioning of people, ideas, and objects with in and outside these boundaries, to create a new community of meaningfulness. For such symbolic reconstruction, ethnicity is a ready context, but not the only one in twenty-first-century Central Africa. Religious congregations in world religions prominently play a similar part.

Ethnicization has yet another role to play. Ethnic identity can become hardened and militant to the point that people are prepared to undergo and inflict violence for its sake. This is when the ethnic identity becomes the focus of modern political history specifically involving the ethnic group, which consolidates itself in the process as a distinct political actor. Individual members of the ethnic group take the injury the group as a whole has suffered as a central personal concern. The awareness of shared historical experience is a powerful mobilizing force, and when it focuses on ethnicity it may lead to such stigmatization of other ethnic groups and to such dramatization of one's own ethnic group's predicament that ethnic identity becomes a folk theory of history, power, and deprivation. The images it conjures up instigate such intransigence that violence becomes an obvious answer, as Central Africa repeatedly showed in the late twentieth century.

See also **Anthropology, Social, and the Study of Africa; Colonial Policies and Practices; Kinship and Affinity; Languages; Military Organizations; Mobutu Sese Seko; Political Systems; Postcolonialism; Urbanism and Urbanization.**

BIBLIOGRAPHY

Amselle, Jean-Loup. *Logiques métisses: Anthropologie de l'identité en Afrique et ailleurs.* Paris: Payot, 1990.

Amselle, Jean-Loup, and Elikia M'Bokolo, eds. *Au coeur de l'ethnie: Ethnies, tribalisme et état en Afrique.* Paris: Découverte, 1985.

Barth, Fredrik, ed. *Ethnic Groups and Boundaries: The Social Organization of Culture Differences.* Boston: Little, Brown, 1969.

Cohen, Abner, ed. *Urban Ethnicity.* London: Tavistock Publications, 1974.

Doornbos, Martin R. *Not All the King's Men: Inequality as a Political Instrument in Ankole, Uganda.* The Hague: Mouton, 1978.

Epstein, A. L. *Ethos and Identity: Three Studies in Ethnicity.* London: Tavistock Publications, 1978.

Fabian, Johannes. *Language and Colonial Power: The Appropriation of Swahili in the Former Belgian Congo, 1880–1938.* Cambridge, U.K.: Cambridge University Press, 1986.

Fardon, Richard. "'African Ethnogenesis': Limits to the Comparability of Ethnic Phenomena." In *Comparative Anthropology*, ed. Ladislav Holy. Oxford: Blackwell, 1987.

Gluckman, H. Max. "Tribalism, Ruralism, and Urbanism in South and Central Africa." In Colonialism in Africa, 1870–1960, Vol. 3: Profiles of Change: African Society and Colonial Rule, ed. Victor Turner. Cambridge, U.K.: Cambridge University Press, 1971.

Gutkind, Peter C. W., ed. The Passing of Tribal Man in Africa. Leiden: Brill, 1970.

Hyden, Gorant, and Michael Bratton, eds. Governance and Politics in Africa. Boulder, CO: Lynne Rienner, 1992.

Lame, Danielle de. Une colline entre mille ou le calme avant la tempête: Transformations et blocages du Rwanda rural. Tervuren, Belgium: Royal Museum for Central Africa, 2005.

Lancaster, C. S. "Ethnic Identity, History, and 'Tribe' in the Middle Zambezi Valley." American Ethnologist 1 (1974): 707–730.

Lemarchand, René. Burundi: Ethnocide as Discourse and Practice. Cambridge, U.K.: Cambridge University Press, 1994.

Mafeje, Archie. "The Ideology of 'Tribalism.'" Journal of Modern African Studies 9 (1971): 253–261.

Newbury, Catharine. The Cohesion of Oppression: Clientship and Ethnicity in Rwanda, 1860–1960. New York: Columbia University Press, 1988.

Prunier, Gerard. The Rwanda Crisis: History of a Genocide. New York: Columbia University Press, 1995.

Romanucci-Ross, Lola; George A. De Vos; and Takeyuki Tsuda. Ethnic Identity: Problems and Prospects for the Twenty-First Century. Lanham, MD: AltaMira Press, 2006.

Rothchild, Donald, and Victor A. Olorunsola, eds. State Versus Ethnic Claims: Ethnic Policy Dilemmas. Boulder, CO: Westview Press, 1983.

Schilder, Kees. Quest for Self-Esteem: State, Islam, and Ethnicity in Northern Cameroon. Aldershot: Avebury: 1994.

Schlee, Gunther. Identities on the Move: Clanship and Pastoralism in Northern Kenya. New York: St. Martin's Press, 1989.

Shaw, Timothy M. "Ethnicity as the Resilient Paradigm for Africa: From the 1960s to the 1980s." Development and Change 17, no. 4 (1986): 587–605.

Tonkin, Elizabeth; Maryon McDonald; and Malcolm Chapman; eds. History and Ethnicity. New York: Routledge, 1989.

Vail, Leroy, ed. The Creation of Tribalism in Southern Africa. Berkeley: University of California Press, 1989.

van Binsbergen, Wim M. J. "From Tribe to Ethnicity in Western Zambia: The Unit of Study as an Ideological Problem." In Old Modes of Production and Capitalist Encroachment: Anthropological Explorations in Africa, ed. Wim M. J. van Binsbergen and Peter Geschiere. London: Routledge, 1985.

van Binsbergen, Wim M. J. Tears of Rain: Ethnicity and History in Central Western Zambia. New York: Kegan Paul, 1992.

Vansina, Jan. Kingdoms of the Savanna. Madison: University of Wisconsin Press, 1966.

Vansina, Jan. Paths in the Rainforests: Toward a History of Political Tradition in Equatorial Africa. Madison: University of Wisconsin Press, 1990.

WIM M. J. VAN BINSBERGEN

EASTERN AFRICA

Ethnicity with reference to eastern Africa has taken on a range of pejorative connotations arising from the horrendous cases of ethnic conflict and genocide, such as have occurred in Rwanda, Democratic Republic of the Congo (DRC), Uganda, and Sudan. But the term *ethnicity* had, over the last few decades, already taken on a number of different usages and meanings, not all of them associated with violence and genocide, and not always noncontentious. First, it largely replaced the discredited term *tribalism*, which carried inappropriate connotations of evolutionary backwardness. Second, it came to refer to a supposedly objective process visible to outsiders by which groups become more and more culturally distinctive. Third, it has been used to denote a subjective process, stressing characteristics that differentiate people from other peoples.

These three meanings of the term are often mutually involved: outsiders may recognize a group by their distinctive habits and dress, whereas the members of the group insist on these same characteristics as evidence of their particular groups membership. Sometimes, however, outsiders may attribute an exaggerated uniqueness to a group whose members do not see such a significance. This is, according to some, what earlier European colonialists did when they divided the peoples under their domination into discrete tribal groups, usually ignoring the complex and crosscutting marriage and trading relations between regions that prevented the development of hard-and-fast differences between peoples. The historical falsity of this rigid demarcation of peoples is another reason why the term *tribalism* has been rejected in favor of *ethnicity*.

Such colonial usages leave their traces, however, and tribalism is still used by people in Kenya,

Tanzania, and Uganda to explain alleged differences among themselves, including political, social, and economic inequalities. The fact that it is often inequalities of access to resources that are really at issue in peoples' conflicts, rather than differences of culture or custom, does not prevent people from explaining such divisions in ethnic terms. Also, in the manner of a self-fulfilling prophecy, disadvantaged peoples often see governments or dominant groups as ethnic in character and recruitment, and react accordingly by organizing themselves along ethnic lines, thereby setting up counter-reactions. In the end, the so-called ethnic groups may each develop distinctive political and economic interests in opposition to one another, with the result that these interests do indeed become broadly isomorphic with cultural differences.

Nevertheless, whatever the consequences of such processes, ethnicity remains fundamentally a method of classification—that is, a set of concepts that divide peoples into stereotyped categories. Such stereotypes consist of beliefs about other ethnic groups concerning their origins, behavior, character, capacities, and even the extent to which they approximate humanity. A people's own ethnic label for itself may imply this. Thus, the so-called Nuer of southern Sudan call themselves *Nath*, which means people, while their neighbors and rivals, the so-called Dinka, call themselves *Jieng*, which also means people. The general term for many of the peoples of eastern Africa is *Bantu*, a linguistic label but one that means people, too.

For many generations, there has developed among Africans an even greater consciousness of the diversity of cultures and peoples in eastern Africa as a result of precolonial long-distance trading, colonial labor migration, and, still later, information spread by radio and television. It is under these changing conditions that new ethnic labels have developed.

In the mid- and late-1940s, numbers of linguistically and culturally similar groups gathered themselves under overarching appellations, especially in Kenya, where soldiers returning from World War II had special influence. Thus, to take a few Kenyan examples, there came into being the Kalenjin (including the Nandi, Turkana, and Pokot), the Mijikenda (the Giriama, Digo, and some seven other subgroups), and the Luhya

(Vugusu, Maragoli, and many others). The subgroup names remain important within smaller, regional contexts, but the more comprehensive terms may be used in wider, especially political, ones. Within subgroups there are likely to be even smaller units known by locality of origin and, in some cases, by descent from a single ancestor.

The classification of peoples thus is often pyramidal, with an overarching differentiation of cultural-linguistic groups throughout eastern Africa subsuming a series of lower-order distinctions according to region, district, and perhaps clan or lineage.

Increasing urbanization is always modifying these ethnic distinctions through intermarriage, through use of such lingua francas as Swahili and English, and through new cultural styles. Nevertheless, they remain dynamically involved in the creation of new categories of interaction.

UGANDA

Uganda can illustrate this modern reorganization of previous classifications. With Uganda's independence in 1962, two political parties—Kabaka Yekka (KY), representing the dominant ethnic group, the Ganda, and the Uganda People's Congress (UPC), with a more Pan-Ugandan constituency—came to power and formed an alliance. The Ganda kingdom was allowed internal autonomy in what was in effect a federated Uganda. The main linguistic-cultural division was between the Bantu-speaking south, many of whose peoples (similar to the Ganda) had kingdoms, and the Nilotic- and Sudanic-speaking north, whose peoples did not. The Ganda king, and head of KY, was made titular president of federal Uganda; the head of the UPC, a northern Nilote, was made prime minister. Within a few years, a struggle for power between the two parties had become too hard to contain. The KY was banned and its leader, the Ganda king, was banished.

There developed a polarization between Ganda and non-Ganda, Bantu-speakers and Nilotic-Sudanic-speakers, southerners and northerners, kingdoms and nonkingdoms, that became mutually reinforcing and essentialized in a way that never existed before colonialism but had been fostered during it through British Indirect Rule, which privileged Ganda authority over other Ugandans. Previously, however, the Ganda kingdom had always absorbed peoples of foreign origins, as had the even earlier great Nyoro-Kitara empire, through trade, settlement, intermarriage, and allowing children to be raised speaking the languages both of their adopted region and of their parents, who might themselves be of diverse linguistic-cultural origins. The sharp and isomorphic distinctions of language, culture, and alleged origins were very much a mid-twentieth-century development.

Under Idi Amin during the 1970s, these polarizations of peoples were crudely exploited as Amin explained his government's failings as the result of the treachery of one ethnic group after another. Only later, under President Yoweri Museveni, did government policy specifically address cultural and linguistic differences among peoples, which were seen as secondary to issues of economic and political privilege.

Where they are not politically exploited, such differences of custom and belief are likely to persist at the domestic level in the form of linguistic vernacular, oral literature, naming systems, systems of marriage and kinship reckoning, myths of origin, rituals of initiation and purification, and beliefs about the cosmos and its forces. By themselves, these cultural differences normally are regarded as aspects of ethnicity only when they are used to demarcate groups' boundaries, territories, and resources in relation to each other. In this sense, cultural differences, whether they are recently invented or long held, are the stuff of which ethnic consciousness, conflict, and cooperation are made.

The question of scale is important in accordance with the pyramidal model of ethnic classification. Thus, the Bantu-speaking neighbors of southern Uganda, the Ganda and Nyoro, may struggle over land at one level but may be united against the Nilotic-speaking Acholi and Lango of northern Uganda at a higher level. Yet, again at a lower level, the Acholi and Lango see themselves as sufficiently linguistically distant (the Lango being identified by linguists as Para-Nilotic rather than Nilotic) for this distinction to be an idiom of conflict between them over land or political representation.

KENYA

In Kenya there is a colonial travesty of ethnic identification. The colonially imposed political border between Kenya and Uganda has assumed, since colonial times and independence, all the significance of a sometimes rigid international barrier, yet it cuts across ethnic groups that once regularly interacted with each other, in particular the Para-Nilotic Teso and the Bantu Samia and other Luhya-speaking subgroups. In addition, the close linguistic and cultural relationship between the Kenya Nilotic Luo and the Uganda Acholi, Alur, and Padhola has been made artificially more distant than it would otherwise have been. The Luo also are divided to their south by the border between Kenya and Tanzania, as are the Para-Nilotic Maasai. To the north of Uganda, Nilotes are further divided by the border with Sudan, and the Uganda–DRC border divides Sudanic speakers, comprising Madi, Lendu, Okebu, and Lugbara, as well as the Nilotic Alur. Other examples exist with regard to Kenya's borders with Ethiopia and Somalia.

In Kenya, the political creation since the 1940s of new ethnic groups comprising smaller ones, such as the Luhya, Mijikenda, and Kalenjin, can be seen in the context of that country's political birth as an independent state. Consolidation into larger groups was viewed as a way for smaller ethnic groups to garner greater political influence, and although Kenya did not achieve its independence until December 1963, African demands for greater political representation and autonomy were intensified beginning in the mid-1940s. They had been expressed as early as the 1920s in Kenya's Central Province, where the numerous and powerful Gikuyu live.

Prior to Kenya's independence, the mainly Gikuyu armed struggle against British domination (the so-called Mau Mau revolt) resulted in the declaration of a state of emergency during the period 1952–1959. There then occurred an interesting political alliance between the Gikuyu leaders, including notably Jomo Kenyatta—most of whom were proscribed, in detention, or in exile in Britain—and Luo leaders, including Oginga Odinga (c. 1911–1994) and Tom Mboya (1930–1969). Whereas the Luo campaigned by means of the law and international opinion, the Gikuyu struggle was focused more directly in their homeland and took the form of protest against land alienation and control by white settlers. The alliance was even reflected at the level of interpersonal relations between Gikuyu and Luo in the major towns of Kenya, where some joint trading and intermarriage occurred.

This alliance between the Bantu-speaking Gikuyu and the Nilotic-speaking Luo culminated in the formation of the Kenya African National Union (KANU), which was victorious in Kenya's independence elections. As in the merging of the KY and UPC in Uganda, this was an example of ethnic groups with sharply contrasting cultures uniting in common national cause. As in Uganda, the alliance did not last long; the majority of the Luo, headed by Odinga, broke away to form their own party, the Kenya Peoples Union (KPU), an avowedly socialist party that was proscribed by the ruling and now Gikuyu-dominated KANU, which clearly had come to espouse the capitalist ethic.

The Luo leader Mboya, however, remained a staunch supporter of KANU. But because of the increasingly ethnic parameters of personal identity, he was regarded by many ordinary Luo as a traitor to their cause, an accusation reinforced by the claim that, because he was born and raised on Rusinga Island in Lake Victoria near the Luhya, he was in fact Bantu in origin.

The Gikuyu and Luo are the two largest groups in Kenya, and it is relevant to ask what role their cultural differences played in the breakup of their union. Unlike in Uganda, none of the Kenyan peoples had kingdoms, so that was not a difference between them. The Luo had a localized, patrilineal, segmentary lineage structure by which any one individual could trace descent back over twelve generations, whereas among the Gikuyu, patrilineal descent groups were rarely remembered beyond the great-grandparents' generation. Instead, the Gikuyu had a system of grading by age-sets and generations that was influenced by the neighboring, more pervasive Maasai system. A Gikuyu's loyalty to his or her descent and kinship groupings was therefore much weaker than among the Luo. Furthermore, during the colonial period, Gikuyu lost much of their land, and they were concentrated in special villages during the state of emergency.

This combination of cultural and political factors appears to have created a marked individualism among Gikuyu that has allowed them to become successful at business, and the Luo frequently observe that their onerous kinship obligations drain the profits accruing from private enterprises and thus hamper individual initiative. These factors are important in the creation of ethnic identity and stereotypes but cannot explain the secession of the Luo from KANU, which is more likely due to what they saw as neglect of their own region in relation to that of Gikuyu.

Most of the other ethnic groups at Kenya's independence were smaller and formed a short-lived, pro-federal opposition party called the Kenya African Democratic Union (KADU); the party's slogan was *majimbo*, meaning district, and it emphasized local and ethnic autonomy. The most important of these groups are the Kalenjin, Maasai, Luhya, Kamba, and Mijikenda, all of which are ethnographically well documented. Consisting of Bantu, Nilotic, and Para-Nilotic peoples, KADU, by representing the interests of these smaller ethnic groups, wished to see the government accommodate such cultural and linguistic differences. In later years, calls for federation were again made in the context of Kenya's post-1992 policy of multiparty democracy, but, although the idea is not completely dead, it remains elusive in practice as successive leaders, including Moi and then Kibaki, grapple with, respectively, their own minority and majority ethnic standing and at the same time address pressing domestic problems, the latter in particular declaring a major policy of eradicating political corruption.

Although ethnic identity may thus be enhanced by political factors, it may also be threatened by the homogenizing influences of urbanization, widespread labor migration, long-distance trade, intermarriage, and the use of Swahili and English in preference to a vernacular. Recognizing such threats, ethnic leaders often launch cultural revivalist movements or at least make ethnic self-awareness a political platform. The Mijikenda of the Kenya coast have a different kind of problem. Although some of them, especially a subgroup called the Digo, are Muslim, most remain non-Muslim and some are Christians. The latter commonly express apprehension that their people may convert to Islam and thereby lose memory of and pride in their own customs, beliefs, and origins. Elders claim that they will lose their ancestors if they convert to Islam and adopt the language and lifestyle of the Muslim Swahili who are found all along the eastern African coast. Leaders among the Giriama, the largest subgroup, try to counter the influence of Islam and modern Western consumerist values brought by European tourism by urging all Giriama to venerate the therapeutic efficacy and cultural essence of a sacred site deep in the heart of Giriamaland, away from the coast.

Being for the most part a maritime people engaged in ocean trade and fishing, the Swahili-speaking peoples live along a thousand-mile stretch of the eastern African coast from Mogadishu in Somalia, in the north, to Maputo in Mozambique, in the south, and are most prevalent in the Kenyan and Tanzanian coastlands. They have a highly complex, literate civilization that spans centuries. Their language and much of their cultural lifestyle have been imitated by inland peoples, despite some opposition by those who fear loss of their own cultural identity. At the same a rising wave of Islamic radicalism under the guidance of Saudi-trained proselytizers called *Wahabi* is more visible than ever before, especially in the Muslim population concentrations of Zanzibar and Mombasa.

TANZANIA

It is quite common, especially in Tanzania, which has a policy of encouraging Swahili as the national and official language, for people to acknowledge themselves as having several ethnic identifies. Thus, a man in Tabora, a center of the nineteenth-century Arab slave trade, may point to distant Arab origins of his father and Sukuma or other Bantu origins of his mother, and may speak both Swahili and the Sukuma language, according to the situation. Such a situational selectivity has been common for generations in Tanzania, where use of Swahili was made easier than in Kenya and Uganda by virtue of its basic structural similarity to the mainly Bantu local vernaculars. Urbanization and labor migration is resulting in ethnolinguistic status becoming a selective matter more recently in Kenya and Uganda.

Indeed, it is a reasonable claim that, in comparison with Kenya and Uganda, Tanzania has no great ethnic divisions, as a relative homogeneity was reinforced by the country's brand of *ujaamaa* (community) socialism. Yet even slight differences can be articulated under conditions of regional conflict, and so it is that the Chagga, living in the foothills of Mount Kilimanjaro, were once envied and discriminated against for their farming and entrepreneurial success, despite speaking Swahili and a vernacular quite close to that of many of their neighbors. As elsewhere in eastern Africa, the separateness of Tanzania's ethnic groups owes more to colonial administrative demarcations than to sharply differing linguistic and cultural divisions. Yet in the early twenty-first century, such large and important groups as the Sukuma, Nyamwezi, and Chagga are often the first points of reference in the ethnic maps that many Tanzanians use to explain national successes and failures.

It would be incorrect to ascribe an irreducible ethnic content to all relationships in eastern Africa. It is clear that changing ethnic identities are among a number of others based on occupation, residence, and religion, which sometimes take priority. However, all people anywhere, including Europe, tend to seek the origins of their present makeup. As a differentiating feature of ordinary, everyday existence, this delineation of ethnic identity need not have overriding significance and is one of several modes of differentiation by which humans make sense of their worlds. If, however, this search for origins provides an identity to individuals and the groups to which they see themselves as belonging, it is not incontrovertible. The origin may be deemed to have changed, and with it the ethnic identity. At one level, persons may seem to exercise choice in such changes, but at another level, wider changes in the distribution of power may force the changes upon them. This negative side of ethnic labeling and stereotyping results in prejudice and discrimination. Striking a balance between the sense of belonging derived from ethnic membership and its politically harmful uses has been one of the great problems confronting humanity. Eastern Africa is no exception.

See also **Amin Dada, Idi; Anthropology, Social, and the Study of Africa; Colonial Policies and Practices; Kinship and Affinity; Languages; Museveni, Yoweri; Postcolonialism; Urbanism and Urbanization.**

BIBLIOGRAPHY

Berman, Bruce, and John Lonsdale. *Unhappy Valley: Clan, Class, and State in Colonial Kenya.* 2 vols. London: James Currey, 1992.

Buckley-Zistel, Susanne. "Remembering to Forget: Chosen Amnesia as a Strategy for Local Coexistence in Post-Genocide Rwanda." *Africa: The Journal of the*

International African Institute 76, no. 2 (2006): 131–150.

Eltringham, Nigel. *Accounting for Horror: Post-Genocide Debates in Rwanda*. London: Pluto Press, 2004.

Finnistroem, Sverker. "Wars of the Past and War in the Present: The Lord's Resistance Movement/Army in Uganda." *Africa: The Journal of the International African Institute* 76, no. 2 (2006): 200–220.

Hansen, Holger Bernt, and Michael Twaddle, eds. *Changing Uganda: The Dilemmas of Structural Adjustment and Revolutionary Change*. London: J. Currey, 1991.

Karege, Anicet. *Les médias Rwandais toujours au service du pouvoir*. Paris: L'Harmattan, 2004.

Mboya, Tom. *Freedom and After*. London: Andre Deutsch, 1963.

Middleton, John. *The World of the Swahili: An African Mercantile Civilization*. New Haven, Connecticut: Yale University Press, 1992.

Moore, Sally Folk. *Social Facts and Fabrications: "Customary Law" on Kilimanjaro, 1880–1980*. Cambridge, U.K.: Cambridge University Press, 1986.

Muriuki, Godfrey. *A History of the Kikuyu, 1500–1900*. Nairobi, Kenya: Oxford University Press, 1974.

Odinga, Oginga. *Not Yet Uhuru: The Autobiography of Oginga Odinga*. New York: Hill and Wang, 1967.

Parkin, David. *The Cultural Definition of Political Response: Lineal Destiny among the Luo*. London: Academic Press, 1978.

Parkin, David. *Sacred Void: Spatial Images of Work and Ritual among the Giriama of Kenya*. Cambridge, U.K.: Cambridge University Press, 1991.

Southall, Aidan W. "The Illusion of Tribe." *Journal of Asian and African Studies* 5, nos. 1–2 (1970): 28–50.

Spear, Thomas, and Richard Waller, eds. *Being Maasai: Ethnicity and Identity in East Africa*. London: James Currey, 1993.

DAVID PARKIN

NORTHERN AFRICA

Ethnicity is an object of social and political contestation in North Africa, both in terms of the particular boundaries of its identity diacritics (race, geography, language, and kinship) and in its general legitimacy as a mode of social organization. Contemporary Northern African states, largely following an Arab nationalist ideology after independence, prioritized national unity through recognition of Islam and Arabic as the official religion and language. Any public acknowledgment of ethnic diversity was considered anathema to state national consciousness, and expressions of cultural difference were decried as feudal survivals, colonial inventions, and de facto threats of secession.

Nevertheless, since the 1960s, a public assertion of cultural differences has occurred throughout North Africa, including cultural movements by Copts (7 million mostly in northern Egypt), Nubians (200,000 in southern and urban Egypt) and Berbers (up to 23 million across North Africa). Most vocally, Berber (or "Amazigh") activists have militated for an official status and institutional inclusion of Tamazight, an Afro-Asiatic language whose multiple dialects are spoken in an area stretching from the Siwa Oasis in western Egypt; east to the Libyan Tripolitania; Djerba in Tunisia; the Algerian regions of the Mzab, Aurès (Chaouia), Kabylia, and Tipaza (Chenoua); the Moroccan Rif, Middle Atlas, and High Atlas mountains, and the southern valleys of the Sous and pre-Saharan oases (Ishlehin); and south among the semi-nomadic Touareg and Zenaga of the Sahel (Mauritania, Mali, Niger, and southern Algeria), with Berber speakers comprising approximately 25 percent of Algeria's population and 40 percent of Morocco's population. Initially, North African states actively suppressed such activism, jailing militants and censoring their publications. Likewise, in Egypt, Nubians were subject to mass displacement following the 1960 construction of the Aswan Dam, and Copts have been subject to repeated communal attacks, particularly from Islamist groups.

Since the late 1990s, however, Northern African governments have gradually acceded to activist demands for inclusion, with Egypt incorporating Copts into high governmental posts, and Algeria and Morocco creating state institutions—the High Amazigh Commission (HCA) and the Royal Institute for Amazigh Culture (IRCAM), respectively—charged with introducing Tamazight into the school system and media. Although many activists have lauded such efforts, others remain suspicious, viewing these compromises as attempts to co-opt ethnic activism into the governments' ongoing battles with the Islamist opposition. They fear that these state institutions will folklorize Berber and Copt heritage rather than protect them from disappearance after decades of official Arabization and Islamization policies.

In the meantime, these debates erase a deeper cultural and religious heterogeneity of North Africa, both within the social categories of Arab, Copt, Nubian, and Berber, as well as in terms of the historical importance and continued existence of a variety of ethnoracial and religious groups in the region. Among them number Bedouins (5.5 million across the Sahara), Domari/Romani (over 1 million in Egypt and Algeria), Sahrawi (500,000 in Western Sahara, Mauritania, Algeria, and Morocco), Haratin/Iqbalin/"Black Maure" (750,000 in southern Morocco, the Western Sahara, and Mauritania), Gnawa (several hundred thousand in Morocco), Kenuzi-Dongola (100,000 in southern Egypt), Greeks (42,000 in Egypt), and Jews (10,000 in Morocco, Tunisia, and Egypt). These groups similarly lack political recognition and confront state marginalization and assimilation.

DIVERSITY

Historically, Northern Africa has been a crossroads of trans-Saharan and trans-Mediterranean commerce, migration, and conquest, linking the region to West Africa, East Africa, the Middle East, and Europe. Since classical times, Phoenician, Roman, Punic, Arab, Portuguese, Spanish, and French invaders have set up imperial outposts and trading entrepôts along the North African coastline and fertile plains, adding to the extant cultural and linguistic diversity of the region. Arabic-speaking populations initially arrived in the seventh century with the Islamic armies of the Umayyad caliphate and later spread out across the western half of North Africa, most significantly with the ninth-century migration of the Banu Hilal from Fatimid Egypt. In the west, they entered a region already divided between multilingual coastal cities, where Latin and Punic remained languages of scholarship and governance, and a Berberophone interior. Not only had many of the Berber tribes already converted first to Judaism and (in many cases) later to Christianity, but they also had culturally and linguistically integrated a number of other marginal groups, including Jewish migrants and African agriculturalists of the pre-Saharan oasis communities. In this respect, if western North Africa has over the last thirteen centuries witnessed a gradual process

of Arabization, it previously had experienced long histories of Christianization and Berberization.

COLONIAL POLICY

A nationalist vision of Arab-Berber fusion under the mantle of Islamic civilization became hegemonic in Tunisia, Algeria, and Morocco after independence, countering a perceived French colonial ethnic policy of divide-and-conquer. French military officers engaged in sustained projects to classify the heterogeneous North African populations they encountered and to devise institutions of mixed governance. While this never constituted a coherent "Berber policy," it did result in a set of educational and legal regimes that differentiated Arab, Berber, and Jewish populations and devolved the management of their internal affairs to recognized ethno-religious bodies.

For North African Jews, the colonial regime granted control of education and civil law to the Alliance Israelite and the rabbinical courts, respectively, and after 1870 granted Algerian Jews full French citizenship rights. Muslims were excluded from political representation in the North African colonies until 1947, and they could access French citizenship only if they renounced their religious "personal status" and accepted the French civil code concerning marriage and property. Otherwise, civil matters for Muslim subjects were under the control of Islamic *shariʿa* courts, but village councils and customary or tribal law had de facto control over local affairs and were officially recognized in the Moroccan Protectorate after 1930. This last change particularly concerned marginal Berber-speaking areas, which had been the last to submit to French "pacification" efforts and had launched repeated rebellions against colonial control. French military officers respected Berbers as redoubtable fighters, and colonial writers consistently lauded the Berbers' democratic spirit, Puritan work ethic, and independence from Islamic orthodoxy, which many colonial ethnologists claimed arose from a common origin of Berbers and Germanic or Latin peoples. Considering Berbers as more potentially assimilable than Arabs, French officials often targeted Berber-speaking areas for labor recruitment and teacher training.

NATIONALISM AND REGIONALISM

In spite of such assimilation efforts, educated Berbers figured among the leaders of the anti-colonial struggle. Berber-speaking areas—particularly Algerian Kabylia and the Moroccan Rif mountains—were sites of some of the earliest and most violent battles in the independence struggle. Nonetheless, Berber leaders were systematically expelled from the nationalist movements, which gradually dismissed intellectual visions of a multiethnic and multiconfessional North Africa in favor of a hegemonic Arabo-Islamic ideology. In the wake of North African independence, a variety of movements for regional autonomy and ethnic self-determination arose in Berber-speaking areas. In Kabylia, Hocine Aït Ahmed led a violently suppressed ten-month insurrection in September 1963 against the ruling National Liberation Front. In the years that followed, the Algerian state remained suspicious of Kabyle regionalism, intervening with force during the student unrest and labor strikes of March–April 1980 (the "Berber Spring") and October 1988. In Morocco, the early years after independence witnessed a similar use of state violence to suppress a series of rebellions in the peripheral Berber-speaking regions (especially the northern Rif and the southeastern Tafilalet) for local autonomy against the ruling, Arab nationalist Istiqlal party.

In spite of such repression, a Berber cultural renaissance has transpired since the late 1960s, with activists operating originally in the diaspora (primarily in France) and increasingly in North Africa proper to make Berber identity an object of political struggle, standardize Tamazight orthography, and disseminate Amazigh consciousness through cultural associations, newspapers, and political song. In Algeria, these actions were directed by the Berber Cultural Movement (MCB) formed in the wake of the 1980 Berber Spring, and later by the rival, Kabylia-based Socialist Forces Front (FFS) and Rally for Culture and Democracy (RCD) political parties legalized after 1989. By the mid-1990s, the state had largely acceded to the demands, agreeing to incorporate Tamazight into the national media and the school system, establishing the HCA, and recognizing Tamazight as "one of the foundations of national identity" in the November 1996 constitutional reforms. In Morocco, while Berber associations have been an active element of urban civil society since the mid–1980s, they were subject to strong state surveillance, with Amazigh activists arrested as late as 1994 for displaying signs written in Tamazight during a May Day parade in Errachidia. Responding to the international outcry protesting these arrests, the government promised a series of reforms that subsequently led to the 2001 establishment of the IRCAM and the planned introduction of Tamazight into the media and primary school classrooms.

These gains on the cultural front have not, however, translated into the institutional self-determination demanded by many Berber activists. During the Algerian civil war of the 1990s, Kabyle villages established local militias to protect their residents from Islamist and military forces. However, the assassinations of political singer Lounès Matoub in June 1998 by unknown assailants and of teenager Mohammed Guermah in April 2001 by military police, provoked a series of violent street protests against ongoing socioeconomic marginalization and the treatment of Kabyles as "second-class citizens." The confrontations between local youth and government forces during the 2001 "Black Spring" resulted in the death of at least sixty young Kabyles, the injuring of over three hundred, and the emergence of a new political actor, the Coordination of Aarouch, Daïras, and Communes (CADC), to transcend extant political divisions between the FFS and the RCD. Additionally, in the wake of the 2001 confrontations, a France-based Movement for the Autonomy of Kabylia (MAK) was formed, advocating regional federalism.

While ethnic activism in the rest of Northern Africa has not had the same violent character as in Kabylia, conflicts in Morocco have pitted Amazigh activists against state officials for the control of regional resources. After the 2001 establishment of IRCAM, a large number of peripheral Berber cultural associations recentered their activities around socioeconomic development and engaged in a series of protests against state efforts to expropriate collective lands. The state responded with legal actions against protesters for threatening the public order and inciting racial hatred and tribalism.

If these state accusations were exaggerated, the protests did amount to ethnoracial contestations over the definition and control of the "local." In pre-Saharan communities, Amazigh activists' claims to autochthony are made at the expense of the former agrarian class of territorially fixed black sharecroppers who anteceded the Berber tribes in the region. These Berber-speaking Haratin—likely the descendants of an earlier migration of Bafour from Mauritania—tilled the oasis fields as dependent clients of the Berber tribes, enjoying neither legal rights nor the ability to own and inherit land. Now full citizens, these former Haratin (or present-day Iqbalin), who are demographically superior in many of the oasis valleys, have challenged local Berber tribal hegemony, using monies earned as migrant workers to purchase land, gain representations in village *djma'at*, and wrest control of local municipal councils. In general, Iqbalin, although Berber-speakers themselves, are understandably suspicious of Amazigh associations and land-claim struggles, seeing them as merely props for tribal politics. Such nonparticipation fuels Berber fears of Iqbalin social mobility, which is often expressed in a form of color racism that persists even among Amazigh activists who promulgate "Africanity" as a constituent element of Berber identity.

Berber/Iqbalin conflict is matched by a lack of solidarity between the Amazigh movement and the fight for Sahrawi self-determination in the disputed Western Sahara. To a great extent, the wide participation of southern Berber speakers in the 1975 Green March—in which King Hasan II mobilized 350,000 Moroccans to occupy lands abandoned by departing Spanish colonizers—established them as loyal citizens in the eyes of the monarchy, and their continued support for the regime's Sahara claims has largely enabled their obtaining of increased cultural and linguistic rights. Such support, combined with persistent racism, marks a black/white ethnoracial divide in North Africa that is often erased or sublimated in the ongoing Arab-Berber or Arab-Nubian or Muslim-Copt identity politics of North Africa.

See also **Anthropology, Social, and the Study of Africa; Hasan II of Morocco; Immigration and Immigrant Groups; Islam; Judaism in Africa; Kinship and Affinity; Nationalism.**

BIBLIOGRAPHY

Brett, Michael, and Elizabeth Fentress. *The Berbers.* Oxford: Blackwell, 1996.

Chaker, Salem. *Berbères aujourd'hui.* Paris: Harmattan, 1997.

Gellner, Ernest, and Charles Micaud. *Arabs and Berbers: From Tribe to Nation in North Africa.* Lexington, MA: Lexington Books, 1972.

Ilahiane, Hsain. *Ethnicities, Community Making, and Agrarian Change: The Political Ecology of a Moroccan Oasis.* Lanham, MD: University Press of America, 2004.

Lorcin, Patricia M. E. *Imperial Identities: Stereotyping, Prejudice, and Race in Colonial Algeria.* London: I. B. Tauris, 1995.

Maddy-Weitzman, Bruce. "Contested Identities: Berbers, 'Berberism,' and the State in North Africa." *Journal of North African Studies* 6, no. 3 (2001): 23–47.

McDougall, James. "Myth and Counter-Myth: 'The Berber' as National Signifier in Algerian Historiographies." *Radical History Review* 86 (2003): 66–88.

Silverstein, Paul. "Martyrs and Patriots: Ethnic, National, and Transnational Dimensions of Kabyle Politics." *Journal of North African Studies* 8, no. 1 (2003): 87–111. Available from www.ethnologue.com.

PAUL SILVERSTEIN

SOUTHERN AFRICA

The study of ethnic identity formation in southern Africa was, until the early 1990s, a neglected field. Debate on the topic was stifled for many years because the government of South Africa used ethnicity to justify apartheid, including measures such as the creation of ethnic homelands for Africans. Furthermore, apologists for apartheid, including some academics, adopted a strongly primordialist approach to ethnicity, arguing that all people were born into culturally bounded and mutually exclusive groups. Many of those opposed to apartheid, and supportive of the African nationalist opposition that rejected tribalism, viewed ethnicity as entirely constructed by the state to serve its racist aims. They believed that debating ethnicity would somehow lend credence to the perception that it was real.

As apartheid crumbled in the 1990s, to be replaced by the country's first democratic government in 1994, ethnic identities showed no sign of disappearing. In some respects they became more acute, with political jockeying for position, and political violence, often manifested in ethnic form. To some, this was a consequence of earlier racist policies that continued to be fostered by racial and class interests. Others believed that as the racial basis of South African society was being dismantled, so ethnicity was being reconfigured and starting to emerge as an important social force.

NEW ENCYCLOPEDIA OF AFRICA

Among academics, ethnicity and related topics such as nationalism started to receive some long-overdue attention from the 1990s onward and resurfaced as matters of public concern and interest. However, the nature of the debate changed. The conventional understanding of ethnicity in southern Africa, documented by Leroy Vail in 1989, pointed to a degree of similarity and coherence across different states within the southern African region, as far as the historical development of ethnic identities was concerned. This, Vail argued, was due to similar colonial experiences and to the establishment of mining and other industries in South Africa. The latter meant that migrant labor was common in most rural parts of the subcontinent. These experiences and developments were the key to understanding ethnicity in the region, and he provided a model of how ethnic groups were constructed across the subcontinent.

According to this model, colonial rule and the development of capitalism led to widespread social disruption throughout southern Africa. The migration of labor to mining and industrial centers in South Africa exacerbated social insecurity in the labor-exporting areas. The British colonial policy of indirect rule divided indigenous people into bounded units; administration of those units was based on the European notion that Africans were inherently tribal and should not become detribalized, which would threaten colonial power by freeing Africans from control by their traditional leaders and enabling them to enter the wider political milieu. Missionaries, historians, and anthropologists helped to define the cultural traits associated with particular ethnic groups, through the codification of languages and the writing of tribal histories and ethnographies. Missionaries also produced educated elites who, as potential future leaders, were keen to construct ethnic ideologies based on local cultural idioms and to propagate these ideologies through administrators and chiefs. The unevenness of the development of ethnic ideologies correlated with the unevenness of educational development.

Fostered by traditional leaders (sometimes appointed and/or manipulated by the colonial power), ethnic ideologies were accepted by ordinary people because of insecurities created by rapid and radical social change. This included land

dispossession, the introduction of new forms of education and religion, and wage labor. Ethnic ideologies were encouraged particularly by migrant workers, because they provided a sense of security and control and helped minimize concerns about family and land back home. In this sense ethnic identity was based on largely invented notions of a golden past and the antiquity of custom but was programmatic in attempting to provide for social coherence in the face of disruption.

However, these insights provide only a partial answer to the question of how one accounts for the emergence of ethnicity after independence from colonial rule, especially where the indigenous population was united in opposition to the colonizers but where ethnic differences emerged in the struggle for power. The case of Zimbabwe is relevant here: the country's two major groups, the Shona and Ndebele, came into conflict after their successful joint bid to defeat the white-dominated government of Ian Smith and to secure independence. In Namibia there have been a number of ethnic claims (e.g., for the recognition of land rights or kingdoms) since independence, and also ongoing public debate about how to reconcile such claims with national unity. In other cases, such as Malawi, ethnic claims were suppressed by Kamuzu Banda's authoritarian rule and started to reemerge with the weakening of his power.

Sometimes it is hard to distinguish ethnicity, in the sense of a strong sense of loyalty to an ethnos, from nationalism. In Swaziland, for example, Swazi identity and tradition were invoked during British rule to assert Swazi nationalism and claims for independence. After independence King Sobhuza II was able to use this to defeat antimonarchical tendencies in the kingdom. Among Swazis in South Africa, however, it has not been easy to call upon Swazi identity as a mobilizing force because of the different political and historical context.

Many elements of Vail's model have been confirmed by studies of contemporary people, at least up to the 1990s. For example, David Coplan demonstrated how migrant workers from Lesotho constructed their identity in terms of a Sotho cultural idiom, in the context of the dangers and hardships of life in the mines and the perceived attractions of their mountain homes. Earlier, Philip Mayer's 1961 work in East London indicated that migrant labor and the conditions of urban life fostered a conservative Xhosa identity. In a 1975 study, Mayer found that ethnicity was of little significance to people in urban Soweto. In the nearby urban hostels, however, where migrant men lived without their families, ethnic identities were strongly developed. The urban conflicts of the late 1980s and 1990s on the Witwatersrand involved, primarily, a struggle for power between the Inkatha Freedom Party and supporters of the African National Congress (ANC) on the eve of democracy's introduction, with Inkatha's strength being based on its control of the hostels housing migrants.

Southern Africa also provides evidence of the difficulties and complexities associated with any attempt at a straightforward definition and understanding of ethnicity. This may be demonstrated by taking two of the better-known groups in the region, the Zulu and Afrikaners, as examples. In both of these cases ethnic identity was constructed under a particular set of historical, political, and economic circumstances. For the Zulu this was the creation of the Zulu state in the early nineteenth century and the amalgamation of a wide variety of linguistically and culturally similar, but politically independent, chiefdoms under the Zulu king. However, as historians have pointed out, the Zulu state was a conquest state in which the conquered chiefdoms retained their original cultural identities. Even after the 1860s and 1870s, when opposition to British colonialism brought a degree of political unity to the kingdom, regional loyalties remained important and most subjects of the state did not regard themselves as Zulu. It was only after about 1920 that a wider sense of Zulu political identity started to emerge, aided by the steady decay of the old social order, threats to the chiefs, migrant labor, and increasing hardships and uncertainties.

In the years from 1806 to 1902 opposition to British colonial rule and linguistic hegemony, among other factors, led to the creation of the group called Afrikaners, forged out of what was originally a heterogeneous European immigrant population, one which eventually identified with a new language that was based on Dutch but included elements of other European languages. The process of ethnic identity formation was a slow and painful one. The idea of Afrikaners speaking a common language, for example, only emerged toward the end of the nineteenth century, when the notion of an Afrikaner volk with a common culture started to develop. And it was only with the election victory of the National Party in 1948 that a degree of Afrikaner unity was achieved. Apartheid and the National Party responsible for it have been widely identified with Afrikaners, and appeals to Afrikaner identity and destiny were regularly used by the party to secure votes. But many Afrikaners never supported apartheid, and many other people, including English speakers, did. Afrikaner identity allowed for a range of political opinion, but it did not allow for a range of racial characteristics. Thus black and "colored" people who spoke Afrikaans as their home language were not considered to be members of the Afrikaner ethnic and cultural group.

In the post-apartheid era Afrikaners are no longer defined in racial terms, and the demand for an independent Afrikaner territory or volkstaat (people's state) represents an ethnic claim that most Afrikaners reject. Similar problems bedevil the current images of Zulu ethnicity, which received official endorsement when KwaZulu was created as one of apartheid's homelands or bantustans, though it never included all the land claimed by Zulu politicians such as Mangosuthu Buthelezi. Buthelezi's party, the Inkatha, made extensive use of Zulu cultural symbols and construed itself as representing the Zulu people, but election results in 1994 and 1996 showed that a large proportion of Zulu people supported the ANC. The territory of KwaZulu included only some of those who speak Zulu, and it also included speakers of other languages, notably Tsonga. The population of KwaZulu as imagined by Inkatha leaders and the real population were very different. In the 1990s, however, Buthelezi and others made appeals to the glorious Zulu past and the greatness of King Shaka to demonstrate the deep historical roots of the Zulu nation and to justify their claim to regional autonomy. There were also demands to reestablish the Zulu kingdom as a sovereign state.

Ethnic identity often has a gender dimension. In his essay on Tsonga ethnicity David Webster showed that among those who claimed Tsonga descent and identity, it was women (who were not labor migrants) who tended to do so. Gender relations among Tsonga are more equitable than among Zulu speakers, and claiming Tsonga identity thus appealed to women. However, their menfolk perceived various advantages in being identified as Zulu and adapted their language and even their clan names accordingly. This allowed them preferential treatment as migrant workers and provided them with an advantage over women at home. The gender dimension of ethnicity is especially evident in the Zulu case, where ideas of masculinity and warriorhood are dominant, as indicated by Gerhard Mare in 1992. Women, too, may think of themselves as Zulu, but not in the same terms. What it means to be Zulu or Tsonga therefore differs according to factors such as gender.

As the Tsonga case indicates, there are identities with a historical and cultural dimension in certain parts of southern Africa that are largely unknown elsewhere, because they have not been used to make wider political claims. The Mfengu (Fingo) people in the Eastern Cape Province are another example of this type. Although some village communities have been divided on a Xhosa/Mfengu basis, and economic and political power at the local level (in the former Ciskei bantustan) was sometimes linked to this ethnic division, there is at the same time a high degree of integration of Mfengu and Xhosa on account of factors such as common race, language, and culture. Only specifics of history and a few current practices, such as minor differences in customs relating to male circumcision, serve to perpetuate the distinction. Members of both groups claim overall Xhosa identity, in the sense of being Xhosa-speaking, as well as a wider South African identity and citizenship.

While elements of earlier explanations of ethnicity in South Africa remained salient in the 1990s, their inadequacies became evident in the context of the political changes that characterized the decade, not only in South Africa but in other parts of the world such as Eastern Europe and the former USSR. As Fredrik Barth showed in 1969, ethnicity often emerges where different groups interact rather than remain isolated. And it is in the process of interaction, especially where this involves competition for power, that ethnic boundaries may emerge and be maintained. This essentially political nature of ethnicity became more and more evident in South Africa's transition to democracy, in the context of the pursuit of power, of competition and conflict, mobilization and reaction, in which some of the participants used the idiom of cultural difference and similarity in pursuit of their goals.

The view that ethnic identities are fixed and unchanging persists in some quarters of post-2000 South Africa. Ethnic divisions remain pertinent, and ethnic tensions rear their ugly heads every now and then in high-visibility incidents, as in the spate of bombings in 2002, attributed to white right wingers, or the controversy in the same year around Mbongeni Ngema's song criticizing Indians in KwaZulu-Natal, which threatened to polarize Africans and Indians in that province and sparked fears of a repeat of the 1949 riots in Durban when Indians were attached by Zulus. However, generally speaking the country has attempted, since 1994, to imagine a future free of racism and ethnic division. The emphasis on reconciliation and nation-building has contributed to this. Inequalities based on race and class remain prominent, but these cut across racial lines and a sizable black middle class has developed. The major political parties emphasize a common, non-racial South African identity (the idea of the "rainbow nation").

The struggle for power that followed the dismantling of apartheid confirmed the principle that political and economic competition and conflict generate ethnicity, explaining the resurgence of both Afrikaner and Zulu ethnicity at that time. Another example of this is the demonstration of Nama ethnicity that took place in 1992 in the context of a land struggle in the northwestern Cape. In this case Nama ethnicity was reformulated and presented in public contexts to demonstrate continuity with the original owners of the land.

In other parts of the subcontinent, too, there have been few major manifestations of ethnic tensions in the 1990s and early twenty-first century. In some this is linked to a high degree of ethnic homogeneity (e.g., Swaziland, Lesotho) while in others (e.g. Mozambique, Botswana, Namibia, Zambia, Angola) it may be due to the existence of stable multiparty democracies coupled, in some cases (e.g., Mozambique), with the absence of a dominant ethnic group or, as in Zambia, with the lack of a strong group identity among the two

Court ruling grants justice to San Bushmen. Roy Sesana (left), lead applicant and leader of the first people of the Kalahari and Bushmen, listens to attorney Gordon Bennett (right), December 13, 2006, explaining the verdict after the final judgment of their case against the Botswana government. The government ruled that hundreds of San Bushmen had been wrongfully forced from their Kalahari Desert homeland and should be allowed to return. GIANLUIGI GUERCIA/AFP/GETTY IMAGES

largest of the country's many ethnic groups, Bemba and Lozi/Barotse.

Even where postindependence power-sharing arrangements have weakened and government has become dominated by an ethnic majority (Ovambo in Namibia, Shona in Zimbabwe) there have been only minor threats to stability that may be called ethnic. In Zimbabwe the significant Matabele minority is aligned with the opposition MDC party, which draws support largely from the country's urban areas, but Robert Mugabe's ZANU-PF has drawn some support from rural Ndebele voters, so the Shona/Matabele conflict, which was manifested largely in the massacres in Matabeleland in the 1980s—and which remains a significant memory and marker of group identity to Ndebele—has been at least partially subsumed under an urban-rural divide. In Namibia, some minorities (e.g. Basters) are concerned about land rights and would

like greater autonomy, and in 1999 there was an armed uprising in the Caprivi region by Lozi-speaking secessionists (reputedly supported by Lozi in Zambia), quickly suppressed by the state.

The most significant case of minority group cooperation that cuts across national boundaries, however, is the case of the Bushmen or San, long marginalized and discriminated against in South Africa, Namibia, Angola, Botswana (where they are also referred to as Basarwa), Zimbabwe, and Zambia. Bushmen in these countries have forged links with each other, established a pan-Southern African Bushman advocacy organization and, with the support of international organizations such as Survival International, have pressed for recognition of land rights or restoration of lost resources.

In Botswana the state forcibly removed two Basarwa groups from their land in the Central Kalahari Game Reserve in 2002, a decision that was challenged and won by the Basarwa in the Botswana High Court in 2006. In a similar case in South Africa, the land and mineral rights of forcibly relocated Nama people of the Richtersveld were recognized by the country's constitutional court in 2003, following an earlier decision that recognized the land rights of Xhomani Bushmen in the Kalahari Gemsbok National Park. In Namibia, Ju'/Hoansi bushmen in the Nyae Nyae area were able to secure their tenancy of their land by getting it proclaimed as a game conservation area in 1998, with themselves as its administrators and guardians. In South Africa itself, the polarization and mobilization along ethnic and racial divisions that threatened to derail the constitutional negotiations in the early 1990s have become less pronounced in the new millennium, and the non-racial democracy that emerged after 1994 has remained stable and unthreatened by sectarian interests.

Scholars have argued that the new constitution and way in which political institutions were reshaped in the new South Africa have played an important role in this respect. The number of political parties with an ethnic basis has declined since the 1990s. The very small Freedom Front still argues for cultural and linguistic self-determination but Afrikaans speakers are politically divided. In the Western Cape there remains tension within the ANC, which is divided on ethnic lines between "Coloureds" and Africans. In Natal, as in the Western Cape, the ANC has increased its support in successive elections, at the expense of its competitors, rather than fissioned along ethnic lines. Inkatha, who many in the 1990s saw as the harbingers of future ethnic strife, has lost support to the ANC and has had to develop more than a simply ethnic appeal. It has participated in a government of national unity and its leader served as the new nation's first vice-president. The same applies to the New National Party, which has attempted to become multiracial. Ethnicity's threat to political stability, which seemed very real before the 1994 elections, has dissipated. The expectations of academics and political commentators, that ethnicity would become more rather than less salient in party politics after the demise of apartheid, have not been realized.

See also **Apartheid; Banda, Ngwazi Hastings Kamuzu; Colonial Policies and Practices; Kinship and Affinity; Mugabe, Robert; Political Systems; Shaka Zulu; Sobhuza I and II.**

BIBLIOGRAPHY

Barth, Fredrik, ed. *Ethnic Groups and Boundaries: The Social Organization of Culture Difference*. Oslo: Scandinavian University Press, 1969.

Coplan, David B. "Eloquent Knowledge: Lesotho Migrants Songs and the Anthropology of Experience." *American Ethnologist* 14, no. 3 (1987): 413–433.

Hamilton, Carolyn, and John Wright. "The Beginnings of Zulu Identity." *Indicator South Africa* 10, no. 3 (1993): 43–46.

Lincoln, Bruce. "Ritual, Rebellion, Resistance: Once More the Swazi Ncwala." *Man* 22, no. 1 (1987): 132–156.

Malan, Johan. "The Foundations of Ethnicity and Some of its Current Ramifications in Namibia." *Africa Insight* 23 (1993): 205–208.

Mare, Gerard. *Brothers Born of Warrior Blood: Politics and Ethnicity in South Africa*. Johannesburg: Ravan Press, 1992.

Mayer, Philip. *Townsmen or Tribesmen? Conservatism and the Process of Urbanization in a South African City*. Cape Town: Oxford University Press. 1961.

Mayer, Philip. "Class, Status, and Ethnicity as Perceived by Johannesburg Africans." In *Change in Contemporary South Africa*, ed. Leonard Thompson and Jeffrey Butler. Berkeley: University of California Press, 1975.

Piombo, Jessica. *Political Institutions, Social Demographics and the Decline of Ethnic Mobilization in South Africa 1994–1999*. CSSR Working Paper No. 63. Cape Town: University of Cape Town, 2004.

Sharp, John. "Ethnic Group and Nation: The Apartheid Vision in South Africa." In *South African Keywords: The Uses and Abuses of Political Concepts*, ed. Emile Boonzaier and John Sharp. Cape Town: David Philip, 1988.

Sharp, John, and Emile Boonzaier. "Staging Ethnicity: Lessons from Namaqualand." *Track Two* 2, no. 1 (1993): 10–13.

Vail, Leroy, ed. *The Creation of Tribalism in Southern Africa*. Berkeley: University of California Press, 1989.

Webster, David. "Abafazi Bathonga Bafihlakala: Ethnicity and Gender in a KwaZulu Border Community." In *Tradition and Transition in Southern Africa*, ed. Andrew D. Spiegel and Patrick A. McAllister. Cape Town: Oxford University Press, 1991.

Wilmsen, Edwin N., and Patrick McAllister, eds. *The Politics of Difference: Ethnic Premises in a World of Power*. Chicago: University of Chicago Press, 1996.

PATRICK MCALLISTER

WESTERN AFRICA

Forms of strong ethnic, cultural, and religious identification are as old as Africa itself. Yet it was only under colonization that the ethnic names and categories that designated different human groups gained a quasi-definitive rigidity. Through the work and writing of missionaries, colonial administrators, ethnographers, and social scientists, especially in the form of ethnic atlases and maps of Africa, ethnic names became codified and came to assume almost axiomatic status. These writings made the categories into veritable performative concepts, that is, concepts that give rise to that which they designate as the people so designated learned to manipulate the categories their colonial rulers applied to them. The tribal conflicts and ethnic confrontations present in West Africa in the early twenty-first century are in part a product of the fixing and reifying of ethnic categories—the imposition of fixed categories upon unstable groups—that was part and parcel of the colonial project.

ETHNICITY BEFORE THE COLONIAL ERA

The various ethnic groups identifiable in precolonial West Africa were hardly bounded, self-contained entities, and should not be thought of in the neatly delineated homogeneous way that ethnic maps portray them (as an assemblage of separate populations existing side by side). They were more akin to the links in a chain, with social groupings overlapping at their edges and sharing significant cultural practices amongst one another. Inhabiting different ecological zones (desert, savanna, forest) with diverse adaptations (nomadic pastoralism, mixed farming, farming), and engaged with histories of trade, war, and political domination, these social clusters remained, by necessity, flexible and porous. Moreover, these blurry totalities were capable of adopting different forms of social organization and diverse monikers over time. For instance, although the Tuareg of the Nigerien Sahara normally led a nomadic existence, during times of extreme drought they withdrew into the cities and even became Hausa—city-dwellers engaged in trade and commerce.

For centuries before the colonial era, West Africa experienced periods of political expansion and contraction, which in turn gave rise to different forms of ethnic belonging and identification. Centers and peripheries—states and their dependencies—rose and fell and redefined relations between groups. On the peripheries of these states, whether empires, kingdoms, or chiefdoms, were buffer or border zones that contained acephalous societies (societies without rulers) that were organized by kinship, and secret societies for men, and sometimes for women. These societies recognized little identification beyond the local unit (lineage/clan/neighborhood). As a result of political expansion and contraction, the people who inhabited these border areas were often known by several ethnic names throughout their history as they passed from acephalous to state-controlled forms and vice versa.

THE COLONIAL RUPTURE

The disruption of commercial patterns, the end of slave wars, and colonial pacification in the decades just before World War I broke the chain of overlapping societies that had resisted rigid, singular ethnic and tribal divisions. As stable ethnic categories were imposed and market economies were developed, relations between previously blurry-bordered West African societies and polities gave way to an ethnic mapping that privileged ties between discrete societies and the colonizing authorities. In northern Togo, for instance, previously unnamed acephalous peoples were assigned names by colonial administrators—Moba, Konkomba, Tamberma, Losso, Kabre—that enabled the Germans and then the French to map colonial subjects and recruit and deploy them in colonial work projects. These ethnic names have persisted into the present.

Three people played a major role in this ethnicizing process: Louis Faidherbe (1818–1889) for France, and Mary Kingsley (1862–1900) and Frederick Lugard for Great Britain. Faidherbe was governor of Senegal from 1854 to 1861, and from 1863 to 1865. Both a raciologist—giving priority to racial type as the key to understanding history—and a republican, he is largely responsible for the spectrum of ethnic groups that live on in Senegal and Mali. Inspired by anthropological theories of race that were in vogue in nineteenth-century Europe, he distinguished three kinds of populations in West Africa: the whites (Arabs and Berbers), the reds (Fulani), and the blacks (Wolof, Serere, Mandinka, and Asante). Faidherbe based his understanding of West African history, particularly the origin of the state, on the idea that certain races, namely whites and reds, were superior—more civilized—and became the driving forces of historical evolution. He also assigned a specific set of characteristics to each population. As a result, Faidherbe is largely responsible for the modern cartographic representation of Senegambian ethnic groups. Moreover, his concern was not merely theoretical. He sought to control the peoples of Senegal and seems, in this respect, to have been a precursor to a line of military officer-ethnographers such as Joseph Simon Gallieni (1849–1916), who claimed that "an officer who succeeds in drawing up a sufficiently large ethnographic map of the territories under his command is close to achieving complete pacification" (Deschamps, 239).

For the British, the politics of races and the ethnicizing of populations were given impetus and shape by the explorer Mary Kingsley, who was one of the first to argue for the cultural singularity of each African society. Her views fed into the doctrine of Indirect Rule, famously implemented in West Africa by Frederick Lugard. Similar to Faidherbe, Lugard founded his theory of indirect administration on a racially based conception of history, seeing certain races as more fit than others to carry out administrative duties. Accordingly, he saw lighter-skinned Hamites and Muslims as more advanced than the aboriginal blacks. The latter, he suggested, had been driven into the mountains and forests and there remained at a primitive stage of development. In northern Nigeria, this racial-hierarchical conception of African societies guided the installation of Indirect Rule by the British, whereby the Fulani—classified as Hamites—were regarded as superior to other groups and allowed to govern using their own chiefs and their own institutions.

Indirect administration made it necessary for the British government to recruit anthropologists to explain the complexities of the conquered societies intended to administer on their own cultural terms. Thus, much of Anglo-Saxon anthropology of the early twentieth century is the product of investigations undertaken for the colonial administration. These early government anthropologists—such as Robert S. Rattray (1881–1938), who worked for the British in the Gold Coast (present-day Ghana)—compiled detailed data on the social practices and cultural mores of local peoples. In so doing, these anthropologists rendered

largely static pictures of the societies they observed, pictures that reflected colonial pacification more than the dynamic histories that had been their precolonial experience. But the description also contributed to creating the reality: an ethnographic mapping of static, bounded ethnic groups.

The Tallensi of the northern Gold Coast (present-day Ghana) offer a good example of this process. After they had been separated by the Pax Britannica from their political overlords, the Mamprusi state, the Tallensi could be studied as an isolated community. Armed with functionalist theory and possessing a romanticized view of supposedly democratic and egalitarian West African societies, Meyer Fortes (1906–1983) became a strong advocate of the perspective that African societies were segmentary and autonomous. But his work reflected more the realities of a colonial situation than anything innately African, and contributed to the view that Tallensi (and African peoples generally) were peoples without history, discrete societies on a timeless ethnographic map.

CONTEMPORARY TRIBALISM

Ironically, this static ethnic division of West Africa—the product of missionaries, colonial administrators and researchers—was adopted after independence by local social actors who used it to suit their own interests. The many ethnic conflicts present in West Africa in the early twenty-first century—in Sierra Leone, Liberia, Senegal, Nigeria, Togo, and Mali—by no means represent a resurgence of ancient hostilities, as commonly assumed. In many cases, these conflicts are the result of the imposition of colonial categories updated to meet postcolonial exigencies. Indirect administration and the practice of divide and conquer, used by both French and British, broke relations between societies and was reinforced and manipulated by authoritarian states after independence. Often tribalism became a preferred way to govern, effectively dividing in order to rule.

Moreover, a tribalist logic coincided with dictatorial single-party rule, itself a product of Cold War geopolitical imperatives, and became a preferred way to govern. Elites, deploying what French political scientist Jean-François Bayart has referred to as a politics of the belly, sought to enrich themselves—to fatten their own bellies—at the expense of the rest of the nation, and did so by deploying ethnicizing frameworks and tribalist categories. Thus, they created intense loyalty among a small group of ethnically similar followers, often small and marginal on the national scale, and shunned those from other ethnic groups, often larger and more central. According to this logic, access to power and resources took place only within the framework of membership in tribal networks.

One might ask whether the wave of democratization that has swept the African landscape since the end of the Cold War has curbed this phenomenon. In fact, however, democracy often exacerbates tribalist thinking and alignments. Thus, at the time of elections in Cameroon, but elsewhere in West Africa as well, political candidates mobilize their support along ethnic and regional lines and play to notions of origin and autochthony—once again performing and creating the concept of ethnicity in its modern sense.

It is important to keep in mind that, despite the pervasiveness and traction of ethnicizing logics across the continent, such categories by no means exhaust the range of human interaction in Africa, nor do they always map the major lines of affiliation. There are myriad counterexamples of ethnic groups that have peacefully coexisted and cross-fertilized one another, exchanging language and ritual as much as labor and marriage partners.

The multiplication of ethnic and border conflicts in Senegal, Mauritania, Sierra Leone, Liberia, Guinea, Mali, and Niger indicates that West Africa has entered into a period of political redefinition expressed by the emergence of new social frameworks. These conflicts represent not the reappearance of old demons but are contemporary phenomena that are forcing researchers to explore new categories of analysis beyond ethnicity to understand them.

See also **Anthropology, Social, and the Study of Africa; Cold War; Colonial Policies and Practices; Kinship and Affinity; Lugard, Frederick John Dealtry; Warfare.**

BIBLIOGRAPHY

Amselle, Jean-Loup. *Mestizo Logics: Anthropology of Identity in Africa and Elsewhere.* Stanford, CA: Stanford University Press, 1998.

Amselle, Jean-Loup. "Ethnies et espaces: Pour une anthropologie topologique." In *Au coeur de l'ethnie: Ethnies, tribalisme et "état" en Afrique,* ed. Jean-Loup Amselle and Elikia M'Bokolo. Paris: La Découverte, 2005.

Banks, Marcus. *Ethnicity: Anthropological Constructions.* London: Routledge, 1996.

Bayart, Jean-François. *The State in Africa: The Politics of the Belly.* London: Longman, 1993.

Bayart, Jean-François. *The Illusion of Cultural Identity.* Chicago: University of Chicago Press, 2005.

Deschamps, Henri. *Gallieni pacificateur.* Paris: Presses universitaires de France, 1949.

Fortes, Meyer. *The Dynamics of Clanship among the Tallensi.* Oxford: Oxford University Press, 1945.

Geschiere, Peter, and Francis Nyamnjoh, "Capitalism and Autochthony: The See-Saw of Mobility and Belonging." *Public Culture* 12, no. 2 (2000): 423–452.

Geschiere, Peter, and Stephen Jackson, eds. "Autochthony and the Crisis of Citizenship." *African Studies Review* 49, no. 2 (2006): 1–7.

Kopytoff, Igor, ed. *The African Frontier: The Reproduction of Traditional African Societies.* Bloomington: Indiana University Press, 1987.

Lovejoy, Paul E., and Stephen Baier. "The Desert-Side Economy of the Central Sudan." *International Journal of African Historical Studies* 8, no. 4 (1975): 551–581.

Lugard, Frederick Dealtry. *The Dual Mandate in British Tropical Africa,* 5th edition. Hamden, CT: Archon Books, 1965.

Piot, Charles. *Remotely Global: Village Modernity in West Africa.* Chicago: University of Chicago Press, 1999.

Rich, Paul B. *Race and Empire in British Politics.* New York: Cambridge University Press, 1986.

JEAN-LOUP AMSELLE
REVISED BY CHARLES PIOT

ETHNOMUSICOLOGY AND THE STUDY OF AFRICA.

Africa has held a special place in ethnomusicology, significantly shaping the development of the field from its late-nineteenth-century origins in comparative musicology and serving as a major site of field work. Africanist ethnomusicology in turn has much to offer African studies, as music (and related dance) is such an important aspect of African life, often acting as a primary source of identity from the very personal through the national levels.

An enormous diversity of musical traditions (including scores of unique instruments used within individual countries), a lack of published documentation (writing and sound recordings), and the growth of new musical forms associated with increasing urbanization and globalization are some of the most important phenomena that have stimulated research in African music. Throughout much of the twentieth century, African music research produced tightly focused accounts of well-defined local traditions as well as ethnographic recordings of such traditions. About the 1970s historical and ethnographic consciousness deepened, and scholars began to study long-term development of musical traditions, music as a window into history, and the individuality of musicians. Beginning about the 1990s, more diverse research began to examine mass-mediated music, constructions of national identity through music, and the transformations of local music in a global marketplace.

EARLY YEARS

Written descriptions of music-making in Africa stem from Arabic travel accounts as early as the eleventh century. Sporadic descriptions increased with the European presence, dating from the early Portuguese accounts of the mid-fifteenth century. It was not until the early twentieth century, with the rise of comparative musicology in Germany, that musicological works were devoted to Africa, initially by so-called armchair musicologists, whose work was based on instruments and recordings brought back from Africa by others. Bernhard Ankermann's 1901 treatise on musical instruments (*Die Afrikanische Musikinstrumente*) was based on the collection in the Berlin Museum, an institution that continues to produce treatises of similar scope in the early twenty-first century.

Erich M. Von Hornbostel (also based at the Berlin Museum), a major figure in the early history of ethnomusicology, published his "African Negro Music" in the very first issue of the journal *Africa* in 1928, propagating some tenacious myths that scholars are still contesting. One of the most problematic issues concerns "an essential contrast between our [European] rhythmic conception and the Africans': we proceed from hearing, they from motion" (p. 53). This mind/body (hearing/motion) dichotomy

is the basis of Négritude, a philosophy that celebrates certain modes of expression and claims them as African, a theory which has been simultaneously propagated and critiqued by Africans. Since the 1959 publication of A. M. Jones's pioneering *Studies in African Music*, which described musicians in Zambia and Ghana, ethnomusicologists have intensively investigated and explicated some of the unique properties of African rhythmic procedures. In the early twenty-first century, researchers recognize rhythmic sophistication as an intellectual endeavor. Similarly, scholars have begun to acknowledge the linguistic (rather than kinetic) basis and significance of many forms of African music.

Other investigative approaches, beginning in the 1930s and 1940s with the French missions of André Schaeffner, Marcel Griaule, Thérèse Rivière, and Gilbert Rouget (all associated with the Musée de l'homme) and the American expedition of Laura Boulton, tended toward the anthropological, gathering data first-hand to show how music functioned in its African context.

MID-TWENTIETH CENTURY

The founding of the Society of African Music (based in South Africa) in 1948, the publication of its journal *African Music* beginning in 1954, and the founding of the International Library of African Music (ILAM) outside Johannesburg the same year were important steps in establishing a central forum for African music research. Hugh Tracey—as honorary secretary of the society, editor of the journal, and founder and director of ILAM—was a major force in promoting the study and especially recording of African music (he recorded and released more than two hundred albums). Early contributors to the journal were a diverse and interdisciplinary group of Europeans, Americans, and Africans. Intense interest in the journal and society gradually dissipated over the next few decades, however, perhaps as a result of the rise of other forums for the dissemination of research.

After Tracey, Ghanaian J. H. Kwabena Nketia pioneered the study of African music by Africans. Since in the 1950s, Nketia has published an enormous number of papers and has exerted a prodigious influence on the field (see Djedje and Carter 1989 for a bio-bibliography, and Nketia 2005 for the first volume of his collected papers). His teaching at the University of California at Los Angeles

(UCLA) in the 1960s led to an influx of Ghanaian drummers who accepted teaching posts in American universities, establishing Ghanaian drumming as the canonical African musical tradition within ethnomusicology. Subsequently, this tradition has enjoyed perhaps the highest and broadest level of critical engagement of any African music within ethnomusicology. Nketia's presence has encouraged generations of Anglophone African scholars to persevere in their research.

Africa played an important role in the early development of the Society for Ethnomusicology (SEM, founded in the United States in 1955), which was marked by a dichotomy between musicological and anthropological approaches. The classic *Anthropology of Music* (1964), by Alan Merriam, a co-founder of SEM and student of pioneer Africanist Melville Herskovits, was significantly informed by Merriam's fieldwork in the Belgian Congo. The index to the book lists about two dozen African peoples as sources, yet rarely references East, Southeast, and South Asian music—traditional favorites of ethnomusicologists. Merriam saw the initial task of ethnomusicologists as consisting of "the collection of data . . . this has most often meant work in the field outside Europe and America" (pp. 7–8). Merriam's exploration of the very concept of music and the fact that it is locally defined drew from the Congo Basongye.

Studies of musical diasporas owe much to Merriam, who posited broad music culture areas in Africa, as well as to Herskovits's student, Richard Waterman (1952), whose five features of African music—multiple meter, off-beat phrasing of melodic accents, dominance of percussion, metronome sense, and overlapping call-and-response patterns—continue to be cited in the early twenty-first century.

MODERN CONCERNS

A general lack of sophistication in musical analyses dramatically changed in the 1970s as ethnomusicologists gained more in-depth access to the intricacies of the music. Learning to play the music became standard practice about this time, a trend led by graduates of UCLA and Wesleyan, universities with the first ethnomusicology programs in the United States. Ironically, however, Africans with university training often came from elite classes that did not have easy access to practical training in indigenous music.

Writing about local traditions has become even more mature since the late twentieth century, with more rigorous standards for linguistic and musical competence, archival research, and ethnographic engagement. The most noticeable development has been in the serious treatment of modern or popular music. Establishing deep linkages between local traditions and more international musical styles has been especially revealing of the unique sensibilities of African syncretic creativity.

Significant variation among the situations of music scholars based in the United States, Europe, and Africa is becoming a contentious issue. Though they agree on many points, researchers from each of the three continents have different concerns, different audiences, and different initial means of access to living African traditions as well as to documentary materials.

See also **Music; Musical Instruments; Tracey, Hugh.**

BIBLIOGRAPHY

Askew, Kelly. *Performing the Nation: Swahili Music and Cultural Politics in Tanzania.* Chicago: University of Chicago Press, 2002.

Berliner, Paul. *The Soul of Mbira.* Berkeley: University of California Press, 1978.

Charry, Eric. *Mande Music: Traditional and Modern Music of the Maninka and Mandinka of Western Africa.* Chicago: University of Chicago Press, 2000.

Djedje, Jaqueline Cogdel, and William G. Carter, eds. *African Musicology: Current Trends, Vol. 1.* Los Angeles: African Studies Center, UCLA, 1989.

Merriam, Alan. *The Anthropology of Music.* Evanston, IL: Northwestern University Press, 1964.

Nketia, J. H. Kwabena. *Ethnomusicology and African Music: Collected Papers, Vol. 1: Modes of Inquiry and Interpretation.* Accra, Ghana: Afram Publications, 2005.

Stone, Ruth, ed. *Garland Encyclopedia of World Music, Vol. 1: Africa.* New York: Garland, 1998.

von Hornbostel, Erich M. "African Negro Music." *Africa* 1, no. 1 (1928): 30–62.

Waterman, Richard Alan. "African Influence on the Music of the Americas." In *Acculturation in the Americas: Proceedings and Selected Papers of the XXIXth International Congress of Americanists,* ed. Sol Tax. Chicago: University of Chicago Press, 1952.

ERIC CHARRY

EUNUCHS.

Eunuchs, or males who have been rendered incapable of reproduction, have often occupied special spaces as gatekeepers to and protectors of sacred or secular honor, virtue, and power. Their singular position stems from their perceived inability either to copulate or to produce progeny. This difference has at times set eunuchs apart in status and position from other members of a society. Nevertheless, eunuchs intersect with other social categories in a variety of ways in Africa and elsewhere.

Men and boys become eunuchs as the result of accident, dysfunction, and either voluntary or forced castration. Neither of the first two cases historically exists in significant numbers, and there is little evidence of the voluntary castration of free individuals in Africa. Rather, in almost all cases eunuchs seem to have been captives or slaves forcibly castrated to act as servants to important households in highly organized states.

Eunuchs as servitors and slaves in Pharaonic Egypt and Islamic African societies inhabited specific niches within a dynamic matrix of power, gender, performance, religion, and status. They began their service as extreme outsiders, usually as slaves imported from other regions and possessing no local ties. Yet their status was often ambivalent. Eunuchs were especially valued as trusted advisers and were often given significant authority for two reasons. First, like other imported slaves, they had no attachment to feuding lineages and thus were more likely to remain loyal to their royal patrons. Second, because they could not propagate, eunuchs were less likely to attempt to establish their own lineage as competitors to those of their patrons. Thus, the fifteenth-century Muslim Hausa rulers of the Kano state balanced the power of noble households and lineages with titled offices occupied by eunuchs. These officials' responsibilities included military leadership, supervision of the city gates and treasury, tax collection, and the execution of criminals.

The Kano state (c. 1000–1809) was succeeded by the jihadist Sokoto (c. 1804–1903) whose rulers maintained semiexclusive positions for eunuchs. In some cases, eunuchs were even able to pass their titles and positions on to adopted sons. Similarly, in the state of Oyo (c. 1380–1835) eunuchs occupied important positions as royal slaves throughout the eighteenth century. Three especially powerful eunuch officers—the Ona Efa, Otun Efa, and Osi Efa—managed the judicial, religious, and administrative offices of the court and acted as patrons to parties and communities throughout the state.

Eunuchs were not only symbols of prestige and useful servitors but also guardians of seclusion. In Mamluk Cairo (c. 1174–1811), eunuchs were detailed to oversee or guard a range of personal and sacred spaces. Some occupied the vestibules of the houses of the wealthy as well as the sultan's palace, allowing or refusing admittance to visitors. Others controlled access to royal tombs. Within the citadel itself, eunuchs served at the highest levels as servants of the wardrobe, as cupbearers, and as guardians of the royal treasury. Eunuch police were responsible for the confiscation of wealthy households. Among the most prominent guardian roles of eunuchs was the position of overseer of the *harim*, or women's quarter. This was especially true in wealthy urban settings in Islamic northern Africa, although eunuch-guarded *harims* could also be found in some Swahili city-states and some Sahelian polities. The perceived sexual neutrality of eunuchs not only guaranteed the inviolability of the women but also safeguarded this sanctuary space within the house from political and civil strife. The *harim* was also a location in which powerful alliances could be contracted between royal wives and eunuchs as happened occasionally in Darfur, where chief eunuchs were sometimes able to determine the succession to the sultanate.

The relationship between eunuchdom and Islam in Africa is far from completely understood. A small percentage of the millions of Africans who entered the trans-Saharan and Indian Ocean slave trades to the Islamic world were eunuchs. Because castration is forbidden under Islamic law, eunuchs were generally produced outside of Dar al-Islam. Islamic sources report that the eunuch guardians of the Ka'aba in Medina in the early modern period were "Tekruris" or West Africans, although some may in fact have originated in Darfur or other regions of the Sudan. In addition, eunuchs were found in many of the Islamic courts of western Africa from the fifteenth century onward, and the practice seems to have spread from these states to savanna and forest-zone polities such as Oyo and Dagomba.

See also **Islam.**

BIBLIOGRAPHY

Bay, Edna. *Wives of the Leopard: Gender, Politics, and Culture in the Kingdom of Dahomey.* Charlottesville: University of Virginia Press, 1998.

Hogendorn, Jan. "The Location of the 'Manufacture' of Eunuchs." In *Slave Elites in the Middle East and Africa*, ed. Miura Toru and John Edward Philips. New York: Columbia University Press, 2000.

Marmon, Shaun E. *Eunuchs and Sacred Boundaries in Islamic Society.* New York: Oxford University Press, 1995.

Stilwell, Sean Arnold. *Paradoxes of Power: The Kano "Mamluks" and Male Royal Slavery in the Sokoto Caliphate, 1804–1903.* Portsmouth: Heinemann, 2004.

TREVOR GETZ

EVOLUTION, HUMAN. *See* **Human Evolution.**

ÉVORA, CESÁRIA

ÉVORA, CESÁRIA (1941–). The singer Cesária Évora was born in the town of Mindelo, on Cape Verde's São Vicente Island. Gifted with a warm voice, she is internationally renowned for her interpretation of Cape Verdean traditional song. Her signature genres are the reflective, bluesy *Morna*, and the more upbeat *Coladera*. Deeply anchored in her island culture, her music has global appeal, and whether in recordings or on stage she frequently brings out collaborators hailing from Cuba to Japan, from Madagascar to Brazil to Europe and North America. Her status as a superstar in the world music universe is the culmination of a halting and nearly abortive career that began when she was a teenager performing in Mindelo's bars and clubs, but did not fully blossom until she was well into her fifties. Now in her mid-sixties, she has millions of albums sold, a Grammy as well as numerous other awards and recognitions, and is an ambassador against hunger for the United Nations' World Food Program. When she is not in a recording studio or on a stage somewhere—in her trademark bare feet—she can be found back in her beloved hometown, entertaining family and friends to whom she remains fiercely loyal.

See also **Music, Modern Popular.**

BIBLIOGRAPHY

Monteiro, João. "From Coal Depot to Cesária's Home: Mindelo at the Crossroads of the World." In *Urbanization and African Cultures*, ed. Toyin Falola and Steve Salm. Durham, NC: Carolina Academic Press, 2005.

Mortaigne, Véronique. *Cesaria Evora: La voix du Cap-Vert.* Arles, France: Actes Sud, 1997.

JOÃO M. MONTEIRO

EXOGAMY. *See* **Kinship and Affinity; Marriage Systems.**

EXPLORATION. *See* **Travel and Exploration.**

EYADEMA, GNASSINGBE (ÉTIENNE)

EYADEMA, GNASSINGBE (ÉTIENNE) (1937–). The military general Gnassingbe (Étienne) Eyadema has been the de facto president of Togo since 1967. Born in Pya in northern Togo to Kabré parents, Eyadema had completed barely six years at elementary school before he enlisted in the French colonial forces, at age sixteen. He fought during World War II, in Indochina (1953–1955), and in Algeria (1956–1961) before returning to newly independent Togo. On his return he joined a veterans' group that petitioned President Sylvanus Olympio to be integrated into an enlarged Togolese army. Their petition was refused, and a coup was planned under the leadership of Emmanuel Bodjolle. Bodjolle withdrew from the plan on the eve of the coup, and Eyadema took over the leadership. President Sylvanus Olympio was assassinated in the coup, and his successor, President Nicolas Grunitzky, acceded to the petition admitting Eyadema and others into the Togolese army.

Eyadema rose rapidly through the ranks, becoming chief of the general staff in 1965. From this position of power he staged a coup of his own in 1967, taking over the offices of president and defense minister. He consolidated his hold on the presidency by rewarding his political base among the peoples of the south to the detriment of the country as a whole. He ordered his image be immortalized in statues and paintings, and suppressed dissent with his rule by censoring the press.

By the 1970s the mismanagement, corruption, and cronyism that characterized his administration was growing ever more apparent. Togo's national revenues, depending primarily on the extraction and export of phosphates, were in serious decline, but the World Bank refused financial aid to the country unless the government instituted economic and political reforms. Unrest among the citizenry grew more outspoken, particularly among the Ewe of the southwestern corner of the country. Eyadema responded with force. Arrests, tortures, and murders became commonplace. By 1980 his administration was bankrupt. Nonetheless, Eyadema was reelected to office in 1972, 1979, and 1986, by means of elections that all outside observers deemed unfair.

In 1990 calls for Eyadema to resign grew increasingly insistent, but the president responded by barricading himself in the presidential palace surrounded by loyal members of the army. He faced a new election in 1993, during which he used open intimidation to dissuade all those who wished to vote for the opposition candidates, and claimed electoral victory. He did, however, promise to step down when his term expired in 2003.

In 2000 Eyadema took over the chairmanship of the Organization of African Unity (OAU), a circumstance that met with grumbling from the European Union (EU) as well as many African nations, particularly because of his stated support of Jonas Savimbi, South African backed challenger in Angola's deadly civil war. The EU suspended all aid to Togo, both in protest of this support and as punishment for the chronic voting irregularities that had marked Togolese elections. In 1998, under pressure from the EU, elections were held but were abruptly halted when opposition candidates appeared to be doing well in the polls. In 2003 Eyadema again reneged on his promise to step down from office and instead used his position to ban his principal rival from campaigning. Other candidates claimed to have been detained and threatened by Eyadema's supporters. He claimed victory, but the EU and some other international observers alleged fraud and malfeasance. Other observers, including a contingent from the United Nations, have disagreed.

See also **Organization of African Unity; Togo; World Bank.**

BIBLIOGRAPHY

Decalo, Samuel. *Historical Dictionary of Togo*, 3rd edition. Lanham, MD: Scarecrow Press, 1996.

GARY THOULOUIS

EZANA (3rd century CE). Ezana, who reigned from c. 330 to c. 356 CE, was the Aksumite (Ethiopian) king whose conversion to Christianity in the fourth century made Christianity Ethiopia's state religion. Ezana is considered the greatest of the Aksumite kings, but his name is not found in Ethiopian oral and manuscript traditions. What scholars know about him comes from numismatic and epigraphic sources and from a letter the Arian Emperor Constantius (c. 356) wrote to him and his brother. There are also a few inscriptions ascribed to Ezana, presenting him as a pagan ruler—as "the son of the invincible god Ares"—and later as a Christian, worshipping the Trinity: "In the faith of God and the power of the Father, and the Son, and the Holy Spirit."

Constantius's letter to Kings Ezana and Shaizana (or Saizana) is preserved in Athanasius's *Apologia ad Constantium*. In it, Constantius demanded that the Aksumite rulers send their first bishop, Frumentius, back to Alexandria so that Frumentius could be indoctrinated in Arianism and consecrated again by George, the Arian archbishop who had temporarily taken the throne of Saint Athanasius.

The local tradition states that two brothers, Abraha and Aṣbǝha, ruled from Aksum (Ṣǝra') at the time Christianity was introduced to Ethiopia. The fact that the local tradition and the letter of Emperor Constantius speak of two brothers ruling Ethiopia when Christianity was introduced into the country is most likely not coincidental.

The most famous of Ezana's inscriptions was written in Greek, Gǝʿǝz (the local language), and Sabaean or Himyaritic. In it, the king identified the regions under his control—Aksum, Ḥǝmer

(Himyar), Räydan (Raydan), Saba (Sheba), Sälḥen, Səyamo, Bəga and Kasu—some of which (specifically, Himyar, Raydan, and Sheba) are on the eastern side of the Red Sea. Furthermore, the inscription describes the king's glorious victory over the Noba, who had been harassing the Mängurto, the ḥasa, the Barya, and the Black and Red people, all of whom were under his protection. Archaeologists have yet to discover the monument or altar, *män-bär*, he set up in the land of the Noba.

See also **Aksum; Christianity.**

BIBLIOGRAPHY

Budge, E. A. Wallis. *A History of Ethiopia: Nubia, and Abyssinia.* The Netherlands: Anthropological Publications, Oosterhout N.B., 1970.

Kobishchanov, Yuri M. *Axum,* trans. Lorraine T. Kapitanoff. University Park and London: Pennsylvania State University Press, 1979.

Litmann, Enno. *Sabäische, griechische und altabessinische Inschriften. Deutsche Aksum-Expedition,* Vol. 4. Berlin: George Reimer, 1913.

Munro-Hoy, Stuart. *Aksum: An African Civilization of Late Antiquity.* Edinburgh: Edinburgh University Press, 1991.

Phillipson, David W. *Ancient Ethiopia: Aksum, Its Antecedents and Successors.* London: British Museum Press, 1998.

Schneider, Roger. "Trois nouvelles inscriptions royals d'Axoum*." In *IV Congresso Internationale di Studi Etiopici.* Rome: Accademia Nazionale dei Lincei, 1974.

Sergew, Hable Sellassie. *Ancient and Medieval Ethiopian History to 1270.* Addis Ababa, Ethiopia: Published privately, 1972.

Szymusiak, Jan M., ed. *Athanase d'Alexandrie: Deux apologies à l'Empereur Constance pour sa fuite.* Paris: Les Éditions du Cerf 1987.

GETATCHEW HAILE

FAMILY

This entry includes the following articles:
ORGANIZATION
ECONOMICS

ORGANIZATION

There is no single African family type, although familial relations are at the center of all major activities—production and work, political affairs, ritual and religious organization. Theoretical treatments have privileged descent and kinship rather than families.

At the heart of African family systems are descent and affinity—genealogical and marital relations. Relations of descent entail inequality between senior and junior generations, ranging from respectful deference to political subordination. Common descent entails the equivalence of siblings, captured in the classificatory kinship terminologies in which words for lineal relatives (father, mother) are the same as those for collaterals (father's brother, mother's sister). The terminological identity posits substitutability in terms of social relations and moral rights and obligations. In some groups, for example, if a wife were barren or died early, her sister was obliged to replace her; a man might be obliged to father children for his deceased brother; and a woman's child might be considered to "be born for" her mother's sister's daughter. Not all of these practices remain dominant but they reveal the broad definition of familial rights and obligations.

There is enormous diversity in forms of alliance, or marriage, in Africa: temporary and permanent relations, single and multiple partners, conveyance of all or some rights in a woman (sexual, procreative, work), and bridewealth transfers that range from token gifts to lifelong series of exchanges. Residence after marriage may be at the husband's home (virilocal), the wife's home (uxorilocal), neither (neolocal), or spouses may live in their respective natal homes. Children may live with their parents until marriage, or at puberty go to live with their grandparents or their mother's brother, or live with age mates. On divorce or a spouse's death, the widow(er) may go to live with natal kin. In consequence, the particular shape of coresidential and neighboring families varies considerably across the continent, as well as within groups over the life cycle.

The structure of marriage is polygynous even though polygyny was/is possible for only a minority of senior, wealthy men and is rare among matrilineal peoples. Polygyny produces identifiable matricentral cells: Each wife has her own hut and associated property, and each is the locus for distinguishing her children, as heirs, from those of other wives. The matricentered unit is also recognized in many groups with matrilineal and bilateral inheritance. Often endowed with semiautonomous socioeconomic and jural roles, it sometimes has a specific name in the group's language. Some scholars use the gloss "hearthhold" to distinguish it from the household. If there is an atom of kinship and family, it is this unit of mother and child rather than the conjugal unit.

In practice, "family" has been used in two different ways in African studies: to refer to the elementary or conjugal family, and to a broader, variously defined kin group or set of relatives. The focus of anthropological theories of kinship and descent in their heyday (1940s–1950s) was on bounded or corporate groups, considered the building blocks of African social structures. The looser aggregation of "family" as a network of relatives did not fit theoretically and usually was not employed, ceding place to terminologies of unilineal groups and descent corporations. An analytical distinction was made between kinship and descent and, in parallel, between the familial and politico-jural domains, with most theorists using the term "family" to refer to the elementary or nuclear family and the domestic unit. However, this use has been contested. The intersection of classificatory kinship terminology, descent groups, and polygyny among African peoples does not produce unitary conjugal or nuclear families as in northern European systems.

In African groups, the conjugal family is not always a conceptual (named) category, and as a social unit is always embedded in larger units of compound, locality, descent group, and so forth. It does not alone fulfill all the activities associated with domestic units (procreation, production, consumption), nor is it the major property-holding unit. These activities and roles are carried out by a range of individuals and groups, only some of whom are co-resident. The particular groups vary greatly but may be drawn from kin living nearby, age groups, gender-based associations, unrelated neighbors, and, increasingly since the 1950s, religious groups (Christian and Muslim).

Rights to land, cattle, and other forms of wealth and productive resources are usually vested in larger groups based on descent, kinship, or locality. Spouses may share rights in certain types of resources (e.g., crops), while retaining access to other resources through their respective natal kinship groups. They may pool part of their income but also keep part (sometimes all) separate in order to fulfill duties to their respective natal families, age groups, or other associations. Marriage does not customarily create a community of property; on the death of a married person, the deceased's property is not inherited by the surviving spouse but by the deceased's kin. This has been challenged in some countries, often on the basis of gender discrimination. Moreover, some richer people will their property to preempt the customary rules, and some civil marriages entail community of property. These remain a minority.

Kinship, marriage, and residence are principles of social organization that are closely tied to those of political organization. The largest residential units (compounds), based on a combination of descent, kinship, and other ties, have been described for some of the agricultural groups of western Africa. Yoruba compounds may contain up to one hundred adult male members, have a formal male head, and constitute political units of the town. Mandinka compounds may contain more than twenty people consisting of a core of agnatically related men with their wives and children; cultivation is carried out by individuals and by groups of men and women that cut across compounds, cooking is done by groups of wives and daughters in turn, and (as in most of the continent) eating is in age- and gender-specific groups. The average Tswana compound is much smaller: It encloses the huts and granaries of a man and his wife (or wives) and children, and perhaps an unmarried sister and her children, an unmarried brother, and an aged mother. Clusters of compounds related through the agnatic line comprise family groups that, in turn, make up a ward (*kgotla*), the smallest administrative unit of the chiefdom or modern-day district.

Some African peoples give a specific term to the set of relatives centered on an individual—an ego-focused family or kindred. The Swahili, for example, refer to the cluster of cognatic and affinal kin centered on a person as *jamaa* (network), and distinguish it conceptually and practically from the household or coresidential unit and from the corporate descent group. Tswana stress agnatic links among compounds for purposes of residence, inheritance, and political affiliation, but a group of close relatives (paternal and maternal kin and affines) provides most advice and support to the constituent married couples.

A characteristic of African family systems is that the classificatory kinship system often goes beyond genealogically traceable links, so acting to incorporate persons unable to trace common descent. A further characteristic is that African systems play havoc with a simple dichotomy between contractual and altruistic relations. Family membership excludes neither semicontractual relations nor exploitation. Among several Gambian peoples, a specific number of days' work due from wives and junior males on the family fields managed by the male elder is required in return for the right to work the rest of the week on their own fields. An example of the second was the right of matrilineal elders among Central Bantu to sell their juniors into slavery. Relations between spouses, between siblings, and between generations are marked by both positive and negative affect (cooperation and competition, love and jealousy, support and sorcery). Witchcraft and sorcery accusations occur between family members, divided as they are by competing interests though conceived as sharing the same substance, derived from either genealogical ties or common locality and shared subsistence.

CHANGE AND TRANSFORMATIONS

Tracing changes in family structures over long periods is particularly difficult in Africa, where written sources for earlier periods are scarce. One trajectory suggested for central Africa is a long past of bilateral kinship groups where the politics of "big men" and accumulation of wealth led to the development of unilineal inheritance and groups defining themselves in terms of lineal descent. This interpretation fits with the better-known view of African politics being about wealth-in-people and, hence, with the necessary intertwining of family and politics. Other ideas are even more speculative, such as the origin of matriliny.

Changes within the time frames of colonialism, commercialization, and political independence do not follow a unidirectional trend. The premise that modernization would lead to the disappearance of the "extended" family and the dominance of the nuclear family has not held up. And while polygyny has greatly decreased (especially the large-scale type associated with chiefs who in the late part of the nineteenth century might have had fifty or more wives), the structural logic of polygyny continues to inform patterns of marriage and sexuality. Family organization has been affected by colonial restructuring of economic, political, and legal systems, through taxation, labor, and housing policies; by Christianity and Islam; and by political and economic change within Africa and between Africa and other regions.

Processes of socioeconomic differentiation divide families and wider kin groups, yet in many places rights to land and other resources continue to depend on ties of real and fictive kinship.

There is much variability. Commercial farming in some places has produced small, nuclear families, sometimes justified through new religious rationales. In other cases, commercial farming generates a resurgence of polygynous, patrilocal families (as in Zimbabwe and Zambia, where wives become the laborers and managers for their husbands). In parts of rural southern Africa, the emergence of smaller families has been described. These are not nuclear families but multigenerational residential groups that in the past would have acted semi-independently but have come to act as one household due to increasing vulnerability in the face of unemployment and land scarcity. In other migrant-laborer areas, such as parts of the Sahel, the periodic return of migrants and their remittances have been described as encouraging the maintenance of families based on large, localized patrilocal descent groups.

Current research reveals intensifying tensions between genders and age groups. One trend among patrilineal groups is that women are remaining or returning to live in their natal homes. In northwest Zambia, groups of agnatic females now characterize Mambwe villages, with implications for labor supply, land claims, and competition between sisters and brothers. In Botswana, a restudy of a ward after some forty years showed its persisting agnatic character, but closer examination of the composition of constituent families revealed a much higher proportion of unmarried female agnates with children than in the earlier generation. Contemporary studies in different countries indicate a reluctance of women to marry or to remarry after a divorce and suggest reasons as lying in the reduced scope for women in control over resources, in access to training and employment, and in returns to their work on family farms. Virtually all women have and want children. What may be happening is that the atom of African families, the mother-child unit or hearth-hold, has found the need and capacity to increase its separation from the encompassing organizational levels of the broader family. This seems to be less a pattern among social elites, among whom the conjugal unit appears to be a more significant social and legal unit. Even then, there are variations. In Kenya, a study found increasing income pooling within the conjugal unit, whereas in Ghana a study showed that part of the separate incomes of the spouses was pooled but part continued to be allocated separately, often to their respective natal kin groups.

Tension and conflict between elder and younger men are intensifying in many places. Research in western Africa found such tension finding expression in mutual accusations of immoral behavior, adultery by the young men and witchcraft by the elders. Another study reports that young people view local systems of land tenure and marriage payments as instruments of exploitation by chiefs and elders, and links these sentiments to the recruitment of young men into armed groups involved in civil wars and more localized mayhem. This is one among many contemporary studies convincingly linking stresses within family and kinship systems with political-economic processes. In Africa, family is not merely a domestic group but part of the overall social and political structure.

See also **Death, Mourning, and Ancestors; Household and Domestic Groups; Kinship and Descent; Marriage Systems; Witchcraft.**

BIBLIOGRAPHY

Cooper, Frederick. "From Free Labor to Family Allowances: Labor and African Society in Colonial Discourse." *American Ethnologist* 16, no. 4 (1989): 745–765.

Guyer, Jane I. "Household and Community in African Studies." *African Studies Review* 24, no. 2–3 (1981): 87–138.

James, Deborah. "Bagagesu (Those of My Home): Women Migrants, Ethnicity and Performance in South Africa." *American Ethnologist* 26, no. 1 (1999): 69–89.

Linares, Olga. *Power, Prayer, and Production: The Jola of Casamance, Senegal.* Cambridge, U.K.: Cambridge University Press, 1992.

MacGaffey, Wyatt. "Lineage, Structure, Marriage, and the Family amongst the Central Bantu." *Journal of African History* 24, no. 2 (1983): 173–187.

Murray, Colin. *Families Divided: The Impact of Migrant Labor in Lesotho.* Cambridge, U.K.: Cambridge University Press, 1981.

Netting, Robert McC.; Richard R. Wilk; and Eric J. Arnould, eds. *Households: Comparative and Historical Studies of the Domestic Group.* Berkeley: University of California Press, 1984.

Pottier, Johan. *Migrants No More: Settlement and Survival in Mambwe Villages, Zambia.* Manchester, U.K.: Manchester University Press for the International African Institute (IAI), 1988.

Richards, Paul. "To Fight or to Farm? Agrarian Dimensions of the Mano River Conflicts (Liberia And Sierra Leone)." *African Affairs* 104, no. 417 (2005): 571–590.

Schapera, Isaac, and Simon Roberts. "Rampedi Revisited: Another Look at a Kgatla Ward." *Africa* 45, no. 3 (1975): 258–279.

Vansina, Jan. "The Peoples of the Forest." In *History of Central Africa*, Vol. 1, ed. David Birmingham and Phyllis M. Martin. London: Longman, 1983.

Yanagisako, Sylvia Junko. "Family and Household: The Analysis of Domestic Groups." *Annual Review of Anthropology* 8 (1979): 161–205.

PAULINE PETERS

ECONOMICS

From Adam Smith to Karl Marx, David Ricardo, and Joseph Schumpeter, virtually all well-known economists from the eighteenth to mid-twentieth centuries have acknowledged the importance of the family in the production and distribution of goods and services. Yet, among these leading thinkers from various schools of thought, Thomas Malthus was one of the very few who carried out an in-depth analysis of the family as a central economic unit. He focused on population growth and analyzed the relationship between fertility, family earnings, and age at marriage. He argued that couples usually marry later in life when economic circumstances are less favorable. It took the work of Gary Becker in the 1960s for economists to start examining the various functions of the family (production of food, production, care, and development of children, and protection against illness and other hazards).

The economic analysis of African families—a burgeoning field in microeconomics but with only a small number of researchers—must overcome several conceptual issues: A first challenge is the (economic) definition of what constitute an African family—its size, criteria for membership, relationship among its members are often different from the typical primary social group (parents and children) considered "family" in the West. Things are made even more complicated by the fact that African families, like many others around the world, have evolved over the past century. Furthermore, even if one could settle on the economic definition of the African family, there is obviously no single model for it: in rural areas, people descending from a common ancestor or even neighbors who have developed close ties across generations tend to consider themselves families. Even families in urban areas where a generally more restrictive definition is used also include people who have a broad conception of kinship with one another. All this makes it a complex task to analyze the functions of African families.

Another difficult issue is whether neo-classical methodology, which has dominated economics for the past several decades—to the point of being called "mainstream economics"—can be used as a framework for the analysis of African families. Anthropologists and sociologists have long questioned the three key assumptions of neoclassical economics, mainly that people have rational preferences among outcomes; that individuals maximize utility and firms maximize profits; and that people act independently on the basis of full and relevant information. While economists have built models that try to relax some of these assumptions, most of the economics of family still rely on them. Three aspects of family behavior are of particular interest in the context of African societies: fertility, labor and income, and resources allocation.

FERTILITY

The question of how the number of children is determined in a typical African family is affected by supply and demand conditions. Supply is determined by the capacity to produce children (age, health, nutrition and other variables), the prevailing social norms, and by knowledge of birth control. Demand is a function of the maximization of the utility of a family, which itself depends on the quantity of children, other "commodities" such as the time of the mothers, and constraints on family resources. Because the net cost of rearing children is reduced when child labor is available, fertility is often much higher in traditional agriculture. Alternatively, in segments of the urban society where women have good education, employment opportunities that raises the relative cost of their time as mothers, and access to birth control, fertility tend to be lower.

LABOR AND FAMILY INCOME

Most people in Africa still live in rural areas where employment opportunities in the formal sector are almost nonexistent. Even those living in urban areas are often employed in the informal sector. In consequence, earnings in the paid labor force outside the household are rarely an important source of family income. In fact, data from surveys consistently show that less than one-third of men and less than 10 percent of women do *any* work at all as employees. Most working people are self-employed or work as "free" labor in family businesses. Therefore, issues such as gender gaps in employment or wages are largely irrelevant for understanding the welfare dynamics in the African family, even though empirical studies generally find substantial differences in the earnings of men and women—which is not surprising given gender gaps in education and labor market experience. Instead, the key issues are how resources are allocated and used within families, and whether women have rights to inherit family wealth or purchase land or own other assets.

RESOURCES ALLOCATION

Initial studies on the economics of the family used the so-called unitary household model, which assumed that households maximize a single utility function given a common household budget constraint—in other words, the distribution of resources within a family had no effect on how allocation decisions were made. Recent economic literature focusing specifically on African families has investigated discrepancies between household welfare and the well-being of individual family members. This approach, which uses "collective" household models and assumes that family members' individual preferences and control over resources influence the sharing rule within the household, is particularly suitable to the African context where anthropologists have found that many households do not pool members' incomes. In fact, in both rural and urban Africa, husbands and wives typically receive different income flows and are responsible for distinct family expenses. The power structure and the distribution of responsibilities within the family are also often such that many women do not even know their husbands' incomes—one reason being that the husbands are often expected to provide financial resources for unforeseen, emergency situations. Recent work on African families using "collective" household models find that women's gaining greater command over resources often give them greater bargaining power within the family, in the form of stronger rights to own assets or to inherit land.

African families have changed over the past century but they still play a central role in the economic process, both as producers of children and human capital, and as buyers of goods and services. They also provide important insurance mechanisms to protect their members against life hazards such as unemployment, health, old age. In order to carry out these tasks, they rely more on altruism and social norms than on the logic of market transactions.

See also **Demography: Fertility and Infertility; Labor.**

BIBLIOGRAPHY

Becker, Gary S. *A Treatise on the Family*, Cambridge, MA: Harvard University Press, 1981.

Becker, Gary S. "Family." In *The New Palgrave: A Dictionary of Economics*, ed. John Eatwell, Murray Milgate, and Peter Newman. New York: Macmillan, 1987.

Malthus, Thomas R. *An Essay on the Principle of Population* [1798]. New York: Modern Library, 1960.

Mammen, Kristin, and Christina Paxson "Women's Work and Economic Development." *Journal of Economic Perspectives* 14, no. 4 (2000): 141–164.

Monga, Célestin. *Je t'aime, moi non plus: Economie politique de la vie conjugale*. Paper presented at the African Studies Association Meeting, Houston, TX, 2001.

Udry, Christopher. "Gender, Agricultural Production, and the Theory of the Household." *Journal of Political Economy* 104 (1996): 1010–1046.

CÉLESTIN MONGA

FAMILY PLANNING. *See* **Demography: Fertility and Infertility.**

FAMINE. Hunger and famine dominate contemporary international images of Africa. The "famine story" is part of the repertoire of every foreign correspondent and is avidly promoted by many voluntary relief agencies. Official statistics also amount to a litany of woe. African hunger is framed in a powerful narrative that implies that only outsiders can save the continent's people. The realities of famine are more complex. However, the basic agenda of research on hunger is set by these powerful representations, and almost every writer at one time or another makes use of the emotive language of helpless starving Africans and their foreign saviors.

The extent of media coverage obscures a remarkable and enduring absence of reliable information about the prevalence of death through famine in Africa. Demographic information concerning famine mortality in Africa is scanty in the extreme; no study approaches European or South Asian standards in terms of sample size or statistical rigor. Only a small number of general conclusions can therefore be forwarded.

One is that most famine deaths in Africa are concentrated among children. A second is that the paramount cause of death is epidemic disease, principally measles (though less so than in past years), malaria, and diarrheal infections. A third is that the decrease in births due to lower fertility as a result of famine is as numerically significant as the rise in deaths. A fourth is that, reflecting their greater biological resilience, women are in general less likely to die than men. Fifth, the most important demographic response to famine is mass migration. Finally, famine deaths are many fewer than are commonly assumed: predictions forwarded by international organizations are invariably exaggerations, and often gross ones. In purely statistical terms, Africans are far less likely to die for famine-related reasons than from one of the range of endemic diseases in the continent. Some famines have even occurred without any excess mortality at all: the Sahelian famine of the early 1970s is arguably a case in point. In the largest famine of the late twentieth century, 1982 to 1985 in Ethiopia, perhaps 400,000 to 600,000 people died.

Overall food production figures such as those produced regularly by the Food and Agriculture Organization of the United Nations and the United States Department of Agriculture are subject to a similar critique. In particular, the importance of many of the foodstuffs that poor people depend upon is minimized, or they are omitted altogether. Wild foods that sustain millions of Africans after every poor harvest are neglected completely. However, it is incontrovertible that African food production has stagnated since the 1970s and malnutrition remains a serious and widespread problem.

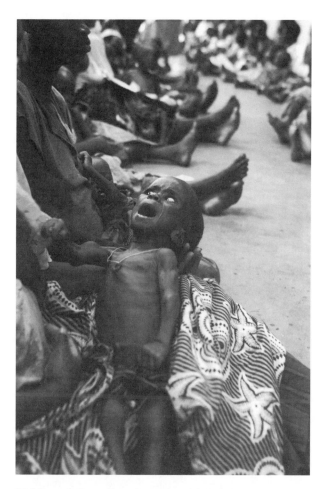

Childhood starvation. A starving child is held by its mother at the pediatric malnutrition ward at the Lilongwe, Malawi, Central Hospital, April 2002. A combination of drought, economic crisis, and HIV/AIDS had plunged Malawi into acute hunger. With increased assistance and better rains, the famine subsided in 2003, but Malawi remains chronically vulnerable to famine. AP PHOTO/OBED ZILWA

conceptions of famine contain important subtleties. For example, famine admits of many degrees, and the social upheaval and economic destitution that it causes may be more significant to the people who suffer than increased hunger and death.

The significance of a famine also depends on who is telling the story. In this regard, there are important differences between rulers and ruled, and between men and women. For example, women may recall a famine as a period in which they were abandoned by their menfolk, who migrated elsewhere, leaving them with the exclusive burden of caring for children. Men may choose to focus on the hardships of unemployment, while administrators concern themselves with problems of mass displacement.

HISTORY
Before the 1970s, the predominant view ascribed African famine to a hostile environment and the continent's social backwardness. In response to the food crises of that decade, a new generation of scholars analyzed famines as the product of new capitalist relations and governmental intrusion into old, robust rural economies. This implied that large-scale famine was an experience new to colonial and postcolonial experience. Subsequently, historical scholarship has uncovered the frequency and depth of precolonial famine, notably the disasters of the last quarter of the nineteenth century that were primarily caused by war. Collaborative work between historians and anthropologists has yielded important insights into the extent and impact of massive social upheaval. The relative absence of acute hunger during the years from 1945 to 1970 makes that period appear in retrospect as unusually bountiful for much of rural Africa.

It is particularly hazardous to draw conclusions about the demographic impact of premodern famines in Africa. Narrative records of contemporary famines invariably suggest a high level of mortality that is not borne out by demographic research. Similar reservations hold true a fortiori for the historical record, and it is improbable that famine was a major constraint on pre-twentieth-century population growth in Africa.

The Millennium Development Goals, adopted by Heads of State at the United Nations in 2000, include a commitment to eradicating extreme poverty and hunger. The Millennium Project, headed by Jeffrey Sachs, envisions an increase in food production through applying Green Revolution technologies as the principal mechanism for achieving this. Critics contend that such approaches have been tried before and have not succeeded, and that research over the recent decades reveals that the causes of hunger and famine are much more complex.

Since the 1980s historical and anthropological literature has revealed many of the complexities of African hunger and famine. African rural livelihoods are designed to manage multiple risks. Indigenous

CREATING FAMINE
Widely differing experiences of famine militate against any single account of causation. Four basic

mechanisms for famine creation can be identified. The mechanisms are not mutually exclusive: severe famines usually arise from a combination of causes.

One type is created by production failure combined with underlying economic crisis. The short-term production failure is commonly caused by drought. The long-term crisis is often caused by environmental degradation and by neglect of social and economic development, notably in agriculture, transport infrastructure, and health services. The geographical scope of production failures is easy to identify, and hence vast resources have been poured into satellite imaging of vegetative growth as an indicator of drought. The socioeconomic profile of the resulting hardship is more complex. Typically, those hardest hit are those most vulnerable to chronic hunger during normal times: small-holder farmers with marginal fields and few if any livestock, female-headed households, pastoralists with few animals, those displaced from the countryside to squatter camps around towns, traditionally disadvantaged minorities such as artisans, and those dependent on casual labor for an income. Examples of this kind of famine include much of the Sahel in the early 1970s, the early 1980s, southern Africa in 1991, Ethiopia in 2002, and Niger in 2005.

The second type of famine is characterized by selective dispossession or repression of certain groups by states or powerful interests associated with them. The most commonly afflicted groups are pastoralists, whose mobility and land rights are often drastically restricted. The alienation of pastures for agriculture has been a major contributor to famine among pastoralists across the continent, for example in Ethiopia and Kenya. Restrictions on movement and access to markets have been instrumental in creating famine in Mali and Uganda. In Mauritania and Somalia, it is farming minorities that have lost land rights, leaving them on the brink of famine.

A third type of famine in Africa is war related. War is the most common cause of famine in Africa and creates famine in several ways. One way is through the destruction and consumption of resources by armies. This can be deliberate, as in the case of scorched-earth policies carried out in order to render areas uninhabitable.

A time-honored way of creating starvation is through laying siege to garrison towns, or sometimes cutting off overland supply to encircled rural areas. Commercial and relief food is prevented from entering, while people are prevented from leaving. This tactic was a fundamental cause of the famine in Biafra during the period from 1968 to 1970 and has been the cause of some of the most extreme suffering seen in modern Africa, such as in besieged towns in Angola in 1993. A noteworthy component of these sieges is that in some instances the besieged army actually connives in the obstruction of food. This is done partly in order to punish the local population, which is often viewed as rebel sympathizers, and partly because army officers may have commercial interests in inflated food prices. This was seen in the siege of Juba in southern Sudan beginning in 1985 and continuing until the ceasefire in 2002 that brought an end to the civil war.

Perhaps the most insidious manner of creating famine is by the use of counterinsurgency strategies designed to prevent civilians from giving support to guerrilla insurrections. As Mao Zedong famously described the liberation fighter as moving through the rural population like a fish through water, army generals have described their response to insurrection as draining the sea to catch the fish. Hence populations are forcibly moved to "protected villages" (ostensibly for their own safety), curfews are enforced, roads, paths, pastures, and wells are mined, movement of people (including migrant workers, petty traders, and herders) is circumscribed, and trade and exchange of foodstuffs is tightly controlled. The rural economy is in effect strangled and the population reduced to dependence on the controlling authority and its unreliable charity. Such strategies have been used in the British suppression of Mau Mau in Kenya, the Rhodesian army campaigns of the 1970s, colonial and postcolonial wars in Angola and Mozambique, imperial and postrevolutionary wars in Ethiopia, and most recently in Darfur, Sudan, to name but a few.

The fourth mechanism for famine creation is the recent emergence of states (or pseudo-states) that are so predatory that the creation of famine becomes intrinsic to the retention of power and prosperity by ruling elites. This model encompasses both countries in which the state has completely broken down, to be replaced by armed factions that sustain themselves by predation, and countries in which the state has become so emasculated in its provision of basic services that it too can be seen as another armed faction, distinguished from the others solely by its possession of the symbols of sovereignty, and also pursuing military strategies to sustain itself that can create widespread famine. The process reached its zenith in Somalia and the Democratic Republic of the Congo. Here, the factions' chief sources of income are from looting, control of looted property, protection rackets imposed upon traders and relief agencies, and smuggling. Many of these activities contribute directly to famine among marginal and vulnerable people. In struggles for basic resources, displacement is no longer a byproduct of conflict: instead it is one of the purposes of waging war.

A central reason that famines develop and relief measures are applied late, if at all, is failure of democratic accountability by governments. Famines are politically sensitive and have often reflected a loss of governmental legitimacy. Emperor Haile Selassie of Ethiopia, overthrown in 1974, is one of several African rulers who lost power at least partly on account of famine. Hence information about famines is subject to political manipulation or complete suppression. Successive Sudanese governments have refused to admit the existence of famines since 1984. The Zimbabwean government was extremely late in acknowledging the drought of 1991–1992 and repeated the denial of hunger when land seizures created a crisis in the early 2000s. Colonel Mengistu Haile Mariam of Ethiopia was willing to admit to drought in 1983–1984, but not to the fact that his own economic policies and counterinsurgency strategies were creating famine, nor that his famine relief policies (such as resettlement of northern populations) served military goals.

In the new millennium, new patterns of acute hunger are evident across Africa. Labeled by Stephen Devereux "the new famines," these are characterized by a marked decay in government services (including provision of basic law and order), the decline of rural livelihoods as they face intersecting concurrent stresses (including collapsing markets for primary goods, environmental crises and unemployment), and the impact of Africa's HIV/AIDS epidemic. In 2002–2003 there were

fears that AIDS was combining with drought to create a "new variant famine" in which afflicted households would be unable to cope. Although the worst predictions failed to materialize, there is no doubt that HIV/AIDS is impoverishing millions and making African production systems much less resilient in the face of stress. The repeated crises in Malawi, suffering simultaneously from declining government capacity, ecological deterioration, collapsing terms of trade for its exports, and a debilitating AIDS epidemic, illustrate this extreme scenario.

RESISTING FAMINE

African governments have it within their power to prevent famine. Despite the general picture of failure, there have been a few noteworthy successes. Colonial famine prevention systems tended to follow one of two models: either they adapted the widely acclaimed Indian famine prevention system, which is based upon provision of paid employment, or they developed village-based relief systems. Sudan, which adopted statutory famine regulations in 1920, is an example of the former; Tanganyika an example of the latter.

Regarded as no longer necessary, many of these systems fell into disuse after independence. Newly independent states saw famine as a legacy of colonial exploitation that would fade into history with independence and development. However, many independent governments made the provision of services a priority, including subsidized food, and developed relief programs when they became needed. Ironically in view of later developments, Somalia, Sudan, and Ethiopia all had effective relief systems in the mid-1970s: Somalia's response to the 1974–1975 drought was rapid if clumsy; Sudan escaped the early 1970s sahelian drought by mobilizing internal surpluses of grain, and the Ethiopian government won acclaim when it set up the Relief and Rehabilitation Commission in 1974 to prevent a recurrence of famine. Unfortunately, the subsequent decline of national famine prevention programs in the Horn is reflected elsewhere. Zimbabwe responded rapidly and effectively to the drought of 1982–1983, with the notable exception of the government's deliberate decision to cut off relief to insurgent Matabeleland. However, its reaction to the drought of 1991–1992 was very slow.

Africa's finest relief system is Botswana, where an ambitious drought relief program was set up after the 1970s droughts. The efficient state provision of relief to the rural populace has prevented recurrent drought-caused famine; in fact, malnutrition rates actually fell during the 1980s droughts. Electoral accountability contributes to this success: providing relief to rural constituencies is a requirement for winning votes. Reflecting another element of accountability, the Botswana drought relief program was set up after an independent investigation into the country's relief needs.

International relief is an increasing part of the response to famine. It is a growing component of the diets of stricken populations, especially in chronic emergencies in which people are compelled to live in displaced camps for year after year. The vast majority of this is provided by bilateral donors and the United Nations, though there is an increasing tendency for these donors to entrust the implementation of their programs to European and North American voluntary agencies. The U.S. government and its main nongovernmental partners continue to dispose of surplus farm produce through relief supplies, while European governments have moved to purchase of food for humanitarian purposes on the open market.

International relief systems are widely studied, with most analyses focusing on technical problems including failures of information, slowness of reaction, or lack of coordination. Consequently, a succession of institutional initiatives, based mainly at the United Nations, has been undertaken. In the 1970s there was a special United Nations (UN) program for the Sahel, in 1984–1985 a special UN Emergency Office for Africa, followed by investment in famine "early warning systems"; based on monitoring the weather and indicators such as cereal prices. More recent, the need for resources and high-level political commitment have been highlighted by the Millennium Project. The failures of international relief tend to be much better publicized than the successes: the late responses to Darfur, Sudan, in 2004 and to Niger in 2005 are cases in point. However, there is strong evidence to suggest that emergency relief technologies are increasingly effective at saving lives. In 2002–2003, Ethiopia suffered the most widespread drought in its history, with more than 13 million people needing food assistance. The evidence suggests that the crisis passed without a significant increase in deaths in the general population. Success at saving lives has not yet translated into effective measures to prevent famine: Ethiopians are no less vulnerable to acute hunger than before.

Increasingly it is recognized that bureaucratic politics and the absence of accountability are major constraints on the ability of the international relief system to live up to its promises. This is particularly the case for war famines, where political sensibilities can be an obstacle to an effective response. To the contrary, famine can be a policy success for some governments, wishing to punish, marginalize or displace insurgent populations.

Most Africans continue to rely on their own survival skills when faced with famine. Coping strategies have been well-studied. Rural Africans eat a range of wild foods, engage in a variety of low-status trades such as selling firewood, or they sell their livestock and possessions and migrate in search of work. They also go very hungry for very long periods of time. There are differential responses by location, livelihood, and gender.

Coping strategies include both a short-term adaptation reflecting rural resilience and a maladaptive long-term response, a slide into "semi-subsistence," in which chronic hunger and intermittent famine have become a fact of life. While keeping people alive, many strategies have severe long-term costs including asset depletion, ecological degradation and insecurity.

Throughout the 1970s, the underlying theme was the banishment of hunger altogether; in the 1980s it was establishing sufficient food security and early warning of impending problems to prevent acute famine. In the early twenty-first century, ambitious hopes for the abolition of extreme poverty have rebounded, alongside fears that Africa's multiple ills spell recurrent famines for years to come.

See also **Agriculture; Desertification, Modern; Disease: HIV/AIDS, Social and Political Aspects; Ecosystems; Haile Selassie I; Mengistu, Haile Mariam; Sudan: Wars; United Nations.**

BIBLIOGRAPHY

Benthall, Jonathan. *Disasters, Relief, and the Media*, London: IB Tauris, 1993.

Davies, Susanna. *Adaptable Livelihoods: Coping with Food Insecurity in the Malian Sahel.* London: Macmillan, 1996.

Devereux, Stephen, ed. *The New Famines.* London: Routledge, 2006.

de Waal, Alex. *Famine Crimes: Politics and the Disaster Relief Industry in Africa.* London: James Currey, 1997.

de Waal, Alex. *Famine That Kills: Darfur, Sudan.* Oxford: Clarendon Press, 2004.

Djurfeldt, Goran; Hans Holmen; Magnus Jirstrom; and Rolf Larsson; eds. *The African Food Crisis: Lessons from the Asian Green Revolution.* Wallingford, U.K., and Cambridge, MA: CABI Publishing, 2005.

Dreze, Jean. "Famine Prevention in Africa: Some Experiences and Lessons." In *The Political Economy of Hunger,* Vol. 2: *Famine Prevention,* ed. Jean Dreze and Amartya Sen. Oxford: Clarendon Press, 1990.

Iliffe, John. *The African Poor: A History.* Cambridge, U.K.: Cambridge University Press, 1987.

Keen, David. *The Benefits of Famine: A Political Economy of Famine and Relief in South-West Sudan.* Princeton, NJ: Princeton University Press, 1994.

Rahmato, Dessalegn. *Famine and Survival Strategies: A Case Study from Northeast Ethiopia.* Uppsala: The Scandinavian Institute of African Studies, 1991.

Seaman, John. "Famine Mortality in Africa." *IDS Bulletin* 24, no. 4 (October 1993): 27–32.

Vaughan, Megan. *The Story of an African Famine: Gender and Famine in Twentieth-Century Malawi.* Cambridge, U.K.: Cambridge University Press, 1987.

Watts, Michael. *Silent Violence: Food, Famine, and Peasantry in Northern Nigeria.* Berkeley: University of California Press, 1983.

ALEX DE WAAL

FANON, FRANTZ

FANON, FRANTZ (1925–1961). The Algerian psychiatrist, writer, and revolution theorist Frantz Fanon was born in Fort-de-France, Martinique, on July 20, 1925, and attended medical school in Lyon, France. In 1953 he was appointed chief psychiatrist at the psychiatric hospital in Blida, Algeria. In 1956 he resigned his position at the hospital and joined the Front de Liberation Nationale (FLN). He died on December 6, 1961, from leukemia while in the United States, where he had gone for medical treatment.

While in France, Fanon's political and philosophical orientation, strongly influenced by Georg Hegel and Karl Marx, began to take form. Fanon was attracted to African intellectuals such as Alioune Diop and Aimé Césaire as well as to Jean-Paul Sartre and Albert Camus. His first book, *Black Skin, White Masks,* was published in 1952. He published his best-known work, *The Wretched of the Earth,* in 1961.

Fanon is considered to be one of the leading theorists of revolution of his time. He had little doubt that the inequalities of colonialism infected the mentalities of both the colonized and the colonizer. By 1961, Fanon was advocating violence as necessary to cleanse the colonized of the mentality of self-hatred that colonialism imposed. After his death, Fanon's theory of revolutionary catharsis became well known in the United States in the Black Liberation movement and in the formation of the Black Panther Party.

See also **Césaire, Aimé; Diop, Alioune.**

BIBLIOGRAPHY

Gibson, Nigel C. *Fanon: The Postcolonial Imagination.* Oxford: Polity Press in association with Blackwell Pub., 2003.

Gordon, Lewis R. *Fanon and the Crisis of European Man: An Essay on Philosophy and the Human Sciences.* New York: Routledge, 1995.

Silverman, Maxim, ed. *Frantz Fanon's Black Skin, White Masks: New Interdisciplinary Essays.* Manchester U.K.: Manchester University Press, 2005.

ROBERT UTTARO

FARAH, NURUDDIN

FARAH, NURUDDIN (1945–). Born in Baidoa, Somalia, Nuruddin Farah is the author of nine novels in English and of *Yesterday, Tomorrow: Voices of Somalis in Exile* (2000). Farah's novels, noted for their poetic style, are all set in Somalia, although many of the characters, like the author, have spent time in exile. Farah's first novel *From a Crooked Rib* (1970), concerns the struggle of a young woman for autonomy and survival. Feminism is also central to many of his later novels. *Naked Needle* (1976), his second novel, concerns a young man who returns to Somalia after higher education abroad. The three novels in the series "Variations on the Theme of an African Dictatorship," *Sweet and Sour Milk* (1980), *Sardines* (1981), and *Close*

Nuruddin Farah (1945–). One of the most prominent African writers, Farah has authored eight books, including two trilogies. Farah lived in exile for 25 years before returning to Somalia and settling in Mogadishu. © DB MATTHIAS SCHUMANN/DPA/CORBIS

Sesame (1983), are set in the period of the early years of the dictatorship of Siad Barre.

The slow collapse of the dictatorship following the war with Ethiopia provides the setting for the novels in the series "Blood in the Sun": *Maps* (1985), *Gifts* (1993), and *Secrets* (1998). Farah's novel *Links* (2003) concerns a Somali exile who has returned to warlord-controlled Mogadiscio after the departure of U.S. troops. Farah was the recipient of the 1998 Neustadt Prize, a major biennial literary prize.

See also **Literature; Somalia.**

BIBLIOGRAPHY

Gray, Stephen. "Nuruddin Farah: The Novelist and the Nomad." *Publishers Weekly* 246, no. 34 (1999): 28–29.

Wright, Derek. *The Novels of Nuruddin Farah*, rev. edition. Bayreuth: Bayreuth University, 2004.

ANN BIERSTEKER

FAROUK, KING OF EGYPT (1920–1965).

Egypt's last monarch, who reigned from 1936 until 1952, Farouk was born on February 11, 1920, in Cairo, the son of King Fuad (1868–1936) and Queen Nazli (1894–1978) and the grandson of Khedive Ismail (1830–1895). Educated in Egypt in a British public school, he continued his studies in England, taking classes as an unenrolled student at the Royal Military College. After the death of his father on April 28, 1936, he ascended the throne as a minor and reigned with the assistance of a regency council until July 1937.

King Farouk I of Egypt (1920–1965). King Farouk was overthrown during the Egyptian Revolution of 1952 and forced to turn over rule to his infant son, Ahmed Fuad. CORBIS

As his father did, Farouk successfully kept the Wafd, the popular nationalist majority party, out of power and tried continuously to enhance the power of the monarchy over parliament, damaging parliamentary democracy in the process. During World War II, he struggled to remain neutral but the British imposed in 1942 the pro-British Wafd leader Mustafa al-Nahhas (1879-1965) as prime minister. Farouk enjoyed some popularity at the beginning of his reign, but this changed around the early 1940s because of corruption, incompetence, autocratic rule, Israel's defeat of Egypt, and Farouk's ostentatious lifestyle. The Committee of the Free Officers led by Gamal Abdel Nasser enforced the king's abdication on July 23, 1952. He went into exile and in 1959 became a citizen of Monaco. Farouk died on March 18, 1965, in Rome.

See also **Egypt, Modern; Fuad, King of Egypt; Nasser, Gamal Abdel.**

BIBLIOGRAPHY

Vatikiotis; Panayiotis J: *The History of Modern Egypt: From Muhammad Ali to Mubarak*, 4th edition. London: Weidenfeld and Nicolson, 1991.

JÖRN THIELMANN

FASILADAS (1602–1667). Fasiladas, emperor of Ethiopia from 1632 to 1667, was the son of the emperor Susenyos, who abdicated in his favor. Fasiladas had opposed his father's policy of bringing the Ethiopian church into line with Roman Catholic doctrine and ritual and at once reversed it. In the process Fasiladas banished the Patriarch Mendez, who had ruthlessly implemented the earlier policy, along with Portuguese Jesuits, while persecuting those Ethiopians who remained committed to Catholicism. His letters to Mendez are impressively authoritative, particularly in his refusal to admit a significant doctrinal difference between the two churches while insisting that only traditional Ethiopian orthodoxy could exist in Ethiopia.

Fasiladas established the normative political and ecclesiastical order of Ethiopia for the next two centuries by founding the new capital of Gondär. This was the first real capital the country had had for centuries; his predecessors had lived a largely nomadic life. He also rebuilt the cathedral of Aksum, which had been in ruins since the Jihad of Grañ a century earlier. Art and music flourished in this period, during which the Ethiopian musical tradition developed its standard notation. Fasiladas also reversed the traditional Ethiopian foreign policy of hostility toward the Muslim states to the north and east. The Portuguese having become the enemy, he was consistently and successfully conciliatory to his Muslim neighbors. Few emperors ruled so long or imposed so considerable a mark upon both the political and the religious tradition of Ethiopia.

See also **Ethiopia and the Horn, History of (1600 to 1910); Susenyos.**

BIBLIOGRAPHY

Abir, M. "Ethiopia and the Horn of Africa." In *The Cambridge History of Africa*, Vol. 4, ed. Richard Gray. Cambridge, U.K.: Cambridge University Press, 1975–1986.

Beccari, Camillo. *Rerum Aethiopicarum scriptores Occidentales inediti a Saeculo.* Vols. 5–12. Rome: Excudebat C. de Luigi, 1903–1917.

ADRIAN HASTINGS

FEMALE GENITAL MUTILATION. *See* **Initiation: Clitoridectomy and Infibulation.**

FERTILITY. *See* **Demography: Fertility and Infertility.**

FESTIVALS AND CARNIVALS. African royal festivals and religious ceremonies have been documented for several centuries, figuring prominently in early Western travel writing, later colonial expositions, museum displays, ethnographic films and monographs, and, more recently, in national dance and theater performances. Nineteenth-century Christian missionaries often portrayed such festivals as heathen practices that catered to primitive instincts, illustrating the depravity of savage idolatry. Throughout the twentieth century, however, this limited perspective yielded to a more informed appreciation of the religious meanings, social values, and historical dynamics of such rituals and festivals as they continued to develop in a range of African societies, and under a variety of colonial and post-colonial conditions, including the expansion of Christianity and Islam.

Due mainly to modern anthropological studies that have investigated the cultural forms of indigenous African festivals while focusing on their sociopolitical functions, scholars can better appreciate their central role as mechanisms not only of social regulation and reproduction, but also of social disruption and change.

A FESTIVAL SURVEY

No reliable definition or typology of African festivals exists, in part because of their complexity—they perform multiple social and religious functions—and also because they change over time, often mixing, blending, or moving between genres. Festivals wax and wane, they remember and forget, they improvise new themes, and even shift between local and national levels. This adaptability to the purposes of their organizers and enactors is important to emphasize because there has been a tendency on the part of scholars and practitioners alike to portray indigenous festivals as fixed traditions, handed down unchanged by the ancestors since the beginning of mythical time. If, in principle, celebrants presume rigid fidelity to the ways of their ancestors, in practice they can innovate substantially, modifying festivals to fit changing circumstances and even using festivals to promote social and political change. With this fluidity and flexibility in mind, we can distinguish a number of general festival forms and processes in Africa.

Royal rituals or festivals of sacred kingship as a genre can be associated with political centralization throughout sub-Saharan Africa, particularly in the historic kingdoms and empires of the western Sahel and the coastal regions, and down through central and southern Africa, following the settling of Bantu-speaking communities that formed the Lovedu, Tsonga, Nguni, Swazi, and Zulu polities. In West Africa, examples include the Odwira festival among the Asante of Ghana, and the Shango festival of the Yoruba in Nigeria, both of which ensure natural, social, and cosmological renewal through the ritual purification and empowerment of the

sacred king. Usually associated with transitions between seasons, harvests, and agricultural cycles, such festivals are often called new yam or first-fruits ceremonies and operate according to a logic—first identified by Sir James Frazer—whereby agricultural productivity and social well being are associated with the king's sacred body that must remain physically and ritually healthy for the kingdom to thrive. In southeast Africa, the royal Swazi Ncwala festival has become a well-known ritual of sacred kingship through Hilda Kuper's detailed account in *An African Aristocracy: Rank among the Swazi* (1980) and subsequent debates over its interpretation. Ritual idioms of fecundity and the restoration of cosmological balance are actually about politics, making sacred kingship a rich focus for the study of political symbolism.

Masquerades are a generic form of African festival. Although they may combine with the celebration of sacred kingship, they more often stand apart, representing lineage-based spirits of the dead, as in Yoruba Egungun festivals; spirits associated with age grades, as in Bamana puppet masquerades in Mali or Afikpo masks in Nigeria; or spirits associated with secret societies and voluntary associations, such as masquerades of the Liberian Poro society, of Yoruba hunters' associations, and of canoe houses among the riverine groups of the Niger Delta, or rites of the Lunda-related peoples of southwestern Congo, western Zambia, and eastern Angola. Whereas royal rituals are generally associated with cosmological renewal, masquerades are usually oriented toward placating the dead, controlling witchcraft, and ostracizing malefactors in the community through ritually sanctioned accusations or parodic displays of antisocial behavior.

Masquerades also play an important role in the organization and representation of gender relations because their membership associations are often segregated by sex, as in the male Poro and the female Sande societies, and because their performances portray gender stereotypes, as in Gelede caricatures of warriors, brides, drummers, and prostitutes. Because of their overtly mimetic routines, masquerades often incorporate figures of power and value from national and global arenas into their costumes and masked superstructures. Some Gelede masks feature Europeans and airplanes. In the Hauka possession cult among the Songhay of Niger, masked dancers embody the power of colonial officers—as portrayed in Jean Rouch's 1955 film *Les maîtres foux*—adding Nigerian military officers to their spirit pantheon when the army came to power.

Muslim festivals are a bona fide festival form associated with the Islamic emirates of West Africa, combining political pageantry with religious feasting and gift exchanges between the sovereign and his subjects. Subjugated and converted by Islamic jihad (holy wars) in the nineteenth century, these kingdoms incorporated elements of preconquest ritual into the annual Sallah festivals, performed on the Muslim high holidays of Id al-Fitr and Id al-Kabir. As described by Siegfried Frederick Nadel in *A Black Byzantium* (1942), during Sallah the ruling emir ritually negotiated the ranks and statuses of his vassal chiefs and courtiers by distributing gifts and kola nuts in lavish public displays. Mobilizing thousands of spectators, the Sallah features a vast procession of political and religious officials on horseback, surrounded by retinues of drummers and praise singers. The high point of the Sallah, called the *jafi* salute, dramatizes the loyalty of the mounted warriors as they charge toward the emir in a mock attack, stopping short, weapons drawn, to proclaim fealty to their commander.

Colonial festivals should also be included in a survey of African festival types, given their historical role in establishing colonial authority by incorporating Africans into wider administrative structures, and by inspiring allegiance to the symbols and centers of the colonial power. In the British colonies, Empire Day provided a festive celebration of colonial overrule, mobilizing the native authorities as collective bodies engaged in competitive school sports, with food and prizes distributed by the district officer. Although secular in function, the British Crown was sanctified by the formal reading of the king or queen's message, followed by throngs singing "God Save the King [Queen]." Another such ceremony of imperial incorporation was the durbar, a colorful spectacle of mounted officers and soldiers, wherein chiefs and emirs were invested with insignia that identified them as agents of the Crown, clearly organized into status grades and ranks. Although durbars were performed to mark special events like the coronation of King George V in 1911 and the Prince of Wales's visit to British West Africa in 1925, they came to celebrate the rank and file of native administration under Indirect Rule.

Wife of a military chief (Balogun Aafin) singing songs of abuse to the king of Ayede-Ekiti and the Yemoja priestesses. A potential beaded crown and staff are marked by red climbing vines, indicating the chief's potential to "climb" toward, and usurp, the kingship. PHOTOGRAPH BY ANDREW APTER

Contemporary national festivals are state-sponsored festivals of arts and culture that emerged with the cultural nationalism of African independence movements and developed into affirmations of postcolonial nationhood. Performed at all levels of political organization, from the local district or province to the nation-state, these festivals adapt traditional ritual and masquerade performances for a more secular stage and a general public, thereby weaving different ethnic identities and traditions into a modern national culture. Increasingly, such festivals are organized on an international scale, celebrating global dimensions of blackness and Africanity, as in Léopold Sédar Senghor's Festival

Yemoja priestess carrying a ritual calabash (*igba Yemoja*) on her head during the annual festival in Ayede-Ekiti, Nigeria. Red parrot feathers arranged in bundles of three represent the ability of the priestesses to depose the king. PHOTOGRAPH BY ANDREW APTER.

the cult, the community, the kingdom, and finally the earth (lower half) and sky (upper half). On the other hand, the political functions or purposes of such festivals, expressed in cultural idioms of purification and fertility, concern the sanctification and reproduction of authority relations. This view has been the classical functionalist one: that whatever the local meaning of the festival, its social value lies in its capacity to uphold the kingship and maintain authority. Taking a closer look at the Swazi Ncwala festival's symbolism, however, anthropologist Max Gluckman (1963) noted that many of the stated and implied festival themes concerned destabilization, opposition, and rebellion against the king by ritually offending and insulting him. To explain this symbolic behavior, Gluckman developed his rituals of rebellion thesis, a perspective that derived from festivals of sacred kingship, but has much broader relevance to all African festival forms, and even European and Latin American carnivals.

Briefly stated, Gluckman argues that the political function of ritual rebellion derives from that of real rebellion, which protects the kingship from the king. A ruler who violates the values of high office will be deposed in a rebellion that changes the incumbent but keeps the principle of kingship and the system of government intact. It is from this critical turning point, focusing on the symbolic inversions of social order acted out in rituals and festivals more generally, that critics of Gluckman have extended his thesis to understand the role of ritual in mobilizing resistance against hegemony or domination, including British colonialism. If Yoruba sacred rituals mobilize the ceremonial opposition of civil and military chiefs, if masquerades like Gelede and Hauka can lampoon colonial officers, if the Sallah contains a cavalry charge against the ruling emir, if colonial durbars mobilized African fighting regiments, and if national festivals contain criticisms of the state, then an overriding theoretical question emerges: under what conditions do the transformative capacities of ritual become actualized? To answer this question, African festivals must be viewed more fully in their historical contexts.

Mondial des Arts Nègres, hosted by Senegal in 1966, in Nigeria's Second World Black and African Festival of Arts and Culture held in 1977 (FESTAC '77), and more recently, in Ghana's Panafest productions, motivated by tourism and neoliberal reform.

RITUALS OF REBELLION

The interpretation of ritual symbolism has become a classical focus of Africanist research, illuminating the study of African festivals in terms of both form and function. On the one hand, sacred kings and ritually charged, or key, symbols lie at the center of cosmologies, from which cultural coherence derives. In royal festivals among the Yoruba, for instance, a ritually charged calabash carried on the head of a priestess signifies the womb, the head,

HISTORY AND MEMORY

African festivals are historical in two senses of the term. As ritual systems, they change over time, but they also invoke historical memories in symbols, songs, drug rhythms, choreographies, and processions to various shrines and altars, honoring the living and the dead. In the past, for example, festivals associated with expanding kingdoms absorbed ritual practices from conquered territories, incorporating new spirits and masquerades into their ritual calendars and choreographies. Thus, the Odwira festival associated with the *asantehene*—the paramount chief of the Asante in Ghana—absorbed ritual representatives of his subordinate chiefdoms in the nineteenth century, as did the Shango festival cycle of the *alaafin* of Oyo in eighteenth-century Yorubaland. But if the Odwira and Shango festivals developed historically to consolidate political control, subordinate towns could resist by asserting themselves as centers of politico-ritual sovereignty. As the Oyo empire expanded, for example, imposing Shango as a cult of administrative control, a counterposed ritual field developed among its vassal kingdoms that asserted their autonomy, mobilizing hidden histories and charters of kingship that controverted Oyo's hegemonic claims. In this important context, political alliances and rebellions were reflected by ritual and also were largely negotiated through them.

Ritual masquerades may be less directly associated with kingship and centralized power, but their political history is no less complex. Masquerade figures may represent eponymous ancestors of groups that migrated to found new communities or settled in towns and cities. In one of the most complex nineteenth-century dramas of forced migration and resettlement, repatriated Yoruba slaves—some of whom returned from Brazil—settled in Freetown, Sierra Leone, where they became Creoles and organized masked Devil or Odelay societies, blending elements of Yoruba Egungun, Gelede, and hunting masquerades with the fancy-dress aesthetic of the New World carnival. In his pathbreaking *Moving with the Face of the Devil* (1987), John Nunley shows how these associations played into urban ethnic relations and national politics, with patronage ties extending into the All Peoples Congress party. One of these associations was commissioned to represent Freetown artists at FESTAC '77 in Nigeria, where it took on pan-African dimensions.

As these and other examples reveal, African festivals are historically dynamic because they both

shape and are shaped by changing social and political relations, from the local and regional to the national and even transnational. How their historical development relates to the histories they profess remains one of the leading questions for future Africanist research.

See also **Art; Dance: Social Meaning; Diasporas; Kingship; Masks and Masquerades; Music; Religion and Ritual; Rouch, Jean; Secret Societies; Senghor, Léopold Sédar; Spirit Possession; Symbols and Symbolism.**

BIBLIOGRAPHY

Apter, Andrew. *Black Critics and Kings: The Hermeneutics of Power in Yoruba Society.* Chicago: University of Chicago Press, 1992.

Apter, Andrew. *The Pan-African Nation: Oil and the Spectacle of Culture in Nigeria.* Chicago: University of Chicago Press, 2005.

Arnoldi, Mary Jo. *Playing with Time: Art and Performance in Central Mali.* Bloomington: Indiana University Press, 1995.

Drewal, Henry John, and Margaret Thompson Drewal. *Gelede: Art and Female Power among the Yoruba.* Bloomington: Indiana University Press, 1983.

Gluckman, Max. "Rituals of Rebellion in South-East Africa." In *Order and Rebellion in Tribal Africa.* New York: Cohen & West, 1963.

Goerg, Odile, ed. *Fêtes urbaines en Afrique. Espaces, identities et pouvoirs.* Paris: Karthala, 1999.

Kuper, Hilda. *An African Aristocracy: Rank among the Swazi.* New York: Africana, 1980.

Lawal, Babatunde. *The Gèlèdé Spectacle: Art, Gender, and Social Harmony in an African Culture.* Seattle: University of Washington Press, 1996.

Lentz, Carola. "Local Culture in the National Arena: The Politics of Cultural Festivals in Ghana." *African Studies Review* 44, no. 2 (2001): 47–72.

McCaskie, T. C. *State and Society in Pre-Colonial Asante.* Cambridge, U.K.: Cambridge University Press, 1995.

Nadel, Siegfried Frederick. *A Black Byzantium; the Kingdom of Nupe in Nigeria.* London: Oxford University Press, 1942.

Nunley, John. *Moving with the Face of the Devil: Art and Politics in Urban West Africa.* Urbana: University of Illinois Press, 1987.

Rosenthal, Judy. *Possession, Ecstasy, and Law in Ewe Voodoo.* Charlottesville: University Press of Virginia, 1998.

Stoller, Paul. *Embodying Colonial Memories: Spirit Possession, Power, and the Hauka in West Africa.* New York: Routledge, 1995.

Strother, Zoe S. *Inventing Masks: Agency and History in the Art of the Central Pende.* Chicago: University of Chicago Press, 1999.

Vail, Leroy, and Landeg White. *Power and the Praise Poem: Southern African Voices in History.* Charlottesville: University Press of Virginia, 1991.

ANDREW APTER

FETISH AND FETISHISM.

The term "fetish," derived from the Portuguese *feitiço*, denotes a European way of thinking about African culture developed in the seventeenth and eighteenth centuries. The term cannot readily be translated into any African language, however, and it does not correspond to any well-defined African concept or class of objects.

Portuguese sailors who arrived on the coast of West Africa in the fifteenth century, finding that the inhabitants were neither "Mohammedans" nor idolaters, as they expected, coined the term *feitiço*—which meant amulets or other spiritually charged, fabricated (in Portuguese, *feito* means "made") objects—to refer to things on which Africans relied to procure good fortune, fend off harm, and enforce contracts. Such objects were not idols, since they were not images of gods located elsewhere but were deemed potent in themselves. In the sixteenth century, Dutch Protestant merchants extended the term to cover what they saw as an African inability to assess material goods at their "true" value. Reports from West Africa asserted that Africans impulsively attributed value and power to objects at random.

In 1760 a French writer, Charles de Brosses, coined the term *fétichisme*; at the end of the century. The eighteenth-century German philosopher Georg Hegel treated "fetishism" as the earliest stage of social evolution before the beginning of civilization and therefore of history—a zero point at which humans were still at one with nature, and therefore rational synthetic thought did not exist. In the nineteenth century, however, European writers began to use "fetishism" in critiques of what they saw as the irrationality of their own civilization or aspects thereof. Karl Marx wrote about the fetishism of commodities; Sigmund Freud, about the fetishization of objects of erotic desire.

In the nineteenth and twentieth centuries, Africa was held to be the natural home of "fetishism," a term commonly applied to any aspect of indigenous religion, including local shrines and movements for the eradication of witchcraft. Gradually, this usage declined. Twenty-first century Africans speaking French or English continue to use the term in this comprehensive sense, however, an idea also conveyed by the words *juju* and *grigri*. Anthropologists, as they accumulated detailed studies of African religion, became increasingly reluctant to dismiss beliefs and practices as the products of irrationality. In a separate movement, many "fetishes" that took the form of wooden sculptures came to be seen as works of art. These sculptures were transferred from ethnographic archives to art museums and became highly valued by collectors.

About 1980, curators of African exhibitions began to replace "fetish" on their labels with "power object." Mindful of the burden of judgment that attaches to the term, anthropologists writing in English usually avoid "fetish" and try to use the appropriate indigenous words. Writers in French have fewer scruples, however. Indeed, neither French nor English scholars have a neutral term to describe portable composite objects that are believed to have power to protect, benefit, or punish people. Stimulating critiques of anthropological theory relative to fetishes, power, and value include those of Jean Bazin (1986) and David Graeber (2001).

During the African colonial period, while anthropological attitudes were changing, administrators and missionaries actively repressed the use of fetishes, especially those sculptures that had been of public importance. In the twenty-first century, fetishes exhibited as works of art are often physically damaged and usually lack documentation of their original composition and use. In Africa, fetishes are by their nature secret and difficult to investigate. Detailed studies are therefore few relative to the past and present importance of fetishes in African life, where today they are widely used by individuals to procure good fortune, by politicians to win elections, and by football teams to secure victory. Public disapproval of fetishism in modern times has meant that in much of Africa, particularly in Congo, spectacular displays and astonishing sculptures have been replaced by covert dealing and furtive packages.

Although sixteenth-century European observers believed fetishes to be trifles chosen at random, modern scholars know that they are in fact complex devices requiring painstaking assembly; that in any given district they are classified according to their nature and purpose; that a fetish's owner-operator is obliged to undergo prolonged training; and that the totality of a fetish includes not only its material substratum but the performance of the ritual that activates it and the obligations it imposes on people associated with it. Ultimately, the fetish is empowered not by its material components but by the correct performance of prescribed behavior on the part of its owner and his clients.

The core element of a fetish is often a mineral associated with spirits of nature, or perhaps dirt from an ancestral grave, which is regarded as the animating force. Many of the other components are chosen because they are linked to animals with desirable qualities; for example, the claw of a hawk, to seize a malefactor. Others are present primarily for linguistic reasons—to represent words denoting the powers attributed to the composite and the desires of the beneficiary. Some are included simply because they are surprising and serve to individuate the whole. The fetish's appearance, as a remarkable assemblage of heterogeneous elements, contributes to its efficacy; while it is used, it accumulates additional materials and related anecdotes reporting its successes, which enhance the respect in which it is held. Some fetishes contain materials that are not apparent to the casual observer but are presumed to be dangerous by those who understand the object's power; these components may be concealed in a deliberately enigmatic exterior (for example, the *boli* found in Mali, a country in West Africa) or, conversely, they may be advertised by an external form that is equally enigmatic but complex and visually striking (such as the celebrated "nail-fetishes," *nkondi*, of Kongo).

Fetish sculptures, particularly anthropomorphic ones, are particularly open to misinterpretation by museum-goers. The Kongo *nkondi*, for example, is not a "portrait" of the target who will suffer from the nails driven into the figure, nor of the force that is being invoked, but of the relationship between the two. In any case, what one is not able to see in a fetish is often as important as what is visible. Unfortunately, the aesthetic dimension of fetishes is often hard to assess because museum collections of them

Nkisi Nkondi. Male figure, Kongo peoples, Democratic Republic of the Congo, late-nineteenth to mid-twentieth century. Made of wood, glass, iron, pigment, cloth, plant fiber, horn, nails. H x W x D: 16 13/16 x 10 1/2 x 7 5/8 in. (42.7 x 26.6 x 19.3 cm). Gift of Dr. and Mrs. Robert Kuhn. PHOTOGRAPH BY FRANKO KHOURY, NATIONAL MUSEUM OF AFRICAN ART, SMITHSONIAN INSTITUTION

are heavily biased by European tastes, which tend to favor sculptures and reject objects such as pots, bundles, and animal horns. When not in use, fetishes are usually concealed; an object that is eventually put on display in a museum would originally have been intended to be shown only on special, emotionally heightened occasions.

Given that the relationship between human interactions and material components is essential to the nature of fetish, one can see that similar principles govern other features of African religion to which "fetish" is not usually applied. The more a fetish is used to treat public problems as opposed to personal situations (for example, in settling disputes, improving agricultural productivity, or combating epidemics), the grander and more animated the performance of the activating ritual and the more prominent the influence of the human element. Masquerades and consecrated chiefs represent two types of public, collective, performance-based human fetishes. Masks, performed as masquerade dances, share some characteristics of fetish objects: an outer appearance empowered by hidden medicines. The dancer, who is usually anonymous, disappears behind the mask, concealing his true identity and becoming a bush-spirit. In contrast, a consecrated chief—inaugurated with rituals that to some extent transform him into an object—continues to be recognized as a human being, although he is characteristically restricted in his mobility and partly concealed from public view. Shrines and graves, distinguished from fetishes by their immobility, nevertheless conform to the same model of unique, self-constituted powers.

In all such rituals, the power attributed to an object (even when that object is a ritually conse-crated human being) derives from that object's relationship to human beings, never solely from the fetish itself or from its physical components. Nor is a fetish's influence derived from a deity located elsewhere, of which the object is a repre-sentation. When the fetish is destroyed, its cult comes to an end; when the rules it imposes are neglected, it reverts to insignificance.

See also **Religion and Ritual; Symbols and Symbolism; Witchcraft.**

BIBLIOGRAPHY

Bazin, Jean. "Retour aux choses-dieux." In *Corps des Dieux*, ed. C. Malamoud and J.-P. Vernant. Paris: Gallimard, 1986.

De Surgy, Albert, ed. *Fétiches: objets enchantés, mots realizes* (Systémes de pensée en Afrique noire, Cahier 8). Paris: Ecole Pratique des Hautes Etudes, 1987.

Graeber, David. *Toward an Anthropological Theory of Value.* New York: Palgrave, 2001.

MacGaffey, Wyatt. *Art and Healing of the Bakongo.* Stockholm: Etnografiska Museet, 1991.

MacGaffey, Wyatt. "Art and Spirituality." In *African Spiri-tuality: Forms, Meanings, and Expressions*, ed. Jacob K. Olupona. New York: Crossroads, 2000.

Pietz, William. "The Problem of the Fetish, I, II, and IIIa." *RES: Anthropology and Aesthetics* 9 (1985): 5–17; 13 (1987): 23–45; 16 (1988): 105–123.

WYATT MACGAFFEY

FEZ. Fez (Arabic, *Fas*) is one of Morocco's four imperial cities, together with Meknes, Rabat, and Marrakesh. Founded by Idris I (ruled 788–791), Fez also hosts the Qarawiyyin mosque uni-versity, one of the oldest centers of learning in North Africa (founded 859). The population of Fez is a combination of Arabs, including refugees from Andalusia (Spain) and Berbers from the Rif-fian mountains to the north, and others from the Middle Atlas to the south. The Jewish contribu-tion to urban life in Fez has traditionally been strong. Most Jews lived in a separate quarter, called the *mallah*, until the early twentieth cen-tury. Only a small Jewish community remains—most having left in the 1960s—although Jews of Fassi origin in France, Canada, and Israel proudly retain strong ties with the city. The older walled city of Fez (*fas al-bali*) is designated as a United Nations Educational, Scientific and Cultural Organization (UNESCO) World Heritage site. Next to the ancient city, or *medina*, is the French-built *ville nouvelle* (new town), with bou-levards, landscaping, and wide streets. Once an international economic crossroads, Fez, with its current population of just over a million as of 2007, has become a regional one. It is econom-ically overshadowed by other Moroccan cities but retains its aura as Morocco's cultural capital. The World Sacred Music Festival, an annual event since 1994, is distinctively linked to Fez.

See also **Judaism in Africa; Marrakesh; Morocco; Rabat and Salé.**

BIBLIOGRAPHY

Deshen, Shlomo. *The Mellah Society: Jewish Community Life in Sherifian Morocco.* Chicago: University of Chicago Press, 1989.

Le Tourneau, Roger. *Fez in the Age of the Marinides*, trans. Besse Alberta Clement. Norman: University of Oklahoma Press, 1961.

DALE F. EICKELMAN

FILM AND CINEMA. Soon after its invention in France in 1895, cinema came to Africa. Over the next century, its development was shaped by European colonialism and its postcolonial after-math. By 2005, however, African cinema had come of age. In the beginning, only Europeans had cameras, but Africans gradually gained control of the medium and the message. Africans began also to make films about Europeans and Americans, reversing a century-old gaze.

The history of African cinema is composed of three strands. First and best known is the commercial cinema: feature films made in Africa for the entertainment market. Second are the documentary films made in Africa by scientists, educators, political activists, and the like. Finally, since independence, a self-consciously African cinema has come into being, created by African directors and shown primarily at film festivals, but also available on DVD. Overwhelmingly, however, the films that reach African viewers are American. Bollywood musicals from India and kung fu films from Hong Kong are also very popular.

This survey of film production will concentrate on three sub-Saharan regions: Southern Africa; the former English colonies of West and East Africa; and the former French and Belgian colonies of West and Central Africa. Space limitations preclude the wider and deeper survey that would have dealt with topics such as the history of Egyptian cinema, the earliest viable film industry on the African continent; the German Encyclopaedia Cinematographica, containing hundreds of filmed "thematic units" from all parts of Africa; the Cuban-backed revolutionary cinema in Portuguese-speaking Angola and Mozambique; or the cinema-in-exile of Ethiopia. Selection criteria for what constitutes "African cinema" are varied and can be invidious; Sembène's disdain for Rouch is one example; South African cinema was contested territory during apartheid. It is therefore important to consult as many sources as possible when researching this topic.

SOUTHERN AFRICA

The bioscope gained a foothold in South Africa early. W. K. L. Dickson (1860–1935) filmed the Boer War, from the British side. Dr. Rudolf Pöch filmed in the Kalahari Desert in 1907. After the Union of South Africa was established in 1910, cinema became a vehicle of national pride. More than a dozen films were produced in South Africa in 1916, among them the epic *De Voortrekkers* (Winning a continent), in Afrikaans and English; it was a huge success in South Africa and in England and was compared to D.W. Griffith's (1875–1948) *Birth of a Nation*. In 1918 an even more ambitious film, *The Symbol of Sacrifice*,

depicted the Zulu wars. South African films were unable to withstand competition from abroad, especially from Hollywood in the 1920s. The number and quality of films declined, and a cinema of apartheid became ensconced, controlled by censorship and by government subsidies.

In the early years of sound, most South African feature films were made in Afrikaans, with plots set in a countryside where sex, violence, big money, outsiders in general, and race agitators in particular were excluded. In the years just before the introduction of television in 1976, the first African language features appeared: *Nogomopho*, directed in Zulu by an Afrikaner, *Tonie van der Merwe*; and *U-Deliwe*, by the first black director, Simon Sabela (1931–1994). Production of cheap, subsidized films in African languages took off.

Many of the films of South African resistance were made by whites, foreigners, or exiles. The Hungarian-born British director Zoltan Korda (1895–1961) filmed Alan Paton's novel *Cry, the Beloved Country* in South Africa in 1951, featuring the American black actors Sidney Poitier (b. 1927) and Canada Lee (1907–1952). Working clandestinely, the American Lionel Rogosin (1924–2000) made *Come Back, Africa* in 1959. The South African journalist Lionel Ngakane (1928–2003) spent years in British exile, where he made *Jemima and Johnny*, and won the first prize at the Venice Film Festival in 1966. Working in London with footage smuggled out of South Africa, Nana Mahomo (b. 1930) made *Last Grave at Dimbaza* (1974). The film was intended for Western audiences, to counter propaganda films made by the South African Information Service. As repression inside South Africa grew, filmmakers grew bolder in their evasions. In 1988, Oliver Schmitz (b. 1960) and his crew hoodwinked township authorities into thinking that they were making a Zulu/Xhosa/Afrikaans/English gangster film. Belatedly banned by South African censors, *Mapantsula* got rave reviews abroad: the New York Times called it "more authentic than any other South African film."

African cinema has always posed the question of authenticity, and none more starkly than the best-known South African film, *The Gods Must Be Crazy*. Its director, Jamie Uys (1921–1996), had been a successful producer of Afrikaans-language films. *The Gods Must Be Crazy* began with a Coke bottle dropped from an airplane, and featured elephants, children, an Afrikaner scientist, a British schoolteacher, Angolan guerrillas, a Land Rover, and a Bushman, most of whom did gently funny things. Because of the cultural blockade against South Africa, the film was released in Botswana in 1980. World audiences, particularly in Sweden and Japan, were enchanted by a lighthearted fable, whereas political activists sharply criticized the film's racism and fakery. But there was nothing inauthentic about its foreign exchange earnings, which surpassed US$84 million.

N!Xau (1944–2003), the !Kung San Bushman in Uys's film, in reality worked as a cook for a mission at Tshumkwe, where John Marshall (1932–2005), an American filmmaker and activist, had a base of operations. Marshall's family, collaborating with Harvard and the Smithsonian Institution, mounted several expeditions to the Kalahari Desert and in 1957 Marshall pulled together his footage into a documentary, *The Hunters*. It became a classic in anthropology courses, but Marshall became convinced that, to give a true picture of !Kung San life, he should have shown women gathering at least as much as men hunting. His concern was in line with developments in anthropology, which after 1968 turned into a public critique of anthropology itself as an imperialist project. In 1978, Marshall refilmed the !Kung San in a desperate state, dispossessed of their hunting lands, subsisting on cornmeal and liquor, dying from tuberculosis, and frayed by domestic violence. *N!ai, the Story of a !Kung Woman*, was heart wrenching, especially when it showed N!ai as a young girl in the 1950s. One of its happier moments showed Uys's film crew directing a N!Xau in a sentimental scene. Marshall's final film, *A Kalahari Family*, showed the grandchildren of the Nyae Nyae !Kung of the 1950s as they prepared to vote in the first Namibian elections.

South African independence in 1994 cleared the way for a more open cinema, with commercial and cultural links to other countries. A production consortium from South Africa, Britain, Cameroon, Ghana, Kenya, and Nigeria produced the first pan-African action thriller, *Critical Assignment* (2003), starring Guinness advertising icon Michael Power as a kinder and gentler African James Bond. The Industrial Development Corporation of South Africa produced *Hotel Rwanda* (2004) and *Tsotsi* (2005). Production in all formats and genres flourished, from TV dramas and children's films to exceedingly frank documentaries, such as Catherine Muller's *Four Rent Boys and a Sangoma* (2003). In this atmosphere of freedom, the young Dumisani Phakathi (b. 1975) developed in a distinctive personal style. His *Christmas with Granny* (2000) and *Waiting for Valdez* (2002) brilliantly showed children's lives in Soweto, where he grew up. *Don't F- with Me I Have 51 Brothers and Sisters* (2004) recorded his efforts to come to terms with the loss of his father. Phakathi told an interviewer: "At first, a lazy eye and mind will have a problem with African cinema. It requires commitment" (Phakathi and Sithole, 117).

WHEN DID AFRICAN CINEMA BEGIN?

Some film historians assume that African cinema didn't exist before independence, which came to many colonies in the 1960s, but clearly it did—in Egypt, which is outside the scope of this work, and even in apartheid South Africa. The principal colonial powers, Britain and France, created two distinct film cultures in the areas under their control. In the British colonies of East and West Africa, a pragmatic and businesslike attitude toward the film medium came in with the colonizers. In the French colonies, the local elites were educated in French philosophy, literature, and art, and filmmakers took on a sense of film as art and an attitude of opposition to Hollywood.

FORMER BRITISH COLONIES

British colonial authorities were concerned to protect African filmgoers from films made for Western audiences, fearing that they would be misinterpreted. But they appreciated film as an educational medium. In 1935, Major L. A. Notcutt directed the *Bantu Educational Cinema Experiment* in Tanganyika. This short-lived unit produced its films on agriculture, hygiene, and folklore entirely in Africa, including film processing and editing. For the first time, African staff was trained in film techniques. In 1939, the Colonial Film Unit was established in Nigeria to help build African support for Britain's war effort; eventually there were eight units located throughout the British colonies. In 1949, a film school was set up in the Gold Coast. When these British colonies became independent, they possessed both film equipment and trained personnel.

A popular hit of 1935, *Sanders of the River*, directed by Zoltan Korda, showed the relationship of a colonial official with Bosambo, a native chief. The American actor Paul Robeson (1898–1976) starred. The story was set in Nigeria, but it was actually filmed in London, with exteriors shot in Kenya and the Belgian Congo. (Jomo Kenyatta, who later became Kenya's first president, had a bit part.) Robeson also appeared in a 1937 Gaumont-British production of *King Solomon's Mines*, based on H. Rider Haggard's (1856–1925) historical fantasy. This story was filmed repeatedly, and in various parts of Africa. The spectacular American version, made in 1950 by MGM, involved its crew in a 12,000-mile journey through Tanganyika, Uganda, Kenya, and the Belgian Congo, accompanied by refrigerated trucks carrying the film stock.

Independent Kenya built up its communications infrastructure in the 1970s, and Nairobi became a center of television production and of satellite distribution. Blessed with wild animals and scenery, in addition to film crews, Kenya became a favored location for Hollywood. *Out of Africa* (1985) was filmed at Isak Dinesen's meticulously restored coffee plantation in the highlands, with the Kenyan novelist Meja Mwangi (b. 1948) serving as assistant director to Sidney Pollack (b. 1934).

Ghana's first president, Kwame Nkrumah, understood the importance of film for cultural and political ends. But state-funded production trailed off as equipment aged and was not replaced. Ghanaian entrepreneurs took up the slack, and the first truly free cinema in Africa was born. The Hollywood-trained playwright and musician Kwah Ansah (b. 1941) set up his own companies to produce commercials and feature films. *Love Brewed in an African Pot* (1980) was a critique of arranged marriage, and *Heritage Africa* (1987) was the poignant tale of Quincy Arthur Bosomfield, a former martinet in the colonial administration, who received a talking-to by his ancestral spirit and went back to being Kwesi Atta Bosomefi, to his family's relief. In the 1990s, theatres disappeared from most African cities as video distribution replaced film. A vibrant Ghanaian video industry sprang up and was soon producing dozens of features a year.

Nigeria, with its population of 125,000,000, is the largest market in Africa, and the Nigerian diaspora is important as well. The preeminent Hausa-language filmmaker was Adamu Alhaji Alilu (b. 1936), who made a film about Shehu Omar in 1977, the Hausa religious leader, and another in 1979 about Kanta of Kebbi, a medieval hero of the Songhay wars. In the south of the country, Ola Balogun (b. 1945) was for many years the most prolific Yoruba-language filmmaker; for about a decade he churned out a film a year, alternating hits and misses. The hits were *Ajani Ogun* (1976), a musical comedy, made with Duro Lapido (1931–1978) and Ade "Love" Afolayan (d. 1996), stars of the Yoruba theater; *Ija Ominira* (1977), with the same group; this was the first Nigerian film to recoup its cost within a year; *Aiye* (1979), with Hubert Ogunde (b. 1916); and *Orun Mooru* (1982), with Moses Olaiya Adejumo ("Baba Sala"). In the 1990s, Nollywood was born in Lagos; as video replaced film, the director Tunde Kelani (b. 1948) has never used any other format. *Saworoide* (1999) and *Agogo Eewo* (2002), his Yoruba village dramas, were veiled critiques of Nigerian politics. *Thunderbolt* (2001) showed the conflicts in a marriage between an Igbo woman and a Yoruba man. In *The Campus Queen* (2002), presidents of rival social clubs at the university fight over the dishy heroine, in an aspirational drama replete with cars and big houses. Indeed, the wide range of cultures and classes depicted in Nigerian films is striking; they range from the working-class dad in Tade Ogidan's *Owo-Blow* (1997), to desperate housewives in Lancelot Imasuen's (b. 1971) *Emotional Crack* (2003), and posh London businessmen in Zina Saro-Wiwa's *Hello Nigeria!* (2004). Distributed on inexpensive DVDs, Nigerian films outsell Hollywood in Nigeria, and reach the remotest parts of Africa and beyond.

FRANCOPHONE AFRICA

The first French films of Africans date from 1895, when a scientist made motion studies of West Africans from Senegal at a colonial exposition in Paris. In 1926, Léon Poirier's (1884–1968) *La Croisière noire* celebrated the Citroën expedition that started in Algeria, crossed French West Africa and the Belgian Congo, and ended up in Madagascar. Julien Duvivier's (1896–1967) *Pépé le Moko* was filmed in the Algiers Casbah in 1936. In 1946, an unemployed French civil engineer, Jean Rouch, floated down the Niger River in a canoe with two friends and a Bell and Howell 16-millimeter camera, stopping occasionally to send dispatches to Agence France-Presse. This was the beginning of a career that catalyzed the film genre of *cinéma-vérité* (with *Chronique d'un été*, 1960), and came to define the field of visual anthropology. Rouch wrote and filmed prolifically on Songhay religion. His wartime experience, during which time he built roads across the interior, impelled Rouch to study the new African religions that were appearing in the cities of the west coast. The most famous, or infamous, of the resulting films was *Les maîtres fous* (1953), about the Hauka cult in Ghana. The intensity of Hauka ritual, and the cruelty of the way it depicted both African and European culture, deeply shocked most viewers. Rouch drew encouragement from the fact that Africans and Europeans equally shared in the offense. Outside of an avant-garde following, his work was greeted with hostility from Africans, and incomprehension from almost everyone else. He made a series of fictional films that dealt in humorous ways with topics such as migrant labor (*Jaguar*, 1957), global business (*Petit à petit*, 1968), avian flu (*Cocorico*, 1974), and drought (*Madame L'Eau*, 1992). However prescient, these films had less critical impact than Rouch's highly emotional psychodrama, *Moi, un noir* (1957). Starring Oumarou Ganda (1935–1981) as a disillusioned Vietnam veteran eking out a living in Côte d'Ivoire, it was named one of the ten best films in history by Cahiers du Cinéma.

The first dramatic film by a black African director was Paulin Soumanou Vieyra's (1925–1987) 1955 *Afrique sur Seine*, which was filmed in Paris while Vieyra was a film student. Vieyra became Africa's first film historian, and wrote the first biography of Ousmane Sembène, who is revered as the father of African film. Born in the Casamance area of Senegal, Sembène served with the French armed forces, joined the labor movement, worked as a longshoreman in Marseilles, and wrote politically-themed novels in French. In 1962–1963, he studied filmmaking in Moscow in order to present his work to a wide African audience. His first feature, *La noire de...* (*Black Girl*, 1966), filmed on the French Riviera and in Dakar, established his reputation as a cultural figure. Based on a true account of the suicide of a desperate African maid in France, the film provoked strong opinions, pro and con, at its festival screening in Cannes.

Sembène returned to Senegal and embarked on a trilogy of social-realist films, *Mandabi* (1968),

Xala (1974), and *Guelwaar* (1992), depicting his characters—often with biting humor—struggling against illiteracy, bureaucracy, corruption, intolerance, impotence, sexual oppression, and international aid. From *Mandabi* onward, Sembène's films were made using African languages, predominantly Wolof. In 1971, Sembène returned to his home province to direct *Emitaï*, depicting the resistance of Jola villagers during World War II. This film became part of a second trilogy on historical themes that included *Ceddo* (1976) and *Camp de Thiaroye* (1988). More somber than the social-realist films, these works dealt with religion, slavery, and ethnic strife, and depicted shocking massacres. In 2004, Sembène turned his attention to the international cause célèbre of genital cutting; his film on this subject, *Moolaadé*, was intended for the widest possible audience. Sembène remains optimistic about African cinema, which, he maintains, employs an original film language, distinct from the rest of the world.

A generation of filmmakers born in the 1940s and 1950s followed Sembène's lead, striving both for high standards and a steady stream of production. Gaston Kaboré (b. 1951) of Burkina Faso made films set in the Burkinabe countryside (*Wend Kuuni*, 1982). Aiming for a broader audience, S. Pierre Yameogo (b. 1955) made comedies out of the complexities of city life: *Silmande* (1998) showed the predicament of Lebanese merchants, whereas *Moi et mon blanc* (*Me and My White Pal*, 2003) set the antics two appealing slackers against the petit bourgeois backdrop of their families in Paris and Ouagadougou. Mweze Dieudonné Ngangura (b. 1950) made the hugely popular *La vie est belle* in Kinshasa in 1987, starring Papa Wemba, before decamping for Brussels along with the rest of the Congolese film industry.

Safi Faye (b. 1943), a Senegalese anthropologist who acted in Rouch's *Petit à petit*, was the only woman filmmaker of this generation; she made several fiction films and also turned her camera on white women and immigrant restaurants in Paris in *As Women See It* and *Ambassades nourricières* (both 1980). Souleymane Cissé (b. 1940) of Mali had a particularly interesting career, making ambitious films while bobbing and weaving to avoid censorship. *Baara* (1978) dealt pointedly with labor problems; *Finye* (1982) showed military repression and intergenerational conflict in an African city (actually Bamako). For his next film, the apocalyptic *Yeelen* (*Brightness*, 1987), Cissé retreated into the safer long ago and far away of esoteric Bambara and Dogon spirituality. In *Waati* (*Time*, 1995), Cissé worked on a Pan-African scale. Lavishly filmed in South, West, and North Africa, with dialogue in seven languages, *Waati* told the story of a young girl's exile, personal growth, and return.

The greatest artistic talent of this generation was the Senegalese Djibril Diop-Mambety (1945–1998), whose early comic promise (*Contras City*, 1968; *Touki Bouki*, 1973) matured in his *Tales of Little People* trilogy, incomplete at the time of his death. *Le franc* (1994) and *La petite vendeuse de soleil* (*The Little Girl who Sold the Sun*, 1999) transfigured the hard reality of life in Dakar. Diop-Mambety also adapted Friedrich Dürrenmatt's (1921–1990) play, *The Visit*, as a Wolof-language film (*Hyenas*, 1992). In the words of Mahen Bonetti (b. 1956), Diop-Mambety moved beyond documenting Africa's victimization toward envisioning the continent's recovery.

The generation of filmmakers born since independence has already shown that it can follow on Diop-Mambety's achievement. The Cameroonian Jean-Pierre Bekolo (b. 1966), having warmed up with gender-bending mockery of traditions in *Quartier Mozart* (1992), was asked in 1995 to make a film to celebrate the centennial of Lumière's cinematograph. The result was *Aristotle's Plot*, in which followers of Schwarzenegger and Sembène, marooned in a dusty South African ghost town, duked it out for control of the town's derelict theater, Cinema Africa. Bekolo followed this cerebral satire with *Les saignantes* (*The Bloodettes*, 2005), a glossy hybrid of action, horror, comedy, pornography, and science fiction. Two delectable femmes fatales, Majolie and Chouchou, used ingenious means to rid their futuristic African country of its corrupt and lecherous powerful men. The reactions of viewers to this film, although both strong and polarized, had nothing to do with its being African. Thus, one can fairly say that by 2005, African Cinema had arrived, and that it is now Cinema.

See also **Media: Cinema; Nkrumah, Francis Nwia Kofi; Paton, Alan; Photography; Popular Culture; Rouch, Jean; Sembène, Ousmane; Theater.**

BIBLIOGRAPHY

"African Film Festival." Available from http://www.africanfilmny.org.

Bonetti, Mahen, and Prerana Reddy. *Through African Eyes: Dialogues with the Directors.* New York: African Film Festival, 2003.

Les Cinémas d'Afrique: Dictionnaire. Paris: Karthala/ATM, 2000.

"Documentary Educational Resources." Available from http://www.der.org.

"Festival Panafricain du Cinéma et de la Television de Ouagadougou." Available from http://www.fespaco.bf.

"International Movie Database." Available from http://www.IMDb.com.

Phakathi, Dumisani, and Xoliswa Sithole, "The Mere Fact of Me Is Political." In *Through African Eyes: Dialogues with the Directors*, ed. Mahen Bonetti and Prerana Reddy. New York: African Film Festival, 2003.

Rouch, Jean. *Cine-Ethnography*, ed. and trans. Steven Feld. Minneapolis: University of Minnesota Press, 2003.

"Sithengi Film and Television Market." Available from http://www.sithengi.co.za.

Tomaselli, Keyan, and Hopeton S. Dunn, eds. *Media, Democracy and Renewal in Southern Africa.* Colorado Springs, Colorado: International Academic Publishers, 2001.

Ukadike, Nwachukwu Frank. *Questioning African Cinema: Conversations with Filmmakers.* Minneapolis: University of Minnesota Press, 2002.

EMILIE DE BRIGARD

FOOD

This entry includes the following articles:
SUPPLIES AND DISTRIBUTION
NUTRITION
MARKETING
PREPARATION AND CUISINES

SUPPLIES AND DISTRIBUTION

Africa's production ecologies are extremely varied, from arid desert regions to deep rainforest, from pastoral savannas to intensive hill terraces and rice paddies. The social organization of food supply from this productive base has varied from localized self-provisioning of communities to centrally administered state distribution and extensive market networks covering large regions. This complex and regionally specific mix of methods, crops, and distribution strategies can best be presented briefly as a history of the ways in which producers and consumers have been linked to each other.

PRECOLONIAL PERIOD

Africa's precolonial food economy has often been depicted as a subsistence economy, implying that the staple foods—yams, cassava, sorghum, rice, millet, banana-plantain, maize, teff (in Ethiopia), groundnuts, melon seed—passed along the intimate pathways of kinship and dependence rather than through markets or state-managed distribution channels. In this model, small communities produced to meet all their own needs: staples from the farm; protein from hunting, fishing, and small-animal husbandry (goats, sheep, and poultry); vegetables and fruit from cultivation and gathering; and very importantly, although not strictly speaking in the food economy, herbs for medical uses and all kinds of raw materials for artisanship. The economic unit managing this self-provisioning was typically much larger than the individual family, encompassing members of a kinship group, dependents, and in some places slaves. Even urban populations such as the Asante city of Kumasi could be largely supplied through the networks of dependence.

Although there is some basis to this depiction, a picture of food supply through networks of dependence within autarchic communities would be misleading for several reasons. Conditions of transport certainly militated strongly against moving heavy and perishable staple crops over long distances, but people were mobile. Seasonally, or in time of crisis, people moved to food sources rather than the food being moved to the people.

The nature of seasonal and famine foods and supply networks in Africa's past is a continuing frontier of research. New work on hunger, for example in Malawi, suggests that there were complex rhythms of daily, seasonal, and interannual supply as conditions fluctuated. Surpluses of some crops were stored for long periods. Some specialized local populations regularly exchanged goods: the hunters of the forest exchanged meat for cultivated staples with the farmers in the equatorial region; herders traded milk products and meat for grain with farmers throughout the pastoral belts. Long-distance trade and exchange were extensive

for specialty and preservable items (dried fish, smoked meat, honey, kola, tobacco, shea butter, ingredients for brewing, and—perhaps most importantly—salt). And even though food staples may not have been extensively marketed for local consumption, new cultigens and their corresponding production and preparation techniques diffused rapidly across ecological and ethnic lines where conditions proved propitious.

The variety of the Africa diet has been substantially enriched from outside the continent: by plantain and groundnuts from Asia around the turn of the first millennium; and throughout the centuries of the Atlantic trade, new cultigens such as cassava, maize, cocoyam and tomatoes, and new varieties of tropical fruit tree such mango, spread from the Americas and the Caribbean throughout the continent. A book series entitled *Lost Crops of Africa* documents a range of food ingredients far beyond the commonly mentioned staples, and is a reminder that wild flora and fauna remained crucial sources of variety and security in food systems up until the end of the twentieth century.

In a few areas staple foods did enter market or administrative channels in substantial amounts: Merchants served the great trading cities of the Sahel from the Middle Ages; markets served the Yoruba city-states from very early on; the Muslim famine-control system of *zakkat* taxes and redistribution in the Hausa city-states was in place from at least the late eighteenth century; there were the tax system of Addis Ababa, Samori Touré's tribute system to support his army, the Dyula traders in the west African Sahel, and slave plantations along the east coast to support an active maritime trade in the nineteenth century. Many of these regional distribution systems were nonmarket; they depended on slave labor or requisitions and tribute payments. Only in a few, such as the Yoruba and Igbo local market systems of Nigeria, were there regular food markets for local consumption.

Markets and prices for food seem to have become institutionalized through trade in other, more valuable items. Currencies have a long and complex history in Africa, but purchase of food was not their primary use. The port cities for the slave trade developed provisioning of boats. It was probably through supplying the passing caravans of hundreds of porters during the growth of legitimate trade after abolition that villages became accustomed to producing food staples for money. Given this variety and mobility, research on the social aspects of food distribution seems increasingly to confirm the suspicion that precolonial hunger and famine was precipitated by politicosocial predations and failures rather than by natural catastrophes such droughts, locusts, savanna fires, or flood.

COLONIAL PERIOD

The growth of colonial urban centers in the twentieth century entailed far-reaching changes as new consumer populations developed: government employees, miners, prisoners, military garrisons, and a growing number of urbanites. Since colonies depended on cheap provisioning for workers, in many places food supply was managed by the state. Roads and railways opened up rural areas as sources of urban food. In the settler economies of Central and southern Africa, colonial governments favored the development of a white large farm sector, while African small farmers were systematically marginalized from the opportunities provided by growing urban demand. In some places, such as the mining town of Kimberley, growth was so rapid that imports from the American plains, brought in by boat and rail, played a part in urban supply from the beginning of the twentieth century. In general, however, food imports were only intermittently important before the 1970s. The salient contest for the urban market was between large and small farmers. Only in parts of West Africa, where food markets and long distance trade had a deep history, was the food sector left more or less to the small operator to respond to increased demand.

The challenge of the rapid urban growth that set in after 1945 was also met from internal sources, but through policies that varied from place to place. In the French colonies the state managed cooperatives (the provident societies) and metropolitan investment funds (Fonds d'Investissement pour le Développement Économique et Social; FIDES) that functioned in food supply as well as other in commodities. In eastern and southern Africa, settler farms were somewhat augmented by African smallholder production. In the Portuguese colonies of Angola and Mozambique, forced labor and requisitions continued well into the 1960s. In British West Africa the indigenous market systems expanded regional wholesale centers, developed associations of traders and transporters,

and institutionalized a larger long-distance cattle trade from the northern savannas to the meat markets of the southern forest. This was the era of the famous "mammy-lorries," the slogan-painted Bedford trucks that were imported after the war and revolutionized transport in the rural areas. Even in these areas, however, colonial policy deeply affected the food economy: farmland was devoted to export crops; *zakkat* was monetized without instituting alternative famine relief. In drought-susceptible areas such as Northern Nigeria, food shortages were acutely felt among the rural population.

The colonial state also started to foster research on the food economy. Centers such as Moor Plantation in Nigeria and the Rhodes-Livingstone Institute in Rhodesia studied production. Research institutes in Ghana and Uganda collected the first urban standard of living data. Production and nutrition studies were promoted. In part this was due to the application in the international context of nutrition and food-distribution principles that had been developed in Europe in the 1930s and during wartime, and in part it was a response to concerns about urban stability during the political unrest of the independence era.

POSTINDEPENDENCE

After independence, from 1957 (in Ghana) onward, the markets for African-produced food products greatly expanded everywhere. Smallholder production was encouraged by populist policies, by rising prices for primary products, and by unusually favorable rainfall patterns from the mid-1950s and to the mid-1960s. In eastern and southern Africa, markets were still regulated and managed by parastatal organizations, whereas in western Africa local commodity chains and transport networks flourished. Until about 1970, the official picture of African food supply was that—apart from in wartime nutritional catastrophes such as Biafra—it worked quite well. There had been intermittent famines, such as in Nyasaland in 1949, and some studies warned of future problems if productivity levels and population growth were not brought into a more promising relationship, but there was no general sense of Africa as in danger of serious chronic shortages.

Then in the 1970s political instability, climate change, a surge in population growth, a shift in the rural-urban terms of trade, and then the economic instabilities of structural adjustment all started to undermine conditions in smallholder production. The highly publicized food failures in the Sahelian and Ethiopian droughts were severe shocks to this image, and brought into play foreign food aid, food-for-work, and other development interventions that both expanded food imports and increased the pressure for innovations in African production.

In some places, innovation has taken the form of more food production for export, such as fresh green beans for Europe. Success in developing African staple equivalents to the Green Revolution crops in Asia and the Americas, however, has been elusive and a sense of urgency has picked up. Some new crops, such as hybrid corns, have been widely introduced before their full effect on disease ecologies can be assessed. Others, such as crops genetically engineered for resistance and productivity, are being tried out amid enormous controversy in scientific and activist circles.

The greatest failures of the late twentieth century—and there were many—were due to the wars and disturbances that rippled out from Cold War politics. Large areas of potentially cultivable land in Angola, in Mozambique, and on the Ethiopia-Eritrea border was land-mined; seed varietal stock was destroyed during the Rwanda genocide; dozens of rice varieties may have been lost in the Liberian and Sierra Leonian civil wars; whole populations of Eastern Congo were unable to sustain productive economies and markets at all and succumbed to famine and disease in untold numbers; sudden price changes as a result of economic policies and the worldwide collapse of primary commodity prices after 1980 produced devastating local penuries; and those who escaped the famines produced in the countryside were fed on an emergency basis by imported rations in refugee camps. Markets in much of West Africa still supply both employment and provisions, but widening inequity is leaving some populations more destitute than ever before.

At the beginning of the twenty-first century—postcolonial and post–Cold War—several systems of food distribution coexist in Africa. As in the past, most landholding rural populations still provide some of their own staples. Small towns are fed by

hinterland markets. Cities depend on both large and small farms, usually marketing through different channels. Women still play a central role in food processing and local trade, while transport and long-distance trade tends to be controlled by men. The state continues to intervene in many places to control the price of the major urban-consumer staples such as imported rice and wheat, which in turn is related to export policies of large producers such as the United States and the European Economic Community. Africa's large refugee-camp populations are fed by the international organizations and food aid in kind.

The formal institutions of a modern food market, however, remain relatively limited: Outside of the settler economies there are no commodity exchanges or trade in futures for locally grown crops; there is little or no regulation of food quality; food preservation is mainly artisanal; consumer price indices, where they are accurate, suggest quite wide regional differences and seasonal fluctuations; and there are few official rubrics for cross-border trade, especially in western and equatorial regions. Political and currency instability have led to "smuggling" in food on a newly expanded scale, which in turn has exacerbated antagonisms between the state and the food sector that in many places have simmered since the 1970s.

What remains remarkable, however, has been the response in one form or another to the unprecedented growth in cities in the last two decades of the century. A key component of resilience, innovation, and also danger has been the expansion of two major New World crops, cassava and maize, and augmentation by imports of others, rice and wheat (for bread). International scientific attention is being applied increasingly to these crops, for better and worse, while others fall into the "lost crops" category.

In the beginning of the twenty-first century, there is on the one hand a sense of the fragility and complexity of food supply in the face of the multiple challenges of turbulent politics, incoherent formal structures, and ecological hazards, including population growth. On the other hand, there are other developments—such as great expansion of food processing by Nigerian women in the environs of one of Africa's largest cities, Ibadan, and the effort to revive crop variety—that build for the future on the basis of past strengths.

See also **Agriculture; Aid and Development; Famine; Kumasi; Plants; Production Strategies; Refugees; Touré, Samori.**

BIBLIOGRAPHY

Bryceson, Deborah Fahy. *Liberalizing Tanzania's Food Trade: Public and Private Faces of Urban Marketing Policy, 1939–1988.* London: UNRISD, 1993.

Freidberg, Susanne. *French Beans and Food Scares. Culture and Commerce in an Anxious Age.* New York: Oxford University Press, 2004.

Guyer, Jane I., ed. *Feeding African Cities: Studies in Regional Social History.* Bloomington: Indiana University Press, 1987.

Jones, William O. *Manioc in Africa.* Stanford, CA: Stanford University Press, 1959.

Jones, William O. *Marketing Staple Food Crops in Tropical Africa.* Ithaca, NY: Cornell University Press, 1972.

Lawson, Rowena. "Engels Law and Its Application to Ghana." *Economic Bulletin* 7, no. 1 (1962): 34–46.

Mandala, Elias C. *The End of Chidyerano: A History of Food and Everyday Life in Malawi 1860–2004.* Westport, CT: Greenwood Press, 2005.

McCann, James. Maize and Grace. *Africa's Encounters with a New World Crop 1500–2000.* Cambridge, MA: Harvard University Press, 2005.

Raikes, Philip. *Modernizing Hunger: Famine, Food Surplus, and Farm Policy in the EEC and Africa.* London: James Currey, 1988.

Vaughan, Megan. *The Story of an African Famine: Gender and Famine in Twentieth-Century Malawi.* Cambridge, U.K.: Cambridge University Press, 1987.

Vennetier, Pierre, ed. *La croissance urbaine dans les pays tropicaux: Dix études sur l'approvisionnement des villes.* Travaux et documents de géographie tropicale, no. 7. Paris: Centre National de la Recherche Scientifique, 1972.

Watts, Michael J. *Silent Violence: Food, Famine, and Peasantry in Northern Nigeria.* Berkeley: University of California Press, 1983.

JANE I. GUYER

NUTRITION

Nutrition plays a crucial role in attaining development, as reflected in the eight Millennium Development Goals of the United Nations. Numerous deficiency diseases continue to persist in Africa, however, especially in the rural areas, as a result of chronic and seasonal food shortages and essential nutrients missing from the daily diet. A new commitment has emerged, among African leaders as well as the international community, to ensure food and nutrition security in Africa by 2020.

NUTRITION ISSUES

The state of food and nutrition of sub-Saharan Africa is as diverse as the geographical and political situation of the region, ranging from relative food abundance to food shortages. Despite strenuous efforts of governments to combat malnutrition, a number of persistent nutritional issues exist. Ensuring food security, access by all people at all times to enough food for an active and healthy life, is a basic condition for a stable society. In sub-Saharan Africa the estimated undernourished population is 33 percent, and it ranges from 9 percent in Nigeria to 73 percent in Eritrea, according to 2004 statistics. Protein-energy malnutrition (PEM) has diminished, but it still remains a serious public health issue. Infants and young children are most susceptible to PEM, a lethal form of malnutrition. The Ghanaian word for protein deficiency is *kwashiorkor.*

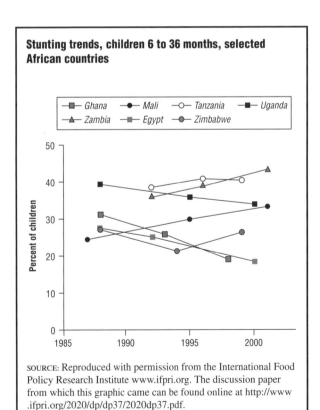

SOURCE: Reproduced with permission from the International Food Policy Research Institute www.ifpri.org. The discussion paper from which this graphic came can be found online at http://www.ifpri.org/2020/dp/dp37/2020dp37.pdf.

Figure 1.

An estimated 200 million people on the continent are undernourished. The result is that more than a third of African children are stunted in their growth and must face a range of physical and cognitive challenges not faced by their better-fed peers (see Figure 1). According to an International Food Policy Research Institute (IFPRI) study by Benson in 2004, the continuing human costs of inadequate food and nutrition are enormous, and the aggregate costs of food and nutrition security at the national level impose a heavy burden on efforts to foster sustainable growth and improved general welfare.

Food insecurity often coincides with micronutrient deficiencies: in particular, a lack of vitamin A, impairing vision; iodine, jeopardizing mental health; iron, causing anemia; and zinc, stunting growth and reducing resistance to infectious diseases (see Figures 2a and 2b).

Vitamin A deficiency causes blindness and renders children susceptible to common childhood diseases and illnesses such as measles, diarrhea, malaria, and pneumonia. A better understanding of the public health importance of vitamin A deficiency began in the 1980s. Community-based studies showed that the rates of morbidity and mortality from diarrhea and respiratory infections were higher in children with mild xerophthalmia than in children without any vitamin-A-deficiency-related eye signs. In the absence of effective policies and programs, an estimated 42 percent of African children from birth to 59 months of age (over 43 million children) are at risk of vitamin A deficiency.

Insufficient supplies of safe drinking water in rural areas and urban slums also adversely affect the nutritional status of the population. Even when enough food is available, rampant diarrhea caused by contaminated drinking water may prevent proper

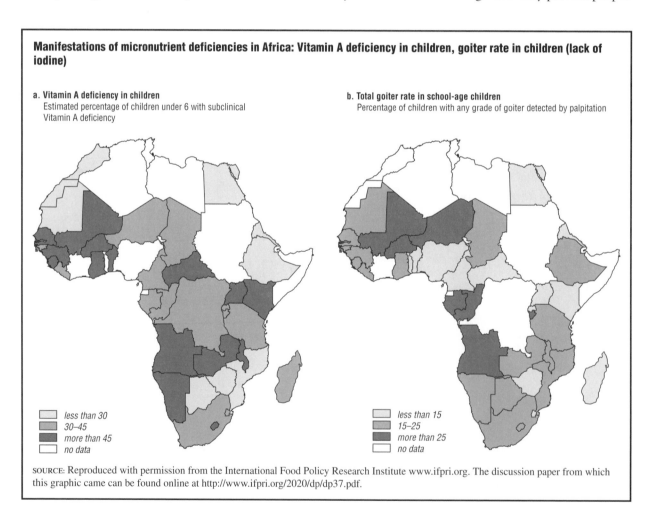

Manifestations of micronutrient deficiencies in Africa: Vitamin A deficiency in children, goiter rate in children (lack of iodine)

a. Vitamin A deficiency in children
Estimated percentage of children under 6 with subclinical Vitamin A deficiency

less than 30
30–45
more than 45
no data

b. Total goiter rate in school-age children
Percentage of children with any grade of goiter detected by palpitation

less than 15
15–25
more than 25
no data

SOURCE: Reproduced with permission from the International Food Policy Research Institute www.ifpri.org. The discussion paper from which this graphic came can be found online at http://www.ifpri.org/2020/dp/dp37.pdf.

Figure 2.

absorption of nutrients, cause dehydration, and result in premature death.

In its early stages, the African HIV/AIDS pandemic was predominantly an urban problem; by the early 2000s the disease had moved to rural areas. HIV/AIDS is undoing decades of rural development and eroding food security. The loss of productive members of society severely affects a household's capacity to produce and buy food, and the deceased heads of households leave behind their elderly relatives and orphaned children. The pandemic also affects the administrative and professional cadres in the government and the economy. A study in Zimbabwe found that maize production fell by 61 percent in households that suffered an AIDS-related death (FAO 2003). The role of nutrition in HIV infection is complex; malnutrition contributes to the progression of the disease, but HIV infection itself also leads to malnutrition. HIV-positive persons have markedly higher energy needs (10 percent higher in asymptomatic HIV patients, and up to 30 percent higher in symptomatic patients). People living with HIV/AIDS need to eat considerably more food to fight the illness, counter weight loss, and extend a productive life. Vitamin A supplementation of HIV-positive children appears to help reduce the incidence, severity, and mortality of diarrhea, one of the leading causes of child mortality. Vitamin A supplements given to HIV-positive pregnant women in the third trimester of pregnancy may reduce incidence of low birth weight and premature births.

In urban areas malnutrition exists in both its forms of under- and overnutrition. The urban slums are characterized by nutritional deficiencies, while among the emerging middle classes, obesity and cardiovascular diseases have become concerns.

AFRICAN FOOD CULTURE

Food insecurity is a persistent problem; however, as the Guinean writer Tierno Monénembo stated in 2002, the image of Africa is focused too much on hunger. People also eat, and they eat well. African food culture is dynamic and through the ages has incorporated new foods into the farming system and diet. It has been estimated that 50 percent of the major food crops originated from the Americas, including cassava, maize, and tomatoes, as well as condiments such as red peppers (*Capsicum*). Crop diversification in Africa started with the Portuguese expansion in the fifteenth century. In many African countries, population growth has caused a shift from indigenous food crops such as sorghum, millet, and yam to cassava and maize. Cassava and maize contribute to food security at household levels, as these foods yield more food energy per acre but are less nutritious than yam, sorghum, and millet. Major gifts from the African food culture to the rest of the world are the red palm oil (*Elaeis guineensis*) and coffee. The red palm oil is the richest known source of biologically active carotenoids and is used in food-based approaches to reduce Vitamin A deficiency, not only in Africa but also in tropical Asia and Central America. West Africa has developed its own indigenous rice, very suitable for dry rice farming (*Oryza glaberrima*).

The main component of a meal in sub-Saharan Africa is a starchy porridge made of tubers or cereals with a stew as an accompaniment. The stew contains cooked vegetables and, depending on the socioeconomic situation of the household, pieces of meat or fish. The starchy porridge combined with a traditional stew (rich in proteins and vitamins) is an excellent basis for a healthy diet. African cuisine is basically a rural cuisine, derived from a rural way of life. This does not mean that dishes are simple, however. West Africa in particular is known for its great variety of elaborated fermented maize dishes. Maize arrived in the sixteenth century at the West African coast.

Food avoidances or food taboos do exist. From a nutritional point of view, it is useful to distinguish between permanent and temporary food avoidances. Muslim Africans avoid pork. Other foods may be avoided when they are closely associated with the history of someone's clan—for instance, certain kinds of antelope or dogs. The pastoral peoples have an aversion to fish, based on their contempt for the way of life in fishing communities. Besides these permanent avoidances, some foods are not consumed during certain critical periods of the life cycle, such as infancy, during pregnancy and lactation, or when suffering from various diseases. Pregnant women may avoid green leafy vegetables and eggs, fearful that these foods may harm the unborn child. Temporary food avoidances can deprive vulnerable groups of nutritious foods, in particular proteins and micronutrients.

Women play a crucial role in the supply and distribution of food at the household level. Household members will not always eat together from the same dish. Sometimes three eating groups can be observed: men, women, and very young children, with the older children under guidance of an elder sister. Foods are not always equally distributed, and men often get the best part of the food, in particular a good piece of the meat or fish. This is not necessarily detrimental to the children's nutrition, but it becomes a point of concern when an insufficient amount of food is available. Data on intra-household food allocation is scanty. A 1988 study in Malawi by Erica F. Wheeler and F. M. Abdullah indicates a priority in food allocation to adult males over adult females. Boys and girls were equally fed, however; girls had better access to snack foods because boys were often absent during the day.

In rural areas infants are breastfed for about a year after birth. The most crucial period is the introduction of weaning foods. At six months, or even later, the infant will receive a soft carbohydrate pap while breastfeeding continues. Poor hygienic conditions and the low protein content of traditional weaning foods cause malnutrition. Mothers in the rural areas and urban slums cannot afford to buy imported, industrially processed infant foods. Governments in several countries have set up small-scale food industries to produce affordable weaning foods based on available local materials.

In addition to infants, the nutritional status of pregnant women has to be taken into account. In the Gambia, locally produced biscuits providing 1,017 calories and 22 grams of protein per day for pregnant women reduced low-birth-weight prevalence by 39 percent, increased birth weight by 136 grams, and reduced infant mortality by about 40 percent, according to a 1997 study by S. M. Ceesay and colleagues.

BEVERAGES

Sub-Saharan Africa has an age-old beer tradition. This explains the presence of flourishing modern breweries producing bottled and draft beer in most African countries. Beer brewing from sorghum, millet, banana, or maize is traditionally a women's business. Apart from being a pleasant beverage, beer plays an indispensable role in ceremonies. In savanna Africa, when assistance is required from neighbors in harvesting crops, beer has to be provided as compensation. In the forest zones, the sugary sap of certain palm trees is drained and left to ferment into palm-wine. In the nineteenth century in West Africa, people began distilling palm-wine together with sugar into a kind of gin, known in Ghana as *akpeteshi*, illicit at first but now produced under license. Ethiopia is well known for its mead, a wine fermented from honey. Alcohol abuse is becoming a serious problem in the fast-growing urban areas and the mining districts of southern Africa. Coffee is indigenous to the highlands of the Horn of Africa. In Ethiopia, coffee preparation is an important ceremony. The beverage tea with sweetened condensed milk and sugar was introduced by the British at the end of the nineteenth century, and in the twenty-first century it remains a preferred drink in the Anglophone countries. In the Francophone countries, coffee with milk (*café au lait*), often combined with a piece of bread, is quite popular.

GEOGRAPHICAL ASPECTS OF FOOD

The foods and beverages that people consume vary by geographic region. In the humid forest zones, the core of the diet is based on roots and tubers supplemented with maize, whereas in the drier zones, cereals form the staple of the diet. Cereals have a higher protein content than do roots and tubers. The daily diet of the dryer Sahelian zone of West Africa contains on an average fewer than 2,200 calories, compared with almost 2,500 calories in the more humid coastal zone. Conversely, protein deficiency is common in the coastal zone and less in the Sahelian zone. Milk and dairy products are absent in the humid tropics, because the climate is unfavorable for cattle, while milk and dairy are part of the cattle-owning nomads and farmers of the Sahel and East African highlands. The importance of insects as a food source (proteins and fat) is underestimated. Edible insects include caterpillars, flying ants, and locusts. Taxonomically, these insects are closely related to shrimp, considered to be a delicacy in Europe and North America. The main fuel for cooking in most households is wood, supplemented with crop residues and sometimes animal dung. Present population growth surpasses the natural increase in wood. Less available wood causes women to spend more time collecting fuel and eliminates healthy foods that require lengthy cooking times, such as protein-rich beans.

SEASONALITY

In zones with a distinct wet and dry season, only one harvest is possible, and households have to build up food stocks. Important social events such as weddings take place after the harvest, when there is plenty of food. Well known is the so-called hungry season, occurring at the beginning of the wet season when food stocks are getting depleted before the new harvest. In northern Bénin, the body weight of rural women fluctuates between seasons. In the pre-harvest period, a temporarily undernourished population must work hard in order to prepare the fields for the coming new agricultural season, causing weight loss. Moreover, according to Michael A. Little and colleagues, during the wet season, several East African pastoral populations consume milk as a percentage of total energy intake at a rate twice as high or higher than that consumed during the dry season. Seasonal weight losses and chronic under-nutrition are intimately linked.

Households have developed a coping mechanism for dealing with seasonal shortages by reducing the number of meals a day, serving smaller portions, and diluting the meals with water. When the shortages last longer, nonconventional foods will be collected in the fields, known as hungry foods. In the savanna zones, it is not unusual for groups of women to search for seeds of wild grasses, tubers, and wild fruits, which would not be consumed otherwise. When the seasonal shortage lasts longer, households may return to an extremely hazardous measure: the consumption of seeds reserved for sowing and planting. Households will also incur debt to buy food. Rules of hospitality, such as offering food and local beer, will disappear at such times.

URBANIZATION AND CHANGING DIETS

In the years to come, the urban factor in African society will increase considerably; in 2000, 38 percent of the population lived in cities and that percentage was expected to increase to 55 percent by 2030, according to a United Nations study. The urban diet is influenced by the richness of food culture of various ethnic groups, the colonial past, and the effects of modern globalization. There has been a shift since the mid-1970s in dietary patterns from coarse grains to nontraditional grains, mainly wheat (bread) and rice. New food habits originally developed in the cities are likely to spread into the rural areas. Urban food habits include a greater demand for imported foods such as wheat (bread, biscuits, and other products based on wheat, such as pasta), canned products (meat, fish, and condensed milk), hard liquor, bottled beer, and soft drinks. The success of local production of bottled soft drinks and beer is striking, but alcohol abuse has become an issue. Small-scale food industries serving the urban consumer are on the increase, but there is a need for governmental support such as credit facilities and technological input from research institutions. As in other parts of the world, the African urbanite is receptive to new foods that are quick and easy to prepare and that require less fuel to cook. Urban food habits comprise basically three components: (1) rural culinary traditions at the household level; (2) effects from working conditions and people with different ethnic backgrounds; and (3) opportunities for more individual food choices. In the city, one can select food outside the household without having to share expensive foods with others.

A striking response to the urban way of life is the rise of street foods in the informal sector. Street foods are ready-to-eat foods and beverages prepared and sold by vendors and hawkers. Women play a major role in the urban food supply, and street foods are largely the domain of women. Men sell the already prepared meat and meat snacks. Street foods are well suited to the urban way of life: they are ready to eat, which means they save time and fuel, and they are often less expensive than the same food prepared at home. From a nutritional point of view, street foods are an indispensable element of the urban diet. In Nigeria the contribution of street foods to the daily energy requirements among adolescents is 24.8 percent, of protein 52.1 percent, and of vitamin A 59.8 percent, according to a 1995 study by Oguntona and Kanye.

For poor households, it can be more economical to purchase daily street foods than to prepare food at home. A point of concern remains the hygiene and quality of the street foods. In essence, the street foods in Africa do not differ significantly from the fast foods of the industrialized countries. Modern fast-food restaurants and supermarkets are prevalent in major African cities. The fast-food restaurant Mr. Biggs has 130 locations in Nigeria and two in Ghana. Similar in concept to McDonald's, it specializes in meat pies. McDonald's opened its first restaurant in Africa in 1995; as of 2006, South Africa had eighty-nine McDonald's locations. Fast food can be considered the modern but more expensive successor of street food; compared to street food, its importance in the urban diet was limited until the early twenty-first century.

Urban agriculture in vacant small lots, along major roads, and in family gardens plays a role in urban food supply. City dwellers grow vegetables and own livestock such as poultry and pigs. In Accra, Ghana, for instance, 90 percent of the city's fresh vegetables consumed by residents are produced within in the city. Urban agriculture faces a number of constraints, however. Polluted water used for watering contaminates vegetables. Animals kept in crowded henhouses and pigpens close to human settlements may cause public health risks. Just as with street foods, urban authorities have become more inclined to protect food safety by means of food control and extension work directed to food producers and vendors.

Compared to country folk, urbanites have a more varied diet, with a greater assortment of fruits and vegetables, more meat, and less seasonal variation. The situation may differ from country to country, however, and between those living in the shantytowns and in the planned urban districts. In African cities, new kinds of food are continually being incorporated into the local food culture. The modern urban diet remains nevertheless in essence an African diet. But the modern urban lifestyle leads to less physical activity, a greater consumption of fat and less fiber, more street foods, and less home-prepared food, resulting in an increase in obesity, diabetes, cardiovascular diseases, and other diet-related diseases. The South African Health Review indicates a level of obesity of 8 percent among men and 30 percent for women, according to 2001 statistics. Epidemiological data from two African countries suggests that the prevalence of diabetes has increased. In Dar-es-Salaam and in South African townships, 5 to 8 percent of the urban adult population is affected by diabetes.

NUTRITION POLICY

Several countries in sub-Saharan Africa have formulated food and nutrition policies and implemented nutrition programs with varying degrees of success. Many countries still have insufficient human, economic, and administrative infrastructures to establish accessible health services and to ensure access for the population to the food needed for a healthy life. Strengthening of the infrastructure will allow the flow of resources to support nutrition activities at the local level.

According to the IFPRI study of 2004, a sustained broad-based economic growth is necessary to end hunger and micronutrient deficiencies by 2050. The region must attain a 3.5 percent of average growth rate in per-capita growth domestic product (GDP). In the preceding decade, however, only half a dozen countries had growth rates above that level. Access to international markets, both within Africa and globally, is a basic necessary condition.

Nongovernmental organizations acting within the context of national food and nutrition policy will enhance the effectiveness of nutrition interventions. Examples are vitamin A supplementation programs, food-based approaches such as home gardens (vegetables), iodized salt, low-cost weaning foods, and nutrition education at health and agricultural centers. Nutrition interventions based on vitamin A supplements are very promising. A sustained policy and large-scale vitamin A supplementation has the potential of a 25 percent reduction in mortality of children from birth to fifty-nine months of age, according to a 2005 study by Victor Aguayo and Shawn Barker. Incorporating HIV prevention, nutritional care for people living with HIV/AIDS, and AIDS mitigation measures into food security and nutrition programs can help to reduce the spread and impact of HIV/AIDS. In the years to come, several African countries must confront the double burden of nutrition: undernutrition in poor rural areas and the urban slums and overnutrition in the rising middle classes.

See also **Agriculture; Ecosystems; Family; Famine; Household and Domestic Groups; Livestock: Domestication.**

BIBLIOGRAPHY

Aguayo, Victor, and Shawn K. Baker. "Vitamin A Deficiency and Child Survival in sub-Saharan Africa: A Reappraisal of Challenges and Opportunities." *Food and Nutrition Bulletin* 26 (2005): 348–355.

Ategbo, Eric-Alain, et al. "Resting Metabolic Rate and Work Efficiency of Rural Beninese Women: A 2-Y Longitudinal Study." *American Journal Clinical Nutrition* 61, (1995): 466–472.

Benson, Todd. *Africa's Food and Nutrition Security Situation; Where Are We and How Did We Get There?* 2020 Discussion Paper no 37. Washington, IFPRI, 2004.

Ceesay, S. M., et al. "Effects on Birth Weight and Perinatal Mortality of Maternal Dietary Supplements in Rural Gambia: 5 Year Randomized Control Trial." *British Medical Journal* 315 (1997): 786–790.

Coutsoudis, Anna. "The Relationship between Vitamin A Deficiency and HIV Infection: Review of Scientific Studies." *Food and Nutrition Bulletin* 22 (2001): 235–247.

Ferro-Luzzi, Anna, et al. "Seasonal Undernutrition in Rural Ethiopia: Magnitude, Correlates, and Functional Significance." *Food and Nutrition Bulletin* 23 (2002): 227–228.

Food and Agriculture Organization of the UN. *The State of Food Insecurity of the World.* Rome: Author, 1999–2004.

Food and Agriculture Organization of the UN. Committee on World Food Security. *The Impact of HIV/AIDS on Food Security.* Rome: Author, 2001.

Honfoga, B., and G. J. M. van den Boom. "Food Consumption Patterns in Central West Africa, 1961–2000, and Challenges to Combat Malnutrition." *Food and Nutrition Bulletin* 24 (2003): 167–182.

International Food Policy Research Institute. *Assuring Food and Nutrition Security in Africa by 2020. Proceedings of an All-African Conference. Kampala, Uganda. April 1–3, 2004.* Washington: Author, 2004.

International Obesity Task Force. *The South African Health Review 2000.* Available from http://www.iotf.org.

Kennedy, Elleen, and Thomas Reardon. "Shift to Non-Traditional Grains in the Diet of East and West Africa: The Role of Women's Opportunity Cost of Time." *Food Policy* 19 (1994): 45–56.

Kydd, Jonathan; Andrew Dorward; and Megan Vaughan. *The Humanitarian Crisis in Southern Africa: Malawi.* Southern Africa Regional Poverty Network. Available from http://www.sarpon.org.

Little, Michael A. "Milk Consumption in African Pastoral Peoples." In *Drinking: Anthropological Approaches,* ed. Igor de Garine and Valery de Garine. New York: Oxford, 2001.

Monénembo, Tierno. "Gombo sec et huile de palme." *Courier International, Hors-Série, Toute le monde à table* 21 (2002): 58–59.

Oguntona, C. R. B., and O. Kanye. "Contribution of Street Foods to Nutrient Intakes by Nigerian adolescents." *Nutrition and Health* 10 (1995): 165–171.

Trèche, Serge, et al. "Les petites industries alimentaires en Afrique de L'Ouest: Situation actuelle et perspectives pour une nutrition saine." *Cahiers Agricultures* 11 (2002): 343–348.

Unwin, Nigel, et al. "Noncommunicable Diseases in Sub-Saharan Africa: Where Do They Feature in the Health Research Agenda?" *Bulletin of the World Health Organization* 79, (2001): 947–953.

Van Huis, Arnold. "Insects as Food in Sub-Saharan Africa." *Insect Science and Its Application* 32 (2003): 163–185.

Van't Riet, Hilde, et al. "The Role of Street Foods in the Dietary Pattern of Two Low-Income Groups in Nairobi." *European Journal of Clinical Nutrition* 55 (2001): 562–569.

Wheeler, Erica, and F. M. Abdullah. "Food Allocation within the Family: Response to Fluctuating Food Supply and Food Needs." In *Coping with Uncertainty in Food Supply,* ed. I. de Garine and G. A. Harrison. New York: Oxford University Press, 1988.

ADEL P. DEN HARTOG

MARKETING

Food marketing involves all steps needed to get produce from the farm gate to the consumer. It includes the exchange of products in the process of assembly, transportation, storage, processing and distribution. These stages may follow a sequence of spot markets or can be organized through alternative forms of vertical coordination, such as flexible supply contracts.

Well-known features of food marketing in sub-Saharan Africa are crowded market places including bazaars and small shops. Most markets in rural areas operate periodically. Many of these markets lack basic facilities such as roofs, fences and storehouses. Some of these markets have developed into rural assembly markets, where farmers and assembling traders sell to wholesalers and retailers coming from urban centers. The market acts not only as a center of commerce but also as a center of social interaction, where people come to meet relatives, friends, or a suitor. Chiefs may settle minor court cases, and local authorities may use the opportunity to make announcements.

When a village evolves into a city, the marketplace tends to become operational more often and, eventually, throughout the week. Specialized retail markets for meat or fish may develop and geographical separation of wholesale and retail trade may be established. Wholesale markets may supply not only retailers operating at markets within the city but also those from other urban centers and rural areas. Produce can also be sold to owners of retail shops and supermarkets. The latter are more and more found in the various quarters of the cities. The assortment of these shops varies with the purchasing power of the customers in their quarter.

ACTORS IN FOOD MARKETING CHANNELS

A food marketing channel is defined as a set of intermediaries involved in the process of making food available for consumption. Since the deregulation of the food trade in sub-Saharan Africa, private traders are the pivot of all food marketing channels. They take title to the produce and, consequently, bear the risks with respect to depreciation of the value of their commercial stock. They may add value by sorting the products into grades, processing, packaging, transport and storage.

In the wholesale segment of food marketing channels, one finds small-scale wholesalers serving local and regional markets, and large-scale wholesalers serving interregional and international markets. Particularly among wholesale traders, a significant share of the transactions may take place outside spot markets. Wholesalers may bypass rural assembly markets and go straight to the villages to deal with either farmers or local purchasing agents. Purchasing agents work on behalf of a wholesaler and receive a commission whereas assembling traders buy independently to supply different wholesalers. The use of agents by wholesalers gives rise to vertical coordination in the marketing channel. Another form of vertical coordination involves wholesalers who buy from farmers through flexible supply contracts. We are dealing with a so-called interlinked market when such a contract (usually an oral agreement) also includes the provision of credit or inputs. This means that the wholesaler receives the right to purchase the harvest in exchange for the delivery of seeds or fertilizer.

Vertical coordination becomes vertical integration when wholesalers produce food crops themselves. Examples of vertical integration are cattle wholesalers who own ranches and slaughterhouses, or dairy cooperatives that run milk factories and retail outlets. Coordination and integration are quite common in the export marketing of fresh food. Many horticultural exporters own large-scale farms, buy also from contract farmers (outgrowers), and supply on contract to foreign importers or retail chains.

Other facilitators in the marketing channel than purchasing agents are transporters, brokers, auctioneers, and credit suppliers. Brokers sell on behalf of wholesalers in large urban markets. They attract customers and negotiate prices and work on a commission basis. Auctions are not very common in the food trade. Nevertheless, auctioneers of cereals operate in some rural assembly markets, auctioneers of vegetables and fruits work in some urban wholesale markets, and cattle auctioneers are to be found in rural cattle auction rings. Commercial banks are reluctant to loan money to traders, due to the trade risks involved and lack of collateral. The main credit suppliers in the food trade are moneylenders, friends, and savings and credit associations. Interest rates can be high due to the opportunity costs of capital and the risks involved.

Many petty traders of food commodities are women trying to earn a little money by selling a household's surplus or small quantities of purchased produce. Trade is one of the rare opportunities for them to obtain cash. Remuneration per hour is low, but it is attractive if no other opportunities exist. Farm revenues are often controlled by the husband, whereas trade revenues may generate a personal income for the women and afford them some autonomy. It has been generally observed that the percentage of male traders is higher when the scale of operation is larger. However, some women managed to accumulate significant amounts of capital. The "Mama-Benz" is a well-known phenomenon in West African societies.

FOOD MARKETS AND TRADE POLICIES

Opinions on the functioning of food markets have shifted in the course of time. During the 1960s market failures got the attention in line with the desire of newly independent states to plan their economic development. Marketing boards were established to regulate and facilitate trade, and to prevent or correct market failures. Regrettably, many of the so-called market failures have been followed by government failures resulting in low prices for farmers and inefficiencies in the organization of trade (1970s). In the 1980s, structural adjustment programs (SAPs) were implemented to address government failures. The role of food marketing boards and state-led food marketing cooperatives has diminished as a result of the liberalization policies.

Food marketing is a policy domain of interest because it is crucial for food security. In most countries of sub-Saharan Africa, the growth in food production has regularly lagged behind population growth. At the same time, a burgeoning urban population has enlarged the market for food. Despite the adjustment policies, marketing or transaction costs remained relatively high and resulted in a large gap between consumer and producer prices. High food marketing costs are the outcome of seasonality of supplies, high transport costs, high storage costs and market imperfections.

Food prices reflect seasonality in production and storage costs. Basically, storage of surpluses reduces the problem of shortages during the lean seasons and limits seasonal price fluctuations. Storage is not an option for farmers when they have to sell their surplus immediately after the harvest to settle debts. For petty traders the opportunity costs of capital are high, and they tend to specialize in buying and selling (spatial arbitrage) rather than storage (temporal arbitrage). Traders are interested in temporal arbitrage on the condition that the seasonal price differences reflect the costs of capital and other storage costs. Uncertainty with regard to future supply is a major element in the cost structure. Spatial arbitrage is driven by price information and the transport costs between surplus and deficit areas. Inadequate infrastructure and deficient market information services inflate these costs in many sub-Saharan countries.

Problems in food marketing in sub-Saharan Africa are often related to various degrees of market imperfection such as: missing markets, thin markets, incomplete markets, interlinked markets, entry barriers, and imperfect information. In the case of missing markets there is no market at all: A supplier is not able to find a buyer or a buyer is not able to find a supplier. If markets are thin, marketing costs are inflated as economies of scale are difficult to realize due to limited supply and/or demand. In incomplete markets a deficient set of commercial services is offered (e.g., credit, transport or storage facilities are lacking). In interlinked markets, the negotiating power of farmers may be seriously affected.

If up-to-date price information is lacking, the market is said to lack transparency. Market transparency can be improved by publishing current prices. Transparency is fostered by standardization of qualities and selling units, but this is, apart from purchases by supermarkets, still not common for fresh food. Traders may sell by the piece, heap, bundle, tin or sack, rather than by weight. Selling units may appear to have standard sizes (for example, a butter cup), but traders tend to manipulate the content to their advantage. In addition to lack of transparency, high entry barriers may impede the performance of food markets. Access to capital was cited above as a possible entry barrier. Informal entry barriers may be erected by market parties in order to gain a larger part of the value added. Another key entry barrier is experience (knowledge). It takes time to develop the market skills needed to compete successfully.

CHALLENGES IN FOOD MARKETING

The relatively high costs of food marketing in sub-Saharan Africa affect food security because it affects both producer and consumer prices. The challenge is to minimize these marketing costs. Governments should facilitate conditions that improve the functioning of the market while fostering both flexibility and competition. No blueprint exists because solutions tend to be product-, region-, and time-specific.

See also **Aid and Development; Capitalism and Commercialization; Gender; Production Strategies; Transportation.**

BIBLIOGRAPHY

Abbott, John. *Agricultural and Food Marketing in Developing Countries.* Wallingford, U.K.: C.A.B. International in association with the Technical Centre for Agricultural and Rural Co-operation ACP-EEC, 1993.

Dijkstra, Tjalling. *Trading the Fruits of the Land: Horticultural Marketing Channels in Kenya.* Aldershot, U.K.: Ashgate, 1997.

Jaffee, Steven, and John Morton. *Marketing Africa's High-Value Foods: Comparative Experiences of an Emergent Private Sector.* Dubuque, IA: Kendall/Hunt, 1995.

Jones, Stephen. *Food Markets in Developing Countries: What Do We Know?* Oxford: Oxford University Press, 1996.

Kherallah, Mylène, et al. *Reforming Agricultural Markets in Africa.* Baltimore: Johns Hopkins University Press, 2002.

Van der Laan, Laurens, Tjalling Dijkstra, and Aad van Tilburg. *Agricultural Marketing in Tropical Africa.* Aldershot, U.K.: Ashgate, 1999.

CLEMENS H. M. LUTZ
REVISED BY AAD VAN TILBURG

PREPARATION AND CUISINES

Compared with Asia and Europe, Africa is a sparsely populated continent. Nevertheless, within its territory a vast range of means of food production, distribution, storage, and consumption is found. City dwellers, dependent for their food on sophisticated industrial technologies, supported by capitalist financing and complex intercontinental networks of distribution, coexist with communities that depend directly on natural resources for their survival. Hunters and gatherers, pastoralists, and many agriculturists exploit these resources by using techniques accessible to all, with differences only according to age and sex. Survival in such societies often depends on access to large expanses of relatively uninhabited land. The population of Africa is growing rapidly, thus increasing the pressures on land, while new political boundaries create barriers to the free movement of populations. Modern political processes are usually accompanied by modern techniques of warfare, which are increasingly destructive and wreak havoc with local food supplies. Among other factors, the combination of expanding population, preindustrial technologies of food production, as well as climatic change have led to a serious food shortage in Africa.

By the beginning of the twenty-first century, famine in diverse parts of Africa had been much publicized. Some of the worst situations were broadcast to a worldwide audience through televised documentation. More often than not, as in the Sudan or Rwanda, famine occurred in the aftermath of warfare. The devastation of war routinely interrupts communication, and with that the distribution of food. However, in much less publicized cases, malnutrition may also result gradually, from less catastrophic events. Drought, as in northern Ghana, may lead to increased cultivation of less nutritious crops that need less water. This is the case of maize, which is displacing the indigenous cultivation of millet and sorghum in northern Ghana.

Maize porridge was rarely eaten in the 1960s but by the 1980s it had become common. Millet and sorghum contain far more protein than maize but require a longer growing season. Another source of pressure on local food resources can result, paradoxically, from improved transport, which in northern Ghana has made it possible to export cattle, sheep, and goats south to the large cities of the coast and the rain forest. Though the farming population in areas formerly remote from the capitalist market economy of the south now receive cash, the depletion of animal resources means that the farmer's diet deteriorates. Warfare in northern Ghana during the 1980s and 1990s also disrupted the local distribution of food, and resources like cattle were sold to buy weapons, which entered the region as part of an international trade.

The indigenous food supply, however, has always been affected by an international market and international political processes. Africa has long been part of intercontinental trade networks involving foodstuffs. From antiquity, salt mined in North Africa was traded for West African gold, and in some parts was of equal value to gold by weight. Kola nuts grown in the rain forests of western Africa are still traded throughout the Islamic world, where they are considered an acceptable stimulant. Food crops from the New World (maize, cassava, chili peppers, tomatoes, cacao) have been in Africa since the sixteenth century. Since British colonization, industrially prepared foods—canned, bottled, and factory made—have been introduced from Europe and America. These were first consumed by European colonizers or settlers, but some, like tinned fish, corned beef, tea, and sugar, are now staples of the indigenous diet in both rural and urban areas. Imported food crops like maize and cassava have tended to displace indigenous sorghum, millet, and yams where these imported plants provide better yields than indigenous ones.

Famine and extreme food shortages in some parts of the continent have made Africa the recipient of food aid through a great diversity of international agencies. This aid is often directed to countries torn by civil war. However, at the same time other African countries export luxury foods (cocoa, coffee, tropical fruits, exotic vegetables) to Europe and North America, and some have begun their own industrial food production. African agriculture is changing rapidly as fertilizers, animal traction, mechanization, and complex irrigation schemes are introduced. Although contemporary commercial and technological developments serve to modernize agriculture in Africa, they also create new problems. In many African countries the cultivation of export crops has displaced cultivation for local consumption, and countries that were once self-sufficient are now importing staple foods.

GENERAL FEATURES

In all human society food has both a nutritional and a symbolic value. Eating, like all human biological needs, is both universal and differently conditioned by custom. The production, storage, distribution, and preparation of food may vary, depending on environmental conditions over which humans have no control, but they also depend on technical knowledge and human choice. Rules vary greatly from one society to another, but all human groups regulate the consumption of food and drink to satisfy social as well as biological needs. Certain substances, through the circumstances surrounding their consumption or the prohibitions with which they are associated, acquire intense symbolic value. However, rules about food and drink are not rigid over time, and diets change, as do the values attached to them.

Given major geographical, political, and economic variation as well as the enormous cultural diversity of Africa's population, the substances consumed differ from one region to another and the symbolic uses of food must be infinitely varied. Urban populations of immigrant origins and indigenous people who have cultivated the cosmopolitan tastes of international urban life may use the same food in the same way as similar populations elsewhere. However, in most of Africa, local conditions and cultural patterns are distinctive. Settled agricultural populations consume different foods than do pastoralists or hunters and gatherers. Because Africa's population is mostly agricultural, some general features of food cultivation, preparation, and use that are common to many agricultural areas are dealt with below.

In most African agriculture the cultivation of food crops is limited by rainfall, which determines the areas appropriate for different cereal crops and tubers. Given the absence of modern networks of food distribution, of a widespread system of refrigerated storage, and of any large-scale production of preserved or synthetic foodstuffs, regional differences in food supply correspond to major differences in diet and cuisine. Further reference to specific cases is meant to illustrate rather than to typify the diversity of practice.

REGIONAL VARIATIONS

Ghana provides an example of marked regional variation within a relatively small territory. As one travels from the northern border south toward the coast, savanna gives way to rain forest that ends at a narrow coastal strip. In this space of five hundred miles, three clearly distinct zones follow one another. Millet and sorghum are basic crops in the northern savanna, and domestic animals include cattle, sheep, goats, domestic fowl, and guinea fowl. In the rain forest and on the coast, yams, cassava, and corn are staples. Small domestic animals are kept in both areas, but cattle do not survive in the rain forest because of the tsetse fly. In the northern savanna nuts from the shea tree (*Butyrospermum parkii*) are made into shea butter, which provides fat for cooking. The basic cooking fat in the forest region and the coast is oil pressed from the nuts of the oil palm (*Elaeis guineensis*). In the north the beer drunk at casual social gatherings and offered in libation at formal ritual occasions is made from millet with specially prepared yeast for fermentation. In the rain forest and on the coast the palm nut tree is tapped and the juice is fermented to make wine that is similarly used. In the savanna food grains are pounded and the resulting flour is boiled to make a cooked porridge. In the rain forest, tubers are boiled, then pounded to produce a sticky dough that is roughly the consistency of cooked porridge. The cumulative effect of very different-tasting cooking fats, different basic carbohydrate staples, and a different alcoholic drink within this relatively small territory is two very distinct regional cuisines. The differences in diet are assimilated to differences in language and culture, and become symbolic of contrasting regional identities.

CYCLE OF AGRICULTURAL PRODUCTION AND FOOD CONSUMPTION

The agricultural calendar of the Tallensi and neighboring peoples of the northern Ghana savanna, with its associated patterns of food consumption, illustrates conditions that are common where hoe agriculture is the basis of subsistence in rural Africa.

The climate of northern Ghana is divided between two well-marked seasons, the rains and the dry season. The rainy season lasts from April to October, and the dry season from November through March. In the rainy season agricultural activity reaches its peak. In the dry season there is much less agricultural work, but social and ceremonial activities become important. The Tallensi arrange marriages and major sacrifices as well as what we might call "commemorative" funerals (second funerals) during the early part of the dry season. Their neighbors, the Mamprusi, perform chiefly installation rituals at this time of year. Between November and February, immediately following the harvests, travel is relatively easy and food is abundant; therefore, the period is particularly appropriate for large social gatherings during which large-scale distributions of food occur.

By the end of the dry season, food is in short supply and people wait anxiously for the first rains. During this period, called "hunger," food is rationed in most households. Hunger foods (*dawa-dawa* [*Parkia filicordea*], pods, shea fruit, peanuts), eaten as a snack or a supplement at other times of the year, are among the few available foods. Similarly, small mammals like mice and voles, which children catch and eat the rest of the year, are eaten by adults. Many people are forced to sell fowl and livestock in order to buy grain. Livestock prices drop as grain prices rise. Wealthier Tallensi travel south, where livestock prices are higher and grain is available, to sell their livestock and to buy grain to resell and to feed themselves. Poorer households live for two or three days a week on vegetable soup, peanuts, and wild fruits, interspersed with a bowl of porridge once every three days. Crops that are drought resistant are particularly important. "Fonio" (*Digitaria exilis*, derived from the wild *Digitaria longiflora*) is cultivated from Cape Verde to Lake Chad and throughout the savanna region. It is drought resistant and can grow wild.

In the hunger season people visit relations in more fortunate areas to obtain food. The slight differences in climate within the area mean that planting and harvesting take place at slightly different times; some areas have better, and others worse,

harvests in a single year. These differences mean that hunger in one area may be somewhat alleviated by help from a neighboring area. In the late twentieth century, when food shortages have reached famine proportions, national government and nongovernmental organizations have intervened with food.

By the time the rains begin, the earth has baked hard. The first rains soften the earth, enabling farmers to clear and sow, and thus to begin the new cycle of production. This is the heaviest phase of agricultural labor. The first planting is of "early millet" and the vegetables women use to make the soup eaten with millet porridge. In the Mamprusi region, early millet should not be eaten in the home until certain rituals are performed by chiefs, but everywhere people on the farms eat millet as the heads begin to ripen. Women dry vegetables, and some meat and fish are kept in dried form to make the relish, soup, or sauce eaten with the cereal porridge. Until the first millet harvest, food is in extremely short supply.

In July early millet is harvested; hoeing, weeding, and planting of other crops continue. Poultry breeding begins. Both men and women own flocks of domestic fowl and guinea fowl; young boys are given poultry to raise as their first independent property, which can become an important source of wealth through careful management. By August cooperative and hired labor is being organized to harvest late millet. In September there are peanut harvests, and the harvesting of roots and vegetables begins. Hoeing and weeding of farms continues for the harvests of guinea corn, rice, root crops, and other vegetables, which occur in October. In November the late millet is harvested, along with cowpeas and bambara beans. As food becomes more plentiful, the price of grain falls and the price of livestock rises. Cooked food is cheap and plentiful in the market. Some late harvesters may still be short of food. Early millet becomes very expensive at the end of the harvest season, but other supplies are abundant and cheap in the market.

The marriage season begins at roughly the same time as the traditional Tallensi harvest festivals, and reaches its peak in December, at the same time as the commemorative "final funeral" ceremonies and the dedication of children to ancestor divinities and shrines. Chiefly installations are also organized for this season. At all of these ritual occasions very large quantities of food and beer are distributed and consumed. Animals are sacrificed to earth shrines and ancestors. It is the period of a maximum annual supply of meat and the season of the greatest consumption of beer. Beer is brewed from millet and is an important source of food. Women and children, who consume less meat than men under normal circumstances, should receive portions at this time.

Grain rationing begins again in January and February. This is the season for building and repairing houses, which require cutting grass and timber. Young men emigrate at this time, to find work in the south. By March the sporadic clearing of fields and hoeing have begun again; the laborers are mainly men, but women help with all other phases of the agricultural cycle and are particularly responsible for the cultivation of the vegetables and spices used in the soups and relishes that accompany the porridge. The rationing of grain since January means that grain is available for only one meal a day. Peanuts and cowpeas supplement the porridge, and women are trading for cereal supplies. Prices start to rise. By March people need food from abroad.

One consequence of the calendar of many agricultural peoples is that the period of hardest physical labor coincides with the period of greatest food shortage. There is no lack of excellent means of storage that enable people to keep food in perfect condition from one year to the next. People are by no means improvident, and they are well aware that food must be preserved for the hunger season. Nevertheless, they still consider that it is more important to consume large quantities of food in ritual expenditures immediately after the harvest than to store as much food as possible for the hunger season. This serves to emphasize how significant the ritual expenditure of food is, and how highly it is valued.

CUISINE

Though it should be eaten with soup in order to constitute a proper meal, throughout Africa the porridge or carbohydrate staple, rather than the soup, which may contain animal protein, is regarded as the true "food" without which no proper meal has been eaten; just as in Europe, bread has been regarded as "the staff of life." Famine or fasting consists in the absence of this basic ingredient of the diet. A list of translations for the words relating to the grains called millet shows the importance of this cereal. In the Buli language of the north Ghanaian savanna, barren millet, early millet, seed of early millet (used for sowing), germinated millet (used for beer), late millet, leaf of late millet, poisonous (black) millet, millet sprouts, threshed millet, upper part of early millet stalk, seed millet, millet beer, fried millet ball, millet cake, fried millet cake, millet chaff, millet gruel, millet porridge, millet stalk, upper part of late millet stalk, small piece of millet stalk, and split millet stalk are all known by distinct words. There are similar, if shorter, lists for guinea corn and sorghum.

In addition to the cultivated plants and the animals that provide food for agricultural communities, there are other vegetables, or delicacies like snails and special insects, that are much appreciated. Some of these, like particular species of snail in the rain forest, or a type of caterpillar that breeds in the savanna and tastes like shrimp, are abundant in particular seasons and particular places known to local people. In times of famine, local knowledge of wild foods and grasses is a significant resource.

FOOD PREPARATION IN THE HOUSEHOLD

Whatever may be the customary division of labor, women rather than men prepare and normally serve food in the home. In most rural areas women also fetch water and firewood. These tasks normally take much longer than the time required to cook and serve a meal. In much of Africa the staple carbohydrate food is prepared by using a long pestle and a standing mortar to pound the grain or tuber. Cereals are reduced to a flour and then boiled to make a thick porridge. Tubers (yam or cassava) are peeled and boiled, then pounded into a thick dough.

Meyer Fortes and S. L. Fortes describe the Tallensi housewife making porridge:

> She mixes some flour with cold water, stirring it to a thin paste with her hand.... When the water boils she pours the paste in, stirring all the while with her stirring-stick...until it thickens.... With a ladle she pours off about a third of the contents into the old calabash and puts it aside. She sprinkles a few handfuls of flour into the porridge in the pot, stirring it swiftly with her stick until it becomes quite thick. Every now and again she dips her hand into cold water and with a brisk movement sweeps the porridge adhering to the stick into the pot. The half-cooked contents of the

calabash is then added to the porridge and stirred again. When it is thick enough for the stick to stand in it the porridge is ready. The time taken to cook a pot full of porridge for 10 people is only about 10 minutes." (266)

Fortes and Fortes calculate that an adult man needs about a pound and a half of porridge to feel he has eaten well.

Tuber and cereal carbohydrates are served with a soup made from vegetables and, if possible, meat or fish. In some societies men are responsible for providing the carbohydrate staple and women provide the soup ingredients, which may be cultivated, collected from the bush, or bought at markets with the proceeds of trade. The relish or soup is classified as slippery or coarse; *ocro* (*Hibiscus esculentis*) soup typifies the first kind, which is more appreciated, and soups made of crushed peanuts and soup made of hibiscus leaves are examples of the coarse type. Women try to vary the soups, though seasonal factors influence what they prepare.

Meat is obtained through hunting in some areas, while in others large game animals are practically extinct. Hunting is usually an exclusively male activity, though both men and women may be involved in fishing. These pursuits are important in some societies for providing basic animal protein in the diet. However, in many societies meat is most commonly consumed in the context of the sacrifice of animals to ancestral and other deities. Although domestic animals are kept for food in northern Ghana, only guinea fowl are killed directly for cooking. The killing of animals is the province of men. Women do not normally kill any animal, even guinea fowl, which they own and may decide to kill for food. It is considered "unbecoming" among some peoples and is simply forbidden among others.

Red pepper and salt are essential for seasoning; ash of grasses or of early millet stalks may be used instead of salt. *Dawadawa* seed, from a wild tree, may be used either as seasoning or as a soup base. The soup is cooked until the meat falls apart and the vegetables have formed a homogeneous sauce. Slices of porridge are served into separate calabashes, or sauce is poured over a calabash of unsliced porridge. Shea butter is rubbed into each portion, and calabashes are distributed to groups of children and adults who eat together. A meal for ten people can be prepared in one hour.

FOOD AVOIDANCE

Within communities that share the same language and culture, individuals and groups may observe distinctive food avoidances. For example, among the Tallensi of northern Ghana, firstborn children in certain families do not eat the domestic fowl. Pregnant women should not eat honey. Bereaved persons, chiefs-elect before their installations, hunters before the hunt, homicides—in general, persons who are regarded as temporarily or permanently distinct from their peers—often observe specific food prohibitions. Members of different family groups are often distinguished by particular food prohibitions. These avoidances identify families as distinct in their origins from other families of the same wider society. Such avoidances often celebrate the experience of an important ancestor. For example, the royal clan of the Mamprusi people in northern Ghana do not eat red pigeon. They avoid it because, they say, in the distant past the red pigeon helped their ancestor win a particular battle.

In *The Web of Kinship Among the Tallensi* (1949), Meyer Fortes records the following myth, which explains why among certain Tallensi lineages firstborn children do not eat fowl:

> A fowl did a great service to our ancestor. He had a wife and many people came to her with slander about her husband trying to persuade her to leave him. This made her very unhappy. One day a broody hen, sitting in her grinding room (the room where she ground her millet to make the daily porridge), spoke to her and told her not to weep. The fowl said that when her husband returned from the farm she must prepare a drink of flour-water for him. The fowl said she would fly up and dash the calabash from his hand as he was about to drink. If the husband killed the fowl in anger, the woman would know that he was a wicked man and if he spared the fowl, she would know that people were slandering him maliciously. The woman did as the fowl suggested, and when the fowl interrupted the husband's drinking, far from being angry, the man merely said "this fowl is thirsty." Thus, the woman knew her husband was a good man and she stayed with him. She bore a daughter and then a son and the man declared that both these first-born children must not eat fowl. Later children could eat it, for if they too were prohibited who would consume the fowls which men sacrifice to the ancestors.

Other Tallensi food prohibitions, typical of those in the savanna region, include land tortoise, water tortoise, squirrel, snake, crocodile, and python. "Totemic" avoidances such as these are often linked, as with the Tallensi, to forms of social organization in which diverse descent groups are interrelated to constitute a single polity, yet the polity as a whole does not possess a set of specialized governmental institutions. Distinct food prohibitions serve to identify individuals with the wider political units of which the society is composed, either as members of particular groups or as different from others who share the same institutions.

FOOD SHARING

In the Domestic Group. Sharing of food within the family is, in all societies, a significant learning experience for young children. Thus, who divides the food, how it is served, and the etiquette of eating form an introduction to important ideas of proper behavior that are significant in many other social situations. In many rural, agricultural communities it is normal for meals to be taken separately by men and women. Boys and men of roughly the same age eat together while women eat with their daughters and small children of both sexes. Those eating together take their portion from a common receptacle, always using the right hand. In some polygynous households co-wives cook separately for their own children and send cooked food to the husband or household head, while in other polygynous communities women observe a rota system with one woman or a group of women cooking a common meal for an entire household. In matrilineal societies, where husbands and wives may live in different households, a wife may send cooked food daily from her house to her husband, who is living elsewhere. Such actions are usually matters of custom and not of individual choice. The cooking and distribution of food are consistent with other features of family organization, and relations of seniority, deference, avoidance, and joking familiarity are learned and expressed at mealtimes.

In a Ritual Context. Animal sacrifice is an element in the ancestor cults that are frequently an essential part of indigenous African social organization. Sacrifices involve the dedication of a live animal to a particular ancestor or set of ancestors, and the subsequent sharing of food, including the flesh of the sacrifice, among living members of a family group (lineage or clan) and the spirits of deceased members. Food offerings are also made to the ancestors in the form of libations (beer, palm wine, water with flour); in some areas kola is

offered. Portions of the flesh and blood of sacrificed animals are placed on shrines as tokens of the creature, which is normally consumed by the living members of the congregation.

Audrey I. Richards notes in *Hunger and Work in a Savage Tribe* (2004) that in some regions of southern Africa the headman divides the slain animal (killed either in the hunt or for sacrifice) so that the elder brother gets a hind leg; the younger brother, a foreleg; and the two eldest sons get the other two limbs. Heart and kidneys go to the wives; relatives-in-law get the rump and tail; and the maternal uncle receives a special part of the loins. She mentions that in eastern Africa, goats, sheep, and oxen are divided according to separate sets of rules.

According to Richards:

> The whole configuration of the community during the division of an animal carcass shows clearly how the family functions as a food-consuming unit. The larger kinship group assembles to get its share of the rarer and more perishable meat food; but each share so divided must be re-allotted within each household according to the rules of precedence of sex and age within that smaller group. The family is the centre of a wider scheme of food distribution, and authority within the family itself depends … on the possession and control of food." (81)

In western Africa, sacrifices to ancestral divinities are performed at regular intervals not only by kin groups tracing common origin from the same ancestors, but also by other kinds of congregations that share dependence on common groups of royal ancestors. Thus, for example, if the king of the former Mamprusi kingdom in northern Ghana sacrifices a cow or sheep to his ancestors, members of the court receive parts of the sacrificed animal according to their office. Warriors receive the chest, drummers receive the feet, the king's speaker and his kin receive the throat, the king's wives receive the back and the waist, and princes receive meat from the legs.

In central Ghana the calendrical feast of Adae is the occasion of an even more elaborate distribution at sacrifices to the royal ancestors of the Okere-Guan people of Akuapem. A sacrifice recorded by Michelle Gilbert was divided as follows. The left foreleg, breast, and thigh were placed before a black stool, the ancestral shrine. Tiny pieces of meat were thrown into the courtyard of the stool house for the ancestors. Small pieces were given to the elders. The queen mother received a thigh and intestines, and the king received a thigh, the backbone, and the loins. A divisional chief received part of the stomach, and elders received half a thigh. Another divisional chief received half a thigh and the heart; the elder who poured the libation received the breast; the senior stool carrier received the neck and part of the left foreleg; other stool carriers received a foreleg and part of the stomach; the former executioner received the head; a chief of the executioner lineage received the back of the neck; the hornblowers' chief received the jaw; drummers received the large intestines; a jester-herald received the lungs; and sword and whisk carriers received the feet. The elder who blesses marriages, the state, and the king, and who pours libation, received part of the large intestine. The child, taster of the king's food and considered to be the "twin" of the king's soul, received the liver.

CONSUMABLES USED IN EXCHANGE

Kola nuts, millet beer, and palm wine are typical of the foods that not only are consumed and shared with divinities but also are formally exchanged among the living. Millet beer and palm wine require elaborate production, and kola nuts, though they are not cooked, as beer is, or fermented, as palm wine is, must be elaborately stored in order to be transported and traded. All of these items, which are offered and consumed in ceremonies of sacrifice, are used in the rituals that establish legitimate marriage.

Another valuable item used in this context is cattle. Among cattle-keeping pastoralists or semi-pastoralists, but also among many African agricultural peoples, cattle serve as bridewealth, to be given by the husband's kin to the wife's kin. Normally, the societies using cattle as bridewealth are patrilineal. The numbers of cattle vary, but the principle of exchange is common. Where kola nuts, beer, or palm wine is used, the inherent value of the substance is perhaps less important than the fact that its consumption by a wide range of persons makes them witnesses to the transaction establishing an ongoing set of obligations between groups of kin linked by the marriage. Although cattle are not consumed immediately, as are kola, millet beer, and palm wine, the distribution of rights over cattle that are received as bridewealth has a similar effect, in that a large number of persons are party to the transaction and witnesses to the marriage. Similarly, in transactions between subjects and chiefs, or landowners and land-users, or where knowledge is to be transmitted from a senior person to a novice, consumable items like kola and palm wine are given by the supplicant as a token of respect.

See also **Agriculture; Aid and Development; Climate; Economic History; Famine; Forestry; Healing and Health Care; Plants; Production Strategies; Queens and Queen Mothers; Religion and Ritual.**

BIBLIOGRAPHY

Arhem, Kaj. *Milk, Meat, and Blood: Diet as a Cultural Code among the Pastoral Maasai.* Uppsala, Sweden: African Studies Program, Department of Cultural Anthropology, University of Uppsala, 1987.

Aunger, Robert. "Are Food Avoidances Maladaptive in the Ituri Forest of Zaire?" *Journal of Anthropological Research* 50 (1994): 277–310.

Aunger, Robert. "Acculturation and the Persistence of Indigenous Food Avoidances in the Ituri Forest." *Human Organization* 55 (1996): 206–218.

Bovill, E. W. *The Golden Trade of the Moors: West African Kingdoms in the Fourteenth Century*, 2nd edition. Princeton, NJ: Marcus Weiner Publishers, 1995.

Drucker-Brown, Susan. "The Court and the Kola Nut: Wooing and Witnessing in Northern Ghana." *Journal of the Royal Anthropological Institute* 1, no. 1 (1995): 129–145.

Fortes, Meyer. *The Web of Kinship among the Tallensi.* London: Oxford University Press, 1949.

Fortes, Meyer, and S. L. Fortes. "Food in the Domestic Economy of the Tallensi." *Africa* 9 (1936): 237–276.

Gilbert, Michelle. "The Person of the King: Ritual and Power in a Ghanaian State." In *The Rituals of Royalty: Power and Ceremonial in Traditional Societies*, ed. David Cannadine and Simon Price. Cambridge, U.K.: Cambridge University Press, 1987.

Goody, J. R., and E. N. Goody. "Changing Patterns of Consumption in Ghana." In *Cambridge Anthropology* 18, no. 3 (1995).

Hartog, A. P. den. *A Selected Bibliography on Food Habits (Socio-Economic Aspects of Food and Nutrition)*. Part 1, *Tropical Africa.* Rome: The Organization, 1974.

Karp, Ivan. "Beer Drinking and Social Experience in an African Society." In *Explorations in African Systems of Thought*, ed. Ivan Karp and Charles S. Bird. Bloomington: Indiana University Press, 1980.

Kröger, Franz. *Buli-English Dictionary.* Munster, Germany: Lit, 1992.

Lewicki, Tadeusz. *West African Food in the Middle Ages: According to Arabic Sources.* Cambridge, U.K.: Cambridge University Press, 1974.

Richards, Audrey Isabel. *Land, Labor, and Diet in Northern Rhodesia: An Economic Study of the Bemba Tribe.* New York: Oxford University Press, 1960.

Richards, Audrey Isabel. *Hunger and Work in a Savage Tribe: A Functional Study of Nutrition among the Southern Bantu.* New York: Routledge, 2004.

Walker, Phillip L., and Barry S. Hewlett. "Dental Health, Diet, and Social Status among Central African Foragers and Farmers." *American Anthropologist* 92 (1990): 383–398.

SUSAN DRUCKER-BROWN

FOREIGN AID. *See* Aid and Development.

FORESTRY

This entry includes the following articles:
OVERVIEW
CENTRAL AFRICA
EASTERN AFRICA
SOUTHERN AFRICA
WESTERN AFRICA

OVERVIEW

Before and since the Rio Earth Summit in 1992, forests and related issues were and continue to be a major concern within the Africa Region and provide many points of contention. Although the governments at Rio de Janeiro were unable to agree on a forest convention, they did agree on a set of nonbinding forest principles under a chapter in Agenda 21 (the official document emanating from the Summit) relating to combating deforestation. The chapter includes the implementation of national forest programs as a tool for addressing deforestation and forest degradation and for achieving sustainable forest management.

The forest and wildlife sectors in Africa face closely linked, if not identical, challenges. Some wild animals live entirely in forests whereas the plains herds commonly found in East and Southern Africa need and make use of the scattered wooded areas and even isolated trees. People depend on forest areas for fruits, firewood, medicines, and, most especially in Equatorial Africa, for bushmeat.

The extent of forest cover varies from one subregion of Africa to another. The African Forestry and Wildlife Commission 2004 states that North Africa has the lowest forest cover of the continent, with most of it either on the Mediterranean coast or in central and southern Sudan. Eastern Africa has most cover in Uganda, with that in Kenya, Eritrea, Ethiopia, Mauritius, and the Seychelles being sparser. The coastal areas of West Africa hold most of this region's forests with the interior either covered in thorny bush or open savanna woodlands. Central Africa has the most forest of all, which covers large areas of Gabon, Cameroon, Rwanda, Burundi, Democratic Republic of the Congo, and Central African Republic. Southern Africa has minimal forested areas, if the high-quality plantations in parts of South Africa, Swaziland, and Zimbabwe are discounted.

Much wildlife depends on forests and other vegetation for its habitat, and its dependence varies from one subregion to the other. In eastern and Southern Africa, wildlife resources form the basis for the tourism sector that is a major source of foreign exchange and employment. In West Africa, the wildlife sector provides bushmeat, an important source of protein. The Food and Agriculture Organization of the United Nations (FAO) has estimated that bushmeat generated about US$110–160 million for Gabon, Togo, Bénin, and Nigeria. Bushmeat production is a major component of the economies of equatorial African countries such as Cameroon, Gabon, Central African Republic, Democratic Republic of the Congo, and Equatorial Guinea.

Africa has the richest and most diverse forest resources in the world. Unfortunately for conservation efforts, the destruction and misuse of this resource continue unabated. Specifically, forest loss has been largely a result of population pressure that at the same time has also reduced the carrying capacity of the forests. Forest resources are declining in many parts of Africa and will be unable in the future to meet the benefits expected by many communities; the destruction of the resource now impacts on climate, water supplies, and wildlife.

On the other hand, ecotourism benefits various African countries. Entrance fees, licenses, and concessions can generate substantial funds that may be used to support conservation and environmental management. In many African countries, tourist spending provides an income for local communities and creates employment opportunities, especially during the peak tourist seasons.

Forests and woodlands are valuable resources. The two provide more than 60 percent of the energy consumed in sub-Saharan Africa and 80 percent of house building materials. Giuseppe Topa (2005) notes that in nineteen African countries forest-related activities account for at least 10 percent of GDP while in some ten African countries, forest products amount to about 10 percent of the national trade.

CHALLENGES ON FOREST AND WILDLIFE SECTORS IN AFRICA

There are several challenges presented to the forest and wildlife sectors in Africa. First is pressure from other land users such as pastoralists and farmers. The latter become less numerous as rural populations move to the towns, but that movement means that fewer farmers have to grow more food to support the urban dwellers. Generally, big fields can be worked more efficiently than small, which implies more clearing of the bushes and trees that often mark boundaries. Second is the lack of good institutional frameworks that give local communities and the private sector a say in forest and wildlife management decisions. Local farmers and pastoralists are often unfairly accused of mismanagement by overgrazing or of slash and burn cultivation when they in fact have little if any say in land use. A third challenge is the low or poor management capacity of some forest users who now use outdated or inappropriate technology that results in waste and destruction, such as charcoal burning. There is evidence in northern Nigeria, Mali, and Niger that many communities manage their trees carefully and have long been aware of the need to do so. However, some scholars argue that it is unrealistic and irresponsible to give local communities responsibility for forests or wildlife when they have neither the resources nor the education to manage them. The fourth difficulty is that destructive traditional agricultural methods, such as shifting cultivation and honey collection, are unsustainable. However, in Mali there is widespread preservation of fruit-bearing tree species that are valuable for sale or for household consumption. Finally, there is a lack of political goodwill and the

presence of corruption in the sustainable exploitation and harvesting of natural resources in countries such as Liberia, Cameroon, and Democratic Republic of the Congo. Various studies confirm that little financial support is given to either forest or wildlife sectors, and the few projects funded by donors and other organizations are unsustainable when the funds are exhausted. This is true with most externally funded projects and programs in Africa.

MEASURES TO ADDRESS EXISTING CHALLENGES

Since independence, many countries in Africa have done much to expand and develop their forests and wildlife sectors, although the pace has been insufficient. The FAO has funded various Tropical Forestry Action plans, and bilateral donors and other institutions such as the World Bank and the European Union have supported these plans. But in all, this support has been modest. However, there are positive lessons to be drawn for future development of these two sectors.

African communities and African governments need to realize the importance of sustainable forest management. Corrupt officials and businessmen, who care nothing for the local people who live there, are destroying the forests for their own benefit. Governments must work with local communities to stop this. Local communities can and should have a major role in the sustainable management of natural resources. However, they have to be helped to gain confidence and other skills if they are to participate in discussions with park managers and field staff from a position of strength.

Many existing forest and wildlife legislative acts need reviewing and updating to be relevant to the current situation. In some African countries, the existing acts, although current, are neither widely publicized nor clearly explained, and the general public does not understand them. The authorities should translate into local languages the main elements of these acts to help local communities and their representatives to comprehend and implement them.

Some peoples have traditional ways of protecting their forests and wildlife resources. These need to be blended with modern conservation strategies to sustain forest and wildlife resources in the most effective manner. However, many countries need their capacity in both areas enhanced. Addressing the capacity constraints in the two sectors should be given priority and should be supported by both African governments and their development partners. Currently, many forest and wildlife ministries or departments are largely ignored and in some cases these services have collapsed. In several countries, the few qualified professionals who were there have left government service to join international organizations. Usually, where forestry and wildlife extension services exist they do not have the basic requirements to make them effective. Overall, African governments and their development partners will have to support more training and more conservation staff if they are to achieve their conservation goals. The governments need to provide job incentives to encourage the development of new working practices, but most important are clear guidelines and standards for conservation agencies to follow.

Most forest and wildlife projects and programs are poorly funded. Despite projects funded by the World Bank, FAO, United Nations Development Programme (UNDP), bilateral donors, international nongovernmental organizations (NGOs), and Global Environment Facility and Foundations, there are still funding gaps. The forestry and wildlife sectors have the potential to generate funds from the private sector (such as tourism and logging) to contribute to national development.

To get Africans to understand that the forestry and wildlife sectors are important to their national economies, the resources must be not only exploited but also protected for succeeding generations. However, many developing countries feel that developed countries do not want them to use their forest and wildlife resources for development. This is despite the advanced countries having become industrialized by depleting their own forests. The current increasing poverty in many African countries may mean that the rural communities will continue to use and deplete the forest and wildlife resources for survival, rather than development. African governments should ensure that the ongoing programs, be they in whatever sector of economy, should filter down to the grassroots.

The FAO Regional Conference for Africa in 2000 proposed that, to minimize illegal trade in African timber, forest products should be certified and eco-labeled. Some countries have developed and adopted certification schemes with advanced countries. Unfortunately, many African countries have yet to take the necessary steps not only to influence the process, but also to develop national guidelines for forest products.

Before sensible planning can take place, existing data on the two sectors must be updated and refined. Research must be done on rates of depletion and of replanting of trees, the size of populations of animals, the number of people who subsist on forest products, and the present habitats and their rate of change. Baseline studies are essential. However, in many African countries investment in forest and wildlife research has been and is minimal. In some postcrisis African countries (e.g., Liberia and others), the research and information system has collapsed or was destroyed. Hence, there is a need for baseline studies to establish the present state and condition of the woodlands that still exist in Africa south of the Sahara.

In short, there are no simple solutions to the problems of sustainable forest and wildlife management in Africa. However, the future of sustainable forest and wildlife management should build on the New Partnership for Africa's Development (NEPAD) policy for stronger democratic processes, peaceful resolution of Africa's conflicts, poverty eradication, and investment in people. This can lead to new proposals for using the forests and wildlife resources as a way to reduce poverty and integrate both resources and environmental protection with other land uses in each country. Up-to-date information is needed to determine the potential of the two sectors. African governments need to find solutions to the problems of blending traditional approaches to forest and wildlife conservation with modern methods. Based on a recent FAO survey of national forestry programs, the challenge remains to find participatory and cost-effective processes that take due account of the socioeconomic characteristics of each country and the best ways to share their knowledge and experience.

See also **Agriculture; Climate; Ecology; Ecosystems; Production Strategies; Wildlife.**

BIBLIOGRAPHY

African Forestry and Wildlife Commission. "Perspectives of Forestry and Wildlife in the Region: Highlights from the Forestry Outlook Study for Africa (FOSA)." 2004. Available from http://www.fao.org/.

Binns, Tony. *Tropical Africa*. London: Routledge, 1994.

Blom, Allard. "A Critical Analysis of Three Approaches to Tropical Forest Conservation Based on Experiences in the Sangho Region." Bulletin Series, Yale University School of Forestry and Environmental Studies no. 102 (1998): 208–215.

Food and Agriculture Organization of the United Nations. "The Challenges of Sustainable Forestry Development in Africa." 2004. Available from http://www.fao.org/.

Inamdar, Amar; David Brown; and Stephen Cobb. "What's Special About Wildlife Management in Forests? Concepts and Models of Rights-Based Management, with Recent Evidence from West-Central Africa." 1999. Available from http://www.odi.org.uk/nrp/44.html.

Kingsburry, Damien. "Environment and Development." In *Key Issues in Development*, ed. Damien Kingsburry et al. New York: Palgrave Macmillan, 2004.

Nelson, John, and Norbert Gami. "Enhancing Equity in the Relationship between Protected Areas and Indigenous and Local Communities in Central Africa, in the Context of Global Change." Theme on Indigenous and Local Communities, Equity and Protected Areas. Bugnaux, Switzerland: World Conservation Union, 2002.

Topa, Giuseppe. "Framework for Forest Resource Management in Sub-Saharan Africa." Africa Region Working Paper Series. 2005. Available at: http://www.worldbank.org/africa/wps/index.htm.

JOHN O. KAKONGE

CENTRAL AFRICA

Central Africa's geography and ecology are marked by two prominent features: river basins and the equatorial rain forest. The Congo and Zambezi River basins dominate the northern and southern parts of this region. The equatorial rain forest, bordered by two savannas, extends from southern Cameroon and the Central African Republic throughout the Congo River basin to below the mouth of the Congo River, where it meets the southern savanna of Angola and Zambia. Covering about 800,000 square miles, the equatorial rain forest experiences high annual rainfall (ranging between 60 and 118 inches per year) and itself contains an enormous diversity of microenvironments, as well as and over 7,000 species of flowering plants.

"The equatorial forest" is in reality a complex mosaic of forest and nonforest formations whose physiognomy and compositions vary greatly. Mono-dominant (single species) forests, dense evergreen and semideciduous forests, raffia palm forests, inundated forests, mountainous forests, patches of savannas, and herbaceous marshy clearings constitute this vast forested expanse of central Africa. Wildlife diversity within central Africa's forests is also high and includes such large species as elephants (*Loxodonta africana*), bongo (*Tragelaphus euryceros*), and lowland and mountain gorillas (*Gorilla gorilla*), but also numerous primate, mongoose and genet, rodent, ungulate, reptile, and avian species.

The variability of equatorial Africa's forests has resulted from a wide range of nonhuman and human activities. Storms, tree fall, high winds, landslides, and river flooding help to create gaps in the forest, to disperse seeds, and to sustain the forest's high plant and animal biodiversity. Seasonal shifts have considerable effects on forests adjacent to some rivers, since trees growing in these locations must be able to tolerate flooding. Forest mammals, too, have affected the structure and composition of the forest. Marshy clearings provide water, minerals, and food to several forest mammals, and in turn, these animals help to maintain the clearings.

People living in the forest have profoundly affected its composition and structure. Human beings have lived in equatorial African forest as far back as since 40,000 to 35,000 BP, and they subsequently recolonized this forest about 12,000 years ago, when conditions in Africa became increasingly humid and the forest expanded. Historians do not know exactly when people began to cultivate within the forest. But by the middle of the last millennium BCE, inhabitants of the forest developed a variety of ways of exploiting it, primarily to supplement their diets: they farmed bananas, yams, and other crops; hunted elephants and other game; raised animals; and gathered fruits, leaves, honey, medicinal plants, and building materials. They thus helped to influence the forest's composition by clearing lands, dispersing seeds, and encouraging particular plants and trees (and perhaps even forest patches) to flourish.

Exploitation and management of the forest continued over the following millennia. During that time forest resources eventually did more than supplement African diets. The forest has long had cultural and social significance, constituting a space within which equatorial Africans created social identities and interacted with forest and ancestral spirits. Africans also developed trades in salt, fish, camwood, and other commodities, taking advantage of varied distribution of resources in the forest and other ecological zones of the Congo River basin. From the late fifteenth century, Africans along the coast of central Africa were also in contact with European traders, who sought to acquire African slaves to work plantations in the Caribbean and the Americas. Africans exploited these new opportunities, trading slaves, ivory, dried fish, ironware, and forest products for highly valued imported goods, such as guns, textiles, and copper goods. And from the sixteenth century through the first half of the nineteenth century, that trade grew, incorporating additional forest products, including hardwoods and cloth made from the leaves of the raffia palm.

During the nineteenth century, many societies in equatorial Africa that had previously remained isolated from this African-European trade increasingly involved themselves in the developing global economy. That economy was strongly driven by European demand for tropical oils, which would fulfill the demands of its burgeoning industries, and for ivory, used for pianos and billiard balls desired by Europe's middle classes. Taking advantage of these new demands for tropical forest products, African specialist traders in the Congo River basin began to form more extensive trading networks, based upon long- and short-distance exchanges of various forest products. African big men accumulated clients, wives, and slaves to cultivate manioc fields in the forest. Manioc, a starchy tuber that grows easily in forest soils, sustained traders and their dependents, who spent many months traveling throughout the river basin. Big men also attracted dependents to collect palm oil and palm wine and to harvest raffia palms and weave them into mats for exchange. They hunted elephants for ivory. Importantly, a trade in slaves within central Africa sustained the acquisition and exchange of these commodities, which big African and European merchants traded for firearms, beads, and cloth.

Through the nineteenth century, some African societies developed extensive means of managing their forests, though historians and anthropologists need to conduct far more research on precolonial forest management in equatorial Africa. In some societies African authorities would dictate when, where, and how people could exploit the forest, especially for hunting and farming. Forest inhabitants elsewhere employed other means of managing their forest environments, including migration to new microenvironments and the development of new techniques with which to exploit those environments. Whether precolonial Africans were inherently conservationist in their uses of forest resources has been debated among scholars. Some argue that very low population densities among hunter-gatherer and farming populations meant that people exerted little pressure on forest lands and resources. They could therefore engage in some activities (such as swidden cultivation) that could become ecologically unsustainable when population densities increased. These same historians point out that some precolonial central Africans did deplete forest resources at certain times, such as ivory and rubber during the nineteenth century economic expansion. Others, however, have contended that some equatorial Africans sought to "optimize" rather than to "maximize" their uses of forest resources, and that they attempted to safeguard these resources for future generations. Despite these differing opinions concerning precolonial forest management and use, historians agree that precolonial Africans could have varied influences on forest ecology.

FOREST USE AND POLICY, 1880–1960

In the late nineteenth century, European interests in gaining a strategic foothold in equatorial Africa and in exploiting its wealth intensified. Perceiving the equatorial forest as a source of untapped riches, Belgian, French, and German powers competed to acquire colonies in the Congo River basin. But once they had laid claim to these lands, resources, and people, European powers realized that exploiting the equatorial forest would require an enormous investment, which they were unwilling to supply. Hence, Leopold II of Belgium and the French and German colonizers who followed his lead sought to administer their equatorial African possessions through concessionary companies. In the last years of the nineteenth century, these companies gained control over substantial tracts of land to extract such commodities as rubber, ivory, palm oil, and animal skins by whatever means available. They later expanded their activities into the cultivation of coffee and cocoa and the mining of diamonds, gold, manganese, and copper. In exchange for a monopoly over forest commodities and African labor, these companies paid a yearly rent to the French, Belgian, and German administrations.

Concessionary companies committed a catalog of abuses against African workers, forcing them to work in the forest for months at a time. The Congo-Ocean railway company, which developed the railroad networks from the Congo River through the equatorial forest to the Atlantic coast, conscripted workers from all over French Equatorial Africa. By 1928 the company had sent well over ten thousand to their deaths; workers had no immunities to forest diseases and received insufficient food. European colonial administrations exercised relatively little control over such companies' activities. Belatedly they tried to rectify these abuses. In 1908, for instance, Belgium assumed control over Léopold II's Congo Independent State, setting up the Belgian Congo, but the abuses continued for many years after. Ultimately, many of the concessionary companies simply went bankrupt, or transformed themselves into other commercial enterprises.

The concessionary companies left disastrous ecological legacies. Concerned with extracting as much as possible within the shortest amount of time, companies generally expressed little concern for exploiting the forest in ecologically sustainable ways. They encouraged the slaughter tapping of rubber trees (extracting so much rubber from a latex-producing tree that it killed the tree), the overexploitation of latex-producing vines, and the massive destruction of elephant populations. Transport companies opened up vast tracts of forest for future exploitation.

Concern for the protection of the equatorial forests developed fitfully and belatedly, and central African forest policy drew much of its inspiration from west African forest policy. Identifying valuable tropical hardwoods in equatorial forests, the concessionary companies set about finding ways of exploiting them. They developed diverse silvicultural techniques that would produce valued timber species for paper production and various kinds of construction. In some locations, foresters relied on enrichment planting as a means of transforming the highly diverse tropical forests into the monoculture of valued species. Elsewhere, they relied on the little-known dynamics of natural regeneration.

Based on their experiences in western Africa, French foresters transplanted ecological concerns about deforestation and environmental degradation to central Africa. They worried that African cultivators were transforming once lush "primary" forests into "secondary" forests, populated by small trees with relatively useless timbers. (Interestingly, contemporary rain forest ecologists maintain that it remains extremely difficult to distinguish between primary and secondary forest, because of the considerable disturbances caused by fauna and climatic conditions.) Foresters and agronomists also bemoaned equatorial Africa's infertile soils, which remained a barrier to increased agricultural production. Generally, however, foresters' knowledge of the forest remained rudimentary; as late as 1947, the inspector general of waters and forests in the French colonies acknowledged that despite their concerns about deforestation and forest destruction in equatorial Africa, foresters knew precious little about the equatorial rain forest's composition, physiognomy, and regeneration processes.

FOREST POLICY, 1960 TO THE PRESENT

Efforts to understand the dynamics of equatorial rain forest growth intensified after independence, when central African states set up their own forestry departments. Initially, these departments were often staffed by French and Belgian forestry agents because so few Africans had acquired forestry training, but this is no longer the case. Increased global demands for tropical hardwoods, as well as the desire of newly independent African states to develop their economies, fueled efforts to expand forest exploitation and to understand the complex ecological relations that constituted the equatorial rain forests.

Nevertheless, all central African states had to contend with conflicting demands on their forests in the postindependence period. Many central African countries with extensive rain forests sold forest concessions to expatriate interests from various countries, including Yugoslavia, France, Italy, Japan, and Libya. The Peoples Republic of Congo, however, nationalized its forests in the early 1970s; later, though, it denationalized the forests and timber industry and sold concessions to expatriate companies. Structural adjustment policies of the early 1980s forced many countries to boost their exports. Selling forest concessions to expatriate firms provided a quick fix for many states seeking to sustain services and to pay civil servants.

Central African states have permitted or encouraged other forms of forest exploitation as well. Some have allowed gold, silver, and coltan mining, which can provide much-needed income, but can also be highly destructive to forest environments. Bushmeat consumption by local populations and urban consumers has also constituted an important use of equatorial African forest resources in recent decades. Timber industries have helped to intensify this game extraction, according to many analysts, because they construct roads and open up less accessible forests to hunters and trappers and because their very presence encourages people to migrate to logging centers for jobs and other economic opportunities.

In the face of increasing global worries over the disappearing tropical rain forests, many Western nations, as well as nongovernmental organizations and multilateral aid organizations such as the World Bank, encouraged African nations to conserve their forests. Efforts to conserve the biodiversity of equatorial rain forests have developed in various central African nations, including Gabon, Cameroon, the Republic of Congo, the Central African Republic, the Democratic Republic of Congo, and Rwanda. Organizations such as the World Wildlife Fund and Wildlife Conservation International have collaborated with African states (or some interests within these states) to set up national parks and other measures to protect forests and wildlife. But protecting the forests has not been trouble-free, because African states and peoples have used the forests in many different ways that do not easily accommodate conservation aims and interventions. Many foresters, for instance, have observed that creating economically and ecologically sustainable exploitation in the very richest forests of equatorial Africa proved very difficult, if not impossible, because of the high cost of transporting logs or finished lumber to the coasts. Some logging companies in the interior in the past and present have struggled to adhere to state regulations for cutting timber, though incentives to bypass these regulations are enormous, particularly when African states do not have the resources to inspect harvesting practices. Moreover, civil wars since the 1990s have complicated efforts to protect the forests and game and indeed have had equivocal effects on

A lone elephant grazes at a clearing in the rain forest of Lope Reserve, Gabon. Forests in the poor central Africa states are faced with twin pressures as governments deal with the conflicting needs to conserve them and also exploit them for much-needed revenues. AP Photo/Saurabh Das

the forests themselves. In the Democratic Republic of Congo, for instance, civil war precipitated the decline of collapse of logging, but encouraged soldiers and refugees to exploit intensively the forest for its fuelwood and game. The bushmeat trade has also precipitated what primatologists and conservationists have called a "catastrophic" decline of certain mammals, including gorillas and chimpanzees. They have also linked opening the forest and game extraction with the transformation and transmission of virulent emerging diseases like ebola, which have devastating impacts on people, but also on certain animal populations.

Hence, African states have faced enormous challenges to resolve violent political conflicts; to respond to conflicting international demands to boost exports; to conserve forests, watersheds, biodiversity, and other natural resources; and to respond to local demands to ensure opportunities for employment, fuelwood, forest game, and agricultural land. In some locations, equatorial Africans' farmers' continued practice of swidden agriculture, their demands for bushmeat and fuelwood, as well as their need to earn income through cash cropping, hunting, trapping, mining, and wage labor have all created significant pressures on forests. Conservation in particular has not always answered to these local demands, and central Africans have not universally embraced conservation efforts, which some believe have interfered with their efforts to make a living and to reproduce themselves socially, culturally, and historically.

See also **Agriculture; Climate; Colonial Policies and Practices; Colonialism and Imperialism: Concessionary Companies; Congo River; Ecology; Economic Systems; Ecosystems; Geography and the Study of Africa; Ivory; Plants; Slave Trades; Textiles; World Bank.**

BIBLIOGRAPHY

Aubreville, A. "Les brousses secondaires en Afrique Equatoriale: Côte d'Ivoire-Cameroun-A.E.F." *Bois et forêts des tropiques* (1947): 24–49.

Aubreville, A. "'Les pays tropicaux' de Pierre Gourou—Le parasolier: La régénération naturelle et l'enrichissement de la forêté quatoriale." *Bois et forêts des tropiques* (1948): 20–30.

Barnes, Richard F.W. "The Bushmeat Boom and Bust in West and Central Africa." *Oryx* 36, no. 3 (2002): 236–242.

Birmingham, David, and Phyllis M. Martin, eds. *History of Central Africa.* 32 vols. New York: Longman, 1983.

Cinnamon, John. "Narrating Equatorial African Landscapes: Conservation, Histories, and Endangered Forests in Northern Gabon." *Journal of Colonialism and Colonial History* 4, no. 2 (2003).

Cleaver Ken, et al., eds. *Conservation of West and Central African Rainforests.* Washington, DC: World Bank, 1992.

Coquery-Vidrovitch, Catherine. *Le Congo au temps des grandes compagnies concessionnaires, 1898–1930.* Paris: Mouton, 1972.

Draulens, Dirk, and Ellen Van Krunkelsven. "The Impact of War on Forest Areas in the Democratic Republic of Congo." *Oryx* 36, no. 1 (2002): 35–40.

Dupré, Georges. *Un ordre et sa destruction.* Paris: Editions de l'Office de la recherche scientifique et technique outre-mer, 1982.

Dupré, Georges. *Les naissances d'un société: Espace et historicité chez les Beembé du Congo.* Paris: Editions de l'Orstom, 1985.

Dupré, Marie-Claude, and B. Pinçon. "Raphia Monies Among the Teke: Their Origin and Control." In *Money Matters: Instability, Values, and Social Payments in the Modern History of West African Communities,* ed. Jane I. Guyer. Portsmouth, NH: Heinemann, 1995.

Dupré, Marie-Claude, and B. Pinçon. *Métallurgie et politique en Afrique Centrale: Deux mille ans de vestiges sur les plateaux Batéké Gabon, Congo, Zaire.* Paris, 1997.

Eves, Heather E.; Rebecca Hardin; and Stephanie Rupp; eds. *Resource Use in the Trinational Sangha River Region of Equatorial Africa: Histories, Knowledge Forms, and Institutions.* Bulletin Series, Yale School of Forestry and Environmental Studies, no. 102, 1998.

Giles-Vernick, Tamara. *Cutting the Vines of the Past: Environmental Histories of the Central African Rain Forest.* Charlottesville: University of Virginia Press, 2002.

Gray, Christopher. *Colonial Rule and Crisis in Equatorial Africa: Southern Gabon Ca. 1850–1940.* Rochester, NY: University of Rochester Press, 2002.

Gray, Christopher, and François Ngolet. "'A Dead People?' Migrants, Land and History in the Rainforests of Central African Republic." Ph.D. diss. Johns Hopkins University, 1996.

Gray, Christopher, and François Ngolet. "Chiefs and their Discontents: The Politics of Modernization in Lambaréné." *Journal of African History* 40, no. 1 (1999): 87–107.

Harms, Robert. "The End of Red Rubber: A Reassessment." *Journal of African History* 16, no. 1 (1975): 73–88.

Harms, Robert. *River of Wealth, River of Sorrow: The Central Zaire Basin in the Era of the Slave and Ivory Trade, 1500–1891.* New Haven, CT: Yale University Press, 1981.

Harms, Robert. *Games Against Nature: An Eco-Cultural History of the Nunu of Equatorial Africa.* Cambridge, U.K.: Cambridge University Press, 1987.

Hochschild, Adam. *King Leopold's Ghost: A Story of Greed, Terror, and Heroism in Colonial Africa.* New York: Mariner, 1998.

Klieman, Kairn A. *"The Pygmies Were Our Compass": Bantu and Batwa in the History of West Central Africa, Early Times to c. 1900 C.E.* Portsmouth, NH: Heinemann, 2003.

Laburthe-Tolra, Philippe. *Les seigneurs de la forêt: Essai sur le passé historique, l'organisation sociale et les normes éthiques des anciens Béti du Cameroun.* Paris: Publications de la Sorbonne, 1981.

MacGaffey, Wyatt. *Kongo Political Culture: The Conceptual Challenge of the Particular.* Bloomington: Indiana University Press, 2000.

Miller, Joseph Calder. *Way of Death: Merchant Capitalism and the Angolan Slave Trade, 1730–1830.* Madison: University of Wisconsin Press, 1988.

Peterson, Richard B. *Conversations in the Rainforest: Culture, Values, and the Environment in Central Africa.* Boulder, CO: Westview Press, 2000.

Vansina, Jan. *Paths in the Rainforest: Toward a History of Political Tradition in Equatorial Africa.* Madison: University of Wisconsin Press, 1990.

Walsh, Peter, et al. "Catastrophic Ape Decline in Western Equatorial Africa." *Nature* 422 (April 2003): 611–614.

TAMARA GILES-VERNICK

EASTERN AFRICA

Human interactions with eastern Africa's forest resources have occurred since time immemorial. People have long depended on trees, wooded land, and forests, along with their associated plants, insects, and animals, to help meet their needs for food, fuel, forage, building materials, medicines, and other items. Forest resources in the early twenty-first century still contribute significantly to livelihoods, providing products for both home consumption and for sale. In the Ethiopian highlands, for example, selling firewood and charcoal in urban centers is a major income source, particularly during droughts. Households often plant trees as a kind of savings bank, to be harvested in hard times. Foragers, herders, and farmers have accumulated, through experimentation and shared experience, a detailed, sophisticated, and dynamic knowledge of forest resources. This knowledge is culturally and socially mediated, reflecting underlying differences based on gender, age, mode of livelihood, area of residence, and other factors. Because women usually collect firewood and prepare meals they often possess greater knowledge about, and well-defined preferences regarding, the burning qualities of different tree species. Forest resources are woven into cultural and social life, reflected in symbolism, rituals, and even identities. Sacred groves have long served as ceremonial sites and places for community tasks such as dispute resolution.

Local environmental knowledge also includes communal and individual strategies for managing forest resources. Based on their needs, livelihood strategies, and available resources (including labor), people have pursued different objectives through time regarding the use, manipulation, and retention of trees and forest. Use of fire and other technology allowed people to reduce tree cover to extend their pastures and farms. People also learned that tree cover could additionally be maintained or increased by land use rotation (pastoralist movements, farm plot fallowing), deliberate protection (for sacred or secular purposes), tree propagation (direct planting or fostering volunteers), and farm practices such as intercropping or pruning (including pollarding and copping). Local decision making over forest resources was usually vested in common property regimes based on descent groups (clans, lineages, and families) or local residential groupings. These common property regimes recognized not only primary right holders but also secondary users. For example, people might be able to collect deadwood or medicinal plants from a neighbor's fallowing plot.

No single narrative captures the sweep of forest resource change for eastern Africa in the millennia before European colonialism. In some places forests were cleared owing to population growth, market pressures, or pasture expansion. In such cases people usually maintained some trees (often multipurpose ones) and wooded areas for economic and cultural purposes. The displacement of human and animal populations through drought, disease, or other disruptions altered vegetation patterns. The ivory trade also had a significant impact on forest resources. Eastern Africa has exported ivory for more than two thousand years, and the trade widened and intensified starting in the 1500s driven by growing linkages with expanding economies along the Indian Ocean and in Europe. As elephant populations declined, dense woods and thickets often replaced open grasslands. In the Serengeti-Mara region, this transition in vegetation began occurring in the late 1800s because of intense elephant hunting combined with rinderpest epizootic that decimated Maasai cattle herds and wild ungulate populations.

THE COLONIAL ERA: LATE 1800S TO THE EARLY 1960S

European colonialism, which was ideologically supported by racial and cultural chauvinism, greatly influenced eastern African forestry. Colonial legal, policy, and administrative arrangements subordinated or extinguished indigenous land rights, rendering the Africans highly vulnerable to official interventions. The Europeans greatly misunderstood African resource use and management, which added to their impulse to intervene. For example, the Europeans portrayed indigenous land tenure as a relic of tribal savagery, unsuited to the demands of a modern economy. Similarly, pastoralism and swidden cultivation (based on rotational fallowing) were seen—mistakenly—as highly irrational and destructive of natural resources. Colonial governments pursued policies that excluded or reduced African forest resource access and use rights.

European private-interest groups obtained control over some forestlands, such as a large tract at Eldama Ravine, Kenya, granted to Ewart Grogan and associates. Colonial authorities, however, mainly relied on state-based custodial management, developed in British India, to oversee commercial development and to promote conservation. Many forests were declared government reserves. Africans were evicted from them without compensation, and their resource use rights were severely curtailed by regulations and user fees that were backed by guards and penalties. These actions generated resentment and resistance, including petitions to officials, willful violations, and sabotage. Loss of forest and farmland were major issues sparking the anticolonial Mau Mau revolt in the 1950s, with Gikuyu insurgents making use of forest cover in central Kenya to wage their struggle. A coerced cooperation also existed, and in some places new forest laborers and entrepreneurs, such as pitsawyers and sawmill operators, emerged. Despite European optimism about timber development, colonial eastern Africa never developed large-scale, export-based forestry industries, and instead wound up with medium- and small-scale enterprises that mainly served local and regional needs.

Most of the region's forest resources—wooded savannas, small patches of moist and dry forests, and farmland and homestead trees—remained under local African control. Colonial provincial officials and technical officers were routinely assigned responsibility for promoting conservation measures in such areas. Coercive strategies, such as compulsory tree planting, cutting bans, and hunting restrictions were highly unpopular among the Africans. Other approaches, which anticipated present-day participatory practices, such as voluntary farm forestry based on decentralized tree nurseries, were more popular. Comanagement agreements between local authorities (as representatives of their African populations) and colonial governments were arranged for some wooded areas, such as Maasai Mara, which became trust lands of the local county council.

FORESTRY SINCE INDEPENDENCE

Both continuity and change are evident in eastern Africa forestry since independence. Governments maintained the command-and-control policies and practices for managing forest reserves and national parks. The harsh eviction in 1988 of Maasai herders from the Mkomazi Game Reserve in Tanzania, for example, showed that fortress conservation based on officially reserved areas controlled by technical experts backed by police powers still prevailed. Official resource managers have been hampered, however, by severe financial and other constraints in the wake of the region's national economic troubles, structural adjustment-induced cutbacks, political turmoil, corruption, rising and completing demand for resources, and armed conflicts. Global conservation organizations, often with the support of multilateral and bilateral development agencies, have sought major roles in the management of the region's forests and parks. Web sites now highlight (and seek further funding for) projects in conservation hotspots such as the coastal forest mosaics, the Eastern Arc Mountains of Tanzania and Kenya, and the Afromountain Region encompassing the highlands of Ethiopia, Kenya, Uganda, and Tanzania. These conservation groups sometimes generate tension at the national level (where officials see them as challenging their policies and even their sovereignty) and at the ground level (when local use and management of forest resources have been curtailed). Local nongovernmental organizations also emerged to address their membership's interests regarding forest resources. Kenyan Wangari Matthai received the Nobel Peace Prize in 2004 for her leadership of the Green Belt Movement, which has mobilized women and men to plant more than 30 million trees, and for her political struggles against the national government on behalf of human rights and environmental issues.

Many officials, organizations, and international donors now recognize that conservation is not possible without the active involvement of rural communities. This shift reflects in part a growing appreciation of the existence of local environmental knowledge, and of local capacity for sustainable resource management. Numerous studies have documented, for example, how higher densities of locally planted and managed trees often accompany rising population pressure (though the trend is by no means universal in the region). It also arises from awareness of pressing local livelihoods needs, as well as concern about long-standing and recent conflicts over natural resources. Governments have tried to alter their national policy frameworks and bureaucracies to varying extents to make them more capable of collaboration with forest resource users. Extension forestry services, comanagement arrangements, and other participatory-oriented approaches have emerged in recent years. Some conservation projects, such as CARE International's efforts in Mgahinga Gorilla National Park in Uganda, try to use multistakeholder negotiations to address conflicting interests. As might be expected in any situation dealing with people and institutions of unequal power and with differing needs, interests, and priorities, the implementation of participation has occurred in many ways (some of them participatory only in name) and with diverse outcomes—with disappointments as well as successes. Nonetheless, participatory natural resource management is likely to offer the most fruitful approach in the future for reconciling the competing interests in East Africa's forest resources.

See also **Agriculture; Climate; Colonial Policies and Practices; Disease; Ecology; Economic History; Ecosystems; Famine; Geography and the Study of Africa;** **Ivory; Maathai, Wangari; Plants; Postcolonialism; Production Strategies.**

BIBLIOGRAPHY

Arnold, J. E. Michael, and Peter A. Dewees, eds. *Tree Management in Farmer Strategies: Responses to Agricultural Intensification.* Oxford: Oxford University Press, 1995.

Brockington, Dan. *Fortress Conservation: The Preservation of the Mkomazi Game Reserve, Tanzania.* Bloomington: Indiana University Press, 2002.

Castro, Alfonso Peter. *Facing Kirinyaga: A Social History of Forest Commons in Southern Mount Kenya.* London: Intermediate Technology Publications, 1995.

Castro, A. Peter, and Erik Nielsen, eds. *Natural Resource Conflict Management Case Studies: An Analysis of Power, Participation and Protected Areas.* Rome: Food and Agriculture Organization of the United Nations, 2003.

Hakansson, N. Thomas. "The Human Ecology of World Systems in East Africa: The Impact of the Ivory Trade," *Human Ecology,* 32 (2004): 561–591.

Niamir, Maryam. *Community Forestry: Herders' Decision-Making in Natural Resources Management in Arid and Semi-Arid Africa.* Rome: Food and Agriculture Organization of the United Nations, 1990.

Shepherd, Gill. *Managing Africa's Tropical Dry Forest: A Review of Indigenous Methods.* London: Overseas Development Institute, 1992.

Weber, William, et al., eds. *African Rain Forest Ecology and Conservation: An Interdisciplinary Perspective.* New Haven, Connecticut: Yale University Press, 2001.

A. PETER CASTRO

SOUTHERN AFRICA

Trees play a central role in the economy and ecology of Southern Africa. Agricultural expansion and, to a lesser degree, demands for construction material and fuelwood, have depleted woodlands and forests in much of the region. The consequences of deforestation for both rural and urban livelihoods, as well as for the ecosystems of the region, are increasingly evident. Since the early colonial period, governments in Southern Africa have attempted to regulate the use of forests and woodlands and to promote tree planting. The results of these efforts have often been limited, in part due to limited government enforcement capacity as well as inadequate understanding of the dynamics of rural society and culture, resulting in inappropriate policies. New efforts to meet the challenges of deforestation in the region focus on combining the goals of conservation with meeting the needs of local communities. Changing political circumstances in the twenty-first century present both promise and peril for these efforts.

Unlike the dense, moist forests of Central Africa and parts of West Africa, the major types of vegetation in Southern Africa are savanna, woodland, scrubland, and grassland. The dominant climatic factor influencing the types of vegetation is the long dry season, which precludes large areas of dense, moist forest. A few high-altitude areas have pockets of moist montane forest, though in these areas plantations of pine and other exotic tree species have replaced much of the original indigenous forest. Most of the remaining dense forests in the region are located in Angola, Mozambique, and Zambia. Scattered remnant patches of forest remain in Botswana, Lesotho, Malawi, South Africa, Swaziland, and Zimbabwe. By far the most common type of vegetation in the region in the early twenty-first century is savanna woodland, ranging from open grassland to closed canopy *miombo* woodland. In places where livestock grazing and overuse have degraded tree cover, extensive thorn scrubland has developed.

Although the woodlands of Southern Africa do not compare with the rich forests of Central Africa or Asia, they play a crucial role in the regional economy and ecology. For the vast majority of the region's population who live in rural areas, woodlands provide vital construction materials for houses and other domestic and agricultural structures, firewood, fruits and nuts, medicine, and fiber. Urban areas continue to rely heavily on wood for cooking and heating. The region has many large plantations of exotic pine and eucalyptus to provide for urban energy needs, but much of the energy consumed in urban areas still comes from indigenous woodlands that have often been cut and transported illegally. Although reliable information is not available for many countries in Southern Africa, the available data show that, although domestic commercial timber production is significant, there is little or no net export of timber from the region (unlike Central or West Africa).

The forests and woodlands of Southern Africa are essential in protecting the fragile ecosystems of the region. From 1990 to 2000, the region's forest area declined by 8 percent. In some countries, such as Malawi, the loss over that decade was as much as 22 percent. In areas that have experienced significant deforestation, soil erosion and reduced soil fertility have accelerated as the old, thin soils of the region are exposed to movement of water and wind. Destruction of vegetation in areas around streams has reduced the water-storage capacity of riparian areas, resulting in reduced flows of water and in some cases in the complete drying of streams that represent important sources of water for people, animals, and fish. Sediment from eroded soils clogs streams and dams, reducing the availability of water and destroying economically and nutritionally important fish breeding grounds. Silting-up of dams associated with deforestation represents an increasingly serious threat to the region's electrical generating capacity.

Commercial timber production is not a primary cause of deforestation in Southern Africa. Rather, the main cause is the conversion of forest and woodland areas to both small- and large-scale commercial agriculture. With increasing smallholder populations competing with commercial producers, the area under cultivation has expanded rapidly at the expense of forest and woodland. Historically, governments in the region have been concerned about the role that demand for firewood and charcoal plays in promoting deforestation. But recent evidence suggests that energy demand plays a major role in deforestation mainly in periurban, and not rural, areas. In rural areas, most people do not cut living trees for firewood. Rather, firewood is harvested by collecting branches from dead and already dried trees, mainly because these are lighter to carry and easier to burn. Where trees are scarce, these residents often prefer to switch to burning crop residues rather than cutting and carrying live trees for fuel. For certain rural industries, such as brickmaking or beer brewing, live trees are sometimes cut, but generally it is only in areas around urban centers and in some severely deforested rural areas that rural energy demand appears to play an important role in deforestation. In some places frequent, deliberate burning of woodland areas to provide increased pasture also contributes to the deforestation.

The consequences of deforestation are felt in the rural areas both in the form of increased labor time expended in collecting tree products, and in reduced crop production due to soil degradation. Throughout the region, rural people report walking much longer distances to collect poles, firewood, fruits and nuts, fiber, and medicine from roots and bark of preferred tree species. In some areas of the region, people report switching from constructing houses with poles and timber to mud brick due to the increased scarcity of trees. Some women report changing their cooking practices to reduce firewood consumption, for example by cooking fewer long-cooking but nutritious foods, such as beans. Reduced crop production is experienced as soils lose fertility and moisture, and in some areas through reduced land area due to gully erosion.

Since the early colonial period, governments in the region have attempted to address problems of deforestation through regulations on tree cutting and through efforts to promote both plantation and smallholder tree planting. As long ago as the late nineteenth century, colonial governments established substantial pine and eucalyptus plantations and established laws and institutions to enforce conservation practices among African populations, as well as on European estates. In Malawi (then Nyasaland), for instance, the British colonial government established laws to prohibit cutting of certain types of indigenous trees and to preserve trees on slopes and in areas around streambeds. Government forest rangers could impose stiff penalties, including substantial prison terms, on Africans caught illegally cutting trees. Forest extension officers required villages to establish forest reserves, which were to be regulated by the local chiefs and could not be converted to agriculture. Similarly, the European estates were required to conserve forests on their land or to establish their own tree plantations. These efforts were substantially constrained, however, by the weak enforcement capacity of the colonial states, and deforestation proceeded largely unchecked in many areas.

More recent efforts to address the problem of deforestation in the region include programs to promote establishment of village woodlots, individual tree planting, agroforestry, and local conservation of indigenous forests. Beginning in the 1970s, many governments attempted to encourage the establishment of community woodlots of exotic tree species,

mainly eucalyptus. These efforts largely failed because most rural people felt that they had no real need for these woodlots that could justify the corresponding loss of time and land that could otherwise be devoted to production of food or more profitable cash crops. Many governments have promoted individual tree planting, programs that also have met with limited success. In addition, some scientists have argued that exotic forestry species represent invasive alien species that threaten local biodiversity.

Because so few people in the region appear able or willing to divert scarce land and other resources to tree cultivation, efforts have shifted to integrated tree and crop production through agroforestry methods. The International Center for Research in Agroforestry (ICRAF) in particular has been active in identifying and promoting soil-enriching tree species that can be planted with crops, with the goal of increasing food yields and producing trees on the same land. The success of these efforts has been limited in part by the additional labor that is required for planting and caring for trees, and also because most agroforestry species reduce crop yields in the first several years after planting.

Much of the failure of older approaches to tree conservation and planting can be understood as a result of inadequate understanding of local economic, social, and cultural conditions. The failure of local people to respond to government-sponsored tree planting programs has, for example, often been attributed to the nature of African land tenure. Because African cultures are said to own land communally rather than individually, it has been suggested that individuals have little incentive to plant trees. In fact, however, in most of Southern Africa individual families securely hold land. Moreover, in many local cultures planting trees is viewed as a way to secure tenure on land. Similarly, governments and outside agencies have sometimes explained the failure of African smallholders to respond to conservation programs as a sign of ignorance about the need for conservation. In reality, the limited response of smallholders more likely reflects the incompatible political and economic objectives of governments and rural people. Many of these programs were designed with the purpose of producing fuelwood for politically important urban constituencies. The smallholder farmers in rural areas, who were supposed to respond to these programs, often found that the benefits and costs of producing commercial fuelwood or timber for urban consumption were much less favorable than producing either food or high-profit cash crops.

Drawing on this experience has led to an increasing awareness that new programs to encourage tree conservation will need to focus more carefully on understanding the needs of local communities and the full complexity of local history and social dynamics. These programs will need to involve communities in the management of forests and woodlands, and to provide incentives for conservation. Efforts toward this goal have produced promising results. In particular, programs have been established to encourage communities to use existing natural forests and woodlands in a sustainable manner. These show considerable promise where communities are granted clear and secure rights to the fruits of their management labors. Efforts are also underway to find species of agroforestry trees that meet the demands of rural populations by requiring little expenditure of labor for management and quickly supplying soil nutrients.

Changing politics in Southern Africa in the 1990s had significant consequences for forestry and conservation. In some countries that have attained functioning democratic forms of government, democracy contributed to the relaxation of highly authoritarian enforcement practices and to increased calls for redistribution of forest reserve areas to local communities. In South Africa and Malawi, for example, the establishment of democratic governments has brought a decline in enforcement in reserved areas, with corresponding increases in illegal harvesting of trees for construction materials and firewood. At the same time, democracy has encouraged local communities to raise their voices in long-standing demands for increased access to forest reserves. In response, governments have initiated public reviews of policies concerning parks and reserved areas, and the question of increased community participation in management of forests has emerged as a central theme.

In other areas of Southern Africa, the end of long and bloody civil wars brought new hope for improved forest management. In Angola and Mozambique, such wars had caused an almost complete breakdown of government capacity to enforce forest policies. That breakdown also prevented the collection of reliable data on issues concerning forests, and little has been known about the situation on the ground. Recently emerging information suggests that the collapse of government forest management led to widespread and rapid destruction of formerly protected areas and plantations. As these nations struggle to rebuild themselves, national governments and nongovernmental organizations are hoping to dramatically improve forest management.

See also **Agriculture; Climate; Colonial Policies and Practices; Ecology; Ecosystems; Land: Tenure; Production Strategies.**

BIBLIOGRAPHY

Anderson, David, and Richard Grove, eds. *Conservation in Africa: People, Policies, and Practice.* Cambridge, U.K.: Cambridge University Press, 1987.

Chenje, Munyaradzi, and Phyllis Johnson, eds. *State of the Environment in Southern Africa.* Harare, Zimbabwe: Southern Africa Research and Documentation Centre, 1994.

Cowling, R. M.; D. M. Richardson; and Shirley M. Pierce. *Vegetation of Southern Africa.* Cambridge, U.K.: Cambridge University Press, 1997.

Lewis, Dale, and Nick Carter, eds. *Voices from Africa: Local Perspectives on Conservation.* Washington, DC: World Wildlife Fund, 1993.

Moyo, Sam; Phil O'Keefe; and Michael Sill. *The Southern African Environment.* London: Earthscan Publications, 1993.

Richardson, David M. "Forestry Trees as Invasive Aliens." *Conservation Biology* 12, no. 1 (1998): 18–26.

Sayer, Jeffrey A.; Caroline S. Harcourt; and N. Mark Collins. *The Conservation Atlas of Tropical Forests: Africa.* Baskingstoke, U.K.: Macmillan Publishers, 1992.

World Resources Institute. *World Resources 2005.* New York: World Resources Institute, 2005.

PETER WALKER

WESTERN AFRICA

Western Africa's major biomes range from coastal tropical forests to woodland and grassland savannas to the arid Sahara Desert. However, regional landscapes have been shaped over a long period by the many cultures that have inhabited, bordered, and formally or informally colonized the region, as well as those institutions—including multilateral development agencies and banks and international conservation organizations—that influence regional environmental management and resource use. Consequently, centuries-long cycles of land use have resulted in the creation of a regional agrosilva-pastoral mosaic of cropland, forest, farm, fallow, and woodland. Indeed, it is widely reported that the region's forest, woodland, and farm tree populations are being rapidly and intensively depleted, threatening, sometimes irreversibly, their regenerative capacity. Anthropogenic processes of vegetation change, however, are not uniformly destructive to the environment, nor are they necessarily of recent origin. They often produce biological diversity and environmental well-being.

The region's forested landscapes have always provided a host of products and services. Most West African urban and rural households still use charcoal and firewood for cooking and heating, for instance. This is true even of Nigeria, Africa's largest petroleum producer. Similarly, businesses such as bakeries and restaurants are often fueled by wood, which is also the major source of cooking energy for a large number of institutions such as prisons, schools, and hospitals. Additionally, across the region, nontimber products (such as game, insects, honey, fruits, nuts, gums, grasses, leaves, bark, and roots) are gathered from forests, woodlands, and grasslands for use as food, fodder, rope, cloth, medicines, drugs, dyes, and for building, fencing, and thatching materials, as well as for the creation of ritual and art objects and musical instruments.

West Africans used many such products for subsistence and exchange long before European trade and colonization reached the coast in the fourteenth century. The kola nut (as well as indigo), for example, has been a consistent feature of forest-savanna trade in the region for centuries. Thus, planted and gathered or collected forestry products have, historically, not simply supplemented local diets. They have also contributed to individual and household income and remain as crucial to the survival of the poor and destitute as to the prosperity of the successful forest commodity producer, transporter, trader, or exporter. The exigencies of structural adjustment programs and measures (such as the cutting of government staff and social services, and the devaluation of national currencies) have reinforced these socioeconomic roles of forests, through limiting both people's access to subsidized goods and services and their ability to earn a living from paid employment. In addition,

Forest rangers surveying a rare forest of bamboo, Mount Oku, Cameroon. The forests of western Africa range from coastal tropical forests to woodland savannas. Trees are endowed with religious, spiritual, and customary meaning throughout the region, and serve as a varied means of livelihood to its inhabitants. © GEORGE STEINMETZ/CORBIS

selected forests, woodlands, and trees are endowed with religious, spiritual, and customary meaning and also play a part in fulfilling complex functions in the local definition of gender roles and spaces.

Not surprisingly, therefore, vegetation (and other natural resource) management and use systems are widespread across western Africa, rather than being restricted to the forest biome and its societies, crops, and products. Frequently complex, usually dynamic, and almost always contested, such systems often have origins that antedate colonial rule. And, unlike much early policy associated with colonial forestry, they demonstrate a conscious desire and willingness on the part of their managers to combine different vegetation and other landscape components and resources into integrated, albeit highly structured, agro-silvapastoral regimes or systems. Colonial forestry policy was predicated, at least initially, on the separation rather than integration of these different land-use and landscape components. Due to this separation, colonial (and postcolonial) policy has been persistently afflicted by difficulties from incompatible directives.

COLONIAL FORESTRY POLICY (1880S–1960S)

Long before the establishment of formal colonial rule, European traders sought a wide range of forestry commodities in western Africa: notably ivory, timber, camwood, and spices from the forests along the coast, and gum arabic from the semiarid Sahelian zone in the north. Indeed, even at the height of the transatlantic slave trade, parts of present-day Sierra Leone and Liberia may have been as well-known for their forest product exports as for their slave cargoes. By the 1800s, therefore, European merchants were attempting to regulate commerce and monopolize the export trade in forestry commodities by collusively fixing prices for products such as gum and timber, imposing production quotas on primary producers of such commodities, and excluding African traders from lucrative European markets for these goods. Gold Coast (present-day Ghana) and Yoruba chiefs, for example, were selling concessions to European timber merchants who were also able to acquire commercial rights over forests through treaty negotiations.

The growth in the volume of exports of gathered products such as palm kernels, rubber, and timber, which resulted in intensive localized deforestation

and the rapid and widespread destruction of rubber vines, led several colonial governments to seriously consider forest conservation strategies, which had already been tried in places such as Mauritius, Burma, the Cape Colony, and particularly India. Further impetus to forest conservation was provided by the impact of riverboat and railway traffic on localized regional forests, which were either cleared during track construction or cut to supply steamboats and trains with fuel. In addition, both rivers and railway lines quickly became conduits for fuelwood and timber, often from the interior to growing coastal cities. Arguably the biggest stimulus to conservation was provided by the systematic demonization of the commonly linked activities of shifting cultivation (involving temporary plots cleared from forests), fuelwood collection, and bush burning. These were perceived to directly threaten future supplies of products such as wild rubber and oil palm, natural gum copal, and indigenous hardwood timber. They were also believed to pose a threat to the economic basis of colonial rule, through assumed causal links to deforestation-induced climate change.

Not surprisingly, early forestry policies were heavily influenced by a perceived need to protect commercial forestry and agricultural interests, even though these policies were routinely justified in environmental rather than fiscal terms. Thus, in 1898, French colonial officials, concerned that deforestation was causing river siltation, set up rotational woodcutting schedules to manage cutting along the Senegal River in a scheme that was never to be enforced. Two years later French West Africa's first forestry code was established by the Colonial Service of Agriculture and Forests. It gave usufructuary rights to local populations while requiring permits for commercial exploitation of all forest products. It also included measures to encourage reforestation where high-value species were cut, and to outlaw deforestation on steep slopes and lands set aside by the governor.

In March 1912, in the midst of a prolonged Sahelian drought and with major export firms voicing concern over the declining productive capacity of Sahelian forests, the governor-general of the colony held a meeting to discuss measures to halt deforestation. One commercial pressure group lobbying the government to pass legislation to conserve local forests noted at the time that the disappearance of forests had not only deprived the colony of a valuable source of production, it has further affected Senegal's climate. Similar concerns were expressed in a 1916 report to the lieutenant governor of Senegal by the chief of the Colonial Service of Agriculture and Forests. The report, which attributed deforestation largely to the combined effect of woodcutting for fuel and indigenous agricultural clearing, and detailed the perceived local consequences of deforestation, also recommended stricter enforcement of existing forestry rules.

Despite concern over the effects of forest exploitation and decline dating to at least the 1800s, it was not until 1923 that an independent French West African Forestry Service was established. In the meantime, the perception of worsening environmental conditions had persisted and assumed increased urgency, while the assumed culpability of indigenous populations and their activities had acquired the status of undeniable fact. Thus, from its inception, the service's primary role was as a paramilitary rural police force, whose responsibility was to restrict local access to forest resources and landscapes.

In justifying such a restrictive policy and its associated recommendation for the establishment of a vast network of forest reserves, the governor cited the necessity to protect forests from abuse and

> to consider above all the principal function that the forest fulfills in the physical and social economy of the land and which gives it public value.... It must be safeguarded, protected and improved, not so much for extracting revenues as for being in condition for best fulfilling its indirect role in the inhabitability and development of the country. (*Journal officiel du Sénégal*, no. 26 S.E. [16 February 1933]: 142–143)

This policy was enshrined in the 1935 Forestry Code with the aim of conserving fuelwood and timber supplies, and restoring ecosystems perceived to be deteriorating. The code reinforced and extended sweeping state powers over forests and forest products which were first asserted in 1990; divided forests into classified (reserves for timber, fuelwood, and game) and protected (all nonclassified forests) zones, with statutes specifying special arrangements for their management; and introduced

or confirmed various use restrictions. It also specified penalties for infractions. The 1935 Code set the tone for forestry policy through the end of the colonial period.

During World War II, the French cut off oil to the colonies, forcing them to rely much more on wood fuels. Woodcutting laws were restructured to increase production of fuelwood (both firewood and charcoal), and fuelwood commerce grew rapidly. Under colonial law, production permits were restricted to French citizens. Because the only Africans granted French citizenship were those living in urban centers, the citizenship laws privileged urban merchants as an occupational group and largely excluded rural dwellers from commercial forestry. This urban control of forestry commerce has endured to the present.

The historian R. R. Grove argued that the methods by which forestry conservation was introduced to western Africa reveal not only that colonial British and French forestry policies were frequently closely intertwined, but that even where important differences existed, the intercolonial and international nature of colonial scientific expertise meant that important cross-connections were retained in the development of policy. For instance, the authors' research, undertaken separately in the drylands of Senegal and in northern Nigeria, provides much evidence of such cross-connections at the local level. Similarly, at the regional scale, a crude synthesis of Anglophone and Francophone policy for the first half of the twentieth century would reveal concern with natural forest protection and management (1900–1920s); the role of silviculture and plantation establishment and management in controlling soil erosion and land degradation (1920s–1940s); and, in the postwar period, the role of forestry administration and management within wider processes of colonial development (1940s–1960s).

Across French and British colonial West Africa, forestry legislation and other forms of intervention predated the formal establishment of forestry services and administrations, which were frequently created before, or at the same time as (and usually as part of), departments with responsibility for agriculture. The design and adoption of coherent forestry policies also tended to follow rather than precede the constitution of forest estates, and a lack of tropical silvicultural knowledge among forestry administrators and technicians merely encouraged practices of utilization before management.

Despite their own continued lack of detailed knowledge and understanding of the structure and dynamics of indigenous agro-silva-pasture, policymakers blamed local populations for deforestation and, on occasion, for even drought and floods. They then disingenuously used this mistaken opinion to justify restrictive policies on forest use, on the grounds that west Africans were in dire need of guidance, training, or education in the ways of scientific or sustainable forestry that, it was hoped, would supplant indigenous land-use practices. Local training of west Africans for employment in regional forestry services, particularly in protecting the regional forest estate from uncontrolled and wasteful use, was thus an integral part of early colonial policy. In this connection, the suggestion made in the 1880s by Alfred Moloney, conservationist and colonial official (ultimately governor) in Lagos Colony, that Africans should be fully trained as forestry technicians and conservation managers, did not gain widespread support. For the most part, as in Northern Nigeria, where a training school was established in the same year that the regional Forestry Service headquarters became operational, Africans in both the British and French colonies were only trained to fill subordinate jobs within forestry departments.

In spite of similarities between different policy traditions, regional policy reflects local institutional and learning processes as well as international influences. Local dynamics help explain the highly effective indigenous challenge to early colonial forest-conservation proposals and plans in both the Gold Coast and Lagos colonies, which had the effect of reasserting, albeit temporarily, indigenous control over local forestry landscapes. Colonial (southern and northern) Nigerian forestry policy grew out of the Indian experience. However, the territory's vast size, its chronic shortage of European supervisory staff, its perpetual lack of operational funds, and arising in part from these, a widespread inability or failure to enforce existing legislation, meant that in practice both tactics and strategies were distinctly local and regional, despite the broad similarity of colonial policy objectives across the territory as a whole.

POSTINDEPENDENCE REGULATION (1960S TO LATE 1980S)

Regional postindependence policies have tended, to varying degrees, to embrace and enlarge on their colonial predecessors. At independence, Francophone west African states inherited the practices of the 1935 forestry code, reproducing these with minor changes. The postcolonial states thus continue to own virtually all forested lands; to regulate access to such land and the resources they support; and to control the retail price of forestry products, notably fuelwood. Rural populations were left with virtually no legal control over the commercial disposition of the resources around them. Indeed, in President Sékou Touré's Guinea (1958–1984), bush burning reportedly carried the death penalty, while in Mali in the 1980s, fines for breaking branches, cutting trees, or starting forest fires were raised well beyond the average annual income.

In contrast, a legacy of indirect rule and forestry management through paramount chiefs and native authorities in the former British colonies bequeathed, at independence, forest estates that were under the dual control of local and central governments. This sometimes led to a confusing overlap of authority that compromised the policing and protection functions of forestry administrations. In Nigeria, poorly financed local government administrations, which were inadequately equipped to sustainably manage forest estates, concentrated on generating income from the issuance of exploitation permits and licenses, while steadfastly resisting attempts by forestry administrators and managers to limit such exploitation. This was tantamount, in the evocative imagery of Nigerian pidgin, to a policy of cut and go. At the same time, both in Nigeria and elsewhere, less accessible areas of forest and woodland (sometimes constituting a part of national forest estates) continued to be subject to local political and patron-client rules of access and use.

Across the region, forest exploitation fees and taxes and forestry commodity prices were sufficiently low to act as a disincentive to conservation of forest resources. In addition, in Cameroon and Liberia, phases of intense forestry (particularly timber) exploitation coincided with political crises, whereas in Nigeria and Senegal powerful pastoral and farming lobbies succeeded in forcing governments to de-reserve sections of the forest estate, sometimes without the knowledge or approval of relevant forestry services, and at times with forest service assistance. Overall, neither logging for timber, felling for firewood and charcoal, nor land use change away from forestry have been guided principally by considerations of physical sustainability.

However, with the extended Sahelian drought episodes of the 1960s, 1970s, and 1980s and, over the same period, a growing (and increasingly globalized) concern with forest destruction, biodiversity loss, and climate change, forestry initiatives designed to halt deforestation and desertification, which were perceived to be major problems across the region, found much favor in national governments and international donor agencies. As in the past, these initiatives consisted, to varying degrees, of tree planting for dune stabilization and windbreaks to reduce soil erosion; encouragement of woodlots and plantations for the supply of fuel and poles; and publicizing the environmental and socioeconomic benefits of farm tree protection and propagation. In addition, there was a concerted attempt to extend regional networks of protected or conservation areas, particularly in the forest zone, and to highlight the significance of nontimber forest products to local and regional livelihood systems.

These initiatives were all actively promoted by local forest services, the international forestry establishment, multilateral development agencies, and environmental nongovernmental organizations, starting in the 1970s. Thus, in a notable reversal of early colonial attitudes, Nigeria, as well as most Francophone countries, issued forestry policy statements making explicit reference to the need to encourage multiple-land-use systems such as agro-forestry and silvi-pasture. Such statements started in the late 1970s, coinciding with a period of federal government and international donor expenditure on environmental and social forestry activities. In Mali, the forest service, the most salient state presence in rural areas, resorted to oppressive and brutal colonial laws and practices in order to demonstrate, for the benefit of foreign donors, the country's commitment to environmental protection. These policies attracted sufficient funds for environmental management that the forest estate was virtually paved with international projects by 1988.

Although much of this intense activity was aimed (albeit often misguidedly) at improving environmental conditions and the quality of rural life, many of its projects and schemes were imposed on rural populations by national forestry services, working with international donor agencies. Few resulted in significant reforestation or noticeable environmental improvement. Some undermined land and tree access and tenure rights or heightened gender and other conflicts. Many underscored the need for a more meaningful role for local participation in forestry planning and management, despite a persistent, albeit residual, inclination toward more restrictive approaches to the management of the regional forest estate.

FORESTRY IN THE PARTICIPATORY ERA
At the height of Mali's democracy revolution of 1991, foresters were reportedly burned alive and chased from the countryside. During a national conference that was subsequently called to discuss post-revolution governance in the country, one of the first demands of rural representatives was the dissolution of the Forest Service. Although these events may have lacked the international significance of the fall of the Berlin Wall, they were no less symptomatic of the predominant mood of the late 1980s and 1990s, which focused attention on relations among civil society, the state, and the market. Within the context of regional forestry, the necessity for mediating between powerful state and private interests on the one hand, and disadvantaged populations on the other, became imperative.

Thus, from about the mid-to-late 1980s, and under pressure from international donors, most West African countries had begun to reassess their forestry policies, recognize the need to revise their forestry sector laws, and reevaluate specific programs and projects. Such debates tended to take place within the context of the formulation of national environmental and forestry action plans, and the 1992 Earth Summit and its outcomes. As a result, by the early 1990s, notions of natural forest management were already challenging the historical preeminence of plantation forestry, while forestry services were publicly voicing their commitment to decentralized and participatory management approaches, and attempting to function less as paramilitary forces and more as technical assistance and extension agencies. Not surprisingly, therefore, the Silver Jubilee Conference of the Forestry Association of Nigeria, held in 1995, was devoted to forestry and the small-scale farmer and had sessions on community participation in forestry development in Nigeria and nonwood forest resources. (For several of the participants in these sessions, however, social or community forestry appeared to recommend itself primarily on grounds of cost effectiveness, rather than meaningful local or popular participation in decision-making.)

As part of their participatory focus, Burkina Faso, the Gambia, Guinea, Mali, Niger, and Senegal have set up local integrated natural resource or commons management schemes. These are organized either through village-level committees or through local councils ostensibly representing rural populations. These schemes are designed to include local populations in forest, pasture, and fisheries management. However, because all decisions require central approval by the forest services of these countries, it is not at all clear that these schemes are more participatory or more decentralized than their predecessors. Further, because neither the committees nor the councils are accountable to or representative of local communities, it is questionable whether these efforts could be considered community participation, even if they created a domain of autonomous local decision making.

In some cases, of course, participatory projects increase local benefits from forestry. In southern Ghana, for example, where the collection of leaves used for wrapping goods contributes to local livelihoods, particularly women's livelihoods, the Forestry Department introduced an experimental system of free permits which has stimulated a positive response from local women, who have set up arrangements for protecting collection sites. Indeed, the country's current forest and wildlife policy speaks of proposals to place particular emphasis on the concept of participatory management and protection of forest and wildlife resources, and of official willingness to seek to develop appropriate strategies, modalities and programs in consultation with relevant agencies, rural communities and individuals. Within forestry circles, institutions, incentives, and adaptive management are major preoccupations.

Elsewhere, particularly in Francophone West Africa, some projects have raised the producer price of wood and increased local control over forestry labor opportunities, giving local villagers access to woodcutting jobs, and rural communities the ability to keep migrant and urban woodcutters out of local forests and woodlands. However, new policies in Burkina Faso, the Gambia, Niger, and Senegal, for example, do not dismantle existing laws that place commercial rights to transport, trade, and distribute wood products with commercial monopolies set up under colonial rule. These most lucrative parts of forest commerce remain beyond the reach of villagers even in the most recent participatory forestry laws. Under the new laws, forest villagers are indeed allowed to participate fully in forest labor, but only marginally in forest profits.

CONCLUSION

Forestry policies in western Africa, while justified as environmental protection and social policy, were developed largely to protect commercial interests. These policies, ranging from permits, licenses, and quotas to managed woodcutting, plantation forestry, protected regeneration, and forest reserves, have rarely been implemented as specified. Had they been fully implemented, most would have served their often-stated environmental and social aims, because they were oriented more toward regulation forestry markets rather than protecting forests. Nevertheless, these policies have had profound effects. Their ecological consequences are difficult to gauge. Their social effects, however, are more clear. Twentieth-century forestry policies in the region have served to put control over commercial forestry into the hands of a limited group of merchants and foresters, while relegating forest villagers to a narrow set of use rights.

The new era of participatory forestry promises to change inequitable patterns of forest regulation. At first glance, however, the new policies seem to be participatory only in name, while carrying forward the highly centralized controls of past policies and practice. The actual social and ecological consequences of these new policies will eventually be gauged through careful analysis of the specific policies being developed and the ways in which they are applied.

See also **Agriculture; Climate; Colonial Policies and Practices; Ecology; Ecosystems; Energy; Ivory; Postcolonialism; Production Strategies; Touré, Sékou; World War II.**

BIBLIOGRAPHY

Adeyoju, S. Kolade. *Forestry and the Nigerian Economy.* Ibadan, Nigeria: Ibadan University Press, 1975.

Barraclough, Solon L., and Krishna B. Ghimire. *Forests and Livelihoods: The Social Dynamics of Deforestation in Developing Countries.* New York: St. Martin's Press, 1995.

Bergeret, Anne, and Jesse C. Ribot. *L'arbre nourricier en pays sahélien.* Paris: Ministère de la coopération et du développement, 1990.

Fairhead, James, and Melissa Leach. *Misreading the African Landscape: Society and Ecology in a Forest-Savanna Mosaic.* New York: Cambridge University Press, 1996.

Freudenberger, Mark Schoonmaker. "The Great Gum Gamble: A Planning Perspective on Environmental Change in Northern Senegal." Ph.D. diss., University of California at Los Angeles, 1992.

Oduwaiye, E. A., ed. *Forestry and the Small-Scale Farmer. Proceedings of the 24th Annual Conference of the Forestry Association of Nigeria, Kaduna.* Ibadan, Nigeria: The Association, 1995.

Ribot, Jesse C. *From Exclusion to Participation: A History of Forest Access Control in Eastern Senegal.* Working Paper 187, African Studies Center, Boston University. Boston, Massachusetts, 1994.

Ribot, Jesse C. "Participation Without Representation: Chiefs, Councils, and Forestry Law in the West African Sahel." *Cultural Survival Quarterly* 20.3 (1996): 40–44.

Richards, Paul. *Fighting for the Rain Forest: War, Youth, and Resources in Sierra Leone.* Portsmouth, NH: Heinemann, 1996.

JESSE C. RIBOT
REGINALD CLINE-COLE

FORESTS AND RAIN FORESTS. *See* Ecosystems: Tropical and Humid Forests.

FREETOWN.

The capital of Sierra Leone, Freetown was founded in 1787 by the Sierra Leone Company, organized by British abolitionists and businessmen seeking to rehabilitate London's black poor and to settle former slaves whom the British had evacuated from North America as they abandoned their former colonies there. The company's officers were convinced that slavery could be replaced by legitimate commerce, and that Christianity could compensate for the moral damage inflicted on Africans by the slave trade. The settlement was tiny at first, and its links with the hinterland were tenuous. With development of a British naval patrol to end Portuguese and Spanish slaving on the Atlantic, the Royal Navy's West Africa Squadron, Africans "recaptured" from the slavers were landed at Freetown and placed under the care of missionaries, who provided them with education. The Fourah Bay Institution (est. 1827) and the Grammar School (est. 1845) were founded for this purpose. Freetown's creole, or "Krio," population of first settlers and later recaptives came to form a distinct ethnic group, possessing their own language and identity. Since there was neither native law nor custom in the colony, many Krio adopted the English way of life and rose to positions of authority within the colonial administration.

When the modern nation of Sierra Leone gained independence in 1961, Freetown was chosen as its capital. The population of Freetown increased from 130,000 in 1963 to more than 1 million in 2004, as people migrated to the city in search of employment. As the city's population grew, leaders from various rural ethnic groups became involved in city politics and in commerce, and the character of the city became increasingly Muslim. Krio continued to dominate most professions, the civil service, and multinational management positions, and a small Lebanese community controlled a significant proportion of wholesale and retail trade. Nonetheless, non-Krio gained influence within the city over time. The politicization of ethnicity occurred because non-Krio leaders in the city maintained ties with their counterparts in the hinterland and used them to influence the national political process, simultaneously earning them a voice within the political parties. Confrontations escalated as ethnic leaders organized challenges to Krio dominance.

In the 1990s a civil war broke out, and in 1997 a military coup ousted Sierra Leone's civilian government, sparking ethnic violence throughout the countryside. The violence displaced vast numbers of people, who fled to the relative safety of the city, vastly swelling the urban population and contributing to Freetown's rapid economic decline. The civil war was brought to an official close in January 2002, and the city began its healing process.

See also **Sierra Leone.**

BIBLIOGRAPHY

Banton, Michael. *A West African City: A Study of Tribal Life in Freetown.* London: Oxford University Press, 1969.

Fyle, C. Magbaily. *Historical Dictionary of Sierra Leone.* Lanham MD: Scarecrow Press, 2006.

Howard, Allen M., and David E. Skinner. "Ethnic Leadership and Class Formation in Freetown, Sierra Leone." In *New Perspectives on Social Class and Socioeconomic Development in the Periphery,* ed. Nelson W. Keith and Novella Z. Keith. New York: Greenwood Press, 1988.

Sikainga, Ahmad A., and Ousseina Alidou, eds. *Postconflict Reconstruction in Africa.* Trenton, NJ: Africa World Press, 2006.

Wyse, Akintola. *The Krio of Sierra Leone: An Interpretive History.* London: Hurst, in association with the International African Institute, 1989.

S. Ademola Ajayi

FRENCH COLONIES. *See* Colonial Policies and Practices: French North Africa; Colonial Policies and Practices: French West and Equatorial Africa.

FRONTIERS.

The map of precolonial sub-Saharan Africa has often been seen as a mosaic of discrete tribes and polities, of clearly bounded cultural, linguistic, and political units. The model such units imply was indeed appropriate to some African societies, and many classic African ethnographies were framed in terms of it. At the same time, most ethnographies have also recognized that the boundaries between the tribes were often fuzzy, that the tribes were usually constituted out of ethnically heterogeneous elements, and that many of them had, historically speaking, emerged usually no more than a few centuries before. A persistent theme in African oral histories speaks of intruders from other societies coming in and founding local polities; these then grew by conquest and assimilation of local populations that had belonged to other groups in the region. When this process of expansion and growth had been sufficiently prolonged, it yielded a society having relatively well integrated institutions and exhibiting a cultural and linguistic unity—in short, a society to which the classic anthropological model is appropriate.

But in reality most African societies did not entirely complete this process and were situated at different points in it. Those at the beginning of the process were small, ambiguous, unimportant, and evidently transient phenomena, shunned by anthropologists as untypical and anomalous. Most of them were indeed eventually dismantled, absorbed by neighboring embryonic polities. But even in a more typical society, the ideal model was most visible at the core of the polity. The peripheries were less integrated. And beyond these there often lay a kind of ethnic and political noman's-land wedged between the established societies and sheltering a culturally and linguistically varied population, clearly heterogeneous in origins and with unclear ethnic and political affiliations: in effect, a frontier land with frontier societies.

This more dynamic picture of African tribes and polities takes it for granted that, over time, societies appeared and grew, and also shrank and vanished, providing fodder for the growth of succeeding societies. When colonial powers occupied Africa in the nineteenth century, they encountered the latest results of an ongoing process of continuous ethnic and political rearrangement, involving emergent and declining societies separated by shifting frontiers.

A frontier is an area over which political control by the regional metropoles is absent or uncertain. It presents an institutional vacuum: Settlers moving into it from the metropoles must create their own institutional arrangements to govern themselves and their relations with neighbors (who are also immigrants from the same or neighboring metropoles). This situation characterized many of the well-known historical frontiers around the world, such as the North American frontier, the Australian outback, the Indian-Spanish frontiers of Latin America, and the Asian frontiers of Russia. The immigrants to these frontiers were utterly foreign outsiders, and the frontiers varied in extent and in the degree of control that the metropoles exercised over the frontiersmen. On some frontiers of continental scope, such as the Russian and the Spanish, metropolitan authority was quite strong. On the equally large North American frontier, metropolitan control was present but relatively mild.

This familiar kind of frontier also existed in Africa, both in prehistory and in modern times. Perhaps the best-known contemporary example involved the movement of European settlers into African territories in South Africa (thus being comparable to the North American frontier). A more unusual version of such a frontier, involving the Africanization of Portuguese incomers and their institutions, occurred in Mozambique. African prehistory provides examples of sweeping frontiers on which historians lack any hard data. Linguistic reconstruction indicates that much of southern sub-Saharan Africa was populated from the north over the past four millennia. There were thus waves of frontiersmen moving ever southward into areas occupied by pygmoid and Khoesan-speaking hunter-gatherers—mainly agriculturists in the west and pastoralists in the east. Historians glimpse some of the dynamics of this moving frontier in its manifestations in the past half-millennium in southern Africa.

But Africa also has exhibited innumerable and systemic instances of a frontier type all its own: what might be called the "internal frontier," which existed at the edge of almost every African society and separated it from neighboring societies. Here, the frontiersmen came not from afar but from the local metropoles, they were indigenous to the immediate area, all the participants were culturally akin, and the peculiar local frontier dynamic was endlessly repeated across the subcontinent.

This special character of internal African frontiers derived from two factors. First, precolonial African population densities were low, and there were large areas open to new settlement. Second, the administrative and policing capacities of African polities were rudimentary, thus confining effective control to their core areas. This kept the peripheral lands open to new settlement and created a full-fledged frontier situation: the immigrant settlers were obliged to construct their own institutions, and they were free to embark upon local expansion by attempting to extend their sway over their neighbors and to build local petty polities. Some of these polities became the embryos of new societies. But such successes were, of course, rare. Rather than absorbing others, most frontiersmen were themselves absorbed into the few embryonic polities that, in time, grew into chiefdoms, kingdoms, and states. This means that most of the mature African societies known to us historically began as "frontier societies."

A frontier does not create frontiersmen unless there are forces that push people out of the metropole into it. The structure of African societies actively encouraged a constant expulsion of people from kin groups, communities, and ruling groups. Since African polities exercised rather limited

political control, kin groups and communities enjoyed great internal autonomy. They had to settle their internal quarrels by themselves and resented outside interference. This meant that internal quarrels tended to fester, usually leading to mutual accusations of witchcraft. Each party was tempted either to expel the other or to flee from it. When African kin groups and political groups became too large, unwieldy, and faction ridden, they consistently resorted to separation: the weaker side left or was expelled. If the ejected group was to reconstitute itself into an effective autonomous group, it was best for it to do so at some distance from its rival. It could move into a neighboring polity (but then it put itself under new political masters) or, better, it could move into a politically open area—that is, into the frontier. These dynamics of ejection to the fringes operated at all levels—in hamlets, villages, larger communities, and the ruling kin groups of kingdoms. African polities seldom had unambiguous rules of succession to the rulership; the death of a ruler usually brought about dynastic quarrels and even civil wars. To the losing faction, moving into a frontier area offered the chance to build a new polity of its own.

Frederick Jackson Turner's original "frontier thesis" suggested that the effect of the North American frontier was innovative, that the frontier experience shaped the egalitarianism and independence of the American national character. But clearly American frontiersmen brought with them the political culture of the coastal metropole—notions about political legitimacy, "natural" social units, the nature of the community, and so on. Indeed, their movement to the frontier was impelled by preexisting ideas (such as those of individual independence and achievement) on which they built the new societies on the frontier. Precisely because the frontier represents an institutional vacuum to the settlers, it gives them an unusual opportunity to erect institutions that express the culturally desirable social order. In this sense, the frontier's function can be culturally "conservative" rather than innovative. It allows reiteration and reassertion, in a pure and naive form, of the model of the ideal society—a model that, in the older metropole, has necessarily been compromised by the contingencies of history.

Settlers came to the African frontiers with a preexisting African political culture. This culture contained certain basic notions: kin groups as essential social units that subsume the individual; kinship as an apt model and metaphor for political relations; hierarchy as a natural regulator of social relations; the primacy of the "first comer" in a region and the need for rulers to adapt this principle to their claims of legitimacy; the patrimonial nature of rulership, in which the polity and its people are regarded as the estate of the rulers; and the related notion that rulers depend on the acceptance of their subjects.

The elements of this political culture were shared by all frontiersmen, both those who built a new embryonic polity and those who submitted to it. They were also well adapted to the frontier situation; having grown out of it, they were easily reinvigorated when reintroduced to it afresh. This process of continuous reinforcement through reintroduction to subsequent frontiers gave continuity over time to the regional political cultures.

In the larger perspective of sub-Saharan Africa as a whole, the process allowed, on a subcontinental scale, the perpetuation of basic Pan-African political ideas. Where, one may ask, did these ideas first arise? One can offer only plausible speculation. The present population of sub-Saharan Africa is overwhelmingly descended, culturally and physically, from the societies that were formed in the smaller (and at that time fertile) saharan-sahelian area some four to five millennia ago. Starting in the third millennium BCE, with the increasing desiccation of the region, populations deriving from these ancestral societies, with their probably kindred cultures, gradually moved south; the last and clearest expression of this movement was the spread of Bantu speakers into the southern third of Africa over the past two and a half millennia. Only within such an historical framework of cultural diffusion can one understand the cultural homogeneity of sub-Saharan Africa, a homogeneity that implies a dispersion of culturally kindred populations. The homogeneity is striking in comparison, say, with Asia or the Americas. The frontier process in turn suggests a mechanism by which cultural reproduction on such a large scale could have been sustained. In this sense, one can broadly speak of African cultures as being rooted in a frontier setting, both in their origins and in their reproduction—in the same way that Western European political culture was rooted in the feudal and manorial arrangements of the post-Roman period and that Chinese political culture was rooted in the organizational necessities of irrigation agriculture.

See also **Anthropology and the Study of Africa; Bantu, Eastern, Southern, and Western, History of (1000 BCE to 1500 CE); Boundaries, Colonial and Modern; Ethnicity; Prehistory.**

BIBLIOGRAPHY

Gerhard, Dietrich. "The Frontier in Comparative Perspective." *Comparative Studies in Society and History* 1, no. 3 (1959): 205–229.

Isaacman, Allen F. *Mozambique: The Africanization of a European Institution: The Zambezi Prazos, 1750–1902.* Madison: University of Wisconsin Press, 1972.

Kopytoff, Igor. "Introduction." In *The African Frontier: The Reproduction of Traditional African Societies,* ed. Igor Kopytoff. Bloomington: Indiana University Press, 1987.

Lamar, Howard, and Leonard Thompson, eds. *The Frontier in History: North America and Southern Africa Compared.* New Haven, CT: Yale University Press, 1981.

Thorpe, Carolyn R. *Hunter-gatherers and Farmers: An Enduring Frontier in the Caledon Valley, South Africa.* Oxford: Archaeopress, 2000.

Turner, Frederick Jackson. "The Significance of the Frontier in American History." In *Frontier and Section: Selected Essays,* ed. Ray Allen Billington. Englewood Cliffs, NJ: Prentice-Hall, 1961.

Wyman, Walker D., and Clifton B. Kroeber, eds. *The Frontier in Perspective.* Madison: University of Wisconsin Press, 1957.

IGOR KOPYTOFF

FUAD, KING OF EGYPT (1868–1936). Ahmad Fuad Pasha was born on March 26, 1868, in Giza as the youngest child of Khedive Ismail. He left Egypt in 1879 for Istanbul and studied in Geneva, Turin, and at the Italian Military Academy. He returned to Egypt in 1892. Fuad became sultan in 1917 when Egypt was still a British protectorate. Having strong popular support, he attempted to lead the government and achieve Egypt's independence. The emerged nationalist movement, the Wafd under Sa'd Zaghlul (1859–1927), blocked his efforts. This led to the collapse of Anglo-Egyptian talks and a unilateral declaration of independence by the British in 1922.

Fuad assumed the title king and promulgated in 1923 a new liberal constitution under which the Wafd won parliamentary majorities in 1923, 1925, and 1929. Nevertheless, Fuad was able to form governments without the Wafd. In 1930 he revoked the 1923 constitution, dissolved the parliament, and changed the electoral law. The next election in 1931 brought a non-Wafdist majority and stability until 1935, when increasing nationalist pressure led to the restoration of the 1923 constitution and, subsequently, a Wafd victory in the 1936 elections. Fuad strongly supported educational institutions in Egypt. Months before the signing of an Anglo-Egyptian treaty for more autonomy, Fuad died on April 28, 1936.

See also **Egypt, Modern.**

BIBLIOGRAPHY

Sayyid-Marsot, Afaf Lutfi al-. *Egypt's Liberal Experiment, 1922–1936*. Berkeley: University of California Press, 1977.

Vatikiotis, Panayiotis J: *The History of Modern Egypt: From Muhammad Ali to Mubarak*, 4th edition. London: Weidenfeld and Nicolson, 1991.

JÖRN THIELMANN

FUELS. *See* **Energy.**

FUGARD, ATHOL   (1932–). The celebrated South African playwright and anti-apartheid activist Harold Athol Lannigan Fugard was born in Middleburg, Cape Province, South Africa, on June 11, 1932. He was raised in Port Elizabeth, and attended the University of Cape Town, but dropped out to travel across Africa before signing on to a merchant ship and sailing the trade routes of Southeast Asia for several years.

When he finally returned to Cape Town, he became involved in the theater. With several fellow actors (including Sheila Meiring, whom he married), he founded Cape Town's Circle Players. He spent the next several years in Cape Town and Johannesberg, writing, acting, and directing plays, and becoming increasingly involved in anti-

King Fuad I of Egypt (1868–1936). In 1923, King Fuad I attempted to strengthen his power by replacing the country's constitution with a new version that limited the role of Parliament to that of mere advisers. Due to public dissatisfaction, he restored the original constitution in 1935. HULTON ARCHIVE/GETTY IMAGES

Athol Fugard (1932-). In Fugard's play *My Children! My Africa!* the South African playwright blasted the African National Congress for boycotting South African schools because he felt the decision hurt a generation of students. CORBIS

apartheid activities. His plays reflected his politics, and in 1961, recognizing that the South African government would not permit the performance of his play *Blood Knot*, he took the production to London. Upon his return to South Africa, the government seized his passport, withholding it for four years. Forced to remain in South Africa, he organized a boycott of actors in protest to the apartheid segregation of theater audiences, further antagonizing the government. In 1971 Fugard was again permitted to leave the country. He began premiering many of his works on the stages of London and at the Yale Reparatory Theater in the United States. His plays could not be produced in South Africa until the end of apartheid in 1994.

Throughout his career, Fugard worked collaboratively with Johannesberg-based actors John Kani and Winston Ntshona. Together they developed a creative style that relied heavily on improvisation and on working out a script before live audiences. His body of work is extensive, much of it powerfully political. With the end of apartheid, however, the political element of his work has become more personal.

Fugard won an Obie Award (1970–1971, for *Roesman and Lena*), a Tony Award (1974–1975, for *Sizwe Banzi Is Dead/The Island*, with Kani and Ntshona), the New York Drama Critics' Circle Award (1980–1981, Best Play for *A Lesson from Aloes*), the 1986 Writers Guild Award for Outstanding Achievement, and an Audie Award (1999, for *The Road to Mecca*). In addition to plays, he has written a novel (*Tsotsi*, 1989) and the nonfiction *Notebooks: 1960–1977* (1983).

See also **Apartheid; South Africa, Republic of: History and Politics (1850–2006); Theater: Southern Africa.**

BIBLIOGRAPHY

Benson, Mary. *Athol Fugard and Barney Simon: A Bare Stage, a Few Props, Great Theater*. Randburg, South Africa: Raven Press, 1997.

Read, John, comp. *Athol Fugard: A Bibliography*. Grahamstown, South Africa: National English Literary Museum, 1991.

NANCY E. GRATTON

GABON

GEOGRAPHY AND ECONOMY

Gabon is located in western Africa, straddling the equator and bordered by the Atlantic Ocean on the west, and Equatorial Guinea, Cameroon, and the Republic of Congo, clockwise, from the northwest. The country's area covers 103,347 square miles, of which 99,486 are land, and 3,861 are its rivers, making it slightly smaller than the American state of Colorado. The economy of Gabon has been shaped by its geography, its heavily forested landscape, its low population density, and its mineral and timber wealth. Its borders correspond to rivers and drainage areas rather than human settlement. The basin of its largest river, the Ogooué, covers 72 percent of the nation's territory. A number of smaller river systems make up the remainder: the Nyanga and Nkomi in the south; and the Komo (Gabon), Upper Woleu, and Upper N'tem in the north. Gabon's low-lying coastal plain rises to a series of inland plateaus, broken by the Monts de Cristal, the Moabi Hills, and the Du Chaillu Massif. The country's lowest point is the Atlantic Ocean; its highest is on Mont Iboundji, just under one mile high. Gabon has seaports and terminals at Libreville, Gamba, Lucinda, Owendo, and Port-Gentil.

Although the Ogooué valley traverses the geographic center of the country, it is at present relatively depopulated. Close to half of Gabon's total population of approximately 1.455 million (2007 estimate) lives in two coastal cities: Libreville, the national capital (2007 estimated population 604,200) and Port-Gentil, the economic capital (114,000 estimated). The most populous rural zones are in the north, near the border of Cameroon, and in the south, near its border with the Republic of the Congo. In the past, people lived in villages scattered along rivers; footpaths through the rain forest were the main transportation routes. In the early twenty-first century most villages lie along government-built roads, where they have moved since the beginning of the twentieth century.

Gabon's climate is invariably hot and humid, nurturing the equatorial rain forest that contains an estimated 8,000 species of plants, of which 400 are trees. The forest covers more than 77,000 square miles, or 75 percent of the country, making it the second largest forest in Africa. The National Gabonese Timber Company, a government-owned monopoly, says that three quarters of the forest may be exploited. The main species harvested is okoumé, which is used all over the world in the manufacture of plywood. It represents more than a quarter of the resources (approximately 360 million cubic feet) exported in 2001. Other types of timber exported include Padouk, Kevazingo, Moabi, Agba, Beli, Azobé, Douka, Izombe, Iroko, and Movingui. Wooded areas along the coast are reserved for Gabonese operators. Forests in the provinces of Nyanga, Ngounié, Moyen-Ogooué

2.2 percent. Gabon's two other major exports in the twenty-first century are uranium and manganese.

Gabon's rich supply of offshore oil and natural gas has made it more prosperous than most nearby nations, with a per capita income four times the average in sub-Saharan Africa. This fact has led to a sharp decline in extreme poverty, but because of a high rate of income inequality, a large proportion of the population remains poor. According to one source, 2 percent of the population enjoys 80 percent of the national income. In 2006, Gabon had a gross domestic product (GDP) of $7.052 billion in U.S. dollars at the official exchange rate, and a per capita GDP of US$7,200. Agriculture employed 60 percent of the work force, industry employed 15 percent, and the service sector accounted for 25 percent, as estimated in 2006. Public debt was 28.6 percent of GDP at that time.

In 2005, the country had 39,100 main telephone landlines in use, and 649,800 mobile cellular phones. At that time it had 67,000 Internet users. There were 56 airports, 11 of which had paved runways, 506 miles of railways, and 5,700 miles of roads, of which 582 were paved. The country is in the happy situation of having a favorable balance of payments. In 2005 it exported US$5.237 million in goods and services, compared to imports worth US$3.820 million.

See also **Ecosystems; Forestry; Libreville.**

BIBLIOGRAPHY

Barnes, James F. *Gabon: Beyond the Colonial Legacy.* Boulder, CO: Westview Press, 1992.

Gardinier, David E. *Historical Dictionary of Gabon.* 2nd edition. Metuchen, NJ: Scarecrow Press, 1994.

Metegue-N'nah, Nicolas. *L'implantation coloniale au Gabon: La résistance d'un peuple, 1839–1960.* Vol. 1. Paris: Harmattan, 1981.

Pourtier, Roland. *Le Gabon.* 2 vols. Paris: L'Harmattan, 1989.

Yates, Douglas. *The Rentier State in Africa: Oil Rent Dependency and Neocolonialism in the Republic of Gabon.* Trenton, NJ: Africa World Press, 1996.

Zomo Yebe, Gabriel. *Comprendre la crise de léconomie gabonaise.* Paris: L'Harmattan, 1993.

MIRYAM EHRLICH WILLIAMSON

and Haut-Ogooué, Ogooué-Lolo, and parts of Ogooué-Ivindo and Woleu-Ntem are available for harvesting by forestry companies. This area is especially desirable because if its link to the railway line. The east-northeast quarter of the country includes the protected Minkébé and the large forest-free savannas of the Batéké plateaus.

Forestry was the backbone of Gabon's export economy until the burgeoning of the oil industry after the country declared its independence in 1961. During the late 1920s and 1930s, the colonial administration introduced cocoa and coffee as export crops, particularly in the northern Woleu-N'tem region. Resulting sales enabled rural cultivators to pay their taxes and school fees, to make marriage payments, to purchase imported goods, and at times to attain a measure of prosperity. Devaluation of the country's currency by 50 percent in 1994 led to an inflationary surge of 35 percent; the rate of inflation then dropped to 6 percent in 1996. Ten years later, in 2006, it was estimated at

SOCIETY AND CULTURES

Archaeological findings of Stone Age tools give evidence that the region now known as Gabon has been inhabited since Paleolithic times. The Baka people (Pygmies) are the earliest known human inhabitants of the area, followed in the thirteenth century by the Myene who established a fishing community along the coast of the Atlantic Ocean. In the 1470s, Portuguese explorers found the estuary of the Ogooué River. Before long, a lively trade was established with European products and salt being imported and slaves and ivory the major exports. Dutch, English, and French traders also found the area profitable. By the end of the eighteenth century, France had achieved a position of dominance in the region. Although the Congress of Vienna abolished the slave trade in 1815, the capture and sale of indigenous people continued until the 1880s. In 1849, the French founded Libreville (free city) as a settlement for freed slaves. In 1886 the French formally assumed governance of Gabon. Gabon became part of French Equatorial Africa in 1910; in 1958 the territory voted to become an autonomous republic while remaining within the French community. Then, in 1961, the country chose independence.

Gabon is one of the least densely inhabited countries in Africa. In 2007, an estimated 1.455 million people inhabited the country, which has an area slightly smaller than the American state of Colorado. It is also one of the most economically successful. Wealth is largely concentrated in the port cities of Libreville, Gabon's capital and largest city, and Port-Gentil, considered the economic capital of the country. Annual population growth in 2007 was estimated at 2.036 percent. Children from birth to fourteen make up 42.1 percent of Gabon's population; the 15–64-year-old age group constitutes 53.9 percent, and those 65 years or over comprise just 4 percent. The number of male and female Gabonese is roughly equal in the population until the age of 65. After that, women outnumber men by nearly 29 percent. A 2007 estimate lists 4.71 children born per woman, with a birth rate of 35.96 births per 1,000 people, and a mortality rate of 53.65 infants per 1,000 live births. Skilled health staff attended more than 85 percent of births. Life expectancy at birth is 52.85 years to 53.99 years for male children, and 55.17 years for females.

Gabon's adult literacy rate in 2007 was 72 percent. Although schooling is compulsory to age sixteen, only 83 percent of children were in school full time. The government pays for every child's schooling from primary school through higher education. The pupil-to-teacher ratio in 2004 was 36 to 1. The Gabonese government places no restrictions on academic freedom, including research.

The risk of infectious disease across all age groups is high. Bacterial diarrhea, hepatitis A, and typhoid fever are carried in food and water; malaria is the primary vector-borne disease. Not all children have access to vaccinations, in some cases because of rural isolation, in others due to cultural norms.

The country is home to more than forty ethnic groups. No group holds a majority. The largest group is the Fang, representing about 40 percent of the population. Other major groups are the Bapunu, the Mayene, the Bateke, the Eshira, the Obamba, the Nzebi, and the Pounou. Ethnic integration is the norm, although the Fang tend to be concentrated in the north and the Myene along the coast, where they have lived since at least the thirteenth century. Urban neighborhoods are not segregated ethnically and interethnic marriages are common. Only a few thousand Pygmies remain, mostly in the rain forest of the northeast. The law grants them the same civil rights as other citizens, but they keep largely to themselves, independent of government authority with their own decision-making apparatus. Because they chose not to participate in government programs that integrated other small communities by building major roads, Pygmies' access to government-funded health and sanitation programs is limited. The Gabonese government has no specific programs directed at Pygmies.

French is the official language in Gabon and is mandatory in the school. Most people under age fifty can speak at least two languages—French and the language of their ethnic group. Linguists have identified eleven Bantu language groups in Gabon: Benga, Fang, Kwele, Myene, Kota-Kele, Tsogo, Punu, Nzabi, Mbama, Teke, and Vili. Pygmies in the north speak Baka, a Ubangian language.

Gabon's constitution provides for religious freedom. There is no state religion, although more than half of Gabonese people are Christian, with

Roman Catholics outnumbering Protestants by approximately three to one. Many Gabonese people practice both a Western religion and Bwiti, an ancient religion involving worship of ancestors, ritual healing, and animism. Muslims make up less than 1 percent of the population. The constitution forbids discrimination based on national origin, race, gender, or opinion. The law provides that women have equal rights of access to education, business, and investment. Women own businesses and property, participate in politics, and work both in government and the private sector. A regulation that requires a woman to obtain her husband's permission to travel abroad is rarely enforced.

Men may legally have more than one wife, but women may have only one husband. Couples must declare at the time of marriage whether the relationship will be monogamous or polygynous. A man may marry more than one woman without his existing wives' consent, but he is required to provide for them equally. A woman in a polygynous marriage who leaves her husband is entitled to half her existing support. If she is the only wife, she gets an equal share of the couple's assets. This applies only, however, to legally sanctioned marriages. In common-law marriage, which is accepted socially and widely practiced, the woman has no property rights. When a marriage is dissolved, children of the marriage are considered to belong to the husband. Probably for this reason, women commonly bear children before marrying; those children are hers in the event of divorce. This view of dependent human beings as property dates back to earlier tribal days, when a man's wealth was measured by the number of his dependents.

Gabonese crafts include carvings, masks, sculpture, and basketry. The Museum of Arts and Traditions in Libreville exhibits traditional artifacts. Casava (manioc) is a staple of the Gabonese diet. Agricultural products include maize and rice, plantains, peppers, taro, yams, tomatoes, eggplant, and squashes. Bananas, guavas, limes, mangoes, oranges, papayas, and pineapples are grown as well. The Gabonese diet also includes meat and fish stews.

Houses in rural areas are built of concrete, brick, wood, and wattle and daub. In contrast, Libreville is a modern city of apartment buildings, high-rise offices, and hotels.

See also **Children and Childhood: Infancy and Early Development; Death, Mourning, and Ancestors; Disease: Viral and Infectious; Ethnicity; Food; Ivory; Marriage Systems.**

BIBLIOGRAPHY

Barnes, James F. *Gabon: Beyond the Colonial Legacy.* Boulder, CO: Westview Press, 1992.

Gaulme, François. *Le Gabon et son ombre.* Paris: Karthala, 1988.

Péan, Pierre. *Affaires africaines.* Paris: Fayard, 1983.

Pourtier, Roland. *Le Gabon.* 2 vols. Paris: L'Harmattan, 1989.

Raponda-Walker, André, and Roger Sillans. *Rites et croyances des peuples du Gabon.* Paris: Presence africaine, 1962.

United States Central Intelligence Agency. *The World Factbook.* Washington, DC: Central Intelligence Agency, 2007.

MIRYAM EHRLICH WILLIAMSON

HISTORY AND POLITICS

The modern history of Gabon, a Central African country, has been shaped largely by French colonial rule and the continued influence of France after independence in 1960. Its natural resources have allowed the country to become one of the wealthiest states in all of Africa, but relatively few Gabonese have received much benefit from the profits.

COLONIAL GABON TO 1930

Gabon emerged as the first French outpost in Central Africa during the late 1830s and 1840s. Coastal communities such as Mpongwe clans along the Gabon Estuary and Orungu settlements in the delta of the Ogooué River had long participated in the Atlantic slave trade. Altercations between these settlements and French naval officers who desired a supply center for their ships led to the establishment of a small colony that consisted only of a few coastal centers. In the interior, southern Gabon was wracked by violent struggles between powerful men along clan lines who competed with one another for access to slaves, ivory, rubber, and control over trade with Europeans. The northern half of Gabon was slowly occupied by decentralized Fang-speaking clans migrating southward from Cameroon and Equatorial Guinea. Like their counterparts to the south, these communities were

République Gabonaise (Gabonese Republic)

Population:	1,454,867 (2007 est.)
Area:	267,658 sq. km (103,347 sq. mi.)
Official language:	French
Languages:	French, Fang, Myene, Bateke, Bapounou/Eschira, Bandjabi
National currency:	CFA franc
Principal religions:	Christian, 55%–75% Muslim, animist
Capital:	Libreville (est. pop. 604,200 in 2007)
Other urban centers:	Port-Gentil, Franceville, Lambaréné
Annual rainfall:	2,540 mm (100 in.) on coast, 3,810 mm (150 in.) in interior
Principal geographical features:	*Mountains:* Monts de Cristal, Du Chaillu Massif, Mount Iboundji, Moabi Hills *Rivers:* Ogooué, Woleu, N'tem, Nyanga *Lagoons:* N'Dogo, M'Goze, M'Komi
Economy:	*GDP per capita:* US$7,200 (2006)
Principal products and exports:	*Agricultural:* cocoa, coffee, sugar, palm oil, rubber; cattle, okoume (a tropical softwood); fish *Manufacturing:* petroleum extraction and refining, chemicals, ship repair, food and beverages, textiles, lumbering and plywood, cement *Mining:* crude oil, uranium, manganese ore, natural gas, gold, iron ore, lead, zinc, diamonds
Government:	Independence from France, 1960. Constitution, 1960 (amended 1961, 1967, 1975, 1983). New constitution approved in 1991, amended in 1995 and 2003. Multiparty presidential democracy. President elected for 7-year term by universal suffrage. Bicameral legislature consists of the Assemblée Nationale, comprising 120 members elected by universal suffrage, and the Senate, comprising 8 members elected by regional and municipal delegates. President appoints prime minister, who appoints Council of Ministers in consultation with the president. For purposes of local government there are 9 provinces headed by governors, 36 prefectures headed by presidentially appointed prefects.
Heads of state since independence:	1960–1961: Prime Minister Léon Mba 1961–1964: President Léon Mba 1964: Jean-Hilaire Aubame 1964–1967: President Léon Mba 1967–: President Albert-Bernard (later El Hadj Omar) Bongo
Armed forces:	President is commander in chief. Voluntary enlistment. *Army:* 3,200 *Navy:* 500 *Air Force:* 1,000 *Paramilitary:* 4,800
Transportation:	*Rail:* 814 km (506 mi.), the Transgabonais railway, begun in 1973 *Waterways:* 1,600 km (994 mi.) (Ogooué River, navigable for 310 km (193 mi.)) *Ports:* Port-Gentil, Owendo, Libreville *Roads:* 9,170 km (5,698 mi.), 10% paved *National airline:* Air Gabon *Airports:* International facilities at Libreville and Port-Gentil; several regional airports
Media:	Main periodicals: *L'Union, Le Quotidien, Dialogue, La Cité, Sept Jours, Le Progressiste, Le Relance, Gabon-Marti, La Griffe, Ngondo, Gabon Libre.* 4 publishing houses. Radiodiffusion-Télévision Gabonais, La Voix de la Renovation, and Africa No. 1 all provide radio services. 4 television stations.
Literacy and education:	*Total literacy rate:* 63% (2006). Education is free, universal, and compulsory for ages 6–16. Postsecondary education provided through Université Nationale Omar Bongo and several technical and vocational schools.

governed by councils of elders and had great difficulty building solidarity beyond clan or even village identity.

Expeditions by French administrators like Pierre Savorgnan de Brazza and other colonial officials into central and southern Gabon from the mid–1870s to the 1890s resulted in even more violence, as guerrilla warfare between French colonial troops and various clan lenders raged throughout the colony until World War I. Until the 1920s, officials struggled to collect taxes and acquire forced laborers, and they had a dismal reputation in French colonial circles for incompetent administrators and perennial budget woes. Mission-educated Africans in Libreville, the capital of the colony, attempted to demand their legal and cultural equality with metropolitan French citizens with little success. Concessionary companies, most notable the Société d'Haut Ogooué (SHO), were allowed from 1900 to the early 1920s to extort natural resources from Gabonese with the backing of colonial troops. Félix Adande Rapontchombo, the leading Mpongwe clan head in the late nineteenth century, spent most of his later career as a fugitive from administrators, despite his formidable mission education and command of the colonial bureaucracy.

World War I and the 1920s proved to be watershed periods in Gabonese history. The war brought on a wave of famine throughout the colony. Fighting with German forces in Cameroon, combined with administrators' demands for more taxes, natural resources, and labor to serve the war effort devastated Gabonese communities and made armed resistance to French officials difficult to continue. On top of these hardships, the influenza epidemic of 1918–1919 and unseasonably rainy dry seasons between 1917 and 1925 also led to hunger. After 1920, the colonial administration handed out concessions to export *okoumé* lumber to large companies and individual investors. Officials supported the timber industry from the boom years of the 1920s through independence in 1960. Administrators encouraged massive recruitment of male laborers from all over Gabon and other colonies to work in timber concessions on the coast and the Ogooué River. These timber camps became the site for new political activity, as many southern Gabonese workers developed new, broader ethnic identities.

From 1910 to 1930, mission-educated Africans in Libreville and the timber port of Port-Gentil pushed for legal equality through lobbying French parliamentary officials, human rights organizations, and by employing local idioms of supernatural power to intimidate other Africans. Some men, like the Libreville-born Fang leader Léon Mba, used the efforts of French officials to appoint African district chiefs to build entourages for themselves in the 1920s.

GABON AFTER 1930

The Great Depression and World War II brought on a series of changes in Gabonese political life. During the Popular Front era in France, when a leftist coalition governed the empire in the late 1930s, Gabonese administrators created a vocal but rather ineffectual African council of notables. In 1940, Governor Georges Masson supported the pro-Nazi Vichy government rather than the Free French under Charles de Gaulle, but the Vichy supporters were defeated in a short invasion by Gaullist forces at the end of the year. By 1946, French officials began to allow elections within the colony. Léon Mba, exiled to the Central African Republic in 1932 on embezzlement charges, returned in 1946 and began to push for a multiethnic political alliance between Fang and coastal groups. Jean-Hilaire Aubame, leader of the Union Sociale et Démocratique Gabonaise (USDG) party and elected as Gabon's representative to the French parliament, became Mba's main rival, especially as administrators manipulated the democratic process to ensure victory for Mba's Bloc Démocratic Gabonais (BDG) party. Mba's loyalty to French colonialism was such that he lobbied to remain in the empire until independence in 1960.

Postcolonial politics in Gabon has been shaped by oil production and continued French influence. Mba greatly curtailed the ability of opposition parties to challenge his authority between 1960 and 1964. When some junior military officers sought to remove President Mba and take power in 1964, the old government was restored by French army units. After Mba's death in 1967, his chief of staff Omar Bongo took power with the blessings of French authorities and formed a one-party state in 1968. With oil and mining profits flooding into the country after the late 1960s, Bongo became one of the wealthiest and most pro-French dictators Africa. Thousands of West African immigrants moved to Gabon to cash in on Gabon's high standard of living, which led to state-supported campaigns against different foreign nationalities in the 1970s and early 1980s. Bongo favored members of his small Teke ethnic community, but he also drew support from a range of political figures, in no small part due to his command over oil revenue.

Opposition parties, such as Mouvement de Redressement National (MORENA) led by Mba Abessole, made little headway against Bongo's

PDG government until the assassination of a political dissident led to riots in 1990. The resulting political unrest led to a 1990 national conference over the future of the government. The drop in global oil prices combined with the conference led Bongo to agree to elections in 1993, which his party won. Allegations of electoral fraud did not weaken Bongo's power, although the PDG consented to end the one-party state. Continued economic problems led to increased poverty and resentment towards the PDG, yet the divided nature of opposition parties and state patronage allowed Bongo to win elections in 1998 and 2005. In 2006, Bongo's party retained control over Gabon.

See also **Brazza, Pierre Paul François Camille Savorgnan de; Human Rights; Ivory; Libreville; Slave Trades; Travel and Exploration; World War I; World War II.**

BIBLIOGRAPHY

Bernault, Florence. *Démocraties ambigües en Afrique Centrale: Congo-Brazzaville et Gabon, 1945–1965.* Paris: Karthala, 1996.

Gray, Christopher. *Colonial Rule and Crisis in Equatorial Africa: Southern Gabon, c. 1850–1940.* Rochester, NY: University of Rochester Press, 2002.

Reed, Michael, and James Barnes, eds. *Culture, Politics, and Ecology in Gabon's Rainforest.* Lewiston, NY: Edwin Mellen, 2003.

Rich, Jeremy. *A Workman Is Worthy of His Meat: Food and Colonialism in the Gabon Estuary, ca. 1840–1960.* Lincoln: University of Nebraska Press, 2007.

Yates, Douglas. *The Rentier State in Africa: Oil Rent Dependency and Neocolonialism in the Republic of Gabon.* Trenton: Africa World Press, 1996.

JEREMY RICH

GABORONE. Gaborone (called Gaberones until 1969) is an entirely new city, built in three years, from 1963 to 1966, as the capital of independent Botswana; the capital of the preceding British protectorate of Bechuanaland had been Mafeking, across the border in the (by-then) Republic of South Africa. The new nation required a new capital symbolizing its hopes for greater autonomy than it had been allowed under the tightly interlinked politics of southern Africa under the domination of the adjoining apartheid regime. The city was built from a British camp adjacent to the town of the BaTlokwa chief Kgosi Gaborone.

Gaborone has since been one of the fastest-growing cities in the world, reaching a population of nearly 210,000 people in 2005. Its central area contains the national government offices and the buildings of the country's central communications facilities. It is also home to the University of Botswana and to the headquarters of the Southern African Development Community (SADC). The country's considerable mineral-driven prosperity (diamonds, manganese, asbestos) have enabled the city to maintain a functioning infrastructure unusual for Africa. The Sir Seretse Khama International Airport is the principal air link for the nation, and Gaborone is one of the significant Southern African nodes modern networks of transportation and communication.

See also **Botswana.**

BIBLIOGRAPHY

Akinboade, Oludele A. "Determinants of Labor Migration to Gaborone, Botswana." In *Social Problems in Africa: New Visions,* ed. Apollo Rwomire. Westport, CT: Praeger, 2001.

Fawcus, Peter. *Botswana: The Road to Independence.* Gaborone, Botswana: Pula Press and the Botswana Society, 2000.

Nyele, Libero. *The Raid on Gaborone, June 14, 1985: A Memorial.* Gaborone, Botswana: L. Nyelele, E. Drake, 1986.

Picard, Louis A. *The Evolution of Modern Botswana: Politics and Rural Development in Southern Africa.* Lincoln: University of Nebraska Press, 1985.

Ramsey, Jeff, Barry Morton, and Fred Morton. *Historical Dictionary of Botswana.* Lanham, MD: Scarecrow Press, 1996.

JOSEPH C. MILLER

GALAWDEWOS (c. 1522–1559). Galawdewos, emperor of Ethiopia from 1540 to 1559, was the son of Emperor Lebna Dengel. In the latter years of Lebna Dengel's reign, Ethiopia was almost completely overrun by the jihad of Ahmad Grañ

(Ahmad ibn Ibrahim al-Ghazi), the imam of Adal, who by 1540 had set up his capital north of Lake Tana and had become the effective ruler of the country. The arrival of a Portuguese expedition led by Cristovão da Gama in 1541 helped save the situation, though da Gama was defeated and executed by Grañ. The remainder of the Portuguese joined forces with Galawdewos; together they defeated and killed Grañ in February 1543 at Woguera.

Galawdewos then had to rebuild the devastated country. Grateful as he was to the Portuguese, he had no intention of altering his religious allegiance to please them and was embarrassed by the arrival of Jesuits who hoped to persuade him to accept the authority of Rome. In reply he composed his Confession of Faith in 1555, a remarkably temperate assertion both of the traditional doctrine of the Ethiopian Orthodox Church and of the practical issues at stake: the celebration of the Sabbath, the rite of circumcision, and the eating of pork. The Jesuits recognized his outstanding qualities in both theological debate and diplomacy. In 1559 Galawdewos was killed in a war with the Muslim kingdom of Adal. He appears as one of the most attractive, intelligent, and humane in Ethiopia's long line of rulers.

See also **Ahmad Ibn Ibrahim al-Ghazi (Ahmad Grañ).**

BIBLIOGRAPHY

Beshah, Girma, and Merid Aregay. *The Question of the Union of the Churches in Luso-Ethiopian Relations.* Lisbon: Junta de Investigaçiões do Ultramar and Centro de Estudos Históricos Ultramarinos, 1964.

ADRIAN HASTINGS

GAMA, VASCO DA (1460–1524).
Vasco da Gama was a Portuguese navigator and the discoverer of the Cape route to India. Having distinguished himself in wars against Castile, in 1497 da Gama was chosen by Portugal's King Manuel I to follow up Bartolomeu Dias's 1488 discovery of the Indian Ocean by making the first sea voyage to India around Africa's Cape of Good Hope. Da Gama departed from Lisbon, rounded the Cape, and reached the location of present-day Natal on Christmas Day, then proceeded slowly up the coast to Mombasa, which he reached on April 7. He clashed with Muslim authorities along the way, but at Malindi he met with a friendly reception. There he obtained a pilot to India, Ahmad ibn Majid, the celebrated author of several treatises on navigation. Sailing across the Indian Ocean, da Gama reached Calicut, on May 20, 1498.

He returned home to great honor, and was sent back to India in 1502–1503. He took tribute from Kilwa and Mombasa on the way, returning from India with immense quantities of spices and other goods, as well as trade treaties. For all this he

Vasco da Gama (1460–1524), from a 1572 woodcut. Da Gama was a Portuguese explorer and commander of the first ships to set sail from Europe to India. He discovered a trade route from Portugal to the East in 1498, causing him to rise to the ranks of admiral and later to India's viceroy, a position he enjoyed for only three months before his death on Christmas Eve, 1524. © BETTMANN/CORBIS

was rewarded with lands, wealth, and the title of Count of Vidigueira. After years of seclusion, in 1524 he was appointed viceroy of India. There he set about reforming the government of Goa but died on Christmas Eve. His body was brought back to Portugal and eventually buried in the Jerónimos monastery church at Belém, beside the poet Camões, whose *Os Lusíadas* celebrated the glory of the Cape route discovery. Da Gama had enriched his country and revolutionized the trade of the Western and Eastern worlds.

See also **Mombasa; Travel and Exploration.**

BIBLIOGRAPHY

Axelson, Eric. *South-East Africa, 1488–1530.* Johannesburg: C. Struik, 1973.

Axelson, Eric, ed. *Vasco da Gama: The Diary of his Travels through African Waters 1497–1499.* Cape Town: Stephan Phillips, 1998.

Disney, Anthony, and Emily Booth, eds. *Vasco da Gama and the Linking of Europe and Asia* (Vasco da Gama Quincentenary Conference, 1997: Melbourne and Fremantle, Australia) Delhi; Oxford: Oxford University Press, 2000.

Freeman-Grenville, G. S. P. "The Coast, 1498–1840." In *History of East Africa,* ed. Roland Oliver et al. Oxford: Oxford University Press, 1963–1976.

Gama, Vasco da. *Vasco Da Gama: The Diary of His Travels through African Waters, 1497–1499,* trans. Eric Axelson. Somerset West, South Africa: Stephan Phillips, 1998.

Watkins, Ronald. *Unknown Seas: How Vasco da Gama Opened the East.* London: John Murray, 2003.

G. S. P. FREEMAN-GRENVILLE

GAMBIA, THE

This entry includes the following articles:
GEOGRAPHY AND ECONOMY
SOCIETY AND CULTURES
HISTORY AND POLITICS

GEOGRAPHY AND ECONOMY

The Republic of the Gambia follows the Gambia River 292 miles eastward from the Atlantic and extends north to south, on average, only 20 miles, making a worm-shaped intrusion into Senegal. The broad river, about one mile wide for a length of over 62 miles up from its mouth, is the country's dominant geographical feature.

Gambian lands differ according to their proximity to water. Along the lower river, where tides are strongest, mangroves and sand dunes dominate. Bordering these and extending farther upriver are *banto faros* (the Mandinka word for "beyond swamp"), areas that are submerged for a month or two in flood season but otherwise are above water. Beyond the river's salinity (108 miles upriver in the dry season), the alluvial soils of the *banto faros* are among the most productive. The rest of the country is a level sandstone plateau (with a highest point of 174 feet) of rolling grasslands that once were heavily wooded. Gambia's 1.7 million people—a population increasing at nearly 3 percent per year—have steadily cleared trees for farming, timber, and firewood. The Gambia experiences two seasons, one hot and humid (July–November) when its annual average of 35 inches of rain falls, and the other hot and dry (December–June) when winds blow off the Sahara. Diminishing rainfall since 1975 has hurt agricultural output.

Despite generally poor soils, Gambians eke out an existence growing cash and subsistence crops, tending cattle and goats, fishing, and harvesting shellfish. Some near the ocean procure salt through solar evaporation of seawater, which they transport by river into the salt-starved interior. Gambians began growing peanuts as a cash crop in the 1830s, and through the colonial period Gambia was Britain's "peanut colony." The subsistence staples, millet and rice, took a back seat, quickly bringing dependence on rice imports. When the Gambia gained independence in 1965, it had a dependent, one-crop economy that its new government made no effort to change. But the economy spiraled downward through the 1970s as drought and falling prices cut peanut revenues and OPEC–induced oil price increases made imports more expensive. Gambia's government borrowed heavily in response, until it owed, by 1985, a sum equal to 114 percent of its gross domestic product (GDP). In that year, following an International Monetary Fund suggestion, the government cut spending,

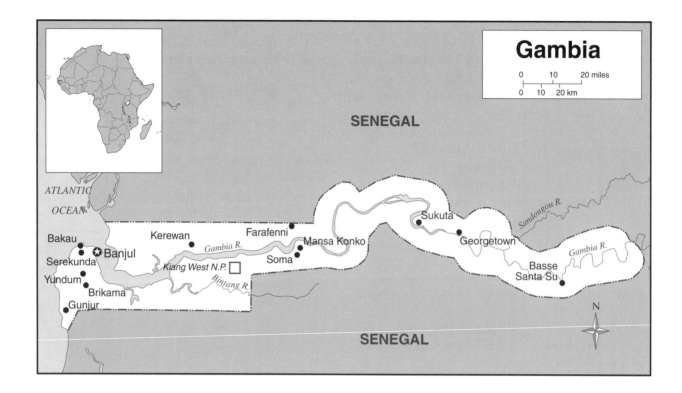

depreciated the currency, and increased government revenues.

Peanut production rallied into the 1990s before falling again, but by then the country was capitalizing on geographical advantages. The Gambia's Atlantic beaches are only a six-hour flight from northern Europe, and tourism has grown steadily from the 1970s. Since 1998, tourism has constituted between 15 and 25 percent of the country's GDP and brought more foreign exchange than any other economic sector. Also, because the Gambia has lower tariffs than its neighbors, a "re-export" trade has become important economically, though it is unstable due to currency fluctuations and border disputes. But local production still meets only one-eighth of the nation's annual rice requirement and food self-sufficiency remains elusive. Since the first decade of the twenty-first century, heavily funded programs to increase rice production along the middle Gambia have achieved mixed success. A Taiwanese mission is working to implement a tidal irrigation system that will enable farmers to produce two rice crops per year. A project to build a bridge to limit the river's salinity and bring more water for rice irrigation is unlikely to be implemented, however,

because of the high cost and predicted negative results.

The Gambia's dependent economy is hampered further by a poor infrastructure. Women gardeners use modern seed and fertilizers to grow healthy vegetables, but cannot transport them forty miles to Atlantic hotel kitchens before spoilage occurs. Lacking good roads, electricity, and refrigeration, they haul their produce to nearby markets via donkey-cart, while the hotels import vegetables from Europe.

See also **Ecosystems; International Monetary Fund; Transporation: Animal.**

BIBLIOGRAPHY

Fyhri, Torgeir. "The Gambia: The Complexity of Modernizing the Agricultural Sector in Africa." Ph.D. diss. University of Oslo, 1998. Available from http://www.afrol.com/library/Fyhri_1998/contents.htm.

McPherson, Malcolm F., and Steven C. Radelet, eds. *Economic Recovery in the Gambia: Insights for Adjustment in Sub-Saharan Africa.* Cambridge, MA: Harvard Institute for International Development, 1995.

Wright, Donald R. *The World and a Very Small Place in Africa: A History of Globalization in Niumi, the Gambia,* 2nd edition. Armonk, NY: M.E. Sharpe, 2004.

DONALD R. WRIGHT

Typical rural shot showing peanut fields ready to be planted. The unremarkableness of the terrain is a good depiction of the Gambia's flat geography, which is increasingly denuded of trees. PHOTOGRAPHY BY DONALD WRIGHT, 2005

SOCIETY AND CULTURES

Three main factors shape contemporary Gambian society: a rapidly growing and rapidly urbanizing population, a relatively large number of local and immigrant ethnic groups that are not regionally concentrated, and the growth of tourism.

URBANIZATION

With a population of 1,688,359 (2007 estimate), the Gambia is one of Africa's most densely populated nations. The capital city of Banjul is effectively capped at about thirty thousand residents because it is located on an island at the mouth of the Gambia River. The urban area connected to Banjul by a causeway, formally designated the Kanifing Municipal Area but more commonly referred to as Serekunda (the oldest settlement at the heart of this city), is the commercial and educational heart of the country. Nearly half of Gambians live in Banjul, Serekunda, or a third, smaller city in the Western Division, Brikama.

This is a relatively recent trend. At independence in 1965, less than 15 percent of the population lived in these urban areas. Thus most urban Gambians have strong ties to relatives in one or more rural communities that they consider home. They visit as often as possible, particularly for major religious holidays.

ETHNICITY AND RELIGION

The Mandinka (42%) is both the largest ethnic group and the most widespread in the Gambia. When European mariners traveled up the Gambia River, they encountered a series of Mandinka kingdoms that had spread out from the ancient Mali Empire. In the early twenty-first century, most rural Mandinkas farm rice and peanuts. The Jaxanke, a major subgroup, were long-distance traders and introduced Islam to the region. Concentrated in eastern Gambia, the Serehuli (9%) speak a related language. They have a reputation for being both successful farmers and astute merchants.

The Wolof, dominant in neighboring Senegal, form about 16 percent of Gambians. Although many are merchants, civil servants, and artisans in the urban areas, there are significant numbers of Wolof farmers in the Saloum region of the country and elsewhere. Serer, a related group, are often involved in artisanal fishing in the Gambia and form about 8 percent of the population.

The Jola (10%) are found on the south bank east of Bintang Creek. Most speakers of the Fogny dialect converted to Islam in the 1930s, whereas speakers of the Karon dialect, found closer to the coast, have more equally converted to Islam and Roman Catholicism. Jolas are well known for a type of rice cultivation based on extensive systems of dikes to retain rainfall and flush salt from the soil. Their colorful male initiation ceremonies are well documented. Manjagos, only 1 percent of the population, also live in this region and are nearly all Catholic.

Living near most farming communities are a smaller settlement of Fulani who specialize in herding cattle. In the upper and middle river regions, many Fulani also farm, particularly millet and sorghum. Fulani distinguish among themselves by dialect and region of origin, either the middle Senegal River region or the Futa Toro region of Guinea.

Concentrated in the urban areas, Aku are the descendants of liberated slaves who maintain strong ties to Sierra Leone. During the colonial period, they had better access to education and are well entrenched in the civil service, the church, education, and the professions.

Part of the Economic Community of West African States (ECOWAS), the Gambia has large numbers of immigrants from neighboring countries. Particularly during the 1990s, Sierra Leoneans and Liberians sought refuge in the Gambia during the wars in those countries. Nigerians and Ghanaians are also found working in many small businesses, teaching in the schools, or filling specialized posts in the government. Mauritanians and Gambians of Lebanese descent run some of the largest businesses. Recently, a number of retirees from Germany and the Netherlands have moved to the Gambia.

In many rural communities, one will find people from multiple ethnic groups living together. Even when one village is mostly of one group, the next town will have a majority from another ethnic group. Certainly in the urban areas, people live and work with people from many backgrounds and speak multiple languages. Although Gambians tend to be quite proud of their own ethnic groups, there is little tension between communities. Part of this pattern can be attributed to the fact that more than 85 percent of Gambians are Muslim and therefore share a common worldview. Nevertheless, respect for the Christian communities is generally high, in part for doctrinal reasons (Islam encourages respect for other "peoples of the Book" including Christians), in part because Christian missions were instrumental in establishing primary and secondary schools, many of which are still recognized for their excellence. In recent years, however, a small but influential group of Muslim clerics have returned to the Gambia from advanced theological studies in Sudan and Saudi Arabia and are trying to spread the less tolerant Wahhabi interpretation of Islam in Gambian society.

TOURISM

As it becomes harder to make a living from farming, many of the young people drawn to the city hope to make a living working in the tourism industry, the fastest growing sector of the Gambian economy. Because European companies own nearly all the major hotels and bring in their own managers, most jobs available to Gambians are lower-paying positions. Young men in particular often wait outside hotels to offer their services as guides and friends to tourists. A significant number, hoping to get a chance to travel to Europe, try to build relationships—sometimes sexual—with European women. Although many Gambians criticize this as a form of prostitution, they also recognized that, for the few young men who can leave the Gambia this way, there are many

Republic of the Gambia

Population:	1,688,359 (2007 est.)
Area:	11,295 sq. km (4,361 sq. mi.)
Official language:	English
Languages:	Mandinka, Wolof, Fula, Jola, other indigenous languages, English
National currency:	dalasi
Principal religions:	Muslim 95%, Christian 4%, animists 1 %
Capital:	Banjul (est. pop. 34,828 excluding suburbs in 2006)
Other urban centers:	Brikama, Basse, Bakua, Farafenni, Serekunda, Kuntaur, Bansang
Annual rainfall:	889 mm (35 in.)
Principal geographical feature:	Gambia River
Economy:	*GDP per capita:* US$2,000 (2006)
Principal products and exports:	*Agricultural:* rice, millet, sorghum, peanuts, corn, sesame, cassava (tapioca), palm kernels, cattle, sheep, goats *Manufacturing:* processing peanuts, fish, and hides, beverages, agricultural machinery assembly, woodworking, metalworking, clothing Tourism is also a major source of income.
Government:	Independence from Great Britain, 1965. Monarchical constitution until 1970, when republican form of government was adopted. Parliamentary democracy until 1994. Beginning in 1982, the President was directly elected by universal suffrage for 5-year terms. Unicameral House of Representatives was the legislative branch. The 51 members of the House included 36 direct electees, 5 chiefs selected by assembly of chiefs, 8 nonvoting appointees, and the attorney general. Prior to 1970, the head of state was prime minister, converted to an executive presidency under the 1970 constitution. Senegambian confederation, uniting Gambia and Senegal, formed on 1 February 1982 and dissolved in September 1989. Military coup in 1994. Government led by Armed Forces Provisional Ruling Council (AFPRC) and a cabinet of military officers and civilians. Pro-military constitution adopted in 1996. Under new constitution, president elected for 5-year term by universal suffrage. Reinstalled House of Assembly comprising 49 members, 45 elected by universal suffrage, 4 appointed by the president, serving 5-year terms.
Heads of state since independence:	1962–1970: Prime Minister Sir Dawda Kairaba Jawara 1970–1994: President Sir Dawda Kairaba Jawara 1994–: Lieutenant (later Colonel) Yahya Jammeh
Armed forces:	No compulsory military service. The army consists of infantry battalions, the national guard, and the navy and comprises about 1,900 people.
Transportation:	*Waterways:* 390 km (242 mi.) Gambia River (river transport is gradually being replaced by road transport) *Port:* Banjul *Roads:* 3,742 km (2,325 mi.), 19% paved *National airline:* Air Gambia (joint government-British Airways venture) *Airport:* International facility at Banjul
Media:	Main periodicals: *The Gambian, Gambia Outlook, Gambia Onward, The Gambian Times, The Nation, The Worker, The Toiler, The Daily Observer, Foroyaa, The Gambian Weekly, Newsmonth, The Point.* The Government Printer produces government documents and reports. However, most educational materials are produced locally. Most major books are still published abroad. Radio Gambia provides radio. There is 1 government-owned television station.
Literacy and education:	*Total literacy rate:* 37.8% (2006) No free, universal, or compulsory education. Gambia College at Brikama provides teacher, agricultural, and health training. There are no universities.

economic opportunities for them in Europe. Meanwhile, these beach boys bring gifts from tourists home to share with their families.

See also **Banjul; Economic Community of West African States (ECOWAS); Tourism.**

BIBLIOGRAPHY

Darboe, Momodou. "Islamism in West Africa: Gambia." *African Studies Review* 47 (2): 73–82. 2004.

Ebron, Paula. *Performing Africa*. Princeton, NJ: Princeton University Press, 2002.

Sanneh, Lamin. *The Crown and the Turban: Muslims and West African Pluralism*. Boulder, CO: Westview, 1997.

Schroeder, Richard A. *Shady Practices: Agroforestry and Gender Politics in the Gambia*. Berkeley: University of California Press, 1999.

DAVID P. GAMBLE
REVISED BY STEVEN K. THOMSON

HISTORY AND POLITICS

The Gambia's earliest political formation was as a vital region of the medieval empire of Mali. The region known as the Gambia was of interest to Malians because it was a highway leading to the salt flats on the tidal reaches of the River Gambia and Saloum River in present-day Senegal. The Gambia and Senegal's separate existence is rooted in the activities of British slave traders who, in 1618, established a fort at the mouth of the River Gambia, from which they gradually spread their commercial and, later, colonial rule upstream to establish the British protectorate of the Gambia. Political development in the colony lagged behind the larger and more populous British colonies in West Africa and it was not until the 1880s when a legislative council formed, primarily of colonial officers and later descendants of freed African slaves, that African political participation increased.

The road to independence was relatively peaceful. Following the London Conference and subsequent general elections in 1962, Dawda Kairaba Jawara (b. 1924) of the Protectorate People's Party (PPP), later renamed the People's Progressive Party (PPP), emerged victorious. This laid the foundation for Jawara's domination of the Gambia's political landscape. With the colonial administration's gradual withdrawal from the colony, self-government was granted in 1963. Jawara was subsequently appointed prime minister and, despite strong recommendations by Britain and the United Nations (UN) for the country to become a part of Senegal, the PPP leadership opted instead for independence on February 18, 1965, amid concern over the Gambia's viability.

President Jawara crafted modest development goals, a moderate foreign policy, and adhered, in principle, to political democracy, human rights, and an open economy. Over time, this ministate of 1.5 million people enjoyed relative peace when the rest of the continent was mired in political instability. This endeared and aligned President Jawara to the West and ultimately won him much respect both within the Gambia and internationally.

The Gambia's political history under Jawara, however, resembled a plateau that was occasionally marred by volcanic eruptions. The image, as projected often to the outside world, was one of a mini-state adept at survival, able despite its underdevelopment to run an open society with a multiparty democracy. Notwithstanding its democratic tradition, or democratic façade, the Gambia under Jawara continued to have one of the lowest living standards in the continent and ranked 166th in the world out of 173 countries according to the United Nations Development Program (UNDP) Human Development.

In 1981, a coup against Jawara's government was staged by elements in the field-force (an unarmed paramilitary force numbering about three hundred), in alliance with civilians. Senegal intervened militarily to restore constitutional order, but at the cost of 400 to 500 lives. Following Senegal's successful intervention and Jawara's resumption of power, he and President Abdou Diouf agreed to the formation of the Senegambia confederation. Characterized as a marriage of confusion, the confederation lasted eight years before a combination of political and economic factors led to its collapse in 1989. In the early twenty-first century, the Gambia National Army (GNA) is the major standing institutional remnant of the Senegambia confederation, which ironically, on July 22, 1994, ousted Sir Dawda Jawara and his ruling PPP Government in a bloodless coup d'etat after Jawara's twenty-nine years in power. The Armed Forces Provisional Ruling Council (AFPRC) was established and headed by Lieutenant Yahya Jammeh (b. 1965), who at the time was less than thirty years old.

Among the various reasons advanced for the 1994 coup d'etat, the most important ones related to the complacency of the ruling PPP and corruption that had permeated every segment of society. Disparity in living conditions between the senior Nigerian officers who headed the army and junior Gambian officers was a major source of discontent. The coup proved to be unpopular among the Gambia's major Western donors and Japan.

In the end, it took combined Western sanctions in November 1994 for the AFPRC to acquiesce to a two-year timetable back to civilian rule. The transition program culminated in a presidential election on October 18, 1996, in which Jammeh, a soldier-turned-presidential-candidate, contested and won a widely condemned election outcome because of its numerous irregularities. In particular, he doctored the new constitution by removing the two five-year term-limit clause for the presidency and lowered the required minimum age for presidential candidates from forty to thirty years. Jammeh also won a second five-year term in 2001, but as before, the outcome was widely criticized and contested by the opposition.

Jammeh was able to succeed because he used a Defiant and Appeasement strategy to cope with Western political and economic pressures for reform. This has enabled him to, on one hand, replace lost economic aid with funds from new friends (Cuba, Libya, Taiwan, and Iraq), and to employ a kind of window dressing to appease Western donors, on the other. Thus, since the coup, he has conducted an assertive foreign policy strategy to circumvent the negative economic fallout from Western aid withdrawal. Jammeh effectively used the Gambia's two-year non-permanent UN Security Council membership from 1998 to 2000 to stem international isolation of his regime and himself, and as a platform on which to advocate the lifting of UN-imposed sanctions on Cuba, Libya, and Iraq.

Relations with the International Monetary Fund (IMF) and the World Bank deteriorated sharply, however, in 2002, following intense pressure on the APRC Government to reform the economy, curb corruption, and improve governance. Additionally, the Gambia was suspended from debt relief assistance given to Highly Indebted Poor Countries (HIPIC), because of its consistently poor human rights record and mismanagement of the national economy. Relations with Washington, D.C., worsened in 2004 following the murder of newspaper editor Deyda Hydara (1946–2004), which many believe was government sponsored. The press continues to be muzzled and trade unions have remained largely ineffective in challenging the status quo. Founded as long as 1929, trade unions since that time have played an enduring, if intermittent role in the affairs of the nation. The post-coup period witnessed their marginalization in political and economic affairs due primarily to a repressive political environment. Because the Gambia is a deeply religious and conservative Sunni Muslim country, women have until the last two decades played traditional roles within society, with little access to education for girls. This is changing, however, primarily because of a "feminist" movement spearheading change in gender roles and relations

and eradication of female circumcision, which remains entrenched among some ethnic groups.

On September 22, 2006, soldier-turned-civilian-president Yahya Jammeh won a third five-year presidential term against a poorly organized and financed opposition. Voter anger over the break up of a five-party coalition, incumbency, intimidation, and voting by Jammeh's Jola co-ethnics who crossed over from Senegal's southern province of Casamance to vote aided him immensely. Despite three presidential elections (1996, 2001), the Gambia has not turned away from its authoritarian past. Political repression, especially of journalists, has intensified and Jammeh continues to use the alleged foiled coup of March 2006 as a pretext to further repress dissidents and journalists.

See also **Colonial Policies and Practices; Diouf, Abdou; Gender; International Monetary Fund; Postcolonialism; World Bank.**

BIBLIOGRAPHY

Ceesay, Ebrima. *The Military and 'Democratisation' in The Gambia, 1994–2003.* London: Trafford Publishing, 2006.

Denton, Fenton. "Foreign Policy Formation in The Gambia, 1964–1994: Small Weak Developing States and their Foreign Policy Decisions and Choices." PhD diss., University of Birmingham, 1998.

Edie, Carlene J. "Democracy in The Gambia: Past, Present and Prospects for the Future." *African Development* 25, nos. 3–4 (2000): 161–99.

Hughes, Arnold, ed. *The Gambia: Studies in Society and Politics.* Birmingham, England: Centre of West African Studies, University of Birmingham, 1991.

Hughes, Arnold. "The Collapse of the Senegambian Confederation." *Journal of Commonwealth and Comparative Politics* 30, no. 2 (1992): 200–222.

Hughes, Arnold, and David Perfect. "Trade Unionism in The Gambia." *African Affairs* 88, no. 353 (1989): 549–572.

Hughes, Arnold, and David Perfect. *A History of The Gambia, 1816–1994.* Rochester, NY: Rochester University Press, 2006.

Loum, Modou. "Bad Governance and Democratic Failure: A Look at Gambia's 1994 Coup" *Civil Wars* 5, no. 1 (2002): 145–174.

Manjang, Ousman. "Marriage of Confusion" *West Africa* 3, July 26, 1986, 2358–2360.

Nyang, Sulayman S. "Politics in Post-Independence Gambia." *A Current Bibliography on African Affairs* 8, no. 2 (1975): 113–126.

Nyang, Sulayman S. "The Gambia: After the Rebellion" *Africa Report* 26, (1981): 47–51.

Perfect, David. "The Political Career of Edward Francis Small." In *The Gambia: Studies in Society and Politics*, ed. Arnold Hughes. Birmingham, England: Centre of West African Studies, University of Birmingham, 1991.

Saine, Abdoulaye. "The Coup d'Etat in The Gambia, 1994: The End of the First Republic." *Armed Forces & Society* 23, no. 1 (1996): 97–111.

Saine, Abdoulaye. "Post-Coup Politics in The Gambia." *Journal of Democracy* 13, no. 4 (2002): 167–172.

Sallah, Tijan M. "Economics and Politics in The Gambia." *Journal of Modern African Studies* 28, no. 4 (1990): 621–648.

Touray, Omar. *The Gambia and the World: A History of the Foreign Policy of Africa's Smallest State, 1965–1995.* Hamburg, Germany: Institute of African Affairs, 2000.

Wiseman, John. "The Gambia: From Coup to Elections." *Journal of Democracy* 9, no. 2 (1998): 64–75.

Wiseman, John, and Elizabeth. Vidler, "The July 1994 Coup d'Etat in The Gambia: The End of an Era." *The Round Table* 333 (1995): 53–65.

Wright, Donald. *The World and a Very Small Place in Africa.* Armonk, New York: M.E. Sharpe, 1997.

Yeebo, Zaya. *State of Fear in Paradise: The Military Coup in The Gambia and Its Implications for Democracy.* London: Africa Research and Information Bureau, 1995.

ABDOULAYE SAINE

GAMES. The origin of the world's oldest game—generically known as "mancala" (from the Arabic verb *naquala* meaning "to move")—has yet to be confirmed. However, variations of this game, involving calculated strategies for capturing game pieces dropped in holes or cups on a board, as well as other strategy games, some resembling checkers, chess, and backgammon, were played in sub-Saharan Africa many centuries ago. For example, remnants of mancala-type games were found in the stone ruins of eleventh-century Great Zimbabwe, in the ruins of the twelfth-century Buganda kingdom (in modern Uganda), and cut into a giant stone megalith in Ethiopia.

More than a form of recreation, mancala—especially in antiquity—was associated with rulers, shrines, and temples, and with concepts of the universe. In the Buganda kingdom the game, here called *omweso*, was kept in the court hall, where the prime minister played it while deciding court cases. Prospective successors to the Buganda throne were required to gather the seeds, *empiki*, used as counters in playing *omweso*. A commemorative statue of Syaam aMbul aNgwoong, founder of the Kuba kingdom (late sixteenth or early seventeenth century in modern Zaire), shows him holding a game board for *lyeel*, the mancala game he introduced symbolizing the monarch's overall supremacy. The Asante kings in the gold-rich area of modern Ghana made boards for a mancala game called *oware* from gold shaped like the Golden Stool, which, according to legend, had descended from heaven to confirm the authority of the kings. The gods themselves were said to play variations of mancala. Introduced into the United States as *wari* by African slaves, this game and many others spread to various parts of the world. A Syrian colony in New York played it under the name *chuba*. Later American commercial versions have included Pitfall, Oh-Wah-Ree, and others.

Reserved in some countries for rulers and their families and often excluding women players (considered intellectually inferior), the game today is played by children, women, and men of all classes. Game equipment varies from lines or holes dug in the ground or on rocks to the beautifully carved and decorated sets found in African art collections. The playing ground might have anywhere from two to four rows with as many as fifty holes in a row. Most common are two-row and four-row games with six to eight holes per row. For counters, children and others playing on the ground might use stones, seeds, or anything handy, whereas adults using permanent boards could choose cowrie shells, seeds, or ivory balls. Rules for mancala, including simplified versions for children, vary as much as the names of the various incarnations of the game. *Okwe*, played by the Igbo (Ibo) people in Nigeria, uses seeds from the okwe tree. In playing *tshisolo* ("chicken"), the Luba people in Zaire call the seeds or nuts *lusolo* (chickens), which when captured are said to be "eaten."

Variations in these games reflect the African environment in which they are played. The game *shisima* (similar to ticktacktoe), meaning "source of water," played by the Tiriki people in Kenya, was inspired by watching *imbalavi* (water insects) crawling toward the *shisima* (water source). The game is played on an octagonal board with lines from all eight corners drawn to a small circle (the water source). Two players, each with three pieces of a different design (representing water insects), compete to be the first to move their pieces in a straight line (through the water) to the center. *Kei*, a chess-type game played in Sierra Leone, uses a board with one hundred squares, twenty black pieces called "black men" and twenty white pieces called "white men."

African games when played in public usually draw a crowd of onlookers, who cheer on the players and closely follow each move. Bystanders have been known to jump in and make the moves for players perceived as being too slow.

In contrast to the individualistic and competitive attitudes that mark so many games and sports in the United States, African games are generally a community affair. Even if there are only two players, a crowd of onlookers is sure to form. In many places the old games are still considered important for developing children's mental and physical skills, and they are sometimes included in coming-of-age ceremonies. African children learn counting, concentration, and socialization through games and other competitive activities such as running and jumping. Games of chance such as *nigbe*, which uses cowrie shells for dice, are popular in west Africa, and *oo*, a guessing game, is played by children as young as four in Côte d'Ivoire. Exchanges of words, songs, dancing, and miming often accompany the games. Singing games include some resembling drop-the-handkerchief, such as *kebele* in Ethiopia. Variations of *kye kye kule*, a Ghanaian call-and-response game with motions, is also found in other countries.

Lacking an abundance of factory-produced goods, many African children excel in inventing their own toys—dolls, spinning tops, boats, flying objects, musical instruments. Materials for such projects have included tree branches, palm leaves, seeds, and other local products. In Zambia in the 1990s a nationally sponsored contest produced an impressive array of childrens' inventions—bicycling figures, cars, trucks, and other vehicles mechanized to move, mostly made of wire, cloth, and scraps of tin. While praising the children for their creativity, many Zambians found large gaps in their wire fences.

See also **Popular Culture; Sports.**

BIBLIOGRAPHY

Adzinyah, Abraham Kobena; Dumisani Maraire; and Judith Cook Tucker. *Let Your Voice Be Heard: Songs from Ghana and Zimbabwe.* Danbury, CT: World Music Press, 1986.

Béart, Charles. *Jeux et jouets de l'ouest africain*, Vol. 2. Dakar, Senegal: IFAN, 1955.

Crane, Louise. *African Games of Strategy*, Urbana: African Studies Program, University of Illinois at Urbana-Champaign, 1982.

LOUISE CRANE

GAO. Gao, in Mali, is one of the oldest cities in West Africa. First called Kawkaw, the city was established on the left bank of the Niger River sometime in the seventh century CE. It constituted one of the earliest centers of trans-Saharan trade, with links to Egypt as well as to North Africa. Until 1009 Gao was politically dependent on the downstream Songhay capital of Kukya. It is reported that the city had a Muslim king by the end of the tenth century and by the twelfth century Arabic literacy had become firmly established. Gao was absorbed into the empire of Mali early in the fourteenth century, but the local Sonni dynasty later managed to detach it from Malian control. Gao thereafter developed as the capital of a regenerated Songhay Empire.

The prosperity of the city in its heyday (fifteenth to sixteenth centuries) depended as much on its extensive trade links as it did on court life and imperial administration. The city may have had up to 70,000 or 100,000 inhabitants at this time and it attracted scholars from the Arab world such as ʿAbd al-Karîm al-Maghîli (d. 1504) and Leo Africanus (d. c. 1527). The prosperity of this period, which ended with the Moroccan conquest of 1592, has been confirmed by archaeology and is manifest in the Mosque of Askia Muhammad (d. 1528), whose step-pyramid minaret is still the city's chief monument. The seventeenth and eighteenth centuries were characterized by decline in all fields but principally in the city's trade links. According to its 1998 census Gao has a population of approximately 35,000. It is not a major administrative center and attracts fewer tourists than Mali's other historic cities, such as Timbuktu, Mopti, and Jenné.

See also **Jenné and Jenné-jeno; Leo Africanus; Mali; Timbuktu.**

BIBLIOGRAPHY

Hunwick, John. "Gao and the Almoravids Revisited: Ethnicity, Political Change and the Limits of Interpretation." *Journal of African History* 35 (1994): 251–273.

Insoll, Timothy. "Iron Age Gao: An Archeological Contribution." *Journal of African History* 38 (1997): 1–30.

Lange, Dierk. "From Mande to Songhay: Towards and Political and Ethnic History of Medieval Gao." *Journal of African History* 35 (1994): 275–301.

ERIC S. ROSS

Black nationalist Marcus Mosiah Garvey (1887–1940). As a proponent of the Back-to-Africa movement, Garvey encouraged people of African descent to return to their homelands. In 1920, he began a program to develop Liberia, but it was ended after European officials showed great interest in the country. CORBIS

GARVEY, MARCUS MOSIAH (1887–1940).

Pan-Africanist Marcus Garvey was born in August 1887 in a Jamaica still under colonial rule. Early in life he recognized the inequities within Jamaican society, rousing him to political activism. Garvey founded the Universal Negro Improvement Association (UNIA) in 1914. A mass movement, the UNIA succeeded in galvanizing blacks in Africa and its diaspora where it had its origins. In 1916 Garvey settled in New York calling for racial unity and for the redemption of Africa by Africans in the diaspora. He incorporated the Black Star shipping line hoping to foster black trade and transport black migrants to Africa. The venture failed, although he succeeded in sending two delegations to Liberia.

Garvey's importance to Africa lies in his impact on the movement for self-determination among colonized populations. His *Negro World* newspaper, read widely in Africa, influenced nationalists across the continent, prompting some colonial governments to ban the paper. Garvey spent two years in jail before being deported from the United States in 1927. He continued his activism in Jamaica and England, publishing other papers and never ceasing his calls for Pan-African unity. Garvey died in June 1940 never having been to Africa, but having greatly influenced its people.

See also **Diasporas; Liberia; Nationalism.**

BIBLIOGRAPHY

Garvey, Amy Jacques, intro. by Robert A. Hill. *The Philosophy and Opinions of Marcus Garvey.* New York: Atheneum, 1992.

Hill, Robert; Emory J. Tolbert; Deborah Forscek; and Barbara Bair; eds. *The Marcus Garvey and Universal Negro Improvement Association Papers, Volumes I–VII.* Berkeley: University of California Press, 1983–1992.

Lewis, Rupert. *Marcus Garvey: Anti-Colonial Champion.* Trenton, NJ: African World Press, 1988.

NEMATA A. BLYDEN

GBAGBO, LAURENT KOUDOU (1945–). Born in Gagnoa in west-central Côte d'Ivoire, Laurent Koudou Gbagbo was raised in a Roman Catholic household. He received a bachelor's degree from the University of Abidjan in 1969 and a master's degree from the Sorbonne in Paris the next year.

In 1970 Gbagbo returned to Côte d'Ivoire to teach history at the University of Abidjan. The following year he was arrested for political and trade union activity and was imprisoned without trial from 1971 to 1974. In 1974 he returned to the University of Abidjan but took time off in 1977 to finish his doctoral work at the Sorbonne, where he received a Ph.D. in 1979. The following year he became director of the Institute of History, Art, and African Archaeology (IHAAA) at the University of Abidjan. In 1982 Gbagbo organized an illegal opposition political party, the moderately socialist Front Populaire Ivoirien (FPI), but because of the resulting government pressure he exiled himself to France in 1985.

In 1990 Gbagbo—whose stronghold was in the southwest—ran for president against Félix Houphouët-Boigny, Côte d'Ivoire's leader since independence. He obtained just 11 percent of the vote but subsequently served as minister of education. In 2000 he ran again, this time against the military ruler Robert Guei (1941–2002), in an election marked by low turnout, violence, and the exclusion of the two biggest parties. Gbagbo was the candidate of the Ivoirian Popular Front (Front Populaire Ivoirien, or FPI). The Democratic Party, which until Guei's coup of December 1999 had a huge majority in parliament, was banned from running a candidate. The Rally of the Republicans was also banned from running its candidate, former Prime Minister Alassane Ouattara.

After early vote tallies put Gbagbo in the lead, Guei stopped the counting and proclaimed he beat Gbagbo. Faced with violent demonstrations, Guei fled and Gbagbo became president in October 2000. In September 2002 hundreds of soldiers, angered at finding that they were to be demobilized, found support for a rebellion in the Muslim north. A compromise agreement between Gbagbo's government and the rebels was reached in 2003 but broke down the following year. A 2005 agreement

Côte d'Ivoire president Laurent Gbagbo (1945–) arrives at peace talks in Accra, Ghana, July 29, 2004. UN Secretary-General Kofi Annan gathered with top African leaders in Ghana to seek African solutions to the continent's crises, including an attempt to revive the peace process in Côte d'Ivoire. © AP Images

ended the fighting, but because the rebels did not disarm, Gbagbo postponed for a year the presidential election scheduled for that fall. In the late summer of 2006, it seemed likely that Gbagbo would again postpone the election on the same grounds

See also **Côte d'Ivoire; Houphouët-Boigny, Félix.**

BIBLIOGRAPHY

"Côte d'Ivoire: Laurent Gbagbo, from Young Firebrand to Silver-haired President." October 18, 2000. Available from http://www.allAfrica.com.

"Ivorian President Gbagbo 'Ordered Media Hijack.'" *Afrol News.* September 9, 2006. Available from http://www.afrol.com/articles.

MICHAEL LEVINE

GENDER

This entry includes the following articles:
OVERVIEW
GENDER ROLES

OVERVIEW

The history of gender is not the history of women, which has a much greater historiographical record. Nevertheless, the list of gender history titles is important. For sub-Saharan Africa alone, up to and including 2005, in terms of history there are more than eighty works or articles with a title that includes the word *gender*, the first appearing in 1978, the second in 1981, and the remainder from 1984 onward. For the same period, on the same topic only one French work, published in 2001, contains the same word (*genre*) in its title. As in the past, very few male historians are interested in or take seriously the significance of gender in history.

What is the difference between the history of African women and an African "gendered" history? Women's history is conceived in classical terms: it is the history of the way women, mostly rural women, lived and thought, the history of mothers, of a few heroines; in short a history in which relations between the sexes are somewhat lacking, so as to devote itself to what is in effect the forgotten half of humanity. Previously, human history had been written asexually, using the masculine for the whole, thus writing about, for example, the peasants, the urbanites, and the workers, in a neutral history, which did not have any regard for the differences between men and women.

Gender is something completely different; to begin with, there are two: masculine and feminine. The idea of gender does not remove that of sex, but it does mean that it is not the most important aspect. Gender is thus an integral part of social history, with all its constraints and how they react to each other, enabling it to function and evolve.

At one time, social history scholars focused largely on class, a form of social history launched by the German political philosopher Karl Marx, studying the rich, the poor, the socially excluded, the workers, without differentiating how genders reacted one from the other. A second approach to social relations developed first in colonial times, and focused on racial, ethnic, and cultural differences, such as whites, Indians, Coloureds, and blacks of apartheid South Africa, where these statistical categories remain despite the change of regime; or with regard to cultural origins and to a lesser degree physical attributes—that is, the Tutsi, Hutu, and Twa in Rwanda and Burundi.

Largely accepted in the twenty-first century is the idea that a third factor is required to understand social relations: gender. Events and milestones do not happen in the same way at every stage of life, depending on whether a person is male or female; this fact is still more visible in African societies, in which most periods and moments of life are highly gendered. In Africa it was for a long time the case that human activities were divided on the basis of gender: women were required to do almost everything that was needed for subsistence and men were specialized in hunting, war, and politics.

HISTORY

The origin of the concept of gender is connected to the history of Western feminism, that is, the struggle of women to be recognized as equal but different, although the very term *feminism* lends itself to discussion. Here one should outline the divergence between the North and South in the time scale and in the purposes of women's struggles for the development of these ideas. Feminism mostly developed in the West from the beginning of the twentieth century with the will from women to vote. It exploded after World War II with the discovery of women's bodies and personal freedom, developed by the French author Simone de Beauvoir.

In Africa feminism and the consciousness of gender differentiation did not experience the same schedule—even if similar movements appeared at a very early stage and at almost the same time in a number of countries of the south, in particular in Egypt from the nineteenth century under the government of Mehemet Ali. The same could be said about Turkey (under Mustapha Kemal) in the 1920s, and about Iran, where the reforms introduced by the Pahlavi dynasty had been assisted by the women's movement following the constitutional revolution during the years 1906 to 1909, heavily influenced by the suffragette movements in the West (there has since been an undoubted retreat because of the pressure of religious fundamentalism).

In the places where the movement has appeared in the late twentieth and early twenty-first centuries, notably Africa south of the Sahara, events have occurred at a different pace. First, because neither men nor women enjoyed political rights under colonization, women in Africa had little to fight for: in Freetown, Sierra Leone, women have had the right to vote in local elections since 1930. In French West Africa (AOF), independence took place in 1960 after the extension of the franchise to French women in 1944, and universal suffrage in 1956. It had been enlarged *de facto* sooner for women than for men, since the reforms of 1951 extended the right to vote to all women over the age of twenty-one who were married with two children, which was almost universally the case for young women.

In contrast, civil rights have been attained only belatedly, and remain nonexistent or rare in the vast majority of cases. Family legislation is generally unfavorable to women. Thus when Europe became liberal at the end of the 1960s there was a mutual lack of understanding between the women of the south and the feminists in the north. The latter have protested strongly and above all with their feeling of colonial superiority against female genital mutilation in Africa. African women claimed from their part against this colonial *suffisance* that they wanted to solve the question by themselves.

Other vital questions were neglected by Western feminists, such as pregnant women and infant mortalities, while they probably needed more attention. A well-known historical event concerning this form of resistance against colonialism was the case in Sudan and Kenya, in 1956, where young girls claimed the right of female circumcision just because the colonial power, Britain, had forbidden the practice as illegal, arguing it was inhumane. The result was that President Jomo Kenyatta reestablished it in 1963, arguing that "no true Kikuyu would accept to marry a non circumcised girl" (Auffret 1983, 151). African women themselves were ambiguous with regard to this uneasy question, and the problem remains only partly solved.

Perhaps one-third of young Sudanese girls still die from female circumcision. Sixty to 80 percent of young Egyptians were circumcised at the dawn of the new millennium, even though the practice was outlawed in 1997 "except by medical necessity," a possibility used by many families. The World Health Organization (WHO) estimates that around 40 percent of African women have undergone operations of this kind in more than thirty-six countries. It takes place over a vast arc, which extends from Mauritania to the Horn of Africa, passing through part of Senegal (except the Wolof and the Sérères), Mali (except the Songhay), and Burkina-Faso, crossing central northern Africa from west to east, passing through Cameroon, Chad, and the Central African Republic as far as Egypt, Kenya, and Tanzania. The Congo Basin and south of the equator are unaffected, except for some places in Botswana, Lesotho, and Mozambique. Although the Islamic regions have been particularly receptive to the practice, it cannot be mistaken as an Arabic custom: the Maghreb ignores it, as does Saudi Arabians and almost 80 percent of contemporary Muslims. Yet the Coptic Christians of Egypt and the Jewish Falashas of Ethiopia know of the practice of excision, as do the Kikuyu in Kenya, while their neighbors the Luo do not. On the contrary certain similar practices can be found in eastern Mexico, in Peru, and in the west of Brazil, where they were exported from Africa at the time of the slave trade.

The origin of these mutilations is as unclear as their geographical distribution, no doubt predating Islam. The awkwardness of British and American feminists has long irritated the African women's movements, and they criticized the former for their interference. Male politicians have taken advantage of this to insist that they have other priorities. Because of these misunderstandings, the World Health Organization has been slow to define its stance: called upon to decide its position by the U.N. Economic and Social Council in 1958 it refused the following year, arguing that it did not regard itself as competent to make a judgment, as these particular ritual operations were social and cultural matters.

Finally, it was African women who once again took the initiative in a United Nations forum, but the first intervention only dates from 1979, with the organization of a conference in Khartoum on "traditional practices affecting the health of women and children." It was only in 1982 that the WHO made its position on the subject clear. Now the taboo has been broken and young women are shown to be much less agreeable than was previously thought. The Senegalese Awa Thiam has created an international organization for the abolition of sexual mutilation. For Malian girls, on which female circumcision was largely practiced, it appears that in the early twenty-first century the custom is more claimed for by migrant parents in France sticking to their traditions than in Mali itself, where local communities come progressively to abandon them thanks to the active militancy of national programs launched by the Union nationale des femmes du Mali (the National Union of Malian Women, UNFM).

In the late twentieth century, however, it was not individual freedom of the body that African women were interested in claiming in the first instance however, it was fair civil legislation and recognition of the glaring inequalities at work, in the home, and in marriage. Considering the gulf between these claims, the initial split that occurred between the women of the north and south from 1970 to 1980 is perfectly clear and understandable.

In contrast to northern Africa, and certainly in French-speaking Africa in particular, where women have been educated more belatedly than elsewhere, the most militant "feminists" in sub-Saharan Africa have often been men. With the exception of the leading female writer in French-speaking Africa, Mariama Bâ, there have been few activist writers like Buchi Emecheta in Nigeria, protesting against all the disadvantages of being a woman: dowry, birthing children, and the grinding job of being a mother and a beast of burden. A few radical male writers were the first to condemn the position of women, such as Ibrahima Ly and Wole Soyinka. For a long time the filmmaker Ousmane Sembène adopted a deliberate "feminist" style, as seen in his works *La noire de …* (On the mistreatment of a domestic servant by her white masters, 1966), his novel and film *Xhala* (1973), in which he makes fun of the male impotence of an old polygamist husband, his film concerning female resistance heroism in Casamance (*Emitaï*, 1971), and his trilogy *L'héroïsme au quotidien* (1999), *Faat kine* (2000), and *Molaadé* (2004), the last title of which contains an angry outburst against ritual excision and women's struggle on this issue.

Differences exist between genders and between individuals as well. Hence the objective of the latest international feminist movements to make people see equality in the face of differences, to make people understand that equality is, but is no more than, a legal concept. And this is indeed where the unquestionable growth in the concept of gender in the field of African social sciences lies. This new phase was initiated by an official international declaration, the Universal Declaration of Human Rights by the United Nations in 1948, whose validity and effectiveness are still a matter of dispute. Even the Convention on the Elimination of All Forms of Discrimination against Women, adopted by the United Nations General Assembly in 1979, has only been accepted with reservations by a number of member states and it does little to prevent the violation of human rights suffered daily by women.

Despite this, a new stage was reached with the United Nations Decade for Women, held between 1975 and 1985, and carried across the world by regular World Conferences on Women organized by the United Nations. Events have evolved quickly since the 1980s. The internationalization of feminist demands has gradually effected a reconciliation between the visions of women in the north and south. Women in the south have adopted a strategy of attaining political power, while those in the north have pressed the demand for women's human rights. They are at one in their criticism of the male-centered nature of the law in general and of human rights in particular.

RESEARCH

These ideas open up an extraordinary area for current research, theoretically at least: all social analysis, on whatever topic, should include a gendered view of its processes. Gender studies is the study of the social relations between men and women. The vast majority of such studies are by women, in Africa just as everywhere else. As elsewhere, very few African male researchers have begun to take any interest in this kind of analysis, under the false pretense that women's matters are only a matter of concern for women themselves. And yet everything in society is gendered. There is very little, indeed too little, study of the relationship between gender and power.

This presupposes a reevaluation of how the political sphere is defined and of the distinction between public and private space. The classical anthropological division, formerly theorized by the Western colonizers and in modern times strongly assumed by most African men, is that the public is the domain of man and the private or domestic sphere is the domain of woman. By opposition, an interesting theory based on linguistic analysis has been proposed by a Nigerian feminist, Oyeronke Oyewumi, who argues that the difference between man and woman strictly defined by biological characteristics limited to sexuality is typically a Western viewpoint. She is in favor of a sociopolitical decision that emphasizes the importance of social processes in the construction of categories. To be a man or a woman becomes a matter of social power and thus of conflict, while the main privilege for both would be seniority rather than gender. This once again comes back to challenging the concept of what is supposed to be universally applicable, because until the twenty-first century the universal subject was, by implication, a man. In this way the main themes are approached differently: In twenty-first-century Africa, the result is impressive: more and more strong women, even if still a relatively tiny minority, are emerging in the public (economic, social, and political) spheres. For the first time in the modern world, an African woman was elected a chief of the state (Liberia).

POLITICAL CITIZENSHIP

Political citizenship, something which in historical terms has only recently been acquired by women, is not the only form of citizenship. There is also civil citizenship, which consists of equality within the family, property rights, and the right to free expression. All these remain unequal in Africa, where family law generally makes a woman a perpetual minor. For example, in Francophone Africa, often polygamy has not been suppressed. In Senegal, the only protection for a women is, when a marriage contract is concluded, to legally choose in advance between monogamy or polygamy with two, three, or four wives. When polygamy is officially forbidden (in most Anglophone or mostly Christianized areas), adultery is usually tolerated from husbands, while it is a crime for a wife. Gender thus influences citizenship.

THE STATE

The state been long neglected in gender relations. The Western women's movement initially took little interest in the state, which was seen as a patriarchal instrument of male domination. The twenty-first-century trend is to stress the crucial role of the state in the institutionalization of gender relations between men and women and in supervising the boundaries between public and private. The relations between the state and gender are multifaceted, with interplay between the state, the market (in an economic sense), and the family. The role of women is different from that of men and state legislation is a direct reflection of those different roles.

Therefore public-private relations are directly relevant to gender relations. If everything about the family is regarded as private, then almost all gender relations are at once excluded from the political sphere. As seen above, a source of inequality between men and women has been in Africa the relegation of women to the realm of subsistence contemptuously described as "domestic." Everywhere that women were the main source of subsistence, that is, almost the entirety of Africa, women were also indispensable economic agents as food producers. It is once again a question of nature versus nature. Were women in old Africa more empowered than in modern societies? It has been argued that female power sometimes was enhanced in precolonial Africa and later dismantled by colonial laws. Nevertheless, most of the time, in spite of a relative protection ensured by matrilinearity (when power was seldom possessed but at least transmitted by women), from the moment that the woman was supposed to provide subsistence for the man in rural preindustrial societies she was at once subject to his commands. Basically, the tangible need for meals, served at regular intervals, under pain of suffering violence from the man, meant that she was inevitably inferior to him.

Therefore, to deal with the relations between the public and the private, it may be assumed that the private space shares at least some part of the political. Some feminists argue that a gendered democratization of the public sphere is only possible with the prerequisite democratization of the private sphere within the family. This needs to be seriously questioned in Africa.

GENDER OF TERRITORIES

As men and women, people live together and apart. This was a striking feature in African rural societies. Male and female territories were clearly gendered. Colonization reinforced gender territorial differences: colonial powers did not send boys and girls to the same schools, they did not use male and female workers in the same fields, they did not speak to male and female Africans in the same way. It has had an influence on the gender relations between colonized men and women inside their own society. The colonizer saw the men only—and not the women—as wage earners. Only men (black men) were "boys," that is, in the domestic service of whites. The African men found themselves organized as paid staff to perform tasks that they would be ashamed to do for themselves at home. The colonizer forcibly confined the women to so-called informal activities that involved providing for the needs of urban black men, since these hired hands had a range of needs: they needed to be fed, to have their clothes washed and ironed, and to have their sexual needs satisfied. There the urban migration of women was not wanted by either the colonizer nor often by the African households, nevertheless they had to be tolerated, while these were officially "invisible," as they did not affect the official accounts. These relationships involving hierarchical domination have had enormous social and mental repercussions, in both town and village, in public and private spheres, between genders, whatever their color. A number of studies have been undertaken on the "construction" of gender from this colonial data (see, for example, Diana Jeater's *Marriage, Perversion and Power* [1993]).

Therefore, political gender can be defined via a vast array of models, and fundamental research still has much to do on this topic. In short, in Africa, given the fact that modern "machism" is usually strongly developed, is for the moment the dream of a neutral (i.e., nongendered) territory a utopia or a myth?

See also **Bâ, Mariama; Émecheta, Buchi; Initiation: Clitoridectomy and Infibulation; Islam; Kinship and Affinity; Marriage Systems; Production Strategies; Prostitution; Religion and Ritual; Sembène, Ousmane; Sexual Behavior; Soyinka, Wole; Textiles.**

BIBLIOGRAPHY

Amadiume, Ifi. *Male Daughters, Female Husbands: Gender and Sex in an African Society.* London: Zed Books, 1987.

Auffret, Séverine. *Des couteaux contre des femmes.* Paris: Éditions des Femmes, 1983.

Ba, Mariama. *So Long a Letter.* London: Heineman, 1989.

Bowman, Cynthia Grant, and Akua Kuenyehia, eds. *Women and Law in Sub-Saharan Africa.* Accra: Sedco Publishing, 2003.

Coquery-Vidrovitch, Catherine. *African Women: A Modern History.* Boulder, CO: Westview Press, 1997.

Denis, Ph., and C. Sappia, eds. *Femmes d'Afrique dans une société en mutation.* Louvain-la-Neuve, Belgium: Academia, 2004.

Emecheta, Buchi. *The Brideprice.* London: Allison & Busby, 1976.

Emecheta, Buchi. *The Slave Girl: A Novel.* London: Allison & Busby, 1977.

Emecheta, Buchi. *The Joys of Motherhood.* New York: G. Braziller, 1979.

Emecheta, Buchi. *Double Yoke.* New York: Braziller, 1982.

Hodgson, Dorothy L., and Sheryl A. McCurdy, eds. *Wicked Women and the Reconfiguration of Gender.* London: James Currey, 2001.

Hunt, Nancy R. Tessie; P. Liu; and Jean Quataert; eds. *Gendered Colonialisms in African History.* Oxford: Blackwell, 1997.

Jeater, Diana. *Marriage, Perversion, and Power: The Construction of Moral Discourse in Southern Rhodesia 1894–1930.* Oxford: Clarendon Press, 1993.

Koso-Thomas, Olayinka. *The Circumcision of Women: A Strategy for Eradication.* London: Zed Books, 1987.

Ly, Ibrahima. *Toiles d'araignées.* Paris: L'Harmattan, 1982.

Mikell, Gwendolyn, ed. *African Feminism: The Politics of Survival in Sub-Saharan Africa.* Philadelphia: University of Philadelphia Press, 1997.

Ouzgane, Lahoucine, and Robert Morrell, eds. *African Masculinities: Men in Africa from the Late Nineteenth Century to the Present.* New York: Palgrave Macmillan, 2005.

Oyewumi, Oyeronke. *The Invention of Women: Making an African Sense of Western Gender Discourse.* Minneapolis: University of Minnesota Press, 1997.

Thomas, L. M. "Ngaitana (I Will Circumsise Myself): The Gender and Generational Politics of the 1956 Ban on Clitoridectomy in Meru, Kenya." *Gender and History* 8, no. 33 (1996): 338–363.

CATHERINE COQUERY-VIDROVITCH

GENDER ROLES

Gender is a culturally defined system of differentiation based on biological and physiological classification. Its fundamental units are men and women. Gender studies are concerned with understanding the rights and duties that order the relations between people defined by gendered differences. The new field grew out of women's studies, a corrective to the mis- or underrepresentation of women in accounts of societies because they were regarded as theoretically uninteresting, the parts they played marginalized or diminished. African women typically entered scholarly accounts in the spheres of kinship and marriage, and they were often depicted as objects of exchange. In the 1970s this changed, as feminist scholars began an exercise to "correct" inadequate disciplinary frameworks of analysis and give women "voice." In recent decades, the field has broadened to examine gender, as a culturally specific interpretation of male-female sexual difference that operates as a structuring principle in all aspects of all societies: of histories, ideologies, economic systems, and political structures. More recently, because men have been represented as homogeneous, work has begun on masculinities, a counter-portrayal of men and their practices. African masculinities "refer to a cluster of norms, values, and behavioral patterns expressing explicit and implicit expectations of how men should act and represent themselves to others" (Miescher and Lindsay 2003, 4); like gender, they cluster around points of power.

What gender, or masculinity, *is* or *means* in any particular culture at any particular moment in time must be *studied*, not *presumed*. This requires close attention to the cultural and historical specificity of both, which leads away from theorizing about women or men as a whole and toward individual cases and comparisons. Because few monographs have been done on African masculinities, and because women had been so marginalized in the literature and there is so much on the part they play in gender relations, most of the following deals primarily with women.

A number of paradigms have been developed to understand African gender relations. While an early central concern was the extent of male dominance and the status of women, scholars began to reconsider the notion of female solidarity, exploring

internal divisions, such as age, ethnicity, religion, that affect the roles that women have assumed in their respective societies. All also note that the impact of colonialism was not neutral. Africanists also look at masculinities, for example in Kenya, Gabra men "becoming" women and Maasai men adapting to modernity. History has helped to refine the understanding of societal institutions and the roles of men and women in their transformation. While there are clearly cases where women are more dominant, less subordinate, than in others, where individual actors have followed different avenues, traditional or innovative, to master a situation, the question is how women and men as social actors have used the system to achieve their ends. In the 1990s, the "gendering of space" became a salient perspective, with the realization that spatial arrangements express and reinforce gender. This holds particularly true for the house, whether one is looking at women Hausa in seclusion or Gabra as nomads.

BECOMING AN ADULT

Both girls and boys go through varying practices of socialization that prepare them for adulthood and its responsibilities in their particular culture. In so-called traditional society, by age six or seven, boys would go off with their fathers while girls stayed with their mothers and the other women in the household. Each gender was then formally and informally taught his/her respective roles. Male initiation rites make boys into men—most famously Turner's Ndembu in Zambia, as well as the Gisu and Maasai of Kenya, Kaguru in Tanzania, Igbo in Nigeria. Similarly, many societies practice puberty rites for girls. The Sande among the Mende of Liberia and Sierra Leone empowers its initiates, because it acts as a marriage broker while cultivating womanliness to bring women initiates access to social and political power. *Chisungu*, a girls' initiation ceremony, is the focus of anthropologist Audrey Richards' classic study among the matrilineal Bemba (Zambia). It is a nubility rite emphasizing the transformation of girls into women.

Missionaries and colonialism reinforced one another on what constituted appropriately male or female roles, and their influence lingers. For example, mission-educated boys in Ghana who became clerks and teachers were crucial as translators of the colonial enterprise. Labor migration became an alternate route for some men to gain power. Those men who fought in World War II in foreign theatres returned home with an ambiguous status, having disrupted their youth. In twenty-first-century Sierra Leone, cohorts of former child soldiers have missed out on the years of socialization into societal roles.

GENDER AND PRODUCTION

African women are celebrated for their economic role as agriculturalists; they have been cocoa producers in Ghana, rice farmers in Liberia, and maize farmers in Kenya. Indeed, in Africa female farming is widely practiced, and most tasks connected to food production are left to women. The standard description of the sexual division of labor in farming is that men clear and prepare the land and (if a plow is used) plow, while women plant, weed, harvest, process, and store crops. This organization is found throughout most of rural Africa. Yet other organizational forms have emerged in the twentieth century. Many African farming societies feature crop combinations, and there are those in which men and women cultivate different crops; Igbo (Ibo) men of southeast Nigeria cultivate yams, the women cassava. Nandi (Kenya) men and women both farm maize, although the crop is split into subsistence (female) and cash (male). In Malawi, all women are involved in most aspects of farming. While the division of labor is framed by marriage, the Western concept of "the family farm" (with husband and wife maximizing utility functions and sharing goods) does not apply in Africa, where husband and wife virtually always have separate incomes and expenditures.

Women constitute 60 to 80 percent of agricultural workers in Africa; yet their work has been undercounted and undervalued in official demographic and economic statistics. This is in part due to definitions of economic activity: unpaid work on family land is statistically "invisible" labor. Moreover, with the change to a cash economy, men gained a monopoly, which is significant if one supports the position that women's contribution to the economy correlates with their status.

Social and economic development has affected the sexes differentially. The conflation of indigenous and colonial sexism has meant that women have been the last to be educated, to gain access to

well-paying positions. With the decline in economic opportunities for rural women, such as the Kpelle in Liberia and the Somali in the Horn of Africa, urban areas became magnets. But life in the city is expensive, especially as compared with the hometown, where one may receive support from the extended family.

In the urban areas, uneducated African women join the informal labor market. Self-employed, they often engage in both licit and illicit economic activities that require minimal training or utilize already existing skills. Occupational choices for illiterates are limited to market trade, domestic service, and prostitution. Throughout West Africa, urbanization flourished under colonialism and market trade did as well. Along the coast, with men taking specialized jobs, the market became the province of women. Urban women's primary trade has been in foodstuff. Women's participation expanded along with the markets. In Accra, the market is still a significant realms of women's influence.

The Asante and Ga in Ghana, the Yoruba in Nigeria, the Krio in Sierra Leone, the Kpelle in Liberia sell even for small profits. Even married Hausa women living in seclusion in northern Nigeria engage in trade, using their young children as runners between compounds. East Africa lacks comparably great centers of market trade. The women there have greater attachments to the land. In Nairobi in the 1980s, a preponderance of women traders still split their time between business and farming. Many urban and peri-urban East African women have engaged in the illicit production and sale of beer. And while the market is largely the domain of women, men have always had their niche—especially as butchers and sellers of meat, and for Muslim populations, as dealers in Islamic paraphernalia, such as prayer beads and scents.

Domestic service, common in West, East, and southern Africa, is largely subsistence work. In areas with a history of European settlement and black domestic workers, African women were incorporated into the economy through domestic service. By 1890 in South Africa, this sector was transformed into a black, female institution, reflecting the changing patterns of racial and sexual exploitation. Economic compulsion was the source of coercion.

In some cases, as in Kisangani, Democratic Republic of the Congo, women have made their mark as entrepreneurs, using their sexuality to gain access to scarce goods. This is a time-honored tradition: in eighteenth-century Senegal, a category of African and European-African women known as *signares* (from the Portuguese *senhora*) were wealthy traders who made life comfortable for European businessmen and in return obtained European merchandise to sell.

Prostitution can be lucrative and requires no investment. A phenomenon of cities and long-distance truck routes, its practitioners include streetwalkers, bar women, and at-home courtesans. Women become prostitutes as a means of survival in the city. During the colonial period, women from southern Togo went to Accra and other colony towns to work as prostitutes. In colonial Nairobi, African women used prostitution to provide a range of domestic services to male migrant laborers. Many such women saw the possibility of buying property and building houses, which, given the instability of marriage, provided considerable security. Among many non-Muslim groups in the early twenty-first century, there is little traditional concern regarding casual sex, and there are even Muslim Hausa women in the towns of northern Nigeria who engage in prostitution.

The dominant construction of masculinity is still mainly of men as economic providers. But what that means has also varied, from the farmer in West Africa to the pastoralist in East Africa, the factory and mine worker in southern Africa, and then of course the doctors, lawyers and other members of the educate elite who also constitute the small band of rich Africans.

MARRIAGE AND THE FAMILY

Anthropological studies of marriage and kinship traditionally focused on males, even though research has always indicated that it is women whose lives are more closely tied to home, marriage, and family. For example, in the classic book *African Systems of Kinship and Marriage*, A. R. Radcliffe-Brown emphasizes the rights and duties of kinship. And while his observation is correct that marriage in Africa is different from that in Europe—involving not just two individuals but two bodies of people—it lacks nuance and has been read to mean that women were married off whether it suited their needs or not. This male bias is part of a theoretical tradition that views women as commodities who are exchanged by others to further those others' political and economic interests.

In fact, African women actively participate in marriage, family, and kin relations and their participation correlates with their power. For both men and women in many societies, the most important ties are not conjugal, but intergenerational—women to children and men to parents. In Tanzania, Barabaig women leave their husbands to live in the households established by their mature sons. The fictive parental links of Sande-society leader Madame Yoko (Sierra Leone) with young women in the Sande society provided her considerable political power in the late nineteenth century. Among the Asante (Ghana) and the Ndembu (Zambia), both matrilineal societies, and the Gonja (Ghana), which is patrilineal, women return to their natal kin to be with their children, to secure their children's future interests, or to pursue their own interests. The Mossi (Burkina Faso) require young men to treat their fathers' wives formally, and grown sons are discouraged from visiting the inside of the fathers' compounds, as the fathers' widows often marry on the death of their much older husband their husbands' sons.

Married women also participate in adulterous relationships that are inimical to the conjugal bond. Nisa, an articulate women of the !Kung (Kalahari Desert), regaled ethnographer Marjorie Shostak with tales of extramarital liaisons. In some African societies, women's solidaristic behavior coalesces around such situations, as women unite in opposition to men's control over their sexuality. Among the Ga of Accra, Ghana, where married men and women traditionally live in separate compounds, female kin report supporting and protecting one another when they engage in adultery. The Maasai (Kenya) are organized in age sets, and women may not marry men their own age (members of the warrior set) but men of the next set up (elders); adultery between the married women and the warriors is common and women never inform on one another. Among the Irigwe (Nigeria), in contrast to many societies, marriage does not guarantee the husband exclusive sexual access to his wife. Rather, women begin and end liaisons at will, pitting men against one another in competing both for sex and for paternity rights over the children.

Unique to Africa is the practice of woman-woman marriage. This highlights the social, economic and political power of the female "husband," who assumes the sociological status of a male. Practiced by peoples in west (the Igbo of Nigeria), east (the Nuer in Sudan, Nandi in Kenya), and southern Africa (the Zulu, Lovedu, and others), this institution is associated with patrilineal descent and provides women opportunities to control important resources. This autonomous female is always pater (the socially defined father) to the children borne by her wife or wives. And then there are elite women, as in Kenya, who in the late twentieth century began to avoid marriage because they said men used their money for mistresses and made the wife vulnerable to AIDS. In Mombasa, a society stuck on social status, there is a coterie of women with money who have marriage-like relationships with younger women. Here, sexual status is less important than socioeconomic status. If one sees these women as active not passive actors, it becomes clear that women have new resources at their disposal.

Men in a variety of African societies also have nontraditional resources for partnership. Marriage is required to attain the ideal of masculinity among Hausa men in Northern Nigeria; yet a group of "men who talk like women" (*'yan daudu*) carry on a parallel lifestyle and by engaging in "gender-bending behaviors" they challenge that norm. In Southern Africa, there are a variety of homosexual identities, which include temporary relations among mine workers and same-sex relationships that are regarded as marriages.

GENDER AND POWER

An archetype in the literature is the African "big man," who gained political and material success, usually by gaining "wealth in people." But there are also women with power or authority to make decisions, and their influence has systemic consequences. In fact, since women hold considerable sway in the home, *domestic* power distribution has consequences for *societal* power distribution: the fission of households and lineages in patrilineal systems often follows matricentric lines, and the rivalry between co-wives can precipitate

separation; mothers accompany and/or support sons who seek to establish households independently of their fathers; the support of women and children can be crucial to men becoming chiefs, as, for example, in central Africa, where men desirous of becoming headmen of their own villages must convince their sisters to leave their maternal uncle by demonstrating greater ability to protect the sisters' interests, and where brothers compete with husbands to attract women and their children.

Women need not sit on the throne to be influential. In northern Nigeria, Hajiya Ma'daki (b. 1907), a Muslim Hausa living in seclusion, married the emir, helped set up a school for girls, pushed her husband to recommend the school to local leaders and later influenced her brother's decisions when he became emir. In Ghana, the Asante queen mother cannot sit on the throne, but within the matrilineal context, she has considerable power as a kingmaker. Among the Nuer (Sudan), many women in conquering lineages adopt male roles and have their husbands come to live with them, while those married to men of aristocratic lineages go to live with them. Women thus gain power by attaching themselves and their daughters to powerful men.

Since the 1970s, using a new lens on the historical and ethnographic record, feminist scholars have unearthed evidence of African women's public political activity. In the nineteenth century, Akyaawa, an Asante royal woman, was present on the *asantehene's* military campaigns in the south and was empowered to sign a treaty with Europeans on behalf of the Asante king. Also during the nineteenth century, among the patrilineal Yoruba, some lineage chiefs were women of wealth, had their own armed forces, supplied lesser chiefs with arms and ammunition, engaged in opposition politics and were regarded as warrior-traders or military chiefs. Many women among the Mende of Sierra Leone became chiefs, lineage heads, and heads of secret societies; and in contemporary society, some women chiefs have political influence in national and international affairs.

A celebrated example of common women's struggle against colonialism was the 1929 Aba Women's War in southeast Nigeria, mounted by Igbo women angered by the perceived threat of taxation. It was based upon a traditional female technique used to discipline recalcitrant men, known as "sitting on a man," and consisted of embarrassing the person through noise and the singing of lewd songs. Similar disciplinary techniques have been found among the Bakweri in Cameroon and the Gikuyu in Kenya. In the continuing fight for independence, there is the example of women in Guinea-Bissau working for the Partido Africano da Independência da Guiné e Cabo Verde (PAIGO), especially to mobilize the war effort against the Portuguese from 1963 to 1974. And in 2002, in a stunning example of petro-politics, hundreds of poor Nigerian women brought oil production to a halt when they occupied five fuel stations owned and operated by Chevron Texaco in the Niger Delta, resulting in a written agreement to provide their communities with basic infrastructure.

Despite a high level of women's participation in independence struggles and contemporary "militance," in the early twenty-first century African women are only marginally involved in government. They and their organizations have played important roles in support of nationalist movements and political parties, but lack success in effecting changes in gender politics and advancing women's interests. Even in South Africa, where women were successful in getting elected in the 1994 election, many felt they were ineffective in Parliament and returned to grassroots activism.

ASSOCIATIONAL LIFE

Women have engaged in associations for generations. Traditionally women came together to promote common interests—economic, social, and political. Facilitating the articulation of women's needs, rights, and interests, the various associations created were based on common denominators such as ethnicity, age, lineage affiliation, and religion. Following colonialism and urbanization, associations helped women deal with diminished roles and opportunities. Among the best known are the rotating credit associations (for example in Cameroon and Côte d'Ivoire), where women meet together periodically, make contributions, and distribute funds to members.

Much research has been conducted on voluntary associations in urban West Africa from the first decade of independence, when migrants to the city sought out others either to reinforce their backgrounds (traditional), to learn the ways of the city (modern), or some mixture of the two. Most of the traditional associations were single sex. Women's groups have included cooperatives and self-help groups, occupational associations (Mathare Valley beer brewers' networks in Nairobi, for example), urban business enterprises, and welfare, church, and entertainment groups. Some have a charter to aid women's economic advancement or political action, while others help support a community of kind in an alien milieu.

Social change has seen associations evolve in their activities and interests. Muslim women along the Swahili Coast had many associations devoted to *lelemama*, a particular form of dance; the women's rationale for attending was entertainment, status, and mutual aid. During the independence period, as *lelemama* declined, new associations dealing with social, educational, and economic issues in the Muslim women's community developed. Similarly among the Gikuyu, initiation and age-set groups were transmuted into women's groups based on economic solidarity.

Educated women also have a history of associational involvement. In some countries, such as Côte d'Ivoire, they have mobilized to impact laws that determine their status. In Ghana, the intestate succession law of 1985 sought to resolve issues of inheritance for widows and children. This has met with some success for women's groups and churches. But non-compliance has made the work of FIDA, International Federation of Women's Lawyers, on behalf of women crucial.

Senegalese Muslim feminist organisation Yeewi-Yeewi is unrestrained in the advocation of gender equality, a marked contrast to the careful conduct and conservative tone taken by Nigeria's Federation of Muslim Women (FOMWAN).

RITUAL AND RELIGION

Women's "religious" engagement is significant and broadly based. Secret societies, which encompass initiation, are found especially in West Africa. Spirit possession, which involves a form of trance (*bori* among the Hausa, Fulani, and other groups in West Africa; *zar* in the Sudan and East Africa; and *tromba* in Madagascar, *orpeko* among Kenya's

Maasai) is commonly blamed for a range of illnesses. In the attempt to placate the spirits, possession becomes an integral part of the process of initiation into a healing cult. The vast majority of adepts are women. Scholars have speculated on the reasons for this, suggesting that, in Muslim societies, where women are excluded from public participation, the cults provide them with an avenue for expression; that spirits are attracted to women because of their femininity; that adepts have ambiguous status identity that the curing (initiation into the cult) mends; that the cults provide a voice for those silenced by Islam; and that the cults are close-knit groups that provide social support in daily life.

Spirit mediumship is a form of possession whereby the individual is perceived as an intermediary between the spirits and people. Such cults (for example, in Tanzania and Uganda) have also been predominantly female, and they deal primarily with female problems.

There has always been a readiness to credit Muslim men with literary and performative abilities and to exclude the women. New research has shown that among Northern Nigerian (Hausa) women, as in North Africa, precolonial knowledge was purveyed in the mode of *oral* traditions, therefore women could be scholars while they were not writers. But there is also the example of Nana Asma'u, daughter of the nineteenth century jihadist Usman dan Fodio, who encouraged her (as a woman) to engage in literary and educational activities. Her writings have had had relevance to contemporary female poets.

The arrival of different forms of Christianity has impacted both men and women.

Syncretic churches include the Christian-based prophetic cults which seek spiritual renewal, direct revelation from God, and charismatic healing. These integrate women and men into the same ritual activities, while specifically offering to women holy communities founded and headed by females (such as the Mai Chaza in Zambia); apostolic-like spirit churches (as in central Africa) in which women are adepts with great access to charismatic or expressive forms of participation; and revivalist groups that are formed throughout the continent. Studies of the church in contemporary African have continued to show the various churches having contradictory results for African women,

sometimes facilitating their oppression and sometimes offering a means of protection or even, on occasion, empowerment, whether through granting women access to Western education, or through women's direct participation in church activities and networks.

Gender has also been a key site for the production and proliferation of Islamic fundamentalist ideologies. For example, in places like Northern Nigeria, a major dimension of militant Islam has been the circumscription and curtailment of women's activities and visibility.

DEVELOPMENT AND CHANGE

Economic development in Africa, initiated by European colonizers, carried with it divergent ideologies and dependency relationships; interaction with indigenous social and economic norms produced or amplified gender hierarchies and systems of social stratification. The European/Christian model of social institutions and its underlying morality—nuclear family living, monogamy, a man-as-breadwinner ethos, Western dress and lifestyle—was embraced by the indigenous elite. The imported values and behaviors that percolated down to the masses included the relegation of women to a subordinate role.

Modernization under the aegis of Western development agencies has also been guided by Western male assumptions about women's "natural" domesticity, dependency, and subordination. It has maximized the differentiation of men's and women's roles, and the status of women relative to men has been eroded. While women farmers may be the main producers of crops, as in the Kenyan highlands, their economic status has changed from being relatively autonomous to relatively dependent. In cities, opportunities are limited by structural constraints (such as shortage of jobs and lack of education) and an ideology that defines women's work fairly narrowly. In Nigeria, women are less skilled than men and occupy positions of less power and authority that offer less money. Instruction in new skills appropriate to increasingly complex technologies is generally denied women throughout Africa. While educational systems in West Africa have expanded considerably, the institutionalization of educational and occupational hierarchies has increased the divergence in academic and professional trajectories of the sexes.

Urban single women (in Ghana, Nigeria, Senegal, and Zambia) are often dependent upon male sex partners to supplement their meager incomes, prompting the "sugar daddy" phenomenon. Elite women may stay in unhappy marriages, some taking lovers, because to divorce would mean to lose one's social position with little hope of recovery.

Women bear the brunt of state crises, which is evident in lower education across the continent and the presence of women in agriculture and other rural enterprises rather than professions, but regardless of their level of education, Nigerian women, for example, have historically produced leaders who are willing to fight for the freedom of other women.

African men and women are dealing with how to respond to new forms of gender hierarchy that have resulted from economic decline, political crises, and globalization. Maasai men who for whom the norm is a nomadic, pastoral life and men who live by the spear understand that in the modern age, "the only source of power now is the power of the pen" (Hodgson in Lindsay, 227). The new African-feminist approach is heterosexual and pronatal, emphasizing culturally linked forms of public participation rather than individual autonomy. In modernizing situations, accusations against women as witches have flourished, and since the late 1980s this has returned Africanist interest to the classic topic of witchcraft. Witchcraft accusations are explicitly linked in Nigeria, Cameroon, Kenya, with globalization and change, nonautocthony, the emergence of new forms of wealth, and men's desire to dominate.

See also **Kinship and Descent; Marriage Systems; Prostitution; Queens and Queen Mothers; Religion and Ritual; Sexual Behavior; Spirit Possession; Women.**

BIBLIOGRAPHY

Amadiume, Ifi. *Male Daughters, Female Husbands: Gender and Sex in and African Society.* London: Zed Books, 1987.

Ciekawy, Diane, and Peter Geschiere. "Containing Witchcraft: Conflicting Scenarios in Postcolonial Africa." Spec. issue, *African Studies Review* 41, no. 3 (1998).

Clark, Gracia. *Onions Are My Husband: Survival and Accumulation by West African Market Women.* Chicago: University of Chicago Press, 1994.

Cooper, Barbara. *Marriage in Maradi: Gender and Culture in a Hausa Society in Niger.* Portsmouth, NH: Heinemann, 1997.

Davison, Jean. *Gender, Lineage, and Ethnicity in Southern Africa.* Boulder, CO: Westview Press, 1996.

Goheen, Miriam. *Men Own the Fields, Women Own the Crops: Gender and Power in the Cameroon Grassfields.* Madison: University of Wisconsin Press, 1996.

Grosz-Ngate, Maria, and Omar H. Kokole, eds. *Gendered Encounters: Challenging Cultural Boundaries and Social Hierarchies in Africa.* London: Routledge, 1997.

Hodgson, Dorothy L. *Gender, Ethnicity and the Cultural Politics of Maasai Development.* Bloomington: Indiana University Press, 2001.

Mack, Beverly B. *Muslim Women Sing: Hausa Popular Song.* Bloomington: Indiana University Press, 2004.

Masquelier, Adeline. *Prayer Has Spoiled Everything: Possession, Power and Identity in an Islamic Town of Niger.* Durham, NC: Duke University Press, 2001.

Miescher, Stephan F., and Lisa A. Lindsay. "Introduction: Men and Masculinities in Modern African History" In *Men and Masculinities in Modern Africa,* ed. L. A. Lindsay and S. F. Miescher. Portsmouth, NH: Heinemann, 2003.

Mikell, Gwendolyn, ed. *African Feminism: The Politics of Survival in Sub-Saharan Africa.* Philadelphia: University of Pennsylvania Press, 1997.

Moore, Henrietta L.; Todd Sanders; and Bwire Kaare, eds. *Those Who Play With Fire: Gender, Fertility and Transformation in East and Southern Africa.* London: Athlone Press, 1999.

Pellow, Deborah "The Architecture of Female Seclusion in West Africa." In *The Anthropology of Space and Place: Locating Culture,* ed. S. M. Low and D. Lawrence-Zunega. Cambridge, MA: Blackwell, 2003.

Prussin, LaBelle. *African Nomadic Architecture: Space, Place and Gender.* Washington DC: Smithsonian, 1995.

Radcliffe-Brown, A. R., and Daryll Forde, eds. *African Systems in Kinship and Marriage.* London; New York: KPI, in association with the International African Institute; New York: Routledge & Kegan Paul, 1987.

Robertson, Claire C. *Sharing the Same Bowl?: A Socio-economic History of Women and Class in Accra, Ghana.* Bloomington: Indiana University Press, 1984.

Robertson, Claire C., and Iris Bergers, eds. *Women and Class in Africa.* New York: Africana Publishing Co., 1986.

Romero, Patricia W., ed. *Life Histories of African Women*. London: Ashfield Press, 1988.

Stichter, Sharon, and Margaret Jean Hay, eds. *African Women South of the Sahara*, 2nd edition. New York: Longman, 1995.

White, Luise. *The Comforts of Home: Prostitution in Colonial Nairobi*. Chicago: University of Chicago Press, 1990.

DEBORAH PELLOW

GENOCIDE. *See* Urbanism and Urbanization; Warfare.

GEOGRAPHY AND THE STUDY OF AFRICA.

Geography, as an institutionalized field of knowledge, figures centrally in both the history of informal and formal colonial rule in Africa and in the ways in which Africa came to be represented in the West, especially from the eighteenth century onward. As an academic discipline, geography has contributed to the knowledge of the continent along two broad dimensions. The first is physical geography, especially the geomorphology of tropical Africa and the desert regions, which explores the physical, climatic, and biological characteristics and dynamics of African ecosystems. Particular sorts of land forms—karsts, inselbergs, and desert surfaces—have drawn much attention, and applied geomorphology has focused on soil erosion and other human-induced problems. Paleogeomorphology (the morphology of sand dune systems in particular), studies of climatic change and climate dynamics, and hydrological and fluvial studies have also become important themes in the physical geographic approach to Africa. Since the 1990s a body of work on global climate change and dynamics of tropical climate has garnered much attention by geographers, in particular how African climatic systems change and are in turn affected by climatic perturbations half a globe away. The other dimension is human geography, which has as its object of study spatial patterns of economic, social, and cultural practice, and the complex relationship between nature and human activity. This discussion will focus on the latter and specifically on the contributions by European, North American, and African geographers to the human geography of Africa in the postcolonial (post–1960) period.

GEOGRAPHY, EMPIRE, AND AFRICANISM

In his important and controversial *Orientalism* (1978), Edward Said reveals how ideas and knowledge, while complex and unstable, are always inseparable from systems of subjection. In his case, orientalism represents a body of European knowledge, a geography of the Orient, which not only helped construct an imperial vision of particular places and subjects but also displaced other voices and indeed had material consequences as such ideas became the basis for forms of rule. Through a web of literary, scholarly, historical, and administrative accounts, orientalism came to be "a scientific movement whose analogue in the world of empirical politics was the Orient's colonial accumulation and acquisition by Europe" (Said 1985, 17).

In an almost identical fashion, the history of geographic scholarship, and of academic geography in particular in the nineteenth and early twentieth centuries, was closely tied to the European imperial mission in Africa. The Royal Geographical Society (RGS) was formed in 1830 as an outgrowth of the Africa Association, and Britain's overseas expansion in the nineteenth century (in which Africa figured prominently, especially after 1870) was by and large orchestrated through the RGS. Similarly, the Franco-Prussian War directly stimulated an increase in French geographical societies, which helped sustain a coherent political doctrine of colonial expansion, not least in Africa. At the Second International Congress of Geographical Sciences held in 1875 and attended by the president of the French Republic, knowledge and conquest of the earth were seen as an obligation, and geography provided the philosophic justification.

Early-nineteenth-century geography in America and Britain was in actuality a heterogeneous set of interests marked by a sharp break between scientists and practitioners. This rupture in pre-Darwinian geography between theory (largely understood in terms of design and teleology) and practice (the adventurer and expeditionary impulses of the RGS) was, however, sutured by the Darwinian revolution. The professionalization of the discipline coupled with its new attachment to a Darwinian natural science was inextricably linked to its central intellectual figures, Sir Halford J. Mackinder and Freidrich Ratzel. An evolution-inspired geography justified Britain's red patches on the globe, as Mackinder put it, and the expansionary impulse of Ratzel's lebensraum. The "new geography" and the "new imperialism" were thus inseparable. Whether in imperial Britain, Nazi Germany, or postwar America, geography and geographical knowledge were forged in the workshop of geopolitics, empire, and militarism. Africa was central to, and to a degree constitutive of, the troika of geography, race, and empire.

European geography, in other words, helped create or, more properly, invent a sort of Africanism, and relatedly a particular set of tropical imaginaries or visions embodied in the emergent field of tropical geography (Driver 2000; Driver and Martins 2005). Equally, Africa played its part in the debates within geography over environmental determinism, race, and civilization, and in what Livingston called the moral economy of climate; Africa helped invent geography. As the geographer Felix Driver properly observed: "The iconography of light and darkness, which embodies powerful images of race, science, and religion, portrayed the European penetration of . . . Africa as *simultaneously* a process of domination, enlightenment, and liberation" ("Geography's Empire," *Society and Space* 10, no. 2 [1992], 31). Geography helped make Africa "dark" in the nineteenth and twentieth centuries as it simultaneously assisted in the means (military cartography) by which the darkness was to be lifted by the *mission civilisatrice*. In a sense, then, the study of Africa lay at the heart of academic geography from its inception, and in so doing nineteenth- and early-twentieth-century geography directly contributed to what Stanley Crouch in his book *Notes of a Hanging Judge* (1990) called "one of the centerpieces of fantasy of our time." It was after all Joseph Conrad's Marlow in *Heart of Darkness* (1902) who says that Africa was "like travelling back to the earliest beginnings of the world" (*The Heart of Darkness*, cited in Chinua Achebe, *Hopes and Impediments*, New York: Doubleday, 1980, 4).

GEOGRAPHY AND THE INVENTION OF DEVELOPMENT

A history of geographers and geographic practice in the service of colonial rule in Africa has yet to be written, but it is quite clear that geographic ideas—most obviously land use and agrarian change, population growth and mobility, and environmental conservation—run through the period from the imperial partition of Africa in the 1870s to the first

wave of independence in 1960. Richard Grove has traced, for example, early conservation thinking in the Cape in southern Africa to the 1811–1844 period, which had produced a "conservation structure" of government intervention by 1888 driven by a triad of interests: scientific botany, the white settler community, and government concerns for security. This tradition of land use and conservation was inherited by various colonial officials in Africa, and it reappeared across much of western and southern Africa in the 1930s in a debate over population growth, deforestation, and the threat of soil erosion. As Paul Richards has noted, in colonial British West Africa the rise of a populist sentiment in agricultural policy singing the praises of the smallholder and the African peasant is very much part of the historiography of cultural ecological thinking in geography as a whole.

The introduction of the concept of development, signaled by the birth of development economics à la Arthur Lewis, Gunnar Myrdal, Albert Hirschmann, and others in the 1940s and 1950s, marked the beginning of wide-ranging theoretical debates about the dynamics of accumulation in the underdeveloped world. These discourses were rooted in part in the postwar establishment of international regulatory and development institutions such as the World Bank, the International Monetary Fund, and the panoply of United Nations (UN) organizations. This is not to suggest that comparative political economy was not studied prior to 1930—these ideas can, of course, be traced back to the classical political economy of the late eighteenth and nineteenth centuries—but theorizing peculiar to a particular space variously called the Third World, the less developed world, or the underdeveloped world as an object of academic scrutiny and public policy debate was enormously expanded and refined from the 1950s onward.

The relevance of geography's concern with land use and human ecology for colonial planning in Africa (and elsewhere) was vastly enhanced by what one might call the "invention of development" in the late colonial period. While the word "development" came into the English language in the eighteenth century with its root sense of unfolding, and was subsequently shaped by the Darwinian revolution a century later, "development" understood as a preoccupation of public and international policy to improve welfare and to produce governable subjects is of much more recent provenance.

Development as a set of ideas and practices was, in short, the product of the transformation of the colonial world into the independent "developing world" in the postwar period. Africa, for example, only became an object of planned development after the Great Depression of the 1930s. The British Colonial Development and Welfare Act (1940) and the French Investment Fund for Economic and Social Development (1946) promoted modernization in Africa through enhanced imperial investment against the backdrop of growing nationalist sentiments.

After 1945, the imperial desire to address development and welfare had a strong agrarian focus, specifically productivity through mechanization, settlement schemes, and various sorts of state interventions (marketing reform, cooperatives), all of which attracted a good deal of geographic attention. Growing commercialization in the peasant sector and new patterns of population mobility and demographic growth (expressed largely in a concern with the disruptive consequences of urbanization and rural-urban migration) pointed to land use as a central pivot of geographic study. British geographers such as Dudley Stamp and W. T. W. Morgan focused singularly on how land-use patterns were changing in rural and peri-urban Africa, a project that revealed striking parallels with the French mapping of traditional rural space through exhaustive, but largely descriptive, microlevel studies. *Atlas des structures agraires en Afrique au sud du Sahara* by Sautter and Pelissier (1962) provided a *morphologie agraire* of the landscape but was largely bereft of a serious investigation of the dynamics of resource use.

The best of the early mobility and land-use studies (conducted by Mansell Prothero, H. Jarrett, and Richard Grove) revealed something of the history of land-use intensity and the dynamics of circular migration in semiarid zones, and criticized the colonial rush to mechanization which seemed to rest on precepts developed in temperate agriculture and which rode roughshod over African indigenous systems of cultivation. Geographic work was particularly critical of the notorious postwar schemes to mechanize agriculture in Africa, many of which were associated with the activities of the Colonial Development Corporation (notably the Tanganyikan groundnut scheme, the irrigated rice scheme in the Gambia, and the Niger agricultural project in Nigeria).

Geography was a central practical field in the mapping of the continent. At the Treaty of Berlin when Africa was partitioned, the maps produced by geographers were for the most part incomplete and inadequate. But the harnessing of cartography to the colonial project was an indispensable component of colonial rule and the exercise of power. Cadastral surveys were the ground on which native authorities and tax collection was to be based, but full cadastral mapping proved to be either too expensive or too political. New critical studies in cartography have provided important accounts not only of the institutionalized role of mapping in colonial (and postcolonial) rule, but such studies have also shed light on cartography as an exercise of power and how it "belongs to the social world in which it is produced" (Harley 1992, 232; see Pickles 2004). The mapping of Africa is still on going and the delimitation of new territories (whether states, local government areas, or chieftaincies) remains a complex process wrapped up with state power and forms of representation that are not captured by the purported objective qualities of scientific map production (Woods 1992; Monmonier 1995).

THE SHOCK OF THE NEW: INDEPENDENCE AND THE FIRST DEVELOPMENT DECADE

Colonial rule in Africa proved to be relatively short, little more than one lifetime long, and produced neither mature capitalism nor a standard grid of imperial rule. Whether settler colonies (Kenya), peasant-based trade economies (Senegal), or mine-labor reserves (Zaire), virtually all the emerging independent African states in the 1960s shared a common imperial legacy: the single-commodity economy. African economies were one-horse towns, hitched to the world market through primary export commodities such as cotton, copper, and cocoa. No matter how distorted or neocolonial their national economies were, African countries' hopes and expectations at independence were high, indeed in some sense almost euphoric. The heady vision of Kwame Nkrumah—of a black Africa utilizing the central-planning experience of the Soviet Union to industrialize rapidly and overcome poverty, ignorance, and disease—captured the popular imagination. Indeed, many of the first generation of African leaders, irrespective of their political stripe, became infatuated with national plans and ambitious long-term planning. Health, education, and infrastructure were heavily funded (typically aided and abetted by "technical" foreign assistance), and government activities were centralized and expanded to facilitate state-led modernization. In spite of the fact that state agencies extracted surpluses from the agrarian sector—peasant production remained the bedrock of most independent states—to sustain import-substitution and industrialization (as well as a good deal of rent-seeking and corruption by elites), African economies performed quite well in the 1960s, buoyed by soaring commodity prices (especially after 1967).

Not surprisingly, much of the geographic scholarship of the 1960s was framed by some variant of modernization theory, or at the very least by the presumption that the processes of modernity (commercialization, urbanization, and transportation) were shaping indigenous institutions and practices. Building upon the so-called quantitative revolution of the late 1950s and mathematical location theory drawn from Max Weber and Hans Christaller, Africanist geographers were among the first to model modernization surfaces. Much of this research attempted to map patterns of modernity—which typically revealed islands of modernity within the urban hierarchy—by charting the diffusion of indices of modernization (schools, mailboxes) through the settlement pattern. Crippled by the weaknesses of the theory itself—a Eurocentric selection of "modern" indices, a teleological and conflict-free vision of change, an inadequate understanding of the dynamics of political economy—modernization surfaces were transitory interests and were ultimately rejected by their practitioners, such as Edward Soja and Barry Riddell. At best, this work raised some important questions about the legacy of colonial transportation systems, the dynamics of diffusion across urban hierarchies, and, more presciently, the character of African urbanism.

Some of the most interesting geographic scholarship of the period was undertaken at subnational levels, grounded if not in an ethnographic approach to fieldwork then at the very least in a careful local empiricism (often by geographers, local and expatriate, located on the continent and engaged in long-term research projects). One focus was marketing systems and indigenous periodic markets in West Africa. By focusing on indigenous exchange, marketing research complemented the work of historians anxious to show the nonsubsistence character of African societies, the historic antiquity of markets and marketplaces, and the relations between periodic markets and the settlement hierarchy. This long-standing concern with trade not only debunked the mythology of the uneconomic or irrational peasant but ultimately fed into a large neoclassical economic literature (the so-called structure-conduct-performance approach associated with the Stanford Food Research Institute), which argued that African marketing systems were open, efficient, and nonexploitative—of the kind much beloved by neoliberal economists. In the 1980s much of this work was critiqued and extended by a Cambridge geographer, Barbara Harriss, working in southern India and West Africa.

A second focus turns on the question of urbanization and human mobility. Urban growth has been an enduring object of scrutiny by French geographers (and is particularly associated in the 1970s with the Department of Geography and Regional Studies at Bordeaux III and the journal Les cahiers d'outremer), but the most innovative scholarship is unquestionably that of Ibadan geographer Akin Mabogunje. Trained in the United Kingdom but influenced by the "new" urban geography of North America, Mabogunje's approach to African urbanism is eclectic, drawing upon urban ethnography, regional theory, urban morphology, and a sensitive grasp of political economy. Writing primarily about his native Yorubaland in southern Nigeria, Mabogunje wrote about precolonial urbanism, laying the foundations for a distinctive theory of West African urbanism (which was drawn upon subsequently in Paul Wheatley's epochal book The Pivot of the Four Quarters [1971] on comparative urbanism). Tracing the genesis of Yoruba towns to sacred geography and cosmogonic mapping, Mabogunje also wrote at length about the transformation of cities—in both social and morphological senses—in the postcolonial period. His monograph on regional mobility draws together a careful analysis of colonial migration patterns, the role of ethnic associations in patterns of urban accommodation and trade, and the implications of migration in resource use. In this latter case, he is able to draw upon some of the studies of geographers who work on land-use changes in Africa to show how migrants are a progressive force and, as Cambridge anthropologist Polly Hill showed in her classic studies of the cocoa belt in Ghana, a source of initiative for local development.

Finally, it is important to mention the land-use scholarship that in many respects predates the 1960s and has been perhaps the central object of study for both British and French geographers in the immediate postwar period. This complex and heterogeneous body of work speaks to the question of traditional patterns of African land use and how they are being shaped and realigned, under local auspices, by post-colonial development. One stream of this scholarship originates in debates over environmental determinism and explores the relationship between African practice and environmental potential, usually drawing upon organic analogies and the adaptive capacities of "traditional farmers and pastoralists." Another and wide-ranging body of work explores through microlevel case studies (typically at the village level) changing intensities of land use, usually couched in Malthusian or Boserupian language of population pressure. This is part of a larger effort to classify systems of land use (long fallow, short fallow, permanent cropping, multicropping) which were seen to be correlated with population density, land-use rights, settlement patterns, labor productivity, and so on. The very best of this work is comparable to the classic ethnographies of agrarian land use undertaken by anthropologists such as Polly Hill in Nigeria in the 1960s and Audrey Richards in the 1930s in Northern Rhodesia. John Hunter's work on the *huza* system in Ghana and his studies of the relations between land use and seasonal hunger are still relevant reading for any graduate student preparing to conduct fieldwork in Africa in the 1990s. Michael Mortimore's twenty-five-year study beginning in 1965 of the close-settled zone of Kano in northern Nigeria is one of the best (indeed one of the only) long-term studies of the complexities of local-level agrarian intensification.

There are perhaps three final observations about the human geography of Africa in the first development decade. First, it is surprising how little direct engagement there was between geographic interests and what one might call the macrotheoretic debates of the period. David Keeble's 1967 review of economic development mechanically inventories W. W. Rostow's stages of growth, big-push theories, unbalanced growth, early structuralism, and so on, but in general human geography appears as sadly distant from the

work of Albert Hirschmann on linkages and sectoral imbalances, Arthur Lewis on labor supply, the ECLA debates over import-substitution, and so on.

The second is that Africa for obvious historic reasons attracted more academic attention in Britain and France than in the United States; indeed, Africa remains the poor sister of regional studies in North America. This geopolitics of knowledge marginalized Africa (primarily through sources of funding) until the 1970s, when a combination of foreign assistance through the U.S. Agency for International Development (USAID) and philanthropic activities (the Rockefeller and Ford Foundations)—as well as changing conditions on the continent itself—drew academics, including geographers, in much larger numbers.

And finally, it is striking how little attention was devoted to political geography. The outbreak of the civil war in Nigeria in 1966 was emblematic of deeper, and darker, political ailments associated with a sort of spoils politics in which governance degenerated into violent, repressive, and corrupt rule crosscut by the manipulation of ethnic difference. The regimes of Idi Amin in Uganda, Jean-Bédel Bokassa in Central Africa, and Francisco Macias Nguema in Equatorial Guinea did not bode well for the future. Geographers, however, had little or nothing to say on the matter.

OIL, DROUGHT, AND AFRICAN CRISIS MANAGEMENT DURING THE 1970S

From the onset of the 1970s the complacency and optimism of the 1960s appeared to be waning. Mounting U.S. deficits, the devaluation of the dollar, and the emergence of floating exchange rates marked the demise of the postwar Bretton Woods financial order. The restructuring of the financial system coincided with the crisis of the "three F's" (price increases in fuel, fertilizer, and food) in 1972–1973, which marked a serious deterioration in Africa's terms of trade. Ironically, the oil crisis also contained a solution. Between 1974 and 1979 the balance-of-payments problems of many African states (which faced not only a quadrupling of oil prices but a general price inflation for imported goods and a sluggish demand for primary commodities) was dealt with through expansionary adjustment: in other words, through borrowing from banks eager to recycle petrodollars or from the special facilities established by the

International Monetary Fund (IMF) and the World Bank. Expansionary adjustment, however, deepened two already problematic tendencies in African political economies. The first was to enhance the politics of public-sector expansion, contributing to waste, inefficiency, and the growing privatization of the public purse. The second was to further lubricate the political machinery, which produced uneconomic investments with cheaply borrowed funds (for example, the Nigeria crusade to produce steel).

Heavy borrowing did little to alter the strong anti-rural bias in African development strategies (systematic undervaluing of agricultural crops by parastatals and limited public investment in infrastructure). Furthermore, the sluggish growth of food output (food output declined in the 1970s) was compounded by devastating droughts in the early 1970s in the Sahelian zone and by rapid population growth. The famines of 1969–1974 threw into dramatic relief the structural vulnerability of African economies, and in some cases prompted a rash of irrational investments in large-scale irrigation as a means of drought-proofing the agricultural sector. Agricultural stagnation, famine, and urban bias occasioned an endless stream of migrants out of the countryside, flooding the vast slums of Nairobi, Lagos, and Kinshasa. In 1967 Lagos held roughly 1 million people; by 1980 it stood at close to 5 million. If the 1960s saw a gradual rise out of urban poverty, the 1970s witnessed a return to penury, declining real wages, and stagnation. In the political realm, the glow of liberation movements in Angola, Mozambique, and Zimbabwe was tarnished by civil wars in the Horn, military coups, arbitrary violence, and gross venality within the public sector.

The crisis of the 1970s helped to precipitate two major changes in the institutional and theoretical climate of Africanist geography. On the one hand, the specter of famine in the Sahel and the Horn drew increased foreign assistance to sub-Saharan Africa as a whole and to rural development in particular. To the extent that this support translated into research and programming activities in the donor countries, academics and consultants were drawn into development and applied work, in the United States through USAID, in Britain through the Ministry of Overseas Development, and in France through the Office de la Recherche Scientifique et Technique d'Outre-Mer (ORSTOM). In the United States in particular, USAID–funded projects permitted some campuses to expand their Africanist activities and encouraged some geographers to systematically explore a number of questions relating to drought, food security, and rural resource use.

On the other, the bleak prospects for Africa in the face of a world recession and deteriorating terms of trade—prospects which contributed to the call for a new international economic order in the first part of the 1970s—were not unrelated to the growing critique of market-oriented modernization theory and the early growth theorists, and to the gradual emergence beginning in the late 1960s of radical dependency theory, and subsequently of Marxist-inspired development theory. Human geography was part and parcel of these transformations, which were both in a sense rooted in the world system: foreign aid in the choppy waters of cold war geopolitics, and theory in the growing sensitivity to the demands imposed by the world market and by dependent locations in the world system of transnational capitalism. In a manner quite unlike the 1960s, Africa appeared central to the often ferocious debates over the political economy of underdevelopment; indeed, one of the central figures in this debate, and one of its great theorists, namely Samir Amin, was himself based in Africa, in Dakar.

Geography's incorporation into the radicalization of development theory during the 1970s was thrown into relief by the drought/famines in the Sahel early in the decade. Critical of the earlier natural-hazards research based primarily on North American environmental perturbations and on a simple perceptual model of hazard response, Ben Wisner and Phil O'Keefe conducted research studying the impact of drought on class relations. Famine was seen not as a mechanical consequence of drought but as a social product. French geographers of a Marxist persuasion had been especially active in pointing out how agricultural and pastoral communities affected by drought had been made vulnerable to both environmental perturbations and reductions in food output, and in so doing built upon the work of Brazilian geographer José de Castro. The key issue, in short, was the manner in which self-provisioning communities were systematically undermined—beginning in the early colonial period—by export commodity production. Michael Watts, working in northern Nigeria, traced the history of famine and food security in northern Nigeria by drawing on the modes-of-production debate to argue that the particular way in which the market developed (the dominant role of merchant capital) left many households vulnerable to drought. This effort to weld natural-hazards research, and earlier cultural ecology, onto a theory of political economy (a theory of resource access and control) marked the onset of a line of scholarship that was to culminate with the "political ecology" approach during the 1980s.

The crisis in semiarid Africa also highlighted several other human geographic developments. One built upon the "agrarian morphology" associated with ORSTOM in France and produced some of the most incisive analyses of agropastoralism in drought-prone environments. Edmond Bernus and Jean Gallais published monographs building on long-term ethnographic research on the land-use practices of the Niger delta and northern Niger (a tradition continued on the other side of the Atlantic in the 1990s by Matt Turner). Each emphasized the complexity of local knowledge (of livestock and the local physical environments) and how pastoral and sedentary communities were organically linked, largely through mobility, social structure, and a fluidity of resource mobilization, in order to survive along the desert edge. The French scholarship that did so much to understand the dynamics of rural space in Sahelian communities was part of a growing concern with local knowledge of the environment (often referred to as ethnogeography or ethnoecology) which pushed the earlier concerns with adaptation into the realm of cross-cultural cognition. The complexities of African farming systems—and in particular their flexibility and robustness—drew considerable attention, in part as a reaction to the recognition that much of what passed as state-led rural development was crudely exploitative of the peasant sector, constrained local initiative and capacity, and undercut indigenous technologies.

Severe drought also helped to highlight desertification as a major global problem. The 1977 UN Conference on Desertification was held in Nairobi, and the semiarid regions of Africa were seen to be especially vulnerable. This marked, of course, the proliferation of environmental histories focused on the reconstruction of climatic variability in Africa and more generally on the relation between human practice and climatic change. Some of the key papers prepared for the UN conference had a strong geographic stamp, although much of the discussion of albedo, greenhouse effects, and global cooling was based on highly inconclusive data, and hence appeared unnecessarily apocalyptic. Indeed, notwithstanding the later debate on global warming and the development of more sophisticated global circulation models, many of the early predictions about rangeland degradation in Africa have proven to be untenable. The resiliency of semiarid ecosystems and complex realignments in land uses along the desert edge suggest that the dynamics of desertification are poorly understood.

Finally, French, or more properly French-speaking, geographers devoted considerable attention in the 1970s to the twin problems of urban growth and health. Francophone geography has a virtual monopoly in both areas, reflecting in some measure a serious funding commitment by state agencies such as ORSTOM. Copiously detailed monographs of specific cities in former French and Belgian colonies, and a long-term interest in food provisioning (*approvisionment*), urban agriculture, and urban marketing networks has distinguished this scholarship. By the late 1970s and early 1980s the urban horizon had been expanded to include urban planning and land use, urban family networks and residential associations, and as one might expect in the context of a deepening political crisis of the state, a closer scrutiny of the public sector in its attempts to control settlements (*bidonvilles*) and services. While largely unconcerned with the political economy of health, the human geography of epidemiology in Africa also garnered attention (building upon a much longer francophonic tradition of medical geography and health represented in the work of Pierre Gourou and culminating in the massive socioecological study of twelve diseases by G. Remy). Some Anglophone research has also successfully integrated medical geography and political economy, most notably the work of Canadian geographer Robert Stock.

In hindsight, the 1970s appear as a sort of watershed in African studies generally. For geopolitical, financial, and other reasons, scholars and policy makers devoted more attention to African underdevelopment as the first blush of independence seemed to wane, and Africa accordingly appeared as a central theater for debates over development theory. In practice this meant a growing concern with various forms of Marxist-inspired political economy, which produced important studies on dependent industrialization, peasant differentiation, state intervention, Africa and global accumulation, and a rewriting of colonial history. Geography was pulled along by this vortex of change, but the confluence of growing theoretical sophistication and a widening of empirical interests was to bear fruit only in the "boom" in Africanist geography in the 1980s, ironically at a moment when the continent was destined, in the view of most analysts, to slide into abject poverty and destitution.

AFRICAN DEVELOPMENT, GEOGRAPHY, AND THE LOST DECADE OF THE 1980s

Commodity prices crashed in the early 1980s, dropping below the historic low point of the Great Depression. Between 1985 and 1988 Africa lost $50 billion to tumbling export prices. In 1986 alone the terms of trade fell so sharply that African import capacity was reduced by 25 percent. By the early 1980s the state-led modernization project of the postcolonial period seemed to have run off the rails. Adjustment in the 1980s occurred without financing, easy money, or concessionary lending. The growth of 1970s debt produced a hideous debt service by the mid–1980s; the ratio of scheduled debt repayment to export earnings in 1988–1989 stood at 70 percent for sub-Saharan Africa as a whole. Many African states faced a massive liquidity crisis—vastly compounded by trade stagnation and high interest rates—and were effectively bankrupt.

The crisis of the 1980s compelled African states to turn to the lenders of last resort—the IMF and the World Bank, in particular—who, in keeping with the radical ideological shift in the advanced capitalist states during the 1980s, spoke the rigid language of market idolatry and economic puritanism. Crisis management was about austerity and stabilization, typically achieved by entering into agreements with the IMF (forty-two letters of intent were signed in sub-Saharan Africa by 1988). The combination of exchange-rate reform, currency devaluation, and public sector cutbacks produced something close to total economic collapse. Sub-Saharan Africa's economic output declined by 20 percent between 1980 and 1986, and many Africans were worse off in 1990 than they were in 1960. State expenditures fell by one-third in the first half of the 1980s, exports by 30 percent, and imports by 65 percent. Taking interest payments into account, private net transfers declined from an average inflow of $2.5 billion in 1980–1982 to an average $7 billion *outflow* in 1985–1987. This was death by strangulation. Several African countries slipped during the 1980s from middle- to low-income status. In 1987 a month's salary for an unskilled laborer in Uganda barely covered his food bill for a week; a secretary's pay in Kinshasha just covered the costs of commuting to work. As Adebayo Adedeji put it, this was the lost decade for Africa.

The precipitous collapse in the 1980s—brought on by the conflation of troubles such as drought, famine, AIDS, bankruptcy, civil strife, and corruption, which led geographer Barry Riddell to claim in 1987 that "the African world has fallen apart"—was matched by an equally dramatic rise of neoliberal theory, what John Toye has called the counterrevolution in development theory. Postcolonial development strategies of most African states championed the powers of free and competitive markets. Although popular in the halls and offices of the World Bank and various development agencies, these tactics sparked considerable theoretical debate. Some geographic scholarship had certainly been critical of state-initiated development schemes, but the myopic prescriptions for free markets were properly criticized for their impact on the poor, for their dismissal of the institutional prerequisites for market capitalism, and as a basis for sustained accumulation. At the same time, the adjustment had devastating consequences on university education in Africa, with the result that research by African geographers was seriously compromised. African scholarship generally withered to the point of collapse as faculty faced the drying up of research monies compounded by declining real wages. Many academics were compelled to engage in second occupations. The most active African geographers were those who were based outside of the continent or who acted as consultants to international development agencies.

Not surprisingly, some of the geographic research of the 1980s addressed conditions and problems that, if not peculiar to the continent, were at the very least endemic. Important work inventorying African environmental crises, the overwhelming refugee problem stemming from the war and civil strife in southern Africa and the Horn, and the social consequences of adjustment appeared by geographers on both sides of the Atlantic. In theoretical terms, however, the 1980s witnessed a retreat from the structural Marxism and cruder forms of dependency theory to more nuanced social history (albeit influenced by British Marxist historiography). Gender- and feminist-inspired theory transformed the understanding of household- and community-level dynamics in Africa and hence the agrarian question more generally, a move which reflected a larger intellectual effort to link cultural and symbolic analysis with political economy. In a still larger sense, the debates within Marxism and political economy marked a growing influence of poststructuralism, and the abandonment of what was purportedly the crude Eurocentric "totalizing vision" of social theory such as Marxism, world systems, and dependency analysis.

Ironically, this postmodern turn in the social sciences occurred precisely at a moment when, within development policy circles, neoclassical economics and World Bank free-market orthodoxy were more hegemonic than ever. Indeed, the events of 1989 suggested to the scions of the World Bank that a particular model of African development had failed irrevocably; according to one World Bank official, "the world knows much better now what policies work and what policies do not. . . . Now we almost never hear calls for alternative strategies based on harebrained schemes."

These broad theoretical shifts have, to varying degrees, shaped the most innovative and enduring human geographic research of the 1980s. This work can be separated into two broad initiatives, which can be called *the agrarian question* and *the space of apartheid*. The agrarian question invokes, of course, the classic debates on the political economy of the rural sector under industrial capitalism, but it has been a centerpiece of the revival of African studies, to which geographers contributed in new and visible ways during the 1980s. One arena has been the long-standing interest in land use. Work by both French- and English-speaking geographers has moved beyond simple morphologies or earlier Boserupian theories to a fuller understanding of the politics of land use. There has been an interesting confluence among Francophone and Anglophone geographers around the complexities of African land tenure, or *foncier*, and land use over the *longue durée*, or long

term, which has produced some extraordinary local studies, most conspicuously Abdellatif Bencherifa and Herbert Popp's study of the oasis of Figuig.

Other themes within the agrarian question include historical and contemporary studies of hunger emphasizing the social organization of farming systems and responses to food shortage, the importance of gender and property rights in shaping technological change and agrarian productivity, the relations between migration and development, a series of populist and radical critiques of rural development, and not least a profusion of excellent studies on environmental change and resource use employing the theoretical insights of political ecology. Much of this latter work starts from literature on the control of and access to resources, and demonstrates how the intersection of institutions with the dynamics of accumulation shapes the capacity of the resource manager (the African peasant or herder) to use the environment in a sustainable manner. Political ecology has, in this sense, permitted geographers to refine such notions as vulnerability and marginalization. Poverty (or, more properly, the social relations of peasant production) can produce soil degradation (it may be situationally rational for the farmer to mine the soil) as much as wealth (or more properly the social relations of timber capital) can account for deforestation.

The emergence of a sophisticated human geography focused on (and largely in) South Africa is, however, perhaps the most striking aspect of the Africanist landscape of the 1980s. Dating back to the emergence of a revisionist interpretation of South African history during the 1970s, human geography was swept along by the wave of Marxist-inspired analysis of the apartheid economy producing what Canadian geographer Jonathan Crush, among others, has referred to as a "new wave" of South African geography. Fueled by a political engagement on and off campus, geographers came to address important economic restructurings, and political struggles, throughout southern Africa. One stream of this work was explicitly spatial and regional, examining industrial decentralization policies, homeland industries, urban apartheid, the informal sector, state politics, and social movements, typically employing theoretical weaponry derived from David Harvey, Doreen Massey, Gillian Hart, Manuel Castells, and proponents of the French regulationist school.

Another body of work, largely rural and agrarian, charts the complex social history of migrations, farm relations, gender politics in town and country, and so on, building upon the exciting "histories from below" of the likes of Charles van Onselen, Colin Bundy, Helen Bradford, and Tim Keegan, who linked apartheid political economy (of various stripes) to the study of popular culture. There is no question that the South African community has been a stronghold of Marxist analysis and of social history recognizing that important tensions and differences reside within their midst. Ferocious debates, political self-righteousness, and a good deal of shallow rhetoric has marred some of this work, but on balance much of the most exciting human geography of Africa emerged from post-Soweto South Africa. What the new postapartheid politics will provide for human geographic analysis is far from clear, but the growing role of geographers in the rough and tumble of South African politics suggests that the Africanist community may do well to look to the southern cone of the continent for its intellectual and theoretical sustenance.

A notable advance in the 1980s was the serious treatment of state theory and state politics. Abdi Samatar provided an original analysis of what he called the "suspended state" in Somalia, drawing upon comparative work in India and East Asia, and this has also been the hallmark of much of the so-called new-wave human and regional geography in South Africa. Deeply influenced by Bayart's Foucauldian approach to power in African politics, the Francophone geographers have also come to address *géopolitiques internés*, apartheid politics, and the problem of weak states and "disengaged statehood," especially around the journal *Herodoyte*. These questions of political geography represented (often from the progressive community) a critical attack on decrepit African states—and to this extent fed into the strongly antistate sentiment typified by the World Bank—and yet was also a response to the crisis of legitimacy that surrounded many African states in the face of structural adjustment and stabilization programs.

By the end of the decade two other issues had, in a curious way, come back to haunt Africa, raising difficult and profound questions about the way Africa is, and has been, inscribed through Western discourse. One is rooted in debates that stretch back to the end of the eighteenth century; the other is relatively new.

The Malthusian specter hangs over the continent and has pride of place in the major policy documents of global development agencies. Some geographers, working largely within a Boserupian problematic, had explored the relations between demographic pressure and land use during the 1980s, but the "new" demographic debate is driven increasingly by the presumption of persistently high fertility rates (in some cases over 4 percent per annum), rapid environmental degradation (the two are seen to be organically linked), and what is widely held to be the extraordinarily bleak economic future in the short term for most African economies. AIDS conversely is of late-twentieth-century provenance, but its history has been, from its inception, linked (often falsely) to Africa. While the statistics are contested on virtually every front, work by geographers has begun to draw out the patterns and consequences of terrifyingly high rural and urban infection rates in the east and central African arc. There seems no question that both reproduction and health—two themes which have always been central to the "invention of Africa"—will be increasingly at the forefront of geographical scrutiny in the 1990s.

GEOGRAPHIC SCHOLARSHIP AND THE NEW MILLENNIUM

Whether the human geography of Africa has approached Edward Said's goal to produce a geography of African historical experience remains an open question. What the most compelling geographies of the 1980s accomplished, nonetheless, was the addition of complexity to our understanding of African places and spaces. To this extent they have contributed to the critical reading of Africa that Said himself aspired to in his treatise on the relations between culture and imperialism. But what will become of the human geography of Africa, and what of its prospects for the twenty-first century?

Doubtless the growing numbers of people and the second wave of global environmentalism will ensure that questions of sustainability will be at the forefront of research and policy (Schroeder 1999; Moore 2005). The rethinking of conservation and national park management around questions of privatization and decentralization is a case in point (Adams and Mortimore 1999; Neumann 1998); the same can be said for new work on decentralized resource management (forests, for example) that focus on the relations between local government capacity and the monitoring role of civic groups (Ribot 1999). Furthermore, the pressing need to revitalize agriculture, coupled with the serious problems of food security, health, and welfare highlighted by economic adjustment, will reinforce the growing literature on poverty, inequality, and gender (Bassett 2001). But it is probably within the fledgling democratic movements and the slow and uneven emergence of civil society that new geographic horizons will emerge. The crumbling of single-party politics and the emergence of new political dialogues of various sorts have opened a space in which grassroots organizations and all manner of civil institutions can flourish. The case of Somalia—and in a quite different way South Africa—reveals that civil society cannot be wished into existence and may well turn out to be a bloody process crosscut by ferocious ethnic or parochial interests.

Nevertheless, the high tide of neoliberalism is passed which, in view of the dismantling of much of the old state-led strategies, suggests that new sorts of public-private contracts and institutional configurations will shape African development—indeed African democracy—in the twenty-first century. This is clear in the way for example that international development agencies, nongovernmental organizations (NGOs), and oil companies are working in new ways around community development in Nigeria and the other Gulf of Guinea states (Zalik 2004). A body of new geographical work that focuses less on Africa declining share of world trade and more on the ways in which the continent is being drawn into retail-driven global commodity chains, especially in the fresh fruit and vegetable sector (Friedberg 2004).

Since 2000 there is no question that Africa has gained a newfound international visibility. Driven in part by the debt question and the efforts of the likes of Bono, Gordon Brown at the British Excheqeur, the New Economic Partnership for Africa (NEPAD), and the so-called anti-globalization movement, Africa is now the focus of substantial global concern. The conjuncture of a number of forces have brought the continent to a sort of impasse: the HIV/AIDS pandemic, the limited success of the austerity and adjustment reforms, a continuing decline in the continent's share of world trade and foreign direct investment, the failure to meet the UN's 2005 Millennium Goals, and

the rise of massive cities (mega-cities) dominated by slums. The Commission on Africa ("Blair Report") and the U.S. Council of Foreign Relations Task Force on Africa Report—both released in 2005—speak in quite different registers to the challenges that geographical scholarship and practice must address. The growing significance of Africa in U.S. "energy security," in which the Gulf of Guinea figures so centrally, is one area in which the longstanding interest of geographers in strategic resources will continue to develop (Watts 2005).

Whether development will build upon distinctive African traditions, institutions, and knowledge—and more generally upon the energies and capacities of peasants, workers, and pastoralists—to forge an "alternative" development is very much an open question. But there is no doubt that the questions of institutions and institutional capacity will be a pivot around which much geographic and social science research will rotate. For geographers, these interests may well speak to the indigenous regulatory and management systems through which resources may be employed in a sustainable fashion, and in a sense look back to the several decades of research on ethnogeography, so-called traditional adaptive strategies of land use, and so on. Informed now by a much more sophisticated sense of the political and institutional conditions under which such knowledge and practices can be harnessed to empower people and develop national economies, this vast body of geographic scholarship on land use, broadly understood, could be part of a renaissance of African agriculture. It would naturally be myopic to push this line of reasoning too far in view of the fluid and heterogeneous politics of sub-Saharan Africa, and not least in view of the fact that some states are in the process of decomposition (such as Congo, Sudan, and Somalia). All of these issues suggest that African politics—and the democracy question more generally—will hold pride of place in the human geography of the new millennium.

See also **Aid and Development; Colonial Policies and Practices; Desertification, Modern; Ecology; Ecosystems; International Monetary Fund; Production Strategies; World Bank.**

BIBLIOGRAPHY

Adams, William. *Wasting the Rain: Rivers, People, and Planning in Africa.* Minneapolis: University of Minnesota Press, 1992.

Adams, William, and Michael Mortimore. *Working the Sahel.* London: Routledge, 1999.

Bascom, Johnathan B. "Food, Wages, and Profits: Mechanized Schemes and the Sudanese State." *Economic Geography* 66, no. 2 (1990): 140–155.

Bassett, Thomas. *The Peasant Cotton Revolution in West Africa.* Cambridge, U.K.: Cambridge University Press, 2001.

Bassett, Thomas J., and Donald E. Crummey. *Land in African Agrarian Systems.* Madison: University of Wisconsin Press, 1993.

Bayart, Jean-François. *The State of Africa.* London: James Currey, 1993.

Beinart, William. "Soil Erosion, Conservationism, and Ideas About Development in South Africa." *Journal of Southern African Studies* 11, no. 2 (1984): 52–83.

Bencherifa, Abdellatif, and H. Popp. *L'oasis de Figuig.* Passau, Germany: Verlag, 1990.

Bernus, Édmond. *Les Illabakan (Niger): Une tribu touarègue sahélienne et son aire de nomadisation.* Paris: ORSTOM, 1974.

Boserup, Ester. *The Conditions of Agricultural Growth: The Economics of Agrarian Change Under Population Pressure.* London: Earthscan, 1965.

Campbell, David. "Response to Drought among Farmers and Herders in Southern Kajaido District, Kenya." *Human Ecology* 12, no. 1 (1984): 35–64.

Crush, Jonathan, and C. Rogerson. "New Wave African Historiography and African Historical Geography." *Progress in Human Geography* 7 (1983): 203–231.

Dalby, David, and R. J. Harrison Church, eds. *Drought in Africa.* London: The Africa Institute, 1973.

Driver, Felix. *Geography Militant: Cultures of Exploration and Empire.* London: Routledge, 2000.

Driver, Felix, and Luciana Martins, eds. *Tropical Visions in an Age of Empire.* Chicago and London: University of Chicago Press, 2005.

Friedberg, Susanne. *French Beans and Food Scares.* Oxford, U.K.: Oxford University Press, 2004.

Gallais, Jean. *Pasteurs et paysans du Gourma: La condition sahélienne.* Paris: ORTSOM, 1975.

Gould, Peter R. "Tanzania 1920–1963: The Spatial Impress of the Modernization Process." *World Politics* 22, no. 2 (1970): 149–170.

Gourou, Pierre. *The Tropical World: Its Social and Economic Conditions and Its Future Status,* 4th edition. London: Longman, 1966.

Grove, A. T. *Land Use and Population in Katsina.* Nigeria: Kaduna, Northwest State Government, 1957.

Grove, Richard. *Green Imperialism: Colonial Expansion, Tropical Island Edens, and the Origins of Environmentalism, 1600–1860.* Cambridge, U.K.: Cambridge University Press, 1995.

Hance, William A. *The Geography of Modern Africa,* 2nd edition. New York: Columbia University Press, 1975.

Harley, Brian. "Deconstructing the Map." In *Writing Worlds,* ed. Trevor Barnes and James Duncan. London: Routledge, 1992.

Hart, Gillian. *Disabling Globalization.* Berkeley: University of California Press, 2004.

Hodder, Bruce. "Some Comments on the Origins of Traditional Markets in Africa South of the Sahara." *Transactions of the Institute of British Geographers* 36 (1965): 97–105.

Jeje, L. "Contributions on the Physical Geography of Tropical Africa." *Singapore Journal of Tropical Geography* 14, no. 2 (1993): 191–211.

Keeble, David. "Models of Economic Development." In *Models in Geography,* ed. Richard J. Chorley and Peter Hagged. London: Methuen, 1967.

Knight, C. Gregory. *Ecology and Change: Rural Modernization in an African Community.* New York: Academic Press, 1974.

May, Jacques M. *The Ecology of Malnutrition in Middle Africa.* New York: Hafner, 1965.

Moore, Donald. *Suffering for Territory.* Durham, NC: Duke University Press, 2005.

Monmonier, Mark. *Drawing the Line.* New York: Henry Holt, 1995.

Mortimore, Michael. *Adapting to Drought: Farmers, Famines, and Desertification in West Africa.* Cambridge, U.K.: Cambridge University Press, 1989.

Mountjoy, Alan B., and Clifford Embleton. *Africa: A New Geographical Study.* New York: Barnes and Noble, 1967.

Mudimbe, V. Y. *The Invention of Africa: Gnosis, Philosophy, and the Order of Knowledge.* Bloomington: Indiana University Press, 1988.

Neumann, Roderick. *Imposing Wilderness.* Berkeley: University of California Press, 1998.

Newman, James L., ed. *Drought, Famine, and Population Movements in Africa.* Syracuse, NY: Syracuse University Press, 1975.

O'Keefe, P., and B. Wismer. "African Drought." In *African Environment, Problems and Perspectives,* ed. Paul Richards. London: Methuen, 1975.

Ominde, S. H. *Land and Population Movements in Kenya.* Evanston, IL: Northwestern University Press, 1968.

Pickles, John. *A History of Spaces.* London: Routledge, 2004.

Porter, Philip W. *Food and Development in the Semi-Arid Zone of East Africa.* Syracuse, NY: Syracuse University Press, 1979.

Remy, G. *Paysages et milieux épidemiologiques dans l'espace ivoiro-burkinabe.* Paris: ORSTOM, 1988.

Ribot, Jesse. "Decentralization, Participation and Accountability in Sahelian Forestry." *Africa* 69, no. 1 (1999): 23–65.

Richards, Paul. *Coping with Hunger: Hazard and Experiment in an African Rice-farming System.* London: Methuen, 1986.

Riddell, Barry. "The Geography of Modernization in Africa: A Re-examination." *Canadian Geographer* 25, no. 3 (1981): 290–299.

Said, Edward W. *Orientalism.* New York: Random House, 1978.

Said, Edward W. "Orientalism Reconsidered." In *Europe and Its Others*, Vol. 1, ed. F. Barker et al. Colchester, U.K.: Essex University Press, 1985.

Said, Edward W. *Culture and Imperialism.* New York: Vintage, 1993.

Samatar, Abdi I. "Social Classes and Economic Restructuring in Pastoral Africa." *Africa Studies Review* 35, no. 1 (1992): 101–128.

Schroeder, Richard. *Shady Practices.* Berkeley: University of California Press, 1999.

Smith, Neil, and Anne Godlewska, eds. *Geography and Empire.* Oxford: Oxford University Press, 1994.

Soja, Edward. *The Geography of Modernization in Kenya: A Spatial Analysis of Social, Economic, and Political Change.* Syracuse, NY: Syracuse University Press, 1968.

Stebbing, E. P. "The Encroaching Sahara: The Threat to the West African Colonies." *Geographical Journal* 85, no. 6 (1935): 506–524.

Swindell, Ken, Jacob Baba, and Michael Mortimore, eds. *Inequality and Development.* London: Macmilllan, 1989.

Thomas, M. F., and G. W. Whittington, eds. *Environment and Land Use in Africa.* London: University of London Press, 1969.

Timberlake, Lloyd. *Africa in Crisis: The Causes, the Cures of Environmental Bankruptcy.* London: International Institute of the Environment, 1985.

Watts, Michael. *Silent Violence: Food, Famine, and Peasantry in Northern Nigeria.* Berkeley: University of California Press, 1983.

Watts, Michael. "The Agrarian Question." *Progress in Human Geography* 13, no. 1 (1989): 1–41.

Watts, Michael. "Visions of Excess: African Development in an Age of Market Idolatry." *Transitions* 51 (1991): 125–141.

Watts, Michael. "Development I: Power, Knowledge, Discursive Practice." *Progress in Human Geography* 17, no. 1 (1993): 257–272.

Watts, Michael. "Righteous Oil." *Annual Review of Environment and Resources* 30 (2005): 9.1–9.35.

Weiner, Daniel. "Agrarian Restructuring in Zimbabwe and South Africa." *Development and Change* 20, no. 3 (1989): 401–428.

Wood, Dennis. *The Power of Maps.* New York: Guilford: 1992.

Zalik, Anna. "The Niger Delta: Petro-Violence and Partnership Development." *Review of African Political Economy* 101, no. 4 (2004): 401–424.

MICHAEL J. WATTS

GEOMETRIES.

Africa is marked by strong geometrical traditions that find their expression in decorative art, craftwork, architecture, pictograms, string figures, and games (for an introduction, see Gerdes 1999). The creativity of the artisans who produce the decorative designs that appear on the raffia pile cloths of the Kuba (Congo), on Bénin bronzes, on the smoking pipes of the Begho (Ghana), on Yoruba *adire* cloths (Nigeria), and *sipatsi* handbags (Mozambique) also expresses itself in the fact that these artists and crafts-workers invented strip patterns belonging to each of the seven different mathematically possible symmetry groups. Figure 1 displays some strip patterns invented by the *sipatsi* weavers—formerly only women.

Symmetries, such as fourfold and fivefold rotational symmetry, are very common in African basketry, art, and architecture. House decoration and mural painting by women continue to be one of the cultural contexts for the development of geometrical ideas, both in southern Africa, for instance among the Ndebele and Sotho women (see Figure 2), and in western Africa, where it is mostly the women who decorate the walls of their houses with geometrical figures. Each year after the harvest, the women gather to restore and paint their mud dwellings, which have been washed clean by the rains of the wet season.

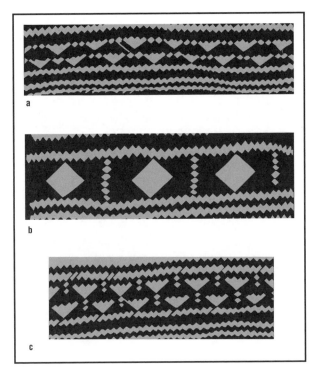

Figure 1. Strip patterns used on woven *sipatsi* hand bags. COURTESY OF PAULUS GERDES

FRACTALS

Fractals are characterized as a geometrical structure by the repetition of similar patterns at ever-diminishing scales. In 1999 Ron Eglash investigated the appearance of fractals in diverse African contexts, from architecture, textiles, hairstyling, and sculpture to cosmology.

DRAWINGS IN THE SAND

Profound mathematical knowledge was embedded in the geometry of the *sona* pictograms that were traditionally drawn in the sand by the Cokwe of northeastern Angola and related peoples—a form of artistic expression that has vanished almost completely. Each boy learned the meaning and execution of the easier *sona* during his period of intensive schooling in the *mukanda* initiation rites. The more complicated *sona* were handed down by drawing experts (*akwa kuta sona*) to their male descendents. These experts were storytellers who used the sand drawings to illustrate proverbs, fables, games, riddles, and animals. The drawings were executed in the following way: After clearing and smoothing the ground, the drawing experts first set out with their fingertips an orthogonal net of equidistant points. They then drew a line figure that embraced the points of the network (see Figure 3). The experts executed the drawings swiftly. Once drawn, the designs were generally extinguished. Symmetry and monolinearity were important aesthetic values: most

Figure 2. Two *literna* wall drawings from Lesotho. COURTESY OF PAULUS GERDES

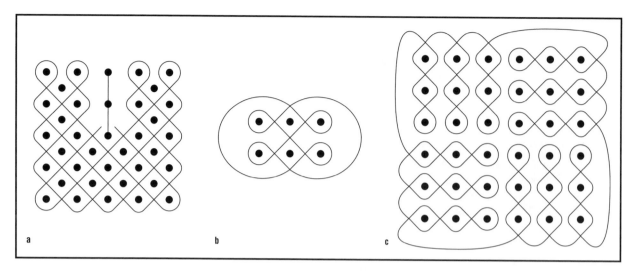

Figure 3. Three *sona* pictograms as traditionally drawn by the Cokwe (Angola). Courtesy of Paulus Gerdes

sona are symmetrical or monolinear or both. ("Monolinear" refers to drawings composed by only one smooth line.)

The drawing experts discovered classes of *sona* and the corresponding geometrical algorithms for their construction. For instance, Figure 4 displays two monolinear *sona* belonging to the same class in the sense that, although the dimensions of the underlying grids are different, both *sona* are drawn by applying the same geometric algorithm.

Sona experts also invented various rules for chaining monolinear *sona* to form bigger ones. Figure 5 illustrates one such chain rule.

Since the late 1990s, the analysis of *sona* by mathematicians has led to the conception of new types of symmetry, and of new areas of mathematics such as Lunda-geometry and new ideas in matrix theory.

Paulus Gerdes and Ahmed Djebbar's *Mathematics in African History and Cultures: An Annotated Bibliography* (2004) contains extensive bibliographic references to geometry in Africa throughout the ages.

See also **Architecture; Art; Arts; Number Systems.**

BIBLIOGRAPHY

Eglash, Ron. *African Fractals. Modern Computing and Indigenous Design.* New Brunswick NJ: Rutgers University Press, 1999.

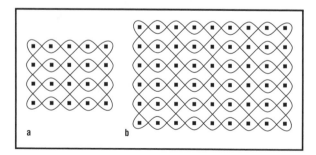

Figure 4. Two monolinear *sona* pictograms. Courtesy of Paulus Gerdes

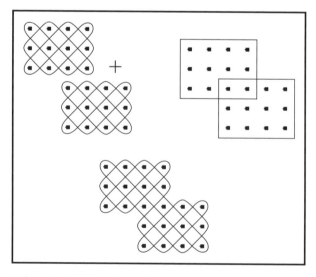

Figure 5. Chaining of monolinear *sona* patterns. Courtesy of Paulus Gerdes

Gerdes, Paulus. *Une tradition géométrique en Afrique—Les dessins sur le sable*. 3 vols. Paris: L'Harmattan, 1995.

Gerdes, Paulus. *Women, Art, and Geometry in Southern Africa*. Trenton, NJ: Africa World Press, 1998.

Gerdes, Paulus. *Geometry from Africa: Mathematical and Educational Explorations*. Washington, DC: The Mathematical Association of America, 1999.

Gerdes, Paulus, and Ahmed Djebbar. *Mathematics in African History and Culture: An Annotated Bibliography*. Cape Town: African Mathematical Union, 2004.

Gerdes, Paulus. *Sona Geometry from Angol: Mathematics of an African Tradition*. Monza: Polimetrica, 2006.

PAULUS GERDES

GERMAN COLONIES. *See* Colonial Policies and Practices: German.

GHANA

This entry includes the following articles:
GEOGRAPHY AND ECONOMY
SOCIETY AND CULTURES
HISTORY AND POLITICS

GEOGRAPHY AND ECONOMY

Formerly known as the Gold Coast, Ghana is located on the Gulf of Guinea along the west coast of Africa. With a total area of about 92,100 square miles and a population of 23 million (according to 2007 estimates), Ghana shares common boundaries with Côte d'Ivoire to the west, Togo to the east, Burkina Faso to the north, and the Atlantic Ocean to the south. From its southernmost point, the country extends some 340 miles north, and is divided into ten administrative regions.

Ghana generally has a tropical climate, but temperatures in the ten geographic regions vary according to season and elevation. It is hot and dry in the north; hot and humid in the southwest, and warm and fairly dry along the southeastern coast. Temperatures usually range between 69 and 95 degrees Fahrenheit with an annual average of about 79 degrees Fahrenheit. In the north, there is one rainy season from April to September and though annual rainfall ranges between 37 and 41 inches,

effective rainfall is far less because this amount may occur within a few months, with a rapid run-off. In the south, there are two distinct rainy seasons, from April to July and from September to November reaching a maximum of about 83 inches per annum, especially in the southeast.

Much of Ghana's natural vegetation has been destroyed over the years due to logging, poor agricultural practices, fuel wood use, and small-scale surface mining operations, especially in the south. However, the savanna grassland of northern Ghana still consists of scattered shrubs and tree such as shea, acacia, and baobabs. The evergreen and semideciduous forests of the south contain trees such as silk cotton, kola, and hardwoods including mahogany, odum, and ebony. Except for the Akuapem-Togo ranges to the eastern border, Ghana is generally a lowland country with rivers such as the Volta, Pra, Ankobra, and Tano and the artificial Lake Volta—the world's largest.

The structure of Ghana's economy in the twenty-first century can be understood in a broader historical context beginning with the British establishment of the Gold Coast Colony in 1874. Great Britain had joined other European nations (Portugal, Netherlands, France, and Denmark) on the Gold Coast in the fifteenth century and, for the next three hundred years, dominated the trade and commerce in slaves on the West African coast. After abolition of slave trade in 1807, Britain continued to extend its sphere of influence in 1901, establishing effective control over the entire country by annexing Asante and the Northern Territories (now northern Ghana) into the Gold Coast Colony.

To consolidate British rule and promote their economic interests, the colonial administration replaced the "traditional" export trade in natural products—such as palm fruits and kernels, kola, and wild rubber—with two major economic activities, gold mining and cocoa production, thereby laying the foundations of Ghana's modern economy. These two activities continued to dominate the country's export economy and dictate the pace of economic growth to this day. The colonial economy's heavy dependence on cocoa and mining made Ghana the leading producer and exporter of cocoa in the world until the 1970s. However, it also laid a pattern of uneven development in the country—stark regional inequalities between the north and south. While the south was opened up

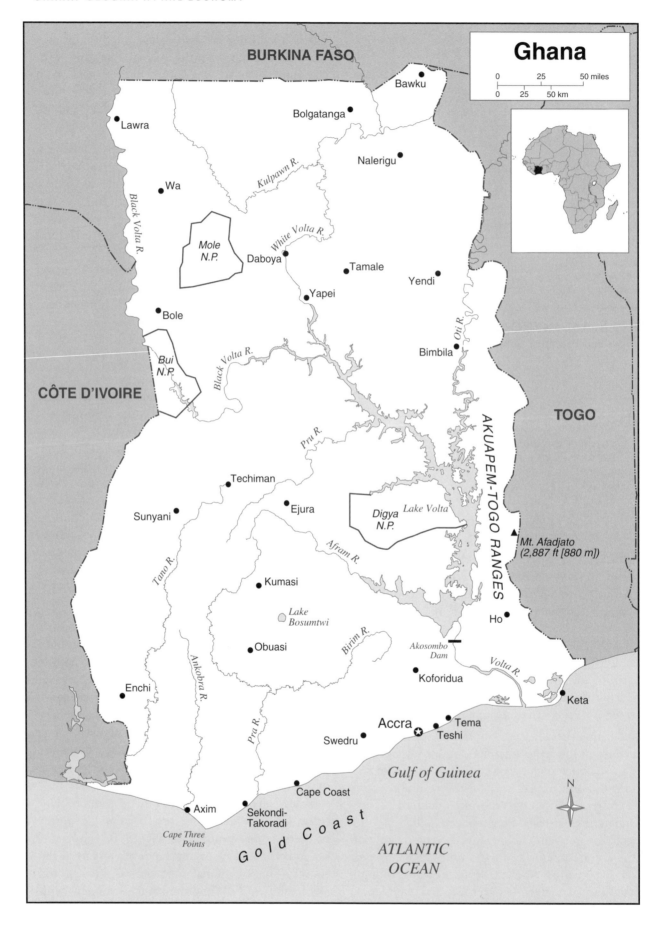

BURKINA FASO

Bawku

Bolgatanga

Lawra

Nalerigu

Wa

Kulpawn R.

Mole
N.P.

White Volta R.

Daboya

Tamale

Yendi

Yapei

Bole

Black Volta R.

Oti R.

Bimbila

CÔTE D'IVOIRE

*Bui
N.P.*

Black Volta R.

TOGO

Pru R.

AKUAPEM-TOGO RANGES

Techiman

Digya
N.P.

Lake Volta

Ejura

Sunyani

*Mt. Afadjato
(2,887 ft [880 m])*

Tano R.

Kumasi

*Lake
Bosumtwi*

Ho

Birim R.

*Akosombo
Dam*

Volta R.

Obuasi

Ankobra R.

Enchi

Koforidua

Keta

Pra R.

Accra

Tema

Teshi

Swedru

Gulf of Guinea

N

Cape Coast

Axim

Sekondi-
Takoradi

*Cape Three
Points*

G o l d   C o a s t

*ATLANTIC
OCEAN*

Ghana

0   25   50 miles
0   25   50 km

and developed because it possessed colonial resources (gold, timber and cocoa), the north was turned into a labor reserve and denied all forms of socioeconomic development.

At independence in 1957, Ghana had a very promising start as one of the richest British colonies in Africa. With accumulated foreign reserves of about £200 million ($392 million), rising cocoa prices, a foreign debt of only £20 million ($39.2 million) and well-formulated development plans, Ghanaians looked forward to an era of self-government that would bring about full employment and economic prosperity. Despite the trade surplus and favorable cocoa prices, the economy at independence was dominated by expatriate companies who exploited the country's natural resources for their own advantage. Although the Nkrumah administration (1957–1966) advocated measures such as economic planning, poverty alleviation, and prohibitions against economic exploitation to reverse the negative consequences of the colonial economic legacy, it achieved very little. Nkrumah's state-centered economic policies left behind a legacy of economic decline–a fragile external sector, heavy debts, and an export sector in which the seeds of destruction had already been sown. Thus the immediate post-Nkrumah period was not only politically unstable but it also witnessed negative economic growth, high rates of inflation, and a general decay of infrastructure.

In the 1980s, as part of measures to revamp the economy, the Jerry Rawlings administration sought assistance from the international donor community in 1983 to implement an Economic Recovery Program (ERP) and its accompanying Structural Adjustment Programs (SAPs). The International Monetary Fund–inspired ERP at least enabled the government to make a significant impact on the lives of Ghanaians by reversing the socioeconomic conditions and to put the country back on the path of moderate economic growth of about 5 percent per annum. However, by 1986 it became obvious that the country required a much more pragmatic development program than what the short-term policies of the ERP were designed to offer. As a result, a National Development Planning Commission (NDPC) was established in 1990 to coordinate the new planning effort and to advise the president on economic development planning.

Though it continues to move forward as a progressive, democratic state, and has made some advances in the economic sector over the past years, Ghana remains heavily dependent on international finance, capital, and assistances in many key sectors of the economy. For example, while the cocoa, timber, and gold mining industries continue to be the main sources of foreign exchange, the domestic economy revolves around subsistence agriculture accounting for 34 percent of gross domestic product (GDP) and employing 60 percent of the work force. Thus while GDP was reported to have grown by 5 percent in 2004, and the value of exports increased by 11 percent, an estimated 40 percent of Ghanaians lived under the poverty level, with a per capita income of less than $1 per day and unemployment remaining high. It comes as no surprise that Ghana opted for debt relief under the Heavily Indebted Poor Country (HIPC) program and was included in a G-8 debt relief program in July 2005—significantly reducing the country's external debt from $6.2 million in 2001 to $2.2 million in 2006. Ghana was also one of sixteen countries awarded funds ($547 million) by the U.S. government through its Millennium Challenge Account toward poverty alleviation in 2006.

See also **Climate; Colonial Policies and Practices; Debt and Credit; Ecosystems; International Monetary Fund; Nkrumah, Francis Kwia Kofi; Rawlings, Jerry.**

BIBLIOGRAPHY

Birmingham, Walter; Isard Neustadt; and E. N. Omaboe. *A Study of Contemporary Ghana*, Vol. 1: *The Economy of Ghana*. Evanston, IL: Northwestern University Press, 1966.

Boahen, Adu A. *Ghana: Evolution and Change in the Nineteenth and Twentieth Centuries*. London: Longman, 1975.

Frimpong-Ansah, Jonathan. *The Vampire State in Africa: The Political Economy of Decline in Ghana*. Trenton, NJ: African World Press, 1992.

GARIBA B. ABDUL-KORAH

SOCIETY AND CULTURES

Ghana can be viewed as divided into two major traditional culture areas that are still meaningful in the early twenty-first century: one belonging to the peoples of the northern savannas, the other to the peoples of the southern forests and the coastal savanna. Northern peoples generally speak languages of the Gur family; southern peoples generally speak Kwa languages, although there are a number of exceptions to both these rules. Similar generalizations can be made about almost every aspect of Ghanaian culture. But the north-south divide is not absolute: There are certain distinctive cultural differences between east and west as well. For example, matrilineal inheritance and political succession is typical of peoples who inhabit western Ghana, particularly the Dagara and to some extent the Dagaba, the Birifor, and also the Akan peoples. Patrilineal inheritance and succession is much more common among eastern peoples, such as the Kusasi, the Dagomba, and the Dangme (Adangbe).

Geographically fragmented ethnic groups inhabit the central part of the country and combine elements of the northern and southern cultures. The northern part of the Volta Region on the Togo border is also populated by many small ethnic groups. Several of the towns and villages of the northwestern Brong-Ahafo Region are composed of two or more distinct ethno-linguistic communities; these may comprise Gur-speaking Kulango; Senufo-speaking Nafana; other, ethnically distinct, Gur-speaking peoples of northern Ghana; the Grusi-speaking Degha (or Mo); the Dumpo, who speak a language related to the languages of southern Ghana; and the various Mande-speaking groups. (The latter are called by different names depending upon their relation to Islam: The traditional Muslims are the Ligby or Djogoh; communities of relatively recent converts to Islam are called Huela; non-Muslim blacksmiths among the Mande-speakers are known by the names Atumfuor and Numu). Small groups on the southeastern border include the Ntrubo and the Chala, who live near the Adele and the Achode peoples and speak Delo (Bogon), a Grusi language closely related to Degha and Vagla. All the exceptions notwithstanding, the chief cultural differences in Ghana exist between the northern and the southern peoples.

NORTHERN GHANA

The peoples of the north residing in the Upper West Region include the Dagaba, the Dagara, the Wala, the Chakali, and the Sissala. Living in the Upper East are the Kasena, the Bulsa, the Nankani, the Farefari, the Talensi, the Nabdam, the Kusasi, and also the Busansi. The Dagaba and the Farefari are probably the largest of these ethnic groups.

The largest group in the Northern Region is the Dagomba; they live in the eastern part of the region. Neighboring the Dagomba are the Mamprusi to the north, the Gonja to the southwest and Nanumba to the south, and the Konkomba to the east. Other peoples of the Northern Region are the Tampulma, or Tampolense; the Bimoba, the Anufo (also known by the Hausa name Chokosi), and the Bassari (Tem speakers), who live along the border with Togo; the Nawuri, in the southern part of the region; the Hanga and the Kamara (the latter are Hanga-speaking Muslims); and in the western part of the region, the Safaliba, the Birifor, the Vagla, and the Deg. Almost all the peoples of the Upper East, Upper West, and Northern Regions speak Central Gur languages that belong to either the Grusi or the Oti-Volta family. The exceptions are the Busansi, who speak a Mande language; the Gonja and the Nawuri, who speak Guang languages; and the Anufo, who speak a Comoe language closely related to the languages of the southern Ghana-Côte d'Ivoire border area.

Marriage in northern Ghana is normally virilocal, that is, the couple lives with the husband's family. It involves public celebration, often including the ritual kidnapping of the bride. Marriage is potentially polygynous, unless the husband is a practicing Christian. Elaborate puberty ceremonies are not common, but several peoples of the far north, among them the Dagaba, the Dagara, the Sissala, the Bulsa, and the Farefari, practiced clitoridectomy before it was made illegal by the Ghana government. (The age at which the procedure was performed varied, from earliest infancy among some of the Sissala to puberty among the Dagaba and the Farefari.) The major *rite de passage* in northern Ghana, as in the rest of the country, is the funeral, which is a major social event and may last for several days. Traditional religious practices in the north focus on domestic ancestor shrines. Islam is also well entrenched in the larger towns, for example Wa and Tamale.

Many of the northern peoples, including the Dagaba, the Sissala, the Kasena, the Bulsa, and the Kusasi, identify with named exogamous patriclans, but the social function of these clans varies. Thus, the Birifor, who live south of the Dagaba (and are closely related to them) and the western Dagaba typically identify more strongly with matriclans. Throughout northern Ghana, however, the right to inherit immovable property and to assume political office usually descends through the paternal line.

Politically, there is a distinction to be made between the many northern ethnic groups that did not form centralized states or have chiefs, at least before colonial times, and those that established centralized kingdoms. Only the latter developed towns. The former live in dispersed settlements organized in large domestic units. For these groups the main authority is the head of the household. There is also a senior person, known by the title "earth priest" or "earth king," who is responsible to and for the local land. (His duties include performing ritual sacrifices to ensure the fertility of the land and also supervising building and burials.) The noncentralized groups also rely for help in understanding and solving their problems on the type of specialists generally known in English as soothsayers. There is little social stratification within such groups. Those who adopted chieftaincy systems, typically in response to colonial rule, maintain them along with the institution of the earth priest.

There are three traditional kingdoms in the eastern part of the Northern Region: Dagomba, which has its capital at Yendi; Mamprusi, which has its capital at Nalerigu; and Nanumba, which has its capital at Bimbila. The three share a common tradition of origin and many characteristic features with the Mossi (Moshi) kingdom in Burkina Faso. The Dagomba, Mamprusi, Nanumba, and Mossi peoples are very closely related, and so are their languages. The system of chieftaincy in the three kingdoms in northern Ghana is based on the ideal of *naam*, or ritual power as it is expressed in political office. Hierarchically graded chieftaincies are open to sons of chiefs of the same patriline; the highest level chieftancies lead to a limited number of "gates" or senior chieftancies, from which an incumbent can aspire to be king. It is only the sons of chiefs who may compete to ascend through ranks of the chieftancies and become king. (In the Upper West the smaller state of Wa has the same sort of chieftancy system.) The system was introduced into northern Ghana in medieval times by a

group from the northeast, which defeated and subordinated the authority of the earth priests.

The kingdom of the Gonja, located in the south-central part of the Northern Region, is different, having been founded by an invading group, probably Mande, from the northwest, which has become wholly assimilated. The Gonja kingdom itself subjugated a number of Gur-speaking peoples to the north and west, including the Vagla and the Hanga, who still predominate in those parts of the kingdom; the Gonja people themselves are mainly concentrated in the eastern part of the Gonja kingdom. Another non-Gur-speaking state in northern Ghana is the small kingdom of Chokosi, which extends beyond the Ghana-Togo border; its capital is actually at Sansanne Mango in Togo. All of the kingdoms in northern Ghana have been strongly influenced by Islam to establish a relatively high degree of social stratification, including occupational castes. None of the kings themselves, however, consistently adhere to Muslim ritual practices.

Metalworking is fairly common in northern Ghana. The Dagaba in particular produce ironwork; brasswork is the specialty of the Farefari. Dyeing and weaving are practiced, especially in the larger towns. Cotton is woven in narrow strips and sewn together to make striped cloths, mainly white, blue and a little black, which women wear as wrappers or as straight dresses and men wear as large smocks. In the towns of northern Ghana some men also wear long cotton gowns that are based on the styles typical of northern Africa, especially the Sahel.

SOUTHERN GHANA

Southern Ghanaians also do weaving that technically is of the same type as that produced by northern Ghanaians, but the patterns and the colors are different, with much red, blue, and yellow. So too is the traditional man's dress in southern Ghana: It consists of a large rectangle of cloth worn over one shoulder, toga-style, with a pair of loose shorts; sometimes a loose shirt is also worn beneath the cloth. The traditional woman's dress in southern Ghana is usually made of printed cotton cloth and typically takes the form of long skirt with overblouse. The peoples of southern Ghana also practice metalworking; Akan brass-casting is particularly well-known.

Major features of the Akan culture are shared by all the Akan-speaking groups of southern Ghana. These include the Asante, the Kwahu, the Akyem, the Brong, the Fante, the Agona, and the Akuapem, mainly in the Ashanti, Central, and Eastern Regions. The Akan culture area also includes the peoples of the Western Region, the Nzema, the Ahanta, the Sehwi, and the Anyi, whose language is very similar to that of the Baule of Côte d'Ivoire and closely related to Akan.

The peoples of the Akan culture area have in common similar matrilineal and patrilineal clan systems, in which members of the same clan are not allowed to marry each other. Whereas the patrilineage dominates in northern Ghana, in the Akan culture area the matrilineage is more typical: Most kinds of property as well as political office are inherited through the maternal line. Marriage is not an occasion of public celebration, and wives often continue to reside with their mothers after marriage. One important celebration is the girls' puberty rite, *bragoro*, also called *braka* or *brato*. Among the Akan-speaking Fante, for example, a girl's reaching menarche is regarded as an occasion of communal rejoicing. *Bragoro* lasts an entire week, during which the girl is bathed, oiled, perfumed, and confined. She and her family and friends eat special foods; the whole ritual often ends with a feast.

Settlements throughout southern Ghana most often take the form of nucleated villages, which are organized into small states, or kingdoms. Unlike the states in northern Ghana, the Akan state system seems to have been an indigenous development, and not the result of invasion or British colonial imposition. In an Akan state there is an elaborate and characteristic system of court officials and regalia, which reached its apogee in the Asante kingdom, whose empire at the end of the nineteenth century included or at least dominated almost the whole of contemporary Ghana. Important features of the Asante court adopted by other southern peoples are the institution of the *okyeame*, or linguist, the king's spokesman, and the shrines made of the stools, i.e. the carved wooden seats, of deceased kings and chiefs.

Although strong Akan influence is detectable in virtually all the cultures of southern Ghana, many of them, including the numerous small Guang groups of the southeast and the Volta Region (whose languages are most closely related to Akan) are patrilineal. The various Guang-speaking peoples are organized into small states based on the Akan model, except that succession to office is often designed to pass through the paternal line. These peoples include the Awutu and the Efutu, who inhabit the eastern part of the Central Region; the Larteh and the Kyerepong, who live in the Eastern Region; the Anum, the Nkonya, the Krachi, the Nchumuru, and the Achode of the Volta Region; the Dwan and the Yeji of eastern Brong-Ahafo; and the Gonja and the Nawuri of the Northern Region.

Other exceptions to the Akan cultural patterns of southern Ghana are manifested by the Ga, who inhabit the western part of the Greater Accra Region, and the Dangme, of eastern Greater Accra. The Ga and the Dangme speak Kwa languages that are closely related to each other but not to the other languages typically spoken in the south. Among the Ga and the Dangme, both land and political offices generally pass through the patriline. While the Ga are organized into seven tiny, loosely associated states, the Dangme are organized into seven small independent states. The traditional public worship of the Ga is based on an annual cycle of cult performances for deities, most of whom are associated with important natural resources. Each Dangme state has its own religious ritual cycle, but all perform the same girls' puberty rite, called *dipo*. The Dangme states are also distinctive for sharing a highly valued body of pentatonic music, lore, and poetry, called *klama*.

Also different from the Akan are the various Ewe-speaking peoples, who dominate the southern part of the Volta Region, and constitute the second largest ethnic group of the country; Ewe speakers include both the Anlo people, who inhabit the coast, and the Northern Ewe groups, who live to the north of them, as well as a large proportion of the population of southern Togo. Religious life on the coast especially has been dominated by a number of large cults. In the hilly parts of the Ewe country and north of it there are also a number of very small ethnic groups whose languages, although they are related to the other languages of southern Ghana, are nevertheless very different from them and from each other. They include

Republic of Ghana

Population:	22,931,299 (2007 est.)
Area:	238,538 sq. km (92,100 sq. mi.)
Official language:	English
Languages:	English, Akan (which includes Asante Twi, Akwapim Twi, Akyem, and Fanti), Mole-Dagbani, Ewe, Ga-Adangbe, Guan
National currency:	cedi
Principal religions:	Christian 63%, Muslim 16 %, traditional and indigenous beliefs 21%
Capital:	Accra (est. pop. 3,000,000 in 2006)
Other urban centers:	Kumasi, Tamale, Takoradi, Cape Coast, Tema, Sekondi
Annual rainfall:	750–1,000 mm (29–39 in.) in southeast coastal savanna to 1,500–2,100 mm (59–83 in.) in extreme southwest
Principal geographical features:	*Mountains:* Akuapem-Togo Mountains, Oti Mountains *Rivers:* White Volta, Black Volta, Tano, Oti, Pra, Ankobra, Daka. *Lakes:* Lake Volta
Economy:	*GDP per capita:* US$2,600 (2006)
Principal products and exports:	*Agricultural:* cocoa, rice, coffee, cassava (tapioca), peanuts, corn, shea nuts, bananas, timber *Manufacturing:* lumbering, light manufacturing, aluminum smelting, food processing, cement, small commercial ship building *Mining:* gold, manganese, bauxite, diamonds
Government:	Independence from Great Britain, 1957. Independence constitution, 1957–1960. New constitution approved in 1969 and another in 1979; suspended in 1981. Present constitution, based on the U.S. constitution, approved in 1992, enacted in 1993. Multiparty parliamentary republic. President elected to a maximum of two 4-year terms by universal suffrage. 200 member parliament elected to 4-year terms by universal suffrage. President advised by 10-member Council of State, elected regionally. Cabinet partially appointed by the president.
Heads of state since independence:	1957–1960: Prime Minister Kwame Nkrumah 1960–1966: President Kwame Nkrumah 1966–1969: Lieutenant-General Joseph A. Ankrah, chairman of the National Liberation Council 1969: General Akwasi O. Afrifa, chairman of the National Liberation Council 1969–1972: Prime Minister Kofi A. Busia 1970–1972: President Edward Akufo-Addo 1972–1978: Colonel (later General) Ignatius K. Acheampong, chairman of the Supreme Military Council (called National Redemption Council until 1975) 1978–1979: General Frederick Akuffo, chairman of the Supreme Military Council 1979: Flight Lieutenant Jerry John Rawlings, chairman of the Armed Forces Revolutionary Council 1979–1981: President Hilla Limann 1981–1992: Flight Lieutenant Jerry John Rawlings, chairman of the Provisional National Defense Council 1993–2001: President Jerry John Rawlings 2001–: President John Agyekum Kuffour
Armed forces:	*Army:* 5,000 *Navy:* 850 *Air Force:* 1,000 *Paramilitary:* 5,000
Transportation:	*Rail:* 950 km (590 mi.), linking Accra-Tema with Takoradi and Kumasi *Ports:* Takoradi, Tema *Roads:* 42,623 km (26,485 mi.), 8% paved *National airline:* Ghana Airways (state-owned) *Airports:* Kotoka International Airport at Accra, domestic airports at Takoradi, Kumasi, Tamale, Sunyani
Media:	Daily newspapers include *Daily Graphic, Ghanaian Times, The Pioneer.* Weeklies include *The Independent, Ghanian Chronicle, Statesman,* and *Mirror.* Publishing houses include the Ghana Publishing Corporation, Ghana University Press, Bureau of Ghana Languages. Ghana Broadcasting Corporation (a state monopoly) broadcasts radio and television. In 1995, government control over broadcasting lifted. There are 49 radio stations and 10 television stations.
Literacy and education:	*Total literacy rate:* 72.6% (2006). 9 years compulsory education. Postsecondary education provided by University of Ghana, University of Science and Technology, University of Cape Coast, and various technical schools.

the Avatime, the Nyangbo, the Tafi, the Logba, the Santrokofi, the Akpafu, the Lolobi, the Likpe, the Balemi, the Bafana, the Animere (which is probably the smallest ethnic group in the country), and the Adele farther north, who live near the Achode.

See also **Body Adornment and Clothing; Ecosystems; Ethnicity; Kingship; Languages; Marriage Systems; Metals and Minerals; Political Systems: Chieftainships.**

BIBLIOGRAPHY

Assimeng, Max. *Social Structure of Ghana: A Study in Persistence and Change.* Accra-Tema, Ghana: Ghana Publishing Corp., 1981.

Drucker-Brown, Susan. *Ritual Aspects of the Mamprusi Kingship.* Cambridge, U.K.: African Studies Center, 1975.

Fortes, M. *Kinship and the Social Order.* London: Routledge and Kegan Paul, 1970.

Goody, Jack. *Death, Property, and the Ancestors: A Study of the Mortuary Customs of the Lodaaga* of West Africa. Stanford, CA: Stanford University Press, 1962.

Huber, Hugo. *The Krobo.* St. Augustin near Bonn, Germany: Anthropos Institute, 1963.

Nukunya, G. K. *Kinship and Marriage among the Anlo-Ewe.* New York: Humanities Press, 1969.

Rattray, R. S. *Ashanti.* Oxford: Clarendon Press, 1923.

Wilks, Ivor. *Wa and the Wala: Islam and Polity in Northwestern Ghana.* Cambridge, U.K.: Cambridge University Press, 1989.

M. E. KROPP DAKUBU

HISTORY AND POLITICS

The post–World War II period serves as the immediate context for postindependent Ghanaian politics. Developments during the period, which witnessed the final phase of the independence struggle, were important in shaping the nature of politics in independent Ghana. It was also remarkable for the formation of the first political parties, the holding of elections, and the design of a constitution to regulate the country after independence. The postindependence political history of Ghana has been marked by alternations between democratic governance and military rule. Until the early 1990s civilians and soldiers jostled for space in the national corridors of power thus undermining attempts at building a democratic nation.

POLITICAL PARTY FORMATION

Political organizing in the Gold Coast predates the post-1945 period; the United Gold Coast Convention (UGCC), formed in 1947, was however the first political party. The party was a grouping of top merchants and professionals and included such individuals as Paa George Grant, J. B. Danquah, William Ofori-Atta, Ako Adjei, and Edward Akufo-Addo. These politicians were to play important roles in independent Ghana either as members of government or the opposition. To this list was added the name of Kwame Nkrumah, who was invited from the United Kingdom (UK) to work for the UGCC as its full-time general secretary in 1947.

Nkrumah's work for the UGCC transformed Gold Coast nationalism from being elitist and conservative to mass-based and radical, as he helped to set up branches of the party throughout the colony and organized rallies that galvanized ordinary people. Nkrumah's mass appeal and radical methods were to get him into trouble with the more conservative members of the UGCC. Ultimately, the disagreements compelled him to leave the UGCC to form his own party, the Convention People's Party (CPP), in 1949.

The formation of the CPP marked a split in the nationalist front that continued until independence. The CPP came to embody radical nationalism that rallied its supporters under the slogan Independence Now, while the UGCC represented a conservative platform with the slogan Independence in the Shortest Possible Time.

The popularity of these two main political groups was tested in elections in 1951, 1954, and 1956, all of which were won by the CPP. Following the CPP's success at the 1951 elections, Nkrumah was appointed the leader of government business (later prime minister), signifying the gradual transfer of power to indigenous leadership. The victories of the CPP also established Nkrumah as the leader whose vision and values had been accepted by the mass of the people. Little wonder then that he and his party formed the first postindependent government under the independence constitution that provided for a multiparty democracy, a national assembly, an independent judiciary, and a prime minister, with the British monarch as the titular head of state.

NKRUMAH'S REGIME

The CPP government under Nkrumah embarked on ambitious programs and schemes that aimed at modernizing all sectors of national life. The centerpiece of his program for economic modernization was the construction of a hydro-electric project on the Volta River which was to provide power for industrialization of the country. Nkrumah also expanded educational facilities and managed to increase enrollment in schools.

Nkrumah implemented a vigorous foreign policy that primarily focused on undermining European colonialism in Africa, the forging of strong intra-African relations, nonalignment, and the pursuit of world peace. In line with his pan-Africanist views, Nkrumah declared that Ghana had a responsibility to help other dependent African peoples to secure their independence from colonialism. Ghana therefore provided both material and moral support to many independence movements across the continent. Nkrumah also played a key role in the formation of the Organization of African Unity (OAU) and sent Ghanaian soldiers on United Nations assignments.

Nkrumah's regime, however, became increasingly authoritarian. He became less and less tolerant of the political opposition and passed laws to stifle dissent. The notorious Preventive Detention Act of 1958, which allowed the government to detain anybody without trial for up to five years, was used against opposition elements. The independence constitution was revised in 1960 to make Ghana a republic. Nkrumah was named president and had his powers increased, enabling him to take further action to silence the opposition. A one-party state was instituted which made the CPP the only legal political party and effectively ended organized political opposition.

These authoritarian measures coupled with deteriorating economic conditions led to some disaffection against the regime. The declining economy was blamed on Nkrumah's ambitious socialist programs and schemes. On February 24, 1966, the military staged a successful coup against the CPP government when Nkrumah was on a visit to the Far East. It is now known that the Ghanaian military had the support of the Central Intelligence Agency (CIA). Clearly, Nkrumah's proactive foreign policy was not well received by some Western powers.

THE POST-NKRUMAH ERA

The intervention of the military in national politics became a regular happening until the early 1990s. The National Liberation Council (NLC), the military junta that overthrew the Nkrumah government, supervised the writing of a new republican constitution and national elections, which ushered in the government of the Progress Party (PP) in 1969 under the leadership of Prime Minister Kofi Abrefa Busia.

Busia's liberal economic policies failed to halt the declining economy. He responded to a precipitous fall in the world price of cocoa, Ghana's lead export, by devaluing the national currency by 44 percent, but this worsened economic conditions. This situation, and the potential and actual cuts in military spending, which resulted in the withdrawal of certain privileges from the military elite, precipitated the second intervention of the military in national politics in 1972.

The coup leader, General Ignatius Acheampong, was also deposed in an in-house coup by his deputy, General Frederick Akuffo, who cited misrule and corruption as his reasons. Another coup by the Armed Forces Revolutionary Council (AFRC) led Flt. Lieutenant Jerry John Rawlings ended the Acheampong/Akuffo Regime in June 1979.

The short-lived AFRC promised to halt the corruption and rot in the national economy and arrest the breakdown in discipline within the military. It also promised to restore the country to democracy, and did so by supervising national elections that ushered in Ghana's third republican government in September 1979.

Ghana's economy was in tatters by now and continuing political instability did not help the situation. The new republican government under the leadership of Dr. Hilla Limann thus faced the enormous task of halting the decline in the economy and achieving some measure of prosperity for the people. This would have required a lot of time, but the military intervened again in 1981, half way into the government's term in office. The new military regime, the Provisional National Defence Council (PNDC), was led by Rawlings.

Rawlings and his PNDC stayed in power until the early 1990s. Though the PNDC broadcast much revolutionary rhetoric, the regime soon became an ardent implementer of International

Monetary Fund (IMF) and World Bank–sponsored Structural Adjustment Programs. While these programs ensured some stability in the national economy, they failed to restructure the economy, while there was an actual decline or worsening in some sectors of the economy such as in the provisioning of health, education, and other social services.

The PNDC, like the other military juntas before it, suspended the constitution and all other democratic institutions guaranteed under it. The regime's human rights record was appalling as extrajudicial killings, abductions, and general intimidation of the civilian populace by the military were commonplace.

RETURN TO DEMOCRACY

In 1993 Ghana returned to constitutional democratic rule as a result of internal and external pressures. The new republican constitution made provision for a multiparty democratic system with an executive presidency, a parliament, and an independent judiciary. The constitution also guaranteed the existence of a free press and protected fundamental human rights. These institutions and the freedoms guaranteed under the constitution have been strengthened over the years, although the economic situation continues to be of concern in the early twenty-first century.

The PNDC regime that metamorphosed into a political party, the National Democratic Congress (NDC), competed with other political parties, including the New Patriotic Party (NPP), the successor to Busia's Progress Party, in the first elections held under the fourth republican constitution in 1992. The NDC under Rawlings won the 1992 elections and also won the next elections held in 1996.

The NDC continued with the neoliberal economic policies implemented by the PNDC under the aegis of the World Bank and the IMF. While some wealth may have been generated at the national center, the policies hardly made a dent in the endemic poverty across the country.

The last two years of the 1990s proved particularly disastrous economically. The economic hardships and the perception that the NDC government was insensitive to the plight of ordinary people or doing very little to ameliorate the hardships prepared the grounds for the leading

opposition party, the NPP, to win the elections held in 2000 with John Agyekum Kufuor as the presidential candidate. President Kufuor was reelected in the 2004 elections.

See also **Busia, Kofi A.; International Monetary Fund; Nationalism; Nkrumah, Francis Nwia Kofi; Organization of African Unity; Rawlings, Jerry; Togo; Warfare: Internal Revolts; World Bank.**

BIBLIOGRAPHY

Boahen, Adu A. *Ghana: Evolution and Change in the Nineteenth and Twentieth Centuries.* London: Longman, 1975.

TAKYIWAA MANUH

GHAZI, AHMAD IBN IBRAHIM AL-. *See* Ahmad ibn Ibrahim al-Ghazi (Ahmad Grañ).

GIDADA, NEGASSO (1943–). The former president of Ethiopia, Negasso Gidada, was born in Dembidollo in Ethiopia's Western Highlands. Gidada attended Addis Ababa University from 1966 to 1971 and then became an elementary school teacher. Gidada went into exile in Germany in 1974 when Emperor Haile Selassie was overthrown. In Germany, he again worked as a teacher while earning his master's and Ph.D. degrees in history.

Still in Germany during the 1980s, Gidada was active in exile groups supporting the struggle for the rights of the Oromo people, his ethnic group, against Ethiopian Marxist dictator Mengistu Haile-Mariam. Gidada returned to Ethiopia in 1991, following the overthrow of Mengistu by the Ethiopian People's Revolutionary Democratic Front (EPRDF), a coalition of ethnic organizations. Gidada served as minister of labor and social affairs and, subsequently, minister of information in a transitional government as Ethiopia attempted to move toward democracy.

In 1995 Gidada was elected president as the EPRDF candidate. Opposition parties, however, boycotted the election. The presidency was an essentially ceremonial office, with real power belonging to Prime Minister Menes Zenawi. Suspected of supporting dissidents within the EPRDF opposed to Zenawi, Gidada was expelled from the Oromo People's Democratic Organization, a constituent member of the EPRDF, during his last year in office.

In 2001 Gidada became the first Ethiopian president to leave office peacefully. Subsequently, he was active in the fight against HIV/AIDS in Ethiopia and sat as an independent member of Ethiopian parliament.

See also **Disease: HIV/AIDS, Social and Political Aspects; Ethiopia, Modern; Haile Selassie I.**

BIBLIOGRAPHY

Parker, Ben. *Ethiopia: Breaking New Ground*, rev. edition. Oxford: Oxfam, 2003.

Pausewang, Siegfried; Kjetil Tronvoll; and Lovise Aalen; eds. *Ethiopia since the Derg: A Decade of Democratic Pretension and Performance.* New York: Zed Books, 2002.

Tesfaye, Aaron. *Political Power and Ethnic Federalism: The Struggle for Democracy in Ethiopia.* Lanham, MD: University Press of America, 2002.

MICHAEL LEVINE

GLOBALIZATION.

Not too long ago, most scholars saw the African continent as divided into separate peoples or societies, each with its distinctive culture and social structure, and each rooted in its own particular territory. These societies were imagined to be essentially closed, internally homogenous, and radically different from Europe and North America. This perspective emerged at the time of European nationalism and was influenced by the German Romantic notion of the *Volk*. It was also fostered by the imposition of tribes as administrative units by colonial governments, and by the production of ethnographic monographs, based upon long-term participant observation within clearly bounded field sites.

Since the 1960s, however, archaeologists, historians, anthropologists, and other scholars of Africa have become increasingly critical of this isolating perspective. Rather than eliciting the distinguishing characteristics particular to various societies, they have documented the enormous impact of intra- and intercontinental connections among them. The former included processes such as warfare, trade, and state formation. The latter connections were forged by the Indian Ocean trade; trans-Saharan contacts with the Mediterranean; European maritime interests; the Atlantic slave trade; the spreads of Christianity and Islam; transfers of technology; the establishment of complex colonial orders; the emergence of African nationalism as a key political idea; desalinization; and the imposition of structural adjustment programs.

ILLUSIONS OF ISOLATION IN THE KALAHARI
Writings on the Bushmen (or San) clearly demonstrate these more contextualized perspectives. Earlier ethnographic texts constructed the Bushmen as egalitarian hunter-gatherers living in uncontaminated purity and primitive affluence in the Kalahari Desert. This vision has come to be seen as a mythical image, invoked by ethnographers to critique of the perils of modernity. More recent writings show Bushmen as central actors in the broader history of southern Africa. For millennia, Bushmen foragers have interacted and traded with pastoralists in the region. In times of Bantu expansion and European invasion, they formed political and economic alliances with the intruders to take advantage of the new circumstances. Bushmen traded ivory, hid in the mercantile world, and worked as shoot-boys for Great White Hunters.

But Bushmen also offered fierce resistance, and they were responsible for the destruction of the Republic of Upingtonia settler polity in 1886. They formed bandit gangs to oppose the imposition of a colonial state, and were literally hunted down by German police and military units. Under the South African occupation of Namibia after World War I, Bushmen were confined to native reserves and missionary stations, worked as farm laborers, and were recruited as trackers and soldiers by the South African Defence Force. The stereotypical image of the Bushmen is now of an underclass resident in squatter camps.

FEATURES OF GLOBALIZATION
Since the 1980s, however, economists and political scientists have gone beyond this vision of African societies as shaped by more encompassing processes. They assert that a major rupture occurred in human history at the dawn of this century: the world entered a new era of globalization and has become a single network of connection and

interdependence. They see this rupture as due to three different, but interconnected, processes. First, the collapse of the former Soviet Union and the fall of the Berlin Wall brought about an end to the Cold War and the final triumph of capitalism. A global commodity market emerged, in which the velocities of flows of finance and goods increased enormously, and in which investments can go anywhere. Second, there was a revolution in electronic media, marked by the advent and spread of e-mail, the Internet, and cellular telephones. This facilitated the formation of solidarities beyond the nation-state. Third, wars, poverty, and the search for new opportunities brought about mass migrations on unprecedented scales. These migrations, when juxtaposed with the rapid flow of images through the media, created diasporic public spheres, connecting people dispersed throughout the world.

One novel feature of the globalized world is time/space compression. The times between investments and profits have shortened, and the distance between viewers and events has decreased. Another feature is the erosion of territorial and national boundaries. Nation states can no longer contain the movements of arms, money, ideologies, and diseases. In this context, new transnational organizations and movements such as Islam play an increasingly important role.

Anthropologists investigate the implications of globalization for the study of culture. Some agree that, in the contemporary world, cultures have become deterritorialized. Communities are detached from local reference and frequently have little sense of place. Likewise, it can no longer be assumed that people living in close proximity share a common culture. Globalization also does not imply cultural homogeneity. At the same time as people in the postcolonial peripheries of the world economy fear Americanization, those in the core areas fear the influx of war criminals and refugees from other countries. Cultural forms have spread not only from the United States but also from Japan, India, and Indonesia.

There are overlapping flows of cultural forms and identities that connect any point to any other point in the system. Like landscapes, these flows have irregular shapes and are without clear structures, regularities, or boundaries. The concept of an ethnoscape may be used to denote the movement of people; technoscape, the global configurations of technology; finanscape, of finance; ideoscape, of political cultures; and mediascape, of images. There are disjunctures between these uncoordinated movements, however.

Hence, in the globalized world, culture is fragmentary and hybrid. Bits of imagery, dress, music, and fantasy are detached from their areas of origin and are often attractive precisely because of the distant associations they evoke. Hollywood images influence people in the African forests, and tropical exorcisms are conducted in Paris.

APPLICATIONS TO AFRICA

Specialists on Africa accept the reality of globalization but fiercely contest its assumed advantages. Whereas bankers celebrate the removal of national trade barriers, social democrats lament the erosion of citizenship rights that have always curbed the brutalities of capitalism. For example, businesses can disaggregate their operations among different countries to take advantage of differing conditions in global markets, and disrupt traditional working class solidarities. There has also been consistent debate on how Africa should meet the challenge of globalization.

In Africanist anthropology, globalization theory has assumed the status of a new paradigm, spawning a host of interesting ethnographic studies on the complexities of global connections. To illuminate transnational flows, ethnographers have found it necessary to conduct multisited fieldwork rather than continue to work in single locales.

Hansen's monograph, *Salaula* (2000), traces the flow of secondhand clothing from the United States and western Europe to Zambia. She argues that such clothes have transnational biographies, and she shows how their movements through various settings reveal different sorts of social relations, political struggles, and cultural issues. A complex chain links the harvesting, retail, and consumption of second hand clothing. Wealthier residents of north Atlantic cities donate unwanted garments to charities and humanitarian aid organizations. European and American sorting plants then collect, recycle, and grade the essentially free raw material. From there, the garments are exported to companies in India, Pakistan,

Singapore, Malaysia, Tunisia, Tanzania, and Uganda. Environmental concerns about the salvaging of textiles and the use of proceeds to support charitable concerns enhance the respectability of the industry. Yet, due to the low wages of immigrant workers in the salvaging industry, and enormous profit margins for owners, perceptions of illegality also pervade the industry.

The secondhand clothing market in sub-Saharan Africa is volatile, being characterized by regional variations in dress styles, constant disruptions by civil wars, strife, import tariffs and bans, and by illicit trading. In Lusaka, wholesale firms sell the clothes in 1,102 pound bales to retailers and small traders, who exchange these in the rural areas for produce and piece work, or sell them in a large open-air market in Lusaka. More than two thousand traders operate in the city, displaying the clothes on the ground, on tables, or on hangers. Zambians may not merely imitate European and North American dress styles. Through consumption they actively recommodify the clothes, giving them new meanings in the contexts of local dress repertoires. In this manner, the market provides a variety and abundance of clothing that enable the urban poor to attain dignity and uniqueness.

Other anthropologists have documented the movements of people who seek refuge from war and/or new economic opportunities. Transnational traders, operating between Congo-Kinshasa and Congo-Brazzaville and the Chateau Rouge neighborhood of Paris, export African foodstuffs to the immigrant communities in Paris and import electrical goods, second hand cars, spare parts, and various other scarce accessories to their home countries. Young men who lack education and fail to secure positions in government may enter the international trade to protest against their exclusion from elite status in central Africa. Operating in a second economy, outside the margins of the law, the traders manipulate the ambiguity of spatial and institutional boundaries, so that these become places of opportunity. They use personal ties of kinship, friendship, and ethnicity, rather than formal bureaucratic processes, to conduct their trade, and evoke normative rather than legal sanctions. The traders emphasize reciprocity and trust, striving to create debt obligations and relations of long term commitment. These instrumentally activated personal networks that lower the costs of business transactions, are remarkably resilient. Traders also establish a reputation for themselves through ostentatious expenditure.

Still other anthropologists argue that any focus on a small, bounded field site is insufficient to understand the dynamics of large-scale events, such as the postindependence war between the FRELIMO government and RENAMO rebels in Mozambique. During this conflict, millions of people were killed, internally displaced, or fled the country. Far from being a local event, the war was fuelled by anger resulting from nationwide processes, such as forced removals and the proscription of chiefs. It was also sustained by a tangled web of international linkages between several governments in the region, war-related industries, mercenaries, and propagandists moving from seemingly local war to seemingly local war around the globe. The concept of a warscape can assist the understanding of the larger dynamics of violence. Not rooted in any particular place, it focuses on the front line, where people's entire beings are determined by war. The front line constantly shifts and is marked by flows of people, as soldiers enter and refugees flee. Nonetheless, it forges common experiences of death and suffering, ways of acting and thinking, strategies for survival, and concepts of humanity.

Front lines also have common actors such as soldiers, splinter groups that break away from the major forces, bandits who prey upon the population, private militias who are used by businesses to protect factories and ports, civilian collaborators, jackals who fend off the kills of others, and movements opposed to the war. Moreover, front lines have spatial features, marked by a territorial division between control areas, where the rebels demand labor and sexual services from the local population; tax areas, where they extract tribute from farmers; and destruction areas, where they seek to execute all inhabitants and destroy all infrastructure.

DOUBTS

In the atmosphere of intellectual excitement surrounding studies like these, few scholars have dared to question the appropriateness of the very concept of globalization. Frederick Cooper (2001, 2005) is perhaps the most notable exception. He suggests that, when examined against the backdrop of

African history, globalization lacks specificity and has rather limited utility. There is little evidence to support the theory of a definite rupture with the past, and any description of African history as a linear movement toward boundless connectivity is a distortion. Global connections are not new. For centuries, linkages of various sorts have shaped Africa. These connections have been constantly reconfigured, and there has been a back and forth movement between territorializing and de-territorializing forces. Portuguese and Dutch voyages of the sixteenth and seventeenth centuries were fired by a global imagination, and organizations such as the Dutch East Indies Company linked the Netherlands, South Africa, Indonesia, and other parts of Asia in vast trade networks. The Atlantic slave trade connected Africa with Europe and with the Americas. The time discipline required by the mass supervision of slave labor subsequently facilitated the English development of industrialism.

Colonization did not necessarily open up the African continent. Instead, colonial regimes imposed borders that disrupted long-distance trade networks crossing western Africa, the Sahara desert, and the Indian Ocean, and isolated Africans from other tribes. Colonialism also forced African protectorates into a world system that focused upon a single metropole, and upon a narrow sphere of production and exchange. In the era of structural adjustment, the lowering of barriers to capital flows is often little more than a discourse. The transnational networks forged by Nigerian and Angolan oil companies are narrowly extractive and reward only gatekeepers. Likewise, networks engaged in the illicit diamond trade mainly involve young people who are detached from local villages.

Some globalization theorists exaggerate the death of the nation-state. In fact, African states are constantly spending an increased proportion of their national GDPs. Uneven political and economic relations, and spatial boundaries to the exercise of power, mean that transnational connections are dense in certain places and more diffuse in others. Bland use of the concept of globalization recognizes no limits to connectivity. Arenas exist where international markets and investors do not go, and they are important barriers to the movement of people. For example, in the early twenty-first century, Africans have found it increasingly difficult to enter Europe.

From the 1980s, Zambians have experienced being disconnected from the global economy. During independence in 1964, there were widespread expectations that Zambia was rapidly becoming a modern industrial nation. Copper mining stood at the forefront of a vibrant economy that connected Zambia to the rest of the world. Zambia had high rates of urbanization and employment, and was commonly described as a middle income country with excellent prospects for entry into the developed world.

However, these expectations of modernity and promises of prosperity failed to materialize. Fiber optics and satellite technology replaced the copper telephone and power lines that had previously connected the world. Between 1965 and 1995, the tons of copper mined in Zambia halved, the GDP shrank to near the bottom of developing countries, and per-capita income fell by more than 50 percent. To alleviate the burden of extreme debt, the Zambian government underwent structural adjustment and abandoned expenditure on health care and education. In this situation, modernity is not something that Zambians look forward to, but something that they remember. Impoverished Zambians have only faint recollections of a time when they owned first-class things, such as suits, neckties, and automobiles. Urbanization gave way to movements back to the land, industrialization to agriculture, and connection to disconnection. Zambian Airlines was liquidated, and most European airlines dropped Lusaka off their routes. In a world of flexible investment and disinvestment, new spaces of accumulation are continuously invented, and older spaces of accumulation rapidly become redundant.

Globalization theorists seldom specify how translocal connections are formed and how actors exercise them. Needed are more precise concepts—such as network, social field, and social situation—to understand the nature of connectivity.

See also **Anthropology, Social, and the Study of Africa; Cold War; Colonial Policies and Practices.**

BIBLIOGRAPHY

Appadurai, Arjun. *Modernity at Large: Cultural Dimensions of Globalization.* Minneapolis: University of Minnesota Press, 1996.

Cooper, Frederick. "What is the Concept of Globalization Good For? An African Historian's Perspective." *African Affairs* 100 (2001): 189–213.

Cooper, Frederick. *Colonialism in Question: Theory, Knowledge, History.* Berkeley: University of California Press, 2005.

Ferguson, James. *Expectations of Modernity: Myths and Meanings of Urban Life on the Zambian Copperbelt.* Berkeley: University of California Press, 1997.

Gordon, Robert J. *The Bushman Myth: The Making of a Namibian Underclass.* Boulder, CO: Westview Press, 1992.

Hannerz, Ulf. *Transnational Connections: Culture, People, Places.* New York: Routledge, 1996.

Hansen, Karen Tranberg. *Salaula: The World of Secondhand Clothing and Zambia.* Chicago: University of Chicago Press, 2000.

Harvey, David. *The Condition of Postmodernity.* Oxford: Blackwell, 1989.

Malkki, Lissa. *Purity and Exile: Violence, Memory, and National Cosmology among Hutu Refugees in Tanzania.* Chicago: University of Chicago Press, 1995.

McGaffey, Janet, and Remy Bazenguissa-Ganga. *Congo-Paris: Transnational Traders on the Margins of the Law.* Oxford: James Currey; Bloomington: Indiana University Press, 2000.

Murdock, George P. *Africa: Its Peoples and Their Culture History.* New York: McGraw-Hill, 1959.

Nordstrom, Carolyn. *A Different Kind of War Story.* Philadelphia: University of Pennsylvania Press, 1997.

Wilmsen, Edwin. *Land Filled with Flies: A Political Economy of the Kalahari.* Chicago: University of Chicago Press, 1989.

ISAK NIEHAUS

GONDÄR. At one time the name Gondär (or Gonder/Gondar) referred to both the province of Bägemdər in Amhara, in the northeast, and to its capital city. Today it is only the name of the old city that is situated at 11° 30' North by 39° 09' East at seven thousand feet above sea level. Gondär was the seat of the Gondärrine dynasty (although it was later rivaled by Däbrä Tabor) and the capital of Ethiopia from the seventeenth to the beginning of the second half of the nineteenth centuries. The gradual decline of Emperor Téwodros's political power and his death in 1868 ended the city's political significance.

Gondär owed its rise to the turmoil in Šäwa (Shewa/Shoa) caused by Imam Aḥmad Graññ's invasion of the country from the east and the Oromo migration from the south during the sixteenth century. The beleaguered imperial palace had to move from Shoa/Amhara to the west, away from the reach of the recurrent Islamic assault. Over a period of more than a century the palace pitched camp in several places until it finally settled in Gondär during the reign of Emperor Fäsiladäs (1632–1667) to whom the city's foundation is credited.

As the subsequent history of Ethiopia shows, there was no real place of escape from the two forces that precipitated the palace's move to Gondär. Nevertheless, because so many church scholars came to Gondär to seek the palace's protection, the city became vibrant in the field of art, literature, church music and architecture. Forty-four churches were built within its boundaries and local clergy competed with one another to excel in academic and other achievements. It is orally reported that a Gondärine emperor once asked the clergy at a banquet he prepared for them the name of the 318 Orthodox Fathers in attendance at the first Nicean Council in 325 CE. In response, a monk stood up and recited, by heart, their names and their bishoprics.

The Gondärine kings' main national preoccupation was defending the empire from the invasion of the Oromo. They also had to contend with the influence of the Portuguese (and Spanish) Catholics who came to Ethiopia during and after the revolt of Imam Aḥmad Graññ. The architecture of the monumental castles in the city, the ruins of which continue to draw visitors, are said to be of Portuguese or European style. In terms of theology, the Portuguese influence manifested itself in a serious schism among the Orthodox clergy regarding the catholic concept of Christology that was propagated by Portuguese and Spaniard missionaries.

The rise of the Mahdist movement in the Sudan in the nineteenth century, in the west, revived and reminded of the old Islamic menace from the east. The army of the Khalifa invaded Gondär in 1887; the devastation inflicted included the burning of churches within and around the city. The last blow to Gondär came in 1866 from its own son: Emperor Téwodros

(1855–1868), rather than surrender the city to his rival Gobeze, pillaged it and then burned it to the ground.

See also **Ahmad ibn Ibrahim al-Ghazi (Ahmad Grañ); Fasiladas; Téwodros.**

BIBLIOGRAPHY

Di Salvo, Mario, et al. *Churches of Ethiopia: The Monastery of Nārgā Śellāśē.* Milan: Skira Editore, 1999.

Jäger, Otto A., and Ivy Pearce. *Antiquities of North Ethiopia.* Stuttgart: F. A. Brockhaus, Abt. Antiquarium, 1974.

Pankhurst, Richard. *History of Ethiopian Towns From the Middle Ages to the Early Nineteenth Century.* Äthiopistische Forschungen. Vol. 8. Stuttgart: Franz Steiner Verlag Wiesbaden, 1982.

Pankhurst, Richard. *History of Ethiopian Towns from the Mid-Nineteenth Century to 1933.* Stuttgart: Franz Steiner Verlag Wiesbaden, 1985.

Rubenson, Sven. *The Survival of Ethiopian Independence.* London: Heinemann, 1976.

Zewde, Gabre-Sellassie. *Yohannes IV of Ethiopia: A Political Biography.* Oxford: Clarendon Press, 1975.

GETATCHEW HAILE

GONDER. *See* Gondär.

GORDIMER, NADINE (1923–). The South African writer Nadine Gordimer was born in the town of Springs on November 20, 1923. Gordimer's father was a Jewish immigrant and her mother was of Jewish descent, but the family's Jewishness, she indicates, played only a minor role in her life. If Gordimer had a childhood religion, it seems, instead, to have been reading. Withdrawn, for medical reasons, from the Convent of Our Lady of Mercy at the age of ten, Gordimer was subsequently educated at home and in her local library, where she read voraciously. By the time she was fourteen she had begun to publish her own short stories in the Johannesburg *Sunday Express* and, as a student at the University of the Witwatersrand, which she attended for a year at the age of twenty-two, she published stories in the *New Yorker.*

Devoted from this early age to a life of writing, Gordimer has, over the years, published twenty-six

Writer Nadine Gordimer (1923–) lectures in the Brunei Gallery, May 27, 2003. Most of Gordimer's work deals with the themes of love and politics with a spotlight on race in South Africa. Gordimer was friends with Nelson Mandela's defense attorneys; upon his release from prison in 1990, she was one of the first people he was eager to see. © RUNE HELLESTAD/CORBIS

volumes of prose, including many collections of short stories (*Face to Face*, 1949; *The Soft Voice of the Serpent and Other Stories*, 1952; *Six Feet of the Country*, 1956; *Friday's Footprint and Other Stories*, 1960; *Not for Publication and Other Stories*, 1965; *Livingstone's Companions*, 1971; *Selected Stories*, 1975; *Some Monday for Sure*, 1976; *A Soldier's Embrace*, 1980; *Town and Country Lovers*, 1980; *Something Out There*, 1984; *Jump and Other Stories*, 1991), ten novels (*The Lying Days*, 1953; *A World of Strangers*, 1958; *Occasion for Loving*, 1963; *A Guest of Honour*, 1970; *The Conservationist*, 1974; *Burger's Daughter*, 1979; *July's People*, 1981; *A Sport of Nature*, 1987; *My Son's Story*, 1990; *None to Accompany Me*, 1994), and several books of essays, including *The Black Interpreters* in 1973 and *The Essential Gesture: Writing, Politics, and Places* in 1988.

With few exceptions, Gordimer's novels and short stories chronicle everyday life in South Africa during the apartheid years. In doing so, they inevitably investigate the brutalization of lives, imaginations, and consciousnesses by meticulously examining the silences, mundane hypocrisies, minor betrayals, and everyday fears on which the South African state built itself. The politics of Gordimer's writing is achieved, not forced. It is something found in the details of individual lives, not asserted on the basis of a systematic philosophy. As such, the political thrust of Gordimer's work seems to flow from her aesthetic convictions and her devotion to close observation and realistic portrayal of what can be seen, heard, and touched. Attuned to the social consequences of the apartheid legislation and policing of intimacy, Gordimer's writing is also aware of the writer's obligation to shape language, to form sentences, to discover the apposite metaphor. Celebrated from early in her writing career, Gordimer has been awarded numerous honors, including honorary degrees from Harvard University, Yale University, Columbia University, and the New School for Social Research, and many literary prizes, among which are the 1974 Booker Prize and the 1991 Nobel Prize in literature.

See also **Apartheid; Literature.**

BIBLIOGRAPHY

Clingman, Stephen. *The Novels of Nadine Gordimer: History from the Inside.* Boston: Allen and Unwin, 1986.

Head, Dominic. *Nadine Gordimer.* New York: Cambridge University Press, 1996.

Roberts, Ronald S. *No Cold Kitchen: A Biography of Nadine Gordimer.* Johannesburg: STE Publishers, 2005.

IAN BAUCOM

GORDON, CHARLES GEORGE

(1833–1885). After service with the Royal Engineers in the Crimean War, the British military commander Charles George Gordon helped to suppress the Taiping rebellion in China in 1863–1864. In 1873 the khedive of Egypt, Ismail Pasha, appointed him governor of Equatoria Province, the huge newly controlled area far up the Nile River. For two years he attempted to establish an ordered administration based on a network of riverine stations as far south as Lake Kyoga, near Lake Victoria in modern Uganda, but with scanty reinforcements he achieved little success. In 1877 Ismail Pasha appointed him governor general of Sudan with orders to suppress the slave trade then raging in the region. Gordon campaigned vigorously against slave traders in the southern reaches of Dar Fur and Kordofan, but his interventions fueled resentment against Egyptian rule among the Baggara Arabs, who soon joined the Islamic reformist Mahdist movement then growing in the area. In 1880 the khedive accepted his resignation, and Gordon served Britain in India and South Africa, being promoted to major general.

Charles George Gordon (1833–1885). The British army officer and administrator was well known for his exploits in China, which would eventually earn him the nickname "Chinese Gordon." Gordon was killed by Mahdists after having been beseiged at Khartoum for several months for trying to defeat the Mahdi in Sudan. LONDON STEREOSCOPIC COMPANY/GETTY IMAGES

In January 1884 the British government sent him to rescue the Egyptian garrisons in Sudan from the insurgent Mahdist forces. He reached Khartoum on February 18 and organized its defense. When the city was under siege, he refused to evacuate. On January 26, 1885, Khartoum fell to the Mahdists, and Gordon was killed. A spectacular commander in war, but privately a skeptical, dissident imperialist, his career and final fate captured the imagination of Victorian England and assisted Britain's reconquest of Sudan from the forces of the Mahdi's successor.

See also **Egypt, Early: Islamic; Islam; Khartoum; Sudan: History and Politics.**

BIBLIOGRAPHY

Allen, Bernard M. *Gordon and the Sudan.* London: Macmillan, 1931.

Hill, Richard. *Gordon: Yet Another Assessment.* Durham, England: Sudan Studies Society of the United Kingdom, 1987.

Zaghi, Carlo. *Gordon, Gessie e la riconquista del Sudan.* Firenze, Italy: Centro Studi Coloniali dell'Università di Firenze, 1947.

RICHARD GRAY

GORÉE. A scenic island and popular tourist site in Dakar harbor, Gorée Island was for centuries a trading entrepôt for various European powers. Barren, small, and uninhabited, it was well situated to become a base for trade with the coast of Senegambia and Upper Guinea. The Dutch occupied it in 1588. The French seized it in 1677 and, though sometimes occupied by the British during various imperial wars, it remained largely a French bastion until Senegal became independent in 1960. Saint-Louis, at the mouth of the Senegal River, was always a more important settlement because it commanded the trade of the Senegal River. For much of the eighteenth and nineteenth centuries, its population ranged between 2,000 and 3,000 people. Until the abolition of slavery, most of the population was composed of slaves who worked as artisans and on boat crews. Small boats worked the opposite coast, called the *Petite Côte* (Lesser Coast), and the rivers from the Saloum down almost to Freetown. They traded in slaves, wax, and hides. An old merchant

house known as *La Maison des Esclaves* has been preserved and become an important tourist location. It is unlikely that many slaves were traded through it. Gorée rarely handled more than 500 slaves per year.

Gorée had no potential for expansion. As a result, in 1857, when French naval officers were thinking of extending their control on to the coast, Dakar was founded. Though it grew slowly at first, it rapidly took over Gorée's function as a trade entrepôt and as a naval basis.

See also **Dakar; Freetown; Saint-Louis; Tourism.**

BIBLIOGRAPHY

UNESCO. *Gorée, Island of Memories.* Paris: UNESCO, 1985.

MARTIN KLEIN

GOVERNMENT

This entry includes the following articles:
HISTORICAL POLITICAL SYSTEMS
LOCAL
MILITARY
PARLIAMENTARY
PRESIDENTIAL

HISTORICAL POLITICAL SYSTEMS

There are four distinct forms of indigenously evolved African governance, distinguished using three criteria: the organization of the governmental system; the polity's size by population and territory; and its forms of economic organization. This classifies them into: hunter-gatherer bands; small-scale villagers and pastoralists; chieftaincies; and states. These abstract types have never existed in isolation from one another or from the outside world. Each has always been more or less interactive with, or integrated into, other governance types. But as abstractions, or types, they define important constitutional frameworks indigenous to Africa.

HUNTER-GATHERER BANDS
Africa has a small number of hunting, gathering, and foraging bands. They are located in the Congo Basin, the Kalahari arid lands, and a congeries of groups in northern Tanzania and western Kenya. For the continent as a whole, there are no more

than 50,000 to 100,000 peoples living within hunting-and-gathering bands. As with other continental land masses, small remnants of this once-ubiquitous form survive in remote areas. Social, economic, and political relations with farmers and graziers, along with complete independence, are characteristic of this adaptation.

Population size per polity is small, averaging about twenty-five. This can vary from a low of one dozen to up to one hundred depending upon the scarcity or abundance of food supplies, the existence of internal conflicts, knowledge of the terrain, seasons of the year, proximity to waterholes and game, and relations to neighboring band and village polities.

The overriding constitutional rule of band government is that of egalitarian ideology and practice. Authoritative officeholders are conspicuously absent. Tendencies to institutionalize authority vary from one band to another in terms of age, gender, personal skills of leaders, and the inherited or acquired rights (through marriage) to a territory or hearth. Specific activities such as hunting, gathering, ritual performances, or dispute settlement may support leaders. But band breakups, aging, and the high value placed upon individual autonomy tend to keep such structuring to a minimum. Long-established bands may develop a headman, albeit with limited authority. These individuals tend to lead discussions over band movement, social order, rituals, and relations to other groups. In everyday terms leadership depends upon successful outcomes. Unsuccessful outcomes result in new leaders. Normal political processes occur when a headman, often aided by a few respected seniors and the most skilled younger members, settle serious quarrels, organize rituals and communal hunts, or help decide on group movements.

Because food sources vary unpredictably, flexibility governs decisions about almost every aspect of band sustenance, except with respect to obligatory food sharing. This allows for rapid adjustments in food-questing plans, in band membership, and in decisions to seek access to another group's territory. Similarly, there are no enforceable rules governing life-cycle issues, such as family size and age spacing, or initiation ceremonies. Flexibility also allows for the territorial separation

of individuals and groups in conflict, minimizing the possibility of violence. Larger bands break up more easily. Peacefulness and order are important, but the lack of mediating authority plus norms of individual autonomy and flexibility can lead to violence when disputes get out of hand. Among the Ituri forest bands, supernatural authority is seen as the spirit (*molimo*) of the home environment, which punishes individuals for serious crimes. Theft and other breaks in social order are settled flexibly by those concerned on a case-by-case basis, with the punishment suiting the crime in the eyes of the Ituri. Shaming deviants through verbal attacks is a widespread form of social control.

Once farming and pastoralism developed (from c. 6500 BP forward), hunting bands were soon linked with villages and pastoralists as periodic traders of forest products and as subordinate workers among labor-hungry food producers. Most bands are able and experienced at political and economic relations with sedentarized villagers. Many were linked individually, through families or by band formations, to more complex polities. Historically, this led to their steady incorporation into surrounding societies, though exceptions continue to survive as independent polities.

SMALL-SCALE VILLAGERS AND PASTORALISTS

There are three forms of small, uncentralized African polities that depend upon renewable and storable foods: independent villages and their outliers; segmentary or allied polities; and age-graded units that use age-sets to organize politically. The degree to which any particular regime fits into an abstract subtype is a matter of sociopolitical isolation and historical relations to other polities.

AUTONOMOUS POLITIES

Autonomous food-producing village polities are widespread throughout Africa. They form a basic sociopolitical format varying from a few families (25–50 people), to up to several thousand, with an average of approximately 300 to 500 per polity. Settlement patterns range from compacted villages to widely dispersed neighborhoods with farm fields and pasture interspersed between households. As population exceeds carrying capacity, settlement areas send off representative members to found new communities. The survival of individuals, families, and households depends upon rightful access to land, animals, and communal institutions across generations. This fundamental constitutional requirement, namely, the need to legitimize and order access rights beyond individual life spans, favors the development of unilineal descent, household rights, and communal governance institutions.

The polity is widely viewed as divided into founders and their lineage descendants, as owners of the land, and later arrivals, who often have lower status, access to more distant farmlands, and less access to political offices. Authority positions are also influenced by factors such as age, gender, kinship, household membership, political skills, and personal success. The most common institution of authority is the headman, elected from the founder lineage, and a council of respected elders from the major or most powerful and established lineages of the community. This eldership assists the headman in the governance of the community. It serves as a court, helps the headman allocate access to resources, carry out rituals, and organize public works. To legitimize these powers the eldership serves as a community memory of legal cases and a registry for all known records of property rights and social relations in the community, including both peaceful and conflictful interactions with other polities.

Another office is that of village priest, which may be differentiated from headman. He links the community ritually to the authority of the local spirits of the land and the ghosts of past leaders whose aid and retributions he interprets. Similar to the headman, he is responsible for the community's political, economic, and general welfare, performing rituals to avoid natural disasters and epidemics, and maintain witch control—the diagnosis and punishment of misfortunes judged to be malevolent outcomes of social conflict. There are also variably institutionalized hunt leaders, leaders of women's organizations, leaders of cooperative work groups, raiding and revenge parties, youth organizations that carry out public works, and, in western Africa, adult male secret societies that enforce social order using threats and punishments from impersonated spirits.

The most ubiquitous office is that of household head. In this sense political activity is an aspect of domestic organization. The general principle is based on size. The larger the household, the greater the political and economic power of its head. Institutions enabling this empowerment are widespread. Thus polygyny, fostering, clientage, pawning, and slavery provide households with extra members, both kin and non-kin, to increase the size, power, and continuity of households as political and socioeconomic units. Households break up through domestic cycling, or segment and divide, increasing their joint power under a senior member as a kin-based faction in village politics. Indigenously, household heads perform rituals recognizing the authority of deceased senior lineage members whose ghosts are concerned with the fates of their descendant members. Over time and generations, servile non-kin members tend to be incorporated into kin groups, ensuring household continuity.

Local authorities (from household heads to lineages to village councils) make up an appeals court system in the adjudication of civil and criminal cases. Precedent, evidence, and swearing or oathtaking are all used. Trial by ordeal, where the experience of the trial is the punishment, is an option for some crimes, especially if a verdict threatens those in authority.

Relations to other polities are carried on through trade, marriage relations, raiding, feuds, joint communal hunts, and inheritable peace treaties between polities. Household heads establish foreign-trade relations with individuals in other polities using such institutional practices as blood-brotherhood and quasi-kinship to protect outsiders. Cross-polity relations emulate kinship, client-age linkages to weaker (including hunting bands) or more powerful (including chieftaincies and states) neighbors, or clanship (that is, putative unilineal descent relations based on a charter of common ancestry).

As with hunting bands, the political culture rewards personal autonomy and individual success, but villages and pastoral communities differ from hunting bands in that the former has a more complex hierarchy and members assume corporate responsibilities. Most offices are open to all competitors within the limits of age and gender, albeit the highest office—village headship—is generally hereditary with some tendencies toward primogeniture, though personal qualities may also play a role. Even with this restriction an ambitious man can migrate, found a new settlement, and become headman. Personal achievements are constrained by traditional principles that legitimize authoritative hierarchies within families, households, and settlements. Identification with the interests of collectivities is made tangible by corporate responsibilities in which individuals are legally obligated by the actions of their fellow group members. Socialization requires learning to live under hierarchical authority, collective responsibilities to households, corporate lineages, villages, and past generations that include spirits and household ghosts. Political skills join individual autonomy, competition, and success with the needs and demands of hierarchical relations and nesting collectivities, including family, household, and village.

SEGMENTARY SYSTEMS

In segmentary systems, unilineal charters among lineages and clans maintain political relations across localized polities. These are tied constitutionally into nested groupings expressed as segmentary oppositions in which social distance and alliances for both peaceful cooperation and warfare are defined by real and putative unilineal descent to common ancestors. This creates two adaptive capacities. First, segmentation allows for the sharing of resources across dispersed groups providing for expansion into marginal environments. Second, it supports the mobilization of separated groupings for social, cultural, and especially political-military purposes. Whether nomadic (Bedouin or Fulani [Fulbe]) or sedentary (the Tiv or Nuer), such polities have a comparative advantage in competition or conflict with localized nonsegmentary villagers. This difference has had profound effects on African political history.

Age-graded polities are located in east, south, and central regions. These are generally pastoral peoples with (such as Nyakyusa) or without (such as Maasai or Boran) permanent villages, whose young people often tend cattle together. All of these societies use an organizing principle of age grades—groups within the polity that are of a similar age and whose responsibilities are age-specific—that defines the life cycle. Each grade is occupied for a time by a group of people—the age-set—who often move together through the grades. As with many aspects

of cultural life, political relations are structured by the age-grading principle.

Age-set relations are the basis for constitutionally defined political relations within and across communities. The principle can be used for settlement purposes, with each new age set forming its own village polity (such as Nyakyusa), or more commonly with each named and ritually entered grade having specified duties to the polity. For men, these grades range from adult-in-training to warrior to decision maker to elder, whose wisdom is tapped but who plays a less active role in everyday affairs. As with segmentary systems, the age-based polities can unite autonomous polities, providing an enabling foundation for chieftaincy if that development is required by events. This occurred when the Zulu resisted European expansion in South Africa. Normally, however, as with autonomous villages, segmentary and age-graded polities expand and fission regularly in relation to population growth, internal conflicts, and migration.

CHIEFTAINCIES

Two forms of supralocal centralized government, chieftaincies and states, evolved throughout Africa. Chieftaincies emerge when a local chief becomes a chief of chiefs, recognized as leader of a dispersed set of sedentarized or nomadic polities. This so-called paramount chief heads a council of leaders, including rival members of his own chiefly lineage. The leader-in-council acts for the entire nonlocal polity in ways reminiscent of the governance of village polities. But it is concerned primarily with coordinating relations among previously independent polities. These include chiefly rituals, public works, and relations with foreign polities. Ritualized exchanges among previously independent co-ethnic leaders shift toward asymmetrical exchanges in which the lower-ranked chiefs send subsistence products to the paramountcy often to provision large gatherings. The paramount in turn sends specialized goods from foreign trade or weapons symbolizing his more central position. He expands his power by channeling resources to followers and the needy.

The primary duty of paramount chiefs is in representing their polity to foreign authorities. In the secular world this means relations through warfare, alliances, traditional ceremonies, and gift exchanges or treaties of nonaggression and rights of passage. The entire polity or representatives gather at the paramount's residence for annual ceremonies, war, and the death or installation of a new chief. Chiefs supplicate spirits of the land to renew its fertility and engage the help of chiefly ancestors to foster polity welfare. The most well-known of such rituals is the *incwala* ceremony of the Swazi.

At the local level, political processes resemble those of village polities. But local units are members of a wider system to which they owe loyalty, tributes, and military duties. Nevertheless, chiefships resemble village polities in two ways: they culturally assimilate newcomers, and they continue to fission regularly. Common culture helps unify the polity; fissioning weakens it. Using close relatives as major advisers in the chiefly council produces constant rivalry and conflict among potential heirs to the chiefly office (such as the Lunda). This leads to inevitable conflicts among factions that ultimately split the polity under rival chiefly heirs, each supported by differing descent groups in the polity. Nguni chiefships expanded, absorbed, and assimilated less powerful villagers and then became too large to administer from the center, allowing for segments to break off as separate chiefships on their own. In Azande the process was institutionalized. Official heirs were enjoined to expand their inheritable segments through warfare. The segments then broke up into new chiefships at the death of the present chief.

The political culture of chiefship, although similar in many ways to village polities, places heavier emphasis on hierarchy and the inheritance of rank. The society is more clearly stratified. Leaders and their close kin are holders of and contenders for inherited offices. Those outside the leadership are "commoners." There are always means to gain access to the leadership class. Age and gender distinctions along with (often inherited) servile status are clearly stratified, but ranked by the status of (usually) male superiors. Thus female children, close kin, and non-kin servile followers have lower ranks than their menfolk, but anyone linked to a leader is ranked by that association. Culturally, chiefships are assimilative. To join a chiefship voluntarily or by force means to take on the language, culture, and customs of the dominant polity. When the Nguni spread northward through central Africa they absorbed smaller groups who were then considered Nguni. Chiefship depends, therefore, upon a common culture to help unify the polity when bonds of governance across local groupings are weak.

STATES

The term state is sometimes used to cover all indigenous African political systems, the term centralized states (population from 250,000 into the millions) being reserved for what elsewhere are called states. This avoids invidious comparisons by lumping distinct constitutional frameworks into one category. For comparative purposes, states are centralized polities with a permanent bureaucracy living in a fortified capital under a hereditary ruler who has sovereign powers over a hinterland area and its peoples. True centralized states evolved within most regions of Africa but proliferated in northern, western, and eastern Africa with incipient or proto-states developing rapidly by 1850 CE in central and southern regions. Each region, and each state within it, are complex and unique societies with rich histories and both regional and original principles and institutions of governance.

The earliest states of Africa are among the oldest in the world, going back to Egypt (c. 5500 BP) and early Aksum (c. 2500 BP) in Ethiopia. The influence of ancient Egypt upon later state development throughout the continent is a matter of ongoing research. Proto-states or chieftaincies in Democratic Republic of the Congo and both central and southern Africa—Barotse and Zulu, for example—had little or no centralized bureaucracies. Important offices in the hands of rival heirs produced instability and fission. Once the step was taken to a non-kin, loyal, and dependent set of central officials, centralized statehood quickly followed. Such steps generally occurred in reaction to local scarcities of essential resources, conquest, migration, control over trade, and contagion, amounting to the formation of centrally organized defenses against nearby predatory states. Principles of African statecraft are most clearly seen in their structures of administration, in foreign relations, and in the political cultures associated with centralized governance.

State administration traditionally involved the central government and its relations to outer or peripheral segments of the state. The pinnacle and central symbol of the state was the monarch and his dynastic lineage, the palace organization, his family, and the other royals. A council of nobles made up the central government, serving as a central executive arm that carried out the decisions of the monarch and a variably constituted inner council of advisers. Within this group was a small group of electors who appointed the next monarch. In addition there were war councils, religious leaders, and representatives of various districts and segments of the state. In a number of African monarchies, high offices were reserved for women royals or so-called queen mothers. Their duties represented the recognition, nurturance, and inevitability of opposing yet complementary interests within the state which must always work together to create its ultimate continuity.

The capital town is highly stratified, with a central place given over to governmental functions—the royal palace and nearby residences of the ruling aristocracy. Market areas, craft specialists, and traders have their special wards, and there is generally a place for foreign traders and emissaries either within the city or close to its walls. The governmental area is also a place for adjudicating civil and criminal cases, for ceremonials, and for public displays of royal pomp and the sumptuary lifestyles of the ruling nobility. The common people are divided by occupation, wealth, ethnicity, and personal patron-client relations with those in the ruling groups. Those of servile status (slaves, pawns, and client servants) are plentiful, but vary in rank from slave nobles in the western Sahel to low-ranking household slaves and pawns.

Relations to the hinterland areas vary by structure and ethnicity, both of which present problems. Structurally, African states allow for consolidated holdings outside the capital under the control of local elites or nobles of the court or both. As with other early states, consolidated holdings were nodes of potential rebellion. Constitutional principles evolved to counteract the problem. Thus, in Buganda, the monarch married polygynously into the local leading lineages of all consolidated districts, giving each one a chance to provide a future monarch through matrifiliation. In Dahomey each district chief was linked to the throne through a queen mother who represented the district chief to the throne and vice versa. In other states—for example, the Islamic emirates of the Sahel—the peripheries were unconsolidated village holdings under subordinates of the noble fief holders who lived permanently in the capital. Holdings could then be used as rewards and punishments for service to the central government.

Whether consolidated or dispersed, peripheral settlements and peoples were linked to the central government through a hierarchy of officials who collected revenues for the rulers at the center and ensured military manpower for frequent predatory or defensive expeditions. Although not universal, the structure of the African states supported the differentiation of ethnicity from citizenship, making for multiethnic capability under uniform principles of state-society relations. Thus, in the Hausa states there were both nomadic and sedentary groups linked to a central government under a common administration and an emergent state religion.

Foreign relations among these states almost always involved some form of control over trade, especially long-distance trade. Thus, states in western Africa arose at entrepôts of trade on the coast (Dahomey) or at the ends of Saharan trade routes (Ghana, Mali, Songhay, Hausa, and Bornu) and the coastal states of eastern Africa. The governments either carried out much of the trade themselves or exacted levies on the trading community. Alliances and tributary relations were in constant flux, varying with the power of a particular state regime at any time period. This, along with the need to control and keep trade routes open, in addition to the need to maintain authority within the state, was associated with the importance of warfare. Multiethnic peripheries and an expanding sovereignty meant a large militia. One writer characterizes these states as predatory war machines. Undoubtedly, warfare was a major organizational feature of centralized state governance. Military strategies, walled defenses, enhanced war technologies including muskets, cavalry, and sieges were commonplace.

Finally, foreign relations included the incursion into Africa of Islam, which connected large sections of the continent, especially states bordering the great Islamic areas of the Near East and the Maghreb. This meant 500 to 1,000 years of common membership in a literate world religion, producing trips from internal Africa to Mecca through the east coast and through Egypt that knit large portions of Africa into the wider Islamic world of learning, diplomacy, trade, jurisprudence, and statecraft.

The political culture of early African states centered on the ideology of statehood itself and a particular state's history compared with other polities. The state was considered a superior, more powerful, more prideful system than others, and each particular state was an ethnizing force in its territories. The penultimate symbol of the state was the monarch, whose health, welfare, and sacred status represented the society as a whole. Thus, the *kabaka* (Uganda) was said to eat the state at his coronation—he was seen as consuming the country and its people so as to become the personification of the polity. The *shehu* of Bornu was considered to be the father of all citizens—he cared for his subjects like a parent for his children or a head of household for those under his care. Widespread as well was the metaphor of monarch as lion—a being of great power among those less powerful.

Even in Islamic areas, there was a universal set of beliefs linking the monarch to the royal ancestors who were prayed to for the welfare of the kingdom, and linking the monarch's well-being to that of the kingdom as a whole. His person was therefore sacred. He could not be spoken to directly or touched, and his subjects' actions toward him were symbolic of extreme deference and subordination, for example, the practice of putting dirt or dust on one's head when coming into his presence. In one case (pre-nineteenth-century Bornu) he appeared in public heavily robed in a cage that separated him from all other mortals.

The leitmotiv of political culture in African states was the primacy placed on inequality and hierarchy—authority, power, and noblesse oblige of superiors, and deference and loyalty of subordinates made for political and economic stability. This could crosscut ethnicity, as with Tutsi-Hutu relations of the far past in Rwanda, where the conquering Tutsi ruling classes had patron-client relations (*ubuhake*) with ambitious underlings including the indigenous Hutu villagers. In Buganda ambitious commoners placed their children as clients of so-called big men in the royal court. This was certainly true as well in the western African states. Personal

achievement was determined by the potentialities of deference and loyalty to a higher-ranked individual, household, or aristocratic lineage.

Finally, multiethnicity and the differences between the capital citadel and the countryside created fundamental distinctions of culture that divided the states into centers of urban court-based life and the more simple life of the countryside. Over time the life of the capital, its language, customs, religion, and patterns of everyday life, strongly influenced the culture of the hinterlands peoples. Thus, an African state could be formed from one culture or many. Central governance produced a sumptuary lifestyle at the center and diffused common elements of this style outward.

See also **Age and Age Organization; Agriculture: Beginnings and Development; Food; Gender; History of Africa; Household and Domestic Groups; Kings and Kingdoms; Kingship; Kinship and Descent; Political Systems: Chieftainships; Queens and Queen Mothers; Secret Societies; Warfare.**

BIBLIOGRAPHY

Apter, David E. *The Political Kingdom in Uganda: A Study in Bureaucratic Nationalism.* Princeton, New Jersey: Princeton University Press, 1961.

Argyle, W. J. *The Fon of Dahomey: A History and Ethnography of the Old Kingdom.* Oxford: Clarendon Press, 1966.

Beidleman, Thomas O. "Swazi Royal Rituals." *Africa* 36, no. 4 (1966): 373–405.

Cohen, Ronald. *The Kanuri of Bornu.* New York: Holt, Rinehart and Winston, 1967.

Cohen, Ronald. "Women, Status, and High Office in African Polities." In *Configurations of Power: Holistic Anthropology in Theory and Practice,* ed. John S. Henderson and Patricia J. Netherly. Ithaca, New York: Cornell University Press, 1993.

Evans-Pritchard, E. E. *The Azande: History and Political Institutions.* Oxford: Clarendon Press, 1971.

Forde, Daryll, and P. M. Kaberry, eds. *West African Kingdoms in the Nineteenth Century.* London: Oxford University Press, 1967.

Kuper, Hilda. *An African Aristocracy: Rank among the Swazi.* New York: Africana Publishing Company, 1980.

Lee, Richard B. *The !Kung San: Men, Women, and Work in a Foraging Society.* Cambridge, U.K.: Cambridge University Press, 1979.

Lemarchand, René, ed. *African Kingships in Perspective: Political Change and Modernization in Monarchical Settings.* London: Cass, 1977.

Middleton, John. *Lugbara Religion: Ritual and Authority Among an East African People.* London: Oxford University Press, 1960.

Njaka, Elechukwu Nnadibuagha. *Igbo Political Culture.* Evanston, Illinois: Northwestern University Press, 1974.

Reyna, Stephen P. *Wars without End: The Political Economy of a Precolonial African State.* Hanover: University of New Hampshire Press, 1990.

Vansina, Jan M. *Kingdoms of the Savanna.* Madison: University of Wisconsin Press, 1966.

RONALD COHEN

LOCAL

Local government, as the lowest tier of formal governance, is characterized by locally accountable executive personnel having authority sufficient to plan, budget, raise, and spend substantial local revenues; and to hire and dismiss personnel. It also involves locally elected and accountable councils with the responsibility and authority to make and implement policies and programs regarding key services such as health, education, sanitation, pubic works, agricultural extension, community development, and the like. If it lacks these features, it is not local government but is merely one or another form of local (deconcentrated or delegated) administration. Considered by these criteria, Africa has experimented much with local administration but experienced little genuine local government. However, there have been significant ebbs and flows in the extent to which Africa has neared genuine local government, and its progress in this has closely paralleled its economic and political fortunes. So, it is an important dimension of the African state.

The colonial era marks the first ebbing of local government in Africa, as top-down, control-focused colonial administrations created dynamics that eroded and corrupted the often thriving precolonial local governance regimes. The elimination of confederal or semi-federal systems that included such regimes, the arbitrary rearrangement of chiefs and chieftaincy systems to suit colonial convenience, and the establishment of chiefs where there hitherto had been none, served to upset indigenous systems of accountability and checks and balances, and effectively ended local governance for most Africans. The colonial powers also frequently corrupted—and enriched—traditional chiefs in the process. Arbitrary, often despotic, and generally upwardly accountable administration of local areas often resulted: but this was not local government.

In the post–World War II era, the United Kingdom—and to a lesser degree, France—took a new direction regarding local government. In response to the gradual delegitimization of colonialism, India's looming independence, and their own shattered economies, the postwar governments began to realize that African colonialism might end in the foreseeable future. This led, among other things, to the British government's Creech-Jones Commission that explored policy options toward Africa, and considered real changes in policy by the British, particularly regarding local government.

Arthur Creech-Jones (1891–1964), the secretary of state for colonial affairs, emphasized three concepts underlying his commitment to reform colonial policy, starting with local government: They should be efficient, democratic, and local. As a result of the subsequent policy shift, democratic (or semi-democratic) councils were established, independent revenue sources were authorized, and specified (if somewhat limited) administrative responsibilities were delegated to the new local governments. Although France's historical commitment to the centralized administrative tradition meant it moved more slowly, particularly in rural areas, nonetheless it granted municipal status to an additional forty-four cities in 1955 (beyond the three granted such status in 1884 in Senegal) and enhanced their capacity as local government entities.

Scholars have described this era as the golden age of local government in Africa. It served as a base from which many of Africa's independence leaders arose. However, its vitality—since largely unmatched—was eroded in the early postindependence era.

The 1960s may be marked as the second ebbing of local government in Africa. During this period the authority, resources, and popular accountability of local governments were badly eroded, for a variety of reasons and through a variety of processes. The two most important dynamics underlying this were the centralization of state power and the consolidation of political control by the newly sovereign leaders. While these are analytically distinct processes, for the most party they occurred simultaneously.

The consolidation of state power occurred through structural reforms that eliminated or reduced the power of subnational governments, enhanced the centralization of administrative authority, and established central economic and development planning. Uganda, Kenya, and Ghana, among others, are examples of this. These were undergirded in many circumstances by socialist ideologies. Ghana under Nkrumah (1909–1972), Tanzania under Nyerere (d. 1999), and Zambia under Kaunda (b. 1924) are all examples of these patterns among Anglophone countries, whereas Guinea and others followed similar paths among Francophone states. In these systems, local governments were seen as administrative tools of national government.

Local governments were frequently eclipsed by various sorts of local planning and coordination boards such as were established by Kenya's District Focus, Tanzania's 1972 decentralization reforms, and similar measures carried out in Zambia and elsewhere. These typically were staffed by administrative personnel from central ministries, members of parliament from the local constituencies, and a few local representatives usually selected from party loyalists, and were chaired by national government appointees. Often established in the name of decentralization, they were in fact only vehicles to consolidate greater central control over local affairs and administration.

At the same time that these structural, administrative and policy changes were weakening local governments, de facto or de jure single-party systems completed the erosion by substituting largely top-down, single-party dominance for local accountability. Even in pragmatic, nonideological states such as Nigeria, Côte d'Ivoire, or Kenya, the centralization of single party systems (in Nigeria in each of the three original regions) greatly eroded the autonomy and local accountability of what local government had hitherto existed. Accountability flowed upward through the party—often through patron-clientage—rather than downward to the local population. Almost without exception the military governments that followed

during these early years in many African states sustained or pushed further these centralizing tendencies.

By the late 1960s and early 1970s, local governments were moribund or nonexistent across most of Africa. At best, localities experienced deconcentrated administration. What local governance (locally accountable mechanisms to manage conflict and/or take collective action) there was occurred where there were still viable and respected traditional authorities and community associations. These were limited to minimal—though at times important—functions by their lack of legal standing and resources.

The political and economic crises of the late 1970s and the 1980s marked a potential watershed for African local government. The economic crises that hit Africa in this era left its leaders searching for ways to reduce the expenditures of national governments. Frequently, this was stimulated by the Structural Adjustment Programs required by the international donors for loans to cover immediate or pending fiscal crises. A variety of initiatives grew from these, most of which amounted, however, only to off-loading hitherto central government-funded responsibilities on local governments, but not giving them comparable resources or local revenue bases. Nor did the central governments give local governments effective control over deconcentrated administrative personnel who retained control over the programs. In effect, while costs and public responsibility for these programs were spun-off to nominal local governments, control over resources and personnel was retained by the center.

Ghana's decentralization reforms of the 1990s are a prime example of this. Begun with much local enthusiasm, the reality was that local taxes—as well as what central grants there were—were devoured by the overhead costs of the local governments (salaries, benefits, buildings, and vehicles), leaving very little for local initiatives. Also, central ministries managed sector (health, and agricultural, for example) personnel and budgets, and presidentially-nominated chief executive officers dominated the district councils. These led only a few years later to steep declines in local voter turnout and enthusiasm for local government.

Côte d'Ivoire's decentralization left most authority in the hands of local mayors who were in reality Abidjan-based notables. Nigeria's several attempts at local government have also been stymied by politicization of local governments, national political instability, serious corruption issues stemming from the oil wealth, and erratic and unreliable national policy toward and treatment of local governments. Kenya and Zambia's local government policies of the 1980s and 1990s were characterized as well by serious politicization, irregular national policies, and ongoing national control of local services. The patrimonial rulership of the Moi era also severely damaged local government in Kenya. Similar patterns were experienced by Cameroon and Côte d'Ivoire in this era, as well as by other states.

Most of these disingenuous policies were pursued under the label of decentralization. Thus, while this era could be construed as a positive one in the changing fortunes of African local government, that is in fact an illusion. In failing to allow for genuine local autonomy, accountability and resources, even within limited responsibilities, these policies ensured local governments would perform badly. This, to some observers, discredited decentralization and local government.

In the early twenty-first century, African local government presents a highly mixed picture. National context has had a decided influence on this. Collapsed states, states torn by war, or states only recently emerging from severe conflict present unclear or uncertain pictures (Somalia, Congo, Sudan, Liberia, Ethiopia, Eritrea, Angola, Sierra Leone, Rwanda, and Côte d'Ivoire). Other states have escaped severely patrimonial, corrupt or military rule (Kenya and Nigeria), but only recently enough that their prospects are still unclear. Others are still gripped by such rule (Gabon, Niger, Togo, and Congo-Brazzaville), and others seem poised at the brink of severe domestic conflict (Zimbabwe). The prospects for some are simply unclear: Zambia, Malawi, and others.

However, others have made general—if at times unsteady—progress in the direction of constitutional and democratic rule. Ghana, Mali, Bénin, Senegal, Mozambique, Namibia, South Africa, and (perhaps) Uganda and Tanzania may be classified in this category. Others, Mauritius and Botswana

among them, have made steady progress since independence toward democratic and constitutional governance.

Local government's fate is still unclear in several of these categories. Except for the last two groups, the national political framework is simply too unstable to generalize with much confidence regarding what will become of it. In Sierra Leone and Rwanda, for example, serious attempts at genuine democratic and devolutionary decentralization are underway, but their prospects are unclear as their respective governments deal with the social and physical damage that remains from their ordeals. Liberia's recovery from severe civil conflict has hardly begun, though a serious future role for some sort of local governance there seems to be likely. Ethiopia has made some groundbreaking efforts at decentralization, but national-level politics are highly conflictual and its wars with Eritrea make its prospects too unstable to regard with confidence.

However, each of the states in the democratic and constitutional categories has made a national commitment to strengthening genuine local government, and there is some evidence to confirm those commitments. Perhaps their most important contribution to this has been their success in sustaining constitutional and democratic governance (though these too are halting at times). Only in a constitutional environment can local government have the legal and policy stability to develop as an effective institution; and only under democratic governance can it develop the local accountability necessary if it is to respond to the priorities of local dwellers, and if they are to take it seriously and contribute their resources to it. Insofar as these conditions are maintained, the future of local government in Africa is encouraging.

Nonetheless, challenges to building genuine local government remain even among these states. They include:

- The continued reluctance of central governments truly to let go of control of local affairs. Even in states where local affairs seem nominally under local control, centrally set minimum standards (Botswana), national final adjudication of local plans (Uganda), or national interference in local accountability (Ghana), serve to limit greatly local autonomy and effectiveness.

In many states, a potentially effective local government structure is in place, but absent central willingness to let it function, it is stymied.

- National government leaders must recognize how genuine local government can be foundational for national democratic and development agendas.

- Lack of personnel and fiscal resources nearly everywhere leave local governments institutionally weak and dependent on national grants, which at times are unreliable, are usually opaque in both criteria and process, and always fraught with the danger of national strings.

- Local councils nearly everywhere are still nascent and frequently ineffective bodies, with personnel who are often poorly educated in general, unfamiliar with government in particular, poorly resourced, poorly trained, and dominated by executive and administrative personnel.

- Local elite capturing and recentralization have been seen in many areas. The relative advantage of administrative and technical personnel over local dwellers in education, proximity to resources and status, along with the relative weakness of local councils, creates difficult principal-agent issues that leave local governments vulnerable to both of these problems. The preference of most locally posted technical and administrative personnel for centralized personnel systems is an open door for recentralization.

- Local governments face severe challenges of working in the least developed, least infrastructure-rich, poorest, and neediest areas, with resources vastly inadequate to their challenges, and with populations frequently frustrated. Often they are so populous that they are not true local governments, but more regional ones. Connections with the grassroots groups are difficult to make and sustain.

- Extralegal structures of influence, patron-clientage, and corruption often leave local government personnel dealing with problems they did not cause and needing resources they do not have.

- National, politically driven decisions can hurt local governments, such as recentralizing control over local government personnel (Nigeria and Ghana), eliminating what few own-source taxes and revenues local governments have (Uganda), dumping massive national wage or universal service obligations on local governments without allocating comparable resources or sufficient skilled personnel (Nigeria and Uganda).

- National government generally does not offer local governments the personnel development and technical assistance they need to fulfill their obligations.

Having noted all this, at least among several of the states noted above, for the first time since the late-colonial era there seems to be a serious and sustained commitment to local government. Senior leaders among the ministries such as finance and local government most critical for local government's success appear to be grappling with these issues, and national associations of local governments are advocating vigorously at the capitals for progress on these problems. Also, high profile African and international donor commitments and efforts to deliver progress to the poorest such as the Millennium Development Goals, and the near universal emphasis on good governance have highlighted the critical role local governments must play if Africa is to make social, economic, and political process. Though serious challenges remain, for now, the future seems favorable for the gradual emergence of genuine local government, at least in some parts of Africa.

See also **Colonial Policies and Practices; Kaunda, Kenneth; Nkrumah, Francis Nwai Kofi; Nyerere, Julius Kambarage; Political Systems.**

BIBLIOGRAPHY

Ayo, S. Bamidele. *Public Administration and the Conduct of Community Affairs among the Yoruba in Nigeria.* Oakland, CA: ICS Press, 2002.

Crook, Richard, and James Manor. *Democracy and Decentralisation in South Asia and West Africa, Participation, Accountability and Performance.* Cambridge, U.K.: Cambridge University Press, 1998.

Hicks, Ursula Kathleen. *Development from Below: Local Government and Finance in Developing Countries of the Commonwealth.* Oxford: Clarendon Press, 1961.

Hyden, Goran. *No Shortcuts to Progress African Development Management in Perspective.* Berkeley: University of California Press, 1983.

Millett, Karin; Dele Olowu; and Robert Cameron; eds. *Local Governance and Poverty Reduction in Africa.* Tunis, Tunisia: Joint Africa Institute, 2006.

Mutahaba, Gelase. *Reforming Public Administration for Development Experiences from Eastern Africa.* West Hartford, CT: Kumarian Press, Inc., 1989.

Olowu, Dele, and James S. Wunsch, eds. *Local Governance in Africa: The Challenges of Democratic Decentralization.* Boulder, CO: Lynn Rienner Publishers, 2004.

Woods, Dwayne. "The Tragedy of the Coco Pod: Rent-Seeking, Land and Ethnic Conflict in Ivory Coast." *Journal of Modern African Studies* 41, no. 4 (2003): 641–655.

JAMES WUNSCH
DELE OLOWU

MILITARY

Coups d'état and military governments have been major features of African political life since the early 1960s, and since the late 1970s organized armed conflict has become a factor in the domestic and international politics of significant numbers of African states. From 1960 to mid-1994, sub-Saharan Africa experienced seventy-one successful military coups and well over twice that number of failed coup attempts. The successful ones have come in waves of different intensities. From 1960 to 1974 they averaged three a year, with a peak average of 3.7 for the years 1974 to 1980. The next wave, from 1986 to 1994, was more a ripple, averaging 1.3 a year.

Only a fine and often imperceptible line seems to distinguish coup-prone countries from those that have avoided direct military intervention, and it is far from certain that the recent diminution in the frequency of coups represents a trend. In general, the armies most likely to plot and initiate a coup, and to succeed in establishing military rule, tend to be large, to take up more of the gross national product and of the total government expenditure, and not to have to share the national territory with troops lent by a major foreign power. They are prone to have factionalized officer corps and tensions over allocations of benefits among ethnic elites reflected in the factional structure. When one considers that the two most coup-prone countries are as different as Nigeria and Burkina Faso (six each), it becomes clear that there is no single pattern of vulnerability. One thoughtful

typology classifies military regimes into four categories, to each of which can be added a civilian counterpart.

The boundary between civilian and military government can itself be uncertain. Most military governments depend on civilian agents at all but the highest levels, and several military regimes have, in appearance, civilianized themselves over time. Were Étienne Eyadema's and Mobutu Sese Seko's regimes still military by the early 1990s? When did they begin to take on a more civilian orientation? Jerry Rawlings's rule in Ghana began as a stern military dictatorship but later was transformed into a civilian government chosen in a somewhat fair election. However great or small the difference between civilian and military rule, the wave of democratization that swept Africa in the first half of the 1990s has severely diminished the legitimacy of all forms of authoritarian rule, and that includes all forms of military rule.

The issue of military versus civilian rule in Africa became a factor in the Cold War competition of the great powers. In the West, where several influential scholars wrote about the militaries of developing countries as agents of technocratic development, Colonel Mobutu Sese Seko was seen by the United States as far preferable to the civilian radical Patrice Lumumba in Democratic Republic of the Congo, and General Joseph Ankrah was preferred over the leftist Kwame Nkrumah in Ghana. The Soviet Union, beginning with its sales to the Nigerian federal government during the Biafran civil war, found that the trade in arms and military training was one sphere in which it could decisively undercut the West. As the Soviet army increased its foreign policy influence in the 1970s, the Soviet government began looking with particular favor on military regimes, and Soviet scholars began discovering progressive virtues in the likes of Bénin's Mathieu Kerekou, Somalia's Siyad Barre, and Ethiopia's Haile Mariam Mengistu. With the end of the Cold War, most such illusions and some of the arms trade faded away.

Since the mid-1970s, the incidence and scale of armed conflict have increased significantly in sub-Saharan Africa. This has both caused and resulted from an increase in military capacity. In the 1960s, most African armies were tiny and hard put to extend their forces beyond national borders. By 1982, however, Ethiopia had a quarter-million men under arms, and modern tank and air forces.

The first, and so far only, successful invasion of one African country by another was accomplished in 1979 when the Tanzanian army defeated the Ugandan army and overthrew Idi Amin. A Somali invasion of Ethiopia failed the same year. The independence of Angola and Mozambique increased the scale of fighting in Southern Africa, most notably through the South African Defense Force's raids into those two countries and its support of armed opponents of their governments. Although the new South Africa is at peace with its neighbors, civil strife has continued in Angola.

If classic interstate armed conflict remains rare in Africa, the use of violence has increased domestically with the rise of politico-military movements, in effect, armed opponents who seek to seize power by the gun. The Frolinat movement in Chad, formed in 1966, was the first of these to make its mark, but Somalia, Rwanda, Liberia, Angola, Mozambique, Ethiopia, and Sudan have all confronted such challenges in the 1990s. Each of these conflicts has its own etiology, but each is helped along by the Cold War legacy of readily available arms across the continent, ineffective or abusive rule by civilian and military governments, and economic desperation. Most such movements benefit from the tolerance, if not the complicity, of neighboring regimes. Unlike the coups d'état of the past, which were mostly limited to the capital's administrative center and over by nightfall, the more recent conflicts between governments and politico-military movements usually begin at the periphery, spread across the country, and result in the killing of large numbers of innocent civilians. Ironically, as governments have learned to protect themselves from coups, they have encouraged armed opposition to take a much more virulent form, one which in some cases has caused both state and civil society to disintegrate.

The troubles in Africa and elsewhere in the post–Cold War world have given many African armies the opportunity to participate in multilateral peacekeeping operations. Troops from Senegal, Botswana, Nigeria, and Tanzania, among others, have become highly skilled at such tasks. However useful, such use of force to discourage armed conflict must be bolstered by political and economic reform if peace is to prevail.

See also **Amin Dada, Idi; Cold War; Ethnicity: Overview; Eyadema, Gnassingbe (Étienne); Lumumba,** **Patrice; Mengistu, Haile Mariam; Military Organizations: National Armies; Mobutu Sese Seko; Nkrumah, Francis Nwia Kofi; Political Systems; Rawlings, Jerry; Warfare.**

BIBLIOGRAPHY

Decalo, Samuel. *Coups & Army Rule in Africa: Motivations & Constraints.* New Haven, Connecticut: Yale University Press, 1990.

Foltz, William J., and Henry S. Bienen, eds. *Arms and the African: Military Influences on Africa's International Relations.* New Haven, Connecticut: Yale University press, 1985.

Howe, Herbert M. *Ambiguous Order: Military Forces in African States.* Boulder, Colorado: Lynne Rienner Publishers, 2001.

Jenkins, J. Craig, and Augustine Kposowa. "The Political Origins of African Military Coups: Ethnic Competition, Military Centrality, and the Struggle over the Postcolonial State." *International Studies Quarterly* 36 (1992): 271–292.

Reno, William. *Warlord Politics and African States.* Boulder, Colorado: Lynne Rienner Publishers, 1998.

WILLIAM J. FOLTZ

PARLIAMENTARY

Most constitutional democracies in present-day Africa are organized in ways that mirror the government of either the presidential system of the United States or the French semi-presidential system. Among Africa's fifty-three countries, only five are based on a parliamentary system of government: Botswana, Ethiopia, Lesotho, Mauritius, and the Republic of South Africa. A number of countries, consisting primarily of former British colonies, tried the parliamentary system during the early postindependence period but opted for presidential systems during the wave of democratization in the 1990s; for example, Ghana, Kenya, Malawi, Nigeria, and Tanzania.

In the parliamentary form of government, the executive head of government is elected by the legislature and there is no separation of powers, making it different from the presidential and semi-presidential systems. In these types of systems, the president is also typically both head of state and head of government, while most parliamentary systems have a nonexecutive head of state such as a king or a ceremonial president. Mauritius, for example, changed its constitution in 1992, creating a ceremonial office of the president as head of state, and Lesotho has a king with essentially no political powers.

In parliamentary systems, the head of government is usually called a prime minister, as in Lesotho, but can also be titled president, as in Botswana and South Africa, and this person has to select the ministers from the legislature, or lawmaking body. In contrast to presidential systems, the legislature can also unseat the government by a majority nonconfidence vote. The head of government may decide to resign if there is no longer a majority in the legislature to support the government's main policies, or if a ruling coalition of parties can no longer agree on major policy issues. As in Mauritius' parliamentary democracy between 1991 and 1995, this resignation may lead to the formation of a new coalition government, but if a new government cannot be formed, the parliament is dissolved and new elections are held, which also happened in Mauritius in 1983.

Botswana, Ethiopia, and Mauritius operate on a British-style electoral system based on plurality vote in single-member constituencies, often referred to as first-past-the-post (FPTP). Lesotho also used the FPTP system from 1993 to 2002 but then decided to switch to a mixed system, in which 80 of the 120 members of Parliament are elected by proportional representation (PR) and the remaining 40 are elected using the FPTP system. A proportional electoral system typically has multi-member constituencies, and each party presents a list of candidates for each constituency. Seats in the legislature are then allocated according to the percentage of votes received at the national level. South Africa uses a PR system based on closed party lists, much like the Swedish system, but unlike most countries in the world using PR, South Africa has no threshold for parties entering parliament. As a consequence, South Africa's parliament contains twelve political parties compared to, for example, Botswana's three legislative parties (according to 2005 statistics).

Research on established democracies as well as on developing nations has tended to support the view that parliamentary systems of governments are more robust than presidential systems, especially in divided societies, and Africa's parliamentary systems corroborate this view. Botswana has been a stable democracy since independence in 1966 and

Mauritius since 1976. Lesotho reintroduced multi-party politics in 1993 and South Africa followed the year after that, and both countries have transitioned into stable democracies. Hence, all of Africa's parliamentary systems of government except Ethiopia's are stable democracies with generally peaceful, free and fair, and inclusive elections whose results have been accepted by all major parties. These four countries are also classified as "free" by Freedom House's ranking of political rights and civil liberties, while Ethiopia is considered "partially free." Political participation as measured by average voter turnout is relatively high in these four countries, hovering around 75 percent. In comparison, among the presidential systems in Africa, democracy has broken down about forty times since 1990; only half of their elections have been classified as substantially free and fair, and about one-third of all their elections have resulted in boycotts. A majority of the presidential systems are classified as only "partially free" or "unfree," and average political participation is much lower, with a voter turnout at around 60 percent.

See also **Botswana: History and Politics; Ethiopia, Modern: History and Politics; Lesotho: History and Politics; Mauritania: History and Politics; Political Systems; South Africa, Republic of: History and Politics (1850–2006).**

BIBLIOGRAPHY

Lijphart, Arendt. *Patterns of Democracy: Government Forms and Performance in Thirty-Six Countries.* New Haven, CT: Yale University Press, 1999.

Lindberg, Staffan I. "Consequences of Electoral Systems in Africa: A Preliminary Inquiry." *Electoral Studies* 24(1), 2005: 41–64.

Lindberg, Staffan I. *Democracy and Elections in Africa.* Baltimore, MD: Johns Hopkins University Press, 2006.

Sisk, Timothy D., and Andrew Reynolds, eds. *Elections and Conflict Management in Africa.* Washington, DC: United States Institute of Peace Press, 1998.

STAFFAN I. LINDBERG

PRESIDENTIAL

Presidential regimes dominate the African political landscape. No pattern has been more prominent in postindependence African politics than executive branch dominance. Indeed, many countries that began as parliamentary systems or mixed systems at independence became executive-dominant systems even as they became less democratic or outright autocratic. Since the end of the Cold War almost all African countries have experienced democratic initiatives in some form, and, in doing so, all but five of these countries (South Africa, Mauritius, Botswana, Lesotho, Ethiopia) have retained executive-dominant political systems that two varying degrees qualify as presidential democracies.

Presidential democracies differ from parliamentary democracies in that legislatures and presidents have separate electoral mandates. Neither is electorally dependent upon the other. While neither a necessary nor a sufficient defining characteristic of presidential democratic regimes, African presidents in these regimes have uniformly been more powerful than the legislative branches, to the point of dominating them in many instances.

The concept of presidential government is complicated, however, both in theory and in African practice by semi-presidential governments. Semi-presidential governments are those dual executive arrangements in which executive power is divided between a president and a prime minister, in contrast to those in which a president is essentially a symbolic figure while the prime minister is the real head of government. More than half of all African presidential regimes are formally semi-presidential in this sense. The powers of prime ministers in semi-presidential regimes are a function of the degree to which they are politically accountable to the legislative branch rather than the president. Prime ministers in almost all African semi-presidential regimes are weak in that both they and their cabinets are accountable to presidents, though they are to be drawn from the legislatures in many cases. The intrinsic ambiguity in semi-presidentialism, concerning where the greater power must lie, as between a president and a prime minister, invites intense political conflict. The role of the prime minister has figured prominently in a near civil war in Côte d'Ivoire that began in 2003 and in a defeated referendum on a new constitution in Kenya in 2005.

In the post–Cold War era of democratic initiatives in Africa, one important accomplishment has the ability of some African countries to limit the duration if not the extent of executive power by imposing two term limits on presidencies. Namibia generated controversy internally and some adverse publicity when founding president Sam Nujoma altered expectations by successfully running for a third term. Elsewhere, when tested, the two-term limit has been upheld de facto in several countries even if not strictly mandated constitutionally. South Africa set an example for African parliamentary regimes in mandating two term limits for its head of state and government.

In retaining presidential systems, African countries have implicitly challenged the prevailing view among scholars that presidential regimes are less stable than parliamentary ones. They contend that parliamentary regimes are more likely to have working majorities needed to implement public policies, enjoy greater capacity to rule where there are multiple parties, better able to restrain heads of government and state from constitutional infringements and to remove those who violate constitutional prescriptions, less prone to overthrow by military coups, and more likely to retain experienced leaders and provide continuity in governance. Some scholars argue, however, that the sources of political stability, or its absence, lie outside these institutional arrangements in electoral systems or other socioeconomic and political variables. African countries have appeared implicitly to contend that presidential systems enjoy a degree of cultural legitimacy that in the early twenty-first century, at least, outweighs the relative instability of these systems.

See also **Cold War; Nujoma, Samuel Shafiishuna; Political Systems.**

BIBLIOGRAPHY

Kuenzi, Michelle, and Gina Lambright. "Party Systems and Democratic Consolidation in Africa's Electoral Regimes." *Party Politics* 11, no. 4 (2005): 423–446.

Linz, Juan, and Arturo Valenzuela, eds. *The Failure of Presidential Democracy.* Baltimore: Johns Hopkins University Press, 1994.

Stepan, Alfred, and Cindy Skach. "Constitutional Frameworks and Democratic Consolidation: Parliamentarism versus Presidentialism." *World Politics* 46 (1993): 1–22.

JOHN W. HARBESON

GOVERNMENT, COLONIAL. *See* Colonial Policies and Practices.

GOWON, YAKUBU (1934–). General Yakubu (Jack) Gowon was born on October 19, 1934, into the minority Angas ethnic group of Plateau State in central Nigeria and grew up in the Christian community of Wusasa on the edge of the capital of the Muslim emirate of Zaria. Educated at Government College in Zaria (1950–1953), he joined the Nigerian colonial army in 1954 and underwent training at Teshie before gaining admission to Sandhurst, the royal military academy in Britain, in 1955. He served with the Nigerian contingent in the United Nations peacekeeping force in the Congo in 1960 and had just completed staff college in Britain when the mutiny of January 15, 1966, erupted in Lagos. Only because he had not reported back for duty did he escape the murder of senior Northern officers that evening. Uninvolved in the Northern countercoup in July, he was called on by the army to take over the drifting national government of Nigeria.

Gowon's intersectarian upbringing and his affection for the give-and-take camaraderie of army life developed an innate integrity into a rare capacity to bridge the troubled chasms of Nigerian national life. Not a dove, and certainly no hawk, in the Biafran War his humanity and tolerance toward the defeated Igbo (Ibo) eased their reintegration into his vision of "One Nigeria." Add his commitment to the Organization of African Unity (OAU) and his creative leadership in establishing the Economic Community of West African States (ECOWAS) in 1975, and one may well wonder why Nigeria ousted Gowon in the bloodless coup of 1975.

Yet behind the sunshine of his leadership lay the cloud of indecisiveness. Was he preeminently fair, or did he fail to be firm enough with his subordinates? Ready to listen, did he listen too much or to the wrong people? Personally honest, was he honorable in his refusal to discipline corrupt governors and, above all, in canceling the scheduled return to civilian rule? Admiration modified by controversy seems set to color history's assessment of Gowon as Nigeria's by-chance, yet most credible, head of state.

Exiled in 1975, Gowon enrolled for a bachelor's degree at Warwick University. He went on to earn a Ph.D. in 1984, researching the founding of ECOWAS. Following his restoration of rank in 1987, he regularly traveled back to Lagos, though his bid for an elective seat in Zaria in 1993 resulted in unexpected rejection. He turned to private industry, and in 2004 served on the board of directors for the Industrial and General Insurance Company, Ltd., one of the largest privately owned insurance companies in Nigeria.

See also **Economic Community of West African States (ECOWAS); Government: Military; Military Organizations: National Armies; Nigeria: History and Politics, Northern Nigeria; Nigeria: History and Politics, Southern Nigeria; Organization of African Unity.**

BIBLIOGRAPHY

Clarke, John D. *Yakubu Gowon: Faith in a United Nigeria.* London: F. Cass, 1987.

Elaigwu, J. Isawa. *Gowon: The Biography of a Soldier-Statesman.* Ibadan, Nigeria: West Books Publisher, 1985.

Kirk-Greene, Anthony H. M. *Crisis and the Conflict in Nigeria: A Documentary Sourcebook.* 2 vols. London: Oxford University Press, 1971.

Oyediran, Oyeleye, ed. *Nigerian Government and Politics Under Military Rule, 1966–1979.* London: Macmillan, 1979.

Major General Yakubu Gowon (1934–). During his rule as Nigerian head of state, Gowon helped prevent Biafran secession. Later he gave amnesty to most of those involved in the Biafran uprising and started a program of "Reconciliation, Reconstruction, and Rehabilitation" to repair the country after years of war. TERRENCE SPENCER/TIME LIFE PICTURES/GETTY IMAGES

Panter-Brick, Keith, ed. *Soldiers and Oil: The Political Transformation of Nigeria*. London: F. Cass, 1978.

ANTHONY KIRK-GREENE

GRAPHIC NOVELS. *See* **Media: Comic Art.**

GRIOT. *See* **Literature: Oral.**

GUINEA

This entry includes the following articles:
GEOGRAPHY AND ECONOMY
SOCIETY AND CULTURES
HISTORY AND POLITICS

GEOGRAPHY AND ECONOMY

Guinea is usually divided into four geopolitical areas or so-called natural regions. This categorization, dating from the end of the nineteenth century, is based primarily on geographical criteria, coupled with sociocultural and historical factors. It has become the usual way of describing Guinea and is now used in political discourse. This division represents an oversimplification of the geography—a juxtaposition of diverse ecological environments that do not coincide with national borders.

The coastal region, known as lower Guinea, consists of plains and mangrove-lined estuaries that stretch from the Gambia to Sierra Leone. Four rivers flow to the sea through this area: Rio Componi, Rio Nunez, Rio Pongo, and the Mellacorée. This region's humid tropical climate makes it well suited to agriculture. Crops such as palm oil, sugarcane, fruit, and rice flourish. Fish and salt are also valuable resources, although marine products are tending to decrease due to the competition of industrial fishing. In the early twenty-first century, pineapple and banana plantations prospered, both for local consumption and for export. The local population consists of the Baga and Nalu and, originating in the hinterland, the Fulani.

Central Guinea consists mainly of a mountainous area rising to about 4,922 feet. In this mountainous region, cattle raising is an important economic activity as the lateritic soil is not fit for cultivation, apart from fonio (*Digitaria exilis*, the smallest species of millet), and except for valleys and some rainy, low-lying regions. Agricultural production has increased since the 1980s, thanks to the efforts of peasant organizations, with the cultivation of potatoes and other market-garden crops such as vegetables and onions that are mainly for the country's capital, Conakry. Formerly, the division between agriculture and cattle-raising reflected an ethnically designated sociopolitical organization, but in the early twenty-first century occupations are much less linked to specific groups, and trade is becoming an important activity. Central Guinea is the most densely populated region in the country, consisting mainly of Fulani, historically the keepers of the region's cattle, with nearly one hundred people per square mile.

Upper Guinea, inhabited mainly by the Malinke (Mande-speaking), has several plateaus 1,312 feet high that are eroded toward the east by the Niger River and its tributaries. The economy combines mainly grains agriculture and livestock raising. Long-distance trade that links the upper Niger Valley to the forest is also important and used to be controlled by Islamized Mande-speaking traders called Jula, who would find fellow Muslims along the trading routes. In the past this trade involved Saharan salt, slaves, and kola nuts, but now it consists of grain, kola nuts, cattle, and fruit.

Finally, the forest region differs from the three other regions both in its ruggedness (hills and mountains that reach as high as 5,578 feet, the summit of Mount Nimba), and in its climate, which is humid and subequatorial. The forests are generally secondary growth. The peoples of the area—Loma, Kpelle, Mano, Kono, and Kissi—practiced a form of shifting agriculture that relied on the ample rainfall, except for the Kissi, whose cultivation of upland rice (*Oryza glaberrima*, or African red rice) required irrigation and sophisticated means of cultivation. Coffee was introduced during colonial times.

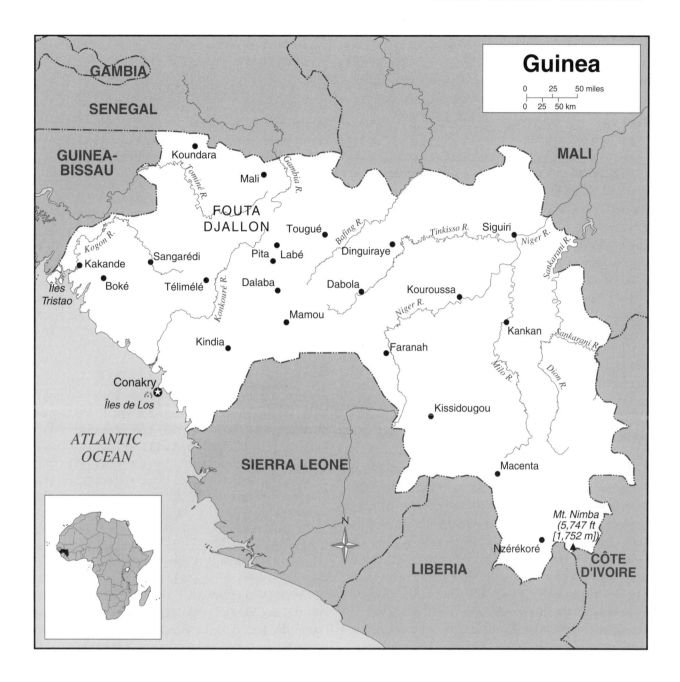

Up to the 1950s the country's main occupation and the primary source of revenue was agriculture. Colonial economic development policies emphasized the opposition between subsistence and cash crops. This artificial divide can still be seen, with some changes. Rice, various species of sorghum, maize, and fonio are the basic staples. Rice is cultivated on the coast as an irrigated crop, as well as a rain-fed crop in the forest. Though greatly valued by the population, production does not suffice for local consumption and its price is higher than imported Asian rice (*Oryza sativa*, or

white rice). At the time of independence, the main cash crops—coffee and bananas—were 80 percent of exports by value. In the early twenty-first century the agricultural sector still employs 70 to 80 percent of the population but contributes a small part of the nation's gross national product (less than 25%). Crops include millet, sorghum, and rice, as well as corn. Export crops decreased in the wake of independence in 1958, but liberalization (the reintroduction of a free market) in the 1980s, however, brought a resurgence of export crops, mainly fruit from the coastal region and coffee from the forest, though declining prices sharply reduced revenues realized, and cotton production increased but depended heavily on international market prices. In 2001, coffee exports equaled 24,000 tons; banana exports rose to more than 150,000 tons; and pineapples exports totaled 72,000 tons.

With the exception of gold (Africans had panned for gold for centuries), the exploitation of mineral products is recent. Diamond exports from the forest region date from 1936. Iron ore of the Kaloum Peninsula in the Conakry region, although discovered earlier, was not exploited until 1953 by the Compagnie Minière de la Guinée Française, which received its concession in 1947 and was financed by U.S. capital. In 1957, over 1 million tons of iron ore were exported, but mining ceased in 1966. Bauxite became the principal resource of independent Guinea. It came from three areas: Kassa (in the Los Islands, near Conakry, in the 1950s), Kindia-Friguiagbé (a mining deposit discovered in 1942), and Fria-Boké (1954). In 1955, roughly 480,000 tons of bauxite were exported from Kassa, an area that was mined from 1952 to 1974. Mineral exports grew significantly after independence in 1958. During Sékou Touré's regime, the bauxite mining areas with their modern technology, Western employees, and adequately sanitary facilities, remained enclaves that contrasted starkly with the rest of Guinea, which was rural and scarcely modernized in spite of projects such as the irrigation of Fuuta Jallon and the dam at Garafiri on the Konkouré River. Mineral exports accounted for about 75 percent of the country's exports in the early 2000s. Guinea's bauxite represents 30 percent of the world reserves but, contrary to Sékou Touré's plans, no aluminum is processed locally. This is primarily due to a lack of electricity and the policies of the international companies in charge of extracting the metal. Rare minerals plus iron ore have been discovered in the forest region, but many factors prevent their exploitation: a difficult environment, high initial investment costs, the distance to the coast, and the political instability of the region. In 2005, minerals represented a quarter of the value added by production in Guinea, equal in value to agriculture. Commerce, retail and wholesale, was the only other category or economic activity in a similar range, at just over one fifth.

Although many people live largely outside the modern cash economy, Guinea's gross domestic product (GDP) in 2006 was approximately US$3.8 billion, or US$2,100 per capita. The GDP has fallen slightly as population increased faster than the 2–3 percent annual rate of economic growth, distributed fairly evenly among agriculture, mining and manufacturing, construction, trade, and transportation.

Since 1945, the population of Guinea has grown rapidly. Statistics are not necessarily accurate, both because censuses have been poorly conducted and because of the large population movements across the country's international boundaries. When Guinea was still a colony, many Guineans went to Senegal to work at peanut cultivation; after independence many fled the country for political reasons combined with worsening economic conditions. There were approximately 3 million inhabitants at the end of the colonial period, 5 or 6 million during the era of Sékou Touré (1958–1984), and at the beginning of the twenty-first century nearly 10 million people. Sixty percent of the population is under twenty years old. Urbanization has accelerated since the 1960s; about 40 percent of the population lives in cities, mainly Conakry. The population of Conakry had been stable at about 10,000 between the two world wars but exceeded 50,000 during the 1950s and reached about 200,000 around 1970. At the beginning of the twenty-first century its population was estimated at 2.2 million out of 9.9 million total for Guinea, and Kankan, the second largest city in Guinea, had about 100,000 inhabitants. Migration to Conakry from rural areas or middle-sized cities in Guinea overwhelmed the infrastructures that were unable to provide the city dwellers with a regular supply of water or electricity, and traffic became a huge problem despite new road construction. Contrasts in living standards increased, with both huge palace-like villas and growing shantytowns.

See also **Conakry; Ecosystems; Forestry; Livestock; Metals and Minerals; Production Strategies; Touré, Sékou.**

BIBLIOGRAPHY

Campbell, Bonnie K. *Les enjeux de la bauxite: La Guinée face aux multinationales de l'aluminium.* Montreal: Presses de l'Université de Montréal, 1983.

Goerg, Odile. *Commerce et colonisation en Guinée. 1850–1913.* Paris: L'Harmattan, 1986.

Lamp, Frederick. *La Guinée et ses héritages culturels.* Conakry, Guinea: U.S. Information Service, 1992.

Lamp, Frederick. *Art of the Baga: A Drama of Cultural Reinvention.* New York: Museum for African Art, 1996; Munich: Prestel, 1996.

Larrue, J. *Fria en Guinée.* Paris: Karthala, 1997.

Toole, Thomas E., and Janice E. Baker. *Historical Dictionary of Guinea.* Metuchen, NJ: Scarecrow Press, 2005.

ODILE GOERG

SOCIETY AND CULTURES

The Republic of Guinea can be considered in four environmental, linguistic, and cultural regions, the "Southern Rivers," "Futa Jallon," "Haute Guinée," and "Guinée Forestière." A mixture of precolonial and colonial designations, these regions represent a reality in present-day Guinea and have been influenced by their indigenous neighbors, Muslim traders and states, and European traders, missionaries, and colonizers.

Coastal Guinea, also called the Southern Rivers, is a swampy, salty area that historically has been isolated by its rivers, seasonal streams, mangrove swamps, torrential rains, mosquitoes, and deadly mosquito-borne diseases. The Nalu and the Baga are its indigenous inhabitants. But these broad ethnic groupings belie much more complicated linguistic identities. First, people who identify themselves ethnically as "Baga" speak seven separate languages: Mandori, Pukur, Sitem, Mbulungish, Kakissa, Koba, and Kalum. Second, although all of the languages are part of the Atlantic language group, some are related to each other only distantly. Pukur and Mbulungish languages are more closely related to Nalu than to any of the other "Baga" languages. Linguistic evidence shows that these three (Nalu, Mbulungish, and Mboteni) languages diverged on the coast, and their linguistic ancestors' occupation of the coastal region can be traced back several millennia. Mandori, Sitem, Kakissa, and Koba are more closely related to Landuma, spoken in Guinea's interior, and Temne, spoken to the south (in modern-day Sierra Leone). These speech communities' migrations from the interior to the coast contributed to the divergence of these languages.

Third, as is characteristic of many coastal Atlantic languages as far north as Senegal, Kalum and possibly Koba have already experienced "language death." Their very small and increasingly elderly populations—Pukur is spoken in just two small villages on a peninsula—exemplify the reality that all "Baga" languages are in danger of extinction in the next few generations, as Susu becomes the *lingua franca* of the coastal Guinea region.

The Susu migrated into the region in the seventeenth century. European traders' accounts recorded between the sixteenth and eighteenth centuries described Nalu and "Baga" as salt-producers and rice farmers who built earthen irrigation systems in their floodplain and mangrove fields to trap and channel fresh water for leaching salinity out of coastal soils. They also reported them as practioners of indigenous spiritual traditions who, in the absence of centralized political authority, were governed by the "Sacred Forest." In oral traditions collected by generations of historians and still retold in the twentieth century by elders who were the first generation to convert to Islam, the Nalu and the Baga construct a common identity, which defies their linguistic differences. They recount their ancestors originating in the Futa Jallon highlands to the east before the Fulbe, refusing to convert to Islam, and fleeing toward the coast. Most historians agree that this common identity has been constructed subsequently in opposition to the prestige and power of Islam and of the interior expansionist state of Futa Jallon.

The rivers that perforate Guinea's coast find their source in the high elevation of the Futa Jallon plateaus, hills, and canyons. Historians have characterized Futa Jallon as a transitional zone for groups migrating from Guinea's interior to the coast, as well as for commerce and Islamic conversion flowing across the Sahara desert into the Senegambia. Two primary ethnic groups have historically inhabited this region, the Jallonke and the Fulbe. Jallonke and Susu are dialects of the same language, a branch of the Mande language family spoken in a large area centered on the headwaters of the Niger River. Linguists estimate that Susu and Jallonke remain dialects of the same language. The out-migration of Susu speakers toward the coast was probably a strong contributing factor to them beginning to diverge. The Fulbe language, like Nalu, Mbulungish, Mboteni, and Sitem spoken on Guinea's coast, is part of the Atlantic language group. Unlike the endangered coastal languages, however, Fulbe boasts more than 1 million speakers, the size and number of its speech communities continuing to grow in Guinea and throughout West Africa.

The Fulbe language has flourished mirroring the expansion of the Fulbe ethnic group. Beginning in the mid-fifteenth century, the nomadic Fulbe pastoralists roamed across West Africa's savanna, a region inhospitable to tsetse flies and therefore hospitable to cattle. The rich grazing land in Futa Jallon attracted the initial waves of Fulbe pastoralists, who subsequently sold livestock and hides into Atlantic trade networks. In the seventeenth century, the trickle became a flood as an influx of Fulbe herders, including Muslim converts, from present-day Senegal and the Sahel stressed environmental resources and social relationships with non-Muslim Jallonke residents. Beginning in 1725, a revolution resulted in the establishment of Guinea's first Islamic state, Futa Jallon, and the absorption of the Jallonke into low-status lineages. The hierarchical nature of the Fulbe's new social order dominated by free Muslim men stands in sharp contrast to the acephalous societies of the coastal region.

East of Futa Jallon lies the grassy savanna of Haute Guinée at the headwaters of the Niger River, once part of the heartland of the ancient empire of Mali, founded in the thirteenth century, and comprehending most of the region's Mande-speaking populations. Trans-Sahara trade in gold gave the empire early contacts with North Africa and early exposure to Islam via Muslim traders, who transported the precious commodity across the sea of sand but never learned its source in the savanna. From the thirteenth to the fifteenth centuries, the Mali empire was the most powerful state in both the western African region, called "Sudan" by Muslim traders, and in the Senegambia. Mande linguistic and cultural influence continues to reverberate in the region. Mande languages are spoken in much of the territory where the precolonial empire formerly reigned supreme—in the modern nations of Mali, Senegal, Gambia, Guinea-Bissau, Guinea representing the core, and Mauritania, Burkina Faso, Sierra Leone, Liberia, and Côte d'Ivoire representing the periphery.

Malinké and Maninka are the Manding dialects spoken in twenty-first-century Guinea, where their speakers number approximately 2 million with more inhabiting Mali. Malinké and Maninka are distantly related to the Mande dialects Susu and Jallonke, spoken respectively in the Southern Rivers and Futa Jallon regions of Guinea. The Mande are heirs to a rich social organization. Like the Fulbe of Futa Jallon, core Mande cultures are hierarchical, historically dividing their population into two classes—the *nyamkalaw*, a class of professional artists of endogamous lineages that includes bards, blacksmiths, weavers, and leatherworkers, and the *horonw*, farmers and nobles. Transmitting oral historical information like the oral epic *Sunjata*, which preserves the Mande's recollection of the Mali Empire and one of its most revered kings, is the charge of the bards, or *griots*, the best-known category of Mande occupational specialists. Traveling east from Guinea's coast into the interior, precolonial Islamization and political centralization ends here.

Guineé Forestière resembles Guinea's coastal region in the abundant rainfall that characterizes this heavily forested region, which is inhabited primarily by Kisi speakers. Their speech communities extend into neighboring Sierra Leone and Liberia. The isolation of Kisi speakers in Guinea's forest resembles the isolation of Nalu, Mbulungish, Mboteni, and Sitem speech communities in Guinea's coast. All of the aforementioned languages belong to the Atlantic language group. And, all are in intense contact with Mande speech communities—Kisi speakers are completely surrounded by Lele, Kuranko, Malinké, Toma/Loma-, Bandi, Mende, and Kono speakers. Lele speakers are even located within the boundaries of traditional Kisi territory. However, despite this intensive contact, the Kisi language boasts more than 500,000 speakers, in robust contrast to the small and endangered Atlantic languages spoken on Guinea's coast.

Kola nuts, found in the forests of Guinea, Sierra Leone, and Liberia, were the principle commodity in both trans-Saharan and trans-Atlantic trade networks. Rice is the inhabitants' principle subsistence crop. In contrast to the floodplain and mangrove rice farming systems practiced in coastal Guinea, farmers in Guinea's rain forests cultivate rice by intercropping several crops within the same field, "slashing" and "burning" brush to add

---

République de Guinée (Republic of Guinea)

Population:	9,947,814 (2007 est.)
Area:	245,856 sq. km (94,925 sq. mi.)
Official language:	French
Languages:	French, Fulani, Malinké, Sousou
National currency:	Guinean franc
Principal religions:	Muslim 85%, Christian (Roman Catholic) 8%, traditional 7%
Capital:	Conakry (est. pop. 2,200,000 in 2005)
Other urban centers:	Kankan, Siguiri, Labé, Kindia
Average annual rainfall:	4,300 mm (170 in.) at the coast to 2,000 mm (80 in.) 200 km inland
Principal geographical features:	*Mountains:* Kakoulima Massif, Futa Jalon Massif, Mount Loura, Mount Nimba
	Rivers: Niger, Rio Nuñez, Cogon (Rio Componi), Rio Pongo, Mellacorée, Konkouré, Tominé, Fatala, Tinkisso, Bafing Rio Kapatchez
	Islands: Tombo, Los Islands
Economy:	*GDP per capita:* US$2,100 (2006)
Principal products and exports:	*Agricultural:* rice, coffee, pineapples, palm kernels, cassava (tapioca), bananas, sweet potatoes, cattle, sheep, goats, timber
	Manufacturing: aluminum, food and beverage processing, textiles, sugar refining
	Mining: bauxite, iron, diamonds, gold
Government:	Independence from France, 1958. Constitution approved 1990. President elected for 5-year term by universal suffrage. The legislature is the 114-member Assemble Nationale. President appoints Council of Ministers. In 2006 President Conte reorganized the government under 6 Ministers of State, each of whom oversees several of the ministries. For purposes of local government the country is divided into 4 geographical regions headed by a minister or governor, 33 administrative regions headed by appointed governors, and a popularly elected 40-member general council, 175 districts headed by district commandants, and local revolutionary authorities at the village level.
Heads of state since independence:	1958–1984: President Sékou Touré
	1984–1993: Colonel (later General) Lansana Conté, president and head of the Comité Militaire du Redressement National
	1993–: President Lansana Conté
Armed forces:	President is commander in chief. Voluntary enlistment with legal provision for draft in times of need.
	Army: 10,000
	Navy: 900
	Air force: 700
	Paramilitary: 9,600
Transportation:	*Rail:* 837 km (520 mi.)
	Waterways: 1,292 km (803 mi.), river transport by poled barge and canoe
	Ports: Conakry, Kamsar, Benty
	Roads: 44,349 km (27,557 mi.), 10% paved
Media:	Three monthly newspapers, several other periodicals, a trade union journal, and one official gazette. Publishing is done through the Government Printer service. Radiodiffusion Télévision de Guinée broadcasts in French, English, Arabic, Portuguese, and local dialects. There is a growing film industry.
Literacy and education:	*Adult literacy rate:* 44.2% (2006).
	Education is free, universal, and compulsory for 8 years, although enrollment is low. Postsecondary education provided by Université de Conakry, Université de Kankan, École Supérieure d'Administration, École Nationale des Arts et Métiers, Institut Polytechnique Gamal Abdul Nasser de Conakry.

---

nutrients to the soil. The forest region's indirect participation in the Muslim trans-Saharan trade networks did not, however, lead to Islamization. Like Guinea's coastal region, large-scale conversion of the indigenous inhabitants' did not occur until Guinea's first independent president sponsored violent Islamization campaigns in 1957.

See also **Ecosystems; Islam; Languages; Travel and Exploration.**

BIBLIOGRAPHY

Barry, Boubacar. *Senegambia and the Atlantic Slave Trade.* Cambridge, U.K.: Cambridge University Press, 1998.

Brooks, George E. *Landlords and Strangers: Ecology, Society, and Trade in Western Africa 1000–1630.* Boulder, CO: Westview, 1993.

Childs, George T. *A Grammar of Kisi: A Southern Atlantic Language.* Berlin: Mouton de Gruyter, 1995.

Conrad, David C., and Barbara E. Frank, eds. *Status and Identity in West Africa: "Nyamakalaw" of Mande.* Bloomington: Indiana University Press, 1995.

Fields-Black, Edda L. *Deep Roots: Rice Farmers in West Africa and the African Diaspora.* Bloomington: Indiana University Press, 2008.

Sarro-Maluquer, Ramon. "Baga Identity: Religious Movements and Political Transformation in the Republic of Guinea." Ph.D. diss. University College of London, 1999.

EDDA L. FIELDS-BLACK

HISTORY AND POLITICS

In such a diverse country, history can only be varied too, with human occupation dating back to several centuries BCE. Most of the political entities before the eighteenth century remained modest in size, with a few notable exceptions. According to archeological diggings, the capital city of the Mali empire, Niani, was situated on the upper Niger within the boundaries of present-day Guinea. Thus, from the thirteenth century, the eastern parts of what is now Guinea lay within the territory of a huge empire that was the heart of a commercial network of Mande-speaking Muslim traders. After the decline of Mali in the fifteenth century, the region broke into smaller states. The coastal region was also divided into many political units, some of them organized in a confederacy; the best known is the Dubreka kingdom that included the site of the future colonial and national capital city, Conakry.

At the beginning of the eighteenth century, a theocratic state in the Fuuta Jallon highlands in the north-central part of the country was founded as the result of a jihad led by Islamized Fulani and Tukulor (from the Senegal valley), allied with local Mande-speaking people who had converted to Islam. Most of the local people, mainly Jalonke, were enslaved. Later on, slaves were acquired through raids on neighboring regions or through trade with those who needed cattle or weapons. At the turn of the twentieth century, captives in Fuuta Jallon amounted to about 50 percent of the population. Settlements reflected the social distinction between the *runde*, which were farming hamlets occupied by slaves, and the *miside*, where the pastoralist Fulani masters lived. The social hierarchy distinguished free from slave and cultivators from pastoralists. Artisans who served the powerful Islamic aristocracy complemented this hierarchy. The Fuuta Jallon state conquered neighboring zones but also faced internal opposition and conflicts between the two branches of the ruling family.

Islam also became the dominant religion at an early stage in Kankan, a city—now in eastern Guinea—famous for its Qur'anic schools and Islamic scholars. In the 1880s, Dinguiraye, the city at the eastern base of the Fuuta Jallon plateau chosen by Umar Tal's son, Amadu Sheku, became another important Islamic center. At about the same time, Samori Touré founded another important state, and he later adopted the title of *almami*, or leader of the Muslim faithful. In the 1860s Samori began building a military regime in this eastern part of Guinea, an empire that reached its apogee in 1887–1888 at a time when the French became more involved in this region. The conflict between the Samori and the French powers lasted for about two decades; it was ended by a brutal French conquest that culminated in the arrest of Samori Touré in 1898 and his exile to France's central African colony of Gabon. The forest zone never contained large states. The terrain and the small size of local political units, allied in certain circumstances, allowed the people to resist both Samori Touré and the French.

COLONIZATION

The Europeans (first the Portuguese, then the British and French) had been on the coast since the fifteenth century. Some of the marine toponymy dates back to this period (Iles des Los, Rio Nunez, for example). During the slave trade era in the eighteenth century, British as well as French ships loaded their human cargo along the Guinean coast. The military rulers of the Fuuta Jallon state played an active role in supplying captives for this trade. Later, as the British attempted to suppress slaving, the tangled network of rivers on the coast harbored the illicit trade and was a boon to the slave traffic until the 1860s. Official French commitment to end this activity served as a pretext for their colonization of this region.

Guinea became a battlefield between France and Great Britain, both countries trying to secure access for their traders. The coastal region was then called the Southern Rivers by the French because it was south of their principal coastal station on Saint-Louis and Gorée islands (present-day Senegal), and the Northern Rivers by the British because it lay to the north of their colony at Freetown (Sierra Leone). The African leaders played one against the other, especially the *almamy* (political leader) of the Fuuta Jallon, who signed treaties with both French and British emissaries. This maneuver postponed French domination only for a while.

French military conquest in pursuit of Samori arbitrarily brought the four above-mentioned regions together into a single administrative unit. The resulting crescent-shaped form of Guinea derives from the successive conquests and political negotiations that led to the formation of the colony. As a result of this distinctive shape, some regions of Guinea are farther from the capital, Conakry, than they are from the principal cities of neighboring countries, such as Monrovia (Liberia) and Freetown. This strained geographical coherence has had grave consequences for national unity, especially because some national borders divide cultural and linguistic communities. It also has affected commerce. The colony earned its revenue through customs duties imposed at Conakry, through which the French attempted to require all trade to pass. Some potential revenue was—and still is—lost, as tea, coffee, and kola nuts from the forested interior were smuggled out of Guinea.

The local political organization, the type of French presence, and the economic and strategic importance accorded to each area determined the pace and the methods of colonial conquest. The French developed two different colonial policies. On the coast, the French presence grew only gradually and incrementally. In the northeast, colonization took the form of brutal and overwhelming conquest. The steadily increasing European presence followed the signing of treaties with local authorities and the needs of commerce. The French first insinuated themselves into the area with the creation of three military posts in 1865–1866 and then began the creation of administrative districts. This only nominal presence was emphasized in negotiations to secure recognition by other European powers. Control was made official (in the eyes of the Europeans) with the foundation of Conakry in 1880, which later became the capital of the colony. Although French military forces from present-day

Mali conquered eastern Guinea in pursuit of Samori Touré (in the 1880s–1890s), a brief military expedition ended negotiations with the theocratic state of Fuuta Jallon in 1896. The forest region was able to resist conquest longer because of the fragmented political power there. It remained under military control as late as 1911–1912.

The French attempted to derive maximum profit from this amalgamation of diverse regions and peoples. As elsewhere in the empire, the economy focused on cash crops for export. The colony of Guinea went through several economic cycles in this regard. A brief phase of peanut exports (1860s–1880s), a crop not suited to the coastal climate, was followed by wild (red) rubber in the 1880s. The latex came from central and upper Guinea and consequently required long, harsh portages by conscripted bearers and peasants. After 1906, rubber was carried to Conakry in part by rail. The export of rubber reached its height in 1909–1912, at 1,700 to 2,000 tons per year and accounted for 73 percent of exports by value between 1892 and 1913. Guinean rubber, highly prized in European markets in that period, was wiped out by sudden competition from Indonesian plantation rubber. After market shocks in 1907 and 1911, the market collapsed in 1913; production in 1914 was only 923 tons, still 28 percent of exports (by value) in that year. Although rubber became unprofitable, certain regions continued to export it for want of an alternative source of cash.

The rubber boom and bust was followed by a depression that lasted until the banana industry began to expand in lower Guinea in the 1930s. Colonial authorities encouraged banana plantations through preferential treatment in customs duties. The introduction of refrigerated ships in 1935 aided the growing industry. European planters dominated production, to the exclusion of African growers, through their control of capital and the support of the French administration, which gave them access to credit, land concessions, and aid in recruiting labor, which came mostly from the forest region. The banana industry also received financial aid from Crédit Agricole de Guinée, a banking institution aimed at helping European planters. Exports reached 114 tons in 1920, more than 20,000 in 1933, and 52,800 in 1938 (which was 81% by weight of all exports from French West Africa, and one-third of French consumption).

Exports peaked at 98,000 tons in 1955, after which a leaf disease damaged the banana industry. Although one crop usually dominated the export economy, other crops were exported, such as palm oil and palm kernels, and, after World War II, coffee and pineapples.

POST-WORLD WAR II POLITICS AND INDEPENDENCE

Political parties appeared in Guinea after 1945. Some were founded by Africans; others by colonial administrators who hoped to control the elections that began to loom throughout western Africa as decolonization gained momentum after World War II. The Guinean branch of the Pan-French West African (Afrique Française Occidentale) political alliance of nationalist politicians, the Rassemblement Démocratique Africain, was founded in 1947 and named the Parti Démocratique de Guinée (PDG) in 1950. It grew rapidly under the leadership of Sékou Touré, who became its secretary-general in 1952. The PDG was instrumental in Guinea's early independence. This independence was acquired in an overwhelming "no" vote (94.7%), rejecting Charles de Gaulle's (1890–1970) proposed French Community in the September 1958 referendum called, de Gaulle expected, to affirm the African colonies' continued close association with France.

After the break with France, the PDG became more radical, at least in its rhetoric. Deprived of support from the former colonial power, Touré established ties with the Eastern bloc nations. Poverty provoked opposition, and soon the regime became dictatorial in tone and intolerant of opposition. PDG used supposed and real external threats (such as that of Portuguese mercenaries of 1970) to increase its internal repression. Political opponents—or anyone accused of being so—were imprisoned in Camp Boiro in Conakry. The camp became infamous through its treatment of Diallo Telli, the first secretary-general of the Organization of African Unity and former Guinean representative to the United Nations, who died there in 1977. It is estimated that between ten- and thirty thousand people suffered repression between 1958 and 1984, the quarter century of Touré's regime.

Without moderating its strong Marxist vocabulary, Guinea signed economic agreements with a wide variety of partners, Western as well as Soviet, for the development of its one great asset: bauxite.

In 1969 the Kindia Office of Bauxite (Guinea) and the Soviet Union set up a joint venture. The Soviet Union financed investment in infrastructure and in return received an advantageous price for the bauxite that came from the mine. Mining began at Débélé in 1974, and in 1975, two million tons of bauxite were exported. Péchiney, with North American funds, had begun mining at Fria before independence. Because of the distance between the mine and the port at Conakry, it was decided to convert bauxite to alumina, an intermediate stage in the processing of aluminum, which is much lighter, at the mine. A railroad 90 miles long was built. The French maintained their investment in spite of Guinea's official political break with France and the government's adoption of virulent anti-imperialist rhetoric. In 1960, 185,000 tons of alumina were exported. In 1962, exports increased to 460,000 tons, and they rose to 700,000 tons in the 1980s.

An American-controlled international consortium, Compagnie des Bauxites de Boké, began mining at Boké Sangarédi in 1973. The company moved all exports through the port of Kamsar north of Conakry. By the first decade of the twenty-first century, exports of bauxite regularly exceeded 12,000,000 tons and, together with alumina, accounted for more than 60 percent of Guinea's exports by value. Gold accounted for another fifth. All mining products (including diamonds) amounted to nearly 90 percent of the total exports by value. Although the government attempted to fix bauxite prices, it was forced to follow the law of the marketplace. Profit in this market was derived from the conversion of bauxite to aluminum and not from the mining of bauxite. The profitable conversion of the ore to metal was never achieved in Guinea, in spite of early attempts to do so.

All other economic sectors (industry, commerce, and agriculture) were gradually subjected to state control and collectivization. These economic constraints, tied to political repression, led to the flight of one million Guineans (out of a population of five or six million in the mid-1980s) and failed to have any positive effect on production. In the 1970s, responding to political pressure, notably from women, some concessions were made. In particular, state monopolies in the commercial sector were relaxed. After a 1977 women's demonstration and its severe repression, private trade and enterprises were allowed again.

Following the death of Sékou Touré in 1984 during heart surgery at a clinic in the United States, the military seized power under the leadership of Lansana Conté (b. 1934) at the head of a Comité Militaire du Redressement National (Military Committee for National Redress). Along with the rest of the continent, Guinea began the laborious process of privatization and political reform. In 1986, the Guinean franc replaced the *syli* (which means elephant, the symbol of the PDG). The syli had been created in 1960 and rapidly lost value. It was nonconvertible and had no value in neighboring countries or in the franc zone. Following a referendum in December 1990, political parties were made legal and the military regime was turned into a civil one. In the 1992 elections, there were forty parties and forty-six in 1996. Elections brought confrontations in certain regions. In the first presidential election in December 1993, Conté was elected president of the Republic of Guinea. Two years later, legislative elections confirmed his party in power (the Parti de l'Unité et du Progrés), but many seats in the National Assembly were won by the opposition, especially Alpha Condé's Rassemblement du Peuple de Guinée, Mamadou Bâ's Union pour la Nouvelle République, and Siradou Diallo's Parti du Renouveau et du Progrès.

Lansana Conté was reelected in 1998 and again in 2003 (until 2010), thanks to a change in the constitution. The opposition, although united in the Front Républicain pour l'Alternance Démocratique (FRAD), cannot win the support of a population that faces harsh repression and censorship. The first general strikes since the colonial era, in 2006 and 2007, led by the trade unions and not by political parties, demonstrated the capacity for mobilization and action of a desperate population in want of profound changes. Political rivalries among the opposition, together with discourse that has no prospect for effecting immediate change, are worth little in view of the increasing difficulties of daily life and the unstable regional environment. Wars in Sierra Leone and Liberia in the 1990s have sent refugees fleeing into the forest area of Guinea, at one point as many as 650,000; most of them returned with the ebbing of the conflicts in 2003–2005.

Guinea remains a land of marked contrasts, with great mineral wealth and other assets. Beyond bauxite, diamonds, iron, and certain rare minerals, it has land suited to agriculture and a dynamic population. Nevertheless, it lies at the bottom of the United Nations' Index of Human Development, with a literacy rate of 30 percent, a poorly developed medical infrastructure, a high infant mortality rate, low wages, a lack of infrastructure, and a high rate of unemployment.

See also **Colonial Policies and Practices: French West and Equatorial Africa; Conakry; Freetown; Gorée; Liberia; Metals and Minerals; Sierra Leone; Touré, Samori; Touré, Sékou; 'Umar ibn Sa'id Tal (al-Hajj).**

BIBLIOGRAPHY

Beavogui, Facinet. *Les Toma (Guinée et Libéria) au temps des négriers et de la colonisation française.* Paris: L'Harmattan, 2001.

Goerg, Odile. *Commerce et colonisation en Guinée. 1850–1913.* Paris: L'Harmattan, 1986.

Goerg, Odile. *Pouvoir colonial, municipalités et espaces urbaines: Conakry-Freetown, des anées 1880 à 1914.* Paris: L'Harmattan, 1997.

Jeanjean, Maurice. *Sékou Touré: Un totalitarisme africain.* Paris: L'Harmattan, 2004.

Nelson, Harold D., et al. *Area Handbook for Guinea.* 3rd edition. Washington DC: United States Government Printing Office, 1976.

O'Toole, Thomas E., and Janice E. Baker. *Historical Dictionary of Guinea.* 4th edition. Lanham, MD: Scarecrow Press, 2005.

Schmidt, Elizabeth. *Mobilizing the Masses: Gender, Ethnicity, and Class in the Nationalist Movement in Guinea, 1939–1958.* Portsmouth, New Hampshire: Heinemann, 2005.

Suret-Canale, Jean. *La République de Guinée.* Paris: Éditions sociales, 1970.

ODILE GOERG

GUINEA-BISSAU

This entry includes the following articles:
GEOGRAPHY AND ECONOMY
SOCIETY AND CULTURES
HISTORY AND POLITICS

GEOGRAPHY AND ECONOMY

Guinea-Bissau is located in West Africa, wedged between Senegal to the north and Guinée to the east and south, with the Atlantic Ocean to the west. Lying between latitudes 12° 20´N and

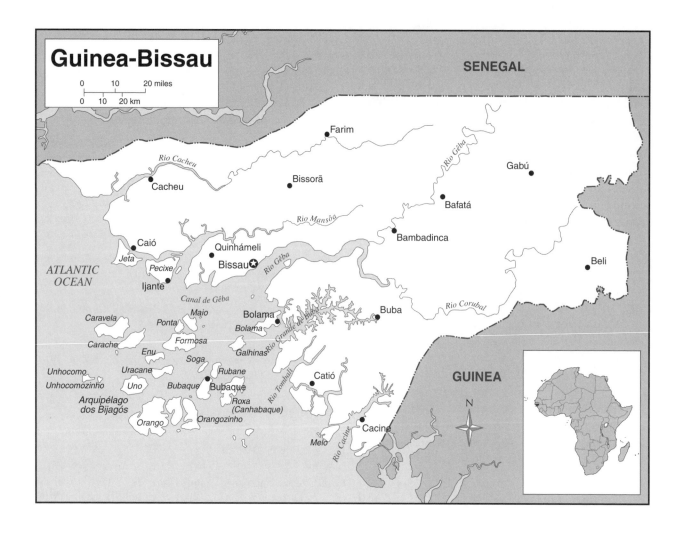

10° 56′N, it has a total surface area of 13,942 square miles, and encompasses a mainland, a string of adjacent islands (including Jeta, Pecixe, and Bolama), and an outlying archipelago of over eighty isles and islets. A great variety of ethnic groups form the population of about 1.5 million inhabitants, as estimated in 2007, the largest, according to 1991 figures, being the Fulas (25.4%), Balantas (23.7%), Mandinkas (13.7%), Manjacos (9.3%), and Pepels (9.0%). Two distinct geographical regions characterize the country: the littoral and the interior.

The littoral region comprises the flat coastal areas, the low-lying adjacent islands, and the equally level Bijagos Archipelago. Thick mangrove forests and palm trees characterize the flora. The major rivers include the Cacheu, Mansoa, Geba, Grande, Corubal, and Cacine. Another characteristic feature is a sunken coastline, known as *ria* (meaning estuary), caused by geological activity that enables ocean waters to flood the coastal areas with the most powerful tides on the West African coast. The tides penetrate inland for significant distances, depositing silt that nourishes verdant vegetation. The relatively abundant rains (June–October) that reach maximums of about 25 inches in the north during August and 40 inches in the south in July, cause erosion of the soil that the tides carry and deposit along the lower channels of rivers and streams.

The lush Bijagos Archipelago, formed from the submerged deltas of the Geba and Grande Rivers, covers an area of about 6,835 square miles and has approximately 27,500 inhabitants living on only twenty-one of the larger islands (including Orango, Canhabaque, Bubaque, Galinhas, Formosa, and Caravela). Characteristic mud flats and sand banks hinder navigation. The rich diversity of ecosystems includes mangrove swamps, palm trees, mixed forests, and savanna grasslands. Several freshwater rivers empty rich nutrients into the sea, which sustains a great variety of aquatic life including crustaceans, mollusks, fish, Nile crocodiles, and a rare species of hippopotamus—the only kind in the world that swim in the open sea. Together with the island of Bolama, the archipelago was designated a UNESCO Biosphere Reserve in 1996. The Biosphere Reserve contains two marine national parks—João Vieira and Poilão—that provide the most important nesting site on the eastern Atlantic for an endangered species of green sea turtles; and Orango, which contains the densest mangrove forests and provides vital habitat for aquatic animals, including some fifty different species of migratory sea birds that annually sojourn there, numbering around a million.

The interior region is a mixed landscape of savanna, forests, plateaus, and low hills. The highest elevation is about 1,000 feet, around the southeastern border area of Madina do Boé. The plateaus of Bafata and Gabu are minor elevations (rising less than 135 feet high) with numerous rivers that form tributaries of the River Geba. The weather is hotter and less humid, with less than half the rainfall of the littoral region. Deforestation, overgrazing, and soil erosion have decreased vegetation cover and the total area of arable land, but the fecundity of the various soils still allows the cultivation of a variety of crops for subsistence and commercial needs.

The economy of Guinea-Bissau is predominantly agricultural, with subsistence farming the major activity. The colonial economy was based on the export of peanuts and palm kernels, and there was surplus production of rice, the staple food. The immediate postindependence attempts at industrialization, beginning with small-scale enterprises including an automobile assembly plant, an oxyacetylene factory, and an agricultural complex to annually process 40,000 tons of peanuts and 23,000 tons of rice, were discontinued following the 1980 coup d'état. Deteriorating economic crises prompted the adoption of a World Bank/International Monetary Fund–funded economic stabilization program, followed four years later with the first structural adjustment package of free-market reforms. However, the restructuring of the economy, which involved drastic reductions of state expenditure on social services and the elimination of subsidies on food and fuel,

produced limited savings and high social costs. Before the destructive eleven-month military revolt in 1998–1999, the country was already among the world's ten poorest nations.

In the early twenty-first century, the major exports are cashew nuts and seafood, although significant deposits of bauxite, phosphate, and oil are known to exist. The maritime waters contain the second richest fishing ground in West Africa, but little benefit is derived from them due to uncontrolled illegal catches by foreign trawlers.

See also **Aid and Development; Climate; Ecosystems; Ethnicity; Forestry: Western Africa; International Monetary Fund; Production Strategies: Agriculture; World Bank.**

BIBLIOGRAPHY

Brooks, George. *Landlords and Strangers: Ecology, Society, and Trade in Western Africa, 1000–1630.* Boulder, CO: Westview Press, 1993.

Da Silva, Aristides. "Dimensão ecológica e socioeconómica das zonas húmidas da Guiné-Bissau." *Soronda Revista de Estudos Guineenses,* Nova Series 3 (2002): 51–76.

Gaillard, Gérald, ed. *Migrations anciennes et peuplement actuel des Côtes Guinéennes.* Paris: Harmattan, 2000.

Galli, Rosemary E. "On Peasant Productivity: The Case of Guinea-Bissau." *Development and Change* 18, no. 1 (1987): 69–98.

Galli, Rosemary E. *Guinea-Bissau: Politics, Economics and Society.* London: F. Pinter Publishers, 1987.

Rodney, Walter. *A History of the Upper Guinea Coast 1545 to 1800.* Oxford: Oxford University Press, 1970.

PETER KARIBE MENDY

SOCIETY AND CULTURES

Guinea-Bissau (or Guiné-Bissau) forms a rough triangle pointing into the forests of far western Africa from a span of 205 miles of the coast, between Senegal and the Republic of Guinea. Known in the seventeenth century as the Rivers of Guinea, both the mainland and the eighteen Bijagos (or Bissagos) islands of the modern country are divided by numerous coastal estuaries, which have been the main entry points of European traders, missionaries, and explorers throughout the recent history of the region. The capital city, Bissau, is located along a watercourse, as are many other major towns in the country.

The society and cultures of Guinea-Bissau are deeply influenced by this riverine-dominated ecology and its long colonial engagement with Portugal. For 93 miles inland, the estuaries exert a strong tidal influence over radical *bulom*, a distinctive ecosystem that consists of rich, alluvial plains, low-lying swampland, and mangroves, and the agro-ecological activities associated with estuarine environments, such as salt extraction and tidal agriculture. The impact of such an ecological environment on human settlements that have received little investment in development projects has meant the continued existence of a dispersed, predominantly rural population that is engaged largely in small-scale agriculture, fishing and forestry practices. Among the thirty-odd ethnic groups of Guinea-Bissau, the Balanta are the largest, but also the most dispersed. The Balanta, who constitute approximately 30 percent of the population, outnumber the Fulani (Fulbe; 20%), the Manjaco (14%), the Mandinka (13%), and the Papel (7%). With the exception of the Mandinka in the eastern savanna portions of the country, the majority of the other inhabitants speak Atlantic languages.

Portuguese traders first explored and established scattered settlements in Guinea-Bissau in 1446. From that period until the 1870s, the country was managed as a dependency of the Cape Verde Islands. *Mestiço* settlers from Cape Verde and their descendants controlled much of the region's trade, and in 1879, when Portugal declared what is present-day Guinea-Bissau its colony, Cape Verdeans constituted a substantial portion of the privileged assimilated population and of the colonial administrators who ran the country from the *praças*.

Colonial rule was most effectively challenged between 1961 and 1973, when Guinea-Bissau and Cape Verde waged together an eleven-year anticolonial people's war (1961–1973) under the leadership of African socialist theorist Amílcar Cabral. As a result, the former colony became in 1974 the first of the African Portuguese colonies to gain independence. This success, however, did not eliminate social and political tensions that had long existed between rural Guinea-Bissauans and the predominantly urban or *praça* dwelling Cape Verdeans and mixed *mestiço* populations. Thus, even though after independence in 1974 Guinea-Bissau and Cape Verde continued to be governed jointly, growing enmity toward Cape Verdean ascendancy and privilege culminated in 1980 in a coup, in which the former vice president, João Bernardo Vieira, popularly known as Nino, assumed power. Subsequently, Guinea-Bissau and Cape Verde suspended plans for unification, Guinea-Bissau's government became all African and many Cape Verdeans and their descendants fled. Mixed urban populations, however, continue into the early twenty-first century to enjoy a disproportionate share of public services and political affiliations are often divided along urban and rural lines.

In cultural and religious terms, Guinea-Bissau stands in contrast to the Francophone and predominantly Muslim populations of Senegal and Guinea. Just over one-third of the 1.5 million inhabitants of Guinea-Bissau are Muslim. Aside from a small but growing percentage of Christians, who are mostly Catholics and celebrate a pre-Lenten carnival, two-thirds of Guinea-Bissauans practice indigenous African religions. Certainly, there has been some assimilation of the coastal peoples to Islamic and Sahelian cultures through the thirteenth-century absorption of refugees from the desiccating Sahelian regions and the twelfth- to fourteenth-century incorporation of Gabu (Kaabu)—present-day Guinea's eastern Gabu district—as a tributary kingdom within the Mali Empire. However, Guinea-Bissau remains an enclave of indigenous religion in the Upper Guinea Coast of West Africa, attracting pilgrims from neighboring countries to its spirit shrines and oracles. Sacrifices and alcohol libations to ancestors and spirits, initiation societies, elaborate life cycle rituals to mark naming, age, grade transitions, circumcision, marriage, death, interrogation of corpses, and other forms of divination feature prominently in the coastal belief systems. Bijagos wild cow masks, wooden spirit figures, fine geometrically woven cloth, regalia of office, and traditional folk and polyrhythmic *gumbe* fusion music often accompany these festivities.

See also **Cabral, Amílcar Lopes; Colonial Policies and Practices; Forestry: Western Africa; Travel and Exploration.**

BIBLIOGRAPHY

Bigman, Laura. *History and Hunger in West Africa: Food Production and Entitlement in Guinea-Bissau and Cape Verde.* Westport, CT: Greenwood Press, 1993.

República da Guiné-Bissau (Republic of Guinea-Bissau)

Population:	1,472,780 (2007 est.)
Area:	36,110 sq. km (13,942 sq. mi.)
Official language:	Portuguese
Languages:	Portuguese, Creole, French, many indigenous languages
National currency:	CFA franc
Principal religions:	indigenous 67%, Muslim 33%, Christian
Capital:	Bissau (est. pop. 388,000 in 2004)
Other urban centers:	Bafatá, Bissorã, Bolama, Cacheu, Teixeira Pinto, Farim, Gabu, Mansôa
Annual rainfall:	635 mm (25 in.) in northeast to 1,016 mm (40 in.) along southern coast
Principal geographical features:	*Rivers:* Cacheu, Mansoa, Geba, Corubal (Rio Grande) *Inlets:* Rio Tombali, Rio Grande de Bolola, Rio Cacine *Islands:* Bijagos Archipelago
Economy:	*GDP per capita:* US$900 (2006)
Principal products and exports:	*Agricultural:* rice, corn, beans, cassava (tapioca), cashew nuts, peanuts, palm kernels, cotton, timber, fish *Manufacturing:* agricultural products processing, beer, soft drinks *Mining:* currently unexploited deposits of bauxite, phosphates, and oil
Government:	Independence from Portugal, 1974. Constitution approved in 1984, revised in 1991 and 1993. Multiparty democracy (single-party prior to 1991). President elected for 5-year term by universal suffrage. 100-member Assembleia Nacional Popular (National Popular Assembly) also directly elected. President appoints prime minister and Council of Ministers. First free elections held in 1994, followed by civil war in 1998, 3 years of control by opposition leaders, and a bloodless coup in 2003. For purposes of local government, there are 9 administrative regions.
Heads of state since independence:	1974–1980: President Luis Cabral 1980–1999: President João Bernardo Vieira 1999–2003: President Kumba Yala 2003–2005: President Henrique Rosa 2005–: President João Bernardo Vieria
Armed forces:	President of Council of State is commander in chief. Compulsory military service. *Army:* 6,800 *Navy:* 350 *Air force:* 100 *Paramilitary:* 2,000
Transportation:	*Waterways:* Extensive inland waterways *Port:* Bissau, Buba, Cacheu, Farim *Roads:* 3,455 km (2,147 mi.), 28% paved *National airline:* Transportes Aéreos da Guin-Bissau (TAGB) *Airports:* International airport in Bissau, 27 smaller airports and airstrips in the interior
Media:	Radio and newspapers are government-owned. Daily newspapers include *Nô Pintcha, Banguerra, Banobero, Expresso-Bissau.* Television, introduced in 1989, is provided in conjunction with the Portuguese Broadcasting System. The National Institute of Studies and Research publishes a journal of Guinean studies (*Soronda*).
Literacy and education:	*Total literacy rate:* 39.6% (2006). Education is free, universal, and compulsory for 4 years. Secondary education is available for teacher, nursing, and vocational training. There are no universities.

Callewaert, Inger, and Tord Olsson. *The Birth of Religion among the Balanta of Guinea-Bissau.* Stockholm, Sweden: Almquiest & Wiksell Intl., 2000.

Einarsdottir, Jonina. *Tired of Weeping: Mother Love, Child Death, and Poverty in Guinea-Bissau,* 2nd edition. Madison: University of Wisconsin Press, 2004.

Forrest, Joshua B. *Guinea-Bissau: Power, Conflict, and Renewal in a West African Nation.* Boulder, CO: Westview Press, 1992.

Galli, Rosemary E., and Jocelyn Jones. *Guinea-Bissau: Politics, Economics, and Society.* London: Frances Pinter, 1987.

Hawthorne, Walter. *Planting Rice and Harvesting Slaves: Transformations along the Guinea-Bissau Coast, 1400–1900.* Portsmouth, NH: Heinemann, 2003.

Lobban, Jr., Richard Andrew, and Peter Karibe Mendy. *Historical Dictionary of the Republic of Guinea-Bissau,* 3rd edition. Lanham, MD: Scarecrow Press, 1997.

Mota, Avelino Teixeira da. *Guineé Portuguesa.* 2 vols. Lisbon, Portugal: Agência Geral do Ultramar, 1954.

EVE L. CROWLEY

HISTORY AND POLITICS

Among the earliest settlers of the Guinea-Bissau savanna were the Diola/Felupe, Pepel/Manjaco/ Mancanha, Balanta, Biafada, Nalu, and Bijago ethnic groups, who belong to the West Atlantic subgroup of African languages. With the thirteenth-century establishment and expansion of the great Mali Empire founded by the legendary Sundiata Keita, the Guinea-Bissau interior came under the rule of Mande-speaking conquerors, which precipitated further emigration of the early settlers to the uninhabited littoral region. The established Mandinka-dominated kingdom of Kaabu, a vassal state of Mali, had its capital in eastern Guinea-Bissau at Kansala. Its political influence extended to the Casamance region of southern Senegal, The Gambia, and neighboring Guinea (Conakry). In 1867, the Fulas—pastoralists who had also settled in the territory from the fourteenth century—finally destroyed Kaabu.

PORTUGUESE PRESENCE AND COLONIAL RULE

The Portuguese were the first Europeans to reach the territory of Guinea-Bissau (*Guiné*), arriving in 1446 with the landing of Alvaro Fernandes at Varela on the northwest coast. The Portuguese Crown claimed exclusive rights over Guiné and other lands of discovery in West Africa, as reflected in the grandiose title of *Senhor da Guiné* (Lord of Guinea) that the monarchs in Lisbon assumed. For centuries, however, their claim was belied by Portugal's influence over only a few fortified coastal trading posts, principally in Cacheu and Bissau. These settlements were largely secured by Cape Verdean traders called *lançados*, although *daxas* (from Portuguese word *taxas*, meaning rates, or taxes) continued to be paid to local rulers until military conquest by Portugal in the early twentieth century.

The colonial period was brief and harsh. The fascist regime established in Portugal during the early 1930s meant iron-fisted colonial rule, characterized by liberal use of violence, forced labor, and a racist mindset that divided the population into civilized and uncivilized. Yet the civilizing mission of the Portuguese was a dismal failure, as evident in the almost total lack of vital infrastructure. At the end of the colonial period, the Portuguese had built only one high school, educated only fourteen university graduates, and left a 99 percent illiteracy rate—the highest among Portugal's African colonies.

Independence movements were formed during the 1950s, the most effective being the African Party for the Independence of Guinea and Cape Verde, *Partido Africano da Independência da Guiné e Cabo Verde* (PAIGC), founded and led by Amilcar Cabral until his assassination on January 20, 1973. Reacting to the massacre of some fifty striking dockworkers in Bissau on August 3, 1959, the PAIGC abandoned its strategy of peaceful negotiation and engaged in an armed liberation struggle. The war of independence (1962–1974) culminated in the declaration of the Republic of Guinea-Bissau on September 24, 1973, and contributed significantly to the downfall of the dictatorship in Lisbon (April 25, 1974) through a coup d'etat led by disaffected young officers of a war-fatigued Portuguese army—thereby hastening the end of Portuguese colonialism in Africa.

POSTINDEPENDENCE DEVELOPMENTS

After the independence of Cape Verde in 1975, Guinea-Bissau and the neighboring island nation were both ruled by the PAIGC until the military coup of November 14, 1980, led by veteran guerrilla commander and Prime Minister João Bernardo Vieira. The coup toppled civilian president Luis Cabral (b. 1931), brother of Amilcar, and ended the planned unification of the two countries. The military would thenceforth assume a role of great importance in politics.

Political factionalism and power struggles came to characterize the postindependence period. Under the first regime of President Vieira (1980–1998), the accumulating political tensions reached several boiling points and resulted in severe repressions, including summary executions. Notwithstanding the introduction of multiparty politics in the early 1990s, factional struggles continued and culminated in the military revolt of June 7, 1998. The implosion that plunged the country into eleven months of devastating civil war was ignited by the attempted arrest of former Armed Forces Chief of Staff Brigadier Ansumane Mane (1940–2000), dismissed for alleged arms trafficking to separatists in Casamance (Senegal). The conflict between Mane's military rebellion and Vieira's loyalist soldiers quickly became regionalized. Neighboring Senegal and Guinea promptly sent troops to support the beleaguered president, while the Casamance separatists rallied to help the rebellious Guinean army. Several West African countries, beginning with The Gambia, attempted to mediate peace, but to no avail.

After several unsuccessful attempts at reconciliation, Vieira and Mane signed the Abuja Peace Accords on November 1, 1998, brokered by the Economic Community of West African States and the Community of Portuguese-Speaking Countries. The accords called for the withdrawal of the foreign troops, the deployment of an international peace-keeping force, and the formation of a government of national unity. Although these requirements were fulfilled, peace did not prevail. The war continued until May 7, 1999, when forces loyal to the president surrendered and Vieira took refuge in the Portuguese Embassy where he was granted political asylum in Portugal. The president of the National Assembly, Malam Bacai Sanha (b. 1947), became interim head of state.

In November 1999, presidential and legislative elections resulted in the defeat of the PAIGC and the election of the populist Social Renovation Party (PRS) leader Kumba Yala (b. 1953) as president. Yala quickly revealed autocratic tendencies. Among other arbitrary measures, he unconstitutionally dissolved the National Assembly, ordered detentions without trial of Supreme Court judges, political opponents, and journalists, and postponed several scheduled elections. On November 30, 2000, soldiers loyal to Yala killed General Ansumane Mane, allegedly for attempting a coup. Yala also refused to promulgate or veto the revised constitution passed by the National Assembly in April 2001. The growing crisis culminated in yet another military takeover, this time led by Armed Forces Chief of Staff General Verissimo Correia Seabra (1947–2004) on September 14, 2003. Seabra's forces toppled Yala and established a military-dominated Committee for the Restoration of Democracy and Constitutional Order. This committee nominated businessman Henrique Rosa (b. 1946) as interim president and named controversial PRS leader Artur Sanha (b. 1965) as prime minister. Sanha, as PRS secretary general and minister of Internal Administration, had been implicated in the mysterious death of a twenty-five-year-old woman who was seven months pregnant and allegedly his mistress.

Legislative elections of March 2004 returned the PAIGC to power, with its president, Carlos Gomes Junior (b. 1949), as prime minister. On October 6, 2004, General Verissimo Correia Seabra was assassinated, yet another victim of factionalism. In the July 2005 presidential election, exiled ex-President Vieira (b. 1939) won the runoff poll over the PAIGC candidate Malam Bacai Sanha. Bacai Sanha strongly complained about electoral fraud and, together with Prime Minister Carlos Gomes Junior, refused to recognize the outcome. Inaugurated on October 1, 2005, President Vieira quickly dismissed the prime minister and replaced him with Aristides Gomes (b. 1954), the suspended first vice president of the PAIGC.

Guinea-Bissau's transition to sustainable peace, democracy, and development remains particularly challenged by the important role of the military in politics and the lack of visionary leadership.

See also **Cabral, Amílcar Lopes; Colonial Policies and Practices; Literacy; Warfare: Civil Wars.**

BIBLIOGRAPHY

Brooks, George. *Landlords and Strangers: Ecology, Society, and Trade in Western Africa, 1000–1630.* Boulder, CO: Westview Press, 1993.

Chabal, Patrick. *Amilcar Cabral: Revolutionary Leadership and People's War.* Cambridge, U.K.: Cambridge University Press, 1983.

Forrest, Joshua. *Lineages of State Fragility: Rural Civil Society in Guinea-Bissau.* Athens: Ohio University Press, 2003.

Koudawo, Fafali, and Peter K. Mendy, eds. *Pluralisme Politique en Guinée-Bissau: une transition en cours.* Bissau, Guiné-Bissau: Instituto Nacional de Estudos e Pesquisa, 1996.

Lobban, Richard A., and Peter K. Mendy. *Historical Dictionary of the Republic of Guinea-Bissau,* 3rd edition. Lanham, MD: The Scarecrow Press, 1994.

Lopes, Carlos. *From Liberation Struggle to Independent Statehood.* London: Zed Books, 1987.

Mendy, Peter K. "Portugal's Civilizing Mission in Colonial Guinea-Bissau: Rhetoric and Reality." *The International Journal of African Historical Studies* 36, no. 1 (2003): 35–58.

Pélissier, René. *Naissance de la Guiné: Portugais et Africains en Senegambie, 1841–1936.* Orgeval, France: Pélissier, 1989.

Rodney, Walter. *A History of the Upper Guinea Coast 1545 to 1800.* Oxford: Oxford University Press, 1970.

Rudebeck, Lars. *Guinea-Bissau: A Study of Political Mobilization.* Uppsala, Sweden: Scandinavian Institute of African Studies, 1974.

Rudebeck, Lars. *On Democracy's Sustainability: Transition in Guinea-Bissau.* Gothenburg, Sweden: SidaStudies, 2001.

PETER KARIBE MENDY

GUNGUNYANA

GUNGUNYANA (c. 1850–1906). Gungunyana was the son of the uMzila, ruler of Gaza in the highlands of southeastern Africa until 1884. That year, he entered into the battle for succession. In 1885 he won the throne as well as many enemies who had wanted the kingship. His defeated rivals took refuge in neighboring countries and remained a threat throughout his reign: In combination with British and Portuguese colonial powers encroaching on Gaza territory, they fomented the struggles of Gungunyana's political life and continually made it difficult for him to hold his regime together. Though successful in repressing internal rebellions, Gungunyana recognized the threats surrounding him and responded by moving the seat of his government in 1889 from the Manica highlands to the mouth of the Limpopo River in the south of present-day Mozambique. With him, he brought some 60,000 people. The relocation proved unsettling: Not only was Gaza's social life destabilized, but so was the economy, which crumbled under added strain after years of warfare.

The Portuguese responded to Gaza's vulnerability by exploiting it. Gungunyana sent representatives to Lisbon in 1885, where they signed documents that recognized Portuguese sovereignty in Gaza. The Portuguese, however, were unable to enforce their rule. Gungunyana, hoping to escape them, hosted an emissary of Cecil Rhodes's British South Africa Company, believing that he was an envoy of the British government. It seemed that Gungunyana was about to enter into a treaty granting the company mining concessions in his territory when, in 1891, Britain and Portugal entered into an agreement that ended their competition in the region as colonial powers. Mozambique was placed under Portuguese influence, and a new campaign was begun to dethrone Gungunyana. Imperialist forces were assisted by Africans opposed to Gungunyana, and he thus stood little chance. In 1895, Gungunyana's army was defeated in battle at Coolela, near his capital of Mandlakaze, and he surrendered. Gungunana was captured, dethroned, and deported to the Azores, where he died.

See also **Mozambique: History and Politics.**

BIBLIOGRAPHY

Bennett, Norman Robert, ed. *Leadership in Eastern Africa: Six Political Biographies.* Brookline, MA: Boston University Press, 1968.

Bennett, Norman Robert. *Zanzibar, Portugal, and Mozambique: Relations from the Late Eighteenth Century to 1890.* Boston: African Studies Center, Boston University, 1987.

Borges de Castro, Eduardo. *Gungunyana.* Lisbon, 1896.

Hedges, David William. "Trade and Politics in Southern Mozambique and Zululand in the Eighteenth and Early Nineteenth Centuries." Ph.D. diss. University of London, 1978.

SARAH VALDEZ

HAILE SELASSIE I (1892–1975). Haile Selassie was emperor of Ethiopia from 1930 to 1974. Born Lij Tafari Makonnen, Haile Selassie came to power in 1916 as regent for Empress Zawditu (r. 1916–1930). To obtain collective security, he engineered Ethiopia's entry into the League of Nations on September 28, 1923, and then undertook development. His success at nation building and his insistence that Ethiopians run their own economy frustrated Italy's imperial ambitions. On December 5–7, 1934, Italy created a crisis at Welwel and then acted as if Ethiopia had been the aggressor. Haile Selassie's trust in collective security was betrayed on October 2, 1935, when Italy attacked Ethiopia. Italy was victorious, and Haile Selassie went into exile on May 2, 1936, remaining abroad until 1940, when Italy joined the Axis side in World War II.

The emperor returned to Addis Ababa in May 1941, after a successful Anglo-Ethiopian operation. Haile Selassie quickly built a relationship with the United States, which provided military and technical assistance and helped to establish the federation of Eritrea to Ethiopia. During the 1950s, Ethiopia's coffee-based economy prospered and permitted the emperor to modernize government. On November 3, 1955, he promulgated a revised constitution, which made the government responsible to the people, although the emperor remained paramount. Some educated officials saw the imperial role as reactionary and mounted an abortive coup on December 14, 1960. The emperor ignored the significance of this attempted coup and reverted to the political status quo ante. As a result he lost the support

Haile Selassie I (1892–1975). The late emperor of Ethiopia is shown in Addis Ababa a few months before he was deposed by a group of army officers seeking an end to oppression and poverty. The coup imprisoned Selassie and eventually murdered him in 1975. STAFF/AFP/ GETTY IMAGES

517

of progressives and students, especially as Eritrea rebelled over the issues of autonomy and cultural discrimination.

By 1973 Haile Selassie was too old to cope with the Eritrean crisis and the inflation brought on by high oil prices. After January 1974, virtually all organized bodies, including the military, demonstrated for higher wages and against the country's economic and social ills, especially the drought and famine in the north. A military leadership, the *derg*, under the chairmanship of Major Mengistu Haile Mariam, gradually took over. The emperor listened to his soldiers' repeated statements of loyalty as they dismantled the monarchy's institutions and arrested his leading supporters. He was deposed on September 12, 1974, and died in Addis Ababa, while under house arrest, on August 27, 1975.

See also **Ethiopia, Modern: History and Politics; Mengistu, Haile Mariam.**

BIBLIOGRAPHY

Getachew, Indrias. *Beyond the Throne: The Enduring Legacy of Emperor Haile Selassie.* Addis Ababa, Ethiopia: Shama Books, 2001.

Marcus, Harold G. *Haile Selassie I: The Formative Years, 1892–1936.* Berkeley: University of California Press, 1987.

HAROLD G. MARCUS

HAJJ. *See* **Pilgrimages, Islamic.**

HAJJ ʿUMAR, AL-. *See* **ʿUmar ibn Saʿid Tal (al-Hajj).**

HAMALLAH OF NIORO (1883–1943). Hamallah of Nioro was a prominent and highly controversial leader of the Tijani Sufi order in western Africa. Born in Nioro (present-day Mali), Hamallah gained a reputation as a pious Muslim ascetic during the first two decades of the twentieth century. In the early 1920s, serious opposition to his leadership in the large sufi Tijaniyya brotherhood emerged in response to the claim that he had

been appointed in Algeria as *khalifa*, or supreme leader, of all Tijanis in western Africa. The challenge to Hamallah was led by the existing Tijani leadership, predominantly the descendants of al-Hajj ʿUmar Tal, nineteenth-century jihadist and proselytizer of the Tijaniyya in the region. The conflict was ritually symbolized by a relatively minor difference in the recitation of the Tijani liturgy of devotional prayers: the Umarians, along with the vast majority of Tijanis everywhere, recited the *jawharat al-kamal* prayer twelve times, whereas Hamallah and his followers recited it eleven times. The underlying political conflicts, however, were very real. Many Umarians saw Hamallah as a threat to their influence and managed to convince the French colonial administration that he opposed their authority. Hamallah, in a sense, played into his enemies' hands by refusing openly to cooperate with the French in any way, thus becoming a rallying point for much political dissent in the region. Blamed for the disruptive and sometimes violent actions of some of his followers, Hamallah was exiled from Nioro in 1925 for ten years; he was again exiled in the early 1940s to France, where he died.

See also **Tijani, Ahmad.**

BIBLIOGRAPHY

Bâ, Amadou Hampaté. *Histoire du Sahel occidental malien: des origines à nos jours.* Bamako, Mali: Editions Jamana, 1989.

Brenner, Louis. *West African Sufi: The Religious Heritage and Spiritual Search of Cerno Bokar Saalif Taal.* Berkeley: University of California Press, 1984.

Dicko, Seïdina Oumar, and Doulaye Konate. *Hamallah:le protégé de Dieu.* Bamako, Mali: Editions Jamana, 1999.

Launay Robert, and B. F. Soares. "The Formation of an 'Islamic Sphere' in French Colonial West Africa." *Economy and Society* 28 (4) (1999): 497–519.

Traoré Alioune. *Islam et colonisation en Afrique: Cheikh Hamahoullah, homme de foi et résistant.* Paris: Maisonneuve et Larose, 1983.

LOUIS BRENNER

HAMPÂTÉ BÂ, AMADOU (1901–1991). Amadou Hampâté Bâ was born in Bandiagara, Mali. He died in Abidjan, Côte d'Ivoire. Bâ came from a distinguished Fulani family and devoted his life to the study and transcribing of the oral traditions of the Fulani and the Bambara. Brought up under French colonial rule, he received a French education. Spiritually, he followed the teaching of Tierno Bokar (1875–1939), a well-known Sufi master. In 1942 he was appointed to the French Institute of Black Africa (Institut Francais de l'Afrique Noire or IFAN) founded by Theodore Monod (1902–2000). It was the perfect position for Bâ, who was able to pursue his passion for the African oral traditions. In 1951 Monod got him a United Nations Educational, Scientific and Cultural Organization (UNESCO) scholarship, which enabled him to spend a year in Paris where he met the great African scholars Marcel Griaule (1898–1956) and Germaine Dieterlen (1903–1999). In 1958 he founded the Institut des Sciences Humaines (Institute of Research in Human Sciences) at Bamako. Two years later he was appointed ambassador to UNESCO, where he pronounced one of his most famous statements: "In Africa the death of an old man is tantamount to the burning of a library."

Bâ was a major contributor to the recognition of African cultures and the importance of the oral traditions. He felt the urgency to preserve in writing the history, folktales, and cosmogony of his people, the Fulani. Among his works to that purpose are *L'empire Peul du Macina* (1955); *Koumen* (1961) with Dieterlen, an anthology of Fulani initiatory tales; and *Kaidara* (1969). In 1973, Bâ published his only novel, *L'etrange destin de Wangrin* (1973), translated as *The Fortunes of Wangrin* (1999). For this remarkable work of fiction he received the *Grand prix littéraire d'Afrique noire*. Finally, two autobiographical books were published posthumously: *Amkoullel, l'enfant Peul* (1991; Amkoullel, the Fulani child) and *Oui, mon commandant!* (1994; Yes, commander).

See also **Colonial Policies and Practices.**

BIBLIOGRAPHY

Adejunmobi, Moradewun. "Disruption of Orality in the Writings of Hampate Ba." *Research in African Literatures* 31, no. 3 (2000): 27–36.

Moura, Jean-Marc. "Textual Ownership in *L'étrange destin de Wangrin* (*The Fortunes of Wangrin*) by Amadou Hampate Ba." *Research in African Literatures* 37, no. 1 (2006): 91–99.

SONIA LEE

HARAR. The capital of Hararege province, in southeastern Ethiopia, the city of Harar is situated on a hilltop near the railroad that links the Ethiopian national capital, Addis Ababa, to its only access to the sea, at Djibouti. Although in the twenty-first century an integral part of the larger Ethiopian state, for most of its history Harar was the capital of an independent kingdom that bore the same name.

Muslim Arabs founded Harar as an inland terminus of the caravan route from the Indian Ocean as early as the seventh century, but certainly no later than the eleventh. By the twelfth century it had emerged as an important center of Islamic culture and learning. Its location, on the edge of the Ethiopian highlands, a major source of gold and slaves, encouraged its growth into a significant commercial center, which it remained until the nineteenth century.

In 1520, a strong Muslim warlord, Ahmad Gran, established an Islamic state in the Ethiopian highlands, and chose Harar as his capital. In 1577, however, the new state was conquered by Oromo invaders, cattle-raising pastoralists from the south. Although the state was destroyed, the city retained its independence, and Gran's successor ordered the great protective walls now encircling the old city to be built in the 1600s. From then until 1887, entrance to the city was forbidden to non-Muslims, although the renowned British explorer, Sir Richard Burton, succeeded in entering the city by a subterfuge in 1854, and the poet Arthur Rimbaud lived there from 1880 until his death in 1891. Harar was conquered by Egypt in 1875, but regained its independence ten years later. In 1887, Ethiopia's Christian king, Menilek II, incorporated the city into his empire and ended its centuries-long exclusion of non-Muslims. Ras Makonnen was appointed governor of the province, and his son, the future emperor Haile Selassie I, became governor in 1910.

Italy invaded Ethiopia in 1936, and Harar was occupied until March 1941. At that time, the first construction outside the city walls was begun. Since then, the city has expanded, and in 2006 newer construction surrounds the old city. In 2004 the city's population was estimated to be just under 100,000. The population includes local Harari (Adari) as well as Christian Amhara, Oromo (Galla), and Somali Muslims.

See also **Addis Ababa; Christianity; Colonialism and Imperialism; Ethiopia and the Horn, History of (1600 to 1910); Haile Selassie I; Islam; Menelik II; World War II.**

BIBLIOGRAPHY

Burton, Richard Francis. *First Footsteps in East Africa of an Exploration of Harar (1854–1855)* [1856]. New York: Dover, 1987.

Gibb, Camilla. "In the City of Saints: Religion, Politics, and Gender in Harar, Ethiopia." Ph.D. diss. University of Oxford, 1996.

Hecht Elisabeth-Dorothea. "City of Harar and the Traditional Harar House." *Journal of Ethiopian Studies* 15 (1982): 57–78.

Steinmetz, Jean-Luc. *Arthur Rimbaud: Presence of an Enigma.* Translated by Jon Graham. New York: Welcome Rain Publishers, 2001.

ALEXANDER GOLDMAN

a city of dusty African townships, spacious and leafy white suburbs, and a multistory downtown, even boasting a university. Urban anticolonial riots in the early 1960s presaged a bitter war waged mainly in the rural areas by nationalist guerrillas. The war ended in 1979, leading to majority elections in 1980. Salisbury was renamed Harare in 1982, and in 2000 its population was approximately 1,500,000.

See also **Zimbabwe.**

BIBLIOGRAPHY

Phimister, Ian. *Economic and Social History of Zimbabwe, 1890–1948: Capital Accumulation and Class Struggle.* London: Longman, 1987.

Yoshikuni, Tsuneo. *African Urban Experiences in Colonial Zimbabwe: A Social History of Harare before 1925.* Harare, Zimbabwe: Weaver Press, 2007.

TERESA BARNES

HARARE. Harare, the capital of Zimbabwe, was founded in 1890 by South African mercenaries with British imperial inspirations. Considered by the indigenous Shona people to be in the land use area of a local chief named Harare, land was peremptorily seized without compensation and the new settlement named Salisbury by the new settlers just as they named their new nation Rhodesia. Seeking a second Rand similar to the gold-laden Witwatersrand in South Africa, the settlers discovered that local gold deposits were scattered and already well worked.

After the defeat of anticolonial African fighters in 1896–1897, Salisbury became a small mining and farming supply town. Always legally segregated, it took on the familiar regional pattern of some early racial mixing, but with vociferous segregationist pressures from white residents by the 1920s. African workers and families lived in service-poor areas called "locations" or townships, characterized by a vibrant associational and political life. Salisbury grew impressively with the advent of large-scale immigration from Britain and local industrialization following World War II: Agricultural processing plants for tobacco and foodstuffs and textile factories were joined by iron and steel production, vehicle assembly, and paper products manufacture. By the 1950s Salisbury had become

HARRIS, WILLIAM WADÉ (1865–1929). A Liberian of Grebo origin, William Harris was a teacher-catechist in the American Episcopalian mission. The Harrist Church, which he founded, was a totally indigenous effort among a population not previously Christianized by missionaries.

Harris led several acts of rebellion against American involvement in the governance of Liberia, for which he was ultimately imprisoned on charges of treason. While still in prison, he claimed to have had a vision of the Archangel Gabriel, who directed him to preach the Christian message. After his release in 1913, Harris went to Côte d'Ivoire, where his message was well received. In a single year he baptized between 100,000 and 120,000 people, enjoying vastly greater success in converting the local peoples than the French Catholic missionaries had experienced in their twenty years in the region. Harris's success may have been due in part to the fact that he spoke very little French and therefore had to preach in indigenous languages. Harris was deported to Liberia in 1914, but his followers remained loyal to his preachings, even in the face of pressure from the Catholic missions.

The Harrist movement also appealed to the indigenous peoples of Côte d'Ivoire and, later, the Gold Coast (Ghana) by emphasizing visionary interpretations of the Bible and the leader's charisma.

Even after his death in 1929, the movement continued to grow. Several offshoots sprang up as well. Among them are Marie Lalou's Deima movement and the Églises Harristes, both in Côte d'Ivoire; the Church of the Twelve Apostles in Ghana; and other more syncretist groups. In 1973 the Harrist Church celebrated its sixtieth anniversary in Côte d'Ivoire with governmental support and recognition. Like the Kimbanquists of Zaire, the Harrists have proceeded from a prophetic movement to an official church with national appeal.

See also **Christianity: Africa and World Christianity; Kimbangu, Simon.**

BIBLIOGRAPHY

Ahui, Paul-William. *Prophete William Wade Harris: Son message d'humilite et de progress.* Abidjan: Les Nouvelles Editions Africaines, 1988.

Haliburton, Gordon Mackay. *The Prophet Harris: A Study of an African Prophet and His Mass-Movement in the Ivory Coast and the Gold Coast, 1913–1915.* New York: Oxford University Press, 1973.

Shank, David A. *Prophet Harris, the "Black Elijah" of West Africa.* Abridged by Jocelyn Murray. Leiden; New York: Brill, 1994.

Walker, Sheila S. *The Religious Revolution in the Ivory Coast: The Prophet Harris and the Harrist Church.* Chapel Hill: University of North Carolina Press, 1983.

S. ADEMOLA AJAYI

HASAN, MUHAMMAD 'ABDALLAH

(1856–1920). Muhammad 'Abdallah Hasan, known by the Islamic honorific as the Sayyid, was born on the eve of the European "scramble" for possession of the Somali coast. Having joined the reformist Salihiyya Muslim brotherhood while on pilgrimage in Mecca, he returned to Somaliland to organize a following of Daraawiish ("dervishes"), who waged war against the British and their local allies (1899–1920). He weathered four British military expeditions sent against him (1901–1904) as well as the denunciation of his leadership by the Salihiyya's founder, which seriously divided the Sayyid's movement. British withdrawal from the interior (1909–1910) created bloody chaos and a political vacuum that allowed the Sayyid to fulfill some of his state-building ambitions. As a successful war leader

enriching his followers with livestock, as a religious leader drawing in followers from all the clans into which the Somali grouped themselves, and as a gifted poet, the Sayyid drew on traditional Somali sources of legitimacy. But he was a modernizer, too. He built forts surrounded by cultivated fields. He sent and received caravans and had a small merchant navy supplying him with guns. He created a standing army, centralized the judiciary, and conducted international diplomacy. This institutionalization of power, however, made him more vulnerable. In 1920 British aerial bombardments of his forts destroyed the dervish movement; the Sayyid died later that year, probably of influenza.

Somalis remember Muhammad 'Abdallah Hasan as the instigator of bloody interclan warfare, the defender of their cultural and religious authenticity, and the proto-nationalist hero of their anticolonial resistance. His powerful poetic legacy shows that he was all of this and more. In his farewell poem he wrote, "If I failed to have a flag flown for me from here to Nairobi, did I fail to win honor in paradise … ?"

See also **Colonial Policies and Practices; Colonialism and Imperialism; Islam; Somalia: History and Politics.**

BIBLIOGRAPHY

Caroselli, Francesco S. *Ferro e fuoco in Somalia.* Rome: Sindacato italiano Arti grafiche, 1931.

Jardine, Douglas. *The Mad Mullah of Somaliland.* London: H. Jenkins, 1923.

Martin, Bradford G. *Muslim Brotherhoods in Nineteenth Century Africa.* Cambridge, U.K.: Cambridge University Press, 1976.

Samatar, Said S. *Oral Poetry and Somali Nationalism: The Case of Sayyid Mahammad 'Abdille Hasan.* New York: Cambridge University Press, 1982.

Sheik-'Abdi. *Divine Madness: Mohammed 'Abdulle Hassan, 1856–1920.* Atlantic Highlands, NJ: Zed Books, 1992.

LIDWIEN KAPTEIJNS

HASAN II OF MOROCCO (1929–
1999). Hasan II, king of Morocco (r. 1961–1999), was the thirteenth sovereign in the 'Alawi dynasty that has ruled Morocco from 1666 until the present. The eldest son of Sultan Muhammad V (r. 1927–1961), Hasan was educated at the

Collège Royal in Rabat and later obtained a law degree at the University of Bordeaux. Hasan emerged as his father's key political adviser after the French exiled the royal family from 1953 to 1955, and played a key role in the February 1956 negotiations that led to Morocco's independence a month later. As army chief of staff in 1956, Prince Hasan led the brutal repression of rebellions in the Rif Mountains, and in 1957 he was instrumental in persuading his father to change his title from sultan to the more modern-sounding king.

Named king on the death of his father in 1961, Hasan made Morocco in 1963 the first North African country to have a constitution and elected parliament. Following widespread unrest in 1965, however, he dissolved parliament and declared a state of emergency. Hasan survived two attempted military coups in 1971 and 1972. The peaceful 1975 Green March, which led to a Moroccan take-over of the Spanish Sahara, proved wildly popular and deflected internal criticism away from regime shortcomings, including heavy political repression that lasted from the 1960s through the late 1980s.

Hasan firmly supported the West during the Cold War, leading him to serve as an intermediary between Arab regimes and Israel and to participate in various Cold War interventions in sub-Sharan Africa, including the Congo. From 1991 until his death, Hasan oversaw the gradual liberalization of Moroccan domestic politics and economic policy, released political prisoners, and established a royal commission on human rights.

See also **Cold War; Congo, Republic of: History and Politics; Morocco.**

BIBLIOGRAPHY

Dalle, Ignace. *Maroc 1961–1999: L'espérance brisée.* Paris: Maisonneuve et Larose, 2001.

Hassan II, and Eric Laurent. *La mémoire d'un roi: Entretien avec Eric Laurent.* Paris: Plon, 1993.

DALE F. EICKELMAN

HEAD, BESSIE EMERY (1937–1986). Though her writing career began as a journalist for the *Golden City Post* in Cape Town, Bessie Head's self-imposed exile from South Africa shaped her later literary career, reflecting the alienation she experienced as a marginalized exile in Botswana, the setting of much of her work. *When Rain Clouds Gather* (1968), based on her experience in a refugee community, articulates the utopian vision characteristic of Head's fiction: alternative, transformative spaces free of racism, sexism, and classism. *Maru* (1987) condemns the evils of caste oppression, while *The Collector of Treasures and Other Botswana Village Tales* (1977) depicts the gendered universe of rural life.

Born on July 6, 1937, in the Fort Napier Mental Institution in Pietermaritzburg, Head lived as a "Coloured" foster child, rejected by the wealthy family of her white mother who died institutionalized, her black father unknown. The specter of madness continued to haunt Head. Her life was interspersed with bouts of mental breakdowns and institutionalization, experiences fictionalized in *A Question of Power* (1974), a philosophical probing

Writer Bessie Head (1937–1986). After moving to Botswana in 1964 as a refugee, Head wrote novels and a number of short stories, most of which focused on ordinary life among humble people. ESTATE OF BESSIE HEAD

of good and evil recorded through a woman's psychological journey through madness.

Head's many works include *Serowe: Village of the Rain Wind* (1981), an oral history of the Bamangwato, and *A Bewitched Crossroads* (1986), an historical novel. Posthumously published writings include *Tales of Tenderness and Power* (1989), *A Woman Alone: Autobiographical Writings* (1990), and *The Cardinals: With Meditations and Stories* (1993). Head's letters and private papers are housed at the Khama III Memorial Museum in Serowe, Botswana.

See also **Literature: Popular Literature.**

BIBLIOGRAPHY

Eilersen, Gillian Stead. *Bessie Head: Thunder behind Her Ears*. Portsmouth, NH: Heinemann, 1996.

Ibrahim, Huma. *Bessie Head: Subversive Identities in Exile*. Charlottesville: University Press of Virginia, 1996.

Sample, Maxine, ed. *Critical Essays on Bessie Head*. Westport, CT: Greenwood, 2003.

Vigne, Randolph, ed. *A Gesture of Belonging: Letters from Bessie Head, 1965–1979*. London: SA Writers, 1991.

MAXINE J. SAMPLE

HEALING AND HEALTH CARE

This entry includes the following articles:
AFRICAN THEORIES AND THERAPIES
HOSPITALS AND CLINICS
ISLAMIC MEDICINE
MEDICAL PRACTITIONERS
MEDICINE AND DRUGS

AFRICAN THEORIES AND THERAPIES

Ideas and practices relating to health, sickness, and healing across the African continent have evolved over millennia in many local, regional, and broader constellations. A continent marked by five distinct language families; sharply contrasting environments of rainforest, savanna, desert, temperate zones and coasts; and broad interaction with the wider world, has an equally complex medical history. Thus, the medicine of ancient Egypt, itself reflecting African impulses, shaped medical ideas and practices of neighboring civilizations,

including classical Greek and Rome. The medicine of the Mediterranean classical antiquity, sharing common humoral ideas identified with Galen, spread back into North Africa, first through Greek traders and Roman legions, then later with Islamic conquest. To this mix were added the medical notions of Persia and Arabia. Christian faith healing spread with early Christianity across North Africa and Ethiopia, then later, with European influence, to sub-Saharan Africa. Post-Enlightenment scientific medicine, building upon ancient Greek and Islamic medicine, brought its ideas of public health and curative medicine to Africa. In the twenty-first century all these perspectives coexist with indigenous perspectives on health, sickness, and healing, themselves dynamic and endlessly hybridized.

Over the centuries the prevailing ideas, practices, and institutions of health, sickness, and healing in Africa have included: (1) empirical therapies based on observation of sickness and the appropriate means of intervention; (2) ritualized therapies that amplify the power of words—formulae, chant, blessing and curse—and the metaphoric uses of natural and cultural objects—as in sacrifices; (3) collective therapies conducted by communities whether kin-based or associations of the commonly afflicted who become healers and mediums; (4) divination, the systematic scrutiny of misfortune within the rubric of distinctive etiologies, epistemologies, and social formations; and (5) ideas and practices of adaptive order, that is, general cultural values and concepts that promote health in the lives of ordinary people living in distinctive ecological niches.

ANCIENT ROOTS, MODERN BRANCHES

Some of the features of African healing are adaptations of ancient hunting and gathering practices that have been retained in current local therapeutic practices. Thus, most healers collected medicinal plants from the wild, assembling fresh medicines for each case. Yet at some point enterprising healers began the cultivation of medicinal plants for a more intentional and controlled use of natural materials. Late-twentieth-century laboratory analysis of medicinal plants and other substances has yielded an even more intensified use and understanding of the natural materia medica.

This process may be seen as a threshold moving in time in the domestication and sedentarization of all aspects of life and society that was well under way by 4000 BCE in West Africa, giving rise to regional healing traditions.

Urban centers and stratified societies emerged on the northern savanna by the early centuries of the first millennium CE, with trade routes to the Mediterranean and Middle East. Late in the first millennium CE, the influences of Islam and Arabia were felt across North Africa, the Sahara, and East Africa. The spread of food cultivation and sedentary communities from the border area of present-day Cameroon and Nigeria southward through and around the equatorial rain forest was associated with the spread of the Bantu, Cushitic, and Nilotic cultures and languages. The study of these languages by historical linguistics yields evidence of a parallel medical tradition. Ecological settings have shaped ideas and practices in African therapeutics.

Both the West African and the Bantu-speaking civilizations, defined primarily by sedentary agriculture, have been obliged to articulate with pastoral nomadism throughout their histories. Where the tsetse fly has been absent—across the Sahel, across the eastern Sudan, in the lake region of east-central Africa, and into moderate southern Africa—pastoralism has conveyed a distinctive set of ideas about health, sickness, and medicine. For example, in the interlacustrine region, where agricultural and pastoral traditions overlap, nearly as many medicinal plants are used in animal husbandry as in human healing. Similarly, zones of desert, tropical rain forest, and savanna have influenced health and healing. In many markets of western and central Africa, separate sections are devoted to the medical plants of the rain forest and of the arid regions. Over the centuries, both ecological settings and cultural traditions have created distinctive emphases within the common core of therapeutic ideas, practices, and institutions that have determined how the therapeutic traditions from the Mediterranean north, the Islamic East, and the Christianized and scientized West would be received.

RECOGNIZING COMMON IDEAS OF HEALTH AND ILL HEALTH

African understandings of health, sickness, and healing are couched in ideas about the nature of the

Nganga Tambwe Antoine, of Katanga province in southern Congo, buys Sahelian West African arid land medicine from a Hausa market woman in Kinshasa's central market. Tambwe also purchased fresh green plants and roots of the savanna and rainforest from Lower Congo merchants. This scene attests to the pan-continental awareness about *materia medica* on the part of Central African *banganga*, the Bantu term for doctors. PHOTOGRAPH BY J. M. JANZEN, 1969

world and life within it that offer powerful metaphors with which to make sense of suffering and uncertainty. These ideas are sometimes discernible in verbal concepts that have a deep history, a broad geographical and cultural distribution, and a continuing use in diagnosis, the formulation of the sickness experience, and therapeutic traditions. Mid-twentieth-century scholarship, typified by Evans-Pritchard and Robin Horton, has often sought to contrast African ideas of sickness and misfortune to Western scientific thinking, characterizing the former as dominated by religion, thus "closed," and the latter as "open." But such broad asymmetrical comparison ignores the dynamic quality of the local response to illness, the complex nature of diverse medical traditions, the richness of popular experience of a vast continent, and the already mentioned pragmatism in healing, and of scientific practitioners within African medical traditions. The most dominant ideas in African medical traditions are noted here, reflecting late twentieth century research and writing.

A first set of examples gives evidence of ideas that structure of the body as health, well-being, or good fortune, and disruption, departure, or negation from that state, which is illness. Anthony Buckley, studying the Yoruba, but echoed more widely, noted that the appearance of "redness" on the otherwise unblemished skin surface (*eela* or *ele*, similar to *beela* in Kongo of western Congo), brings into play the widespread color code of red as transition and danger, against white chalk as purity and wholeness and charcoal black as human chaos. Phillip Guma's research of ideas used in the diagnosis and treatment of childhood diarrhea, and thus experiences of health and illness, among Nguni of the Western Cape indicates a dynamic tripartite relationship between *umoya* (vital force), *inyongo* (gall), and *ithongo* (ancestral dream). Christopher Davis, in her research among the Tabwa on the Congo shores of Lake Tanganyika, finds clearly discerned verbal concepts of order and disorder articulated as inside and outside, individual and society, and heat (the fire of passion, anger, and affliction) and coolness (of health, grace, and harmony).

These latter contrasts reveal a second prevalent idea in African medicine, "balance" or "harmony" that is deemed necessary to a state of health. This is true of relationships between persons as well as between the human community and the natural and spiritual environment (*lunga*, in Zulu of South Africa and Kongo of western Congo, where this is also an attribute of God). An elaborate notion of color and plant balance is often present in Kongo compounds and medicines, combining opposites—wild and domesticated, male and female, purgatives and fats, white and red flowers or fluids—that would balance and purify the body to counteract the diseased condition. In regions and societies influenced by Greek humoral theory via Islamic medicine, an equilibrium between the humors, and between heat and cold, leads to health; imbalance, to disease.

A third idea expresses purity as a ritual state in which the dimensions of the human world are in order or right. Its opposite, a state in which these affairs are out of order, causes ritual pollution or sickness. Edward Green, in connection with the incorporation of healers into health education programs, considers that purity and pollution concepts represent a traditional set of natural contrasts that are not bound by spirit or human forces, and may have served in the past as a foundation for ideas of health and the prevention of disease.

Fourth, the concept of "flow and blockage" is very widespread, often as a homology between the physical realm of the body and exchanges in society; flow in both realms is necessary for life and health. Christopher Taylor suggests of Rwandan society that "flow and blockage" is a dominant metaphor by which milk, honey, and money flow within the body physical and social. Envy, stinginess, and ill will may lead to constipation, infertility, witchcraft, and disease.

Fifth, the widespread notion of "contagion" used to explain disease, is a relatively old idea, suggests Edward Green, that goes back well before an understanding of microbial vectors of disease. In his research in Southeast African societies, that which spreads and infects may include ill will, poison, malefic medicines, and a variety of forces that cause harm. Quite possibly this thinking was applied to specific diseases and comes to resemble the modern idea of infection. Thus, for example, in nineteenth-century examples of East Africa, smallpox-infested communities were quarantined as a health measure, and the healthy were immunized with a bit of fluid from the pustules of an infected individual. More generally, the incorporation and subduing of the "ill" rather than its expulsion, is a common idea in African etiology and healing.

The foregoing ideas or idea-complexes contribute to a widely noted, sixth, concept of causal dualism that contrasts illnesses that just happen, are "of God," and those that are caused by an agency, either spirit, ancestor, or most often living persons within the immediate social environment of the individual or community sufferer. This dichotomy thus recognizes the natural world and its effects on humans and animals, and that affliction may occur for reasons of climate, bad food, bad practices, old age, or even for no apparent reason at all—akin to Aristotle's sense of nature, in philosopher-ethnographer Brian Morris's rendering based on research in Malawi. However, the other side of the dichotomy recognizes the impact of relationships, enemies, ancestors, and mischievous spirits on the health of persons and communities. Although informants may readily draw up lists of particular diseases and conditions that are "natural" or "person-willed," in practice the causes of particular misfortunes are interpreted in the light of ongoing circumstances in the life and society of the afflicted.

The foregoing ideas, singly or in combination, often provide the imagery by which sickness and impaired health are articulated, and treatment is determined. Scholars of African medicine try to understand how these higher-level ordering principles are invoked to organize or explain the pragmatism reflected in particular diagnoses and therapies. Steven Feierman, studying healing among the Shaamba in Tanzania, speaks of a process of "addition" in diagnosis that brings to a case layer upon layer of probable cause and related therapy to understand and deal with the disorder at hand. Increasingly, too, scholars of health and healing in Africa recognize the pluralism of medical ideas and practices in one and the same community. As this author found in Kongo society of Lower Congo, there is much shopping or shuttling on the part of therapy managers for their suffering kin. In a 1992 study of health and health-seeking in a suburb of Dakar, Didier Fassin identifies and describes traditional, Islamic, and biomedical knowledge and practices, that people bring to bear—singly or multiply—to make sense of their perplexing and troubling experiences.

The disparities and pluralisms seen in much scholarship on sickness, health, and healing in Africa are incorporated by Rwandan physician-scholar Pierre-Claver Rwangabo into a single modern reality rather than a perplexing combination of fossilized tradition at odds with "modern" medicine. For Rwangabo, the causal domains of Rwandan sickness and healing are divided between "physical and mystical causes." Diseases range across a variety of types that may be attributed to either category, depending on the context. Rwangabo's medical training is evident in his listing of disease classes that include parasitic disease, microbial disease, systemic diseases and bodily accidents, gynecological and obstetrical diseases, and psycho-

mental and behavioral diseases. Under the latter group he identifies current psychopathologies that entail abnormal behavior as understood even in traditional thought, and diseases believed to be caused by broken prohibitions and beliefs about ancestors and other spirits that often are identified in relation to mental illnesses. He places the diseases resulting from "poisoning" into yet another category, separate from that brought on by the breach of social rules, which have a "mystical" though not mysterious etiology. Rwangabo noted that most pathology may have a physical dimension and a "mystical" dimension, and that in African thinking this affects the way therapy will be arranged. The decision to seek physical or other therapy has to do with the context in which the pathology occurs, its severity, and its response to treatment.

THE SHIFT FROM MUNDANE TO RITUALIZED THERAPIES

The principles enumerated provided the basis of many practical diagnoses and interventions and specialties, including bone setting and midwifery, and in a host of specific interventions for such ailments as fever, rheumatism, intestinal disorders, parasites, lactation deficiency, earache, toothache, headache, epilepsy, and menstrual disorders. Medications are based on a wide array of mineral, animal, and vegetable substances from the desert, savanna, and rain forest. Many studies have been conducted to discover and analyze the active ingredients of African medicines, such as John M. Watt and Maria G. Breyer-Brandwijk's heavy tome *The Medicinal and Poisonous Plants of Southern and Eastern Africa* (1962), or Raimo Harjula's study of healer *Mirau and His Practice: A Study of the Ethnomedicinal Repertoire of a Tanzanian Herbalist* (1980). National institutes in Nigeria, Zimbabwe, South Africa, Tanzania, and Rwanda, to name a few, have undertaken intensive research and developed programs often in collaboration with healer-herbalists.

Anecdotal and laboratory evidence demonstrate the effectiveness of medications used singly and in compounds, deriving from plant, animal, and inorganic sources. For example, mamiso (Bidens pilosa L.), one of the many plants with which Tanzanian healer Mirau, as described by Harjula, treats children's diarrhea, is described by Watt and Breyer-Brandwijk as an antibacterial substance effective against microorganisms, including five enteric pathogens. Since economic liberalization of the 1990s, drugs of global manufacture are more widely available in markets and pharmacies. Patients and their families often use them interchangeably with traditional medicines.

However, the reduction of African herbal preparations and pharmaceuticals of global manufacture to efficacious treatments of single diseases, though possible, would miss the common strategy of African healers and their patient's expectations to address concurrently the multiple sources of distress, most importantly human relationships. Kongo healer Mama Mankomba treats bodily swelling. She distinguishes between swelling thought to be due to heart

Mama Mankomba, Luozi region, Lower Congo, collects sap of the "finger cactus" (Euphorbia tirucalli L.= Euphorbiaceae). Finger cactus is one of several ingredients in a medicine that is ingested orally for treatment of edema swelling. The mixture is based on the idea of complementary opposition of the cactus sap (a poison) with a fatty substance (a base) that is intended to dry the body of excess liquids. PHOTOGRAPH BY J. M. JANZEN, 1969

congestion and swelling due to poisoning, the result of anger or animosity between people. Her basic treatment for both begins with a powerful emetic from the sap of a cactus, mixed with soapy water. Congestive swelling requires a thrice-daily intake of medicine made of the roots of six savanna plants, and dietary restrictions. Swelling from poisoning requires a single plant purge. Mankomba's approach to poisoning stopped short of dealing with the root causes, anger. The complicated process of identifying the aggressor, and mediating the conflict, she left to other healers and judges.

Ritualized therapies, or the ritualization of therapy, may be defined as the purposeful amplification of mundane or empirical therapies with highly charged affective symbols. Where and when such therapies are invoked depends on the understanding of the cause of the misfortune and on what may be deemed appropriate in handling it. The shift from mundane to ritualized therapy to deal with the shift from "low density" to "high density" cases—as historian Gwynn Prins has phrased it—occurs because the misfortune or affliction is perceived to be fraught with tension, anxiety, and fear of pollution through both human and supernatural conflict. The stakes are higher; the symbolic realms of human and mystical relations need to be reordered. Consecrated persons, recognized by society and the spirit world, are capable of handling such powerful therapies as the purification of polluted persons and settings, making sacrifices to ancestors, and neutralizing menacing spirits. The social dimension of misfortune is highly appreciated in the African setting. Analysis of this dimension is often the first item of the therapy management group's agenda, or of the diviner to whom they refer a case. Sjaak Van der Geest, Susan Reynolds Whyte, and Anita Hardon (2003) have analyzed the creation of meaning and metaphors in medicines at the time of their preparation, use, and perceived efficacy as a "biographical" approach.

DIVINATION

The pervasiveness of divination in relation to sickness and misfortune in Africa attests to the importance of the general questions about causation, especially the suspected shift from a mundane to a highly charged cause in the human or spirit realm. Over a wide region of Africa, etiological imputation

Ngoma novice with goat prior to initiation sacrifice, Guguleto, Western Cape, South Africa. The sacrifice of an animal embodies the exchange of the life and health of the animal for the sickness and suffering of the novice-patient. The novice will wear the gall bladder of the goat on his head with a string of white beads, the first element of a more elaborate costume that will grow as dreams, experience, and learning are added. PHOTOGRAPH BY J. M. JANZEN, 1982

Usually consultation with a diviner is not undertaken until there is sufficient reason for the kin group of the sufferer to suspect causes other than the natural. Such a precipitating factor may be the worsening condition of a sick person, a sudden and inexplicable death, the juxtaposition of a sickness with a conflict in close social proximity to the sufferer, or the puzzling incidence of a disease that strikes one side of a family and not another. In such cases the clients are looking for an answer to their questions: "Why did it happen?" "Why did it happen to us?" "Who caused it?" "What should we do about it?"

Most often these questions will be answered by pointing to the human causes of a misfortune, including error in judgment by the sufferer, excesses of various kinds, inconsistencies, contradictions, rivalries and conflicts in the immediate social field around the sufferer, willful gossip, the power of harmful words, poisonings, and attempted mystical killings. The advancement of health and scientific understanding in a community may not necessarily lay to rest these questions, which are of a different order from the ideas in natural causation. A community of individuals may know very well that the spores transmitted by the bite of an infected Anopheles mosquito causes malaria in the blood of a human. But the diviner may shed light on the question of why some people in a kin group are infected and not others, or why some died and not others when all were infected. Divination also may clarify the human causes behind accidents or provide an explanatory pattern.

As pervasive as divination is across the African continent, its particular instrumentalities vary enormously. In the broad West Africa belt from central Nigeria to Ghana, the prevailing mode of divination is known as Ifa, or one of its variants. Using a cup or tray, a set of cowries or pods is thrown out whose combination of "ups" and "downs" is coded to indicate a set of verses, numbering in the thousands, that illuminate the life situation before the diviner. On the southern savanna, from the Kongo coast southeastward to the Copperbelt, the Ngombo basket mode of divination is common. Carved figurines and natural objects, representing human situations and predicaments, lie together in the basket. As the basket is shaken, one of the objects emerges at the basket's rim between two lumps of clay, one red and the other

of misfortune allows for that which "just happens," translated by some as "natural cause." Many African glosses of this etiology are translated as misfortune caused "by God"—not the divine retribution of Islam or Christianity but part of the order of creation. The diviner may thus tell the client that his or her case does not entail anything to worry about, that it is "of God"—that is, in the nature of creation. This is helpful to the client, for it lifts the case and its diagnosis to a more general level of thought and representation that ties together the many approaches of African therapeutics.

white, suggesting the liminality of the threshold between the visible and the invisible, spirit world. The diviner then "reads" the case in the light of the emergent object or the constellation in the basket.

In southern Africa a favorite mode of divination is a bag of animal vertebrae that are thrown onto a mat before the client. The bones, whose constellation represents issues in human life, relationships, and the world of spirits, may be combined with trance to indicate a complex hierarchy of causation behind the surface realities of a misfortune. These and many other types of divination are predicated on the assumption that sickness or other misfortunes may be caused by an untoward turn of events in the human or related spirit world. An immediate proximal cause may act within the prism of human or spirit agents. Thus, despite widespread acceptance of scientific medicine in Africa, divination continues to be common as a means of unscrambling the human factor that is seen as important in the cause of misfortune and suffering.

RULES, WORDS, AND WILL IN THE CAUSE OF SICKNESS AND MISFORTUNE

A few examples will suffice to illustrate the role of agency as believed cause of misfortune in the extremely rich and nuanced world of African healing. The verbal concept, *gidu*, widespread in western Bantu-speaking societies, refers to the role of social prohibitions and taboos, and the consequences of their violation. Sometimes this is mentioned with reference to the restriction on eating or killing one's clan or individual totems and familiars. Other observers, especially well-versed African physicians, note that these prohibitions help individuals adhere to social codes in general, including health-promoting restrictions on such things as excessive consumption of alcohol, overeating, or health-destroying excesses of any kind. Another widespread notion of the human cause of sickness or misfortune encompasses both anger or ill will toward another and the instrument expressing it, be that an injurious word, a blow to the head, or a bit of poison in drink or food. This notion is so ancient in Africa that its radical (reconstructed as *-dog* or *-dok*) is included in Proto-Bantu lexica of at least 3,000 years ago. Because of its centrality to the African worldview, modern derivations of it are found from Cameroon and the Kongo coast in the west, to

the Swahili coast in the east, to the Nguni speakers in South Africa, and everywhere in between (*kuloka* in KiKongo; *kuroga* in Kinyarwanda; *kuthaka* in Zulu). The notion is not always associated with ill will; sometimes it is used to refer to the power of words, or the use of powerful words as in oaths or spells, which may well be its original and central semantic core.

In contemporary diagnosis of misfortune, victims often identify a string of misfortunes and try to recall the exact words spoken by others prior to or in association with the events, drawing the logical inference that these utterances caused, or could have led to, the misfortunes. Words of warning or injurious words spoken in anger are especially suspect. Therefore, in divination, these moments are recalled so that the affected individuals or relationships may be treated, to get at the root causes of an affliction.

HEALING THE BODY POLITIC

If sickness and other misfortunes can be caused by the utterance of hurtful or condemning words, as well as other acts of aggression, then the injuries they cause can be healed through the purging of bodies of their poisons, the intervention of blessed powerful words (including songs and gestures), the assertion of legitimate authority, or the enactment of justice. This is the logic behind the myriad ritual therapies, shrine communities, and cults in all corners of the African continent. Sometimes they are gender-divided, as in the widespread Sande (female) and Poro (male) associations of the Guinea forest region. Elsewhere they take on a more focused, specialized quality, centering on such issues as twinship (as in the Ibeji of Yorubaland), particular forms of disease (Ipona, the cult of smallpox), institutions of central authority or individual achievement (the cult of the hand in Igboland).

In the Hausa region of Northern Nigeria, the ancient Bori cult subsumes many types of issues, especially in women's affairs. In the Sudan, Egypt, Ethiopia and Somalia, the Zar cult brings mostly women together to articulate their unique afflictions and circumstances. Janice Boddy's scholarship exemplifies the close attention by many researchers to women's unique status in Islamic societies and to the distinctive way that their agency is voiced often through the spirits marginal to or outside of the dominant socio-religious order. Across equatorial Africa this type of therapeutic ritual assembly often centers on particular issues, such as fertility and the reproduction of the lineage, twinship, women's reproductive issues, the health and well-being of infants and children, debilitating chronic conditions, fortune and misfortune for men in hunting, mental illnesses, and a range of social and even environmental issues such as poisonous snakes.

Membership in these "drums of affliction"—Victor Turner's translation of the widespread term *ngoma*, literally drum, also song-dance, cult, network, carrier of the voice of the ancestors—usually consists of the afflicted and formerly afflicted, who undergo a phased therapeutic initiation through stages from sufferer-novice to healer-priest. The drum connotes the voice of the ancestors and spirits that inhabit the celebrants, expressed in the song-dances at the core of the ritual performances. Often the mark of growth or healing in the sufferer-novice is the articulation of a personal song based on the ordeal of suffering, a dream vision, or other powerful transforming experience. Such a song constitutes a unique set of "powerful words" that offset the destructive forces of disintegration, misfortune, sickness, and chaos of the previous period of the individual's life.

Where such a "drum of affliction" addresses community issues, society itself becomes the body that is cured. Leaders or segments of society such as households may be the "sufferers," and the "medicines" may be symbols of authority or titles of leadership. This was the case with the seventeenth- to nineteenth-century coastal equatorial African cult Lemba, which arose in response to the destructiveness of the forces of the Atlantic slave trade to lineage-based society. The sufferers were elite households who feared the envy of their subordinates. Their "therapy" included ritual purification and the distribution of wealth obtained in the trade. The result of this therapy was the reconciliation of lineages within the class-exacerbating economy of mercantilism. In Nkita, another example of the *ngoma* type of therapeutic ritual in western equatorial Africa that has reached Haiti in the New World, the gynecological aspects of reproduction within the clan are emphasized, along with the reconciliation of the community of the living with the ancestors. The title of Rene Devisch's study of Nkita highlights the dominant metaphors of Nkita as *Reweaving the Threads of Life*.

African "public healing" has become the focus of significant research from the late twentieth century on. Historian of African healing Steven Feierman has been concerned with the accurate identification of healers and mediums in the resistance to colonial repression of indigenous institutions and practices. He noted that the study and affirmation

Street ngoma for new *igqira* novice, Guguleto, Western Cape, South Africa. Senior *igqira* healers (at left, in colorful costumes) perform ngoma for new novice (at right, in white), at the close of a weekend opening event in his initiatory therapy. PHOTOGRAPH BY J. M. JANZEN, 1982

Novice patients in "doing ngoma" (sangoma) song-dance sessions in Guguleto, Western Cape, South Africa. Ngoma is a term of wide-ranging meaning that refers to drum (the instrument), the sound and rhythm of the drumming, and the accompanying dancing and singing, as well as the cells of healers and networks between them. PHOTOGRAPH BY J. M. JANZEN, 1982

Kongo Christian healing, Church of the Holy Spirit in Africa, Manianga region, Lower Congo, Democratic Republic of Congo. As in many African independent churches, healing is an important focus of this church, along with blessings, all-night vigils, prayers, and a sense of close community. PHOTOGRAPH BY J. M. JANZEN, 1969

Writing Islamic prayers, Taiba, Central Sudan. Assistants of the sheikh, the head of the community, prepare amulets by writing Qurʾanic verses on slips of paper that will be worn or placed under beds or in auspicious places. Verses may also be written on tea leaves that are dissolved in hot water and ingested as medicine. PHOTOGRAPH BY J. M. JANZEN, 2004

of "traditional healing" in the postcolonial era has too often presented it as a static individualized practice that is subsumed under a narrative of Western and scientific domination. His review of the history of scholarship on the cult and figure of Nyabingi in the Great Lakes demonstrates the power of this alternative public healing tradition throughout precolonial, colonial, and postcolonial eras. A symposium and volume produced by a group of Dutch scholars inspired by Professor Matthew Schofeleers has raised similar issues. *The Quest for Fruition through Ngoma: Political Aspects of Healing in Southern Africa* (2000) brings together essays on research into the historical and contemporary "cults of affliction" in Tanzania, Zambia, Malawi, Zimbabwe, and South Africa.

Especially in the twentieth century, the ritual therapeutic attributes of these African cults and shrines have related dynamically to Christianity and Islam. Sometimes the African institution has absorbed the outside idea or symbol, at other times Christian and Islamic institutions have recreated the African forms and substance. Especially widespread in sub-Saharan Africa are the independent African Churches, many of which encourage healing, exorcisms, and incorporation of rites of

purification, protection, and sanctification. Prophet-founders play the role of ancestor-mediators, and prominent or especially talented members assume the diagnostic role of diviners. These roles are not unknown in the mainstream mission churches where, for nearly half a century, theologians have researched ways to Africanize the form and substance of Christianity.

Islam has similarly penetrated African therapeutic culture, and vice versa. Although orthodox Muslims, like some Christians, frown on syncretistic blending of African and Near Eastern religion, the interpenetration of Islam and African ritual healing is marked. In many and varied Sufi movements across West Africa, the Sahel, Sudan, and East Africa, local saints and ancestors, *jinn* and *sheitani* spirits widely inhabit the worldviews of adepts. Local sheikhs provide a range of services—schools, orphanages mosques, healing centers, mediation to ancestors—that establish the public order often lacking in poor states. These sheikhs may adhere to historic movements or *tariqa* founded by memorable leaders of the past, or they may be their own unique blend of social service, public religious authority. Purification symbolism of African healing merges with that of the ritual ablutions of Islam in connection with prayer.

In northern Swahili towns such as Lamu, early-twentieth-century ngoma Maulidi was introduced for performance in the mosque; its songs celebrated the prophet Muhammad. In the twenty-first century reform Muslims are trying to extricate it from this setting, because of its use of drumming, dancing, and a ritual form associated with "pagan" Africa. Studies of medicine and healing in the Hausa region of Northern Nigeria by Lewis Wall and Ishmail Abdalla have shown the active incorporation of the teachings of Islam as virtue and expression of the moral order. Across the Sahel, from Senegal to Sudan, this incorporation of African healing and social visions occurs within local or regional Sufi movements, often founded by local sheikhs who were instrumental in resisting the colonial order and defining a way of life. Successor sheikhs organize a combination of medicine of the prophet and biomedicine in local communities.

HEALING IN THE AFTERMATH OF WAR

A noteworthy feature of postcolonial African healing has been its widespread role in healing the wounds of war. Warfare, perhaps the ultimate form of the "malicious power of words and deeds," requires a solution that purifies individuals and communities and restores harmonious ties with the ancestors. Scholars on healing the wounds of war have provided important new insights. Sidonie Matokot-Mianzenza has examined the impact of rape on women in the civil war in Congo-Brazzaville, one of the many settings in Africa and worldwide of the use of this technique of terror. As a therapist, she has practiced, and advocated for, family therapies in the tradition of the therapy management group found in Kongo society. Mariane Ferme has explored social ambiguity, memory, and materiality in everyday life in Sierra Leone as a way to understand the outbursts of violence in that country's civil war, and the way that metaphors and materials reincorporate these cultural ambiguities or secrets in complex ritual memories. Marian Tankink has with colleagues examined the all too common condition of the aftermath of war where the destruction of a public social space for sharing experiences has led to a "conspiracy of silence" in which no one speaks of the trauma of war.

Pierre-Claver Rwangabo, in his book published a year before the Rwandan genocide of 1994, and a year before his own violent death, discusses at some length precisely those dimensions with which the postwar healing has to cope: overcoming "poisoning" (*uburozi*) and dealing with the ancestors (*abazimu*, a general sub-Saharan term). He noted that the use of chemical poisons had been a very serious problem in Rwandan society, involving siblings, the lineage, and rivals in the office or institution, even spouses. Poisoning was, however, an extension of the harmful powerful words. In the postwar period, attention has been given to remembering the dead killed in the war. The ancestors are accorded power both to inflict disease and to overcome, indeed prevent, disease and misfortune. They safeguard the health of their descendants and punish those who forget to remember them. Ancestors are considered to be the mediators to Imaana, God, and it is to them that prayers are given.

Other wars approaching the Rwandan war in horror have been studied in the longer term. Years and decades, rather than months, are required to see the progress from mass dislocation and deep shock to emotional acknowledgment of the events, grieving, and the eventual reconstruction of a memory, including the recognition of the morally restorative ancestors. Richard Werbner's *Tears of the Dead*, on the aftermath of war in Zimbabwe, shows that part of the response to war was to reestablish memory of the prewar ancestors—the *mizimu*—and to bring them closer, while laying to rest the memory of those who died a violent death and were not properly buried—the ngozi. In the Kalanga lineage of southern Zimbabwe that Werbner had known from before the war, and revisited in the late 1980s, these ancestors were reconnected to the community of the living within the Ndebele-inspired *ngoma* rituals. In this revival of *ngoma*, the dead were sorted into good and useful mediums versus threatening or harmful mediums—that is, those who had died a violent death or had not been properly buried, or those who had killed others wantonly.

This ten-year sorting out of spirits following a war recalls the spirit categories in Swaziland, where *ngoma* spirits who possess mediums are differentiated into four categories: victims of Swazi wars, those who died by drowning and received no proper burial, nature spirits, and the lineal ancestors. The "victims of Swazi wars" category recalls the early-nineteenth-century wars of southern Africa, but the whole constellation of memories, stories, divination, and healing rituals offers a paradigm for dealing with lesser traumas of today. The focused ritual of reconnecting to the prewar ancestors and marginalizing the *ngozi*, thereby creating a nuanced worldview of healing, exorcism, and mediumship, is a powerful trauma treatment procedure. The ancestors are an extension of living humans who have suffered all the horrors of war—indeed, these ancestors are the icons of those terrible moments, some having been killed, others having done the killing. The open wounds of war that need attention are the fear, shock, denial, and blaming of others—all the emotions Western therapists associate with long-term psychological damage that takes years, if not lifetimes, to heal. The collective trauma is so great, and this healing process is so momentous, that the resulting spirit paradigms may continue, as in Swaziland, for decades or even centuries.

PUBLIC HEALTH AND THE RELEGITIMATION OF AFRICAN MEDICINE

African ways of perceiving health, sickness, and healing as described here came under severe assault by most colonial regimes and the missionaries who came to evangelize Africa from the late nineteenth to the mid-twentieth century. Just as Muslim crusaders had attacked "pagan" African forms of healing and religion, so Western Christian missionaries discredited the basis of knowledge as well as the overall approach to ritual healing. Assumptions that human relations could cause sickness were dismissed as superstition or "witchcraft" at a time when the first steps of positive science were discovering the causes of contagious diseases, and the first public health campaigns were being waged to make Africa safe and healthy for "progress." With their dramatic cures for such diseases as yaws, leprosy, and later malaria and dysentery, Christian missionaries and their hospitals contributed to the conversion of many Africans.

Yet, in the postcolonial era, although Christianity and Islam have gained an ever-wider following, the marks of a distinctive African worldview of misfortune have persisted, and therapeutic techniques and material medica have received new

Pharmacist Byamungu Lufungula wa Chibanga-banga in his medicine factory Bukavu, Eastern Democratic Republic of Congo. Trained in France as a pharmacist, he was part of the early post-colonial initiative to find value in African herbal and therapeutic knowledge. After having researched herbal and ritual healing in the Kivu region of Eastern Congo in the 1960s and 1970s, he opened a research institute to develop products based on traditional and research-based insights. PHOTOGRAPH BY J. M. JANZEN, 1994

legitimacy. National research centers and national associations of healers are expressions of the state's legitimacy extended to African healing. The financial constraints of African states and the search for an infrastructure of health have led planners and developers to take a second look at African healing ideas and institutions. Research initiatives have focused on major health scourges such as malaria, childhood diarrhea, and river blindness. Researchers have examined the way that ideas of misfortune have informed social behavior in epidemic outbreaks such as ibola. The HIV/AIDS pandemic has received focused attention both from researchers and planners. The sharp divisions between "traditional" and "modern" medicines have dissolved in favor of a more integrated use of any and all available resources in the resolution of health crises or health dimensions of social, political, and economic crises.

Health, sickness, and healing thus form a rich and highly developed dimension of African civilization that has grown both as it meets the needs of its peoples and as it incorporates ideas and techniques from the outside.

See also **Death, Mourning, and Ancestors; Disease; Divination and Oracles; Ecosystems; Food; Religion and Ritual; Slave Trades; Spirit Possession; Symbols and Symbolism; Urbanism and Urbanization: Historic; Witchcraft.**

BIBLIOGRAPHY

Abdalla, Ishmail H. "Diffusion of Islamic Medicine into Hausaland." In *The Social Basis of Health and Healing in Africa*, ed. Steven Feierman and John M. Janzen. Berkeley: University of California Press, 1992.

Boddy, Janice. *Wombs and Alien Spirits: Women, Men, and the Zar Cult in Northern Sudan.* Madison: University of Wisconsin Press, 1989.

Buckley, Anthony. *Yoruba Medicine.* Oxford: Oxford University Press, 1985.

Buxton, Jean. *Religion and Healing in Mandari.* Oxford: Oxford University Press, 1973.

Chavunduka, Gordon. *Traditional Healers and the Shona Patient.* Gwelo: Mambo, 1978.

Davis, Christopher O. *Death in Abeyance: Illness and Therapy among the Tabwa of Central africa.* Edinburgh: Edinburgh University Press, International African Library, 2000.

Devisch, René. *Weaving the Threads of Life: The Khita Gyn-Eco-Logical Healing Cult among the Yaka.* Chicago: University of Chicago Press, 1993.

Douglas, Mary. *Purity and Danger: An Analysis of Concepts of Pollution and Taboo.* New York: Praeger, 1966.

Evans-Pritchard, E. E. *Witchcraft, Oracles, and Magic among the Azande.* Oxford: Oxford University Press, 1937.

Fassin, Didier. *Pouvoir et maladie en Afrique: Anthropologie sociale dans la banlieue de Dakar.* Paris: Presses Universitaires de France, 1992.

Feierman, Steven. "Colonizers, Scholars, and the Creation of Invisible Histories." In *Beyond the Cultural Turn: New Directions in the Study of Society and Culture.* Berkeley: University of California Press, 1999.

Feierman, Steven. "Explanation and Uncertainty in the Medical World of Ghaambo." *Bulletin of the History of Medicine* 74 (2000): 317–344.

Feierman, Steven, and John M. Janzen, eds. *The Social Basis of Health and Healing in Africa.* Berkeley: University of California Press, 1992.

Ferme, Mariane C. *The Underneath of Things: Violence, History, and the Everyday in Sierra Leone.* Berkeley: University of California Press, 2001.

Green, Edward C. *AIDS and STDs in Africa: Bridging the Gap between Traditional Healing and Modern Medicine.* Boulder, CO: Westview Press, 1994.

Green, Edward C. *Rethinking AIDS Prevention: Learning from Successes in Developing Countries.* Westport, CT: Praeger, 2000.

Guma, Mthobeli Phillip. "The Politics of Umoya: Variation in the Interpretation and Management of Diarrheal Illnesses among Mothers, Professional Nurses, and Indigenous Health Practitioners in Khayelitsha, South Africa." Ph.D. diss. University of North Carolina at Chapel Hill, 1998.

Harjula, Raimo. *Mirau and his Practice: A Study of the Ethnomedical Repertoire of a Tanzanian Herbalist.* London: Tri-Med Books, 1980.

Janzen, John M. *Lemba, 1650–1930: A Drum of Affliction in Africa and the New World.* New York: Garland Publishers, 1982.

Janzen, John M. *The Quest for Therapy: Medical Pluralism in Lower Congo.* Berkeley: University of California Press, 1987.

Janzen, John M. *Ngoma: Discourses of Healing in Central and Southern Africa.* Berkeley: University of California Press, 1992.

Janzen, John M. *The Social Fabric of Health: An Introduction to Medical Anthropology.* New York: McGraw-Hill, 2002.

Janzen, John M., and Edward C. Green. "Continuity, Change, and Challenge in African Medicine." In *Medicine across Cultures: History and Practice of Medicine in Non-Western Cultures*, ed. Helaine Selin. Boston: Kluwer Academic Publishers, 2003.

Janzen, John M., and Reinhild Kauenhoven Janzen. *Do I Still Have a Life? Voices from the Aftermath of War in Rwanda and Burundi.* Lawrence: University of Kansas Publications in Anthropology 20, 2000.

Katz, Richard. *Boiling Energy: Community Healing among the Kalahari Kung.* Cambridge, MA: Harvard University Press, 1982.

Last, Murray, and Gordon Chavunduka, eds. *The Professionalization of African Medicine.* Manchester, U.K.: Manchester University Press in association with the International African Institute, 1986.

Matokot-Mianzenza, Sidonie. *Viol des femmes dans les conflits armés et thérapies familiales: Cas du Congo-Brazzaville.* Paris: L'Harmattan, 2003.

Mendonsa, Eugene L. *The Politics of Divination: A Processual View of Reactions to Illness and Deviance among the Sisala of Northern Ghana*. Berkeley: University of California Press, 1982.

Morris, Brian. *The Power of Animals: An Ethnography*. Oxford: Berg, 1998.

Ngubane, Harriet. *Body and Mind in Zulu Medicine: An Ethnography of Health and Disease in Nyuswa-Zulu Thought and Practice*. New York: Academic Press, 1977.

Pfeiffer, James T. "African Independent Churches in Mozambique: Healing the Afflictions of Inequality." *Medical Anthropology Quarterly* 16, no. 2 (2002): 176–199.

Prins, Gwynn. "A Modern History of Lozi Therapeutics." In *The Social Basis of Health & Healing in Africa*, ed. Steven Feierman and John M. Janzen. Berkeley: University of California Press, 1992.

Rwangabo, Pierre-Claver. *La médecine traditionnelle au Rwanda*. Paris: Karthala, 1993.

Tankink, Marian. "Silence: Coping with War Memories in Southwest Uganda." *Medische Antropologie* 12, no. 2 (2000).

Taylor, Christopher. *Milk, Honey, and Money: Changing Concepts in Rwandan Healing*. Washington, DC: Smithsonian Institution Press, 1992.

Teixeira, Maria. *Rituels divinatoires et thérapeutiques chez les Manjak de Guinee-Bissau et du Senegal*. Paris: L'Harmattan, 2001.

Turner, Victor. *Drums of Affliction*. Oxford: Clarendon Press, 1968.

Van Dijk, Rijk; Ria Reis; and Maria Spierenburg; eds. *The Quest for Fruition through Ngoma: The Political Aspects of Healing in Southern Africa*. Athens: Ohio University Press, 2000.

Vaughan, Megan. *Curing Their Ills: Colonial Power and African Illness*. Stanford, CA: Stanford University Press, 1991.

Wall, Lewis. *Hausa Medicine: Illness and Well-Being in a West African Culture*. Durham, NC: Duke University Press, 1988.

Wastiau, Boris. *Mahamba: The Transforming Arts of Spirit Possession among the Luvale-Speaking People of the Upper Zambezi*. Fribourg: University Press, 2000.

Watt, John Mitchell, and Mary Gerdina Breyer-Brandwijk. *The Medicinal and Poisonous Plants of Southern and Eastern Africa*. Edinburgh: Livingstone, 1962.

Werbner, Richard. *Tears of the Dead*. Edinburgh: Edinburgh University Press, International African Institute, 1991.

Whyte, Susan Reynolds. *Questioning Misfortune: The Pragmatics of Uncertainty in Eastern Uganda*. Cambridge, U.K.: Cambridge University Press, 1997.

Whyte, Susan Reynolds; Sjaak van der Geest; and Anita Hardon. *The Social Lives of Medicines*. Cambridge, U.K.: Cambridge University Press, 2003.

JOHN M. JANZEN

HOSPITALS AND CLINICS

During the colonial era, hospitals and clinics were shaped by the colonizing countries: Britain, France, Germany, Portugal, Spain, Germany, Belgium, and Italy. In South Africa there were also subtle influences from Holland and Islamic influences from Indonesia. Postindependence, during the Cold War, the United States and the Soviet Union also had an effect on health care in Africa. Trade unions pressured the government for improved services in different ways in different countries. Each of these factors influenced the pattern of health care and establishment of hospitals and clinics for the very varied population in each country.

The distribution of health services between urban and rural areas, the emphasis on attitudes to family planning and services for women and children, and the degree of linkage between biomedical and traditional services differs depending largely on these colonial precedents. For example, the former French colonies in the west of Africa developed their maternal and child health services more slowly than those on the largely English-speaking eastern half as evidenced by differences in immunization rates in the 1980s. There was perhaps closer understanding between biomedical and traditional services in countries with an Islamic influence. This could possibly have been because of some similarity of religious components between Muslim and traditional health care.

The political and economic stability of a country, the languages, as well as ethnic groups and the physical and social environments of African countries all influenced the establishment of health care. Wars and civil disturbance have had a deleterious effect on developing effective health services greatly influenced by the duration of conflict before peace. Wars and civil disturbances have had very serious effects on the development of effective health services for the increased ill health and disabilities that they cause. There are many examples of this; perhaps the most devastating are the civil wars in Darfur, Sudan and in Somalia. The very process of liberation toward independence was often traumatic, with adverse consequences for health services in Mozambique, Zimbabwe, South Africa, and northern Namibia. Two world wars also had deleterious effects on many African countries.

Corruption affects the economy and the distribution and functioning of health services. Wars and famines lead to more movement of people, disruption of family and social networks, and increases in sexually transmitted infections including HIV/AIDS. Wars and civil disturbances increase trauma and levels of stress and uncertainty, which coupled with deteriorating biomedical health care can lead to increased reliance on traditional therapy.

Economic disaster with repercussions for health services has overtaken some countries with dictatorship, political mismanagement, and corruption such as in Zimbabwe, Congo, and the Central African Republic. Uganda went through this process with Idi Amin as president but has since recovered sufficiently to deal with the rising AIDS epidemic.

Natural disasters such as famines (usually from drought) have periodically devastated countries, including Ethiopia, Karamoja in Uganda, Niger, and Mauritania, northern Kenya. Floods, for example in Mozambique, have led to malnutrition, suffering, and death.

Pandemic or epidemic disease has had major effects on individuals, families, communities, and countries. Ebola and other hemorrhagic fevers, river blindness, bilharzias, cholera, and ever-present malaria have caused dramatic emergencies, heaped on the chronically present death toll from diarrhea, malnutrition, and childbearing. In South Africa the influenza pandemic of 1918 left as many orphans as AIDS is creating in the early twenty-first century. The AIDS pandemic affects predominantly Africa and is the overarching reality of health care in the continent.

HOSPITALS

In Africa there are numerous organizations, administrations, and partnerships involved in healing and health care. While most governments attempt to provide some type of care for all, both private and not-for-profit organizations provide an important component of health care in most African countries.

Hospitals are built and run by governments at national, provincial, and district or municipal levels. In South Africa the so-called Bantustans with new "independent" governments nationalized existing hospitals, to the distinct disadvantage of quality care. In Tanzania there was a phased takeover, with the government putting a chief executive officer in place while maintaining the staff and religious aspects of faith-based hospitals. State-aided hospitals are often run and partly financed by a faith or community organizations but subsidized by funds from government, as in much of Malawi in the twenty-first century.

A new type of service in response to wars, coups, civil disturbances, famines, epidemics, and disasters is the international hospital (for example, Doctors without Borders). This type of hospital has the specific aim of being short term, using international donor funds, using a trained international professional staff, and dealing with a specific problem. Examples have been in Goma after the Rwandan genocide in 1994, in Somalia, Liberia, and Sierra Leone during civil wars, and in famine areas of Ethiopia.

Since independence many commercial private hospitals that run on business principles and cater to wealthy patients or those who have medical-aid insurance have been built. Health care "companies" often have hospitals in several major cities providing the best and most advanced medical care with a strong component of quality control. The staff are more highly qualified and better paid, leading to siphoning off of lower-paid professionals from the government.

Another category is the public-private partnership (PPP) hospital with the contract between inferior technology government hospitals and high-quality, better-equipped private hospitals. Often there is an old, deteriorating poorly staffed and poorly financed public government hospital that no longer meets the public needs. A public outcry for better facilities together with patients who have medical insurance or who can afford to pay but do not find it convenient to go far to other cities for more complex medical care has led to this trend. The private consortium finances alterations to the buildings and provides better equipment and specialized staff, which also improves care for the poor served by the same facility.

Most countries have specialized hospitals for mental illness, tuberculosis, or local priorities; for example, leprosy, eye diseases, and vesico-vaginal fistula (as in Addis Ababa). These may be government or philanthropic. Military hospitals are usually situated in relation to army barracks. Subspecialty hospitals exist for forensic psychiatry and for multi-drug-resistant tuberculosis.

Yet another category of hospital is for special age groups—the children's hospitals and the geriatric hospitals. They have specialized staff and equipment dealing with the particular problems of the age group.

A category of small "hospital" exists where a private general practitioner or a traditional or alternative healer becomes famous and sets up a unit with beds. These facilities can deal with addiction, psychoneurosis, and traditional local-named syndromes, and can provide counseling, herbal treatment, and acupuncture. Some overlap into the category of being called "health centers," though most do not provide the full range of services of a primary health-care clinic.

Teaching hospitals often have evolved from a small hospital, initially training various categories of medical assistants. After independence governments were driven by the need to produce their own doctors, nurses, and other health workers. Often a new, big teaching hospital was built; examples include the Nelson Mandela Teaching Hospital, Groote Schuur Hospital, Muhimbili Hospital, and Mulago Hospital. Examples of small hospitals that trained assistant medical officers and then expanded into big medical schools are Dar es Salaam School of Health Services and Makerere Medical School. Sometimes the big hospital subsumed the national health budget and rapidly fell into disrepair, like the John F. Kennedy Hospital in Liberia, or in Zambia. The costs of running large specialized urban hospitals can overwhelm a previously balanced health budget, resulting in deterioration of primary services for the dispersed rural population.

Some governments have started step-down facilities adjacent to or near hospitals. These cater to patients not yet fully fit who still need better nutrition, more counseling, adherence to drug regimes, and/or physiotherapy. Such patients include children recovering from severe malnutrition or adults placed on antiretroviral treatment but still needing care. The step-down facility is useful in decompressing an over-full hospital and it allows for more rapid turnover. It is likely that in such facilities integrating traditional therapies would lead to more rapid healing.

CLINICS

Clinics come in all sizes and functions, from the old dispensary, which literally only dispensed medicines, to health centers that provide a wide range of services and have a wider spectrum of staff. The health centers usually provide the full range of curative and preventive care, including obstetrics, simple surgery, mental health, and some rehabilitation of disabilities. Small clinics serve local communities—either rural or urban—and are run by nurses or midwives receiving technical support from either a health center, a hospital, or a district health management team. The support required is for supplies, logistics, quality control training, and referral both upward to specialists and downward back to community workers. Another type of clinic is the mobile clinic, which is especially needed for remote rural areas with too few and scattered population to merit a fixed facility. Periodic visits provide at least a modicum of curative care and assure higher coverage of preventive services.

The essential services provided by clinics often are divided into two streams: the sick or morbid and the preventive/promotive, including maternal and child care, antenatal care, immunization, growth monitoring and improvement of faltering growth, family planning, cervical smears, voluntary counseling and testing for HIV, and tuberculosis detection and treatment. With much of the morbidity having its roots in adolescence (substance abuse and HIV in particular), services have to be adolescent friendly to promote healthy behavior (nutrition, exercise, family planning, use of condoms, and counseling on smoking, alcohol, and drugs). This requires a new focus on the approach to youth, rather than the old "do what I say" authoritarian type of health worker.

Most African health systems evolved from colonial hospitals with limited outreach services but have since embraced the concepts of the primary healthcare center, building the system from below and starting at communities with volunteer or low-paid community health workers (CHWs). These CHWs are, in turn, linked to clinics and through them to health centers and hospitals beyond.

INTEGRATION OF TRADITIONAL THERAPIES

Traditional practitioners inherently integrate healing and health promotion, and modern hospitals and clinics have sometimes tried to integrate their work by allowing joint treatment. The traditional healer has a holistic approach that views the social, emotional, physical, and spiritual aspects of the illness and at the same time may employ herbal or physical treatment. Inhalations, scarifications, and herbal infusions are all part of traditional treatments, but it is the social environment in which healing takes place that is less easy to integrate within hospital or clinic centers. The strong belief systems of most Africans make careful study of local healers and working partnerships a key strategy for good health care. At a minimum, health workers must know and respect local language, beliefs, and practices if they are to succeed.

In South Africa in 1994 the Medical Association published the booklet "Bridging the Gap," which explained the potential for partnership between African traditional healers and biomedical personnel. It was followed in 2006 by an addendum with additional references. Professional associations and legislation have been established in many countries, such as South Africa, Nigeria, and Ghana. Universities have also been involved in research (e.g., Nairobi University in Kenya and Ibadan and LFE Universities in Nigeria). Emphasis has been especially on psychiatry, obstetrics, sexually transmitted diseases, parasitic infections, and in research into drugs obtained from plants.

HIV/AIDS is one of the most dominant considerations in the healing and health care process in most countries in Africa. Its association with increasing spread of tuberculosis and also poor levels of adherence to medication with evolution of resistant strains of virus and mycobacterium all pose an escalating threat. In this situation the need for a holistic approach to health and healing is very apparent. All the physical, social, mental, emotional, and spiritual aspects have to be dealt with, and a combination of working together with family, friends, and local helpers in the language of the individual is needed. It is here that most interaction between state health services and community organizations has occurred.

The interrelationship between type of community and use of traditional health care is complex and changing. Rural communities with poor biomedical services will always use traditional practitioners but in urban areas educated Africans with jobs also use them to obtain a diagnosis of social causation.

GOVERNANCE

One aspect of growing importance is the extent of community involvement in the running of hospitals and clinics. This usually occurs through hospital governing boards and clinic/community committees. In South Africa there is legislation relating to the composition, responsibilities, and roles of these bodies. Aspects of importance are fundraising, community adherence and participation in recommended practices (immunization, antenatal and delivery care, family planning, HIV testing, STI contact tracing, environmental clean-up), monitoring of quality of care at the facility, assuring good communications, and friendliness/patient centeredness of staff. Communities especially expect prompt treatment of midwifery cases and ill children. Adverse judgments and complaints from the public usually relate to lack of cleanliness and lack of friendliness of staff as well as delays in being treated. Initially, medical professionals felt threatened by community oversight, but this partnership is key to success of the health facility and to the health of the people served. Good governance leads to good health, and in realizing this medical professionals have begun to welcome community interest and involvement.

See also **Disease; Famine; Food: Nutrition; Postcolonialism; Sudan: Wars; Warfare.**

BIBLIOGRAPHY

Baguma, P. "The Traditional Treatment of AIDS in Uganda: Benefits and Problems; Key Issues and Debates; Traditional Healers." *Sociétés d'Afrique & SIDA* 13 (July 1996): 4–6.

Bannerman, R. H.; J. Burton; and C. Wen-Chieh. *Traditional Medicine and Health Care Coverage: A Reader for Health Administrators and Practitioners.* Geneva: World Health Organization, 1983.

Feierman S., and J. M. Jansen. *The Social Basis of Health and Healing in Africa.* Berkeley: University of California Press, 1992.

Kark, Sidney L., and G. W. Stewart. *A Practice of Social Medicine: A South African Teams Experience in Different African Communities.* Edinburgh: E. and S. Livingstone, 1962.

Rohde Jon, Meera Chatterjee, and David Morley. *Reaching Health for All.* New York: Oxford University Press, 1993.

South African Medical Association. *Bridging the Gap* and *Addendum to Bridging the Gap.* Pretoria: South African Medical Association, 1994 and 2006.

Van der Geest, S. "Is There a Role for Traditional Medicine in Basic Health Services in Africa?" *Tropical Medicine and International Health* 2 (September 1997): 903–911.

F. JOHN BENNETT
JON ROHDE

ISLAMIC MEDICINE

Since the mid-seventh century CE, Muslim conquerors, traders, travelers, itinerant preachers, and medical practitioners brought Islam and popular and literate Islamic medical tradition to Africa. Itself a synthesis of Greek, Indian, Persian, and pre-Islamic Arab healing practices, Islamic medicine gradually developed into a multifarious health care delivery system in North Africa where Muslim culture became dominant, or in communities elsewhere in the continent where Islam was a formidable competitor to local beliefs. In Egypt and North Africa, it was the clinical, empirical, and scholastic Islamic medical practice that flourished, with full-time physicians, endowed teaching hospitals, and pharmacies. In tropical Africa, the Islamic medical empiricism of the Mediterranean littoral was eclipsed by a largely spiritual therapeutic system dependent on the medicine of the Prophet Mohammad and the local, pre-Islam healing traditions. Muslim health care deliverers in both regions managed to carve out for themselves a successful profession of dispensing medicine to the needy among Muslims and non-Muslims alike.

The early conversion to, or the subsequent close association with, Islam of sultans, kings, and courtiers was possible largely because of the effective healing and protective gear made available to these political dignitaries by Islamic medicine as it crossed the religious ethnic or cultural boundaries. The complex pluralistic medical system that evolved in Muslim Africa has prevailed to the present time. The introduction and proliferation of Western biomedicine to the continent, sanctioned and financed by the colonial and postcolonial independent states, has only partially displaced the alternative multi-approach, open-ended Islamic healing tradition, rather than abolishing it completely.

There are three categories of the medical repertoire termed Islamic medicine. First, there are the familial popular remedies inherited from the local pre-Islamic healing traditions. These include tested herbal recipes as well as limited surgery. Healers in this category deal generally with the minor ailments of headache, stomach ache, toothache, skin rash, recurrent fevers, and injuries, and may use diagnostic procedures in which supernatural powers are instrumental.

Second is Prophetic medicine. This is an extensive and literate therapeutic genre that includes simple or compound medicaments extracted from fauna and flora, as well as magical formulae, astrological divination, prayer, spells, and incantations. In addition to familial remedies, practitioners of Prophetic medicine utilize therapeutic strategies derived directly or indirectly from the Qur'an, or the sayings and practice of the Prophet Muhammad. Chief among the medicinal ingredients frequently mentioned in extant sources are honey, vinegar, tamarind, black cumin, and natron (sodium carbonate), alongside proper dieting, fasting, supplication, bloodletting, and cauterization. Medical practitioners who claim descent from the Prophet (the *sharifs*), or who are leaders of religious fraternities, (the *sufis*), or clerics renown for piety and learning, (the *faqis*, the marabouts, and the *malams*), use their personal *baraka* (spiritual power) to effect healing, foretell the future, or provide needed protection against unpredictable calamities.

The third category is Greek humoralism as articulated by Galen (d. c. 216) and systemized later by the Muslim physician Ibn Sina (Avicenna, d. 1037). This theory underscores balance in nature and health. Accordingly, a body is healthy when the four humors of blood, phlegm, yellow bile, and black bile and their respective corresponding qualities of moist, cold, heat, and dryness remain in equilibrium. Illness is the absence of such balance. By prescribing drugs that are hot to counter cold illnesses, or moist to offset the dryness of certain ailments, the physician reestablishes the balance necessary for restoring health. To optimize the conditions needed for a speedy recovery, medical practitioners must take into account such factors as sleep, emotional stress, diet, exercise, retention and evacuation of bodily solids or fluids, and the prevailing environmental conditions that influence the patient's response to treatment.

Ecological conditions were considered so important that the Egyptian physician 'Ali ibn Ridwan (d. 1068) wrote a whole treatise blaming Egypt's debilitating climate and terrain for the country's endemic fevers and recurring pestilences.

Islamic medicine in Africa has been a quest for a hybridized therapy that underscored the physical, physiological, and social dimensions of well-being. It has utilized complex hygienic regimes, dietary and drug prescriptions, and supernatural intervention. Within this open-ended, overarching healing tradition, specialized scholastic physicians and pharmacologists, ordinary herbalists, barbers, midwives, bonesetters, the sharifs, the sufis, or the spirit mediums are at liberty to utilize whatever subtherapeutic system or systems they believe will bring immediate relief or benefits to their patients. Hygienic practices deemed necessary for the maintenance or the restoration of health included socially mandated dos and don'ts concerning the intake of food or drink, and the general daily activities of the individual. Certain foods were tabooed, tolerated, or encouraged because of their perceived negative or positive effect on health. The yellow of the egg, for example, is thought to be bad for children among the contemporary Hamar, a Muslim group in Western Sudan. Gender inequality dictates that pregnant and old women among these people consume only the pancreas of slaughtered animals, the least desirable internal organ. Good oral and physical hygiene are regarded as healthy practices on the strength of both local custom and Prophetic medicine. Working or traveling in the midday sun is a health risk that must be avoided, whereas drinking or eating in moderation is the ultimate safeguard against ill health and general indisposition.

For many Muslims in Africa, recipes of herbs, minerals, and animal products or parts prepared in accordance with guidelines found in extant Islamic medical books are the preferred remedies against many internal illnesses. The preparation and application of such remedies, and the timing and quantities of doses taken, are based on extended local experience as well as on concepts and norms derived from humoralism or Western biomedicine. They are, however, legitimized and rendered efficacious because of

their association with the sanctified medicine of the Prophet.

ISLAMIC MEDICINE AND POLITICS

Historically, the close relationship between the political and the medical hegemony is illustrated by the special attention Muslim rulers in Africa gave to the healthcare delivery system in their domains. The Abbasid provincial governor of Egypt, Ahmed ibn Tulun, founded the first hospital at Old Cairo in 872 CE to cater for the sick and the insane. Sultan Salah al-Din (Saladin, c. 1138–1193) built a bigger and better endowed hospital in the twelfth century, the Nasiri Hospital, surpassed in size, elegance, and specialization only by the Mansuri hospital of Sultan Qalawun, completed in 1284 CE.

These and similar hospitals in other urban centers in North Africa developed into centers not only for healing but also for medical education. They had their different wards for the various diseases, each with separate sections for men and women. They were equipped with teaching halls, pharmacies where prescriptions were filled, hot and cold bathing facilities, even musicians to soothe patients' spirit. Patients of all walks of life, age, or religious persuasion found good medical treatment in these institutions. The hospitals also doubled as an asylum for the mentally unstable, a shelter for the aged and the homeless, and a convalescent home for the infirm.

Though there were no hospitals in Africa south of the Sahara, politics and medical practice still reinforced one another. Sultan Muhammad Bello of the nineteenth century Fulani Caliphate in Northern Nigeria was not only an accomplished physician in his own right, but also a teacher of Islamic medical tradition, a subject on which he authored several treatises that are still circulating in Nigeria and neighboring countries. Similarly, Muslim medical practitioners were held in high esteem in other courts in the tropics, and their intercession with the deity on behalf of their royal clients is documented among the Asanti of Ghana, the Ganda of Uganda, as well as the kings of Darfur, Taqali, and Sennar in present-day Sudan.

Where the healing repertoire of pre-Islamic origin held its ground against the expanding Islamic medical tradition, local healers nonetheless acquiesced to a position of subordination. The spirit mediums of the Bori cult in Northern Nigeria have Islamized their healing practice sufficiently to avoid rancorous attacks from the Muslim establishment. They expressed deference to political Islam by holding healing sessions on days other than Friday, the Muslim Sabbath, by giving Muslim names and titles to some powerful but friendly pagan spirits, and by slaughtering sacrificial animals in a fashion sanctioned by Muslim law. This is also the case among the Hufriyaat residents of northern Sudan, the Berti of Darfur, or the Songhay of Mali where the behavior of non-Muslim spirits in *bori* or *zar* dancing rituals is indistinguishable from that of Muslim spirits, and consumption of alcoholic beverages in such rituals is a thing of the past.

At present, there is a strong drive in the Muslim world, especially in countries experiencing exclusionary revivalist Islam such as Sudan, to Islamize knowledge, including medicine. Sudanese authorities, for example, have made it illegal to import drugs known to contain traces of alcohol or some other ingredients considered *haram*, or unlawful. On the other hand, the Sudanese government officially encourages research on the efficacy of honey and other medicinal ingredients recommended by the Prophet Mohammad. Political legitimation of therapeutic regimens is by no means limited to the Islamization of practice or the substitution of the medicinal ingredients used. It also involves rivalry among the different players in the field. The Hausa/Fulani male medical practitioners, for instance, attempted without much success to undermine the popularity of the women spirit mediums of the Bori cult by characterizing the cult as a heathen practice. The Halali Sunna, an orthodox reform Muslim movement among the Swahili communities in east Africa, challenges the power of sharifs (descendents of the Prophet) in dispensing medicine to the needy. The Halali reformists, as their counterparts in West Africa, the Wahhabists, reject the concept of spirits intruding into a person's body to cause illness. The introduction and adoption of Western biomedicine has only intensified such contestation.

The more flexible practitioners of the Islamic medical tradition have already adopted certain therapeutic procedures derived from the new system. For example, they prescribe taking medication three times daily, prepare recipes in powder, tablets, or liquids, and bottle them in recycled biomedicine plastic or glass containers. To the traditional ingredients in their repertoire they may add medicinal tablets, ointments, or syrups they purchase from Western-type pharmacies, and direct patients with complicated cases to see doctors in hospitals. However, there are practitioners of the Islamic tradition who remain resistant to change. They opt, instead, to overstress the healing property of the Prophetic medicine, or the supernatural power of certain verses from the Qur'an.

To conclude, medical and historical studies of sub-Saharan communities show that the evolution of medical practice as a strategy for healing or a means for religious or political empowerment is lively and multifaceted. The confluence of Islamic and humoral concepts of disease and cure with local customs and traditions has exhibited a profound dynamism in content, method, and geographic spread. Medical treatises and compilations are being produced and circulated now as they had always been over the centuries. As of 2007 there is no indication that this complex and open-ended medical pluralism in Muslim Africa that meets the health needs of millions of Africans is likely to disappear any time soon.

See also **Gender; Islam; Spirit Possession.**

BIBLIOGRAPHY

Abdalla, Ismail. *Islam, Medicine and Practitioners in Northern Nigeria.* Lewiston, New York: E. Mellen Press, 1997.

Beckerleg, Susan. "Medical Pluralism and Islam in Swahili Communities in Kenya." *Medical Anthropology Quarterly* 8, no. 3 (1994): 299–313.

Dols, Michael W. *Medieval Islamic Medicine: Ibn Ridwan's Treatise "On the Prevention of Bodily Ills In Egypt."* Berkeley: University of California Press, 1984.

Du Toit, Brian, and Ismail H. Abdalla, eds. *African Healing Strategies.* New York: Trado-Medic Books, 1985.

Lewis, I. M.; Ahmed Al-Safi; and Sayyid Hurreiz; eds. *Women's Medicine: The Zar-Bori Cult in Africa and Beyond.* Edinburgh: Edinburgh University Press for the International African Institute, 1991.

Slikkerveer, Leendert Jan. *Plural Medical Systems in the Horn of Africa: The Legacy of the "Sheikh" Hippocrates.* London: Kegan Paul International, 1990.

Swantz, Marja-Liisa. "Manipulation of Multiple Health Systems in the Coastal Regions of Tanzania." In *Culture, Experience, and Pluralism: Essays on African Ideas of*

Illness and Healing, ed. Anita Jacobson-Widding and David Westerlund. Uppsala, Sweden: Academiae Upsaliensis, 1989.

ISMAIL H. ABDALLA

MEDICAL PRACTITIONERS

Western allopathic medicine entered most of Africa with European global expansion, conquest, and colonization. Doctors accompanied the soldiers and sailors, explorers and traders, and missionaries and settlers who appeared along its coasts from the fifteenth century on—although until the late eighteenth century there was little that distinguished their medical skills from those they encountered among the continent's indigenous inhabitants, who had their own healing cosmologies and practices that were often born of careful empirical observation and an intimate knowledge of the environment. Until well into the twentieth century, the vast majority of Africans depended on the expertise of a variety of indigenous healers, and, in the absence of biomedical health workers, many still do.

On the northern and southern littorals, Western medicine has had a longer and more sustained presence than in most of the rest of Africa, reflecting these regions' more intensive and diverse contact with the European world. Moreover, until the eighteenth century, Islamic and European medical traditions had much in common, built as they were on a common literate Hippocratic tradition, and this was to mediate the subsequent experience of biomedicine in North and, to some extent, East Africa.

THE EXPANSION OF BIOMEDICINE IN AFRICA

Western biomedicine expanded all over Africa in the last third of the nineteenth century, with the simultaneous annexation of African territories by competing European powers, the mineral revolution in southern Africa, and the microbiological revolution. The development of more effective treatments for malaria and yellow fever was not only an essential precondition of European conquest and white settlement in parts of the continent hitherto avoided as "the white man's grave"; it also provided a major justification for European rule. "La seule excuse de la colonisation, c'est la médecine

[Medicine is the only justification for colonization]" declared Hubert Lyautey (1854–1934), the conqueror of Madagascar and Morocco and founder of the French colonial medical service (Porter 1997, 463).

The record was, however, far more ambiguous than advocates of the "civilizing role" of allopathic medicine allowed. The disruptions caused by the scramble for African territories and the mineral revolution were the source of much of the increased morbidity in Africa that so shocked European observers at the turn of the nineteenth century; until the 1920s, Western practitioners who followed in the wake of colonial rule were far more concerned with the health of soldiers, settlers, and officials than that of the empire's indigenous subjects, while public health based on racial science provided legitimization for segregationist policies and new modes of control in the name of "tropical hygiene."

MISSION MEDICINE

Until well into the twentieth century in sub-Saharan Africa, African health was largely left to the ministrations of indigenous healers or missionaries, who were also responsible for the training of the first African doctors and nurses. Initially, few missionaries were medically qualified. In the mid-nineteenth century, there were only forty medical missionaries anywhere in the world, and even David Livingstone, the most famous nineteenth-century medical missionary, had little clinical training. The Church Missionary Society (CMS) in West and East Africa was unusual in providing every mission station with a resident physician. Toward the century's end, however, the majority of the mission societies came to support medically qualified missionaries, although their main concern remained saving souls. By the beginning of the twentieth century, missionary doctors, many of them inspired by Livingstone, were establishing small cottage hospitals and clinics across rural Africa.

With the advent of colonial rule, mission doctors were joined by an increasing number of private practitioners and doctors in the colonial service, who brought with them the ethos, traditions, and professional organizations of their home countries. By the turn of the nineteenth century, schools of "tropical medicine," in part inspired by the advances in microbiology, were established in most of the colonial metropoles to prepare doctors wishing to practice in the colonies. After initial appalling mortality rates, large-scale enterprises—such as mining and plantations—also established health services, generally headed by doctors, for their workers—black and white.

BIOMEDICAL TRAINING FOR AFRICANS

In sub-Saharan Africa, the first Africans to train in Western biomedicine were mission converts, whether in Anglophone or—slightly later—in Francophone Africa. Initially the number of physicians trained was small, because of both the expense and the psychosocial demands of overseas training; the pioneers usually came from affluent elite families, although the first British-trained West African doctors were the mission-educated sons of ex-slaves in Sierra Leone. In the 1850s, the high death rate of its men persuaded the British army to train African doctors to serve its troops. Among the medical students was the renowned writer and thinker, James Africanus Beale Horton, who trained in London and Edinburgh. This early policy was short-lived but by the last three decades of the nineteenth century, West African doctors were finding their way to medical schools in Britain, often supported by wealthy relatives or the CMS; one of this generation, Dr. J. F. Easmon, rose to head the Gold Coast's Colonial Medical Service from 1892 until 1897, when the rising tide of racism and an increasingly impermeable color bar put an end to his employment and more widely to the prospects of educated Africans, including the small number of British-trained African doctors, in the colonial civil service.

In the Cape Colony and Natal, a handful of Africans sought medical training in the United States and Britain in the late nineteenth century. In an increasingly segregated and color-conscious South Africa, however, they were barred from government employment, and although some were consulted by whites, few African patients could afford private treatment. Everywhere, Western-qualified African doctors remained few in number until after World War II.

In many parts of Africa, physicians were often among the earliest nationalists, a function both of the discrimination they suffered personally and their awareness of the gap between the pretensions and the realities of colonial rule, as well as their relative economic independence. Thus, in West Africa, Africanus Horton was not only one of the earliest of the British-trained doctors, but he also signaled his nationalist sentiments by his choice of name and writings. Elsewhere, too, doctors were often among the most outspoken critics of colonialism and leaders in the anticolonial struggle; in many countries they became the first ministers of health after independence. Nevertheless, most African doctors accepted the individualized health care promoted by their Western training, and they largely rejected indigenous healing practices.

RURAL HEALTH AND THE TRAINING OF PARAPROFESSIONALS

In all the colonial territories, Western-type hospitals and the small number of qualified medical professionals were urban-based, and rural areas were woefully underserved despite missionary endeavors. This situation changed during and after World War I, as colonial authorities were faced with a crisis in health that seemed to threaten their future labor supply. The casualties of the war, the result of both the ruthless deployment of African carriers in the combat zones and the great influenza pandemic, compounded mortality from widespread sleeping sickness (which preoccupied colonial authorities in central Africa from the early 1900s), and fanned fears of African depopulation through syphilis and other sexually transmitted diseases.

Thus, starting with the Uganda Native Medical Corps in 1914 (which became the East African Native Medical Corps in 1916), colonial authorities began to extend their medical services to increasing numbers of Africans. Small clinics were established; extensive vaccination and immunization campaigns were undertaken against smallpox, yaws, and syphilis; and all the colonial powers began to train medical auxiliaries known variously as hospital and health assistants, "tribal dressers," sanitation aides, male orderlies and—on a very small scale, except in South Africa—female nurses.

In the interwar years, the success of the School of Applied Medicine in Dakar (Senegal, founded in 1918) in producing a cadre of rural health workers made it the model for the establishment of medical training by colonial administrations in Yaba (Nigeria, 1930), Fort Hare (South Africa,

1936–1940), Mengo (Uganda, 1948), and Leopoldsville (Belgian Congo, 1936). Most of these training centers evolved into full-fledged medical schools after World War II. Graduates of these institutions in the early years, however, were not treated well. They received lesser promotion prospects, income, and status compared to physicians; they were granted only limited qualifications after a lengthy period of study; and they suffered from condescension and racism at the hands of white medical supervisors.

The training of medical auxiliaries was often opposed by white doctors who feared what they termed unfair competition, and by black physicians who condemned what they saw as the devaluing of their skills and the training of second-class doctors for second-class people. In most of rural Africa, however, medical auxiliaries and nurses provide the bulk of biomedical health care, and it was through their endeavors that many Africans were introduced to Western medicine.

The training of local cadres of paraprofessionals in the interwar period reflected a broader shift, as Western doctors in Africa began to understand the social and environmental causes of ill health and the complexities of treatment in multicultural societies. Not until after World War II, however, did colonial powers looked to develop their African territories and promote colonial welfare vigorously enough that the number of indigenous private practitioners increased substantially. Despite this expansion, these physicians remained few in number and mostly urban-based.

DECOLONIZATION: DURING AND AFTER
For the elites who took over power in Africa after decolonization, Western medicine remained the touchstone of modernity and underpinned the benefits they promised their supporters. In the years just before, during, and after independence, health services were greatly expanded, new medical schools built, and major health campaigns mounted. Students were sent to study medicine not only at former imperial universities but also in the Communist bloc, with greater emphasis on public health care. The World Health Organization joined the Rockefeller Foundation, which had long been active in scientific research and medical training in Africa, in emphasizing primary health care. Neither

this effort, however, nor the various attempts to enlist traditional healers in the health services remedied the budgetary imbalance between high-tech curative biomedicine and preventative family and community health care.

Apart from a few exceptions, postindependence new governments found it as difficult to address the problems of rural health as had their colonial predecessors. Doctors remained concentrated in the urban areas, and the majority of the continent's rural inhabitants remained dependent on indigenous healers for their health.

NURSING
Except in South Africa, the history of nursing in Africa is astonishingly underresearched, while even the history of the British Colonial Nursing Association awaits its historian. The terminology is confusing, and nurses' terms of service and backgrounds are largely unknown; their history has to be pieced together from scattered paragraphs in accounts written by or about male doctors.

In sub-Saharan Africa, nursing care was generally part of a complex set of reciprocal rights and obligations among kin. Nor was it specifically associated with women. Caregivers were usually the elderly, regardless of gender, except for childbirth assistance, which was left to experienced older women. This was very different from Western models of professional nursing which involved the care of strangers.

EUROPEAN NURSES IN AFRICA
The first Western nurses, daughters of the reform of European and American nursing in the second half of the nineteenth century, also arrived in the wake of colonialism but slightly later than their medical counterparts. Most of them accompanied Protestant missionaries or came to Africa under the aegis of Catholic and Anglican sisterhoods in the last three decades of the century; a handful of them accompanied imperial armies in the late nineteenth century, combining sacrifice and service to others with a sense of imperial mission and adventure.

In 1896 the Colonial Nursing Association (CNA; renamed the Overseas Nursing Association in 1919 and taken under the wing of the Colonial Office in 1940 as the unified Colonial Nurses' Service) was formed in Britain to send nurses across the empire; by the turn of the century, several of these nurses were employed in colonial hospitals in Africa. During the South African War (1899–1902), nurses also made their way to the battlefields, forbears of the British nurses who served at the front in World War I.

While many of the CNA nurses shared the Christian vocation of the sisterhoods, British women found in overseas service independence, adventure, and travel, and upward mobility through marriage. They also found a more challenging hospital environment, and they performed a range of duties that had normally been the preserve of house officers in Britain. Initially responsible for nursing the expatriate community, they increasingly also treated the African population, and they became responsible for training a small number of female nursing assistants on the job.

Nevertheless, the legacy of the sisterhoods left an enduring mark on nursing in Africa, as it did in Europe. Premised on the subordination of nursing

to medical authority, their practice was based on tight discipline, seen as essential in the confused and ambiguous world of the colonial hospital. In an environment in which domestic labor was associated not only with the lower classes but also with the inferior races, class and race distinctions were jealously preserved through rigid hierarchies and careful delineation of roles and status, which were marked on nurses' bodies in the shape of uniforms, badges, and insignia. Innumerable rules regulated every aspect of their behavior. Their battles to achieve respectability and professional status had racial as well as gender and class consequences, distancing them from the vast majority of women in the subcontinent.

THE TRAINING OF AFRICAN NURSES
By the early 1900s male missionaries in the Cape Colony began training African nurses to the demanding standards required for state registration. Drawn from the Christian elite, they were

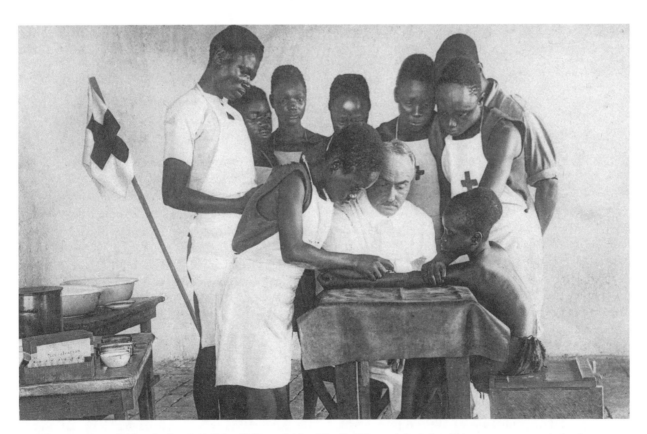

Red Cross nurses being trained. Until the 1940s, outside of South Africa, relatively few African women were trained as western-style professional nurses. Most rural health clinics were staffed by African male primary health care workers, shown here being trained in basic Red Cross skills. © RYKOFF COLLECTION/CORBIS

intended to be harbingers of progress and healing in black society, and—as importantly in a racially divided settler society—to relieve white women from having to nurse black men. In 1908 Cecilia Makiwane became the first African nurse registered with the Colonial Medical Council. In the rest of Africa (as in the South African mines), most nursing was done by male hospital assistants, tribal dressers, or orderlies, who began to be trained systematically after World War I.

In the rest of sub-Saharan Africa, the systematic training of African women as nurses was slower to develop, often occurring after midwifery training. Although missionaries had trained a few in a somewhat haphazard fashion in the nineteenth century and more methodically in the twentieth, formal courses for registered nurses were unavailable in most African countries until the late 1930s and 1940s, when the war spurred the implementation of the female nurse training. A greater number of midwifery colleges were established in the interwar years. In Ghana, for example, the majority of practicing nurses were men until a nursing college was opened at Kumasi in 1948, although there were almost four hundred trained midwives at work by 1953.

As in the case of medics, the training of African women as nurses was part of the modernizing agenda of the postcolonial state, and their numbers increased exponentially during the years just before and after independence. Together with teaching, nursing became the most important profession for women, many of whom were or became leading members of their communities. Student nurses constituted the labor force of the expanding hospital system, and they were paid while in training: this was particularly important for young women from poorer families. Similar to nurses in other parts of the world, they were drawn into the profession by a mixture of motives: a sense of vocation, a desire for adventure and upward mobility, or the attractions of a uniform, although their wages were low and the work demanding.

HEALTH CARE SINCE THE 1970S

Since the 1970s, the lives of Westernized health workers have been profoundly affected by the general context in which they have worked—from the extremes of war, torture, and genocide in Rwanda,

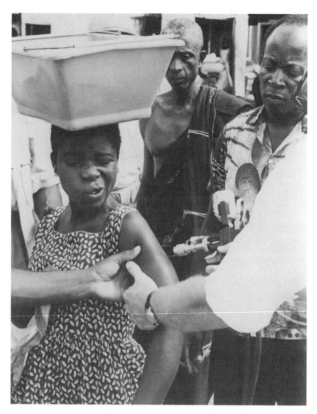

Nigerian girl being vaccinated against smallpox. In colonial times, vaccination was the main encounter of many Africans with biomedicine. This picture was taken in 1969, a year before the international eradication of smallpox, perhaps the most important triumph of the World Health Organization. © BETTMANN/CORBIS

Angola, Mozambique, the Congo, and Sierra Leone to the socialist experiment in Tanzania, the capitalist free market of Kenya, and apartheid and post-apartheid South Africa, where the Western medical profession has the strongest presence on the continent. Economic collapse has affected the lives of doctors and nurses, undermining their status and at times even their sense of professionalism, as transport infrastructures have collapsed, drugs have been in short supply, hospitals have deteriorated, and corruption has found a ready foothold among poverty-stricken health demands. These factors have sidelined public health and preventive medicine and left most countries without the necessary infrastructure or human resources to stem the contemporary outbreak of the HIV/AIDS pandemic. HIV/AIDS has not only claimed a high number of health workers since the 1970s; it has also contributed to the huge brain drain of African nurses and doctors, leaving those behind over-worked and demoralized. African leaders decry this brain drain not only because of its effects on health care in their country, but because impoverished African countries bear a substantial part of the costs of training health workers for the developed world.

According to the World Health Organization, in 2006 there were some 590,198 health workers (doctors, nurses, and midwives) in Africa, and 36 of the 46 countries in Africa suffered from a critical shortage of health workers. To achieve 80 percent coverage (estimated as between 2 and 2.5 health workers per 1,000 head of population) would require an expansion of nearly 140 percent. Twenty-five percent of Africa's doctors and 5 percent of its nurses are working in North America and Europe. In the early twenty-first century, Africa has 11 percent of the world's population and 24 percent of the global burden of disease but only 3 percent of the world's health workers.

See also **Decolonization; Disease; Horton, James Africanus Beale; Kumasi; Livingstone, David.**

BIBLIOGRAPHY

Doctors

Deacon, Harriet; Howard Phillips; and Elizabeth van Heyningen; eds. *The Cape Doctor in the Nineteenth Century: A Social History.* Wellcome Institute Series in the History of Medicine. Atlanta: Rodopi, 2003.

Etherington, Norman. "Education and Medicine." In *Missions and Empire*, ed. Norman Etherington. History of the British Empire Companion Series. Oxford: Oxford University Press, 2005.

Gallagher, Nancy Elizabeth. *Medicine and Power in Tunisia, 1780–1904.* Cambridge, U.K.: Cambridge University Press, 1983.

Iliffe, John. *East African Doctors: A History of the Modern Profession.* Cambridge, U.K.: Cambridge University Press, 1997.

Janssens, P. G.; M. Kivits; and J. Vuylsteke, J.; eds. *Health in Central Africa since 1885: Past, Present and Future*, Vol. 1. Brussels: King Baudouin, 1997.

Kuhnke, LaVerne. *Lives at Risk: Public Heath in Nineteenth-Century Egypt.* Berkeley: University of California Press, 1990.

Patterson, K. David. *Health in Ghana: Disease, Medicine and Socio-Economic Change.* Waltham, MA: Crossroads Press, 1981.

Patton, Adell. *Physicians, Colonial Racism, and Diaspora in West Africa.* Gainesville: University of Florida Press, 1996.

Porter, Roy. *The Greatest Benefit to Mankind. A Medical History of Humanity from Antiquity to the Present.* London: Fontana Press, 1997.

WHO. *The World Health Report 2006—Working Together for Health.* Geneva: WHO Press, 2006.

Nurses

Holden, Pat. "Colonial Sisters: Nurses in Uganda." In *Anthropology and Nursing*, ed. Pat Holden and Jenny Littlewood. New York: Routledge, 1991.

Kuper, Hilda. "Nurses." In *An African Bourgeoisie: Race, Class, and Politics in South Africa*, ed. Leo Kuper. New Haven, CT: Yale University Press.

Marks, Shula. *Divided Sisterhood: Race, Class, and Gender in the South African Nursing Profession.* New York: St. Martin's Press, 1994.

SHULA MARKS

MEDICINE AND DRUGS

The use of medicinal products in Africa involves a long and complex history of local knowledge and practice, the utilization of indigenous plants, and the assimilation of Western pharmaceuticals into what constitutes a series of highly dynamic and pluralistic medical systems across the continent. Medicines themselves, whether plant-, animal-, or mineral-based, have been incorporated into diverse medical and healing cosmologies. Local knowledge of medicinally useful plants handed down through generations has informed regionally specific healing practices across the continent.

Many modern pharmaceuticals are derivative of both the natural products found across Africa and the existing indigenous knowledge of their identification, cultivation, and usage. Many of these medicinal plants have been in use by local healers for generations, prompting a greater awareness that the development of pharmaceutical products owes a debt to these communities for what constitutes intellectual property. Such protections were written into the 2006 draft of the United Nations Declaration on the Rights of Indigenous Peoples, although it remains to be seen how such rights will be ensured.

It is estimated that twenty-five percent of modern medicines are derived from plant-based traditional medicines found across the globe. Plants such as *Artemesia annua*, an ancient Chinese herbal remedy used to treat malaria, have been laboratory tested and are recommended as effective treatments by global public health bodies such as the World Health Organization (WHO).

Malaria remains an overwhelming source of morbidity and mortality in Africa, with up to 500 million infections each year. It is clear that the cost of treating malaria with exclusively external sources would be far too great. However, with more than 1,000 plant species identified for use in the treatment of malaria globally, it is clear that the primary responsibility for treating the disease has remained with families, communities, and locally based traditional healers. Although the increased accessibility of drugs such as chloroquine have had a significant impact on the treatment of malaria in Africa, drug resistant strains

of the malarial parasite have become a concern in recent years. The WHO estimates that traditional medicine still remains the first line of defense for the majority of Africans. Current debates about the extent to which African traditional medicines should be incorporated into national healthcare systems have been aided by the increasing standardization and regulation of some traditional healers within their own national professional associations. In 2003, South Africa passed the Traditional Health Practitioners Bill that created a council to regulate the activities of traditional healers. The recognition that 75 percent of people living with HIV/AIDS may also use some form of traditional or complementary alternative medicine is a global phenomenon that corresponds not only to African countries, but also the United States and Great Britain. As a result, research programs designed to test the efficacy of herbal treatments for a variety of conditions, including malaria, have been successfully implemented in countries across Africa such as Zimbabwe, Kenya, Uganda, Burkina Faso, Mali, and Nigeria.

Although medicines in Africa have existed for millennia, the emergence of modern, laboratory-produced drug therapies is a development of the twentieth century, a period in African history roughly corresponding to European colonial rule. Early depictions of Africa as the white man's grave gave way at the turn of the century to a new optimism ushered in by the emerging discipline of tropical medicine and the realization that anti-malarial drugs such as quinine (from *Cinchona*) would allow for the successful settlement of European colonists in the African territories. Europeans were the primary users of quinine and its derivatives for malaria, but as colonial governments expanded, other drugs became part of health campaigns directed at African populations, often on a massive scale. Drug treatments for syphilis and yaws were often well received in some regions. However, other campaigns, such as those against sleeping sickness in the Belgian Congo, used force and incarceration as a means of making diagnoses and administering treatment with atoxyl, a drug associated with severe side effects that included blindness.

In the early twenty-first century, the pharmaceutical industry is one of the most profitable in the world and the increasingly high cost of drugs and drug development has had a significant impact on

A man sells vines and roots in Lagos, Nigeria, January 2004. More than 60 percent of the population in Africa rely heavily on traditional plant medicines. Increasingly, consumers in even the most industrialized countries are making room for alternative remedies and herbal products. AP Photo/George Osodi

substantially rising healthcare costs globally. From the early twenty-first century, drug pricing has become increasingly controversial as industry critics claim that pharmaceutical companies spend vast sums on marketing and lobbying efforts, rather than on the science of drug development. Such tactics suggest that the high price of drugs cannot be justified. This issue has been magnified across the African continent as infectious diseases that have impacted the continent, such as malaria, tuberculosis, and HIV/AIDS, continue to debilitate or kill millions each year. Essential medicines for treatment or prevention remain too expensive for the vast majority of the population, or access is limited due to poor healthcare infrastructure.

In general, drugs research and development is driven generally by the needs and interests of countries in the Europe and North America, despite a much greater burden of disease felt throughout the developing world, including most African countries. Increasingly, issues of access to essential medications and affordability have been tied to the issue of drug patents and restrictions on the importation of cheaper alternative drugs to poor countries. In 1994, the Trade Related Aspects of Intellectual Properties (TRIPS) agreement stipulated that corporations' intellectual property (patents) could be protected, but "in a manner conducive to social and economic welfare, and to a balance of rights and obligations" (TRIPS, Article 7). Some provisions in the Act were intended to guard against the potentially negative effects of a trade monopoly on life-saving medications. The agreement allows for a revocation of the monopoly privilege in the event of public health crises, or for the importation of cheaper alternatives from countries with lower-priced drugs.

However, in some instances such attempts have been met with lawsuits brought by multinational drug companies or pressure from governments in the West arguing against the relaxation of patents or the importation of generic drugs. With the development of antiretroviral drugs for the treatment of AIDS, the tensions between multinational pharmaceutical interests and consumers in countries such as South Africa have come to the fore as the Treatment Action Campaign (TAC) and other activist organizations have begun to lobby on a national and international level for more equitable access to essential medications.

Despite the high priority placed on research and clinical trials designed to test new drugs, recruiting the high numbers of research subjects necessary for successful clinical trials conducted in the West has been difficult. As a result, there has been a significant trend to ship experimental drug trials overseas to impoverished countries where the ethical standards required for research may be relaxed substantially. In 2001, the pharmaceutical company Pfizer came under fire for their sponsorship of an experimental trial for the drug Trovan conducted in 1996 involving children with meningitis in Nigeria. The company was charged with employing coercive methods, failing to implement a credible system of informed consent, and exposing research participants to considerable risk. The Pfizer drug trial in Nigeria served to highlight the attitude that, in such poverty-stricken environments, whatever scientists opt to do is better than paying no attention at all to such populations. As a result of the drug trial, thirty Nigerian families filed a class action lawsuit against Pfizer claiming that the company violated medical ethics as stipulated by the Nuremberg Code. In 2005 the suit against Pfizer was dismissed when the courts decided that United States law did not cover the types of claims being made. The Pfizer case has drawn attention to the ongoing debates about the portability of ethical standards that may be applied by law in the West, but have been more malleable when applied to African countries. Additional questions surround experimental trials that may not in themselves pose significant risks or skirt standard ethical requirements, but the results of which are designed to benefit populations outside of Africa. Thus, two of the most pressing issues related to the development of new medicines in Africa remain a greater provision of accessible and affordable drugs for the majority populations, and the establishment of research trials that target diseases and conditions that significantly impact the continent.

See also **Disease; Divination and Oracles; Food; Plants; Religion and Ritual; Witchcraft.**

BIBLIOGRAPHY

Rugemalila, J.B., and Wen L. Kilama, eds. "Proceedings Seminar on Health Research Ethics in Africa." *Acta Tropica* 78 (2001): S1–S126.

Shah, Sonia. "Globalization of Clinical Research by the Pharmaceutical Industry." *International Journal of Health Services* 33, no. 1 (2003): 29–36.

Whyte, Susan Reynolds; Sjaak van der Geest; and Anita Hardon. *Social Lives of Medicines.* Cambridge, U.K.: Cambridge University Press, 2002.

Willcox, Merlin; Gerard Bodeker; and Philippe Rasoanaivo; eds. *Traditional Medicinal Plants and Malaria.* London: CRC Press, 2004.

World Health Organization. *Traditional Medicine, Fact Sheet No. 134.* Geneva: World Health Organization, 2003.

SLOAN MAHONE

HERITAGE, CULTURAL

This entry includes the following articles:
MANAGEMENT AND PRESERVATION
TRADE

MANAGEMENT AND PRESERVATION

Cultural heritage can mean both tangible (monumental) and intangible (the dramatic arts, languages, traditional music, and informational, spiritual, and philosophical components) that a particular people view as meaningful to their history and identity. Many institutions in the early twenty-first century are involved in the management and preservation of cultural heritage or patrimony. They include the United Nations Educational, Scientific and Cultural Organization (UNESCO), and national government ministries of culture. Within nations, national museums, antiquities departments, community cultural centers, national park services, and lately, community and nongovernmental organizations are organizations involved with cultural heritage management and preservation. In Africa, however, national museums are the primary bodies responsible for management and preservation of the national cultural patrimony.

As African nations gained independence, the political leadership was confronted with new challenges: fostering governments and national unity, and preserving cultural patrimony. As a result, governments created national museums and parks and granted them the mandate to investigate and identify sites of national and global significance for preservation. Museums, national galleries, and cultural theatres became the focal points of promoting these ideals. Governments invested in the preservation of archaeological, historical, and ethnographic sites of local and national significance. Expeditions and campaigns to collect important culture materials to fill the museums and galleries were undertaken. National galleries and cultural centers were developed to promote the performing arts, including traditional museums, poetry, and drama. The goal was to promote national unity and pride in the new nations.

In the early twenty-first century, most African nations boast a number of historical and archaeological sites and monuments that have become symbols of both humankind's and national unity. These sites and monuments include the early hominid sites of Africa in Tanzania, Kenya, and Ethiopia; the Great Pyramids of Egypt; the rock churches of Lalibäla, Ethiopia; and the Great Zimbabwe ruins of Zimbabwe. They are a source of cultural pride for Africans and give meaning to the belief that Africans have indeed played an important role in the evolution of humankind. Since the designation of those sites as significant cultural locations, heritage management has become more diversified and now includes community organizations and private museums and galleries. UNESCO is more engaged in the management and protection of both movable and nonmovable cultural patrimony, and more engaged than ever with indigenous notions of heritage. Likewise, national museums and other institutions now work more closely with local communities to manage both tangible and intangible cultural heritage.

MUSEUMS AS AGENTS OF CULTURAL HERITAGE PRESERVATION AND MANAGEMENT IN AFRICA

Museums house the earth's natural and cultural heritage for humankind. Most museums in Africa are government funded and are managed by curators and researchers who collect, curate, study, and develop permanent and temporary exhibits for the public. Museums mount exhibitions on many topics in the natural, life, and cultural sciences, organize traveling exhibitions in outstations or provincial centers, and publish guides and catalogues on the exhibits. They use audio, visual, and audio-visual media such as radio, transparencies, slides, movie films, video films, and television programs to educate the public about their work. Education officers in museums spread knowledge on cultural and scientific work carried out in the museum.

AFRICAN MUSEUMS AS CENTERS OF MANAGEMENT AND PRESERVATION CULTURAL HERITAGE

The International Commission of Museums (ICOM) defined the museum, in its Eleventh General Assembly at Copenhagen, 1974, as "a non-profit making, permanent institution in the service of society and its development, and open to the public which acquires, conserves, researches, communicates, and exhibits, for purposes of study, education, and enjoyment of material evidence of man and his environment" (Aykac 1989, 84). Do African museums meet this mandate? What are the limitations of African museums? And, how can these limitations be corrected in order to permit them to successfully carry out their mission? As elsewhere, curators manage museums in Africa. Curators ensure that the museum's mandate—including the proper collections, curations, and exhibitions of cultural archaeological, ethnographic, and artistic objects. The curators promote the goals of the nation, including cultural and national unity through research on cultural, social, technological, and political achievements of its people. They promote the care of collections held at museum from piracy and damage, especially by art dealers, the environment, and vermin. They sponsor exhibitions and displays on technological and historical achievements of the people.

Most museums have an education department that develops teaching and learning materials for school children on exhibitions and museum collections. Museums' education staff assists children and their teachers to understand and appreciate the cultural heritage of various ethnic groups, intra- and interethnic relationships, and the specific contributions each community makes to the nation and to the world. Education officials print pamphlets that are distributed to children when they visit the museum. The officials also give lectures, show educational films, and provide guided tours of the museum. Many museums in Africa also have archaeology and/or history departments that are responsible for conducting research into various aspects of cultures, dissemination of cultural information, and promotion and development of culture. For example, the archaeology department in

Kenya conducts research on the evolution of humankind, the origins of urbanism, and the cultural and economic relationships between Kenyan communities and foreign traders.

Museum conservators carry out the preservation of sites and monuments, and care for all sites in the country including those gazetted and nongazetted. They monitor and repair, when necessary, all collections held in galleries and storage, and maintain stable temperatures and humidity levels in the museum and storerooms. Conservators consult with museum researchers and assist them in preparing protocols of handling collections in field and laboratory contexts. Museum conservators also work in consultation with other agencies. For example, the conservation departments in Kenya and Tanzania are involved in large conservation programs of the UNESCO World Heritage Sites at the ancient cities of Kilwa, Lamu, and Mombasa.

CHALLENGES OF CULTURAL PRESERVATION AND MANAGEMENT IN AFRICA

Africans have made major contributions to global history. The earliest fossil evidence for emergence of humankind has been found only in Africa. From architecture and settlement planning to water management, Africans developed appropriate technologies that were well adapted to the functional and symbolic requirements of Africans. Unfortunately, Africa is not presently able to fully protect its cultural heritage, nor is it able to stop the destruction of the sites. Archaeological and monumental sites that were once marvels of architecture, sites with beautiful and elegant old houses, and sites that hold rare and priceless fossils and artifacts that bear the earliest evidence of human ancestors are in danger of being lost to natural and human destructive forces. Antiques and art dealers and developers illegally excavate many sites and monuments. Ethnographic and art objects are illicitly procured from their owners or from museums and are exported to be sold at art auctions in more wealthy countries and displayed, out of context, in private collections.

How can national museums successfully meet their mandate to preserve cultural heritage? Few African museums have enough resources, because African governments no longer fully financially support museums. For example, the National Museums of Kenya (NMK), considered one of the top museum systems in Africa, receives 28 percent of its budget of US$3 million from the government. The NMK must raise the rest of its required revenue from donor nations and agencies. This shortfall in funding and manpower affects museums' ability to manage their responsibilities. Consequently, exhibits have not been changed in many museums for years and are thoroughly outdated. Displays behind glass show-cases that have become so unpopular in Western museums remain the norm in African museums.

Although conservators should regularly visit all the sites and monuments to monitor their condi-tion, in practice few have resources to visit them and sadly only do so after sites have been com-pletely destroyed by vandals or developers. Other sites have succumbed to natural forces, such as erosion and flooding. Still other sites have fallen victim to resettlement by local people. Yet others are victim to art dealers and collectors who finance illegal looting expeditions.

CONCLUSION

Museums in Africa are guardians of the continent's peoples' priceless cultural heritage. They have been mandated by national governments to research, manage, preserve, and educate the public about this heritage. African governments must, therefore, pro-vide sufficient funding to museums and other cul-tural institutions to enable them to carry out their mandate. The vandalism and destruction of archaeo-logical sites is a much larger problem that will require the cooperation of all peoples of the world.

See also **Archaeology and Prehistory; Lalibäla; Libraries; Mombasa; Museums; Zimbabwe, Great.**

BIBLIOGRAPHY

Ardouin, Claude Daniel. "Protection without Encasement: An African Argument." *Museum* 37, no. 2 (1985): 77–80.

Aykac, Ahmet. 1989 "Elements for an Economic Analysis of Museums." *Museum* 162, no. 2 (1989): 84–87.

Etherington, R. "Schole: Deschooling Children Museum Activities." *Museum*, no. 2 (1989): 69–71.

Ndegwa, L. "Extending Museum Education in Kenya." *Museum* 36, no. 4 (1984): 228–232.

Nurse, Derek, and Thomas Spear. *The Swahili: Reconstruct-ing the History of an African Society.* Philadelphia: University of Pennsylvania Press, 1985.

Odak, Osaga. "Kenya: The Museum Functions of KAERA (the Kenya Archaeological and Ethnographic Research Agency." *Museum* 40, no. 3 (1988): 150–154.

Price, Sally. *Primitive Art in Civilized Places*, 2nd edition. Chicago: University of Chicago Press, 2001.

Robert, Adèle. "Children Don't Like Museums? Visit the Inventorium and Find Out" *Museum* 2, no. 162 (1989): 72–75.

Schåvelzon, Daniel. "The History of Mesoamerican Archaeology at the Crossroads: Changing Views of the Past." In *Tracing Archaeology's Past: The Historiog-raphy of Archaeology*, ed. Andrew L. Christenson. Car-bondale: Southern Illinois University Press, 1989.

Wandibba, Simiyu. "Archaeology and Education in Kenya." Paper read at the World Archaeology Congress, South-ampton, 1987.

CHAPURUKHA M. KUSIMBA

TRADE

Since the seventeenth century, in the context of overseas trade, colonialism, and globalization, an ever-growing stream of ritual objects has flowed from African villages, shrines, and graves to Western nations. The objects have moved to and through trading, administrative and missionary posts, cabinets of curiosity, museums, monasteries, private collections, antique shops, art galleries, and auction houses, and sometimes back to the regions of origin.

Along the way, various, often conflicting, values and meanings have been lent to these items by their animist, Islamic, and Christian owners; commercial undertakings; traditional and modernist European art; anthropological scholarship; as well as ethnic and nationalist articulations of identity and the cul-tural property discourse. Literally millions of ritual objects labeled as "idols," "rarities," "trophies," "curios," "ethnographics," "souvenirs," or "objets d'art," have been commodified and traded. In increasingly transnational markets that connected African hinterlands to Western metropoles in the late nineteenth century, such items occupied a somewhat special place alongside the developing commodity flows of rubber, ivory, minerals, and tropical wood. They were not infrequently taken by force or ruse, but more typically were exchanged for beads, mirrors, clothing, iron nails, tools, or currency. In the Belgian Free State of Congo, for example, between 1906 and 1909 the Hungarian ethnographer Emil Torday acquired and carefully documented more than three thousand Kuba and other items, which he sold primarily to the British Museum.

In the course of the twentieth century, Christian missionaries have financed their activities by removing hundreds of thousands of African objects from their original contexts of cult and selling them through temporary exhibitions in the West. Other objects were destined for permanent missionary museums and often ended up in museums of ethnography or the market for "tribal art." At least as many objects as were traded were burnt by zealous missionaries, a practice that occasionally continues in the twenty-first century.

FANG *BYERI*

Telling examples of the reception history of African ritual art in the West are the *byeri* guardian figures or heads that surmounted human relic containers among the Fang of Gabon, Equatorial Guinea, and Cameroon. They are among the most sought-after and high-priced genres of art from Africa. The first examples were collected in the late nineteenth century, when they were generally seen as backward, ugly curiosities or superstitious idols. But around the turn of the twentieth century, modernist artists in the colonial metropoles began to view and collect these reliquary figures as high art, testifying to imagined African primordial purity and a natural unaffectedness felt to have been lost in Europe. The figures were among the earliest African art objects to be handled by gallery owners such as Paul Guillaume and Daniel-Henry Kahnweiler in Paris, Alfred Stieglitz in New York, and Carel van Lier in Amsterdam, who combined European avant-garde art with *art nègre*.

One of the best-known "tribal art" collectors of the twentieth century, cosmetics tycoon Helena Rubinstein, had thirteen Fang reliquary guardian heads and figures in her collection when it was auctioned in New York in 1966. Armand Arman, the renowned French *nouveau realisme* artist and collector of African art from the 1960s until his death in 2005, owned about as many. As an artist,

he specialized in so-called accumulations, or series of all sorts of objects, and as a collector he applied the same aesthetic principle, accumulating Fang *byeri* in quantity, among other classes of African art.

Early in the twenty-first century, fine Fang figures fetch hundreds of thousands of dollars at auction. Even more is paid for them when early collectors and dealers of repute figure in their pedigrees, spelled out in the auction catalogs that constitute important sources documenting the multifarious itineraries of African art. The most expensive *byeri* yet, a 29-centimeter female torso, was sold at auction in 1999 for $1.5 million to a London dealer bidding for a private collector. Additional prestige was lent to the object and its new owner by the fact that it had been part of a landmark exhibition: *African Negro Art*, the first comprehensive show of African art in the United States. An initiative of the Museum of Modern Art in New York in 1935, it featured more than six hundred objects and established a canon of "classical" African art. *Fang: An Epic Journey* (2001), a short fictional film based on real events by Susan Vogel, traces the itinerary of one statue from Gabon through Paris and Berlin to New York. The film addresses fundamental theoretical issues, such as what constitutes "art" and how aesthetic values are transformed into market values. Similar cases could be made for quite a few other highly valued traditions of African art, such as Dogon, Yoruba, Bangwa, Vili, or Chokwe.

CÔTE D'IVOIRE ART TRADE

In 1994 Christopher Steiner studied another aspect of tribal-art trading in a ground-breaking ethnographic and economic account of the Côte d'Ivoire trade in mostly, but not exclusively, low-grade and fake artwork of the Baule, Dan, Akan, Asante, Senufo, among others, or in their style. Several hundred traders with their families and networks, predominantly Mande, Wolof, and Hausa, operate from or are connected to market stalls and store houses in the capital, Abidjan. These middlemen are Muslims, who attach no religious value to the masks, statues, and utensils they handle. They mediate between non-Muslim local producers in hinterland villages and secluded workshops on the one hand and non-Muslim consumers in Western metropoles on the other hand, "adding economic value to what they sell by interpreting and capitalizing on the cultural values and desires from two different worlds" (Steiner 1994, 14). Value emerges through bargaining and cultural brokerage. Stereotypical meanings are invented, and a mystique of African "authenticity," a purely Western canon, is created by feigning or adding to signs of use: wear, dirt, and patina.

ETHNOGRAPHY VERSUS AESTHETICS

Anthropologists tend to deride the categorization and decontextualization of African ritual objects as primarily "fine art" and look down upon the "tribal art" market as ethically dubious. At the same time, curators cannot always escape from being actors in this market, such as when accepting donations of private collections with the help of dealers, or when borrowing exhibits from collectors.

On the other side, there are art historians and curators who take a predominantly aesthetic approach and see no reason to treat African fine art differently from the fine arts of European or other expressions. Particularly in the United States, the ties between academia and commerce are narrow in the case of art museums, which often have acquired substantial parts of their collections directly or indirectly from dealers and galleries and continue to do so. The goings-on around exhibitions, donations, and auctions of African art constitute Trobriand *kula*-like personal "tournaments of value." Pedigree and prestige are all important, and the biographies of objects, dealers, socialite-collectors, and institutions are intertwined. Ironically, in authentic African contexts, the identity of the donor of an object is primary in constituting its value to a recipient. Anthropologists, however, seem to apply a double standard by stressing African contexts and neglecting subsequent non-African travels and owners of objects.

A salient recent example of the conflict between aesthetic and ethnographic views, as well as interconnections between scholarship and commerce, is the Musée du Quai Branly in Paris, which opened in 2006. It was a project of the French president, a collector himself, to relocate the national collections of *arts premiers*—a phrase that tries to avoid, but revealingly still resonates in the ear, the derogatory *art primitive*—in one huge venue in the heart of the former colonial metropole. The endeavor was masterminded by a prominent tribal art connoisseur and upmarket dealer, a close friend of the president, who was confronted by anthropologists in charge of ethnographic contextualization. The spectacular museum came about amidst continuous conflicts over how and what to exhibit.

CULTURAL HERITAGE

Another landmark was the entrance into the Louvre of 117 pieces of tribal art a few years earlier, presented as high art but fiercely resisted by the museum's art historians. Some pieces that entered the Louvre as objets d'art had unclear provenances. Some were bought from, and others donated by, dealers. Four objects were from an exquisite Swiss private collection of Nigerian art, bought in 1997 for the new museum. This purchase sparked much discussion in an era of growing concern with illicit trade in cultural heritage, in the sense that these objects have social, religious, aesthetic, or scientific significance for the people who created them and should be seen as those people's inalienable property.

Most fine African art can now be found in the West, not in African countries plagued by poverty, disease, and civil strife. Theft from African museums by impoverished employees and others is endemic, and archaeological sites, such as the Nok sites in Nigeria and the Djenné sites in Mali, continue to be looted by local residents. In the last few decades new ethical and legal standards have emerged regarding the protection, acquisition, restitution, and international traffic of "cultural property," but these guidelines have not yet been ratified by all nations or museums. "The story of the illicit trade in African art," Dele Jegede commented, "is, in large measure, the story of the unscrupulous Western exploitation of loopholes . . . within the organizational and social structure in Africa for personal gratification or for corporate, institutional, or national aggrandizement" (Schmidt and MacIntosh 1996, 126).

See also **Art; Globalization; Trade, National and International Systems.**

BIBLIOGRAPHY

Corbey, Raymond. *Tribal Art Traffic: A Chronicle of Taste, Trade, and Desire in Colonial and Post-Colonial Times.*

Amsterdam: Kit Publishers/Royal Tropical Institute, 2000.

Fang: An Epic Journey. Directed by Susan Vogel. Prince Street Pictures, Inc., 2001.

Prélever, exhiber: La mise en musées. Special issue of *Cahiers d'Etudes Africaines* 34 no. 155–156 (1999).

Schildkrout, Enid, and Curtis A. Keim, eds. *The Scramble for Art in Central Africa.* New York: Cambridge University Press, 1998.

Schmidt, Peter R., and Roderick J. McIntosh, eds. *Plundering Africa's Past.* Bloomington: Indiana University Press, 1996.

Steiner, Christopher B. *African Art in Transit.* New York: Cambridge University Press, 1994.

RAYMOND CORBEY

HERITAGE TOURISM. *See* **Heritage, Cultural: Trade; Tourism.**

HISTORIOGRAPHY

This entry includes the following articles:
WESTERN AND AFRICAN CONCEPTS
EUROPEAN
ISLAMIC
ORAL

WESTERN AND AFRICAN CONCEPTS

Deeper issues of conceptualizing historical thinking itself underlie the progression of themes, including "trade and politics," "resistance," and "underdevelopment," that have marked the writing of African history in its first half century. History as a disciplined academic field is an expression of the post-Enlightenment West's empiricism and humanism with a distinctive epistemology, of logic of inquiry and explanation. It contrasts, as such, with parallel but different, heuristic principles in earlier eras in Europe and also everywhere else in the world, including Africa.

The modern discipline of history took shape in the nineteenth century, led by German philosophers following with Georg Wilhelm Friedrich Hegel (1770–1831), as a moralistic exploration of human (rather than divine) virtues. It was history's background in moral philosophy that inclined the paradigm-defining historians of that century to focus on exemplary individuals and to puzzle over how so perfected an ancient model of Europe's imperialistic ambitions in that era as the Roman Empire might have "declined and fallen," as Edward Gibbon's epic classic phased so forbidding a prospect. It was a time of uninhibited triumphalism in Europe as the continent, already wealthy by world standards, delighted in the productivity and power of its unprecedented Industrial Revolution and aggressively assumed the burden of "civilizing" the rest of the world through its commerce, conquest, and Christian charity. Since literacy figured prominently among these virtues, it was axiomatic that the documentary record was the only sort of evidence necessary for so noble a narrative, since exemplary men—seldom women—were assumed to have recorded their best thinking in writing, as indeed did many political and military leaders of the generation that give formed modern historical thought, concerned thus to record their contributions to the glorious progress of modern man.

The discipline of history thus emerged as part and parcel of the surge of national pride in the nineteenth century. It's two major components, "ancient history" and "modern history," mirrored one another, with the ancient Greeks and Romans, as well as early Christianity, scanned for the origins of the virtues that Europeans fancied in themselves and modern Europeans perfecting ancient practices of all-but-invincible military power, republican forms of government that had replaced the absolute monarchy of the dark days in between (the "medieval" or "middle" ages), democratic and increasingly populist politics, and virtuous benevolence to the unenlightened and inherently less able, darker-skinned peoples of the world. A rampant racism was the downside of history's culmination in the modern West. This "modern history" was conceptualized fundamentally in terms of the "nations" then also taking shape in Europe and in the United States, groups of citizens joined in a fundamental civic and spiritual equality. The word itself—"nation"—came from the Latin word for "birth," so that nationality was inherent by virtue of common ancestry in a figurative if not also literal sense. Antiquity of national or "civilizational" histories replaced aristocratic lineage as a prime mark of precedence in the present. This epistemological muddling of present and past was not without its glaring contradictions.

By these self-celebratory standards, as is all too well known, Africa had no "history." It had no known documentary record. It stood, for Hegel and virtually all other respectable historians until the middle of the twentieth century, as the living polar opposite of progressive Europe and the United States; it was a continent where time seemed to have stood still, its people "primitives" either in a racist sense of perpetual children or in a liberal sense of "noble savages" representing humanity before the biblical Fall, awaiting redemption as Christians, and perhaps also updatable in time. Only the most courageous and brilliant African American scholars challenged this turn-of-the-twentieth-century exclusion of their ancestors from history itself, and with sense of racial identity as proud and strong as the national identities that excluded them, began to detect the in-fact readily available written records of African military prowess in the past and wrested credit for the "ancient empires" of Ghana, Mali, and Songhay in western Africa away from mythical "Hamites" or Arabs and the monumental building in stone in southeastern Africa—Great Zimbabwe—from Phoenecians or King Solomon or other honorary "whites." In the racial conceptualization of the world at that time they could express local sources in Africa only as "black."

The historical discipline has been in recovery ever since from what is now understood to have been the radically ahistorical characteristics of its birth. History's distinctive epistemology rests on three fundamental premises, and none of them feature the past. The "past," that is human experiences through time, may be summoned in the service of other, usually behavioral, academic disciplines, for example economics, sociology, or political science. "Economic history" vacillates between epistemologically historical study of past economic behaviors and simply mining data from the past selectively to test economic modeling. Political history shifts subtly between epistemologically historical study of particular political dynamics and mining data from the past to test models intended to be predictive of general tendencies in political behavior. All data are in fact "past," in fact, by the time researchers collect them, and so epistemologically the degree of remoteness in time (as Westerners see it) is not an issue.

Historians distinctively study human behaviors not so much "through time" as with by centering attention on the dynamic dimension of temporality, ephemerality, momentariness, the constant becoming-ness of human existence. Further, they distinctively explain human actions as creativity enabled and motivated by the contexts in which actors have found themselves. Historians deeply embed their subjects in their contexts of time and place. They never abstract a concept or isolate it by "holding other things equal" (the key strategy of scientific methods) but rather identify and interpret every possible scrap of data that they can plausibly bring to bear on the times and places of the actions they study. Other people on these scenes are vital and dynamic parts of this rich contextualization of every action, since they always react to every initiative, no matter how subtle. Their reactions generate endless strings of dialectical tensions and resolutions, and then new tensions generated by every solution. Historians thus do not study "change" in some philosophical sense but rather the incremental, dialectical sequences, or processes, produced by the ways in which people have reacted to each another, generating the modern linear sense of time as they go. They constitute their own identities mutually, as well as contesting territory or women or other limited values. People have always interacted in these ways as fundamentally social creatures, for better and for worse.

Africa finally entered the mainstream of the academic discipline through its "social history revolution" in the 1960s, in which the civil rights generation discovered and championed the cause of the neglected "people without history" (in the old sense) within their own national cultures and elsewhere around the world. The great leap forward over the sanctity of the authorial documentary record of Dead Great White Men was propelled by statistical analytic techniques, drawing heavily on the available precedents in economic modeling, as well as sociology, demography, and other behavioral social sciences, of the vast quantities of neglected bureaucratic records of governments attempting to record, if not also regulate, the behavior of their subjects, or citizens: notarial archives, tax and property records, censuses, parish books of births and baptisms, and the like.

Records of this sort were exclusively European and rare to nonexistent for Africa, with the exception of government records of the sailing vessels that had carried Africans to the Americas. But the idea of studying aggregates of people who had not written about themselves, rather than the heroic individuals in the authorial literate elite, provided the conceptual bridge over the barrier of literacy into an African past conceived fundamentally in parallel aggregative terms of "peoples." This initial historicization of Africa in terms of its "peoples and (corresponding) cultures" coincided (not coincidentally) with the ethnic framework of the ethnography of the colonial era, then ending. Other than rejecting the then-pejorative label of "tribe" to designate these unproblematized groups, the first generation in the 1960s of professional historians of Africa grasped, somewhat uncritically of necessity, at every possible straw that they might spin into the historian's gold—"evidence."

But these first straws, blowing in on the winds of very inventive uses of nonliterate sources (oral traditions, taken more or less at face value, or by analogy with documents copied over and over through time; archaeology; historical linguistics; ethnographic descriptions), were nowhere nearly sufficient to break through to the sort of densely contextualized understanding of past contexts in Africa needed to infer motivation for actors in an epistemologically historical way. Action was by ethnic aggregates, "peoples" "migrating" through space, and nearly always enduring through time. For want of direct evidence of action, historians studied the results of whatever people might have done, however they might actually have done it. For historiographical reasons (the nationalist euphoria of the time), these outcomes were pre-eminently "states" (or kingdoms, or empires, not analytically distinguished) and other social or intellectual structures (a.k.a. "cultures") always (again, of necessity) taken as single-dimensioned, abstracted, relatively static practices and institutions (including the ethnic populations themselves).

Although historians managed to contemplate past times in Africa by these historically dubious premises, subtle aspects of their practice implicitly assumed a very ahistorical stability through time. Africans, they confirmed, had formed large centralized and powerful political systems as precedents for the political responsibilities of modern independence as nations striving for the respectability of the primary modern standard of historical existence. Others in Africa, negatively conceptualized as "stateless,"

had in fact also worked out sophisticated political systems. Most had engaged in "long-distance" trade with sophistication bordering on modern commercial enterprise. These structures and systems of thought—stabilized as coherent "cultures" or "religions"—were shown to have been efficacious, and hence stable, leaving the actual dialectical historical dynamics of these organic institutions, their tensions and contradictions, their sheer multiplicity, unacknowledged, or at best muted. With only scattered "data points" as yet on the historical screen, historians tended to connect them by sketching abstracted models of their regularities in sound sociological style rather than focusing on the particularities and peculiarities of strategies and tactics accessible and effective at specific times and in specific places.

The paucity of evidence, in spite of the steady recognition of finding vast ranges of previously unsuspected information borrowed from the methods of other disciplines, permitted no more historically refined interpretive method. The other academic disciplines from which the pioneer professional historians of Africa borrowed—ethnography, archaeology, linguistics, oral expressive arts, and so on—all had their own epistemologies that oriented scholars working in them to develop data focused on their materials—customs, potsherds, languages, cosmologies—that did not probe the motivations behind human actions and the dynamics of the ensuing reactions; they were not historical. But, as with all historical sequences, things have a way of working out in spite of themselves or—to define the process in terms of human historical actions—the best intentions can have the worst of unintended outcomes, and the most naïve of beginnings can, with enough mistakes made along an infinitely iterative path, produce a viable outcome. Such was the case with modern historical epistemology in Africa by the end of the twentieth century.

The array of research across many disciplines, leading in the most diverse of directions, and a succession of determined historians barking up one theoretical tree after another (neo-Marxism, neo-liberal economics, and more recently and definitively, cultural history) to try to make use of the only moderately less than random data generated, produced a sufficiently dense array of evidence, stretching back over more than 20,000 years, by the opening decade of the twenty-first century that historians stood on the verge of having contexts rich enough to think historically about Africa's past. The general late-twentieth-century "turn" in intellectual thinking away from "modern" preoccupations with regularities and rationality toward felt experiences, subjectivities, and particularities, brought people and perceptions to the forefront of historians' thinking and crystallized a cultural sense for the premises and priorities of Africans' thinking, and hence motivations, as distinct from the older abstractions like "systems or modes of thought," "states" and other structures.

This sense for distinctive African cognitive premises and values and the strategies of human action that they motivate is revealing an African historical epistemology that largely contrasts with the epistemology of modern western history. Rather than progressive history's heroic individuals isolated from their historical contexts—the now derided paradigm of "kings and generals," or the general individuation of modernity—for Africans the collectivity of inter-related individuals is the primary human identity. They think in terms of a "communal ethos" rather than an ethos of individualism. Oral traditions personalize the collectivities at the center of their concern as historical entities, or personages, and thus narrate the formation, consolidation, and ongoing composition of groups as the deeds of personified entities.

The valence of African historical thinking is restorative rather than progressive. That is, rather than the modern West's linear sense of time as a continuum, and the historical responsibility of actors to move forward along it, for Africans time is a sense of eroding integrity, coherence, solidarity, functionality, and mutual respect toward dissolution, disorder, and dissension, that is, toward dispersal of the group, leaving its members alone and vulnerable to the world around them. The historical responsibility of members of these groups or communities, with which everyone primarily identifies, is to save the group from the fallibility (primarily disloyalty, selfishness, or greed) of its living custodians in the present.

Rather than the modern and abstract temporal sense of "present" as opposed to "past," Africans instead experientially distinguish proximate from distant; proximate means relationships with many people in one another's midst functioning to mutual satisfaction, while distant means everyone and everything not related, not relational, not experientially in touch. Restorative historical strategies are meant to keep the living in touch with those who have gone before—personal ancestors, predecessor holders of authority (hence the need for lists of "kings")—and who become absent only through neglect. Since contact with protective ancestors depends on the integrity of the group of the living, and the historical world consists of those with whom one can define and enact a relationship (of kin, of hierarchy, of patronage, of marriage) there is a pervasive suspicion of anyone who might withdraw from such relationships. They thereby become uncontrollable, and dangerous; because unrelated; much African thought characterized as about "witchcraft" focuses on those suspected of acting alone, by definition at the expense of the community, and metaphorically represented as endangering the collective future by "eating" the group's children.

The same metaphor describes strangers, outsiders unrelated to the group, threatening to attract members of the community away and to incorporate them—ingest them socially—as "eating people"; the Europeans who appeared from beyond Atlantic horizons to buy slaves thus more than fulfilled the behavior expected of such remote, itinerant, and unintelligible beings as "cannibals." Within Africa communities routinely described others just beyond the range of the neighbors with whom they maintained coherent and reliable relationships through marriages and other exchanges similarly as "cannibals."

Africans do not share the modern felt need to homogenize, to standardize, to normalize, thus condemning the unavoidable variations of every individual (the modern obsession) from these highly singular paradigms as deviations, if not deviant. Rather they compose their communities or collectivities to cultivate diversity among people included in them. The greater the range of experience, talents, knowledge, and capacities the group can incorporate, the greater its collective ability to mobilize around someone capable of rising to an unexpected occasion. This compositional strategy, this celebration of mosaic-like multiplicity, means that the past does not recede but rather becomes the base to which novelties are added, welcomed as potentially useful in a mental space that westerners would characterize as "the future"; for Africans, it more a question of the undetectable potentialities of the present. By thus aggressively adding, the complexity of communities—including political ones—grows through time. Intricacy becomes the hallmark of success, of size, of endurance, of incorporating ("eating") challengers rather than becoming recent (and hence less respectable) food nurturing others.

These—and many other—general tendencies of non-Muslim African historiographies (and also African versions of Islamic theology) differ fundamentally from the premises of the modern historical epistemology of individuals acting, motivated by their perceived contexts of times and places, usually conservatively trying to preserve familiar existing practices by intensifying them to the point of necessitating changes in other aspects of their lives in failing attempts to hold back the "tides of time," that is the (witchlike?) uncontrollable actions of everyone else involved. Africans instead decontextualize, hence unmotivated, personages to emphasize the outcomes of past actions, additively preserved into the present, rather than recovering the no-longer relevant particular circumstances of their initiation. Past actions for them are less important than the outcomes they have managed to preserve into the compositional mosaics that define success. Historical performers therefore represent whatever may have happened by whatever stories convey their relevance to the moments of their performance, rather than attempting specific reconstructions of circumstances in the past.

Features of African historical thinking like these, once dismissed as hopeless "presentism," are instead components of groups' ongoing historical composition carefully preserved into ongoing presents. Languages grow in similarly additive ways, and thus historical linguistics can unpack deep past sequences of language differentiation, where sufficient numbers of languages and degrees of differentiation exist. Western historians, recognizing the compositional processes of African historical creation in time—political ones, primary communities, languages, and much else—can unpack and sequence the components of the present along the linear arrays of conventional historiography, thus refashioning them as changes through time. However, doing so depends on first acknowledging the separate epistemological enterprises of modern Western history and history in Africa.

See also **Communications: Oral; History and the Study of Africa; Zimbabwe, Great.**

BIBLIOGRAPHY

Baum, Robert Martin. *Shrines of the Slave Trade: Diola Religion and Society in Precolonial Senegambia.* New York: Oxford University Press, 1999.

Du Bois, W. E. B. *The Negro.* New York: Henry Holt, 1915.

Eltis, David; David Richardson; Stephen D. Behrendt; and Herbert S. Klein; eds. *The Atlantic Slave Trade: A Database on CD-ROM Set and Guidebook.* Cambridge, U.K.: Cambridge University Press, 1999.

Finley, Moses I. *Ancient Slavery and Modern Ideology.* New York: Viking Press, 1980.

Gibbon, Gibbon. *The History of the Decline and Fall of the Roman Empire.* London: W. Strahan and T. Cadell, 1776.

Giles-Vernick, Tamara. *Cutting the Vines of the Past: Environmental Histories of the Central African Rain Forest.* Charlottesville: University of Virginia Press, 2002.

Guyer, Jane I., et al. "Wealth in People: Wealth in Things." *Journal of African History* 36, no. 1 (1995): 83–140.

Hegel, Georg Wilhelm Friedrich. *Lectures on the Philosophy of History,* trans. J. Sibree. London: Henry G. Bohn, 1857.

History in Africa: A Journal of Method. New Brunswick, NJ: African Studies Association, 1974–.

Hofmeyr, Isabel. *"We Spend our Years as a Tale that Is Told": Oral Historical Narrative in a South African Chiefdom.* Portsmouth, NH: Heinemann, 1994.

Isichei, Elizabeth. *Voices of the Poor in Africa.* Rochester, NY: University of Rochester Press, 2002.

Miller, Joseph C. "History and Africa/Africa and History." *American Historical Review* 104, no. 1 (1999): 1–32.

Shaw, Rosalind. *The Dangers of Temne Divination: Ritual Memories of the Slave Trade in West Africa.* Chicago: University of Chicago Press, 2002.

Skaria, Ajay. *Hybrid Histories: Forests, Frontiers and Wildness in Western India.* Delhi: OUP, 1999.

Vansina, Jan. *Paths in the Rainforests: Toward a History of Political Tradition in Equatorial Africa.* Madison: University of Wisconsin Press, 1990.

Vansina, Jan. *How Societies are Born: Governance in West Central Africa Before 1600.* Charlottesville: University of Virginia Press, 2004.

JOSEPH C. MILLER

EUROPEAN

Separated only by the Mediterranean Sea from Europe, North Africa was well within the European historical consciousness from at least the time of Herodotus (fifth century BCE), who had much to say about Egypt and also the north African littoral. Herodotus also introduced the concept of a mysterious Africa by initiating the question of the sources of the Nile, which he ascribed to snowmelt from the areas south of Egypt—a view that has held up well until the search shifted from reasons to regions. Soon after Herodotus, Thucydides named "Ethiopia beyond Egypt" as the source for the plague of Athens in 430 BCE.

Other ancient historians and others, like Pliny the Younger (second century CE) also turned their attention to Africa, as did the Byzantine historian Procopius (sixth century CE) who, echoing Thucydides, saw the African interior, about which he knew nothing, as the incubator of epidemic diseases, specifically the so-called plague of Justinian. For nearly two millennia, the picture of Africa in Europe was one characterized by apprehension.

The Muslim conquest of all of north Africa—and the increasing desiccation of the Sahara—prevented Europe from advancing its knowledge of "beyond Egypt" for several centuries, although the constant stream of gold to north Africa and Europe was a reminder of Africa's mineral wealth. It was the desire to establish direct access to this wealth that finally precipitated Europe's slow advance down the west coast and then up the east coast of Africa beginning in the fifteenth century and continuing apace, if at first very slowly, into the twentieth century.

This early expansion was not accompanied by much historiography since the Europeans were almost entirely ensconced along the coasts, leaving the continent's vast interior to be the subject of hearsay and legend. Just the same, the growth of the slave trade ineluctably led to a view of Africa that was consistent with the notion that slavery was an appropriate fate for its inhabitants. Thus, even when "histories" of African entities began to be written from the late seventeenth century, they proved to be strong on predispositions and weak on observed or inferred facts, and provided time-depth largely by connecting African societies to biblical theories of origins.

By the mid-nineteenth century, ambitions of political control replaced the slave trade as the primary interest of Europeans, including those who wrote what they thought of as history. In this scheme, Africans still remained objects, rather than subjects, of scholarly inquiry and the study of the continent was suffused with the popular notion that Africans were "the white man's burden." who could not be allowed pasts—and presents—that they controlled. Such signs of "'civilization'" that the Europeans discerned (e.g., Great Zimbabwe or "divine kingship") were typically attributed to unknown predecessors of existing African societies, usually and conveniently termed "Hamites," who had come from northeast Africa or the Near East—areas long recognized at early centers of eligible civilizations.

Denied a past, whether or not discernible, Africans began to take the initiative under colonial rule to write their own histories, which often took Eurocentric notions (particularly by assimilating biblical history or "Western" narrative strategies) as points of departure. This made them more acceptable to Europeans, but hardly served to advance historical knowledge of the continent, and in the mid-twentieth century the interpretations of the sub-Saharan past most of it was unworthy of extended study and treatment beyond that which was concerned with European activities. This was the result of a belief that Africans could not—and therefore did not—develop sophisticated societies and political structures, but remained, rather like American Indians, in a constant state of benignity, watching time pass without being interested in doing anything about it. Combined with—and probably deriving from—this was the conjoined belief that in any case there was virtually a total lack of suitable source materials to plumb much farther back than the eighteenth century—no familiar written documents, just oral tradition and a smattering of archeological remains. Thus even a desire to study the African past was not only misplaced, but could only be stillborn.

The coming of nationalism and then independence brought dramatic changes in scale and orientation to African historiography, all but eradicating this long-held set of beliefs in scarcely more than a decade. For the first time the study of the African past was upgraded to a legitimate stand-alone scholarly enterprise rather than regarded as a backwater subset of

European colonial history. Once maligned, oral tradition was brought to center stage as a prolific and reliable source for gathering information about the past, while overdue attempts at archeological excavation began to show that far more existed than previously thought. The same proved true for written documents, which proved to exist in quantities heretofore unsuspected.

It did not take long for some scholars to suspect that this attempt to redress the historiographical was going too far, too fast. Apologists for oral tradition, for instance, were not able to withstand some of the criticisms of their methods and materials; grandiose attempts to explain the linguistic map of Africa led to hurried and defective comparisons and interpretations; many archeological explanations proved premature. Nonetheless, much of this early work remains valid or at least defensible, and it can now be said that the practice of African historiography went from nonexistent to academically respectable more quickly than any other segment of western historiography.

Accordingly, the study of the African past has taken its place as an equal partner in various historical methodologies. Every European nation, as well as the United States and other Western Hemisphere countries, have contributed to this enterprise, most for the first time because, before this rapid growth, the non-African historiography of the continent had been largely confined to the former colonial powers.

See also **History of Africa; Zimbabwe, Great.**

BIBLIOGRAPHY

Curtin, Philip D. *The Image of Africa: British Ideas and Action, 1780–1850.* Madison: University of Wisconsin Press, 1964.

Disney, Anthony, ed. *Historiography of Europeans in Asia and Africa.* Brookfield, VT: Variorum, 1995.

Heintze, Beatrix, and Adam Jones, eds. *European Sources for Sub-Saharan Africa: Use and Abuse.* Stuttgart: n.p., 1887.

Jewsiewicki, Bogumil, and Davis S. Newbury, eds. *African Historiographies? Which History for Which Africa?* Beverly Hills, CA: Sage, 1986.

Neale, Caroline. *Writing "Independent" History: African Historiography, 1960–1980.* Westport, CT: Greenwood, 1985.

DAVID HENIGE

ISLAMIC

All writing about the past occurs within specific frameworks of cultural and intellectual values peculiar to particular times and places. The meanings ascribed to the past depend on the standpoint of the historian. Acts of historical composition are what we call historiography, which simply means writing about the past and can be thought of as distinct from history as such, which commonly refers to the past itself. Writings about the past are, of course, great sources of information and interpretation about past events and people, but such writings are also valuable for what they reveal about the contemporary social and cultural context of the historical moment in which the historian lived.

The Islamization of parts of Africa brought with it new tools and a new cultural system of meaning through which the past would be organized and interpreted. Although historical writing had been produced by people in Africa long before the introduction of Islam—most famously perhaps by the third century BCE Egyptian writer Manetho—it is not an exaggeration to say that, for many parts of Africa, the writing of history was made possible by the introduction of Islam. This is not to say that writing made consciousness of the past possible; in more or less structured ways, Africans had employed oral methods to pass along stories of origin and migration, lists of rulers and prominent people, as well as parables and stories of wisdom drawn from the past. Not only did the technology of writing act as a mnemonic device for such oral (more properly, aural) histories, but it also gave information about the past a more permanent character, fixing the standpoint of the author for later readers in a much more obvious way than oral traditions, which have to be reconstrued to some extent with each retelling.

The more important change that Islamization brought to Africans who became Muslims was the absorption and adoption of a specifically Islamic moral and cosmological framework within which the flow of events on earth could be understood. Similar to the process of Islamization itself, the development of a specifically Islamic historical consciousness was a slow and complex procedure that produced different results in different environments.

Because Egypt and much of North Africa were rapidly conquered by Arab Muslim armies in the decades after the birth of Islam in the seventh century CE, people here came to belong to the core area of Islamic political power and cultural development from the beginning.

Islam was introduced to Saharan and sub-Saharan Africa much later and by different means. The first Muslims crossed the Sahara in the eighth century CE, but it was traders and missionaries from North Africa, rather than conquering armies, that introduced Islam into Saharan and Sudanic regions of the continent. The pace of Islamization was most rapid among pastoralist, seminomadic populations in the Sahara and in the coastal lowlands of the Horn of Africa, beginning in the eighth century CE; it was much slower and largely confined to expatriate trading communities and small circles of political elites in the Sudanic regions, and along the Indian Ocean coast of East Africa. It is only in the fourteenth century CE that there is evidence of significant numbers of indigenous sub-Saharan Muslims for the first time. sub-Sahara

Extant historical writings by Muslims in Saharan and sub-Saharan Africa date back only as far as the sixteenth century CE. Three phases of history writing in Islamic Africa can be distinguished:

1. Early Islamic African historiography: During the sixteenth and seventeenth centuries, most Islamic scholarly production was concentrated in a few intellectual and cultural centers, among which the most important were Chinguetti, Walāta, Timbuktu, Katsina, Bornu, the Upper Nile Valley, Harar, and Kilwa. The histories written in these sites reflect clearly the particular values and interests of a Muslim scholarly strata (the *ulamā*) in regions where these scholars often felt themselves to be isolated from the central Islamic lands and surrounded by non-Muslims on all sides. The histories that were written in these circumstances reflect a strong sense of Muslim identity coupled with ethical rejections of non-Muslim practice, especially in politics.

2. Reformist Islamic African historiography: By the middle of the eighteenth century, there was a much wider distribution of Islamic scholarship in areas which hitherto had felt little

Muslim presence. The spread of Islam in this period to rural areas, and the much wider extent of Islamization amongst non-elite populations, led to an increased production of historical chronicles of even relatively unimportant chiefdoms and local events. The various Islamically inspired reformist political movements (usually described as jihads) of the last quarter of the eighteenth century and much of the nineteenth century produced a significant body of historical accounts of particular wars and campaigns.

3. Colonial Islamic African historiography: The advent of European colonial occupation at the end of the nineteenth century led to a new genre of Islamic historiography in Africa meant to explain particular Muslim encounters and relationships with Europeans. Much of this historiography is influenced by simultaneous European-language historiography, especially in the second half of the twentieth century.

The relationship between historians in Saharan and sub-Saharan Africa and the wider tradition of Islamic historiography is not always easy to determine with any precision. Classical Islamic historiography was fully mature by the tenth century CE, by which time the major works of early Islamic history had been compiled. The main feature of these early histories is their use of narrative accounts of past events, and their reliance on oral reports (*akhbār*) of the testimony by firsthand witnesses passed down through time by authenticated chains of transmission (*isnād*). Although they often overlap, there are three principal forms of Islamic historiography:

1. Chronology (*ta'rīkh*): This includes the narrative accounts of particular stretches of time of early Islamic history and universal histories written by authors such as al-Tabarī (d. 923). In the postclassical period (after the tenth century), there was a greater focus on didactic texts concerned with political prudence and moral admonition, as well as the development of new genres such as the dynastic chronicle and local histories of particular cities and regions. Ibn Khaldūn's (d. 1406) universal history (*Kitāb al-'ibar*) is the crowning achievement in this genre.

2. Prosopography (*tabaqāt*): This is the compilation of biographical materials for individuals who

belong to the same group. Examples include collections of biographical information about the scholars or notables of a particular place or era, and the companions of the Prophet Muhammad. The biographical dictionary (*mu'jam*) is an important subset of prosopography.

3. Biography (*sīra*): By far the most important subject of individual biographical works was the Prophet Muhammad, although he was by no means the only subject of this genre of literature. Other examples include the biographies of Saladin (d. 1193).

It is obvious from the form and content of the most sophisticated works of Islamic African historiography that many of the classical historical works were known in Saharan and sub-Saharan Africa. For example, there is a surviving parchment copy of al-Mas'ūdī's (d. 955) *Murūj al-dhahab* (Meadows of Gold), which is a universal history of the world until the advent of Islam, after which it is an Islamic political history down to the tenth century. Evidence that this work was read in sub-Saharan Africa also comes from the fact that it was cited in several of the larger chronicles. However, the principal sources of wider Islamic historical information seem to have been later authors such as the Egyptian scholar 'Abd al-Rahmān al-Suyūtī (d. 1505) and his *Ta'rīkh al-khulafā'* (History of the Caliphs), copies of which are found today in almost every manuscript collection in West Africa. In a similar way, the principal source of historical information on the life of the Prophet Muhammad came not from the more sober classical *sīra* of Ibn Hishām (d. 835), but from al-Qadī 'Iyād's (d. 1149) more devotional and fantastic recension (in his *Kitāb al-shifā' bi'ta'rīf huqūq al-mustafa*). The influence of Ibn Khaldūn is difficult to measure because, although there are few manuscript copies of his writings in sub-Saharan manuscript collections today, he is quoted by some sub-Saharan writers such as the celebrated Timbuktu scholar Ahmad Baba (d. 1627).

Scholars associated with the town of Timbuktu produced the first historical works written in West Africa. The first known written history was composed in the sixteenth century by an otherwise unknown author named Bābā Gūru b. al-hājj Muhammad b. al-hājj al-Amīn Gānīū. This text, which is not extant, is called the *Durar al-hisān fī akhbār ba'd mulūk al-*

sūdān (The Pearls of the Beauties in the History of Some of the Kings of the Blacks). It was the first of many chronicles written about Timbuktu and the kingdoms that controlled it. By far the most important are two lengthy chronicles, which cover the history of the same region, and which became influential across the whole of Islamic West Africa. Both the *Ta'rīkh al-fattāsh* (The History of the Investigator), written by Mahmūd Ka'ti (d. 1593), and the *Ta'rīkh al-sūdān* (The History of the Blacks) by 'Abd al-Rahmān al-Sa'dī (d. 1656) provide detailed regional chronologies of Timbuktu, its sister town of Jenné, and the wider region.

The core of these works are the chronologies of the reign of Sunni 'Alī Ber (r. 1464–1492), the Askia dynasty that ruled the Songhay Empire after him until 1591, and (in the case of the *Ta'rīkh al-sūdān*) the Moroccan-descended dynasty that controlled Timbuktu after 1591. Both chronicles were composed in the wider Islamic tradition of local and dynastic histories discussed above. They also include elements of prosopography in their listing of obituaries of prominent people of Timbuktu. Both are written from the point of view of Muslim scholars and partisans for Muslim Timbuktu. As such, they denounce rulers who attempted to impose strict control over Timbuktu and those who failed to heed the advice of Timbuktu's Muslim scholars or accord them fiscal privileges such as tax exemption and state stipends. Conversely, they hail those rulers who sought and followed their advice and granted them privileges.

The Timbuktu chronicles spawned a wider West African tradition of chronicle writing. Chronicles still exist that were originally written in the eighteenth century in present-day Ghana, northern Nigeria, and Mauritania, and the so-called Funj Chronicle written in Sudan at the beginning of the nineteenth century. There are at least twelve known manuscripts of the Funj Chronicle, each of which reflects different recensions and multiple authors. This text is a chronicle of the Funj Sultanate of Sinnār (1504–1820), and in some versions, an account of the beginnings of the Turco-Egyptian rule in Sudan (beginning in 1820). The other major historical work from Sudan is a prosopographical work called the *Kitāb al-tabaqāt fī khusūs al-awliyā' wa'l-sālihīn wa'l-'ulamā' wa'l-shu'arā' fī 'l-sūdān* (The Generation of the Saints, the Pious, the Learned and the Poets in the Sudan) compiled by Muhammad al-Nūr b. Dayf Allah (d. 1809/10). In this work, there are 270 biographical notices of prominent eighteenth-century Sudanese Muslims. Other well-known prosopographical works were produced in the Mauritanian town of Walāta, in Timbuktu, and Sokoto. There are also historical chronicles from East African sites such as Kilwa.

Historical accounts of Islamically inspired reformist movements are quite common from the nineteenth century. Each of the successful jihads in West Africa, and the Mahdist Movement in Sudan, produced historical accounts that painted the actions of the reformers in righteous religious terms. The earliest example of this genre of historical literature in sub-Saharan Africa comes from Ethiopia in the sixteenth-century account of the successful jihad of Ahmad Grañ against the Christian Solomonid kingdom (1529–1543). Although the Muslim tradition in the Horn of Africa was distinct from West Africa, there are broad similarities in the wider African reformist historiography. At the beginning of this book, titled the *Futūh al-habasha* (The Conquest of Ethiopia), written by a Yemeni participant in the jihad named Shihāb al-dīn Ahmad, the author aligns himself with the histories of al-Suyūtī and al-Mas'ūdī as models for his own composition. The author attributes the successes of the Muslims in these campaigns to God's favor. An example from the text gives an idea of its larger argument:

> How excellent are these Muslims and their imām [Ahmad Grañ]! They waged the holy war for God whose due it was. They were patient and resolute in confronting the enemy. They made the sacrifice of their jihad in order to please God. They did not hold back until they had torn Faithlessness from its throne, and plunged it into its grave. Islam was raised up, and manifested; and Faithlessness was humiliated, and forced to take flight. (Shihāb ad-Dīn Ahmad, 26)

Historical texts such as this reflect a militant, reformist perspective in which true Muslims destroy a corrupt or unbelieving enemy as the result of divine favor. In this case the enemy is Christian; in Saharan and Sudanic Africa, the enemy was usually construed as a corrupt and lax Muslim ruler or idolater.

Another important feature of Islamic African historiography is biography. In many cases, biographical works were composed about leaders of

Islamic reform movements: There are biographies of 'Uthman dan Fodio (d. 1817), leader of the Sokoto jihad, by his son and successor Muhammad Bello (d. 1837). The work is titled the *Infāq al-maysūr* (The Expenses of the Fortunate). There are also biographies of more pacific figures such as the Arabophone Sufi leader of the Azawad region north of Timbuktu, Sīdī al-Mukhtār al-Kuntī (d. 1811). Sīdī al-Mukhtār's biography, together with his wife, was written by his son, Sīdī Muhammad al-Kuntī (d. 1826) and titled the *Kitāb al-tarā'if wa-'l-talā'id* (The Book of Uncommon and Inherited Qualities). Sīdī Muhammad credits his father and mother with being Muslim saints (*awliyā' allāh*), who lived lives of great piety and were blessed with many saintly miracles (*karāmāt*). In these two cases of biography, and in others examples similar to them, the author is keen to demonstrate the authority of their subject in Islamic terms, as scholars in possession of advanced learning, and often, as people blessed with signs of God's favor manifested in their lives. Such biographies often served as foundational documents for multi-generational claims to political and religious authority.

Confronted with European colonial invasion and occupation, Muslims in Saharan and sub-Saharan Africa produced many histories written in Arabic describing confrontation and resistance to, in their terms, Christians. Unlike the reformist histories, these colonial-era works always ended in defeat or accommodation of some kind with the colonial power. For some writers, resistance to the colonial occupation was heroic and laudatory for the particular groups that fought; for others, accommodation with the colonial state was presented as an alliance that allowed African groups to administer themselves internally. When such arrangements were violated by the colonial state—as they often were to judge by many local histories—Muslim writers invoked ethical arguments about justice (*'adl*). As such, some colonial-era Muslim histories are critical of European rule. However, there are also a number of histories that are not, and seem to share more in common with a wider process across Africa of so-called ethnohistories produced by Africans at least in part for reasons of political positioning in postcolonial politics. The Timbuktu writer Muhammad Mahmoud ould Cheikh's (d. 1973) history of Northern Mali (the *Kitāb al-turjumān fī ta'rīkh al-sahrā' wa'l-sūdān*) is one example of an Arabic ethnohistory with the explicit purpose of narrating a coherent and distinct past for a particular group of people with political goals of attaining autonomy. In this example, the French colonial state is actually praised for bringing peace and justice.

The Arabic-language historiographical tradition is still alive in Islamic Africa in the early twenty-first century. Formal education opportunities in Arabic have expanded significantly and new generations of Muslim Africans are reading—and writing—the specifically Islamic histories of their regions.

See also **Bello, Muhammad; Harar; Islam; Jenné and Jenné-jeno; Timbuktu; Travel and Exploration; 'Uthman dan Fodio; Walāta.**

BIBLIOGRAPHY

Austen, Ralph A., and Jan Jansen. "History, Oral Tradition and Structure in Ibn Khaldun's Chronology of Mali Rulers." *History in Africa* 23 (1996): 17–28.

Batran, 'Abd al-'Aziz 'Abd Allah. *The Qadiryya Brotherhood in West Africa and the Western Sahara: The Life and Times of Shaykh al-Mukhtar al-Kunti, 1729–1811.* Rabat, Morocco: Université Muhammad V, Institut des Etudes Africaines, 2001.

Cleaveland, Timothy. *Becoming Walāta: A History of Saharan Social Formation and Transformation.* Portsmouth, New Hampshire: Heinemann, 2002.

de Moraes Farias, P.F. *Arabic Medieval Inscriptions from the Republic of Mali: Epigraphy, Chronicles, and Songhay-Tuareg History.* Oxford: British Academy, 2003.

El Hamel, Chouki. *La vie intellectuelle islamique dans le Sahel Ouest-Africain (XVIe-XIX siècles).* Paris: Harmattan, 2002.

Hodgkin, Thomas. *Nigerian Perspectives: An Historical Anthology.* London: Oxford University Press, 1960.

Humphreys, R. Stephen. *Islamic History: A Framework for Inquiry.* Princeton, New Jersey: Princeton University Press, 1991.

Hunwick, John O. "Not yet the Kano Chronicle: King-Lists with and without Narrative Elaboration from Nineteenth-Century Kano." *Sudanic Africa* 4 (1993): 95–130.

Hunwick, John O. *Arabic Literature of Africa*, vol. 2. *Writings of Central Sudanic Africa.* Leiden, The Netherlands: Brill, 1995.

Hunwick, John O. *Timbuktu and the Songhay Empire.* Leiden, The Netherlands: Brill, 1999.

Hunwick, John O. *Arabic Literature of Africa*, vol. 4. *Writings of Western Sudanic Africa.* Leiden, The Netherlands: Brill, 2003.

Khalidi, Tarif. *Arabic Historical Thought in the Classical Period.* New York: Cambridge University Press, 1994.

Levtzion, Nehemia. "Merchants vs. Scholars and Clerics in West Africa." In *Rural and Urban Islam in West Africa*, eds. Nehemia Levtzion and Humphrey J. Fisher. Boulder, Colorado: Lynne Rienner Publishers, 1987.

Mahmout Kati ben El-Hadj El-Motaouakkel Kati. *Tarikh el-fettach*, trans. O. Houdas. Paris: Adrien-Maisonneuve, 1964.

McHugh, Neil. *Holymen of the Blue Nile: The Making of an Arab-Islamic Community in the Nilotic Sudan, 1500–1850.* Evanston, Illinois: Northwestern University Press, 1994.

O'Fahey, R.S. *Arabic Literature of Africa*, vol. 1. *Writings of eastern Sudanic Africa to c. 1900.* Leiden, The Netherlands: Brill, 1994.

O'Fahey, R.S. *Arabic Literature of Africa*, vol. 3, fasc. A. *Writings of the Muslim peoples of Northeastern Africa.* Leiden, The Netherlands: Brill, 2003.

Robinson, Chase F. *Islamic Historiography.* New York: Cambridge University Press, 2003.

Shihāb ad-Dīn Ahmad bin 'Abd al-Qāder bin Sālem bin 'Uthmān. *Futūh al-habasha. The Conquest of Abyssinia*, trans. Paul Lester Stenhouse. Hollywood, California: Tsehai Publishers, 2003.

Zouber, Mahmoud A. *Ahmad Baba de Tombouctou (1556–1627). Sa vie et son oeuvre.* Paris: G.-P. Maisonneuve et Larose, 1977.

BRUCE S. HALL

ORAL

Modern African historiography stands on three legs of a tripod: the tradition of African orality, the Islamic written tradition, and the written tradition of the Latin Christian West. The early Egyptian hieroglyphic written tradition, one of the first in world history, developed within the continent from the oral tradition. Several internal written systems also came into use over limited areas during particular periods of time. These included the Meroitic script of the Eastern Sudan late in the first millennium BCE, the Punic and Libyan scripts of North Africa of similar date, the Coptic or Sahidic successor of hieroglyphics in Egypt in the early first millennium CE, Ethiopic of the Ethiopian Highlands at about the same time, the various subsequent Somali scripts, and the nineteenth-century scripts of the Mende (Sierra Leone), the Vai, Basa, Kapelle/Kpelle, Toma, and Gerze of Guinea, the Bamum of Cameroon, and the Nigerian Nsibidi and Oberi Okaime scripts, among others. The historiographical impact of these internal systems of writing in Africa has yet to be adequately assessed but should not be discounted.

The oral tradition embraces a wide category of cultural phenomena in societies without writing. Where all communication is carried out orally, oral literature always satisfied aesthetic ends in a variety of forms, such as myth, legends, poetry. Those forms, which focus on the past, have been classified into the two categories: "oral tradition" and "oral history." Oral tradition has been specified to mean those oral testimonies about the past that are performed by historians/performers/raconteurs/*griots* who were not themselves participants, eyewitnesses, or contemporaries of the events reported. Such accounts are transmitted from one person to another over periods of time, sometimes considerable, with each transmitting historian and generation interpreting the accounts in terms relevant to their own times and contemporary conditions. In contrast, oral history refers to testimonies concerning the past told by participants in the events, or by persons who were eyewitnesses to them, or by those who belonged to the generation or period in which the events took place. In these cases, the historians/informants/raconteurs/*griots* assume the posture of first-hand reporters and interpreters of the events.

In cultures with writing, material culture and general patterns of behavior provide other information. In African societies, much information bearing on the past was also embedded in ritual acts, festivals, dances, and masking practices, drumming, declamatory utterances, and in various economic, social and political institutions and activities.

The oral historiographical tradition once existed everywhere in the world, even in cultures that subsequently came to include literacy. This tradition continued to influence their subsequent written historiography, as oral histories were transformed into some of the first written accounts. The Homeric epics of the Greeks, for example, represent the transformation of ancient Greek oral traditions; the Bible codified the oral tradition of the Jews and the early Christians. In Africa, different African communities that acquired the literary traditions of the Christian West and of Islam similarly wrote their histories by transcribing and interpreting local oral traditions.

AFRICAN ORAL CONCEPTUALIZATION OF THE PAST

African peoples from antiquity have conceived of the past as continuous with the present and also as flowing on into the future. They kept their past alive in the present by preserving concrete evidence of it and through practical activities, as well as in their thought systems and worldview. The ancient Egyptians built pyramids to preserve the memory of their dead and kept records in a variety of materials, lists, and genealogies, and they added monumental inscriptions, annals, day-books, and literary texts. The oral Ijo people of the Niger Delta built ancestral houses over their revered ancestors, kept memorabilia of the ancestors, and even carved wooden figures to represent their lives. Accordingly, the dead were not gone but continued to live in the present and to participate in the lives of their descendants. Indeed, the present was occupied not only by the ancestors from the past but also by the gods and other spiritual entities conceived in historical terms, such as the settled earth, the deified heroes, and the communal spirits.

The African concept recognized change as the essence of historical time. The present was the validation of the past, and people were enjoined to take account of the future in their everyday planning and actions. The concept also acknowledged eternity, but the future could be imagined only imperfectly, and eternity lay only in the knowledge of God. It is instructive to note that the first modern philosophy of time, propounded by Saint Augustine of Hippo (354–430 CE), was similarly grounded on the African concept as preserved in the African proverbs and ancient Egyptian wisdom literature; he defined time as conceivable only on the basis of the impression it makes on the mind in the present as memory (the past), intuition (the present), and expectation (the future). St. Augustine ruled out the possibility of exact measurement of time, since the present, which alone has reality, does not occupy space and is always in the process of changing into the past and passing out of existence, while the future, which has no existence, is constantly becoming manifest as the present. The African oral tradition of history is similarly not marked by the delineated chronologies of the Western historiographical tradition.

A firm concept of the past, of history, was thought to be the possession of the elders, gained through the lengthy experience they brought into the present. According to the Egyptian wisdom literature, "a man learns from his father," and African proverbs stress the importance of hindsight as the basis of foresight, and experience as the basis of right action in the present.

THE UTILITY OF HISTORY IN THE PRESENT

In African oral societies, the utility of history in the present was never in doubt, since the ancestors were always present and still active in the lives of their descendants, the living. In the defining ideology of literate societies, history, or a sense of the past, of origins, is central. In Africa it means even more. History is the definition of humanity. Consciousness of continuity, and responsibility for it, differentiates human beings from animals and from the rest of creation. According to the Niger Delta (Nembe) proverb, one who is ignorant of his origins is nonhuman, a nondescript creature of fable. The same corpus of oral tradition defines history as that body of knowledge that nurtures the competent citizen, one who is aware of community custom, mores, and morality and thus is able to live an upright life.

Since the past provides a mirror, even if imperfect, of the future and a guide for action in the present, the elders who know history deserve the respect of the community, and the persons chosen to be rulers and leaders must possess such knowledge. They are expected to use their knowledge to adjudicate justly in disputes over rights to land, office, position, or status in the community. The African oral history defined the individual and one's group affiliations in time and space: to family, lineage, community, to land and environment, and, eventually, to humanity and the spirit world.

The person without historical knowledge is, thus, less than human, incompetent as a citizen, and without status in the community. A responsible person had to have such clear knowledge of one's place in space and in time in a historiographical tradition where the past, present, and future were so closely interrelated.

MEMORY AND CONSTRUCTION OF THE PAST

In oral cultures, time and history reside in memory, not in writing, as well as in concrete objects, in the language and culture, and in the deliberate efforts of communities to preserve what is essential to define relationships, rights, duties and a worldview that expresses this past in everyday life. Fathers and other elders, even in the most decentralized societies, assume the responsibility of remembering and teaching. In other societies, professional historians, cultural experts, and specialists of various types bear the burdens of remembrance for larger groups. These specialists devise cultural mnemonic devices in literature, song, legends, and varied forms of memorized formulaic fixed texts to support the variable free literary texts, and to remember the past. Eventually, the frequency of performance of such texts provides the best means of remembrance from generation to generation, and the aesthetics of the drum, dance, and musical forms encourage frequency of performance.

Reenactment of history at festivals, coronations, funerals and jubilees was supported by the construction of monuments, from the pyramids of Egypt to groves of trees and sacred cemeteries and grounds, regalia, and symbols. Artists produced clay, stone, metal, ivory, and wooden representations of gods, heroes, kings, and queens. These were often preserved in special structures, together with trade goods and other cultural icons. But these material witnesses to the past could only testify to the past through the spoken words of the historian informant and interpreter.

Did the African oral historiography operate with a rigorous method and philosophy? It did, indeed, observe an internal code defining the truth value of testimonies and standards of authority. Eyewitness evidence was respected, and so was evidence supported by a second or third witness. But a historical account always stood the test of reason: was the testimony in accordance with the nature of things in the real world of experience? The standards of evidence were thus ultimately empirical according to the consensus of all those present, and statements of the past acquired their importance from the presence of as many confirming witnesses as possible.

CONCLUSION

The basically oral historiography of Africa was a lived, practical guide to the past for use in the present to secure a future. Its chronology was relative, embracing all dimensions of time and space, and it included the worlds of the living, the dead, and the unseen dimensions of life. It may thus be contrasted with the modern Western view of an abstracted linear concept separating the past from the present and the future.

Modern academic African historiography now supplements the Christian Western written tradition as well as the Islamic, and it uses the insights of many other disciplines to interpret the ethnographic material and other varied forms in which evidence of the African past manifests itself.

See also **Augustine of Hippo, Saint; Death, Mourning, and Ancestors; Festivals and Carnivals; Literature: Oral.**

BIBLIOGRAPHY

Alagoa, E. J. "Towards a History of African Historiography." In *Etudes d'Historiographie*, ed. Lucian Boia. Bucharest: University of Bucharest, Department of History and Philosophy, 1985.

Alagoa, E. J. "The Encounter Between African and Western Historiography Before 1800." *Storia della Storiografia* 19 (1991): 73–87.

Alagoa, E. J. "An African Philosophy of History in the Oral Tradition." In *Paths Towards the Past: African Historical Essays in Honor of Jan Vansina*, ed. Robert W. Harms, Joseph C. Miller, David S. Newbury, and Michele D. Wagner. Atlanta, GA: The African Studies Association Press, 1994.

Gelb, I. J. *A Study of Writing: The Foundations of Grammatology*. Chicago: University of Chicago Press, 1963.

Jewsiewicki, Bogumil, and David Newbury. *African Historiographies: What History for Which Africa?* Beverly Hills, CA: Sage Publications, 1986.

Simpson, William Kelly, ed. *The Literature of Ancient Egypt: An Anthology of Stories, Instructions, and Poetry*. New Haven, CT: Yale University Press, 1973.

Vansina, Jan. *Oral Tradition: A Study in Historical Methodology*. Chicago: Aldine, 1965.

Vansina, Jan. *Oral Tradition as History*. Madison: University of Wisconsin Press, 1985.

E. J. ALAGOA

HISTORY, WORLD: AFRICA IN.

From very early times Nilotic, Mediterranean, and Indian Ocean Africa figured in the chronicles, geographies, and then histories, of the literate cultures of southwestern Asia. The Axumite rulers of the present-day Ethiopian highlands in northeastern Africa controlled the Red Sea and parts of the Arabian peninsula in the middle of the first millennium of the Common Era. These same parts of the continent became core parts of the Islamic ecumene from the eighth century on, and at times—the tenth- through thirteenth-century caliphate in Fatimid Egypt—its center. Mansa Musa, of the "Mali empire" along the upper Niger River, attracted worldwide attention for the gold that he spent in Egypt in the thirteenth century. Muslim geographers—notably the famous Ibn Khaldun—reported on the upper Niger region in western Africa and on the Swahili coasts as carefully as they did on any other part of far-flung Muslim trading networks and conquests reaching to central Asia, Iberia, and the Philippines. Early European Christians also took respectful account of Africans whom they encountered on the Atlantic shores of the continent in the fifteenth century.

However, modern disciplined historical thinking at the end of the eighteenth century in Europe excluded Africans philosophically from their emerging sense of secular time, based on the idea of linear progress leading exclusively toward their own commercial, increasingly technology-based economies and highly militarized monarchies. Africa, in the seminal metaphysical phrasings of the philosopher Georg Wilhelm Friedrich Hegel (1770–1831), thus became the continent "without history." Although Hegel's exclusion of Africa from European historical thinking carried a primarily moral sense, later generations of scholars developed the discipline in terms of military power, industrialized wealth, and modern civic nations that they found entirely wanting in Africa. They increasingly invoked the pseudoscientific racial myths of the late nineteenth and early twentieth centuries to account for what they imagined as the timeless fossilization of presumed origins of humankind into modern times in "darkest Africa." Africans were accessible to modern scholarship primarily through the lenses of the several European schools of ethnographic observation and reporting that, while emphasizing the rationality of Africans' cultures, tended to maintain their isolation from history.

DIFFERING HISTORIOGRAPHIES

From the beginning of the twentieth century African American historians, led by the brilliant and indefatigable African American thinker W. E. B. Du Bois, set about destroying these figments of the modern imagination of outsiders, including missionaries intent on educating and on saving the souls of Africans they saw as ignorant in spiritual as well as secular terms. But they redeemed Africans for the progressive history of their era primarily by emphasizing the location, in northeastern Africa, of the ancient Egyptian "civilization" glorified since Hegel's era as ancestral to that of modern Europe. They also claimed as "African" the evident military strength and occasional monumental architectures of thirteenth- and fourteenth-century military rulers in Sudanic western Africa (primarily Ghana, Mali, and Songhay) and the great stone ruins in southeastern Africa at Zimbabwe. Strongly nationalistic schools of history in European and North America focused primarily on their respective national narratives and only after World War II elevated their sights to integrate their progressive celebration of themselves together as "western civilization." The "world historical" thinkers of the era—Arnold J. Toynbee (1889–1975) and others—maintained one version or another of Hegel's omission of Africa from whiggish celebrations of "world" civilization, led by and all but limited to Europeans.

The late-twentieth-century wave of "world history" thinking developed with decolonization in Africa and Asia in the 1960s and attempted a more inclusive coverage of the world's growing complement of recognized nations. It thus remained rooted in the nationalism and progressivism at the heart of the historical discipline. The first major achievement along these new and more comprehending lines, by William H. McNeill, could contextualize *The Rise of the West* only in its Asian setting and, with regard to Africa, faintly echo Du Bois' and others' accents on the exceptional moments in its past that appeared to resemble the militarism or monumentality of the modern West. The subsequent very considerable "world-historical field" within American historiography, deriving from the pioneering efforts of McNeill and others— notably led by Africanist historians, many of them trained in the 1960s under Philip D. Curtin at the University of Wisconsin—has continued to include Africa primarily through the Ghana–Mali–Songhay sequence, before shifting uneasily to Africans' suffering at the hands of European slavers (sixteenth through nineteenth centuries), then imperial conquest and colonial domination (1880s–1950s), and finally economic, political, epidemiological, and even genocidal catastrophe in the last half century. Other (European) historiographies have been slower to develop the field, with German historians—heirs to Hegel—taking a more epistemological approach that takes less specific account of particular parts of the world, including Africa. The highly selective and profoundly distorting image of Africa's victimization in world history dominates, sometimes apologetically, the continent's very limited presence in school texts everywhere in the world outside of the continent itself.

At the threshold of the twenty-first century a growing chorus of African scholars voicing a critique of xenophobically modernist and European national pretensions were starting to form an alternative vision that centered Africa on the world-historical stage rather than marginalizing it. This African historical epistemology contrasts with the post-Enlightenment emphasis on the individual, the modern social sciences based on that premise, and the corresponding national civic societies based on the presumed homogeneity of the social or political persons in them. This alternative vision highlights the existential isolation of modern individualism and its consequent unrestrained competitiveness and material consumption, industrial technologies' massive extraction of irreplaceable environmental resources, and the potential destruction of human life, or even the habitability of the planet, of atomic and biological weapons against their undeniable personal benefits in physical comfort, at least for the privileged.

This African vision of humans in their social and natural environments replaces these paragons of conventional progressive history with integration of human activity in its environmental contexts, valuation of the community and its preservation, distributed political responsibilities rather than centralized political authority, and reconciliatory rather than retributive resolutions of conflict. The Truth and Reconciliation Commission in postapartheid South Africa, after a century of divisive racial alienation, is the best known implementation of this widespread

African philosophy. An aphorism popular among scholars of Africa expresses the idea of social relatedness: there "people were wealth, and people were power." By this ethos, productive (not strongly distinguished from reproductive) technologies were focused on female fecundity, the fertility of the land, and the moral health and hence continuation of the community. People were valuable for the individual knowledge and experiences they could bring to their communities. Relationships, including marriage alliances among the reproductive groups of kin, were the primary forms of investment, with women often constituting the most valuable—because the most reproductive—tokens of mutual commitment.

These characteristically African values—of course, achieved in practice no more often than the corresponding moralities of any community anywhere in the world—provide a basis for a world history conceptualized in terms of small-scale community and continuity that contrast with the massive scales, attained nearly always only by military force, that lie beneath the veneer of the literate "civilizations" in the master narrative of conventional world histories. In them, discussion never abandons the premises of militarism, monumentality, and eventually mercantilism, and debates develop only around the relative excellence of various regions of the world in these terms. In the early twenty-first century, for example, discussion swirls around Europe's dependence on the Asian counterparts of modern "empires" before the nineteenth century.

AFRICA'S PLACE IN EARLY HISTORY

World history viewed from the alternative perspective of classical Africa produces a narrative of recurrent losses of the human intimacy it emphasizes, and also personal security to the always-partial extent that the communal ethos has ever been realized in practice. It is not a history of human perfectibility, through historical progress, but rather a study in trade-offs and humility. In this "African" view of the history of the world, the relatively low-labor inputs of the foraging (hunting-and-gathering) economies of 10,000 years ago (at that point prevailing everywhere in the world) were abandoned in the alluvial river valleys in the dry latitudes ($25°–30°$) of the Northern Hemisphere in the interests of sustaining populations crowded together in them during periods of desiccation (on millennial time-scales) that alternated with demographically favorable eras of

greater moisture. Domestication of the horse, in eastern Europe or central Asia some 5,000 or 6,000 years ago, exposed these densely settled, and hence vulnerable, agricultural populations from China west to Mesopotamia to the depredations of highly mobile horse-riding raiders from the steppes. War leaders emerged in these agrarian regions to coordinate defensive preparations on unprecedentedly large and continuing scales. Their successors then found themselves burdened with the high costs of the military establishments they inherited and resorted to ongoing conquests in evermore remote regions to support them.

The need to integrate remote conquests in turn supported the development of communities of merchants, who handled the logistical support of centrally controlled military operations on scales that transcended most individuals' personal experiences or contacts. To coordinate commerce on these scales, increasingly anonymous, they invented methods of communicating by writing and standardized currencies. Operating over ranges far beyond the capabilities of cavalry-based military power, merchants became vital sources of wealth—and of exotic markers of rank and power—for rulers increasingly dependent on elaborate, abstract ideological depictions of themselves as far above—and thus removed from—the populations they defended, or claimed to defend. Rulers, supported by cadres of priests as acolytes, celebrated themselves as quasi-divine, or divine, and built stone structures of monumental proportions—especially tombs—to accent the power they claimed as durable, even eternal, beyond the death inevitable for individual mortals. Thus taking account of the costs of scale, the monumental "civilizations" on which conventional world history centers were very expensive, defensive, and artificial impositions on the productive and reproductive agricultural families and villages who grew what everyone—"divine" or not—ate.

Africans south of the Sahara Desert mostly escaped the horse and its monumental consequences during these early millennia.

By five or six thousand years ago, the third or fourth millennium before the Common Era, Africans developed less vulnerable, mobile tropical agricultural technologies based on the principle of integrating diverse communities of specialists across their growing range of technologies—except in the subtropical highlands of Ethiopia and the lower valley of the Nile River, which lay within range of the chariot-based militaries of southwestern Asia. Sub-Saharan Africans could not incorporate large draft animals into their cultivating regimes owing to a tropical disease environment in which the tsetse-fly vector of a disease lethal to equids (horses) bovids (hollow-horned hoofed ruminants, antelopes as well as cattle) flourished. But pastoralist herders of cattle south of the desert moved seasonally from the drier Saharan latitudes through the agricultural regions to the south. Recent work has described this integration of dispersed specialized communities as a "heterarchical" form of social, political, and economic organization that enabled transport of substantial production surpluses, from grains to metals, leather, salt and other minerals, over hundreds of miles without significantly centralized—and thus lower-cost—coordination. It was differentiated in terms of parallel culturally and ethnically defined communities that all contributed to a shared welfare rather than vertically in terms of power, as in hierarchical Asian (and later European) systems developed originally to defend against the threat of raiders on horseback or riding chariots. It may be argued further, from heretofore neglected archaeological evidence, that such dispersed, or composite, forms of large-scale organization—collaboration without centralization—also predated the large Asian military empires of the last millennia before the Common Era.

Without the need to support the costly and destructive defensive measures that Asian "civilizations" had raised against marauding horsemen from the steppes of Asia, African fishermen and canoe transporters, hoe cultivators, cattle pastoralists, networks distributing rare and valuable products, and others elsewhere in Africa elaborated many other composite, or dispersed, forms of political integration as they confronted novel circumstances and opportunities during the following two or three millennia. These networks facilitated widespread distribution of material products and ideas, and the words for them that linguistic historians now use to trace the resulting patterns through modern Africa's hundreds of languages. Hierarchical, horse-driven military organization reached northern Africa with Roman military expansion, at the same time that it reached Europe to

the north. At the same time, merchants—but not military governments—from the increasingly commercialized Mediterranean Sea appropriated camels to cross the Sahara to the western sudan, Arab and Persian dhows sailed down along the eastern African coast, and Red Sea merchants searched the Ethiopian highlands in search of the gold needed as currencies in the growing merchant sectors of these maritime economies. In no case, however, did they arrive with the military backing of the imperial systems beyond the seas that they supplied.

However, the commercial credit that these merchants introduced to Africans from the beginning stimulated a tendency toward indebtedness beyond what buyers of their wares in Africa could pay in the tropical exotica in demand in distant temperate-latitude markets: the familiar list of oils and other fragrances, dyestuffs, and animal products—pelts, ivory, and rhinoceros horn. All of these exports came from wild sources that did not readily sustain increased rates of extraction to cover increased borrowing stimulated by competition among the many components of composite African polities and distribution networks. African communities built around such trading found themselves compelled to try to cover these growing trade deficits with the primary forms of asset that they had organized themselves to create and to accumulate: human beings, ideally members of communities of others, disruptive members of their own, or dependents of rivals. This tendency to give up people to buy commercial goods has appeared everywhere in the world that merchants have introduced commercial credit into small dispersed communities, from Italian merchants in the Slavic-speaking regions of eastern Europe to the southeastern Asian archipelago to the Native Americas. The people "sold" into the commercial sectors of agrarian, priestly, warlord "civilizations" of the sort predominating in Asia and around the Mediterranean staffed communities of merchants otherwise isolated from local peasant farmers, who were claimed almost entirely by the terrestrial military and ecclesiastical institutions there.

The horse reached sub-Saharan latitudes only belatedly, in the tenth or eleventh centuries, long after Africans had consolidated communities of this heterarchical sort and consolidated wide-ranging contacts among them. The military efficacy of powerful and speedy horses in the western southern margins of the Sahara provoked a rapid escalation in military costs from the Mali cavalry in the west to other polities in the so-called sudan eastward beyond Lake Chad to Ethiopia. Military costs rose further owing to the mobility of the farmers raided, who withdrew to defensible locations and formed new communities, often in less arable or otherwise less productive terrain. Moreover, the horses imported were themselves extremely costly for the warriors to buy and maintain, and so raiders who ran down and captured remote populations sold their captives as a significant means of paying off the indebtedness resulting from the animals imported to sustain this escalating arms race.

The ancient and worldwide pattern of small dispersed communities selling captives to cover debts created by the waves of commercial merchandise that traders could introduce, on credit, intensified by an order of magnitude in the sixteenth century on the Atlantic coasts of Africa. Two circumstances enabled the European merchants who sailed then along African shores to make so significant a difference. One was that they came as representatives of military monarchies in Europe, caught in the same bind as the contemporary warlords in Mali, Songhay, and Kanem in Africa: military costs escalating faster than local sources of revenue could cover. No previous merchants had reached Africa with comparable backing of terrestrial military powers.

The second novelty was the fortuitous flood of gold and silver into Europe brought by contact with, first, African and then American sources of specie. European merchants henceforth had the wealth both to support their military backers in Europe and to invest in production, beyond their historically limited concentration of assets in inventories, equipment, artisanal production, lavish households, and other familiar components of the commercial sectors within which military and ecclesiastical authorities, who controlled local productive peasant populations, confined them. In the Atlantic, they encountered effectively empty lands in which they themselves were free to invest in large-scale agricultural production, starting with the islands just off the shores of Africa—principally the Madeiras and the Canaries. The tropical Americas, largely emptied of their native populations by European diseases and military aggression,

then became the principal sites of commercially grown agricultural commodities—mostly sugar, but also rice, indigo, and eventually coffee and cotton—on large rural industrial sites (plantations) worked by Africans whom they purchased and collateralized as slaves.

Africans in contact with the rapidly growing commercial economy of the Atlantic first sold extracted commodities—primarily gold, but in regions lacking the primary commodity of interest to the Europeans also hides, ivory, copper, textiles, and much else—in order to acquire distinctive imports that they could distribute through the usual channels to attract and display dependents: wives, clients, and slaves. But—without pausing here to mention the particular circumstances recounted elsewhere in this work—the Europeans also accepted criminals, refugees from drought, and war captives when they could. With the explosive seventeenth-century growth of sugar production in the New World they—particularly the Dutch and English—began to stimulate supplies of captives from Africa with commercial credit. They pumped in trade goods on "trust" much faster than local populations could grow to absorb them without resorting to violence. The eighteenth century saw hostilities break out everywhere along the cutting edges of this inflationary inflow of commercial credit, from the upper Niger to the heart of Central Africa. Highly—and, as always, expensive—military regimes emerged to bring a kind of tense peace to the regions torn by violence, and then found that they had to raid outlying populations in order to sustain themselves. The same phrasing would describe equally well the consolidation of the contemporaneous "absolute" military monarchies in Europe, and the naval forces that they built to extract the wealth they needed from outlying portions of the globe.

In Africa, many of the people captured were retained to populate growing commercial sectors: diaspora of trading villages, networks of brokers, and canoe transporters, "enforcers" and security guards, and agricultural villages provisioning these new nonproductive populations. Within two generations, these commercial communities—or, in the larger polities, factions—had grown to a prominence that enabled them to place their representatives in positions of leadership bequeathed by an earlier generation of war leaders. This "bourgeois revolution" marked many of Africa's well-known "slaving states" of the second half of the eighteenth or in some cases early nineteenth centuries, from Asante and Dahomey south to Kasanje and Lunda in Central Africa. Africa's engagement with the Atlantic economy thus produced a contemporaneous sequence of military expansion and commercial consolidation (though terrestrial rather than maritime) that paralleled those of both Europe and the more commercialized parts of the Americas. Eastern Africa followed the same path from longstanding extraction of gold and ivory, overstimulated by Asian merchants in the eighteenth century, to violence that produced the large numbers of captives sold as slaves in the nineteenth.

Atlantic commerce and African slaves thus became the motors that propelled baroque European monarchies of the seventeenth and eighteenth centuries to build the navies that Spanish, Portuguese, Dutch, English, and French used to extend their competition for artisan products, and later strategic resources, around the globe. The large global markets that they thus created stimulated the development of hydraulic and fossil-fuel technologies in Europe to construct the weaponry and to fabricate textiles and other manufactured products that—by the nineteenth century—consolidated the modern commercially integrated world of heavily armed national states and industrial technology, centered in Europe and North America. Before the nineteenth century, from a world-historical perspective centered in Africa (or, similarly, also Asia and the Native Americas), these expensive and risky ventures were the strategies of monarchs on Europe's northwestern maritime fringe, marginal to the great Eurasian equestrian military powers, from China and northern Indian military aristocracies to Alexander to the Romans to Persia to the many Muslim contenders over a millennium since the eighth century, culminating by the sixteenth century in the Ottomans then seriously threatening the chilly Christian fringes of the known world. The costly mounted militarism and monumentality had been interrupted, over its five-thousand-year history, only by new waves of warriors on horses who repeatedly streamed out of central Asia. Tropical Africa, except for the southern edges of the Sahara, had been spared these costs.

MODERN HISTORY: TRANSATLANTIC SLAVE TRADE TO THE PRESENT

The mercantile powers of maritime western Europe drew a succession of raw resources from Africa, each one critical to the phase of commercial and then industrial growth that propelled it. European interests in Asia until the middle of the nineteenth century were focused instead on the artisan and agricultural production of that continent's large, sedentary, agrarian populations. The Americas provided specie and an opportunity for mercantile investment in tropical production and, in temperate North America, immigrant settler agriculture and timbering. Africans tended to move in pursuit of extractive resources, including human beings, rather than to dig in and invest in stabilized production. The Africans captured, sold as slaves, supported the initial European investments in American agricultural production in two senses: (1) their productive labor; and (2) their financial value as the (human) collateral that backed the initial large European investments in the plantations where they worked. In the eighteenth century, these captive markets for crude early European manufactures, still not remotely a match for Asian artisanry in quality or quantities, supported key start-up phases of what later became widespread industrialization in the nineteenth century. Africans, among others around the world, preferred Indian cottons over European woolens and linens until the middle of the nineteenth century, but the silver and then gold from the Americas had paid for all the textiles that European merchants could sell.

When proto-industrial techniques of plantation management, the stimulants (coffee, cocoa, tea, tobacco) that they produced for exhausted workers in European factories, and the profits they generated had gradually allowed European manufacturers to move into the robust phases of the industrial revolution after 1800, Africa provided key industrial lubricants (palm oil, peanuts, or groundnuts), Victorian consumer luxuries (ivory, ostrich plumes, wax for votive candles in Catholic countries), and eventually wild ("red") rubber, as well as diamonds and gold from the southern part of the continent that propelled Europe into the twentieth century. Industrial technologies also brought modern weaponry (rifles, machine guns) and medical technology and public sanitation worked out, in significant part, to maintain European armies in tropical latitudes, that enabled the military conquest of the continent from the 1880s, in an initial series of remote skirmishes that culminated in World War I. That unprecedented conflagration, the first near-global conflict of the twentieth century, was fought with several significant theatres in Africa. The European colonies thus consolidated by the end of the war rewarded the victors with the strategic mineral resources of modern, twentieth-century steel-based industrial age, from copper to tin and bauxite, and with agricultural commodities from coffee to cocoa to plantation sisal and rubber. The uniquely western European alliance of mercantile interests with monarchical, and then national, military power had conquered the world, including Africa.

Throughout world history merchants have accumulated wealth faster than military powers have conquered territories, and especially more effectively than conquerors have managed to consolidate control and rebuild after the first, relatively low-cost destructive phases of their conquests. And so it was for the Europeans in colonial Africa from the 1890s through the 1950s. Africa's dispersed military regimes, even after two centuries of gaining strength from Atlantic, Indian Ocean, and Saharan trades in slaves, fell easily before modern European weapons, communications, and logistics. But the resulting colonies were impossible to control without strengthening the Africans who survived the older military regimes—the "chiefs" (or equivalents) recognized as local authorities in nearly every colony. These chiefs were effectively in charge of most colonial populations on a day-to-day basis in all but the industrial—mostly mining—sites that the Europeans developed around male labor migrants, seldom permanently resident families. There, and along critical infrastructural components of the colonies—ports and railroads—colonial administrators and employers faced protests and strikes in spite of draconian restrictions that they imposed on the workers they had recruited, often forcibly.

Almost nowhere were metropolitan regimes willing to make the investments that might have attracted willing volunteer workers for wages. Colonial rule everywhere in the world was meant to extract resources, not to invest them. European nations drained their colonies to support the ever-more costly investments in modern weaponry, and social welfare for the voting citizens of civic nations. Farmers, herders, and others thus strained in Africa and Asia found few opportunities in the commercialized economies and turned to their historic, local, often community resources to survive. Most Africans survived their integration into the "modern world" by adapting—"reinventing," in the name of "tradition," as they had always done—cultural and human resources of their own.

Meanwhile, after World War II early-twentieth-century international mining consortia and trading companies had been succeeded by modern multinational corporations, operating well beyond the national domains of the early colonial era, including the colonies in Africa and elsewhere. At the same time, politicians in the African colonies looked to the nationalist political model of the European nations that had conquered them as the route to a respected, and they hoped also prosperous, future for themselves in the liberal, democratic world that the Europeans believed they were making. That is to say that African politicians turned to the nation-state model of political organization and won independence in these terms in the 1960s, precisely as the essentially nineteenth-century dynamic of nationalism was playing out in the supranational industrial world it had enabled.

On a world scale, the resulting half century of Africa's national/political independence has been marked by the failure of its own national governments, vastly weaker from the start than their European models, to withstand the pressures of foreign corporate investment and then Cold War–era militarization by superpowers trying to protect or gain access to strategic resources. By the 1970s, petroleum reserves from Nigeria to Gabon to Angola to the southern Sudan and central Sahara had become the principal magnets for foreign investment. Multinational arms merchants, drug cartels, the International Monetary Fund, and the World Bank, in one way or another have all stepped in to support one or another competing African interest in dealing with the ballooning debt taken on to stave off fiscal collapse. The pattern of ruinous borrowing to attempt to cover the sequence of global commercial, industrial, and now financial investment, dating from Africa's earliest contacts with commercial economies, continues.

Globalization for Africa has meant not only a growing lust for the excesses of the modern western culture of consumption but also sometimes desperate struggles by very poor people for the riches to be gained through the shadowy transnational networks dealing in diamonds, drugs, and AK-47s. Health has suffered from the vulnerabilities of populations weakened by eroding local community integrity and too little food for far too long. The victims of these sometimes brutal struggles, ordinary people, have appropriated other resources—mostly cultural, which after all are almost free—from the consolidating world in the form of Islamic Sufism, and toleration of Islamist regimes, as well as evangelical Christianity, and popular media entertainments, including football.

This popular retreat into globally derived populist versions of Africans' historical devotion to community solidarity and self-sufficiency derives from the continent's costly experience with heavily armed, commercially driven, nation-state modernity. It also has generated the critique of modernity that is starting to emanate from intellectuals with formative backgrounds in Africa. Far from lingering somewhere beyond the fringes of history, as Hegel defined it for Europeans at the threshold of their nineteenth-century move toward modernity, Africans' continuing, seemingly ever-renewable reliance on themselves much more closely resembles the long course of human history throughout the world. On this global scale, the millennia-long, and hardly millennial, diversion of African community solidarity and mutual—if also highly differentiated—respect into Asian-European militarism, monumentality, and material accumulation, mercantile distractions from production of whatever it takes to sustain viable local communities, and ultimately the existential isolation of modernist individualism is the historical aberration. The limits of such "civilization," though celebrated in conventional world histories, have become apparent to those onto whom their costs have been displaced. An inclusive, truly global history of the world includes the alternative strategies that Africans, and most of the world, have tried, and often failed, to preserve.

See also **Cold War; Colonial Policies and Practices; Du Bois, W. E. B.; Globalization; International Monetary Fund; Mansa Musa; Slave Trades; Slavery and Servile Institutions; Transportation: Caravan; Warfare; World Bank; World War I; World War II.**

BIBLIOGRAPHY

Eckert, Andreas. "Fitting Africa into World History: A Historiographical Exploration." In *Writing World History 1800–2000*, ed. Benedikt Stuchtey and Eckhardt Fuchs. New York: Oxford University Press, 2003.

Ehret, Christopher. *An African Classical Age: Eastern and Southern Africa in World History, 1000 B.C. to 400 A.D.* Charlottesville: University Press of Virginia, 1998.

Feierman, Steven. "African Histories and the Dissolution of World History." In *Africa and the Disciplines*, ed. Robert H. Bates, V. Y. Mudimbe, and Jean O'Barr, pp. 167–212. Chicago: University of Chicago Press, 1993.

"Forum: Africa and World History." *Historically Speaking* 5. no. 2 (2004).

Gilbert, Erik, and Jonathan K. Reynolds. *Africa in World History from Prehistory to the Present.* Upper Saddle River, NJ: Pearson Education, 2004.

Gilbert, Erik; Jonathan Reynolds; Candice Gaucher; and R. Hunt Davis. "Forum: Teaching Africa in World History: Issues and Approaches." *World History Connected* 2, no. 1 (November 2004). Available from worldhistory connected.press.uiuc.edu

Gomez, Michael A. *Reversing Sail: A History of the African Diaspora.* Cambridge, U.K.: Cambridge University Press, 2005.

Manning, Patrick. *Navigating World History: Historians Create a Global Past.* New York: Palgrave Macmillan, 2003.

Manning, Patrick. *The African Diaspora: A History through Culture.* New York: Columbia University Press, 2008.

McIntosh, Roderick J. *Ancient Middle Niger: Urbanism and the Self-Organizing Landscape.* New York: Cambridge University Press, 2005.

Northrup, David. *Africa's Discovery of Europe, 1450–1850.* New York: Oxford University Press, 2002.

Reynolds, Jonathan T., ed. "Africa in World History." In *World History Bulletin* 22, no. 1 (Spring 2006): 3–30.

Wright, Donald R. *The World and a Very Small Place in Africa.* Armonk NY: M. E. Sharpe, 1997.

JOSEPH C. MILLER

HISTORY AND THE STUDY OF AFRICA.

In most of Africa the demand for a professional study of history came late. Whereas the study of geography, for example, had been intimately linked with the whole work of African exploration and colonization, and that of African languages with the earliest propagation of the Christian gospel, and whereas anthropology had been seen as an essential tool of successful colonial administration at least from the 1920s, the quest for African as distinct from colonial history came to the fore only after World War II, when the progress of colonial education had made possible the creation of university colleges in the tropical African colonies. The first teachers of history in those colleges were inevitably expatriates, recruited from the universities of the European colonial powers, and trained at best to research in some kind of colonial history. But faced by African students, and with thoughts of political independence already in the air, it did not take them long to realize that the Africa of the future would need to know more about coherent regions of the continent than about the scattered possessions of this or that colonial empire, and would wish to extend the study of those regions as far back as was possible into the history of the precolonial past.

Such ideas, coming out of tropical Africa, were first publicized at a series of international conferences held at the School of Oriental and African Studies in London University between 1953 and 1961. These brought together the teachers of history and other relevant scholars from British, French, Belgian, and Portuguese universities and research organizations. The discussions made it clear that the first step was to search the materials already in print, in the literature of travel and exploration, of missionary work, of colonial administration, of ethnography and anthropology, of linguistic classification and, above all, of recent, Iron Age archaeology—all with an eye to the evidence that they could yield about the history of the African peoples. The next step was to study the traditions recorded in writing by the first generation of literate Africans and to explore, before it was too late, what further sources might still exist in the minds and memories of nonliterate informants.

These ideas developed a wider impact as the budding African universities began to send the best of their early graduates to study for higher degrees in the universities of Europe. Their presence alongside European research students inspired supervisors to help them to find topics in which they could employ their inherited knowledge of their own

languages and cultures, and these efforts did much to broaden prevailing concepts of what constituted valid historical research. The first experiments were necessarily cautious in order to keep the confidence of the rest of the profession. These sent them in search of the archival collections that carried materials relating to the precolonial period, such as those of the Dutch and British trading companies, the missionary societies, and the European consulates established around the coasts of Africa during the nineteenth century to discourage the slave trade and encourage legitimate commerce. Most of the early doctoral students from West Africa, such as Kenneth Dike, Saburi Biobaku, Jacob Ajayi, Adu Boahen, Kwame Daaku, and John Fynn, began their research careers in this way, and they did so in company with British research students such as Richard Gray, John Flint, Anthony Hopkins, David Birmingham, and Richard Rathbone.

The next step was to locate and make available the archives created within Africa by early colonial governments in their correspondence with provincial and district officials and with African notables, which proved to be much richer than those preserved in the metropolitan archives of the colonial powers. Finally, for the brave and the linguistically gifted, there was the possibility of recording, translating and analyzing the unwritten memoranda handed down by word of mouth by the courtiers of African chiefs and clan-heads, as well as by elders to their descendants.

One outstanding pioneer of the last method was a young Belgian research student, Jan Vansina, who worked among the Kuba people of the Kasai from 1953 until 1956 and later in Rwanda from 1957 until 1960. Another was a Kenyan, Allan Ogot, who studied his own Luo people and became the first student in London University to complete a doctoral thesis based almost entirely on oral evidence. The student who carried this method to perfection was an American student in London, David William Cohen, who presented a thesis on the historical tradition of Busoga, Uganda, and followed it by publishing a selection of his recorded and transcribed texts in the Soga language, complete with English translations. It was hoped that, with the proliferation of African universities and their ability to train their own students for higher degrees, perhaps a hundred monographs designed on the Cohen model might emerge to bear permanent witness to Africa's oral traditions. But sadly this was not to be.

Nearly all of the African research students trained in Britain returned to teach in the universities of their own countries, and gradually the expatriate teachers returned from Africa to universities in their countries of origin. Thus, for example, John Fage, after ten years service in the University of Ghana, returned to found the Center of West African Studies in the University of Birmingham. Kenneth Ingham, after a similar period at Makerere University in Uganda, returned via Sandhurst to the University of Bristol, G. N. Sanderson returned from the University of Khartoum to Royal Holloway College in the University of London. Eric Stokes returned from the University College of Rhodesia and Nyasaland to Cambridge University. When the African Studies Association of the United Kingdom was founded in 1965, no fewer than ninety of its approximately five hundred founding members were teachers of African history, of whom the majority had previously served in universities in Africa. Such an accretion of competent personnel could not fail to attract the notice of historians of other regions of the world.

In Francophone tropical Africa a parallel movement took place, starting with the foundation of the University of Dakar in 1955 and the Universities of Lovanium and Elizabethville in the Belgian Congo in 1956. In both cases progress was accelerated by the preexistence of colonial research institutes—in Dakar the French Institute for Black Africa (IFAN), and in the Belgian Congo the Institute for Research in Central Africa (IRSAC). The archaeologist and historian Raymond Mauny was employed for twenty-two years at IFAN before returning to France in 1960 as the first professor of African archaeology at the Sorbonne, which simultaneously appointed the historian of Madagascar, Governor Hubert Deschamps, to fill its first chair of African history. In the Congo, Vansina carried out his first two major projects of field research under the auspices of IRSAC, of which the most resounding result was a treatise on the methodology of collecting oral tradition, first published in French in 1961.

Meanwhile, during the early years of Lovanium, African history was served by ecclesiastical historians from the University of Louvain, and notably by Louis Jadin, who had worked in the Vatican archives on the ancient kingdom of Kongo, while a younger colleague, Jean-Luc Vellut, was later to initiate the teaching of African history at the new Belgian Francophone university at Louvain-la-Neuve. The first rector of the University of Elizabethville was the archaeologist and ethnologist, Jean Hiernaux, whose excavations of sites in Rwanda and Kivu, had done much to establish the chronology of the Iron Age in central Bantu Africa, whereas the same years saw the exciting excavations by Jacques Nenquin of a sequence of much more advanced Iron Age sites around Lake Kisale in the valley of the upper Lualaba.

At the same time the approach of political independence in most of the tropical African countries between 1957 and 1963 provided the signal for a greatly enhanced American involvement in African affairs and African studies. The U.S. government funded the Peace Corps, and American universities soon counted a multitude of returned volunteers with first-hand experience of some African countries. The great U.S. foundations responded by funding African Studies Centers at some of the leading universities, including Boston, Columbia, Northwestern, Wisconsin, Indiana and the constituent campuses of the University of California. These centers led the way in developing research and teaching in African history, both by American postgraduate students and by students from many African countries who came to America on scholarships provided by the U.S. government on a scale that far surpassed those available in European countries. Many of these African students remained in America after completing their studies, finding academic posts in universities and colleges that were happy to employ a single teacher qualified to contribute a course or two in African history alongside other more mainline subjects. In many of these institutions a significant part of the demand for African history came from African american students, who saw them in the context of black studies and expected a concentration on the Atlantic slave trade and the African diaspora, which sometimes led on to claims that African history could be properly taught only by teachers who were black.

All this gave a somewhat different flavor to African history as practiced in America from that prevailing in Africa and in Europe. Nevertheless, there can be no doubt that by the early 1970s America was leading the world in this subject, both in the number of participating institutions and in the quality of the research and publication being undertaken at the best of them. Academic salaries in America and support for research were generous compared with those of Europe, and some key posts in the United States were filled by importation. Thus, the leading archaeologist of Africa, Desmond Clark, was recruited by Berkeley from the Rhodes-Livingstone Museum in Zambia, Leonard Thompson from the University of Cape Town by the University of California at Los Angeles (UCLA), Graham Irwin from the University of Ghana by Columbia, Phyllis Martin from SOAS by Indiana.

Meanwhile, at the University of Wisconsin Philip Curtin successfully converted his earlier teaching program in comparative tropical history to one in African history and capped it by patiently wooing and winning Vansina as his most distinguished colleague. Many well-known scholars emerged from the Wisconsin African Studies seminar, including Joseph Miller, Martin Klein, Paul Lovejoy, Robert Harms, David Henige, Thomas Spear, and Andrew Roberts, and a much larger penumbra of assistant professors who went out to teach in universities and colleges nationwide. By Curtin's estimate, in 1973 some 350 historians of Africa were in academic employment in the United States, of whom some 300 had been trained in American universities. Curtin himself, and later Miller, became well enough recognized by the profession to be elected presidents of the American Historical Association. In 1983 Vansina was chosen as the first recipient of the Distinguished Africanist award of the African Studies Association of the United States, an organization that represented all the academic disciplines.

The great problem for the further development of the subject lay in Africa itself, and it was that, with rapidly growing populations and nearly static economies, African countries found that they could no longer support universities and colleges of the standard established during the late colonial period. Student numbers increased remorselessly, while university revenues steadily declined. Research time for staff disappeared, and soon university libraries fell far behind the current state of knowledge. University teachers with extended families to support were tempted to take on second jobs. In many African countries academic life was deeply affected by political and civil disturbances. In 1966 Kenneth Dike, by then vice chancellor of Ibadan University, was among those who had to flee, first to his native Biafra and later to a chair at Harvard. Many of his colleagues were less fortunate.

In Uganda during the presidencies of Amin and Obote, all the well-qualified historians at Makerere University, including Mathias Kiwanuka, Samwiri Karugire, and Patrick Kakwenzire, fled abroad. In this most unfortunate country some eighteen years passed without the possibility of serious research in either history or archaeology. In circumstances like these, which were nearly replicated in many other African countries, it became difficult for outsiders to help. While international conferences on African history, and universities like Wisconsin, were insisting that doctoral students should command an African language and undertake field work in Africa, they were in reality limiting the advancement of knowledge to a handful of the most politically stable African countries and excluding huge areas of the continent from the mainstream of ongoing research.

Tropical Africa apart, there remained the question of the place to be given in the study of African history to the regions north and the south of the tropics. Each had long possessed its own universities, from which there had issued a respectable body of historical literature. In North Africa, the main tradition was Francophone, and its founding father was Ch.-A. Julien, professor of history at the University of Algiers and later at the Sorbonne, whose *History of North Africa from the Arab conquest to 1830* was first published in 1931. It was revised in 1952 by his successor, Roger Le Tourneau, who ten years later added a history of the political evolution of Muslim North Africa from 1920 to 1961. The work of both men amounted to much more than colonial history, but it was also something less than African history, since it scarcely touched on the historical connections with the peoples of the Sahara or the Muslim populations to the south of it. It was in fact only with the conclusion of the Algerian civil war of

1957 to 1963 that Algeria assumed its pan-African role as a supplier of arms and military training for liberation movements all over the continent and so became, along with Egypt, Libya, and Morocco, a major player in the African scene, whose modern history, at least, had to be regarded as fundamentally important for the rest of Africa.

Likewise, in Africa south of the Limpopo there had long existed a local historiography, based upon the richest documentary evidence available for any region of the continent, at least from the early nineteenth century onward. But it remained until the mid-twentieth century essentially a historiography of white settlement and conquest, in which the local African peoples figured mainly as the uncivilized subjects of white expansion and domination, the study of whose strange beliefs and customs were best left in the safe hands of archaeologists and anthropologists, leaving historians free to concentrate on the rivalries of Boer and Briton. As lately as 1957, the standard and frequently revised work on Southern African history by Eric Walker of Cape Town and later of Cambridge University affirmed that the settlement of the Bantu peoples in Southern Africa was not much older than that of the Europeans, and in the western Cape Province much later.

The approach to a less blinkered view was bravely pioneered by Leonard Thompson from his chair of history at Cape Town during the 1960s and later embodied in the *Oxford History of South Africa*, which he edited with Monica Wilson from 1969 to 1972. Briefly, he argued that, just as the oral historiography of Rwanda was essentially that of a Tutsi minority which had formerly dominated the majority population of Hutu, so in the rigidly stratified society of South Africa a written historiography was not merely a reflection of social inequality but also a powerful instrument for the maintenance of inequality. Before departing Cape Town for UCLA, he steered his star pupil, Shula Marks, toward SOAS London, from where, in a long and successful career as a research supervisor of white South African doctoral students, she led the necessary reform of South African historiography.

It could perhaps be argued, however, that the most powerful factor in the stitching together of tropical African history with that of its northern and southern extremities arose from two major

collaborative works of reference, which were planned in the 1960s and published during the 1970s and 1980s, one by the Cambridge University Press on a normal commercial basis and the other under the auspices of the United Nations Education, Scientific, and Cultural Organization (UNESCO) and with access to large subsidies for preparatory seminars, the collection of documents, translations, and the pricing of ultimate sales. The contents of each series filled eight stout volumes, of which five were allocated to the precolonial period and three to the colonial period and after. However, whereas the Cambridge series was planned and supervised by two general editors with the assistance of six more volume editors, the UNESCO series was controlled by an international scientific committee of thirty-nine members, two-thirds of them chosen from African countries, and the remaining third from non-African historians selected to represent all philosophies of history. Members of the committee were convened in different African venues over the course of a decade during the planning stages, and all theoretically participated in reading and amending the contributions that came in. All the volume editors were Africans, and in the choice of contributors, preference was given to Africans residing in Africa.

One obvious effect of this competition was to attract nearly all of the potential African contributors away from the Cambridge enterprise into that of UNESCO. Another and more fortunate effect followed from the location of the UNESCO headquarters in Paris and from the fact that its director general from 1974 to 1987 was a Senegalese. It was to ensure a proper representation of Francophone scholarship in the African historical field, especially in the treatment given to North and West Africa and Madagascar. The Cambridge series was correspondingly stronger than the UNESCO series in its treatment of Central and Southern Africa. Due probably to the inevitable ten years gap between planning and production, American scholarship was the most under-represented feature of both series. Of 230 chapters in the UNESCO series, only eight were contributed by American authors, and of 96 chapters in the Cambridge series, only ten. It may be concluded, however, that the main merit of both series was that they attempted serious coverage of every region of Africa, thus showing where the gaps in existing knowledge were greatest. And, taken together, they presented a fair summary of what had been achieved by scholars in Africa and Europe during the forty years from 1950 and 1990.

Meantime, first-hand research in history and historical archaeology was moving forward, even if conducted mostly by outsiders. In Francophone West Africa, IFAN carried on with its excavations at Koumbi Saleh, the presumed site of the capital of ancient Ghana, under the direction of Jean Devisse, who later succeeded Mauny at the Sorbonne. IFAN likewise sponsored the astonishingly copious biography of the late nineteenth century Mandinka warlord Samori by Yves Person, published in four large volumes between 1968 and 1975. Then there was the marvelous work carried out by the American couple, Ann and Roderick McIntosh, at Jenné-jeno on a tributary of the upper Niger, proving that a walled city had existed there since the beginning of the Iron Age around 250 BCE, and had been trading far up and down the Niger river system, thus antedating by more than a thousand years the opening of the trans-Saharan caravan routes. There was the discovery and excavation by Bernard Fagg of sites bearing pottery figurines of the Nok culture of the Jos plateau in northern Nigeria, dating to the early Iron Age of the last six centuries BCE, which was clearly ancestral to the plastic art of later Ife and Bénin.

From Ivor Wilks of the University of Ghana and later of Northwestern University, there came the majestic monograph on the Asante empire in the nineteenth century, which provided a telling example of the kind of political enlargement and development that might have occurred elsewhere in Africa, had there been no European intervention. From the other side of the continent there was all the work of the British Institute in Eastern Africa, led first by Neville Chittick and later by John Sutton, on the medieval harbor towns of the Indian Ocean coast, at Kilwa Kisiwani, Manda and Pate, which was to be completed by Mark Horton's excavations at Shanga. There were the five seasons of rigorous excavations by David Phillipson at the site of Aksum, the ancient capital city of Christian Ethiopia, and the two outstanding monographs on medieval and modern Ethiopia by the local scholars, Taddesse Tamrat and Mohammed Hassen.

There were the definitive excavations of Great Zimbabwe by Roger Summers and others, which established the existence of a stone-built capital city, the population of which may have grown to 20,000 between the eleventh and the fifteenth century CE. And there were the patient excavations by Merrick Posnansky and John Sutton at the capital sites of a pastoral dynasty at Bigo and Ntusi in western Uganda dating to the eleventh century CE.

Work on the history of Western Equatorial Africa was, unsurprisingly, dominated by Vansina, whose two outstanding contributions were, first, the radically revised version of his early fieldwork on the Kuba, and secondly his riveting account of the economic and political history of the Western Bantu farmers and fishermen of the River Congo and its tributaries, entitled *Paths in the Rainforest*. Following in Vansina's footsteps, Robert Harms studied the Bobangi people, who lived by fishing and long distance trading beside the banks of the Congo River and its two great tributaries the Ubangi and the Kasai. His great book *River of Wealth, River of Sorrow*, showed how the Bobangi of precolonial times bought slaves in the far interior, using the best of them as paddlers and selling the remainder into the Atlantic trading system. Their commerce survived the suppression of the Atlantic trade by turning from slaves to ivory, but it was finally destroyed by the introduction of the colonial river steamer.

Meanwhile, another early disciple of the Wisconsin school, Joseph Miller, spent the last few years of Portuguese rule in Angola studying the traditional history of the Mbundu people, and especially of that section of them called the Imbangala, who emerged in southern Angola in the seventeenth century as raiding bands, who sold their captives to the Portuguese, but later settled to form the kingdom of Kasanje, claiming descent from the Lunda kingdoms much further inland. The resulting book, *Kings and Kinsmen*, was a landmark in the methodology of interpreting oral traditions in the whole region. Miller's next and most magisterial work, *Way of Death*, which followed in 1988, carried the history of the African diaspora into the southern hemisphere with a definitive study of the slave trade between Angola and Brazil during the years from 1730 to 1830.

Perhaps the most difficult problem in African historiography has been that of how to treat the traffic in African captives to other continents. Whereas the circumstances of their capture and deportation belong obviously to the history of Africa, as do the demographic consequences for Africa of their removal, from that point on their history belongs mainly to that of the new lands to which they went. More important for African history is the continued survival of slavery in Africa itself long after its nominal suppression by the colonial powers that partitioned and occupied the continent in the 1880s and 1890s, for it is this which shows how fundamental was the role of indigenous slavery in most African societies. Here, the works of Suzanne Miers and her several collaborators lead the field. Moreover, the excessive concentration of slavery studies upon the Atlantic and Indian Ocean components of the trade have mostly ignored the dimensions of the trans-Saharan trade from the Muslim countries of the Sudanic belt to the Muslim countries of North Africa, which have been estimated by Paul Lovejoy to have accounted for two-thirds of the export trade.

As was only to be expected, the most contentious performance by historians of Africa has been in relation to the colonial period, which can be seen most clearly by comparing the relevant volumes of the UNESCO and Cambridge histories. It is that most African eyes see the colonial period predominantly in terms of conquest and resistance to conquest, whereas to most outsiders conquest and resistance were separated by some fifty years of more or less unchallenged colonial rule, during which the states of modern Africa had their schooling for survival in the modern world—not only at the hands of colonial governments but also through the education provided by Christian missions and by daily interaction with immigrant minorities from Europe and Asia.

During this brief period, the multitudinous statelets and ethnicities of precolonial Africa were amalgamated into some forty workable political/administrative units, introduced to a monetary economy, to modern means of transport, to western concepts of law and justice, to education in languages of wider communication and to worldwide religious faiths. Taken together, influences so fundamental are not easily dismissed by any process of selective amnesia. It was in the field of warfare and violence that the postcolonial state differed most significantly from its colonial predecessor, as the end of colonial rule quickly led to a quintupling of armed forces and their re-equipment with modern weaponry, and not only at governmental level, but also at that of insurgent warlords and their outside abettors. It may be that with the end of the Cold War and the emergence of the African Union there will be a reduction of violence, but the omens do not look good, especially along the fault-line running east along the southern fringes of the Sahara Desert from the Atlantic to the Red Sea, where Muslim and Christian Africa meet and conflict.

See also **Historiography; Research; Slave Trades.**

BIBLIOGRAPHY

Ajayi, J. F. Ade, ed. *General History of Africa*, Vol. 6. Paris: UNESCO, 1989.

Boahen, A. A., ed. *General History of Africa*, Vol. 7. Paris: UNESCO, 1985.

Cohen, David William. *The Historical Tradition of Busoga*. Oxford: Clarendon Press, 1972.

Cohen, David William. *Womunafu's Bunafu*. Princeton, NJ: Princeton University Press, 1977.

Ehret, Christopher. *The Civilizations of Africa*. Oxford: James Currey, 2002.

El Fasi, M., and I. Hrbek, eds. *General History of Africa*, Vol. 3. Paris: UNESCO, 1988.

Miers, S., and Richard Roberts, eds. *The End of Slavery in Africa*. Madison: University of Wisconsin Press, 1986.

Oliver, Roland. *In the Realms of Gold*. Madison: University of Wisconsin Press, 1997.

Oliver, Roland. *The African Experience*, 2nd edition. Boulder, CO: Westview Press, 2000.

Phillipson, David. *African Archaeology*. Cambridge, U.K.: Cambridge University Press, 1985.

Roberts, A., ed. *Cambridge History of Africa*, Vol. 7: *1905–1940*. Cambridge, U.K.: Cambridge University Press, 1986.

Thornton, John Kelly. *Africa and Africans in the Making of the Atlantic World 1460–1680*. Cambridge, U.K.: Cambridge University Press, 1992.

Vansina, Jan. *Oral Tradition as History*, 2nd edition. Madison: University of Wisconsin Press, 1985.

Vansina, Jan. *Paths in the Rainforest*. Madison: University of Wisconsin Press, 1990.

Vansina, Jan. *Living with Africa*. Madison: University of Wisconsin Press, 1994.

ROLAND OLIVER

HISTORY OF AFRICA

This entry includes the following articles:
TO SEVENTH CENTURY
SEVENTH TO SIXTEENTH CENTURY
SIXTEENTH TO NINETEENTH CENTURY
NINETEENTH AND TWENTIETH CENTURIES

TO SEVENTH CENTURY

Africa's history goes back more than 4 million years ago. Humanity has its origins in the terminal Miocene-early Pliocene geological period, from around 5.3 to 2 million years ago. Throughout the entire Pleistocene, from 2 million to 10,000 years ago, and during the subsequent period, humanity developed and adapted to the varied and ever-changing African environments and landscapes. Generally, around the seventh century CE, sub-Saharan Africa was consolidating newly acquired iron and pottery technologies. Farmers had occupied much of the continent of the Sahara. The food they produced saw population concentrations in some regions such as the Inland Niger Delta, the Upemba Depression and Lake Chad basin. The spread of Islam from the Arabian Peninsula, as a religion, a culture, a form of governance, and as an economic market force, resulted in the Arab conquest of Egypt, the Mediterranean Rim, and the Saharan and Sahelian northern and western Africa. New commercial relationships developed between eastern Africa and Asia.

AFRICAN PHYSIOGRAPHY

Plateaus and basins dominate Africa's topography. High Africa consists of those plateaus, high mountains, and steep escarpments that are over 3,281 feet above sea level, found mainly in eastern and southern Africa. Here, the landscape is a complex maze of tectonic, volcanic, and residual mountains: the Ruwenzori Range, Virunga Range, Kirinjaya, Kilimanjaro, the Ethiopian Highlands, and the Drakensberg/Maluti. Faulting has formed the East African Rift valley, that occupies the lower Zambezi basin, the entire Shire–Lake Malawi trough, the African plateau on either side of Lake Victoria, parts of Ethiopia up to the Red Sea, the Gulf of Aquaba, and the Jordan Valley in western Asia. The sedimentation process of the last 4 million years has preserved some evidence of early humans and their environments,

and volcanic activity has also preserved trace fossils of our human ancestors. In northern, central, and western Africa, both basins and mountains dominate. The Atlas Mountains, the Ahaggar Plateau, the Tibesti Massif, and the Ennedi and Marra mountains stand prominently in a complex maze of landscapes that is largely surrounded by basins—Djouf, Chad, and Sudan. This Low Africa extends to western and central Africa, in Sahelian, savanna, and equatorial zones, occupied respectively by the Niger-Benuë Basin, and the Congo Basin.

There is considerable climatic variability in Africa. Northern Africa experiences desert climate conditions and receives little to no rainfall. Perennial rivers that flow through it such as the Nile, or underground artesian water systems that emerge on the surface as oases, sustain the resultant apparently harsh environment. These have attracted considerable human settlement since the desertification process started some 3,000 years ago. In contrast, sub-Saharan Africa's climate is mainly tropical and equatorial with the equator running roughly in between these broad regions found in both hemispheres. Low rainfall and semidesert conditions exist in the Sahel region, northern and eastern Kenya and Somalia, and in parts of Angola, Namibia, the northern Cape of South Africa, and Botswana. High altitude regions over 4,921 feet above sea level such as the Drakensberg/Maluti mountains, southern Malawi, Rwanda, Burundi, Kilimanjaro, central Kenya, and Ethiopia experience montane climates.

As a result of the diversity of topography and climate, Africa has vegetation ranging from desert to tropical savanna (woodland, bushland, trees, and grasses), equatorial hardwood forest to montane forest, tussock grassland, and woodland. The high rainfall received in the equatorial areas and montane forest zones is responsible for high species diversity found in these regions. Major regions of crop diversity include the Ethiopian highlands, the Sahel, the Internal Niger Delta, and the humid forest zone of West and Central Africa. In these regions African rice, oil palm, yams, cowpeas, sorghum, finger and pearl millets, teff, fonio, Bambara groundnut, watermelon, melon, gourds, sesame, noug, Hausa potato, and coco-yam contribute significantly to subsistence requirements. Crops introduced from outside the continent such as maize, rice, cassava, beans, and cacao also contribute significantly to African agriculture.

About a billion people live in Africa, the majority concentrated on fertile volcanic plateaus, riverine lowlands and deltas, and high rainfall highland regions, where they depend directly on the land for their sustenance. In the rainforests of equatorial Central Africa and the drylands of the Kalahari, communities subsist on hunting and gathering. In favorable environments, vast arrays of agricultural systems have evolved, ranging from nomadic and transhumant livestock production to intensive smallholder mixed crop/livestock systems. Although less than 10 percent of Africa's land is under cultivation, agriculture—predominantly small-scale subsistence farming—is the largest source of employment and sustenance.

AFRICAN TECHNOLOGIES

About four principal technological systems were instrumental in the growth of African cultures from early times. These technologies shaped the development of Africa with varying degrees of intensity and impact. Technology revolves around a complex maze of settlement units and patterns built in a manner that has shaped African ways of thinking and social behavior.

The working of stone appeared as the earliest humans emerged in Africa, sometime between 2 and 3 million years ago. Wood, which rarely survives in the archaeological record, was used for the construction of shelters, settlements, and the manufacture of utilitarian tools and sailing crafts. A durable product of the past is pottery. The earliest pottery in Africa is still unidentified. However, in southern and eastern Africa, pottery manufacture is associated with the expansion of Bantu speakers, although the industry was long established in the northern parts of the continent prior to this. Pottery not only indicates the physical presence of its makers, but ethno-archaeological studies have contributed to an understanding of the technical, as well as symbolic, elements behind raw material acquisition, clay preparation, vessel construction, ornamentation, drying, and firing of the finished products. Pottery provided a durable capacity to store, transport, and heat liquids and dispersible solids better and more economically than ostrich eggshells, gourds, or ground stone bowls did. This usefulness inspired its rapid acceptance and dissemination. The ability to heat water permitted cooking of a wide range of plant foods, encouraging not

only cultivation, but also investments in long-term settlements and storage facilities near garden sites. As a result, permanent hamlets of pole and dried clay daubed house walls, agriculture, ceramic manufacture, and metallurgy became a constant part of the African scene.

Iron and copper dominate the metal technologies of Africa. In northern Africa, coppersmithing was probably practiced in Egypt from the fourth millennium BCE. Ancient copper mines and factories occur throughout the regions of Mauritania, Mali, Niger, and in parts of Nigeria, western Uganda, and much of the western half of Central and Southern Africa. The earliest copper artifacts in sub-Saharan Africa were a mixture of utilitarian and ornamental forms. The origins of iron technology are unknown, but by the middle of the first millennium BCE, iron was widely used in the forest zones of West and Central Africa, and the region of Buhaya in eastern Africa. By the first half of the first millennium CE, ironworking had reached southern Africa.

THEMES

Human Origins. Humanity evolved in Africa. Fossil hominine remains in southern African cave deposits are sealed in geological matrices that are often difficult to disentangle. Eastern African contexts, in ancient lake and volcanic sediments, are also hard to work on. That the record is so extensive is testament to the dedication of the generations of investigators. The localities of Lake Turkana in Kenya and Afar in Ethiopia are producing hominine species that show that *Australopithecus* and *Homo* were near contemporaries. Dating remains imprecise, but it seems that humanity's African ancestors originated about 1.8–4 million years ago during the terminal Pliocene and early Pleistocene periods. Perceived differences between some australopithecines and early forms of Homo may be artificial, and, indirectly, related to a toolmaking ability.

Specimens of incipient humans from Chad suggest these hominids lived during the terminal Miocene. However, it would appear that an assortment of hominines, including the australopithecines, living in East and Southern Africa during the Pliocene-Early Pleistocene interface, exhibited cranial and postcranial features suggesting bipedal locomotion, as well as a gait similar to that of later humans. Hominines of the genus Homo (the *habilines*, *ergaster*, or *erectus* with enhanced cranofacial and postcranial features) appeared just after 2 million years ago. Homo and australopithecines appear to have been exploiting the same ecological habitats around this time. Climatic changes between 2 and 2.5 million years ago influenced an adaptive diversification of human lineages that in turn initiated their spread toward more arid and open environments.

Tools of an Olduwan type appear at Sterkfontein, Olduvai Gorge, Koobi Fora, Gona, and Omo, indicating a substantial geographical range for early tool making hominines. *H. erectus/ergaster* spread its range beyond East and Southern Africa about 1.5 million years ago, reaching eastern Europe, western Asia, and Indonesia. By about 1 million years ago, it had settled in northern China and western Europe. In Africa, groups of premodern humans began occupations at Bodo (Ethiopia), Ndutu (Tanzania), and Kabwe (Zambia). Dating remains sketchy, but this post-H. erectus, archaic form of *H. Sapiens* has similarities to both the Neanderthal type and modern humans. Some paleontologists argue for the taxon *Homo Heidelbergensis*, distinguishing between *H. neanderthalensis* in Europe and H. sapiens in Africa. Whatever happened during the Early Pleistocene, there were changes that eventually saw the emergence of modern kinds of humanity. By about 100,000 years ago, modern humans inhabited most parts of Africa. Key sites, dating from 130,000 to 200,000 years ago, include Border Cave, Klasies River Mouth (South Africa), Kabwe (Zambia), Mumba (Tanzania), and Omo (Ethiopia).

Pliocene and Early Pleistocene hominids seem to have preferred forested or wooded environments near lakes, where they foraged on a variety of plant floods. Flakes and worked core implements associated with them were useful to butcher game for meat and hides, breaking bones, opening nuts and hard fruits, as well as digging for tubers. Sticks were certainly used, but these do not survive under African conditions. Early humans moved about in small groups from one place to another, collecting food and raw materials in a manner that prefigures the more orchestrated annual rounds of later advanced forgers. Their camps may have been visited repeatedly, but were not occupied for long periods. Indications at Olduvai and Kalambo Falls suggest that grass shelters or hedge fences were set up during the periodic visits. H. erectus and H. sapiens, using bifacial Acheulean hand axes and cleavers, occupied the African continent, except the forested western and central zones, between 1.5 million years ago to about 200,000 years ago. In time, they were able to exploit even these habitats using versatile assemblages of flaked tools from prepared cores. Foraging was still characterized by seasonal reoccupation of favored sites, located in the open for the most part, but caves and rock shelters modified by the construction of structures were used from this time onward.

Fire became important for roasting meat and tubers, for warmth, and for burning brush on a seasonal basis. As a result, bands of human foragers secured territories where they knew well and regularly exploited the resources. Intersections of different territories served to encourage exchange necessities from zone to zone, moving valued commodities over long distances. At this time, the development of modern behaviors seems to emerge. This includes regular long-distance movement of raw materials (mainly stone and shell), ritual behavior (including art and formal burial of humans and artifacts), fishing, specialized hunting and food storage, and population densities more comparable to those of modern foragers living in similar environments.

Developments from about 40,000 to 20,000 years ago pose serious interpretative problems, as it is still difficult to explain the gradual transition to the advanced stoneworking techniques that become evident during the Holocene period. Available archaeological record suggests no such smooth transition because there is palpable overlap of the terminal Pleistocene and the early versions of Holocene assemblages. Individual, group, and/or regional preferences in these technologies need to be examined, particularly in assisting humans to cope with increasingly colder climatic conditions culminating with the Last Glacial Maximum around 18,000 years ago.

Art, Ritual, and Ceremony. An important development in virtually all parts of Africa during the terminal Pleistocene and much of the Holocene periods was the appearance of rock art in the form of paintings and engravings found in caves, rock shelters, and open spaces. Generally, art of different regional traditions carries a combination of social, religious, and educative values. The art expressed the local cosmological world of myths and symbolism. Some depict intergroup rivalries or conflicts, seemingly recording historical events.

In Southern Africa, natural earth colors were used to depict women and men with equipment, sometimes fighting. Also shown are large and small animals in a naturalist or schematic state. Figures that are half-human and half-animal (therianthropes) are also shown. Studies of stylistic typology have not proved useful, and dating has been problematic. The earliest known rock art site in southern Africa is Apollo II Cave in Namibia dated to 27,000 years ago. Recent studies question previously held simplistic notions of interpretation that ranged from depictions of sympathetic magic to art for art's sake. An ethnographic study of the now extinct !Xam (San foragers) shows a cognitive world of the artists centered on shamanistic trance as an avenue of healing, hunting, fertility, and rainmaking rituals. Many related paintings emphasize the eland, an animal important to the ritual life of San.

Much of the rock art in Central and East Africa is naturalistic representations of animals and humans painted in red. Sometimes these are covered by later geometric patterns of various shapes and patterns, which in turn are covered by paintings of geometric shapes and stylized animals in thick white paint. A later style is of schematic red and white designs. It is thought that hunter-foragers created the naturalistic paintings, whereas the later schematic ones were the product of farming communities. The art is poorly dated, the earliest known being that from Kisese II rock shelter in Tanzania dating 19,000 years ago. It appears that this art was critical to hunter-forager economic and sacerdotal activities, portraying the forager's cosmology and their cultural and natural landscape. In the Horn of Africa, the more than one hundred carving and engraving sites from Ethiopia, Eritrea, Djibouti, and Somalia are associated with pastoralist communities that have occupied the area during the past millennium.

Western African rock art remains poorly studied, but offers interesting prospects. The little art that is known comes from the Sahelian and savanna regions. This art probably dates from the inception of the food producers from the Sahara,

suggesting that the tradition had a northern origin. Its production continues to the early twenty-first century.

The rock art found in the Sahara is clearly a product of food producers. Despite its complexity, it sheds light on a world that existed in what is now a desolate part of the continent, yielding to the largest desert in the world. Most of the art, which displays considerable regional variation, is found in the mountain regions of Fezzan, Tassili-n-Ajjer, Hoggar, Atlas, Tibesti, Ennedi, and Jebel Uweinat. It remains poorly understood but serves as a powerful archaeological and historical source, particularly on environmental and cultural developments in the Sahara from early to late Holocene times.

The polished engravings formerly attributed to the Bubaline Phase are naturalistic in character, and depict mainly wild animals such as the rhinoceros, elephant, hippopotamus, giraffe, ostrich, lion, antelope, and extinct buffalo (*Bubalus antiquus*). They also show cattle, sheep, and donkeys. Human figures are shown, some carrying wild animal heads. Dated from 6,000 years ago, this tradition ended at different times in different regions of the Sahara, probably between 4,500 and 3,000 years ago. These engravings were contemporaneous with paintings formerly attributed to the Round Head Phase. Characterized by human figures of varying sizes and colors, these paintings normally show black and white faces and a range of wild animals (as found in the polished engravings, although without the extinct buffalo).

Within the Sahara has also been identified another painting, and to a lesser extent, engraving tradition depicting cattle, sheep, and goats accompanied by herdsmen, scenes of hunting, conflict, camping, traveling, dancing, and milking of cows. Material culture items such as pots, bows, throwing sticks, shields, and spears are shown as well. Formerly ascribed to the Bovidean Phase, they date from 6,000 to 3,500 years ago and are widespread and contemporaneous with the other traditions described above. This artistic tradition shows the life of herders and the process of domestication of cattle, sheep, goats, donkeys, and dogs in what is now the Sahara.

The later paintings and engravings dating from approximately 2,700 years ago are mainly schematic representations of horses and sometimes oxen, pulling two- or four-wheeled vehicles, chariots, or carts. Human figures are shown mounted on horses. The art, which is spread in some kind of linear tracks across the Sahara, is indicative of contacts between the Mediterranean and the southerly sections of the desert. Previous categorized as the Horse Phase, the art also depicts the Libyco-Berber script, mounted armed men, domestic cattle, and wild animals. Depictions of the camel reflect events of the last 2,000 years when the animal was introduced in increasingly arid regions. Also shown are schematic representations of humans, wild animals, cattle, and goats. Tifinagh or Arabic script that appears in some areas reflect post-seventh century CE developments.

Food Production.   Africa has its own centers of domestication, and these include the Horn and adjoining southern fringes of the Sahara. Botanical studies of the present distribution of wild species are indicative of the origins of modern domesticates. About 18,000 to 12,000 years ago in the eastern Sahara and the Nile Valley, experimentation and intensified exploitation of native plants resulted in their adoption as domesticates. Wild sorghum occurs in a broad band between the Nile Valley and Lake Chad. Finger millet (*Eluesine*) was probably domesticated in the Ethiopian Highlands, along with ensete, teff, and noug. Sorghum, lentil, coffee, wheat, and barley were brought from elsewhere. Bulrush millet (*Pennisetum*) was domesticated on the savanna, south of the Sahara from Senegal across to the Sudan, and African rice (*Oryza glaberrima*) in the Interior Niger Delta, as well as the Benue Valley. Yam (*Dioscorea*) cultivation began in the forest fringes of western Africa, and oil palm was domesticated elsewhere in that region. Cowpeas (*Vigna unguiculata*) are also grown in western Africa. Though Africa has many different wild animals, few animals were domesticated. Animals kept by African pastoralists and agriculturists, such as sheep and goats, derive from western Asia, but wild forms of cattle (*bos promigenius*) are known from southern Libya. The domesticated species of cattle seem to derive from the Near East. However, western Africa is the probable home of the modern dwarf short-horned breed of cattle.

Whatever their origins, the domestication of animals and cultivation of crops in Africa is well attested by the presence of domestic animal bones,

including cattle, sheep or goats, pigs, and sometimes donkey, and of grinding stones, pottery, and permanent settlements. In Africa, the process of socioeconomic structuring, comparable to the Neolithic era, began in the Sahara regions during the wet periods of the Early Holocene (8,000–5,500 years ago). It is thought that the process spread to other parts of sub-Saharan Africa, encouraged by this climatic episode. During this time, Lake Chad was 5–6 times larger than its present size, the vegetation in the region was largely savanna, and most of the highlands experienced a Mediterranean climate.

Early food producers in the southern Sahara spread eastwards into the Nile Valley where they merged with people still dependent on fishing and hunting, about 9,000–9,600 years ago. Full-time pastoralism and mixed agriculture developed later. For a time, two threads trace through the history of the Sahel—one of flourishing hunter-fishers, and the other establishing fully fledged pastoralists and mixed farmers. This suggests that, although the idea of food production was available, it was not a practicable alternative to the natural harvest of the humid belt south of the Sahara. Rock art in southern Libya and Algeria depicts wild cattle of the long-horned bos promigenius type, whereas cattle of the *bos africanus* type were certainly domesticated. Tichitt in southern Mauritania, dated to around 4,500 years ago, has considerable remains of settled village life. By 3,000 years ago, these villages housed agriculturists. In the Sudanese Nile Valley, animal domestication and crop production is dated from the first half of the fifth millennium CE, with sites such as Kadero showing evidence of sheep or goats, cattle, and sorghum. In Nubia, similar sites date from 4,000 years ago. From about 4,300 to 2,900 years ago, cattle become more important in a number of sites. Developments within these sites led to the rise of the Kush civilization that conquered and ruled Egypt a century later, setting up the kingdom of Meroë.

In the Egyptian desert, Napta Playa and Bir Kiseba show grinding equipment, wild millet and sorghum, and permanent villages dating from 7,900 to 10,000 years ago. In Egypt, some food production sites date back to the seventh millennium BCE. Three predynastic cultural traditions characterize the Egyptian section of the Nile—Badarian, Amratian, and Gerzean. These saw the development of sizeable towns representing small states, with some of them having a population of around 5,000 people. They exhibited a high level of artistry in flint working, pottery production, copper smelting and casting. One of these early states established rule in the area north of Aswan and set up the first Egyptian dynasty.

The Malian Sahara housed early fishing settlements on ancient lakeshores 6,400–9,500 years ago, comparable to those found to the east. The effort to harvest this bounty found in these ancient lakes (fish and aquatic mammals and crocodiles) was, presumably, less than required to engage in farming or the tending of stock. As a result, the introduction of food production was delayed until the advent of arid conditions after 6,500 years ago. Hunting and fishing continued, supplemented with pastoralism. In western Africa, cereal cultivation arrived at Karkarichinkat Sud in the Tilemsi Valley in Mali, and Seyyid Ouinquil (Dar Tichitt) in Mauritania, sometime between 3,000 and 2,500 years ago.

In eastern Africa, animal domestication and crop cultivation first appeared around Lake Victoria, in areas east of Lake Turkana and the Rift Valley, on the Serengeti Plains, and in central parts of Kenya around 5,000 years ago. This was in response to the drying up of the Sahara causing pastoralists to move south. The pastoralist Kansyore (Oltome), Olmalenge, Narosura (Oldishi), and Elmentaitan traditions had cattle, made pottery, ground stone axes, and flaked microlithic stone tools. The makers of the Oldishi tradition constructed large settlements that they occupied periodically. Sites such as Ele Bor show evidence of sheep or goats and camel, as well as grindstones and wild cereal seeds, suggesting continued exploitation of wild plants. Later developments around this and other places in the region point toward an increased use of pottery and a more settled lifestyle of farming communities. Whether these were new arrivals replacing preexisting pastoralist-foragers or part of the same continuously changing socioeconomic way of life remains a subject of debate.

In Southern Africa at this time, prior to the introduction of domestic stock and plants from elsewhere, there is a pattern of intensified hunting and gathering, elaboration of ritual activity, and exchange by resident hunter-foragers. The causes of this are unknown, as is the question of the origin and impact of introducing cattle-keeping into Southern Africa. There are difficulties in correlating Khoe-speakers and various Khoekhoen groups with the spread of prehistoric livestock and pottery. The western half of the region, ethnographically and historically populated by Khoekhoen, has livestock bones in hunter-gatherer contexts, along with pottery. The archaeological record seemingly suggests complex interaction and shifting identities between resident hunter-gatherers and newly fledged or arrived pastoralists and hunter-herders. Such shifting identities and attempts to relate the archaeological past to an ethnographic present are difficult to discern in the archaeological record. Domestic animals in Southern Africa appear slightly more than 2,000 years ago, with the Cape region of South Africa and parts of Namibia showing the presence of cattle and sheep or goats in apparently hunter-gatherer contexts.

The domestication of animals and the growing of crops were an adaptive exercise involving effective husbanding of animals, once hunted in the wild, and cultivation of plants, once harvested from natural stands. The implication is that early pastoralists or farmers already understood the properties of animals and plants they undertook to domesticate. The question has always been: why undertake a task requiring increased effort and a time investment to reach an end already achievable through time-tested methods. It is suggested that the period of increased aridity in northern Africa made the effort worthwhile, and having accomplished the socioeconomic and population changes associated with this way of life, their ability to return to full-time foraging was limited. This process resulted in the creation of altered social formations, technologies, and ecological niches.

The investment in permanent settlements changed the forager life considerably, forcing on them the need to find new ways of social management and the need to earn new technologies related to the keeping of stock and the cultivation of plants in drought environments. Fluctuations in seasonal patterns, such as droughts and dry periods, enforced social answers to increasingly intensified labor intensive production, distribution of produce, and the enfranchisement of authority, ensuring greater economic and social security. This was a marked departure from the usual forager annual cycle of activities. What evolved was a system that took advantage of the altered set of economic opportunities and constraints. These developments engendered an increased population in the Sahel region, leading to the expansion of farming communities there and elsewhere.

The emergence of iron-using, pottery-making, agro-pastoral societies in East and Southern Africa just prior to and around the beginning of the first millennium CE unites these regions to with the complex developments in the Sahel and savanna regions associated with the growing of crops and domestication of animals. The expansion and spread of agro-pastoral societies is identified by archaeological sites with pottery that is well-fired and has a thickened lip, thick bodied forms, a slightly concave neck, and decoration motifs on the rim-neck-shoulder-body region that are either channeled (grooved) or comb-stamped. A few places exhibit metalworking, livestock keeping, and pole-and-daub structures of permanent settlement. This pottery has been recovered from around Lake Victoria in Uganda, in Rwanda, Burundi, Tanzania, much of southern and coastal Kenya, the southern part of Democratic Republic of the Congo (DRC), parts of Angola, Zambia, Malawi, Mozambique, and much of the northern highveld of South Africa, Swaziland, and the eastern coastal zones of the province of KwaZulu-Natal.

The association of specific archaeologically known groups with the complex dynamics of language is a thorny issue. However, there was some form of movement from one part of the continent to the other. Bantu speakers who populate most of sub-Saharan Africa are widely assumed, for example, to have expanded from the northern part of the equatorial forests as part of the southward movement of agro-pastoralists. This may have taken the form of slash-and-burn whereby, after three to five years, communities would leave a piece of land due to marginal fertility of the soils and move on to another. Here they would clear and burn the vegetation to get nutrient-filled ash. This practice dictated repetitive movement; with the consequent result that population was always small, as were their production yields. In this way, large areas of Southern and East Africa were rapidly occupied. In some cases, this process generated large population concentrations. Modest farmer settlements grew into towns, a scenario already witnessed in the Nile Valley some 3,000 years earlier.

Urbanism and Social Complexity. Apart from triggering a process of domesticating of some wild animals and crop varieties, the initiation of food production also led toward new social formations associated with ranked societies, usually referred to as chiefdoms and states, and enhanced networks of interaction and trade. These processes initially took place in areas bordering the Sahara, including the Nile Valley, the Horn, the Sahelian-Sudanic belt, and in the Inland Niger Delta and the forested regions immediately to the south. Egypt is the oldest and historically most well-documented example of emerging complexity in Africa, going back more than 5,000 years. The bases of this civilization date to 6,500–5,000 years ago and lie in Egyptian agricultural societies that emerged as a growing response to increased aridity in the adjacent Sahara, founding a most successful civilization in Africa.

The Nile River was the key to the success of this civilization, as it provided water for irrigation-rich silt that fertilized the crops and the grazing that saw cattle, sheep, and goats being raised. Wheat, barley, and sorghum were grown, such that the Nile valley was able to produce enough food to feed a growing population. The Nile also became a channel of communication between farmers and other groups living along the river. Soon, trading contacts were established with Nubia, Ethiopia, Palestine, and Syria.

The Egyptian state emerged from among competing polities. A sacred leadership emerged around the pharaoh, the head of the state. Pharaohs centralized state authority, were able to mobilize considerable labor resources, and accumulate wealth. Some of this wealth is reflected in monumental architecture such as the pyramids, temples, causeways, sphinxes, and palaces. Some pharaohs had rich possessions. Most of the pharaohs' history is well documented. They were supported by a large public service that was well trained and able to communicate its tasks and decisions. This was facilitated by the use of written scripts such as hieroglyphics, hieratic, and demotic. Although the Egyptian state went through periods of decline referred to in written sources as Intermediate Periods (2200–2040, 1785–1552, and c. 1069–656 BCE), its essential character remained the same for many centuries. Its imperial ventures beyond its traditional frontiers brought it to the realm of the Greeks and the Romans. The spread of Christianity and Islam toward the eastern Mediterranean brought about additional changes to Egyptian society.

The emergence of stratified societies in northeastern Africa from the fourth to the second millennium BCE resulted in several kingdoms in the Middle Nile Valley and the Horn. Kerma was the earliest state in the Middle Nile Valley—in Upper Nubia, which arose following the collapse of the Egyptian state and its withdrawal from adjacent Lower Nubia between 2200 and 2040 BCE. Kerma acted as an intermediary between regions to the south and the Lower Nile Valley. The revival of the Egyptian state during Middle Kingdom times (2040–1785 BCE) saw the state's return to Lower Nubia to face the growing threat of Kerma, with whom the Egyptians traded extensively. Kerma reached its peak during the period 1785–1552 BCE, when it traded with the Hyksos who had conquered the Egyptians. The final demise of Kerma came with the revival of Egypt during New Kingdom times (1552–1069 BCE).

Another decline of the Egyptian state (c. 1069–656 BCE) saw the rise of a polity at Napata in Upper Nubia. Known as Kush, this kingdom ruled Egypt from 747 to 646 BCE. In the Horn, the kingdoms of Daamat during the mid-first millennium BCE and Aksum in the first millennium CE were responses to commercial opportunities. This regional network involved Nubia with Egypt from the mid-fourth millennium BCE, with economic expansion into regions to its south during the first millennium BCE, and with Roman trade through the Red Sea to the Indian Ocean in the early first millennium CE.

AFRICA BY THE SEVENTH CENTURY CE

Developments in the Eastern Roman Empire from the fourth century CE saw Egypt weakened politically, divided internally, and under Byzantine control. When the Arabs invaded in 630 CE, Egypt offered little resistance. The Arabs extended their conquest to the rest of northern Africa, reaching Tunis by 647 CE. Their advancing frontier was later extended to Morocco and across the Mediterranean to Spain. This conquest saw the introduction of a new religion, culture, politics, architecture, science, and literature. New networks of trade came into effect, linking western Africa with the Mediterranean world, and Islam spread rapidly to western Africa.

In the Sudanese Nile Valley, the production of iron at Meroë enhanced trading contacts with the Red Sea and Ethiopia. Connections with Egypt are seen in Meroë's monumental architecture. Iron production took place on a large scale during the last centuries BCE and the fist millennium CE. Meroë was destroyed by the rising civilization in the Horn of Africa, based at Axum, in 350 CE. Axum became the capital of an extensive state, subsuming southern Arabian and indigenous Ethiopian cultural elements. It traded with the Roman Empire, had a unique form of writing, and constructed monumental stelae and other colossal architecture. The conquest of Meroë ensured effective control of the Red Sea trade as well as the Sudanese Nile Valley—a source of ivory. Axumite kings controlled parts of southern Arabia in the sixth century CE until the seventh century when Arabs gained captured the Red Sea ports.

In East and Southern Africa, iron-using farmers consolidated agricultural production, and increasingly opened direct trading links via the Indian Ocean, the Red Sea, and the Persian Gulf. Enhanced agricultural and iron production from the sixth or seventh century CE ushered in an urban tradition, blending foreign and local architectural styles and other elements. The Toutswe state in the eastern Kalahari sandveld is an example of a complex society that consolidated wealth in cattle, agriculture, and regional networks of trade. Western Africa also experienced similar developments, with an urban tradition much earlier than that of East and Southern Africa. Regional networks of exchange brought in raw materials such as iron and copper. Jenné-jeno, Daima, and other centers laid the foundations of later complex societies mainly in the savanna and Sahel regions. By the seventh century CE, it appears the state of ancient Ghana was founded and had profound effects on the subsequent histories of the region.

See also **Agriculture; Archaeology and Prehistory; Bantu, Eastern, Southern, and Western, History of (1000**

BCE to 1500 CE); Ceramics; Early Human Society, History of (c. 50,000 BP to 19,000 BCE); Ecosystems; Egypt, Early; Human Evolution; Jenné and Jenné-jeno; Metals and Minerals; Nile River; Prehistory; Production Strategies; Technological Specialization Period, History of (c. 19,000 to 5000 BCE).

BIBLIOGRAPHY

Connah, Graham. *Forgotten Africa: An Introduction to its Archaeology.* London: Routledge, 2004.

Davidson, Basil. *The Search for Africa: History, Culture, Politics.* New York: Times Books, 1994.

Ehret, Christopher. *The Civilizations of Africa: A History to 1800.* Charlottesville: University Press of Virginia, 2002.

Fage, John D., ed. *The Cambridge History of Africa*, Vol. 2. *From c. 500 BC to AD 1050.* London: Cambridge University Press, 1978.

Fage, John Donnelly, ed. *The Cambridge History of Africa*, Vol. 1. *From the Earliest Times to 500 BC.* London: Cambridge University Press, 1982.

Martin, Phyllis M. and Patrick O'Meara, eds. *Africa*, 2nd edition. Bloomington: Indiana University Press, 1986.

Mayer, Ruth. *Artificial Africas: Colonial Images in the Times of Globalization.* Hanover, NH: University Press of New England, 2002.

McIntosh, Susan Keech, ed. *Beyond Chiefdoms: Pathways to Complexity in Africa.* Cambridge, U.K.: Cambridge University Press, 1999.

Phillipson, David W., *African Archaeology*, 3rd edition. Cambridge, U.K.: Cambridge University Press, 2005.

Shaw, Thurstan, et al., eds. *The Archaeology of Africa: Food, Metals, and Towns.* London: Routledge, 1993.

Stahl, Ann Brower, ed. *African Archaeology: A Critical Introduction.* Malden, MA: Blackwell, 2005.

Vogel, Joseph O., ed. *Encyclopedia of Precolonial Africa: Archaeology, History Languages, Cultures, and Environments.* Walnut Creek, CA: Altamira Press, 1997.

INNOCENT PIKIRAYI

SEVENTH TO SIXTEENTH CENTURY

Strictly speaking no single periodization can be valid for every single region within a continent as vast and as diverse as Africa. Yet the introduction of Islam in the seventh century is used to signal a new era because of its long-term influence on much of the continent. The arrival of Europeans on the West African coast in the later fifteenth century and the conquest of most of North Africa by the Ottomans in the sixteenth century are considered turning points for the same reasons. More important than these, however, are the shared influences and particular processes marking the emergence and consolidation of major sociocultural regional traditions that have existed on the continent ever since. In most places these traditions emerged between the seventh and twelfth centuries and blossomed during the following ones. This emergence was not caused by either of the three major new external influences noted above or the development of a thriving intercontinental trade based on gold during this same period. Rather, the links lie in the other direction: Islam made headway and the trade flourished only because, and in so far as, larger regional traditions were already emerging.

NORTHERN AFRICA

In December 639 a small Arab force entered Egypt and introduced Islam. Seventy years later and with the active participation of a sizeable fraction of the local populations recruited as clients (*mawali*), all of northern Africa, except for the Nile valley south of Egypt, had been won for the Umayyad caliphate. The parochial fragmentation of Berber societies first facilitated this conquest and then expressed itself by embracing a range of different doctrinal varieties of Islam (Sunni, Khariji-Sufri, Khariji 'Ibadi and later Shi'a). Scattered Christian communities survived until about 1200 and a new monotheistic revealed religion (*barghawata*) arose in the far west of Morocco. In Egypt and Tunisia the older regional cultures reasserted themselves as larger political entities only imperfectly controlled by the caliphs. But new centralizing movements sustained by reformist religious goals appeared during the tenth and twelfth centuries and struggled to overcome such regionalisms.

In a bid for the mastery of the whole Muslim world, the Fatimid caliphs, standard-bearers of the Shi'a doctrine established first a base in Tunisia and then conquered Egypt (969), mostly with Berber troops. But by 1050 they had lost Tunisia and by 1100 most Egyptians had returned to the Sunni dispensation (the caliphate did not collapse until 1771). Meanwhile around 1050 Berber Almoravids found a following in the far western Sahara and raised the banner of Sunni doctrine and its Maliki school of law in the Maghri. Although their caliphate in Morocco and Spain lasted but a century, it permanently secured the supremacy of Sunnism and of Maliki law both in the Maghrib and in West Africa.

Despite all these particularisms, the early Muslim conquests created a single vast economic world in which trade flowed unfettered fueling rapid development and creating much wealth, at least among the urban elites. Because they had access to gold from West Africa and soon struck gold currencies, North African rulers benefited especially from this. Among other commodities gold provided the financial backbone for the rapid growth of trans-Saharan trade after about 750, but especially from Fatimid and Almoravid times onward as the yellow metal became a vital weapon in the struggle for supremacy between the North African caliphates and sustained North Africa's advantage in its trade relations with Europe until about 1200 when, in the Maghrib at least, that advantage shifted to the European shores as a result of Europe's richer resources and environments which weighed more and more in the balance as its internal economic structures became more efficient. Meanwhile the population of the Maghrib declined, partly by emigration and partly by food shortages, and its economy weakened. The devastation wrought by the turbulent immigration of Arab nomads who had been cast forth from Egypt around 1050 and slowly overran and Arabized the Maghrib and much of the western Sahara may be partly responsible, for Egypt itself remained prosperous and Cairo remained the foremost hub of long-distance trade until almost 1500. But clearly climatic deterioration did play a role as well.

By 1200 centrifugal forces once again gained the upper hand in North Africa, and new or old social groups of all sorts again began to expressed their identity in religious terms, albeit it within the common Sunni fold. Various Sufi (mystical) brotherhoods, appeared often allied to a cult for deceased holy men. They legitimized collective identities based on common genealogy, local devotion, or/and associations of various kinds. The influence of various competing strata in the "civil society," such as urban 'ulama lawyers, administrators, traders and guilds as well as, regional aggregations, or nomadic coalitions (saff) soon weakened central government to the extent that at times the public realm almost vanished. Only Egypt retained a strong centralized government based on military rule by Mamluk officers, although even

these military had to curry favor with the intellectual elite, the corporations of traders, various organized groups in the countryside and even local Cairene guilds.

The initial Muslim conquest failed to overcome the Christian kingdoms along the Nile. But from Fatimid times (969–1171) onward Arab nomads continually infiltrated from Egypt into the deserts of the Sudan and ultimately led to the Arabization of the Nile valley and the adoption of Islam. By 1317 the ruler of the northern kingdom of Makuria in Nubia was a Muslim. Nevertheless Christianity survived in isolated pockets in Nubia and beyond until about 1500. Meanwhile in Ethiopia Christian Axum abruptly collapsed during the seventh century, and little is known about its successors until around 1270 including a shadowy non-Christian polity called Damut. Nevertheless monasteries continued to spread Christianity southwards over most of the highlands while Muslim traders were creating a new mercantile networks at the same time in the eastern and southern lowlands where small sultanates appeared. The main Christian Ethiopian kingdom revived after 1270. From 1315 onward its rulers succeeded in raising such an efficient army that they obtained supremacy over all the surrounding polities. They then structured the realm as a confederation of kingdoms, put it on a new feudal and militaristic footing, and maintained their hegemony over the Ethiopian highlands until the waning of the next century.

WESTERN AFRICA

By the middle of the first millennium CE the farming populations in the western part of western Africa were rapidly increasing, assisted by favorable climatic conditions, especially in the vast inner Niger-Delta, where cities such as Jenné-jeno and Ja appeared as early as 400 CE. These lands were becoming a demographic hub that affected a large part of West Africa. Economic production increased, spurred on by the specialization of whole communities into farmers, fishermen, herders, hunters, metallurgists, potters, weavers (after about 1000 CE), and traders. A trading network supported by its accompanying institutions (lodgings, marketing, transport, and probably currencies) crossed and linked the lateral ecological zones that stretched from ocean to desert. The basic commodities traded were foodstuffs, salt, iron, and textiles, while the demand for luxury goods and exotic items such as copper alloy, kola nuts, mala-guetta (African pepper), and gold was increasing in the towns and political capitals. Gold had been exported as far as Tunisia from perhaps as early as the third century CE. Major social innovations and spatial reorganizations accompanied the economic developments. Two major kingdoms, Ghana and Kanem (Kanembu), had already appeared in the Sahel before 700 CE, but their internal organization remains unclear. It is not even known whether they were centralized enough to be called states or whether they were merely a confederation of smaller territorial groups that accepted the theoretical supremacy of a single leader among them. Historians do know that elsewhere, decentralized forms of government did flourish. Thus the dense population of the Inner Niger Delta was not central-ized; each city was probably ruled by a "power asso-ciation" backed by religious legitimacy or because clear-cut occupational distinctions were well on the way to solidifying as sub-ethnicities or "castes" by an emerging set of professional associations with inter-secting memberships.

Hence the region was flourishing around 750 when the first Khariji Berber merchants arrived in search of gold. Since the necessary infrastructure was already in place the trans-Saharan trade soon blossomed and began to quicken ongoing proc-esses of economic and social change. Trading net-works reached farther and farther, while towns or other commercial hubs were founded in new areas. Thus, by the ninth century Igbo Ukwu, a non-urban hub was linked to a mining industry along the Benue river, to northern Africa, perhaps by way of Gao and to the nearby coast of the Gulf of Bénin. By 1100 all the major regions of western Africa seem to have been linked by trading routes, and new cities were appearing just north of the Akan goldfields (Nyarko and Begho), near Accra (Ladoku), in Yorubaland and Bénin in present-day Nigeria, in the lower Shari region, and in Hausa land. These trading centers were also political cap-itals whose cultures strongly influenced their hin-terlands. In this way these dynamics fostered the spread and dominance of less than a dozen major regional sociocultural traditions over nearly all of western Africa.

The eleventh and twelfth centuries saw dramatic climatic deterioration as the favorable wet climate (700–1100) became much drier (1100–1500) and triggered major population and political shifts. About 1000 Fulani (Fulbe) herders squeezed between the encroaching desert and the tsetse belt in the south, began to migrate eastward from Senegal to the inner Niger Delta and eventually to Bornu. The drier climate led to a considerable population decline in the inner Niger Delta, large groups of Tuareg immigrated southwards of the Niger bend and all the major political centers shifted southwards: Mali as the successor to old Ghana; the Mossi kingdoms as successors to ear-lier polities in today's northeastern most Burkina Faso and nearby Niger; and Bornu as successor to Kanem.

As North African traders settled in the mercantile cities along the river Niger they brought Islam with them and gradually convinced other inhabitants there to adopt their religion. Then just before 1100 and the climatic deterioration, the rulers of the Sahelian king-doms as well as of Mali adopted Sunnism and the Maliki school of law. Thus Islam could spread farther south, and the trading routes opened up to Muslim merchants and itinerant cleric-healers alike particu-larly during the apogee of the Mali Empire (1250–1450) when much of westernmost Africa came under its political cultural, and linguistic sway.

EASTERN, SOUTHERN, AND CENTRAL AFRICA

Well before 750, agriculture accompanied by much gathering and some herding had become the main source of food production over nearly all of east-ern, southern, and central Africa. Substantial pop-ulation growth followed between 750 and 1100, accompanied by the emergence of a dozen or so distinct regional clusters of similar cultures. At the same time the social and political complexity of most of the component societies of these clusters and their polities grew. Although a few large king-doms and some city-states (Swahili coast) appeared many other forms of governance emerged as well. Some of these were based on age groups (Kenyan pastoralists, southern Ethiopians) others on egali-tarian councils of household leaders (southeast Africa), or on deep lineages (Somali, some groups in the rain forests), or on coalitions of houses (rain forests) and on a variety of associations. The internal institutions of the kingdoms were just as variable. In some of these (e.g., Luba) ritual associations played a major role; in others complementary communities based on specialized occupations arose (Ethiopia, Great Lakes area, some groups in the rain forests); and wherever cattle were a valued resource, social classes arose and patron-client links became crucial.

During the same period long distance trading links for the distribution of rare or coveted resources were established all over the savannas and along the main Congo river at least as far upstream as the lower Ubangi river. Intercontinental trade inland from the Indian ocean began to flourish after the spread of Islam to the Middle and Near East and reached its full maturity during the eleventh century. Gold (from Zimbabwe), slaves, ivory, some luxury goods and basic commodities such as timber and iron were exchanged for textiles, beads, and preciosities, including many fine ceramics.

By 900, or perhaps even earlier, the goldfields in southern Zimbabwe became the fulcrum for the whole system. They were joined to emporia on the coast north of the Limpopo River and those were linked by sea to the main harbors along coasts northwards from Kilwa. Trade inland from the coast, probably on a small scale, reached as far as Lake Baringo and the shores of Lakes Tanganyika and Malawi (Nyasa) before 1000. Indeed a few cowries and beads have been found as far inland as the valley of the Lualaba in Katanga and the outskirts of Durban. By 1200 the coastal network began to mesh with another large commercial network in the interior that was structured around the trade in copper ingots and ran from the Lualaba river in Katanga to Great Zimbabwe and beyond. Indeed by then trading routes covered all of Africa south of the rainforests and south of central Tanzania.

The Indian Ocean trade also brought innovations such as a suite of new crops: sugarcane, taro, cotton and eggplants—that eventually spread all over eastern and central Africa. Plantains and bananas were either the earliest among these or had already been introduced before 750. They revolutionized agriculture in the wet forested regions and on humid mountain slopes and soon became the major staple there. Plantains provided farmers in Equatorial Africa with considerable food surpluses, allowed them to settle anywhere in the region, and provided the means to develop a fully symbiotic relationship with local foragers. Eventually bananas became a staple crop in East African highlands such as in the Kilimanjaro region and in Buganda where their cultivation in groves led to increased population densities.

Islam was adopted only in the Swahili regional cluster. The first humble mosques for the use of a few Muslim traders appeared in coastal settlements there between 780 and 800. As larger towns with some stone buildings (a technique imported from the Red Sea region) grew during the tenth century and as city states were founded by Muslims (to judge by the names of their rulers) during the next century, Islam spread and was adopted by most of the urban population. Thus by the end of the eleventh century the main features of a complex Swahili urban way of life had been well established. Apart from the Swahili cities the Indian Ocean, trade played a major role only in the kingdom of Mapungubwe and its successor Zimbabwe. Preciosities monopolized by the rulers of Mapungubwe probably raised their prestige and facilitated to a certain extent the concentration of power in their hands. Later Muslim traders operated in Zimbabwe itself but neither Islam nor any significant feature of the Swahili way of life found favor there.

See also **Agriculture; Christianity; Egypt, Early; Egypt, Modern; Islam; Jenné and Jenné-jeno; Zimbabwe; Zimbabwe, Great.**

BIBLIOGRAPHY

Brooks, George E. *Landlords and Strangers: Ecology, Society, and Trade in Western Africa 1000–1630.* Boulder, CO: Westview Press, 1993.

Devisse, Jean; J. Polet; and S. Sidibe; eds. *Vallees du Niger.* Paris: Editions de la Réunion des musées nationaux, 1993.

El Fasi, Mohammad, and I. Hrebk, eds. *UNESCO General History of Africa*, Vol. 3: *Africa from the Seventh to the Eleventh Century.* London: Heinemann, 1988.

Fage, John, ed. *The Cambridge History of Africa*, Vol. 2: *From c. 500 BC to A.D. 1050.* Cambridge, U.K.: Cambridge University Press, 1978.

Horton, Mark, and John Middleton. *The Swahili: The Social Landscape of a Mercantile Society*. Malden, MA: Blackwell, 2000.

Keech, McIntosh Susan. *Beyond Chiefdoms: Pathways to Complexity in Africa*. Cambridge, U.K.: Cambridge University Press, 1999.

Moraes, Farias de. *Arabic Medieval Inscriptions from the Republic of Mali: Epigraphy, Chronicles, and Songhay-Tuareg History*. New York: Oxford University Press, 2003.

MacEachern, Scott. "Two Thousand Years of West African History." In *African Archaeology: A Critical Introduction*, ed. Ann Bower Stahl. Malden, MA: Blackwell, 2005.

Mar, Leslie, and Tim Maggs, eds. *African Naissance:The Limpopo Valley 1000 Years Ago*. Cape Town: South African Archaeological Society, 2000.

McIntosh, Roderick J. *The Peoples of the Middle Niger*. Malden, MA: Blackwell, 1998.

Niane, Djibril Tamsir, ed. *UNESCO General History of Africa*, Vol. 4: *Africa from the Twelfth to the Sixteenth Century*. London: Heinemann, 1981.

Oliver, Roland, ed. *The Cambridge History of Africa*, Vol. 3: *From c. 1050 to c. 1600*. Cambridge, U.K.: Cambridge University Press, 1987.

Phillipson, David, W. "The Axumite Roots of Medieval Ethiopia." *Azania* 39 (2004): 77–89.

JAN VANSINA

SIXTEENTH TO NINETEENTH CENTURY

Between 1500 and 1800 the most important factor shaping events within Africa was the demand for African slaves in the Americas. Parts of eastern and southern Africa were also influenced by the growth of European empires in Asia. In spite of this, much of Africa was touched only marginally and continued to evolve according to its own internal rhythms. The period in question saw in much of Africa an increase in violence, rising exports of human beings, and efforts of threatened societies to protect themselves. It also saw increases in state formation, the extension of trade routes, and the development of markets for the exchange of local products.

Europe knew relatively little of Africa before the arrival of Portuguese navigators in the fifteenth century, but Africa was not isolated. North Africa was part of a Mediterranean world linked to Christian Europea by both trade and conflict. The East African coast had been involved in commerce on the Indian Ocean for at least 1,500 years. Many societies of Northeast Africa were long linked to civilizations in Egypt, the Mediterranean, and the Arabian Peninsula. Further west, along the sand sea of the Sahara, the empires of western and Central Sudan had commercial, intellectual, and religious links with North Africa, and via North Africa provided gold and leather goods for Europea.

ATLANTIC SLAVE TRADE

The Portuguese, who moved down the African coast in the 1440s, were more interested in gold than in slaves. They did, however, seize Africans to show their king and often found that raiding coastal villages for slaves helped them pay the costs of an expedition. Slaves were sought for large estates in southern Portugal, for plantations on Atlantic islands like Madeira and São Tomé, and in the Mediterranean trade. Most Mediterranean slaves came from Slavic eastern Europe, but when the fall of Constantinople to the Turks in 1453 blocked many of those markets, Africa became the major source. The trade was still relatively small in the fifteenth century, but as European diseases decimated native people in the Americas, sugar planters there replaced them with Africans, who experienced a lower mortality.

The resultant loss of population in Africa has been much debated. The number exported from Africa in the Atlantic trade may have been as high as 12 million, with between 10 and 11 million landing in the Americas. Estimates of the trans-Saharan trade suggest that more than 3 million may have made it across the Sahara in the same period. Evidence is not as good on population loss within Africa from warfare, slave raids, and the movement of slaves. Some estimates of such losses run as high as five times the number shipped out. At least as important as the losses was the effect on African people: the development of military structures capable of enslaving large numbers of people and marketing systems capable of draining slaves from the far interior. These made it possible for African slavers to provide increasingly large numbers of slaves to European traders. At the height of the trade, between 1700 and 1810, more than 6 million were exported. Trading networks also made slaves available for use within Africa, probably more than were exported. Africans kept most of the women and children and exported primarily men.

NORTH AFRICA

North Africa was overwhelmingly Muslim with small Christian and Jewish minorities, and by the sixteenth century had largely become Arabic-speaking. Berber languages and cultures remained important in the western Maghreb. In 1517, the Ottoman Turks defeated the Mamluks of Egypt and then gradually brought most of the rest of North Africa under their control. Only Morocco remained independent of Ottoman control. With time, each of the North African provinces of the Ottoman Empire established their autonomy: Tunisia in the sixteenth century, Algeria in the seventeenth, Tripoli and Egypt in the eighteenth. All continued to recognize Ottoman suzerainty, but the exercise of power was controlled by dynasties based in the Ottoman troops in the Maghreb and the Mamluks in Egypt. In Morocco, the Sa'di Dynasty arose in the early sixteenth century to lead a resistance to Iberian inroads. The Sa'dis and their seventeenth century Alawite successors maintained Moroccan independence and several times were able to send armies across the Sahara.

North Africa was important to areas south of the Sahara as a source both of a new religion and of trade. Islam was carried south by Arab traders. Some lived and established families in Sudanic regions. The first converts were often their trading partners. Muslims from the sub-Saharan societies often studied in northern Africa, particularly at Egypt's Al-Azhar University and in Morocco. Arabic became the language of literacy in large parts of Africa. African Muslims also visited northern Africa on the pilgrimage to Mecca. Arab traders who crossed the Sahara did so largely in a quest for gold, slaves, and ivory. They provided in exchange horses, metal goods, cloth, and books. They also brought with them North African architecture, clothing, the narrow loom used in weaving, and new crops like onions and tomatoes. There was also some reverse influence as African slaves brought with them African music and spirit possession cults, both of which have in some ways been incorporated into Muslim practice.

WESTERN AFRICA

Although the slave trade incorporated western Africa into an Atlantic trading system, there was little European settlement because of the high mortality for Europeans on the coast. The trade was conducted from ships or at coastal trading stations. Europeans dealt with local rulers or with middlemen, such as the Cape Verdeans who settled along the upper Guinea coast. Further east, middlemen were usually indigenous trading peoples. The slave trade had varying effects on its participants. The two largest states the Portuguese confronted in the fifteenth century were Bénin and Kongo. The Kongo kings welcomed the Portuguese, accepted Christianity, and were eager to learn new skills. Royal authority was, however, eroded when Portuguese personnel at the Kongo court traded in slaves and commercial interests in São Tomé encouraged warfare and civil strife. In 1568 Kongo was sacked by *jagas*, mercenaries hired by the Portuguese and seven years later, the Portuguese founded Luanda in 1575. The Kongo state reestablished itself, but by the beginning of the eighteenth century, Kongo was the mere shell of a state and Luanda had become the major base for the Portuguese slave trade in Central Africa. Bénin, by contrast, never allowed Europeans to live in Benin City. It allowed foreigners to trade only at a licensed trading center under royal administration. Bénin sold slaves, but never became a major slave producer. For a long time, the export of males was prohibited. Bénin lost control of more distant tributaries, but remained powerful until 1897.

Others developed more predatory state systems. The late seventeenth century saw a sharp increase in the demand for slaves in the West Indies and the beginning of a large trade in guns. None of the new slaving powers were based on the coast and none had European residents at court. Oyo, a Yoruba cavalry state in what is now Nigeria, became a large exporter in the late seventeenth century. Asante emerged from a struggle for power in the Gold Coast when it bested Denkyera, its major rival, in 1702. It expanded throughout the eighteenth century and came to control an area of three to five million people. The Segu Bambara formed a military state about 1712.

Decentralized societies often resisted the attractions of the slave trade, sometimes with great success, but many found that they had to sell slaves to more effectively defend themselves. If nothing else, they needed to be able to buy weapons or iron to make weapons. The threat of slavers created insecurity over large areas and radically changed the way people lived. Villages were surrounded by walls or stockades and houses were built close together. In hilly areas, people retreated into strong defensive positions sometimes, far from the most fertile fields. People stayed close to home or went to market or to work their fields in groups.

It is more difficult to define with precision the economic effects of the trade. Certainly, the export of gold and hides declined after 1700 as slave exports rose, and slave raiding contributed to insecurity on trade routes. Many writers argue that slave raiding increased vulnerability to the famines of the eighteenth century. The eighteenth century also saw more exploitation of slave labor. Nomadic tribes in Mauritania used slaves to produce gum used to make dyes for the European textile industry. Dyula and Hausa traders used slaves to produce commodities and to serve as porters on their caravans. In the Niger Delta and along the Congo River, male slaves paddled canoes and female slaves worked in the fields.

The slave trade was a giant vortex, sucking in peoples over 600 miles from the coast. During the eighteenth century, the Lunda Empire in the heart of the Congo basin provided three thousand slaves a year. Further north, Bobangi fisherman on the Congo River became slave traders. Canoe men of the Niger Delta, traditionally fishermen and salt producers, bought slaves in the markets and along the creeks and river of southern Nigeria. The Aro, an Igbo sub-group, developed alliances and trade routes that made it possible for them to deliver large numbers of slaves to the Delta traders. Asante demanded slaves from its northern tributaries, who were forced to raid in what is now northern Ghana and Burkina Faso. In Senegambia, the major source of slaves was the Bambara states, more than 600 miles from the coast.

SOUTHERN AND EASTERN AFRICA

Southern and eastern Africa were less affected by demand for slaves, though in the eighteenth century eastern and southeastern Africa provided some slaves for Indian ocean sugar producers. Others were moved to India and the Middle East, but in relatively small numbers. Destruction of an Arab fleet by the Portuguese in 1509 and the seizure of

Sofala, which was the major entrepot for the gold trade from Zimbabwe, ended a prosperous and creative period for the Swahili coast. The Swahili cities collaborated with Omani Arabs in by passing Portuguese efforts to control the trade and then in ousting them from the northern coast. In 1698, Fort Jesus in Mombasa fell to the Arabs. Further south, the Portuguese penetrated the interior only in the Zambezi valley, where they tapped the gold trade from Zimbabwe. Land grants called *prazos* created new feudal title-holders, vassals both of the king of Portugal and the Shona rulers of Zimbabwe.

In 1652 the Dutch created a supply station at the Cape of Good Hope for ships traveling to Asia. They soon found the Khoesan hunters and gatherers unable or unwilling to provide the supplies they wanted and settled a small number of Dutch and German farmers. In the favorable climate of the Cape, this settlement grew rapidly. Frontier farmers staked out very large farms and took over the livestock and many of the cattle-raising methods of the Khoe. The Khoesan, decimated by European diseases or defeated by Dutch arms, either retreated into the interior or accepted a subservient position on settler estates. The Dutch also imported slaves from eastern Africa, Madagascar, and the East Indies, most of whom worked in the urban economy of Capetown and on the commercial grain and wine farms that surrounded it.

In the 1770s the rapidly expanding Dutch frontier found itself confronting a more densely populated Bantu frontier. In 1779 the first of a series of eight wars broke out with the Xhosa. These wars ended with the incorporation of the Xhosa into a European colony. Further east, changes were stirring among other Nguni-speakers. In the early eighteenth century, the Nguni were organized in small states, which mixed cattle-herding and agriculture and were marked by limited social differentiation. Gradually some chiefs imposed themselves on others, using new military techniques. The process culminated with the emergence of a powerful Zulu state under Shaka after 1818. The Zulu replaced their spears with short stabbing knives and were organized in regiments that lived, worked, and drilled together.

The Indian Ocean trade had a limited effect on the peoples of the interior. The Dutch settlement was small. In eastern Africa, the hinterland of the Swahili was very poor. The Swahili were more interested in coastal commerce than in long distance caravan routes. Except in the Zambezi valley, they depended on "relay" trade, which brought trade goods from the interior in short stages. Increasingly, however, the relay traders covered longer distances. In the seventeenth and eighteenth centuries, Yao from Lake Malawi and Nyamwezi from West Central Tanzania began carrying ivory to the coast. Both also searched out new sources of ivory. Traditions of Buganda state that Chinese porcelain first arrived on the shores of Lake Victoria in the late eighteenth century. This marks the beginning of direct trade between the coast and southern Uganda. In 1735 the French started buying slaves at Kilwa in present-day Tanzania and the Yao ivory caravans began increasingly meeting that demand.

NORTHEAST AFRICA

During the sixteenth century the Ottomans extended their control over northern Africa and the coast of northeastern Africa. Arab infiltration into the Nilotic Sudan continued as did the Arabization of existing inhabitants. 'Alwa, the last of the Christian kingdoms of Nubia, fell to the Arabs early in the sixteenth century. Arab expansion was stopped by the rise of the Funj Sultanate of Sinnar. Originally cattle nomads who had moved up from the south, the Funj profited from their position at the junction of east-west and north-south trade routes. As in the medieval empires of West Africa, the Funj became Muslim though Islam co-existed with many of the pre-Islamic institutions of divine kingship.

Highland Ethiopia remained the last bastion of Christianity in northeastern Africa. Stable in the early sixteenth century, Ethiopia collected tribute from smaller Muslim states. During the 1530s, Ahmad al-Ghazi, known as Ahmad Grañ (the Left-Handed), united the Muslims and overan the highlands. Aided by the timely intervention of Portuguese musketeers, the Ethiopians defeated and killed Ahmad Grañ in 1543. Nevertheless, isolated by Muslim control of the coast, Ethiopia never completely regained the prosperity of the fourteenth and fifteenth centuries. The monarchy continued to exist, but by the late eighteenth century, it had little control over the church or the more powerful nobles. During the sixteenth and seventeenth centuries, many of the Muslim states in what is now southern Ethiopia were overrun by cattle-herding Oromo. The Oromo also took over Ethiopian areas, but because they sought land rather than the overthrow of the Ethiopian monarchy, they proved less of a threat than the Muslims.

ISLAM AND THE DESERTSIDE

One of the effects of the long distance slave trade in West Africa is that trade increasingly moved toward the coast rather than the desert. The Saharan trade remained important, but the era of the Sudanic empires came to an end. The Songhay Empire, founded in the mid-fifteenth century, remained strong through most of the sixteenth, but in 1591 the army of the Askia of Songhay was defeated by Moroccan musketeers. The Moroccans were not able to establish a new hegemony and the Western Sudan remained deeply divided until conquered by the French at the end of the nineteenth century. Timbuktu, the most important center of religious learning in the region, fell under the domination of Tuareg nomads in the eighteenth century, but it remained the terminus of important transsaharan trade routes.

Further east in Borno, the introduction of muskets by Mai (king) Idris Aloma at the end of the sixteenth century led to a brief period of expansion, but by the end of the seventeenth century, Borno too was in decline. By contrast, the Hausa states grew. Islam had been important among the Hausa since the fourteenth century, but in the late fifteenth century, a group of Muslim rulers used Islamic and Arab models to form more bureaucratic and centralized states. The best known of these rulers, Mohammed Rumfa of Kano, enforced Qur'anic law, introduced royal seclusion, and built a new palace and market. These reforms provided a framework for economic growth. Kano became a major industrial center, important in textile and leather production.

A number of Islamic sultanates were created between the Nile and Lake Chad. The most important were Darfur and Wadai, formed in the early seventeenth century. In these states, trade introduced Islam, which brought with it political models and a law code conducive to trade and to the formation of more centralized states. Darfur became in the eighteenth century a source of slaves for Ottoman markets. The late seventeenth and eighteenth centuries also saw the growth of commercial cities in West Africa. Many were twinned cities, a Muslim city dominated by merchant elites and the king's city, dominated by warrior elites. These groups had different values but were linked by self-interest. The Muslim merchant families also developed around each city a closely cropped zone of slave-worked plantations.

Until the eighteenth century, Muslim Africans were generally tolerant of the traditional religious beliefs of their neighbors. Many Muslim clerics participated in the political life of religiously pluralist states. Increasingly, however, in the late seventeenth and eighteenth century, there was a split between clerics who profited from court life and reformers who provided an alternate leadership for those alienated by more exploitative rulers. In this process, the slave trade was a double edged sword. Many Muslim merchants were slave traders and slave users. At the same time, in many areas, Muslim clerics rallied rural populations victimized by slave raiding. Jihads led by the reformers were to transform West Africa in the nineteenth century. The first was led by Nasr al-Din, a marabout from southwest Mauritania, who attacked ruling elites for selling Muslims as slaves, for corruption and luxurious living. His *jihad*, begun in 1674, briefly controlled much of northwest Senegal and southwest Mauritania, but in 1677, he was defeated by an alliance of the French and the traditional elites. In 1690, some of his former allies founded a Muslim state at Bundu in the upper Senegal river. In the 1720s, an alliance of Muslim clerics in the Futa Jallon (Guinea) began a jihad that prevailed only after a half century, during which Futa Jallon became an important source of slaves. Finally, a jihad begun in the Futa Toro (middle Senegal river) in 1776 was motivated by the failure of existing rulers to protect local populations from slave raiders. Once in power, the jihadist regime restricted the trade in Fulbe slaves, but eventually made its peace with the French.

THE INTERIOR

Although the slave trade extended far into the interior, many African peoples were not affected by it until the nineteenth century. For eastern, southern, and parts of Central Africa, the period from 1500 to 1800 was one of gradual change. There were few mass migrations, but much slow

movement. Famine was more of a danger to human life than warfare. As population grew, more complex political systems evolved to deal with conflicts. Many peoples, however, resisted or ignored the state. On the high grasslands of eastern Africa, for example, the most dramatic movements were those of Maasai pastoralists who established a loose hegemony over a vast area without centralized institutions and absorbed members of many earlier pastoral societies.

The most complex states in eastern Africa developed in the interlacustrine area through interaction between cattle-herders and agriculturalists. North of Lake Nyanza, Bunyoro emerged in the sixteenth century and imposed tributary obligations on its smaller neighbors. Further south, other kingdoms emerged, of which the most powerful was Rwanda. Here there was a rigid differentiation between two social strata, the cattle-herding BaTutsi minority and a larger population of BaHutu agriculturalists. In both Bunyoro and Rwanda, cattle were distributed from the king's huge herds to those who served him loyally. By the late seventeenth century, Buganda established its independence from Bunyoro and began a steady process of expansion. An agricultural society dependent on bananas, Buganda imposed appointed chiefs on conquered areas, gradually developing a bureaucratic state, in which the *kabaka* (king) promoted young men to political office from a corps of pages. By the late eighteenth century, Buganda was the most centralized and wealthiest state in the interior of East Africa. Further south, the Rozvi empire of Changamire broke away from the Mwene Mutapa and took most of its territory. The Rozvi confined the Portuguese to several trading bases on the Zambezi River and eliminated Catholic religious influence.

During the eighteenth century long distance trade affected more and more Africans, moving slaves, ivory, and various other commodities to markets within Africa, in the Middle East, and within the continent itself. Patterns changed dramatically in the nineteenth century. British abolition of the slave trade in 1807 was the beginning of the end of the export slave trade. At this time, the industrial revolution had begun in Europe, creating both new demands and opportunities. The nineteenth century saw dramatic changes in both the modes of production and the modes of destruction.

See also **Ahmad ibn Ibrahim al-Ghazi (Ahmad Grañ); Cape Colony and Hinterland, History of (1600 to 1910); Islam; Menelik II; Mombasa; Shaka Zulu; Slave Trades; Téwodros; Tippu Tip; 'Uthman dan Fodio; Zambezi River.**

BIBLIOGRAPHY

Barry, Boubacar. *Senegambia and the Atlantic Slave Trade.* Cambridge, U.K.: Cambridge University Press, 1998.

Birmingham, David, and Phyllis Martin, eds. *History of Central Africa.* 2 vols. London: Longman, 1983.

Curtin, Philip. *Atlantic Slave Trade. A Census.* Madison: University of Wisconsin Press, 1969.

Elphick, Richard, and Hermann Giliomee, eds. *The Shaping of South African Society, 1652–1840.* Capetown, South Africa: Maskew Miller Longman, 1989.

Gray, Richard, ed. *Cambridge History of Africa.* Vol. 4. Cambridge, U.K.: Cambridge University Press, 1975.

Hopkins, Anthony G. *An Economic History of West Africa.* London: Longman, 1973.

Law, Robin. *The Slave Coast of West Africa, 1550–1750.* Oxford: Clarendon, 1991.

Levtzion, Nehemia, and Randall Pouwels, eds. *The History of Islam in Africa.* Athens: Ohio University Press, 2000.

Lovejoy, Paul. *Transformations in Slavery: A History of Slavery in Africa.* Cambridge, U.K.: Cambridge University Press, 1983.

Manning, Patrick. *Slavery and African Life.* Cambridge, U.K.: Cambridge University Press, 1990.

Ogot, B.A., ed. *UNESCO General History of Africa*, Vol. 5: *Africa from the Sixteenth to the Eighteenth Century.* London: Heinemann, 1992.

Robinson, David. *Muslim Societies in African History.* Cambridge, U.K.: Cambridge University Press, 2004.

MARTIN A. KLEIN

NINETEENTH AND TWENTIETH CENTURIES

The history of Africa can be written in terms of internal rhythm or external forces. Various internal dynamics continued to operate in the nineteenth century, but Africa was increasingly shaped by global forces such as the end of the Atlantic slave trade, the changing market for African commodities, new weapons, more efficient transport, and the interest of European capital in African mineral wealth and commodity exports.

INTERNAL FORCES: MFECANE AND JIHAD

Two internal developments that took place were a period of revolutionary change among the Nguni-speaking peoples of South Africa and a series of Muslim jihads that took place across the northern tier of sub-Saharan Africa. Well into the eighteenth century, the Nguni were largely cattle herders living in small and minimally differentiated chiefdoms. In the late eighteenth century, trade with the Cape Colony and the Portuguese led to control struggles for scarce resources, and to increased social differentiation and larger more centralized political units. Age sets were increasingly forged into regiments in which young men lived together and fought in close order formations until free to marry. The most successful ruler was Shaka, who dominated Natal and forged diverse microstates into the Zulu kingdom. Similar groups, some of them defeated by Shaka, founded kingdoms elsewhere, for example Mzilikazi's Ndebele in Zimbabwe and Ngoni states as far north as central Tanzania. Closer to the expanding European settlement at Cape Town, other statebuilders used guns and horses to create new polities. The outstanding figure and probably the ablest statesman in nineteenth century South Africa was Moshoeshoe, who created the kingdom of Lesotho and often took under his umbrella refugees from other conflicts.

Farther north, Islam had spread gradually by peaceful means, but starting in the 1670s some Muslims became dissatisfied either with the commitment of existing rulers to Islam or the inability of these rulers to protect Muslim communities from the ravages of the slave trade. During the nineteenth century, revolts took place all over the Sudanic zone. The most important of the jihad states was in northern Nigeria, where 'Uthman dan Fodio led a jihad between 1804 and 1810 that created the Sokoto Caliphate. The caliphate was the most economically dynamic society in the interior of nineteenth-century Africa. Another major revolt took place in the Egyptian-run Sudan, where Mohammed Abdullah proclaimed himself *Mahdi* (the rightly-guided one), and in 1885 defeated an Anglo-Egyptian military force. The Mahdist state lasted until defeat by the British in 1898.

INDUSTRY AND ABOLITION

In 1807 Great Britain abolished the slave trade, which led to efforts by the British navy to stop the slave trade in the Atlantic and Indian oceans. Slaves freed by the Atlantic squadron were sent to Sierra Leone, where many became Christians, sought education, and served British commerce, Christian missions, and the colonial state effectively throughout the nineteenth century. In 1833 the British abolished slavery itself and in 1848 the French did the same. By the 1860s, thanks both to British persistence and better steamships, the Atlantic slave trade had effectively been ended. This did not, however, end slaving or the use of slaves within Africa. Many African states had become efficient slave-producing organizations. More important, the industrial revolution created a demand for new commodities such as palm and peanut oil, the manufacture of which often used slave labor. In East Africa, slave traders first penetrated the interior in the early nineteenth century to find labor for coastal plantations. There was also increased demand for slaves in the Middle East, where sources of East European slaves had been cut off.

Technological progress in Europe also produced cheaper consumer goods, particularly cotton cloth, which motivated African cultivators to produce for European markets. Steamships reduced the price of transport. The most disastrous innovations, however, were more efficient weapons. Breech-loading rifles, first introduced in the 1860s, had greater range and accuracy than the muskets they replaced. Within a decade even better weapons were available, first repeating rifles, then field artillery, and then machine guns. Though few African leaders obtained field artillery, accurate rapid-firing rifles fueled the emergence of a series of warlords whose state-building efforts made the last third of the nineteenth century the bloodiest period in African history.

TOWARD PARTITION

Throughout Africa, leaders sought to exploit new technologies and commercial opportunities, sometimes with unintended consequences. In Egypt, Muhammad 'Ali, appointed viceroy in 1805, launched a comprehensive program of modernization. The tragic aftermath was the extension of trade routes into the more remote sections of southern Sudan that extended the quest of ivory, but eventually focused on slaving. Sa'id ibn Sultan, who became Sultan of Oman and Zanzibar in 1806, began a different kind of economic development: He encouraged clove plantations on Zanzibar, other commodities on the coast, and a commercial empire that extended into the eastern part of the Congo Basin. It too became heavily involved in a new slave trade. In Ethiopia, a series of reforming emperors restored the position of the Ethiopian state and extended it farther south. Elsewhere, African statebuilders often got caught in a scissors crisis because the quickest way for most to pay for the weapons they needed was to sell slaves, but slave raiding made it difficult for them to create larger states. Samori Touré, a brilliant strategist in West Africa, was able to hold the French off for fifteen years, but an effort to destroy a rival, Tieba Traoré of Sikasso (d. 1893), led to revolts and the failure of his enterprise. Others, such as Rabih bin Fadlallah, originally a commander in the forces of Sudan's most powerful slave dealer, did not even try to establish a state but rather lived off the spoils from pillage and slaving.

For most of the nineteenth century, Britain was the dominant European power in Africa, but it preferred as much as possible to avoid the costs of colonization and to maintain its hegemony through a policy of informal empire. Toward 1880, that was being challenged. Other nations were industrializing. Major elements in all countries were convinced that colonies were essential to world power. Soldiers sought military experience, and, along with imperialist ideologues, the prestige of empire. Some commercial interests became convinced that warfare and the tolls collected by African rulers were inhibiting economic growth. The discovery in South Africa of diamonds in 1867 and gold in 1884 whetted the appetite for anticipated mineral wealth. It led the British to take over increasing parts of South Africa and attracted capital and immigration to South Africa. From 1880, the French began moving into the western Sudan and Léopold II, king of the Belgians (1835–1909), was staking out a claim to the Congo Basin. In 1884 and 1885 the German chancellor Otto von Bismarck (1815–1898) claimed four colonies in places where German explorers had signed treaties with African chiefs.

The race was on. The Berlin Conference of 1884–1885 staked out the ground rules, which required effective occupation and meant raising the flag and establishing a small garrison. Individual boundaries were often worked out in meetings between competing powers. Believing that there was some profit to be made in colonizing areas where they had no interests, European powers often claimed colonies only to keep their rivals out. The real problem was informing the African peoples. In some cases, African rulers recognized superior military power and yielded quickly. In others, there was a scramble for protection as Africans sought protection from an African rival by aligning themselves with a European power, only to find later that they had lost independence. Many of the more powerful states, such as the Sokoto Caliphate conquered by Sir Frederick Lugard in 1903, had to be defeated in battle. Often, valiant African warriors with no experience of European weaponry charged against European machine guns and submitted after having their youth decimated.

The most effective opposition came after conquest through what is called secondary resistance. In Rhodesia (present-day Zimbabwe), massive expropriation of land and cattle after the defeat of the Ndebele in 1893 led to a more effective revolt in 1896. In German East Africa (present-day Tanganyika), the Maji-Maji rebellion of 1905 occurred after the introduction of taxation and forced cultivation; it took the Germans two years to reestablish control. Africans quickly learned the methods of guerrilla warfare. In distant and isolated areas, resistance continued into the interwar era. Only at Adowa and in South Africa were Europeans unable to impose themselves. The British won a pyrrhic victory in the South Africa War (1899–1902), but were forced to concede self-government to the two formerly independent Afrikaner states, the Orange Free State and the Transvaal, which led to the formation of an Afrikaner-dominated Union of South Africa after their absorption into it. Thanks to wealth in diamonds and gold, South Africa became a powerful modern industrial state. A large white minority maintained effective control over African workers and peasants. With the victory of Afrikaner nationalists in 1948, this was tightened into apartheid, one of the harshest and most exploitative forms of racial segregation ever known.

COLONIAL RULE

By 1907 or 1908, most of Africa had submitted to European masters. The nature of colonial rule was shaped by the values of the colonizers and the reluctance of European parliaments to underwrite their aspirations. European parliaments were willing to allow the colonial interests to have their colonies, but they generally insisted that colonies pay all or most of their own expenses. That posed problems: European administrators had to be paid salaries high enough to attract them to African posts. Even with a thin administrative service, salaries and pensions for European staff took up about half of the budget of West African colonies.

Budgetary limitations also meant a reliance on African staff. There were two key groups. The first was the chiefs. British practice differed from French or Belgian in that they often preserved the structure, ritual, and titles of the traditional African state ways. This was called Indirect Rule. The French, however, although also relying mostly on traditional chiefs, treated these men as modern functionaries. Chiefs were expected to collect taxes, enforce laws, and were usually the lowest level of the judiciary. They had to support a body of retainers to carry out the administration's desires. Chiefs were sometimes illiterate, especially in the early years, and rarely well educated. The administration also depended on a cadre of clerks, interpreters, guards, and messengers. Most administrators did not speak the languages of those they administered, though the British made a serious effort in major language areas. This increased the foreigners' dependence on their intermediaries.

The system of colonial rule had several characteristics. First, it was highly arbitrary: At each level, the governor, the administrator, and the chief could generally do what they wanted. Second, the social system was marked by social distance. Administrators rarely socialized with either chiefs or the educated intermediaries. Third, the system was unspecialized. Both the administrator and the chief were jacks-of-all-trades. The administrator had to be a judge, a road-builder, and an agronomist. Fourth, the career options of African males were highly limited. Only in the early years, and again in the late ones, was it possible for a clerk to become an administrator, and even then often only through a European patron. Finally, colonial administrations tended to be torn between development priorities and the maintenance of stability. Both administrators and chiefs were often reluctant to encourage any development that might undermine their fragile authority.

In this, the consent of the governed was irrelevant. There were no significant electoral institutions except in the Four Communes, urban communities in Senegal that elected municipal governments and sent a deputy to the French parliament. In British West Africa, powerless legislatures councils contained some Africans, but these representatives had little influence and no power. European democracies did not think Africans were mature enough to choose their own leaders. Traditional consultative structures were shut down as chiefs were incorporated in the colonial autocracy in the name of imagined traditions.

Development was, however, essential to fund the system. This took several forms, all marked by a focus on export of commodities. In much of Southern African, the existence of reserves of gold, copper, and other minerals led to the development of a network of railroads to move mineral wealth to the ports. A major concern for such areas was labor. Some regions were kept underdeveloped so that men would have to migrate to earn money to pay their taxes. In the Belgian Congo, facilities for family life were developed to attract workers. In South Africa, by contrast, housing was available only for men, and families were left in rural areas. In Kenya and Rhodesia, settler agriculture was the basis of the economy. The colonial state in such areas had to provide labor for the settlers and to protect them from African competition. Finally, in large areas, peasant agriculture produced small surpluses, which made it possible for the state to run itself on customs duties and the head tax.

DECOLONIZATION

During the years between the wars, Africans increasingly formed organizations, including religious communities such as the Kimbanguists in the Congo and the Watchtower in the Rhodesias, that challenged their colonial rulers. The Kikuyu Central Association sent Jomo Kenyatta to England to lobby for their interests. The National Congress of British West Africa articulated the unhappiness of educated West Africans who had

been shunted aside during the early colonial period. Workers went on strike for better wages and working conditions, though few organized formal labor unions. Labor conflict and the articulation of grievances became more intense during the Depression as the drop in exports and colonial expenditures cut into African living standards. In spite of this, there was nothing that could be called a nationalist political party until after World War II. Some colonial officials, however, began to realize that change was inevitable.

The war effected many changes. African soldiers served in European and Asian military campaigns and were influenced by the democratic propaganda of the allies. European parliaments swung sharply to the left after the war, giving power to people who wanted a reformed colonialism and the extension of more rights to Africans. The new constitution of the French Fourth Republic allowed colonial peoples to send representatives to the French parliament and to elect local legislative councils. In British West Africa, new constitutions set up consultative institutions. Nationalist parties became increasingly assertive at a time when many Europeans began to question whether colonialism conferred benefits that justified the wars the Dutch faced in Indonesia, the French in Indochina and Algeria, and the British in Malaysia, Cyprus, and Kenya.

Between the independence of the Sudan in 1955 and Swaziland in 1968, most of colonial Africa acceded to independence. In the present-day Democratic Republic of the Congo, independence came only four years after formation of the first political party and eighteen months after the Belgians reconsidered their desire to hang on to authority. By 1965, the only white-ruled states were the three Portuguese colonies (Angola, Mozambique, and Guinea), Rhodesia (present-day Zimbabwe), and South Africa. In 1974 the Portuguese army, embittered by losses in African guerrilla wars, brought down the fascist dictatorship in Portugal and freed the three Portuguese colonies. In Rhodesia, the settler state yielded in 1979. In South Africa, the state had powers of repression much greater than elsewhere, but by the 1980s, apartheid and repression was getting more and more costly, particularly during the Soweto riots of 1976 and an insurrection from 1984 to 1986. In 1990 Nelson Mandela was released from prison and African nationalist parties were recognized. A new constitution was negotiated and in 1994 an elected African-led government took power.

INDEPENDENCE AND NEOCOLONIALISM

The period between World War II and independence was a time of reformed colonialism. Prices for African commodities were high, wages were rising, representative institutions were being created, and colonial regimes were granting rights to the colonized. Africans took over the state with independence, but they had no control over the means of production, which were owned by Europeans or by expatriate minorities from India or Lebanon. Where African states tried to take over these areas, the results were generally disastrous. Only Tanzania had limited successes, but it too had to back away from its *ujama* socialism in the 1980s. African states also had to look to international capital for any new investment.

The failure of state-controlled economies was due in part to the lack of experienced personnel. There were almost no trained economists or administrators at the time of independence. African governments often had to either rely on Europeans or to promote young men quickly to senior positions. They also faced problems of national integration. Boundaries negotiated by European diplomats cut across ethnic boundaries and grouped together disparate peoples. Colonial rulers were generally not interested in creating a sense of national identity. Africa's largest states all had bloody civil wars: In Sudan two wars between the Muslim North and the Christian South; in the Democratic Republic of the Congo, five years of civil conflict ended only by the creation of a military dictatorship; and in Nigeria a brutal four-year civil war. The most serious problem, however, was that soldiers often did not feel any loyalty to the new nation or to its leaders.

To deal with these problems, African leaders often created single-party systems that entrenched ruling groups. However, the people in power often became corrupt and were hard to remove. Such systems often squelched discussion of issues, expecting members to support whatever the party line was. Similar to single parties elsewhere, they often became gerontocracies in which aging leaders held on to power long after their skills had

declined. When these systems faltered, military coups often brought soldiers to power. Generally, the military rulers proved more corrupt and less competent than their civilian counterparts. By the late 1980s, African states started moving away from both single-party regimes and from military rule.

In spite of their problems, progress was made in many areas, particularly health and education. Medical schools were created, doctors were trained, and medical care became more widely available. Life expectancy rates rose rapidly until AIDS began decimating populations in many parts of Africa, particularly in the east and south. Schools were also built, universal primary education becoming a goal for many African countries. At the end of World War II there were only three universities between South Africa and the Sahara; by the end of the twentieth century Nigeria alone had more than fifty. The expansion of education has opened up a wide range of careers to Africans, male and female. In almost all spheres of life, African countries can call upon a class of trained professional that did not exist at independence.

In the 1980s inflation in the United States led to a sharp rise in interest rates. African nations, many of which had accumulated debts without seeing significant growth in productivity, found themselves required to renegotiate those debts at prohibitive rates. This had a disastrous effect on African economies. During the subsequent decade, the vast majority of African countries were forced to turn to the International Monetary Fund for aid and accept structural adjustment programs that forced them to cut expenditures, privatize state companies, and reduce the number of civil servants. Health expenditures were reduced and school fees often raised. With commodity prices low, this was, for most Africans, a difficult time.

For some, this was a time of disaster. The 1990s saw a failed state in Somalia, bitter social conflict in Sierra Leone and Liberia, genocide in Rwanda that killed an estimated 800,000, and a civil war that that followed the flight of Mobutu in the Democratic Republic of the Congo. It was also, however, a time of renewal. Long-standing conflicts were resolved in Mozambique, Angola, Sudan, and the Democratic Republic of the Congo. With the collapse of apartheid, South Africa ceased to destabilize its neighbors and became a force of economic cooperation. Single-party systems were rejected and military regimes were pushed out in many African states. By 2005, many of the new democracies had held several elections; for example, Mali, Ghana, Nigeria, Tanzania, Zambia, and Mozambique.

See also 'Ali, Muhammad; Boundaries, Colonial and Modern; Cape Town; Christianity; Colonialism and Imperialism; Decolonization; Education, School; History, World: Africa in; Ibadan; International Monetary Fund; Kenyatta, Jomo; Labor; Lugard, Frederick John Dealtry; Mandela, Nelson; Mobutu Sese Seko; Moshoeshoe I; Neocolonialism; Postcolonialism; Rabih bin Fadlallah; Shaka Zulu; Slave Trades; Slavery and Servile Institutions; Téwodros; World War II.

BIBLIOGRAPHY

Ajayi, Jacob Festus Ade, and Michael Crowder, eds. *History of West Africa*, 3rd edition. Harlow, U.K.: Longmans, 1985.

Birmingham, David, and Phyllis Martin, eds. *History of Central Africa*, Vol. 2. Harlow, U.K.: Longmans, 1983.

Boahen, A. Adu, ed. *Africa under Colonial Domination, 1880–1935*. Berkeley: University of California Press, 1985.

Cooper, Frederick. *Africa since 1940: The Past of the Present*. Cambridge, U.K.: Cambridge University Press, 2002.

Davenport, T. R. H., and Christopher Saunders, eds. *South Africa: A Modern History*. 5th edition. New York: St. Martin's Press, 2000.

Falola, Toyin. *Africa*, 5 vols. Durham, NC: Carolina Academic Press, 2000–2003.

Freund, William. *The Making of Contemporary Africa*. Bloomington: Indiana University Press, 1984.

Gann, Lewis, and Peter Duignan, eds. *Colonialism in Africa*, 4 vols. Cambridge, U.K.: Cambridge University Press, 1969–1975.

Mazrui, Ali, ed. *Africa since 1935*. Berkeley: University of California Press, 1993.

MARTIN KLEIN

HOMINIDS. *See* Early Human Society, History of (c. 50,000 BP to 19,000 BCE); Prehistory.

HOMO ERECTUS. *See* Prehistory.

HOMO SAPIENS. *See* Prehistory.

HORTON, JAMES AFRICANUS BEALE (1835–1883). James Africanus Beale Horton was a Sierra Leonean physician, political scientist, and businessman. Born in Sierra Leone of Igbo (Ibo) recaptive parentage (his father had been set free from a slave ship there), Horton grew up in Freetown, the capital, at a time when skin color was not a barrier to advancement. Educated at mission schools, he went on to train in Britain as an army medical doctor. He qualified in 1859 and served for twenty years in British West Africa as a medical officer and administrator, retiring with the rank of lieutenant colonel. Having studied geology, he prospected for gold, and upon retirement from the army in 1879, he formed a mining company and subsequently opened a bank in Freetown. Death at the age of forty-eight cut short his entrepreneurial schemes.

Horton's doctoral thesis, a medical topography of West Africa, was published along with eight other works on medical and political subjects, including a textbook on tropical diseases. His best-known work, *West African Countries and Peoples* (1868), subtitled *A Vindication of the Negro Race*, contested the racial theories then current and set out a blueprint for the future political evolution of West Africa on lines that anticipated those that were to be followed at decolonization in the 1950s and 1960s.

See also **Literature; Literature and the Study of Africa.**

BIBLIOGRAPHY

Fyfe, Christopher. *Africanus Horton (1835–1883): West African Scientist and Patriot*. New York: Oxford University Press, 1972.

Horton, James Africanus Beale. *Africanus Horton: The Dawn of Nationalism in Modern Africa*, ed. Davidson Nicol. Harlow: Longmans, 1969.

Porter, A. T. *The Concept of the African University: Horton's Dream and Today's Reality*. Edinburgh: Center of African Studies, University of Edinburgh, 1983.

CHRISTOPHER FYFE

HOTTENTOTS. *See* **Languages: Khoesan and Click.**

HOUPHOUËT-BOIGNY, FÉLIX

(1905–1993). Félix Houphouët-Boigny was born as Dia Houphouët into a Baule chief's family at Yamoussoukro, the present-day capital city of Côte d'Ivoire. Educated in the French colonial system, he attended the local École Primaire Supérieure at Bingerville (1916–1917), the École Normale William Ponty at Dakar, Senegal (1918–1925), and the École de Médecine et de Pharmacie at Dakar, where he graduated as *médecin africain* (African physician) in 1925. As a member of the numerically and socially dominant ethnic group, and endowed with a high traditional social status, Houphouët-Boigny became a prominent member of the African elite in Côte d'Ivoire and earned a successful living as a doctor (1925–1940), chief of his home district (1940), and a coffee planter. He worked to organize African planters in an effort to end the institution of forced labor and other social inequities generated by colonialism, including inequalities that disadvantaged African planters vis-à-vis their European competitors.

He founded and presided over the African Agricultural Syndicate (Syndicat Agricole Africain, SAA; est. 1944); the Democratic Party of Côte d'Ivoire (Parti Démocratique de la Côte d'Ivoire, PDCI; est. April 1946); and the African Democratic Assembly (Rassemblement Démocratique Africain, RDA; est. October 1946), a Francophone inter-territorial political movement, of which the PDCI was a local branch. With the first territorial elections of 1945, he embarked on his political career, which, judged by any standard, was one of the longest, richest, and most brilliant of African history. He held office at five different levels (traditional, municipal, territorial, regional, and metropolitan). His positions were as follows: member of the French Constituent Assemblies (1945–1946); member of the French National Assembly (1946–1959); member of the General Council (1946–1952); member of the Territorial Assembly (1952–1959); mayor of Abidjan; (1956–1960); president of the Territorial Assembly (1957–1958); grand counselor for French West Africa (1957–1959); member of the Legislative

Félix Houphouët-Boigny (1905–1993), the first president of Côte d'Ivoire. Houphouët-Boigny aided in the development of the country's expansive cocoa industry, and under his strong leadership, Côte d'Ivoire prospered economically. ISSOUF SANOGO/AFP/GETTY IMAGES

Assembly (1959–1960); minister in six successive French governments (1956–1959); prime minister of Côte d'Ivoire (1959–1960); president of the independent republic (1960–1993); and between 1963 and 1973, head of the ministries of Foreign Affairs, Agriculture, Defense, Interior, and Education.

A genuinely skillful politician, Houphouët-Boigny was one of the most powerful and influential statesmen in Africa. He was praised for the success of his economic policy in the 1960s and 1970s, the "Ivoirian miracle"—the social peace and political stability at home, made possible partially by spectacular economic growth. Declining economic conditions after the mid-1970s led to growing social and political unrest in the 1980s, obliging Houphouët-Boigny to retreat from the one-party political system and to reestablish political pluralism in April 1990. He was reelected for a seventh five-year term in October 1990 at age eighty-five, and with his strategy of the "heir with no name," he astutely managed the problem of succession until his death in office on Independence Day (December 7, 1993). He is also remembered for his building of the enormous Catholic Cathedral at Yamoussoukro.

See also **Aid and Development; Côte d'Ivoire: History and Politics; Postcolonialism; Yamoussoukro.**

BIBLIOGRAPHY

Naka, Leon. *La démocratie économique et sociale en Côte d'Ivoire: Les idées de Félix Houphouët-Boigny et Henri Konan Bédié.* Abidjan, Côte d'Ivoire: CEDA, 1996.

Rencontres avec Félix Houphouët-Boigny: Uuvrage collectif réalisé sous la direction de Frédéric Grah Mel. Abidjan, Côte d'Ivoire: Frat Mat Éditions, 2005.

TESSY D. BAKARY

HOUSEHOLD AND DOMESTIC GROUPS.

The etymology of the word "household" combines the idea of a physical habitat with its social context. It is closely related to the way domestic African peasant societies pragmatically represent their own basic structure. Many African societies have a vernacular word to express the idea of the household, such as *ya* among the Tiv, *ka* among the Soninke, and *efako* among the Nupe. When there is no generic term for it, a household is called after the proper name of its inhabitants, as among the Guro of Côte d'Ivoire.

THE OPERATION OF THE HOUSEHOLD

In practice, a household stands forth as a community assembled in one or more common buildings on shared land. Its members are of different ages, genders, and statuses. They may or may not be related.

The notion of "household" suggests the way its members live, work, and eat together, as well as the relations of interdependence and hierarchy associated with the organization of tasks and the allotment of the common product. Even though its size may vary, the household operates most efficiently when it satisfies the subsistence needs of all its members, productive or not, and manages its social reproduction. The traditional model of organization is the self-sustaining domestic community. It constantly reproduces lifelong relationships through various channels of reciprocity between the age groups.

A household's self-sustenance is contingent upon the physical reproduction of the group. The productive adults work in agricultural and domestic activities to the benefit of the whole community. It requires, for a given level of productivity, a constant and appropriate ratio of these active adults of both sexes to the unproductive population: children under age, the elderly, and the disabled. Self-sustenance favors the emergence of a central authority who presides over the redistribution of subsistence goods between all the household members. This responsibility, which is carried out through management of the granaries and herds, is generally entrusted to the head (the eldest male) of the community. He is representative of the dead ones who have preceded him in the cycle of production and circulation of subsistence goods. His authority creates links between generations stretching back through the ancestors.

Because it is organized and hierarchized as an operational unit, the household acquires a social and political identity. Through this identity, it is recognized as a partner with homologous households in a larger social and territorial whole, such as, for example, the village. In this setting, the household contributes to collective tasks and participates in material exchanges and in common cultural and religious activities.

Through its political existence, the household also gains access to the means of its demographic and institutional reproduction. The household recruits most of its members from those who are born and raised within it. Kin make up what is called a family, a parental framework with an exogamous constitution. The family stands as a partner in matrimonial alliances with other households to exchange their marriageable (nubile) children.

At the level of the family, natural growth does not guarantee the required demographic ratio between age groups and sexes. By enlarging its nuptial population, matrimonial alliances alleviate potential demographic imbalance, though they do not thoroughly correct it. It is often beneficial to introduce foreigners into the household. The institutional ties among the household's members are different, depending upon whether one is born into the household, adopted, or captured. The degree to which outsiders are integrated varies from complete assimilation to servitude. Children, and sometimes even adults, may be introduced by adoption or fosterage. Distant relatives may be invited to settle permanently, but in a dependent position toward their hosts.

In patrilineal societies, a foreign young man may sometimes be married to a girl of the household without paying bride-wealth; he would then set himself under the authority of the lineage of his wife and give up his ascendancy over her offspring. Outsiders may also be brought in, without invoking kinship ties, as servants, serfs, or slaves. Whether they marry, or whether they breed their own offspring, depends upon the master's will. Thus, the household, facing the conflicting demands of production and social requirements, must call upon several patterns of integration in order to correct the imbalance of age and sex imposed by demography. Hence, the household is not identical to the kin group. Its composition, as well as its size and growth, depend upon the solutions adopted to meet its requirements.

SEGMENTATION

The continuous growth of the household leads to decentralization. The head may entrust a senior under him with the management of the household's granaries or herds, while keeping to himself control over the matrimonial policy of the entire household and his authority over dependent members. If, nevertheless, "there are too many people around the household dish," or if the youngest branches are too far removed from the succession, or if cohabitation hinders the possibility of marriages between distant members of the same household, then a segment may be allowed to settle aside. The head of the new household is granted authority over his own descendents. The new segment may keep harmonious relationships with the original unit, which may be manifested in the celebration of communal rituals, in gifts and loan of seeds or animals, in food exchanges during dearth, and in preferential marriages when the matrimonial rules allow them.

Segmentation may also occur through conflict, when through lack of a friendly agreement relationships between the two groups are partially or entirely severed. The household generated through segmentation can accommodate kin groups of every size, from a married couple to a large extended family. In its turn, it acquires dependents and servants. Although it will not immediately have the social weight of the household from which it came, it enters into a comparable cycle of development.

With segmentation, kinship extends beyond the original household in abstract networks. It symbolically and ideologically unifies larger and deeper parental entities, such as lineages, clans, or dynasties. The preservation of knowledge relative to membership in a kin group and to the sequence of births constitutes a genealogical charter of ancestral ties and successions. It also supplies the information necessary to identify the prohibited or prescribed partners in case of marriages. It sets the structural perception of the domestic society, to which ethnology sometimes limits itself even though kinship cannot be considered separately from its material basis, namely, the household.

MODERNIZATION

Under the influence of colonization and the monetary economy, the function of the traditional household as described above has been altered. Its structure has proven itself to be helpful for confronting the market economy, but within short limits. The household is increasingly threatened by the weakening capacity of its members for managing matrimonial affairs and, eventually, by the loss of its agents of reproduction. Household sizes and internal structures could be highly variable in the past, and in some places they remain so as of the early twenty-first century. Within communities, there could be successful households comprised of dozens of people while others were the size of a nuclear family. And there have always been certain differences between peoples. Yoruba compounds were architecturally and socially impressive enough to have been referred to in English as compounds. Married siblings of the household head, married children, spouses and descendants, plus varying numbers of non-kin, made up the large *ile* (houses), Poor households would be much smaller.

In trading societies, the house could be the basis of the business.

Participation in the market economy, which the politics of development encourages, requires the production of commodities or the sale of one's labor. The household may offer an infrastructure and an organization for cash-cropping (in addition to or instead of subsistence), but only as long as it can have free or cheap access to land, due to its low labor productivity. The extension of modern farming drives peasants out of the market. Subsistence agriculture, as the economic and social substratum of kinship, is carried on under unsatisfactory commercial conditions. In the competitive context of the international market economy, attempts at modernization of subsistence agriculture almost inevitably lead to bankruptcy. Any activity in the monetary sector is bound to be more profitable than subsistence agriculture. Climatic vicissitudes or monetary fluctuations encourage adults to migrate and sell their labor power in the monetary sector. But exile and wage earning offer little security.

The household may remain for some time a refuge against unemployment, illness, or old age. A division takes place between those of its members who migrate for varying periods of time, supplying the household with monetary income, and those who stay in the countryside managing, looking after, and trying to regenerate the household. The monetization of bridewealth deprives the elders of means formerly at their disposal to control the young men's marriage. Among the men who leave, some marry outside traditional alliances and do not return. The young women, whom the elders try to retain home in order to induce the return of the male emigrants, depart in their turn to work and settle down in the city. The servants take advantage of the new social arrangements to gain full emancipation. The household survives, but solely as a symbolic support of local social security.

Should the international economy thrive and should migrant workers be locally protected by social security systems of their employers, the traditional peasant household would lose its raison d'être as a refuge. Should the household survive as a refuge within the new market economy, however, its persistence would be less evidence of its vitality than of deep international economic and social crises.

See also **Agriculture; Death, Mourning, and Ancestors; Family; Kinship and Affinity; Marriage Systems; Peasants; Production Strategies.**

BIBLIOGRAPHY

Bender, Donald R. "A Refinement of the Concept of Household: Families, Co-Residence, and Domestic Functions." *American Anthropologist* 69 (1967): 493–504.

Bohannan, Paul. *Tiv Farm and Settlement.* London: Her Majesty's Stationery Office, 1954.

Firth, Raymond. *Elements of Social Organization*, 2nd edition. Boston: Beacon Press, 1963.

Goody, Jack, ed. *The Developmental Cycle in Domestic Groups.* Cambridge, U.K.: Cambridge University Press, 1958.

Little, Kenneth L. "The Mende Family Household." *Sociological Review* 48 (1948): 37–56.

Lowie, R. H. *Social Organization.* New York: Rinehart, 1948.

Meillassoux, Claude. *Maidens, Meal, and Money: Capitalism and the Domestic Community.* Cambridge, U.K.: Cambridge University Press, 1981.

Middleton, John. *Lugbara Religion: Ritual and Authority among an East African People.* New York: Oxford University Press, 1960.

Nadel, Siegfried. *A Black Byzantium: The Kingdom of Nupe in Nigeria.* New York: Oxford University Press, 1942.

Poller, Eric, and Grace Winter. *La société soninke.* Brussels: Éditions de l'Institut de sociologie, Université libre de Bruxelles, 1972.

CLAUDE MEILLASSOUX
REVISED BY JANE I. GUYER

HUDDLESTON, TREVOR (1913–1998). Ordained in 1937, one-time Bishop of Masasi (Tanzania), Stepney (England), and Mauritius, also Archbishop of the Indian Ocean, Huddleston was knighted in 1998 as Bishop Trevor of Sophiatown. His monastic order, the Community of the Resurrection, sent Huddleston in 1943 to the racially mixed suburb of Sophiatown near Johannesburg. Subsequently, he became one of the most influential clergymen in Africa. There and at St. Peter's School in Rosettenville, he had profound personal impact on many key South Africans, including Desmond Tutu, Oliver Tambo (1917–1993), Nelson Mandela, jazz musician

Father Trevor Huddleston (1913-1998). Father Trevor Huddleston stands on the grounds of Howick Hall, Northumberland, shortly after the announcement that he has been appointed Bishop of Masasi in Tanganyika, August 6, 1960. Father Huddleston was a staunch opponent of apartheid. KEYSTONE/HULTON ARCHIVE/GETTY IMAGES

Hugh Masekela, and writers Ezekiel Mphahlele (b. 1919) and Alan Paton.

\When Sophiatown was bulldozed by apartheid authorities in 1955 to make way for a white neighborhood, Huddleston wrote a powerful denunciation in *Naught for Your Comfort*, a work that brought him worldwide attention. Called *Makhalipile*, the dauntless one, he was bestowed in 1955 at the historic Congress of the People in Kliptown with the exceptional title of Isitwalandwe, the African National Congress' highest honor, and the first of many. Motivated by deep religious convictions, Huddleston fought against apartheid because he saw its impact on the people for whom he had responsibility—a link between pastoral care and social engagement that echoes in an African context the origins of Latin American liberation theology.

See also **Apartheid; Mandela, Nelson; Masekela, Hugh; Paton, Alan; Tutu, Desmond Mpilo.**

BIBLIOGRAPHY

Denniston, Robin. *Trevor Huddleston: A Life.* New York: St. Martin's Press, 2000.

Honore, Deborah Duncan, ed. *Trevor Huddleston: Essays on His Life and Work.* Oxford: Oxford University Press, 1988.

Huddleston, Trevor. *Naught for Your Comfort.* London: Collins, 1956.

McGrandle, Piers. *Trevor Huddleston: Turbulent Priest.* London: Continuum, 2004.

JAMES R. COCHRANE

HUMAN EVOLUTION

This entry includes the following articles:
PATTERNS OF EVOLUTION
ORIGINS OF MODERN HUMANS
HUMAN BIOLOGICAL DIVERSITY

PATTERNS OF EVOLUTION

Africa, Charles Darwin postulated, was where human beings evolved. With characteristic reservation, in 1871 he wrote in *The Descent of Man*: "It is therefore probable that Africa was formerly inhabited by extinct apes closely allied to the gorilla and chimpanzee; and as these two species are now man's nearest allies, it is somewhat more probable that our early progenitors lived on the African continent than elsewhere." In 1871 almost none of the early human progenitors were known; there was fossil evidence of a small apelike creature and some of the first Neanderthals that Darwin knew little about. This, however, came from Europe, not Africa. Nor did the next set of fossil discoveries substantiate Darwin's belief. They were found in Indonesia and China. It was not until 1925 that the first hard evidence appeared that suggested that early progenitors of humans lived on the African continent. And since then, evidence has accumulated showing that not only did the earliest progenitors live in Africa, but that most of the extinct species of humans evolved and first lived there. Practically all the major morphological changes in the human lineage took place on that continent, and the evidence for it comes almost exclusively from fossil sites in sub-Saharan Africa.

The evidence for human ancestry is generally in the form of fossils. These are pieces of the skeleton that have in one way or another been preserved and lasted over time. They are mostly fragmentary; rarely are complete skulls found, and even more rarely do anthropologists find different parts of the skeleton of a single individual together. Such fossil materials have become known in relatively large quantities since Darwin's time. They now make it possible to sketch an outline of human evolution that is most likely broadly accurate.

The human lineage is characterized by the propensity to walk habitually on two legs. This is one of the main morphological features that distinguish humans from apes and identify the human zoological family, the Hominidae. Additionally, humans belonging to the present-day genus, *Homo*, are distinguished by a relatively large brain. Present fossil evidence suggests that a variety of now extinct apelike creatures lived in Africa from at least 25 million years ago. One of these apes became bipedal, maybe sometime between 8 and 6 million years ago. Subsequently, a variety of different species of hominids evolved. *Homo* appears around 2.5 million years ago, and just after 2 million years ago a minimum of four distinct kinds of hominid lived in eastern Africa alone.

All but one lineage eventually became extinct. This one, represented by the species *Homo erectus*, had developed a larger brain than the others, and it expanded its range out of Africa into parts of Asia at least one and three quarter million years ago. More modern kinds of human also probably evolved in Africa, from *H. erectus*, subsequently moving into the rest of the Old World. Here they gave rise to such distinctive types as the Neanderthals that inhabited much of Europe and the Near East. These forms of humans were eventually replaced by another product of Africa, *Homo sapiens*, the surviving species. *Homo sapiens*, too, moved out of Africa, replaced the other existing kinds of human throughout the Old World, and eventually came to inhabit much of the globe.

That is the broad picture, but it is probably worth cataloging the evidence for this succession of hominids and events in more detail. The earliest hominid known is named *Sahelanthropus tchadensis*.

It comes from Chad and is between 6 and 7 million years old. A slightly later species, *Ardipithecus kadabba*, is found in the Middle Awash region of Ethiopia, dated at about 5.8 million years. It is followed by *Ar. ramidus*, and there may be a fossil specimen or two from Kenya belonging to this species as well, both occurrences around 4.4 million years in age. A little later in time another species is known from sites in northern Kenya, referred to as *Australopithecus anamensis*. What is known of the head and teeth of these early species is extremely similar to that of apes. However, they are believed to be bipedal, indicating that they are on an evolutionary lineage that had already diverged from those leading to the modern African gorilla and chimpanzee. Although *S. tchadensis* is represented by a whole cranium, the fossil evidence of these early hominid species retrieved by the end of the twentieth century was fragmentary, and relatively little is known about them.

A far better-known species, *Australopithecus afarensis*, lived from at least 3.6 to about 2.8 million years ago, and its remains are known from Ethiopia, Tanzania, and possibly as far west as Chad. This too had an apelike head and teeth, but as shown by its limbs and other postcranial bones, was clearly bipedal. The most convincing evidence of its bipedality, however, comes from tracks of its footprints preserved in volcanic ash at the site of Laetoli, northern Tanzania. These show that *Au. afarensis* walked in an upright manner with a striding gait essentially similar to *Homo sapiens*. However, analysis of hand and foot bones suggests to some that the species still spent a considerable amount of time in the trees. It is difficult to estimate the height and weight of these fossil creatures with any precision, but they were certainly small. Plausible estimates for *Au. Afarensis* range from sixty-four to ninety-nine pounds, and they may have been about four feet tall. They were also sexually dimorphic, with males being considerably larger than females. A similar species, *Au. africanus*, occurred in South Africa at roughly the same time.

There is no evidence that any of these species made stone tools. However, it is possible that they used rocks to help process food as do modern chimpanzees, and in any case there would be no remnants of implements made from perishable materials such as wood.

By about 2.5 million years ago there is evidence for two contemporaneous species in eastern Africa, and they are different. One is another australopithecine, sometimes called *Paranthropus aethiopicus*, characterized by a massive broad face and extremely large molar teeth. The other is the first indication of *Homo*, with the suggestion of an expanded brain cavity. Specimens are known from Kenya and from Ethiopia near this age, but they are so scant that it is not possible to allocate them to a particular species. This coincides with the first appearance of stone artifacts, which are known at this time period from sites in Ethiopia and northern Kenya. Most archaeologists prefer to designate *Homo* as the hominid responsible for the artifacts, but it is not impossible that both species made tools.

By just after 2 million years ago, however, relatively more specimens are known, and it is clear that in eastern Africa there were several species inhabiting the area at this time. The species *P. boisei* is similar to the earlier *P. aethiopicus*, and is almost certainly its descendant. Another similar form, *P. robustus*, occurs in South Africa. In addition, there are three separate species of the genus *Homo* in eastern Africa. *H. habilis* is known from Olduvai Gorge, Tanzania, from Lake Turkana in northern Kenya, and probably South Africa. At the Kenyan site there is also *H. rudolfensis* and *H. erectus*. The first two of these early species of *Homo* are only known over a short time period in the fossil record, but *P. boisei* lasted until at least 1.4 million years ago.

Again, for most of these species there is only tentative information about body weight and stature, but all were small. Estimates for *P. boisei* are about seventy-five pounds, five feet tall, and there are similar judgments for the species in the genus *Homo*. However, there are much better data for *H. erectus*. A remarkably complete skeleton of a young male individual found to the west of Lake Turkana in northern Kenya makes possible accurate estimates. He was about ten or twelve years in age, and calculations based upon limb bone lengths show that he was five foot three inches tall at death. Based on plausible projections to adult stature he would have grown to more than six feet in height. Weight estimates using different methods all fall around 110

pounds, probably exceeding 150 pounds when adult. This specimen lived 1.6 million years ago.

H. erectus is significant as the first hominid known outside Africa. This range expansion was long thought not to have taken place until 1 million years ago, but recently there is good evidence that *H. erectus* may have reached the Caucasus of eastern Georgia by 1.8 million years ago, and even perhaps Indonesia by about the same time.

There is some controversy of opinion about subsequent events, but most scientists believe that a hominid more like *H. sapiens* than *H. erectus* evolved in Africa, and once again moved into the rest of the Old World. Modern *H. sapiens*, morphologically indistinguishable from humans of the early twenty-first century, again evolved in Africa, possibly as long ago as one hundred thousand years, and again migrated into the rest of the world, where it replaced such archaic forms as the Neanderthals.

What caused this succession of transformations in human evolutionary lineage, transformations that involved some remarkable morphological alterations such as the adoption of an upright striding posture and the development of a large brain? Evolutionary shifts are generally thought of as responses to alterations in environment, ranging from climatic ones on a large scale to changes in vegetation, and to the interactions among different species of animals more locally.

Some have suggested that major shifts in human evolution are correlated with large-scale global climatic episodes that can be detected in the history of the earth. For example, at about 6 million years ago the Mediterranean Sea more or less completely dried up, one in a series of related events known as the Messinian crisis. This is approximately the time when bipedal hominids are thought to have appeared. Similarly, some have thought that an alleged intense pulse of global aridity at 2.5 million years ago was responsible for the origin of *Homo* and the beginning of stone tools. These are plausible and attractive ideas. They are linked to even older ideas that bipedality and the development of a larger brain were the product of a shift in African environments from forest to grassland savannas.

There are problems with ascertaining the validity of these ideas. It had been difficult to know how global climatic variability, detectable mainly from evidence in the oceans, affected environments in the interior of a continent such as Africa. But recent discoveries clearly show this cyclical climatic change in the east African Rift Valley, driven by predictable astronomical perturbations. However, despite this, and although there is good evidence for increasing aridity on a global scale between 3 and 1.5 million years ago, it is less clear that there is any particular event at 2.5 million years ago near the apparent origin of the current genus and the first stone tools. It would be helpful to have associated evidence of vegetation, but fossil plants over this period in Africa are about as rare as human fossils. It is possible, however, to get a notion of vegetation from analyzing isotopes in fossil soils. Work such as this has shown, at least for the eastern part of Africa where hominid fossils occur, that there is no sign of a large-scale and sudden shift from forest to open savannas. This does not mean, of course, that evolution in the human lineage has been unaffected by environmental and ecological variations. It is simply hard to isolate possibly subtle yet significant former environmental effects precisely in time and space. Even if detectable, correlating them with particular morphological changes in hominids as convincing causes is difficult.

This makes looking at the development of human behaviors on a finer scale even more problematic. Some information can be derived from archaeological sites. The earliest tools, attributed to the Oldowan Industry, are relatively unsophisticated technologically. It is not clear which of the several early hominid species possessed this technological ability. Possibly all of them did. By about 1.7 million years ago, stone hand-axes and cleavers appear in increasing numbers, signaling the Acheulian Industry that lasted for about a million years. It is unknown what these various artifacts were used for, although the presence of animal bones at many of these sites, some of which bear cut-marks made by tools, suggest that the hominids were using them for processing meat at least occasionally. Some scientists have suggested that carcasses killed by carnivores were scavenged by hominids, and that organized hunting of large prey came much later in human evolution. Moreover, analyses of the wear on the edges of some of these artifacts show that

they were also used to cut wood, grass, and other vegetable items. Plant food is likely to have been important to early hominids, although evidence for it is less conspicuous.

Issues involving the social behavior of these extinct species are even less tangible. Most of the early species appear to have been sexually dimorphic. Socioecological theory and comparative observations of modern species of animals suggest that this implies they were unlikely to be monogamous or solitary. Groups probably defended from others the area over which they ranged and were no doubt aggressive in certain situations. More advanced hominids, such as *Homo erectus*, had a large brain capacity when adult. This meant that offspring had to be born at a early stage of development in order to be able to pass through the mother's birth canal, just as in modern humans. Consequently, this would have entailed a relatively long period of infant care.

An important general point is that nearly all the evidence for early human evolution and behavior comes from a few sites in South Africa and a series of localities on the eastern edge of the continent, nearly all associated with the Great Rift Valley. Scholars have almost no knowledge about what was happening in those areas comprising the vast extent of the rest of Africa. There are many unanswered issues in human evolution. Some questions will remain unanswered, including some of the most interesting and obvious ones. The remarkable thing is that anything at all is known about the remote human ancestry. And a great deal more now is known than since the time when Darwin, correctly as it happens, postulated Africa as the place of origin of humankind.

See also **Archaeology and Prehistory; Climate; Leakey, Louis and Mary; Prehistory.**

BIBLIOGRAPHY

Brunet, Michel, et al. "A New Hominid from the Upper Miocene of Chad, Central Africa." *Nature* 418 (2002):145–151.

Dart, Raymond. "*Australopithecus africanus*, the Man-ape of South Africa." *Nature* 115 (1925):195–199.

Darwin, Charles. *The Descent of Man, and Selection in Relation to Sex.* London: John Murray, 1871.

Gibbons, Ann. *The First Human.* New York: Doubleday, 2006.

Haile-Selassie, Yohannes; Gen Suwa; and Tim D. White. "Late Miocene Teeth from Middle Awash, Ethiopia, and Early Hominid Dental Evolution." *Science* 303 (2004): 1503–1505.

Hill, Andrew, et al. "Earliest *Homo*." *Nature* 335 (1992): 719–722.

Johanson, Donald C., and Blake Edgar. *From Lucy to Language*. New York: Simon and Schuster, 1996.

Johanson, Donald C., and Tim D. White. "A Systematic Assessment of Early African Hominids." *Science* 202 (1979): 321–330.

Johanson, Donald C., Tim D. White, and Yves Coppens. "A New Species of *Australopithecus* (Primates: Hominidae) from the Pliocene of Eastern Africa." Kirtlandia 28 (1978): 1–14.

Leakey, Louis S. B. "A New Fossil Skull from Olduvai." *Nature* 184 (1959): 491–493.

Leakey, Louis S. B., Philip V. Tobias, and John R. Napier. "A New Species of the Genus *Homo* from Olduvai Gorge." *Nature* 202 (1964): 5–7.

Leakey, Mary D., et al. "Fossil Hominids from the Laetolil Beds at Laetoli, Northern Tanzania." *Nature* 262 (1976): 460–466.

Leakey, Meave G., et al. "New Four-Million-Year-Old Hominid Species from Kanapoi and Allia Bay, Kenya." *Nature* 376 (1995): 565–571.

McBrearty, Sally, and Alison Brooks. "The Revolution That Wasn't: A New Interpretation of the Origin of Modern Human Behavior." *Journal of Human Evolution* 39, no. 5 (2000): 453–563.

Reader, John. *Missing Links: The Hunt for Earliest Man*, 2nd edition. London: Penguin Books, 1988.

Tattersall, Ian. *The Fossil Trail: How We Know What We Think We Know about Human Evolution*. Oxford: Oxford University Press, 1995.

Walker, Alan, and Richard Leakey. *The Nariokotome* Homo erectus *Skeleton*. Cambridge, MA: Harvard University Press, 1993.

Walker, Alan, et al. "2.5 Myr *Australopithecus boisei* from West of Lake Turkana, Kenya." *Nature* 322 (1986): 517–522.

White, Tim D.; Gen Suwa; and Berhane Asfaw. "*Australopithecus ramidus*, a New Species of Early Hominid from Aramis, Ethiopia." *Nature* 371, no. 6495 (1994): 306–312.

ANDREW HILL

ORIGINS OF MODERN HUMANS

In *The Descent of Man* (1871), the English naturalist (1809–1882) Charles Darwin hypothesized that Africa was humankind's evolutionary homeland because it was the continent where humans' closest relatives, the African apes, could be found. It took another fifty years, however, before fossil evidence supporting his theory began to be discovered. Before then, Europe—with the Neanderthals, "Heidelberg Man," and the spurious "Piltdown Man"—and Asia, with "Java Man," had been the foci of scientific attention concerning human ancestry. But the 1921 discovery of the Broken Hill cranium in Northern Rhodesia (present-day Zambia) and the 1924 discovery of the Taung skull (from South Africa) slowly began to give Africa its rightful paramount importance in the story of human evolution. Even so, the critical evolutionary role of the australopithecines, primitive hominids (members of the human family) mainly dating from 1.5 to 4 million years ago, was not generally accepted until at least another thirty years after that first discovery from Taung. Since then, a profusion of ancient fossils and species has been discovered, and what follows is necessarily a simple summary of what must have been a complex evolutionary story.

Even though it is now known from fossils and ancient tracks that the australopithecines were bipedal, like humans, they are not usually regarded as true humans, that is, members of the human genus, *Homo*. For that status, a brain size above the 350 to 550-milliliter volume of australopithecines and modern African apes would be expected, along with features such as a less projecting face, a more prominent nose, and a humanlike body shape. Where it could be determined, it might also be expected that other human features such as regular tool production and a relatively long period of growth and development might be present. For the australopithecines, these human features cannot definitely be recognized. But while the last australopithecines still lived in southern and eastern Africa, more advanced hominids had appeared and were living alongside them; these are usually regarded as the first humans and are assigned to the species *Homo habilis*.

HOMO HABILIS

By about 2.4 million years ago, new types of hominids had appeared in the fossil record of eastern and southern Africa. The finds are isolated and incomplete but significant, including a lower jaw from Uraha, Malawi, and the side of a cranium from Chemeron (near Baringo), Kenya. At about the same time, the first recognizable stone tools were manufactured, and these evolutionary and

COURTESY OF CHRIS STRINGER/*NATURE*

behavioral events may have marked the advent of the earliest true humans, known to scientists as *Homo habilis* ("Handy Man"). This species of the genus *Homo* was named in 1964 by Louis B. Leakey and his colleagues on the basis of fossils found at Olduvai Gorge in Tanzania, known to date to between 1.5 and 1.8 million years old. *H. habilis* was regarded as intermediate between australopithecines and *Homo sapiens*, and fragments of skull were used to estimate a brain size of about 700 milliliters, larger than those

of australopithecines and the largest-brained apes. The back teeth were large but narrow compared with those of earlier hominids.

There was immediate argument about *H. habilis*, because many scientists felt that the fossil material was not distinct enough to be placed in a separate species. Some researchers believed that it was merely an advanced australopithecine; others felt that some of the material represented an early form of another species, *Homo erectus*. It took the discovery of fossils of similar age and type from Koobi Fora in northern Kenya to produce general acceptance of such an early and primitive species of human.

The material from Koobi Fora was mostly recovered between 1969 and 1976 and includes a number of partial skulls, mandibles, and, from the same sites, a hip bone and various limb bones. In addition, there were simple stone tools, all dating from the period between about 1.6 and 2.0 million years ago. The specimens are generally known from their Kenya National Museum catalog numbers and the initials of the original site name, East Rudolf (later renamed East Turkana).

The most famous of all these fossils is KNM-ER 1470, found in 1972. This skull had a large brain (volume about 750 milliliters) and was originally dated to more than 2.5 million years ago, subsequently revised to about 1.9 million years. The braincase had a more human shape than is found in australopithecines, but the face was flat and very high, with prominent and wide australopithecine-like cheekbones. Although no teeth are preserved, the spaces for them were large by human standards. There are correspondingly large jaws and teeth in other specimens from the same levels at Koobi Fora, and some skull fragments indicate an even larger brain than in KNM-ER 1470. If hip and leg bones found in the same deposits belong to the species, they indicate that some of these very early humans were large and apparently rather similar to the later species *Homo erectus* in aspects of their body structure.

The specimens from Koobi Fora discussed so far have often been assigned to *H. habilis*. However, there are further finds from Koobi Fora that complicate the picture of early human evolution. These include specimen KNM-ER 1813, a small skull with a brain volume of only 510 milliliters, which nevertheless looks more "human" in its face and upper jaw than does 1470, and KNM-ER 1805, which has teeth like 1813, a face like 1470, a brain capacity of about 580 milliliters, and a braincase with a primitive crest along the midline—a feature otherwise only found in large australopithecines among early hominids. The meaning of this great variation in morphology is still unclear, but it may be that *H. habilis* was not the only human-like inhabitant of eastern and southern Africa about 2 million years ago.

Further evidence of this complexity has come from a more recent discovery at Olduvai of parts of a skull and a skeleton of a small-bodied hominid (OH 62) from the lowest levels, which had previously yielded *Homo habilis* fossils. Features of the fragmentary skull are similar to those of some *Homo habilis* fossils, yet the rest of the skeleton more closely resembles that of the much older australopithecine "Lucy" (*Australopithecus afarensis*) from Hadar in Ethiopia. While some experts still believe that *Homo habilis* had a very variable body size, it now seems more likely that there were at least two kinds of early *Homo*, one large and the other small, with the small species retaining australopithecine features in the limbs. One suggestion is that the large forms, such as 1470, represent another species, *Homo rudolfensis*, while the smaller ones would still be classified in the original species, *Homo habilis*. If this view is accepted, the oldest finds mentioned, from Uraha and Chemeron, would represent *H. rudolfensis*.

HOMO ERECTUS

About 1.8 million years ago, a new type of human appeared in the fossil record of eastern Africa, a species that lasted for well over a million years and also became the first human type known to have spread out of Africa to Asia. Most scientists believe that the African and Asian fossils represent a single species called *Homo erectus* ("Erect Man"), but others feel that the earliest African fossils represent a more primitive, and presumably ancestral, species called *Homo ergaster*.

If one accepts the majority view, the earliest examples of African *H. erectus* are from northern Kenya, on the previously mentioned east side (Koobi Fora) and west side (Nariokotome) of Lake Turkana. At the Koobi Fora site, two skulls (KNM-ER 3733 and 3883) and various other fragments have been found, while at Nariokotome the nearly complete skeleton of a boy (KNM-WT 15000) was discovered in 1984. These fossils are characterized by brain sizes of about 800 to 900 milliliters (considerably above those of *Homo habilis* fossils), but the braincase was relatively longer, flatter, and more angular. The browridges were prominent, but the face was less projecting than in typical *H. habilis* fossils and had a more prominent, and human, nose. The Nariokotome boy's skeleton shows that although he was perhaps only ten years old at death, he was already about 5 feet, 6 inches tall and well built. He had the long-legged but narrow-bodied build found in many of today's tropical humans, but he also had some unusual features in his spinal column and rib cage. Nevertheless, his skeleton was unmistakably that of a human.

Other examples of early *H. erectus* are known from Olduvai Gorge, where a skull dated to about 1.2 million years ago was discovered in 1960. This strongly built skull (OH 9) has a brain volume of about 1,050 milliliters, a flat forehead, and a very thick brow ridge. Later finds from Olduvai (less than 1 million years old) include jaw fragments, a robustly built hip bone and partial thigh bone (OH 28), and a small and more lightly built skull (OH 12), which represents either an extreme variant of the *erectus* type or perhaps even an entirely separate species. Elsewhere in Africa, fossils classified as *H. erectus* have been found in Kenya (Baringo), and further afield in Buia (Eritrea), Algeria (Tighenif), Morocco (Aïn Marouf, Salé, and the Thomas quarries), Ethiopia (Daka and Melka Kontoure), and South Africa (Swartkrans).

By 1.5 million years ago, *H. erectus* was also present in western and eastern Asia, with particularly rich finds dating from about 1.7 million years ago from Dmanisi in Georgia. These latter finds are primitive and varied enough to even raise fundamental issues about the supposed African origins of the species. The East Asian populations are best known from the finds of "Java Man" in the 1890s and "Peking Man" in the 1930s, although many additional finds have since been made in both Indonesia and China. The Javanese finds are mostly earlier in date, with recent evidence that some could even be close in age to the oldest African examples, at about 1.6 million years. They are robust, with relatively small brain volumes, although there is also an enigmatic sample of shin bones and skulls, lacking faces, from Ngandong (Solo) in Java, which seems to represent a late-surviving descendant form.

The East Asian finds show some consistent differences from the African fossils of *H. erectus*; the skulls are more strongly reinforced with ridges of bone, and the walls of the skulls are generally thicker. The fragmentary bones of the rest of the skeleton known from Zhoukoudian (the "Peking

Man" cave site) are strongly built, like their equivalents from Africa. One of the thigh bones found in the Javanese excavations in the 1890s looks rather more modern, but research suggests that it may be geologically younger than the *H. erectus* skulls.

Information about the way of life of *H. erectus* has been gathered from both caves and open sites. The early African and the Asian representatives used flake tools manufactured from local materials such as lava, flint, and quartz, but from 1.4 million years ago African groups produced larger, multipurpose tools, such as hand axes and cleavers. These were also used in Europe and western Asia from at least 500,000 years ago. The *Homo erectus* peoples were nomadic hunters and gatherers, although living more simply and opportunistically than any hunter-gatherers alive today. Like those of the earlier *H. habilis*, the teeth of *H. erectus* were similar to our own, albeit larger, and indicate a mixed diet of meat and plant foods.

HOMO HEIDELBERGENSIS

By about 600,000 years ago, there had been enough changes in some *Homo erectus* populations for a new species of early human to be recognized. The applicable fossil remains are often known by the unsatisfactory term "archaic *Homo sapiens*" (implying that they belong to the same species as modern humans), but it is much more likely that they represent a species distinct from both *H. erectus* and *H. sapiens*, often named *Homo heidelbergensis*, after the 1907 discovery of a lower jaw at Mauer, near Heidelberg, Germany.

This species had a larger brain (around 1,100–1,300 milliliters in volume) than *H. erectus*, with a taller, parallel-sided braincase. There were also reductions in the reinforcements of the skull and in the projection of the face in front of the braincase, an increase in the prominence of the face around the nose, and changes in the base of the skull that might indicate the presence of a vocal apparatus of modern type. Little is known of the rest of the skeleton, but what evidence there is suggests that *H. heidelbergensis* was at least as strongly built as *H. erectus*.

It is not generally agreed which particular fossils from 200,000 to 600,000 years ago actually represent *H. heidelbergensis*, although African fossils such as the skulls from Broken Hill or Kabwe (Zambia),

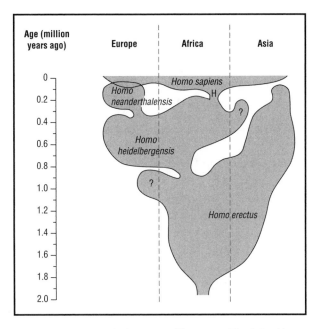

Possible evolutionary history of the genus Homo over the last two million years. The letter H represents the African origin of Homo sapiens about 200,000 years ago. COURTESY OF CHRIS STRINGER/*NATURE*

Elandsfontein (South Africa) and Bodo (Ethiopia) are usually included. Similarly, in Europe there is dispute about whether the fossils from Mauer (Germany), Vértesszöllös (Hungary), Petralona (Greece), Bilzingsleben (Germany), and Boxgrove (England) represent "advanced" *erectus*, *Homo heidelbergensis*, or ancestral Neanderthals. It appears that *H. erectus* persisted in the Far East, until at least 400,000 years ago, and the Ngandong (Solo) remains from Java may be as young as 50,000 years. In China, however, there is evidence that after 400,000 years *H. erectus* was succeeded by more advanced populations which might also represent *H. heidelbergensis*, exemplified by the skull from Dali and the partial skeleton from Jinniushan.

NEANDERTHALS AND MODERN HUMANS

By about 300,000 years ago, further evolutionary changes in *Homo heidelbergensis* led to the differentiation of a distinct lineage in Europe: that of the Neanderthals (*Homo neanderthalensis*), as recognized from sites such as Swanscombe (England), Atapuerca (Spain), and Ehringsdorf (Germany). By 100,000 years ago, the late Neanderthals displayed large brains housed in a long and low braincase, and their most distinctive feature was in their face, which was dominated by an enormous and projecting nose. The most characteristic Neanderthals were European, but closely related peoples lived in western Asia, at least as far east as Uzbekistan, and in Iraq, Syria, and Israel. The physique of the Neanderthals was ideally suited to the conditions of Ice Age Europe, yet by about 30,000 years ago they had apparently become extinct over their whole range.

The disappearance of the Neanderthals from Europe and Asia may have had much to do with the arrival of early modern people (*Homo sapiens*), who would have competed with them for the available resources, and growing climatic instability between 30,000 and 50,000 years ago may have exacerbated the situation. These first modern humans were anatomically distinct from Neanderthals, with less prominent brow ridges; higher, shorter, and more rounded skulls; shorter lower jaws with a bony chin (at best only slightly developed in some Neanderthals); and a taller, relatively narrower, and less robust skeleton.

The first modern people known in Asia, from the Israeli sites of Qafzeh and Skhul, had a way of life superficially little different from that of the Neanderthals, although there is some evidence from the structure of their skeletons that they exploited their environment more efficiently. However, thermoluminescence and electron spin resonance dating tests suggest that they are about 110,000 years old, and therefore the same age or even older than many Neanderthal fossils. If this is so, there potentially was a long period of coexistence or alternating occupation of the region by early *H. sapiens* and Neanderthals. By 40,000 years ago, however, modern people seem to have been the sole occupants left in the Middle East.

The dispersal of early modern people (the Cro-Magnons) into Europe probably occurred about 40,000 years ago, and there is more evidence of behavioral differences between Neanderthals and early modern people by this time. Although most Neanderthals are associated with Middle Paleolithic (Middle Old Stone Age) or Mousterian tool industries, the Cro-Magnons are associated with Upper Paleolithic industries. These contain narrow blade tools of stone, which could be used to work bone, antler, and ivory, and even to produce engravings and sculptures. However, some of the last Neanderthals in Europe also briefly developed tool industries with Upper Paleolithic characteristics, suggesting possible contact and even intermixture with the contemporaneous Cro-Magnons.

The ancestors of present-day Europeans, Asians, and the native populations of the American and Australian continents probably shared common ancestors within the past 80,000 years. The early modern people who reached Australia by at least 40,000 years ago must have needed boats or rafts, even when sea level was at its lowest because of water locked up in the expanded ice caps of the last Ice Age. On their way to Australia they perhaps encountered surviving archaic humans such as the dwarfed humanoid form known as *Homo floresiensis*, from the island of Flores, which may have survived until as recently as 12,000 years ago. For people to reach the Americas, it would then have been possible to walk from Asia across the land bridge between Siberia and Alaska, or to travel along a more southerly coastal route by island hopping. However, it is still uncertain whether this had happened before or after 15,000 years ago, and there is evidence that distinct populations may have been involved.

If early modern people did not evolve from the Neanderthals of Europe and Asia, where did they originate? Modern people had appeared in China at least 30,000 years ago; they arrived in Australia by boat at least 40,000 years ago. However, there are no fossils that show a convincing local evolution from more archaic predecessors, although this has been claimed by proponents of "multiregional evolution" for China and Australia.

Only Africa has credible transitional fossils between premodern and modern humans, and it is here that *Homo heidelbergensis* was apparently transformed into *Homo sapiens*. Fossil remains of modern type have been discovered that are as early as, or even older than, those in Israel. These early modern fossils are from sites such as Border Cave and Klasies Caves (South Africa), Guomde (Kenya), and Omo-Kibish and Herto (Ethiopia). The South African remains are between 70,000 and 120,000 years old, while the Guomde skull and femur and the Omo and Herto fossils are probably all more than 150,000 years old. Although they can be classified as modern in anatomy, these people still retained some primitive features and were apparently not yet fully modern in behavior. The transition from *Homo heidelbergensis* to these early *Homo sapiens* may be represented by fossils of even greater antiquity, such as the Florisbad skull from South Africa, skulls from Ngaloba (Tanzania) and Eliye Springs (Kenya), and several fossils from Djebel Irhoud (Morocco).

The way in which the evolution of modern people proceeded in Africa, and why the transition happened at all, is still uncertain. There is some evidence of an increasing sophistication in African Middle Stone Age industries, which could have promoted evolutionary change, including the beginning of symbolism and art, or following severe climatic changes, geographical isolation may have been responsible. As discussed below, genetic evidence indicates that all living people are closely related and share a common ancestor who lived in Africa during the last 300,000 years (the time range of the last *Homo heidelbergensis* and the first *Homo sapiens*).

THE "OUT OF AFRICA" MODEL AND THE "EVE HYPOTHESIS"

Most paleoanthropologists believe that *Homo erectus* was directly or indirectly ancestral to *Homo sapiens*, but the manner of the transition is one of the most hotly disputed topics in science. Two extreme views can be contrasted, although there are also a number of intermediate viewpoints.

One view is the "multiregional model," which posits that *Homo erectus* gave rise to *Homo sapiens* across its whole range, which included Africa, China, Java (Indonesia), and perhaps Europe. From this model *Homo erectus*, following its presumed African origin about 1.8 million years ago, dispersed around the Old World and in the process began to develop regional variation. This is seen as lying at the roots of modern "racial" variation, so that particular features of *Homo erectus* in a given region are believed to have persisted in local descendant populations of today. For example, Chinese *Homo erectus* specimens supposedly had the same flat faces, with prominent cheekbones, that are found in modern Asian populations. Javanese *Homo erectus* had, in contrast, robustly built cheekbones and faces that jutted out from the braincase, traits that, it is argued, are also found in recent native Australians. In Europe no definite representatives of *Homo erectus* have yet been discovered, because the fossil record does not yet extend back as far as those of Africa and Asia, but the multiregional model posits that European *Homo erectus* existed and evolved into the Neanderthals, who is turn were the ancestors of modern Europeans. Features of continuity in this European lineage supposedly include prominent noses and midfaces. The multiregional model was first articulated in detail by the German anatomist Franz Weidenreich and was developed further by the American Carleton Coon, who tended to regard the regional lineages as genetically separate.

In the twenty-first century, the model has become associated with researchers such as Milford Wolpoff in the United States and Alan Thorne in Australia, who have reemphasized the importance of gene flow between the regional lines. In fact, they regard the continuity in time and space between the various forms of *Homo erectus* and their regional descendants to be so complete that they should not be regarded as separate species but as representing only one species—*Homo sapiens*—dating back to 1.8 million years ago.

The alternative idea that *Homo sapiens* represents a distinct lineage from forms such as Asian *Homo erectus* and the Neanderthals also has a long history. The more specific idea of a recent and restricted origin for modern *Homo sapiens* was dubbed the "Garden of Eden," or "Noah's Ark," model by the American anthropologist William Howells in 1976 because of its concept that all modern human variation had a localized origin from one center (a concept comparable to the biblical Ark or the Garden of Eden). Howells did not specify the center of origin, but Africa now has the strongest claim. The consequent "Out of Africa" model posits that an evolutionary transition from the descendants of African *Homo erectus* to *Homo sapiens* took place between about 120,000 and 300,000 years ago. Part of the African stock of early modern humans then began to disperse out of the continent into adjoining regions by about 100,000 years ago. Regional ("racial") variation only developed during and after the dispersal event, which means that there was no genuine continuity of regional features between *Homo erectus* and present populations in the same areas outside of Africa.

In common with the multiregional model, it is accepted that *Homo erectus* evolved into new forms of humans in inhabited regions outside of Africa, but in contrast to that model, it is argued that these non-African lineages became extinct without evolving into modern people. Some, such as the Neanderthals, were directly replaced by the spread of modern humans into their regions. Since 2000, the "Out of Africa" theory has been bolstered by fossil and dating evidence from sites such as Omo-Kibish and Herto in Ethiopia for the existence of modern humans there more than 150,000 years ago.

In 1987, research on mitochondrial DNA (mtDNA), a special genetic material passed on by females, led to the reconstruction of a hypothetical female ancestor for all present-day human mtDNA variation. This "Eve" was believed to have lived in Africa about 200,000 years ago. Re-examination of the "Eve" research by other scientists raised doubts about the reliability of the conclusions and also emphasized that there was an ancestral population, not a single ancestor. Nevertheless, further support for an "Out of Africa" model has come from a number of other mtDNA studies and from parallel research on the male-inherited Y-chromosome, and the much more extensive nuclear DNA, which is inherited from both parents. Estimates of genetic evolutionary rates and examination of fossil remains both indicate that "racial" differences in the genes and skeleton have developed only during the last 100,000 years, in line with the "Out of Africa" model and at odds with the million-year-plus time span expected from the multiregional model. Thus, the shared features of *Homo sapiens* appear to have evolved first, in Africa, while the differences between modern populations evolved subsequently and globally.

What remains unclear, however, is whether modern human origin was entirely an African process, or whether there was some genetic input from populations outside of Africa as modern humans dispersed. While mtDNA and Y-chromosome data largely support the former idea, other DNA data are more ambiguous. The recovery of mtDNA from several Neanderthal fossils has confirmed their distinctiveness as an evolutionary lineage, with no evident sign of a genetic contribution to modern humans, but more genetic data are required to settle the question definitively.

See also **Anthropology, Social, and the Study of Africa; Archaeology and Prehistory; Leakey, Louis and Mary; Prehistory.**

BIBLIOGRAPHY

Klein, Richard G. *The Human Career: Human Biological and Cultural Origins.* Chicago: University of Chicago Press, 1999.

Klein, Richard G., and Blake Edgar. *The Dawn of Human Culture.* Chicester, U.K.: Wiley, 2002.

Lewin, Roger. *Human Evolution: An Illustrated Introduction.* Maiden, MA: Blackwell, 2005.

Lewin, Roger, and Robert Foley. *Principles of Human Evolution;* 2nd edition. Maiden, MA: Blackwell, 2004.

"New Look at Human Evolution." *Scientific American* special issue (June 2003).

Stringer, C. "Modern Human Origins: Progress and Prospects." *Philosophical Transactions of the Royal Society, London* (B) 357 (2002): 563–579

Stringer, Chris, and Peter Andrews. *The Complete World of Human Evolution.* London: Thames & Hudson, 2005.

CHRIS STRINGER

HUMAN BIOLOGICAL DIVERSITY

The distribution of biological variation in the human species is among the most contentious issues in contemporary science because of its abuse throughout modern history as a rationalization for social injustice. Though the concept of race was never clearly defined, anthropologists traditionally grouped people into hierarchically organized clusters of populations, or races. It is presently clear,

however, that such a practice does not afford an optimal description of human biodiversity.

It is obvious that human beings differ from one another, that local human populations differ from one another, and that such differences are patterned geographically. This does not indicate, however, that the human species is naturally partitionable into a fairly small group of reasonably discrete races, nor how such entities might be distinguished from one another. What is clear, rather, is that populations of humans are each variable, and are generally more similar to populations nearby than to populations far away. Not only are local populations the most natural units of the human species, but they are also bioculturally constituted—the result of marriage patterns, migrations, wars, trade, and adoption. The human species is best understood biologically "as constituting a widespread network of more-or-less interrelated, ecologically adapted and functional entities" (Weiner 1957).

Further, the identification of significant clusters of human populations is not itself a strictly biological enterprise, for many areas are biologically heterogeneous, and cultural classifications (especially linguistic) are commonly imposed upon human populations as well. Sub-Saharan Africa contains an extraordinary amount of human biological diversity—by some measures, more than the rest of the human species. The distribution of these human populations is the result of biological, demographic, and historical forces, and has resulted in a complex geographical pattern.

In 1758 a Swedish naturalist formalized the classification of the human species into subspecies (later made equivalent to races), grouping all Africans together and juxtaposing them against Europeans, Asians, and Americans. The criteria were often nonbiological, however, using stereotypes of dress, law, and personality. Although subsequent generations of anthropologists invoked more obviously constitutionally based features when attempting to formalize natural divisions of the species, they nevertheless generally ignored the real extent of African biological diversity and presented Africans as a homogeneous biological entity, often derived from a stereotype.

Explorers and anthropologists undermined the idea that the diverse aboriginal peoples of Africa could readily be subsumed under a single biological category. Africa contains both the shortest and the tallest peoples of the world, as well as the greatest breadth of skin color and body build. The diverse biological populations of Africa can be grossly contrasted, although the specific number of groups is not intended to be significant, and it must be borne in mind that considerable heterogeneity exists within each of these categories and in each of these areas: 1) The North Africans generally resemble other Mediterranean peoples; 2) West-Central Africans are most deeply pigmented; 3) Peoples of eastern Africa range from resembling other populations of the Middle East to the tall, thin, dark peoples of the Nile Valley, and encompass peoples of varying complexion, facial features, and body builds; 4) Pygmy denotes the short-statured people of the central African rainforest; and 5) Khoesan designates the lighter-skinned and small-jawed aboriginal peoples of southern Africa. It should be noted when making these distinctions that these may not be biologically equivalent categories. They are neither qualitative identifiers of individuals nor representations of distinct differences among primordial populations. These categories are simply constructs to help visualize the contrasts among indigenous Africans drawn from different parts of the continent, and to highlight the considerable biological diversity present.

Some populations tend to be characterized by particular anatomical or genetic variations, but these are generally neither universal within a given area nor distinct from populations in other areas. Rather, biological traits are found to be distributed as clines, or gradients. This is true regardless of whether the feature under study is a complex phenotype or a specific allele.

Skin color is clinally distributed, such that aboriginal populations far from the equator tend to be more lightly pigmented than those close to the equator. Likewise, specific alleles, such as that for sickle-cell anemia, reach frequencies of up to 25 percent in malarial regions of western Africa, gradually descending as one proceeds outward.

MICROEVOLUTIONARY PROCESSES IN HUMAN POPULATIONS

The detectable patterns of biological variation across human populations are due to the operation of four forces, each of which has different effects upon the human biological landscape. The first is

natural selection, the more efficient survival or proliferation of people with particular inherited qualities. If such a bias in survival or reproduction is consistent over many generations, the composition of the population will gradually reflect the preponderance of those favored qualities. Ultimately, this is the way that biological populations evolve adaptively and come to track the demands of their environment. This is also a manner by which populations come to differ from other populations, adapting to other local conditions. Natural selection is generally invoked to explain the stature of pygmies, the linear body build of Nilotics, and the clinal variation in skin color. Recent studies have also shown that the ability to digest milk through adulthood, or lactase persistence, is caused by a genetic change that is far more common in East African dairying peoples than in other African populations.

The second force is genetic drift, the propensity for gene pools to diverge from each other purely at random. Here, populations become biologically differentiated from one another, but in nonadaptive ways, for these genetic changes do not result in the gene pool's being molded to track its environment. These genetic changes are as likely to be harmful as they are to be beneficial, although they are generally benign. Genetic drift operates in inverse proportion to the size of the population, for small populations will have the largest stochastic fluctuations from the mathematical expectations of population genetics. Here, features such as flatness of the face, shape of the nose, and many other qualities that vary without providing a significant advantage for their bearers may be the result of genetic drift.

The third force is gene flow, or the result of intermarriage between populations. Here the net effect is to make neighboring populations genetically similar to one another in adaptive or nonadaptive ways, and to increase the diversity within any particular population.

The last force is cultural selection, by which populations with nongenetic advantages (generally technological) expand demographically at the expense of other indigenous populations. Although the technology responsible for this spread is not a genetic feature, it results in the proliferation of the people bearing it and consequently mimics natural selection in promoting the survival and reproduction of people possessing certain cultural traits at the expense of other populations. Obviously, the biological peculiarities borne by those peoples will spread along with their technologies.

The clinal pattern of variation is principally the result of two factors: first, the gradual variation in climate and geography to which human populations adapt, and second, gene flow.

GENETIC VARIATION IN AFRICA

The study of biological variation is impeded by a general lack of historical knowledge of sufficient depth over most of the world. Without such knowledge it is often difficult to tell whether a particular biological feature found in a particular area requires an adaptive explanation, a nonadaptive explanation, or is simply the result of sociohistorical (nonbiological) processes.

Perhaps the greatest difficulty, however, is the biologically ephemeral nature of the cultural categories in which human groups identify themselves. These categories are continually submerged and reinvented, which creates a sampling problem for the biologist interested in studying intergroup differences: who biologically represents the named group, and what does the group itself represent? Two paradigmatic cases from Africa demonstrate this.

Aboriginal populations of Southern Africa are classically designated by the linguistic category Khoesan subsuming Hottentots (Khoe) and Bushmen (San). Their history prior to the last few centuries is conjectural, and their history in early colonial times is controversial. The Khoe are noteworthy in the classical literature for steatopygia (enlarged buttocks) and lengthening of the labia in females—attributes that were of sufficient interest in the early 1800s to have merited the 1817 dissection of Saartje Baartman (1789–1815), the so-called Hottentot Venus, by Georges Cuvier (1769–1832), the leading anatomist in France. Although the Khoe and San cluster together linguistically, historically high amounts and complex patterns of gene flow result in discovering the Khoe to be more genetically similar to the Bantu speakers to the north than to the San. Thus, the category Khoesan is a construct and not a valid representation of the true patterns of biological similarity of the contemporary peoples.

If the Khoesan exemplify the constructed fusion of cultural groups in contrast to their patterns of biological differentiation, the Hutu and Tutsi of Rwanda exemplify the opposite, the constructed division of peoples in contrast to their biological or genetic identity. Again, generations of gene flow obliterated whatever clear-cut physical distinctions may have once existed between these two Bantu peoples—renowned to be height, body build, and facial features. With a spectrum of physical variation in the peoples, Belgian authorities legally mandated ethnic affiliation in the 1920s, based on economic criteria. Formal and discrete social divisions were consequently imposed upon ambiguous biological distinctions. To some extent, the permeability of these categories in the intervening decades helped to reify the biological distinctions, generating a taller elite and a shorter underclass, but with little relation to the gene pools that had existed a few centuries ago. The social categories are thus real, but there is little if any detectable genetic differentiation between Hutu and Tutsi.

THE INTERPRETATION OF GENETIC DATA

Surprisingly, there is little systematic data available on the peoples of Africa. As a result, much of what exists involves unjustifiable generalization. For example, in an ostensibly global study, Pygmies from Democratic Republic of the Congo and the Central African Republic were presented as representing Africa.

Another major problem is typology. The earliest genetic studies were carried out on the classic ABO blood group markers, now known to be coded by a single gene on chromosome 9. The three major alleles are present in all populations of the world, with the exception of some New World populations, which appear to have lost B. Because nonhuman primates possess this polymorphism, and nearly all known human populations do, may easily be inferred that all ancestral human populations were polymorphic as well. This is, however, not the way the work was originally interpreted. Geneticists assumed genetic purity of ancestral populations and consequently imaginatively reconstructed a primordially *O* human species invaded by an *A* race from northern Europe and a *B* race from south Asia.

There seems to be no basis on which to infer the interbreeding of genetically homogeneous archaic races as the cause of present-day polymorphisms. It appears as though many human polymorphisms are ancient (such as ABO) and have been carried through the biohistory of the human species for hundreds of thousands of years. The complex processes of microevolution must be invoked to explain the current distribution of these variations.

Unfortunately, it is still common to find geneticists naively treating the polymorphic genes in a typological manner. Thus, an allele whose frequency ranges from 30 percent to 80 percent in a small sample of Africans, and 10 percent to 20 percent in a small sample of Europeans, casually becomes an African allele, and one found in 20 percent to 60 percent of Europeans sampled, but in less than 10 percent of Africans sampled, becomes a Caucasoid allele.

From cavalier treatment of such data emerge comparably cavalier conclusions, such as scientifically inferring that Caucasians are the admixed products of 65 percent African and 35 percent Asian genetic contributions. Unfortunately, the technologically most sophisticated data are often bound to the most conceptually primitive interpretations. This is probably the major handicap to biological studies of African populations in the early twenty-first century.

A related set of problems involves the interpretation of patterns in the genetic data. Because the analytic units of population genetics are populations, sampling is commonly done for tribes, which has the consequence of reifying them as stable genetic entities. The odd properties of mitochondrial DNA have made it a valuable commodity for companies marketing recreational genetic services, some of which match an American client's DNA to that of Africans, although the significance of such a match, and its relationship to the client's ancestry, may be far from clear. Finally, the relationship between population genetic patterns and ethnohistory may be far more complex than geneticists commonly assume.

MITOCHONDRIAL EVE

One of the most influential studies of the 1980s was the genetic survey of the small bit of DNA possessed by a subcellular organelle known as the mitochondrion. Passed on from mother to child (rather than biparentally, as nuclear or Mendelian genes are), mitochondrial DNA, or mtDNA, has several other significant properties: it accumulates mutations rapidly and thus will detect differences among populations; it is easy to isolate and study; and it is inherited as a single unit. Studies indicated that Africans subsumed more genetic diversity than Europeans or Asians. This was initially interpreted as evidence that the human lineage originated in Africa, but it is also compatible with other interpretations, such as the idea that for most of their existence, human populations in Africa were generally larger than those elsewhere.

Mitochondrial Eve was the name given to the African possessor of the hypothetical ancestral DNA sequence from which all other modern mtDNA sequences have evolved. In its crudest form, a scientific origin myth of the 1980s held that Mitochondrial Eve was the founder of the modern human lineage in Africa, and her descendants spread across Europe and Asia 200,000 years ago, supplanting the archaic aboriginal populations of those continents. The relationship between the ancestral mtDNA sequence and the ancestral population of modern human beings is, however, exceedingly unclear.

BIOLOGICAL IMPLICATIONS OF OUT OF AFRICA

Contemporary interpretations of genetic diversity acknowledge three things. First, if compared to the genetic diversity encountered in humans to that encountered in their closest relatives, the apes, humans are much more similar genetically to one another than the apes are to their conspecifics. Second, there is more genetic diversity among Africans than among Europeans or Asians. And third, the genetic variation in Europe and Asia appears to be a subset of the African diversity, and thus appears to have originated in Africa.

Nuclear DNA can be analyzed as haplotypes, that is, as a physically contiguous series of variable genetic sites. For example, two genes, A and B, can be imagined to be located nearby one another on a specific human chromosome. Over time, mutations occur and spread throughout the population, so at some later time there might be two variants of A (A1 and A2), and four variants of B (B1, B2, B3, and B4). There are thus eight possible haplotypes:

A1B1, A1B2, A1B3, A1B4, A2B1, A2B2, A2B3, and A2B4. In general, there is a considerably more restricted range of haplotypes in populations outside of Africa, and a fuller range of haplotypes within sub-Saharan Africa. The simplest interpretation is that the restricted range of variation outside Africa is a result of comparatively recent origin of these populations, from a subset of the diversity still found in contemporary Africans, in harmony with the mitochondrial Eve story.

The interpretations of these data, however, are still somewhat primitive, as it is also clear that different processes could account for these patterns. A regimen of strong selection would also reduce genetic variation. The correctness these interpretations hinges on the ability to infer demographic properties of the prehistoric populations of Africa—notably, their size, mobility, and migration rates.

The fossil record suggests the development of modern human features about 200,000 years ago, first in Africa, then elsewhere. Modern human features, however, incorporate a general overall reduction in skeletal robusticity, which may not be entirely genetic in origin and may instead be related to lifestyle. Anatomically, modern humans do not appear to have been so different from archaic humans as to preclude the possibility of interbreeding. Indeed, in some parts of the world a few specific skeletal features of modern populations are arguably found in the archaic fossils. Whether this represents genetic continuity or similar selective pressures acting on different populations in the same place is unclear.

See also **Archaeology and Prehistory: Historical; Baartman, Sara; Knowledge: Overview; Prehistory; Research.**

BIBLIOGRAPHY

Ayala, Francisco J. "The Myth of Eve: Molecular Biology and Human Origins." *Science* 270 (1995): 1930–1936.

Bowcock, Anne M., et al. "Drift, Admixture, and Selection in Human Evolution: A Study with DNA Polymorphisms." *Proceedings of the National Academy of Sciences* 88 (1991): 839–843.

Cann, Rebecca L.; Mark Stoneking; and Allan C. Wilson. "Mitochondrial DNA and Human Evolution." *Nature* 325 (1987): 31–36.

Cavalli-Sforza, Luigi Luca; Paolo Menozzi; and Alberto Piazza. *The History and Geography of Human Genes.* Princeton, New Jersey: Princeton University Press, 1994.

Cuvier, Georges. "Extrait d'observations faites sur le cadavre d'une femme connue à Paris et à Londres sous le nom de Vénus Hottentotte." *Mémoires du Muséum d'Histoire Naturelle* 3 (1817): 259–274.

Hiernaux, Jean. *The People of Africa.* London: Weidenfeld and Nicholson, 1974.

MacEachern, S. "Genes, Tribes, and African History." *Current Anthropology* 41 (2000): 357–384.

Marks, Jonathan. "The Legacy of Serological Studies in American Physical Anthropology." *History and Philosophy of the Life Sciences* 18 (1997): 345–362.

Relethford, John H. "Genetics and Modern Human Origins." *Evolutionary Anthropology* 5 (1996): 53–63.

Spurdle, Amanda B.; M. F. Hammer; and T. Jenkins. "The Y Alu Polymorphism in Southern African Populations and Its Relationship to Other Y-Specific Polymorphisms." *American Journal of Human Genetics* 54 (1994): 319–330.

Tishkoff, Sarah., et al. "Convergent Adaptation of Human Lactase Persistence in Africa and Europe." *Nature Genetics* 39 (2007): 31–40.

Weiner, Joseph S. "Physical Anthropology: An Appraisal." *American Scientist* 45 (1957): 79–87.

JONATHAN MARKS

HUMAN RIGHTS. Human rights are defined in international law as rights that every individual possesses equally with every other individual, merely by virtue of being human; such rights do not depend on one's social status, accomplishments, or fulfilment of social duties, except to respect others' rights. Internationally recognized human rights include civil, political, economic, cultural, and social rights. This entry uses international law as the standard for the discussion of human rights in Africa.

In the early decades of independence, there was much debate about whether the international standard of human rights should apply to Africa. Some scholars, activists, and politicians argued that human rights were a Western colonial imposition, reflecting a preoccupation with individual autonomy that was at odds with Africans' traditional embeddedness in the community. Others argued that different cultures evolved different concepts of human rights, and

African concepts of rights were not synonymous with Western or "universal" concepts. The West, these Africans argued, stressed rights, whereas Africans stressed duties and obligations to others. Influenced by their contact with socialism or Marxism, some African thinkers prioritized the collective right to economic progress or development over individual civil and political rights. Nevertheless, many African participants in this debate accepted the international standard and advocated protection of individual civil and political rights, regardless of African tradition or the imperative to develop.

The African human rights record during the early postindependence period (c. 1960 to 1990) was very poor. This was to be expected in an economically deprived continent in which the state system was newly established. The need for economic development took priority over protection of human rights.

After 1990, however, many states began to democratize and pay more attention to civil and political rights as well as to economic development. Nevertheless, even these states found it very difficult to protect their citizens' economic rights.

AFRICAN CHARTER OF HUMAN AND PEOPLES' RIGHTS

This regional Charter of the then–Organization of African Unity (OAU), later renamed the African Union, entered into force in 1986. By 2005 it had been signed or ratified by all fifty-three of the African Union's member states. It adds indigenous force to the 1948 United Nations' Universal Declaration of Human Rights and other international human-rights documents. Of these, the two most important are the International Covenant on Civil and Political Rights and the International Covenant on Economic, Social, and Cultural Rights, ratified as of June 9, 2004, by forty-nine and fifty-one African states, respectively. In 1987 the OAU established an African Commission on Human and Peoples' Rights, whose role is to supervise implementation of the charter. A protocol to establish an African Court of Human Rights was agreed upon in January 2004, but as of October 2005 the court had not yet been set up.

The African Charter contains several unique features, some of which reflect the communitarian orientation of many Africa thinkers about human

rights. The charter stresses economic rights and the right to development. Until the independence of the last colonized country, Namibia, in 1990, a major human rights preoccupation of the OAU was the collective right to self-determination. The charter also includes clauses on individuals' duties to the family, community, and state.

THE RIGHT TO LIFE

The most basic human right is the right to life. The worst human rights abuses in Africa are, therefore, found in situations of civil and international war, genocide and famine, of which only some examples can be offered here. In Uganda, under the rule of Idi Amin (1972–1979) and the second regime of Milton Obote (1981–1985), perhaps half a million people died. In 1994 extremist elements of the majority Hutu in Rwanda committed a full-scale genocide of ethnic Tutsi: upwards of one million Tutsi and tens of thousands of Hutu who opposed the genocide were murdered. The Rwanda genocide was followed by an international war in the Great Lakes region, centered in Congo, where by 2005 an estimated 3.8 million people had been killed. An estimated 2 million people died in war between Southern and Northern Sudan, from 1955 to 1972 and again from 1983 to 2004. In 2003, as peace was being negotiated between the South and the North, "Arab" militias in the Darfur region of western Sudan began mass slaughter of "Africans," apparently with the support of the central government.

During the Cold War the Soviet Union, the United States, and some members of the North Atlantic Treaty Organization flooded Africa with weapons. In Angola and Mozambique, long struggles between different factions wishing to take over from the Portuguese colonizers were exacerbated by Cold War rivalries. Other civil wars were caused by political or military manipulations of ethnic hostilities or by favoritism toward one particular ethnic group. In the 1990s, brutal civil wars, sometimes fought by criminal gangs, caused the breakdown of both state and civil society in Sierra Leone and Liberia; by 2002, civil war also threatened the previously stable Côte d'Ivoire.

The right to life implies respect for the right to food, which is most severely undermined by famine. Famines were often the result of warfare or political decisions. In the 1980s the Marxist regime in Ethiopia forcibly relocated members of rebel ethnic groups from food-productive to drought-ridden areas. In Somalia 300,000 people died of war-induced famine in the early 1990s. In the early twenty-first century, state-induced malnourishment, if not outright famine, occurred in Zimbabwe, where President Robert Mugabe forcibly "redistributed" white-owned land, causing massive disruption of food production and unemployment of farm workers; he also withheld food from Zimbabwans who supported the political opposition.

The OAU Refugee Convention, which preceded the Human Rights Charter, entered into force in 1974. In 2004 there were more than 3 million refugees and close to 14 million displaced persons in Africa. Many African states willingly bore the extremely high costs of supporting refugees, with some assistance from the United Nations High Commission for Refugees, other United Nations organizations, and many private international organizations.

CIVIL AND POLITICAL RIGHTS

Civil and political rights include inter alia freedom from arbitrary arrest, torture, or slavery; the right to legal due process; the right to vote; the right to participate in government; freedom of religion; freedom of the press; trade union rights; and citizenship rights.

Torture and arbitrary execution were widespread in Africa in the first three decades after independence, affecting not only political prisoners but also common criminals. Prison conditions were dreadful, partly because governments lacked resources to properly maintain prisons: prisoners often died of starvation or preventable disease. In other instances, governments deliberately underfunded prisons because the resulting conditions were deemed appropriate for criminals and political opponents. After 1990 civil society advocates for prisoners' rights emerged in some countries. A new openness to freedom of speech, assembly, and the media reduced the rate of political imprisonment.

Slavery has been outlawed in international law since 1926, yet in Mauritania there was widespread de facto enslavement of hundreds of thousands of black Africans by lighter-skinned "Arabs," well into the early twenty-first century. Some southerners

were taken as slaves by northerners during the Sudanese civil war.

From the independence era to about 1990 most countries were governed by military rulers, one-party regimes, or personal dictators, ranging from the relatively benign, such as Jomo Kenyatta in Kenya (1963–1978) to the extremely abusive, such as Mobutu Sese Seko in Zaire/Congo (1965–1997). Only a few countries, notably Senegal and Botswana, practiced continuous multiparty democracy.

Dissidents in some countries, such as Guinea, Zaire, and Malawi, could expect arbitrary arrest, torture, and imprisonment without trial. Preventive detention laws, frequently holdovers from colonial rule, were used to repress political debate. In most countries the press was censored, judiciaries were at best semifree, and judges were frequently killed, imprisoned, or exiled. Trade unions were usually suppressed or incorporated into state labor organizations.

Migrants from one African country to another were often denied rights to land, employment, and political participation. Some mass expulsions from one country to another occurred, usually as a result of political quarrels or popular pressures for job protection. As countries democratized in the 1990s, quarrels began in some countries over which groups were citizens and which residents could vote.

Freedom of religion was generally upheld, although in several countries small Christian sects such as the Jehovah's Witnesses were banned. Sudan and Nigeria introduced conservative Islamic (*shari'a*) law in 1983, to be applied to non-Muslim as well as Muslim citizens; elsewhere, social despair fed Christian-Muslim hostility. Some states of Northern Nigeria introduced *shari'a* in the 1990s or early twenty-first century, sometimes also applying it to non-Muslims.

In the late 1980s, internal pressures resulted in what was hoped to be a continental transition to democracy. Simultaneously, the end of the Cold War meant that Western powers had fewer interests in propping up abusive but pro-Western rulers. Russia, the successor state to the Soviet Union, had no further significant interest in Africa. International financial institutions and individual Western governments began to demand moves to democracy, rule of law, and human rights as conditions for foreign aid.

Thus, in the 1990s and early twenty-first century many countries, such as Nigeria, Tanzania, and Zambia, made the transition to formal multiparty democracy. Even formerly war-torn areas such as Angola and Mozambique followed the multiparty path. But in some cases, democratically elected rulers became as corrupt as the dictators they had succeeded.

In South Africa, the apartheid system, which denied human rights to everyone not classified as "white," was abolished in 1991. The first elections based on universal suffrage were held in 1994. By 2005 multiparty democracy and civil and political rights appeared firmly entrenched in South Africa, although crime rates were extremely high and violence against women was endemic. Poverty and unemployment also remained distressingly high.

ECONOMIC RIGHTS

Economic rights include inter alia the rights to food, health care, education, and an adequate standard of living. The view formerly popular in Africa that economic rights must precede the entrenchment of civil and political rights had largely disappeared by about 1990: the relevance of civil and political rights to the protection of universal economic rights was generally acknowledged. Severe economic problems, however, continued to inhibit the possibility of everyone's enjoying fundamental economic rights. Indigenous African economies had been undermined in the late nineteenth and early twentieth centuries by colonialists who destroyed intra-African trade; replaced subsistence agriculture with production of export crops such as cocoa, tea and coffee; and introduced labor migration to towns and mines. After independence many governments adopted economic policies that did more harm than good. Overinvestment in state-owned corporations and underpayment of peasants for food and cash crops undermined indigenous entrepreneurship. Export-oriented agriculture encountered highly competitive world markets, while industrialization failed because of lack of expertise, technology, and infrastructure.

One result of these policies was declining rates of growth in gross national product; in sub-Saharan Africa as a whole, the gross national product declined by 1.2 percent annually from 1980 to 1991. Burgeoning population growth rates exacerbated ecological devastation, especially deforestation and overuse of fertile lands. Structural adjustment programs imposed by international financial institutions as conditions for development aid resulted in decreased government spending on education and health and drastically reduced employment opportunities in the public sector. These disadvantages were partially offset in some countries by increased producer prices for food and export crops, and by new opportunities for entrepreneurs and exporters.

Foreign aid donors and international financial institutions promoted market economies, on the assumption that market economies would generate surpluses that could be used to protect citizens' economic rights. But by the early twenty-first century, Africa was still struggling to make profits in the global economy. Although African states joined the World Trade Organization, they could not bargain on equal terms with stronger states. Attempts to export African products floundered because of tariff barriers in developed countries and subsidized production of crops such as cotton that Africa might otherwise have been able to sell. Africa lacked professional skills (in part because many professionals had gone into exile to escape political persecution and/or economic decline), communications technology, and computer capacity. Debt relief did assist some poor countries, with massive relief announced, but not yet delivered, by wealthier countries in 2005.

Despite these severe difficulties, during the first three decades of independence the continent witnessed improvements in the basic material quality of life. Life expectancy increased from 39 years in 1960 to 51 years in 1991; the adult illiteracy rate fell from 84 percent in 1960 to 50 percent in 1991; and infant mortality fell from 144 deaths per thousand in 1970 to 104 in 1991. But in the last decade of the twentieth century many of these improvements were eroded, in part because of HIV/AIDS, but also because of continued severe threats to the right to health from such diseases as malaria and tuberculosis. By 2005 life expectancy across the continent had not increased, remaining at 51.2 years. For most sub-Saharan countries, the probability at birth that a child born between 2000 and 2005 would not survive to age 40 was between 25 and 75 percent. By 2005 West Africa had yet to experience HIV/AIDS' peak, while in East and Central Africa national infection rates were as high as 25 to 35 percent. While there were international efforts to control the disease, American promotion of abstinence over condom use encouraged its spread. President Mbeki of South Africa refused to acknowledge the seriousness of HIV/AIDS for some years, thus undermining early attempts to control the disease.

RIGHTS OF SOCIALLY MARGINALIZED GROUPS

Almost everywhere in Africa, women's political rights were formally equal to men's, but women were not well incorporated into the political process. By June 2004, for example, fifty-one African countries had signed the United Nations' Convention on the Elimination of All Forms of Discrimination against Women (1979). Yet ever since the colonial period, as the market economy replaced subsistence agriculture and land was registered as male property, women had lost much of their traditional authority, status, and security.

Within the household, women continued to be subordinate to men. In those countries protecting *shari'a* law, women did not enjoy equal legal rights with men, nor did customary and Europeanized legal systems necessarily grant equality to women. In the late 1980s and early 1990s, as more women had access to higher education, women leaders began to mobilize against domestic violence, unequal inheritance rights, and traditional customs such as child betrothal. Through health and educational campaigns, women activists and governments tried to eliminate female genital mutilation. In 2003 the OAU added a Protocol on the Rights of Women to the African Charter: by August 2005, however, the protocol had not yet entered into force, as it had received only twelve of the necessary fifteen state ratifications.

In the 1990s and beyond, activists and policymakers began to focus on children's rights. In some war-torn countries, rebel groups recruited or kidnapped children: boys were used as soldiers and torturers, while girls performed domestic labor, were abused as sex slaves, and were also used as soldiers. More attention was paid to child labor in household and farm production, as well as to sale of children to work on plantations producing cash crops such as cocoa. The African Charter on the Rights and Welfare of the Child entered into force in 1999, and by 2005 thirty-seven countries had ratified it.

Rights for gays and lesbians faced considerable hostility, although in South Africa their rights were entrenched in the constitution. Elsewhere, as in Namibia and Zimbabwe, politicians denounced gay and lesbian rights in attempts to foment popular hostility against an allegedly imperialist, culturally insensitive Western human rights agenda. Nevertheless, a community of gay and lesbian human rights activists emerged.

THE HUMAN RIGHTS MOVEMENT

Although both during and after the colonial period large numbers of Africans advocated human rights, the movement was hampered during the first three decades of independence by severe political repression, resulting in death, torture, imprisonment, and exile for hundreds of thousands of people. During these decades, those sectors of society most concerned with human rights were academics and students; professionals, especially lawyers; and leaders of Christian churches. A much larger segment of the populace engaged in human rights advocacy in the 1990s and beyond. Many indigenous human rights organizations were formed, and other citizen organizations were increasingly involved in human rights campaigns.

Internationally, several influential organizations such as Africa Watch and African Rights were formed in the late 1980s and early 1990s. These monitoring, reporting, and advocacy organizations both cooperated with and protected African human rights actors. But there were concerns that foreign governments, independent foundations, and nongovernmental organizations often set the agenda for African civil society groups, and that employment in organizations funded by foreigners simply became an attractive career option, regardless of an individual's commitment to human rights.

See also **Amin Dada, Idi; Apartheid; Cold War; Government: Military; Kenyatta, Jomo; Mobutu Sese Seko; Mugabe, Robert; Obote, Milton; Organization of African Unity; Refugees; Sudan: Wars; United Nations; Warfare: Civil Wars.**

BIBLIOGRAPHY

An-Na'im, Abdullahi Ahmed, ed. *Human Rights under African Constitutions: Realizing the Promise for*

Ourselves. Philadelphia: University of Pennsylvania Press, 2003.

Center for Human Rights, University of Pretoria. *Compendium of Key Human Rights Documents of the African Union.* Pretoria, South Africa: Pretoria University Law Press, 2005.

Dunton, Chris, and Mai Palmberg, *Human Rights and Homosexuality in Southern Africa.* Uppsala: Nordiska Africaininstituet, 1996.

Howard, Rhoda E. *Human Rights in Commonwealth Africa.* Totowa, NJ: Rowman and Littlefield, 1986.

Ibhawoh, Bonny. *Imperialism and Human Rights: Colonial Discourses of Rights and Liberties in African History.* Albany: State University of New York Press, 2006.

Murray, Rachel. *Human Rights in Africa: From the OAU to the African Union.* Cambridge, U.K.: Cambridge University Press, 2004.

Mutua, Makau. *Human Rights: A Political and Cultural Critique.* Philadelphia: University of Pennsylvania Press, 2002.

Shivji, Issa G. *The Concept of Human Rights in Africa.* London: CODESRIA Book Series, 1989.

Welch, Claude E., Jr. *Protecting Human Rights in Africa: Strategies and Roles of Non-Governmental Organizations.* Philadelphia: University of Pennsylvania Press, 1995.

Wiredu, Kwasi. *Cultural Universals and Particulars: An African Perspective.* Bloomington: Indiana University Press, 1996.

RHODA E. HOWARD-HASSMANN

HUNTING, SPORT. *See* Wildlife: Hunting, Sport.

HUTU. *See* Burundi; Rwanda.

HYDROLOGY.

Africa is the world's second largest continent after Asia, having an area of more than 11 million square miles, approximately 20 percent of the earth's land surface. It is a continent of climatic, and hydrological extremes, extending as it does from the southern Mediterranean at 37 degrees North to its southern tip, the Cape of Good Hope at 35 degrees South. The climate and hydrology of Africa are complex, being affected by global pressure and wind fields (the northeasterly and southeasterly trades), by sea surface temperatures and currents in the Atlantic Ocean to the west and Indian Ocean to the east, and by the seasonally north and southward migration of the sun across the equator. A key feature of sub-Saharan Africa's climate is the Intertropical Convergence Zone (ITCZ), a trough of low pressure between northerly and southerly air masses that migrates northward and southward following the sun's migration. Space does not permit a full explanation of the complexities of the ITCZ, but readers are referred to numerous references on the climatology of Africa. Figure 1 illustrates the position of the ITCZ in January and July and its impact upon rain-bearing winds.

The seasonal migration of the ITCZ has a profound effect upon the nature and timing of rainfall across Africa, with some parts of the continent near the equator having either rainfall in most months, or two separate wet seasons; one as the ITCZ passes toward the north, and a second as it returns southward. However, other regions have just one rainy season during summer months, with much of southern Africa receiving the bulk of its rainfall (more than 70 to 85%) during November to March or April, and parts of northeastern Africa getting most of its rainfall during June to August. There are many transitional zones where regions experience two rainfall seasons, although one is generally wetter than the secondary season.

This complex rainfall seasonality has a marked effect upon river flows because of the effects of evaporation on soil moisture. Evaporation is relatively conservative, varying little from year to year, whereas annual rainfalls are generally variable. Given an annual rainfall of 40 inches for example, where perhaps 80 percent of this were to occur in a single four- to five-month rainfall season, potential evaporation losses might typically be 5 to 6 inches per month, or some 24 to 31 inches over the wet season, leaving perhaps 8 to 15 inches for groundwater recharge and streamflow. However, in two rainfall season regions, with the same annual rainfall occurring over perhaps seven to nine months, evaporation effects are more marked, soil moisture deficits will absorb more of the rainfall, and groundwater recharge and streamflow will be significantly less.

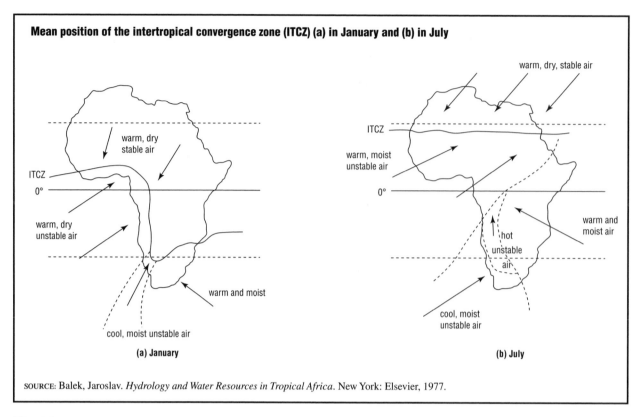

Mean position of the intertropical convergence zone (ITCZ) (a) in January and (b) in July

warm, dry
stable air

ITCZ

0°

warm, dry
unstable air

warm and moist

cool, moist unstable air

(a) January

warm, dry, stable air

ITCZ

warm, moist
unstable air

0°

hot
unstable
air

warm and
moist air

cool, moist
unstable air

(b) July

SOURCE: Balek, Jaroslav. *Hydrology and Water Resources in Tropical Africa.* New York: Elsevier, 1977.

Figure 1.

The variability of annual rainfall over Africa shows the huge regions of northern Africa, including the Sahara, with annual totals of less than 4 inches, and also the large zone of West and Central Africa where totals of 40 to 49 inches occur. The variability of seasonal rainfall and its spatial variability was illustrated by John V. Sutcliffe and D. G. Knott (1987), who considered rainfall along a south to north transect from Abidjan at 5 degrees North to Timbouctou at 16 degrees North in West Africa. A diagram from this paper, reproduced here as Figure 2(a), shows how annual average rainfall decreases from more than 78 inches near the coast to less than 8 inches some 807 miles to the north. The seasonal distribution of rainfall is shown in Figure 2(b), where the changing pattern in response to the migration of the ITCZ is apparent.

Another key feature of rainfall, and resulting runoff, over much of Africa is its extreme variability from year to year, with Makindu in Kenya being a prime example; recorded annual rainfalls have ranged from 2 inches to 77 inches. This variability may well be influenced by external global factors such as sea surface temperatures in the Atlantic and Indian Oceans, and by *El Niño* and *La Niña* in the eastern Pacific, and by the North Atlantic Oscillation. The marked variability in rainfall over much of Africa is one of the causes of the well-publicized devastating droughts that have affected many countries over the years; not only are annual rainfall totals variable, the distribution of annual totals is highly skewed, with there being many more years with below average rainfall than years above average. In a heavily skewed distribution, the mean is a poor indicator of "normal" conditions, as it is "dragged up" above the "norm" by occasional very high values that are many times larger than average. This is illustrated in Figure 3, where the majority of years have rainfall totals less than the mean, and hence the mode, what might be termed a "normal" annual rainfall, being significantly less than the mean, or arithmetic average. This skewed distribution of annual rainfall totals is even more marked in the case of annual runoff totals, particularly in drier regions, with the relationship between rainfall and runoff being markedly nonlinear..

The average annual rainfall over Africa as a whole is 27 inches, but there are huge disparities between

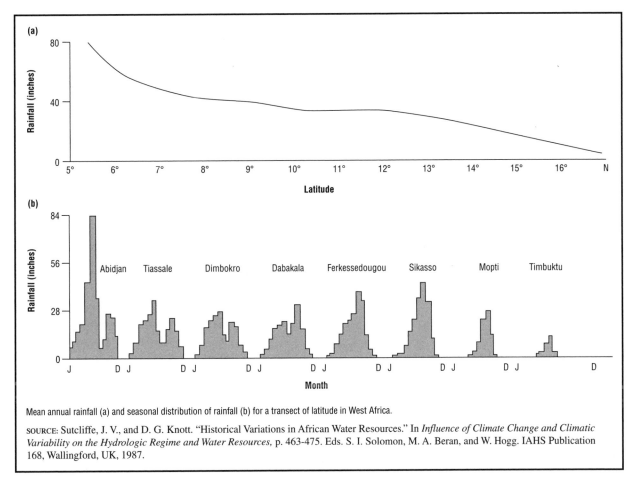

(a)

Rainfall (inches)

Latitude

(b)

Rainfall (inches)

Abidjan   Tiassale   Dimbokro   Dabakala   Ferkessedougou   Sikasso   Mopti   Timbuktu

Month

Mean annual rainfall (a) and seasonal distribution of rainfall (b) for a transect of latitude in West Africa.

SOURCE: Sutcliffe, J. V., and D. G. Knott. "Historical Variations in African Water Resources." In *Influence of Climate Change and Climatic Variability on the Hydrologic Regime and Water Resources,* p. 463-475. Eds. S. I. Solomon, M. A. Beran, and W. Hogg. IAHS Publication 168, Wallingford, UK, 1987.

Figure 2.

countries and regions. The northern region of Mediterranean rim and Sahelian countries, comprising about 20 percent of the continental area, receives less than 3 percent of the total, whereas the central region, with a similar area, receives 37 percent of the rainfall, but generates a massive 48 percent of the continent's renewable resources. Overall however, renewable water resources (river flows and groundwater recharge) represent less than 9 percent of the rainfall input due to evaporation losses, but regional variations are again large.

It is misleading to consider renewable water resources on a countrywide basis, because of the numerous international, or transboundary, river basins. For example, Egypt has internally generated natural resources of only about 25 m^3/person/ year, or only 68 l/s/day/person even if all this resource could be captured. However, the Nile

River flowing northward through Egypt "imports" 55 km^3 annually from the nine southern riparian countries, and increases available water resources to almost 800 m^3/person/year as of 2006, although over time there are likely to be increasing demands upon water resources in upstream riparian countries. Water resources cannot be considered solely at the national level, but must be planned at the river basin scale.

Africa has sixty international river basins, with more than 70 percent of the continent being drained by transboundary rivers, and just nine of these basins—the Congo, Nile, Lake Chad, Niger, Zambezi, Orange, Senegal, Limpopo, and Volta—drain more than 42 percent of the continent. This makes the concept of Integrated Water Resources Management (IWRM), where the conflicting needs of all stakeholders within the basin must be considered

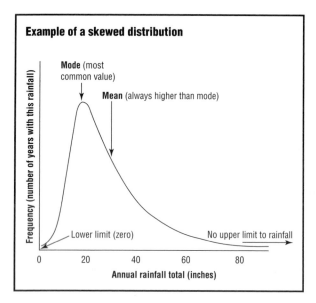

Example of a skewed distribution

Mode (most common value)

Mean (always higher than mode)

Frequency (number of years with this rainfall)

Lower limit (zero)

No upper limit to rainfall

Annual rainfall total (inches)

Figure 3.

when drawing up sustainable management plans for land and water, very challenging. Achieving equitable and sustainable IWRM is even difficult within a single country, and one of the greatest constraints can often be between competing governmental bodies, with the Ministry of Agriculture's needs often very different to those of urban water supply, the Ministry of Energy etc, and with environmental flow requirements often being very low on the national agenda. Developing effective river basin management plans for large international basins is even more difficult, although for all the nine basins mentioned above except the Volta, some form of collaborative basin authority has been established.

One key feature of African hydrology is the seasonality of rainfall, and hence resultant river flows and groundwater recharge. With significant parts of the continent receiving the bulk of its annual rainfall total in a four- to five-month rainy season, access to reliable surface water for drinking water or irrigation is limited unless wet season runoff is stored in reservoir. Africa has a large number of dams; the World Commission on Dams suggests 1,272, of which only 53 of the largest store more than 90 percent of the total capacity of almost 800 km^3. Approximately two thirds of all dams were built to supply irrigation water, one quarter for water supply, and about 20 percent for hydroelectricity. According to a number

of groups, many of these dams have failed to deliver the expected benefits, and in many cases the beneficiaries have been urban "rich" communities or large commercial farming operations, while displaced rural populations have often been disadvantaged. However, given the seasonal nature of river flows, significant sustainable utilisation of river flows in parts of Africa is only possible through use of dams, and there is little doubt that there have been significant economic and social benefits from dam construction in Africa, although how fairly such benefits have been shared is a matter for debate.

Climate change will affect Africa just as it is doing elsewhere in the world. The IPCC will publish its fourth Assessment Report in mid 2007, which will provide the most up-to-date scientific evidence. However, the magnitude of climate changes on a continent as large as Africa is difficult to summarize, and is still far from certain. Indeed some of the current climate models even contradict one another, with some suggesting particular parts of the continent will become wetter whereas other models indicate the same region becoming drier. There is thus still considerable uncertainty over the directions and magnitudes of change throughout Africa, although it is likely that those regions already vulnerable to marked inter-annual variability will become even more vulnerable.

In conclusion, the climate and hydrology of Africa is complex and highly variable. The continent has the world's largest desert, where renewable water resources are extremely small, yet it also has some of the world's largest rivers, the Nile being the world's longest, the Congo being in the top five or six in terms of discharge, and basins such as the Volta, Niger, and Zambezi being significant rivers in world terms. In absolute terms, it could be argued that Africa is not a water scarce continent, but only because of the huge resources contained in the Congo and other West African rivers. However, this resource is too remote from many of the regions of demand, and because of the seasonal nature of rainfall and runoff, and their marked interannular variability, many parts of Africa certainly do experience significant water stress, and millions of people, particularly those living in rural areas, have inadequate access to safe freshwater. Improving this poor water supply and sanitation situation are among the aims of the Millennium Development Goals, and many African countries can only begin to emerge from their dependence upon aid through a massive program of investment in water.

See also **Climate; Ecosystems; Water and Irrigation.**

BIBLIOGRAPHY

Balek, Jaroslav. *Hydrology and Water Resources in Tropical Africa.* New York: Elsevier, 1977.

Gleick, Peter H. *Water in Crisis: A Guide to the World's Freshwater Resources.* New York: Oxford University Press, 1993.

Gleick, Peter H. *The World's Water, 2000–2001: The Biennial Report on Freshwater Resources.* Washington, DC: Island Press, 2000.

Griffiths, John F. *World Survey of Climatology,* Volume 10: *Climates of Africa.* New York: Elsevier Publishing, 1972.

Shiklomanov, Igor A., ed. *Comprehensive Assessment of the Freshwater Resources of the World: Assessment of Water Resources and Water Availability in the World.* Geneva: World Meteorological Organization, 1997.

Sutcliffe, John V., and D. G. Knott. 1987. "Historical Variations in African Water Resources." In *Influence of Climate Change and Climatic Variability on the Hydrologic Regime and Water Resources,* ed. S. I. Solomon, Max A. Beran, and W. D. Hogg, 463–475. Wallingford, U.K.: IAHS Press, 1987.

United Nations. *World Water Assessment Program.* Paris and New York: UNESCO and Berghahn Books, 2006.

FRANK FARQUHARSON

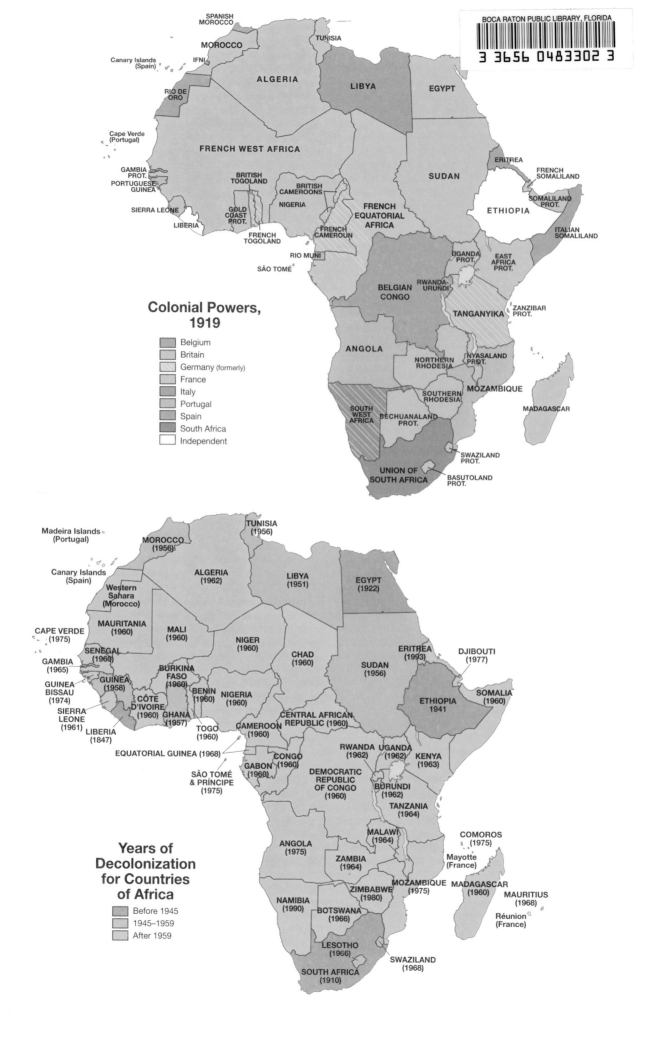

BOCA RATON PUBLIC LIBRARY, FLORIDA

3 3656 0483302 3

SPANISH MOROCCO

MOROCCO

Canary Islands (Spain)

IFNI

RIO DE ORO

Cape Verde (Portugal)

ALGERIA

TUNISIA

LIBYA

EGYPT

FRENCH WEST AFRICA

SUDAN

ERITREA

FRENCH SOMALILAND

GAMBIA PROT.

PORTUGUESE GUINEA

SIERRA LEONE

LIBERIA

BRITISH TOGOLAND

BRITISH CAMEROONS

NIGERIA

GOLD COAST PROT.

FRENCH TOGOLAND

FRENCH CAMEROUN

RIO MUNI

SÃO TOMÉ

FRENCH EQUATORIAL AFRICA

BELGIAN CONGO

ETHIOPIA

SOMALILAND PROT.

ITALIAN SOMALILAND

UGANDA PROT.

RWANDA-URUNDI

EAST AFRICA PROT.

TANGANYIKA

ZANZIBAR PROT.

ANGOLA

NORTHERN RHODESIA

NYASALAND PROT.

MOZAMBIQUE

SOUTHERN RHODESIA

MADAGASCAR

SOUTH WEST AFRICA

BECHUANALAND PROT.

SWAZILAND PROT.

UNION OF SOUTH AFRICA

BASUTOLAND PROT.

Colonial Powers, 1919

- Belgium
- Britain
- Germany (formerly)
- France
- Italy
- Portugal
- Spain
- South Africa
- Independent

Madeira Islands (Portugal)

TUNISIA (1956)

MOROCCO (1956)

Canary Islands (Spain)

Western Sahara (Morocco)

ALGERIA (1962)

LIBYA (1951)

EGYPT (1922)

MAURITANIA (1960)

CAPE VERDE (1975)

MALI (1960)

NIGER (1960)

CHAD (1960)

SUDAN (1956)

ERITREA (1993)

DJIBOUTI (1977)

SENEGAL (1960)

GAMBIA (1965)

GUINEA BISSAU (1974)

GUINEA (1958)

BURKINA FASO (1960)

SIERRA LEONE (1961)

CÔTE D'IVOIRE (1960)

GHANA (1957)

BENIN (1960)

NIGERIA (1960)

LIBERIA (1847)

TOGO (1960)

CAMEROON (1960)

CENTRAL AFRICAN REPUBLIC (1960)

ETHIOPIA 1941

SOMALIA (1960)

EQUATORIAL GUINEA (1968)

SÃO TOMÉ & PRÍNCIPE (1975)

GABON (1960)

CONGO (1960)

DEMOCRATIC REPUBLIC OF CONGO (1960)

RWANDA (1962)

UGANDA (1962)

KENYA (1963)

BURUNDI (1962)

TANZANIA (1964)

COMOROS (1975)

ANGOLA (1975)

MALAWI (1964)

ZAMBIA (1964)

ZIMBABWE (1980)

MOZAMBIQUE (1975)

MADAGASCAR (1960)

Mayotte (France)

MAURITIUS (1968)

Réunion (France)

NAMIBIA (1990)

BOTSWANA (1966)

Years of Decolonization for Countries of Africa

- Before 1945
- 1945–1959
- After 1959

LESOTHO (1966)

SWAZILAND (1968)

SOUTH AFRICA (1910)